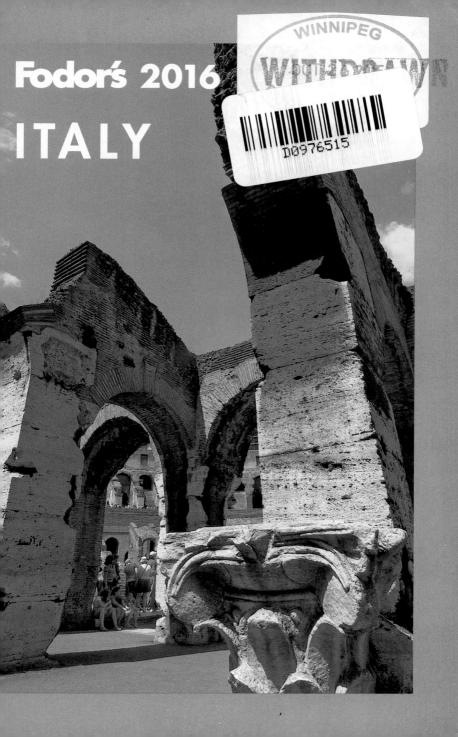

Fodor's 2016

ITALY

WELCOME TO ITALY

Italy is the kind of destination that travelers return to over and over. They come for awe-inspiring art and architecture that influenced Western civilization, and stunning historical ruins—as well as for some of the world's best food and wine. Also beckoning irresistibly are Italy's sun-kissed olive groves and vineyards, the sparkling waters of Lake Como and the Mediterranean, and atmospheric monasteries, castles, and farmhouses. And if you seek vibrant cities with renowned museums, restaurants, and shopping opportunities, Rome, Florence, and Milan await.

TOP REASONS TO GO

★ **Food:** Italy is a pasta lover's paradise; but don't forget the pizza and the gelato.

★ **Romance:** Whether you're strolling atmospheric Venice or sipping wine, Italy enchants.

★ **History:** The ruins of ancient Pompeii and the leaning tower of Pisa breathe antiquity.

★ **Art:** The big hitters—Botticelli, Michelangelo, Raphael, Caravaggio, and more.

★ **Shopping:** Few things say quality or style like "made in Italy."

★ **Stunning landscapes:** Tuscany, the Amalfi Coast, the Cinque Terre, to name just a few.

Fodor's ITALY 2016

Publisher: Amanda D'Acierno, *Senior Vice President*

Editorial: Arabella Bowen, *Editor in Chief*; Linda Cabasin, *Editorial Director*

Design: Tina Malaney, *Associate Art Director*; Chie Ushio, *Senior Designer*

Photography: Jennifer Arnow, *Senior Photo Editor*; Mary Robnett, *Photo Researcher*

Production: Linda Schmidt, *Managing Editor*; Evangelos Vasilakis, *Associate Managing Editor*; Angela L. McLean, *Senior Production Manager*

Maps: Rebecca Baer, *Senior Map Editor*; David Lindroth and Mark Stroud, Moon Street Cartography, *Cartographers*

Sales: Jacqueline Lebow, *Sales Director*

Marketing & Publicity: Heather Dalton, *Marketing Director*; Katherine Punia, *Publicity Director*

Business & Operations: Susan Livingston, *Vice President, Strategic Business Planning*; Sue Daulton, *Vice President, Operations*

Fodors.com: Megan Bell, *Executive Director, Revenue & Business Development*; Yasmin Marinaro, *Senior Director, Marketing & Partnerships*

Copyright © 2016 by Fodor's Travel, a division of Penguin Random House LLC

Writers: Robert Andrews, Peter Blackman, Lorna Holland, Liz Humphreys, Fergal Kavanagh, Bruce Leimsidor, Megan McCaffrey-Guerrera, Patricia Rucidlo, Amanda Ruggeri, Margaret Stenhouse, Jonathan Willcocks, Dante Zambrano-Cassella.

Editors: Róisín Cameron (lead editor), Bethany Beckerlegge, Alexis C. Kelly, Daniel Mangin.

Editorial Contributor: Nicholas McNallen

Production Editor: Jennifer DePrima

ISBN 978-1-101-87836-1

ISSN 0361–977X

All details in this book are based on information supplied to us at press time. Always confirm information when it matters, especially if you're making a detour to visit a specific place. Fodor's expressly disclaims any liability, loss, or risk, personal or otherwise, that is incurred as a consequence of the use of any of the contents of this book.

SPECIAL SALES

This book is available at special discounts for bulk purchases for sales promotions or premiums. For more information, e-mail specialmarkets@penguinrandomhouse.com.

PRINTED IN THE UNITED STATES OF AMERICA

10 9 8 7 6 5 4 3 2 1

CONTENTS

Fodor's Features

MAPS

ABOUT THIS GUIDE

Fodor's Recommendations

Everything in this guide is worth doing—we don't cover what isn't—but exceptional sights, hotels, and restaurants are recognized with additional accolades. Fodor'sChoice★ indicates our top recommendations. Care to nominate a new place? Visit Fodors.com/contact-us.

Trip Costs

We list prices wherever possible to help you budget well. Hotel and restaurant price categories from **$** to **$$$$** are noted alongside each recommendation. For hotels, we include the lowest cost of a standard double room in high season. For restaurants, we cite the average cost of a meal. The meal includes three courses: *primo* (usually pasta or an appetizer), *secondo* (meat or fish main course), and *dolce* (dessert). For attractions, we always list adult admission fees; discounts are usually available for children, students, and senior citizens.

Hotels

Our local writers vet every hotel to recommend the best overnights in each price category, from budget to expensive. Unless otherwise specified, you can expect private bath, phone, and TV in your room. For expanded hotel reviews, facilities, and deals visit Fodors.com.

Top Picks

★ Fodor'sChoice

Listings

- Address
- Branch address
- Telephone
- Fax
- Website
- E-mail
- Admission fee
- Open/closed times
- Subway
- Directions or Map coordinates

Hotels & Restaurants

- Hotel
- Number of rooms
- Meal plans
- Restaurant
- Reservations
- Dress code
- No credit cards
- Price

Other

- See also
- Take note
- Golf facilities

Restaurants

Unless we state otherwise, restaurants are open for lunch and dinner daily. We mention dress code only when there's a specific requirement and reservations only when they're essential or not accepted. To make restaurant reservations, visit Fodors.com.

Credit Cards

The hotels and restaurants in this guide typically accept credit cards. If not, we'll say so.

EUGENE FODOR

Hungarian-born Eugene Fodor (1905–91) began his travel career as an interpreter on a French cruise ship. The experience inspired him to write *On the Continent* (1936), the first guidebook to receive annual updates and discuss a country's way of life as well as its sights. Fodor later joined the U.S. Army and worked for the OSS in World War II. After the war, he kept up his intelligence work while expanding his guidebook series. During the Cold War, many guides were written by fellow agents who understood the value of insider information. Today's guides continue Fodor's legacy by providing travelers with timely coverage, insider tips, and cultural context.

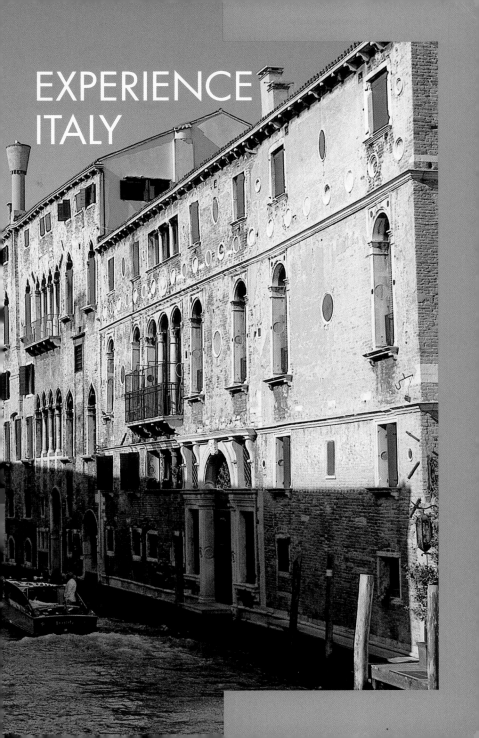

EXPERIENCE
ITALY

ITALY TODAY

Enduring Cuisine

The old joke goes that three-quarters of the food and wine served in Italy is good—and the rest is amazing. In some sense, that's still true, and the "good" 75% has gotten even better. Those pundits would claim that ingredients that in the past were available only to the wealthy can now be found even in the remotest parts of the country at reasonable prices. Dishes originally conceived to make the most of inferior cuts of meat or the least flavorful part of vegetables are now made with the best.

But many Italians would say—pause, gesture, exclamation—that the food in Italy is getting worse. There's a proliferation of fast-food establishments, and increasing tourism has allowed many restaurants to lower their standards while raising their prices. This is true not only in Rome, but in most other tourist centers as well. The good news is Italy is home to one of the world's greatest cuisines, and its traditional favorites still put meat on bones and smiles on faces. Italian restaurateurs seem determined to make the most of the country's reputation for good food. Though quaint, family-run trattorias with checker tablecloths, traditional dishes, and informal atmosphere are still common but on the decline, nearly every town has a newer eatery with matching flatware, a proper wine list, and an innovative menu.

The same is true of Italian wine. Today, through investment and experimentation, Italy's winemakers are figuring out how to get the most from their gorgeous vineyards. It's fair to say that Italy now produces more types of high-quality wine from more different grape varieties than any other country in the world.

Soccer Rules

Soccer (or, as the Italians say, "*calcio*"—which means "kick") stands without rival as the national sport of Italy, but recent years have seen some changes to the beautiful game. On the positive side, Italy won its fourth World Cup in 2006 (though another major success has since proved elusive), giving the country more world titles than any other this side of Brazil. The game is still played at a high level and its teams do well in international tournaments. In the past few years, however, soccer lovers have had to come to terms with a series of unwelcome developments, including more violence around the stadium, rigged referee selections to favor some major teams, and, worst of all, match fixing at all levels (and throughout Europe) financed by betting consortia in Asia. More games in the schedule and a dwindling fan base mean fewer people are seen at the stadium. Still, fans can't stop watching the game on television.

An Aging Population

Italy's population is the oldest in Europe (worldwide, only Japan's is older)—the result of its low birth rate, relatively strict immigration laws, and one of the highest life-expectancy rates in the world. The median age of an Italian is 44.5 years old (compared to 37.6 in the United States), and the number keeps rising.

The result is a remarkably stable population: the number of Italian residents barely rises most years, and, according to the most recent estimates, is projected to start contracting by 2020. But the situation is putting a strain on the country's pension system and on families, because elderly family members are likely to live with their children or grandchildren in a country where retirement homes are rare.

The trend also has an impact in other areas, including politics (where older politicians are eager to promote policies aimed at older voters), the popular culture (where everything from fashion to television programming takes older consumers into consideration), and a kind of far-reaching nostalgia. Thanks to a long collective memory, it's common to hear even younger Italians celebrate or rue something that happened 50 or 60 years earlier as if it had just taken place.

The Black-Market Economy

Nobody knows how big Italy's black-market economy is, though experts all agree it's massive. Estimates place it at anywhere from a fourth to a half of the official, legal economy.

Put another way, if the highest estimates are correct, Italy's black market is about as large as the entire economy of Switzerland or Indonesia. If the estimated black-market figures were added to the official GDP, Italy would likely leapfrog France and the United Kingdom to become the world's fifth-largest economy.

The presence of the black market isn't obvious to the casual observer, but whenever a customer isn't given a printed receipt in a store or restaurant, tobacco without a tax seal is bought from a street seller, or a product or service is exchanged for another product or service, that means the transaction goes unrecorded, unreported, and untaxed. But that's all penny-ante stuff compared to what many professionals evade by neglecting to declare all they earn. Austerity measures imposed in 2012 have led to much disgruntlement among the population; now most shopkeepers insist that you take a receipt. If you don't, you could be fined, as could the shopkeeper.

A Growing Parks System

Italy boasts 24 national parks covering a total of around 1.5 million hectares (58,000 square miles), or about 5% of the entire surface area of the country—more than twice as much as 25 years ago. And a new park is added or an existing park is expanded every few months.

Part of the reason for the expansion has been a growing environmental movement in Italy, which has lobbied the government to annex undeveloped land for parks, thus protecting against development. But the trend is a boon for visitors and nature lovers, who can enjoy huge expanses of unspoiled territory.

Staying Home in August

Italy used to be the best example of Europe's famous August exodus, when city dwellers would spend most of the month at the seaside or in the mountains, leaving the cities nearly deserted. Today the phenomenon continues, but is much less prevalent, as economic pressures have forced companies to keep operating through August. As a result, vacations are more staggered and vacationers' plans are often more modest.

The loss of shared vacation time for Italian workers means good things for visitors: in August there's more room (or a little more room, at any rate) at the seaside and in the mountains; in addition, cities have taken to promoting local events designed to appeal to nonvacationing natives. These days, summers in Italy offer a plethora of outdoor concerts and theatrical events, extended museum hours, and local festivals.

WHAT'S NEW

Steeped in history and tradition, and bearing a lustrous patina of antiquity, Italy luxuriates in the illusion that change comes slowly—or maybe not at all—in the *bel paese*. Despite the ravages of war and urban renewal, Italians have skillfully retained so much of the past that it seems the historical centers of many Italian cities would be easily recognizable to residents of 350 years ago. The present and the past merge seamlessly. Tiny cars and whining scooters in Italian cities and towns maneuver without missing a beat through narrow cobblestone streets designed for horses and carriages.

The Hot, the Hip, and the New

The pervasiveness of the past also makes us forget that Italy, not by breaking with tradition but rather by continuing it, has been in the forefront of producing major monuments of contemporary style. By creating everything from skyscrapers to sports cars, raincoats to coffeepots, today's Italian designers and architects have infused beauty into the everyday lives of people around the world. In so doing, they have proved themselves to be true sons and daughters of the Renaissance, heirs to Brunelleschi and Leonardo da Vinci, who combined beauty and functionality to create marvelous works of art.

Despite Italy's ties to the past, "modern" and "Italian design" have become almost synonymous. Perhaps because Italy (or more exactly, Milan) has become the epicenter of the fashion and design world, Italians seem to be more obsessed with fashion and the "new" than other Europeans are. While you'll easily be able to buy your choice of a classic suit or dress for business wear, for casual wear you'll have to look hard for a sweater or shirt that's not in the very latest season's color or cut.

And be forewarned: there's zero tolerance for even slightly worn or frayed clothing.

Italy's Youngest Prime Minister

Visitors also tend to forget that Italy is one of Western Europe's newest countries, having been unified only in 1861. Before that, Italy was divided into myriad states, some at times independent and glorious, but, since the Renaissance, mainly under the domination of Spain, France, Austria, or part of the Papal States. To this day, most Italians identify more strongly with their region or city than with the Italian nation, and local cultural and even linguistic differences are still valued. The variety and contrast between Italian regions, an inheritance from its centuries-long division, while making Italy a fascinating place to visit, has hindered its development as a modern nation-state. Many Italians thought new man Silvio Berlusconi would usher in reform. Others thought progress would come from submitting to an ever-stronger guiding hand from the European Union. Then Berlusconi embarrassed himself out of power, just as the 2008 financial crisis left Italy's economy reeling. For the first time, the government was without recourse to an expedient devaluation of its currency to support exports, because the euro was the common currency and exchange rates were out of Italian hands. By insisting on austerity at all costs, even the EU has lost favor with most Italians. As of this writing, Italy's prime minister is still the relatively new-kid-on-the-block and former mayor of Florence, Matteo Renzi. A canny political operator, Renzi is finding he has little room for maneuver in electoral or economic reform. Italians are not holding their breath, forecasts for 2016 are gloomy, and the national mood remains pessimistic.

Handling Immigration

Italians long enjoyed a reputation for being friendly and hospitable to those down on their luck, but lately this has changed. Although Italy has received more migrants than it has exported since the 1970s, this trend has grown to alarming proportions over the last two decades. This increased immigration has had no effect either on crime or the unemployment rate. Nevertheless, xenophobes and opportunists fanned the flames of fear and promoted policies that brought Italy under the scrutiny of European human rights monitors. Italian friendliness and hospitality, however, haven't entirely disappeared; even those who complain about immigrants will then contribute generously to charities assisting them, and incidents of violence against immigrants remain less frequent in Italy than in neighboring countries, where recently governments have also been bolting their doors, as the financial situation in Europe remains precarious.

A Secular State? Well, Maybe . . .

Rome is still the spiritual home of the world's 1.1 billion Catholics, but, as in other European countries, church attendance in Italy has been eroding since the 1950s, and today fewer than one in five Italians attend church regularly. The April 2013 papal election of the Argentinean cardinal Jorge Mario Bergoglio, who took the name of Francis, appears to have burnished the image of the church, even in the eyes of many non-Catholics. Meanwhile, the Conference of Bishops still wields considerable political influence and is not expected to alter its conservative stance on birth control, same-sex relationships, and a greater participation of women in the Church any time soon.

And although the Italian Constitution (1948) proclaims that Italy is a secular state, a crucifix still adorns all courts and schoolrooms, and if you're unlucky enough to land in jail, a statue of the Madonna is likely to greet you as you enter. The Italian courts have ruled crucifixes can stay where they are, reasoning that they are merely innocuous symbols of Italy's cultural heritage, and not symbols of religious allegiance.

Getting Connected in Rome

Romans are still patiently awaiting the completion of the new Metro C subway line (started in 2007), which will cut through the city center with stops at Piazza Venezia and link with both the A and the B lines at Ottaviano for St. Peter's and the Colosseum, respectively. Expected to considerably ease on-surface traffic congestion, the new line progresses slowly, because every time a shaft is sunk in Roman ground, some important archaeological site comes to light and all work halts while it is investigated. The planned station at Piazza Torre Argentina, in fact, had to be canceled due to the wealth of material uncovered. In November 2014, the surface rail part out to Monte Compatri and a few underground stations to the still relatively peripheral Parco di Centocelle were opened. The section through central Rome, with connection to the other lines is still a ways off, however.

WHAT'S WHERE

1 Rome. Italy's capital is one of the greatest cities in Europe. It's a large, busy metropolis that lives in the here and now, yet there's no other place on earth where you'll encounter such powerful evocations of a storied and spectacular past, from the Colosseum to St. Peter's.

2 Northern Italy. The prosperous north has Italy's most diverse landscape. **Venice** is a rare jewel of a city, while **Milan** and **Turin** are centers of commerce and style. Along the country's northern border, the mountain peaks of the **Dolomites** and **Valle d'Aosta** attract skiers in winter and hikers in summer, while the **Lake District** and the coastline of the Italian **Riviera** are classic summer-time playgrounds. Food here is exceptional, from the French-influenced cuisine of **Piedmont** to Italian classics prepared with unrivaled skill in **Emilia-Romagna**.

3 Central Italy. No place better epitomizes the greatness of the Renaissance than **Florence**, where there's a masterpiece around every corner, from Michelangelo's *David* to Botticelli's *Venus*. Elsewhere, the central regions of **Tuscany** and **Umbria** are characterized by midsize cities and small hilltop towns, each with its own rich history and

art treasures. Highlights include the walled city of **Lucca**; **Pisa** and its Leaning Tower; **Siena**, home of the Palio; and **Assisi**, the city of St. Francis. In between, the gorgeous countryside produces some of Italy's finest wine.

4 Southern Italy. The region of **Campania** is a popular place both to unwind—on the tiny island of **Capri** or in the resort towns of the **Amalfi Coast**—and to explore the past—at the ruins of **Pompeii, Hercu-laneum**, and **Paestum**. In the middle of everything is the vibrant, chaotic city of **Naples**. Farther south, in the off-the-beaten-path regions of **Puglia, Basili-cata**, and **Calabria**, you'll find attractive beaches, mysterious ancient dwell-ings, and the charming town of **Lecce**. Across a narrow strait from Calabria is **Sicily**. Baroque church-hopping could be a sport on the bustling streets of **Palermo** and **Siracusa**, while one of the world's best-preserved Greek ruins stand amid the almond groves of **Agrigento**. The island of **Sardinia**, meanwhile, provides a thrill of discovery to beach lovers and those who appreciate luxurious seclusion and wild natural beauty.

Elevation	
15,577	4,748
10,825	3,300
9,840	3,000
8,860	2,700
7,875	2,400
6,900	2,100
5,900	1,800
4,920	1,500
3,940	1,200
2,920	900
1,970	600
980	300
490	150
250	75
100	30
feet	meters

AUSTRIA

TRENTINO-ALTO ADIGE

Bolzano

Trento

Lake Garda

THE DOLOMITES

FRIULI-VENEZIA GIULIA

Udine

VENETO

Treviso

Trieste

SLOVENIA

Bergamo

LOMBARDY

Verona

Vicenza

Padua

Venice

Gulf of Venice

CROATIA

Parma

Modena

Ferrara

Bologna

EMILIA-ROMAGNA

Ravenna

Rimini

SAN MARINO

3 Florence

Pistoia

La Spezia

Lucca

Pisa

Livorno

Arno

Arezzo

TUSCANY

SAN MARINO

Ancona

THE MARCHES

Adriatic Sea

ELBA

Siena

Perugia

Assisi

UMBRIA

Orvieto

Tiber

Terni

MONTENEGRO

1

ROME

Tivoli

LATIUM

ABRUZZO

Pescara

MOLISE

Foggia

CAMPANIA

Bari

Naples

VESUVIUS

ISCHIA

Amalfi

CAPRI

Paestum

Potenza

BASILICATA

PUGLIA

Taranto

Brindisi

Lecce

Tyrrhenian Sea

Gulf of Taranto

AEOLIAN ISLANDS

4

Cosenza

Catanzaro

CALABRIA

Palermo

Messina

Reggio

Ionian Sea

EGADI ISLANDS

SICILY

ETNA

Mediterranean Sea

Agrigento

Catania

Siracusa

TUNIS

TUNISIA

PANTELLERIA

SICILY

0   100 miles

0   150 km

NEED TO KNOW

AT A GLANCE

Capital: Rome

Population: 60,920,000

Currency: Euro

Money: ATMs are common; cash is more common than credit.

Language: Italian

Country Code: 29

Emergencies: 112

Driving: On the right

Electricity: 200v/50 cycles; electrical plugs have two round prongs.

Time: Six hours ahead of New York

Documents: Up to 90 days with valid passport; Schengen rules apply.

Mobile Phones: GSM (900 and 1800 bands)

Major Mobile Companies: Vodafone, TIM, Wind, Tre

WEBSITES

Italy: ⊕ *www.italia.it*

Farmstays: ⊕ *www. agriturismo.it*

Culture: ⊕ *www. beniculturali.it*

GETTING AROUND

✈ **Air Travel:** The major airports are Rome, Milan, Bergamo, and Venice.

🚌 **Bus Travel:** Good for smaller towns and the best way to travel the Amalfi coast.

🚗 **Car Travel:** Rent a car to explore at your own pace, but never to use in the cities themselves (including Rome and Florence). Always rent a GPS along with the car, as Italy's roads can be confounding. Gas is very expensive.

🚆 **Train Travel:** Excellent and fast between major cities. Slower regional trains connect many smaller towns, as well.

PLAN YOUR BUDGET

	HOTEL ROOM	MEAL	ATTRACTIONS
Low Budget	€140	€25	Visiting Florence's Duomo, free
Mid Budget	€290	€45	Ticket to the Vatican and the Sistine Chapel, €16
High Budget	€350	€60	Evening gondola ride in Venice, €150

WAYS TO SAVE

Stay at an *agriturismo*. Farm-stays are Italy's best-kept secret. In beautiful settings, they sometimes include meals and are often for half the price of a hotel.

Drink from the free fountains. No need to buy bottled water; fill up at the free public fountains, especially in Rome.

Book rail tickets in advance. Book online at least a week in advance for half the price. ⊕ *www.trenitalia.com.*

Enjoy aperitivo. This northern Italian tradition entails getting a drink and access to a buffet which can be light or heavy for about €8–€10.

PLAN YOUR TIME

Hassle Factor	Low. Flights to Rome, Milan, and Venice are frequent, and Italy has great transport elsewhere.
3 days	You can see some of the magic of Rome and perhaps take a day trip to Pompeii or Florence.
1 week	Spend time in Rome with a one-day trip to Pompeii, Umbria, or the Amalfi coast, as well as an additional day or two in Florence. Alternatively, tour the main cities with three days in Rome, two in Florence, and one in Venice.
2 weeks	You have time to move around and for the highlights, including stops in Rome, Florence, and Venice, excursions to Pompeii, Naples, and the Amalfi coast, and a trip to beautiful Tuscany or Umbria.

WHEN TO GO

High Season: June through September is expensive and busy. In August, most Italians take their own summer holidays; cities are less crowded, but many shops and restaurants close. July and August can be uncomfortably hot.

Low Season: Unless you are skiing, winter offers the least appealing weather, though it's the best time for airfare and hotel deals and to escape the crowds. Temperatures are still mild, especially in the south.

Value Season: By late September, temperate weather, saner airfares, and more cultural events can make for a happier trip. October is also great, but November is often rainy and (hence) quiet. From late April to early May, the masses have not yet arrived but cafés are already abuzz. March and early April can be changeable and wet.

BIG EVENTS

February: Carnival kicks off across Venice and around Italy. ⊕ www.carnevaleitaliano.it

April: Religious processions commemorate Easter. On Pasquetta (Easter Monday), most Italians picnic.

June: The Festa della Repubblica commemorates Italy's 1946 vote for the republic. ⊕ www.festadellarepubblica.it

October: Alba's Fiera del Tartufo is devoted to the area's white truffles. ⊕ www.fieradeltartufo.org

READ THIS

■ *Delizia! The Epic History of the Italians and Their Food,* John Dickie. A history of Italian flavors.

■ *Under the Tuscan Sun,* Frances Mayes. The memoir that launched a thousand Tuscan trips.

■ *La Bella Figura,* Beppe Severgnini. A humorous introduction to modern Italy.

WATCH THIS

■ *Roman Holiday.* The 1953 classic starring Audrey Hepburn—and, of course, Rome.

■ *La Dolce Vita.* Fellini's famous study of glitzy 1950s Italy.

■ *Il Postino.* Romance in an Italian fishing village.

EAT THIS

■ *Mozzarella di bufala*: a specialty of Campania and the south.

■ *Prosciutto crudo*: tender, dry-cured ham, especially from Parma and San Daniele.

■ *Pasta carbonara*: a Roman dish of eggs, *guanciale* (cured pork jowl), cheese, and pepper.

■ *Bistecca fiorentina*: the classic Tuscan T-bone.

■ *Wine*: from Barolo to Chianti.

■ *Sfogliatelle*: a layered and filled southern Italian pastry.

ITALY
TOP ATTRACTIONS

The Vatican
(A) The home of the Catholic Church, Vatican City, a tiny independent state tucked within central Rome, holds some of the city's most spectacular sights, including St. Peter's Basilica, the Vatican Museums, and Michelangelo's Sistine Chapel ceiling. (⇨ *Chapter 1.*)

Ancient Rome
(B) The Colosseum and the Roman Forum are remarkable ruins from Rome's ancient past. Sitting above it all is the Campidoglio, with a piazza designed by Michelangelo and museums containing one of the world's finest collections of ancient art. (⇨ *Chapter 1.*)

Venice's Grand Canal
A trip down Venice's "Main Street," whether by water bus or gondola, is a signature Italian experience. (⇨ *Chapter 3.*)

Palladio's Villas and Palazzi
The 16th-century genius Andrea Palladio is one of the most influential figures in the history of architecture. You can visit his creations in his hometown of Vicenza, in and around Venice, and outside Treviso. (⇨ *Chapter 4.*)

Ravenna's Mosaics
This town off the Adriatic Sea, once the capital of the Western Roman Empire and seat of the Byzantine Empire in the West, is home to 5th- and 6th-century mosaics that rank among the greatest art treasures in Italy. (⇨ *Chapter 9.*)

Galleria degli Uffizi, Florence
The Uffizi—Renaissance art's hall of fame—contains masterpieces by Leonardo, Michelangelo, Raphael, Botticelli, Caravaggio, and dozens of other luminaries. (⇨ *Chapter 10.*)

Duomo, Florence

(C) The massive dome of Florence's Cathedral of Santa Maria del Fiore (aka the Duomo) is one of the world's great feats of engineering. (⇨ *Chapter 10.*)

Piazza del Campo, Siena

(D) Siena is Tuscany's classic medieval hill town, and its heart is the Piazza del Campo, the beautiful, one-of-a-kind town square. (⇨ *Chapter 11.*)

Basilica di San Francesco, Assisi

(E) The giant basilica—made up of two churches, one built on top of the other—honors St. Francis with its remarkable fresco cycles. (⇨ *Chapter 12.*)

Palazzo Ducale, Urbino

No other building better exemplifies the principles and ideals of the Renaissance than this palace in the Marches region, east of Umbria. (⇨ *Chapter 12.*)

The Ruins of Pompeii

(F) When Vesuvius erupted in AD 79, its fallout froze the town of Pompeii in time. Walking its streets brings antiquity to life. (⇨ *Chapter 13.*)

Ravello, on the Amalfi Coast

(G) Nowhere else better captures the essence of the gorgeous Amalfi Coast than Ravello. Perched high above the Tyrrhenian Sea, it's the place to go for your blissful *dolce vita* moment. (⇨ *Chapter 13.*)

Lecce, Puglia

With its lavish Baroque architecture and engaging street life, Lecce takes the prize for the most appealing town in Italy's deep south. (⇨ *Chapter 14.*)

Valle dei Templi, Sicily

(H) The Greek influence in Sicily dates to ancient days, as is borne out by these well-preserved temple ruins. (⇨ *Chapter 15.*)

TOP EXPERIENCES

Il Dolce Far Niente

"The sweetness of doing nothing" has long been an art form in Italy. This is a country in which life's pleasures are warmly celebrated, not guiltily indulged.

Of course, doing "nothing" doesn't really mean nothing. It means doing things differently: lingering over a glass of wine for the better part of an evening as you watch the sun slowly set; savoring a slow and flirtatious evening *passeggiata* (stroll) along the main street of a little town; and making a commitment—however temporary—to thinking that there's nowhere that you have to be next, and no other time but the magical present.

In the quiet, stunningly positioned hilltop village **Ravello**, above the Amalfi Coast (⇨ Chapter 13), it's easy to achieve such a state of mind. The same holds true for **Bellagio**, on Lake Como (⇨ Chapter 6), where you can meander through stately gardens, dance on the wharf, or just watch the boats float by in the shadow of the Alps.

And there's still nothing more romantic than a **gondola ride** along Venice's canals (⇨ Chapter 3), watched over by Gothic palaces with delicately arched windows.

Driving the Back Roads

If you associate Italian roads with unruly motorists and endless traffic snarls, you're only partly right. Along the rural back roads, things are more relaxed.

You might stop on a lark to take a picture of a crumbling farmhouse, have a coffee in a time-stood-still hill town, or enjoy an epic lunch at a rustic *agriturismo* inaccessible to public transportation. Driving, in short, is the best way to see Italy.

Among the countless beautiful drives, these are three of the most memorable: the legendary mountain ascent on **SS48, the Grande Strada delle Dolomiti** (⇨ Chapter 5), takes you through the heart of the Dolomites, the famous Passo di Sella, and into the Val Gardena, passing unforgettable, craggy-peaked views. Every time the A1 Autostrada tunnels through the mountains, the smaller **SS1, Via Aurelia** (⇨ Chapter 8), stays out on the jagged coastline of the Italian Riviera, passing terraced vineyards, cliff-hanging villages, and shimmering seas. **SS222, the Strada Chiantigiana** (⇨ Chapter 11), between Florence and Siena, meanders through classic Tuscan landscapes. Be aware that Italian roads are often poorly marked. It helps to know a little geography, as many signs indicate the town the road leads to, but not what the road number is.

Hiking the Hills

Even if you don't fancy yourself a disciple of Reinhold Messner (the favorite son of the Dolomites and the first man to reach the peak of Everest without oxygen), you'll find great summer hiking aplenty all over Italy.

The **Vie Ferrate (Iron Paths)** are reinforced trails through the mountains of Trentino–Alto Adige (⇨ Chapter 5), once forged by the Italian and Austro-Hungarian armies; they're a great way to get off the beaten path in the Dolomites.

The **Cinque Terre**—five cliff-clinging villages along the Italian Riviera (⇨ Chapter 8)—are spectacular, and they're all connected by hiking trails with memorable views of the towns, the rocks, and the Ligurian Sea. (And they are always overcrowded in summer.)

In Umbria (⇨ Chapter 12) you can hike the **Paths of St. Francis** outside Assisi. An easy half-hour walk takes you from the town of Cannara to Pian d'Arca, site of

St. Francis's sermon to the birds; with a bit more effort you can make the walk from Assisi to the Eremo delle Carceri, and from here to the summit of Monte Subasio, which has views for miles in every direction.

Tasting the Wine

When it comes to wine making, the Italian Renaissance is happening right now: from tip to toe, vintners are challenging themselves to produce wines of ever-higher quality. You can taste the fruits of their labor at wine bars and restaurants throughout the country, and in many areas you can visit the vineyards as well.

For the lowdown on Italy's "King of Wines," see **On the Trail of Barolo** (⇨ *Chapter 7*). For a full primer on the wines of Tuscany, see **Grape Escapes** (⇨ *Chapter 11*).

Picking up Some Italian Style

"Made in Italy" is synonymous with style, quality, and craftsmanship, whether it refers to high fashion or Maserati automobiles.

Every region has its specialties: Venice is known for glassware, lace, and velvet; Milan and Como for silk; and the Dolomites and the mountains of Calabria and Sicily for hand-carved wooden objects.

Bologna and Parma are the places for cured meats and cheeses; Modena for balsamic vinegar; Florence for straw goods, gold jewelry, leather, and paper products (including beautiful handmade notebooks); Assisi for embroidery; and Deruta, Gubbio, Vietri, and many towns in Puglia and Sicily for ceramics.

In Milan, Italy's fashion capital, the streets of the **Quadrilatero** district (⇨ *Chapter 6*) are where to go for serious shopping—or just for taking in the chic scene. Rome's **Piazza di Spagna** (⇨ *Chapter 1*) is another mecca for high-fashion shopping, and a few steps away is the Via del Corso, with more than a mile of stores of all varieties.

To be overwhelmed by the aromas of Emilia-Romagna's legendary food, head to **Tamburini** in Bologna (⇨ *Chapter 9*), where you can get vacuum-packed delicacies to take home with you.

Church or Museum?

Few images are more identifiable with Italy than the country's great churches, amazing works of architecture that often took centuries to build. The name "Duomo" (derived from the Latin *domus,* or house) is used to refer to the principal church of a town or city. Generally speaking, the bigger the city, the more splendid its Duomo.

Still, impressive churches inhabit some unlikely places—in the Umbrian hill towns of **Assisi** and **Orvieto,** for example (⇨ *Chapter 12*).

In Venice the Byzantine-influenced **Basilica di San Marco** (⇨ *Chapter 3*) is a testament to the city's East-meets-West character. **Milan's Duomo** (⇨ *Chapter 6*) is the largest, most imposing Gothic cathedral in Italy. The spectacular dome of **Florence's Duomo** (⇨ *Chapter 10*) is a work of engineering genius. The **Basilica di San Pietro** in Rome (⇨ *Chapter 1*) has all the grandeur you'd expect from the seat of the Roman Catholic Church. And Italy's classical past is on display at **Siracusa's Duomo** (⇨ *Chapter 15*), which incorporates the columns of a 6th-century-BC Greek temple.

QUINTESSENTIAL ITALY

Il Caffè (Coffee)

The Italian day begins and ends with coffee, and more cups of coffee punctuate the time in between. To live like the Italians do, drink as they drink, standing at the counter or sitting at an outdoor table of the corner bar. (In Italy, a "bar" is a coffee bar.) A primer: *caffè* means coffee, and Italian standard issue is what Americans call espresso—short and strong. *Cappuccino* is a foamy half-and-half of espresso and steamed milk; cocoa powder (*cacao*) on top is acceptable, and sometimes cinnamon, too.

If you're thinking of having a cappuccino for dessert, think again—some Italians drink only caffè or caffè *macchiato* (with a spot of steamed milk) after lunchtime. However, if that's what you want, by all means order it: many Italians do, too. Confused? Homesick? Order caffè *americano* for a reasonable facsimile of good-old filtered joe. Note that you usually pay for your coffee first, then take your receipt to the counter and order.

Il Calcio (Soccer)

Imagine the most rabid American football fans—the ones who paint their faces on game day and sleep in pajamas emblazoned with the logo of their favorite team. Throw in a dose of melodrama along the lines of a tear-jerking soap opera. Ratchet up the intensity by a factor of 10, and you'll start to get a sense of how Italians feel about their national game, soccer— known in the mother tongue as *calcio*. On Sunday afternoons during the long September-to-May season, stadiums are packed throughout Italy.

Those who don't get to games in person tend to congregate around televisions in restaurants and bars, rooting for the home team with a passion that feels like a last vestige of the days when the country was a series of warring medieval city-states. How calcio mania affects your stay in

If you want to get a sense of contemporary Italian culture and indulge in some of its pleasures, start by familiarizing yourself with the rituals of daily life. These are a few highlights—things you can take part in with relative ease.

Italy depends on how eager you are to get involved. At the very least, you may notice an eerie Sunday-afternoon quiet on the city streets, or erratic restaurant service around the same time, accompanied by cheers and groans from a neighboring room. If you want a memorable, truly Italian experience, attend a game yourself. Availability of tickets may depend on the current fortunes of the local team, but they often can be acquired with help from your hotel concierge.

Il Gelato (Ice Cream)

During warmer months, *gelato*—the Italian equivalent of ice cream—is a national obsession. Though it's often on restaurant menus, it's usually considered more of a snack rather than dessert, bought at stands and shops in piazzas and on street corners, and consumed on foot, usually at a leisurely stroll. Gelato is softer, less creamy, more intensely flavored, and less sugar-y than its American counterpart. It comes in simple flavors that capture the essence of the main ingredient. Pick from conventional choices like pistachio, *nocciola* (hazelnut), caffè, and numerous fresh-fruit varieties, or try new flavors, such as Chianti gelato in Florence. Quality varies; the surest sign that you've hit on a good spot is a line at the counter.

La Passeggiata (Strolling)

A favorite Italian pastime is *la passeggiata* (literally, "the promenade"). In the late afternoon and early evening, especially on weekends, couples, families, and packs of teenagers stroll the main streets and piazzas of Italy's towns. It's a ritual of exchanged news and gossip, window-shopping and flirting that adds up to a uniquely Italian experience. To join in, simply hit the streets for a bit of wandering. You may feel more like an observer than a participant, until you realize that observation is what la passeggiata is all about.

MAKING THE MOST OF YOUR EUROS

Transportation

Italy's state-sponsored train system has been given a run for its money by a private competitor. Sadly, the competitor (Italo) competes only on major, high-speed connections (such as Rome to Naples, Florence to Venice, Milan to Bologna) and not on the local routes. Because of this competition, Trenitalia and Italo engage in price wars—which only plays to the consumer's advantage. Depending on time of day and how far in advance you purchase the tickets, great bargains can be had.

No such good news exists for the *regionali* trains. These are trains connecting cities, highly frequented by commuters, and used often by visitors who want to get to less-visible towns. These trains are habitually late, frequently cancelled, and almost always crowded. Patience is a virtue, and much needed when taking them, particularly during high season.

Food and Drink

Always remember, when you enter a bar, that there is almost always a two-tier pricing system: one if you stand, and one if you sit. It's always cheaper to stand, but sometimes sitting is not only necessary, but fun: you can relax and watch the world go by. Italians love a good sandwich for lunch. Seek out popular sandwich shops (long lines signify that the place is worth visiting) or go to a *salumeria* (delicatessen) and have them make a sandwich for you. It will be simple—cheese and/or cold cuts with bread, no trimmings—but it will be made while you wait: fresh, delicious, and inexpensive.

Sights

There's plenty of free wonderful stuff to see. Visit the Musei Vaticani, the Uffizi, and the Accademia in Florence (book ahead whenever possible), but don't forget that many artistic gems are found in churches, most of which are free (some of Caravaggio's best work can be found in various churches in Rome). Also consider renting audio guides if you want direction to any specific place; if you find the idea of joining an organized tour daunting, most museums sell official guidebooks that can help you target what to see. Walking in *centri storici* (historic centers) is also a joy, and free. Seek out piazzas, climb towers, and look for views.

Lodging

High season in Italy runs from Easter to mid-October. If you want to have Florence practically to yourself, come in November or February (most Italian cities are very crowded during the Christmas holidays, which begin around Christmas, and finish on January 6). Many hotels in cities offer bargain rates in July and August because most people are off to the beach or to the mountains. Remember to factor in great heat and massive crowds, along with the money you'll save. If you decide to travel then, ensure that you either had access to a pool and/or air-conditioning.

A great budget-conscious way to travel is via Airbnb (⊕ *www.airbnb.com*). You can sleep on someone's couch, rent a private room in an apartment (sometimes with en-suite bathroom), or rent an entire apartment or house. One of the best things about Airbnb is that many of these accommodations come with refrigerators and kitchens, which means you don't have to spend all your money eating out.

In general, book sooner rather than later. You'll often find better deals that way.

A GREAT ITINERARY

VENICE, FLORENCE, ROME, AND HIGHLIGHTS IN BETWEEN

This itinerary is designed for maximum impact. Think of it as a rough draft for you to revise according to your own interests and time constraints.

Day 1: Venice

Arrive in Venice's Marco Polo Airport (there are direct flights from the United States), hop on the bus into the main bus station in Venice, then check into your hotel, get out, and get lost in the back canals for a couple of hours before dinner. If you enjoy fish, you should indulge yourself at a traditional Venetian restaurant. There's no better place for sweet, delicate Adriatic seafood.

Logistics: At the airport, avoid the Alilaguna boat into Venice on arrival. It's expensive, slow, and singularly unromantic. The bus is quick and cheap—save the romance for later. When you get to the main station, transfer to the most delightful main-street "bus" in the world: the *vaporetto* ferry. Enjoy your first ride up the Grand Canal, and make sure you're paying attention to the *fermata* (or stop) where you need to get off. As for water taxis from the airport to the city, they're very expensive, although they'll take you directly to your hotel.

Day 2: Venice

Begin by skipping the coffee at your hotel and have a real Italian coffee at a real Italian coffee shop. Spend the day at Venice's top sights, including the Basilica di San Marco, Palazzo Ducale, and Galleria dell'Accademia; don't forget Piazza San Marco, which is probably the densest concentration of major artistic and cultural monuments in the world. The intense anticipation as you near the giant square through a maze of tiny shop-lined alleys and streets climaxes in the stunning view of the piazza (return at 7 am the next morning to see it *senza popolo* [without people], when it will look like a Canaletto painting come alive). Stop for lunch, perhaps sampling Venice's traditional specialty, *sarde in saor* (sardines in a mouthwatering sweet-and-sour preparation that includes onions and raisins), and be sure to check out the fish market at the foot of the Rialto Bridge; then sunset at the Zattere before dinner. Later, stop at one of the bars around the Campo San Luca or Campo Santa Margarita, where you can toast to being free of automobiles.

Logistics: Venice is best seen by wandering. The day's activities can be done on foot, with the occasional vaporetto ride if you feel the urge to be on the water. Never leave your lodgings without a city map: Venice is very easy to get totally lost in.

Day 3: Ferrara/Bologna

Get an early start and leave Venice on a Bologna-bound train. The ride to Ferrara, your first stop in Emilia-Romagna, is about an hour and a half. Visit the Castello Estense and Duomo before grabbing lunch. A panino and a beer at one of Ferrara's cafés should fit the bill. Wander Ferrara's cobblestone streets, then hop on the train to Bologna (a ride of less than an hour). Once you've arrived, check into your hotel and walk around Piazza Maggiore before dinner. Later you can check out some of northern Italy's best nightlife.

Logistics: In Ferrara, the train station lies a bit outside the city center, so you may want to take a taxi or a less-expensive city bus into town (though the distance is easily walkable, too). Going out, there's a taxi stand near the back of the castle, toward Corso Ercole I d'Este. In Bologna the walk into town from the station is more manageable, particularly if you're staying along Via dell'Indipendenza.

Day 4: Bologna/Florence

After breakfast, check out some of Bologna's churches and piazzas, including a climb up the leaning Torre degli Asinelli for a red-rooftop-studded panorama. After lunch, head back to the train station and take the short ride to Florence. You'll arrive in time for an afternoon siesta and an evening passeggiata.

Logistics: Florence's Santa Maria Novella train station is within easy access to some hotels, and farther from others. Florence's traffic is legendary, but taxis at the station are plentiful. (The taxi stand is just outside the station.)

Day 5: Florence

This is your day to see the sights of Florence. Start with the Uffizi Gallery (reserve your tickets in advance), where you'll see Botticelli's *Primavera* and *Birth of Venus*. Next, walk to Piazza del Duomo, the site of Brunelleschi's spectacular dome, which you can climb for an equally spectacular view. By the time you descend, you'll be more than ready for a simple trattoria lunch. Depending on your preferences, either devote the afternoon to art or hike up to Piazzale Michelangelo, overlooking the city. Either way, finish the evening in style with a traditional *bistecca alla fiorentina* (grilled T-bone steak with olive oil).

Day 6: Lucca/Pisa

After breakfast, board a train for Lucca. It's an easy 1½-hour trip to see this walled medieval city. Don't miss the Romanesque Duomo, or a walk along the city's ramparts. Have lunch at a trattoria before continuing on to Pisa, where you'll spend

TIPS

■ The itinerary can also be completed by car on the modern *autostrade* (four-lane highway system), although you'll run into dicey traffic in Florence and Rome. For obvious reasons, you're best off waiting to pick up your car until Day 3, when you leave Venice.

■ When it comes to trains, aim for the reservations-only Eurostar Italia or the relative newcomer to the scene, Italo.

■ The sights along this route are highly touristed; you'll have a better time if you make the trip outside the busy months of June, July, and August.

an afternoon seeing—what else?—the Leaning Tower, along with the equally impressive Duomo and Battistero. Walk down to the banks of the Arno River, contemplate the majestic views at sunset, and have dinner at one of the many inexpensive local restaurants in the real city center—a bit removed from the most touristy spots.

Logistics: Lucca's train station lies just outside the walled city—it's a very easy walk. Pisa's train station isn't far from the city center, although it is on the other side of town from the Campo dei Miracoli (site of the Leaning Tower). Since Lucca and Pisa are only 15 minutes apart by train, you may want to return from Pisa to spend the night in more-charming Lucca.

Day 7: Orvieto/Rome

Three hours south of Pisa is Orvieto, one of the prettiest and most characteristic towns of the Umbria region, conveniently situated right on the Florence–Rome train line. Check out the memorable cathedral before a light lunch accompanied by one

of Orvieto's famous white wines. Get back on a train bound for Rome, and in a little more than an hour you'll arrive in the Eternal City in time to make your way to your hotel and relax for a bit before you head out for the evening. When you do, check out Piazza Navona, Campo de' Fiori, and the Trevi Fountain—it's best in the evening—and have a stand-up *aperitivo* (Campari and soda is a classic) at an unpretentious local bar before dinner. It's finally pizza time; you can't go wrong at any of Rome's popular local pizzerias.

Logistics: To get from Pisa to Orvieto, you'll first catch a train to Florence and then get on a Rome-bound train from here. Be careful at Rome's Termini train station, a breeding ground for pickpockets. Keep your possessions close, and only get into a licensed taxi.

Day 8: Rome

Rome took millennia to build, but on this whirlwind trip you'll only have a day and a half to see it. In the morning, head to the Vatican Museums to see Michelangelo's glorious frescoes at the Sistine Chapel. See St. Peter's Basilica and Square before heading back into Rome proper for lunch around the Pantheon, followed by a coffee from one of Rome's famous coffee shops. Next, visit ancient Rome: first see the magnificent Pantheon, and then head across to the Colosseum, stopping along the way along Via dei Fori Imperiali to check out the Roman Forum from above. From the Colosseum, walk or take a taxi to Piazza di Spagna, a good place to see the sunset and shop at stylish boutiques. Taxi to Piazza Trilussa at the entrance of Trastevere, a beautiful old working-class neighborhood where you'll have a relaxing dinner.

Day 9: Rome/Departure

Head by taxi to Termini station and catch the train to the Fiumicino airport.

Logistics: The train from Termini station to the airport is fast, and easy—for most people, it's preferable to an exorbitantly priced taxi ride that, in bad traffic, can take twice as long and cost much, much more.

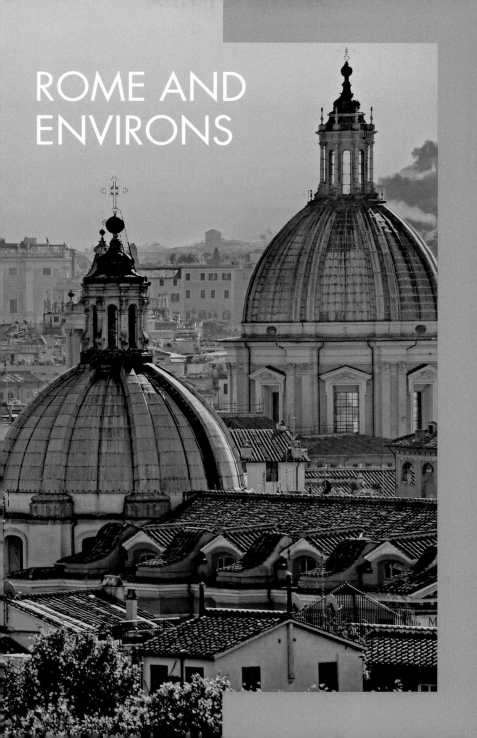

ROME AND ENVIRONS

WHAT'S WHERE

1 Ancient Rome. Backed by the most stupendous monument of ancient Rome—the Colosseum—the Roman Forum and Palatine Hill were once the hub of Western civilization.

2 Piazza Navona and Campo de' Fiori. The *cuore*, or heart, of the *centro storico* (historic quarter), revolves around the Pantheon, the Campo de' Fiori, and the Piazza Navona.

3 The Jewish Ghetto. Once a Jewish quarter, the gentrified Ghetto still preserves the flavor of Old Rome.

4 Piazza di Spagna. Travel back to the days of the Grand Tour in this glamorous area. After people-watching at the Spanish Steps, shop along Via dei Condotti, then be sure to throw a coin in the Trevi Fountain.

5 Repubblica and Quirinale. A largely 19th-century district, Repubblica lets art lovers "go for Baroque" with a bevy of Bernini works, including his *Ecstasy of St. Theresa* at Santa Maria della Vittoria. To the south looms the Palazzo Quirinale, Italy's presidential palace.

6 Villa Borghese and Piazza del Popolo. Rome's most famous park is home to playful fountains, sculptured gardens, and the treasure-packed Galleria Borghese. Piazza del Popolo—a beautiful place to watch the world go by—lies south.

7 The Vatican. The Vatican draws millions of pilgrims and art lovers to St. Peter's Basilica, the Vatican Museums, and the Sistine Chapel.

8 Trastevere. Rome's left bank has kept its authentic roots thanks to mom-and-pop trattorias, medieval alleyways, and Santa Maria in Trastevere, stunningly spotlighted at night. Nearby is the Isola Tiberina (Tiber Island), so picturesque it will click your camera for you.

9 The Catacombs and the Via Appia Antica. Follow in the footsteps of St. Peter to this district, home to the spirit-warm catacombs and the Tomb of Cecilia Metella.

10 Monti, Esquilino, and San Lorenzo. Near Termini station, these are some of Rome's least touristy neighborhoods, with plenty of trattorias.

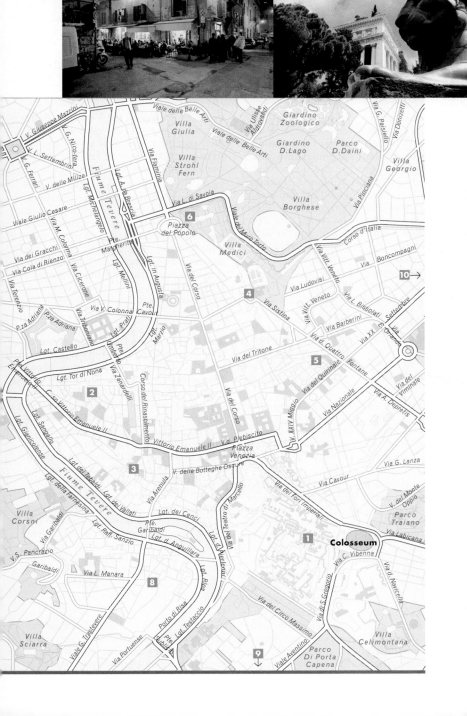

Villa Giulia

Viale delle Belle Arti

Viale delle Belle Arti

Villa Strohl Fern

Giardino Zoologico

Giardino D.Lago

Parco D.Daini

Villa Georgio

V. Giuseppe Mazzini

V. G. Nicotera

V. G. Ferrari

V. L. Settembrini

Fiume Tevere

Lgt. Michelangelo

Via A. da Brescia

Via Flaminia

V. delle Milize

Viale Giulio Cesare

Via M. Colonna

Via del Gracchi

Via Cola di Rienzo

Via Cicerone

Via Terenzio

Lgt. Mellini

Lgt. in Augusta

Pte. Margherita

Piazza del Popolo **6**

Via del Corso

Villa Medici

Villa Borghese

Viale del Muro Torto

Via L. di Savoia

Corso d'Italia

Via Boncompagni

Via Vitt. Venelo

Corso d'Italia

Via.

10 →

P.za Adriana

Pza Adriana

Via V. Colonna

Via Triboniano

Pte. Cavour

Via Mazzini

Lgt. Prati

Lgt. Umberto

Via Zanardelli

Pte. Umberto

Lgt. Castello

Lgt. Tor di Nona

4

Via Sistina

Via Ludovisi

Viale Vitt. Veneto

Via Vitt. Veneto

Via L. Bissolati

Via Barberini

Via XX Settembre

Via del Tritone

Via d. Quattro Fontane

5

Via del Quirinale

Via XXIV Maggio

Via Nazionale

Via del Viminale

Via A. Depretis

Piazzale Vitt.rio E. Emanuele

Lgt. C.so Vittorio Emanuele II

Corso del Rinascimento

2

Via del Corso

Vittorio Emanuele II

V.d. Plebiscito

Piazza Venezia

Lgt. Sangallo

Lgt. Gianicolense

Fiume Tevere

Lgt. dei Tebaldi

Lgt. dei Vallati

Via Arenula

V. delle Botteghe Oscure

3

Via G. Lanza

Via Cavour

Villa Corsni

Lgt. della Farnesina

Lgt. Raff. Sanzio

Lgt. dei Cenci

Pte. Garibaldi

Lgt. d. Anguillara

Via del Teatro d'Marcello

Via d. Marcello

Via dei Fori Imperiali

1 **Colosseum**

V. del Monte Oppio

Parco Traiano

Via Labicana

Via d. Navicella

Via Garibaldi

V. S. Pancrazio

Garibaldi

Via L. Manara

8

Via G. Trastevere

Porto di Risa

Lgt. Testaccio

Pte. Sublicio

Via Portuense

Via del Circo Massimo

Viale Aventino

Via di S. Gregorio

Via C. Vibenna

Parco Di Porta Capena

9 ↓

Villa Sciarra

Villa Celimontana

PLANNER

Fortunately for tourists, many of Rome's main attractions are concentrated in the *centro storico* (historic center) and can be covered on foot. Some sights that lie nearer the border of this quarter can be reached via the Metro Line A, nicknamed the *"linea rossa"* (red line) and include: the Spanish Steps (Spagna stop), the Trevi Fountain (Barberini stop), St. Peter's Square (Ottaviano stop), and the Vatican Museums (Ottaviano or Cipro–Musei Vaticani stop), to name a few.

Tickets for the bus, tram, and Metro can be purchased at many *tabacchi* (tobacco shops), at some newsstands, and from machines inside Metro stations. These tickets are good for 100 minutes for a single Metro ride and on any number of buses and trams. Day passes can be purchased for €4, and weekly passes, which allow unlimited use of buses, trams, and the Metro, for €16.

For a fuller explanation of Metro routes, pick up a free map from a tourist information booth or log on to the website of Rome's public transportation system, the ATAC (⊕ *www.atac.roma.it*).

Making the Most of Your Time

"Roma, non basta una vita" ("Rome, a lifetime is not enough"). This famous saying should be stamped on the passport of every first-time visitor to the Eternal City. On the one hand, it's a warning: Rome is so packed with sights that it's impossible to take them all in; it's easy to run yourself ragged trying to check off the items on your "bucket list." On the other hand, the saying is a celebration of the city's abundance. There's so much here, you're bound to make discoveries you hadn't anticipated. To conquer Rome, strike a balance between visits to major sights and leisurely neighborhood strolls.

In the first category, the Vatican and the remains of ancient Rome loom the largest. Both require at least half a day; a good strategy is to devote your first morning to one and your second to the other.

Leave the afternoons for exploring the neighborhoods that comprise "Baroque Rome" and the shopping district around the Spanish Steps and Via Condotti. If you have more days at your disposal, continue with the same approach. Among the sights, Galleria Borghese and the multilayered church of San Clemente are particularly worthwhile, and the neighborhoods of Trastevere and the Ghetto make for great roaming.

Great Savings

There's a lot of ground to cover in Rome, so it's wise to plan your busy sightseeing schedule with possible savings in mind. Purchasing the Roma Pass (⊕ *www. romapass.it*) can allow you to do just that, depending on your plans. The three-day pass costs €36 and is good for unlimited use of buses, trams, and the metro (like the three-day public transportation pass). It adds free admission to two of more than 40 participating museums or archaeological sites, including the Colosseum (bumping you to the head of the long line there), plus discounted tickets to many other museums. As they're not Rome museums per se, it's worth noting that Vatican museums are not included. The Roma Pass can be purchased at tourist information booths across the city, at Termini Station, at Fiumicino Airport, or online at the Roma Pass website.

When to Go

Not surprisingly, spring and fall are the best times to visit, with mild temperatures and many sunny days; the famous Roman sunsets are also at their best. Summers

are often sweltering. In July and August, learn to do as the Romans do—get up and out early, seek refuge from the afternoon heat, resume activities in early evening, and stay up late to enjoy the nighttime breeze. Come August, many shops and restaurants close as locals head out for vacation. Remember that air-conditioning, though increasingly available, is still not ubiquitous in this city. Roman winters are relatively mild, with persistent rainy spells.

Hop-On, Hop-Off

Rome has its own "hop-on, hop-off" sightseeing buses. The Rome Open Tour bus operates from the front of Termini Station every 20 to 25 minutes, taking in St. Mary Major, the Colosseum, Piazza Venezia, St. Peter's, Castel Sant'Angelo, the Trevi Fountain and Via Veneto. Commentaries in eight languages are available. The first departure from Termini is at 9 am and the last at 5 pm. A ticket valid for 24 hours costs €18. For more, see ⊕ *www. romeopentour.it.*

Roman Hours

Much of the city shuts down on Sunday, although civic museums and many restaurants are closed Monday. Most stores in the centro storico, the part of town that caters to tourists, remain open. Shop hours generally run from 10 am to 1 pm, then reopen around 3 pm until 7 or 7:30 pm. Unless advertised as having *orario continuato* (open all day), most businesses close from 1 to 3. On Monday, shops usually don't open until around 3 or 4 pm. Pharmacies tend to have the same hours of operation as stores unless they advertise *orario notturno* (night hours); two can be found on Corso Rinascimento and Piazza dei Cinquecento (near Termini Station). As for churches, most open at 8 or 9

in the morning, close from 12:30 to 3 or 4, then reopen until 6:30 or 7. St. Peter's, however, is open 7 to 7 (until 6:30 October to March).

Information, Please

Rome's main Tourist Information Office is at Via Leopardi 24 (☎ *06/0608*), near Piazza Vittorio.

Green information kiosks with multilingual personnel are located near the most important sights and squares, as well as at Termini Station and Leonardo da Vinci Airport. These kiosks, called Tourist Information Sites (Punti Informativi Turistici, or PIT) can be found at:

PIT Castel S. Angelo, Piazza Pia; open 9:30–7

PIT Ciampino, Aeroporto Ciampino, Arrivi Internazionali Baggage Claim; open 9–6:30

PIT Fiumicino, Aeroporto Leonardo da Vinci, Arrivi Internazionali Terminal C; open 9–7:30

PIT Minghetti, Via Marco Minghetti (corner of Via del Corso); open 9:30–7

PIT Navona, Piazza delle Cinque Lune (north end of Piazza Navona); open 9:30–7

PIT Nazionale, Via Nazionale (Palazzo delle Esposizioni); open 9:30–7

PIT Santa Maria Maggiore, at Via dell'Olmata; open 9:30–7

PIT Termini, Stazione Termini, at Via Giovanni Giolitti 34; open 8–8

PIT Trastevere, on Piazza Sidney Sonnino; open 9:30–7

ROME
TOP ATTRACTIONS

The Pantheon

Reputedly constructed to honor all pagan gods, the best-preserved building of ancient Rome was rebuilt in the 2nd century AD by Emperor Hadrian. The vast dome of perfect dimensions (142 feet high by 142 feet wide) was the largest freestanding dome until the 20th century.

The Vatican

Though its population numbers are just shy of a thousand, the Vatican—home base for the Catholic Church and the pope—has millions of visitors each year. Savor Michelangelo's Sistine Ceiling, attend Papal Mass, and marvel at St. Peter's Basilica, embraced by the colonnades of St. Peter's Square.

The Colosseum

(A) Legend has it that as long as the Colosseum stands, Rome will stand; and when Rome falls, so will the world. One of the "new" seven wonders of the world, the mammoth amphitheater was begun by Emperor Vespasian and inaugurated by the next emperor, his son Titus, in year AD 80. For "the grandeur that was Rome," this yardstick of eternity can't be topped.

Piazza Navona

(B) You couldn't concoct a more Roman street scene: cafés and crowded tables at street level, coral- and rust-color houses above, most lined with wrought-iron balconies, and at the center of this urban "living room" Bernini's spectacular Fountain of the Four Rivers and Borromini's supertheatrical Sant'Agnese.

Roman Forum

(C) Set between the Capitoline and Palatine hills, this fabled labyrinth of ruins variously served as a political playground, a commerce mart, and a place where justice was dispensed during the days of the Republic and Empire (509 BC to AD 476). Once adorned with stately buildings, triumphal arches, and impressive

temples, the Forum today is a silent ruin: *sic transit gloria mundi* ("so passes away the glory of the world").

The Campidoglio

(D) Catch an emperor's-eye view of the Roman Forum from beside Michelangelo's Palazzo Senatorio, situated atop one of the highest spots in Rome, the Capitoline Hill. Next door you'll find the Vittoriano, the Capitoline Museums, and beloved Santa Maria in Aracoeli.

Trevi Fountain

(E) One of the few fountains in Rome that's actually more absorbing than the people crowding around it, the Fontana di Trevi was designed by Nicola Salvi in 1732. Immortalized in *Three Coins in a Fountain* and *La Dolce Vita*, this fountain may be your ticket back to Rome—that is, if you throw a coin into it.

The Spanish Steps

(F) Byron, Shelley, and Keats all drew inspiration from this magnificent "Scalinata," constructed in 1723. Connecting the shops at the bottom with the hotels at the top, this is the place for prime people-watching. The steps face beautiful sunsets.

Galleria Borghese

(G) Only the best could satisfy the aesthetic taste of Cardinal Scipione Borghese, and that means famed Bernini sculptures, great paintings by Titian and Raphael, and the most spectacular 17th-century palace in Rome.

Trastevere

Just across the Tiber River, this charming neighborhood is a maze of jumbled alleyways, cobblestone streets, and medieval houses. The area also boasts one of the oldest churches of Rome, Santa Maria in Trastevere.

TOP ROME EXPERIENCES

Say "Cheese," Spartacus

Taking a photo with one of those ersatz gladiators in front of Rome's ancient sights will win some smiles and give your eight-year-old a great souvenir to show off at home. Some of these Russell Crowe lookalikes have helmets and cloaks for tourists to try on and a sword to brandish to complete the picture. Remember to fix the "photo fee" beforehand. It shouldn't be more than €5. These Spartacus characters are not authorized to pose for shots, but police tolerate them because tourists like them. You'll find them around the Forum, Colosseum, and along Via dei Fori Imperiali. A few venture as far as the Trevi Fountain and Piazza Navona.

A Whole World Underground

From opulent villas to Mithraic temples, an entire ancient world lies beneath ground-level Rome. No, it's not because ancient Romans had a penchant for the subterranean. It's because, two millennia ago, the ground level stood 30 to 40 feet lower than it does today.

As a result, every time someone goes to dig a hole in Rome, they get a surprise. That's been a source of both pride and frustration, as most recently seen with the ongoing project for Line C. Rome's third Metro line is supposed to go through the heart of the centro storico—but several subway stops have had to be scrapped when workers hit (surprise!) ancient ruins. Most famously, a desired stop at Piazza Venezia had to come to a halt when workers discovered ruins of an ancient auditorium built by Emperor Hadrian in the 2nd century AD.

For a great glimpse of how modern Rome sits atop the ancient, book a tour at Palazzo Valentini, just around the corner from that doomed Piazza Venezia stop.

In 2007, excavations beneath the 16th-century Palazzo Valentini—today the seat of the Province of Rome—turned up ruins of two 2nd- and 3rd-century villas. On an automated tour experience beneath the Renaissance palazzo, visitors are brought through the opulent rooms and, with light shows, shown how they once would have looked—all without ever emerging aboveground.

Through a Keyhole

Head to the Aventine hill, just across the Circus Maximus from the Palatine, for a quirky surprise. The Order of the Knights of Malta, the only private entity to also be a sovereign state, has its headquarters here. Although the building is closed to the public unless you're on a prebooked tour, its most charming facet is open to anyone: the keyhole. Peek through for a perfectly framed view of the dome of St. Peter's Basilica—and the chance to see three countries (Vatican City, Italy, and the Order of the Knights of Malta) in one glance.

Lights, Camera, Action!

The Festival Internazionale del Cinema di Roma (Rome International Film Festival; ⊕ *www.romacinemafest.it*), founded in 2006, has hosted the likes of Martin Scorsese, Robert De Niro, Meryl Streep, and Scarlett Johansson. Though Rome is far from reclaiming the long-lost glories of the Cinecittà studios where Fellini and others turned out movie masterpieces, the festival draws important players in the world of film and sees its share of world premieres. The festival is held at the Auditorium Parco della Musica during a full week in the fall.

Three Coins in the Fountain

Rome has always been in love with *amore*. But romance is certainly nowhere more contagious than around its famous fountains. If a besotted couple can spare the time, a trip up to Tivoli's Villa D'Este (an hour outside Rome via bus) is nirvana. Its seductive garden and endless array of fountains (about 500 of them) provide the perfect setting to put anyone in the mood for love.

That's your cue to return to Rome and make a beeline for the luminous Trevi Fountain, even more enchanting at night than in the daytime. Make sure you and that special someone throw your coins into the fountain for good luck. Legend has it that those who do so are guaranteed a trip back to Rome.

L'Aperitivo

Borrowed from *i Milanesi*, the trend of *l'aperitivo* has become *moda* in Rome. Not to be confused with happy hour, l'aperitivo is not about discounts or heavy drinking, but rather a time to meet up with friends and colleagues after work or on weekends—definitely an event in which to see and be seen. Aperitivo hours are usually from 7 to 9 pm.

Depending on where you go, the price of a drink often includes an all-you-can-eat appetizer buffet of finger foods, sandwiches, and pasta salads. Some aperitivo hot spots on the *trendissimo* list are Enoteca Palatium (Via Frattina) near the Piazza di Spagna; L'Angolo Divino (Via del Balestrari) near the Campo de' Fiori; Freni e Frizioni (Via del Politeama) in Trastevere; and the 5th Floor Terrace at Il Palazzetto, set on a magical balcony right over the Spanish Steps.

Rome's Coolest Artisans

Despite the encroachment of chain stores and big brands, many of Rome's finest artisans are still hanging on—barely. Locals hope the artisans will be able to withstand globalization's assault, because they still produce some of the finest (and best-value!) handmade clothes, shoes, leather goods, and more, in the city. Top-notch artisans can be found in neighborhoods like Trastevere and Via del Governo Vecchio, near Campo dei Fiori, as well as in many side streets off the Corso. For a glimpse of how tradition and trend can combine, wander through Monti, a neighborhood chockablock with young jewelers, fashion designers, and artists, many of whom use traditional artisanal techniques (and often handcraft their products right in the store)—but with an eye toward contemporary style.

Walk Like a Roman

Rome was made for wandering, with relentlessly picturesque streets and alleyways, leading you past monuments, down narrow *vicoli*, through ancient Roman arches, and into hidden piazzas. A stroll is the best way to become attuned to the city's rhythm and, no matter how aimlessly you wander, chances are you'll end up somewhere magical.

The best walking tours in Rome are given by Context (⊕ *www.contexttravel.com*). Also getting rave reviews from the public and media are the truly wonderful walking tours offered by Through Eternity (⊕ *www.througheternity.com*).

GETTING HERE AND AROUND

Getting Here by Air

Rome's principal airport is Leonardo da Vinci Airport (☎ 06/65951 ⊕ www.adr. it), commonly known by the name of its location, Fiumicino (FCO). It's 30 km (19 miles) southwest of the city but has a direct train link with downtown Rome. Rome's other airport, with no direct train link, is Ciampino (☎ 06/65951 ⊕ www. adr.it) or CIA, 15 km (9 miles) south of downtown and used mostly by low-cost airlines.

Two trains link downtown Rome with Fiumicino. Inquire at the PIT counter in the International Arrivals hall (Terminal 2) or at the train information counter near the tracks to determine which takes you closest to your destination in Rome. The 30-minute nonstop Airport–Termini line (called the "Leonardo Express") goes directly to Termini Station, Rome's main train station; tickets cost €14. The FM1 train stops in Trastevere and Ostiense. Always stamp your tickets in the little machines near the track before you board. As for Ciampino, COTRAL buses connect to trains that go to the city and Terravision (☎ 06/97610632 ⊕ www.terravision. eu) buses link the airport to Termini Station for €4 each way. Taxi transport to and from Fiumicino carries a flat fee of €48; to and from Ciampino is €30. The price includes all luggage.

Getting Here by Bus

Bus lines cover Rome's surrounding Lazio region and are operated by the Consorzio Trasporti Lazio, or COTRAL (☎ 800/174471 ⊕ www.cotralspa.it). These bus routes terminate either near Tiburtina Station or at outlying Metro stops, such as Laurentina and Ponte Mammolo (Line B) and Anagnina (Line A). COTRAL buses are good options for

short day trips from Rome, such as those that leave daily from Rome's Ponte Mammolo Metro station (Line B) for the town of Tivoli, where Hadrian's villa and Villa D'Este await.

Getting Here by Car

The main access route from the north is the A1 (Autostrada del Sole) from Milan and Florence. The same A1 continues south to Naples and beyond. All roads in and out of the city connect with the Grande Raccordo Anulare (GRA) ring road, which channels traffic into the city center. For driving directions, check out ⊕ www.autostrade.it and ⊕ www. tuttocitta.it. Note: parking in Rome can be a nightmare—private cars are not allowed access to the centro storico weekdays 6:30 am–8 pm and Saturday 2 pm–6 pm, except for residents. Contact your hotel to ask about parking facilities.

Getting Here by Train

State-owned Trenitalia (☎ 892021 in Italy, 06/68475475 abroad ⊕ www. trenitalia.it) trains also serve some destinations on side trips outside Rome. The main Trenitalia stations in Rome are Termini, Tiburtina, Ostiense, and Trastevere. On long-distance routes (to Florence and Naples, for instance) you can either travel on the cheap but slow regionali trains, or on the fast but more expensive Intercity, Eurostar Alta Velocità. The state railways' website is user-friendly. The privately run Italo high-speed train (⊕ www.italotreno. it) has two lines serving Rome. The Turin–Salerno line stops in Bologna, Florence, Rome, Naples, and Salerno, and the Venice–Napoli line serves Padova, Bologna, Florence, and Rome.

Getting Around by Bus and Tram

ATAC city buses and trams are orange, gray and red, or blue and orange. Remember to board at the front or rear and to exit at the middle; in most cases, you must buy your ticket before boarding, and always stamp it in a machine as soon as you enter. The ticket is good for a single Metro ride and unlimited buses and trams within the next 100 minutes.

ATAC has a website (⊕ *www.atac.roma. it*) that will help you calculate the number of stops and bus routes needed.

Getting Around by Metropolitana

The Metropolitana (or Metro) is the easiest and fastest way to get around Rome. Street entrances are marked with red and white "M" signs.

The Metro Line A, known as the "*linea rossa,*" will take you to a chunk of the main attractions in Rome: Piazza di Spagna (Spagna stop), Piazza del Popolo (Flaminio), St. Peter's Square (Ottaviano–San Pietro), the Vatican Museums (both Ottaviano and Cipro–Musei Vaticani), and the Trevi Fountain (Barberini).

Line B ("*linea blu*") will take you to the Colosseum (Colosseo stop), Circus Maximus and Aventino (Circo Massimo stop), the Pyramid (Piramide stop for Testaccio, Ostiense Station, and trains for Ostia Antica), and Basilica di San Paolo Fuori le Mura (San Paolo stop). The two lines intersect at Rome's main station, Termini.

Getting Around by Public Transportation

Rome's integrated transportation system is ATAC (☎ *06/57003, 06/46951, or 800/431784* ⊕ *www.atac.roma.it*), which includes the Metropolitana subway, city buses, and municipal trams. A ticket (BIT) valid for 100 minutes on any combination of buses and trams and one entrance to the Metro costs €1.50. Day-long *giornaliero* passes are €6, three-day passes are €16.50, and weekly passes are €24.

Tickets (singly or in quantity—it's a good idea to keep a few tickets handy so you don't have to hunt for a vendor) are sold at tobacconists, newsstands, some coffee bars, ticket machines in Metro stations, some bus stops, and ATAC ticket booths. Some buses also have ticket machines onboard.

Time-stamp tickets at Metro turnstiles and in little yellow machines on buses and trams when boarding the first vehicle. The expiration date and time will be printed on the reverse side of the ticket.

Getting Around by Scooter

As bikes are to Beijing, so scooters are to Rome; they're everywhere. Riders are required to wear helmets. You can rent a scooter at Bici & Baci (✉ *Via del Viminale 5* ☎ *06/48986162* ⊕ *www.bicibaci.com*) from between €7 to €15 per hour, €32 to €65 per day, according to the model. A bike rental costs €12.50 per day.

Getting Around by Taxi

Taxis in Rome do not cruise, but if free they'll stop if you flag them down. They wait at stands, but can also be called by phone (☎ *0609, 06/5551, 06/6645, 06/3570, 06/4994, or 06/0609*). You will be asked to give an address when you phone. If you are on the street, give the street number of the nearest building.

Always ask for a receipt (*ricevuta*) to make sure the driver charges you the correct amount, and ensure the driver is running the meter (unless you're coming from the airport, when it's the flat fare). Use only licensed cabs with a plaque next to the license plate reading "*Servizio Pubblico.*"

ROME
TODAY

Multiculturalism

Spend a day in Rome's Esquilino neighborhood and you'll see just how multicultural the Eternal City is becoming. Once famous for its spice market at Piazza Vittorio, the neighborhood has fast become a multiethnic stomping ground.

In fact, finding a true Roman restaurant or a local shopkeeper is hard to come by in this area, now that Chinese, Indian, African, and Middle Eastern restaurants have moved in (a typical example: the Syrian restaurant Zenobia, perched on Piazza Dante, even includes a weekend belly-dancing show).

Homegrown and locally produced, the Orchestra di Piazza Vittorio, founded in 2002, is a perfect picture of the neighborhood's growing ethnic population.

The multiethnic troupe got its start in the ramshackle district just steps away from Rome's Termini train station and has gone on from strength to strength. Their repertoire includes a highly acclaimed version of Mozart's *Magic Flute* and their *Carmen* won accolades when it was performed in the summer at Rome's Baths of Caracalla.

Breaking New Ground

With a big push to modernize those parts of Rome particularly lacking in the luster department, visitors will notice some new and novel aspects to the city. First, that former eyesore, the Tiburtina train station, was completely overhauled, to the tune of some €330 million, to become the new avant-garde Tiburtina Stazione, the first rail hub in Italy to handle superhigh-speed (Alstom AGVs) trains.

The opening of 15 stations on the new Metro Line C took Romans by surprise. It has been in the pipeline for nearly 20 years, and many people believed it would never be finished, due to endless problems and hold-ups caused by galloping expenses and unexpected archaeological finds. For now, brand spanking new trains run from the town of Montecompatri in the Castelli Romani to the suburb of Centocelle. Additionally, if all goes well, the line will be connected to St. John Lateran some time in 2016 and then to the Colosseum, creating a link with both the existing A and B lines. Romans hope this new facility will ease the city's chronic traffic problems.

The Domus Aurea, Nero's Golden House beside the Colosseum, was closed in 2006

CREATING NEW "IT" NEIGHBORHOODS

The leader among Rome's "It" neighborhoods is Pigneto, the working-class area once immortalized as the backdrop for Roberto Rossellini's magnificent Academy Award–nominated *Roma Città Aperta* (*Rome, Open City*).

Set in the northwestern part of the city on the other side of the Porta Maggiore walls, Pigneto has come a long way since the black-and-white days of the 1950s. This hot new *quartiere* has undergone a major transformation into a colorful hub for hipsters who

tuck into the many wine bars and bookshops along main drags like Fanfulla da Lodi and Via del Pigneto.

To channel the days when legends Pier Paolo Pasolini and Luchino Visconti spent time filming here, enjoy an aperitivo at the historic Bar Necci (Via

for safety reasons. During the last five years, it has been treated to a €31 million restoration program involving reinforcing the structure, dealing with water infiltration, lightening the weight of the soil that covers the roof and protecting the remaining grotesque decorations that inspired Raphael. Although no one can predict exactly when in 2016 restoration will finally be finished, guided tours upon prior booking can be arranged. (☎ 06/39967700)

Political Limbo

The winds of change have been blowing through the Italy since 2014, bringing a new pope, a new President of the Republic and Matteo Renzi, a new dynamic Prime Minister. With Silvio Berlusconi banned from public office due to tax evasion and other offences, and his party, Forza Italia, in sharp decline, Renzi's PD (Democratic Party of the Left) has had a relatively clear run. Italian politics, however, never move fast and many of the sweeping reforms that Renzi vows to implement have had a slow and difficult start. Attempts to stir up the sluggish labor market and the drowsy and outmoded civil service sector have run up against fierce opposition from Italy's powerful trade unions.

Renzi has also had to cope with dissidence within his own party. In spite of his critics, Renzi forges ahead, making abundant use of the media and web to put his ideas across. This tenacity has won him grudging respect from the notoriously cynical Italian electorate.

Since not even politics can be dreary in Italy, the scene has been livened up by a new movement called Cinque Stelle (Five Stars), founded by the comedian Beppe Grillo. It follows a policy of unconstructive opposition, expressed largely in strings of curses and oaths and broadcast over the web. Initially, Grillo gathered considerable support from Italians disillusioned by the traditional Right and Left Wing parties, but his movement now shows signs of running out of steam.

On the positive side, the new Italian government appears to be making a serious effort to combat organized crime and has already scored some spectacular successes by rounding up some of the most notorious bosses and confiscating their property.

Fanfulla da Lodi 68), where Pasolini once filmed scenes for his 1961 *Accatone* (an award-winning depiction of how a pimp living in the slums of Rome attempts to go straight).

Another young neighborhood, San Lorenzo, is just a stone's throw from the Termini train station. Just beyond the city walls near Via Tiburtina, Rome's new "Left Bank" is filled with students and a young bohemian crowd, thanks to its proximity to La Sapienza University. The area has an *alternativa* feel to it, with its plethora of starving artists, tattoo parlors, and hippie musicians. In fact, if you don't know what you're looking for, you could easily get lost in this maze of dark, narrow streets, many now lined with underground cafés, bars, hip restaurants, and music clubs.

EATING AND DRINKING WELL IN ROME

In Rome, traditional cuisine reigns supreme. Most chefs follow the mantra of freshness over fuss, and simplicity of flavor and preparation over complex cooking methods.

So when Romans continue ordering the standbys, it's easy to understand why. And we're talking about *very* old standbys: some restaurants re-create dishes that come from ancient recipes of Apicius, probably the first celebrity chef (to Emperor Tiberius) and cookbook author of the Western world. Today Rome's cooks excel at what has taken hundreds, or thousands, of years to perfect.

Still, if you're hunting for newer-than-now developments, things are slowly changing. Talented young chefs are exploring new culinary frontiers, with results that tingle the taste buds: fresh pasta filled with carbonara sauce, cod "tiramisù," and mozzarella gelato with basil sorbet and semisweet tomatoes are just a few recent examples. Of course, there's grumbling about the number of chefs who, in a clumsy effort to be *nuovo*, end up with collision rather than fusion. That noted, Rome *is* the capital city, and the influx of residents from other regions of the country allows for many variations on the Italian theme.

FOODIE FINDS

Via Cola di Rienzo is home to two of Rome's best specialty shops: Franchi (✉ *Via Cola di Rienzo 200, Prati* ☎ *06/6874651*), pictured above, is a gastroshop that sells high-quality cured meats, Italian cheeses, wines, pastas, and fresh truffles. Next door, Castroni (✉ *Via Cola di Rienzo 196/198, Prati* ☎ *06/6874383*) is well known among expats for its imported foreign foods from the United States, Great Britain, Japan, India, and Mexico, as well as for its impressive selection of candies, preserves, olive oils, and balsamic vinegars. Castroni has a branch in Via Nazionale, the thoroughfare that leads from Termini Station to Piazza Venezia.

ARTICHOKES

If there's one vegetable Rome is known for, it's the artichoke, or *carciofo*. The classic Roman preparation, carciofo *alla romana*, is a large, globe-shape artichoke stripped of its outer leaves, stuffed with wild mint and garlic, then braised. It's available at restaurants throughout the city from February to May, when local artichokes are in season. For the excellent Roman-Jewish version, carciofo *alla giudia*—artichoke deep-fried until crisp and brown—head to any restaurant in the Ghetto.

BUCATINI ALL'AMATRICIANA

What may appear to the naked eye as spaghetti with red sauce is actually *bucatini all'amatriciana*—a spicy, rich, and complex dish that owes its flavor to an important ingredient: *guanciale*, or cured pork jowl. Once you taste a meaty, guanciale-flavor dish, you'll understand why Romans swear by it. Along with guanciale, the simple sauce features crushed tomatoes and red pepper flakes. It's served over *bucatini,* a hollow, spaghetti-like pasta, and topped with grated pecorino Romano cheese.

CODA ALLA VACCINARA

Rome's largest slaughterhouse in the 1800s was housed in the Testaccio neighborhood. That's where you'll find dishes like *coda alla vaccinara,* or "oxtail in the style of the cattle butcher." This dish is made from ox or veal tails stewed

with tomatoes, carrots, celery, and wine, and seasoned with cinnamon, pancetta, and myriad other flavorings. The stew cooks for hours then is finished with the sweet-and-sour element—often raisins and pine nuts or bittersweet chocolate.

GELATO

For many travelers, the first taste of gelato is a memorable moment. Italians shun the mass-produced ice cream that most street vendors sell. They go for the *gelaterie artigianale,* ice-cream shops that produce their own each day in a vast variety of delicious flavors. You usually get to choose three different tastes to put on your cone, topped with a generous dollop of whipped cream. In Rome a few common flavors are caffè, *pistacchio* (pistachio), *nocciola* (hazelnut), *fragola* (strawberry), and *cioccolato fondant* (dark chocolate).

PIZZA

Roman pizza comes in two types: pizza *al taglio* (by the slice) and pizza *tonda* (round pizza). The former has a thicker focaccia-like crust and is cut into squares. These slices are sold by weight and available all day. In Rome, pizza tonda has a thin crust. It's cooked in wood-burning ovens that reach extremely high temperatures. Because they're so hot, the ovens are usually fired up in the evening, which is why Roman pizzerias are only open for dinner.

A GREAT ITINERARY

Rome wasn't built in a day, and even locals themselves will tell you that it takes a lifetime to discover all its treasures. Jam-packed with monuments, museums, fountains, galleries, and picturesque neighborhoods, Mamma Roma makes it hard for visitors to decide which to tackle first during their adventurous Roman holiday. This one-day itinerary will give you a taste of some of the marvels the Eternal City has to offer.

Rome 101

"Rome in a Day" requires stamina, so start off early with a good breakfast and your most comfortable sneakers.

Everything pivots round **Piazza Venezia,** Rome's principal square. The **Campidoglio Hill** is on the right, somewhat dwarfed by the enormous **Victor Emmanuel Memorial** (unofficially known as "the wedding cake"). Take Michelangelo's stairway to the top of the Campidoglio for a photo shot of the equestrian statue of Emperor Marcus Aurelius—it looks great, even though it's a copy: the original is inside the museum. Then walk past Rome City Hall to the panoramic terrace where you'll find Ancient Rome, with the **Forum,** the **Palatine,** and the **Colosseum** all spread out before you.

The Colosseum is probably on your mustsee list. Regrettably, a lot of other people want to see it as well, so resign yourself and join the line. Otherwise, settle for a stroll among the temples of the gods in the Roman Forum.

Head next for Baroque Rome, clustered round the **Corso** at the opposite end of Piazza Venezia. A short detour left at Via dell'Umiltà leads to the **Trevi Fountain,** while the **Pantheon** is tucked away in the labyrinths of alleyways on the right of the Corso. Admire Bernini's Elephant Obelisk in front of Rome's only Gothic church, **Santa Maria Sopra Minerva,** where aspiring artists leave letters on the tomb of Fra Angelico, and pop into **San Luigi dei Francesi** to see the Caravaggios.

Cut across to **Piazza Navona,** with Bernini's spectacular Four Rivers fountain, where you've earned a coffee break or a gelato, It's a short hop from there to the Tiber embankment. Turning right along the riverside, you'll come to the **Bridge of the Angels** (Bernini and school) that leads to **Castel Sant'Angelo** and **St. Peter's.**

After you've admired the treasures of St. Peter's, including Michelangelo's *Pietà* and Bernini's baldacchino, grab something to eat in the old Vatican Borgo to sustain you for your visit to the **Vatican Museum.** You'll have to walk round the perimeter walls of Vatican City to get to the entrance (about half a mile) and there's another fair walk through rooms filled with some of the world's most amazing antiquities and works of art to get to the **Sistine Chapel.**

By now, you'll be glad to take a ride (Metro Line A at Ottaviano or Cipro stations) to the next stop—**Piazza del Popolo** (Flaminia station)—where you can head past the antiques shops in Via del Babuino to reach **Piazza di Spagna.** You'll be just in time to give a perfect ending to your day. Take your seat on the **Spanish Steps** to drink in the incomparable sight of the glorious Roman sunset tingeing the vista of rooftops with golden light.

ROME

Updated
by Amanda
Ruggeri

The timeless city to which all roads lead, Mamma Roma, enthralls visitors today as she has since time immemorial. Here the ancient Romans made us heirs-in-law to what we call Western Civilization; where centuries later Michelangelo painted the Sistine Chapel; and where Gian Lorenzo Bernini's Baroque nymphs and naiads still dance in their marble fountains.

Today the city remains a veritable Grand Canyon of culture. Ancient Rome rubs shoulders with the medieval, the modern runs into the Renaissance, and the result is like nothing so much as an open-air museum.

But always remember: *"Quando a Roma vai, fai come vedrai"* ("When in Rome, do as the Romans do"). Don't feel intimidated by the press of art and culture. Instead, contemplate the grandeur from a table at a sun-drenched café on Piazza della Rotonda; let Rome's colorful life flow around you without feeling guilty because you haven't seen everything. It can't be done, anyway. There's just so much here that you'll have to come back again, so be sure to throw a coin in the Trevi Fountain.

EXPLORING ROME

Most visitors to Rome begin by discovering the grandeur that was Rome: the Colosseum, the Forum, and the Pantheon. Then many move on to the Vatican, the closest thing to heaven on Earth for some.

The historical pageant continues with the 1,001 splendors of the Baroque era: glittering palaces, jewel-studded churches, and Caravaggio masterpieces. Arrive refreshed—with the help of a shot of espresso—at the foot of the Spanish Steps, where the picturesque world of the classic Grand Tour (peopled by such spirits as John Keats and Tosca) awaits you.

Thankfully, Rome provides delightful ways to catch your historic breath along the way: a walk through the cobblestone valleys of Trastevere or

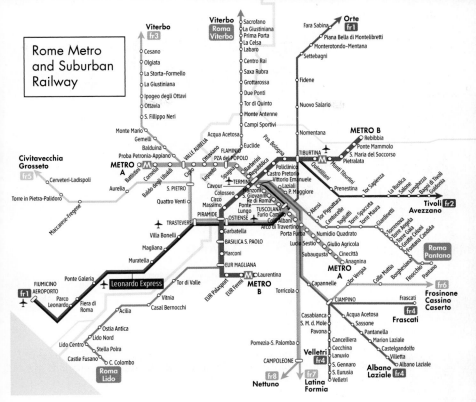

Rome Metro and Suburban Railway

an hour stolen alongside a splashing Bernini fountain. Keep in mind that an uncharted ramble through the heart of the old city can be just as satisfying as the contemplation of a chapel or a trek through marbled museum corridors. No matter which aspect of Rome you end up enjoying the most, a visit to the Eternal City will live up to its name in memory.

PIAZZA NAVONA AND THE CAMPO DE' FIORI

Set between Via del Corso and the Tiber bend, these time-burnished districts are some of the city's most beautiful. They're filled with narrow streets bearing curious names, airy piazzas, and half-hidden courtyards. Some of Rome's most coveted residential addresses are nestled here. So, too, are the ancient Pantheon and the Renaissance square of Campo de' Fiori, but the spectacular, over-the-top Baroque monuments of the 16th and 17th centuries predominate.

The hub of the district is the queen of squares, Piazza Navona—a cityscape adorned with the most jaw-dropping fountain by Gian Lorenzo Bernini, father of the Baroque. Streets running off the square lead to many historic must-sees, including noble churches by Borromini and Caravaggio's greatest paintings at San Luigi dei Francesi. This district has been an integral part of the city since ancient times, and its

Continued on page 60

CAPITOLINE HILL: The ancient Romans built their most important temples here, and it's been the seat of city government since the Middle Ages. It now holds the Capitoline Museums, chock-full of the treasures of antiquity.

ROMAN FORUM: Downtown Ancient Rome. People from all corners of the empire crowded into the Forum to do business, to hear the latest news, and to worship.

PALATINE HILL: Home of the empire's rich and famous. Luxurious villas lined Palatine Hill; emperors held court on its heights and vied with their predecessors for lasting renown.

CAMPIDOGLIO FORO ROMANO COLLE PALATINO

ANCIENT ROME
GLORIES OF
THE CAESARS

Time has reduced ancient Rome to fields of silent ruins, but the powerful impact of what happened here, of the genius and power that made Rome the center of the Western world, echoes across the millennia.

In this one compact area of the city, you can step back into the Rome of Cicero, Julius Caesar, and Virgil. Walk along the streets they knew, cool off in the shade of the Colosseum that loomed over the city, and see the sculptures poised above their piazzas. At the end of a day of exploring, climb one of the famous hills and watch the sun set over what was once the heart of the civilized world.

Today, this part of Rome, more than any other, is a perfect example of that layering of historic eras, the overlapping of ages, of religions, of a past that is very much a part of the present. Christian churches rise from the foundations of ancient pagan temples. An immense marble monument to a 19th-century king shares a square with a Renaissance palace built by a pope. Still, the history and memory of ancient Rome dominate the area. It's fitting that in the aftermath of centuries of such pageantry Percy Bysshe Shelley and Edward Gibbon reflected here on the meaning of *sic transit gloria mundi* (so passes away the glory of the world).

COLOSSEUM: Gladiators fought for the chance to live another day on the floor of the Colosseum, iconic symbol of ancient Rome.

COLOSSEO

CAMPIDOGLIO

The Capitoline Museums are closed on Monday. Late evening is an option for this area. Though the Santa Maria d'Aracoeli church is closed, the museums are open until 8 pm, and the views of the city lights and the illuminated Altare della Patria (aka the Victor Emmanuel II monument) and the Foro Romano are striking.

CLIMB MICHELANGELO'S DRAMATIC RAMP TO THE SUMMIT of one of Rome's famous hills, the Campidoglio (also known as Capitoline Hill), for views across the rooftops of modern Rome in one direction and across the ruins of ancient Rome in the other. Check out the stellar Musei Capitolini, crammed with a collection of masterpieces rivaled only by the Vatican museums.

★ **Piazza del Campidoglio.** In Michelangelo's piazza at the top of the Campidoglio stands a bronze equestrian statue of Marcus Aurelius (AD 121–180). A legend foretells that some day the statue's original gold surface will return, heralding the end of the world. Pending the arrival of that day, the original 2nd century statue was moved inside the Musei Capitolini; a copy sits on the piazza. Stand with your back to it to survey central Rome.

The Campidoglio, the site of the Roman Republic's first and holiest temples, had fallen into ruin by the Middle Ages and was called *Monte Caprino* (Goat Hill). In 1536 Pope Paul III (1468–1549) decided to restore its grandeur for the triumphal entry into the city of Charles V (1500–1558), the Holy Roman Emperor. He called upon Michelangelo to create the staircase ramp, the buildings and facades

on the square, the pavement decoration, and the pedestal for the bronze statue.

The two buildings that make up the **Musei Capitolini** are on the piazza, flanking the **Palazzo Senatorio**. The Campidoglio has long been the seat of Rome's government; its Latin name is the root for the word capitol. Today, Rome's city hall occupies the Palazzo Senatorio. Head to the vantage points in the belvederes on the sides of the palazzo for great views of the ruins of ancient Rome.

★ **Musei Capitolini** (Capitoline Museums). Housed in the twin Palazzo dei Conservatori and Palazzo Nuovo buildings, this is a greatest hits collection of Roman art through the ages, from the ancients to the baroque.

Lining the courtyard of the **Palazzo dei Conservatori** are the colossal fragments

AN EMPEROR CHEAT SHEET

OCTAVIAN/AUGUSTUS (27 BC–AD 14)
After the death of Julius Caesar, Octavian gained control of Rome following a decade-long civil war that ended with the defeat of Antony and Cleopatra at Actium. Later known as Caesar Augustus, he was Rome's first emperor. His rule began a 200-year period of peace known as the Pax Romana.

Colle Palatino

CALIGULA (AD 37–41)
Caligula was tremendously popular when he came to power at the age of 25, but he very soon became infamous for his excessive cruelty, immorality, and erratic behavior. His contemporaries universally considered him to be insane. He was murdered by his own guard within four years.

of a head, leg, foot, and hand—all that remains of the famous statue of the emperor Constantine. These immense effigies were much in vogue throughout the Roman Empire. The renowned symbol of Rome, the *Capitoline Wolf*, a medieval bronze (long thought to be Etruscan), holds a place of honor in the museum; the suckling twins were added during the Renaissance to adapt the statue to the legend of Romulus and Remus.

The Palazzo also contains some of baroque painting's great masterpieces, including Caravaggio's *La Buona Ventura* (1595) and *San Giovanni Battista* (1602), Peter Paul Rubens's *Romulus and Remus* (1615), and Pietro da Cortona's sumptuous portrait of Pope Urban VIII (1627). When museum fatigue sets in, enjoy the view and refreshments on a large open terrace in the Palazzo dei Conservatoria.

The **Palazzo Nuovo** contains hundreds of Roman busts of philosophers and emperors—a fascinating Who's Who of the ancient world. A dozen Roman emperors are represented. Unlike the Greeks, whose portraits are idealized, the Romans preferred a more realistic representation.

Other notable sculptures include the poignant *Dying Gaul* and the regal *Capitoline Venus*. In the Capitolino courtyard is a gigantic, reclining sculpture of Oceanus, found in the Roman Forum and later dubbed *Marforio*. This was one of Rome's "talking statues" to which citizens from the 1500s to the 1900s affixed anonymous satirical verses and notes of political protest. ☎ *06/0608* ⊕ *www. museicapitolini.org* ⊗ *Tues.–Sun. 9–8.* *€14*

Santa Maria in Aracoeli. Seemingly endless, steep stairs climb from Piazza Venezia to the church of Santa Maria. There are 15th-century frescoes by Pinturicchio (1454–1513) in the first chapel on the right. ✉ *Scala dell'Arce Capitolina 14* ⊗ *May–Sept., daily, 9–12:30 and 3–6:30; Oct.–Apr., daily 7–12:30 and 3–6:30.*

NERO (AD 54–68)

Nero is infamous as a violent persecutor of Christians. He also murdered his wife, his mother, and countless others. Although it's certain he didn't actually fiddle as Rome burned in AD 64, he was well known as a singer and a composer of music.

Domus Aurea

DOMITIAN (AD 81–96)

The first emperor to declare himself "Dominus et Deus" (Lord and God), he stripped away power from the Senate. After his death, the Senate retaliated by declaring him "Damnatio Memoriae" (his name and image were erased from all public records).

Colle Palatino

FORO ROMANO

⌚ **TIMING TIPS**

It takes about an hour to explore the Roman Forum. There are entrances on the Via dei Fori Imperiali and from the Palatine Hill. A 30-minute walk will cover the Imperial Fora. You can reserve tickets online or by phone—operators speak English. If you are buying tickets in person, remember there are shorter lines here than at the Colosseum and the ticket is good for both sights.

EXPERIENCE THE ENDURING ROMANCE OF THE FORUM. Wander among its lonely columns and great, broken fragments of sculpted marble and stone— once temples, law courts, and shops crowded with people from all corners of the known world. This was the heart of ancient Rome and a symbol of the values that inspired Rome's conquest of an empire.

★ **Foro Romano** (Roman Forum). Built in a marshy valley between the Capitoline and Palatine hills, the Forum was the civic core of Republican Rome, the austere era that preceded the hedonism of the emperors. The Forum was the political, commercial, and religious center of Roman life. Hundreds of years of plunder and the tendency of later Romans to carry off what was left of the better building materials reduced it to the series of ruins you see today. Archaeological digs continue to uncover more about the sight; bear in mind that what you see are the ruins not of one period but of almost 900 years, from about 500 BC to AD 400.

The **Basilica Giulia**, which owes its name to Julius Caesar who had it built, was where the Centumviri, the hundred-or-so judges forming the civil court, met to hear cases. The open space before it was the core of the forum proper and prototype of Italy's

famous piazzas. Let your imagination dwell on Mark Antony (circa 83 BC–30 BC), who delivered the funeral address in Julius Caesar's honor from the rostrum left of the **Arco di Settimio Severo**. This arch, one of the grandest of all antiquity, was built several hundred years later in AD 203 to celebrate the victory of the emperor Severus (AD 145–211) over the Parthians, and was topped by a bronze equestrian statuary group with four horses. You can explore the reconstruction of the large brick senate hall, the **Curia**; three Corinthian columns (a favorite of 19th-century poets) are all that remains of the **Tempio di Vespasiano el Tito**. In the **Tempio di Vesta**, six highly privileged vestal virgins kept the sacred fire, a tradition that dated back to the very earliest days of Rome. Their luxurious villa beside the temple was opened to the public in 2011. The cleaned and restored **Arco di Tito**, which stands in a slightly

AN EMPEROR CHEAT SHEET

TRAJAN (AD 98–117)

Trajan, from Southern Spain, was the first Roman emperor not born in Italy. He enlarged the empire's boundaries to include modern-day Romania, Armenia, and Upper Mesopotamia.

Colonna di Traiano, Foro di Traiano, Mercati di Traiano

HADRIAN (AD 117–138)

He expanded the empire in Asia and the Middle East. He's best known for rebuilding the Pantheon, constructing a majestic villa at Tivoli, and initiating myriad other constructions across the empire, including the famed wall across Britain.

elevated position on a spur of the Palatine Hill, was erected in AD 81 to honor the recently dead Emperor Titus. It depicts the sacking of Jerusalem 10 years earlier, after the great Jewish revolt. A famous relief shows the captured contents of Herod's Temple—including its huge seven-branched menorah—being carried in triumph down Rome's Via Sacra. The temple of Venus and Roma sits between the arch and the Colosseum. Making sense of the ruins isn't always easy; consider renting an audio guide (€4) or buying a booklet that superimposes an image of the Forum in its heyday over a picture of it today. ☎ 06/39967700 ⊕ www.pierreci.it ☾ Daily, Jan.–Feb. 15 and last Sun. in Oct.–Dec., 8:30–4:30; Feb. 16–Mar. 15, 8:30–5; Mar. 16–last Sat. in Mar., 8:30–5:30; last Sun. in Mar.–Aug., 8:30–7:15; Sept., 8:30–7; Oct.1–last Sat. in Oct., 8:30–6:30. €12

THE OTHER FORA

Fori Imperiali (Imperial Fora). These five grandly conceived squares flanked with columnades and temples were built by Caesar, Augustus, Vespasian, Nerva, and Trajan. The original Roman Forum, built up over 500 years of Republican Rome, had grown crowded, and Julius Caesar was the first to attempt to rival it. He built the **Foro di Cesare** (Forum of Caesar), including a temple dedicated to the goddess Venus. Four emperors followed his lead, creating their own fora. The grandest was the **Foro di Traiano** (Forum of Trajan) a veritable city unto itself built by Trajan (AD 53–117). Here you find the 100-ft Colonna di Traiano (Trajan's Column, AD 110), carved with 2,600 figures in relief. In the 20th century, Benito Mussolini built the Via dei Fori Imperiali directly through the Imperial Fora area. Marble and limestone maps on the wall along the avenue portray the extent of the Roman Republic and Empire, and many of the remains of the Imperial Fora lay buried beneath its surface.

Mercati di Traiano (Trajan's Markets). This huge multilevel brick complex of 120 offices was one of the marvels of the ancient world. It provides a glimpse into Roman daily life and offers a stellar view from the belvedere at its top. ☎ 06/0608 ⊕ www.mercatiditraiano.it ☾ Daily 9–7. €15

MARCUS AURELIUS (AD 161–180)

Remembered as a humanitarian emperor, Marcus Aurelius was a Stoic philosopher and his *Meditations* are still read today. Nonetheless, he was an aggressive leader devoted to expanding the empire.

Piazza del Campidoglio

CONSTANTINE I (AD 306–337)

Constantine changed the course of history by legalizing Christianity. He legitimized the once-banned religion and paved the way for the papacy in Rome. Constantine also established Constantinople as an Imperial capital in the East.

Arco di Constantino

COLLE PALATINO

A stroll on the Palatino, with a visit to the Museo Palatino, takes about two hours. The hill was once home to several major imperial palaces. Domitian's 1st-century AD palace is the best preserved. The Colle Palatino entrances are from the Roman Forum and at Via S. Gregorio 30.

IT ALL BEGAN HERE. ACCORDING TO LEGEND, ROMULUS, THE FOUNDER OF ROME, lived on the Colle Palatino (Palatine Hill). It was an exclusive address in ancient Rome, where emperors built palaces upon the slopes. Tour the Palatine's hidden corners and shady lanes, take a welcome break from the heat in its peaceful gardens, and enjoy a view of the Circo Massimo fit for an emperor.

★ **Colle Palatino** (Palatine Hill). A lane known as the Clivus Palatinus, paved with worn stones that were once trod by emperors and their slaves, climbs from the Forum area to a site that historians identify as one of Rome's earliest settlements. The legend goes that the infant twins Romulus and Remus were nursed by a she-wolf on the banks of the Tiber and adopted by a shepherd. Encouraged by the gods to build a city, Romulus chose this site in 753 BC. Remus preferred the Aventine. The argument that ensued left Remus dead and Romulus Rome's first king.

During the Republican era the hill was an important religious center, housing the Temple of Cybele and the Temple of Victory, as well as an exclusive residential area. Cicero, Catiline, Crassus, and Agrippa all had homes here. Augustus was born on the hill, and as he rose in power, he built libraries, halls, and temples here; the **House of Augustus,** opened in 2008, preserves exquisite 1st-century BC frescoes. Emperor Tiberius was the next to build a palace here; others followed. The structures most visible today date back to the late 1st century AD, when the Palatine experienced an extensive remodeling under Emperor Domitian. During the Renaissance, the powerful Farnese family built gardens in the area overlooking the ruins of the Forum. Known as the **Orti Farnesiani,** they were Europe's first botanical gardens. The **Museo Palatino** charts the history of the hill. Splendid sculptures, frescoes, and mosaic intarsia from various imperial buildings are on display. ☎ 06/39967700 ⊕ *www.pierreci.it* 🕐 *Daily, Jan.–Feb. 15 and last Sun. in Oct.– Dec., 8:30–4:30; Feb. 16–Mar. 15, 8:30–5; Mar. 16–last Sat. in Mar., 8:30–5:30; last Sun. in Mar.–Aug., 8:30–7:15; Sept., 8:30–7; Oct.1–last Sat. in Oct., 8:30–6:30.*

THE RISE AND FALL OF ANCIENT ROME

218 BC

ca. 800 BC	Rise of Etruscan city-states.
509–510	Foundation of the Roman republic; expulsion of Etruscans from Roman territory.
343	Roman conquest of Greek colonies in Campania.
264–241	First Punic War (with Carthage): increased naval power helps Rome gain control of southern Italy and then Sicily.
212–202	Second Punic War: Hannibal's attempted conquest of Italy, using elephants, is eventually crushed.

NEAR THE COLLE PALATINO

Circo Massimo (Circus Maximus). Ancient Rome's oldest and largest racetrack lies in the natural hollow between the Palatine and Aventine hills. From the imperial box in the palace on Palatine Hill, emperors could look out over the oval course. Stretching about 660 yards from end to end, the Circus Maximus could hold more than 200,000 spectators. On certain occasions there were as many as 100 chariot races a day, and competitions could last for 15 days. The central ridge was framed by two Egyptian obelisks. Check out the panoramic views of the Circus Maximus from the Palatine Hill's Belvedere. You can also see the green slopes of the Aventine and Celian hills, as well as the bell tower of Santa Maria in Cosmedin.

Terme di Caracalla (Baths of Caracalla). For the Romans, public baths were much more than places to wash. The baths also had recital halls, art galleries, libraries, massage rooms, sports grounds, and gardens. Even the smallest public baths had at least some of these amenities, and in the capital of the Roman Empire, they were provided on a lavish scale. Ancient Rome's most beautiful and luxurious public baths were opened by the emperor Caracalla in AD 217 and were used until the 6th century.

Taking a bath was a long process, and a social activity first and foremost. You began by sweating in the *sudatoria*, small rooms resembling saunas. From these you moved on to the *calidarium* for the actual business of washing, using an olive-oil-and-sand exfoliant, then removing it with a *strigil* (scraper). Next was the *tepidarium*, where you gradually cooled down. Finally, you splashed around in the *frigidarium*, in essence a cold–water swimming pool. There was a nominal admission fee, often waived by officials and emperors wishing to curry favor with the plebeians. The baths' functioning depended on the slaves who cared for the clients and stoked the fires that heated the water. ☎ *06/39967700* ⊕ *www.pierreci.it* ⊗ *Tues.–Sun., 9-4.30 (6.30 in summer). All Mondays, 9–1. €6*

150 BC	Roman Forum begins to take shape as the principal civic center in Italy.
149–146	Third Punic War: Rome razes city of Carthage and emerges as the dominant Mediterranean force.
133	Rome rules entire Mediterranean Basin except Egypt.
58–52	Julius Caesar conquers Gaul.
44	Julius Caesar is assassinated.
27	Rome's Imperial Age begins; Octavian (now named Augustus) becomes the first emperor and is later deified. The Augustan Age is celebrated in the works of Virgil (70–19 BC), Ovid (43 BC–AD 17), Livy (59 BC–AD 17), and Horace (65–8 BC).

44 BC

COLOSSEO

⏱ **TIMING TIPS**

You can give the Colosseum a cursory look in about 30 minutes, but it deserves at least an hour. Make reservations by phone (there are English-speaking operators) or online at least a day in advance to avoid long lines. Or buy your ticket at the Roman Forum or Palatine Hill, where the lines are usually shorter.

LEGEND HAS IT THAT AS LONG AS THE COLOSSEUM STANDS, ROME WILL STAND; and when Rome falls, so will the world. No visit to Rome is complete without a trip to the obstinate oval that has been the iconic symbol of the city for centuries.

★ **Colosseo.** A program of games and shows lasting 100 days celebrated the opening of the massive and majestic Colosseum in AD 80. On the opening day Romans claimed that 5,000 wild beasts perished. More than 50,000 spectators could sit within the arena's 596-yard circumference, which had limestone facing, hundreds of statues for decoration, and a *velarium*—an ingenious system of sail-like awnings rigged on ropes manned by imperial sailors—to protect the audience from the sun and rain. Before the imperial box, gladiators would salute the emperor and cry, "*Ave, imperator, morituri te salutant*" ("Hail, emperor, men soon to die salute you"); it is said that one day they heard the emperor Claudius respond, "Or maybe not," they were so offended that they called a strike.

Originally known as the Flavian Amphitheater, it took the name Colosseum after a truly colossal gilt bronze statue of Nero that stood nearby. Gladiator combat ended by the 5th century and staged animal hunts

by the 6th. The arena later served as a quarry from which materials were looted to build Renaissance churches and palaces, including St. Peter's Basilica. Finally, it was declared sacred by the Vatican in memory of the many Christians believed martyred here. (Scholars now maintain that Christians met their death elsewhere.) During the 19th century, romantic poets lauded the glories of the ruins when viewed by moonlight. Now its arches glow at night with mellow golden spotlights.

Expect long lines at the entrance and actors dressed as gladiators who charge a hefty fee to pose for pictures. (Agree on a price in advance if you want a photo.) Once inside you can walk around about half of the outer ring of the structure and look down into the exposed passages under what was once the arena floor, now represented by a small stage at one end. Climb the steep stairs for panoramic views in the Colosseum and out to the Palatine and Arch of Constantine. A museum

THE RISE AND FALL OF ANCIENT ROME

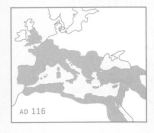

AD 116

58 AD	Rome invades Britain.
50	Rome is the largest city in the world, with a population of possibly as much as a million.
64–68	Emperor Nero begins the persecution of Christians in the Empire; Saints Peter and Paul are executed.
72–80	Vespasian begins the Colosseum; Titus completes it.
98–117	Trajan's military successes are celebrated with his Baths (98), Forum (110), and Column (113); the Roman Empire reaches its apogee.

space on the second floor holds temporary archaeological exhibits. ☎ *06/39967700* ⊕ *www.pierreci.it* ⊙ *Daily, 9–sunset. €12, includes Forum.*

Arco di Costantino. The largest (69 feet high, 85 feet long, 23 feet wide) and the best preserved of Rome's triumphal arches was erected in AD 315 to celebrate the victory of the emperor Constantine (280–337) over co-emperor Maxentius (died 312). According to legend, it was just before this battle that Constantine, the emperor who legalized Christianity, had a vision of a cross in the heavens and heard the words "In this sign, thou shalt conquer."

NEAR THE COLOSSEO

Domus Aurea. At this writing, Nero's "Golden House"was closed, with the prospect of reopening uncertain. The site gives a good sense of the excesses of Imperial Rome. After fire destroyed much of the city in AD 64, Nero took advantage of the resulting open space to construct a lavish palace so large that it spread over a third of the city. It had a facade of marble, sea-

water piped into the baths, gilded vaults, decorations of mother-of-pearl, and vast gardens. Not much of this ornamentation has survived; a good portion of the building and grounds was buried under the public works with which subsequent emperors sought to make reparation to the Roman people for Nero's phenomenal greed. As a result, the site of the Domus Aurea itself remained unknown for many centuries. A few of Nero's original halls were discovered underground at the end of the 15th century. Raphael (1483–1520) was one of the artists who had themselves lowered into the rubble-filled rooms, which resembled grottoes. The artists copied the original painted Roman decorations, barely visible by torchlight, and scratched their names on the ceilings. Raphael later used these models—known as *grotesques* because they were found in the so-called grottoes—in his decorative motifs for the Loggia of Julius II in the Vatican. The palace remains impressive in scale, even if a lot of imagination is required to envision the original. ⊠ *Via della Domus Aurea* ☎ *06/39967700* ⊕ *www.pierreci.it.*

AD 450

238 AD	The first wave of Germanic invasions penetrates Italy.
293	Diocletian reorganizes the Empire into West and East.
330	Constantine founds a new Imperial capital (Constantinople) in the East.
410	Rome is sacked by Visigoths.
476	The last Roman emperor, Romulus Augustus, is deposed. The western Roman Empire falls.

position between the Vatican and Lateran palaces, both seats of papal rule, put it in the mainstream of Rome's development from the Middle Ages onward. Craftsmen, shopkeepers, and famed artists toiled in the shadow of the huge palaces built to consolidate the power of leading figures in the papal court. Artisans and artists still live here, but their numbers are diminishing as the district becomes increasingly posh and—so critics say—"Disneyfied." But three of the liveliest piazzas in Rome—Piazza Navona, Piazza della Rotonda (home to the Pantheon), and Campo de' Fiori—are lodestars in a constellation of some of Rome's finest cafés, stores, and wine bars.

GETTING HERE AND AROUND

To bus it from Termini train station or the Vatican, take the No. 40 Express or the No. 64 and get off at Corso Vittorio Emanuele II, a two-minute stroll from either Campo de' Fiori or Piazza Navona, or take little electric No. 116 from Via Veneto to Campo de' Fiori. Bus nos. 87 and 571 link the area to the Forum and Colosseum. Tram No. 8 runs from Largo Argentina to Trastevere.

TOP ATTRACTIONS

Campo de' Fiori. A bustling marketplace in the morning (Monday to Saturday 8 am–2 pm) and a trendy meeting place the rest of the day (and night), this piazza has plenty of earthy charm. By sunset, all the fish, fruit, and flower vendors disappear and this so-called *piazza trasformista* takes on another identity, becoming a circus of bars particularly favored by study-abroads, tourists, and young expats. Brooding over the piazza is a hooded statue of the philosopher Giordano Bruno, who was burned at the stake here in 1600 for heresy. His was the first of the executions that drew Roman crowds to Campo de' Fiori in the 17th century. ⊠ *Intersection of Via dei Baullari, Via Giubbonari, Via del Pellegrino, and Piazza della Cancelleria.*

Fodor'sChoice
★

Palazzo Altemps. Containing some of the finest ancient Roman statues in the world, the collection here formerly made up the core of the Museo Nazionale Romano. In 1995, it was moved to these new, suitably grander digs. The palace's sober exterior belies a magnificence that appears as soon as you walk into the majestic courtyard, studded with statues and covered in part by a retractable awning. The restored interior hints at the Roman lifestyle of the 16th through 18th century while showcasing the most illustrious pieces from the Museo Nazionale, including the Ludovisi family collection. In the frescoed salons you can see the *Galata,* a poignant work portraying a barbarian warrior who chooses death for himself and his wife rather than humiliation by the enemy. Another highlight is the large Ludovisi sarcophagus, magnificently carved from marble. In a place of honor is the Ludovisi Throne, which shows a goddess emerging from the sea and being helped by her acolytes. For centuries, this was heralded as one of the most sublime Greek sculptures, but today at least one authoritative art historian considers it a colossally overrated fake. Look for the framed explanations of the exhibits that detail (in English) how and exactly where Renaissance sculptors, Bernini among them, added missing pieces to the classical works. In the lavishly frescoed Loggia stand busts of the Caesars. In the wing once occupied by early-20th-century poet Gabriele D'Annunzio

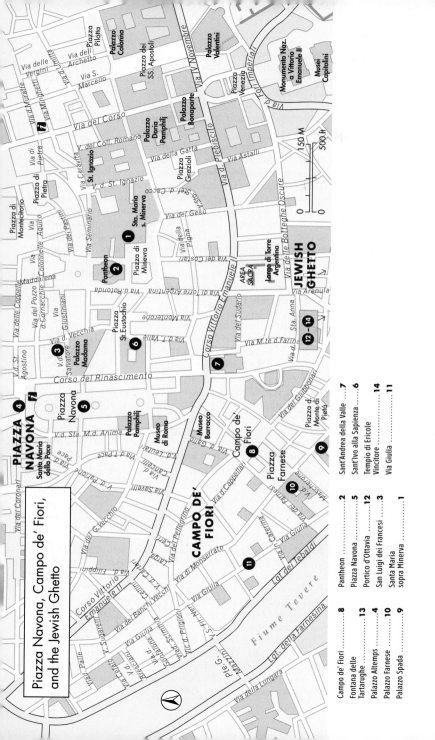

Piazza Navona, Campo de' Fiori, and the Jewish Ghetto

(who married into the Altemps family), three rooms host the museum's Egyptian collection. ✉ *Piazza Sant'Apollinare 46, Piazza Navona* ☎ *06/39967700* ⊕ *www.coopculture.it* 🎫 *€7, includes 3 other Museo Nazionale Romano sites (Crypta Balbi, Palazzo Massimo, Museo Diocleziano); €10 if any one of them has a special exhibit ⊙ Tues.–Sun. 9–7:45; ticket office closes 1 hr early* Ⓜ *Bus 70, 81, 87, 116T, 186, 492, 628.*

Palazzo Farnese. The most beautiful Renaissance palace in Rome, the Palazzo Farnese is fabled for the Galleria Carracci, whose ceiling is to the Baroque age what the Sistine ceiling is to the Renaissance. The Farnese family rose to great power and wealth during the Renaissance, in part because of the favor Pope Alexander VI showed to the beautiful Giulia Farnese. The massive palace was begun when, with Alexander's aid, Giulia's brother became cardinal; it was further enlarged on his election as Pope Paul III in 1534. The uppermost frieze decorations and main window overlooking the piazza are the work of Michelangelo, who also designed part of the courtyard, as well as the graceful arch over Via Giulia at the back. The facade on Piazza Farnese has recently been cleaned, further revealing geometrical brick configurations that have long been thought to hold some occult meaning. When looking up at the palace, try to catch a glimpse of the splendid frescoed ceilings, including the **Galleria Carracci** vault painted by Annibale Carracci between 1597 and 1604. The Carracci gallery depicts the loves of the gods, a supremely pagan theme that the artist painted in a swirling style that announced the birth of the Baroque. Other opulent salons are among the largest in Rome, including the Salon of Hercules, which has an overpowering replica of the ancient *Farnese Hercules* front and center. The French Embassy, which occupies the palace, offers weekly tours in English; be sure to book at least eight days in advance (book online at ⊕ *www.inventerrome.com*) and bring photo ID. ✉ *French Embassy, Servizio Culturale, Piazza Farnese 67, Campo de' Fiori* ☎ *06/686011* 🎫 *€5 ⊙ By tour only (no children under 10); English tour Wed. at 5.*

Palazzo Spada. In this neighborhood of huge, austere palaces, Palazzo Spada strikes an almost frivolous note, with its upper stories covered with stuccos and statues and its pretty, ornament-encrusted courtyard. While the palazzo houses an impressive collection of old-master paintings, it is most famous for its trompe-l'oeil garden gallery, a delightful example of the sort of architectural games rich Romans of the 17th century found irresistible. Even if you don't go into the gallery, step into the courtyard and look through the glass window of the library to the colonnaded corridor in the adjacent courtyard. See—or seem to see—Borromini's 8-meter-long gallery quadrupled in depth, a sort of optical telescope taking the Renaissance's art of perspective to another level, as it stretches out for a great distance with a large statue at the end. In fact the distance is an illusion: the corridor grows progressively narrower and the columns progressively smaller as they near the statue, which is just 2 feet tall. The Baroque prided itself on special effects, and this is rightly one of the most famous. It long was thought that Borromini was responsible for this ruse; it's now known that it was designed by an Augustinian priest, Giovanni Maria da Bitonto. Upstairs

CLOSE UP

1

Going Baroque

Flagrantly emotional, heavily expressive, and visually sensuous, the 17th-century artistic movement known as Baroque was born in Rome. It was the creation of three geniuses: the sculptor and architect Gian Lorenzo Bernini (1598–1680), the painter and architect Pietro da Cortona (1596–1669), and the architect and sculptor Francesco Borromini (1599–1667). From the drama found in the artists' works to the jewel-laden, gold-on-gold detail of 17th-century Roman palaces, the Baroque style was intended both to shock and delight by upsetting the placid, "correct" rules of proportion and scale of the Renaissance. If a building looks theatrical—like a stage or a theater, especially with curtains being drawn back—it's usually Baroque. Look for over-the-top, curvaceous marble work, trompe-l'oeil, allusions to other art, and high drama to identify the style. Baroque's appeal to the emotions made it a powerful weapon in the hands of the Counter-Reformation.

is a seignorial picture gallery with the paintings shown as they would have been, piled on top of each other clear to the ceiling. Outstanding works include Brueghel's *Landscape with Windmills,* Titian's *Musician,* and Andrea del Sarto's *Visitation.* Look for the fact sheets that have descriptive notes about the objects in each room. ⊠ *Piazza Capo di Ferro 13, Campo de' Fiori* ☎ *06/6861158* ⊕ *www.galleriaborghese. it* ⊠ *€5* ⊗ *Tues.–Sun. 8:30–7:30.*

Fodor's Choice
★

Pantheon. One of the wonders of the ancient world, this onetime pagan temple, a marvel of architectural harmony and proportion, is the best-preserved ancient building in Rome. It was entirely rebuilt by the emperor Hadrian around AD 120 on the site of an earlier pantheon (from the Greek *pan*—all—and *theon*—gods) erected in 27 BC by Augustus's general Agrippa. It's thought that the majestic circular building was actually designed *by* Hadrian, as were many of the temples, palaces, and lakes of his enormous villa at Tivoli. Hadrian nonetheless retained the inscription over the entrance from the original building (today, unfortunately, replaced with modern letters) that named Agrippa as the builder. This caused enormous confusion among historians until, in 1892, a French architect discovered that all the bricks used in the Pantheon dated from Hadrian's time.

The most striking thing about the Pantheon is not its size, immense though it is—until 1960 the dome was the largest ever built—nor even the phenomenal technical difficulties posed by so vast a construction; rather, it's the remarkable unity of the building. You don't have to look far to find the reason for this harmony: the diameter described by the dome is exactly equal to its height. It's the use of such simple mathematical balance that gives classical architecture its characteristic sense of proportion and its nobility and why some call it the world's only architecturally perfect building. The great opening at the apex of the dome, the oculus, is nearly 30 feet in diameter and was the temple's only source of light. It was intended to symbolize the "all-seeing eye of heaven."

To do the interior justice defied even Byron. He piles up adjectives, but none seems to fit: "Simple, erect, severe, austere, sublime." Not surprising, perhaps, when describing a dome 141 feet high and the same across. Although little is known for sure about the Pantheon's origins or purpose, it's worth noting that the five levels of trapezoidal coffers represent the course of the five then-known planets and their concentric spheres. Then, ruling over them, comes the sun represented symbolically and literally by the 30-foot-wide eye at the top. The heavenly symmetry is further paralleled by the coffers themselves: 28 to each row, the number of lunar cycles. Note how each coffer takes five planetary steps toward the wall. Then in the center of each would have shone a small bronze star. Down below the seven large niches were occupied not by saints, but, it's thought, by statues of Mars, Venus, the deified Caesar, and the other "astral deities," including the moon and sun, the "sol invictus." (Academics still argue, however, about which gods were most probably worshipped here. We may never know for sure.)

The Pantheon is by far the best preserved of the major monuments of imperial Rome, a condition that is the result of it being consecrated as a church in AD 608. (It's still a working and Mass-holding church today, and it's the church name, the Basilica of Saint Mary and the Martyrs, that you'll see on the official signs.) No building, church or not, escaped some degree of plundering through the turbulent centuries of Rome's history after the fall of the empire. In 655, for example, the gilded bronze covering the dome was stripped. Similarly, in the early 17th century, Pope Urban VIII removed the bronze beams of the portico. Although the legend holds that the metal went to the *baldacchino* (canopy) over the high altar at St. Peter's Basilica, the reality may be worse—it went to cannons at Castel Sant'Angelo. Most of its interior marble facing has also been stripped and replaced over the centuries. Nonetheless, the Pantheon suffered less than many other ancient structures.

One-hour tours (€10) are run regularly in English; check at the information desk on your right as you enter. ⊠ *Piazza della Rotonda, Piazza Navona* ☏ *06/68300230* ⊕ *www.pantheonroma.com* ⧠ *Free; audio guides €5* ☯ *Mon.–Sat. 9–7:30, Sun. 9–6, public holidays that fall on a weekday 9–1* Ⓜ *Closest bus hub: Argentina (Bus 40, 85, 53, 46, 64, 87, 571; Tram 8).*

Piazza Navona. Here, everything that makes Rome unique is compressed into one beautiful Baroque piazza. Always camera-ready, Piazza Navona has Bernini sculptures, three gorgeous fountains, a magnificently Baroque church (Sant'Agnese in Agone), and, best of all, the excitement of so many people strolling, admiring the fountains, and enjoying the view. The piazza has been an entertainment venue for Romans ever since being built over Domitian's circus (pieces of the arena are still visible near adjacent Piazza Sant'Apollinare). Although undoubtedly more touristy today, the square still has the carefree air

1

of the days when it was the scene of medieval jousts and 17th-century carnivals. Today, it's the site of a lively Christmas "Befana" fair. The piazza still looks much as it did during the 17th century, after the Pamphili pope Innocent X decided to make it over into a monument to his family to rival the Barberini's palace at the Quattro Fontane.

At center stage is the Fontana dei Quattro Fiumi, created for Innocent X by Bernini in 1651. Bernini's powerful figures of the four rivers represent the four corners of the world: the Nile; the Ganges; the Danube; and the Plata, with its hand raised. One story has it that the figure of the Nile—the figure closest to Sant' Agnese in Agone—hides its head because it can't bear to look upon the church's "inferior" facade designed by Francesco Borromini, Bernini's rival. In fact, the facade was built after the fountain, and the statue hides its head because it represents a river whose source was then unknown.

Fodor'sChoice ★ **San Luigi dei Francesi.** A pilgrimage spot for art lovers everywhere, San Luigi's Contarelli Chapel is adorned with three stunningly dramatic works by Caravaggio (1571–1610), the Baroque master of the heightened approach to light and dark. At the altar end of the left nave, they were commissioned for San Luigi, the official church of Rome's French colony (San Luigi is St. Louis, patron of France). The inevitable coin machine will light up his *Calling of St. Matthew, Matthew and the Angel,* and *Matthew's Martyrdom,* seen from left to right, and Caravaggio's mastery of light takes it from there. When painted, they caused considerable consternation to the clergy of San Luigi, who thought the artist's dramatically realistic approach was scandalously disrespectful. A first version of the altarpiece was rejected; the priests were not particularly happy with the other two, either. Time has fully vindicated Caravaggio's patron, Cardinal Francesco del Monte, who secured the commission for these works and stoutly defended them. They're now recognized to be among the world's greatest paintings. ✉ *Piazza San Luigi dei Francesi, Piazza Navona* ☎ *06/688271* ⊕ *www.saintlouisrome.net* ⊗ *Fri.–Wed. 10–12:30 and 3–6:45, Thurs. 10–12:30* Ⓜ *Bus 40 or 87.*

Santa Maria sopra Minerva. The name of the church reveals that it was built *sopra* (over) the ruins of a temple of Minerva, ancient goddess of wisdom. Erected in 1280 by the Dominicans on severe Italian Gothic lines, it has undergone a number of more or less happy restorations to the interior. Certainly, as the city's major Gothic church, it provides a refreshing contrast to Baroque flamboyance. Have a €1 coin handy to illuminate the **Cappella Carafa** in the right transept, where Filippino Lippi's (1457–1504) glowing frescoes are well worth the small investment, opening up the deepest azure expanse of sky where musical angels hover around the Virgin. Under the main altar is the tomb of St. Catherine of Siena, one of Italy's patron saints. Left of the altar you'll find Michelangelo's *Risen Christ* and the tomb of the gentle artist Fra Angelico. Bernini's unusual and little-known monument to the Blessed Maria Raggi is on the fifth pier from the door on the left as you leave the church. In front of the church, the little obelisk-bearing elephant carved by Bernini is perhaps the city's most charming sculpture.

An inscription on the base of **Bernini's Elephant Obelisk,** which was recently cleaned and restored, references the church's ancient patroness, reading something to the effect that it takes a strong mind to sustain solid wisdom. ✉ *Piazza della Minerva, Piazza Navona* ☎ *06/6793926* ⊕ *www.basilicaminerva.it* ⊙ *Weekdays 6:45–7, Sat. 6:45–12:30 and 3:30–7, Sun. 8–12:30 and 3:30–7.*

Fodor's Choice
★

Via Giulia. Still a Renaissance-era diorama and one of Rome's most exclusive addresses, Via Giulia was the first street in Rome since ancient times to be laid out in a straight line. Named for Pope Julius II (of Sistine Chapel fame) who commissioned it in the early 1500s as part of a scheme to open up a grandiose approach to St. Peter's Basilica (using funds from the taxation of prostitutes), it became flanked with elegant churches and palaces. Though the pope's plans to change the face of the city were only partially completed, Via Giulia became an important thoroughfare in Renaissance Rome. Today, after more than four centuries, it remains the "salon of Rome," address of choice for Roman aristocrats, although controversy has arisen about a recent change—the decision to add a large parking lot along one side of the street—that meant steamrolling through ancient and medieval ruins underneath. A stroll will reveal elegant palaces and old churches (one, **San Eligio,** at No. 18, reputedly designed by Raphael himself). The area around Via Giulia is a wonderful section to wander through and get the feel of daily life as carried on in a centuries-old setting. Among the buildings that merit your attention are **Palazzo Sacchetti** (No. 66), with an imposing stone portal (inside are some of Rome's grandest state rooms, still, after 300 years, the private quarters of the Marchesi Sacchetti), and the forbidding brick building that housed the **Carceri Nuove** (New Prison; No. 52), Rome's prison for more than two centuries and now the offices of Direzione Nazionale Antimafia. Near the bridge that arches over the southern end of Via Giulia is the church of **Santa Maria dell'Orazione e Morte** (Holy Mary of Prayer and Death), with stone skulls on its door. These are a symbol of a confraternity that was charged with burying the bodies of the unidentified dead found in the city streets. Home since 1927 to the Hungarian Academy, the **Palazzo Falconieri** (No. 1) was designed by Borromini—note the architect's rooftop belvedere adorned with statues of the family "falcons," best viewed from around the block along the Tiber embankment. With reservations and a €5 fee, you can visit the Borromini-designed salons and loggia. ✉ *Between Piazza dell'Oro and Piazza San Vincenzo Palloti, Campo de' Fiori.*

WORTH NOTING

Sant'Andrea della Valle. Topped by the highest dome in Rome (designed by Maderno) after St. Peter's, this huge and imposing 17th-century church is remarkably balanced in design. Fortunately, its facade, which had been turned a sooty gray from pollution, has been cleaned to a near-sparkling white. Use the handy mirror that's provided to examine the early-17th-century frescoes by Domenichino in the choir vault and those by Lanfranco in the dome. One of the earliest ceilings done in full Baroque style, its upward vortex was influenced by Correggio's dome in Parma, of which Lanfranco was also a citizen. (Bring a few coins to light the paintings, which can be very dim.) The three massive paintings of

Saint Andrew's martyrdom are by Maria Preti (1650–51). Richly marbled and decorated chapels flank the nave, and in such a space, Puccini set the first act of *Tosca*. ⊠ *Piazza Vidoni 6, Corso Vittorio Emanuele II, Campo de' Fiori* ☎ *06/6861339* ⊕ *www.sant-andrea-roma.it* ☉ *Daily 7:30–12:30 and 4:30–7:30.*

Sant'Ivo alla Sapienza. The main facade of this eccentric Baroque church, probably Borromini's best, is on the stately courtyard of an austere building that once housed Rome's university. Sant'Ivo has what must surely be one of the most delightful domes in all of Rome—a golden spiral said to have been inspired by a bee's stinger. The bee symbol is a reminder that Borromini built the church on commission from the Barberini pope Urban VIII (a swarm of bees figure on the Barberini family crest). The interior, open only for three hours on Sunday, is worth a look, especially if you share Borromini's taste for complex mathematical architectural idiosyncrasies. "I didn't take up architecture solely to be a copyist," Borromini once said. Sant'Ivo is certainly the proof. ⊠ *Corso Rinascimento 40, Piazza Navona* ☎ *06/6864987* ⊕ *www.060608.it* ☉ *Sept.–June, Sun. 9–noon* Ⓜ *Bus 130, 116, 186, 492, 30, 70, 81, or 87.*

THE JEWISH GHETTO

A warren of twisting, narrow streets, the Jewish Ghetto, was where Rome's Jewish community was at one time confined. It's now a combination of medieval, Renaissance, and modern structures.

GETTING HERE AND AROUND

From Termini station, nab Bus No. 40 Express or No. 64 to Largo Torre Argentina, where you can get off to visit the Jewish Ghetto area.

TOP ATTRACTIONS

Fontana delle Tartarughe. Designed by Giacomo della Porta in 1581 and sculpted by Taddeo Landini, this 16th-century fountain, set in venerable Piazza Mattei, is Rome's most charming. The focus of the fountain is four bronze boys, each grasping a dolphin spouting water into a marble shell. Bronze turtles held in the boys' hands drink from the upper basin. The turtles are thought to have been added in the 17th century by Bernini. ⊠ *Piazza Mattei, Jewish Ghetto.*

Jewish Ghetto. Rome has had a Jewish community since the 2nd century BC, and from that time until the present its living conditions have varied widely according to its relations with the city's rulers. In 1555 Pope Paul IV Carafa established Rome's Ghetto Ebraico in the neighborhood marked off by the Portico d'Ottavia, the Tiber, and the Piazza dei Cenci. It measured only 200 yards by 250 yards. Jews were obligated to live there by law and the area quickly became Rome's most densely populated and least healthy. The laws were rescinded when Italy was unified in 1870 and the pope lost his political authority, but German troops tragically occupied Rome during World War II and in 1943 wrought havoc here. Today there are a few Judaica shops and kosher groceries, bakeries, and restaurants (especially on Via di Portico d'Ottavia), but the neighborhood mansions are now being renovated and much coveted by rich and stylish expats. The Museo Ebraico arranges tours of the Ghetto. The museum has exhibits detailing the millennial history of Rome's Jewish community.

Portico d'Ottavia. Looming over the district, this huge porticoed enclosure, with a few surviving columns, stands as one of the Ghetto's most picturesque set pieces, with the time-stained church of Sant'Angelo in Pescheria built right into its ruins. Named by Augustus in honor of his sister Octavia, it was originally 390 feet wide and 433 feet long, encompassed two temples, a meeting hall, and a library, and served as a kind of grandiose foyer for the adjacent Teatro di Marcello. The ruins of the portico became Rome's *pescheria* (fish market) during the Middle Ages. A stone plaque on a pillar, a relic of that time, admonishes in Latin that the head of any fish surpassing the length of the plaque was to be cut off "up to the first fin" and given to the city fathers or else the vendor was to pay a fine of 10 gold florins. The heads were used to make fish soup and were considered a great delicacy. After restoration, the lovely medieval church of Sant'Angelo in Pescheria has reopened to the public *(Wed., Sat., and 1st Mon. of month 2–5; 06/68801819).* ⊠ *Via Tribuna di Campitelli 6, Jewish Ghetto.*

WORTH NOTING

Tempio di Ercole Vincitore. All but one of the 20 original Corinthian columns in Rome's most evocative small ruin remain intact. It was built in the 2nd century BC. Long considered a shrine to Vesta, it's now believed that the temple was devoted to Hercules by a successful olive merchant. ⊠ *Piazza Bocca della Verità, Jewish Ghetto.*

PIAZZA DI SPAGNA

In spirit (and in fact) this section of the city is its most grandiose. The overblown Vittoriano monument, the labyrinthine treasure-chest palaces of Rome's surviving aristocracy, even the diamond-draped denizens of Via Condotti's shops—all embody the exuberant ego of a city at the center of its own universe. Here's where you'll see ladies in furs gobbling pastries at café tables, and walk through a thousand snapshots as you climb the famous Spanish Steps, admired by generations from Byron to Versace. Cultural treasures abound around here: gilded 17th-century churches, glittering palaces, and the greatest example of portraiture in Rome, Velázquez's incomparable *Innocent X* at the Galleria Doria Pamphilj. Have your camera ready—along with a coin or two—for that most beloved of Rome's landmarks, the Trevi Fountain.

GETTING HERE AND AROUND

One of Rome's handiest subway stations, the Spagna Metro station is tucked just to the left of the Spanish Steps. Bus nos. 117 (from St. John Lateran and the Colosseum) and 119 (from Largo Argentina) hum through the neighborhood.

TOP ATTRACTIONS

Fodor'sChoice
★
Ara Pacis Augustae *(Altar of Augustan Peace).* This vibrant monument of the imperial age has been housed in one of Rome's newest architectural landmarks: a gleaming, rectangular glass-and-travertine structure designed by American architect Richard Meier. Overlooking the Tiber

on one side and the ruins of the marble-clad **Mausoleo di Augusto** (Mausoleum of Augustus), on the other, the result is a serene, luminous oasis right in Rome's center. Opened in 2006, after a decade of bitter controversy over the monument's relocation, the altar itself dates back to 13 BC; it was commissioned to celebrate the Pax Romana, the era of peace ushered in by Augustus's military victories. It is covered with spectacular and moving relief sculptures. Like all ancient Roman monuments of this type, you have to imagine them painted in vibrant colors, now long gone. The reliefs on the short sides show myths associated with Rome's founding and glory; the long sides display a procession of the imperial family. It's fun to try to play "who's who"—although half of his body is missing, Augustus is identifiable as the first full figure at the procession's head on the south frieze—but academics still argue over exact identifications. ✉ *Lungotevere in Augusta, Piazza di Spagna* ☎ *06/0608* ⊕ *www.arapacis.it* 🖅 *€10.50* ☾ *Tues.–Sun. 9–7; last admission 1 hr before closing* Ⓜ *Flaminio (Piazza del Popolo).*

Monumento a Vittorio Emanuele II, or Altare della Patria (*Victor Emmanuel Monument, or Altar of the Nation*). The huge white mass of the "Vittoriano" is an inescapable landmark—Romans say you can avoid its image only if you're actually standing on it. Some have likened it to a huge wedding cake; others, to an immense typewriter. Though not held in the highest esteem by present-day citizens, it was the source of great civic pride at the time of its construction, at the turn of the 20th century. To create this elaborate marble monster and the vast piazza on which it stands, architects blithely destroyed many ancient and medieval buildings and altered the slope of the Capitoline Hill, which abuts it. Built to honor the unification of Italy and the nation's first king, Victor Emmanuel II, it also shelters the eternal flame at the tomb of Italy's Unknown Soldier killed during World War I. The flame is guarded day and night by sentinels, while inside the building there is the (rather dry) Institute of the History of the Risorgimento. You can't avoid the Monumento, so enjoy neo-imperial grandiosity at its most bombastic.

The views from the top are some of Rome's most panoramic. The only way up is by elevator (located to the right as you face the monument); stop at the museum entrances (to the left and right of the structure) to get a pamphlet identifying the sculpture groups on the monument itself and the landmarks you will be able to see once at the top. ✉ *Entrance at Piazza Ara Coeli, next to Piazza Venezia, Piazza di Spagna* ☎ *06/0608* ⊕ *www.060608.it* 🖅 *Free, elevator €7* ☾ *Elevator: Mon.–Thurs. 9:30–6:30; Fri. and weekends 9:30–7:30; last entrance 45 mins before closing. Stairs: winter, daily 9:30–4:30; summer, daily 9:30–5:30.*

Fodor'sChoice
★ **Palazzo Colonna.** Rome's grandest family built itself Rome's grandest palazzo in the 18th century—it's so immense, it faces Piazza Santi Apostoli on one side and the Quirinal Hill on the other (a little bridge over Via della Pilotta links the palace with the gardens on the hill). While still home to some Colonna patricians, the palace also holds the family picture gallery, open to the public one day a week. The galleria is itself a setting of aristocratic grandeur; you might recognize the **Sala Grande** as the site where Audrey Hepburn meets the press in *Roman Holiday*. At one end looms the ancient red marble column

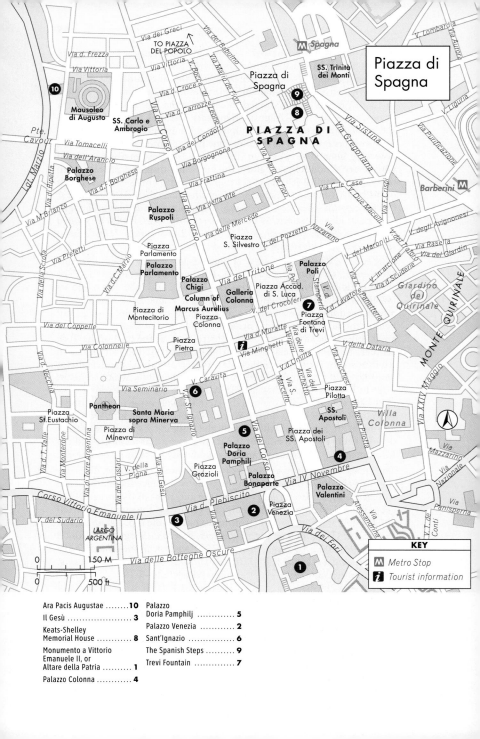

Piazza di Spagna

PIAZZA DI SPAGNA

KEY

M *Metro Stop*

i *Tourist information*

(*colonna*), the family's emblem; above the vast room is the spectacular ceiling fresco of the Battle of Lepanto painted by Giovanni Coli and Filippo Gherardi in 1675—the center scene almost puts the computer-generated special effects of Hollywood to shame. Adding redundant luster to the opulently stuccoed and frescoed salons are works by Poussin, Tintoretto, and Veronese, and a number of portraits of illustrious members of the family such as Vittoria Colonna—Michelangelo's muse and longtime friend—and Marcantonio Colonna, who led the papal forces in the great naval victory at Lepanto in 1577. Lost in the array of madonnas, saints, goddesses, popes, and cardinals is, spoon at the ready, with mouth missing some front teeth, Annibale Carracci's lonely *Beaneater.* As W. H. Auden put it, "Grub first, art later." At noon, there's a guided tour in English, included in your entrance fee. In 2013 the gallery opened a new wing, including its tapestry room, to the public. ⊠ *Via della Pilotta 17, Piazza di Spagna* ☎ *06/6784350* ⊕ *www.galleriacolonna.it* ⊠ *€12* ⊗ *Sat. 9–1:15; tour in English at noon, private tours available on request.*

Fodor's Choice
★

Palazzo Doria Pamphilj. Along with the Palazzo Colonna and the Galleria Borghese, this spectacular family palace provides the best glimpse of aristocratic Rome. Here, the main attractions are the legendary old master paintings, including treasures by Velázquez and Caravaggio; the splendor of the main galleries; and a unique suite of private family apartments. The beauty of the graceful 18th-century facade of this patrician palace may escape you unless you take time to step to the opposite side of the street for a good view; it was designed by Gabriele Valvassori in 1730. The foundations of the immense complex of buildings probably date from classical times. The current building dates from the 15th century, with the exception of the facade. It passed through several hands before it became the property of the famous seafaring Doria family of Genoa, who had married into the Roman Pamphilj (also spelled Pamphili) clan. As in most of Rome's older patrician residences, the family still live in part of the palace.

Housed in four wings that line the palace's courtyard, the picture gallery contains 550 paintings, including three by Caravaggio—a young *St. John the Baptist, Mary Magdalene,* and the breathtaking *Rest on the Flight to Egypt.* Off the eyepopping **Galleria degli Specchi** (Gallery of Mirrors)—a smaller version of the one at Versailles—are the famous Velázquez *Pope Innocent X,* considered by some historians to be the greatest portrait ever painted, and the Bernini bust of the same Pamphilj pope. Elsewhere you'll find a Titian, a double portrait by Raphael, and some noted 17th-century landscapes by Claude Lorrain and Gaspar Dughet. ⊠ *Via del Corso 305, Around Piazza Navona* ☎ *06/6797323* ⊕ *www.dopart.it* ⊠ *€11* ⊗ *Daily 9–7; last entrance 1 hr before closing.*

Fodor's Choice
★

Sant'Ignazio. Rome's largest Jesuit church, this 17th-century landmark harbors some of the most city's magnificent trompe-l'oeil. To get the full effect of the marvelous illusionistic ceiling by priest-artist Andrea Pozzo, stand on the small disk set into the floor of the nave. The heavenly vision above you, seemingly extending upward almost indefinitely, represents the *Allegory of the Missionary Work of the Jesuits* and is part of Pozzo's cycle of works in this church exalting the early history of the Jesuit

Order, whose founder was the reformer Ignatius of Loyola. The saint soars heavenward, supported by a cast of thousands; not far behind is Saint Francis Xavier, apostle of the Indies, leading a crowd of Eastern converts; a bare-breasted, spear-wielding America in American Indian headdress rides a jaguar; Europe with crown and scepter sits serene on a heftily rumped horse; while a splendid Africa with gold tiara perches on a lucky crocodile. The artist repeated this illusionist technique, so popular in the late 17th century, in the false dome, which is actually a flat canvas—a trompe-l'oeil trick used when the budget ran dry. The overall effect of the frescoes is dazzling (be sure to have coins handy for the machine that switches on the lights) and was fully intended to rival that produced by Baciccia in the nearby mother church of Il Gesù. ⊠ *Piazza Sant'Ignazio, Around Piazza Navona* ☎ *06/6794406* ⊕ *www.chiesasantignazio.it* ☉ *Mon.–Sat. 7:30–7 (Aug. 9–7), Sun. and holidays 9–7.*

FAMILY **The Spanish Steps.** That icon of postcard Rome, the Spanish Steps (often called simply *"la scalinata"*—"the staircase"—by Italians) and the Piazza di Spagna from which they ascend both get their names from the Spanish Embassy to the Vatican on the piazza—even though the staircase was built with French funds in 1723. In honor of a diplomatic visit by the king of Spain, the hillside was transformed by architect Francesco de Sanctis to link the church of Trinità dei Monti at the top with the Via dei Condotti below. In an allusion to the church, the staircase is divided by three landings (beautifully banked with azaleas from mid-April to mid-May). For centuries, the scalinata and its neighborhood have welcomed tourists, dukes, and writers in search of inspiration—among them Stendhal, Honoré de Balzac, William Makepeace Thackeray, and Byron, along with today's enthusiastic hordes. Bookending the bottom of the steps are two monuments to the 18th-century days when the English colonized the area: to the right, the Keats-Shelley House, and to the left, Babington's Tea Rooms—both beautifully redolent of the Grand Tour era. For weary sightseers, there is an elevator at Vicolo del Bottino 8 (next to the adjacent Metro entrance), but those with mobility problems should be aware that there is still a small flight of stairs after (it also is sometimes closed for repair). Be aware, too, that this area is in a constant state of work through 2016: although the lovely Barcaccia (or "little boat") fountain has been restored and was unveiled in September 2014 to its current, gleaming-white loveliness, the entire staircase is getting a facelift throughout 2015 and 2016, thanks to a €1.5-million contribution by Rome jeweler Bulgari. ■TIP→ **In recent years, a low-grade but annoying scam has proliferated in the piazza. This is the "rose scam," where a man comes up to a female tourist with a rose and insists he's giving it to her for free. When she takes it, he waits a couple of beats and then goes to a gentleman in her party, asking for just a few euros for the flower. Often, everyone concerned is too embarrassed not to pay. If this happens to you, simply firmly refuse the rose from the beginning, or hand it back when you're asked for money. Unless you want it, of course!** ⊠ *Intersection of vias Condotti, del Babuino, and Due Macelli, Piazza di Spagna* Ⓜ *Spagna.*

Fodor's Choice **Trevi Fountain.** Alive with rushing waters commanded by an imperious
★ Oceanus, the Fontana di Trevi (Trevi Fountain) earned full-fledged
iconic status in 1954 when it starred in 20th-Century Fox's *Three Coins
in the Fountain.* As the first color film in Cinemascope to be produced
on location, it caused practically half of America to pack their bags for
the Eternal City.

From the very start, however, the Trevi has been all about theatrical effect. An aquatic marvel in a city filled with them, the fountain's
unique drama is largely due to the site: its vast basin is squeezed into
the tight meeting of three little streets (the *"tre vie,"* which may give
the fountain its name) with cascades emerging as if from the wall of
Palazzo Poli. The conceit of a fountain emerging full-force from a palace
was first envisioned by Bernini and Pietro da Cortona for Pope Urban
VIII's plan to rebuild the fountain (which marked the end-point of the
ancient Acqua Vergine aqueduct, created in 18 BC by Agrippa). Only
three popes later, under Pope Clement XIII, did Nicolo Salvi finally
break ground with his winning design.

Salvi had his cake and ate it, too, for while he dazzles the eye with
Baroque pyrotechnics—the sculpted seashells, the roaring seabeasts, the
divalike mermaids—he slyly incorporates them in a stately triumphal
arch (in fact, Clement was then restoring Rome's Arch of Constantine).
Salvi, unfortunately, did not live to see his masterpiece completed in
1762: working in the culverts of the aqueduct 11 years earlier, he caught
his death of cold.

The fountain has been undergoing a long-overdue restoration that has
left most of it under scaffolding; the €2.18 million bill is being picked
up by Rome fashion house Fendi. The scaffolding should be off, and
a gleaming Trevi Fountain unveiled, by late 2016. In the meantime, a
temporary basin has been built to allow visitors to continue the Trevi's
most famous tradition—tossing coins in the fountain. ⊠ *Piazza di Trevi,
Piazza di Spagna* Ⓜ *Barberini–Fontana di Trevi.*

WORTH NOTING

Il Gesù. The mother church of the Jesuits in Rome is the prototype of
all Counter-Reformation churches. Considered the first fully Baroque
church, it has spectacular interior that tells a lot about an era of religious triumph and turmoil. Its architecture (the overall design was by
Vignola, the facade by della Porta) influenced ecclesiastical building in
Rome for more than a century and was exported by the Jesuits throughout the rest of Europe. Though consecrated as early as 1584, the interior
of the church wasn't decorated for another 100 years. It was originally
intended that the interior be left plain to the point of austerity—but,
when it was finally embellished, no expense was spared. Its interior
drips with gold and lapis lazuli, gold and precious marbles, gold and
more gold, all covered by a fantastically painted ceiling by Baciccia.
Unfortunately, the church is also one of Rome's most crepuscular, so its
visual magnificence is considerably dulled by lack of light.
⊠ *Piazza del Ges, off Via del Plebiscito, Campo de' Fiori* ☎ *06/697001*
⊕ *www.chiesadelgesu.org* ⊙ *Daily 7–12:30 and 4–7:45.*

Keats-Shelley Memorial House. Sent to Rome in a last-ditch attempt to treat his consumption, English Romantic poet John Keats lived—and died—in this house at the foot of the Spanish Steps. At that point, this was the heart of the colorful bohemian quarter of Rome that was especially favored by the English. Keats had become celebrated through such poems as "Ode to a Nightingale" and "She Walks in Beauty," but his trip to Rome was fruitless. He breathed his last here on February 23, 1821, aged only 25, forevermore the epitome of the doomed poet. In this "Casina di Keats," you can visit his rooms, although all his furnishings were burned after his death as a sanitary measure by the local authorities. You'll also find a rather quaint collection of memorabilia of English literary figures of the period—Lord Byron, Percy Bysshe Shelley, Joseph Severn, and Leigh Hunt as well as Keats—and an exhaustive library of works on the Romantics. ⊠ *Piazza di Spagna 26* ☏ *06/6784235* ⊕ *www.keats-shelley-house.org* ☙ *€5* ☾ *Mon.–Sat. 10–1 and 2–6* Ⓜ *Spagna.*

REPUBBLICA AND THE QUIRINALE

This sector of Rome stretches down from the 19th-century district built up around the Piazza della Repubblica—originally laid out to serve as a monumental foyer between the Termini train station and the rest of the city—and over the rest of the Quirinale. The highest of ancient Rome's famed seven hills, it's crowned by the massive Palazzo Quirinale, home to the popes until 1870 and now Italy's presidential palace. Along the way, you can see ancient Roman sculptures, Early Christian churches, and highlights from the 16th and 17th centuries, when Rome was conquered by the Baroque—and by Bernini.

Although Bernini's work feels omnipresent in much of the city center, the Renaissance-man range of his work is particularly notable here. The artist as architect considered the church of Sant'Andrea al Quirinale one of his best; Bernini the urban designer and water worker is responsible for the muscle-bound sea god who blows his conch so provocatively in the fountain at the center of whirling Piazza Barberini. And Bernini the master gives religious passion a joltingly corporeal treatment in what is perhaps his greatest work, the *Ecstasy of St. Teresa,* in the church of Santa Maria della Vittoria.

GETTING HERE AND AROUND
Bus No. 40 will get you from Termini station to Via Nazionale, an artery of the Quirinale, in one stop; from the Vatican, take Bus No. 64 or Metro Line A to the very busy and convenient Repubblica metro stop on the piazza of the same name. Bus No. 62 and the metro also run from the Vatican to Piazza Barberini.

TOP ATTRACTIONS
Capuchin Crypt. Not for the easily spooked, the crypt under the Church of Santa Maria della Concezione holds the bones of some 4,000 dead Capuchin monks. Arranged in odd decorative designs around the shriveled and decayed skeletons of their kinsmen, a macabre reminder of the impermanence of earthly life, the crypt is strangely touching and beautiful. As one sign proclaims, "What you are, we once were. What we are,

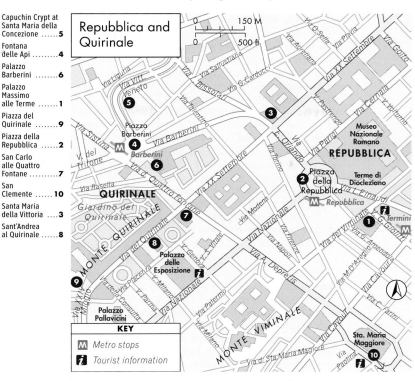

Republica and Quirinale

REPUBBLICA

QUIRINALE

Piazza Barberini

Piazza della Repubblica

Museo Nazionale Romano

Terme di Diocleziano

Giardino del Quirinale

Palazzo delle Esposizione

Palazzo Pallavicini

Sta. Maria Maggiore

KEY

Ⓜ *Metro stops*

🛈 *Tourist information*

you someday will be." After a recent renovation, the crypt was reopened to the public with a new museum devoted to teaching visitors about the Capuchin order; the crypt is now located at the end of the museum circuit. Upstairs in the church, the first chapel on the right contains Guido Reni's mid-17th-century *St. Michael Trampling the Devil*. The painting caused great scandal after an astute contemporary observer remarked that the face of the devil bore a surprising resemblance to the Pamphilj Pope Innocent X, archenemy of Reni's Barberini patrons. Compare the devil with the bust of the pope that you saw in the Palazzo Doria Pamphilj and judge for yourself. ☒ *Via Veneto 27, Quirinale* ☎ *06/88803695* ⊕ *www.cappucciniviaveneto.it* ☒ *€6, includes museum and crypt* ☾ *Fri.–Wed. 9–7* Ⓜ *Barberini.*

Palazzo Barberini. One of Rome's most splendid 17th-century palaces, the recently renovated Palazzo Barberini is a landmark of the Roman Baroque style. Pope Urban VIII had acquired the property and given it to a nephew, who was determined to build an edifice worthy of his generous uncle and the ever-more-powerful Barberini clan. The result was, architecturally, a precedent-shattering affair—a "villa suburbana" set right in the heart of the urban city and designed to be strikingly open to the outdoors. Note how Carlo Maderno's grand facade seems almost entirely composed of window tiers rising up in proto–20th century fashion.

Ascend Bernini's staircase to the Galleria Nazionale d'Arte Antica, hung with famed paintings including Raphael's *La Fornarina*, a luminous portrait of the artist's lover (a resident of Trastevere, she was reputedly a baker's daughter)—study the bracelet on her upper arm bearing Raphael's name. Also noteworthy are Guido Reni's portrait of the doomed Beatrice Cenci (beheaded in Rome for patricide in 1599)—Hawthorne called it "the saddest picture ever painted" in his Rome-based novel, *The Marble Faun*—and Caravaggio's *Judith and Holofernes*.

But the showstopper here is the palace's Gran Salone, a vast ballroom with a ceiling painted in 1630 by the third (and too-often neglected) master of the Roman Baroque, Pietro da Cortona. It depicts the *Glorification of Urban VIII's Reign* and has the spectacular conceit of glorifying Urban VIII as the agent of Divine Providence and escorted by a "bomber squadron" (to quote art historian Sir Michael Levey) of some huge, mutantlike Barberini bees, the heraldic symbol of the family. ✉ *Via Barberini 18, Quirinale* ☎ *06/32810* ⊕ *www.galleriaborghese.it* 🎟 *€7* ⊙ *Tues.–Sun. 8:30–7; ticket office closes 1 hr early* Ⓜ *Barberini; Bus 52, 56, 60, 95, 116, 175, or 492.*

Fodor'sChoice **Palazzo Massimo alle Terme.** Come here to get a real feel for ancient
★ Roman art—the collection rivals even the Vatican's. The Roman National Museum, with a collection ranging from striking classical Roman paintings to marble bric-a-brac, has been organized in four locations: here, Palazzo Altemps, Crypta Balbi, and the Museo delle Terme di Diocleziano. The vast structure of the Palazzo Massimo holds the great ancient treasures of the archaeological collection and also the coin collection. Highlights include the *Niobid*, the famous bronze *Boxer*, and the *Discobolus Lancelloti*. Pride of place goes, however, to the great ancient frescoes on view, stunningly set up to "re-create" the look of the homes they once decorated. These include stuccos and wall paintings found in the area of the Villa della Farnesina (in Trastevere) and the legendary frescoes from Empress Livia's villa at Prima Porta, delightful depictions of a garden in bloom and an orchard alive with birds. Their colors are remarkably well preserved. These delicate decorations covered the walls of cool, sunken rooms in Livia's summer house outside the city. ■TIP→ **Admission includes entrance to all four national museums, good for three days.** ✉ *Largo Villa Peretti 1, Repubblica* ☎ *06/39967700* ⊕ *www.coopculture.it* 🎟 *€7* ⊙ *Tues.–Sun. 9–7:45* Ⓜ *Repubblica.*

Piazza del Quirinale. This strategic location atop the Quirinal Hill has long been of great importance. It served as home of the Sabines in the 7th century BC, then deadly enemies of the Romans, who lived on the Capitoline and Palatine Hills (all of 1 km [½ mile] away). Today it's the foreground for the presidential residence, Palazzo del Quirinale, and home to the **Palazzo della Consulta,** where Italy's Constitutional Court sits. The open side of the piazza has an impressive vista of the rooftops and domes of central Rome and St. Peter's. The **Fontana di Montecavallo,** or Fontana dei Dioscuri, is composed of a huge Roman statuary group and an obelisk from the tomb of the emperor Augustus. The group of the Dioscuri trying to tame two massive marble steeds was found in the Baths of Constantine, which occupied part of the summit of the Quirinal Hill. Unlike just about every other ancient statue in Rome, this group survived the Dark Ages intact and accordingly became one of the city's great sights, especially during the Middle Ages. Next to the figures, the ancient obelisk from the Mausoleo di Augusto (Tomb of Augustus) was put here by Pope Pius VI at the end of the 18th century. ⊠ *Quirinale* Ⓜ *Barberini*.

FodorśChoice
★

San Carlo alle Quattro Fontane. Sometimes identified with the diminutive San Carlino because of its tiny size, this is one of Borromini's master-pieces. In a space no larger than the base of one of the piers of St. Peter's Basilica, he created a church that is an intricate exercise in geometric perfection, with a coffered dome that seems to float above the curves of the walls. Borromini's work is often bizarre, definitely intellectual, and intensely concerned with pure form. In San Carlo, he invented an original treatment of space that creates an effect of rippling movement, especially evident in the double-S curves of the facade. Characteristically, the interior decoration is subdued, in white stucco with no more than a few touches of gilding, so as not to distract from the form. Don't miss the **cloister**, a tiny, understated Baroque jewel, with a graceful portico and loggia above, echoing the lines of the church. ⇨ *For more on Borromini and this church, see our special photo feature, "Baroque and Desperate: The Tragic Rivalry of Bernini and Borromini" in this chapter.* ⊠ *Via del Quirinale 23, Quirinale* ☎ *06/4883109* ⊕ *www.sancarlino-borromini. it* ⊙ *Weekdays 10–1 and 3–6, Sat. 10–1, Sun. noon–1* Ⓜ *Barberini*.

FodorśChoice
★

San Clemente. One of the most impressive archaeological sites in Rome, San Clemente is a historical triple-decker. A 12th-century church was built on top of a 4th-century church, which in turn was built over a 2nd-century pagan temple to the god Mithras and 1st-century Roman apartments. The layers were rediscovered in 1857, when a curious prior, Friar Joseph Mullooly, started excavations beneath the present basilica. Today, you can descend to explore all three.

The **upper church** (at street level) is a gem even on its own. In the apse, a glittering 12th-century mosaic shows Jesus on a cross that turns into a living tree. Green acanthus leaves swirl and teem with small scenes of everyday life. Early Christian symbols, including doves, vines, and fish, decorate the 4th-century marble choir screens. In the left nave, the Castiglioni chapel holds frescoes painted around 1400 by the Florentine artist Masolino da Panicale (1383–1440), a key figure in the introduction of realism and one-point perspective into Renaissance painting. Note the large Crucifixion and scenes from the lives of Sts. Catherine, Ambrose, and Christopher, plus an Annunciation (over the entrance).

To the right of the sacristy (and bookshop), descend the stairs to the **4th-century church,** used until 1084, when it was damaged beyond repair during a siege of the area by the Norman prince Robert Guiscard. Still intact are some vibrant 11th-century frescoes depicting stories from the life of St. Clement. Don't miss the last fresco on the left, in what used to be the central nave. It includes a particularly colorful quote (including "Go on, you sons of harlots, pull!")—not only is it unusual for a religious painting, but one of the earliest examples of written vernacular Italian.

Descend an additional set of stairs to the **mithraeum**, a shrine dedicated to the god Mithras. His cult spread from Persia and gained a hold in Rome during the 2nd and 3rd centuries AD. Mithras was believed to have been born in a cave and was thus worshipped in underground, cavernous chambers, where initiates into the all-male cult would share a meal while reclining on stone couches, some visible here along with the altar block. Most such pagan shrines in Rome were destroyed by Christians, who often built churches over their remains, as happened here. ⊠ *Via San Giovanni in Laterano 108, Celio* ☎ *06/7740021* ⊕ *www.basilicasanclemente.com* ⊠ *Archaeological area €5* ⊙ *Mon.– Sat. 9–12:30 and 3–6, Sun. noon–6* Ⓜ *Colosseo.*

Santa Maria della Vittoria. Like the church of Santa Susanna across Piazza San Bernardo, this church was designed by Carlo Maderno, but this one is best known for Bernini's sumptuous Baroque decoration of the **Cappella Cornaro** (Cornaro Chapel), on the left as you face the altar, where you'll find his interpretation of heavenly ecstasy in his statue of the *Ecstasy of St. Theresa (*⇨ *For more on Bernini, see our special photo feature, "Baroque and Desperate: The Tragic Rivalry of Bernini and Borromini" in this chapter).* Your eye is drawn effortlessly from the frescoes on the ceiling down to the marble figures of the angel and the swooning saint, to the earthly figures of the Cornaro family (who commissioned the chapel), to the two inlays of marble skeletons in the pavement, representing the hope and despair of souls in purgatory.

Evident in other works of the period, the theatricality of the chapel is the result of Bernini's masterly fusion of elements. This is one of the key examples of the mature Roman high Baroque. Bernini's audacious conceit was to model the chapel as a theater: Members of the Cornaro family—sculpted in colored marbles—watch from theater boxes as, center stage, the great moment of divine love is played out before them. The swooning saint's robes appear to be on fire, quivering with life, and the white marble group seems suspended in the heavens as golden rays illuminate the scene. An angel assists at the mystical moment of Theresa's vision as the saint abandons herself to the joys of heavenly love. Bernini represented this mystical experience in what, to modern eyes, may seem very earthly terms. ⊠ *Via XX Settembre 17, Largo Santa Susanna, Repubblica* ☎ *06/42740571* ⊕ *www.chiesasantamariavittoriaroma.it* ⊙ *Daily 7–noon and 3:30–7* Ⓜ *Repubblica.*

WORTH NOTING

Fontana delle Api (*Fountain of the Bees*). Decorated with the famous heraldic bees of the Barberini family, the upper shell and the inscription are from a fountain that Bernini designed for Pope Urban VIII; the rest was lost when the fountain had to be moved to make way for a new street. The inscription was the cause of a considerable scandal when the fountain was first put up in 1644. It said that the fountain had been erected in the 22nd year of the pontiff's reign, although in fact the 21st anniversary of Urban's election to the papacy was still some weeks away. The last numeral was hurriedly erased, but to no avail—Urban died eight days before the beginning of his 22nd year as pope. The superstitious Romans, who had immediately recognized the inscription as a foolhardy tempting of fate, were vindicated. Thanks to a recent restoration and cleaning, the once-dirty fountain has been returned to its former glory. ⊠ *Via Veneto at Piazza Barberini, Quirinale* Ⓜ *Barberini.*

Piazza della Repubblica. Often the first view that spells "Rome" to weary travelers walking from the Stazione Termini, this broad square was laid out in the late 1800s and includes the exuberant **Fontana delle Naiadi** (Fountain of the Naiads). This pièce de résistance is draped with voluptuous bronze ladies wrestling happily with marine monsters. The nudes weren't there when the pope unveiled the fountain in 1870, sparing him any embarrassment. But when the figures were added in 1901, they caused a scandal. It's said that the sculptor, Rutelli, modeled them on the ample figures of two musical comedy stars of the day. The piazza owes its curved lines to the structures of the Terme di Diocleziano; the curving, colonnaded Neoclassical buildings on the southwest side trace the underlying form of the ancient baths. Today, one of them is occupied by the superdeluxe Hotel Exedra—which shows you how much the fortunes of the formerly tatterdemalion part of the city have changed. Ⓜ *Repubblica.*

Sant'Andrea al Quirinale. Designed by Bernini, this is an architectural gem of the Baroque. His son wrote that Bernini considered it one of his best works and that he used to come here occasionally just to sit and enjoy it. Bernini's simple oval plan, a classic of Baroque architecture, is given drama and movement by the church's decoration, which carries the story of St. Andrew's martyrdom and ascension into heaven, starting with the painting over the high altar, up past the figure of the saint over the chancel door, to the angels at the base of the lantern and the dove of the Holy Spirit that awaits on high. ⊠ *Via del Quirinale 29, Quirinale* ☎ *06/4740807* ⊕ *www.gesuitialquirinale.it* ☉ *Mon.–Sat. 8:30–noon and 2:30–6, Sun. 9–noon and 3–6* Ⓜ *Barberini.*

VILLA BORGHESE AND PIAZZA DEL POPOLO

Touring Rome's artistic masterpieces while staying clear of its hustle and bustle can be, quite literally, a walk in the park. Some of the city's finest sights are tucked away in or next to green lawns and pedestrian piazzas, offering a breath of fresh air for weary sightseers, especially in the Villa Borghese park. One of Rome's largest, this park can alleviate gallery gout by offering an oasis in which to cool off under the ilex, oak, and umbrella pine trees. If you feel like a picnic, have an *alimentari* (food shop) make you some panini before you go; food carts within the park are overpriced.

GETTING HERE AND AROUND

Electric Bus No. 119 does a loop that connects Largo Argentina, Piazza Venezia, Piazza di Spagna, and Piazza del Popolo. The No. 117 connects Piazza del Popolo to Piazza Venezia and the Colosseum. The No. 116 motors through the Villa Borghese to the museum and connects the area with Piazza Navona, Campo de' Fiori, and the Pantheon. Piazza del Popolo has a metro stop called Flaminio.

Fodor's Choice
★ **Galleria Borghese.** It's a real toss-up as to which is more magnificent: the villa built for Cardinal Scipione Borghese in 1612, or the art that lies within. Despite its beauty, the villa never was used as a residence. Instead, the luxury-loving cardinal built it as a showcase for his fabulous collection of both antiquities and more "modern" works, including those he commissioned from the masters Caravaggio and Bernini. Today, it's a monument to Roman interior decoration at its most extravagant. With the passage of time, however, the building has become less celebrated than the collections housed within, including one of the finest collections of Baroque sculpture anywhere in the world.

Like the gardens, the casino and its collections have undergone many changes since the 17th century. The building was largely redecorated in the late 18th century, when the villa received many of its eye-popping ceiling frescoes (although some original decorations also survive). The biggest change to the collection, however, came thanks to Camillo Borghese. After marrying Napoléon's sister Pauline, he sold 154 statues, 170 bas-reliefs, 160 busts, 30 columns, and a number of vases, all ancient pieces, to his new brother-in-law. Today, those sculptures, including the so-called Borghese Gladiator and Borghese Hermaphroditus, are in the Louvre in Paris. At the end of the 19th century, a later member of the family, Francesco Borghese, attempted damage control with his fellow Romans (outraged that many of their art treasures had been shipped off to Paris) with some new acquisitions; he also transferred to the casino the remaining works of art then housed in Palazzo Borghese. In 1902 the casino, its contents, and the estate were sold to the Italian government.

One of the most famous works in the collection is Canova's Neoclassical sculpture of Pauline Borghese as Venus Victrix. Scandalously, Pauline reclines on a Roman sofa, bare-bosomed, her hips swathed in classical drapery, the very model of haughty detachment with a sly come-hither stare. You can imagine what the 19th-century gossips were saying!

The next three rooms hold three key early Baroque sculptures: Bernini's *David, Apollo and Daphne,* and *Rape of Proserpina.* All were done when the artist was in his 20s, and all illustrate Bernini's extraordinary skill. Other Berninis on view in the collection include a large, unfinished figure called *Verità,* or Truth. Bernini began work on this brooding figure after the death of his principal patron, Pope Urban VIII. It was meant to form part of a work titled *Truth Revealed by Time.* The next pope, Innocent X, had little love for the ebullient Urban, and, as was the way in Rome, this meant that Bernini would be excluded from the new pope's favors. However, Bernini's towering genius was such that the new pope came around with his patronage with almost indecent haste.

The Caravaggio Room holds works by this hotheaded genius, who died of malaria at age 37. All of his paintings, even the charming *Boy with a Basket of Fruit,* seethe with an undercurrent of darkness. The disquieting *Sick Bacchus* is a self-portrait of the artist who, like the god, had a penchant for wine. *David and Goliath,* painted in the last year

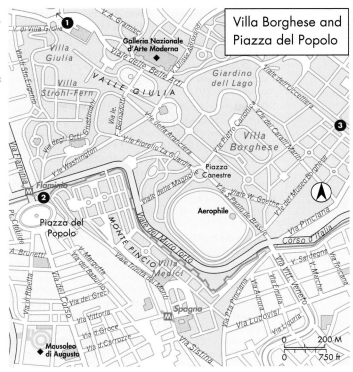

Villa Borghese and Piazza del Popolo

of Caravaggio's life—while he was on the lam for murder—includes a self-portrait in the head of Goliath. Upstairs, the Pinacoteca (Picture Gallery) boasts paintings by Raphael (including his moving *Deposition*), Pinturicchio, Perugino, Bellini, and Rubens. Probably the gallery's most famous painting is Titian's allegorical *Sacred and Profane Love,* a mysterious and yet-unsolved image with two female figures, one nude, one clothed.

■TIP➡ **Admission to the Museo is by reservation only.** Visitors are admitted in two-hour shifts from 9 to 5. Prime-time slots can sell out days in advance, so in high season reserve by phone or directly through the Borghese's website. You need to collect your reserved ticket at the museum ticket office a half hour before your entrance. However, when it's not busy, you can purchase your ticket at the museum for the next entrance appointment. ⊠ *Piazza Scipione Borghese 5, off Via Pinciana, Villa Borghese* ☎ *06/32810 for reservations, 06/8413979 for info* ⊕ *www.galleriaborghese.it* ⧉ *€11, including a €2 reservation fee; audio guide €5* ⊙ *Tues.–Sun. 8:30–7:30* Ⓜ *Bus No. 910 from Piazza della Repubblica, or Tram No. 19 or Bus No. 3 from Policlinico.*

Fodor's Choice **MAXXI—Museo Nazionale delle Arti del XXI Secolo** (*National Museum of ★ 21st-Century Arts*). It took 10 years and cost some €150 million, but for art lovers, Italy's first national museum devoted to contemporary art and architecture was worth it. The building alone impresses, as it should: the design, by Anglo-Iraqi starchitect Zaha Hadid, triumphed over 272 other contest entries. The building plays with lots of natural light, curving and angular lines, and big open spaces, all meant to question the division between "within" and "without" (think glass ceilings and steel staircases that twist through the air). While not every critic adored it at its 2010 unveiling, it's hard not to feel delighted by the surprisingly playful space.

The MAXXI hosts temporary exhibits on art, architecture, film, and more. Past shows have included a retrospective on top Arte Povera artist Michelangelo Pistoletto and an exhibit of works by architect and engineer Pietro Nervi. From the permanent collection, rotated through the museum, more than 350 works represent artists including Andy Warhol, Francesco Clemente, and Gerhard Richter. ⊠ *Via Guido Reni 4, Flaminio* ☎ *06/32810* ⊕ *www.fondazionemaxxi.it* 💶 *€11* 🕙 *Tues.–Fri. and Sun. 11–7, Sat. 11–10; ticket office closes 1 hr early* Ⓜ *Flaminio, then Tram 2 to Apollodoro; Bus 53, 217, 280, 910.*

Fodor's Choice
★
Santa Maria del Popolo. Standing inconspicuously in a corner of the vast Piazza del Popolo, this church often goes unnoticed, but the treasures inside make it a must for art lovers, as they include an entire chapel designed by Raphael and one adorned with striking Caravaggio masterpieces. Bramante enlarged the apse of the church, which had been rebuilt in the 15th century on the site of a much older place of worship. Inside, in the first chapel on the right, you'll see some frescoes by Pinturicchio from the mid-15th century; the adjacent **Cybo Chapel** is a 17th-century exercise in marble decoration. Raphael's famous **Chigi Chapel,** the second on the left, was built around 1513 and commissioned by the banker Agostino Chigi (who also had the artist decorate his home across the Tiber, the Villa Farnesina). Raphael provided the cartoons for the vault mosaic—showing God the Father in benediction—and the designs for the statues of Jonah and Elijah. More than a century later, Bernini added the oval medallions on the tombs and the statues of Daniel and Habakkuk, when, in the mid-17th century another Chigi, Pope Alexander VII, commissioned him to restore and decorate the building.

The organ case of Bernini in the right transept bears the Della Rovere family oak tree, part of the Chigi family's coat of arms. The **choir,** with vault frescoes by Pinturicchio, contains the handsome tombs of Ascanio Sforza and Girolamo delle Rovere, both designed by Andrea Sansovino. The best is for last: The **Cerasi Chapel,** to the left of the high altar, holds two Caravaggios, the *Crucifixion of St. Peter* and the *Conversion of St. Paul.* ⊠ *Piazza del Popolo 12, near Porta Pinciana, Piazza del Popolo* ☎ *06/3610836* ⊕ *www.santamariadelpopolo.it* 🕙 *Mon.– Thurs. 7:15–12:30 and 4–7, Fri. and Sat. 7:30–7, Sun. 7:30–1:30 and 4:30–7:30* Ⓜ *Flaminio.*

THE VATICAN

Capital of the Catholic Church, this tiny walled city-state is a place where some people go to find a work of art—Michelangelo's frescoes, rare ancient Roman marbles, or Bernini's statues. Others go to find their souls. Whatever the reason, thanks to being the seat of world Catholicism and also address to the most overwhelming architectural achievement of the 16th and 17th centuries—St. Peter's Basilica—the Vatican attracts millions of travelers every year. In addition, the Vatican Museums are famed for magnificent rooms decorated by Raphael, sculptures such as the *Apollo Belvedere* and the *Laocoön*, paintings by Giotto, frescoes by Raphael, and the celebrated ceiling of the Sistine Chapel. The Church power that emerged as imperial Rome declined gave impetus to a profusion of artistic expression and shaped the destiny of the city for a thousand years. Allow yourself an hour to see St. Peter's Basilica, at least two hours for the museums, an hour for Castel Sant'Angelo, and an hour to climb to the top of the dome. Note that ushers at the entrance of St. Peter's Basilica and the Vatican Museums bar entry to people with "inappropriate" clothing—which means no bare knees or shoulders.

Outside the Vatican, the Borgo and Prati neighborhoods have restaurants, lots of souvenir shops, and a few hotels.

GETTING HERE AND AROUND

From Termini station, hop on Bus No. 40 Express or No. 64 to be delivered to Piazza San Pietro. Metro stops Cipro or Ottaviano will get you within about a 10-minute walk of the entrance to the Vatican Museums (use Ottaviano for St. Peter's Basilica).

TOP ATTRACTIONS

Fodor's Choice
★

Basilica di San Pietro. The world's largest church, built over the tomb of St. Peter, is the most imposing and breathtaking architectural achievement of the Renaissance (although much of the lavish interior dates to the Baroque). The physical statistics are impressive: it covers 18,000 square yards, runs 212 yards in length, and is surmounted by a dome that rises 435 feet and measures 138 feet across its base. Its history is equally impressive. No fewer than five of Italy's greatest artists—Bramante, Raphael, Peruzzi, Antonio Sangallo the Younger, and Michelangelo—died while striving to erect this new St. Peter's.

The history of the original St. Peter's goes back to AD 349, when the emperor Constantine completed a basilica over the site of the tomb of St. Peter, the Church's first pope. The original church stood for more than 1,000 years, undergoing a number of restorations and alterations, until, toward the middle of the 15th century, it was verging on collapse. In 1452 a reconstruction job began but was quickly abandoned for lack of money. In 1503, Pope Julius II instructed the architect Bramante to raze all the existing buildings and to build a new basilica, one that would surpass even Constantine's for grandeur. It wasn't until 1626 that the basilica was completed and consecrated.

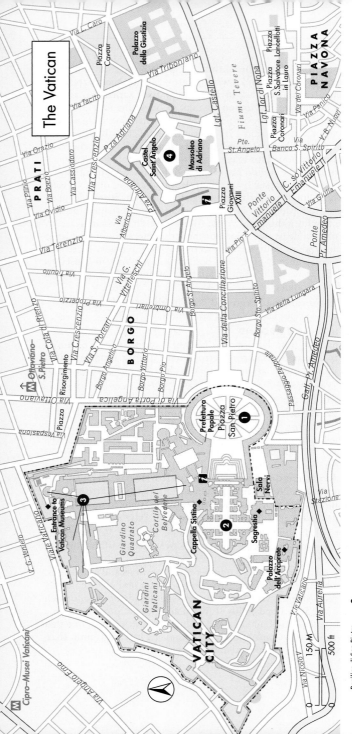

The Vatican

PRATI

Via L. Caro
Via Tacito
Via Orazio
Via Plinio
Via Boezio
Via Cassiodoro
Via Ovidio
Via Terenzio
Via Tibullo
Via G. Vitelleschi
Via G. Vitelleschi
Via Properzio
Via S. Porcari
Via Crescenzio
Via Cola di Rienzo
Via Cicerone
Piazza Cavour
Palazzo della Giustizia
Via Tribonjano
P.za Adriana
Via Terenzio
Via Alberico II

Fiume Tevere
Lgt. Castello
Lgt. Tor di Nona
Piazza di Nona
Piazza S.Salvatore Lancellotti in Lauro
Via dei Coronari
Piazza Coronari
Via B. Nubon
Via Panico

PIAZZA NAVONA
Piazza S.Salvatore Lancellotti in Lauro

Ponte Vittorio Emanuele I
C. so Vittorio Emanuele I
Via Giulia

Castel Saint'Angelo ❹
Mausoleo di Adriano

Piazza Giovanni XXIII
Pte. St.Angelo
Piazza Banco S. Spirito
Via Banco S. Spirito

Via Pio X
Via della Conciliazione

Borgo Sto. Spirito
Via della Lungara

BORGO
Via Ombrellari
Borgo Vittorio
Borgo Angelico
Borgo Pio
Borgo S.Angelo
Via di Porta Angelica

Ottaviano–S. Pietro
Piazza Risorgimento
Via Ottaviano
Piazza Vespasiano

V. G. Veneto
Viale Vaticano
Entrance to Vatican Museums ❸

Giardino Quadrato
Cortile del Belvedere
Cappella Sistina
Sagrestia
Palazzo dell'Arciprete

Prefettura Papale
Piazza San Pietro ❶
Sala Nervi

Giardini Vaticani

VATICAN CITY

Via Stazione
V.le Vaticano
V.le Aurelia
Via Nicolo V

150 M
500 ft

Cipro–Musei Vaticani
V. Angelo Emo

St. Peter's Crossing and Dome

Though Bramante made little progress in rebuilding St. Peter's, he succeeded in outlining a basic plan for the church. He also, crucially, built the piers of the crossings—the massive pillars supporting the dome. After Bramante's death in 1514, Raphael, the Sangallos, and Peruzzi all proposed, at one time or another, variations on the original plan. In 1546, however, Pope Paul III turned to Michelangelo and forced the aging artist to complete the building. Michelangelo returned to Bramante's first idea of having a centralized Greek-cross plan—that is, with the "arms" of the church all the same length—and completed most of the exterior architecture except for the dome and the facade. His design for the dome, however, was modified after his death by Giacomo della Porta (his dome was much taller in proportion). Pope Paul V wanted a Latin-cross church (a church with one "arm" longer than the rest), so Carlo Maderno lengthened one of the arms to create a longer central nave.

Works by Giotto and Filarete

As you climb the shallow steps up to the great church, flanked by the statues of Sts. Peter and Paul, you'll see the **Loggia delle Benedizioni** (Benediction Loggia) over the central portal. This is the balcony where newly elected popes are proclaimed, and where they stand to give their apostolic blessing on solemn feast days. The vault of the vestibule is encrusted with rich stuccowork, and the mosaic above the central entrance to the portico is a much-restored work by the 14th-century painter Giotto that was in the original basilica. The bronze doors of the main entrance also were salvaged from the old basilica. The sculptor Filarete worked on them for 12 years; they show scenes from the martyrdom of St. Peter and St. Paul, and the life of Pope Eugene IV (1431–47), Filarete's patron.

Pause a moment to appraise the size of the great building. The people near the main altar seem dwarfed by the incredible dimensions of this immense temple. The statues, the pillars, and the holy-water stoups borne by colossal cherubs are all imposing. Walk over to where the cherub clings to a pier and place your arm across the sole of the cherub's foot; you will discover that it's as long as the distance from your fingers to your elbow. It's because the proportions of this giant building are in such perfect harmony that its vastness may escape you at first. Brass inscriptions in the marble pavement down the center of the nave indicate the approximate lengths of the world's other principal Christian churches, all of which fall far short of the 186-meter span of St. Peter's Basilica. In its mega scale—inspired by the spatial volumes of ancient Roman ruins—the church reflects Roman *grandiosità* in all its majesty.

As you enter the great nave, immediately to your right, behind a protective glass partition, is **Michelangelo's *Pietà*,** sculpted when the artist was only 25. The work was of such genius, some rivals spread rumors it was by someone else, prompting the artist to inscribe his name, unusually for him, across Mary's sash. Farther down, with its heavyweight crown barely denting its marble cushion, is Carlo Fontana's monument to Catholic convert and abdicated Queen Christina of Sweden (who is buried in the Grotte Vaticane below). Just across the way, in the **Cappella di San Sebastiano**, now lies the **tomb of Blessed Pope John Paul II.** The beloved pope's remains were moved into the chapel after his beatification on May 1, 2011. Exquisite bronze grilles and doors by Borromini open into the third chapel in the right aisle, the **Cappella del Santissimo Sacramento** (Chapel of the Most Holy Sacrament), generally open to visitors only from 7 am to 8:30 am, with a Baroque fresco of the Trinity by Pietro da Cortona. The lovely carved angels are by Bernini. At the last pillar on the right (the pier with Bernini's statue of St. Longinus) is a bronze statue of St. Peter, whose right foot is ritually touched by lines of pilgrims. In the right transept, over the door to the **Cappella di San Michele** (Chapel of St. Michael), usually closed, Canova created a brooding Neoclassical monument to Pope Clement XIII.

Bernini's Baldacchino

In the central crossing, Bernini's great bronze *baldacchino*—a huge, spiral-columned canopy—rises high over the *altare papale* (papal altar). At 100,000 pounds, it's said to be the largest, heaviest bronze object in the world. Circling the baldacchino are four larger-than-life statues of saints whose relics the Vatican has; the one of St. Longinus, holding the spear that pierced Christ's side, is another Bernini masterpiece. Meanwhile, Bernini designed the splendid gilt-bronze **Cattedra di San Pietro** (throne of St. Peter) in the apse above the main altar to contain a wooden and ivory chair that St. Peter himself is said to have used, though in fact it doesn't date from farther back than medieval times. (You can see a copy of the chair in the treasury.) Above, Bernini placed a window of thin alabaster sheets that diffuses a golden light around the dove, symbol of the Holy Spirit, in the center.

Two of the major papal funeral monuments in St. Peter's Basilica are on either side of the apse (and unfortunately are usually only dimly lighted). To the right is the **tomb of Pope Urban VIII**; to the left is the **tomb of Pope Paul III**. Paul's tomb is of an earlier date, designed between 1551 and 1575 by Giacomo della Porta, the architect who completed the dome of St. Peter's Basilica after Michelangelo's death. Many believed the nude figure of Justice to be a portrait of the pope's beautiful sister, Giulia. The charms of this alluring figure were such that in the 19th century, it was thought that she should no longer be allowed to distract worshippers from their prayers, and she was thenceforth clad in marble drapery. It was in emulation of this splendid late-Renaissance work that Urban VIII ordered Bernini to design his tomb. The real star here, however, is *la Bella Morte* ("Beautiful Death") who, all bone and elbows, dispatches the deceased pope above to a register of blue-black marble. The **tomb of Pope Alexander VII**, also designed by Bernini, stands to the left of the altar as you look up the nave, behind the farthest pier of the crossing. This may be the most haunting memorial in the basilica, thanks to another frightening skeletonized figure of Death, holding an hourglass in its upraised hand to tell the pope his time is up. Pope Alexander, however, was well prepared: he kept a coffin (also designed by Bernini) in his bedroom and made a habit of dining off plates embossed with skulls.

1

Subsidiary Attractions

Under the Pope Pius V monument, the entrance to the sacristy also leads to the **Museo Storico-Artistico e Tesoro** (*Historical-Artistic Museum and Treasury; 06/69881840; €10, includes audio guide; Apr.–Sept., daily 9–6:15; Oct.–Mar., daily 9–5:15*), a small collection of Vatican treasures. They range from the massive and beautifully sculptured 15th-century tomb of Pope Sixtus IV by Pollaiuolo, which you can view from above, to a jeweled cross dating from the 6th century and a marble tabernacle by Donatello. Continue on down the left nave past Algardi's **tomb of St. Leo.** The handsome bronze grilles in the **Cappella del Coro** (Chapel of the Choir) were designed by Borromini to complement those opposite in the Cappella del Santissimo Sacramento. The next pillar holds a rearrangement of the Pollaiuolo brothers' monument to Pope Innocent VIII, the only major tomb to have been transferred from the old basilica. Lacking in bulk compared to many of its Baroque counterparts, it more than makes up in Renaissance elegance. The next chapel contains the handsome bronze monument to Pope John XXIII by contemporary sculptor Emilio Greco. On the last pier in this nave stands a monument by the late-18th-century Venetian sculptor Canova to the ill-fated Stuarts—the 18th-century Roman Catholic claimants to the British throne, who were long exiled in Rome and some of whom are buried in the crypt below.

Above, the vast sweep of the basilica's dome is the cynosure of all eyes. Proceed to the right side of the Basilica's vestibule; from here, you can either take the elevator or climb the long flight of shallow stairs to the **roof** (*06/69883462, elevator €7, stairs €5; Apr.–Sept., daily 8–6; Oct.–Mar., daily 8–5; closed during Papal Audience (Wed. until noon); closed during other ceremonies in piazza*). From here, you'll see a surreal landscape of vast, sloping terraces, punctuated by domes. The roof affords unusual perspectives both on the dome above and the piazza below. The terrace is equipped with the inevitable souvenir shop and restrooms. A short flight of stairs leads to the entrance of the *tamburo* (drum)—the base of the dome—where, appropriately enough, there's a bust of Michelangelo, the dome's principal designer. Within the drum, another short ramp and staircase give access to the gallery encircling the base of the dome. (You also have the option of taking an elevator to this point.) From here, you have a dove's-eye view of the interior of the church. If you're overly energetic, you can take the stairs that wind around the elevator to reach the roof.

Only if you're of stout heart and strong lungs should you then make the taxing climb from the drum of the dome up to the *lanterna* (lantern) at the dome's very apex. A narrow, seemingly interminable staircase follows the curve of the dome between inner and outer shells, finally releasing you into the cramped space of the lantern balcony for an absolutely gorgeous panorama of Rome and the countryside on a clear day. There's also a nearly complete view of the palaces, courtyards, and gardens of the Vatican. Be aware, however, that it's a tiring, slightly claustrophobic climb. There's one stairway for going up and a different one for coming down, so you can't change your mind halfway and turn back. ⊠ *Piazza di San Pietro, Vatican* ⊗ *Apr.–Sept., daily 7–7; Oct.–Mar., daily 7–6:30;*

closed during Papal Audience (Wed. until noon); closed during other ceremonies in piazza Ⓜ *Ottaviano–San Pietro.*

Necropoli Vaticana (*Vatican Necropolis*). With advance notice you can take a 1¼-hour guided tour in English of the Vatican Necropolis, under the basilica, which gives a rare glimpse of Early Christian Roman burial customs and a closer look at the tomb of St. Peter. Apply by fax or email at least 2–3 weeks in advance, specifying the number of people in the group (all must be age 15 or older), preferred language, preferred time, available dates, and your contact information in Rome. ✉ *Piazza di San Pietro, Vatican* ☏ *06/69885318* 🖷 *06/69873017* ✉ *scavi@fsp.va* ⊕ *www.vatican.va* 💲 *€12* ⊙ *Ufficio Scavi Mon.–Sat. 9–6, visits 9–3:30* Ⓜ *Ottaviano–San Pietro.*

Grotte Vaticane (*Vatican Grottoes*). The entrance to the Grotte Vaticane is to the right of the Basilica's main entrance. The crypt, lined with marble-faced chapels and tombs occupying the area of Constantine's basilica, stands over what is believed to be the tomb of St. Peter himself, flanked by two angels and visible through glass. Among the most beautiful tombs leading up to it are that of Borgia pope Calixtus III with its carving of the Risen Christ, and the tomb of Paul II featuring angels carved by Renaissance great Mino da Fiesole. ✉ *Piazza di San Pietro, Vatican* 💲 *Free* ⊙ *Weekdays and Sat. 9–4, Sun. 1:30–3:30; closed during Papal Audience (Wed. until noon); closed during other ceremonies in piazza.*

FAMILY **Castel Sant'Angelo.** Standing between the Tiber and the Vatican, this circular and medieval "castle" has long been one of Rome's most distinctive landmarks. Opera lovers know it well as the setting for the final scene of Puccini's *Tosca*; at the opera's end, the tempestuous diva throws herself from the rampart on the upper terrace. In fact, the structure began life many centuries before as a mausoleum for the emperor Hadrian. Started in AD 135, it was completed by the emperor's successor, Antoninus Pius, about five years later. It initially consisted of a great square base topped by a marble-clad cylinder on which was planted a ring of cypress trees. Above them towered a gigantic statue of Hadrian. From the mid-6th century the building became a fortress, a place of refuge for popes during wars and sieges. Its name dates from 590, when Pope Gregory the Great, during a procession to plead for the end of a plague, saw an angel standing on the summit of the castle, sheathing his sword. Taking this as a sign that the plague was at an end, the pope built a small chapel at the top, placing a statue next to it to celebrate his vision—thus the name, Castel Sant'Angelo.

Enter the building through the original Roman door of Hadrian's tomb. From here, you pass through a courtyard enclosed in the base of the classical monument. You enter a vaulted brick corridor that hints at grim punishments in dank cells. On the right, a spiral ramp leads up to the chamber in which Hadrian's ashes were kept. Where the ramp ends, the Borgia pope Alexander VI's staircase begins. Part of it consisted of a wooden drawbridge, which could isolate the upper part of the castle completely. The staircase ends at the Cortile dell'Angelo, a courtyard that has become the resting place of neatly piled stone cannonballs as well as the marble angel that stood above the castle (it was replaced by a bronze sculpture in 1753). In the rooms off the Cortile dell'Angelo, look for the **Cappella di Papa Leone X** (Chapel of Pope Leo X), with a facade by Michelangelo.

In the courtyard named for Pope Alexander VI, a wellhead bears the Borgia coat of arms. The courtyard is surrounded by gloomy cells and huge storerooms that could hold great quantities of oil and grain in case of siege. Benvenuto Cellini, the rowdy 16th-century Florentine goldsmith, sculptor, and boastful autobiographer, spent some time in Castel Sant'Angelo's foul prisons; so did Giordano Bruno, a heretical monk who was later burned at the stake in Campo de' Fiori, and Beatrice Cenci, accused of patricide and incest and executed just across Ponte Sant'Angelo.

Take the stairs at the far end of the courtyard to the open terrace for a view of the Passetto, the fortified corridor connecting Castel Sant'Angelo with the Vatican, which recently featured in the book and 2009 film *Angels and Demons* (it's possible to request a visit; call for more information). Pope Clement VII used the Passetto to make his way safely to the castle during the Sack of Rome in 1527. Near here is a café for refreshments. Continue your walk along the perimeter of the tower and climb the few stairs to the *appartamento papale* (papal apartment). As if times of crisis were no object, the Sala Paolina (Pauline Room), the first you enter, was decorated in the 16th century by Pierino del Vaga and assistants with lavish frescoes of scenes from the Old Testament and the lives of St. Paul and Alexander the Great. Look for the trompe-l'oeil door with a figure climbing the stairs. From another false door, a black-clad figure peers into the room. This is believed to be a portrait of an illegitimate son of the powerful Orsini family. Out on the upper terrace, at the feet of the bronze angel, take in a magnificent view of the city below. ⊠ *Lungotevere Castello 50, Prati* ☎ *06/6819111 (central line), 06/6896003 for tickets* ⊕ *www.castelsantangelo.com* 🎫 *€10.50* ☉ *Tues.–Sun. 9–7:30; ticket office closes 6:30, open until 10 on Fri.* Ⓜ *Lepanto.*

Fodor'sChoice
★

Musei Vaticani (*Vatican Museums*). Besides the pope and his papal court, the occupants of the Vatican include some of the most famous artworks in the world. The museums that contain them are part of the **Vatican Palace,** residence of the popes since 1377. The palace consists of an estimated 1,400 rooms, chapels, and galleries. The pope and his household occupy only a small part of the palace; most of the rest is given over to the Vatican Library and Museums. Beyond the glories of the Sistine Chapel, the collection is so extraordinarily rich you may just wish to skim the surface, but few will want to miss out on the great antique sculptures, the Raphael Rooms, and the old master paintings, such as Leonardo da Vinci's *St. Jerome.*

Subsidiary Museums

Among the collections on the way to the chapel, the **Egyptian Museum** (in which Room II reproduces an underground chamber tomb of the Valley of Kings) is well worth a stop. The **Chiaramonti Museum** was organized by the Neoclassical sculptor Canova and contains almost

Continued on page 98

HEAVEN'S ABOVE:
THE SISTINE CEILING

Forming lines that are probably longer than those waiting to pass through the Pearly Gates, hordes of visitors arrive at the Sistine Chapel daily to view what may be the world's most sublime example of artistry:

Michelangelo: *The Creation of Adam*, Sistine Chapel, The Vatican, circa 1511.

Michelangelo's Sistine Ceiling. To paint this 12,000-square-foot barrel vault, it took four years, 343 frescoed figures, and a titanic battle of wits between the artist and Pope Julius II. While in its typical fashion, Hollywood focused on the element of agony, not ecstasy, involved in the saga of creation, a recently completed restoration of the ceiling has revolutionized our appreciation of the masterpiece of masterpieces.

By Martin Bennett

MICHELANGELO'S
MISSION IMPOSSIBLE

Designed to match the proportions of Solomon's Temple described in the Old Testament, the Sistine Chapel is named after Pope Sixtus VI, who commissioned it as a place of worship for himself and as the venue where new popes could be elected. Before Michelangelo, the barrel-vaulted ceiling was an expanse of azure fretted with golden stars. Then, in 1504, an ugly crack appeared. Bramante, the architect, managed do some patchwork using iron rods, but when signs of a fissure remained, the new Pope Julius II summoned Michelangelo to cover it with a fresco 135 feet long and 44 feet wide.

Taking in the entire span of the ceiling, the theme connecting the various participants in this painted universe could be said to be mankind's anguished waiting. The majestic panel depicting the Creation of Adam leads, through the stages of the Fall and the expulsion from Eden, to the tragedy of Noah found naked and mocked by his own sons; throughout all runs the underlying need for man's redemption. Witnessing all from the side and end walls, a chorus of ancient Prophets and Sibyls peer anxiously forward, awaiting the Redeemer who will come to save both the Jews and the Gentiles.

POCALYPSE NOW

he sweetness and pathos of his Pietà, carved
y Michelangelo only ten years earlier, have
een left behind. The new work foretells an
pocalypse, its congregation of doomed sin-
ers facing the wrath of heaven through hang-
g, beheading, crucifixion, flood, and plague.
ichelangelo, by nature a misanthrope, was
ready filled with visions of doom thanks
o the fiery orations of Savonarola, whose
underous preachments he had heard be-
ore leaving his hometown of Florence. Va-
ari, the 16th-century art historian, coined the
ord "terrabilità" to describe Michelangelo's
ension-ridden style, a rare case of a single
ord being worth a thousand pictures.

ichelangelo wound up using a *Reader's Di-
est* condensed version of the stories from
enesis, with the dramatis personae overseen
y a punitive and terrifying God. In real life,
oor Michelangelo answered to a flesh-and-
lood taskmaster who was almost as venge-
ul: Pope Julius II. Less vicar of Christ than
tter-day Caesar, he was intent on uniting
aly under the power of the Vatican, and was
ager to do so by any means, including rid-
g into pitched battle. Yet this "warrior pope"
onsidered his most formidable adversary to
e Michelangelo. Applying a form of black-
ail, Julius threatened to wage war on Mi-
elangelo's Florence, to which the artist had
ed after Julius canceled a commission for a
rand papal tomb unless Michelangelo agreed

to return to Rome and take up the task of
painting the Sistine Chapel ceiling.

MICHELANGELO, SCULPTOR

A sculptor first and foremost, however, Michelangelo considered painting an inferior genre—
"for rascals and sissies" as he put it. Second,
there was the sheer scope of the task, leading
Michelangelo to suspect he'd been set up by a
rival, Bramante, chief architect of the new St.
Peter's Basilica. As Michelangelo was also a
master architect, he regarded this fresco commission as a Renaissance mission-impossible.
Pope Julius's powerful will prevailed—and six
years later the work of the Sistine Ceiling
was complete. Irving Stone's famous novel
The Agony and the Ecstasy—and the granitic
1965 film that followed—chart this epic battle
between artist and pope.

THINGS ARE LOOKING UP

To enhance your viewing of the ceiling, bring
along opera-glasses, binoculars, or just a
mirror (to prevent your neck from becoming bent like Michelangelo's). Note that no
photos are permitted. Insiders know the
only time to get the chapel to yourself is
during the papal blessings and public audiences held in St. Peter's Square. Failing that,
get there during lunch hour. Admission and
entry to the Sistine Chapel is only through
the Musei Vaticani (Vatican Museums).

CHEMATIC OF THE SISTINE CEILING

PAINTING THE BIBLE

The ceiling's biblical symbols were ideated by three Vatican theologians, Cardinal Alidosi, Egidio da Viterbo, and Giovanni Rafanelli, along with Michelangelo.

As for the ceiling's painted "framework," this *quadratura* alludes to Roman triumphal arches because Pope Julius II was fond of mounting "triumphal entries" into his conquered cities (in imitation of Christ's procession into Jerusalem on Palm Sunday).

THE CENTER PANELS

Prophet turned art-critic or, perhaps doubling as ourselves, the ideal viewer, Jonah the prophet (painted at the altar end) gazes up at the

Creation, or Michelangelo's version of it.

1 The first of three scenes taken from the Book of Genesis: God separates Light from Darkness.

2 God creates the sun and a craterless pre-Galilean moon while the panel's other half offers an unprecedented rear view of the Almighty creating the vegetable world.

3 In the panel showing God separating the Waters from the Heavens, the Creator tumbles towards us as in a self-made whirlwind.

4 Pausing for breath, next admire probably Western Art's most famous image—God giving life to Adam.

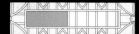

The Creation of Eve from Adam's rib leads to the sixth panel.

6 In a sort of diptych divided by the trunk of the Tree of Knowledge of Good and Evil, Michelangelo retells the Temptation and the Fall.

7 Illustrating Man's fallen nature, the last three panels narrate, in un-chronological order, the Flood. In the first Noah offers a pre-Flood sacrifice of thanks.

8 Damaged by an explosion in 1794, next comes Michel-

angelo's version of Flood itself.

9 Finally, above the monumental Jonah, you can just make out the small, wretched figure of Noah, lying drunk—in pose, the shrunken anti-type of the majestic Adam five panels down the wall.

THE CREATION OF ADAM

Michelangelo's Adam was partly inspired by the Creation scenes Michelangelo had studied in the sculpted doors of Jacopo della Quercia in Bologna and Lorenzo Ghiberti's Doors of Paradise in Florence. Yet in Michelangelo's version Adam's hand hangs limp, waiting God's touch to impart the spark of life. Facing his Creation, the Creator—looking a bit like the pagan god Jupiter—is for the first time ever depicted as horizontal, mirroring the Biblical "in his own likeness." Decades after its completion, a crack began to appear, amputating Adam's fingertips. Believe it or not, the most famous fingers in Western art are the handi-work, at least in part, of one Domenico Carnevale.

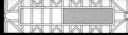

1,000 copies of classical sculpture. The gems of the Vatican's sculpture collection are in the **Pio-Clementino Museum,** however. Just off the hall in Room X, you can find the *Vatican Apoxyomenos* (the "Scraper"), a beautiful 1st-century AD copy of the famous bronze statue of an athlete. There are other even more famous pieces in the **Octagonal Courtyard,** where Pope Julius II installed the pick of his private collection. On the left stands the celebrated Apollo Belvedere. In the far corner, on the same side of the courtyard, is the *Laocoön* group. Found on Rome's Esquiline Hill in 1506, this antique sculpture group influenced Renaissance artists perhaps more than any other.

In the **Hall of the Muses,** the Belvedere Torso occupies center stage: this is a fragment of a 1st-century BC statue, probably of Hercules, all rippling muscles and classical dignity, much admired by Michelangelo. The lovely Neoclassical room of the **Rotonda** has an ancient mosaic pavement and a huge porphyry basin from Nero's palace.

The room on the Greek-cross plan contains two fine porphyry *sarcophagi* (burial caskets), one for St. Constantia and one for St. Helena, daughter and mother of the emperor Constantine, respectively.

Upstairs is an **Etruscan Museum,** an **Antiquarium,** with Roman originals; and the domed **Sala della Biga,** with an ancient chariot. In addition, there are the **Candelabra Gallery** and the **Tapestry Gallery,** with tapestries designed by Raphael's students. The incredibly long **Gallery of Maps,** frescoed with 40 maps of Italy and the papal territories, was commissioned by Pope Gregory XIII in 1580. Nearby is the **Apartment of Pius V.**

The Raphael Rooms

Rivaling the Sistine Chapel for artistic interest—and for the number of visitors—are the recently restored **Stanze di Raffaello** (Raphael Rooms). Pope Julius II moved into this suite in 1507, four years after his election. Reluctant to continue living in the Borgia apartments downstairs, with their memories of his ill-famed predecessor Alexander VI, he called in Raphael to redecorate his new quarters. When people talk about the Italian High Renaissance—thought to be the very pinnacle of Western art—it's probably Raphael's frescoes they're thinking about.

The **Stanza della Segnatura,** the first to be frescoed, was painted almost entirely by Raphael himself (his assistants painted much of the other rooms). The theme of the room, which may broadly be said to be "enlightenment," reflects the fact that this was meant to be Julius's private library. Instead, it was used mainly as a room for signing documents, hence "*segnatura*" (signature). Theology triumphs in the fresco known as the *Disputa,* or *Debate on the Holy Sacrament,* on the wall in front of you as you enter. Opposite, the *School of Athens* glorifies philosophy in its greatest exponents. Plato (likely a portrait of Leonardo da Vinci), in the center, debates a point with Aristotle. The pensive, gloomy figure on the stairs is thought to be modeled after Michelangelo, who was painting the Sistine ceiling at the same time Raphael was working here. Michelangelo does not appear in preparatory drawings, so Raphael may have added his fellow artist's portrait after admiring his work. In the foreground on the right, the figure with the compass is

Euclid, depicted as the architect Bramante; on the far right, the handsome youth just behind the white-clad older man is Raphael himself. Over the window on the left is Mt. Parnassus, the abode of the Muses, with Apollo, famous poets (many of them likenesses of Raphael's contemporaries), and the Muses themselves. In the lunette over the window opposite, Raphael painted figures representing and alluding to the Cardinal and Theological Virtues, and subjects showing the establishment of written codes of law. Beautiful personifications of the four subject areas—Theology, Poetry, Philosophy, and Jurisprudence—are painted in circular pictures on the ceiling above.

However, the rooms aren't arranged chronologically. Today, for crowd-management purposes, you head down an outdoor gallery to loop back through them; as you go, look across the way to see, very far away, the Pinecone Courtyard near where you entered the museums. The first "Raphael Room" is the **Hall of Constantine**—actually decorated by Giulio Romano and Raphael's other assistants after the master's untimely death in 1520. The frescoes represent various scenes from the life of Emperor Constantine, including the epic-sized *Battle of the Milvian Bridge*. Guided by three low-flying angels, Constantine charges to victory as his rival Maxentius drowns in the river below.

The **Room of Heliodorus** is a private antechamber. Working on the theme of Divine Providence's miraculous intervention in defense of the faith, Raphael depicted Leo the Great's encounter with Attila; it's on the wall in front of you as you enter. The *Expulsion of Heliodorus from the Temple of Jerusalem,* opposite, refers to Pope Julius II's attempt to exert papal power to expel the French from Italy. The pope himself appears on the left, watching the scene. On the window wall, the *Liberation of St. Peter* is one of Raphael's best-known and most affecting works.

After the Room of the Signature, the last room is the **Room of the Borgo Fire.** The final room painted in Raphael's lifetime, it was executed mainly by Giulio Romano, who worked from Raphael's drawings for the new pope, Leo X. It was used for the meetings of the Segnatura Gratiae et Iustitiae, the Holy See's highest court. The frescoes depict stories of previous popes called Leo, the best of them showing the great fire in the Borgo (the neighborhood between the Vatican and Castel Sant'Angelo) that threatened to destroy the original St. Peter's Basilica in AD 847; miraculously, Pope Leo IV extinguished it with the sign of the cross. The other frescoes show the coronation of Charlemagne by Leo III in St. Peter's Basilica, the *Oath of Leo III,* and a naval battle with the Saracens at Ostia in AD 849, after which Pope Leo IV showed clemency to the defeated.

Downstairs, enter the recently restored **Borgia apartments,** where some of the Vatican's most fascinating historical figures are depicted on elaborately painted ceilings. Pinturicchio designed the frescoes at the end of the 15th century, though the paintings were greatly retouched in later centuries. It's generally believed that Cesare Borgia murdered his sister Lucrezia's husband, Alphonse of Aragon, in the **Room of the Sibyl.** In the Room of the Saints, Pinturicchio painted his self-portrait in the figure to the left of the possible portrait of the architect Antonio da Sangallo. (His profession is made clear by the fact that he holds a T-square.) The lovely St. Catherine of Alexandria is said to represent Lucrezia Borgia herself.

In the frescoed exhibition halls, the **Vatican Library** displays precious illuminated manuscripts and documents from its vast collections. The **Aldobrandini Marriage Room** contains beautiful ancient frescoes of a Roman nuptial rite, named for their subsequent owner, Cardinal Aldobrandini. The **Braccio Nuovo** (New Wing) holds an additional collection of ancient Greek and Roman statues, the most famous of which is the Augustus of Prima Porta, in the fourth niche from the end on the left. It's considered a faithful likeness of the emperor Augustus, who was 40 years old at the time. Note the workmanship in the reliefs on his armor.

The Vatican Pinacoteca

Equally celebrated are the works on view in the **Pinacoteca** (Picture Gallery). These often world-famous paintings, almost exclusively of religious subjects, are arranged in chronological order, beginning with works of the 12th and 13th centuries. Room II has a marvelous Giotto triptych, painted on both sides, which formerly stood on the high altar in the old St. Peter's. In Room III you'll see Madonnas by the Florentine 15th-century painters Fra Angelico and Filippo Lippi. Room VIII contains some of Raphael's greatest creations, including the exceptional *Transfiguration,* the *Coronation of the Virgin,* and the *Foligno Madonna,* as well as the tapestries that Raphael designed to hang in the Sistine Chapel. The next room contains Leonardo's beautiful (though unfinished) *St. Jerome* and a Bellini *Pietà.* A highlight for many is Caravaggio's gigantic *Deposition,* in Room XII. In the courtyard outside the Pinacoteca you can admire a beautiful view of the dome of St. Peter's, as well as the reliefs from the base of the now-destroyed column of Antoninus Pius. A fitting finale to your Vatican visit can be found in the **Museo Pio Cristiano** (Museum of Christian Antiquities), where the most famous piece is the 3rd-century AD statue of the Good Shepherd, much reproduced as a devotional image.

■ TIP→ **The best way to avoid long lines into the museums, which can be three hours long in the high season, is to arrive between noon and 2, when lines will be very short or even nonexistent (except Sunday when admissions close at 12:30). Even better, schedule your visit during the Wednesday Papal Mass, held in the piazza of St. Peter's or at Aula Paolo Sesto, usually at 10:30 am. Also consider booking your ticket in advance online (⊕ biglietteriamusei.vatican.va); there is a €4 surcharge.**

For those interested in guided visits to the Vatican Museums, tours start at €32, including entrance tickets, and can also be booked online. Other offerings include a regular two-hour guided tour of the Vatican gardens and the semiregular Friday night openings, allowing visitors to the museums until 11 pm; call or check online to confirm. For more information, call ☎ *06/69884676* or go to ⊕ *mv.vatican.va.* For information on tours, call ☎ *06/69883145* or *06/69884676*; visually impaired visitors can arrange tactile tours by calling ☎ *06/69884947.* Wheelchairs are available (free) and can be booked in advance by emailing *accoglienza.musei@scv.va* or by request at the "Special Permits" desk in the entrance hall.

⚠ **Ushers at the entrance of St.** Peter's and sometimes the Sistine **Chapel will bar entry to people with bare knees or bare shoulders.** ✉ *Viale Vaticano, near intersection with Via Leone IV, Vatican* ⊕ *www. museivaticani.va* ⌨ *€16 (free last Sun. of month)* ☾ *Mon.–Sat. 9–6 (last entrance at 4), last Sun. of month 9–12:30* ☾ *Closed Jan. 1 and 6, Feb. 11, Mar. 19, Easter and Easter Mon., May 1, June 29, Aug. 14 and 15, Nov. 1, and Dec. 8, 25, and 26* Ⓜ *Cipro–Musei Vaticani or Ottaviano– San Pietro. Bus 64 or 40.*

Piazza di San Pietro. Mostly enclosed within high walls that recall the papacy's stormy history, the Vatican opens the spectacular arms of Bernini's colonnade to embrace the world only at St. Peter's Square, scene of the pope's public appearances. One of Bernini's most spectacular masterpieces, the elliptical Piazza di San Pietro was completed in 1667 after only 11 years' work and holds 400,000 people.

Surrounded by a pair of quadruple colonnades, it is gloriously studded with 140 statues of saints and martyrs. Look for the two disks set into the piazza's pavement on either side of the central obelisk. If you stand on either disk, a trick of perspective makes the colonnades look like a single row of columns.

Bernini had an even grander visual effect in mind when he designed the square. By opening up this immense, airy, and luminous space in a neighborhood of narrow, shadowy streets, he created a contrast that would surprise and impress anyone who emerged from the darkness into the light, in a characteristically Baroque metaphor.

At the piazza center, the 85-foot-high Egyptian obelisk was brought to Rome by Caligula in AD 37 and moved here in 1586 by Pope Sixtus V. The emblem at the top of the obelisk is the Chigi star, in honor of Pope Alexander VII, a member of the powerful Chigi family, who commissioned the piazza. Alexander demanded that Bernini make the pope visible to as many people as possible from the Benediction Loggia and to provide a covered passageway for papal processions.

Officially called "*Informazioni per turisti e pellegrini,*" the Main Information Office is just left of the basilica as you face it, a couple of doors down from the Braccio di Carlo Magno bookshop. On the south side of the Piazza Pio XII you'll find another Vatican bookshop, which contains the Libreria Benedetto XVI. ✉ *West end of Via della Conciliazione, Vatican* ☎ *06/69881662* ☾ *Daily 6:30 am–11 pm (midnight during Christmas)* Ⓜ *Cipro–Musei Vaticani or Ottaviano–San Pietro.*

TRASTEVERE

Across the Tiber from the Jewish Ghetto is Trastevere (literally "across the Tiber"), long cherished as Rome's Greenwich Village and now subject to rampant gentrification. In spite of this, Trastevere remains about the most tightly knit community in the city, the Trasteverini proudly (and erroneously!) proclaiming their descent from the ancient Romans. Ancient bridges, the Ponte Fabricio and the Ponte Cestio, link the Ghetto to Tiber Island, the diminutive sandbar that's one of Rome's most picturesque sights.

GETTING HERE AND AROUND

From Termini station, nab Bus No. 40 Express or No. 64 bus to Largo Torre Argentina; switch to Tram No. 8 to get to Trastevere. Bus No. 75 departs from Termini, passes the Colosseum, runs through Trastevere, and later ascends the Janiculum Hill.

TOP ATTRACTIONS

Isola Tiberina. It's easy to overlook this tiny island in the Tiber. Don't. In terms of history and sheer loveliness, the charming Isola Tiberina—shaped like a boat about to set sail—gets high marks.

Cross onto the island via Ponte Fabricio, constructed in 62 BC, Rome's oldest remaining bridge; on the north side of the island crumbles the romantic ruin of the Ponte Rotto (Broken Bridge), which dates back to 179 BC. Descend the steps to the lovely river embankment to see the island's claim to fame: a Roman relief of the intertwined-snakes symbol of Aesculapius, the great god of healing. In 291 BC, a temple to Aesculapius was erected on the island. A ship had been sent to Epidaurus in Greece, heart of the cult of Aesculapius, to obtain a statue of the god.

As the ship sailed back up the Tiber, a great serpent was seen escaping from it and swimming to the island—a sign that a temple to Aesculapius should be built here. In imperial times, Romans sheathed the entire island with marble to make it look like Aesculapius's ship, replete with a towering obelisk as a mast. Amazingly, the ancient sculpted ship's prow still exists. You can marvel at it on the downstream end of the embankment. ⊠ *Isola Tiberina can be accessed by the Ponte Fabricio or the Ponte Cestio, Trastevere.*

Fodor'sChoice
★

Santa Maria in Trastevere. Originally built sometime before the 4th century, this is certainly one of Rome's oldest and grandest churches. With a nave framed by a processional of two rows of gigantic columns (22 in total) taken from ancient Roman temples and an altar studded with gilded mosaics, the interior conjures up the splendor of ancient Rome better than any other in the city. Larger Roman naves exist, but none seem as majestic as this one, bathed in a sublime glow from the 12th- and 13th-century mosaics and Domenichino's gilded ceiling (1617). Supposedly Rome's first church dedicated to the Virgin Mary, it was rebuilt in the 12th century by Pope Innocent II (who hailed from Trastevere). The 19th-century portico draws attention to the facade's 800-year-old mosaics, which represent the parable of the Wise and Foolish Virgins. They enhance the whole piazza, especially at night, when the church front and bell tower are illuminated. Back inside, the church's most important mosaics, Pietro Cavallini's six panels of the *Life of the Virgin,* cover the semicircular apse. Their new sense of realism is said to have inspired the great Giotto. Note the little building labeled "Taberna Meritoria" just under the figure of the Virgin in the Nativity scene, with a stream of oil flowing from it. It recalls the legend that on the day Christ was born, a stream of pure oil flowed from the earth on the site of the piazza, signifying the coming of the grace of God. Off the piazza's northern side lies a little street called Via delle Fonte

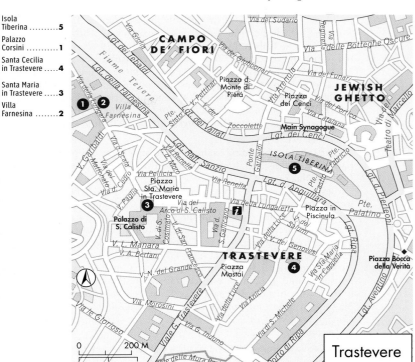

Trastevere

dell'Olio in honor of this miracle. ✉ *Piazza Santa Maria in Trastevere, Trastevere* ☎ *06/5814802* ⏰ *Daily 7:30 am–9 pm.*

Fodor's Choice ★ **Villa Farnesina.** Money was no object to the extravagant Agostino Chigi, a banker from Siena who financed many a papal project. His munificence is evident in this elegant villa, built for him about 1511. He was especially proud of the delicate fresco decorations in the airy loggias, now glassed in to protect their artistic treasures. When Raphael could steal a little time from his work on the Vatican Stanze, he came over to execute some of the frescoes himself, notably a luminous *Galatea*. In his villa, Agostino entertained the popes and princes of 16th-century Rome. He delighted in impressing his guests at alfresco suppers held in riverside pavilions by having his servants clear the table by casting the precious silver and gold dinnerware into the Tiber. His extravagance was not quite so boundless as he wished to make it appear, however: he had nets unfurled a foot or two under the water's surface to catch the valuable ware.

In the magnificent **Loggia of Psyche** on the ground floor, Giulio Romano and others worked from Raphael's designs. Raphael's lovely *Galatea* is in the adjacent room. On the floor above you can see the trompe-l'oeil effects in the aptly named **Hall of Perspectives** by Peruzzi. Agostino Chigi's bedroom, next door, was frescoed by Sodoma with scenes from the life of Alexander the Great, notably the *Wedding of Alexander and Roxanne*, which is considered to be the artist's best work. The palace also houses the **Gabinetto Nazionale delle Stampe,** a treasure house of old prints and drawings. When the Tiber embankments were built in 1879, the remains of a classical villa were discovered under the Farnesina gardens, and their decorations are now in the Museo Nazionale Romano's collections in Palazzo Massimo alle Terme. ⊠ *Via della Lungara 230, Trastevere* ☎ *06/68027268 for info, 06/68027397 for guided tour reservations* ⊕ *www.villafarnesina.it* 🎫 *€6* ☾ *Mon.–Sat. 9–2.*

WORTH NOTING

Palazzo Corsini. A brooding example of Baroque style, this palace houses part of the 16th- and 17th-century sections of the collection of the Galleria Nazionale d'Arte Antica and is across the road from the Villa Farnesina. Among the most famous paintings in this large, dark collection are Guido Reni's *Beatrice Cenci* and Caravaggio's *St. John the Baptist.* Stop in, if only to climb the 17th-century stone staircase, itself a drama of architectural shadows and sculptural voids. Behind, but separate from, the palazzo is the **Orto Botanico** (☾ *Summer, Mon.–Sat. 9:30–6:30; winter, Mon.–Sat. 9:30–4:30* 🎫 *€8*), Rome's only botanical park, containing 3,500 species of plants. Explore the various greenhouses around a recently restored stairway/fountain with 11 jets. Or, if you prefer, just enjoy it as a peaceful park where kids can run and play. ⊠ *Via della Lungara 10, Trastevere* ☎ *06/68802323 for Galleria Corsini, 06/32810 for tickets; 06/49912436 for Orto Botanico* ⊕ *www. galleriaborghese.it* 🎫 *€5* ☾ *Wed.–Mon. 8:30–7:30.*

Fodor'sChoice
★

Santa Cecilia in Trastevere. The basilica commemorates the aristocratic St. Cecilia, patron saint of music. One of ancient Rome's most celebrated Early Christian martyrs, she was put to a supernaturally long death by the emperor Diocletian around the year AD 300. After an abortive attempt to suffocate her in the baths of her own house (a favorite means of quietly disposing of aristocrats in Roman days), she was brought before the executioner. But not even three blows of the executioner's sword could dispatch the young girl. She lingered for several days, converting others to the Christian cause, before finally dying. In 1595, her body was exhumed. It was said to look as fresh as if she still breathed—and the heart-wrenching sculpture by eyewitness Stefano Maderno that lies below the main altar was, the sculptor insisted, exactly how she looked. Time your visit to enter the cloistered convent to see what remains of Pietro Cavallini's *Last Judgment,* dating from 1293. It's the only major fresco in existence known to have been painted by Cavallini, a forerunner of Giotto. ⊠ *Piazza Santa Cecilia in Trastevere 22, Trastevere* ☎ *06/5899289* 🎫 *Church free, frescoes €2.50, underground €2.50* ☾ *Basilica and underground, daily 9:15–12:45 and 4–6; frescoes, daily 10–12:30.*

THE CATACOMBS AND VIA APPIA ANTICA

Early Christian sites on the ancient Appian Way are some of the religion's oldest. The catacombs, where ancient pagans, Jews, and early Christians buried their dead, lie below the very road where tradition

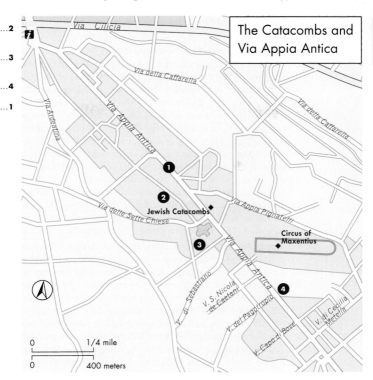

The Catacombs and Via Appia Antica

says Christ appeared to Saint Peter. The Via Appia Antica, built 400 years before, is a quiet, green place to walk and ponder the ancient world. There's a helpful office around the first milestone (at No. 58/60) that provides informative pamphlets and bicycle rentals.

GETTING HERE AND AROUND

You can take Bus No. 118 from Circo Massimo, No. 218 from Piazza San Giovanni in Laterano, or No. 660 from the Colli Albani Metro station (Line A). There's also an Archeobus OpenTram bus from Termini (⊕ *www.trambusopen.com*).

TOP ATTRACTIONS

Catacombe di San Sebastiano (*Catacombs of St. Sebastian*). The 4th-century church was named after the saint who was buried in the catacomb, which burrows underground on four different levels. This was the only Early Christian cemetery to remain accessible during the Middle Ages, and it was from here that the term "catacomb" is derived—it's in a spot where the road dips into a hollow, known to the Romans as *catacumbas* (Greek for "near the hollow"). The Romans used the name to refer to the cemetery that had existed here since the 2nd century BC, and it came to be applied to all the underground cemeteries discovered in Rome in later centuries. ⊠ *Via Appia Antica 136* ☎ *06/7850350* ⊕ *www.*

catacombe.org ⌨ €8 ⊙ *Mid-Dec.–mid-Nov., Mon.–Sat. 10–4:30* Ⓜ *Bus 118, 218, or 660.*

Tomba di Cecilia Metella. For centuries, sightseers have flocked to this famous landmark, one of the most complete surviving tombs of ancient Rome. One of the many round mausoleums that once lined the Appian Way, this tomb is a smaller version of the Mausoleum of Augustus, but impressive nonetheless. It was the burial place of a Roman noblewoman, wife of the son of Crassus, one of Julius Caesar's rivals and known as the richest man in the Roman Empire (infamously entering the English language as "crass"). The original decoration includes a frieze of bulls' skulls near the top. The travertine stone walls were made higher and the medieval-style crenellations added when the tomb was transformed into a fortress by the Caetani family in the 14th century. An adjacent chamber houses a small museum of the area's geological phases. ✉ *Via Appia Antica 162* ☎ *06/39967700* ⊕ *archeoroma. beniculturali.it* ⌨ *€6, includes Terme di Caracalla and Villa dei Quintili* ⊙ *Tues.–Sun. 9–1 hr before sunset; last entrance 1 hr earlier.*

Via Appia Antica. This Queen of Roads, "Regina Viarium," was the most important of the extensive network of roads that traversed the Roman Empire, a masterful feat of engineering that made possible the Roman control of a vast area by allowing for the efficient transportation of armies and commercial goods. Begun in 312 BC by Appius Claudius, the road was ancient Europe's first major highway. The first part reached as far as Capua near Naples, ultimately being extended in 191 BC to Brindisi 584 km (365 miles) southeast of Rome on the Adriatic Coast. The ancient roadway begins at Porta San Sebastiano, southeast of the Circus Maximus, passing through grassy fields and shady groves and by the villas of movie stars (Marcello Mastroianni and Gina Lollobrigida had homes here). The area of primary interest lies between the second and third milestones and is still paved with the ancient *basoli* (basalt stones) over which the Romans drove their carriages—look for the wheel ruts. Pick a sunny day for your visit, wear comfortable shoes, and bring a bottle of water. The Appia Antica is best reached with public transportation (there are no sidewalks along the road); ⇨ *See Getting Here, above.* For more information, or bike rentals for exploring the Via Appia, visit the Information Point (✉ *Via Appia Antica 58/60* ☎ *06/5135316* ⊙ *Winter, daily 9:30–4:30; summer, weekdays 9:30–5, weekends 9:30–6; Aug., daily 9:30–5* ⊕ *www. parcoappiaantica.it).*

WORTH NOTING

Catacombe di San Callisto (*Catacombs of St. Calixtus*). Burial place of many popes of the 3rd century, this is the oldest and best-preserved underground cemetery. One of the (English-speaking) friars who act as custodians of the catacomb will guide you through its crypts and galleries, some adorned with Early Christian frescoes. Watch out for wrong turns: this is a five-story-high catacomb! ✉ *Via Appia Antica 110/126, Via Appia Antica* ☎ *06/5310151* ⊕ *www.catacombe.roma.it* ⌨ *€8* ⊙ *Mar.–mid-Jan., Thurs.–Tues. 9–noon and 2–5* Ⓜ *Bus 118 or 218.*

MONTI, CELIO, AND ESQUILINO

Monti is the oldest *rione* in Rome. Gladiators, prostitutes, and even Caesar made their homes in this area that stretches from Santa Maria Maggiore down to the Forum. Today, Monti is one of the best-loved neighborhoods in Rome, known for its appealing mix of medieval streets, old-school trattorias, and hip boutiques. Bordering it is **Celio,** named after the same hill—the one across from the Palatine and from the Colosseum—which has residential cobblestone streets, ancient churches, and some good authentic restaurants and wine bars. **Esquilino,** covering Rome's most sprawling hill—the Esquiline—lies at the edge of the tourist maps, near the Termini station. Today it's where inhabitants of many nationalities live and work. It's not the cobblestone-street atmosphere that most think of when they think of Rome.

AVENTINO AND TESTACCIO

The **Aventino** district is somewhat rarefied, where some houses still have their own bell towers and private gardens are called "parks," without exaggeration. Like the emperors of old on the Palatine, the fortunate residents here look out over the Circus Maximus and the river, winding its way far below. **Testaccio** is perhaps the world's only district built on broken pots: the hill of the same name was born from discarded pottery used to store oil, wine, and other goods loaded from the nearby Ripa, when Rome had a port and the Tiber was once a mighty river to an empire. It's quiet during the day, but on Saturday buzzes with the loud music from rows of discos and clubs.

WHERE TO EAT

Rome has been known since ancient times for its great feasts and banquets, and though the days of the triclinium and the Saturnalia are long past, dining out is still the Romans' favorite pastime. The city is distinguished more by its good attitude toward eating out than by a multitude of world-class restaurants. Simple, traditional cuisine reigns, although things are slowly changing as talented young chefs explore new culinary frontiers. Many of the city's restaurants cater to a clientele of regulars, and atmosphere and attitude are usually friendly and informal. The flip side is that in Rome the customer isn't always right—the chef and waiters are in charge, and no one will beg forgiveness as they deny you a cappuccino after your meal. Be flexible—and steer clear of touristy spots—and you're sure to *mangiar bene* (eat well). Lunch is served from approximately 12:30 to 2:30 and dinner from 8 until about 10:30, though some restaurants stay open later, especially in summer, when patrons linger at sidewalk tables to enjoy the parade of people and the *ponentino* (evening breeze).

	WHAT IT COSTS			
	$	$$	$$$	$$$$
AT DINNER	under €15	€15–€24	€25–€35	Over €35

Restaurant prices are the average cost of a main course at dinner or, if dinner is not served, at lunch.

Use the coordinate (✣ B2) at the end of each listing to locate a site on the Where to Eat in Rome map.

PIAZZA NAVONA AND THE CAMPO DE' FIORI

PIAZZA NAVONA

$$ ROMAN 🍴 **Armando al Pantheon.** In the shadow of the Pantheon, this trattoria (open since 1961) delights the tourists who tend to come for lunch. There's an air of authenticity, witnessed by Roman antique shopowners who've been regulars here for a generation—well-dressed older gentlemen who come here to enjoy a leisurely meal and scold the waitress (by name) when she brings coffee before the profiteroles. This is the place to try Roman artichokes or *vignarola* (a fava bean, asparagus, pea, and guanciale stew) in the spring, or the wild-boar bruschetta in winter. Pastas are filling and great, and the secondi deliver all the Roman staples: oxtail, lamb chops, tripe, meatballs, and other hearty fare. [$] *Average main: €15* ✉ *Salita dei Crescenzi 31, Piazza Navona* ☎ *06/68803034* 🌐 *www.armandoalpantheon.it* ⏲ *Closed Sun., and Dec.–Jan. 6. No dinner Sat.* ✣ *1:E4.*

$ CAFÉ 🍴 **Caffè Sant'Eustachio.** Traditionally frequented by Rome's literati, this has what is generally considered Rome's best cup of coffee. Servers are hidden behind a huge espresso machine, vigorously mixing the sugar and coffee to protect their "secret method" for the perfectly prepared cup. (If you want your caffè without sugar here, ask for it "*amaro.*") [$] *Average main: €2* ✉ *Piazza Sant'Eustachio 82, Piazza Navona* ☎ *06/68802048* 🌐 *www.santeustachioilcaffe.it* ✣ *1:E4.*

$ WINE BAR Fodor's Choice ★ 🍴 **Cul de Sac.** This popular wine bar near Piazza Navona is among the city's oldest and offers a book-length selection of wines from Italy, France, the Americas, and elsewhere. The food is eclectic, ranging from a huge assortment of Italian meats and cheeses (try the delicious *lonza,* cured pork loin, or *speck,* a northern Italian smoked prosciutto) to various Mediterranean dishes, including delicious baba ghanoush, a tasty Greek salad, and a spectacular wild-boar pâté. Outside tables get crowded fast, so arrive early, or come late—they serve until about 12:30 am, though they're closed from about 4 to 5:30 pm. [$] *Average main: €14* ✉ *Piazza Pasquino 73, Piazza Navona* ☎ *06/68801094* 🌐 *www.enotecaculdesacroma.it* ✍ *Reservations not accepted* ✣ *1:D4.*

$ MEDITERRANEAN Fodor's Choice ★ 🍴 **Etablì.** On a narrow *vicolo* (alley) off beloved Piazza del Fico, this multifunctional space has a beautifully finished bar room done in modern Italian farmhouse chic, with vaulted wood-beam ceilings, wrought-iron touches, plush leather sofas, and chandeliers. In the restaurant section, it's minimalist Provençal hip (*etabli* is French for the regionally typical tables within). The food is clean and Mediterranean, with touches of Asia in the *crudi* (raw fish appetizers). Pastas are more traditional Italian, and the secondi run the gamut from land to sea. The place fills up by *dopo cena* ("after dinner") when it becomes a popular spot for sipping and posing, usually overlooking the tiny cobblestone street out front. [$] *Average main: €12* ✉ *Vicolo delle Vacche 9/a, Piazza Navona* ☎ *06/97616694* 🌐 *www.etabli.it* 🕒 *7 days a wk for breakfast, lunch, and dinner* ✣ *1:D3.*

$$$$ **MODERN ITALIAN** **Fodor's Choice** ★

🍴 **Il Convivio.** In a tiny, nondescript alley north of Piazza Navona, the three Troiani brothers—Angelo in the kitchen, and brothers Giuseppe and Massimo presiding over the dining room and wine cellar—have quietly been redefining the experience of Italian eclectic *alta cucina* (haute cuisine) for many years. Antipasti include "speck" of amberjack fish, herbs, pears, pomegranate, nuts and raspberry oil, while pastas include spelt spaghetti with shrimp, mint, cocoa beans, and chili pepper. Or opt for one of the famed secondi, with offerings like Ischian-style rabbit or "cannoli" of sole, artichokes, and saffron. Service is attentive without being overbearing, and the wine list is exceptional. [$] *Average main: €40* ✉ *Vicolo dei Soldati 31, Piazza Navona* ☎ *06/6869432* 🌐 *www.ilconviviotroiani.it* ✍ *Reservations essential* 🕒 *Closed Sun. and 2 wks in Aug. No lunch* ✣ *1:D3.*

$$ **ITALIAN**

🍴 **La Ciambella.** The sprawling space evokes a U.S. restaurant, with a bar up front and a bartender mixing specialty cocktails, but the structure itself is all Roman, with brick archways, high ceilings, and a skylight in one of the dining rooms that allows guests to gaze at the fantastic Roman sky. The emphasis here is on high-quality primary ingredients and Italian culinary traditions, evident in the incomparable Pugliese burrata cheese, thin-crust pizzas, flavorful pastas (both classic and seasonal specialties), and grilled meats on offer. [$] *Average main: €17* ✉ *Via dell'Arco della Ciambella 20, Piazza Navona* ☎ *06/6832930* 🌐 *www.laciambellaroma.com* ✣ *1:E4.*

$ **CAFÉ**

🍴 **Tazza d'Oro.** Many admirers contend this is the city's best cup of coffee. The hot chocolate in winter, all thick and gooey goodness, is a treat. And in warm weather, the coffee granita is the perfect cooling alternative to a regular espresso. [$] *Average main: €4* ✉ *Via degli Orfani 84, Piazza Navona* ☎ *06/6789792* 🌐 *www.tazzadorocoffeeshop.com* ✣ *1:E4.*

CAMPO DE' FIORI

$$ **ITALIAN**

🍴 **Ditirambo.** Don't let the country-kitchen ambience fool you. At this little spot off Campo de' Fiori, the constantly changing selection of offbeat takes on Italian classics is a step beyond ordinary Roman fare. Antipasti can be delicious and unexpected, like Gorgonzola-pear soufflé drizzled with aged balsamic vinegar, or a mille-feuille of mozzarella, sun-dried tomatoes, and fresh mint. But people really love this place for rustic dishes like roast lamb, suckling pig, and hearty pasta with guinea fowl and porcini mushrooms. Vegetarians will adore the cheesy potato gratin with truffle shavings. [$] *Average main: €16* ✉ *Piazza della Cancelleria 74, Campo de' Fiori* ☎ *06/6871626* 🌐 *www.ristoranteditirambo.it* 🕒 *Closed 2 wks in Aug. No lunch Mon.* ✣ *1:D4.*

$ **ITALIAN**

🍴 **Filetti di Baccalà.** For years, Dar Filettaro a Santa Barbara (to use the hole-in-the-wall's official name) has been serving just that—battered,

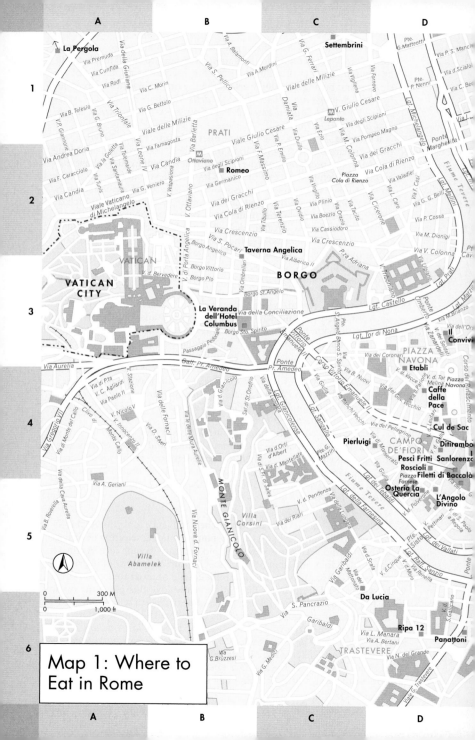

Map 1: Where to Eat in Rome

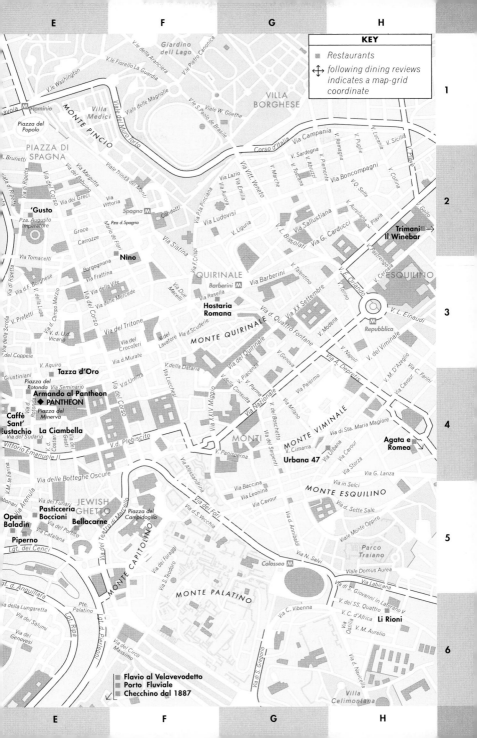

deep-fried fillets of salt cod—and not much else. You'll find no-frills starters such as *bruschette al pomodoro* (garlic-rubbed toast topped with fresh tomatoes and olive oil), and sautéed zucchini. In winter months, the cod is served alongside *puntarelle,* chicory stems tossed with a delicious anchovy-garlic-lemon vinaigrette. The location, down the street from Campo de' Fiori in a little piazza in front of the beautiful Santa Barbara church, begs you to eat at one of the outdoor tables, weather permitting. Be prepared for service as Roman as the food: that is, brusque. $ *Average main: €12* ⊠ *Largo dei Librari 88, Campo de' Fiori* ☎ *06/6864018* ▭ *No credit cards* ☉ *Closed Sun. and Aug. No lunch* ✛ *1:D5.*

$$$$
SEAFOOD
Fodor'sChoice
★

✕ **Il Sanlorenzo.** This gorgeous space, with chandeliers and soaring original brick ceilings, houses one of the better seafood spots in the Eternal City. The eight-course tasting menu is extremely tempting—think cuttlefish-ink tagliatelle with mint, artichokes and roe, or shrimp from the island of Ponza with rosemary, bitter herbs and porcini mushrooms—and (for Rome) a relative bargain at €85. There are also plenty of à la carte items like a wonderful series of small plates including *crudi,* like the perfectly seasoned fish tartare trio, sweet *scampi* (local langoustines), and wispy-thin carpaccio of red shrimp. The restaurant's version of spaghetti with sea urchin is exquisite and delicate; follow it with a main course of freshly caught seasonal fish prepared to order. $ *Average main: €36* ⊠ *Via dei Chiavari 4/5, Campo de' Fiori* ☎ *06/6865097* ⊕ *www.ilsanlorenzo.it* ⌟ *Reservations essential* ☉ *No lunch Sat.–Mon.* ✛ *1:D4.*

$$
WINE BAR

✕ **L'Angolo Divino.** There's something about this cozy wine bar that feels as if it's in a small university town instead of a bustling metropolis. Serene blue-green walls lined with wood shelves of wines from around the Italian peninsula add to the warm atmosphere. Along with several hot plates including fresh pasta, you can order smoked fish, cured meats, cheeses, and salads to make a nice lunch or light dinner. The kitchen stays open until the wee hours on weekends. $ *Average main: €15* ⊠ *Via dei Balestrari 12, Campo de' Fiori* ☎ *06/6864413* ⊕ *www. angolodivino.it* ☉ *Closed 1 wk in Aug.* ✛ *1:D5.*

$
ITALIAN

✕ **Open Baladin.** The craft beer movement has really taken hold in Italy of late. The Baladin label owns this sceney beer-and-burger joint in a gorgeous, sprawling space down the road from Campo de' Fiori. Staff members take their jobs—and brews—seriously, and they're helpful with recommendations from the more than 40 interesting options on tap, from Baladin's own domestic beers to imports from Belgium, Germany, and beyond. There are also more than 100 bottled beers on offer. Burgers can be a little too complicated for their own good, but if Piemontese beef topped with, say, 'nduja or mozzarella di bufala appeals, this is your place—and don't miss the hand-cut potato chips (try the licorice or paprika flavors). $ *Average main: €14* ⊠ *Via Degli Specchi 5–6, Campo de' Fiori* ☎ *06/6838989* ⊕ *www.baladin.it* ✛ *1:E5.*

$$
ROMAN

✕ **Osteria La Quercia.** Diners can sit under a gorgeous looming oak tree at this casual trattoria. The menu is simple—the usual suspects include fried starters like stuffed zucchini flowers, as well as Roman pasta dishes like spaghetti carbonara. Main dishes include *saltimbocca alla romana* (veal with prosciutto and sage) and meatballs in tomato sauce. The ubiquitous Roman sautéed *cicoria* (chicory) with olive oil and chili pepper is a good choice for a green side. Service is friendly and allows for lingering on balmy Roman afternoons and evenings—so close, and yet so seemingly far from the chaos of nearby Campo de' Fiori. $ *Average main: €15* ⊠ *Piazza della Quercia 23, Campo de' Fiori* ☎ 06/68300932 ✚ *1:D5.*

$$
SOUTHERN
ITALIAN

✕ **Pesci Fritti.** This cute jewel box of a restaurant on the amphitheater-shape street behind Campo de' Fiori serves the namesake fried fish, and much more. It feels like an escape to the Mediterranean, all whitewashed with touches of pale sea blue. Much of the cuisine echoes this, with heavy incorporation of seaside favorites like octopus, *spigola* (sea bass) and *bottarga* (roe). Especially delicious are the pasta with clams and fish prepared many different ways. The few missteps happen when the cooks try to get too creative, so stick to the southern classics and enjoy this virtual seaside escape. $ *Average main: €18* ⊠ *Via della Grottapinta 8, Campo de' Fiori* ☎ 06/68806170 ☾ *Closed Sun. and Mon.* ✚ *1:D5.*

$$$
ITALIAN

✕ **Pierluigi.** This perennial seafood favorite is quite the scene on balmy summer evenings, and interior renovations have made Pierluigi a year-round dining destination. As at many Italian fish ristoranti, antipasti featuring crudi are smart choices here: delicious tartare, carpaccio, shrimp, clams, and oysters are all in abundance. So are pasta and risotto with seafood, and secondi like roasted turbot with potatoes, cherry tomatoes, and black olives are delicious. Traditional Roman meat dishes are also on offer for the landlubbers among the group. No matter your preference, ask for a nice *sgroppino* (lemon sorbet, vodka, and prosecco) to end the meal. Just don't be afraid to put your foot down regarding what you do and don't want to order, and if you are ordering fresh fish, always double-check its cost *after* it has been weighed: in recent years, the servers have gotten a bit of a reputation for upselling, particularly to foreign clients. $ *Average main: €28* ⊠ *Piazza de Ricci 144, Campo de' Fiori* ☎ 06/6861302 ⊕ *www.pierluigi.it* ⌦ *Reservations essential* ☾ *Closed Mon.* ✚ *1:D4.*

$$
WINE BAR
Fodor'sChoice
★

✕ **Roscioli.** More like a Caravaggio painting than a place of business, this food shop and wine bar is dark and decadent. The store in front beckons with top-quality comestibles: wild Alaskan smoked salmon, hand-sliced cured ham from Italy and Spain, more than 300 cheeses, and a dizzying array of wines. Venture farther inside to a cavelike room where you can sit and order artisanal cheeses and smoked meats, as well as an extensive selection of unusual dishes and interesting takes on classics. Try the burrata cheese with Norwegian herring caviar, pasta with sardines, or Sicilian linguini with red prawns and cumin. The menu features meats, seafood (including a nice selection of raw fish preparations), and vegetarian-friendly items. ■TIP➜ **Reserve a table in the cozy wine cellar beneath the dining room. After your meal, head around the corner to their bakery for rightfully famous breads and sweets.** $ *Average main: €22* ⊠ *Via dei Giubbonari 21/22, Campo de' Fiori* ☎ 06/6875287 ⊕ *www.salumeriaroscioli.com/restaurant* ⌦ *Reservations essential* ☾ *Closed Sun.* ✚ *1:D5.*

BARBERINI

$
ROMAN
Fodor's Choice ★

🍴 **Hostaria Romana.** In an area best known for its touristy, overpriced restaurants, Hostaria Romana is a well-priced Roman trattoria with dependably good food and friendly, professional servers. Start with a mixed antipasti platter with temptations like mozzarella, roasted red peppers and eggplant, and in season, don't miss the Roman artichokes, served either in a succulent *romana* (braised) or crispy *giudia* (fried) style. Pastas come in abundant portions and cooked, of course, perfectly *al dente;* if you haven't yet tried *bucatini all'amatriciana* or *spaghetti alla carbonara* while in Rome, this is the place. [$] *Average main: €13* ✉ *Via del Boccaccio 1, Barberini* ☎ *06/4745284* 🌐 *www.hostariaromana.it* ✍ *Reservations essential* ⏲ *Closed Sun.* ✢ *1:G3.*

THE JEWISH GHETTO

$$
ROMAN

🍴 **Bellacarne.** *Bellacarne* means "beautiful meat," and that's the focus of this Jewish Ghetto newcomer (though the double entendre is that it's also what a Jewish Italian grandmother might say while pinching her grandchild's cheek). The kosher kitchen makes its own pastrami—a decent version of what one might find in Jewish delis in NYC. The difference is that the meat is served on its own, thinly sliced, at room temperature, and on a platter with mustard—much like cured meats are served in Italy. It's culturally on point, though it might leave you longing for two slices of rye bread to make a sandwich. Try the fried artichokes (perhaps the best in Rome!), the shawarma with hummus, or the chopped Israeli salad. The dining room is tranquil and lovely, too. [$] *Average main: €17* ✉ *Via Portico d'Ottavia 51, Jewish Ghetto, Roma* ☎ *06/6833104* 🌐 *www.bellacarne.it* ⏲ *Closed Jewish holidays. No dinner Fri.; no lunch Sat.* ✢ *1:E5.*

$
CAFÉ

🍴 **Pasticceria Boccioni.** *Forno* means "oven" in Italian, but it's also the word for a bakery that specializes in bread and simple baked goods, like biscotti and pine nut tarts. A *pasticceria,* on the other hand, specializes in more complicated Italian sweets, like fruit tarts, *montebianco* (a chestnut-cream creation resembling an alpine mountain), and *millefoglie* (puff pastry layered with pastry cream). Straddling the line between a forno and a pasticceria, on the "main drag" of the Ghetto, Pasticceria Boccioni—commonly known as "Forno del Ghetto" (aka "The Burnt Bakery," for the dark brown crust most everything here seems to acquire)—is famous for being the only establishment that makes Roman Jewish specialties. Try the delicious ricotta cheesecake, filled with cherries or chocolate, baked in an almond crust. Get here early on Friday as they sell out before closing for the Sabbath. [$] *Average main: €4* ✉ *Via del Portico d'Ottavia 1, Jewish Ghetto* ☎ *06/6878637* ✢ *1:E5.*

$$
ROMAN

🍴 **Piperno.** *The* place to go for Rome's extraordinary *carciofi alla giudia* (fried whole artichokes), Piperno has been in business since 1860. The location, up a tiny hill in a piazza tucked away behind the palazzi of the Jewish Ghetto, lends the restaurant a rarefied air. Try the exquisite prosciutto and buffalo mozzarella plate, the *fiori di zucca ripieni e fritti* (fried stuffed zucchini flowers), and *filetti di baccalà* (fillet of cod) to start. The display of fresh local fish is enticing enough to lure diners to try offerings from sea instead of land. Service is in the old-school style of dignified formality. This is a very popular destination for Sunday lunch. Ⓢ *Average main: €20* ✉ *Monte dei Cenci 9, Jewish Ghetto* ☎ *06/68806629* ⊕ *www.ristorantepiperno.it* ⚭ *Reservations essential* ⊗ *Closed Mon. and Aug. No dinner Sun.* ✛ *1:E5.*

PIAZZA DI SPAGNA

$$
WINE BAR

✕ **'Gusto.** There's an urban-loft feel to this trendy two-story space, a bit like a Pottery Barn exploded in Piazza Augusto Imperatore. The ground floor trattoria has a busy, buzzing atmosphere and serves typically Roman and Italian staples, done well. The ground-floor wine bar in the back has a casual-but-hopping vibe, where a rotating selection of wines by the glass and bottle are served alongside a vast array of cheeses, salumi, and breads. Lunchtime features a great-value salad bar. And for the kitchen enthusiast, the 'Gusto "complex" includes a store, selling everything from cookware to cookwear. Upstairs is a more upscale restaurant, where some dishes work, some don't. Ⓢ *Average main: €22* ✉ *Piazza Augusto Imperatore 9, Piazza di Spagna* ☎ *06/3226273* ⊕ *www.gusto.it* ✛ *1:E2.*

$$$
ITALIAN
Fodor'sChoice
★

✕ **Nino.** A favorite among international journalists and the rich and famous for decades (Tom Cruise and Katie Holmes had their celeb-studded rehearsal dinner here), Nino is Rome's best-loved dressed-up trattoria. The interior is country rustic *alla toscana*, and, along with its look—and waiters!—Nino sticks to the classics when it comes to its food: basically Roman and Tuscan staples. Start with a selection from the fine antipasto spread, or go for the cured meats or warm *crostini* (toasts) spread with liver pâté. Move on to pappardelle *al lepre* (a rich hare sauce) or hearty Tuscan *ribollita* soup, and go for the gold with a piece of juicy grilled beef. ⚠ **If you're not Italian or a regular or a celebrity, the chance of brusque service multiplies—insist on good service and you'll win the waiters' respect.** Ⓢ *Average main: €28* ✉ *Via Borgognona 11, Piazza di Spagna* ☎ *06/6786752, 06/6795676* ⊕ *www. ristorantenino.it* ⊗ *Closed Sun. and Aug.* Ⓜ *Spagna* ✛ *1:F2.*

REPUBBLICA

$$
WINE BAR

✕ **Trimani Il Winebar.** Operating nonstop from 11 am to midnight, this wine bar serves hot food at lunch and dinner. The interior is in minimalist style, and the second floor provides a subdued, candlelit space to sip wine. There's always a choice of soup and pasta plates, as well as second courses and *torte salate* (savory tarts). Around the corner is a wine shop, one of the oldest in Rome, of the same name; call about tastings and classes (in Italian). Ⓢ *Average main: €15* ✉ *Via Cernaia 37/b, Repubblica* ☎ *06/4469630* ⊕ *www.trimani.com* ⊗ *Closed Sun. and 2 wks in Aug.* Ⓜ *Castro Pretorio* ✛ *1:H2.*

AROUND THE VATICAN: BORGO AND PRATI

$$
MODERN ITALIAN

✕ **Romeo.** In the front, a bakery sells breads and pizza by the slice, created by Rome's famed Roscioli bakery; in the back, a contemporary restaurant serves up dishes every bit as eclectic as the space's style. Dishes range from creative (like a poached egg in a Parmesan fondue with toasted hazelnuts, or pumpkin soup with beetroot) to the more classic (like *rigatoni alla carbonara* or tortellini soup). Make sure to get started with something from the long list of *salumi*; this is a restaurant that prides itself on its ingredients, so from the *mortadella bolognese* to the Spanish hams, you can be sure you're tasting the best cured meats Italy (and, in some cases, Europe) has to offer. $ *Average main: €16* ✉ *Via Silla 26/a, Vatican* ☎ *06/32110120* ⊕ *www.romeo.roma.it* ⏱ *9 am to midnight* ✛ *1:B2.*

BORGO

$$$
ROMAN
Fodor'sChoice
★

✕ **La Veranda dell'Hotel Columbus.** Deciding where to sit at La Veranda isn't easy, because both the shady courtyard, torch-lit at night, and the frescoed dining room are among Rome's most spectacular settings. While La Veranda is known for classic Roman cuisine, some dishes are served with refreshing twists on the familiar. The seasonal menu may include an eggplant *caponata* with *burrata* (fresh cheese made from mozzarella and cream) and Sardinian bottarga; Piedmontese oxtail soup; or a risotto with Barolo wine, blue cheese, and quail carpaccio with mustard seeds. Call ahead, especially on Saturday, because the hotel often hosts weddings, which close the restaurant. $ *Average main: €25* ✉ *Hotel Columbus, Borgo Santo Spirito 73, Borgo* ☎ *06/6872973* ⊕ *www.laveranda.net* ✍ *Reservations essential* ⏱ *Closed Mon.* ✛ *1:B3.*

$$
MODERN ITALIAN

✕ **Taverna Angelica.** The Borgo area near St. Peter's Basilica hasn't been known for culinary excellence, but this is starting to change, and Taverna Angelica was one of the first of a handful of more refined dining outposts in this part of town. The dining room is small, which allows the chef to create a menu that's inventive without being pretentious: think pasta with pistachio pesto, and shrimp or turbot with crushed almonds and white-wine sauce. Spaghetti with crunchy pancetta and leeks is practically addictive, as is the warm seafood soup. Fresh sliced tuna in a pistachio crust with orange sauce is light and delicious. And desserts here go beyond the same-old tiramisù and panna cotta. $ *Average main: €22* ✉ *Piazza A. Capponi 6, Borgo* ☎ *06/6874514* ⊕ *www.tavernaangelica.it* ✍ *Reservations essential* ⏱ *No lunch Mon.–Sat.* Ⓜ *Ottaviano* ✛ *1:B2.*

PRATI

$$
MODERN ITALIAN
Fodor'sChoice
★

✕ **Settembrini.** The modern, intimate dining room hints at what's to come from the kitchen and the staff: elegant and restrained cooking, friendly yet unobtrusive service, and an interesting and well-curated wine list. The menu puts creative twists on classic Italian ingredients—think risotto with sea urchins, basil and licorice, or cod with burrata, watermelon, and cardamom. This is a gem in a quiet neighborhood. $ *Average main: €20* ✉ *Via Luigi Settembrini 27, Prati* ☎ *06/3232617* ⊕ *www.viasettembrini.com* ✍ *Reservations essential* ⏱ *Closed Sun. No lunch Sat.* Ⓜ *Lepanto* ✛ *1:C1.*

1

TRASTEVERE

$ ROMAN 🍴 **Da Lucia.** There's no shortage of old-school trattorias in Trastevere, but Da Lucia seems to have a strong following among them. Both locals and expats enjoy the brusque "authentic" service and hearty Roman fare, like classic *bombolotti* (short, fat tubed pasta) all'amatriciana and spaghetti *cacio e pepe* (cheese and pepper), and meat dishes like beef *involtini* with peas and Roman-style tripe. Snag a table outside in warm weather for the true Roman experience of dining on the cobblestones. [$] *Average main: €14* ✉ *Vicolo del Mattonato 2b, Trastevere* ☎ *06/5803601* ⏲ *Closed Mon.* ✥ *1:C5.*

$ PIZZA FAMILY 🍴 **Panattoni.** Nicknamed "Ai Marmi" for its marble-slab tables (and usually referred to that way by locals), Panattoni is actually about as lively as you can get. Packed every night, it serves crisp pizzas that come out of the wood-burning ovens at top speed. The fried starters here, like a nice baccalà, are light and tasty. Panattoni stays open well past midnight, convenient for a late meal after the theater or a movie nearby. [$] *Average main: €12* ✉ *Viale Trastevere 53–57, Trastevere* ☎ *06/5800919* ✍ *Reservations not accepted* 💳 *No credit cards* ⏲ *Closed Wed., and 3 wks mid-Aug. No lunch* ✥ *1:D6.*

$$$ ITALIAN 🍴 **Ripa 12.** This classic Roman seafood spot is an old standard in the neighborhood, and renovations a few years ago spiffed it up and made the environs as elegant as the food. Fresh ingredients and simple preparations make this a great place for going for broke with a mixed antipasto of crudi, including delicious tartares, carpaccios, and the like. Or, pick fresh shellfish and mollusks to slurp down with some spumante, always the perfect accompaniment to light, bright seafood. Pastas like a classic spaghetti *con le vongole* (white clam sauce) are expertly prepared, and main courses are inventive, like black cod cooked on a rock with pistachios and pink salt. [$] *Average main: €28* ✉ *Via San Francesco a Ripa 12, Trastevere* ☎ *06/5809098* 🌐 *www.ripa12.com* ✍ *Reservations essential* ⏲ *Closed Sun.* ✥ *1:D6.*

MONTI, CELIO, AND ESQUILINO

MONTI

$$ MODERN ITALIAN 🍴 **Urbana 47.** Open breakfast through dinner, Urbana 47 represents a relatively new concept for Rome's culinary landscape: *kilometro zero.* Referring to the lack of distance food travels to get to the kitchen and onto your plate, this restaurant highlights local ingredients from the surrounding Lazio region, which appeals to locavore hipsters and the boho Monti crowd. In the morning there is a Continental or "American" breakfast with free Wi-Fi; lunch means tasty "fast slow-food" options like grain salads and healthy panini. From 6 pm onward there are tapas and drinks, plus leisurely dinners like homemade pasta with broccoli, anchovies, and orange zest, or a local free-range chicken stuffed with potatoes and chicory. [$] *Average main: €15* ✉ *Via Urbana 47, Monti* ☎ *06/47884006* 🌐 *www.urbana47.it* [M] *Cavour* ✥ *1:H4.*

CELIO

$ 🍴 **Li Rioni.** One of the best pizzerias in the Rome center, Li Rioni is
PIZZA an institution among locals and in-the-know tourists alike. The lively
FAMILY atmosphere (if you want to see Roman families with children in their element, come around 8:30 pm on a Sunday) is made even more fun by the décor, as the interior is designed to look like you're dining outside on a piazza. (There are a handful of outdoor tables, too.) The *fritti* (fried appetizers) here are fairly good, but the real draw is the pizza: it's the best of the classic Roman-style thin crust from a wood-burning oven, piled with fresh toppings and very little grease. Do note that those not in a pizza-eating mood may struggle, however; the menu's only other option is a small section of salads and, depending on the day, the occasional pasta. Reservations are essential at night, when there's often a line out the door. [$] *Average main: €11* ✉ *Via dei Santi Quattro Coronati, 24, Celio* ☎ *06/70450605* 🌐 *www.lirioni.it* ✍ *Reservations essential* ✥ *1:H6.*

ESQUILINO

$$ 🍴 **Agata e Romeo.** For the perfect marriage of fine dining, creative cui-
MODERN ITALIAN sine, and rustic Roman tradition, the husband-and-wife team of Agata
Fodor's Choice Parisella and Romeo Caraccio is the top. Chef Agata was perhaps the
★ first in the capital to put a gourmet spin on Roman ingredients and preparations, elevating dishes like cacio e pepe with the addition of an even richer Sicilian aged cheese and saffron to the pecorino; "baccalà 5 ways" showcases salt cod of the highest quality; and many dishes are the best versions of classics you can get. Prices are a little steep, but for those who appreciate extremely high-quality ingredients and an incredible wine cellar, dining here is a real treat. [$] *Average main: €20* ✉ *Via Carlo Alberto 45, Esquilino* ☎ *06/4466115* 🌐 *www.agataeromeo.it* ✍ *Reservations essential* ⏲ *Closed Sun., and 2 wks in Aug. No lunch Sat. and Mon.* [M] *Vittorio Emanuele* ✥ *1:H4.*

TESTACCIO

$$ 🍴 **Checchino dal 1887.** Literally carved out of a hill of ancient shards of
ROMAN amphorae, Checchino remains an example of a classic, upscale family-run Roman restaurant, with one of the best wine cellars in the region. Though the slaughterhouses of Testaccio are long gone, an echo of their existence lives on in the restaurant's soul food—mostly offal and sundry cuts like *trippa* (tripe), *pajata* (intestine with the mother's milk still inside), and *coratella* (sweetbreads and beef heart) are all still on the menu for Roman purists. For the less adventuresome, house specialties include braised milk-fed lamb with seasonal vegetables. It's always a classic, but note that Checchino is really beginning to show its age. [$] *Average main: €23* ✉ *Via di Monte Testaccio 30, Testaccio* ☎ *06/5746318* 🌐 *www.checchino-dal-1887.com* ✍ *Reservations essential* ⏲ *Closed Sun. and Mon., Aug., and 1 wk at Christmas* ✥ *1:F6.*

$$ 🍴 **Flavio al Velavevodetto.** It's all the things you want a real Roman eating
ROMAN experience to be: authentic, in a historic setting, filled with Italians eat-
Fodor's Choice ing good food at good prices. In this very "romani di Roma" working-
★ class neighborhood, and surrounded by discos and bars sharing Monte

Testaccio, you can enjoy a meal of classic Roman pasta dishes (carbonara, amatriciana, etc.) or a delicious fettucine with baby calamari and cherry tomatoes, along with some very good antipasti (try the mixed vegetable plate), and great meat secondi like meatballs and beef stew. It's simple, seasonal, and served either in the cozy cavelike indoor dining rooms or outside under the umbrellas. A second location for the increasingly popular restaurant, called Velavevodetto ai Quiriti, is just around the corner from the Vatican. $ *Average main: €16* ⊠ *Via di Monte Testaccio 97, Testaccio* ☎ *06/5744194* ⊕ *www.ristorantevelavevodetto.it* ⌂ *Reservations essential* Ⓜ *Piramide* ✥ *1:F6.*

$
ITALIAN
Fodor'sChoice
★
✕ **Porto Fluviale.** This massive structure is on a stretch of street that's gone from gritty clubland to popular night spot, thanks largely to Porto Fluviale's arrival here. It means all things to all people: bar-café, pizzeria and lunch buffet, lively evening restaurant, and private dining spot. And, in true Italian fashion, it features cuisine from up and down the peninsula, with service as organized as one might expect in a cavernous space in Rome (which is to say, not very). Still, it's quite a convivial spot, and the food is tasty, from pizza made in wood-burning ovens to pasta and grilled meats and interesting salads. Cocktails at the bar, if you can swing a spot, are a fun option. $ *Average main: €14* ⊠ *Via del Porto Fluviale 22, Testaccio* ☎ *06/5743199* ⊕ *www.portofluviale.com* ✥ *1:F6.*

BEYOND THE CITY CENTER

$$$$
MODERN ITALIAN
Fodor'sChoice
★
✕ **La Pergola.** La Pergola's rooftop location offers a commanding view of the city and a three–Michelin star experience. The difficulty comes in choosing from among Chef Heinz Beck's *alta cucina* (haute cuisine) specialties, though most everything will prove to be incredibly special: expect such temptations as a John Dory fillet with white truffles, pumpkin puree and mushrooms, or deep-fried zucchini flower with caviar in a shellfish-and-saffron consommé. The dessert course is extravagant, including tiny petits fours, and the wine list is as thrilling as one might expect from such a high-class establishment. $ *Average main: €65* ⊠ *Rome Cavalieri, Via Cadlolo 101, Monte Mario* ☎ *06/35092152* ⊕ *www.romecavalieri.com/lapergola.php* ⌂ *Reservations essential* ⌂ *Jacket and tie* ✆ *Closed Sun. and Mon., 2 wks in Aug., and most of Jan. No lunch* ✥ *1:A1.*

WHERE TO STAY

Lodging options in Rome are abundant. Over the past decade or so there's been an upswing in the number of bed-and-breakfasts, stylish boutique hotels, and lodgings with over-the-top opulence. At the same time, there continue to be many modest, budget hotels and *pensioni* (small family-run accommodations).

If swanky is what you're after, the best place to look is in the Spanish Steps and Via Veneto areas. On the flip side, many of the city's lower-cost accommodations are scattered near the Stazione Termini. But for the most convenient Roman experience, stay in or near the centro storico, where you'll be able to cover most of the main attractions on foot.

WHAT IT COSTS			
$	**$$**	**$$$**	**$$$$**
FOR TWO PEOPLE			
under €125	€125–€200	€201–€300	over €301

Exact prices listed are for a standard double room in high season.

Hotel reviews have been shortened. For full information, visit Fodors. com. Use the coordinate (✛ B2) at the end of each listing to locate a site on the Where to Stay in Rome map.

PIAZZA NAVONA AND THE CAMPO DE' FIORI

PIAZZA NAVONA

$$$
HOTEL
Fodor'sChoice
★

Albergo Santa Chiara. If you're looking for a good location (right behind the Pantheon) and top-notch service at great prices—not to mention comfortable beds and a quiet stay—look no further than this historic hotel, run by the same family for some 200 years. **Pros:** great location; free Wi-Fi; lovely terrace/sitting area in front, overlooking the piazza. **Cons:** rooms in need of updating; service is iffy; Wi-Fi can be slow; some rooms can be noisy. $ *Rooms from: €240* ⊠ *Via Santa Chiara 21, Piazza Navona* ☎ *06/6872979* ⊕ *www.albergosantachiara. com* ☞ *96 rooms, 3 suites, 3 apartments* ✎ *Breakfast* ✛ *2:E4.*

$$$
HOTEL

Hotel Genio. Just outside one of Rome's most beautiful piazzas—Piazza Navona—this pleasant hotel has a lovely rooftop terrace perfect for enjoying a cappuccino or glass of wine and taking in the view. **Pros:** friendly staff; the included breakfast buffet is abundant; free Wi-Fi; spacious, elegant bathrooms. **Cons:** rooms facing the street can be noisy; European-size (read: small) showers; beds can be too firm for some. $ *Rooms from: €230* ⊠ *Via Giuseppe Zanardelli 28, Piazza Navona* ☎ *06/6832191* ⊕ *www.hotelgenioroma.it* ☞ *60 rooms* ✎ *Breakfast* ✛ *2:D3.*

$$
HOTEL

Relais Palazzo Taverna. This little hidden gem on a side street behind the lovely Via dei Coronari is a good compromise for those looking for boutique-style accommodations on a budget. **Pros:** centrally located; free Wi-Fi; friendly, responsive staff; spacious rooms. **Cons:** staff are on duty only until 11 pm (they can be contacted after-hours in an emergency). $ *Rooms from: €180* ⊠ *Via dei Gabrielli 92, Piazza Navona* ☎ *06/20398064* ⊕ *www.relaispalazzotaverna.com* ☞ *11 rooms* ✎ *Breakfast* ✛ *2:D3.*

CAMPO DE' FIORI

$$$
B&B/INN
Fodor'sChoice
★

Casa di Santa Brigida. The friendly sisters of Santa Brigida oversee simple, straightforward, and centrally located accommodations in one of Rome's loveliest convents, with a rooftop terrace overlooking Palazzo Farnese. **Pros:** no curfew in this historic convent; insider papal tickets; location in the Piazza Farnese; large library and sunroof; free Wi-Fi; 15% discount for those coming in February, July, August, and December. **Cons:** weak a/c; no TVs in the rooms (though there is a common TV room); not equipped for guests with disabilities; breakfast is unexciting; 3% extra fee for credit cards (cash or cheque preferred). [$] *Rooms from: €210* ✉ *Piazza Farnese 96 (entrance around the corner at Via Monserrato 54), Campo de' Fiori* ☎ *06/68892596* 🌐 *www.brigidine.org* 🛏 *20 rooms* 🍴 *Multiple meal plans* ✥ *2:D4.*

$$$$ HOTEL Fodor's Choice ★ 🏨 **D.O.M. Hotel.** Rome's newest luxury hotel raises the bar for the city's boutique accommodations, proving that old can be contemporary, small can be sumptuous, and discreet can be chic. **Pros:** thoughtful amenities, like iPads in each room, 24-hour room service, and Acqua di Parma toiletries; beautiful rooftop terrace, which becomes a restaurant and bar in warmer months; very professional, friendly staff. **Cons:** Some rooms can be noisy when there are popular nights or special events at the bar (request a room on one of the floors farther upstairs); no gym or spa. [$] *Rooms from: €400* ✉ *Via Giulia 131, Campo de' Fiori* ☎ *06/6832144* 🌐 *www.domhotelroma.com* 🛏 *24 rooms* 🍴 *Breakfast* ✥ *2:C4.*

$$$ HOTEL Fodor's Choice ★ 🏨 **Hotel Ponte Sisto.** Situated in a restored Renaissance palazzo with one of the prettiest patio-courtyards in Rome, this hotel is a relaxing retreat inches from Trastevere and Campo de' Fiori. **Pros:** staff are friendly; rooms with views (and some with balconies and terraces); luxury bathrooms; discount for groups; can find very good deals on hotel's website (even in high season), often with extras like limoncello or an archaeological book; beautiful courtyard garden. **Cons:** streetside rooms can be a bit noisy; some rooms are small; carpets starting to show signs of wear; aside from breakfast, restaurant only caters to groups and must be booked in advance. [$] *Rooms from: €260* ✉ *Via dei Pettinari 64, Campo de' Fiori* ☎ *06/6863100* 🌐 *www.hotelpontesisto.it* 🛏 *103 rooms, 4 suites* 🍴 *Breakfast* ✥ *2:D5.*

$$ B&B/INN 🏨 **Maison Giulia.** This little hotel is a rare gem: a comfortable budget spot on the beautiful, upscale Via Giulia. **Cons:** at the hotel, the rooms tend to be on the small side; the hotel's rooms can be a bit dim; no elevators, and there can be several staircases to climb (although staff will usually help with your bags). [$] *Rooms from: €140* ✉ *Via Giulia 189/A, Campo de' Fiori* ☎ *06/68808325* 🌐 *www.maisongiulia.it* 🛏 *6 rooms in hotel, 13 apartments* 🍴 *Breakfast* ✥ *2:D5.*

JEWISH GHETTO

$$ HOTEL 🏨 **Arenula.** A hefty bargain by Rome standards (especially in low season, when some rooms go down to €70), Hotel Arenula has an almost unbeatable location, an imposingly elegant stone exterior, and simple but comfortable rooms with pale-wood furnishings and double-glazed windows, but alas, no elevator. **Pros:** a real bargain; conveniently located, close to Campo de' Fiori and Trastevere; spotless. **Cons:** totally no-frills accommodations; no elevator; can still be a bit noisy despite the double-glazed windows. [$] *Rooms from: €140* ✉ *Via Santa Maria dei Calderari 47, off Via Arenula, Jewish Ghetto* ☎ *06/6879454* 🌐 *www.hotelarenula.com* 🛏 *50 rooms* 🍴 *Breakfast* ✥ *2:E5.*

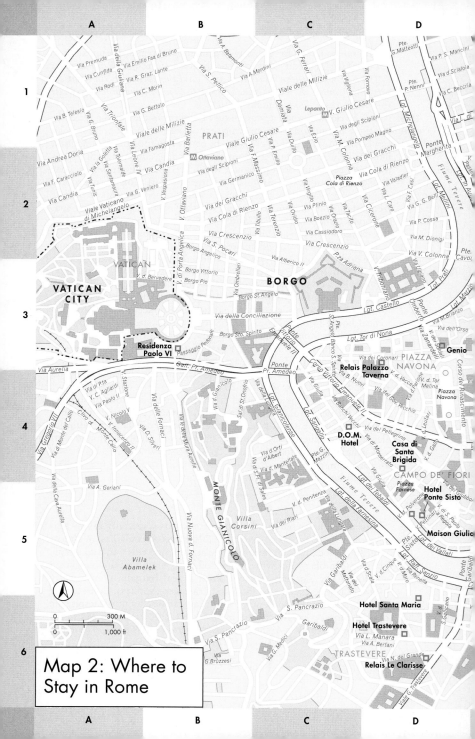

Map 2: Where to Stay in Rome

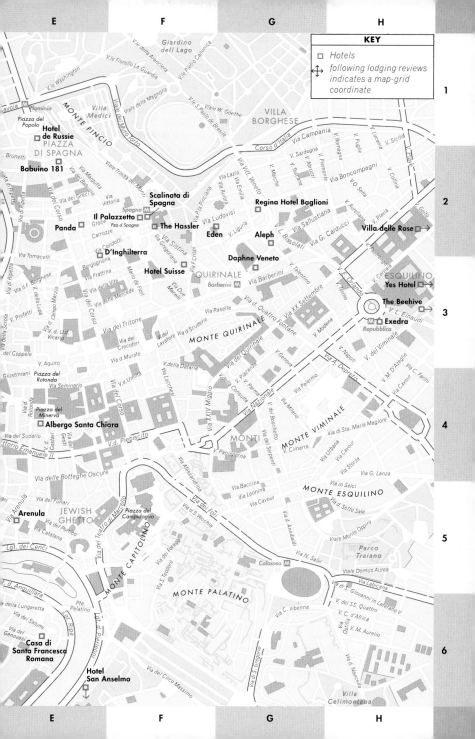

KEY

☐ Hotels

⤢ following lodging reviews indicates a map-grid coordinate

PIAZZA DEL POPOLO

$$$
HOTEL
Fodor's Choice
★

Babuino 181. Located on Rome's most stylish street a stone's throw from Piazza del Popolo, Babuino 181 is a luxurious boutique hotel with a particularly personal connection to Rome: its gracious owner, Alberto Moncada di Paternò, hails from a noble Roman family that's lived in the neighborhood for 160 years. **Pros:** spacious rooms and bathrooms; personalized, discreet service from friendly staff and owner; 24-hour front desk service; rooftop bar and terrace; free Wi-Fi. **Cons:** breakfast costs extra; no spa or gym. $ *Rooms from: €250* ⊠ *Via del Babuino 181, Piazza del Popolo* ☎ *06/32295* ⊕ *www.romeluxurysuites.com* ⤳ *24 rooms* ⦿*No meals* ✛ *2:E2.*

PIAZZA DI SPAGNA

$$$$
HOTEL
Fodor's Choice
★

Aleph. If you're wondering where the beautiful people are, look no further than the Aleph, the most unfalteringly fashionable of Rome's design hotels. **Pros:** free access to the spa for hotel guests; award-winning design; free Wi-Fi. **Cons:** rooms are too petite for the price; cocktails are expensive; there is a buffet breakfas, but it costs extra; although the terrace is huge, the views aren't of Rome's most flattering side. $ *Rooms from: €320* ⊠ *Via San Basilio 15, Piazza di Spagna* ☎ *06/422901* ⊕ *aleph-roma.boscolohotels.com* ⤳ *90 rooms, 6 suites* Ⓜ *Barberini–Fontana di Trevi* ⦿*No meals* ✛ *2:G2.*

$$$
B&B/INN
Fodor's Choice
★

Daphne Veneto. This "urban B&B" is run by people who love Rome and want to make sure you do, too—the staff will happily act as your personal travel planners, helping you map out your destinations, plan day trips, choose restaurants, and organize transportation. **Pros:** the opportunity to see Rome "like an insider"; friendly, helpful staff; beds have Simmons mattresses and fluffy comforters; free Wi-Fi. **Cons:** no TVs; some bathrooms are external, and two rooms at the Trevi share one bathroom. $ *Rooms from: €230* ⊠ *Via di San Basilio 55, Piazza di Spagna* ☎ *06/87450087* ⊕ *www.daphne-rome.com* ⤳ *11 rooms (Veneto), 10 rooms (Trevi)* ⦿*Breakfast* Ⓜ *Barberini–Fontana di Trevi* ✛ *2:G3.*

$$$$
HOTEL
Fodor's Choice
★

Eden. A recent refurbishment of the Hotel Eden has put it back in the running for one of Rome's top luxury lodgings: once a favorite haunt of Hemingway, Ingrid Bergman, and Fellini, this superlative hotel combines dashing elegance, exquisitely lush décor, and stunning vistas of Rome with true Italian hospitality. **Pros:** gorgeous mirrored roof-terrace restaurant; you could be rubbing elbows with the stars; 24-hour room service. **Cons:** breakfast not included in the price (and, at €42 per day, is very expensive); although basic Wi-Fi is free, a faster connection costs extra; some say the staff can be hit-or-miss. $ *Rooms from: €490* ⊠ *Via Ludovisi 49, Piazza di Spagna* ☎ *06/478121* ⊕ *www.dorchestercollection.com/en/rome/hotel-eden* ⤳ *121 rooms, 13 suites* ⦿*No meals* Ⓜ *Spagna* ✛ *2:G2.*

$$$$
HOTEL
Fodor's Choice
★

The Hassler. When it comes to million-dollar views, this exclusive hotel atop the Spanish Steps has the best seats in the house, so it's no surprise that generations of fans, many rich and famous (Tom Cruise, Jennifer Lopez, Gwenyth Paltrow, and the Beckhams included), are willing to pay top dollar to stay here. **Pros:** charming old-world feel; prime location and panoramic views; stunning rooms. **Cons:** VIP prices (and the 10% V.A.T. isn't included in the rack rates listed); high-speed Wi-Fi costs extra; breakfast isn't included [$] *Rooms from: €795* ✉ *Piazza Trinità dei Monti 6, Piazza di Spagna* ☎ *06/69934755, 800/223–6800 toll-free from U.S.* 🌐 *www.hotelhasslerroma.com* 🛏 *82 rooms, 14 suites* 🍴 *No meals* [M] *Spagna* ✥ *2:F2.*

$$$$ HOTEL 🏨 **Hotel d'Inghilterra.** Situated in a 17th-century guesthouse and founded in 1845, Hotel D'Inghilterra has a long, storied history. **Pros:** distinct character and opulence; turndown service (with chocolates); genuinely friendly and attentive staff. **Cons:** elevator is small and slow; although Wi-Fi is free, it costs more for high-speed or for more than four hours a day; some rooms badly in need of renovations; the location, despite soundproofing, is still noisy. [$] *Rooms from: €550* ✉ *Via Bocca di Leone 14, Piazza di Spagna* ☎ *06/699811* 🌐 *www.hoteldinghilterrarome.com* 🛏 *81 rooms, 7 suites* 🍴 *Breakfast* [M] *Spagna* ✥ *2:E3.*

$$$$ HOTEL FAMILY Fodor's Choice ★ 🏨 **Hotel de Russie.** A ritzy retreat for government bigwigs and Hollywood high rollers, the Hotel de Russie is just steps away from the famed Piazza del Popolo and occupies a 19th-century hotel that once hosted royalty, Picasso, and Cocteau. **Pros:** big potential for celebrity sightings; activities for children; extensive gardens (including a butterfly reserve); first-rate luxury spa; Wi-Fi included. **Cons:** some rooms need updating; breakfast is not included. [$] *Rooms from: €691* ✉ *Via del Babuino 9, Piazza del Popolo* ☎ *06/328881* 🌐 *www.hotelderussie.it* 🛏 *89 rooms, 33 suites* 🍴 *No meals* [M] *Flaminio* ✥ *2:E1.*

$$ HOTEL 🏨 **Hotel Suisse.** Located on a picturesque street around the corner from the Spanish Steps is a warm and inviting hotel that's been run by the same family for three generations. **Pros:** good value; the rooms are obviously cared for; great location. **Cons:** breakfast selection isn't that ample and is served in your room; bathrooms are on the small side. [$] *Rooms from: €195* ✉ *Via Gregoriana 54, Piazza di Spagna* ☎ *06/6783649* 🌐 *www.hotelsuisserome.com* 🛏 *12 rooms* 🍴 *Breakfast* [M] *Barberini–Fontana di Trevi, Spagna* ✥ *2:F3.*

$$$$ B&B/INN Fodor's Choice ★ 🏨 **Il Palazzetto.** This 15th-century house, once a retreat for one of Rome's richest noble families, is one of the most intimate and luxurious hotels in Rome, with gorgeous terraces where you can watch the never-ending theater of la scalinata. **Pros:** location and view; free Wi-Fi; guests have full access to sister hotel the Hassler's services; continental breakfast, served at the Hassler, is included. **Cons:** restaurant is often rented out for crowded special events; bedrooms do not access the communal terraces; often books up far in advance. [$] *Rooms from: €350* ✉ *Vicolo del Bottino 8, Piazza di Spagna* ☎ *06/699341000* 🌐 *www.ilpalazzettoroma.com* 🛏 *4 rooms* 🍴 *No meals* [M] *Spagna* ✥ *2:F2.*

$$ HOTEL 🏨 **Panda.** You couldn't possibly find a better deal in Rome than here at the Panda, especially given its key location just behind the Spanish Steps. **Pros:** 10% discount if you pay cash; free Wi-Fi; on a quiet street, but still close to the Spanish Steps; very high ceilings. **Cons:** dim lighting; no elevator directly to floor; breakfast is not included. [$] *Rooms from: €130* ✉ *Via della Croce 35, Piazza di Spagna* ☎ *06/6780179* 🌐 *www.*

hotelpanda.it ⟿ *28 rooms (20 with bath)* ⊤◎⊥ *No meals* Ⓜ *Spagna* ✛ *2:E2.*

$$
B&B/INN
Fodor's Choice
★

⛢ **Scalinata di Spagna.** Perched atop the Spanish Steps, this charming boutique hotel makes guests fall in love over and over again (in fact, it's often booked far in advance). **Pros:** friendly and helpful concierge; fresh fruit in the rooms; free Wi-Fi throughout. **Cons:** it's a hike up the hill to the hotel; small rooms; no porter and no elevator. Ⓢ *Rooms from:* €195 ⊠ *Piazza Trinità dei Monti 17, Piazza di Spagna* ☎ *06/45686150* ⊕ *www.hotelscalinata.com* ⟿ *16 rooms* ⊤◎⊥ *Breakfast* Ⓜ *Spagna* ✛ *2:F2.*

REPUBBLICA

$
B&B/INN
Fodor's Choice
★

⛢ **The Beehive.** Living the American dream *dolce vita*–style is exactly what one Los Angeles couple started to do in 1999, when they opened the Beehive, a hip, alternative budget hotel near Termini station. **Pros:** massage and other therapies offered on-site; convenient to Termini station; very good prices, even in high season. **Cons:** some rooms do not have private baths; standard rooms lack TV and a/c; breakfast is not included. Ⓢ *Rooms from: €100* ⊠ *Via Marghera 8, Repubblica* ☎ *06/44704553* ⊕ *www.the-beehive.com* ⟿ *8 rooms, 1 dormitory, 3 apartments* ⊤◎⊥ *No meals* Ⓜ *Termini* ✛ *2:H3.*

$$$$
HOTEL
Fodor's Choice
★

⛢ **Exedra.** Located in one of the most spectacular piazzas in the city, this is the It Girl of Rome's hotel scene, where high-rollers come to party by the rooftop pool and pamper themselves in the spa. **Pros:** spacious and attractive rooms; terrace with cocktail service; top-notch service; free Wi-Fi; close to Termini station. **Cons:** food and beverages are expensive; beyond the immediate vicinity of many sights. Ⓢ *Rooms from:* €385 ⊠ *Piazza della Repubblica 47, Repubblica* ☎ *06/489381* ⊕ *www. exedra-roma.boscolohotels.com* ⟿ *220 rooms, 18 suites* ⊤◎⊥ *Breakfast* Ⓜ *Repubblica, Termini* ✛ *2:H3.*

AROUND THE VATICAN: BORGO

BORGO

$$$
HOTEL
Fodor's Choice
★

⛢ **Residenza Paolo VI.** Set in a former monastery that is still an extraterritorial part of the Vatican and magnificently abutting Bernini's colonnade of St. Peter's Square, the Paolo VI (pronounced "Paolo Sesto," Italian for Pope Paul VI) is unbeatably close to St. **Pros:** unparalleled views of St. Peter's from the rooftop terrace; quiet rooms; huge breakfast spread. **Cons:** the small rooms are really small; bathrooms are small; the atmosphere at night is a little too quiet. Ⓢ *Rooms from: €295* ⊠ *Via Paolo VI 29, Borgo* ☎ *06/684870* ⊕ *www.residenzapaolovi.com* ⟿ *35 rooms* ⊤◎⊥ *Breakfast* Ⓜ *Ottaviano* ✛ *2:B3.*

TRASTEVERE

$$
HOTEL
Fodor's Choice
★

⛢ **Casa di Santa Francesca Romana.** In the heart of Trastevere but tucked away from the hustle and bustle of the medieval quarter, this cheap, clean, comfortable hotel in a former monastery is centered on a lovely green courtyard. **Pros:** the price can't be beat; excellent restaurants nearby; away from rowdy side of Trastevere. **Cons:** thin walls; interior is a bit bland; Wi-Fi is spotty. $ *Rooms from: €129* ✉ *Via dei Vasceillari 61, Trastevere* ☎ *06/5812125* ⊕ *www.sfromana.it* ↻ *37 rooms* ⃝❘ *Breakfast* Ⓜ *Piramide, Circo Massimo* ✛ *2:E6.*

$$$
HOTEL
Fodor'sChoice
★
🏨 **Hotel Santa Maria.** A Trastevere treasure with a pedigree going back four centuries, this ivy-covered, mansard-roof, rosy brick-red, erstwhile Renaissance-era convent—just steps away from the glorious Santa Maria in Trastevere church and a few blocks from the Tiber—has sweet and simple guest rooms: a mix of brick walls, "cotto" tile floors, modern oak furniture, and matching bedspreads and curtains. **Pros:** a quaint and pretty oasis in a central location; relaxing courtyard; stocked wine bar; free bicycles to use during your stay. **Cons:** hotel is tricky to find; some of the showers drain slowly; finding a cab is not always easy in Trastevere. $ *Rooms from: €259* ✉ *Vicolo del Piede 2, Trastevere* ☎ *06/5894626* ⊕ *www.hotelsantamariatrastevere.it* ↻ *20 rooms* ⃝❘ *Breakfast* ✛ *2:D6.*

$
HOTEL
🏨 **Hotel Trastevere.** This tiny hotel captures the villagelike charm of the Trastevere district and offers basic, clean, comfortable rooms in a great location. **Pros:** cheap with a good location; convenient to transportation; free Wi-Fi; friendly staff. **Cons:** no frills; rooms are a little worn around the edges; few amenities. $ *Rooms from: €105* ✉ *Via Luciano Manara 24/a–25, Trastevere* ☎ *06/5814713* ⊕ *www.hoteltrastevere.net* ↻ *18 rooms* ⃝❘ *Breakfast* ✛ *2:D6.*

$$
B&B/INN
Fodor'sChoice
★
🏨 **Relais Le Clarisse.** Set within the former cloister grounds of the Santa Chiara order, with beautiful gardens, Le Clarisse makes you feel like a personal guests at a friend's villa, thanks to the comfortable size of the accommodations and personalized service. **Pros:** spacious rooms with comfy beds; high-tech showers/tubs with good water pressure; free Wi-Fi. **Cons:** this part of Trastevere can be noisy at night; rooms fill up quickly; reception unavailable after 10:30 pm. $ *Rooms from: €150* ✉ *Via Cardinale Merry del Val 20, Trastevere* ☎ *06/58334437* ⊕ *www.leclarisse.com* ↻ *13 rooms, 3 suites* ⃝❘ *Breakfast* ✛ *2:D6.*

MONTI AND SAN LORENZO

SAN LORENZO

$
HOTEL
Fodor'sChoice
★
🏨 **Yes Hotel.** This chic hotel may fool you into thinking these digs are expensive, but the contemporary coolness of Yes Hotel, located around the corner from Termini station, comes at a bargain rate. **Pros:** discount if you pay cash; great value and doesn't feel budget. **Cons:** rooms are small; fee for Wi-Fi in rooms. $ *Rooms from: €114* ✉ *Via Magenta 15, Repubblica* ☎ *06/44363836* ⊕ *www.yeshotelrome.com* ↻ *38 rooms, 2 suites* ⃝❘ *Breakfast* Ⓜ *Termini, Castro Pretorio* ✛ *2:H3.*

AVENTINO

$$$$
HOTEL
🏨 **Hotel San Anselmo.** This refurbished 19th-century villa is a romantic retreat from the city, set in a molto charming garden atop the Aventine Hill. **Pros:** free Wi-Fi; historic building with artful interior; great showers with jets; a garden where you can enjoy breakfast. **Cons:** a bit of a hike to sights; limited public transportation. $ *Rooms from: €314* ✉ *Piazza*

San Anselmo 2, Aventino ☎ *06/570057* 🌐 *www.aventinohotels.com* 🛏 *35 rooms* 🍴 *Breakfast* [M] *Circo Massimo* ✥ *2:E6.*

VIA VENETO

$$$$ HOTEL Fodor's Choice ★ **Regina Hotel Baglioni.** This five-star property on the Via Veneto is, quite literally, fit for a queen: Queen Margherita of Savoy stayed here while she was waiting for the completion of her palazzo, located across the street (and now home to the American Embassy). **Pros:** very good spa and small gym; impeccable service; luxurious Italian design; in-hotel restaurant and bar; ample buffet breakfast; excellent attention to detail (like a turndown service with chocolates, and high-end toiletries). **Cons:** Wi-Fi costs extra; rooms vary in in the date of their last renovation, and some could use a face-lift. [$] *Rooms from: €500* ✉ *Via Veneto 72, Via Veneto* ☎ *06/421111* 🌐 *www.baglionihotels.com/category/regina-hotel-baglioni-rome* 🛏 *118 rooms* 🍴 *Breakfast* ✥ *2:G2.*

NIGHTLIFE AND PERFORMING ARTS

NIGHTLIFE

Rome's nightlife is decidedly more happening for locals and insiders who know which palms to grease and when to go where. The "flavor of the month" factor is at work here, and many places fade into oblivion after their 15 minutes of fame. Smoking has been banned in all public areas in Italy (that's right, it actually happened), and Roman aversion to clean air has meant a decrease in crowds at bars and clubs. Trastevere and the area around Piazza Navona are both filled with bars, restaurants, and, after dark, people. In summer, discos and many bars close to beat the heat (although some simply relocate to the beach, where many Romans spend their summer nights). The city-sponsored Estate Romana (Rome Summer) festival takes over, lighting up hot city nights with open-air concerts, bars, and discos. Pick up the event guide at newsstands.

PIAZZA NAVONA AND CAMPO DE' FIORI

BARS

Antico Caffè della Pace. It doesn't get any more Rome than this: a cappuccino or cocktail alfresco at a turn-of-the-20th-century-style café nestled among the picturesque side streets behind Piazza Navona. Celebrities and literati hang out at the coveted outdoor tables of Antico Caffè della Pace, also known as Bar della Pace, where the atmosphere ranges from peaceful to percolating. Its location is equally enchanting, in the *piazzatina* (tiny piazza) of Santa Maria della Pace, by Baroque architect Pietro da Cortona. ✉ *Via della Pace 3/7, Piazza Navona* ☎ *06/6861216* 🌐 *www.caffedellapace.it.*

L'Angolo Divino. Nestled on a quiet side street around the corner from the ever-vivacious Campo de' Fiori, this wood-paneled enoteca is a hidden treasure of wines. Its extensive selection lists more than 1,000 labels to go along quite nicely with its quaint menu of delicious homemade pastas

1

and local antipasti, and since it's open every night until 1:30 am, it's the ideal place for a late-night tipple. ⊠ *Via dei Balestrari 12, Campo de' Fiori* ☎ *06/6864413* ⊕ *www.angolodivino.it.*

Fodor's Choice
★ **Roof Garden Bar at Grand Hotel della Minerve.** During the warm months, this lofty perch offers up perhaps the most inspiring view in Rome—directly to the Pantheon's dome. The Roof Garden has an equally impressive cocktail menu. Take advantage of summer sunsets and park yourself in a front-row seat as the dome glows. ⊠ *Grand Hotel della Minerve, Piazza della Minerve 69, Piazza Navona* ☎ *06/695201* ⊕ *www.grandhoteldelaminerve.com.*

Vinoteca Novecento. A lovely, tiny enoteca with a very old-fashioned vibe, Vinoteca Novecento has a seemingly unlimited selection of wines, proseccos, vin santos, and grappas along with salami-and-cheese tasting menus. Inside is standing-room only; in good weather, sit outside on one of the oak barriques. ⊠ *Piazza Delle Coppelle 47, Piazza Navona* ☎ *06/6833078.*

NIGHTCLUBS AND DISCOS

Fodor's Choice
★ **La Cabala.** Atop the medieval Hostaria dell'Orso, La Cabala is an after-dinner club and late-night dance party whose VIP room hosts wannabe models. Depending on the evening, vibe can be chic, hipster, or clubby. Rome's version of a supper club, La Cabala is part of the Hostaria dell'Orso trio of restaurant, disco, and piano bar. Dress code is stylish. ⊠ *Hostaria dell'Orso, Via dei Soldati 23, Piazza Navona* ☎ *06/68301192* ⊕ *www.hdo.it.*

PIAZZA DI SPAGNA

BARS

Fodor's Choice
★ **Enoteca Palatium.** Just down the street from the Piazza di Spagna hub is this modern gem run by Lazio's Regional Food Authority as a chic showcase for the best of Lazio's pantry and wine cellar. You can sample fine vintages, olive oils, cheeses, and meats, and also a full seasonal menu of Lazio cuisine, including classics from top-notch ingredients (think gnocchi with mutton ragù) and dishes with a twist (like lentil and calamari soup, or durum wheat rigatoni with zucchini sauce). Located where famed aesthete and poet Gabriele d'Annunzio once lived, this is not your garden-variety corner wine bar. ■ TIP➡ **Stop by during aperitivo hour, from 6:30 pm onward (reservations recommended) to enjoy this burst of local flavor.** ⊠ *Via Frattina 94, Piazza di Spagna* ⊕ *www.enotecapalatium.com.*

Wine Bar at the Palazzetto. The prize for perfect aperitivo spot goes to the Palazzetto, with excellent drinks and appetizers and a breathtaking view of Rome's domes and rooftops, all from its fifth-floor rooftop overlooking Piazza di Spagna. Keep an eye on the sky, as any chance for a rainy day will close the terrace (as do special events). ⊠ *Palazzetto, Piazza Trinità di Monti, Piazza di Spagna* ☎ *06/69934711* ⊕ *www.ilpalazzettoroma.com* Ⓜ *Spagna.*

REPUBBLICA

Fodor's Choice
★ **Champagnerie Tazio.** A chic champagne bar named after the original Italian *paparazzo* Tazio Secchiaroli, this spot brings a very *dolce vita* vibe with its red, black, and white lacquered interior with crystal chandeliers.

The favorite pastime at Tazio is sipping champagne while watching people parade through the colonnade of the lobby. In summer, the hotel's rooftop Posh bar is the place to be, with its infinity pool and terrace view overlooking downtown. ⊠ *Hotel Exedra, Piazza della Repubblica 47, Repubblica* ☎ *06/48938061* ⊕ *exedra-roma.boscolohotels.com* Ⓜ *Repubblica–Teatro dell'Opera.*

PIAZZA DEL POPOLO

Stravinskij Bar at the Hotel de Russie. The Stravinskij Bar, in the Hotel de Russie's garden, is the best place to catch a glimpse of *la dolce vita.* Celebrities, blue bloods, and VIPs hang out in the private courtyard garden where mixed drinks and cocktails are well above par (as are the prices). ⊠ *Hotel de Russie, Via del Babuino 9, Popolo* ☎ *06/328881* ⊕ *www.hotelderussie.it* Ⓜ *Flaminio.*

TRASTEVERE

Fodor'sChoice ★ **Freni e Frizioni.** This hipster hangout has a cute artist vibe, great for an afternoon coffee, tea, or aperitifs, or for late-night socializing. In warmer weather, the crowd overflows the large terrazzo overlooking the Tiber and the side streets of Trastevere. ⊠ *Via del Politeama 4, Trastevere* ☎ *06/45497499* ⊕ *www.freniefrizioni.com.*

MONTI

Ai Tre Scalini. A rustic wine bar in the center of Monti, Rome's trendiest 'hood, Ai Tre Scalini has a warm and cozy menu of delicious antipasti and light entrées to go along with its enticing wine list. After about 8 pm, if you haven't booked, be prepared to wait—this is one extremely popular spot with locals. ⊠ *Via Panisperna 251, Monti* ☎ *06/48907495* ⊕ *www.aitrescalini.org* Ⓜ *Cavour.*

TESTACCIO

The Manhattan. A new entry to Testaccio's club line up on Via Galvani, The Manhattan combines lounge style with disco vibes. Great for late-night dancing. ⊠ *Via Galvani 20, Testaccio* ☎ *39/3931818498.*

PERFORMING ARTS

Rome has a good range of publications with timely information regarding events and happenings in the city. Begin with the city's official website (⊕ *www.comune.roma.it*). Events listings can also be found in the Cronaca and Cultura sections of Italian newspapers, as well as in *Metro* (the free newspaper). Flip to the back for the brief yet detailed English-language section. Check out events website ⊕ *www.inromenow.com* and ⊕ *www.romeing.it* (*in English*), as well as *The American* (⊕ *www.theamericanmag.com*). In addition, consult the monthly English-language periodical (with accompanying website) *Wanted in Rome* (⊕ *www.wantedinrome.com*), available at many newsstands.

TICKETS

Orbis. An in-person, cash-only ticket vendor, Orbis stocks a wide array of tickets for music, cultural, and performance events. ⊠ *Piazza dell'Esquilino 37, Repubblica* ☎ *06/4827403.*

VivaTicket. One of Italy's largest ticket vendors (both online and at ticket offices), VivaTicket covers major musical performances and cultural events in Rome and throughout Italy. ⊕ *www.vivaticket.it.*

MAIN VENUES

Fodor'sChoice ★ **Teatro Argentina.** A gorgeous, turn-of-the-last-century theatre, Teatro Argentina evokes glamour and sophistication with its velvet upholstery, large crystal chandeliers and beautifully dressed theatergoers who come to see international productions of stage and dance performances. ✉ *Largo di Torre Argentina 52, Campo de' Fiori* ☎ *06/684000311* ⊕ *www.teatrodiroma.net.*

Teatro Olimpico. Part of Rome's theater circuit, the 1930s-era Teatro Olimpico is one of the main venues for contemporary dance companies, visiting international ballet companies, touring Broadway shows, and TEDxRoma. ✉ *Piazza Gentile da Fabriano 17, Flaminio* ☎ *06/3265991* ⊕ *www.teatroolimpico.it.*

OPERA

Fodor'sChoice ★ **Teatro dell'Opera.** Rome has recently stepped into the spotlight for opera aficionados thanks to Maestro Riccardo Muti's ongoing support of Rome's Teatro dell'Opera. Though considered a far younger sibling of Milan's Scala and Venice's Fenice, the company commands an audience during its mid-November–May season. In the hot summer months, the company moves to the Baths of Caracalla for its outdoor opera series. As can be expected, the oft-preferred performance is *Aida* for its spectacle, which has been known to include real elephants. The company has taken a new direction, using projections atop the ancient ruins to create cutting-edge sets. ✉ *Piazza Beniamino Gigli 8, Repubblica* ☎ *06/481601, 06/48160255 for tickets* ⊕ *www.operaroma.it* Ⓜ *Repubblica–Teatro dell'Opera.*

SHOPPING

They say, "When in Rome, do as the Romans do"—and the Romans love to shop. After all, this is the city that gave us the Gucci "moccasin" loafer, the Fendi bag, and the Valentino dress that Jackie O wore when she became Mrs. Onassis. Stores are generally open from 10 to 1 and from 3:30 or 4 to 7 or 7:30 (with the exception of Monday, when most are closed in the morning). There's a tendency for shops in central districts to stay open all day, and hours are becoming more flexible throughout the city. Many places close all day Sunday, though this is changing, too, especially in the city center. Some stores also close Saturday afternoon from mid-June through August.

You can stretch your euros by taking advantage of the Tax-Free for Tourists V.A.T. (value-added tax) refunds, available at most large stores on purchases of more than €155. Or hit Rome in January and early February or in late July and August, when stores clean house with the justly famous biannual sales, or *saldi.* There are so many hole-in-the-wall boutiques selling top-quality merchandise in Rome's center that even just wandering, you're sure to find something that catches your eye.

SHOPPING DISTRICTS

The city's most famous shopping district, **Piazza di Spagna,** is conveniently compact, fanning out at the foot of the Spanish Steps in a galaxy of boutiques selling gorgeous wares with glamorous labels. Here you can prance back and forth from Gucci to Prada to Valentino to Versace with less effort than it takes to pull out your credit card. If your budget is designed for lower altitudes, you also can find great clothes and accessories at less extravagant prices. But here, buying is not necessarily the point—window displays can be works of art in themselves, and dreaming may be satisfaction enough. Via dei Condotti is the neighborhood's central axis, but there are shops on every street in the area bordered by Piazza di Spagna on the east, Via del Corso on the west, between Piazza San Silvestro and Via della Croce, and extending along Via del Babuino to Piazza del Popolo. Via Margutta, a few blocks north of the Spanish Steps, is a haven for contemporary art galleries.

Running from Piazza Venezia to Piazza del Popolo, the **Via del Corso** has more than a mile of shops. Unfortunately, these days most of it is taken up by the same chain stores you find worldwide (including Gap, H&M, and even an Athlete's Foot), rendering it little more interesting than a trip to one's local shopping mall. Running west from Piazza Navona, Via del Governo Vecchio has numerous women's boutiques and secondhand-clothing stores.

The Termini train station has become a good one-stop place for many shopping needs, although again, most stores are the same you see worldwide. Its 60-plus shops are open until 10 pm and include a Nike store, the Body Shop, Sephora, Mango (women's clothes), a UPIM department store, a grocery store, and a three-story bookstore with selections in English. For local designers and independent boutiques, don't miss the trendy shopping districts of **Monti** near the Forum and **Trastevere** across the Tiber from the centro storico.

PIAZZA NAVONA

CLOTHING

Arsenale. Arsenale has a sleek layout and a low-key elegance that stands out, even in Rome. Rest your feet awhile in an overstuffed chair before sifting through the racks. Whether you are looking for a wedding dress or a seductive bustier, you are bound to find something unconventional here. Designer and owner Patriza Pieroni creates many of the pieces on display, all cleverly cut and decidedly captivating. ⊠ *Via del Pellegrino 172, Piazza Navona* ☎ *06/68802424* ⊕ *www.patriziapieroni.it.*

Le Tartarughe. Designer Susanna Liso, a Rome native, adds suggestive elements of playful experimentation to her haute couture and ready-to-wear lines, which are much loved by Rome's aristocracy and intelligentsia. With intense and enveloping designs, she mixes raw silks or cashmere and fine merino wool together to form captivating garments that are a mix of seduction and linear form. ⊠ *Via Piè di Marmo 17, Piazza Navona* ☎ *06/6792240* ⊕ *www.letartarughe.eu.*

Mado. Still a leader in nostalgia styling, Mado has been vintage cool in Rome since 1969. The shop is funky, glamorous, and often over-the-top wacky. Whether you are looking for a robin's-egg-blue empire-waist dress or a '50s gown evocative of a Lindy Hop, Mado understands the challenges of incorporating vintage pieces into a modern wardrobe. ✉ *Via del Governo Vecchio 89/a, Piazza Navona* ☎ *06/6798660.*

FOOD AND WINE

Enoteca al Parlamento Achilli. The tantalizing smell of truffles from the snack counter, where a sommelier waits to organize your wine-tasting session, is enough alone to lure you into Enoteca al Parlamento Achilli, filled with gastronomic treasures. The proximity of this traditional enoteca to Montecitorio, the Italian Parliament building, makes it a favorite with journalists and politicos, who often stop in for a glass of wine after work—its prices are not for the faint of heart. Ask to take a look at the wine shop's most prized possessions: bottles of Brunello di Montalcino, vintages 1891 and 1925, strictly not for sale. ✉ *Via dei Prefetti 15, Piazza Navona* ☎ *06/6873446* ⊕ *www.enotecaalparlamento.it.*

Moriondo e Gariglio. The Willy Wonka of Roman chocolate factories opened its doors in 1850. The shop uses the finest cocoa beans and adheres strictly to family recipes passed down from generation to generation. Known for rich, gourmet chocolates, they soon were the favored chocolatier to the House of Savoy. In 2009, the shop partnered with Bulgari and placed 300 pieces of jewelry in their Easter eggs to benefit cancer research. While you may not find diamonds in your bonbons, marrons glacés, or dark-chocolate truffles, you'll still delight in choosing from more than 80 delicacies. ✉ *Via Piè di Marmo 21, Piazza Navona* ☎ *06/6990856.*

JEWELRY

MMM—Massimo Maria Melis. Drawing heavily on ancient Greek, Roman, and Etruscan designs, Massimo Maria Melis jewelry will carry you back in time. Working with 21-carat gold, he often incorporates antique coins acquired by numismatists or pieces of ancient bronze and polychromatic glass. Some of his pieces are done with an ancient technique much loved by the Etruscans in which tiny gold droplets are soldered together to create intricately patterned designs. ✉ *Via dell'Orso 57, Piazza Navona* ☎ *06/6869188* ⊕ *www.massimomariamelis.com.*

Quattrocolo. This historic shop dating to 1938 showcases exquisite antique micro-mosaic jewelry painstakingly crafted in the style perfected by the masters at the Vatican mosaic studio. You'll also find 18th- and 19th-century cameos and beautiful engraved stones. Their small works were beloved by cosmopolitan clientele of the Grand Tour age and offer modern-day shoppers a taste of yesteryear's grandeur. ✉ *Via della Scrofa 48, Piazza Navona* ☎ *06/68801367* ⊕ *www.quattrocolo. com.*

SHOES AND ACCESSORIES

Spazio IF. In a tiny piazza alongside Rome's historic Via dei Coronari, designers Irene and Carla Ferrara have created a tantalizing hybrid between fashion paradise and art gallery. Working with unconventional designers and artists who emphasize Sicilian design, the shop has more to say about the style of Sicily and the creativity of the island's inhabitants than flat caps, puppets, and rich pastries. Perennial favorites include handbags cut by hand in a *putia* (shop) in Palermo, swimsuits, designer textiles, jewelry, and sportswear. ⊠ *Via dei Coronari 44a, Piazza Navona* ☎ *06/64760639* ⊕ *www.spazioif.it.*

TOYS

Fodor'sChoice **Bartolucci.** Bartolucci attracts shoppers with a life-size Pinocchio ped-
★ aling furiously on a wooden bike. Inside is a shop that would have warmed Geppetto's heart. For more than 60 years and three generations, this family has been making whimsical, handmade curiosities out of pine, including clocks, bookends, bedside lamps, and wall hangings. You can even buy a child-size vintage car entirely made of wood, including the wheels. ⊠ *Via dei Pastini 98, Piazza Navona* ☎ *06/69190894* ⊕ *www.bartolucci.com.*

PIAZZA DI SPAGNA

ACCESSORIES

Furla. Furla has 12 franchises in Rome alone. Its flagship store, to the left of the Spanish Steps, sells bags like hot cakes. Be prepared to fight your way through crowds of passionate handbag lovers, all anxious to possess one of the delectable bags, wallets, or watch straps in ice-cream colors. ⊠ *Piazza di Spagna 22* ☎ *06/69200363* ⊕ *www.furla. com* Ⓜ *Spagna.*

CLOTHING

Dolce & Gabbana. Dolce and Gabbana met in 1980 when both were assistants at a Milan fashion atelier and opened their first store in 1982. With a modern aesthetic that screams sex appeal, the brand has always thrived on its excesses. The Rome store can be more than a little overwhelming, with its glossy glamazons, but at least there is plenty of eye candy, masculine and feminine, with a spring line heavy of stars and sequins as well as enthusiastic fruits, flowers, and veggies. There is a second location on Via Condotti. ⊠ *Piazza di Spagna 94–95* ☎ *06/6991592* ⊕ *www.dolcegabbana.it* Ⓜ *Spagna.*

Elena Mirò. Elena Mirò is an absolutely delectable Italian atelier making its mark designing clothes specifically for those who don't have the proportions of a 14-year-old. If your DNA gave you the curves of *Mad Men*'s Joan Holloway you will love the fact that this designer specializes in beautifully sexy clothes for curvy, European-styled women size 46 (U.S. size 12, UK size 14) and up. There are eight locations in Rome. ⊠ *Via Frattina 11–12, Piazza di Spagna* ☎ *06/6784367* ⊕ *www. elenamiro.it* Ⓜ *Spagna.*

Fodor'sChoice **Fendi.** Fendi has been a fixture of the Roman fashion landscape since
★ "Mamma" Fendi first opened shop with her husband in 1925. With an eye for crazy genius, she hired Karl Lagerfeld, who began working with the group at the start of his career. His furs and runway antics have made him one of the world's most influential designers of the 20th century and brought international acclaim to Fendi along the way. Recent Lagerfeld triumphs include new collections marrying innovative

textures, fabrics (cashmere, felt, and duchesse satin) with exotic skins like crocodile. Keeping up with technology, they even have an iPad case that will surely win a fashionista's seal of approval. The atelier, now owned by the Louis Vuitton group, continues to symbolize Italian glamour at its finest, though the difference in owners is noticeable; it's also gotten new life in the Italian press for its "Fendi for Fountains" campaign, which includes funding the restoration of Rome's Trevi Fountain. ⊠ *Largo Carlo Goldoni 419–421, Piazza di Spagna* ☎ *06/3344501* ⊕ *www.fendi.com* Ⓜ *Spagna.*

Giorgio Armani. One of the most influential designers of Italian haute couture, Giorgio Armani creates fluid silhouettes and dazzling evening gowns with décolletés so deep they'd make a grown man blush, his signature cuts made with the clever-handedness and flawless technique that you only achieve working with tracing paper and Italy's finest fabrics over the course of a lifetime. His menswear collection uses traditional textiles like wide-wale corduroy and stretch jersey in nontraditional ways while staying true to a clean, masculine aesthetic. It's true that exotic runway ideas and glamorous celebrities give Armani saleability, but his staying power is casual Italian elegance with just the right touch of whimsy and sexiness. ⊠ *Via Condotti 77–79, Piazza di Spagna* ☎ *06/6991460* ⊕ *www.giorgioarmani.com* Ⓜ *Spagna.*

Fodor's Choice ★ **Gucci.** As the glamorous fashion label approaches its centennial, the success of the double-G trademark brand is unquestionable. Survival in luxury fashion depends on defining market share, and new creative director Alessandro Michele now must prove knows the soul of the House of Gucci. Tom Ford may have made Gucci the sexiest brand in the world, but it's today's reinterpreted horsebit styles and Jackie Kennedy scarves that keep the design house on top. And while Gucci remains a fashion must for virtually every A-list celebrity, their designs have moved from heart-stopping sexy rockstar to something classically subdued and retrospectively feminine. There's another store on Via Borgognona. ⊠ *Via Condotti 8, Piazza di Spagna* ☎ *06/6790405* ⊕ *www.gucci.com* Ⓜ *Spagna.*

Fodor's Choice ★ **Laura Biagiotti.** For 40 years Laura Biagiotti has been a worldwide ambassador of Italian fashion. Considered the Queen of Cashmere, her soft-as-velvet pullovers have been worn by Sophia Loren and her snow-white cardigans were said to be a favorite of the late Pope John Paul II. Princess Diana even sported one of Biagiotti's cashmere maternity dresses. Be sure to indulge in her line of his-and-her perfumes. ⊠ *Via Mario de' Fiori 26, Piazza di Spagna* ☎ *06/6791205* ⊕ *www.laurabiagiotti.it* Ⓜ *Spagna.*

Fodor's Choice ★ **Patrizia Pepe.** One of Florence's best-kept secrets for up-and-coming fashions, Patrizia Pepe emerged on the scene in 1993 with designs both minimalist and bold, combining classic styles with low-slung jeans and jackets with oversize lapels that are bound to draw attention. Her line of shoes are hot-hot-hot for those who can walk in stilts. It's still not huge on the fashion scene as a stand-alone brand, but take a look at this shop before the line becomes the next fast-tracked craze. ⊠ *Via Frattina 44, Piazza di Spagna* ☎ *06/6781851* ⊕ *www.patriziapepe.com.*

Fodor's Choice   **Prada.** Not just the devil, but also serious shoppers wear Prada season
★   after season, especially those willing to sell their souls for one of their
ubiquitous handbags. If you are looking for that blend of old-world
luxury with a touch of fashion-forward finesse, you'll hit paydirt here.
Recent handbag designs have a bit of a 1960s Jackie Kennedy feel, and
whether you like them will hinge largely on whether you find Prada's
signature retro-modernism enchanting. You'll find the Rome store more
service-focused than the New York City branches—a roomy elevator
delivers you to a series of thickly carpeted rooms where a flock of
discreet assistants will help you pick out dresses, shoes, lingerie, and
fashion accessories. The men's store is located at Via Condotti 88/90,
and women's is at down the street at 92/95. ⊠ *Via Condotti 88/90 and
92/95, Piazza di Spagna* ☎ *06/6790897* ⊕ *www.prada.com* Ⓜ *Spagna.*

Salvatore Ferragamo. One of the top 10 most-wanted men's footwear
brands, Salvatore Ferragamo has been providing Hollywood glitterati
and discerning clients with unique handmade designs for years. Ferragamo fans will think they have died and followed the white light when
they enter this store. The Florentine design house also specializes in
handbags, small leather goods, men's and women's ready-to-wear, and
scarves and ties. Men's styles are found at Via Condotti 65, women's at
73/74. ⊠ *Via Condotti 65 and 73/74, Piazza di Spagna* ☎ *06/6781130*
⊕ *www.ferragamo.com* Ⓜ *Spagna.*

Save the Queen!. A hot Florentine design house with exotic and creative
pieces for women and girls with artistic and eccentric frills, cutouts, and
textures, Save the Queen! has one of the most beautiful shops in the
city, with window displays that are works of art unto themselves. The
store is chock-full of Baroque-inspired dresses, shirts, and skirts that
are ultrafeminine and not the least bit discreet. Pieces radiate charming
excess, presenting a portrait of youthful chic. ⊠ *Via del Babuino 49,
Piazza di Spagna* ☎ *06/36003039* ⊕ *www.savethequeen.com* Ⓜ *Spagna.*

Schostal. At the end of the 19th century when ladies needed petticoats,
corsets, bonnets, or white or colored stockings made of cotton thread,
wool, or silk, it was inevitable for them to stop at Schostal. A Piazza
di Spagna fixture since 1870, the shop still preserves that genteel ambience. Fine-quality shirts come with spare collars and cuffs. Ultraclassic
underwear, handkerchiefs, and pure wool and cashmere are available
at affordable prices. There's a second location at Piazza Euclide. ⊠ *Via
Fontanella Borghese 29, Piazza di Spagna* ☎ *06/6791240* ⊕ *www.
schostalroma.com* Ⓜ *Spagna.*

Fodor's Choice   **Valentino.** Since taking the Valentino reins a few years ago, creative
★   directors Maria Grazia Chiuri and Pier Paolo Piccioli have faced numerous challenges, the most basic being keeping Valentino true to Valentino after the designer's retirement in 2008. Both served as accessories
designers under Valentino for more than a decade and understand
exactly how to make the next generation of Hollywood stars swoon.
Spagna's sprawling boutiques showcase designs with a romantic edgi-
ness: think kitten heels and or a show-stopping prêt-à-porter evening
gown worthy of the Oscars. ⊠ *Via Condotti 15, Piazza di Spagna*
☎ *06/6739420* ⊕ *www.valentino.com* Ⓜ *Spagna.*

Versace. Versace's new Rome flagship, which opened in a palazzo at the Piazza di Spagna in fall 2013, is a gem both of architecture and design—with Byzantine-inspired mosaic floors and futuristic interiors—and of fashion. Here shoppers will find apparel, jewelry, watches, fragrances, cosmetics, and home furnishings in designs every bit as flamboyant as Donatella and Allegra (Gianni's niece), drawing heavily on the sexy rocker gothic underground vibe. There's also a smaller boutique on the Via Veneto with pret-à-porter and jewelry. ⊠ *Piazza di Spagna 12* ☎ *06/6691773* ⊕ *www.versace.com* Ⓜ *Spagna.*

CLOTHING: MEN'S

Fodor's Choice ★

Brioni. Founded in 1945 and hailed for its impeccable craftsmanship and flawless execution, the Brioni label is known for attracting and keeping the best men's tailors in Italy where the exacting standards require that custom-made suits are designed from scratch and measured to the millimeter. For this personalized line, the menswear icon has 5,000 spectacular fabrics to select from. As thoughtful as expensive, one bespoke suit made from wool will take a minimum of 32 hours to create. Their prêt-à-porter line is also praised for peerless cutting and stitching. Past and present clients include Clark Gable, Donald Trump, Barack Obama and, of course, James Bond. And they say clothing doesn't make the man? There also are two other central locations, one on Via Condotti 21/a and the other on Via Veneto 129. ⊠ *Via del Babuino 38/40, Piazza di Spagna* ☎ *06/484517* ⊕ *www.brioni.com* Ⓜ *Spagna.*

DEPARTMENT STORES

La Rinascente. Italy's best-known department store, La Rinascente is where Italian fashion mogul Giorgio Armani got his start as a window dresser. Recently relocated inside the Galleria Alberto Sordi, the store has a phalanx of ready-to-wear designer sportswear and blockbuster handbags and accessories. The upscale clothing and accessories are a hit with the young and well dressed, while retail turf is geared toward people on lunch breaks and the ubiquitous tourist. The Piazza Fiume location has more floor space and a wider range of goods, including a housewares department. ⊠ *Galleria Alberto Sordi, Piazza Colonna* ☎ *06/6784209* ⊕ *www.rinascente.it* Ⓜ *Spagna.*

JEWELRY

Bulgari. Every capital city has its famous jeweler, and Bulgari is to Rome what Tiffany is to New York and Cartier to Paris. The jewelry giant has developed a reputation for meticulous craftsmanship melded with noble metals and precious gems. In the middle of the 19th century, the great-grandfather of the current Bulgari brothers began working as a silver jeweler in his native Greece and is said to have moved to Rome with less than 1,000 lire in his pocket. Today the megabrand emphasizes colorful and playful jewelry as the principal cornerstone of its aesthetic. Popular collections include Parentesi, Bulgari-Bulgari and B.zero1. In honor of its 130th anniversary in 2015, Bulgari commissioned American architect Peter Marino to refurbish its Rome flagship store; reopened to the public in spring 2014, the restoration was hailed by critics as a savvy update that stays true to the store's 1930s modernist style. ⊠ *Via Condotti 10, Piazza di Spagna* ☎ *06/696261* ⊕ *www.bulgari.com* Ⓜ *Spagna.*

SHOES

A. Testoni. Amedeo Testoni was born in 1905 in Bologna, the heart of Italy's shoemaking territory. In 1929 he opened his first shop and began producing shoes as artistic as the Cubist and Art Deco artwork of the period. His shoes have adorned the art-in-motion feet of Fred Astaire and proved that lightweight shoes could be comfortable and luxurious and still make heads turn. Today the Testoni brand includes an extraordinary women's collection and a sports line that is relaxed without losing its artistic heritage. The soft, calfskin sneakers are a dream, as are the matching messenger bags. ⊠ *Via Condotti 80, Piazza di Spagna* ☎ *06/6788944* ⊕ *www.testoni.com* Ⓜ *Spagna.*

Fodor's Choice
★

Braccialini. Founded in 1954 by Florentine stylist Carla Braccialini and her husband, Braccialini—currently managed by their sons—makes bags that are authentic works of art in delightful shapes, such as little gold taxis or Santa Fe stagecoaches. The delightfully quirky beach bags have picture-postcard scenes of Italian resorts made of brightly colored appliquéd leather: be sure to check out their eccentric Temi (Theme) creature bags; the opossum-shape handbag made out of crocodile skin makes a richly whimsical fashion statement. There's a second location at the Galleria Alberto Sordi. ⊠ *Via Mario De' Fiori 73, Piazza di Spagna* ☎ *06/6785750* ⊕ *www.braccialini.it* Ⓜ *Spagna.*

Bruno Magli. Bruno Magli has high-end, well-crafted, classically styled shoes for both men and women. Magli and his siblings Marino and Maria learned the art of shoemaking from their father and grandfather. From its humble family origins to the corporate design powerhouse it has become today, Bruno Magli footwear always has kept the focus on craftsmanship: it's not uncommon for 30 people to touch each shoe during the course of its manufacture. ⊠ *Via Condotti 6, Piazza di Spagna* ☎ *06/69292121* ⊕ *www.brunomagli.it* Ⓜ *Spagna.*

Fausto Santini. Fausto Santini gives a hint of extravagance in minimally decorated shoes that fashion mavens love. For 45 years, Santini has successfully attracted an avant-garde clientele of both men and women who flock to his preppy-hipster/nerdy-chic shoes, which are bright and colorful and sport deconstructed forms in plush, supple leathers that scream to be tried on. ■TIP➔ An outlet at Via Cavour 106 sells last season's shoes at a deep discount. ⊠ *Via Frattina 120, Piazza di Spagna* ☎ *06/6784114* ⊕ *www.faustosantini.it* Ⓜ *Spagna.*

Fodor's Choice
★

Saddlers Union. Reborn on the mythical artisan's street, Via Margutta, across the street from Federico Fellini's old house, Saddlers Union first launched in 1957 and quickly gained a cult following among those who valued Italian artistry and a traditional aesthetic. Jacqueline Kennedy set the trend of classical elegance by sporting their rich saddle-leather bucket bag. Closed in 2004, one of Italy's finest labels is back, representing everything for which Rome leatherwork has become famous. If you're searching for a sinfully fabulous handbag in a graceful, classic shape or that "I have arrived" attorney's briefcase, you will find something guaranteed to inspire envy. Items are made on-site with true artistry and under the watchful eye of Angelo Zaza, one of Saddlers Union's original master artisans. The prices are high, but so is the quality. ⊠ *Via Margutta 11, Piazza di Spagna* ☎ *06/32120237* ⊕ *www. saddlersunion.com* Ⓜ *Flaminio, Spagna.*

Fodor'sChoice ★ **Tod's.** With just 30 years under its belt, Tod's has grown from a small family brand into a global powerhouse so wealthy that it has donated €20 million to renovate the Colosseum. Tod's has gathered a cult following among style mavens worldwide, due in large part to owner Diego Della Valle's equally famous other possession: Florence's soccer team. The shoe baron's trademark is simple, understated design. Sure to please are his light and flexible slip-on Gommini driving shoes with rubber-bottom soles for extra pedal grip—now you just need a Ferrari. There are also locations on Via Condotti and Via Borgogona. ⊠ *Via Fontanella di Borghese 56a–57, Piazza di Spagna* ☎ *06/68210066* ⊕ *www.tods.com* Ⓜ *Spagna.*

MONTI AND SAN LORENZO

CLOTHING

Hydra. An avant-garde clothing shop for older teens and twentysomethings who believe clothing should make a statement, Hydra has styles that range from voluptuous Betty Boop retro dresses to indie underground to in-your-face T-shirts that would make your grandmother blush. ⊠ *Via Urbana 139* ☎ *06/48907773* Ⓜ *Cavour.*

Fodor'sChoice ★ **Le Gallinelle.** This tiny boutique lives in a former butcher's shop—hence the large metal hooks. Owner Wilma Silvestri transforms vintage, ethnic, and contemporary fabrics into retro-inspired clothing with a modern edge without smelling like mothballs from your great aunt Suzie's closet. ⊠ *Via Panisperna 61, Monti* ☎ *06/4881017* ⊕ *www.legallinelle. it* Ⓜ *Cavour.*

TRASTEVERE

FLEA MARKETS

Porta Portese. Rome's biggest flea market is at Porta Portese, which welcomes 100,000 visitors every Sunday from 7 am until 2 pm. Larger than the St. Ouen in Paris, this mecca of flea markets is easily accessible by Tram No. 8. Like one vast yard sale, the market disgorges mountains of new and secondhand clothing, furniture, pictures, old records, used books, vintage clothing, and antiques—all at rock-bottom prices (especially if you're adept at haggling). There is a jovial atmosphere, with the aroma of food wafting in the air and people crowding around the stalls, hoping to pick up a 1960s Beatles album or a rare Art Deco figurine. Bring your haggling skills, and cash—stallholders don't accept credit cards and the nearest ATM is a hike. ■ TIP→ **Keep your valuables close; pickpockets lurk around here.** ⊠ *Via Portuense and adjacent sts. between Porta Portese and Via Ettore Rolli, Trastevere.*

SHOES

Fodor'sChoice ★ **Joseph DeBach.** The best-kept shoe secret in Rome and open only in the evenings (or by appointment), Joseph DeBach has weird and wonderful creations that are more art than footwear. Entirely handmade from wood, metal, and leather in his small and chaotic studio, his abacus wedge is worthy of a museum. Styles are outrageous "wow" and sometimes finished with hand-painted strings, odd bits of comic books, newspapers, or other unexpected baubles. Individually signed and dated, his shoes are distributed, in very small numbers, in London, Paris, Tokyo, and New York. ✉ *Piazza de' Renzi 21, Trastevere* ☎ *3460255265* ⊕ *www.josephdebach.it.*

SIDE TRIPS FROM ROME

WELCOME TO
SIDE TRIPS FROM ROME

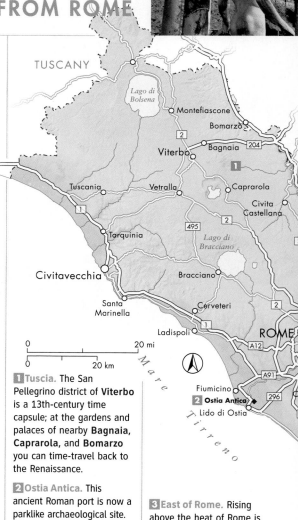

TOP REASONS TO GO

★ **Ostia Antica:** Perhaps even more than Pompeii, the excavated port city of ancient Rome conveys a picture of everyday life in the days of the empire.

★ **Tivoli's Villa d'Este:** Hundreds of fountains cascading and shooting skyward (one even plays music on organ pipes) will delight you at this spectacular garden.

★ **Castelli Romani:** Be a Roman for a day and enjoy an escape to the ancient hilltop wine towns on the city's doorstep.

★ **Get "Middle-Aged" in Viterbo:** This town may be modern, but it has a Gothic papal palace, a Romanesque cathedral, and the magical medieval quarter of San Pellegrino.

★ **Gardens bizarre and beautiful:** The 16th-century proto-Disneyland Parco dei Mostri (Monster Park) is famed for its fantastic sculptures; the Villa Lante, a few miles away, remains the stateliest Renaissance garden of them all.

1 **Tuscia.** The San Pellegrino district of **Viterbo** is a 13th-century time capsule; at the gardens and palaces of nearby **Bagnaia, Caprarola,** and **Bomarzo** you can time-travel back to the Renaissance.

2 **Ostia Antica.** This ancient Roman port is now a parklike archaeological site.

3 **East of Rome.** Rising above the heat of Rome is cool, green **Tivoli,** a fitting setting for the regal Villa Adriana and the unforgettable Villa d'Este, a park filled with the most gorgeous fountains in the world.

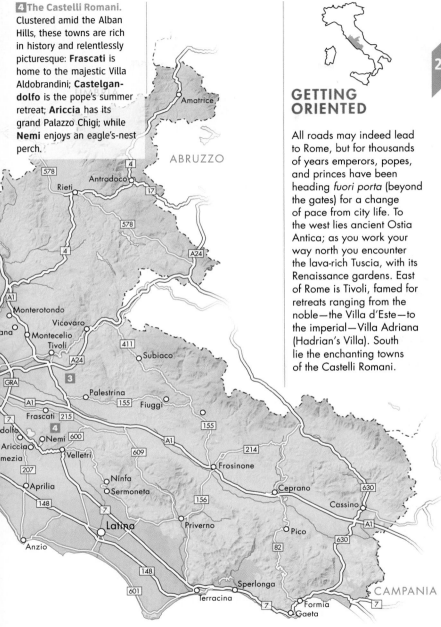

4 The Castelli Romani.
Clustered amid the Alban Hills, these towns are rich in history and relentlessly picturesque: **Frascati** is home to the majestic Villa Aldobrandini; **Castelgandolfo** is the pope's summer retreat; **Ariccia** has its grand Palazzo Chigi; while **Nemi** enjoys an eagle's-nest perch.

GETTING ORIENTED

All roads may indeed lead to Rome, but for thousands of years emperors, popes, and princes have been heading *fuori porta* (beyond the gates) for a change of pace from city life. To the west lies ancient Ostia Antica; as you work your way north you encounter the lava-rich Tuscia, with its Renaissance gardens. East of Rome is Tivoli, famed for retreats ranging from the noble—the Villa d'Este—to the imperial—Villa Adriana (Hadrian's Villa). South lie the enchanting towns of the Castelli Romani.

Updated by
Margaret
Stenhouse

Lazio, the region that encompasses Rome, the capital, is often bypassed by foreign visitors. This is a pity, since the area, which stretches from the Apennine mountain range to the Mediterranean coast, holds dozens of fascinating towns and villages, as well as scenic lakes, national parks, and forests. A trip outside of Rome introduces you to a more intimate aspect of Italy, where local customs and feast days are still enthusiastically observed, and local gastronomic specialties take pride of place on restaurant menus.

Despite these small towns' proximity to the capital and the increased commuter traffic congestion of today, they still each manage to preserve their individual character. Ostia Antica, ancient Rome's seaport, is one of the region's top attractions—it rivals Pompeii in the quality of its preservation, and for evocativeness and natural beauty, it easily outshines the Roman Forum. Emperors, cardinals, and popes have long escaped to green and verdant retreats in nearby Tivoli, Viterbo, and the Alban Hills, and their amazing villas, palaces, and gardens add to nature's allure. So if the screeching traffic and long lines at the Colosseum start to wear on you, do as the Romans do: get out of town. There's plenty to see and do.

PLANNING

MAKING THE MOST OF YOUR TIME

Ostia Antica is in many ways an ideal day trip from Rome: it's fascinating, it's not far from the city, it's reachable by public transit, and it takes about half a day to do. Villa d'Este and Villa Adriana in Tivoli also make for a manageable, though fuller, day trip. There's so much to see at these two sights alone, but also be sure to visit Tivoli's picturesque gorge, which is strikingly crowned by an ancient Roman temple to Vesta

S. Lorenzo Nuovo

Orvieto

A1

448

E45

Spoleto

Lago di Corbara

74

UMBRIA

3

209

Bolsena

71

Lago di Bolsena

2

Montefiascone

A1

Terni

E45

Bomarzo

204

Orte

578

Rieti

Antrodoco

17

Viterbo

Bagnaia

uscania

674

Norchia

Vetralla

Lago di Vico

Caprarola

Tevere

Lago di Salto

674

Civita Castellana

Lago di Turano

Tarquinia

495

2

Monterosi

3

Carsoli

Tolfa

Lago di Bracciano

A1

Civitavecchia

Bracciano

493

550

Monterotondo

Mentana

Vicovaro

Santa arinella

1

Cerveteri

2

Montecelio

411

A12

Villa d'Este

Tivoli

Ladispoli

A12

ROME

Villa Adriana

Subiaco

GRA

A24

Fiumicino

A91

Tevere

Ciampino

A1

Palestrina

155

Frascati

215

Castelgandolfo

Lido di Ostia

296

7

Lago di Albano

Nemi

A1

Ariccia

600

Ostia Antica see detail map

148

Pomezia

Velletri

609

Tor Vaianica

207

Ninfa

Aprilia

148

Sermoneta

601

7

Lido di Pini

Latina

Anzio

Nettuno

TO SPERLONGA

148

601

Mare Tirreno

0   15 mi
0   15 km

Side Trips from Rome

(now it's part of the famed Sibilla restaurant). Other destinations can be visited in a day, but you'll get more out of them if you stay the night.

One classic five-day itinerary that takes in the area's grand villas, ancient ruins, and pretty villages begins with Ostia Antica, the excavated port town of ancient Rome. Then head north to explore Viterbo's medieval streets on Day 2. On Day 3, take in the hot springs or the gardens of Bomarzo, Bagnaia, and Caprarola. For Day 4, head to Tivoli's delights. Then on Day 5 take a relaxing trip to the Castelli Romani, where Frascati wine is produced. Admire the monumental gardens of the aristocrats of yore and explore the narrow streets of these small hill towns—what more could any vacationer want?

GETTING HERE AND AROUND

There's reliable public transit from Rome to Ostia Antica, Tivoli, and Viterbo. COTRAL is the regional bus company. For other destinations, having a car is a big advantage—going by bus or a Trenitalia train can add hours to your trip, and the routes and schedules are often puzzling.

COTRAL ☎ 800/174471 ⊕ www.cotralspa.it ☯ Call center weekdays 8–6 (English speakers available).

Trenitalia ☎ 892021, 06/68475475 outside Italy ⊕ www.trenitalia.com.

RESTAURANTS

Prices in the dining reviews are the average cost of a main course at dinner, or, if dinner is not served, at lunch.

HOTELS

Former aristocratic houses with frescoed ceilings, agriturismi farmhouses, luxury spas and cozy bed-and-breakfasts are just a few of the lodging options here. You won't find much in the way of big chain hotels, though.

WHAT IT COSTS				
	$	$$	$$$	$$$$
RESTAURANTS	under €15	€15–€24	€25–€35	over €35
HOTELS	under €125	€125–€200	€201–€300	over €300

Prices in the dining reviews are the average cost of a main course at dinner, or, if dinner is not served, at lunch. Prices in the reviews are the lowest cost of a standard double room in high season.

VISITOR INFORMATION

Tourist information kiosks, which are scattered around Rome's main squares and tourist sights, can give you information about the Castelli Romani, Ostia Antica, and Tivoli. The Tuscia area is served by the central tourist office in Viterbo.

Visit Lazio ☎ 8000/12283 ⊕ www.visitlazio.com ☯ Call center weekdays 8–6.

OSTIA ANTICA

30 km (19 miles) southwest of Rome.

Founded around the 4th century BC, Ostia served as Rome's port city for several centuries until the Tiber changed course, leaving the town high and dry. What has been excavated here is a remarkably intact Roman town. To get the most out of a visit, fair weather and good walking shoes are essential. To avoid the worst extremes of hot days, be here when the gates open or go late in the afternoon. A visit to the excavations takes two to three hours, including 20 minutes for the museum. Inside the site, there's a snack bar and a bookshop.

GETTING HERE AND AROUND

The best way to get to Ostia Antica is by train. The Ostia Lido train leaves every half hour from the station adjacent to Rome's Piramide Line B Metro station, stopping off at Ostia Antica en route. The trip takes 35 minutes. By car, take the Via del Mare that leads off from Rome's EUR district. Be prepared for heavy traffic, especially at peak hours, on weekends, and in summer.

EXPLORING

Castello della Rovere. The distinctive Castello della Rovere, easily spotted as you come off the footbridge from the train station and part of the medieval *borgo* (town), was built in 1483 by Pope Julius II when he was the cardinal bishop of Ostia. The structure's triangular form is unusual for military architecture. As of 2015 the castle was closed for a lengthy restoration. ⊠ *Piazza della Rocca* ☎ *06/56358013.*

Fodor'sChoice ★ **Scavi di Ostia Antica** (*Ostia Antica excavations*). Tidal mud and wind-blown sand covered the ancient port town, which lay buried until the beginning of the 20th century, when it was extensively excavated. A cosmopolitan population of rich businessmen, wily merchants, sailors, slaves, and their respective families once populated the city. The great warehouses were built in the 2nd century AD to handle huge shipments of grain from Africa; the *insulae* (forerunners of the modern apartment building) provided housing for the city's growing population. The combined assaults of the barbarians and the malaria-carrying mosquito, as well as the Tiber changing course, led to the port's abandonment. The **Ostiense Museum** inside the ruined city displays sculptures, mosaics, and objects of daily use found on the site. A cafeteria is at the entrance. ⊠ *Viale dei Romagnoli 717* ☎ *06/56350215* ⊕ *www. ostiaantica.beniculturali.it* ▧ *€8, includes Museo Ostiense (€11 when there is a special exhibition; free 1st Sun. of month)* ⊘ *Late Mar.–Aug., Tues.–Sun. 8:30–6:15; Sept., Tues.–Sun. 8:30–6; Oct. (through last Sun. of month), Tues.–Sun. 8:30–5:30; late Oct.–late Mar., Tues.–Sun. 8:30–3:30 (until 4 or 4:30 in late Feb. and Mar.).*

WHERE TO EAT

$$$
ROMAN

✕ **Sora Margherita al Borghetto.** Under the shadow of the castle in medieval Ostia Antica, this trattoria is decorated with reproductions of fresco fragments from a Roman palace. The owners operate another restaurant in the Rome Ghetto and follow the culinary traditions of Rome's Jewish community. Expect homemade pastas, *carciofi alla*

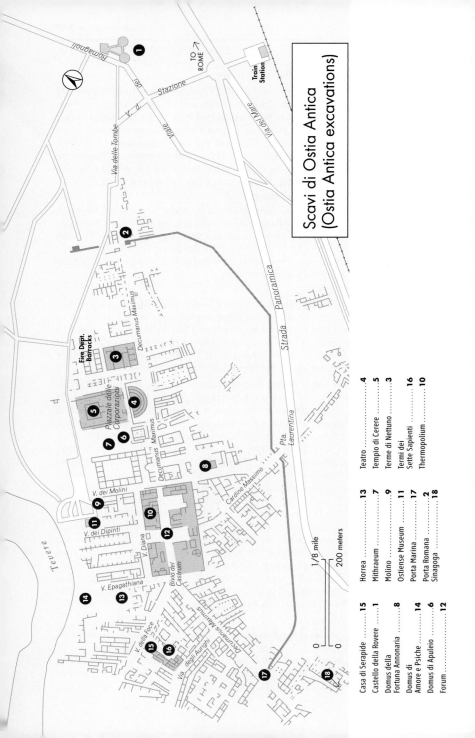

Scavi di Ostia Antica
(Ostia Antica excavations)

TO ROME

Train Station

Fire Dept. Barracks

Piazzale delle Corporazioni

Tevere

Pta. Laurentina

Strada Panoramica

Via delle Tombe

Stazione

Viale

Via del Mare

V. d. Stazione

Romagnoli

Decumanus Maximus

Decumanus Maximus

Cardine Massimo

V. dei Molini

V. dei Dipinti

V. Diana

Bivio del Castrum

V. Epagathiana

V. della Foce

V. degli Aurighi

Decumanus Maximus

1/8 mile

200 meters

giudia (deep-fried artichokes), and traditional "pluck" dishes (heart, liver, and other innards transformed into savory stews) not easily come by nowadays. Take the plunge—you might be pleasantly surprised. [$] *Average main: €30* ✉ *Via del Forno 11* ☎ *06/56352956* ⏲ *Closed Tues. No dinner Sun. in winter.*

TUSCIA

Tuscia (the modern name for the Etruscan domain of Etruria) is a region of dramatic beauty punctuated by deep, rocky gorges and thickly forested hills, with dappled light falling on wooded paths. This has long been a preferred locale for the retreats of wealthy Romans, a place where they could build grand villas and indulge their sometimes-eccentric gardening tastes. The provincial capital, Viterbo, which overshadowed Rome as a center of papal power for a time during the Middle Ages, lies in the heart of Tuscia. The farmland east of Viterbo conceals small quarries of the dark, volcanic *peperino* stone, which shows up in the walls of many buildings here. Lake Bolsena lies in an extinct volcano, and the sulfur springs still bubbling up in the spas were used by the ancient Romans. Bagnaia and Caprarola are home to palaces and gardens; the garden statuary at Bomarzo is in a league of its own—somewhere between the beautiful and the bizarre.

The ideal way to explore this region is by car. From Rome you can reach Viterbo by train and then get to Bagnaia by local bus. If you're traveling by train or bus, check schedules carefully; you may have to allow for an overnight if you want to do a round of the region's sights.

VITERBO

104 km (64 miles) northwest of Rome.

Viterbo's moment of glory was in the 13th century, when it became the seat of the papal court. The medieval core of the city still sits within 12th-century walls. Its old buildings, with windows bright with geraniums, are made of dark *peperino*, the local stone that colors the medieval part of Viterbo a dark gray, contrasted here and there with the golden tufa rock of walls and towers. Peperino is also used in the characteristic and typically medieval exterior staircases that you see throughout the old town.

Viterbo has blossomed into a regional commercial center, and much of the modern city is loud and industrial. However, in Viterbo's San Pellegrino district you'll get the feel of the Middle Ages—daily life is carried on here in a setting that has remained practically unchanged over the centuries. The Palazzo Papale and the cathedral enhance the effect. The city has remained a renowned spa center for its natural hot springs just outside town, which have been frequented by popes and mere mortals alike since medieval times.

GETTING HERE AND AROUND

Viterbo is well served by public transport from Rome. Direct train service takes an hour and 40 minutes. Try to avoid peak hours, as many commuters live in towns along the line. By road, take either the old Roman consular road, the Via Cassia, which passes near Caprarola, or, if you are in a hurry, the A1 toll highway to the Orte exit and then the 204 highway, with a detour to Bomarzo. The trip can take a couple of hours or even more, depending on traffic.

VISITOR INFORMATION

Viterbo Tourism Office ✉ *Via Ascenzi 4* ☎ *0761/325992* ⊕ *www.comune. viterbo.it* ✆ *Jan. and Feb., Tues.–Sun. 10–1 and 3–5; Mar., Apr., and Oct.–Dec., Tues.–Sun. 10–1 and 3–6; May–Sept., Tues.–Sun. 10–1 and 3–7.*

EXPLORING

Cattedrale di San Lorenzo. Viterbo's Romanesque cathedral was built over the ruins of the ancient Roman Temple of Hercules. During World War II, the roof and the vault of the central nave were destroyed by a bomb. Subsequently the church was rebuilt to its original medieval design. Three popes are buried here, including Pope Alexander IV (1254–61), whose body was hidden so well by the cannons, out of fear that it would be desecrated, that it has never been found. The small adjoining **Museo del Colle del Duomo** has a collection of 18th-century reliquaries, Etruscan sarcophagi, and a painting of the Crucifixion that has been attributed to Michelangelo. ✉ *Piazza San Lorenzo* ☎ *338/1336529* ⊕ *www.museocolledelduomo.com* 🖭 *Museum €3* ✆ *Mid-Mar.–Aug., Tues.–Sun. 8–6:15; Sept.–Dec. and mid-Jan.–mid-Mar., Tues.–Sun. 8–4. Closed 1st 2 wks in Jan.*

Palazzo Papale (*Papal Palace*). This Gothic palace was built in the 13th century as a residence for popes looking to get away from the city. At the time, Rome was notoriously unhealthful, ridden with malaria and plague, not to mention rampaging factions of rival barons. In 1271 the palace was the scene of a novel type of rebellion. A conclave held that year to elect a new pope dragged on for months. The people of Viterbo were exasperated by the delay, especially as custom decreed that they had to provide for the cardinals' board and lodging for the duration of the conclave. To speed up the deliberations the townspeople tore the roof off the great hall where the cardinals were meeting, and put them on bread and water. A new pope, Gregory X, was elected in short order. ✉ *Piazza San Lorenzo* ☎ *3381336529* ⊕ *www.museocolledelduomo. com* 🖭 *€9, includes tour of Cattedrale di San Lorenzo and Museo del Colle del Duomo* ✆ *Mid-Mar.–Aug., Tues.–Sun. 8–6:15; Sept.–Dec. and mid-Jan.–mid-Mar., Tues.–Sun. 8–4.*

San Pellegrino. One of the best preserved medieval districts in Italy, San Pellegrino has charming vistas of arches, vaults, towers, exterior staircases, worn wooden doors on great iron hinges, and tiny hanging gardens. You pass many antiques shops and craft workshops as you explore the little squares and byways. The **Fontana Grande** in the piazza of the same name is the largest and most extravagant of Viterbo's Gothic fountains. ✉ *Via San Pellegrino* ⊕ *www.comune.viterbo.it.*

Fodor's Choice ★ **Terme dei Papi.** Viterbo has been a spa town for centuries, and this excellent spa continues the tradition, providing the usual health and beauty treatments with an Etruscan twist: try a facial with local volcanic mud, or a steam bath in an ancient cave, where scalding hot mineral water direct from the spring splashes down a waterfall to a pool beneath your feet. The Terme dei Papi's main draw, however, comes from the *terme* (baths) themselves: a 21,000-square-foot outdoor limestone pool, into the shallow end of which Viterbo's famous hot water pours at 59°C (138°F)—and gives a jolt with its sulfurous odor. Floats and deck chairs are available for rent, but bring your own bathrobe and towel unless you're staying at the hotel. **TIP→ Shuttle buses operate between Rome and the Terme. Return tickets cost €8; call or check website for travel times.** ✉ *Strada Bagni 12, 5 km (3 miles) west of town center* ☎ *0761/3501* 🌐 *www.termedeipapi.it* 🎟 *Pool €12 weekdays, €18 weekends* ⏲ *Pool Sun., Mon., and Wed.–Fri. 9–7, Sat. 9–7 and 9:30 pm–1 am.*

WHERE TO EAT

$$ ROMAN 🍴 **Ristorantino La Torre.** You get a good value at this little trattoria in the heart of town, an offshoot of the super-elegant Enoteca La Torre, which has now transferred to Rome. The carefully edited menu changes according to what's in season, but the pasta sprinkled with grated black truffles and the *pasta e fagioli* (pasta and bean soup) are regular favorites. The restaurant is popular with local businesspeople, so it can get quite busy. The service is friendly and informal. [$] *Average main: €16* ✉ *Via della Torre 5* ☎ *0761/226467* ⏲ *Closed Tues.*

$ ITALIAN 🍴 **Tre Re.** Viterbo's oldest restaurant—and one of the most ancient in Italy—has been operating in the *centro storico* (historic center) since 1622. The kitchen focuses on traditional local dishes, such as *zuppa ceci e castagne* (chickpea and chestnut soup), stuffed chicken "Viterbo-style," and roasted porchetta. Some great Italian wines are on the list here. The small, wood-paneled dining room, chummily packed with tables, was a favorite haunt of movie director Federico Fellini and, before that, of British and American soldiers during World War II. Local diners make a point of touching the old inn sign of the "Three Kings," now hanging inside, as this is supposed to bring good luck. **TIP→ Tre Re can get very busy at lunch, so reservations are a good idea.** [$] *Average main: €12* ✉ *Via Macel Gattesco 3* ☎ *0761/304619* 🌐 *www.ristorantetrere.com* ⏲ *Closed Thurs.*

WHERE TO STAY

$$$ HOTEL 🏨 **Hotel Niccolò V.** The relaxed, country-house elegance and the comfortable rooms at this spa hotel are a sharp contrast to the brisk and clinical atmosphere of the Terme dei Papi spa itself, which bustles with doctors, bathers in bathrobes, and uniformed staff. **Pros:** friendly staff; comfortable rooms; relaxing. **Cons:** guests lounging in the lobby in bathrobes; several miles out of town. [$] *Rooms from: €300* ✉ *Strada Bagni 12, 5 km (3 miles) west of town center* ☎ *0761/350555* 🌐 *www.termedeipapi.it* 🛏 *20 rooms, 3 suites* 🍽 *Breakfast.*

$ B&B/INN Fodor's Choice ★ 🏨 **La Terrazza Medioevale.** The historic Palazzo Perotti in the center of old Viterbo's San Pellegrino district is the setting for three stylish, elegantly furnished rooms. **Pros:** elegant surroundings at bargain price.

Cons: no credit cards accepted; accessible only by flight of stairs. [$] *Rooms from: €80* ✉ *Via S. Pellegrino 1* ☎ *0761/307034* 🌐 *www.laterrazzamedioevale.it* 🛏 *3 rooms* 💳 *No credit cards* 🕒 *Closed Aug. 1–25* 🍴 *Breakfast.*

CAPRAROLA

21 km (13 miles) southeast of Bagnaia, 19 km (12 miles) southeast of Viterbo.

The wealthy and powerful Farnese family took over this sleepy village in the 1500s and had the architect Vignola design a huge palace and gardens to rival the great residences of Rome. He also rearranged the little town of Caprarola to enhance the palazzo's setting.

GETTING HERE AND AROUND

Caprarola is served by COTRAL bus, leaving from Rome's Saxa Rubra station on the Roma Nord suburban railway line.

EXPLORING

Fodor's Choice ★ **Palazzo Farnese.** When Cardinal Alessandro Farnese, Pope Paul III's grandson, retired to Caprarola, he intended to build a residence that would reflect the family's grandeur. In 1559, he entrusted the task to the leading architect Jacopo Barozzi da Vignola, who came up with some innovative ideas. A magnificent spiral staircase, lavishly decorated with allegorical figures, mythical landscapes, and grotesques by Antonio Tempesta, connected the main entrance with the cardinal's apartments on the main floor. The staircase was gently inclined, with very deep but low steps, so that the cardinal could ride his horse right up to his bedchamber. A tour includes the Hall of Farnese Triumphs, the Hercules Room, and the Antechamber of the Council of Trent, all painted by the Zuccari brothers. Of special interest is the Hall of the Maps, with the ceiling depicting the zodiac and the walls frescoed with maps of the world as known to 16th-century cartographers. The palace is surrounded by a formal Renaissance garden. ✉ *Piazza Farnese 1* ☎ *0761/646052* 🌐 *www.caprarola.com* 🎟 *€5* 🕒 *Palazzo: Tues.–Sun. 8:30–7:30; last entry at 6:45. Garden: mid-Mar.–mid-Oct., Tues.–Sun. 8:30–4; mid-Apr.–mid-Oct., Tues.–Sun. 8:30–5.*

WHERE TO EAT

$$$ ROMAN ✕ **Antica Trattoria del Borgo.** Visitors to Caprarola's landmark Palazzo Farnese often round out the experience with a hearty meal at this celebrated trattoria. Lovers of game delight in grilled selections that might include wild boar, venison, and roe deer. The restaurant also does well with pastas such as fettuccine with porcini mushrooms, and there are gluten-free pasta dishes on the menu. Among the noteworthy desserts is an exquisite hazelnut mousse. [$] *Average main: €28* ✉ *Via Borgo Vecchio 107* ☎ *0761/645252* 🌐 *www.anticatrattoriadelborgo.it* 🕒 *Closed Mon.*

BOMARZO

15 km (9 miles) northeast of Viterbo.

GETTING HERE AND AROUND

Bomarzo is easily reached by car from the A1 autostrada. If you want to go there directly, carry on to the Attigliano exit. Parco dei Monstri is some 6 km (4 miles) from that point. Alternatively, come out at Orte and branch off at Casalone on the Viterbo road. A public bus also goes here, from Viterbo.

EXPLORING

FAMILY **Parco dei Mostri** (*Monster Park*). This eerie fantasy, originally known as the Village of Marvels, or the Sacred Wood, was created in 1552 by Prince Vicino Orsini, with the aid of the famous artist Pirro Ligorio. It's populated with weird and fantastic sculptures of mythical creatures intended to astonish illustrious guests. The sculptures, carved in outcroppings of mossy stone in shady groves and woodland, include giant tortoises and griffins and an ogre's head with an enormous gaping mouth. Children love it, and there are photo ops galore. The park has a self-service café (closed in winter) and a gift shop. ⊠ *1½ km (1 mile) west of Bomarzo* ☎ *0761/924029* ⊕ *www.parcodeimostri.com* 🎟 *€10* ⊗ *Daily 8:30–sunset.*

TIVOLI AND PALESTRINA

Tivoli is a five-star draw, its main attractions being its two villas. There's an ancient one in which Hadrian reproduced the most beautiful monuments in the then-known world, and a Renaissance one, in which cardinal Ippolito d'Este put a river to work for his delight. Unfortunately, the Via Tiburtina from Rome to Tivoli passes through miles of industrial areas with chaotic traffic. Grit your teeth and persevere—it'll be worth it. In the heart of this gritty shell lie two pearls that are rightly world-famous. You'll know you're close to Tivoli when you see vast quarries of travertine marble and smell the sulfurous vapors of the little spa, Bagni di Tivoli. Both sites in Tivoli are outdoors and entail walking. With a car, you can continue your loop through the mountains east of Rome, taking in the ancient pagan sanctuary at Palestrina, spectacularly set on the slopes of Mt. Ginestro.

TIVOLI

36 km (22 miles) northeast of Rome.

In ancient times, just about anybody who was anybody had a villa in Tivoli, including Crassus, Trajan, Hadrian, Horace, and Catullus. Tivoli fell into obscurity in the medieval era until the Renaissance, when popes and cardinals came back to the town and built villas showy enough to rival those of their extravagant predecessors.

Nowadays Tivoli is small but vibrant, with winding streets and views over the surrounding countryside. The deep Aniene River gorge runs through the center of town and comes replete with a romantically sited bridge, cascading waterfalls, and two jewels of ancient Roman architecture that crown its cliffs—the round Temple of Vesta (or the Sybil, the prophetess credited with predicting the birth of Christ) and the ruins of the rectangular Temple of the hero-god Tibur, the mythical founder of the city. These can be picturesquely viewed across the gorge from the Villa Gregoriana park, named for Pope Gregory XVI, who saved Tivoli from chronic river damage by diverting the river through a tunnel, weakening its flow. An unexpected side effect was the creation of the Grande Cascata (Grand Cascade), which shoots a huge jet of water into the valley below. You may also want to set your sights on the Antico Ristorante Sibilla, set right by the Temple of Vesta. From its dining terrace you can take in one of the most memorably romantic landscape views in Italy.

GETTING HERE AND AROUND

Unless you have nerves of steel, it's best not to drive to Tivoli. Hundreds of businesses line the Via Tiburtina from Rome and bottleneck traffic is nearly constant. You can avoid some, but not all, of the congestion by taking the Roma–L'Aquila toll road. Luckily, there's abundant public transport. Buses leave every 15 minutes from the Ponte Mammolo stop on Metro Line A; the ride takes an hour. Regional Trenitalia trains connect from both Termini and Tiburtina stations and will have you in Tivoli in under an hour. Villa d'Este is in the town center, and there is bus service from Tivoli's main square to Hadrian's Villa.

VISITOR INFORMATION

PIT (Punto Informativo Turistico) (*Tivoli tourist office*). ⊠ *Piazzale Nazioni Unite* ☎ *0774/313536* ⊕ *www.comune.tivoli.rm.it/pit* ☯ *Summer, Tues.–Sun. 9:30–5:30; winter, Tues.–Sun. 9:30–3.*

EXPLORING

Fodor's Choice
★

Villa Adriana (*Hadrian's Villa*). An emperor's theme park, this astonishingly grand 2nd-century villa was an exclusive retreat below the ancient settlement of Tibur where the marvels of the classical world were reproduced for a ruler's pleasure. Hadrian, who succeeded Trajan as emperor in AD 117, was a man of genius and intellectual curiosity, fascinated by the accomplishments of the Hellenistic world. From AD 125 to 134, architects, laborers, and artists worked on the vast villa, re-creating some of the monuments and sights that the emperor had seen on his travels in Egypt, Asia Minor, and Greece.

During the Middle Ages, the site was sacked by barbarians and Romans alike, and many of the statues and architectural features ended up in the Vatican Museums. Nonetheless, the colossal remains are impressive: the ruins rise in a garden setting of green lawns framed with oleanders, pines, and cypresses. Not surprisingly, Villa Adriana is a UNESCO World Heritage Site, and it's one that has not yielded up all of its secrets. Archaeologists recently discovered the site of the Temple of Isis, complete with several sculptures, including one of the falcon-headed god Horus. ■TIP→ **A visit to the villa takes at least two hours (carry water on hot days); maps dispensed at the ticket office will help you get your bearings.** ⊠ *Largo Margherite Yourcenar 1, 6 km (4 miles) southwest of Tivoli* ☎ *0774/530203* ⊕ *www.villaadriana.beniculturali.it* 🎟 *€8 (free 1st Sun. of month)* ☯ *Daily 9–1 hr before sunset.*

Fodor's Choice ★ **Villa d'Este.** One of Italy's UNESCO World Heritage Sites, Villa d'Este was created by Cardinal Ippolito d'Este in the 16th century. This villa in the center of Tivoli was the most amazing pleasure garden of its day, and it still stuns visitors with its beauty. Este (1509–72), a devotee of the Renaissance celebration of human ingenuity over nature, was inspired by the excavation of Villa Adriana. He paid architect Pirro Ligorrio an astronomical sum to create a mythical garden with water as its artistic centerpiece and diverted the Aniene River to water the garden and feed the several hundred fountains that cascade, shoot skyward, imitate birdsong, and simulate rain. The musical **Fontana dell'Organo** has been restored to working order: the organ plays a watery tune every two hours. Romantics will love the night tour of the gardens and floodlit fountains that takes place on Friday and Saturday in summer. **TIP→ Allow at least an hour for a visit, which involves many stairs. No refreshments are available inside the garden.** ✉ *Piazza Trento 1* ☎ *0774/312070* 🌐 *www.villadestetivoli.info* 🎟 *€8 (€11 for night tour)* ⏲ *Villa: Tues.–Sun. 8:30 am–1 hr before sunset. Night tour: July–Sept., Fri. and Sat. 8:30–11.*

WHERE TO EAT AND STAY

$$$ ITALIAN Fodor's Choice ★ 🍴 **Antico Ristorante Sibilla.** Count this famed restaurant among the most beautiful sights of Tivoli. Built in 1730 beside the circular Roman Temple of Vesta and the Sanctuary of the Sybil, the terrace garden has a spectacular view over the deep gorge of the Aniene River, with the thundering waters of the waterfall in the background. The standard of food, wine, and service is high, and seasonal produce and local dishes are a major part of the menu. Be sure to sample the house specialty—a lavish choice of antipasti served on individual three-tier trays that resemble old-fashioned cake stands. Dishes for the first course might include pappardelle made with spelt and dressed with garlic, olive oil, and tiny "datterini" tomatoes. For the second course, local lamb, suckling pig, and a salad with ricotta, herbs, honey, and prunes are all possible. Despite the filling courses that precede them, the desserts vie for attention. [$] *Average main: €25* ✉ *Via della Sibilla 50* ☎ *0774/335281* 🌐 *www.ristorantesibilla.com* ⏲ *Closed Mon.*

$ B&B/INN 🏨 **Adriano.** Gabriella and Patricia Cinelli operate this hotel and restaurant beside the entrance to Villa Adriana. **Pros:** wonderful location; peaceful garden; attentive service. **Cons:** busloads of tourists disembark under the windows; some rooms are small. [$] *Rooms from: €80* ✉ *Largo Yourcenar 2* ☎ *348/3029144* 🌐 *www.hoteladriano.it* 🛏 *10 rooms, 3 suites* ⏲ *Closed mid-Dec.–mid-Jan.* 🍴 *Breakfast.*

$$ HOTEL 🏨 **Hotel Torre Sant'Angelo.** A former monastery and residence of the Massimo princes now contains comfortable guest rooms equipped with modern amenities. Best of all, it overlooks the old town, the Aniene Falls, and the Temple of the Sybil. **Pros:** 21st-century comfort in a historic mansion; pool; competitive rates. **Cons:** a mile outside town. [$] *Rooms from: €140* ✉ *Via Quintilio Varo* ☎ *0774/332533* 🌐 *www.hoteltorresangelo.it* 🛏 *25 rooms, 10 suites* 🍴 *Breakfast.*

PALESTRINA

27 km (17 miles) southeast of Tivoli, 37 km (23 miles) east of Rome.

Except to students of ancient history and music lovers, Palestrina is little known outside Italy. Its most famous native son, Giovanni Pierluigi da Palestrina, born here in 1525, is considered the master of counterpoint and polyphony. He composed 105 masses, as well as madrigals, Magnificats, and motets. There is a small museum dedicated to his life and work in the town center.

Ancient Praeneste (modern Palestrina) flourished much earlier than Rome. It was the site of the Temple of Fortuna Primigenia, which dates from the 2nd century BC. This was one of the largest, richest, most frequented temple complexes in all antiquity—people came from far and wide to consult its famous oracle. In modern times no one had any idea of the extent of the complex until World War II bombings exposed ancient foundations occupying huge artificial terraces, which stretch from the upper part of the town as far downhill as its central Duomo.

GETTING HERE AND AROUND

COTRAL buses leave from the Anagnina terminal on Rome's Metro Line A and from the Tiburtina railway station. Alternatively, you can take a train to Zagarolo, where a COTRAL bus takes you on to Palestrina. The total trip takes 40 minutes. By car, take the A1 Autostrada del Sole to the San Cesareo exit and follow the signs to Palestrina. Expect it to take about an hour.

VISITOR INFORMATION

Palestrina Tourism Office ⊠ *Piazzale Caduti Senza Croce* ☎ *06/95302318* ⊕ *www.comune.palestrina.rm.it* ☉ *Daily 8–1:30 and 4–8.*

EXPLORING

Palazzo Barberini. A bomb blast during World War II uncovered the remains of the immense Temple of Fortune that covered the entire hillside under the present town. Large arches and terraces are now visible and you can walk or take a local bus up to the imposing Palazzo Barberini, which crowns the highest point. The palace was built in the 17th century along the semicircular lines of the original temple. It now contains the **Museo Nazionale Archeologico di Palestrina,** with material found on the site that dates from throughout the classical period. A well-labeled collection of Etruscan bronzes, pottery, and terra-cotta statuary as well as Roman artifacts take second place to the main event, a 1st-century BC mosaic showing ancient Egyptian pleasure craft and African animals. This highly colorful and detailed work is worth the trip to Palestrina by itself. But there's more: a model of the temple as it was in ancient times helps you appreciate the immensity of the original construction. ⊠ *Piazza della Cortina 1* ☎ *06/9538100* ⊕ *www.comune. palestrina.rm.it* ☎ *€5* ☉ *Museum daily 9–8; archaeological zone daily 9–1 hr before sunset.*

WHERE TO EAT

$$ ✕ **Il Piscarello.** Tucked away at the bottom of a steep side road, this
ITALIAN elegant dining room immersed in a garden comes as a bit of a surprise. The high quality of the menu and the impeccable service make this a

favorite choice for wedding parties and anniversaries, which are usually accommodated in one of the private rooms. In summer, you can eat outside on the small patio overlooking the garden. Specialties of the house include meat carpaccio and fish, seafood, and meat dishes with white and black truffles. $ *Average main: €20* ✉ *Via del Piscarello 2* ☎ *06/9574326* ⊕ *www.ristoranteilpiscarello.it* ⊘ *Closed Mon. No dinner Sun.*

THE CASTELLI ROMANI

The *"castelli"* aren't really castles, as their name would seem to imply. They're little towns that are scattered on the slopes of the Alban Hills near Rome. And the Alban Hills aren't really hills, but extinct volcanoes. There were castles here in the Middle Ages, however, when each of these towns, fiefs of rival Roman lords, had its own fortress to defend it. Some centuries later, the area became given over to villas and retreats, notably the pope's summer residence at Castelgandolfo, and the 17th- and 18th-century villas that transformed Frascati into the Beverly Hills of Rome. Arrayed around the rim of an extinct volcano that encloses two crater lakes, the string of picturesque towns of the Castelli Romani are today surrounded by vineyards, olive groves, and chestnut woods—no wonder overheated Romans have always loved to escape here.

Ever since Roman times the Castelli have been renowned for their wine. In the narrow, medieval alleyways of the oldest parts you can still find old-fashioned taverns where the locals sit on wooden benches, quaffing the golden nectar straight from the barrel. Traveling around the countryside, you can also pop into some of the local vineyards, where they will be happy to give you a tasting of their wines. Exclusive local gastronomic specialties include the bread of Genzano, baked in traditional wood-fire ovens, the *porchetta* (roast suckling pig) of Ariccia, and the *pupi* biscuits of Frascati, shaped like women or mermaids with three or more breasts (an allusion to ancient fertility goddesses). Each town has its own feasts and saints' days, celebrated with costumed processions and colorful events. Some are quite spectacular, like Marino's annual Wine Festival in October, where the town's fountains flow with wine; or the Flower Festival of Genzano in June, when an entire street is carpeted with millions of flower petals, arranged in elaborate patterns.

FRASCATI

20 km (12 miles) south of Rome.

It's worth taking a stroll through Frascati's lively old center. Via Battisti, leading from the Belvedere, takes you into Piazza San Pietro with its imposing gray-and-white cathedral. Inside is the cenotaph of Prince Charles Edward, last of the Scottish Stuart dynasty, who tried unsuccessfully to regain the British Crown, and died an exile in Rome in 1788. A little arcade beside the monumental fountain at the back of the piazza leads into Market Square, where the smell of fresh baking will entice you into the Purificato family bakery to see the traditional pupi biscuits, modeled on old pagan fertility symbols.

Take your pick from the cafés and trattorias fronting the central Piazzale Marconi, or do as the locals do: buy fruit from the market gallery at Piazza del Mercato, then get a huge slice of porchetta from one of the stalls, a hunk of *casareccio* bread, and a few *ciambelline frascatane* (ring-shape cookies made with wine), and take your picnic to any one of the nearby *cantine* (homey wine bars), and settle in for some sips of tasty, inexpensive vino.

GETTING HERE AND AROUND

An hourly train service along a single-track line through vineyards and olive groves takes you to Frascati from Termini station. The trip takes 45 minutes. By car, take the Via Tuscolano, which branches off the Appia Nuova road just after St. John Lateran in Rome, and drive straight up.

VISITOR INFORMATION

Frascati Point (tourism office) ✉ *Piazza G. Marconi 5* ☎ *06/94015378* ⊕ *www.prontocastelli.it/frascati* ⊗ *Weekdays 8–8, weekends 10–8.*

EXPLORING

Abbey of San Nilo. In Grottaferrata, a busy village a couple of miles from Frascati, the main attraction is a walled citadel founded by St. Nilo, who brought his group of Basilian monks here in 1004, when he was 90. The order is unique in that it's Roman Catholic but observes Greek Orthodox rites.

The fortified abbey, considered a masterpiece of martial architecture, was restructured in the 15th century by Antonio da Sangallo for the future Pope Julius II. The abbey church, inside the second courtyard, is a jewel of Oriental opulence, with glittering Byzantine mosaics and a revered icon set into a marble tabernacle designed by Bernini. The Farnese chapel, leading from the right nave, contains a series of frescoes by Domenichino.

If you make arrangements in advance you can visit the library, which is one of the oldest in Italy. The abbey also has a famous laboratory for the restoration of antique books and manuscripts, where Leonardo's *Codex Atlanticus* was restored in 1962 and more than a thousand precious volumes were saved after the disastrous Florence flood in 1966. ✉ *Corso del Popolo 128, Grottaferrata* ☎ *06/9459309* ⊕ *www.abbaziagreca.it* 🎫 *Free* ⊗ *Daily 6:30–12:30 and 3:30–8.*

Villa Aldobrandini. Frascati was a retreat of prelates and princes who built magnificent villas, the most spectacular being the 16th-century Villa Aldobrandini, which dominates the town's main square from atop its steeply sloped park. The villa isn't open for touring, but the garden is a public park where you can stroll sweeping pathways lined with stone balustrades, box hedges, and the Baroque Teatro d'Acqua—the sort of showy sculpture group with water features that was a must-have garden adornment for every 16th-century millionaire, in this case Cardinal Pietro Aldobrandini, Pope Clement VIII's favorite nephew. The half circle of sculptures of mythical figures that adorn the "theater" reflect the grandeur and wealth of a prince of the church who thought nothing of diverting the entire water supply of the surrounding area to make his fountains perform. These days the fountains only play on special occasions. The villa is often rented out for private receptions; the gardens may be closed at these times. ✉ *Via Cardinale Massaia, off Via del Tuscolo* ☎ *06/9421434* 🌐 *www.aldobrandini.it* 🎟 *Free* 🕒 *Garden weekdays 9–5:30.*

WHERE TO EAT AND STAY

$$$ ROMAN 🍴 **Antica Fontana Grottaferrata.** Across the road from the Abbey of San Nilo lies one of Grottaferrata's most esteemed restaurants, run by the Consoli family since 1989. The décor is rustic but stylish, with plants hanging from the ceiling and rows of polished antique copper pans and molds decorating the walls. Tables are well spaced, and the soft lighting helps make meals here relaxing and congenial. In summer, you can eat outside. Dishes worth considering include the special antipasti, fettuccine with porcini, and gnocchi with radicchio. [$] *Average main: €25* ✉ *Via Domenichino 24–26, Grottaferrata* ☎ *06/9413687* ✍ *Reservations essential* 🕒 *Closed Mon.*

$$ ROMAN 🍴 **Il Grottino Frascati.** This former wine cellar just beyond Frascati's market square is now an old-fashioned and cheerful trattoria serving traditional Roman dishes. The pasta and gnocchi are all homemade, and you'll also find old favorites on the menu—among them pasta carbonara, fettuccine with porcini, and saltimbocca—all lovingly supervised by the owner, Alfredo. In summer you can sit under an awning outside and can enjoy the sweeping view over the plain and hills. [$] *Average main: €16* ✉ *Viale Regina Margherita 41–43* ☎ *06/94289772* 🌐 *www.trattoriailgrottino.it* 🕒 *Closed Thurs.*

$$ ITALIAN Fodor's Choice ★ 🍴 **Osteria Del Fico Vecchio.** This coaching inn dating to the 16th century is on an old Roman road a couple of miles outside Frascati. The old fig tree that gave the place its name shades the restaurant's charming garden. The dining room has been tastefully renovated, preserving many of its old-fashioned features. The chef prepares typical Roman dishes, among them spaghetti *cacio e pepe* (with sheep's cheese and pepper) and *abbacchio allo scottadito* (literally "burn-your-fingers-grilled lamb"). Do not confuse this with the more modern Ristorante Al Fico across the road. [$] *Average main: €20* ✉ *Via Anagnini 257* ☎ *06/9459261* 🌐 *www.alfico.it.*

$$ HOTEL Fodor's Choice ★ 🏨 **Park Hotel Villa Grazioli.** One of the region's most famous residences, this patrician villa halfway between Frascati and Grottaferrata is now a first-class hotel, though the standard-issue guest rooms are a bit of a let-down amid the frescoed salons. **Pros:** wonderful views of the countryside; elegant atmosphere; professional staff. **Cons:** difficult to find; some rooms could use updating. [$] *Rooms from: €160* ✉ *Via Umberto Pavoni 19, Grottaferrata* ☎ *06/9454001* 🌐 *www.villagrazioli.com* 🛏 *60 rooms, 2 suites* 🍽 *Breakfast.*

CASTELGANDOLFO

8 km (5 miles) southwest of Frascati, 25 km (15 miles) south of Rome.

This little town is the pope's summer retreat. It was the Barberini Pope Urban VIII who first headed here, eager to escape the malarial miasmas that afflicted summertime Rome; before long, the city's princely families also set up country estates around here.

The 17th-century **Villa Pontificia** has a superb position overlooking Lake Albano and is set in one of the most gorgeous gardens in Italy; unfortunately, neither the house nor the park is open to the public (although crowds are admitted into the inner courtyard for papal audiences). On the little square in front of the palace there's a fountain by Bernini, who also designed the nearby Church of San Tommaso da Villanova, which has works by Pietro da Cortona.

The village has a number of interesting craft workshops and food purveyors, in addition to the souvenir shops on the square. On the horizon, the silver astronomical dome belonging to the Specola Vaticana observatory—one of the first in Europe—where the scientific Pope Gregory XIII indulged his interest in stargazing, is visible for miles around.

GETTING HERE AND AROUND

There's an hourly train service for Castelgandolfo from Termini station (Rome–Albano line). Otherwise, buses leave frequently from the Anagnina terminal of Metro Line A. The trip takes about 30 minutes. By car, take the Appian Way from San Giovanni in Rome and follow it straight to Albano, where you branch off for Castelgandolfo (about an hour, depending on traffic).

EXPLORING

FAMILY   **Lakeside Lido.** Lined with restaurants, ice-cream parlors, and cafés, this is a favorite spot for Roman families to relax. No motorized craft are allowed on the lake, but you can rent paddleboats and kayaks. In summer, you can also take a short guided boat trip to learn about the geology and history of the lake, which lies at the bottom of an extinct volcanic crater. The waters are full of swans, herons, and other birds, and there is a nature trail along the wooded end of the shore for those who want to get away from the throng. Deck chairs are available for rent; you might also want to stop for a plate of freshly prepared pasta or a gigantic Roman sandwich at one of the little snack bars under the oak and alder trees. There's also a small, permanent fairground for children. ⊠ *Lake Albano.*

WHERE TO EAT AND STAY

$$$ ✕ **Antico Ristorante Pagnanelli.** One of most refined restaurants in the
ITALIAN   Castelli Romani has been in the same family since 1882. The present generation—Aurelio Mariani, his Australian wife, Jane, and their four sons—has lovingly restored this old railway inn perched high above Lake Albano. The dining-room windows open onto a breathtaking view across Lake Albano to the conical peak of Monte Cavo. In winter a log fire blazes in a corner; in summer you can dine on the flower-filled terrace. Many of the dishes are prepared with produce from the family's own farm. The wine cellar, carved out of the local tufa rock, boasts more than 3,000 labels. Ⓢ *Average main: €25* ⊠ *Via Gramsci 4* ☎ *06/9361740* ⊕ *www.pagnanelli.it.*

$$ ⌂ **Hotel Castelgandolfo.** Overlooking the volcanic crater of Lake Albano
HOTEL   and a minute's walk from the Pope's summer palace, this intimate hotel in the heart of Castelgandolfo makes an ideal retreat for romantics. **Pros:**

convenient location; intimate; ideal for romantics. **Cons:** some rooms have street views; balconies are small and narrow. [$] *Rooms from: €160* ✉ *Via de Zecchini 27* ☎ *06/9360521* 🌐 *www.hotelcastelgandolfo.com* 🛏 *18 rooms* 🍴 *Breakfast.*

ARICCIA

8 km (5 miles) southwest of Castelgandolfo, 26 km (17 miles) south of Rome.

Ariccia is a gem of Baroque town planning. When millionaire banker Agostino Chigi became Pope Alexander VII, he commissioned Gian Lorenzo Bernini to redesign his country estate to make it worthy of his new station. Bernini restructured not only the existing 16th-century palace, but also the town gates, the main square, with its loggias and graceful twin fountains, and the round church of Santa Maria dell'Assunzione (the dome is said to be modeled on the Pantheon). The rest of the village was coiled around the apse of the church down into the valley below.

Ariccia's splendid heritage was largely forgotten in the 20th century, and yet it was once one of the highlights of every artist's and writer's Grand Tour. Corot, Ibsen, Turner, Longfellow, and Hans Christian Andersen all came to stay here.

GETTING HERE AND AROUND

For Ariccia, take the COTRAL bus from the Anagnina terminal of Metro Line A. Buses on the Albano–Genzano–Velletri line stop under the monumental bridge that spans the Ariccia Valley, where an elevator whisks you up to the main town square. If you take a train to Albano, you can proceed by bus to Ariccia or go on foot (it's just under 3 km [2 miles]). If you're driving, follow the Via Appia Nuova to Albano and carry on to Ariccia.

EXPLORING

Fodor's Choice ★ **Palazzo Chigi.** Here is a true rarity: a Baroque residence whose original furniture, paintings, drapes, and decorations are largely intact. The Italian film director Luchino Visconti used the villa for most of the interior scenes in his 1963 film *The Leopard*. The rooms of the **piano nobile** (main floor), which like the rest of the palazzo's sections that are open to the public can only be viewed on guided tours, contain intricately carved pieces of 17th-century furniture, as well as textiles and costumes from the 16th to the 20th century. The Room of Beauties is lined with paintings of the loveliest ladies of the day, and the Nuns' Room with portraits of 10 Chigi sisters, all of whom took the veil.

Open for touring only on weekends are **Le stanze del Cardinale** (Cardinal's Rooms), suites occupied by the pleasure-loving Cardinal Flavio Chigi. The upper floors contain the **Museo del Barocco** (Baroque Museum), with an important collection of 17th-century paintings. The park stretching behind the palace is the last remnant of the ancient Latium forest, where herds of deer still graze under the trees. **TIP→ Tours in English are possible if you book ahead.** ✉ *Piazza di Corte 14* ☎ *06/9330053* 🌐 *www.palazzochigiariccia.it* 🎟 *€14 full villa* *tour (when possible), €8 piano nobile and park, €6 Cardinal's Rooms, €6 Baroque Museum, €4 park* ⏲ *Piano nobile: tours year-round, Tues.–Fri. at 11, 4, and 5:30, weekends and public holidays at 10:30, 11:30, 12:30, 4, 5, and 6 (and other times by season). Cardinal's Rooms: Apr.–Sept., weekends 10–1:30 and 3:30–7; Oct.–Mar., weekends 10–1:30 and 3–6:30. Museum: Apr.–Sept., Tues.–Sun. 10–1 and 3:30–6:30; Oct.–Mar., Tues.–Sun. 10–1 and 3–6. Park: Apr.–Oct., weekends and public holidays 10–1 and 3:30–7 (also early July–mid-Aug., Tues.–Fri. 5–7 pm).*

WHERE TO EAT

A visit to Ariccia isn't complete without tasting the local gastronomic specialty: *porchetta,* a delicious roast whole pig stuffed with herbs. The shops on the Piazza di Corte will make up a sandwich for you, or you can do what the Romans do: head for one of the *fraschette* wine cellars, which also serve cheese, cold cuts, pickles, olives, and sometimes a plate of pasta. You sit on a wooden bench at a trestle table covered with simple white paper, but there's no better place to make friends and maybe join in a sing-along.

$ ITALIAN 🍴 **L'Ariccíarola.** This place near Palazzo Chigi is great for for people-watching, which you can do while enjoying a platter of cold cuts and mixed cheeses, washed down with a carafe of local Castelli wine. At informal L'Ariccíarola you'll be sitting on wooden benches with a paper tablecloth, surrounded by Roman families who come to Ariccia for its famous porchetta. Be sure to try it. [$] *Average main: €10* ✉ *Via Borgo S. Rocco 9* ☎ *06/9334103* ⏲ *Closed Mon.*

NEMI

8 km (5 miles) west of Ariccia, 34 km (21 miles) south of Rome.

A bronze statue to Diana the Huntress greets you at the entrance to Nemi, the smallest and prettiest village of the Castelli Romani. It's perched on a spur of rock 600 feet above the little oval-shaped lake of the same name, which is formed from a volcanic crater. Nemi has an eagle's-nest view over the rolling Roman countryside as far as the coast, some 18 km (11 miles) away. The one main street, Corso Vittorio Emanuele, takes you to the baronial Castello Ruspoli (not open to the public), where there's an 11th-century watchtower, and the quaint Piazza Umberto 1, lined with outdoor cafés serving the tiny wood strawberries harvested from the crater bowl.

If you continue on through the arch that joins the castle to the former stables, you come to the entrance of the dramatically landscaped public gardens, which curve steeply down to the panoramic **Belvedere terrace,** with a café that's open in summer. A pedestrian-only road runs down the crater side to the Roman Ships Museum. Otherwise, car access is from the town of Genzano on the opposite side of the lake.

GETTING HERE AND AROUND

Nemi is difficult to get to unless you come by car. Buses from the Anagnina station on Metro Line A go to the town of Genzano, where a local bus travels to Nemi every two hours. If the times aren't convenient, you can take a taxi or walk the 5 km (3 miles) around Lake Nemi. By car, take the panoramic route known as the Via dei Laghi (Road of the Lakes). Follow the Appia Nuova from St. John Lateran and branch off on the well-signposted route after Ciampino airport. Follow the Via dei Laghi toward Velletri until you see signs for Nemi.

EXPLORING

Museo delle Navi Romani (*Roman Ship Museum*). Nemi may be small, but it has a long and fascinating history. In Roman times it was an important sanctuary dedicated to the goddess Diana, drawing thousands of pilgrims from all over the Roman Empire. In the 1930s the Italian government drained the lake to recover two magnificent ceremonial ships, loaded with sculptures, bronzes, and art treasures, that were submerged for 2,000 years.

The Museo delle Navi Romani, on the lakeshore, was built to house the ships, but they were burned during World War II. Inside are scale models and finds from the sanctuary and the area nearby. There's also a colossal statue of the infamous Roman Emperor Caligula, who had the ships built. Italian police snatched it just in time from tomb robbers as they were about to smuggle it out of the country. ✉ *Via del Tempio di Diana 9* ☎ *06/9398040* 🌐 *www.museonaviromane.it* 🎟 *€3* 🕒 *Mar.–Dec., daily 9–6:30; Jan. and Feb., daily 9–6.*

WHERE TO EAT

$$ ITALIAN 🍴 **La Fiocina.** With its privileged position on the tranquil shores of Lake Nemi next to the Museum of Roman Ships, La Fiocina makes for a relaxing lunchtime stopover. The dining room is elegant and welcoming, and there's a terrace on which you can dine alfresco, overlooking the small lakeside garden. Coregone, a local freshwater fish, is among the specialties, as is linguine with river shrimp, but meat and game are prepared as well. If they're being served for dessert, don't miss the tiny woodland strawberries Nemi is famous for. [$] *Average main: €15* ✉ *Via delle Navi Di Tiberio 9* ☎ *06/9391120* 🕒 *Closed Tues.*

$ ITALIAN 🍴 **Specchio di Diana.** Halfway down the main street is the town's most historic inn—Byron may have stayed here when visiting the area. A wine bar and café are on street level, while the restaurant proper on the second floor offers marvelous views, especially at sunset. Megapizzas (they stretch over two plates) are a specialty of the house, but don't neglect Nemi's regional specialties: *fettuccine al sugo di lepre* (fettuccine with hare sauce), roasted porcini mushrooms, and the little wood-strawberries with whipped cream. [$] *Average main: €14* ✉ *Corso Vittorio Emanuele 13* ☎ *06/9368805* 🌐 *www.specchiodidiana.it.*

NORTHERN ITALY

WHAT'S WHERE

1 **Venice.** One of the world's most unusual—and beautiful—cities, Venice has canals where the streets should be and an atmosphere of faded splendor. It's also a major international cultural center.

2 **The Veneto and Friuli–Venezia Giulia.** The green plains stretching west of Venice hold three of northern Italy's most artistically significant midsize cities: Padua, Vicenza, and Verona. Farther north and east, Alpine foothills are dotted with welcoming villages and some of Italy's finest vineyards.

3 **The Dolomites.** Along Italy's northeast border, the Dolomites are the country's finest mountain playground, with gorgeous cliffs, curiously shaped peaks, lush meadows, and crystalline lakes. The skiing is good, and the scenery is different, and often more spectacular, than what you find in the Austrian, Swiss, or French Alps.

4 **Milan, Lombardy, and the Lakes.** The lakes of Lombardy—Como, Garda, and Maggiore—have been attracting vacationers since the days of ancient Rome. At the center of Lombardy is Milan, Italy's second-largest city and its business capital. It holds Italy's most renowned opera house, and as the hub of

AUSTRIA

TRENTINO-
ALTO ADIGE

Cortina
d'Ampezzo

FRIULI-VENEZIA
GIULIA

Bolzano

Belluno

Udine

Trento

Trieste

Lake
Garda

VENETO

Treviso

Verona

Vicenza

Padua

Venice

ntua

Adige

Gulf of
Venice

Po

Ferrara

EMILIA-ROMAGNA 7

Modena

Bologna

Ravenna

Adriatic Sea

Pistoia

Rimini

SAN MARINO

SAN MARINO

Florence

Arno

TUSCANY

Arezzo

THE
MARCHES

Ancona

Macerata

Siena

Perugia

Assisi

UMBRIA

Grosseto

Orvieto

Italian fashion and design, it's a shopper's paradise.

5 Piedmont and Valle d'Aosta. A step off the usual tourist circuit, these regions are well worth a visit. You'll find here great Alpine peaks along the French and Swiss borders, one of the most highly esteemed food-and-wine cultures in Italy (think of the famed white truffles of Alba!), and an elegant regional capital in Turin.

6 The Italian Riviera. Northern Italy's most attractive coastline runs along the Italian Riviera in the region of Liguria. The best beaches and temperate winter climate are west of Genoa, but the main appeal lies to the east, where fishing villages are interspersed along beautiful seaside cliffs and coves.

NORTHERN ITALY PLANNER

Getting Here

Aeroporto Malpensa, 50 km (31 miles) northwest of Milan, is the major northern Italian hub for intercontinental flights and also sees substantial European and domestic traffic. Venice's **Aeroporto Marco Polo** also serves international destinations. There are regional airports in Turin, Genoa, Bologna, Verona, Trieste, Treviso, Bolzano, and Parma, and Milan has a secondary airport, Linate. You can reach all of these on connecting flights from within Italy and from other European cities. If you fly into Malpensa, but Milan isn't your final destination, you can also get where you're going by train, using the Italian national rail system, **Ferrovie dello Stato** (☎ 199303060 toll-free within Italy ⊕ www.trenitalia.com). Shuttle buses run three times an hour (less often after 10 pm) between Malpensa and Milan's main train station, Stazione Centrale; the trip takes about 75 minutes, depending on traffic. The Malpensa Express Train, which leaves twice an hour, takes 40 minutes and delivers you to Cadorna metro station in central Milan.

When to Go

Spring: Late April, May, and early June are ideal times to tour northern Italy: the weather is mild, and the volume of tourists (Venice excepted) isn't as large as it is in summer.

Although there's some rain, springtime is generally drier in northern Italy than it is in northern Europe or the east coast of North America. By May the coastal towns of Liguria are beginning to come to life. Meanwhile, in the mountains hiking trails can remain icy well into June.

Summer: Anywhere away from the mountains, summers are warm and humid, but not nearly as humid as in the eastern or southern United States. It seldom rains, and when it does, it's mainly in the late afternoon and at night. Summer is prime hiking season in the Alps, and the lakes and the Riviera are in full swing (meaning lodging reservations are a must).

Note that a large portion, maybe even the majority, of tourists in northern Italy are not foreigners; they're Italians seeing their own country, and they come in summer, when the kids are out of school and families can travel together.

Fall: Much like spring, autumn, with its mild weather, is an ideal time for touring most of the region. Much of northern Italy enjoys pleasant, sunny weather through September and well into October. Most years it doesn't really begin to get cold until mid-November, though in the mountains temperatures drop sharply in September. Many of the mountain tourist facilities close down entirely until the ski season kicks in.

Winter: In the Dolomites most ski resorts are open from mid-December through April, but snowfall in early winter is unreliable, and the best conditions often aren't seen until late February.

Likewise, in Piedmont and Valle d'Aosta snow conditions vary drastically year to year—some years there's good snow beginning in November, while others don't see much more than a flake or two until February.

In Venice winters are relatively mild, with fewer but still substantial numbers of tourists. There are frequent rainy spells, and at the beginning and end of the season there's the threat of *acqua alta*, when tides roll in and flood low-lying parts of the city. (The floods last at most three hours.)

The larger cities are active year-round, but the resort towns of the Lake District and the Riviera are all but shut down.

TYPICAL TRAVEL TIMES		
	HOURS BY CAR	**HOURS BY TRAIN**
Milan–Venice	3:30	2:35
Milan–Turin	2:00	2:00
Milan–Genoa	2:00	1:45
Milan–Bologna	2:30	1:00
Venice–Bologna	2:15	1:25
Venice–Turin	5:00	4:20
Venice–Genoa	4:45	4:30
Bologna–Genoa	3:15	3:00
Bologna–Turin	3:30	2:00
Genoa–Turin	2:00	2:00

On the Calendar

From December through June, the **opera season** is in full swing, most notably in Milan, Venice, Turin, Parma, and Genoa. In Milan the **Festa di Sant'Ambrogio** in early December officially launches the season at La Scala; it's celebrated by a huge street fair around the Castello Sforzesco.

Venice's **Carnevale**, during the 10 days preceding Lent (usually falling in February), includes concerts, plays, masked balls, fireworks, and indoor and outdoor happenings of every sort. It's probably Italy's most famous festival, attracting hundreds of thousands.

The **Festa del Redentore** (Feast of the Redeemer) in Venice on the third Sunday in July commemorates the end of the plague of 1575. Venetians eat a traditional dinner in boats on San Marco Basin or along the water and then watch the spectacular fireworks.

Venice's **Mostra del Cinema,** the oldest of the international film festivals, takes place in late August and early September.

L'Arena di Verona Stagione Lirica (Arena of Verona Outdoor Opera Season), from early July to late August, is known for its grand productions, performed in Verona's 22,000-seat Roman amphitheater.

Speaking the Language

Even in the cosmopolitan north, although knowledge of foreign languages is increasing, often highly educated Italians speak only Italian. Many are slightly offended if a foreigner assumes they speak English without first asking politely, *"Parla Lei inglese?"* If you do ask, most Italians, even those with no English, will try to be helpful. Perhaps because of their own linguistic limitations, Italians are tolerant of foreigners who try to speak their language and do wonders in understanding fractured Italian.

Even if you do speak Italian, don't be surprised if you can't understand conversations going on around you, which may be in local dialect. Because of television and mass education, now almost everyone speaks standard Italian, and in cities such as Milan dialect has almost died out, but it still thrives in the Veneto and in areas that have not had a large influx of residents from other parts of Italy. Among friends, at home, and in moments of high emotion, standard Italian gives way to the local language.

NORTHERN ITALY
TOP ATTRACTIONS

Giotto's Frescoes in the Scrovegni Chapel, Padua

(A) A contemporary of Dante, Giotto decorated this chapel with an eloquent and beautiful fresco cycle. Its convincing human dimension helped to change the course of Western art.

Lake Como

(B) Just a short drive or train ride north of Milan, Lake Como combines spectacular mountain scenery with the elegance of Baroque and Neoclassical villas and gardens and the charm of picturesque villages. It's great any time of year, but best in the spring, when the azaleas are in bloom in the gardens of Villa Carlotta.

Leonardo's *Last Supper*

(C) On the refectory wall of Santa Maria della Grazie in Milan one of the world's most famous paintings still evokes wonder, not at all trivialized by millions of reproductions or dulled by its poor state of conservation.

Mantua

(D) This charming town, slightly off the beaten track in Lombardy, contains a high point of 15th-century painting: Mantegna's frescoes in the wedding chamber of the Palazzo Ducale, a masterpiece of spatial illusion. On the outskirts of town, Giulio Romano's Palazzo Te is an elegant pleasure palace, frescoed with illusionistic painting that carried the tradition established by Mantegna several steps further.

Palladio's Villas and Palazzi

(E) The great 16th-century architect Palladio created harmoniously beautiful buildings that were influential in spreading the Neoclassical style to northern Europe, England, and, later, America. He did most of his work in and around his native city of Vicenza. If a visit to Vicenza simply whets your appetite for Palladio, you can see another wonderful Palladian villa outside Venice (La Malcontenta) and

his famous collaboration with Veronese outside Treviso (Villa Barbaro).

Ravenna's Mosaics

(F) This small, out-of-the-way city houses perhaps the world's greatest treasure trove of early-Christian art. After the decline of Rome, Ravenna was the capital of the Western Roman Empire and, a bit later, the seat of the Byzantine Empire in the West. The exquisite and surprisingly moving 5th- and 6th-century mosaics decorating several churches and other religious buildings still retain their startling brilliance.

Venice's Grand Canal

(G) No one ever forgets a first trip down the Grand Canal. The sight of its magnificent palaces, with the light reflected from the canal's waters shimmering across their facades, is one of Italy's great experiences.

Venice's Piazza San Marco

(H) Perhaps nowhere else in the world gathers together so many of man's noblest artistic creations. The centerpiece of the piazza is the Basilica di San Marco, arguably the most beautiful Byzantine church in the West, with not only its shimmering Byzantine Romanesque facade, but also its jewel-like mosaic-encrusted interior. Right next door is the Venetian Gothic Palazzo Ducale, which was so beloved by the Venetians that when it burned down in the 16th century they rejected projects by the greatest architects of the Renaissance and had their palace rebuilt *come era, dove era*—exactly how and where it was.

TOP EXPERIENCES

Discovering the Cinque Terre

Along the Italian Riviera east of Genoa are five fishing villages known collectively as the Cinque Terre. The beauty of the landscape—with vine-covered hills pushing against an azure sea—and the charm of the villages have turned the area into one of Italy's top destinations. The number-one activity is hiking the trails that link the villages—the views are once-in-a-lifetime gorgeous—but if hiking isn't your thing, you can still have fun lounging about in cafés, admiring the water, and wandering through the medieval streets.

Taking Part in Venice's Festivals

Few people love a good party as much as the Venetians. The biggest is, of course, **Carnevale,** culminating on Fat Tuesday, but with revelry beginning about 10 days earlier. Visitors from the world over join the Venetians in a period of institutionalized fantasy, dressing in exquisitely elaborate costumes. The program changes each year and includes public, mostly free cultural events in all districts of the city.

The **Redentore,** on the third weekend in July, is a festival essentially for Venetians, but in recent years more and more guests have come to view the festivities. The Venetians pack a picnic dinner and eat in boats decorated with paper lanterns in the Bacino di San Marco or on tables set up for private parties along the canals. Just before midnight, there's a magnificent fireworks display. After the fireworks, young people head for the Lido, where there is dancing on the beach until dawn. The next day (Sunday), everyone crosses a temporary bridge spanning the Canale della Giudecca to Palladio's Redentore church to light a candle.

Venice Biennale is a cutting-edge international art exposition held in odd-numbered years from June to November in exhibition halls in the Venice Public Gardens (Giardini) and in the 14th-century industrial complex (Le Corderie) in the Arsenale. It's the most important exhibition of contemporary art in Italy and one of the three most important in Europe. On even numbered years the Biennale devotes itself to architecture, and the Biennale di Architettura has become a must for those interested in contemporary architecture.

Feasting in Bologna

Italians recognize Emilia as the star of its culinary culture and Bologna as its epicenter. Many dishes native to Bologna, such as the slow-cooked meat-and-tomato sauce *sugo alla Bolognese,* have become so famous that they're widely available throughout Italy and abroad. But you owe it to yourself to try them in the city where they were born, and where they remain a subject of local pride. Take note, however: in Bologna, a sugo is never served with spaghetti, but rather with tagliatelle, lasagna, or tortellini.

Fashion and Style in Milan

Italian clothing and furniture design are world famous, and the center of the Italian design industry is Milan. The best way to see what's happening in the world of fashion is to browse the showrooms and boutiques of the fabled *quadrilatero della moda,* along and around Via Montenapoleone. The main event in the world of furniture design is Milan's annual Salone Internazionale del Mobile, held at the Milan fairgrounds for a week in April. Admission is generally restricted to the trade, but the Salone is open to the general public for one day, generally on a Sunday, during the week of the show.

NORTHERN ITALY TODAY

The Influence of Immigration

The population of northern Italy, especially the western regions, has undergone a substantial transformation due to immigration. Starting with the economic boom of the 1960s and continuing to the 1980s, Italians from the south moved to the industrial centers of Turin and Milan, changing the face of those cities. The southerners, or at least their children, adopted most northern customs—few now go home for a nap at midday—but their presence has had a clear influence on the culture of the north. Especially in the cities, local dialects died out, and at the dinner table traditional polenta and risotto now share space with pasta, and southern dishes often appear on menus.

Prosperity, and immigration, came later to the northeast. Venetians still enjoy the 18th-century dialect comedies of Goldoni, and it's not uncommon to hear dialect spoken by elegant operagoers at La Fenice.

Northern Italy, like the rest of the country, has recently experienced an influx of foreign immigrants, although their numbers are smaller relative to the local population than in many other European countries. Their welcome has varied: proudly cosmopolitan Venice is fairly open to newcomers, while in cities where the government is controlled by the overtly xenophobic Northern League integration has been contentious. In recent years some politicians have exploited the issue for their own gain, drawing criticism from internationally respected human rights organizations. With the current economic crisis, the xenophobic attitudes have become even stronger, even though it has been repeatedly shown that the immigrants represent no economic threat and, actually, are a benefit to the economy. The latest political changes in Italy have, unfortunately, not done much to counteract the xenophobic trend set by the former government. Many Middle Eastern and African immigrants choose to leave Italy, since both economic conditions and social acceptance are stronger in northern Europe.

The Global Economy

Parts of northern Italy are among Europe's most prosperous areas, but even these economic powerhouses have run into trouble. The industrial base consists mainly of small and midsize businesses, many of which have had to close or outsource to Eastern Europe or Asia. Restrictive labor laws that impede hiring staff while remaining competitive are the crux of the problem. It remains to be seen whether Italians will accept economic and social reforms that will allow Italy to regain its competitive status.

The Effects of Global Warming

Venice has long suffered from a natural phenomenon called *acqua alta*—flooding that occurs when especially high tides coincide with a strong *sirocco,* a wind that blows north from Africa, forcing more water into the lagoon. Occurring mostly between mid-October and December, the floods are temporary, lasting only for three or four hours around high tide. However, it has become clear that climate change is affecting the frequency and intensity of the flooding. While the city is equipped to cope with flooding, more buildings are being affected, and there is concern over the long-term damage to a city already under threat.

A GREAT ITINERARY

Day 1: Bellagio

If you're flying to northern Italy from overseas, there's no better way to rest up after a long flight than with a day on Lake Como, combining some of Italy's most beautiful scenery with elegant historic villas and gardens.

At the center is **Bellagio,** a pretty village with world-class restaurants and hotels, as well as more economical options. From Bellagio you can ferry to other points along the lake, take walking tours, hike, or just sit on a terrace watching the light play on the sapphire water and the snow-capped mountains.

Logistics: There are inexpensive bus/train combinations from Milan's Malpensa airport. A limousine service, Fly to Lake (☎ *0341/286887* ⊕ *www.flytolake.com*), leaves Malpensa four times per day (€35–€70 per person depending on the number of travelers; no service Sunday, late fall, or winter). The trip takes a little over two hours. In Bellagio you won't need a car, since most of your touring will be on foot, by ferry, or by bus.

Day 2: Milan

After a leisurely breakfast in Bellagio, take the ferry to Varenna (15 minutes) and then the train (1¼ hours) to Milan's Central Station. **Milan** is a leading center of fashion and design, and many visitors keep to the area of elegant shops around **Via Montenapoleone.**

But the city also houses some of Europe's great art treasures in the **Brera Gallery** and has two churches by Bramante, perhaps the most refined of the Italian High Renaissance architects. And then, of course, there's Leonardo's *Last Supper.* You may want to spend your evening taking in an opera at Italy's most illustrious opera house, **La Scala.**

Logistics: Central Milan is compact, with excellent public transportation. Milan does have its share of crime; keep an eye on your possessions, especially around the train station and avoid hotels in that area.

Days 3 to 5: Verona/Mantua/Vicenza

Take an early express train to Verona (1½ hours from Milan) and settle into your hotel, where you'll stay for three nights; you'll be using this stately medieval city as your base to see three of the most important art cities in northern Italy.

Verona, with its ancient Roman arena, theater, and city gates, its brooding medieval palaces and castle, and its graceful bridge spanning the Adige, is probably the most immediately impressive of the three, and you'll want to spend the first day exploring its attractions. But the real artistic treasures are in the two smaller cities you'll see on day trips out of Verona.

The next day, take a short train trip to **Mantua** (30–45 minutes). Be sure to arrive in time for lunch, because Mantua has one of the most interesting local cuisines in northern Italy. The great specialty is *tortelli di zucca* (pumpkin-, cheese-, and almond paste–filled ravioli), served with sage butter and Parmesan cheese.

The top artistic attractions are the Mantegna frescoes in the **Palazzo Ducale,** and you should also pay a visit to Giulio Romano's **Palazzo Te,** a 16th-century pleasure palace, on the outskirts of town. Take the train back to Verona in time for dinner, and perhaps catch an opera performance in Verona's Roman amphitheater.

The day after, take a short train trip to **Vicenza** (30 minutes) to see the palaces, villas, and public buildings of the lion of late-16th-century architecture, Andrea Palladio. Don't miss his **Teatro Olimpico** and his most famous villa, **La Rotonda,**

slightly out of town. For lunch, try the *baccalà alla vicentina,* the local version of salt cod, which is surprisingly good and not at all salty.

Also be sure to see the frescoes by Gianbattista and Giandomenico Tiepolo in the **Villa Valmarana ai Nani**, near the Rotonda. In spring and summer there are concerts in the **Teatro Olimpico**; if you want to attend, you'll have to book a hotel in Vicenza, since you'll miss the last train back to Verona.

Day 6: Padua

Most people visit this important art and university center on a day trip out of Venice, but then they miss one of Padua's main attractions: the nightlife that goes on in the city's wine bars and cafés from evening until quite late.

Most cities in northern Italy, even Venice and Milan, have surprisingly little to offer after dinner or the theater, but in Padua going out for a nightcap or coffee with friends is a tradition, not only for students but also for older folks, too.

Arrive early enough to see at least the Giotto frescoes in the **Cappella degli Scrovegni** and the **Basilica di San Antonio** before lunch, then spend a relaxing afternoon at the **Villa Pisani**, enjoying its gardens and important Tiepolo fresco.

Logistics: Trains are frequent to Padua from Verona (1 hour) and Vicenza (30 minutes); you don't really have to schedule ahead.

Day 7: Venice

Three days are hardly enough to see one of the world's most beautiful cities, and one of the cradles of modern Western civilization. But rushing from sight to sight would be a mistake, since Venice is a wonderful place to stroll or just hang out, taking in some of the atmosphere that inspired such great art.

The first things you'll probably want to do in Venice are to take a vaporetto ride down the **Grand Canal** and see the **Piazza San Marco**. These are best done in the morning. If you go before 8:30, you'll avoid rush hour on the vaporetto, and although there's likely to be a line at San Marco when it opens, it'll be shorter than later in the day. After that, move on to the adjacent **Palazzo Ducale** and Sansovino's **Biblioteca Marciana**, facing it in the Piazzetta.

For lunch, take vaporetto No. 1 to the Ca' Rezzonico stop and have a sandwich and a *spritz* in the **Campo Santa Margherita**, where you can mingle with the university students in one of Venice's most lively squares. From there, make your way to

the **Galleria dell'Accademia** and spend a few hours taking in its wonderful collection of Venetian paintings.

In the evening, take a walk up the Zattere and have a drink at one of the cafés overlooking the **Canale della Giudecca.**

Logistics: Be careful selecting your early train from Padua to Venice; some can be very slow. The 7:50 am (weekdays) is one of the fastest (27 minutes), and will get you into Venice in time to beat rush hour on the Grand Canal vaporetto. To get an early start, unless your hotel is very near San Marco, deposit your luggage at the station, and pick it up later, after you've seen the Piazza. Seeing the Grand Canal and Piazza San Marco in relative tranquillity will be your reward for getting up at the crack of dawn and doing a little extra planning.

Day 8: Venice

If the Accademia has just whetted your appetite for Venetian painting, start the day by visiting churches and institutions where you can see more of it.

For Titian, go to **Santa Maria Gloriosa dei Frari** church and **Santa Maria della Salute;** for Tintoretto, **Scuola Grande di San Rocco** and **Madonna dell'Orto;** for Bellini, the **Frari** and **San Giovanni e Paolo;** for Tiepolo, **Ca' Rezzonico, Scuola Grande dei Carmini,** and the **Gesuati;** for Carpaccio, **Scuola di San Giorgio;** and for Veronese, **San Sebastiano.**

If your taste runs to modern art, there are the Guggenheim Collection and, down the street, the Pinault Collection in the refashioned **Punta della Dogana.**

In the afternoon, head for the Fondamenta Nuova station to catch a vaporetto to the outer islands: **Murano,** where you can shop for Venetian glass and visit a glass museum and workshops; **Burano,** known for lace-making and colorful houses; and **Torcello,** Venice's first inhabited island and home to a beautiful cathedral.

Day 9: Venice

Venice is more than a museum—it's a lively city. The best way to see that aspect of La Serenissima is to pay a visit to the **Rialto Market,** where the Venetians buy their fruits and vegetables and, most important, their fish, at one of Europe's largest and most varied fish markets. Note that the Rialto Market is closed on Sunday and Monday; since there is no fishing on Sunday, there can be no fresh fish available on Monday. In Venice, it is unthinkable to buy fish that is more than a day out of the sea.

Have lunch in one of the excellent restaurants in the market area.

On your last afternoon in Venice, allow time to sit and enjoy a coffee or spritz in one of the city's lively squares or in a café along the **Fondamenta della Misericordia** in Cannaregio, simply watching the Venetians go about their daily lives.

There's certainly a good deal more art and architecture to see in the city, and if you can't resist squeezing in another few churches, you may want to see Palladio's masterpiece, the Redentore church on the **Giudecca,** or Tullio Lombardo's lyrical **Miracoli,** a short walk from the San Marco end of the Rialto Bridge.

Day 10: Venice/Departure

Take one last vaporetto trip up the Grand Canal to **Piazzale Roma** and, after saying good-bye to Venice, catch Bus No. 5 to the airport.

VENICE

WELCOME TO VENICE

TOP REASONS TO GO

★ **Cruising the Grand Canal:** The beauty of its palaces, enhanced by light playing on the water, make a trip down Venice's "main street" unforgettable.

★ **Basilica di San Marco:** Don't miss the gorgeous mosaics inside—they're worth standing in line for.

★ **Santa Maria Gloriosa dei Frari:** Its austere, cavernous interior houses Titian's *Assunta*—one of the world's most beautiful altar-pieces, plus several other spectacular art treasures.

★ **Gallerie dell'Accademia:** Legendary masterpieces of Venetian painting will overwhelm you in this fabled museum.

★ **Sipping wine and snacking at a bacaro:** For a sample of tasty local snacks and excellent Veneto wines in a uniquely Venetian setting, head for one of the city's many wine bars.

1 San Marco. The neighborhood at the center of Venice is filled with fashion boutiques, art galleries, and grand hotels. Its Piazza San Marco is one of the world's most beautiful and elegant urban spaces.

2 Dorsoduro. This graceful residential area is home to the Santa Maria della Salute, the Gallerie dell'Accademia, the Peggy Guggenheim Collection, and François Pinault Collection at the Punta della Dogana, and the Campo Santa Margherita, a lively hangout for students from Venice's three Universities. The sunny Zattere promenade is one of the best spots to stroll with a gelato or linger at an outdoor café.

3 Santa Croce and San Polo. These bustling sestieri are both residential and commercial, with all sorts of shops and artisan studios, several major churches and museums, and the Rialto fish and produce markets.

4 Cannaregio. Brimming with residential Venetian life, this sestiere provides some of the sunniest open-air canalside walks in town. The Fondamenta della Misericordia is a strand of restaurants and cafés interspersed among gothic, Renaissance and Baroque residences, and the Jewish Ghetto has a fascinating history and tradition.

5 Castello. Along with Cannaregio, this area is home to most of the residents. With its gardens, park, and narrow, winding walkways, it's the sestiere least influenced by Venice's tourist culture.

THE JEWISH GHETTO

Fond. d.

Canal

Stazione Ferrovia Santa Luca

Santa Maria Gloriosa dei Frari

Canal Del

LA GIUDECCA

6 **San Giorgio Maggiore
and the Giudecca.** San
Giorgio Maggiore, across
from Piazza San Marco,
is graced with Palladio's
magnificent church. His
elegant Church of the
Santissimo Redentore is
the major landmark on the
Giudecca, where the main
attractions are the wonderful views of Venice.

7 **Islands of the Lagoon.**
Torcello, Burano, and Murano
are the islands of Venice's
northern lagoon; each has
its own allure. The Lido
is the barrier island that
closes the Venetian lagoon
off from the Adriatic—it's
Venice's beach.

GETTING
ORIENTED

Venice proper is divided
into six *sestieri,* or districts
(the word *sestiere* means,
appropriately, "sixth"):
Cannaregio, Santa Croce,
San Polo, Dorsoduro,
San Marco, and Castello.
More sedate outer islands
float around them—San
Giorgio Maggiore and the
Giudecca just to the south;
beyond them to the east,
the Lido, the barrier island;
and to the north, Murano,
Burano, and Torcello.

7

4

Misericordia

CANNAREGIO

rande

**SANTA
CROCE**

3

Canal Grande

Ca' d'Oro

SAN POLO

**SAN
MARCO**

1

Basilica di
San Marco

5

Piazza ◆
San Marco

CASTELLO

Palazzo Ducale

Gallerie dell'
Accademia

Grande

Peggy ◆
Guggenheim
Collection

2

Santa Maria
◆ della Salute

DORSODURO

*Zatterre
Promenade*

Giudecca

6

6

**SAN
GIORGIO
MAGGIORE**

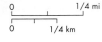

0   1/4 mi

0   1/4 km

3

EATING AND DRINKING WELL IN VENICE

The catchword in Venetian restaurants is "fish." How do you learn about the catch of the day? A visit to the Rialto's *pescheria* (fish market) is more instructive than any book, and when you're dining at a well-regarded restaurant, ask for a recommendation.

Traditionally, fish is served with a bit of salt, maybe some chopped parsley, and a drizzle of olive oil—no lemon; lemon masks the flavor. Ask for an entire sea-caught fish; it's much more expensive than its farmed cousin, but certainly worth it. Antipasto may be *prosciutto di San Daniele* (cured ham of the Veneto region) or *sarde in saor*, (fresh panfried sardines marinated with onions, raisins, and pine nuts). Risotto—a rice dish cooked with shellfish or veggies—is a great first course. Pasta? Enjoy it with seafood sauce: this is *not* the place to order spaghetti with tomato sauce. Other pillars of regional cooking include *pasta e fagioli* (thick bean soup with pasta), polenta, often with *fegato alla veneziana* (liver with onion), and that dessert invented in the Veneto: *tiramisù*.

GOING BACARO

You can sample regional wines and scrumptious *cicheti* (small snacks) in *bacari* (wine bars), a great Venetian tradition. *Crostini* (toast with toppings) and *polpette* (meat, fish, or vegetable croquettes) are popular cicheti, as are small sandwiches, seafood salads, *baccalà mantecato* (creamy whipped dried cod), and toothpick-speared items such as roasted peppers, marinated artichokes, and mozzarella balls.

SEAFOOD

Granseola (crab), *moeche* (tiny, locally caught soft-shell crabs), sweet *canoce* (mantis shrimp), *capelunghe* (razor clams), calamari, and *seppie* or *seppioline* (cuttlefish) are all prominently featured, as well as *rombo* (turbot), *branzino* (sea bass), *San Pietro* (John Dory), *sogliola* (sole), *orate* (gilthead), and *triglia* (mullet). Trademark dishes include *sarde in saor*, *la frittura mista* (tempura-like fried fish and vegetables), and baccalà mantecato.

RISOTTO, PASTA, POLENTA

Although legend has it that Venetian traveler Marco Polo brought pasta back from China, it isn't a traditional staple of Venetian cuisine. As a first course, Venetians favor the creamy rice dish risotto *all'onda* ("undulating," as opposed to firm), prepared with vegetables or shellfish. When pasta is served, it's generally accompanied by seafood sauces, too: *pasticcio di pesce* is lasagnatype pasta baked with fish, and *bigoli* is a strictly local whole wheat pasta shaped like thick spaghetti, usually served *in salsa* (an anchovy-onion sauce with a dash of cinnamon), or with *nero di seppia* (cuttlefish-ink sauce). A classic first course is *pasta e fagioli* (bean and pasta soup). *Polenta* (cornmeal gruel) is another staple that's served creamy or fried in wedges, generally as an accompaniment to stews or seppie in nero.

VEGETABLES

The larger islands of the lagoon are legendary for fine vegetables, such as the Sant'Erasmo *castraure,* sinfully expensive but heavenly tiny white artichokes that appear for a few days in spring. Other regions produce baby artichokes, but only Sant'Erasmo has true castraure. Spring treats are fat white asparagus from neighboring Bassano or Verona, and artichoke bottoms (*fondi*), usually sautéed with olive oil, parsley, and garlic. From December to March the prized *radicchio di Treviso,* a local red endive, is grilled and served frequently with a bit of melted *taleggio* cheese from Lombardy. Fall brings small wild mushrooms called *chiodini,* and *zucca di Mantova,* a yellow squash with a gray-green rind used in soups, puddings, and to stuff ravioli.

SWEETS

Tiramisù lovers will have ample opportunity to sample this creamy delight made from ladyfingers soaked in espresso and rum or brandy and covered with mascarpone cream and cinnamon—a dessert invented in the Veneto. Gelati, *sgropini* (prosecco, vodka, and lemon sorbet), and *semifreddi* (soft, homemade ice cream) are other sweets frequently seen on Venetian menu, as are almond cakes and dry cookies served with dessert wine. Try *focaccia veneziana,* a sweet raised cake made in the late fall and winter.

Updated
by Bruce
Leimsidor

It's called La Serenissima, "the most serene," a reference to the majesty, wisdom, and power of this city that was for centuries a leader in trade between Europe and the Orient, and a major center of European culture. Built on water by a people who saw the sea as a defense and ally, and who constantly invested in her splendor with magnificent architectural projects, Venice is a city unlike any other.

No matter how often you've seen it in photos and films, the real thing is more dreamlike than you could ever imagine. Its most notable landmarks, the Basilica di San Marco and the Palazzo Ducale, are exotic mixes of Byzantine, Romanesque, Gothic, and Renaissance styles, reflecting Venice's ties with Constantinople in the east and the rest of Italy. Shimmering sunlight and silvery mist soften every perspective here; it's easy to understand how the city became renowned in the Renaissance for its artists' use of color. It's full of secrets, inexpressibly romantic, and frequently given over to pure, sensuous enjoyment.

You'll see Venetians going about their daily affairs in *vaporetti* (water buses), in the *campi* (squares), and along the *calli* (narrow streets). They're quite skilled—and remarkably tolerant—in dealing with the veritable armies of tourists who fill the city's streets.

VENICE PLANNER

MAKING THE MOST OF YOUR TIME

The hordes of tourists visiting Venice are legendary, especially in spring and fall, but during other seasons, too—there's really no "off-season" in Venice. Unfortunately, tales of impassable, tourist-packed streets and endless queues to get into the Basilica di San Marco are not exaggerated. A little bit of planning, however, will help you avoid the worst of the crowds.

The large majority of tourists do little more than take the vaporetto down the Grand Canal to Piazza San Marco, see the piazza and the basilica, and walk up to the Rialto and back to the station. You'll want to visit these areas, too, but do so in the early morning, before most tourists have finished their breakfast cappuccinos. Since many of the tourists are other Italians who come for a weekend outing, you can further decrease your competition for Venice's pleasures by choosing weekdays to visit the city.

Away from San Marco and the Rialto, the streets and quays of Venice's beautiful medieval and Renaissance residential districts receive only a moderate amount of traffic. Besides the Grand Canal and the Piazza San Marco, and perhaps Torcello, the other historically and artistically important sites are seldom overcrowded. Even on weekends you probably won't have to queue up to get into the Gallerie dell'Accademia.

Venice proper is quite compact, and you should be able to walk across it in a couple of hours, counting even a few minutes for getting lost. The water buses will save wear and tear on tired feet, but won't always save you much time.

PASSES AND DISCOUNTS

Avoid lines and save money by booking services and venue entry online with **Venezia Unica City Pass** (⊕ *www.veneziaunica.it*). The seven-day pass costs €39.90 (discounts for those under 30) and gives you free entry to the Palazzo Ducale, ten of Venice's Civic Museums, the Quirini-Stampalia museum, and the Jewish Museum. Note that the Gallerie dell'Accademia, the Guggenheim, the Ca' d'Oro, the Scuola di San Rocco and the Scuola di San Giorgio, and the Pinault collection at the Punta della Dogana are not Civic Museums, and thereby not included. It also gives you access to 15 of the most important churches in Venice, There is a reduced version of this pass, which gives you, for €25.90, access to the Palazzo Ducale, three museums in Piazza San Marco, three churches of your choice, and the Quirini-Stampalia museum.

Fifteen of Venice's most significant churches covered by the Venezia Unica City Pass are part of the **Chorus Foundation** umbrella group (☎ *041/2750462* ⊕ *www.chorusvenezia.org*), which coordinates their administration, hours, and admission fees. Churches in this group are open to visitors all day except Sunday morning. Single church entry costs €3; you have a year to visit all 15 with the €12 **Chorus Pass** (family and student discounts are available). Get a pass at any participating church or online.

The **MUVE Pass** (€45) from **Musei Civici** (☎ *041/2715911* ⊕ *www.museicivicieveneziani.it*) includes multiple entry to 12 Venice city museums for one year. Since the Venezia Unica City Pass is limited to one week, visitors who plan an extended stay, or who plan more than one visit to Venice in a year, may prefer to take the MUVE Pass plus the Chorus Pass, which would provide most of the same privileges as the Venezia Unica pass, but valid for multiple entries for a year, instead of only for one week.

GETTING HERE AND AROUND

AIR TRAVEL

Aeroporto Marco Polo. Venice's Aeroporto Marco Polo is on the mainland, 10 km (6 miles) north of the city. It's served by domestic and international flights, including connections from 21 European cities, plus direct flights from New York's JFK and other U.S. cities. To avoid substantial queues at check-in, it's highly advisable to use online check-in services if provided by your airline. It is reachable from Venice either by bus or by special vaporetto (Alilaguna). ☎ *041/2609260* ⊕ *www.veniceairport.it.*

LAND TRANSFERS   **ATVO.** Buses run by ATVO make a quick (20-minute) and cheap (€6) trip from the airport to Piazzale Roma, from where you can get a vaporetto to the stop nearest your hotel. Tickets are sold from machines and at the airport ground transportation booth (daily 9–7:30), and on the bus when tickets are otherwise unavailable. The public ACTV Bus No. 5 also runs to the Piazzale Roma in about the same time. Tickets (€6) are available at the airport ground transportation booth. A taxi to Piazzale Roma costs about €35. ☎ *0421/383672* ⊕ *www.atvo.it.*

WATER TRANSFERS   From Marco Polo terminal, it's a mostly covered seven-minute walk to the dock where boats depart for Venice's historic center.

Alilaguna. This company has regular, scheduled ferry service from pre-dawn until nearly midnight. During most of the day there are two departures from the airport to Venice every hour, at 15 and 45 minutes after the hour. Early-morning and evening departures are less frequent, but there is at least one per hour. The charge is €15, including bags, and it takes about 1½ hours to reach the landing near Piazza San Marco; some ferries also stop at Fondamente Nove, Murano, Lido, the Cannaregio Canal, and the Rialto. Slight reductions are possible if you book a round trip online. ☎ *041/2401701* ⊕ *www.alilaguna.it.*

CAR TRAVEL

Venice is at the end of SR11, just off the east–west A4 autostrada. There are no cars in Venice; if possible, return your rental when you arrive.

A warning: don't be waylaid by illegal touts, often wearing fake uniforms, who try to flag you down and offer to arrange parking and hotels. Use one of the established garages and consider reserving a space in advance. The **Autorimessa Comunale** (☎ *041/2727211* ⊕ *www.asmvenezia.it*) costs €26–€29 for 24 hours (slight discounts if you book on line.) The **Garage San Marco** (☎ *041/5232213* ⊕ *www.garagesanmarco.it*) costs €26 for up to 14 hours and €30 for 24 hours, slight discounts for prepaid online reservations. On its own island, **Tronchetto** (☎ *041/5207555*) charges €21 for 5 to 24 hours. Watch for signs coming over the bridge—you turn right just before Piazzale Roma. Many hotels and the casino have guest discounts with San Marco or Tronchetto garages. A cheaper alternative is to park in Mestre, on the mainland, and take a train (10 minutes, €1) or bus into Venice. The garage across from the station and the Bus No. 2 stop costs €8–€10 for 24 hours.

PUBLIC TRANSPORTATION

WATER BUSES **ACTV.** The ACTV operate the land bus and *vaporetto* (water bus) service in Venice. A single tourist ticket valid for 60 minutes costs €7, but there are also one-, two-, and three-day tickets plus a one-week ticket available, which represent considerable savings if you plan to move frequently around the city by public transportation. Vaporetti run 24 hours in Venice, because there are parts of the city that are accessible only by water; service is quite frequent during the day. Routes and schedules are available on the ACTV website, or at individual vaporetto stations. Tickets are available at main vaporetto stops, at tobacconists, and at some newspaper kiosks. They are valid on both the vaporetti in Venice and on the bus lines to Mestre and on the Lido. Controls are frequent, and fines for traveling without a valid ticket are steep.

If you plan an extended stay in Venice, or plan to make several trips, and have a local address (not a hotel or B&B), you can apply for a Carta Venezia (€50), valid for several years, which will give you substantially reduced rates on public transportation. ☎ *041/2424* ⊕ *www.actv.it.*

WATER TAXIS A *motoscafo* isn't cheap: you'll spend about €60 for a short trip in town, €80 to the Lido, and €90 or more per hour to visit the outer islands. It is strongly suggested to book through the Consorzio Motoscafi Venezia (☎ *041/5222303* ⊕ *www.motoscafivenezia.it*) to avoid having to argue with the driver over prices. A water taxi can carry up to 10 passengers, with an additional charge of €10 per person more than five people, so if you're traveling in a group, it may not be that much more expensive than a vaporetto.

TRAIN TRAVEL

Venice has rail connections with many major cities in Italy and Europe. Note that Venice's train station is **Venezia Santa Lucia,** not to be confused with Venezia Mestre, which is the mainland stop prior to arriving in the historic center. Some trains don't continue beyond the Mestre station; in such cases you can catch the next Venice-bound train. Get a €1 ticket from the newsstand on the platform and validate it (in the yellow time-stamp machine) to avoid a fine.

TOURS

If you want some expert guidance around Venice, you may opt for private, semiprivate, or large group tours. Any may include a boat tour as a portion of a longer walking tour. For private tours, make sure to choose an authorized guide.

LARGE-GROUP TOURS

Venice Tourism Office. Visit any Venice tourism office to book walking tours of the San Marco area (no Sunday tour in winter). There's also an afternoon walking tour that ends with a gondola ride, and a daily serenaded gondola ride. Check the main branch of the city's tourist office or their website for additional scheduled offerings, meeting places, prices, and times. ✉ *San Marco 2637* ☎ *041/5298711* ⊕ *www.turismovenezia.it.*

PRIVATE TOURS

A Guide in Venice. This popular company offers a wide variety of innovative, entertaining, and informative themed tours for groups of up to eight people. Tours generally last two to three hours. Guide fee is €70 per hour, and does not include admissions or transporatation fees. ☎ *3477876846 for Sabrina Scaglianti* ⊕ *www.aguideinvenice.com.*

Walks Inside Venice. For a host of particularly creative group and private tours, from historic to artistic to gastronomic, opt for one run by Walks Inside Venice. Tours are for groups up to six people and guides include people with advanced university degrees and published authors. ☎ *041/5241706 for Roberta, 041/5202434 for Cristina* ⊕ *www. walksinsidevenice.com.*

VISITOR INFORMATION

The multilingual staff of the **Venice tourism office** (☎ *041/5298711* ⊕ *www.turismovenezia.it*) can provide directions and up-to-the-minute information. Their free, quarterly *Show and Events Calendar* lists current happenings and venue hours. Tourist office branches are at Marco Polo Airport; the Venezia Santa Lucia train station; Garage Comunale, on Piazzale Roma; at Piazza San Marco near Museo Correr at the southwest corner; the Venice Pavilion (including a Venice-centered bookstore), on the *riva* (canalfront street) between the San Marco vaporetto stop and the Royal Gardens; and at the main vaporetto stop on the Lido. The train-station branch is open daily 8–6:30; other branches generally open at 9:30.

EXPLORING VENICE

Venice proper is divided into six sestieri: Cannaregio, Castello, Dorsoduro, San Marco, San Polo, and Santa Croce. More-sedate outer islands float around them—San Giorgio Maggiore and the Giudecca just to the south, beyond them the Lido, the barrier island; to the north, Murano, Burano, and Torcello.

SAN MARCO

Extending from the Piazza San Marco to the Rialto bridge, San Marco comprises the historical and commercial heart of Venice. Aside from the Piazza itself—San Marco is the only square in Venice given full stature as a "piazza" and accordingly is often known simply as "the Piazza"—this sestiere is graced with some of Venice's finest churches and best-endowed museums. San Marco is also the shopping district of Venice, and its mazes of streets are lined with Venetian glass, fine clothing, and elegantly wrought jewelry. Most of the famous Venetian glass producers from Murano have boutiques in San Marco, as do most Italian designers.

TIMING

You can easily spend several days seeing the historical and artistic monuments in and around the Piazza San Marco alone, but at a bare minimum, plan on at least an hour for the basilica, with its wonderful

Continued on page 194

CRUISING THE GRAND CANAL

THE BEST INTRODUCTION TO VENICE IS A TRIP DOWN MAIN STREET

Venice's Grand Canal is one of the world's great thoroughfares. It winds its way from Piazzale Roma to Piazza San Marco, passing 200 palazzi built from the 13th to the 18th centuries by Venice's richest and most powerful families. There's a theatrical quality to a boat ride on the canal: it's as if each pink- or gold-tinted façade is trying to steal your attention from its rival across the way.

In medieval and Renaissance cities, wars and sieges required defense to be an element of design; but in rich, impregnable Venice, you could safely show off what you had. But more than being simply an item of conspicuous consumption, a Venetian's palazzo was an embodiment of his person—not only his wealth, but also his erudition and taste.

The easiest and cheapest way to see the Grand Canal is to take the Line 1 vaporetto (water bus) from Piazalle Roma to San Marco. The ride takes about 35 minutes. Invest in a day ticket and you can spend the better part of a day hopping on and off at the vaporetto's many stops, visiting the sights along the banks. Keep your eyes open for the highlights listed here; some have fuller descriptions later in this chapter.

FROM PIAZZALE ROMA TO RIALTO

Palazzo Labia
Tiepolo's masterpiece, the cycle of Antony and Cleopatra, graces the grand ballroom in this palazzo. The Labia family, infamous for their ostentation, commissioned the frescos to celebrate a marriage and had Tiepolo use the face of the family matriarch, Maria Labia, for that of Cleopatra. Luckily, Maria Labia was known not only for her money, but also for her intelligence and her beauty.

Santa Maria di Nazareth

Ponte di Scalzi

R. DI BIASIO

FERROVIA

SANTA CROCE

Stazione Ferrovia Santa Lucia

After you pass the Ferrovia, the baroque church immediately to your left is the baroque **Santa Maria di Nazareth**, called the Chiesa degli Scalzi (Church of the Barefoot).

After passing beneath the Ponte di Scalzi, ahead to the left, where the Canale di Cannaregio meets the Grand Canal, you'll spy **Palazzo Labia**, an elaborate 18th-century palace built for

the social-climbing Labia family. Known for their ostentation even in this city where modesty was seldom a virtue, the Labias chose a location that required three façades instead of the usual one.

A bit farther down, across the canal, is the 13th-century **Fondaco dei Turchi**, an elegant residence that served as a combination commercial center and ghetto for the Turkish

community. Try not to see the side towers and the crenellations; they were added during a 19th-century restoration.

Beyond it is the obelisk-topped **Ca' Belloni-Battagia**, designed for the Belloni family by star architect Longhena. Look for the family crest he added prominently on the façade.

On the opposite bank is architect Mauro Codussi's magnificent **Palazzo Vendramin-Calergi**, designed just before 1500. Codussi ingeniously married the fortress-like Renaissance style of the Florentine Alberti's Palazzo Rucellai to the lacy delicacy of the Venetian Gothic, creating the prototype of

Palazzo Vendramin-Calergi
Venice's first Renaissance palazzo. Immediately recognized as a masterpiece, it was so highly regarded that later, when its subsequent owners, the Calergi, were convicted of murder and their palace was to be torn down as punishment, the main building was spared.

Ca' d'Oro
Inspired by stories of Nero's Domus Aurea (Golden House) in Rome, the first owner had parts of the façade gilded with 20,000 sheets of gold leaf. The gold has long worn away, but the Ca' D'Oro is still Venice's most beautiful Gothic palazzo.

GHETTO

S. MARCUOLA

Ca' Belloni-Battagia

Ca' da Mosto
Venice's oldest surviving palazzo gives you an idea of Marco Polo's Venice. More than any other Byzantine palazzo in town, it maintains its original 13th-century appearance.

S. STAE

Ca' Pesaro

Fondaco dei Turchi

Depositi del Megio

San Stae Church

CA' D'ORO

SAN POLO

Ca' Corner della Regina

Rialto Mercato

Pescheria
Stop by in the morning to see the incredible variety of fish for sale. Produce stalls fill the adjacent fondamenta. Butchers and cheesemongers occupy the surrounding shops.

Fondaco dei Tedeschi

Ca' dei Camerlenghi

RIALTO

SAN MARCO

the Venetian Renaissance palazzo. The palazzo is now Venice's casino.

The whimsically baroque church of **San Stae** on the right bank is distinguished by a host of marble saints on its façade.

Farther along the bank is one of Longhena's Baroque masterpieces, **Ca' Pesaro**. It is now the Museum of Modern Art.

Next up on the left is **Ca' d'Oro** (1421-1438), the canal's most spendid example of Venetian Gothic domestic design. Across from this palazzo is the loggia of the neo-Gothic **pescheria**, Venice's fish market.

Slightly farther down, on the bank opposite from the vegetable market, is the early 13th-century **Ca' da Mosto**, the oldest building on the Grand Canal. The upper two floors are later additions, but the ground floor and piano nobile give you a good idea of a rich merchant's house during the time of Marco Polo.

As you approach the Rialto Bridge, to the left, just before

the bridge, is the **Fondaco dei Tedeschi**. German merchants kept warehouses, offices, and residences here; its façade was originally frescoed by Titian and Giorgione.

FROM RIALTO TO THE PONTE DELL' ACCADEMIA

SAN POLO

Ponte di Rialto

RIALTO

Palazzo Barzizza

Ca' Loredan

S. SILVESTRO

Ca' Farsetti

Ca' Foscari
The canal's most imposing Gothic masterpiece, Ca' Foscari was built to blot out the memory of a traitor to the Republic.

Ca' Grimani

Palazzo Pisani Moretta

S. ANGELO

TOMA

Ca' Garzoni

Palazzo Grassi

Ca' Rezzonico

REZZONICO

SAN MARCO

ACCADEMIA

Gallerie dell'Accademia

DORSODURO

The shop-lined **Ponte di Rialto** was built in stone after former wooden bridges had burned or collapsed. As you pass under the bridge, on your left stands star architect Sansovino's Palazzo Dolfin Manin. The white stone–clad Renaissance palace was built at huge expense and over the objections of its conservative neighbors.

A bit farther down stand **Ca' Loredan** and **Ca' Farsetti**, 13th-century Byzantine palaces that today make up Venice's city hall.

Along the same side is the **Ca' Grimani**, by the Veronese architect Sanmichele. Legend has it that the palazzo's oversized windows were demanded by the young Grimani's fiancée, who insisted that he build her a palazzo on the Canale Grande with windows larger than the portal of her own house.

At the Sant'Angelo landing, the vaporetto passes close to Codussi's **Ca' Corner-Spinelli**. Back on the right bank, in a lovely salmon color, is the graceful **Palazzo Pisani Moretta**, built in the mid-15th century and typical of the Venetian Gothic palazzo of the generation after the Ca' D'Oro.

A bit farther down the right bank, crowned by obelisks, is **Ca' Balbi**. Niccolò Balbi built this elegant palazzo in order to upstage his former landlord, who had insulted him in public.

Farther down the right bank, where the Canale makes a sharp turn, is the imposing **Ca' Foscari**. Doge Francesco Foscari tore down an earlier palazzo on this spot and built this splendid palazzo to erase memory of the traitorous former owner. It is now the seat of the University of Venice.

Continuing down the right bank you'll find Longhena's **Ca' Rezzonico**, a magnificent baroque palace. Opposite stands the Grand Canal's youngest palace, Giorgio Massari's **Palazzo Grassi**, commissioned in 1749. It houses part of the François Pinot contemporary art collection.

Near the canal's fourth bridge, is the former church and monastery complex that houses the world-renowned **Gallerie dell'Accademia**, the world's largest and most distinguished collection of Venetian art.

ARCHITECTURAL STYLES ALONG THE GRAND CANAL

BYZANTINE: 13th century
Distinguishing characteristics: high, rounded arches, relief panels, multicolored marble.

Examples: Fondaco dei Turchi, Ca' Loredan, Ca' Farsetti, Ca' da Mosto

GOTHIC: 14th and 15th centuries
Distinguishing characteristics: pointed arches, high ceilings, and many windows.

Examples: Ca' d'Oro, Ca' Foscari, Palazzo Pisani Moretta, Ca' Barbaro (and, off the canal, Palazzo Ducale)

RENAISSANCE: 16th century
Distinguishing characteristics: classically influenced emphasis on harmony and motifs taken from classical antiquity.

Examples: Palazzo Vendramin-Calergi, Ca' Grimani, Ca' Corner-Spinelli, Ca' dei Camerlenghi, Ca' Balbi, Palazzo Corner della Ca' Granda, Palazzo Dolfin Manin, and, off the canal, Libreria, Sansoviniana on Piazza San Marco

BAROQUE: 17th century
Distinguishing characteristics: Renaissance order wedded with a more dynamic style, achieved through curving lines and complex decoration.

Examples: churches of Santa Maria di Nazareth, San Stae, and Santa Maris della Salute; Ca' Belloni Battaglia, Ca' Pesaro, Ca' Rezzonico

FROM THE PONTE DELL'ACCADEMIA TO SAN ZACCARIA

Ca' Barbaro
John Singer Sargent, Henry James, and Cole Porter are among the guests who have stayed at Ca' Barbaro. It was a center for elegant British and American society during the turn of the 20th century.

Santa Maria Della Salute
Baldessare Longhena was only 26 when he designed this churc which was to become one of Ve ice's major landmarks. Its rotund form and dynamic Baroque decoration predate iconic Baroc churches in other Italian cities.

SAN MARCO

Ponte dell' Accademia

Casetta Rossa

Ca' Pisani-Gr

ACCADEMIA

S. M. DEL GIGLIO

DORSODURO

Ca' Barbarigo

SALUTE

Palazzo Venier dei Leoni
Eccentric art dealer Peggy Guggenheim's personal collection of modern art is here. At the Grand Canal entrance to the palazzo stands Marino Marini's sexually explicit equestrian sculpture, the Angel of the Citadel. Numerous entertaining stories have been spun around the statue and Ms. Guggenheim's overtly libertine ways.

Palazzo Salviati

S. Maria della Salute

Ca' Dario
Graceful and elegant Ca' Dario is reputed to carry a curse. Almost all its owners since the 15th century have met violent deaths or committed suicide. It was, nevertheless, a center for elegant French society at the turn of the 20th century.

Down from the Accademia bridge, on the left bank next door to the fake Gothic Ca' Franchetti, is the beautiful **Ca' Barbaro**, designed by Giovanni Bon, who was also at work about that time on the Ca' D'Oro.

Farther along on the left bank Sansovino's first work in Venice, the **Palazzo Corner della Ca' Granda**, begun in 1533, still shows the influence of his Roman Renaissance contemporaries, Bramante and Giulio Romano. It faces the uncompleted **Palazzo Venier dei Leoni**, which holds the Peggy Guggenheim Collection, a good cross-section of the visual arts from 1940 to 1960.

Ca' Dario a bit farther down, was originally a Gothic palazzo, but in 1487 it was given an early Renaissance multicolored marble façade.

At this point on the canal the cupola of **Santa Maria della Salute** dominates the scene. The commission for the design of the church to celebrate the Virgin's rescuing Venice from the disastrous plague of 1630, was given to the 26-year-old

Longhena. The young architect stressed the new and inventive aspects of his design, likening the rotunda shape to a crown for the Virgin.

Across from the Salute, enjoying the magnificent view across the canal, are a string of luxury hotels whose historic

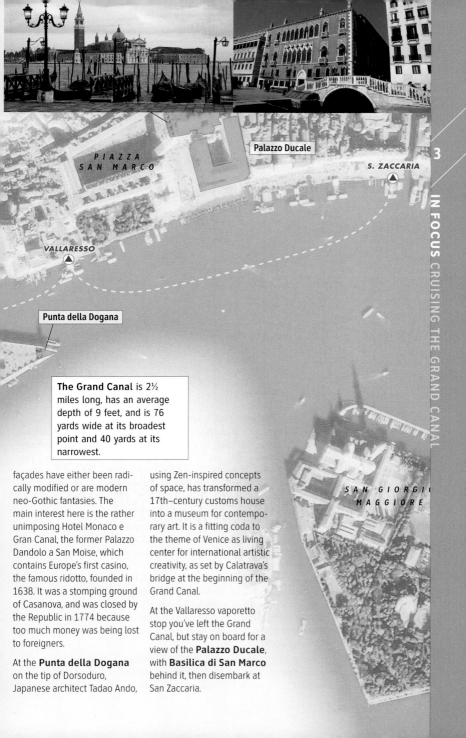

PIAZZA SAN MARCO

Palazzo Ducale

S. ZACCARIA

VALLARESSO

Punta della Dogana

SAN GIORGIO MAGGIORE

The Grand Canal is 2½ miles long, has an average depth of 9 feet, and is 76 yards wide at its broadest point and 40 yards at its narrowest.

façades have either been radically modified or are modern neo-Gothic fantasies. The main interest here is the rather unimposing Hotel Monaco e Gran Canal, the former Palazzo Dandolo a San Moise, which contains Europe's first casino, the famous ridotto, founded in 1638. It was a stomping ground of Casanova, and was closed by the Republic in 1774 because too much money was being lost to foreigners.

At the **Punta della Dogana** on the tip of Dorsoduro, Japanese architect Tadao Ando, using Zen-inspired concepts of space, has transformed a 17th–century customs house into a museum for contemporary art. It is a fitting coda to the theme of Venice as living center for international artistic creativity, as set by Calatrava's bridge at the beginning of the Grand Canal.

At the Vallaresso vaporetto stop you've left the Grand Canal, but stay on board for a view of the **Palazzo Ducale**, with **Basilica di San Marco** behind it, then disembark at San Zaccaria.

mosaics. Add on another half hour if you want to see its Pala d'Oro,
Galleria, and Museo di San Marco. You'll want at least an hour to
appreciate the Palazzo Ducale. Leave another hour for the Museo Correr, through which you also enter the archaeological museum and the
Libreria Sansoviniana. If you choose to take in the piazza itself from a
café table with an orchestra, keep in mind there will be an additional
charge for the music.

TOP ATTRACTIONS

Fodor's Choice
★

Basilica di San Marco. The Basilica di San Marco is not only the religious
center of a great city, but also an expression of the political, intellectual,
and economic aspiration and accomplishments of a city that for centuries was at the forefront of European culture. It is a monument not just
to the glory of God, but also to the glory of Venice. The basilica was
the doges' personal chapel, linking its religious function to the political life of the city and was endowed with all the riches the Republic's
admirals and merchants could carry off from the Orient (as the Byzantine Empire was known), earning it the nickname "Chiesa D'Oro,"
or "Golden Church."

The dim light, the galleries high above the naves—they served as the
matroneum, the women's gallery—the massive altar screen, or *iconos-
tasis*, the single massive Byzantine chandelier, even the Greek cross

ground plan give San Marco an exotic aspect quite unlike that of most Christian churches. The effect is remarkable: here the pomp and mystery of Oriental magnificence are wedded to Christian belief, creating an intensely awesome impression.

The original church, consecrated in 832, was built to house the body of St. Mark, which, according to legend, had been stolen by two Venetians in 828. The whole enterprise, however, was intended to establish Venice's prominence over neighboring Aquileia, a city with a glorious ancient Roman past. When the present church was begun in the 11th century, rare colored marbles and gold leaf mosaics were used in its decoration. When Venice's sons returned from their military exploits, especially when Venice conquered and sacked her former ruler, Constaninople, in 1204, the trophies of the conquest were not just displayed but rather permanently integrated into the facades and the altar.

During the 11th century, when the construction of the present church was begun, Venice was still under the rule of the Byzantine Empire, and the new church was patterned after the Church of the Twelve Apostles (now demolished) in Constantinople, rivaling the Hagia Sophia in religious and political importance. The building was, therefore, a political statement, informing Venice's Byzantine masters that her new basilica was equal to that in Constantinople and housed a relic of an apostle and evangelist.

When the basilica was consecrated in the late 11th century, like many early Christian churches, it had an unadorned brick facade. The 12th and 13th centuries were, however, a period of intense military expansion, and by the early 13th century, the facades began to bear testimony to Venice's conquests. The apse of the portal of St. Alipio, the farthest north (left) of the five west facade portals, bears a 13th-century mosaic showing how the church looked at that time: the facade is already decorated with precious marbles, and the gilt-bronze ancient Roman horses taken from Constantinople in 1204 are already in place on the facade's upper register.

The glory of the basilica is, of course, its medieval mosaic work; about 30% of the mosaics survive in something close to their original form. The earliest date from the late 12th century, but the great majority date from the 13th century. The taking of Constantinople in 1204 was a deciding moment for the mosaic decoration of the basilica. Large amounts of mosaic material were brought in, and a Venetian school of mosaic decoration began to develop. Moreover, a 4th- or 5th-century treasure—the Cotton Genesis, the earliest illustrated Bible—was brought from Constantinople and supplied the designs for the exquisite mosaics of the Creation and the stories of Abraham, Joseph, and Moses that adorn the *narthex* (entrance hall). They are among the most beautiful and best preserved in all the basilica.

The earliest mosaics, bearing the graceful lines of high Byzantine art, are in the first dome of the interior, the Dome of the Pentecost, and date from the 12th century. It is probably the work of Byzantine artisans. The central dome, the Dome of the Ascension, is from the 13th century, and shows the development of a particularly Venetian style.

In the Sanctuary, the main altar is built over the tomb of Saint Mark, its green marble canopy lifted high on 6th-century carved alabaster columns—again, pillaged art. The Pala d'Oro, a dazzling gilt-silver, gem-encrusted screen containing 255 enameled panels, was commissioned in 976 in Constantinople by the Venetian Doge Orseolo I and enlarged over the subsequent four centuries.

■ TIP→ **To skip the line at the basilica entrance, reserve your arrival—at no extra cost—on the website. If you check a bag at the nearby checkroom, you can show your check stub to the guard, who will wave you in. Remember that this is a sacred place: guards will deny admission to people in shorts, sleeveless dresses, and tank tops.** ⊠ *Piazza San Marco, San Marco 328* ☎ *041/2413817 for tour info, 10–noon weekdays* ⊕ *www.basilicasanmarco.it* ⊠ *Basilica free, Treasury €3, sanctuary and Pala d'Oro €2, museum €5* ⊗ *Basilica Mon.–Sat. 9:45–5, Sun. and holidays 2–5 pm (2–4 pm in winter); Treasury, sanctuary, Pala d'Oro, and museum close a few mins earlier. Free guided tours to the Basilica, Apr.–Oct.* Ⓜ *Vallaresso/San Zaccaria.*

Fodor's Choice **Palazzo Ducale** (*Doge's Palace*). Rising majestically above the Piazzetta
★ San Marco, this Gothic fantasia of pink-and-white marble is a majestic expression of Venetian prosperity and power. Although the site was the doges' residence from the 10th century, the building began to take its present form around 1340; what you seen now is essentially a product of the first half of the 15th century. It served not only as a residence, but also as the central administrative center of the Venetian Republic.

The Palazzo Ducale took so long to finish that by the time it was completed, around 1450, it was already a bit out of fashion. It barely predates the main gate of the Arsenale, built in 1460 in fully conceived Renaissance classical style. The Venetians, however, even later on, were not disturbed by their palazzo's dated look. In the 1570s the upper floors were destroyed by fire and Palladio submitted an up-to-date design for its reconstruction, but the Venetians refused his offer and insisted on reconstruction "*come era, dove era*" ("as it was, where it was").

Unlike other medieval seats of authority, the Palazzo Ducale is free of any military defenses—a sign of the Republic's self-confidence. The position of the loggias below instead of above the retaining wall, and the use of pink marble to emphasize the decorative function of that wall, gave the palazzo a light and airy aspect, one that could impress visitors—and even intimidate them, though through opulence and grace rather than fortresslike bulk. Near the basilica you'll see Giovanni and Bartolomeo Bon's Gothic **Porta della Carta** (Gate of the Paper), built between 1438 and 1442, where official decrees were traditionally posted, but you enter the palazzo under the portico facing the water. You'll find yourself in an immense courtyard that holds some of the first evidence of Renaissance architecture in Venice, such as Antonio Rizzo's **Scala dei Giganti** (Stairway of the Giants), erected between 1483 and 1491, directly ahead, guarded by Sansovino's huge statues of Mars and Neptune, added in 1567. Though ordinary mortals must use the central interior staircase, its upper flight is the lavishly gilded

Scala d'Oro (Golden Staircase), also designed by Sansovino in 1555. The palace's sumptuous chambers have walls and ceilings covered with works by Venice's greatest artists. Visit the **Anticollegio**, a waiting room outside the Collegio's chamber, where you can see the *Rape of Europa* by Veronese and Tintoretto's *Bacchus and Ariadne Crowned by Venus*. Veronese also painted the ceiling of the adjacent **Sala del Collegio.** The ceiling of the **Sala del Senato** (Senate Chamber), featuring *The Triumph of Venice* by Tintoretto, is magnificent, but it's dwarfed by his masterpiece *Paradise* in the **Sala del Maggiore Consiglio** (Great Council Hall). A vast work commissioned for a vast hall, this dark, dynamic piece is the world's largest oil painting (23 feet by 75 feet). The room's carved gilt ceiling is breathtaking, especially with Veronese's majestic *Apotheosis of Venice* filling one of the center panels. Around the upper walls, study the portraits of the first 76 doges, and you'll notice one picture is missing near the left corner of the wall opposite *Paradise*. A black painted curtain, rather than a portrait, marks Doge Marin Falier's fall from grace; he was beheaded for treason in 1355, which the Latin inscription bluntly explains.

A narrow canal separates the palace's east side from the cramped cell blocks of the **Prigioni Nuove** (New Prisons). High above the water arches the enclosed marble **Ponte dei Sospiri** (Bridge of Sighs), which earned its name in the 19th century, from Lord Byron's *Childe Harold's Pilgrimage.* ■TIP➜ Reserve your spot for the palazzo's popular Secret Itineraries tour well in advance. You'll visit the doge's private apartments, through hidden passageways to the interrogation (torture) chambers, and into the rooftop *piombi* (lead) prison, named for its lead roofing. Venetian-born writer and libertine Giacomo Casanova (1725–98), along with an accomplice, managed to escape from the piombi in 1756; they were the only men ever to do so. ✉ *Piazzetta San Marco, Piazza San Marco* ☏ *041/2715911, 041/5209070 for Secret Itineraries tour* ⊕ *www.museicivicivenezians.it* ✉ *Museums of San Marco Pass €16, includes entry to Museo Correr, Museo Archeologico, and Biblioteca Nazionale Marciana (free with MUVE Pass).* "Secret Itineraries" tour €20 ☉ *Apr.–Oct., daily 8:30–7; Nov.–Mar., daily 8:30–5:30; last entry 1 hr before closing.* "Secret Itineraries" tour in English at 9:55 and 11:35 Ⓜ *Vaporetto: San Zaccaria, Vallaresso.*

Fodor'sChoice
★
Piazza San Marco. One of the world's most beautiful squares, Piazza San Marco (Saint Mark's Square) is the spiritual and artistic heart of Venice, a vast open space bordered by an orderly procession of arcades marching toward the fairytale cupolas and marble lacework of the Basilica di San Marco. From midmorning on, it is generally packed with tourists. (If Venetians have business in the piazza, they try to conduct it in the early morning, before the crowds swell.) At night the piazza can be magical, especially in winter, when mists swirl around the lampposts and the campanile.

If you face the basilica from in front of the Correr Museum, you'll notice that rather than being a strict rectangle, the square is wider at the basilica end, creating the illusion that it's even larger than it is. On your left, the long, arcaded building is the **Procuratie Vecchie**, renovated to their present form in 1514 as offices and residences for the powerful procurators (magistrates).

On your right is the **Procuratie Nuove,** built half a century later in a more imposing, classical style. It was originally planned by Venice's great Renaissance architect Jacopo Sansovino (1486–1570), to carry on the look of his Libreria Sansoviniana (Sansovinian Library), but he died before construction on the Nuove had begun. Vincenzo Scamozzi (circa 1552–1616), a pupil of Andrea Palladio (1508–80), completed the design and construction. Still later, the Procuratie Nuove was modified by architect Baldassare Longhena (1598–1682), one of Venice's Baroque masters.

Piazzetta San Marco is the "little square" leading from Piazza San Marco to the waters of Bacino San Marco (Saint Mark's Basin); its *molo* (landing) once served as the grand entrance to the Republic. Two imposing columns tower above the waterfront. One is topped by the winged lion, a traditional emblem of Saint Mark that became the symbol of Venice itself; the other supports Saint Theodore, the city's first patron, along with his dragon. (A third column fell off its barge and ended up in the bacino before it could be placed alongside the others.) Though the columns are a glorious vision today, the Republic traditionally executed convicts between them. Even today, some superstitious Venetians avoid walking between the two. ⊠ *San Marco.*

Fodor'sChoice
★
Ponte di Rialto (*Rialto Bridge*). The competition to design a stone bridge across the Grand Canal attracted the best architects of the late 16th century, including Michelangelo, Palladio, and Sansovino, but the job went to the less famous (but appropriately named) Antonio da Ponte (1512–95). His pragmatic design, completed in 1591, featured shop space and was high enough for galleys to pass beneath. Putting practicality and economy over aesthetic considerations, and unlike the classical plans proposed by his more famous contemporaries, Da Ponte's bridge essentially followed the design of its wooden predecessor; it kept decoration and cost to a minimum at a time when the Republic's coffers were low due to continual wars against the Turks and the competition brought about by the Spanish and Portuguese opening of oceanic trade routes. Along the railing you'll enjoy one of the city's most famous views: the Grand Canal vibrant with boat traffic. ⊠ *San Marco* Ⓜ *Vaporetto: Rialto.*

WORTH NOTING

Campanile. Construction of Venice's famous brick bell tower (325 feet tall, plus the angel) began in the 9th century, and took on its present form in 1514. During the 15th century, the tower was used as a place of punishment: immoral clerics were suspended in wooden cages from the tower, some forced to subsist on bread and water for as long as a year; others were left to starve. In 1902, the tower unexpectedly collapsed, taking with it Jacopo Sansovino's marble loggia (1537–49) at its base. The largest original bell, called the *marangona,* survived. The crushed loggia was promptly reconstructed, and the new tower, rebuilt to the old plan, reopened in 1912. Today, on a clear day the stunning view includes the Lido, the lagoon, and the mainland as far as the Alps,

VENICE THROUGH THE AGES

BEGINNINGS

Venice was founded in the 5th century when the Veneti, inhabitants of the mainland region roughly corresponding to today's lower Veneto, fled their homes to escape invading Germanic and other barbarian tribes. The unlikely city, built on islands in the lagoon and later atop wooden posts driven into the marshes, would evolve into a maritime republic lasting over a thousand years. After liberating the Adriatic from marauding pirates, its early fortunes grew as a result of its active role in the Crusades, beginning in 1095 and culminating in the Venetian-led sacking of Constantinople in 1204. The defeat of rival Genoa in the Battle of Chioggia (1380) established Venice as the dominant sea power in Europe.

EARLY GOVERNMENT

As early as the 7th century, Venice was governed by a ruler, the *doge*, elected by the nobility to a lifetime term; however, since the common people had little political input or power, the city wasn't a democracy by modern definition. Beginning in the 12th century, the doge's power was increasingly subsumed by a growing number of councils, commissions, and magistrates. In 1268 a complicated procedure for the doge's election was established to prevent nepotism, but by that point power rested foremost with the Great Council, which at times numbered as many as 2,000 members.

A LONG DECLINE

Venice reached the height of its wealth and territorial expansion in the early 15th century, during which time its domain included all of the Veneto region and part of Lombardy, but the seeds of its decline were soon to be sown, with the fall of Constantinople to the Turks in 1453 and the opening up of Atlantic trade routes, starting, of course, with Columbus in 1492.

By the beginning of the 16th century, the pope, threatened by Venice's mainland expansion, organized the League of Cambrai, defeated Venice in 1505, and effectively put a stop to the Republic's mainland territorial designs. The Ottoman Empire blocked Venice's Mediterranean trade routes, and newly emerging sea powers such as Britain, Spain, Portugal, and the Netherlands ended Venice's monopoly.

When Napoleon arrived in 1797, he first offered Venice an alliance and then, having been betrayed by the Venetians' violation of a pledge of neutrality, took the city without a fight. Venice was ceded again to the Austrians at the Council of Vienna in 1815, and they ruled (save for a brief Venetian revolt in 1848) until the formation of the Italian Republic in 1866. During their occupation, the Austrians helped themselves to many of the city's artistic treasures—very few of them have been returned. Ironically, Venice's greatest contributions to western culture, and those that leave a lasting impression upon the visitor, took place during her periods of political humiliation and economic decline. While some of the Romanesque and Gothic palaces along the Grand Canal were built during her period of undisputed power, its most marvelous palaces and churches, were built after her sun had begun to set.

3

but, strangely enough, none of the myriad canals that snake through the city. Currently, the Campanile is undergoing foundation restoration due to deterioration caused by the occasional acqua alta; however, this hasn't affected visiting hours. ⊠ *Piazza San Marco* ☎ *041/5224064* 🎫 *€8* 🕐 *Easter–June, Oct., and Nov., daily 9–7; July–Sept., daily 9–9; Nov.–Easter, daily 9–3:45; last entry 1 hr before closing* Ⓜ *Vaporetto: Vallaresso, San Zaccaria.*

Fodor'sChoice
★ **Museo Correr.** This museum of Venetian art and history contains an important sculpture collection by Antonio Canova and important paintings by Giovanni Bellini, Vittore Carpaccio (Carpaccio's famous painting of the Venetian courtisans is here), and other major local painters. It's the main repository of Venetian drawings and prints, which, unfortunately, can be seen only by special arrangement, or during special exhibitions. It also houses curiosities such as the absurdly high-sole shoes worn by 16th-century Venetian ladies (who walked with the aid of a servant). The city's proud naval history is evoked in several rooms through highly descriptive paintings and numerous maritime objects, including ships' cannons and some surprisingly large iron mast-top navigation lights. The museum also has a significant collection of antique gems. The Correr exhibition rooms lead directly into the **Museo Archeologico**, which houses the Grimani collection—an important 16th- and 17th-century collection of Greek and Roman art, still impressive even after the transfer of many objects to Paris and Vienna during the Napoleonic and Austrian occupations—and the **Stanza del Sansovino**, the only part of the **Biblioteca Nazionale Marciana** open to visitors. ⊠ *Ala Napoleonica, opposite basilica, Piazza San Marco* ☎ *041/2405211* ⊕ *www.museicivicivenezaini.it* 🎫 *Museums of San Marco Pass €16, includes entry to Museo Archeologico, Biblioteca Nazionale Marciana, and Palazzo Ducale (free with MUVE Pass)* 🕐 *Apr.–Oct., daily 10–7; Nov.–Mar., daily 10–5; last entry 1 hr before closing* Ⓜ *Vaporetto: Vallaresso, San Zaccaria.*

Palazzo Grassi. Built between 1748 and 1772 by Giorgio Massari for a Bolognese family, this palace is one of the last of the great noble residences on the Grand Canal. Once owned by auto magnate Giovanni Agnelli, it was bought by French businessman François Pinaut in 2005 to showcase his highly important collection of modern and contemporary art (which has now grown so large that Pinaut rented the Punta della Dogana, at the entryway to the Grand Canal, for his newest acquisitions). Pinaut brought in Japanese architect Tadao Ando to remodel the Grassi's interior. Check online for a schedule of temporary art exhibitions. ⊠ *Campo San Samuele, San Marco* ☎ *041/5231680* ⊕ *www.palazzograssi.it* 🎫 *€15 (€20, includes the Punta della Dogana)* 🕐 *Wed.–Mon. 10–7* Ⓜ *Vaporetto: San Samuele.*

DORSODURO

The sestiere Dorsoduro (named for its "hard back" solid clay foundation) is across the Grand Canal to the south of San Marco. It is a place of meandering canals, the city's finest art museums, monumental churches and *scuole* (Renaissance civic institutions) filled with works by Titian, Veronese, and Tiepolo, and a promenade called the Zattere, where on sunny days you'll swear half the city is out for a *passeggiata*, or stroll. The eastern tip of the peninsula, the Punta della Dogana, is capped by the dome of Santa Maria della Salute and was once the city's customs point; the old customs house is now a museum of contemporary art.

Dorsoduro is home to the Gallerie dell'Accademia, with an unparalleled collection of Venetian painting, and the gloriously restored Ca' Rezzonico, which houses the Museo del Settecento Veneziano. Another of its landmark sites, the Peggy Guggenheim Collection, has a fine selection of 20th-century art.

TIMING

You can easily spend a full day in the neighborhood. Devote at least a half hour to admiring the Titians in the imposing and monumental Santa Maria della Salute, and another half hour for the wonderful Veroneses in the peaceful, serene church of San Sebastiano. The Gallerie dell'Accademia demands a few hours, but if time is short an audio guide can help you cover the highlights in about an hour. Ca' Rezzonico deserves at least an hour, as does the Peggy Guggenheim collection.

TOP ATTRACTIONS

Fodor's Choice ★ **Ca' Rezzonico.** Designed by Baldassare Longhena in the 17th century, this gigantic palace was completed nearly 100 years later by Giorgio Massari and became the last home of English poet Robert Browning (1812–89). Stand on the bridge by the Grand Canal entrance to spot the plaque with Browning's poetic excerpt, "Open my heart and you will see graved inside of it, Italy" on the left side of the palace. The spectacular centerpiece is the eyepopping Grand Ballroom, which has hosted some of the grandest parties in the city's history, from its 18th-century heyday to the 1969 Bal Fantastica (a Save Venice charity event that attracted every notable of the day, from Elizabeth Taylor to Aristotle Onassis) to the balls recreated for Heath Ledger's 2005 *Casanova*. Today the upper floors of the Ca' Rezzonico are home to the especially delightful **Museo del Settecento** (Museum of Venice in the 1700s). Its main floor successfully retains the appearance of a magnificent Venetian palazzo, decorated with period furniture and tapestries in gilded salons, as well as Tiepolo ceiling frescoes and oil paintings. The upper floors contain a fine collection of paintings by 18th-century Venetian artists, including the famous genre and Pucinella frescoes by Gianbattista Tiepolo's son, Giandomenico, moved here from the Villa di Zianigo. There's even a restored apothecary, complete with powders and potions. ✉ *Fondamenta Rezzonico, Dorsoduro 3136* ☎ *041/2410100* ⊕ *www.museicivicivenezziani.it* 🎫 *€8 (free with MUVE Pass)* ☉ *Wed.–Mon. 10–6* Ⓜ *Vaporetto: Ca' Rezzonico.*

Fodor's Choice ★ **Gallerie dell'Accademia.** The greatest collection of Venetian paintings in the world hangs in these galleries founded by Napoleon back in 1807 on the site of a religious complex he had suppressed. They were carefully and subtly restructured between 1945 and 1959 by the renowned architect Carlo Scarpa.

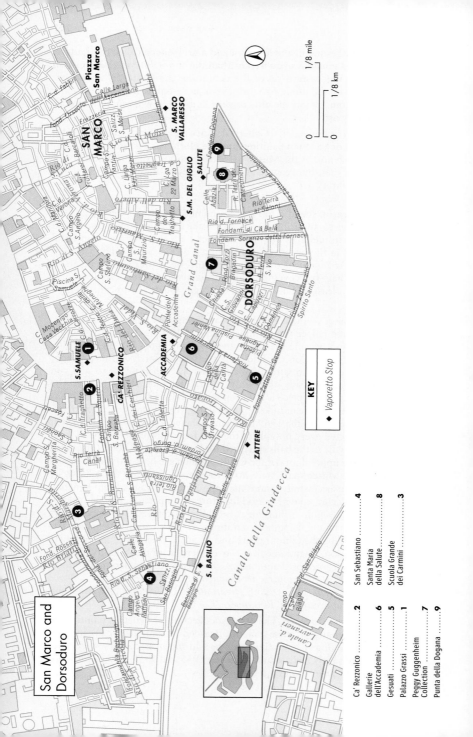

San Marco and Dorsoduro

KEY

♦ Vaporetto Stop

Jacopo Bellini is considered the father of the Venetian Renaissance, and in Room 2 you can compare his *Madonna and Child with Saints* with such later works as *Madonna of the Orange Tree* by Cima da Coneg-liano (circa 1459–1517) and *Ten Thousand Martyrs of Mt. Ararat* by Vittore Carpaccio (circa 1455–1525). Jacopo's more accomplished son Giovanni (circa 1430–1516) attracts your eye not only with his subject matter but also with his rich color. Rooms 4 and 5 have a good selection of his madonnas. Room 5 contains *Tempest* by Giorgione (1477–1510), a revolutionary work that has intrigued viewers and critics for centuries. It is unified not only by physical design elements, as was usual, but more importantly by a mysterious, somewhat threatening atmosphere. In Room 10, *Feast in the House of Levi*, commissioned as a Last Supper, got Veronese summoned to the Inquisition over its depiction of dogs, jesters, and other extraneous figures. Room 10 also houses several of Tintoretto's finest works, including three paintings from the life of Saint Mark. Titian's *Presentation of the Virgin* (Room 24) is the collection's only work originally created for the building in which it hangs. Don't miss Rooms 20 and 21, with views of 15th- and 16th-century Venice by Carpaccio and Gentile Bellini (1429–1507), Giovanni's brother— you'll see how little the city has changed. (Note: The arrangement of the paintings described above may be changed during special exhibitions.)

■TIP→ Booking tickets in advance isn't essential but helps during busy seasons and costs only an additional €1.50. Booking is necessary to see the Quadreria, where additional works cover every inch of a wide hallway. A free map notes art and artists, and the bookshop sells a more informative English-language booklet. In the main galleries a €4 audio guide saves reading but adds little to each room's excellent annotation. ✉ *Dorsoduro 1050, Campo della Carità just off Accademia Bridge* ☎ *041/5222247 for Quadreria reservations, 041/5200345 for reservations* ⊕ *www.gallerieaccademia.org* ✆ *€9, subject to increase for special exhibitions* ☉ *Galleria: Tues.–Sun. 8:15–7:15, Mon. 8:15–2. Quadreria: Fri. 11–1, Sat. 11–noon* Ⓜ *Vaporetto: Accademia.*

QUICK BITES | **Gelateria Nico.** Enjoy the Zattere's most scrumptious treat—Nico's famous *gianduiotto*, a slab of chocolate-hazelnut ice cream floating on a cloud of whipped cream—and relax on the big, welcoming deck. Nico's is one of the few places still serving authentic *artiginale* (homemade) ice cream, seducing Venetians since 1935. ✉ *Dorsoduro 922* ☎ *041/5225293* ⊕ *www. gelaterianico.com.*

FAMILY **Peggy Guggenheim Collection.** Housed in the surprisingly small and charming Palazzo Venier dei Leoni, this choice selection of 20th-century painting and sculpture represents the taste and extraordinary style of the late heiress Peggy Guggenheim. Through wealth and social connec-tions, Guggenheim (1898–1979) became an important art dealer and collector from the 1930s through the 1950s, and her personal collec-tion here includes works by Picasso, Kandinsky, Pollock, Motherwell, and Ernst (at one time her husband). The museum serves beverages, snacks, and light meals in its refreshingly shady, artistically sophisti-cated garden. On Sunday at 3 pm (except in August) the museum offers a free tour and art workshop for children 10 and under; conducted in Italian, anglophone interns are generally on hand to help those who don't *parla italiano.* ⊠ *Fondamenta Venier dei Leoni, Dorsoduro 701* ☎ *041/2405411* ⊕ *www.guggenheim-venice.it* ⊒ *€14* ⊘ *Wed.–Mon. 10–6* Ⓜ *Vaporetto: Accademia.*

Fodor's Choice ★ **Punta della Dogana.** Funded by the billionaire who owns Christie's Auction House, the François Pinault Foundation had Japanese architect Tadao Ando redesign this fabled customs house—sitting at the *punta,* or very head, of the Grand Canal—and now home to a changing roster of eyepopping works from Pinault's collection of contemporary art. The streaming light, polished surfaces, and clean lines of Ando's design contrast beautifully with the brick, massive columns, and sturdy beams of the original Dogana. Even if you are cool to contemporary art, a visit is worthwhile just to see Ando's amazing architectural transformation. Be sure to walk down to the *punta* (point) for a magnificent view of the Venetian basin. Check online for a schedule of temporary exhibitions. ⊠ *Punta della Dogana* ☎ *041/5231680* ⊕ *www.palazzograssi.it* ⊒ *€15 (€20 includes the Palazzo Grassi)* ⊘ *Wed.–Mon. 10–7; last entry 1 hr before closing* Ⓜ *Vaporetto: Salute.*

Fodor's Choice ★ **San Sebastiano.** Paolo Veronese (1528–88), although still in his twenties, was already the official painter of the Republic when he began the oil panels and frescoes at San Sebastiano, his parish church, in 1555. For decades he continued to embellish the church with very beautiful illusionistic scenes. The cycles of panels in San Sebastiano are considered to be his supreme accomplishment. Veronese is buried beneath his bust near the organ. The church itself, remodeled by Antonio Scarpagnino and finished in 1548, offers a rare opportunity to see a monument in Venice where both the architecture and the pictorial decoration all date from the same period. Be sure to check out the portal of the ex-convent, now part of the University of Venice, to the left of the church; it was designed in 1976–78 by Carlo Scarpa, one of the most important Italian architects of the 20th century. ⊠ *Campo San Sebastiano* ☎ *041/2750462* ⊕ *www.chorusvenezia.org* ⊒ *€3 (free with Chorus Pass)* ⊘ *Mon.–Sat. 10–5* Ⓜ *Vaporetto: San Basilio.*

Fodor's Choice ★ **Santa Maria della Salute.** The most iconic landmark of the Grand Canal, La Salute (as this church is commonly called) is most unforgettably viewed from the Riva degli Schiavoni at sunset, or from the Accademia Bridge by moonlight. En route to becoming Venice's most important Baroque architect, 32-year-old Baldassare Longhena won a competition in 1631 to design a shrine honoring the Virgin Mary for saving Venice from a plague that in the space of two years (1629–30) killed 47,000 residents, or one-third of the city's population. It was not completed, however, until 1687—five years after Longhena's death. Outside, this ornate, white Istrian stone octagon is topped by a colossal cupola with snail-like ornamental buttresses—in truth, piers encircled by finely carved "ropes," an allusion to the sail-making industry of the city (or so say today's art historians). Inside, a white-and-gray color scheme is echoed by a polychrome marble floor and the six chapels. The Byzantine icon above the main altar has been venerated as the Madonna della Salute (Madonna of Health) since 1670, when Francesco Morosini brought it here from Crete. Above it is a sculpture showing Venice on her knees before the Madonna as she drives the wretched plague from the city.

Do not leave the church without visiting the **Sacrestia Maggiore,** which contains a dozen works by Titian, including his *San Marco Enthroned with Saints* altarpiece. You'll also see Tintoretto's *The Wedding at Cana.* For the Festa della Salute, held November 21, a votive bridge is constructed across the Grand Canal, and Venetians pilgrimage here to light candles in prayer for another year's health. ✉ *Punta della Dogana* ☎ *041/2411018* 🖙 *Church free, sacristy €2* 🕙 *Daily 9–noon and 3–5:30* Ⓜ *Vaporetto: Salute.*

Campo Santa Margherita. Lined with cafés and restaurants generally filled with students from the nearby university, Campo Santa Margherita also has produce vendors and benches where you can sit and take in the bustling local life of the campo. Also close to the Ca' Rezzonico and the Scuola dei Carmini, and only a 10-minute walk from the Gallerie dell'Accademia, the square is the center of Dorsoduro social life. It takes its name from the church to one side, closed since the early 19th century and now used as an auditorium. On weekend evenings it sometimes sometimes attracts hordes of high school students from the mainland.

Il Caffè. For more than a portable munch, bask in the sunshine at the popular Caffè, commonly called Bar Rosso for its bright red exterior. It dishes up the best *tramezzini* (snack sandwiches) in the campo, is open until midnight, and serves drinks and other light refreshments every day except Sunday. ✉ *Campo Santa Margherita, Dorsoduro 2963* ☎ *041/5287998.*

WORTH NOTING

Gesuati. When the Dominicans took over the church of Santa Maria della Visitazione from the suppressed order of Gesuati laymen in 1668, Giorgio Massari, the last of the great Venetian baroque architects, was commissioned to build this structure between 1726 and 1735. It has an important Gianbattista Tiepolo (1696–1770) illusionistic ceiling and several other of his works, plus those of his contemporaries, Giambattista Piazzetta (1683–1754), and Sebastiano Ricci (1659–1734). ✉ *Zattere* ☎ *041/2750462* ⊕ *www.chorusvenezia.org* 🖙 *€3 (free with Chorus Pass)* 🕙 *Mon.–Sat. 10–5* Ⓜ *Vaporetto: Zattere.*

Scuola Grande dei Carmini. When the order of Santa Maria del Carmelo commissioned Baldassare Longhena to finish the work on the Scuola Grande dei Carmini in the 1670s, their brotherhood of 75,000 members was the largest in Venice and one of the wealthiest. Little expense was spared in the decorating of stuccoed ceilings and carved ebony paneling, and the artwork was choice, even before 1739, when Gianbattista Tiepolo began painting the **Sala Capitolare.** In what many consider his best work, Tiepolo's nine great canvases vividly transform some rather conventional religious themes into dynamic displays of color and

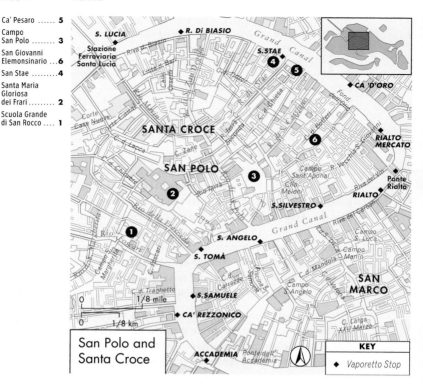

San Polo and
Santa Croce

movement. ✉ *Campo dei Carmini, Dorsoduro 2617* ☎ *041/5289420*
💶 *€5* ⊙ *Daily 11–5* Ⓜ *Vaporetto: Ca' Rezzonico.*

SAN POLO AND SANTA CROCE

The two smallest of Venice's six sestieri, San Polo and Santa Croce, were
named after their main churches, though the Chiesa di Santa Croce
was demolished in 1810. The city's most famous bridge, the Ponte di
Rialto, unites San Marco (east) with San Polo (west). The Rialto takes
its name from Rivoaltus, the high ground on which it was built. Shops
abound in the area surrounding the Ponte di Rialto. On the San Marco
side you'll find fashions, on the San Polo side, food.

TIMING

To do the area justice requires at least half a day. If you want to take
part in the food shopping, come early to beat the crowds. Campo San
Giacomo dell'Orio, west of the main thoroughfare that takes you from
the Ponte di Rialto to Santa Maria Gloriosa dei Frari, is a peaceful place
for a drink and a rest. The museums of Ca' Pesaro are a time commitment—you'll want at least two hours to see them both.

TOP ATTRACTIONS

Fodor's Choice
★
Santa Maria Gloriosa dei Frari. Completed in 1442, this immense Gothic church of russet-color brick—known locally as *I Frari*—is famous worldwide for its array of spectacular Venetian paintings. Visit the sacristy first, to see Giovanni Bellini's 1488 triptych *Madonna and Child with Saints* in all its mellow luminosity, painted for precisely this spot. The Corner Chapel on the other side of the chancel is graced by Bartolomeo Vivarini's (1415–84) 1474 altarpiece *St. Mark Enthroned and Saints John the Baptist, Jerome, Peter, and Nicholas,* which is much more conservative, displaying attention to detail generally associated with late medieval painting. In the first south chapel of the chorus, there is a fine sculpture of Saint John the Baptist by Donatello, dated 1438 (perhaps created before the artist came to Venice), which displays a psychological intensity rare for early Renaissance sculpture. You can see the rapid development of Venetian Renaissance painting by contrasting Bellini with the heroic energy of Titian's *Assumption,* over the main altar, painted only 30 years later. Unveiled in 1518, it was the artist's first public commission and, after causing a bit of controversy, did much to establish his reputation.

Titian's beautiful *Madonna di Ca' Pesaro* is in the left aisle. The painting took seven years to complete (finished in 1526), and in it Titian disregarded the conventions of his time by moving the Virgin out of center and making the saints active participants. The composition, built on diagonals, anticipates structural principals of baroque painting in the following century. ⊠ *Campo dei Frari, San Polo* ☏ *041/2728618, 041/2750462 for Chorus Foundation* ⊕ *www.chorusvenezia.org* ⌨ *€3 (free with Chorus Pass)* ⊘ *Mon.–Sat. 9–6, Sun. 1–6* Ⓜ *Vaporetto: San Tomà.*

Fodor's Choice
★
Scuola Grande di San Rocco. Saint Rocco's popularity stemmed from his miraculous recovery from the plague and his care for fellow sufferers. Throughout the plague-filled Middle Ages, followers and donations abounded, and this elegant example of Venetian Renaissance architecture, built between 1517 and 1560—including the work of at least four architects—for the essentially secular charitable confraternity bearing the saint's name, was the result. Although San Rocco is bold and dramatic outside, its contents are even more stunning: a series of more than 60 paintings by Tintoretto. In 1564 Tintoretto edged out competition for a commission to decorate a ceiling by submitting not a sketch, but a finished work, which he moreover offered free of charge. *Moses Striking Water from the Rock, The Brazen Serpent,* and *The Fall of Manna* represent three afflictions—thirst, disease, and hunger—that San Rocco and later his brotherhood sought to relieve. ⊠ *Campo San Rocco, San Polo 3052* ☏ *041/5234864* ⊕ *www.scuolagrandesanrocco.it* ⌨ *€10, includes audio guide* ⊘ *Daily 9:30–5:30; last entry ½ hr before closing* Ⓜ *Vaporetto: San Tomà.*

QUICK BITES

Caffè dei Frari. Just over the bridge in front of the Frari church is this old-fashioned place where you'll find an assortment of sandwiches and snacks, but it is the atmosphere, and not the food, that is the main attraction. Established in 1870, it's one of the last Venetian tearooms with its original décor. It's frequented more by residents and students than by tourists. Prices are a bit higher (€3.50 for a spritz) than in cafés in nearby Campo Santa Margherita, but the décor and the friendly "retro" atmosphere seem to make the added cost worthwhile. ✉ *Fondamenta dei Frari, San Polo 2564* ☎ *No phone* ⊙ *Open Sun. and Mon. 9–4, Tues.–Sat. 9 am–10 pm.*

Pasticceria Tonolo. Venice's premier confectionary has been in operation since 1886. During Carnevale it's still one of the best places in town for *fritelle*, fried doughnuts (traditional raisin, or cream-filled), and before Christmas and Easter, Venetians order their *focaccia*, a traditional raised cake eaten especially at holidays, from here well in advance. Closed Monday; no seating any time. ✉ *Calle Crosera, Dorsoduro 3764* ☎ *041/5237209.*

WORTH NOTING

Ca' Pesaro. Baldassare Longhena's grand Baroque palace, begun in 1676, is the beautifully restored home of two impressive collections. The **Galleria Internazionale d'Arte Moderna** has works by 19th- and 20th-century artists such as Klimt, Kandinsky, Matisse, and Miró. It also has a collection of representative works from Venice's Biennale art show that amounts to a panorama of 20th-century art. The pride of the **Museo Orientale** is its collection of Japanese art, and especially armor and weapons, of the Edo period (1603–1868). It also has a small but striking collection of Chinese and Indonesian porcelains and musical instruments. ✉ *San Stae, Santa Croce 2076* ☎ *041/721127 for Galleria, 041/5241173 for Museo Orientale* ⊕ *www.museicivicivenezianiit* 🎫 *€10, includes both museums (free with MUVE Pass)* ⊙ *Apr.–Oct., Tues.–Sun. 10–6; Nov.–Mar., Tues.–Sun. 10–5* Ⓜ *Vaporetto: San Stae.*

Campo San Polo. Campo San Polo once hosted bull races, fairs, military parades, and packed markets, and now comes especially alive on summer nights, when it's home to the city's outdoor cinema. The **Chiesa di San Polo** has been restored so many times that little remains of the original 9th-century church, and sadly, 19th-century alterations were so costly that the friars sold off many great paintings to pay bills. Though Gianbattista Tiepolo is represented here, his work is outdone by 16 paintings of his son Giandomenico (1727–1804), including the *Stations of the Cross* in the oratory to the left of the entrance. The younger Tiepolo also created a series of expressive and theatrical renderings of the saints. Look for altarpieces by Tintoretto and Veronese that managed to escape auction. San Polo's bell tower (begun 1362) remained unchanged through the centuries—don't miss the two lions playing with a disembodied human head and a serpent that guard it. Tradition has it that the head refers to that of Martin Falier, the Doge executed for treason in 1355. ✉ *Campo San Polo* ☎ *041/2750462 for Chorus Foundation* ⊕ *www.chorusvenezia.org* 🎫 *€3 (free with Chorus Pass)* ⊙ *Church Mon.–Sat. 10–5* Ⓜ *Vaporetto: San Silvestro, San Tomà.*

San Giovanni Elemosinario. Storefronts make up the facade, and the altars were built by market guilds—poulterers, messengers, and fodder merchants—at this church intimately bound to the Rialto Market. The original church was completely destroyed by a fire in 1514 and rebuilt in

1531 by Antonio Abbondi, who had also worked on the Scuola di San Rocco. During a recent restoration, workers stumbled upon a frescoed cupola by Pordenone (1484–1539) that had been painted over centuries earlier. Don't miss Titian's *St. John the Almsgiver* and Pordenone's *Sts. Catherine, Sebastian, and Roch,* which in 2002 were returned after 30 years by the Gallerie dell'Accademia. ⊠ *Rialto Ruga Vecchia San Giovanni, Santa Croce* 🕾 *041/2750462 for Chorus Foundation* 🌐 *www. chorusvenezia.org* 📧 *€3 (free with Chorus Pass)* 🕗 *Mon.–Sat. 10–5* Ⓜ *Vaporetto: San Silvestro, Rialto.*

San Stae. The church of San Stae—the Venetian name for San Eustacchio (Eustace)—was reconstructed in 1687 by Giovanni Grassi and given a new facade in 1707 by Domenico Rossi. Renowned Venetian painters and sculptors of the early 18th century decorated this church around 1717 with the legacy left by Doge Alvise Mocenigo II, who's buried in the center aisle. San Stae affords a good opportunity to see the early works of Gianbattista Tiepolo, Sebastiano Ricci, and Piazzetta, as well as those of the previous generation of Venetian painters, which whom they had studied. ⊠ *Campo San Stae, Santa Croce* 🕾 *041/2750462 for Chorus Foundation* 🌐 *www.chorusvenezia.org* 📧 *€3 (free with Chorus Pass)* 🕗 *Mon.–Sat. 9–5* Ⓜ *Vaporetto: San Stae.*

CANNAREGIO

Seen from above, this part of town seems like a wide field plowed by several long, straight canals that are linked by intersecting straight streets—not typical of Venice, where the shape of the islands usually defines the shape of the canals. Cannaregio's main thoroughfare, the Strada Nova (literally, "New Street," as it was converted from a canal in 1871), is the longest street in Venice; it runs parallel to the Grand Canal. Today the Strada Nova serves as a pedestrian walkway from the train station almost to the Rialto. Cannaregio, first settled in the XIV century, is one of the more "modern" of Venice's neighborhoods, with walkways, or *fondamente,* along its major canals north of the Strada Nova, making it ideal for canalside strolls where you can view some spectacular gothic and Baroque facades.

TOP ATTRACTIONS

Fodor's Choice ★

Ca' d'Oro. One of the postcard sights of Venice, this exquisite Venetian Gothic palace was once literally a "Golden House," when its marble traceries and ornaments were embellished with gold. It was created by Giovanni and Bartolomeo Bon between 1428 and 1430 for the patrician Marino Contarini, who had read about the Roman emperor Nero's golden house in Rome, and wished to imitate it as a present to his wife. Her family owned the land and the Byzantine *fondaco* (palace–trading house) previously standing on it; you can still see the round Byzantine arches on the entry porch incorporated into the Gothic building. The last proprietor, Baron Giorgio Franchetti, left Ca' d'Oro to the city, after having had it carefully restored and furnished with the antiquities, sculptures, and paintings that today make up the **Galleria Franchetti.** Besides Andrea Mantegna's *St. Sebastian* and other Venetian works, the Galleria Franchetti contains the type of fresco that once adorned the

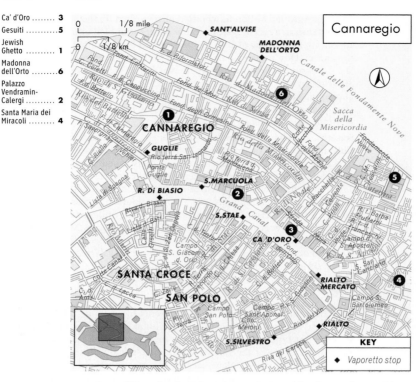

exteriors of Venetian buildings (commissioned by those who could not afford a marble facade). One such detached fresco displayed here was made by the young Titian for the facade of the Fondaco dei Tedeschi near the Rialto. ⊠ *Calle Ca' d'Oro, Cannaregio 3933* ☎ *041/5238790* ⊕ *www.cadoro.org* ⊒ *€6, plus €1.50 reservation fee; €9.50 when there is a special exhibition (free 1st Sun. of the month)* ⊗ *Tues.–Sun. 8:15– 7:15, Mon. 8:15–2* Ⓜ *Vaporetto: Ca' d'Oro.*

Fodor'sChoice   **Jewish Ghetto.** The neighborhood that gave the world the word "ghetto"
★   is today a quiet neighborhood surrounding a large campo. It is home to Jewish institutions, two kosher restaurants, a rabbinical school, and five synagogues. Present-day Venetian Jews live all over the city, and the contemporary Jewish life of the ghetto, with the exception of the Jewish museum and the synagogues, is an enterprise conducted almost exclusively by American Hassidic Jews of Eastern European descent and tradition.

Though Jews may have arrived earlier, the first synagogues weren't built and a cemetery (on the Lido) wasn't founded until the Askenazim, or Northern European Jews, came in the late 1300s. Dwindling coffers may have prompted the Republic to sell temporary visas to Jews, who were over the centuries alternately tolerated and expelled. The Rialto commercial district, as mentioned in Shakespeare's *The Merchant of*

Venice, depended on Jewish moneylenders for trade, and to help cover ever-increasing war expenses.

In 1516 relentless local opposition forced the Senate to confine Jews to an island in Cannaregio, then on the outer reaches of the city, named for its *geto* (foundry). The term "ghetto" also may come from the Hebrew *ghet,* meaning separation or divorce. Gates at the entrance were locked at night, and boats patrolled the surrounding canals. Jews were allowed only to lend money at low interest, operate pawnshops controlled by the government, trade in textiles, or practice medicine. Jewish doctors were highly respected and could leave the ghetto at any hour when on duty. Though ostracized, Jews were nonetheless safe in Venice, and in the 16th century the community grew considerably—primarily with refugees from the Inquisition, which persecuted Jews in southern and central Italy, Spain, and Portugal. The ghetto was allowed to expand twice, but it still had the city's densest population and consequently ended up with the city's tallest buildings. Although the gates were pulled down after Napoleon's 1797 arrival, the ghetto was reinstated during the Austrian occupation. The Jews realized full freedom only in 1866 with the founding of the Italian state. Many Jews fled Italy as a result of Mussolini's 1938 racial laws, so that on the eve of World War II, there were about 1,500 Jews left in the ghetto. Jews continued to flee, and the remaining 247 were deported by the Nazis—only eight returned.

The area has Europe's highest density of Renaissance-era synagogues, and visiting them is interesting both culturally and aesthetically. Though each is marked by the tastes of its individual builders, Venetian influence is evident throughout. Women's galleries resemble those of theaters from the same era, and some synagogues were decorated by artists who were simultaneously active in local churches; Longhena, the architect of Santa Maria della Salute, renovated the Spanish synagogue in 1635. ⊠ *Campo del Ghetto Nuovo* ⌇ *€8.50 Synagogue tour (arranged through Jewish Museum in Campo del Ghetto Nuovo), museum €4; combination ticket €10* ⊘ *Synagogue tours (in English or Italian): June–Sept., Sun.–Fri., hourly 10:30–5:30; Oct.–May, Sun.–Fri., hourly 10:30–4:30.*

Museo Ebraico. The small but well-arranged museum highlights centuries of Venetian Jewish culture with splendid silver Hanukkah lamps and Torahs, and handwritten, beautifully decorated wedding contracts in Hebrew. Hourly tours in Italian and English (on the half hour) of the ghetto and its five synagogues leave from the museum. ⊠ *Campo del Ghetto Nuovo, Cannaregio 2902/B* ☎ *041/715359* ⊕ *www.museoebraico.it* ⌇ *Museum €3, guided tour and museum €8.50* ⊘ *June–Sept., Sun.–Fri. 10–7; Oct.–May, Sun.–Fri. 10–6. Tours hourly starting at 10:30* Ⓜ *Vaporetto: San Marcuola, Guglie*

Fodor'sChoice ★ **Madonna dell'Orto.** Though built toward the middle of the 14th century, this church is characterized by its beautiful late-Gothic facade, added between 1460 and 1464; it's one of the most beautiful Gothic churches in Venice. Tintoretto lived nearby, and this, his parish church, contains some of his most powerful work. Lining the chancel are two huge (45 feet by 20 feet) canvases, *Adoration of the Golden Calf* and *Last*

Judgment. In glowing contrast to this awesome spectacle is Tintoretto's *Presentation of the Virgin at the Temple* and the simple chapel where he and his children, Marietta and Domenico, are buried. Paintings by Domenico, Cima da Conegliano, Palma il Giovane, Palma il Vecchio, and Titian also hang in the church. A chapel displays a photographic reproduction of a precious *Madonna with Child* by Giovanni Bellini. The original was stolen one night in 1993. ■ TIP→ **Don't miss the beautifully austere late-Gothic cloister (1460), which you enter through the small door to the right of the church; it is frequently used for exhibitions but may be open at other times as well.** ✉ *Campo della Madonna dell'Orto, Cannaregio* ☎ *041/2750462 for Chorus Foundation* ⊕ *www. chorusvenezia.org* 🎫 *€3 (free with Chorus Pass)* ⊙ *Mon.–Sat. 10–5* Ⓜ *Vaporetto: Orto.*

Fodor'sChoice ★ **Santa Maria dei Miracoli.** Tiny yet harmoniously proportioned, this Renaissance gem, built between 1481 and 1489, is sheathed in marble and decorated inside with exquisite marble reliefs. Architect Pietro Lombardo (circa 1435–1515) miraculously compressed the building into its confined space, then created the illusion of greater size by varying the color of the exterior, adding extra pilasters on the building's canal side, and offsetting the arcade windows to make the arches appear deeper. The church was built to house *I Miracoli,* an image of the Virgin Mary by Niccolò di Pietro (1394–1440) that is said to have performed miracles—look for it on the high altar. ✉ *Campo Santa Maria Nova, Cannaregio* ☎ *041/2750462 for Chorus Foundation* ⊕ *www. chorusvenezia.org* 🎫 *€3 (free with Chorus Pass)* ⊙ *Mon.–Sat. 10–5* Ⓜ *Vaporetto: Rialto.*

WORTH NOTING

Gesuiti. The interior walls of this early-18th-century church (1715–30) resemble brocade drapery, and only touching them will convince skeptics that rather than embroidered cloth, the green-and-white walls are inlaid marble. This trompe-l'oeil décor is typical of the late Baroque's fascination with optical illusion. Toward the end of his life, Titian tended to paint scenes of suffering and sorrow in a nocturnal ambience. A dramatic example of this is on display above the first altar to the left: Titian's daring *Martyrdom of St. Lawrence* (1578), taken from an earlier church that stood on this site. ✉ *Campo dei Gesuiti, Cannaregio* ☎ *041/5286579* ⊙ *Apr.–Oct, Thurs., Fri., and Sat. 10–noon* Ⓜ *Vaporetto: Fondamente Nove.*

Palazzo Vendramin-Calergi. Hallowed as the place of Richard Wagner's death, and today's Venice's most glamorous casino, this magnficent edifice found its fame centuries before: Venetian star architect Mauro Codussi (1440–1504) essentially invented Venetian Renaissance architecture with this design. Built for the Loredan family around 1500, Codussi's palace married the fortresslike design of the Florentine Alberti's Palazzo Ruccelai with the lightness and delicacy of Venetian Gothic. Note how Codussi beautifully exploits the flickering light of Venetian waterways to play across the building's facade and to pour in through the generous windows.

Venice has always prized the beauty of this palace. In 1652 its owners were convicted of a rather gruesome murder, and the punishment would have involved, as was customary, the demolition of their palace. The murderers were banned from the Republic, but the palace, in view of its beauty and historical importance, was spared. Only the newly added wing was torn down. ✉ *Cannaregio 2040* ☎ *041/5297111, 338/4164174 for Sala di Wagner tours* ⊕ *www.casinovenezia.it* 💳 *Casinò €10, Sala di Wagner tour €5 suggested donation* ☺ *Casinò: Sun.–Thurs. 3:30 pm–2:30 am, Fri. and Sat. 3:30 pm–3 am; slot machines daily from 3 pm. Opens 30 mins later in summer. Sala di Wagner tours Tues. and Sat. at 10:30, Thurs. at 2:30 (call by noon the day before to reserve)* Ⓜ *Vaporetto: San Marcuola.*

CASTELLO

Castello, Venice's largest sestiere, includes all of the land from east of Piazza San Marco to the city's easternmost tip. Its name probably comes from a fortress that once stood on one of the eastern islands. Not every well-off Venetian family could find a spot or afford to build a palazzo on the Grand Canal. Many who couldn't instead settled in western Castello, taking advantage of its proximity to the Rialto and San Marco, and built the noble palazzos that today distinguish this area from the fishermen's enclave in the more easterly streets of the sestiere. During the days of the Republic, eastern Castello was the primary neighborhood for workers in the shipbuilding Arsenale, which is located in its midst.

TOP ATTRACTIONS

Arsenale. Visible from the street, the impressive Renaissance gateway, the **Porta Magna** (1460), was the first classical structure to be built in Venice. It is guarded by four lions—war booty of Francesco Morosini, who took the Peloponnese from the Turks in 1687. The interior is not regularly open to the public, since it belongs to the Italian Navy, but it opens for the Biennale and for Venice's festival of traditional boats, **Mare Maggio** (⊕ *www.maremaggio.it*), held every May. If you're here during those times, don't miss the chance for a look inside; you can enter from the back via a northern-side walkway leading from the Ospedale vaporetto stop.

The Arsenale is said to have been founded in 1104 on twin islands. The immense facility that evolved—it was the largest industrial complex in Europe built prior to the Industrial Revolution—was given the old Venetian dialect name *arzanà*, borrowed from the Arabic *darsina'a*, meaning "workshop." At the height of its activity, in the early 16th century, it employed as many as 16,000 *arsenalotti*, workers who were among the most respected shipbuilders in the world. The Arsenale's efficiency was confirmed time and again—whether building 100 ships in 60 days to battle the Turks in Cyprus (1597) or completing one perfectly armed warship, start to finish, while King Henry III of France attended a banquet. ✉ *Campo dell'Arsenale, Castello* Ⓜ *Vaporetto: Arsenale.*

FodorsChoice ★ **Santi Giovanni e Paolo.** A venerated jewel, this gorgeous church looms over one of the most picturesque squares in Venice: the Campo

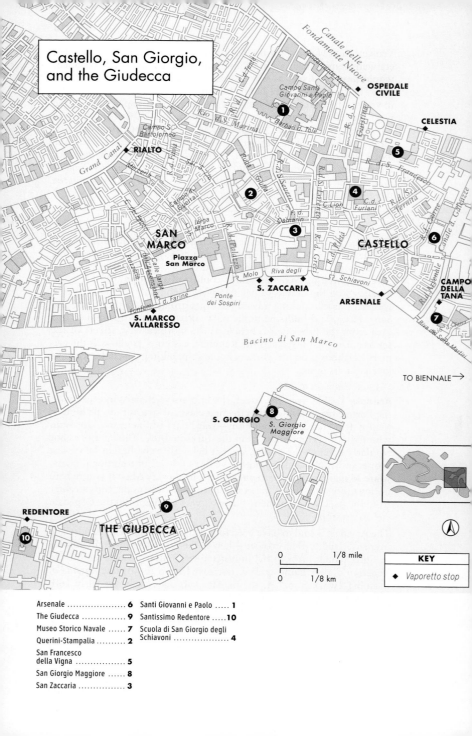

Castello, San Giorgio, and the Giudecca

TO BIENNALE →

0   1/8 mile

0   1/8 km

KEY

◆ *Vaporetto stop*

Giovanni e Paolo, centered on the magnificent 15th-century equestrian statue of Bartolomeo Colleoni by the Florentine Andrea Verrocchio. Also note the beautiful facade of the Scuola Grande di San Marco (now the municipal hospital), begun by Pietro Lombardo and completed after the turn of the 16th century by Mauro Codussi. The massive Italian Gothic church itself is of the Dominican order and was consecrated in 1430. Bartolomeo Bon's portal, combining Gothic and classical elements, was added between 1458 and 1462, using columns salvaged from Torcello. The 15th-century stained-glass window near the side entrance is breathtaking for its brilliant colors and beautiful figures; it was made in Murano from drawings by Bartolomeo Vivarini and Gerolamo Mocetto (circa 1458–1531). The second official church of the Republic after San Marco, San Zanipolo is the Venetian equivalent of London's Westminster Abbey, with a great number of important people, including 25 doges, buried here. Artistic highlights include an early (1465) polyptych by Giovanni Bellini (right aisle, second altar), where the influence of Mantegna is still very evident, Alvise Vivarini's *Christ Carrying the Cross* (sacristy), and Lorenzo Lotto's *Charity of St. Antonino* (right transept). Don't miss the *Cappella del Rosario* (Rosary Chapel), off the left transept, built in the 16th century to commemorate the 1571 victory of Lepanto, in western Greece, when Venice led a combined European fleet to defeat the Turkish Navy. However quick your visit, don't miss the Pietro Mocenigo tomb to the right of the main entrance, by Pietro Lombardo and his sons. Note also Tullio Lombardo's tomb of Andrea Vendramin, the original home of Tullio's Adam, which has been restored in New York City's Metropolitan Museum. ✉ *Campo dei Santi Giovanni e Paolo, Castello* ☎ *041/5235913* 💶*€3* 🕐 *Mon.–Sat. 9:30–6, Sun. 1–6* Ⓜ *Vaporetto: Fondamente Nove, Rialto.*

Didovich Pastry Shop. To satisfy your sweet tooth, head for Campo Santa Marina and the family-owned and -operated shop. It's a local favorite, especially for Carnevale-time *fritelle* (fried doughnuts). There is limited seating inside, but in the warmer months you can sit outside. ✉ *Campo Santa Marina, Castello 5909* ☎ *041/5230017* 🕐 *Closed Sun.*

WORTH NOTING

FAMILY **Museo Storico Navale** (*Museum of Naval History*). The boat collection here includes scale models such as the doges' ceremonial *Bucintoro,* and full-size boats such as Peggy Guggenheim's private gondola, complete with romantic *felze* (cabin). There's a range of old galley and military pieces, and also a large collection of seashells. A visit to the **Padiglione delle Navi,** a part of the museum, allows you to see a portion of the interior of the Arsenale otherwise closed to visitors. ✉ *Campo San Biagio, Castello 2148* ☎ *041/2441399* 💶*€5* 🕐 *Mon.–Thurs. 8:45–1:30, Fri. and Sat. 8:45–5:30 (until 5 in winter), Sun. and holidays, 10–5. Visits to Padiglione delle Navi (Pavilion of the Ship) in Arsenale Sat. at 2:30 and 4, Sun. at 11, 12:30, 2:30, and 4* Ⓜ *Vaporetto: Arsenale.*

Querini-Stampalia. A connoisseur's delight, this art collection at this late-16th-century palace includes Giovanni Bellini's *Presentation in the Temple* and Sebastiano Ricci's triptych *Dawn, Afternoon, and Evening.*

Portraits of newlyweds Francesco Querini and Paola Priuli were left unfinished on the death of Giacomo Palma il Vecchio (1480–1528)—note the groom's hand and the bride's dress. Original 18th-century furniture and stuccowork are a fitting background for Pietro Longhi's portraits. Nearly 70 works by Gabriele Bella (1730–99) capture scenes of Venetian street life. Downstairs is a café. The entrance hall and the beautiful rear garden were designed by famous Venetian architect Carlo Scarpa during the 1950s. ⊠ *Campo Santa Maria Formosa, Castello 5252* ☎ *041/2711411* ⊕ *www.querinistampalia.org* ⌸ *€10* ⊙ *Tues.– Sun. 10–6* Ⓜ *Vaporetto: San Zaccaria.*

San Francesco della Vigna. Although this church contains some interesting and beautiful paintings and sculptures, it's the architecture that makes it worth the hike through a lively, middle-class, residential neighborhood. The Franciscan church was enlarged and rebuilt by Jacopo Sansovino in 1534, giving it the first Renaissance interior in Venice; its proportions are said to reflect the mystic significance of the numbers three and seven dictated by Renaissance neo-Platonic numerology. The soaring, but harmonious facade was added in 1562 by Palladio. The church represents, therefore, a unique combination of the work of the two great stars of Veneto 16th-century architecture. As you enter, a late Giovanni Bellini *Madonna with Saints* is down some steps to the left, inside the Cappella Santa. In the Giustinian chapel to the left is Veronese's first work in Venice, an altarpiece depicting the Virgin and child with saints. In another, larger chapel, on the left, are bas-reliefs by Pietro and his son Tullio Lombardo. ⊠ *Campo di San Francesco della Vigna, Castello* ☎ *041/5206102* ⌸ *Free* ⊙ *Daily 8–12:30 and 3–7* Ⓜ *Vaporetto: Celestia.*

San Zaccaria. Practically more a museum than a church, San Zaccaria has a striking Renaissance facade, with central and upper portions representing some of Mauro Codussi's best work. Most of the church was 14th-century Gothic, with its facade completed in 1515 (some years after Codussi's death in 1504), and it retains the proportions of the rest of the essentially Gothic structure. Inside is one of the great treasures of Venice, Giovanni Bellini's celebrated altarpiece, *La Sacra Conversazione,* easily recognizable in the left nave. Completed in 1505, when the artist was 75, it shows Bellini's ability to incorporate the esthetics of the High Renaissance into his work. The three outstanding Gothic polyptychs attributed to Antonio Vivarini earned it the nickname "the Golden Chapel." ⊠ *Campo San Zaccaria, Castello 4693* ☎ *041/5221257* ⌸ *Church free, chapels and crypt €1* ⊙ *Mon.–Sat. 10– noon, Sun. 4–6* Ⓜ *Vaporetto: San Zaccaria.*

Scuola di San Giorgio degli Schiavoni. Founded in 1451 by the Dalmatian community, this small scuola was—and still is—a social and cultural center for migrants from what is now Croatia. It contains one of Italy's most beautiful rooms, harmoniously decorated between 1502 and 1507 by Vittore Carpaccio. While Carpaccio generally painted legendary and religious figures against backgrounds of contemporary Venetian architecture, here is perhaps one of the first instances of "Orientalism" in western painting. In this scuola for immigrants, Carpaccio focuses on "foreign" saints especially venerated in Dalmatia: Sts. George,

Tryphone, and Jerome. He combined keen empirical observation with fantasy, a sense of warm color, and late medieval realism. (Look for the priests fleeing Saint Jerome's lion, or the body parts in the dragon's lair.) ■ TIP→ **Opening hours are quite flexible. Since this is a "must see" site, check to confirm, so you won't be disappointed.** ⊠ *Calle dei Furlani, Castello 3259/A* ☎ *041/5228828* 🎫 *€3* ☉ *Tues.–Sun. 9–noon and 3–6* Ⓜ *Vaporetto: Arsenale, San Zaccaria.*

SAN GIORGIO MAGGIORE AND THE GIUDECCA

3

Beckoning travelers across Saint Mark's Basin is the island of San Giorgio Maggiore, separated by a small channel from the Giudecca. A tall brick campanile on that distant bank nicely complements the Campanile of San Marco. Beneath it looms the stately dome of one of Venice's greatest churches, San Giorgio Maggiore, the creation of Andrea Palladio. To the west, on the Giudecca, is Palladio's other masterpiece, the Church of the Santissimo Redentore.

You can reach San Giorgio Maggiore via Vaporetto Line 2 from San Zaccaria. The next three stops on the line take you to the Giudecca. The island's past may be shrouded in mystery, but despite recent gentrification by artists and well-to-do bohemians, it's still down to earth and one of the city's few remaining primarily working-class neighborhoods. Interestingly, you find that most Venetians don't even consider the Giudecchini Venetians at all.

TIMING

A half day should be plenty of time to visit the area. Allow about a half hour to see each of the churches and an hour or two to look around the Giudecca.

TOP ATTRACTIONS

Fodor'sChoice
★
San Giorgio Maggiore. There's been a church on this island since the 8th century, with a Benedictine monastery added in the 10th century. Today's refreshingly airy and simply decorated church of brick and white marble was begun in 1566 by Palladio and displays his architectural hallmarks of mathematical harmony and classical influence. *The Last Supper* and the *Gathering of Manna,* two of Tintoretto's later works, line the chancel. To the right of the entrance hangs *The Adoration of the Shepherds* by Jacopo Bassano (1517–92); his affection for his home in the foothills, Bassano del Grappa, is evident in the bucolic subjects and terra-firma colors he chose. The monks are happy to show Carpaccio's *St. George and the Dragon,* hanging in a private room, if they have time. The campanile dates from 1791, the previous structures having collapsed twice.

Adjacent to the church is the complex now housing the **Cini Foundation**, containing a very beautiful cloister designed by Palladio in 1560, his refectory, and a library designed by Longhena. Guided tours are given on weekends (10–4), reservations not required. ⊠ *Isola di San Giorgio Maggiore* ☎ *041/5227827* 🎫 *Church free, campanile €3* ☉ *Mon.–Sat. 9:30–12:30 and 2–6, Sun. 2–6 (hrs tend to be flexible)* Ⓜ *Vaporetto: San Giorgio.*

Santissimo Redentore. After a plague in 1576 claimed some 50,000 people—nearly one-third of the city's population (including Titian)—Andrea Palladio was asked to design a commemorative church. Giudecca's Capuchin friars offered their land and services, provided the building was in keeping with the simplicity of their hermitage. Consecrated in 1592, after Palladio's death, the Redentore (considered Palladio's supreme achievement in ecclesiastical design) is dominated by a dome and a pair of slim, almost minaretlike bell towers. Its deceptively simple, stately facade leads to a bright, airy interior. There aren't any paintings or sculptures of note, but the harmony and elegance of the interior makes a visit worthwhile.

For hundreds of years, on the third weekend in July the doge would make a pilgrimage here to give thanks to the Redeemer for ending the 16th-century plague. The event has become the Festa del Redentore, a favorite Venetian festival featuring boats, fireworks, and outdoor feasting. It's the one time of year you can walk to Giudecca—across a temporary pontoon bridge connecting Redentore with the Zattere. ⊠ *Fondamenta San Giacomo* ☎ *041/5231415, 041/2750462 for Chorus Foundation* 🎫 *€3 (free with Chorus Pass)* ☉ *Mon.–Sat. 10–5* Ⓜ *Vaporetto: Redentore.*

ISLANDS OF THE LAGOON

The perfect vacation from your Venetian vacation is an escape to Murano, Burano, and sleepy Torcello, the islands of the northern lagoon. Torcello is legendary for its beauty and offers ancient mosaics, greenery, breathing space, and picnic opportunities (remember to pack lunch). Burano is an island of fishing traditions and houses painted in a riot of colors—blue, yellow, pink, ocher, and dark red. Visitors still love to shop here for "Venetian" lace, even though the vast majority of it is machine-made in Asia; visit the island's Museo del Merletto (Lace Museum) to discover the undeniable difference between the two.

Murano is renowned for its glass, plenty of which you can find in Venice itself. It's also notorious for high-pressure sales on factory tours, even those organized by top hotels. Vaporetto connections to Murano aren't difficult, and for the price of a boat ticket (included in any vaporetto pass) you'll buy your freedom and more time to explore. The Murano "guides" herding new arrivals follow a rotation so that factories take turns giving tours, but you can avoid the hustle by just walking away. ■ TIP→ **Don't take a "free" taxi to Murano: it only means that should you choose to buy (and you'll be strongly encouraged), your taxi fare and commission will be included in the price you pay.**

San Michele, a vaporetto stop on the way to Murano, is the cemetery island of Venice, the resting place of many international artists who have chosen to spend eternity in this beautiful city. It also hosts Venice's first church to exhibit features of Renaissance architecture.

The Lido is Venice's barrier island, forming the southern border of the Venetian Lagoon and protecting Venice from the waters of the Adriatic. It forms the beach of Venice, and is home to a series of bathing establishments both public and private—some luxurious and elegant,

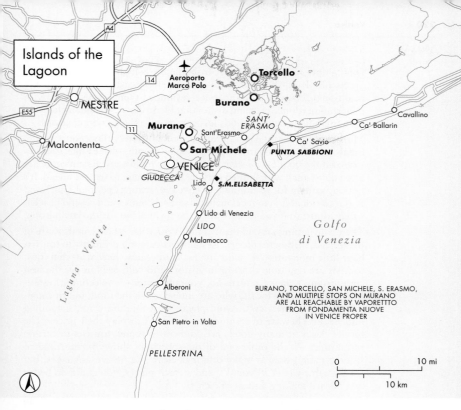

Islands of the
Lagoon

A4

14 Aeroporto
Marco Polo

Torcello

MESTRE

E55

Burano

SANT'
ERASMO

Cavallino

Murano

11

Sant'Erasmo

Ca' Ballarin

Malcontenta

San Michele

Ca' Savio
PUNTA SABBIONI

VENICE

GIUDECCA

Lido

S.M.ELISABETTA

Golfo
di Venezia

Lido di Venezia

LIDO

Malamocco

Alberoni

BURANO, TORCELLO, SAN MICHELE, S. ERASMO,
AND MULTIPLE STOPS ON MURANO
ARE ALL REACHABLE BY VAPORETTTO
FROM FONDAMENTA NUOVE
IN VENICE PROPER

San Pietro in Volta

Laguna Veneta

PELLESTRINA

0   10 mi
0   10 km

some quite simple and catering to Venetian families and their children.
Buses run the length of the island.

TIMING

Hitting all the sights on all the islands takes a busy, full day. If you limit
yourself to Murano and San Michele, you can easily explore for an
ample half day; the same goes for Burano and Torcello. In summer the
express Vaporetto Line 7 will take you to Murano from San Zaccaria
(the Jolanda landing) in 25 minutes; Line 3 will take you from Piazzale
Roma to Murano via the Canale di Cannaregio in 21 minutes; otherwise, local Line 4.1 makes a 45-minute trip from San Zaccaria every 20
minutes, circling the east end of Venice, stopping at Fondamente Nove
and San Michele island cemetery on the way. To see glassblowing, get
off at Colonna; the Museo stop will put you near the Museo del Vetro.

Line 12 goes from Fondamente Nove direct to Murano and Burano
every 30 minutes (Torcello is a five-minute ferry ride—Line 9—from
there); the full trip takes 45 minutes each way. To get to Burano and
Torcello from Murano, pick up Line 12 at the Faro stop (Murano's
lighthouse).

WHERE TO EAT

Dining options in Venice range from the ultra–high end, where jackets are required and shorts are a no-go, to the very casual. Once staunchly traditional, many restaurants have revamped their menus along with their dining rooms, creating dishes that blend classic Venetian elements with ingredients and methods less common to the lagoon environs.

Mid- and upper-range restaurants are often more willing to make the break, offering innovative options while keeping dishes like *sarde in saor* and *fegato alla veneziana* available as mainstays. Restaurants are often quite small with limited seating, so make sure to reserve ahead. It's not uncommon for restaurants to have two seatings per night, at 7 and 9. A traditional Italian meal includes several courses and should be a leisurely affair; so if you don't want to be rushed, opt for the later sitting.

There's no getting around the fact that Venice has more than its share of overpriced, mediocre eateries. Restaurants catering primarily to tourists have little motivation to maintain quality, because they know that most tourists are one-time short-term visitors and will, even under the best circumstances, never return. So, you are better off selecting a restaurant frequented by locals, who are interested in the food, not in canal-side dining or the views. Avoid places with cajoling waiters standing outside, and beware of restaurants that don't display their prices. The service desks at many hotels are paid off to funnel tourists to certain restaurants. At the other end of the spectrum, showy *menu turistico* (tourist menu) boards make offerings clear in a dozen languages, but for the same €15–€20 you'd spend at such places, you could do better at a bacaro making a meal of cicheti.

Use the coordinate (✛ B2) at the end of each listing to locate a site on the Where to Eat and Stay in Venice map.

WHAT IT COSTS			
$	$$	$$$	$$$$
AT DINNER up to €15	€15–€24	€25–€35	over €35

Prices in the dining reviews are the average cost of a main course at dinner, or, if dinner is not served, at lunch.

SAN MARCO

$
CAFÉ ✕ **Bar all'Angolo.** This corner of Campo Santo Stefano is one of the most pleasing locations to sit and watch the Venetian world go by. The constant motion of the café staff assures you'll receive your coffee, spritz, panino, or *tramezzino* (sandwich on untoasted white bread, usually with a mayonnaise-based filling) in short order; consume it at your leisure either at one of the outdoor tables, at the bar, or take refuge at the tables in the back. They'll whip you up a fresh salad, and they offer a delectable tiramisù for dessert—homemade, just like the sandwiches. The pasta, however, is not homemade; as in most bars, it is better to stick to cold dishes. Closing time is 9 pm, making the Angolo

a good alternative to a more elaborate evening meal. [$] *Average main: €8* ✉ *Campo Santo Stefano (just in front of Santo Stefano church), San Marco 3464* ☎ *041/5220710* ⏲ *Closed Sun., and Jan.* [M] *Vaporetto: Sant'Angelo* ✥ *C4.*

$$$ CAFÉ Fodor's Choice ★ 🍴 **Caffè Florian.** Because of the prices and the tourist mobs, Venetians tend to avoid the cafés in Piazza San Marco. But when they want to indulge and regain control of their city, they go to Florian. Founded in 1720, it's not only Italy's first café, but with its glittering neo-Baroque décor and attractive 19th-century wall panels depicting Venetian heroes, it's undisputedly the most beautiful. Florian is steeped in local history: favored by Venetians during the long Austrian occupation, it was the only café to serve women during the 18th century (hence Casanova's patronage), and it was the café of choice for artistic notables like Wagner, Goethe, Goldoni, Lord Byron, Marcel Proust, and Charles Dickens. It was also the birthplace of the international art exhibition, which later blossomed into the Venice Biennale. The coffee, drinks, and snacks are quite good (think chocolate, hot or otherwise), but you really come here for the atmosphere and to be part of Venetian history. There's a surcharge for music; so savvy Venetians and travelers in a hurry opt for lower prices at the comfortable bar in the back. [$] *Average main: €27* ✉ *Piazza San Marco, San Marco 56* ☎ *041/5205641* 🌐 *www.caffeflorian.com* ⏲ *Daily 9 am–midnight* ✥ *E4.*

$ WINE BAR 🍴 **Enoteca al Volto.** A short walk from the Rialto Bridge, this bar has been around since 1936; the satisfying cicheti and primi have a lot to do with its staying power. Grab one of the tables out front, or take refuge in one of the two small, dark rooms with ceilings plastered with wine labels that provide a classic backdrop for simple fare, including a delicious risotto served daily at noon. The place prides itself on its solid wine list of both Italian and foreign selections. If you stick to a panino or some cicheti at the bar, you'll eat well for relatively little. If you take a table and opt for one of the day's exceptional primi, the price category goes up a notch; however, this is still a good bargain for San Marco. There are, of course, traditional secondi, like the very good seppie in nero. Al Volto is open every day of the year but Christmas (and closes a bit early on Christmas Eve). [$] *Average main: €12* ✉ *Calle Cavalli, San Marco 4081* ☎ *041/5228945* 🌐 *www.alvoltoenoteca.it* 💳 *No credit cards* ⏲ *Daily 10–4 and 6–10* [M] *Vaporetto: Rialto* ✥ *E3.*

$$$$ VENETIAN Fodor's Choice ★ 🍴 **Harry's Bar.** For those who can afford it—and despite its recently having become the favorite watering hole of Russian oligarchs and their female spike-heeled retinues—lunch or dinner at Harry's Bar is as much a part of a visit to Venice as a walk across the Piazza San Marco or a vaporetto ride down the Grand Canal. Harry's is not just a fine restaurant; it's a cultural institution. When founder Giuseppe Cipriani opened the doors in 1931, the place became a favorite of almost every famous name to visit Venice (including Charlie Chaplin, Orson Welles, and Ernest Hemingway) and still attracts much of Venetian high society as regulars. Today, many still remember Harry's as one of the few restaurants in town that continued to serve Jewish patrons during the period of the Fascist racial laws. Inside, the suave, subdued beige-on-white décor is unchanged from the 1930s, and the classic Venetian fare

is carefully and excellently prepared. Try the delicate baked sea bass with artichokes, and don't miss the Harry's signature crêpes flambées or his famous Cipriani chocolate cake for dessert. Because a meal at Harry's is as much about being seen, book one of the cramped tables on the ground floor—the upper floor of the restaurant is the Venetian equivalent of "Siberia" (but take heart: the second floor does have windows with views that look like framed paintings). And be sure to order a Bellini cocktail—a refreshing mix of white-peach purée and sparking prosecco—this is its birthplace, after all. On the other hand, true to its "retro" atmosphere, Harry's makes one of the best Martini cocktails in town. $ *Average main: €38* ⊠ *Calle Vallaresso, San Marco 1323* ☎ *041/5285777* ⊕ *www.harrysbarvenezia.com* ⌗ *Reservations essential* 🎩 *Jacket required* ☉ *Daily 10:30 am–11 pm* Ⓜ *Vaporetto: San Marco (Calle Vallaresso)* ✛ *E4.*

$$$$
VENETIAN
Fodor's Choice
★

✕ **Ristorante Quadri.** Located above the famed café of the same name sits one of the most widely discussed restaurants in Italy: Quadri, a name steeped in history (as a café, it was the first to introduce Turkish coffee to an already overcaffeinated city in the 1700s), and its dark-wood furnishings, lush burgundy damask walls, and sparkling chandeliers create a typical Venetian ambience. The Alajmo family (of the celebrated Le Calandre restaurant near Padua) has taken over the restaurant and put their accomplished sous-chef from Padua in charge of the kitchen. The menu, bearing the creative mark of the Alajmos, has developed in the direction of increasing complexity, which runs contrary to the inherent simplicity and directness of classic Italian cuisine. For tasting menus that range from €170 to €235 (exclusive of wine), you can savor such delights of creative cuisine as pumpkin lasagnetta noodles with lobster, squid, ginger and almonds, or you can be more conservative and enjoy *burrata* ravioli with a seafood-tomato sauce spiked with oregano. Downstairs, the simpler **abcQuadri** (located next to the café)—with impeccably restored neo-Rococo wall paintings—serves more traditional Venetian fare and some of the best Martinis in town; however, a three-course dinner will still set you back €100 without wine. As for Quadri itself: the prices, cuisine, and décor are all *alta,* so beware: some food critics find the fare doesn't measure up. Be sure to book one of the few tables with a Piazza San Marco view; otherwise, the ambience offered is lavish, but not really extraordinary, considering the price. $ *Average main: €65* ⊠ *Piazza San Marco 121* ☎ *041/5222105* ⊕ *www.caffequadri.it* ⌗ *Reservations essential* ☉ *Closed Mon.* ✛ *E4.*

DORSODURO

$
CAFÉ

✕ **Caffè Bar Ai Artisti.** Sitting on a campo made famous in films with Katharine Hepburn and Indiana Jones, Caffè Ai Artisti gives locals, students, and travelers alike good reason to pause and refuel. The location is central, pleasant, and sunny—perfect for people-watching and taking a break before the next destination—and the hours are long: you can come here for a morning cappuccino, or drop by late for an after-dinner spritz. The panini are composed on-site from fresh, seasonal ingredients, their names scribbled in front of each on the glass case. There's a varied selection of wines by the glass, as well as herbal teas, and even caffè with ginseng. $ *Average main: €8* ⊠ *Campo San Barnaba, Dorsoduro 2771* ☎ *041/5238994* ▤ *No credit cards* Ⓜ *Vaporetto: Ca' Rezzonico* ✛ *C4.*

$ ✕ **Cantinone già Schiavi.** A mainstay for anyone living or working in the
WINE BAR area, this beautiful, family-run 19th-century bacaro across from the *squero* (gondola repair shop) of San Trovaso has original furnishings and one of the best wine cellars in town—the walls are covered floor to ceiling with bottles for purchase. Cicheti here are some of the most inventive and freshest in Venice (feel free to compliment the Signora, who makes them up to twice a day). Try the crostini-style layers of bread, smoked swordfish, and slivers of raw zucchini, or pungent slices of Parmesan, fig, pistachio, and toast. They also have a creamy version of baccalà mantecato spiced with herbs, and there are nearly a dozen open bottles of wine for experimenting at the bar. You'll have no trouble spotting the Cantinone as you approach: it's the one with throngs of chatty patrons enjoying themselves. $ *Average main: €2* ⊠ *Fondamenta Nani, Dorsoduro 992* ☎ *041/5230034* ▤ *No credit cards* ☾ *Closed Sun., and 2 wks in Aug.* Ⓜ *Vaporetto: Zattere, Accademia* ✛ *C5.*

$ ✕ **Impronta Cafe.** This sleek café is a favorite lunchtime haunt for pro-
VENETIAN fessors from the nearby university and local businesspeople. Unlike in
Fodor'sChoice more traditional places, it's quite acceptable to order only pasta or a sec-
★ ondo, without an antipasto or dessert. Although the restaurant is also open for dinner—and you can dine well and economically in the evening—the real bargain is lunch, where you can easily have a beautifully prepared primo or secondo, plus a glass of wine, for around €12–€18. There's also a good selection of sandwiches and salads. The attentive staff speak English, although you may be the only non-Venetian in the place. Unlike most local eateries, this spot is open from breakfast through late dinner (with tea and chocolate served late afternoon). $ *Average main: €12* ⊠ *Crosera–San Pantalon, Dorsoduro 3815–3817* ☎ *041/2750386* ⊕ *www.improntacafevenice.com* ☾ *Closed Sun.* ✛ *B3.*

$$ ✕ **La Bitta.** The décor is more discreet, the dining hours longer, and the
NORTHERN service friendlier and more efficient here than in many small restaurants
ITALIAN in Venice—and the nonfish menu (inspired by the cuisine of the Venetian
Fodor'sChoice terra firma) is a temptation at every course. Market availability keeps
★ the menu changing almost every day, although typically you can start with a savory barley soup or gnocchi with winter squash and aged ricotta cheese. Then choose a secondo, such as lamb chops with thyme, *anatra in pevarada* (duck in a pepper sauce), or guinea hen in cream. The homemade desserts are all luscious, and it's been said that La Bitta serves the best panna cotta in town. Trust owner Deborah Civiero's selection from her excellent wine and grappa lists. $ *Average main: €20* ⊠ *Calle Lunga San Barnaba, Dorsoduro 2753/A* ☎ *041/5230531* ⟁ *Reservations essential* ▤ *No credit cards* ☾ *Closed Sun. No lunch* Ⓜ *Vaporetto: Ca' Rezzonico* ✛ *B5.*

$$$$ ✕ **L'Incontro.** This trattoria between San Barnaba and Campo Santa Mar-
ITALIAN gherita has a faithful clientele of Venetians and visitors, attracted by flavorful Sardinian food, sociable service, and reasonable prices. Starters include Sardinian sausages, but you might skip to the delicious traditional primi, such as *culingiones* (large ravioli filled with pecorino, saffron, and orange peel). The selection of secondi is heavy on herb-crusted

meat dishes such as *coniglio al mirto* (rabbit baked on a bed of myrtle sprigs) and the *costine d'agnello con rosmarino e mentuccia* (baby lamb ribs with rosemary and wild mint). This is one of the few restaurants in Venice that is meat only—no fish at all. The accommodating cook will make up a veggie plate, but this is really a place for carnivores. $ *Average main: €35* ⊠ *Rio Terà Canal, just off Campo Santa Margherita, Dorsoduro 3062/A* ☎ *041/5222404* ⊘ *Closed Mon. in winter* Ⓜ *Vaporetto: Ca' Rezzonico* ✛ *B4.*

$
WINE BAR
Fodor'sChoice
★

✕**Osteria al Squero.** It wasn't long after this lovely little locale appeared across from the Squero San Trovaso that it became a neighborhood—and citywide—favorite. The Venetian owner of this reimagined bacaro has created a personal vision of what a good one should offer: a variety of sumptuous cicheti, panini, and cheeses to be accompanied by just the right regional wines (ask for his recommendation). You can linger along the fondamenta outdoors, and there are places to perch and even sit inside, in front of a sunny picture window that brings the outside view in. $ *Average main: €12* ⊠ *Fondamenta Nani, Dorsoduro 943/944* ☎ *335/6007513* ⊕ *osteriaalsquero.wordpress.com* ⊘ *Closed Mon.* Ⓜ *Vaporetto: Accademia, Zattere* ✛ *C5.*

$$
VENETIAN
Fodor'sChoice
★

✕**Osteria alla Bifora.** A beautiful and atmospheric bacaro, alla Bifora has such ample and satisfying food and wine selections that most Venetians consider it a full-fledged restaurant. Most of the offerings consist of overflowing trays of cold, sliced meats and cheeses, various preparations of baccalà, or Venetian classics such as polpette, sarde in saor, or marinated anchovies; there's a good selection of regional wines by the glass as well. La Bifora also serves up a couple of excellent hot dishes, and the seppie in nero is among the best in the city. Owner and barman Franco Bernardi and his sister Mirella are warm and friendly; after a few visits, you'll be greeted like a member of the family. Always open for dinner, you may find this place is also open for lunch—if you're lucky. $ *Average main: €18* ⊠ *Campo Santa Margherita, Dorsoduro 2930* ☎ *041/5236119* ⌘ *Reservations essential* ▭ *No credit cards* ✛ *B4.*

SAN POLO

$$$
MODERN ITALIAN
Fodor'sChoice
★

✕**Al Paradiso.** In a small dining room made warm and cozy by its pleasing and unpretentious décor, proprietor Giordano makes all diners feel like honored guests. Pappardelle "al Paradiso" takes pasta with seafood sauce to new heights, while risotto with shrimp, champagne, and grapefruit puts a delectable twist on a traditional dish. The inspired and original array of entrées includes meat and fish selections, such as salmon with honey and balsamic vinegar in a stunning presentation. Unlike many elegant restaurants, Al Paradiso serves generous portions; you may want to follow the traditional Italian way of ordering and wait until you've finished your antipasto or your primo before you order your secondo. $ *Average main: €26* ⊠ *Calle del Paradiso, San Polo 767* ☎ *041/5234910* ⌘ *Reservations essential* ⊘ *Closed Mon., and 3 wks in Jan. and Feb.* Ⓜ *Vaporetto: San Silvestro* ✛ *D3.*

$
CAFÉ

✕**All'Arco.** Just because it's noon and you only have time between sights for a sandwich doesn't mean that it can't be a satisfying, even awe-inspiring one. There's no menu at All'Arco, but a scan of what's behind the glass counter is all you need. Order what entices you, or have Roberto or Matteo (father and son) suggest a cicheto or panino. Options here are broad enough to satisfy both conservative and adventurous eaters. Wine options are well suited to the food. Arrive early or at the tail end of lunchtime to snag one of the few tables in the calle. $ *Average main: €6* ⊠ *Calle Arco, San Polo 436* ☎ *041/5220619* ⊙ *Closed Sun.* Ⓜ *Vaporetto: San Silvestro* ✛ *D3.*

$$$$
VENETIAN

✕ **Alla Madonna.** "The Madonna" used to be world-famous as "the" classic Venetian trattoria, but in the past decades she has settled into middle age. Owned and run by the Rado family since 1954, this Venetian institution looks like one, with its wood beams, stained-glass windows, and panoply of paintings on white walls. It is frequented more often by regular Italian visitors to Venice and people from the provinces than it is by Venetians themselves. Folks still head here to savor the classic Venetian repertoire and, as most dishes are properly prepared (for the stiff prices, they should be), the rooms here are usually bustling. Get ready to enjoy a festive and lively meal. $ *Average main: €60* ⊠ *Calle della Madonna, San Polo 594* ☎ *041/5223824* ⊕ *www. ristoranteallamadonna.com* ⌸ *Reservations essential* ⊙ *Closed Wed., Jan., and 2 wks in Aug.* Ⓜ *Vaporetto: San Silvestro* ✛ *D3.*

$$$
VENETIAN
Fodor's Choice
★

✕ **Antiche Carampane.** Judging from its rather modest and unremarkable appearance, you wouldn't guess that Piera Bortoluzzi Librai's trattoria is among the finest fish restaurants in the city, both because of the quality of the ingredients and because of the chef's creative magic. Antiche Carampane's kitchen explores the more complex and interesting, but lesser known, dishes from the traditional Venetian repertoire. Embark on a culinary journey with St. Peter's fish with radicchio di Treviso; mullet in red wine; or an unusual spaghetti with spicy shellfish sauce from the town of Chioggia, the major fishing port on the Venetian lagoon. If you prefer simpler fare, stick with the perfectly grilled fish—always wild-caught and fresh—or, in spring, try the fried local soft-shell crabs. $ *Average main: €26* ⊠ *Rio Terà della Carampane, San Polo 1911* ☎ *041/5240165* ⊕ *www.antichecarampane.com* ⌸ *Reservations essential* ⊙ *Closed Sun. and Mon., 10 days in Jan., and 3 wks in July and Aug.* Ⓜ *Vaporetto: San Silvestro* ✛ *D3.*

$
WINE BAR

✕ **Cantina Do Mori.** This is the original bacaro—in business continually since 1462. Cramped but warm and cozy under hanging antique copper pots, it has been catering to the workers of the Rialto Market for generations. In addition to young, local white and red wine, the well-stocked cellar offers reserve labels, many available by the glass. Between sips you can choose to munch the myriad cicheti on offer, or a few tiny, well-stuffed tramezzini, appropriately called *francobolli* (postage stamps). Don't leave without tasting the delicious baccalà mantecato, with or without garlic and parsley. If you choose to create a light lunch, snag one of the stools at the bar that lines the wall across from the banco. $ *Average main: €2* ⊠ *Calle dei Do Mori, San Polo 429* ☎ *041/5225401* ▬ *No credit cards* ⊙ *Closed Sun., 3 wks in Aug., and 1 wk in Jan.* Ⓜ *Vaporetto: Rialto Mercato* ✛ *D3.*

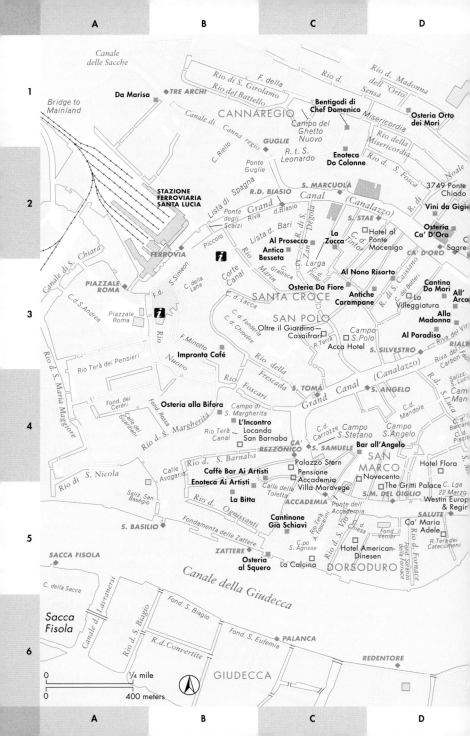

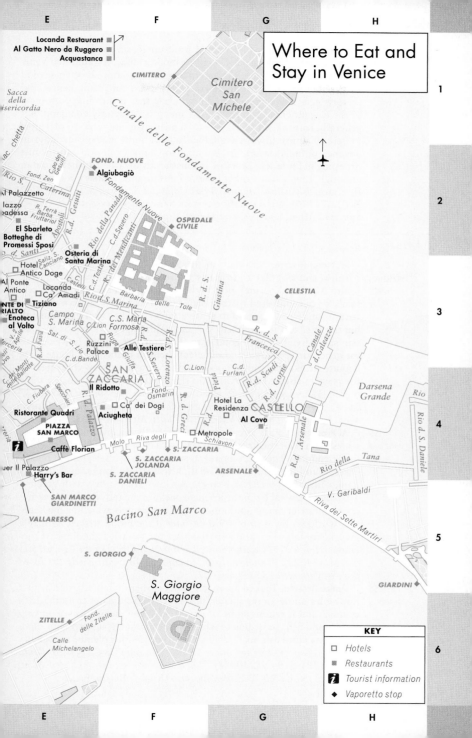

$$$ VENETIAN Fodor's Choice ★ 🍴 **Osteria Da Fiore.** The understated atmosphere, simple décor, and quiet elegance featured alongside Da Fiore's modern take on traditional Venetian cuisine certainly merit its international reputation. It offers several moderately priced (€50), three-course, prix-fixe luncheon menus, and the prix-fixe dinner menu is €80, which brings it into line with most of the elegant choices in town. The menu is constantly changing, but generally fritto misto or Da Fiore's tender, aromatic version of seppie in nero is almost always available. Reservations, made a few days in advance in high season, are essential for dinner, but you can try just dropping in for lunch. Da Fiore is consistently awarded a Michelin star, although, unlike many other honored restaurants, it does not publicize that fact. [$] *Average main: €34* ✉ *Calle del Scaleter, San Polo 2002* ☎ *041/721308* 🌐 *www.dafiore.net* ✍ *Reservations essential* 🕒 *Closed Sun. and Mon., and 3 wks in Jan.* [M] *Vaporetto San Tomà* ✥ *C3.*

SANTA CROCE

$ VENETIAN FAMILY 🍴 **Al Nono Risorto.** Although in the Santa Croce neighborhood, this friendly and popular trattoria is really only a short walk from the Rialto Market. You may not be the only tourist here, but you'll certainly be outnumbered by the locals (and if just a couple or a trio, the friendly staff may ask you to share a table). There's no English menu, but a server can usually help you out. Although pizza is not a Venetian specialty, it's pretty good here. The star attractions, however, are the generous appetizers and excellent shellfish pastas. The house wine is quite drinkable, and in good weather you can enjoy your meal in the pergola-covered courtyard (do reserve if you want to snag a table there). [$] *Average main: €9* ✉ *Ramo de l'Arsenal, Santa Croce 2337* ☎ *041/5241169* ✍ *Reservations essential* 💳 *No credit cards* 🕒 *Closed Wed. No lunch Thurs.* [M] *Vaporetto: Rialto Mercato* ✥ *D3.*

$$ WINE BAR 🍴 **Al Prosecco.** Locals stream into this friendly bacaro both to explore wines from their own region and to discover new ones from elsewhere in the country. They accompany a carefully chosen selection of meats, cheeses, and other food from small, artisanal producers, used in tasty panini like the *porchetta romane verdure* (roast pork with greens). There are a few tables in the intimate back room, and when the weather cooperates you can sit outdoors on the lively campo, watching the Venetian world go by. It's open 9 to 9, later if the mood strikes. Mostly a favorite for lunch, it's also a special place for an early light dinner. [$] *Average main: €20* ✉ *Campo San Giacomo dell'Orio, Santa Croce 1503* ☎ *041/5240222* 🌐 *www.alprosecco.com* 💳 *No credit cards* 🕒 *Closed Sun.* [M] *Vaporetto: San Stae* ✥ *C2.*

$$ SEAFOOD 🍴 **Antica Besseta.** Tucked away in a quiet corner of Santa Croce, with a few tables under an ivy shelter, the Antica Besseta dates from the 18th century, and it retains some of its old feel. The menu focuses on vegetables and fish, according to what's at the market: spaghetti with *caparozzoli* or cuttlefish ink, *schie* (tiny shrimp) with polenta, and plenty of grilled fish. [$] *Average main: €15* ✉ *Salizzada de Ca' Zusto, Santa Croce 1395* ☎ *041/5240428* 🌐 *www.anticabesseta.it* 🕒 *Closed Mon. and Tues. No lunch Wed.* [M] *Vaporetto: Rive di Biasio* ✥ *C2.*

$$
NORTHERN
ITALIAN
✕ **La Zucca.** What makes La Zucca special is the use of fresh, local ingredients (many of which, like the particularly sweet *zucca* itself, aren't normally found outside northern Italy), and simply great cooking. Though the menu does have superb meat dishes such as the *piccata di pollo ai caperi e limone con riso* (sliced chicken with capers and lemon served with rice), more attention is paid to dishes from the garden: try the radicchio *di Treviso con funghi e scaglie di Montasio* (with mushrooms and shavings of Montasio cheese), the *finocchi piccanti con olive* (fennel in a spicy tomato-olive sauce), or the house's signature dish— the *flan di zucca,* a luscious, naturally sweet, pumpkin pudding topped with slivered, aged ricotta cheese. Ⓢ *Average main: €18 ⊠ Calle del Tintor, at Ponte de Megio, Santa Croce 1762 ☎ 041/5241570 ⊕ www. lazucca.it ⌂ Reservations essential ⊙ Closed Sun., and 1 wk in Dec.* Ⓜ *Vaporetto: San Stae ✛ C2.*

CANNAREGIO

$$$
ITALIAN
✕ **Algiubagiò.** A waterfront table is more affordable at lunchtime here on Venice's northern Fondamente Nove, where instead of a grand palazzo, the wide-open lagoon is the backdrop—on a clear day, the majestic Dolomites put on quite a show. Algiubagiò has a dual personality: big salads at lunch (a better bet than the pizza); at dinner, creative primi like ravioli stuffed with *pecorino di fossa* (a hard sheep's-milk cheese) are followed by elegant secondi such as Angus filets with vodka and Gorgonzola. The young, friendly staff also serve ice cream, drinks, and sandwiches all day. A lunch table is an airy respite; while quite romantic, dinnertime sees a considerable rise in prices. Ⓢ *Average main: €26 ⊠ Fondamente Nove, Cannaregio 5039 ☎ 041/5236084 ⊕ www. algiubagio.net ⌂ Reservations essential ⊙ Closed Sun.* Ⓜ *Vaporetto: Fondamente Nove ✛ E2.*

$$
VENETIAN
✕ **Bentigodi di Chef Domenico.** Many claim that owner Domenico Iacuzio is one of Venice's best chefs, even though he hails from Italy's deep south. The chef marries delicious Venetian culinary traditions with southern accents; try the sarde in saor, which perfectly balances sweet and savory, and the diced raw tuna *cipolata,* enlivened by sautéed onions and oranges. His seafood risottos are always made to order, and his preparations of freshly caught—never farmed—fish are magical. For the Venetian traditionalist, Domenico prepares a first-class fritto misto. If you've missed his southern accent up to now, you'll find it at dessert with homemade southern specialties such as cannoli or *cassata* (candied Sicilian cake). Portions are ample, the atmosphere is informal, and the service is helpful. Ⓢ *Average main: €22 ⊠ Calesele, Cannargio 1423 ☎ 041/8223714 ⊕ www.bentigodi.com ⌂ Reservations essential ✛ C1.*

$
VENETIAN
✕ **Botteghe di Promessi Sposi.** Join locals at the *banco* (counter) premeal for an *ombra* (small glass of wine) and a cicheto, like polpette croquettes or violet eggplant rounds, or reserve a sit-down meal in the dining room or intimate courtyard. A varied, seasonal menu includes local standards like calf's liver or grilled *canestrelli* (tiny Venetian scallops), along with creative regional fusions incorporating classic Venetian fare, like homemade ravioli stuffed with *radicchio di Treviso* (red chicory leaves) or *orecchiette* (small ear-shape pasta) with a scrumptious sauce

of minced duck. The service is friendly and helpful. Be sure to make a reservation (later is better for a more relaxed environment). [$] *Average main: €13* ✉ *Calle de l'Oca, just off Campo Santi Apostoli, Cannaregio 4367* ☎ *041/2412747* ✍ *Reservations essential* ⏲ *Closed Mon. No lunch Wed.* [M] *Vaporetto: Ca' d'Oro* ✥ *E2.*

$$ VENETIAN Fodor's Choice ★

🍴 **Da Marisa.** This is the most famous working-man's restaurant in Venice. If you can get a table for lunch, you'll eat, without any choice, what Marisa prepares for her workmen clientele—generally enormous portions of excellently prepared pasta, followed by a hearty roast-meat course (frequently game, more infrequently fish) for the unbelievably inexpensive fixed price (€15). Dinner is a bit more expensive, and you may have a bit more choice, but not much. But for the authentic "Marisa" experience, go for lunch: it is as essential a part of Venice, on one end of the social spectrum, as dinner at Harry's Bar is at the other. In good weather, you'll have a better chance getting a table, since additional tables are set up along the fondamenta. Don't be put off by the occasionally gruff service; it's part of the scene. [$] *Average main: €15* ✉ *Fondamenta di San Giobbe,Cannaregio 625b,* ☎ *041/720211* ✍ *Reservations essential* 💳 *No credit cards* ⏲ *No dinner Mon. and Tues.* ✥ *B1.*

$ WINE BAR

🍴 **El Sbarlefo.** This odd name is Venetian for "smirk," although you'd be hard-pressed to find one of those around this cheery, familiar wine bar with a selection as ample as the cicheti on offer. Making the most of their limited space, owners Alessandro and Andrea have installed counters and stools inside, tables outside, and external banco access for ordering a second round. And order you will—selecting from a spread of delectable cicheti ranging from classic polpette of meat and tuna to tomino cheese rounds to speck and robiolo rolls, and more. They've paid equal attention to their wine selection—ask for a recommendation and you're likely to make a new discovery. [$] *Average main: €4* ✉ *Salizzada del Pistor, off Campo Santi Apostoli, Cannaregio 4556/C* ☎ *041/5233084* 💳 *No credit cards* [M] *Vaporetto: Ca d'Oro* ✥ *E2.*

$ WINE BAR

🍴 **Enoteca Do Colonne.** Venetians from this working-class neighborhood frequent this friendly bacaro, not just for a glass of very drinkable wine, but also because of its excellent selection of traditional Venetian cicheti for lunch. There's not only a large selection of sandwiches and panini, but also luscious tidbits like grilled vegetables, breaded and fried sardines and shrimp, and a superb version of baccalà mantecato. For the more adventurous, there are Venetian working-class specialties such as *musetto* (a sausage made from pigs' snouts served warm with polenta) and *nervetti* (veal tendons with lemon and parsley). These dishes are worth trying at least once when in Venice, and Do Colonne offers the best musetto in town. [$] *Average main: €8* ✉ *Rio Terà Cristo, Cannaregio 1814* ☎ *041/5240453* 🌐 *www.docolonne.it* 💳 *No credit cards* ⏲ *Closed Sun.* [M] *Vaporetto: San Marcuola* ✥ *C2.*

$ VENETIAN

🍴 **Osteria Ca' d'Oro (alla Vedova).** "The best polpette in town," you'll hear fans of the venerable Vedova say, and that explains why it's an obligatory stop on any *giro d'ombra* (bacaro tour). The polpette are always hot and crunchy, and also gluten-free, as they're made with polenta. Ca' d'Oro is a full-fledged trattoria as well, but make sure to reserve ahead, as it's no secret to both locals and travelers seeking traditional Venetian fare at a reasonable cost. Vedova is one of the few places that still serves house wine in tiny, traditional *palline* glasses; never fear, if you order a bottle, you'll get a fancier glass. $ *Average main: €12* ⊠ *Calle del Pistor, off Strada Nova, Cannaregio 3912* ☎ *041/5285324* ▭ *No credit cards* ☾ *Closed Thurs., and Aug.* Ⓜ *Vaporetto: Ca d'Oro* ⊕ *D2.*

$$ ✕ **Osteria Orto dei Mori.** A small and popular Cannaregio neighborhood
ITALIAN restaurant specializing in creative versions of classic Italian dishes. The attentive expertise of chef and co-owner Lorenzo is evident in every dish: try the *fagotti* (bundles of beef marinated in Chianti with goat cheese) or a seafood version with prawns, zucchini, and ricotta. Risotto with scampi and savory *fenferli* mushrooms won't disappoint, nor will the signature parchment-baked monkfish. Co-owner Micael has artfully created a regional wine list. The osteria is just under the nose of the campo's famous corner statue. $ *Average main: €16* ⊠ *Campo dei Mori, Fondamenta dei Mori, Cannaregio 3386* ☎ *041/5235544* ⌂ *Reservations essential* ☾ *Closed Tues.* Ⓜ *Vaporetto: Orto, Ca' d'Oro, or San Marcuola* ⊕ *D1.*

$ ✕ **Tiziano.** A fine variety of excellent tramezzini lines the display cases
ITALIAN at this *tavola calda* (roughly the Italian equivalent of a cafeteria) on the main thoroughfare from the Rialto to Santi Apostoli; inexpensive salad plates and daily pasta specials are also served. This is a great place for a light meal or snack before a performance at the nearby Teatro Malebran. Whether you choose to sit or stand, it's a handy—and popular—spot for a quick meal or a snack at very modest prices. Service is efficient, if occasionally grumpy. $ *Average main: €8* ⊠ *Salizzada San Giovanni Crisostomo, Cannaregio 5747* ☎ *041/5235544* ▭ *No credit cards* Ⓜ *Vaporetto: Rialto* ⊕ *E3.*

$$$ ✕ **Vini da Gigio.** Deservedly popular with Venetians and visitors alike,
VENETIAN this is one of the best values in the city. Indulge in pastas such as riga-
Fodor's Choice toni with duck sauce and arugula-stuffed ravioli. The seafood risotto
★ has patrons raving. Fish is well represented—try the sesame-encrusted tuna—but the meat dishes steal the show. The steak with red-pepper sauce and the *tagliata di agnello* (sautéed lamb filet with a light, crusty coating) are both superb, and you'll never enjoy a better *fegato alla veneziana* (Venetian-style liver with onions). This is a place for wine connoisseurs, as the cellar is one of the best in the city. Come at lunch or for the second sitting in the evening for more relaxed service. $ *Average main: €25* ⊠ *Fondamenta San Felice, Cannaregio 3628/A* ☎ *041/5285140* ⊕ *www.vinidagigio.com* ⌂ *Reservations essential* ☾ *Closed Mon. and Tues., 2 wks in Jan., and 3 wks in Aug.* Ⓜ *Vaporetto: Ca' d'Oro* ⊕ *D2.*

CASTELLO

$ ✕ **Aciugheta.** Almost an institution, the "tiny anchovy" (as the name
WINE BAR translates) doubles as a pizzeria-trattoria, but here the stars are the tasty cicheti offered at the bar, like the eponymous anchovy minipizzas, the *arancioni* rice balls, and the polpette. Wines by the glass change daily, but there are always a good selection of local wines on hand, as well as some Tuscan and Piedmontese choices thrown in for good measure. Don't miss the *tonno con polenta* (tuna with polenta) if it's offered.

$ *Average main: €12* ✉ *Campo SS. Filippo e Giacomo, Castello 4357* ☎ *041/5224292* Ⓜ *Vaporetto: San Zaccaria* ✛ *F4.*

$$$
VENETIAN

✕ **Al Covo.** For years, Diane and Cesare Binelli's Al Covo has set the standard of excellence for traditional, refined Venetian cuisine. The Binellis are dedicated to providing their guests with the freshest, highest-quality fish from the Adriatic, and vegetables, when at all possible, from the islands of the Venetian lagoon and the fields of the adjacent Veneto region. Although their cuisine could be correctly termed "classic Venetian," it always offers surprises like the juicy crispness of their legendary fritto misto—reliant upon a secret, nonconventional ingredient in the batter—or the heady aroma of their fresh anchovies marinated in wild fennel, an herb somewhat foreign to the Veneto. The main exception to Al Covo's distinct local flavor is Diane's wonderful Texas-inspired desserts, especially her dynamite chocolate cake. $ *Average main: €28* ✉ *Campiello Pescaria, Castello 3968* ☎ *041/5223812* ⊕ *www.ristorantealcovo.com* ✍ *Reservations essential* ⊙ *Closed Wed. and Thurs.* Ⓜ *Vaporetto: Arsenale* ✛ *G4.*

$$$
VENETIAN
Fodor's Choice
★

✕ **Alle Testiere.** The name is a reference to the old headboards that adorn the walls of this tiny, informal restaurant, but the food (and not the décor) is undoubtedly the focus. Local foodies consider this one of the most refined eateries in the city thanks to Chef Bruno Cavagni's gently creative take on classic Venetian fish dishes. The chef's artistry seldom draws attention to itself, but simply reveals new dimensions to familiar fare, creating dishes that stand out for their lightness and balance. A classic black risotto with cuttlefish, for example, is surrounded by a brilliant coulis of mild yellow peppers; tiny potato gnocchi are paired with tender newborn squid. The menu changes regularly to capitalize on the freshest produce of the moment, and the wine selection is top-notch. To enjoy a more leisurely meal, be sure to book the second dinner sitting. $ *Average main: €26* ✉ *Calle del Mondo Novo, Castello 5801* ☎ *041/5227220* ⊕ *www.osterialletestiere.it* ✍ *Reservations essential* ⊙ *Closed Sun. and Mon., 3 wks in Jan. and Feb., 4 wks in July and Aug.* ✛ *F3.*

$$$
MODERN ITALIAN
Fodor's Choice
★

✕ **Il Ridotto.** Longtime restaurateur Gianni Bonaccorsi (proprietor of the popular Aciugheta nearby) has established an eatery where he can pamper a limited number of lucky patrons with his imaginative cuisine and impeccable taste in wine. *Ridotto,* "reduced" in Italian, refers to the size of this tiny, gracious restaurant. The innovative menu employing traditional elements is revised daily, with the offerings tending toward lighter, but wonderfully tasty versions of classic dishes. The €70 tasting menus—one meat, one fish—where Gianni "surprises" you with a selection of his own creations, never fail to satisfy. Ask for a wine recommendation from the excellent cantina. $ *Average main: €28* ✉ *Campo SS. Filippo e Giacomo, Castello 4509* ☎ *041/5208280* ⊕ *www.ilridotto.com* ✍ *Reservations essential* ⊙ *Closed Wed. No lunch Thurs.* Ⓜ *Vaporetto: San Zaccaria* ✛ *F4.*

$$$
VENETIAN
Fodor's Choice
★

✕ **Osteria di Santa Marina.** The candlelit tables on this romantic campo are inviting enough, but it's this intimate restaurant's imaginative kitchen creations that are likely to win you over. Star dishes include *tortino di baccalà mantecato* (cod torte) with baby arugula and fried polenta; *passatina di piselli* (fresh pea puree with scallops and tiny calamari); scampi in saor, a turn on a Venetian classic with leeks and ginger; and fresh ravioli stuffed with mussels and turbot in a creamed celery sauce. You can also opt for one of the rewarding tasting menus (fish or meat, €55–€85). The wine list is ample and well-thought-out. Service is gracious and cordial—just don't be in a terrible rush or expect the server to be your new best friend. $ *Average main:* €26 ⊠ *Campo Santa Marina, Castello 5911* ☎ *041/5285239* ⊕ *www. osteriadisantamarina.com* ⌕ *Reservations essential* ♥ *Closed Sun. No lunch Mon.* Ⓜ *Vaporetto: Rialto* ✛ *E2.*

ISLANDS OF THE LAGOON

$$
VENETIAN

⨉ **Acquastanca.** Grab a seat among locals at this charming, intimate eatery—the perfect place to pop in for a lunchtime primo or embark on a romantic evening. Tasteful décor sets the mood, with exposed brick, iron and glass accents, and charming fish sculptures. Giovanna Arcangeli, changing course after years as an event planner for Harry's Bar, offers up gnocchi with scallops and zucchini, and curried scampi with black *venere* rice; you might even ask for a beef *tagliata* and mushroom plate for the table to share. The name, referring to the tranquillity of the lagoon at the turn of the tide, reflects this restaurant's approach to food and service. $ *Average main:* €20 ⊠ *Fondamenta Manin 48, Murano* ☎ *041/3195125* ⊕ *www.acquastanca.it* ⌕ *Reservations essential* ♥ *Closed Sun. Dinner Mon. and Fri. only, other evenings drinks and cicheti until 8 pm* Ⓜ *Vaporetto: Murano Colonna, Murano Faro* ✛ *F1.*

$$$
SEAFOOD

⨉ **Al Gatto Nero da Ruggero.** Even cats know that this restaurant dedicated to one of their own offers the best fish on Burano. The fish is top-quality and couldn't get any fresher; all pastas and desserts are made in-house; the fritto misto is outstanding in its lightness and variety of fish. Risotto *de Gò* (*ghiozzo*) is a Burano *cucina povera* standard that had almost disappeared from local menus until Anthony Bordain introduced it to travelers. No matter what you order, though, you'll savor the pride owner Ruggero and his family have in their lagoon, their island, and the quality of their cucina (maybe even more so when enjoying it on the picturesque fondamenta). $ *Average main:* €26 ⊠ *Fondamenta della Giudecca 88, Burano* ☎ *041/730120* ⊕ *www. gattonero.com* ⌕ *Reservations essential* ♥ *Closed Mon., and 3 wks in Nov.* Ⓜ *Vaporetto: Burano* ✛ *F1.*

$$$
VENETIAN

⨉ **Locanda Restaurant.** A nearly legendary restaurant established by a nephew of Arrigo Cipriani (the founder of Harry's Bar), this inn profits from its idyllic location on the island of Torcello. Hemingway, who loved the silence of the lagoon, came here often to eat, drink, and brood under the green veranda. The food is not exceptional, especially considering the high prices, but dining here is more about getting lost in Venetian magic. The menu features pastas, *vitello tonnato* (chilled poached veal in a tuna and caper sauce), baked *orata* (gilthead) with potatoes, and lots of other seafood. Vaporetto Line 10 runs every 30 minutes until 11:30 pm—afterward upon request, and service is sporadic. $ *Average main:* €34 ⊠ *Piazza Santa Fosca 29, Torcello*

☎ 041/730150 ⋞ *Reservations essential* ⊙ *Closed Tues., and early Jan.– early Feb.* Ⓜ *Vaporetto: Torcello* ⊕ *F1.*

WHERE TO STAY

Venetian magic can still linger when you retire for the night, whether you're staying in a grand hotel or budget *locanda* (inn). Some of the finest Venetian hotel rooms are lighted with Murano chandeliers and swathed in famed fabrics of Rubelli and Bevilacqua, with gilded mirrors and furnishing styles from Baroque to Biedermeier and Art Deco.

Even if well-renovated, most hotels occupy very old buildings. Preservation laws prohibit elevators in some, so if climbing stairs is an issue, check before you book. In the lower price categories, hotels may not have lounge areas, and rooms may be cramped, and the same is true of standard rooms in more expensive hotels. Space is at a premium in Venice, and even exclusive hotels have carved out small, dowdy, Cinderella-type rooms in the "standard" category. It's not at all unusual for each room to be different even on the same floor: windows overlooking charming canals and bleak alleyways are both common. En-suite bathrooms have become the norm; they're usually well equipped but sizes will range from compact to more than ample; tubs are considered a luxury but are not unheard-of, even in less expensive lodging. Air-conditioning is rarely a necessity until mid-June. A few of the budget hotels make do with fans.

WHAT NEIGHBORHOOD TO STAY IN?

"Only a stone's throw from Saint Mark's square" is the standard hotel claim. Whether that's the case, it's not necessarily an advantage. In Venice, you can't go terribly wrong in terms of "good" areas in which to stay, and once you get your bearings, you'll find you're never far from anything.

You may, however, want to consider how close your hotel is to a vaporetto stop, and how many bridges there are to cross between your hotel and the vaporetto station. If you have lots of heavy baggage, carrying them over the bridges to and from your hotel can be quite a chore.

The area in and around San Marco will always be the most crowded and touristy and almost always more expensive: even two- and three-star hotels cost more here than they do in other parts of town. If you want to stay in less-trafficked surroundings, consider still convenient but more tranquil locations in Dorsoduro, Santa Croce, and Cannaregio (though hotels near the train station in Cannaregio can have their own crowd issues), or even Castello in the area beyond the Pietà church. A stay on the Lido in shoulder season offers serenity and beaches for the kids, but it also includes about a half-hour boat ride to the centro storico, and in summer it's crowded with beachgoers.

Substantial savings can be had by staying in a hotel in Mestre or Marghera, or near the airport, but you must count on at least an hour each way until you get into the centro storico. Touring in Venice can be physically taxing, involving a lot of walking on stone pavement, climbing stairs and foot bridges, and a paucity of places to sit down unless you've ordered a drink or a snack at a café. You may want to return to your hotel for a brief rest, or for a shower on a hot, humid summer day. Booking a hotel in the historic center will make a brief rest possible; a hotel on the mainland simply won't.

Venice is saturated with lodging options, but it is also one of the most popular destinations on earth—so book your lodging as far in advance as possible.

FINDING YOUR HOTEL

It is *essential* to have detailed arrival directions along with the address, including the sestiere and preferably a nearby landmark; conveniently, most hotels include maps on their websites. Even if you choose a pricey water taxi, you may still have a walk, depending on where the boat leaves you. Nothing is obvious on Venice's streets (even if you have GPS); turn-by-turn directions can help you avoid wandering back and forth along side streets and across bridges, luggage in tow.

Hotel reviews have been shortened. Visit Fodors.com for full information.

Use the coordinate (✥ B2) at the end of each listing to locate a site on the Where to Eat and Stay in Venice map.

PRICES

Hotel rates are about 20% higher than in Rome and Milan but can be reduced by as much as half off-season, from November to March (excluding Christmas, New Year's, and Carnevale), and likely in August as well.

WHAT IT COSTS				
	$	$$	$$$	$$$$
FOR TWO PEOPLE	under €125	€125–€200	€201–€300	over €300

Prices in the reviews are the lowest cost of a standard double room in high season.

SAN MARCO

$$$$
HOTEL

Bauer Il Palazzo. This palazzo with an ornate, 1930s neo-Gothic facade facing the Grand Canal has lavishly decorated guest rooms (large by Venetian standards) featuring high ceilings, tufted walls of Bevilacqua and Rubelli fabrics, Murano glass, marble bathrooms, damask drapes, and replica antique furniture. **Pros:** pampering service; high-end luxury. **Cons:** in one of the busiest areas of the city; you will pay handsomely for a room with a canal view; Wi-Fi is additional; furnishings are, as is the facade, imitations. $ *Rooms from: €700* ⊠ *Campo San Moisè, San Marco 1413/D, San Marco* ☎ *041/5207022* ⊕ *www.ilpalazzovenezia. com* ⇱ *38 rooms, 34 suites* ⭘| *Breakfast* Ⓜ *Vaporetto: Vallaresso* ✥ *E4.*

$$$$
HOTEL
Fodor'sChoice
★

The Gritti Palace. Reopened in 2013 after an extensive renovation, the Gritti Palace represents aristocratic Venetian living at its best, complete with hand-blown chandeliers, sumptuous textiles, and sweeping canal views. **Pros:** historic setting; white-glove service; Grand Canal location;

classic Venetian experience. **Cons:** major splurge; some extra fees (not for Wi-Fi). $ *Rooms from: €600* ✉ *Campo Santa Maria del Giglio, San Marco 2467* ☎ *041/794611* 🌐 *www.thegrittipalace.com* 61 *rooms, 21 suites* 🍴 *No meals* ⊕ *D5.*

$$$ HOTEL Fodor's Choice ★ **Hotel Flora.** The elegant and refined facade announces truly special place; the hospitable staff, the tastefully decorated rooms, and magical garden do not disappoint. **Pros:** central location; lovely garden; fitness center; excellent breakfast; free Wi-Fi. **Cons:** some rooms can be on the small side. $ *Rooms from: €240* ✉ *Calle Bergamaschi, just off Calle Larga XXII Marzo, San Marco 2283/A* ☎ *041/5228217* 🌐 *www.hotelflora.it* *40 rooms* 🍴 *Breakfast* Ⓜ *Vaporetto: San Marco (Vallaresso)* ⊕ *D4.*

$$$ HOTEL **Novecento.** A stylish yet intimate retreat tucked away on a quiet calle midway between Piazza San Marco and the Accademia Bridge offers exquisite rooms tastefully decorated with original furnishings and tapestries from the Meditteranean and Far East. **Pros:** intimate, romantic atmosphere; free Wi-Fi. **Cons:** some rooms are small, and some can be noisy. $ *Rooms from: €240* ✉ *Calle del Dose, off Campo San Maurizio, San Marco 2683/84* ☎ *041/2413765* 🌐 *www.novecento.biz* *9 rooms* 🍴 *Breakfast* Ⓜ *Vaporetto: Santa Maria del Giglio* ⊕ *C4.*

$$$$ HOTEL Fodor's Choice ★ **Westin Europa & Regina.** Spread across five historic palazzi (is there anything else in Venice?) in the lee of San Marco, this amalgamation of the former Hotel Britannia and Hotel Regina is easily one of Venice's still-undiscovered gems. **Pros:** ideal location, with the überboutiques of Via XXII Marzo and the Piazza San Marco a stone's throw away. **Cons:** slightly dated public areas and restaurants. $ *Rooms from: €550* ✉ *Corte Barozzi, San Marco 2159* ☎ *041/240 0001* 🌐 *www.westineuropareginavenice.com* *185 rooms* 🍴 *No meals* ⊕ *D5.*

DORSODURO

$$$$ HOTEL **Ca' Maria Adele.** One of the city's most intimate and elegant getaways immerses guests in a mix of classic style (terrazzo floors, dramatic Murano chandeliers, antique-style furnishings) and touches of the contemporary, found in the African-wood reception area and breakfast room. **Pros:** quiet and romantic; imaginative contemporary décor; free Wi-Fi; tranquil yet convenient spot near Santa Maria della Salute. **Cons:** small rooms, even for Venice; few good restaurants nearby. $ *Rooms from: €420* ✉ *Campo Santa Maria della Salute, Dorsoduro 111* ☎ *041/5203078* 🌐 *www.camariaadele.it* *12 rooms, 4 suites* 🍴 *Breakfast* Ⓜ *Vaporetto: Salute* ⊕ *D5.*

$$$$ HOTEL **Hotel American–Dinesen.** The exceptional service here will help you feel at home in spacious guest rooms furnished in Venetian brocade fabrics with lacquered Venetian-style furniture; some front rooms have terraces with canal views. **Pros:** high degree of personal service; on a bright, quiet, exceptionally picturesque canal; free Wi-Fi. **Cons:** no elevator; rooms with canal views are more expensive; some rooms could stand refurbishing. $ *Rooms from: €330* ✉ *San Vio, Dorsoduro 628* ☎ *041/5204733* 🌐 *www.hotelamerican.com* *28 rooms, 2 suites* 🍴 *Breakfast* Ⓜ *Vaporetto: Accademia, Salute, and Zattere* ⊕ *C5.*

$$ HOTEL Fodor's Choice ★ 🏨 **La Calcina.** Time-burnished and elegant rooms with parquet floors, original 19th-century furniture, and firm beds enjoy an enviable position along the sunny Zattere, with front rooms offering vistas across the wide Giudecca Canal; a few have private terraces. **Pros:** panoramic views from some rooms; elegant, historic atmosphere. **Cons:** not for travelers who prefer ultramodern surroundings; no elevator; rooms with views are appreciably more expensive. [$] *Rooms from: €180* ✉ *Zattere, Dorsoduro 780* ☎ *041/5206466* 🌐 *www.lacalcina.com* 🛏 *27 rooms (26 with bath), 5 suites* 🍴 *Breakfast* [M] *Vaporetto: Zattere* ⊕ *C5.*

$$ HOTEL 🏨 **Locanda San Barnaba.** This family-run, value-for-money establishment is housed in a 16th-century palazzo and, if you're lucky, you'll bag one of the superior rooms or the double that has original 18th-century wall paintings; one junior suite has two small balconies and is exceptionally luminous. **Pros:** garden and terrace; close to vaporetto stop; traditional furnishings make spacious rooms attractive and welcoming. **Cons:** no elevator, minibar, or Internet access. [$] *Rooms from: €175* ✉ *Calle del Traghetto, Dorsoduro 2785–2786* ☎ *041/2411233* 🌐 *www.locanda-sanbarnaba.com* 🛏 *11 rooms, 2 junior suites* 🍴 *Breakfast* [M] *Vaporetto: Ca' Rezzonico* ⊕ *B4.*

$$$$ HOTEL 🏨 **Palazzo Stern.** This opulently refurbished neo-Gothic palazzo features marble-columned arches, terrazzo floors, frescoed ceilings, mosaics, and a majestic carved staircase and some rooms have tufted walls and parquet flooring, but the gracious terrace that overlooks the Grand Canal is almost reason alone to stay here. **Pros:** excellent service; lovely views from many rooms; modern renovation retains historic ambience; steps from vaporetto stop. **Cons:** multiple renovations may turn off some Venetian architectural purists; rooms with a Grand Canal view are much more expensive; terrace bar and service are substandard; quality of the rooms varies and inferior rooms are not offered at reduced prices. [$] *Rooms from: €400* ✉ *Calle del Traghetto, Dorsoduro 2792* ☎ *041/2770869* 🌐 *www.palazzostern.com* 🛏 *18 rooms, 5 junior suites, 1 suite* 🍴 *Breakfast* [M] *Vaporetto: Ca' Rezzonico* ⊕ *C4.*

$$$ HOTEL Fodor's Choice ★ 🏨 **Pensione Accademia Villa Maravege.** Behind iron gates in one of the most densely packed parts of the city you'll find yourself in front of a large and elegant garden and Gothic-style "villa" where accommodations are charmingly decorated with a connoisseur's eye. **Pros:** a unique "villa" in the heart of Venice; one of the city's most enchanting hotels. **Cons:** standard rooms are smaller than is usual in Venice, and seem to be more sparsely decorated than the more expensive options. [$] *Rooms from: €290* ✉ *Fondamenta Bollani, Dorsoduro 1058* ☎ *041/5210188* 🌐 *www.pensioneaccademia.it* 🛏 *27 rooms, 2 suites* 🍴 *Breakfast* [M] *Vaporetto: Accademia* ⊕ *C4.*

SAN POLO

$$ HOTEL 🏨 **La Villeggiatura.** If eclectic Venetian charm is what you seek, this luminous residence offers six individually decorated rooms, each with its own original, theatrically themed fresco by a local artist. **Pros:** relaxed atmosphere; meticulously maintained; well-located near markets, artistic monuments, and restaurants. **Cons:** positioned high over a popular and busy thoroughfare; no elevator and lots of stairs; modest breakfast;

no view to speak of, despite the climb. $ *Rooms from: €195* ⊠ *Calle dei Botteri, San Polo 1569* ☎ *041/5244673* ⊕ *www.lavilleggiatura.it* ⇗ *6 rooms* ⦿*Breakfast* Ⓜ *Vaporetto: Rialto Mercato* ✛ *D3.*

$$$
HOTEL

🖫 **Oltre il Giardino–Casaifrari.** It's easy to overlook—and it can be a challenge to find—this secluded palazzo, sheltered as it is behind a brick wall just over the bridge from the Frari church, but the search is well worth it: airy, individually decorated guest rooms face a large garden, an oasis of peace (especially in high season). **Pros:** a peaceful, gracious, and convenient setting; walled garden. **Cons:** a beautiful but not particularly Venetian ambience. $ *Rooms from: €250* ⊠ *Fondamenta Contarini, San Polo 2542* ☎ *041/2750015* ⊕ *www.oltreilgiardino-venezia. com* ⇗ *6 rooms* ⦿*Breakfast* Ⓜ *Vaporetto: San Tomà* ✛ *C3.*

SANTA CROCE

$$
HOTEL
Fodor'sChoice
★

🖫 **Hotel al Ponte Mocenigo.** A columned courtyard welcomes you to this elegant, charming palazzo, former home of the Santa Croce branch of the Mocenigo family (which has a few doges in its past), and the canopied beds, striped damask fabrics, lustrous terrazzo flooring, and gilt-accented furnishings keep the sense of Venice's past strong in the guest rooms. **Pros:** enchanting courtyard; water access; friendly and helpful staff; free Wi-Fi; very reasonable prices. **Cons:** beds are on the hard side; standard rooms are small; rooms in the annex can be noisy. $ *Rooms from: €145* ⊠ *Fondamento de Rimpeto a Ca' Mocenigo, Santa Croce 2063* ☎ *041/5244797* ⊕ *www.alpontemocenigo.com* ⇗ *10 rooms, 1 junior suite* ⦿*Breakfast* Ⓜ *Vaporetto: San Stae* ✛ *C2.*

CANNAREGIO

$$
B&B/INN

🖫 **3749 Ponte Chiodo.** Attractively appointed guest rooms handy to the Ca' d'Oro vaporetto stop look past geranium-filled windows to the bridge leading to its entrance (one of the only ones without hand railings remaining) and canals below or the spacious enclosed garden. **Pros:** highly attentive service; warm, relaxed atmosphere; private garden; good value; very low prices in off-season. **Cons:** no elevator; some bathrooms are smallish. $ *Rooms from: €180* ⊠ *Calle Racchetta, Cannaregio 3749* ☎ *041/2413935* ⊕ *www.pontechiodo.it* ⇗ *6 rooms* ⦿*Breakfast* Ⓜ *Vaporetto: Ca' d'Oro* ✛ *D2.*

$
B&B/INN

🖫 **Al Palazzetto.** Understated yet gracious Venetian décor, original open-beam ceilings and terrazzo flooring, spotless marble baths, and friendly, attentive service are hallmarks of this intimate, family-owned guest house. **Pros:** stand-out service; owner on site; quiet; free Wi-Fi; very good value for money. **Cons:** not for amenity seekers or lovers of ultramodern décor. $ *Rooms from: €100* ⊠ *Calle delle Vele, Cannaregio 4057* ☎ *041/2750897* ⊕ *www.guesthouse.it* ⇗ *6 rooms, 1 suite* ⦿*Breakfast* Ⓜ *Vaporetto: Ca' d'Oro* ✛ *E2.*

$$$$
HOTEL
Fodor'sChoice
★

🖫 **Al Ponte Antico.** This 16th-century palace inn has lined its Gothic windows with tiny white lights, creating an inviting glow that's emblematic of the hospitality and sumptuous surroundings that await you inside: rich brocade-tufted walls, period-style furniture, and hand-decorated beamed ceilings. **Pros:** upper-level terrace overlooks Grand Canal; family

3

run; superior service; Internet is free. **Cons:** in one of the busiest areas of the city, although not particularly noisy. §️ *Rooms from: €315* ✉️ *Calle dell'Aseo, Cannaregio 5768* ☎️ *041/2411944* ⊕ *www.alponteantico. com* 🛏️ *12 rooms, 1 junior suite* ⭗ *Breakfast* Ⓜ️ *Vaporetto: Rialto* ✛ *E3.*

$$$$
HOTEL
Fodor's Choice
★

🖥️ **Ca' Sagredo Hotel.** A study in Venetian opulence, this expansive palace has been the Sagredo family residence since the mid-1600s and has the décor to prove it: the massive staircase has Longhi frescoes soaring above it and the large common areas are adorned with original art by Tiepolo, Longhi, and Ricci, among others. **Pros:** excellent location; authentic yet comfortable renovation of Venice's patrician past; about as close as you can get to an authentic 17th-century Venetian experience. **Cons:** more opulent than intimate; views of the Grand Canal are fine, but they can't match those from the hotels on the Bacino di San Marco. §️ *Rooms from: €400* ✉️ *Campo Santa Sofia, Cannaregio 4198/99* ☎️ *041/2413111* ⊕ *www.casagredohotel.com* 🛏️ *42 rooms, 2 junior suites, 3 suites* ⭗ *Breakfast* Ⓜ️ *Vaporetto: Ca' d'Oro* ✛ *D2.*

$$
HOTEL

🖥️ **Hotel Antico Doge.** Once the home of Doge Marino Falier, the XIV century doge who was executed for treason, this palazzo has been attentively modernized in elegant 18th-century Venetian style: all rooms are adorned with brocades, damask tufted walls, gilt mirrors, and parquet floors and even the breakfast room comes fitted out with a stuccoed ceiling and Murano chandelier. **Pros:** romantic, atmospheric décor; convenient to the Rialto and beyond. **Cons:** on a busy thoroughfare; no outdoor garden or terrace; no elevator. §️ *Rooms from: €170* ✉️ *Campo Santi Apostoli, Cannaregio 5643* ☎️ *041/2411570* ⊕ *www.anticodoge. com* 🛏️ *19 rooms, 1 suite* ⭗ *Breakfast* Ⓜ️ *Vaporetto: Ca' d'Oro or Rialto* ✛ *E3.*

$$
HOTEL

🖥️ **Locanda Ca' Amadi.** A historic palazzo is a welcome retreat on a tranquil *corte*, and individually decorated rooms have tufted walls and views of a lively canal or a quiet courtyard. **Pros:** classic Venetian style; personal service, free Wi-Fi; handy for sightseeing. **Cons:** standard rooms are small; not ideal for guests with mobility issues; staff present only during hours of reception (though always available by phone and on request). §️ *Rooms from: €140* ✉️ *Corte Amadi, Cannaregio 5815* ☎️ *041/5285210* ⊕ *www.caamadi.it* 🛏️ *6 rooms* ⭗ *Breakfast* Ⓜ️ *Vaporetto: Rialto* ✛ *E3.*

$$$
HOTEL

🖥️ **Palazzo Abadessa.** At this late-16th-century palazzo, you can experience gracious hospitality, a luxurious atmosphere, and unusually spacious guest rooms well appointed with antique-style furniture (although the hotel's website claims that they are original antiques), frescoed or stuccoed ceilings, and silk fabrics. **Pros:** enormous walled garden, a rare and delightful treat in crowded Venice; superb guest service. **Cons:** some bathrooms are small. §️ *Rooms from: €295* ✉️ *Calle Priuli off Strada Nova, Cannaregio 4011* ☎️ *041/2413784* ⊕ *www.abadessa.com* 🛏️ *10 rooms, 5 suites* ⭗ *Breakfast* Ⓜ️ *Vaporetto: Ca' d'Oro* ✛ *E2.*

CASTELLO

$$ ⊞ **Ca' dei Dogi.** A quiet courtyard secluded from the San Marco melee
HOTEL offers an island of calm in six individually decorated guest rooms (some
with private terraces) that feature contemporary furnishings and acces-
sories. **Pros:** some rooms have terraces with views of the Doge's Palace.
Cons: rooms are on the small side; furnishings are spartan and look
a bit cheap; located in the middle of the most tourist-frequented part
of Venice. Ⓢ *Rooms from: €150* ⊠ *Corte Santa Scolastica, Castello
4242* ☎ *041/2413751* ⊕ *www.cadeidogi.it* ↴ *6 rooms* ☾ *Closed Dec.*
Ⓞ *Breakfast* Ⓜ *Vaporetto: San Zaccaria* ✛ *F4.*

$$ ⊞ **Hotel La Residenza.** Most rooms at this renovated Gothic-Byzantine
HOTEL palazzo are spacious and elegant, with imitation period furnishings and
18th-century paintings as well as modern amenities. **Pros:** free Wi-Fi;
quiet, residential area. **Cons:** not super-close to a vaporetto stop; a
few of the rooms are indeed small; not the warmest staff. Ⓢ *Rooms
from: €190* ⊠ *Campo Bandiera e Moro (or Bragora), Castello 3608*
☎ *041/5285315* ⊕ *www.venicelaresidenza.com* ↴ *15 rooms* Ⓞ *Breakfast* Ⓜ *Vaporetto: Arsenale* ✛ *G4.*

$$$$ ⊞ **Metropole.** Atmosphere prevails in this labyrinth of intimate, opulent
HOTEL spaces featuring classic Venetian décor combined with exotic Eastern
Fodor's Choice influences. The owner, a lifelong collector of unusual objects, fills com-
★ mon areas and the sumptuously appointed guest rooms with an assortment of antiques and curiosities. **Pros:** hotel harkens back to a gracious
Venice of times past; fine bar (great Martinis!); good (but expensive)
restaurant. **Cons:** one of the most densely touristed locations in the city,
although noise is not a serious problem; rooms with views are considerably more expensive, although the views are spectacular. Ⓢ *Rooms
from: €400* ⊠ *Riva degli Schiavoni, Castello 4149* ☎ *041/5205044*
⊕ *www.hotelmetropole.com* ↴ *67 rooms, 13 junior suites, 9 suites*
Ⓞ *Breakfast* Ⓜ *Vaporetto: San Zaccaria* ✛ *F4.*

$$$$ ⊞ **Ruzzini Palace Hotel.** Public rooms are Renaissance- and Baroque-
HOTEL style, with soaring spaces, Venetian terrazzo flooring, frescoed and
open-beam ceilings, and Murano chandeliers, while guest rooms are
essays in historic style but come integrated with contemporary furnishings and appointments. **Pros:** excellent service; a luminous, aristocratic
ambience; near some good restaurants and artistic attractions; located
on a lively Venetian campo not frequented by tourists. **Cons:** the 5-
to 10-minute walk from San Zaccaria or Rialto includes two bridges
and can be cumbersome for those with mobility issues or significant
amounts of luggage; relatively far from a vaporetto stop; no restaurant.
Ⓢ *Rooms from: €380* ⊠ *Campo Santa Maria Formosa, Castello 5866*
☎ *041/2410447* ⊕ *www.ruzzinipalace.com* ↴ *19 rooms, 6 junior suites,
3 suites* Ⓞ *Breakfast* Ⓜ *Vaporetto: San Zaccaria or Rialto* ✛ *E3.*

NIGHTLIFE AND PERFORMING ARTS

NIGHTLIFE

Venice's offerings for nightlife are, even by rather sedate standards, fairly tame. Most bars must close by midnight, especially those that offer outdoor seating. Piazza San Marco is a popular meeting place in nice weather, when the cafés stay open relatively late and all seem to compete to offer the best live music. The younger crowd, Venetians and visitors alike, tend to gravitate toward the area around Rialto Bridge, with Campi San Bartolomeo and San Luca on one side and Campo Rialto Nuovo on the other. Especially popular with university students and young people from the mainland are the bars around Campo Santa Margherita. Pick up a booklet of *2Night* or visit ⊕ *venezia.2night.it* for nightlife listings and reviews.

SAN MARCO AND DORSODURO

Al Chioschetto. While this popular place consists only of a kiosk set up to serve some outdoor tables, it is located on the Zattere, and thus provides panoramic views. It's a handy meet-up for locals and a stop-off for tourists in nice weather for a spritz, panini, or a sunny read as the Venetian world eases by. But go for the view and the sunshine; the food and drink, while acceptable, are not exceptional. ⊠ *Near Ponte Lungo, Dorsoduro 1406/A* ☎ *338/1174077* Ⓜ *Vaporetto: Zattere.*

Corte dell'Orso. It is easy to see why this place is popular with the locals, offering fairly priced cocktails, a reasonable assortment of cicheti, and a good selection of Italian wine, but the warm ambience, a friendly staff, and live music every Wednesday (beginning around 8 pm) are the main draws. The kitchen stays open late. ⊠ *Tucked away in an alley across from Church of San Giovanni Grisostomo, San Marco 5495* ☎ *041/5224673* Ⓜ *Vaporetto: Rialto.*

Fodor'sChoice ★ **Il Caffè.** Commonly called "Bar Rosso" for its bright-red exterior, Il Caffè has far more tables outside than inside. A favorite with students and faculty from the nearby university, it's a good place to enjoy a *spritz*—the preferred Venetian aperitif of white wine, Campari or Aperol, soda water, an olive, and a slice of orange. It has excellent tramezzini (among the best in town) and panini, and a hip, helpful staff. Its closing time depends on the always-changing noise laws, but typically around midnight. It's been recently frequented by high school students from the mainland on week end nights. It's more enjoyable around lunch time, or in the early evening. ⊠ *Campo Santa Margherita, Dorsoduro 2963* ☎ *041/5287998* ⊘ *Closed Sun.*

Fodor'sChoice ★ **Imagina.** Just off Campo Santa Margherita toward the Ponte dei Pugni, this bar draws a more mature and sophisticated Venetian clientele than the student-oriented places in the campo itself. The friendly fellows running the place make an excellent (and generous) spritz, serve decent wine, and some American regulars have taught them to make a rather palatable Martini. A great place for a light lunch. Sandwiches and snacks are limited, but what's offered is fresh and tasty. The salads are particularly good, generous and reasonably priced. Outdoor and indoor seating are available. The bar hosts regular art exhibitions by local, yet-to-be-established artists. ⊠ *Campo Santa Margherita, Dorsoduro 3126* ⊕ *www.imaginacafe.it* ⊙ *Daily* Ⓜ *Vaporetto: Ca'Rezzonico.*

Orange. Modern, hip, and complemented by an internal garden, this welcoming bar anchors the south end of Campo Santa Margherita, the liveliest campo in Venice. You can have *piadine* sandwiches, salads, and drinks while watching soccer games on a massive screen inside, or sit at the tables in the campo. Despite being close to the university, Orange is frequented primarily by young working people from the mainland and tourists. ⊠ *Campo Santa Margherita, Dorsoduro 3054/A* ☎ *041/5234740.*

SAN POLO

Naranzaria. At the friendliest of the several bar-restaurants that line the Erbaria, near the Rialto Market, enjoy a cocktail outside along the Grand Canal or at a cozy table inside of the renovated 16th-century warehouse. Although the food is acceptable, the ambience is really the main attraction. After the kitchen closes at 10:30, light snacks are served until midnight, and live music (usually jazz, Latin, or rock) occasionally plays on Sunday evening. ⊠ *L'Erbaria, along Grand Canal, San Polo 130* ☎ *041/7241035* Ⓜ *Vaporetto: Rialto Mercato.*

CASTELLO

Zanzibar. This kiosk bar is very popular on warm summer evenings with upper-class Venetians and tourists. It offers food, but that is mostly limited to conventional Venetian sandwiches and commercial ice cream. The most interesting thing about the place is its location with a view of the church of Santa Maria Formosa, which makes it a pleasant place for a drink and a good place for people-watching. ⊠ *Campo Santa Maria Formosa, Castello 5840* ☎ *041/962640* Ⓜ *Vaporetto: San Zaccaria.*

PERFORMING ARTS

Visit ⊕ *www.aguestinvenice.com* for a preview of musical, artistic, and sporting events. *Venezia News* (*VENews*), available at newsstands, has similar information but also includes in-depth articles about noteworthy events. The tourist office publishes a handy, free quarterly *Calendar* in Italian and English, listing daily events and current museum and venue hours. *Venezia da Vivere* is a seasonal guide listing nightspots and live music. For a Venice website that allows you to scan the cultural horizon before you arrive; try ⊕ *www.turismovenezia.it,* And don't ignore the posters you see plastered on the walls as you walk—they're often the most up-to-date information you can find.

CARNEVALE

Although Carnevale has traditionally been associated with the time leading up to the Roman Catholic period of Lent, it originally started out as a principally secular annual period of partying and feasting to celebrate Venice's victory over the patriarch of Ulrich Aquileia in 1162. To commemorate the annual tribute Ulrich was forced to pay, a bull and 12 pigs were slaughtered each year on the day before Lent in Piazza San Marco. The use of masks for Carnevale was first mentioned in 1268, and its direct association with Lent was not made until the end of the 13th century. Since then, for centuries the city marked the days preceding *quaresima* (Lent) with abundant feasting and wild celebrations. The word *carnevale* is derived from the words *carne* (meat) and *levare* (to remove), as eating meat was restricted during Lent.

Venice earned its international reputation as the "city of Carnevale" in the 18th century, when partying would begin several months before Lent and the city seemed to be one continuous masquerade. During this time, income from tourists became a major source of funds in La Serenissima's coffers. With the Republic's fall in 1797, Carnevale was prohibited by the French and the Austrians. From Italian reunification in 1866 until the fall of fascism in the 1940s, the event was alternately resumed and banned, depending on the government's stance.

It was revived for good in the 1970s, when residents began taking to the calli and campi in their own impromptu celebrations. It didn't take long for the tourist industry to embrace the revival as a means to stimulate business during low season. The efforts were successful. Each year over the 10- to 12-day Carnevale period (ending on the Tuesday before Ash Wednesday), more than a half million people attend concerts, theater and street performances, masquerade balls, historical processions, fashion shows, and contests. Since 2008 Carnevale has been organized by **Venezia Marketing & Eventi** (⊕ *www.carnevale.venezia.it*). *A Guest in Venice* is also a complete guide to public and private Carnevale festivities. Stop by the **tourist office** (☎ *041/5298711* ⊕ *www.turismovenezia.it*) or Venice Pavilion for information, but be aware they can be mobbed. If you're not planning on joining in the revelry, you'd be wise to choose another time to visit Venice. Crowds throng the streets (which become one-way, with police directing foot traffic), bridges are designated "no-stopping" zones to avoid gridlock, and prices skyrocket.

FESTIVALS

The **Biennale** (⊕ *www.labiennale.org*) cultural institution organizes events year-round, including the **Venice Film Festival,** which begins the last week of August. **La Biennale di Venezia,** an international exhibition of contemporary art, is held in odd-numbered years, usually from mid-June to early November, at the Giardini della Biennale, and in the impressive Arsenale.

Fodor's Choice ★ **Festa del Redentore.** On the third Sunday in July, crowds cross the Canale della Giudecca by means of a pontoon bridge, built every year to commemorate the doge's annual visit to Palladio's Chiesa del Redentore, to offer thanks for the end of a 16th-century plague. The evening before, Venetians set up tables and chairs along the canals. As evening falls, practically the whole city takes to the streets and tables, and thousands more take to the water. Boats decorated with colored lanterns, well provisioned with traditional Redentore meals, jockey for position to watch the grand event. Half an hour before midnight, Venice kicks off a fireworks display over the Bacino, with the fireworks reflecting in its waters. Anywhere along the Riva degli Schiavoni you'll find good viewing; or try Zattere, as close to Punta Dogana as you can get, or on the Zitelle end of the Giudecca. After the fireworks you can join the young folks in staying out all night and greeting sunrise on the Lido beach, or rest up and make the procession to Mass on Sunday morning. If you're on a boat, allow for a couple of hours to dislodge yourself from the nautical traffic jam when the festivities break up.

SHOPPING

Globalization has made most goods available in Venice and items like Venetian glass widely available in major cities throughout the world. While the selection of Italian and Venetian made goods may be a bit better in Venice than at home, the prices may actually be lower in the United States, especially considering that U.S. retailers discount sale goods quite radically. Venetian antiques, especially antique Venetian glass, is almost invariably cheaper in other places, because Venetians are ready to pay high prices for their own heritage. So, before your trip, check the prices at home on what you may wish to buy abroad before you leave.

Alluring shops abound in Venice. You'll find countless vendors of trademark Venetian wares such as glass and lace. The authenticity of some goods can be suspect, but they're often pleasing to the eye regardless of their place of origin. There are also some interesting craft and art studios, where you can find high-quality, one-of-a-kind articles, but Venice is a design center only for glass, lace, and high-end textiles. You will probably find a better choice of leather, clothing, and furnishings in other Italian cities.

Regular store hours are usually 9 to 12:30 and 3:30 or 4 to 7:30; some stores close Saturday afternoon or Monday morning. Food shops are open 8 to 1 and 5 to 7:30, and may close Wednesday afternoon and all day Sunday. Supermarkets are generally open every day, including Sunday, and have longer opening hours than independent stores. Many tourist-oriented shops are open all day, every day. Some shops close for both a summer and a winter vacation.

The **San Marco** area is full of shops and couture boutiques such as Armani, Missoni, Valentino, Fendi, and Versace. Le Mercerie, the Frezzeria, Calle dei Fabbri, and Calle Larga XXII Marzo, all leading from Piazza San Marco, are some of Venice's busiest shopping streets. Other good shopping areas surround Calle del Teatro and Campi San Salvador, Manin, San Fantin, and San Bartolomeo. You can find somewhat less expensive, more varied and imaginative shops between the Rialto Bridge and San Polo and in Santa Croce, and art galleries in Dorsoduro from the Salute to the Accademia.

SAN MARCO AND DORSODURO

GIFTS

Giuliana Longo. A hat shop that's been around since 1901 offers an assortment of Venetian and gondolier straw hats, Panama hats from Ecuador, caps and berets, and some select scarves of silk and fine wool; even a special corner dedicated to accessories for antique cars. ⊠ *Calle*

Venetian Art Glass

The glass of Murano is Venice's number-one product, and you'll be confronted by mind-boggling displays of traditional and contemporary glassware—much of it kitsch and not made in Venice. Traditional Venetian glass is hot, blown glass, not lead crystal; it comes in myriad forms that range from the classic ornate goblets and chandeliers, to beads, vases, sculpture, and more. Beware of paying "Venetian" prices for glass made elsewhere. A piece claiming to be made in Murano may guarantee its origin, but not its value or quality; the prestigious Venetian glassmakers—like Venini, Seguso, Salviati, and others—sign their pieces, but never use the "made in Murano" label. To make a smart purchase, take your time and be selective. You can learn a great deal without sales pressure at the Museo del Vetro on Murano; unfortunately you'll likely find the least-attractive glass where public demonstrations are offered. Although prices in Venice and on Murano are comparable, shops in Venice with wares from various glassworks may charge slightly less.

■TIP→ A "free" taxi to Murano always comes with sales pressure. Take the vaporetto that's included in your transit pass, and, if you prefer, a private guide who specializes in the subject but has no affinity to any specific furnace.

del Lovo, San Marco 4813 ☎ *041/5226454* ⊕ *www.giulianalongo.com* Ⓜ *Vaporetto: San Marco.*

GLASS

Ma.Re. Collectors head here for the one-of-a-kind objects created by leading glass artists. If you've broken a piece out of a set of out of production Venetian glasses, the friendly staff will try to help you replace it, either by finding a substitute, or having one made for you. A visit to this shop will give you a good overview of premium Venetian production. ✉ *Via XXII Marzo, San Marco 2088* ☎ *041/5231191* 🖷 *041/5285745* ⊕ *www.mareglass.com* Ⓜ *Vaporetto: San Marco.*

Marina and Susanna Sent. The beautiful and elegant glass jewelry of Marina and Susanna Sent has been featured in *Vogue*. Look also for vases and other exceptional design pieces. Other locations are near San Moise in San Marco and on Murano on the Fondamenta Serenella. ✉ *Campo San Vio, Dorsoduro 669* ☎ *041/5208136 in Dorsoduro, 041/5204014 in San Marco, 041/5274665 in Murano* ⊕ *www.marinaesusannasent.com* Ⓜ *Vaporetto: Accademia/Zattere, Giglio, Murano Serenella.*

Pauly & C. Established in 1866, Pauly & C features a truly impressive selection of authentic Murano art glass (both traditional and contemporary styles) by the most accomplished masters. The showroom at No. 73 houses the more traditional collection; at No. 77 you can find works by artists and designers. ✉ *Piazza San Marco, San Marco 73 and 77* ☎ *041/5235484, 041/2770279* ⊕ *www.pauly.it.*

Venini. When connoisseurs of Venetian glass think of the firms who have restored Venice to its place as the epicenter of artistic glass production,

Venini is, without any major discussion, the firm that immediately comes to mind. Since the beginning of the 20th century, Venini has found craftsmen and designers that have made their trademark synonymous with the highest quality both in traditional and in creative glass design. A piece of Venini glass, even one of modest price and proportions, will be considered not only a charming decorative object, but also a work of art that will maintain its value for years to come. While Venini's more exciting and innovative pieces may cost thousands of euros, the Venini showrooms in the Piazza San Marco and on Murano also have small, more conventional designs for prices as low as €100. ⊠ *314 Piazzetta Leoncini, San Marco* ☎ *041/5224045* ⊕ *www.venini.com.*

LEATHER

Il Grifone. Very few artisan leather shops remain in Venice, and Il Grifone is the standout with respect to quality, tradition, and a guarantee for an exquisite product. For more than 30 years, Antonio Peressin has been making bags, purses, belts, and smaller leather items that have a wide following because of his precision and attention to detail. His prices remain reasonable and accessible. ⊠ *Fondamenta del Gaffaro, Dorsoduro 3516* ☎ *041/5229452* ⊕ *www.ilgrifonevenezia.it* ⊗ *Closed Sun. and Mon., and Sat. pm* Ⓜ *Vaporetto: Piazzale Roma.*

TEXTILES

Fodor'sChoice
★

Bevilacqua. This renowned studio has kept the weaving tradition alive in Venice since 1875, using 18th-century hand looms for its most precious creations. Its repertoire of 3,500 different patterns and designs yields a ready-to-sell selection of hundreds of brocades, Gobelins, damasks, velvets, taffetas, and satins. You'll also find tapestry, cushions, and braiding. Fabrics made by this prestigious firm have been used to decorate the Vatican, the Royal Palace of Stockholm, and the White House. This listing is for the main retail outlet of the Bevilacqua establishment; there's another behind the San Marco Basilica. ■TIP➜ **If you're interested in seeing the actual 18th century looms in action making the most precious fabrics, request an appointment at the Luigi Bevilacqua production center in Santa Croce.** ⊠ *Campo di Santa Maria del Giglio, San Marco 2520* ☎ *041/2410662 for main retail outlet, 041/5287581 for retail outlet behind the Basilica, 041/721566 for Santa Croce production center* ⊕ *www.bevilacquatessuti.com* Ⓜ *Vaporetto: Giglio.*

Fodor'sChoice
★

Jesurum. A great deal of so-called "Burano-Venetian" lace is now machine-made in China; so, unless you have some experience—and there really is a difference—you're best off going a trusted place. Jesurum has been the major producer of handmade Venetian lace since 1870. Its lace is, of course, all modern production, but if you want an antique piece, the people at Jesurum can point you in the right direction. ⊠ *Calle Larga XII Marzo, San Marco 2401* ☎ *041/5238969* ⊕ *www. jesurum.it.*

THE VENETO AND
FRIULI–VENEZIA GIULIA

WELCOME TO THE VENETO AND FRIULI-VENEZIA GIULIA

TOP REASONS TO GO

★ **Giotto's frescoes in the Cappella degli Scrovegni:** In this Padua chapel, Giotto's expressive and innovative frescoes foreshadowed the Renaissance.

★ **Villa Barbaro in Maser:** Master architect Palladio's graceful creation meets Veronese's splendid frescoes in a one-time-only collaboration.

★ **Opera in Verona's ancient arena:** The performances may not be top-notch, but even serious opera fans can't resist the spectacle of these shows.

★ **Roman and early Christian ruins at Aquileia:** Aquileia's beautiful ruins offer an image of the transition from pagan to Christian Rome, and are almost entirely free of tourists.

★ **The wine roads north of Treviso:** A series of routes takes you through beautiful hillsides to some of Italy's finest wines.

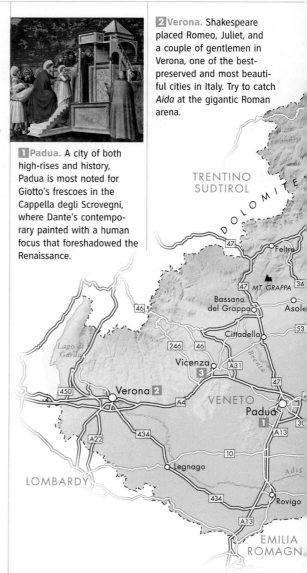

1 Padua. A city of both high-rises and history, Padua is most noted for Giotto's frescoes in the Cappella degli Scrovegni, where Dante's contemporary painted with a human focus that foreshadowed the Renaissance.

2 Verona. Shakespeare placed Romeo, Juliet, and a couple of gentlemen in Verona, one of the best-preserved and most beautiful cities in Italy. Try to catch *Aida* at the gigantic Roman arena.

3 **Vicenza.** This elegant art city, on the green plain reaching inland from Venice's lagoon, bears the signature of the great 16th-century architect Andrea Palladio, including several palazzi and other important buildings.

4 **Treviso and the Hillside Towns.** Treviso is a prosperous, busy town with more than a touch of Venetian style. Asolo (the City of a Hundred Horizons) is the most popular destination in a series of towns that dot the wine-producing hills north of Treviso.

GETTING ORIENTED

The Venetian Arc is the sweep of land curving north and east from the River Adige to the Slovenian border. It's made up of two Italian regions—the Veneto and Friuli–Venezia Giulia—that were once controlled by Venice, and the culture is a mix of Venetian, Italian, Alpine, and Central European sensibilities.

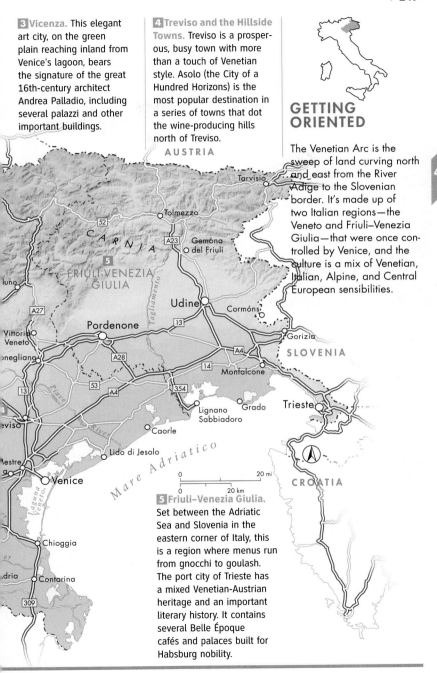

5 **Friuli–Venezia Giulia.** Set between the Adriatic Sea and Slovenia in the eastern corner of Italy, this is a region where menus run from gnocchi to goulash. The port city of Trieste has a mixed Venetian-Austrian heritage and an important literary history. It contains several Belle Époque cafés and palaces built for Habsburg nobility.

EATING AND DRINKING WELL IN THE VENETO AND FRIULI–VENEZIA GIULIA

With the decisive seasonal changes of the Venetian Arc, it's little wonder that many restaurants shun printed menus. Elements from field and forest define much of the region's cuisine, including white asparagus, herbs, chestnuts, radicchio, and wild mushrooms.

Restaurants of the Venetian Arc tend to cling to tradition, not only in the food they serve, but also when they serve it. From 2:30 in the afternoon until about 7:30 in the evening most places are closed (though you can pick up a snack at a bar during these hours), and on Sunday afternoon restaurants are packed with Italian families and friends indulging in the weekly ritual of lunching out.

Meals are still sacred for most Italians, so don't be surprised if you get disapproving looks when you gobble down a sandwich or a slice of pizza while seated on the church steps or a park bench. In many places it's actually illegal to do so. If you want to fit in with the locals, snack while standing at the bar or seated in a café, and they may not even notice that you're a tourist.

THE BEST IN BEANS

Pasta e fagioli, a thick bean soup with pasta, served slightly warm or at room temperature, is made all over Italy. Folks in the Veneto, though, take special pride in their version, made from particularly fine beans grown around the village of Lamon, near Belluno.

Even when they're bought in the Veneto, the beans from Lamon cost more than double the next most expensive variety, but their rich and delicate taste is considered well worth the added expense. You never knew that bean soup could taste so good.

FISH

The catch of the day is always a good bet, whether it's sweet and succulent Adriatic shellfish, sea bream, bass, or John Dory, or freshwater fish from Lake Garda, near Verona. A staple in the Veneto is *baccalà,* dried salt cod, introduced to Italy during the Renaissance by northern European traders. Dried cod is soaked in water or milk and then prepared in a different way in each city. In Vicenza, baccalà *alla vicentina,* is cooked with onions, milk, and cheese, and is generally served with polenta.

MEAT

Because grazing land is scarce in the Veneto, beef is a rarity, but pork and veal are standards, and goose, duck, and guinea fowl are common poultry options. In Friuli–Venezia Giulia, menus show the influences of Austria-Hungary: you may find deer and hare on the menu, as well as Eastern European-style goulash. Throughout the Veneto an unusual treat is *nervetti*—cubes of gelatin from a calf's knee prepared with onions, parsley, olive oil, and lemon.

PASTA, RISOTTO, POLENTA

For *primi* (first courses), the Veneto dines on *bigoli* (thick whole-wheat pasta), generally served with an anchovy-onion sauce delicately flavored with cinnamon, or risotto, creamy rice generally flavored with vegetables or shellfish. *Polenta* (cornmeal gruel) is

everywhere, whether it's a stiff porridge topped with Gorgonzola, or a stew, or a patty grilled alongside meat or fish. Spaghetti and other types of pasta are widely available, but they are considered practically foreign. The same holds true for pizza. You can find fairly good pizza in the Veneto, but it has little in common with the local cuisine.

RADICCHIO DI TREVISO

In fall and winter be sure to try the radicchio di Treviso, *pictured above,* a red endive grown near that town but popular all over the region. Cultivation is very labor-intensive, so it can be expensive. It's best in a stew with chicken or veal, in a risotto, or just grilled or baked with a drizzle of olive oil and perhaps a little taleggio cheese from neighboring Lombardy.

WINE

The Veneto produces more D.O.C. (Denominazione di Origine Controllata) wines than any other region in Italy. Amarone, the region's crowning achievement, is a robust, full-bodied red. The best of the whites are Soave, prosecco, and *pinot bianco* (pinot blanc). In Friuli–Venezia Giulia the local wines include *tocai friulano,* a dry, lively white made from the sauvignon vert grape, and *piccolit,* perhaps Italy's most highly prized dessert wine.

Updated
by Bruce
Leimsidor

The arc around Venice—stretching from Verona to Trieste, encompassing the Veneto and Friuli–Venezia Giulia regions—is undisputedly one of most culturally rich areas in Italy, an intellectual and spiritual feast of architecture, painting, and sculpture. Since the 16th century, the art, architecture, and way of life here have all reflected Venetian splendor. Whether coastal or inland, the emblem of Venice, Saint Mark's winged lion, is emblazoned on palazzi and poised on pedestals.

It wasn't always this way. Back in the Middle Ages, Padua and Verona were independent cities that developed substantial cultural traditions of their own, leaving behind many artistic treasures. And even while it was under Venice's political domination, 16th-century Vicenza contributed more to the cultural heritage of La Serenissima than it took from her, in large part because of its master architect, Andrea Palladio.

The area is primarily flat, green farmland. As you move inland, though, you encounter low hills, which swell and rise in a succession of plateaus and high meadows, culminating in the snowcapped Dolomite Alps. Much of the pleasure of exploring here comes from discovering the variations on the Venetian theme that give a unique character to each of the towns. Some, such as Verona, Treviso, and Udine, have a solid medieval look. Padua, with its narrow arcaded streets, is romantic; Vicenza, ennobled by the architecture of Palladio, is more elegant. Udine, in Friuli–Venezia Giulia, is a genteel, intricately sculpted city that's home to the first important frescoes by Gianbattista Tiepolo. In Trieste, once the main port of the Austro-Hungarian Empire, you can find survivors of those days in its Viennese-inspired coffeehouses and *buffets*—hole-in-the-wall eateries serving sausages and other pork dishes.

Unlike the western regions of northern Italy, the Veneto and Friuli–Venezia Giulia were slow to move from an agricultural to an industrial economy, and even now depend upon small and medium businesses, many of which are still family-run. The area, therefore, attracted far fewer migrants from elsewhere in Italy, and it was able to maintain its local cultures to a substantial degree. Local dialects may have all but died out in places like Milan and Turin, but they still thrive in the Veneto and Friuli–Venezia Giulia, and even when the residents speak standard Italian, it is frequently laced with local words and usage.

THE VENETO AND FRIULI–VENEZIA PLANNER

PLANNING

Several of the most interesting and important sights in the Venetian Arc require reservations or are open only at limited times. If you want to make the most of your visit, it's important to plan ahead. For instance, reservations are required to see the Giotto frescoes in Padua's Cappella degli Scrovegni—though if there's space, you can "reserve" on the spot.

On the outskirts of Vicenza, the Villa della Rotonda, one of Palladio's masterpieces, is open to the public only from mid-March through mid-November, and only on Wednesday and Saturday. (Hours for visiting the grounds are less restrictive.) Another important Palladian villa, Villa Barbaro near Maser, is open weekends and several days during the week from March to October. From November to February, it's open only on weekends.

MAKING THE MOST OF YOUR TIME

Lined up in a row west of Venice are Padua, Vicenza, and Verona—three prosperous small cities that are each worth at least a day on a northern Italy itinerary. Verona has the most charm and the widest selection of hotels and restaurants, so it's probably the best choice for a base in the area, even though it also draws the most tourists. The hills north of Venice make for good drives, with appealing villages set amid a visitor-friendly wine country.

East of the Veneto, the region of Friuli–Venezia Giulia is off the main tourist circuit. You probably won't go here on a first trip to Italy, but by your second or third visit you may be drawn by its caves and castles, its battle-worn hills, and its mix of Italian and Central European culture. The port city of Trieste, famous for its elegant cafés, has a quiet character that some people find dull but others find alluring.

GETTING HERE AND AROUND

BUS TRAVEL

There are inter-urban and inter-regional connections throughout the Veneto and Friuli, handled by nearly a dozen private bus lines. To figure out which line will get you where, the best strategy is to get assistance from local tourist offices.

CAR TRAVEL

Padua, Vicenza, and Verona are on the highway (and train line) between Venice and Milan. Seeing them without a car isn't a problem; in fact, having a car can complicate matters. The cities sometimes limit access, permitting cars only with plates ending in an even number on even days, odd on odd, or prohibiting cars altogether on weekends. There's no central source for information about these sporadic traffic restrictions;

the best strategy is to check with your hotel before arrival for an update. You'll need a car to get the most out of the hill country that makes up much of the Venetian Arc, and it will be particularly useful for visiting Aquileia, since public transportation to that quite interesting site is limited.

The two main access roads to the Venetian Arc from southern Italy are both linked to the A1 (Autostrada del Sole), which connects Bologna, Florence, and Rome. They are the A13, which ends in Padua, and the A22, which passes through Verona running north–south. Linking the region from east to west is the A4, the primary route from Milan to Trieste, skirting Verona, Padua, and Venice along the way. The distance from Verona to Trieste via A4 is 263 km (163 miles; 2½ hours), with one break in the autostrada near Venice/Mestre. Branches link the A4 with Treviso (A27), Pordenone (A28), and Udine (A23).

TRAIN TRAVEL

Trains on the main routes from the south stop almost hourly in Verona, Padua, and Venice. From northern Italy and the rest of Europe, trains usually enter via Milan or through Porta Nuova station in Verona. Treviso and Udine both lie on the main line from Venice to Tarvisio. Unfortunately, there are no daytime express trains between Venice and Tarvisio, only the slower inter-regional and regional service. There is also no through train service between this region and neighboring Slovenia, only an inconvenient and uncomfortable minibus. To the west of Venice, the main line running across the north of Italy stops at Padua (30 minutes from Venice), Vicenza (1 hour), and Verona (1½ hours); to the east is Trieste (2 hours). Local trains link Vicenza to Treviso (1 hour) and Udine to Trieste (1 hour).

Be sure to take express trains whenever possible—a local "milk run" that stops in every village along the way can take considerably longer. The fastest trains are the Eurostars, but reservations are mandatory and fares are much higher than on regular express trains.

Information ☎ *892021* ⊕ *www.trenitalia.com.*

RESTAURANTS

Prices in the dining reviews are the average cost of a main course at dinner, or, if dinner is not served, at lunch.

HOTELS

Rates tend to be higher in Padua and Verona; in Verona especially, seasonal rates vary widely and soar during trade fairs and the opera season. There are fewer good lodging choices in Vicenza, perhaps because more overnighters are drawn to the better restaurant scenes in Verona and Padua. *Agriturismo* (farm stay) information is available at tourist offices and sometimes on their websites. Ask about weekend discounts, often available at hotels catering to business clients. Substantial savings can sometimes be had by booking through reservation services on the Internet.

Hotel reviews have been shortened. For full information, visit Fodors. com.

WHAT IT COSTS				
	$	$$	$$$	$$$$
RESTAURANTS	under €15	€15–€24	€25–€35	over €35
HOTELS	under €125	€125–€200	€201–€300	over €300

Prices in the dining reviews are the average cost of a main course at dinner, or, if dinner is not served, at lunch. Prices in the reviews are the lowest cost of a standard double room in high season.

PADUA

A romantic warren of arcaded streets, Padua is a major cultural center in northern Italy. It has first-rate artistic monuments and, along with Bologna, is one of the few cities in the country where you can catch a glimpse of student life.

Its university, founded in 1222 and Italy's second oldest, attracted such cultural icons as Dante (1265–1321), Petrarch (1304–74), and Galileo (1564–1642), thus earning the city the sobriquet "La Dotta" (The Learned). Padua's Basilica di Sant'Antonio, begun around 1238, attracts droves of pilgrims, especially on his feast day, June 13. Three great artists—Giotto (1266–1337), Donatello (circa 1386–1466), and Mantegna (1431–1506)—left significant works in Padua. Giotto's Capella degli Scrovegni here is one of the best-known and most meticulously preserved works of art in the country. Today, a bicycle-happy student body—some 50,000 strong—flavors every aspect of local culture. Don't be surprised if you spot a *laurea* (graduation) ceremony marked by laurel leaves, mocking lullabies, and X-rated caricatures.

GETTING HERE AND AROUND

Many people visit Padua from Venice: the train trip between the cities is short, and regular bus service originates from Venice's Piazzale Roma. By car from Milan or Venice, Padua is on the Autostrada Torino–Trieste A4/E70. Take the San Carlo exit and follow Via Guido Reni to Via Tiziano Aspetti into town. From the south, take the Autostrada Bologna–Padova A13 to its Padua terminus at Via Ballaglia. Regular bus service connects Venice's Marco Polo airport with downtown Padua.

Padua is a walker's city—parking is difficult, and cars are prohibited in much of the city center. If you arrive by car, leave your vehicle in one of the parking lots on the outskirts, or at your hotel. Unlimited bus service is included with the Padova Card (⊕ *www.padovacard.it*; €16 or €21, valid for 48 or 72 hours), which allows entry to all the city's principal sights (€1 extra for a Capella degli Scrovegni reservation). It's available at tourist information offices and at some museums.

VISITOR INFORMATION

Padua Tourism Office ⊠ *Padova Railway Station* ☎ *049/2010080* ⊕ *www. turismopadova.it* ☉ *Mon.–Sat. 9–7, Sun. 10–4* ⊠ *Galleria Pedrocchi* ☎ *049/8767927* ⊕ *www.infopadova.it* ☉ *Weekdays 9–noon and 3–6, Sat. 9–noon.*

EXPLORING

TOP ATTRACTIONS

Fodor'sChoice **Basilica di Sant'Antonio** (*Basilica del Santo*). Thousands of faithful make
★ the pilgrimage here each year to pray at the tomb of Saint Anthony,
while others come to admire works by the 15th-century Florentine master Donatello. His equestrian statue (1453) of the *condottiere* (mercenary general) Erasmo da Narni, known as Gattamelata, in front of the
church is one of the great masterpieces of Italian Renaissance sculpture.
It was inspired by the ancient statue of Marcus Aurelius in Rome's Campidoglio. Donatello also sculpted the beautiful series of bronze reliefs
in the imposing interior illustrating the miracles of Saint Anthony, as
well as the bronze statues of the Madonna and saints, on the high altar.

The huge church, which combines elements of Byzantine, Romanesque,
and Gothic styles, was probably begun around 1238, seven years after
the death of the Portuguese-born saint. It was completed in 1310, with
structural modifications added from the end of the 14th century into
the mid-15th century. Because of the site's popularity with pilgrims,
masses are held in the basilica almost constantly, which makes it difficult
to see these works. More accessible is the restored **Cappella del Santo**
(housing the tomb of the saint), which dates to the 16th century. Its
walls are covered with impressive reliefs by various important Renaissance sculptors, including Jacopo Sansovino (1486–1570), the architect of the library in Venice's Piazza San Marco, and Tullio Lombardo
(1455–1532), the greatest in a family of sculptors who decorated many
churches in the area, among them Venice's Santa Maria dei Miracoli.
✉ *Piazza del Santo* ☎ *049/8225652* ⊕ *www.basilicadelsanto.it* ☾ *Oct.–
Apr., daily 6:20 am–7 pm; May–Sept., daily 6:20 am–7:45 pm.*

Fodor'sChoice **Cappella degli Scrovegni** (*The Arena Chapel*). The spatial depth, emo-
★ tional intensity, and naturalism of the frescoes illustrating the lives of
Mary and Jesus in this world-famous chapel—note the use of blue
sky instead of the conventional, depth-destroying gold background of
medieval painting—broke new ground in Western art. Enrico Scrovegno
commissioned these frescoes to atone for the sins of his deceased father,
Reginaldo, the usurer condemned to the Seventh Circle of the Inferno
in Dante's *Divine Comedy.* Giotto and his assistants worked on the
frescoes from 1303 to 1305, arranging them in tiers to be read from
left to right. Opposite the altar is a *Last Judgment,* most likely designed
and painted by Giotto's assistants, where Enrico offers his chapel to the
Virgin, celebrating her role in human salvation—particularly appropriate, given the penitential purpose of the chapel.

▪TIP➜ Mandatory reservations, nonrefundable and for a specific
time, can be made in advance at the ticket office, online, or by phone.
Payments online or by phone by credit card must be made one day in
advance. Reservations are necessary even if you have a Padova Card.
In order to preserve the artwork, doors are opened only every 15 minutes. A maximum of 25 visitors at a time must spend 15 minutes in an
acclimatization room before making a 15-minute (20-minute in winter,
late June, and July) chapel visit. Punctuality is essential; tickets should
be picked up at least one hour before your reservation time. If you don't

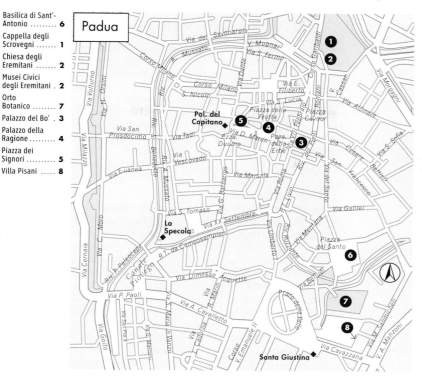

have a reservation, it's sometimes possible to buy your chapel admission on the spot—but you might have to wait a while until there's a group with an opening. You can see fresco details as part of a virtual tour at the Musei Civici degli Eremitani. A good place to get some background before visiting the chapel is the multimedia room, where there are films and interactive computer presentations. Between Christmas and Epiphany (January 6), the chapel sometimes has special late hours. ⊠ *Piazza Eremitani 8* ☏ *049/2010020 for reservations* ⊕ *www. cappelladegliscrovegni.it* 🎫 *€13, includes Musei Civici (€1 with Padova Card)* ⊘ *Daily 9–7.*

Palazzo della Ragione. Also known as Il Salone, the spectacular arcaded reception hall in Padua's original law courts is as notable for its grandeur—it's 85 feet high—as for its colorful setting, surrounded by shops, cafés, and open-air fruit and vegetable markets. Niccolò Miretto and Stefano di Ferrara, working from 1425 to 1440, painted the frescoes, following the plan of frescoes by Giotto destroyed by a fire in 1420. The stunning space hosts art shows, and an enormous wooden horse, crafted for a public tournament in 1466, commands pride of place. It is patterned after the famous equestrian statue by Donatello in front of the Basilica di San Antonio, and may, in fact, have been designed by Donatello himself in the last year of his life. ⊠ *Piazza della Ragione*

THE VENETIAN ARC, PAST AND PRESENT

Long before Venetians made their presence felt on the mainland in the 15th century, Ezzelino III da Romano (1194–1259) laid claim to Verona, Padua, and the surrounding lands and towns. He was the first of a series of brutal and aggressive rulers who dominated the cities of the region until the rise of Venetian rule.

After Ezzelino was ousted, powerful families such as Padua's Carrara and Verona's della Scala (Scaligeri) vied throughout the 14th century to dominate these territories. With the rise of Venetian rule came a time of relative peace, when noble families from the lagoon and the mainland commissioned Palladio and other accomplished architects to design their palazzi and villas. This rich classical legacy, superimposed upon medieval castles and fortifications, is central to the identities of present-day Padua, Vicenza, and Verona.

The region remained under Venetian control until the Napoleonic invasion and the fall of the Venetian Republic in 1797. The Council of Vienna ceded it, along with Lombardy, to Austria in 1815. The region revolted against Austrian rule and joined the Italian Republic in 1866.

Friuli–Venezia Giulia's complicated history is reflected in its architecture, language, and cuisine. It's been marched through, fought over, hymned by patriots, and romanticized by writers that include James Joyce, Rainer Maria Rilke, Ernest Hemingway, Pier Paolo Pasolini, Italo Svevo, and Jan Morris. The region has seen Fascists and Communists, Romans, Habsburgs, and Huns. It survived by forging sheltering alliances—Udine beneath the wings of San Marco (1420), Trieste choosing Duke Leopold of Austria (1382) over Venetian domination.

Some of World War I's fiercest fighting took place in Friuli–Venezia Giulia, where memorials and cemeteries commemorate the hundreds of thousands who died before the arrival of Italian troops in 1918 finally liberated Trieste from Austrian rule. Trieste, along with the whole of Venezia Giulia, was annexed to Italy in 1920. During World War II, Germany occupied the area and placed Trieste in an administrative zone along with parts of Slovenia. The only Nazi extermination camp on Italian soil, the Risiera di San Sabba, was in a suburb of Trieste. After the war, during a period of Cold War dispute, Trieste was governed by an allied military administration; it was officially re-annexed to Italy in 1954, when Italy ceded the Istrian peninsula to the south to Yugoslavia. These arrangements were not finally ratified by Italy and Yugoslavia until 1975.

☎ *049/8205006* ✉ *Salone €4 (free with Padova Card)* ⊗ *Feb.–Oct., Tues.–Sun. 9–7; Nov.–Jan., Tues.–Sun. 9–6.*

Piazza dei Signori. Some fine examples of 15th- and 16th-century buildings line this square. On the west side, the **Palazzo del Capitanio** (facade constructed 1598–1605) has an impressive **Torre dell'Orologio,** with an astronomical clock dating from 1344 and a portal made by Falconetto in 1532 in the form of a Roman triumphal arch. The 12th-century **Battistero del Duomo** (Cathedral Baptistry), with frescoes by Giusto de' Menabuoi (1374–78), is a few steps away. ✉ *Piazza dei Signori* ☎ *049/656914* ⚑ *Battistero €3 (free with Padova Card)* ☉ *Daily 10–6.*

FAMILY **Villa Pisani.** Extensive grounds with rare trees, ornamental fountains, and garden follies surround this extraordinary palace in Stra, 13 km (8 miles) southeast of Padua. Built in 1721 for the Venetian doge Alvise Pisani, it recalls Versailles more than a Veneto villa. This was one of the last and grandest of many stately residences constructed along the Brenta River from the 16th to 18th century by wealthy Venetians for their *villeggiatura*—their vacation and escape from the midsummer humidity. Gianbattista Tiepolo's (1696–1770) spectacular fresco on the ballroom ceiling alone is worth the visit. For a relaxing afternoon, explore the gorgeous park and maze. To get here from Venice, take Bus No. 53 from Piazzale Roma. The villa is a five-minute walk from the bus stop in Stra. ■TIP➡ **Mussolini invited Hitler here for their first meeting, but they stayed only one night because of the mosquitos—which remain. If visiting on a late afternoon in summer, carry bug repellent.** ✉ *Via Doge Pisani 7, Stra* ☎ *049/502074* ⊕ *www.villapisani. beniculturali.it* ⚑ *€7.50 villa and park, €4.50 park only* ☉ *Villa and park: Apr.–Sept., Tues.–Sun. 9–7; Oct., Tues.–Sun. 9–5; Nov.–Mar., Tues.–Sun. 9–4. Maze closed Nov.–Feb. Hrs vary subject to weather conditions.*

WORTH NOTING

Chiesa degli Eremitani. This 13th-century church houses substantial fragments of Andrea Mantegna's frescoes (1448–50), which were damaged by Allied bombing in World War II. Despite their fragmentary condition, Mantegna's still beautiful and historically important depictions of the martyrdom of Saint James and Saint Christopher show the young artist's mastery of extremely complex problems of perspective. ✉ *Piazza degli Eremitani* ☎ *049/8756410* ☉ *Winter Sun. 9–12:30 and 4–7, Mon.–Sat. 7:30–12:30 and 3:30–7; summer, Sun. 10–1 and 4:30–7, Mon.–Sat. 8:15–6:45.*

Medieval towns. For a fascinating and delightful day excursion out of Padua, take a drive (or a bus ride) to see several medieval towns. **Monselice,** 23 km (14 miles) south of Padua, has a castle perched on a hilltop that is everything a 13th-century castle should be, both inside and out. It also has the Villa Duodo, designed by Palladio's disciple and collaborator, Scamozzi. **Este,** 10 km (6 miles) west of Monselice, is another example of a medieval walled city. Farther west, the walls surrounding the town of **Montagnana,** 50 km (30 miles) southwest of Padua, are some of the best preserved in Italy; they enclose a market square, a 500-year-old cathedral, a Palladian Villa, and a medieval castle.

Musei Civici degli Eremitani (*Civic Museum*). This former monastery now houses works of Venetian masters, as well as fine collections of archaeological finds and ancient coins. Notable are the Giotto Crucifix, which once hung in the Capella degli Scrovegni, and the *Portrait of a Young Senator,* by Giovanni Bellini (1430–1516). ✉ *Piazza Eremitani 8* ☎ *049/82045450* ⚑ *€10, €13 with Scrovegni Chapel (free with Padova Card)* ☉ *Tues.–Sun. 9–7 (9–6 in winter).*

Orto Botanico (*Botanical Garden*). The Venetian Republic ordered the creation of Padua's botanical garden in 1545 to supply the university with medicinal plants, and it retains its original layout. You can stroll the arboretum—still part of the university—and wander through hothouses and beds of plants that were introduced to Italy in this late-Renaissance garden. A St. Peter's palm, planted in 1585, inspired Goethe to write his 1790 essay "The Metamorphosis of Plants." ✉ *Via Orto Botanico 15* ☎ *049/8272119* 🌐 *www.ortobotanico.unipd.it* 🎫 *€10 (€5 with Padova Card)* 🕒 *Apr.–May, Tues.–Sun. and holiday Mon. 9–7; June–Sept., Tues.–Sun. 9–7; Oct., Tues.–Sun. 9–6; Nov.–Mar., Tues.–Sun. 9–5.*

COCKTAIL HOUR ON PADUA'S PIAZZAS

A great Padua tradition is the outdoor consumption of aperitifs—a *spritz* (a mix of Aperol or Campari, soda water, and wine), prosecco, or wine—in the Piazza delle Erbe and Piazza delle Frutta. Several bars there provide drinks in plastic cups, so you can take them outside and mingle among the crowds. The ritual, practiced primarily by students, begins at 6 or so, at which hour you can also pick up a snack from an outdoor vendor. In recent years police have begun enforcing the mandated closing time for outside consumption, so bars generally close shortly after midnight.

Palazzo del Bo'. The University of Padua, founded in 1222, centers around this predominantly16th-century palazzo with an 18th-century facade. It's named after the Osteria del Bo' (*bo'* means "ox"), an inn that once stood on the site. It's worth a visit to see the perfectly proportioned anatomy theater (1594), the beautiful "Old Courtyard," and a hall with a lectern used by Galileo. You can enter only as part of a guided tour. Most guides speak English, but it is worth checking ahead by phone. ✉ *Via VIII Febbraio* ☎ *049/8275111 for University switchboard* 🌐 *www.unipd.it* 🎫 *€5* 🕒 *Nov.–Feb., Mon., Wed., and Fri. at 3:15 and 4:15, Tues., Thurs., and Sat. at 10:15 and 11:15; Mar.–Oct., Mon., Wed., and Fri. at 3:15, 4:15, and 5:15; Tues., Thurs., and Sat. at 9:15, 10:15, and 11:15.*

WHERE TO EAT

$$ ITALIAN

🍴 **Enoteca dei Tadi.** In this cozy and atmospheric cross between a wine bar and a restaurant you can put together an inexpensive dinner from the various classic dishes from all over Italy on offer. Portions are small, but so are the prices—just follow the local custom and order a selection. Dishes are made with first-rate ingredients and are coupled with a fine selection of wines. Start with fresh *burrata* (mozzarella's creamier cousin) with tomatoes, or choose from a selection of prosciutto *crudo* or salami. Don't pass up the house specialty, lasagna; there are several kinds on the menu. Main courses are limited, but they include a savory Veneto stew with polenta. [$] *Average main: €18* ✉ *Via dei Tadi 16* ☎ *049/8364099, 388/4083434 (cell phone)* 🌐 *www.enotecadeitadi.it* ✍ *Reservations essential* 🕒 *Closed Mon. No lunch.*

$$$ MODERN ITALIAN Fodor's Choice ★ 🍴 **La Finestra.** One of Padua's trendier restaurants, La Finestra is cozy yet elegant. The carefully prepared and creatively presented dishes may not always stick to tradition, but no one can claim that owners Carlo Vidali and Hélène Dao don't know what they're doing in the kitchen. Try their wonderful black bean soup with ginger, prawns, and sour cream—it's heavenly—followed by seared tuna with saffron and onions, or a more traditional beef *tagliata* (sliced steak) with rosemary. The service is attentive and helpful. [$] *Average main: €28* ✉ *Via dei Tadi 15* ☎ *049/650313* 🌐 *www.ristorantefinestra.it* ✍ *Reservations essential* ⏲ *Closed Mon., 1 wk in Jan., and 1 wk in Aug. No lunch Tues.–Thurs; no dinner Sun.*

$$ WINE BAR 🍴 **L'Anfora.** This mix between a traditional *bacaro* (wine bar) and an *osteria* (tavernlike restaurant) is a local institution. Stand at the bar shoulder to shoulder with a cross section of Padovano society, from construction workers to professors, and let the friendly and knowledgeable proprietors help you choose a wine. The reasonably priced menu offers simple *casalinga* (home-cooked dishes), plus salads and a selection of cheeses. Portions are ample, and no one will look askance if you don't order the full meal. The place is packed with loyal regulars at lunchtime, so come early or expect a wait. [$] *Average main: €20* ✉ *Via Soncin 13* ☎ *049/656629* ⏲ *Closed Sun. (except in Dec.), 1 wk in Jan., and 1 wk in Aug.*

$$$$ MODERN ITALIAN 🍴 **Le Calandre.** If you are willing to shell out around €600 for a dinner for two and are gastronomically adventurous but not very hungry, then consider this quietly elegant restaurant that critics often rave about. Traditional Veneto recipes are given a highly sophisticated and creative treatment—traditional squid in its ink comes as a "cappuccino," in a glass with a crust of potato foam—while dishes such as sole with grapefruit and curry sauce leave the Veneto far behind. Owner-chef Massimiliano Alajmo's creative impulses, together with seasonal changes, augment the signature dishes, but Alajmo considers food to be an art form rather than nourishment, so be prepared for minuscule portions. Reserve well in advance. [$] *Average main: €250* ✉ *Via Liguria 1, Sarmeola di Rubano, 7 km (4 miles) west of Padua* ☎ *049/630303* 🌐 *www.calandre.com* ✍ *Reservations essential* ⏲ *Closed Sun. and Mon., and Jan. 1–15.*

$$ VENETIAN 🍴 **Osteria Dal Capo.** A friendly trattoria in the heart of what used to be Padua's Jewish ghetto serves almost exclusively traditional Veneto dishes, and it does so with refinement and care. The liver with onions is extraordinarily tender. Even the accompanying polenta is grilled to perfection—slightly crisp on the outside and moist on the inside. The desserts are nothing to scoff at, either. ■ **TIP→ This tiny place fills up quickly, so reservations are a must.** [$] *Average main: €20* ✉ *Via degli Oblizzi 2* ☎ *049/663105* ✍ *Reservations essential* ⏲ *Closed Sun.*

WHERE TO STAY

$ HOTEL 🏨 **Al Fagiano.** The delightfully funky surroundings in this boutique hotel include sponge-painted walls, brush-painted chandeliers, and some views of the spires and cupolas of the Basilica di Sant'Antonio. **Pros:** large rooms; relaxed atmosphere; convenient location; free Wi-Fi. **Cons:**

no room service or help with baggage; some find the eccentric decoration a bit much. $ *Rooms from: €80* ✉ *Via Locatelli 45* ☎ *049/8750073* ⊕ *www.alfagiano.com* ⤴ *40 rooms* ⦿⦿ *No meals.*

$$ ⛛ **Albergo Verdi.** One of the best-situated hotels in the city provides
HOTEL tastefully renovated rooms that tend toward the minimalist without being severe; they also have the rare virtue of being absolutely quiet. **Pros:** excellent location close to the Piazza dei Signori; attentive staff; pleasant and warm atmosphere; discounts available depending on time of year. **Cons:** rooms are not that large; few views; charge for Wi-Fi; hefty parking fee. $ *Rooms from: €150* ✉ *Via Dondi dell'Orologio 7* ☎ *049/8364163* ⊕ *www.albergoverdipadova.it* ⤴ *14 rooms* ⦿⦿ *Breakfast.*

$ ⛛ **Methis.** Four floors of sleekly designed guest rooms reflect the ele-
HOTEL ments: gentle earth tones, fiery red, watery cool blue, and airy white in the top-floor suites. **Pros:** attractive rooms; helpful and attentive staff; pleasant extras such as umbrellas; better breakfast than usual for Italy. **Cons:** a 15-minute walk from major sights and restaurants; uninviting public spaces. $ *Rooms from: €120* ✉ *Riviera Paleocapa 70* ☎ *049/8725555* ⊕ *www.methishotel.com* ⤴ *52 rooms, 7 suites* ⦿⦿ *Breakfast.*

NIGHTLIFE

CAFÉS AND WINE BARS

Fodor's Choice **Caffè Pedrocchi.** No visit to Padua is complete without taking time to sit
★ in this massive café, as the French novelist Stendhal did shortly after it was established, in 1831. Nearly 200 years later, it remains central to the city's social life. The café was built in the Egyptian Revival style, which became popular after Napoléon's expeditions in Egypt. The accomplished restaurant serves only lunch and is proud of its innovative menu. ✉ *Piazzetta Pedrocchi* ☎ *049/8781231* ⊕ *www.caffepedrocchi.it* ⊙ *Café 8:30 am–midnight, restaurant 12:30 pm–2:30 pm.*

VICENZA

A visit to Vicenza is a must for any student or fan of architecture. This elegant, prosperous city bears the distinctive signature of the architect Andrea Palladio (1508–80), whose name has been given to the "Palladian" style of architecture.

Palladio emphasized the principles of order and harmony using the classical style of architecture established by Renaissance architects such as Brunelleschi, Alberti, and Sansovino. He used these principles and classical motifs not only for public buildings but also for private dwellings. His elegant villas and palaces were influential in propagating classical architecture in Europe, especially Britain, and later in America—most notably at Thomas Jefferson's Monticello.

In the mid-16th century Palladio was commissioned to rebuild much of Vicenza, which had been greatly damaged during wars waged against Venice by the League of Cambrai (1505), an alliance of the papacy, France, the Holy Roman Empire, and several neighboring city-states.

He made his name with the renovation of the Basilica, begun in 1549 in the heart of Vicenza, and then embarked on a series of noble buildings, all of which adhere to the same principles of classicism and harmony.

GETTING HERE AND AROUND

Vicenza is midway between Padua and Verona, and several trains leave from both cities every hour. By car, take the Autostrada Brescia–Padova/Torino–Trieste A4/E70 to SP247 North directly into Vicenza.

VISITOR INFORMATION

Vicenza Tourism Office ✉ *Piazza Giacomo Matteotti 12* ☎ *0444/320854* ⊕ *www.vicenzae.org* ⊗ *Daily 9–1 and 2–5:30.*

EXPLORING

TOP ATTRACTIONS

Palazzo Barbaran da Porto (Palladio Museum). Palladio executed this beautiful city palace for the Vicentine noble Montano Barbarano between 1570 and 1575. The noble patron, however, did not make things easy for Palladio; the plan had to incorporate at least two preexisting medieval houses, with irregularly shaped rooms, into his classical, harmonious plan, and to support the great hall of the *piano nobile* above the fragile walls of the original medieval structure. The wonder of it is that this palazzo is one of Palladio's most harmonious constructions; the viewer has little indication that this is actually a transformation of a medieval structure. The palazzo also contains a museum dedicated to Palladio and is the seat of a center for Palladian studies. ✉ *Contra' Porti 11* ☎ *0444/323014* 💶 *€6, €10 combination ticket with Palazzo Chiericati and Teatro Olimpico* ⊗ *Tues.–Sun 10–6.*

Fodor'sChoice ★ **Teatro Olimpico.** Palladio's last, and perhaps most spectacular work, was begun in 1580 and completed in 1585, after his death, by Vincenzo Scamozzi (1552–1616). Based closely on the model of ancient Roman theaters, it represents an important development in theater and stage design and is noteworthy for its acoustics and the cunning use of perspective in Scamozzi's permanent backdrop. The anterooms are frescoed with images of important figures in Venetian history. One of the few Renaissance theaters still standing, it is used for concerts, operas, and other performances. ✉ *Piazza Matteotti* ☎ *0444/222800* ⊕ *www. teatrolimpico.it* 💶 *€11* ⊗ *July–early Sept., Tues.–Sun. 10–6; early Sept.– June, Tues.–Sun. 9–5.*

Fodor'sChoice ★ **Villa della Rotonda** (*Villa Almerico Capra*). This beautiful Palladian villa, commissioned in 1556 as a suburban residence for Paolo Almerico, is the purest expression of Palladio's architectural theory and aesthetic. More a villa-temple than a residence, it contradicts the rational utilitarianism of Renaissance architecture and demonstrates the priority Palladio gave to the architectural symbolism of celestial harmony over practical considerations. A visit to view the interior can be difficult to schedule—the villa remains privately owned—but this is a worthwhile stop, if only to see how Palladio's harmonious arrangement of smallish, interconnected rooms around a central domed space paid little attention to the practicalities of living. The interior decoration, mainly later Baroque stuccowork, contains some allegorical frescoes in the cupola by Palladio's contemporary, Alessando Maganza. Even without a peek inside, experiencing the exterior and the grounds is a must for any visit to Vicenza. The villa is a 20-minute walk from town or a short ride on Bus No. 8 from Vicenza's Piazza Roma. ⊠ *Via della Rotonda* 🕾 *0444/321793* ⊕ *www.villalarotonda.it* 🎟 *€10 villa and grounds, €5 grounds only* ⊙ *Villa interior: mid-Mar.–early Nov., Wed. and Sat. 10–noon and 3–6. Grounds: mid-Mar.–early Nov., Tues.–Sun. 10–noon and 3–6; early Nov.–mid-Mar., Tues.–Sun. 10–noon and 2:30–5. Hrs vary during inclement weather.*

Fodor'sChoice
★
Villa Valmarana ai Nani. Inside this 17th- to 18th-century country house, named for the statues of dwarfs adorning the garden, is a series of frescoes executed in 1757 by Gianbattista Tiepolo depicting scenes from classical mythology, *The Iliad,* Tasso's *Gerusalemme Liberata,* and Ariosto's *Orlando Furioso.* They include his *Sacrifice of Iphigenia,* a major masterpiece of 18th-century painting. The neighboring *foresteria* (guest house) is also part of the museum; it contains frescoes showing 18th-century life at its most charming, and scenes of chinoiserie popular in the 18th century, by Tiepolo's son Giandomenico (1727–1804). The garden dwarves are probably taken from designs by Giandomenico. You can reach the villa on foot by following the same path that leads to Palladio's Villa della Rotonda. ⊠ *Via dei Nani 2/8* 🕾 *0444/321803* ⊕ *www.villavalmarana.com/en* 🎟 *€10* ⊙ *Tues.–Sun. 10–12:30 and 3–6.*

WORTH NOTING

Palazzo Chiericati. This imposing Palladian palazzo (1550) would be worthy of a visit even if it didn't house Vicenza's **Museo Civico.** Because of the ample space surrounding the building, Palladio combined elements of an urban palazzo with those he used in his country villas. The museum's important Venetian holdings include significant paintings by Cima, Tiepolo, Piazzetta, and Tintoretto, but its main attraction is an extensive collection of rarely found works by painters from the Vicenza area, among them Jacopo Bassano (1515–92) and the eccentric and innovative Francesco Maffei (1605–60), whose work foreshadowed important currents of Venetian painting of subsequent generations. ⊠ *Piazza Matteotti* 🕾 *0444/325071* 🎟 *€5* ⊙ *July–early Sept., Tues.–Sun. 9–5; early Sept.–June, Tues.–Sun. 10–6.*

Piazza dei Signori. At the heart of Vicenza, this square contains the **Palazzo della Ragione** (1549), the project with which Palladio made his name by successfully modernizing a medieval building, grafting a graceful two-story exterior loggia onto the existing Gothic structure. Commonly known as Palladio's basilica, the palazzo served as a courthouse and public meeting hall (the original Roman meaning of the term "basilica") and is now open only when it houses exhibits. The main point of interest, though, the loggia, is visible from the piazza. Take

Palazzo Barbaran da Porto (Palladio Museum) **7**
Palazzo Chiericati **3**
Piazza dei Signori **1**
Santa Corona **6**
Teatro Olimpico **2**
Villa della Rotonda **4**
Villa Valmarana ai Nani **5**

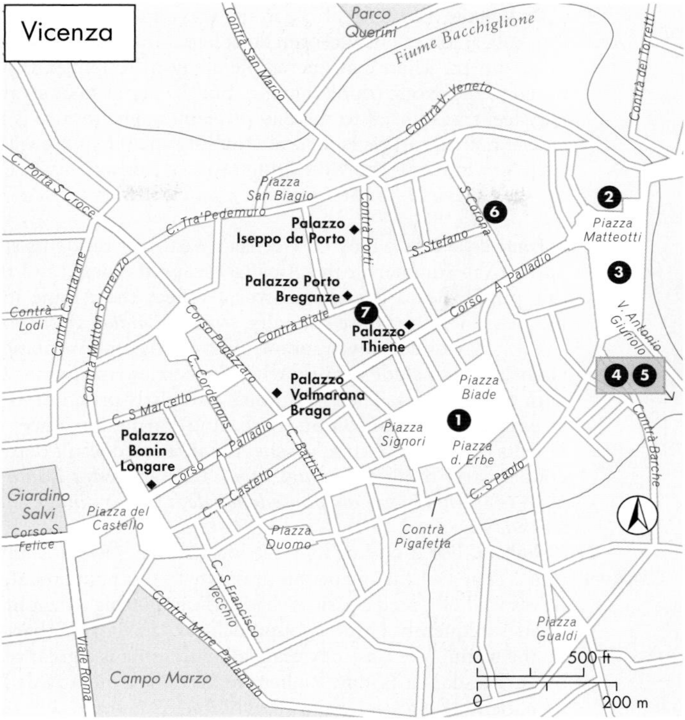

a look also at the **Loggia del Capitaniato,** opposite, which Palladio designed but never completed.

Santa Corona. An exceptionally fine *Baptism of Christ* (1502), a work of Giovanni Bellini's maturity, hangs over the altar on the left, just in front of the transept. The church also houses the elegantly simple Valmarana chapel, designed by Palladio. ✉ *Contrà S. Corona* ☎ *0444/222811* 🕓 *Tues.–Sun. 8:30–noon and 2:30–6:30.*

WHERE TO EAT

$$ VENETIAN

🍴 **Antico Ristorante agli Schioppi.** When they want to eat well, Vicentini generally head to the countryside, so it is telling that this is one of the few restaurants in the city frequented by local families and the business community. Done in Veneto country style, with enormous murals, agli Schioppi serves simple, well-prepared regional cuisine with some modern touches. Order the risotto, delicately flavored with wild mushrooms and zucchini flowers, creamy and beautifully textured, or try the Vicenza specialty *baccalà* (salt cod). The "Menu Palladiana" presents 16th-century dishes featuring spices common during that period, such as cinnamon and cloves, and omitting New World items like tomatoes and potatoes. [$] *Average main: €18* ✉ *Contrà Piazza del Castello 26* ☎ *0444/543701* 🕓 *Closed Mon. No dinner Sun.*

$ PIZZA 🍴 **Da Vittorio.** You'll find little in the way of atmosphere or style at this tiny, casual place, but Vicentini flock here for what may be the best pizza in the north. There's an incredible array of toppings, from the traditional to the exotic (think mango), but the pizzas taste so authentic you may feel transported to the Bay of Naples. The service is friendly and efficient. **TIP→ This is a good stop for lunch if you're walking to Palladio's Rotonda or the Villa Valmarana.** [$] *Average main: €12* ✉ *Borgo Berga 52* ☎ *0444/525059* 💳 *No credit cards* 🕒 *Closed Tues., and 2 wks in July.*

$$ NORTHERN ITALIAN 🍴 **Ponte delle Bele.** Many of Vicenza's wealthier residents spend at least part of the summer in the Alps to escape the heat, and the dishes of this popular and friendly trattoria reflect the Alpine influences on local cuisine. The house specialty, *stinco di maiale al forno* (roast pork shank), is wonderfully fragrant, with herbs and aromatic vegetables. Game dishes include venison with blueberries, and guinea fowl roasted with white grapes. The restaurant's also justly proud of its *baccalà alla vicentina* (cod in an onion, herb, and Parmesan sauce, served with polenta). Though a little kitschy, the interior doesn't detract from the good, hearty food. [$] *Average main: €22* ✉ *Contrà Ponte delle Bele 5* ☎ *0444/320647* 🌐 *www.pontedellebele.it* 🕒 *No dinner Sun.; no lunch weekdays.*

$ ITALIAN 🍴 **Righetti.** For a city of its size, Vicenza has few outstanding restaurants. That's why many people gravitate to this popular cafeteria, which serves well prepared classic dishes without putting a dent in your wallet. There's frequently a hearty soup, such as *orzo e fagioli* (barley and bean) on the menu. The classic baccalà alla vicentina is a great reason to stop by on Tuesday or Friday. Righetti tends to be a bit crowded at lunch, so be patient. [$] *Average main: €12* ✉ *Piazza Duomo 3* ☎ *0444/543135* 💳 *No credit cards* 🕒 *Closed weekends, and 1 wk in Jan. and Aug.*

WHERE TO STAY

During annual gold fairs in January, May, and September, it may be quite difficult to find lodging. If you're coming then, be sure to reserve well in advance and expect to pay higher rates.

$$ HOTEL 🏨 **Campo Marzio.** Rooms at this comfortable, full-service hotel, a five-minute walk from the train station and right in front of the city walls, are ample and furnished in various styles, from modern to traditional and romantic. **Pros:** central; more amenities than its competitors; set back from the street, so it's quiet and bright; free Wi-Fi in rooms. **Cons:** public spaces are uninspiring; expensive during fairs. [$] *Rooms from: €140* ✉ *Viale Roma 21* ☎ *0444/5457000* 🌐 *www.hotelcampomarzio.com* 🛏 *36 rooms* 🍽 *Breakfast.*

$ HOTEL Fodor's Choice ★ 🏨 **Due Mori.** Rooms at one of the oldest hotels in the city (1883), just off the Piazza dei Signori, are filled with turn-of-the-20th-century antiques, and regulars favor the place because the high ceilings in the main building make it feel light and airy. **Pros:** comfortable, tastefully furnished rooms; friendly staff; central location; rate same year-round; free Wi- Fi. **Cons:** no a/c (ceiling fans minimize the need for it); no help with baggage; no TVs. [$] *Rooms from: €90* ✉ *Contrà Do Rode 24*

Continued on page 272

PALLADIO COUNTRY

Wealthy 16th-century patrons commissioned Andrea Palladio to design villas that would reflect their sense of cultivation and status. Using a classical vocabulary of columns, arches, and domes, he gave them a series of masterpieces in the towns and hills of the Veneto that exemplify the neo-Platonic ideals of harmony and proportion. Palladio's creations are the perfect expression of how a learned 16th century man saw himself and his world, and as you stroll through them today, their serene beauty is as powerful as ever. Listen closely and you might even hear that celestial harmony, the music of the spheres, that so moved Palladio and his patrons.

TOWN & COUNTRY

Although the villa, or "country residence," was still a relatively new phenomenon in the 16th century, it quickly became all the rage once the great lords of Venice turned their eyes from the sea toward the fertile plains of the Veneto. They were forced to do this once their trade routes had faltered when Ottoman Turks conquered Constantinople in 1456 and Columbus opened a path to the riches of America in 1492. In no time, canals were built, farms were laid out, and the fashion for *villeggiatura*—the attraction of idyllic country retreats for the nobility—became a favored lifestyle. As a means of escaping an overheated Rome,

villas had been the original brainchild of the ancient emperors and it was no accident that the Venetian lords wished to emulate this palatial style of country residence. Palladio's method of evaluating the standards, and standbys, of ancient Roman life through the eye of the Italian Renaissance, combined with Palladio's innate sense of proportion and symmetry, became the lasting foundation of his art. In turn, Palladio threw out the jambalaya of styles prevalent in Venetian architecture—Oriental, Gothic, and Renaissance—for the pure, noble lines found in the buildings of the Caesars.

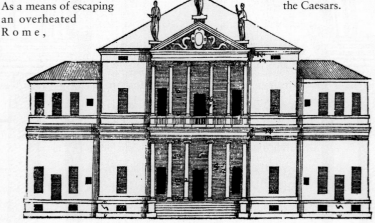

PALLADIO, STAR ARCHITECT

Andrea Palladio (1508–1580)

"Face dark, eyes fiery. Dress rich. His appearance that of a genius." So was Palladio described by his wealthy mentor, Count Trissino. Trissino encouraged the young student to trade in his birth name, Andrea di Pietro della Gondola,

for the elegant Palladio. He did, and it proved a wise move indeed. Born in Padua in 1508, Andrea moved to nearby Vicenza in 1524 and was quickly taken up by the city's power elite. He experienced a profound revela-

THE OLD BECOMES NEW

La Malcontenta

Studying ancient Rome with the eyes of an explorer, Palladio employed a style that linked old with new—but often did so in unexpected ways. Just take a look at Villa Foscari, nicknamed **"La Mal-contenta"** (Mira, 041/5470012, www.lamalcontenta.com €10. Open May–Oct., Tues. and Sat. 9–noon; from Venice, take an ACTV bus from Piazzale Roma to Mira or opt for a boat ride up on the Burchiello). Shaded by weeping willows and mirrored by the Brenta Canal, "The Sad Lady" was built for Nicolò and Alvise Foscari and is the quintessence of Palladian poetry. Inspired by the grandeur of Roman public buildings, Palladio applied the ancient motif of a temple facade to a domestic dwelling, topped off by a pediment, a construct most associated with religious structures. Inside, he used the technique of vaulting seen in ancient Roman baths, with giant windows and immense white walls ready-made for the colorful frescoes painted by Zelotti. No one knows for certain the origin of the villa's nickname—some say it came from a Venetian owner's wife who was exiled there due to her scandalous behavior. Regardless of the name, it's hard today to associate such a beautiful, graceful villa with anything but harmony and contentment.

tion on his first trip, in 1541, to Rome, where he sensed the harmony of the ancient ruins and saw the elements of classicism that were working their way into contemporary architecture. This experience led to his spectacular conversion of the Vicenza's Palazzo della Ragione (1545) into a basilica recalling the great meeting halls of antiquity. In years to come, after relocating to Venice, he created some memorable churches, such as S. Giorgio Maggiore (1564). Despite these varied projects, Palladio's unassailable position as one of the world's greatest architects is tied to the countryside villas, which he spread across the Veneto plains like a firmament of stars. Nothing else in the Veneto illuminates more clearly the idyllic beauty of the region than these elegant residences, their stonework now nicely mellowed and suntanned after five centuries.

VICENZA, CITY OF PALLADIO

Palazzo della Ragione

La Rotonda

To see Palladio's pageant of palaces, head for Vicenza. His **Palazzo della Ragione**, or "Basilica," marks the city's heart, the Piazza dei Signori. This building rocketed young Palladio from an unknown to an architectural star. Across the way is his redbrick **Loggia dei Capitaniato.**

One block past the Loggia is Vicenza's main street, appropriately named Corso Andrea Palladio. Just off this street is the Contrà Porti, where you'll find the **Palazzo Barbaran da Porto** (1570) at No. 11, with its fabulously rich facade erupting with Ionic and Corinthian pillars. Today, this is the Centro Internazionale di Studi di Architettura Andrea Palladio (0444/323014, www.cisapalladio. org), a study center which mounts impressive temporary exhibitions. A few steps away, on the Contrà San Gaetano Thiene, is the Palazzo Thiene (1542-58), designed by Giulio Romano and completed by Palladio.

Doubling back to Contrà Porti 21, you find the **Palazzo Iseppo da Porto** (1544), the first palazzo where you can see the neoclassical effects of young Palladio's trip to Rome. Following the Contrà Reale, you come to Corso Fogazzaro 16 and the **Palazzo Valmarana Braga** (1565). Its gigantic pilasters were a first for domestic architecture.

Returning to the Corso Palladio, head left to the opposite end of the Corso, about five blocks, to the Piazza Mattoti and **Palazzo Chiericati** (1550). This was practically a suburban area in the 16th century, and for the palazzo Palladio combined elements of urban and rural design. The pedestal raising the building and the steps leading to the entrance—unknown in urban palaces—were to protect from floods and to keep cows from wandering in the front door. (For opening times and details, see the main text).

Across the Corso Palladio is Palladio's last and one of his most spectacular works, the **Teatro Olimpico** (1580). By careful study of ancient ruins and architectural texts, he reconstructed a Roman theater with archaeological precision. Palladio died before it was completed, but he left clear plans for the project. (For opening times and details, see the main text.)

Although it's on the outskirts of town, the **Villa Almerico Capra**, better known as **La Rotonda** (1566), is an indispensable part of any visit to Vicenza. It's the iconic Palladian building, the purest expression of his aesthetic. (For opening times, details, and a discussion of the villa, see the main text.)

A MAGNIFICENT COLLABORATION

Villa Barbaro

At the **Villa Barbaro** (1554) near the town of Maser in the province of Treviso, 48 km (30 miles) northeast of Vicenza, you can see the results of a one-time collaboration between two of the greatest artists of their age.

Palladio was the architect, and Paolo Veronese decorated the interior with an amazing cycle of trompe l'oeil frescoes—walls dissolve into landscapes, and illusions of courtiers and servants enter rooms and smile down from balustrades.

Legend has it a feud developed between Palladio and Veronese, with Palladio feeling the illusionistic frescoes detracted from his architecture; but there is prac-tically nothing to support the idea of such a rift.

It's also noteworthy that Palladio for the first time connected the two lateral granaries to the main villa. This was a working farm, and Palladio thus created an architectural unity by connecting with graceful arcades the working parts of the estate to the living quarters, bringing together the Renaissance dichotomy of the active and the contemplative life.

ALONG THE BRENTA CANAL

During the 16th century the Brenta was transformed into a landlocked version of Venice's Grand Canal with the building of nearly 50 waterside villas.

Back then, boating parties viewed them in *"burchielli"*—beautiful boats. Today, the Burchiello excur-sion boat (Via Orlandini 3, Padua, 049/8206910, www.ilburchiello. it) makes full- and half-day tours along the Brenta, from March to November, departing from Padua and Venice Tues.–Sun., running in both directions; tickets are €55–€95 and can also be bought at travel agencies. You visit three houses, including the Villas Pisani and Foscari, with a lunchtime break in Oriago (€30 extra). Note that most houses are on the left side coming from Venice, or the right from Padua.

☎ *0444/321886* ⊕ *www.hotelduemori.com* ⤳ *53 rooms* ☉ *Closed 1st 2 wks in Aug., 2 wks in late Dec.* ⦿ *No meals.*

VERONA

On the banks of the fast-flowing River Adige, enchanting Verona, 60 km (37 miles) west of Vicenza, has timeless monuments, a picturesque town center, fascinating museums, and a romantic reputation as the setting of Shakespeare's *Romeo and Juliet.* Verona grew to power and prosperity within the Roman Empire as a result of its key commercial and military position in northern Italy. With its Roman arena, theater, and city gates, it has the most significant monuments of Roman antiquity north of Rome. After the fall of the empire, the city continued to flourish under the guidance of barbarian kings such as Theodoric, Alboin, Pepin, and Berenger I. It reached its cultural and artistic peak in the 13th and 14th centuries under the della Scala (Scaligeri) dynasty. (Look for the *scala*, or ladder, emblem all over town.) In 1404 Verona traded its independence for security and placed itself under the control of Venice. (The other recurring architectural motif is the lion of Saint Mark, a symbol of Venetian rule.)

With its lively Venetian air and proximity to Lake Garda, Verona attracts many tourists, especially Germans and Austrians. Tourism peaks during summer's renowned season of open-air opera in the arena and during spring's Vinitaly, one of the world's most important wine and spirits expos.

If you're going to visit more than one or two sights, it's worth purchasing a VeronaCard, available at museums, churches, and tobacconists for €15 (for 24 hours) or €20 (72 hours). It buys a single admission to most of the city's significant museums and churches, plus you can ride for free on city buses. If you're mostly interested in churches, a €6 Chiese Vive Card is sold at Verona's major houses of worship and gains you entry to the Duomo, San Fermo Maggiore, San Zeno Maggiore, and Sant'Anastasia (all also covered also by the Verona Card). Verona's churches enforce a dress code: no sleeveless shirts, shorts, or short skirts. See ⊕ *www.turismoverona.eu* for more information.

GETTING HERE AND AROUND

Verona is midway between Venice and Milan. Its small Aeroporto Valerio Catullo accommodates domestic and European flights, though many travelers fly into Venice or Milan and drive or take the train to Verona. Several trains per hour depart from any point on the Milan–Venice line. By car, from the east or west, take the Autostrada Trieste–Torino A4/E70 to the SS12 and follow it north into town. From the north or south, take the Autostrada del Brennero A22/E45 to the SR11 East (initially, called the Strada Bresciana) directly into town.

EVENTS

Vinitaly. This widely attended international wine and spirits event takes place for five days, generally in late March. Recent editions have attracted more than 4,000 exhibitors from two dozen countries. The festivities kick off with Opera Wine (⊕ *www.operawine.it*), a showcase for the top 100 Italian wines, as chosen by *Wine Spectator* magazine, that takes place in the Palazzo della Gran Guardia, in Piazza Bra. ⊠ *Fiera di Verona, Viale del Lavoro 8* ☎ *045/8298854* ⊕ *www.vinitaly. com* ⤳ *€60 daily.*

EXPLORING

TOP ATTRACTIONS

Fodor's Choice ★ **Ancient City Gates/Triumphal Arch.** In addition to ancient Verona's famous arena and Roman theater, two of its city gates and a beautiful triumphal arch have survived. These graceful and elegant portals provide an idea of the high aesthetic standards of the time. The oldest portal, the **Porta dei Leoni** (on Via Leoni, just a few steps from Piazza delle Erbe), dates from the 1st century BC, but its original earth-and-brick structure was sheathed in local marble during early Imperial times. The other, the **Porta dei Borsari,** was, as its elegant decoration suggests, the main entrance to ancient Verona, and, in its present state, dates from the 1st century AD. It's at the beginning of Corso Porta Borsari, a few steps from the opposite side of Piazza della Erbe. Continuing down Corso Cavour, which starts on the other (front) side of the Porta dei Borsari, you can find the **Arco dei Gavi,** which is simpler and less imposing, but also more graceful, than the triumphal arches in Rome. It was built in the 1st century AD by the architect Lucius Vitruvius Cerdo to celebrate the accomplishments of the patrician Gavia family. It was highly esteemed by several Renaissance architects, including Palladio. ⊠ *Via Leoni.*

FAMILY
Fodor's Choice ★ **Arena di Verona.** Only Rome's Colosseum and Capua's arena would dwarf this amphitheater, built for gymnastic competitions, choreographed sacrificial rites, and games involving hunts, fights, battles, and wild animals. Though four arches are all that remain of the arena's outer arcade, the main structure is complete and dates from AD 30. In summer, you can join up to 16,000 people packing the stands for spectacular opera productions. Even those not crazy about opera can sit in the stands and enjoy Italians enjoying themselves—including, at times, singing along with their favorite hits. ■TIP➜ **The opera's the main thing here: when there is no opera performance, you can still enter the interior, but the arena is less impressive inside than the Colosseum or other Roman amphitheaters.** ⊠ *Piazza Brà 5* ☎ *045/596517* ⊕ *www.arena.it* ⤳ *€6 (free with Chiese Vive or VeronaCard)* ⊗ *Daily 8:30–7:30 (closes at 5 on opera days); hrs sometimes reduced in late fall and winter.*

Fodor's Choice ★ **Castelvecchio.** This crenellated, russet brick building with massive walls, towers, turrets, and a vast courtyard was built for Cangrande II della Scala in 1354 and presides over a street lined with attractive old buildings and palaces of the nobility. Only by going inside the **Museo di Castelvecchio** can you really appreciate this massive castle complex with its vaulted halls. You also get a look at a significant collection of Venetian and Veneto art, medieval weapons, and jewelry. The interior of the castle was restored and redesigned as a museum between 1958 and 1975 by Carlo Scarpa, one of Italy's most accomplished architects. Behind the castle is the Ponte Scaligero (1355), which spans the River

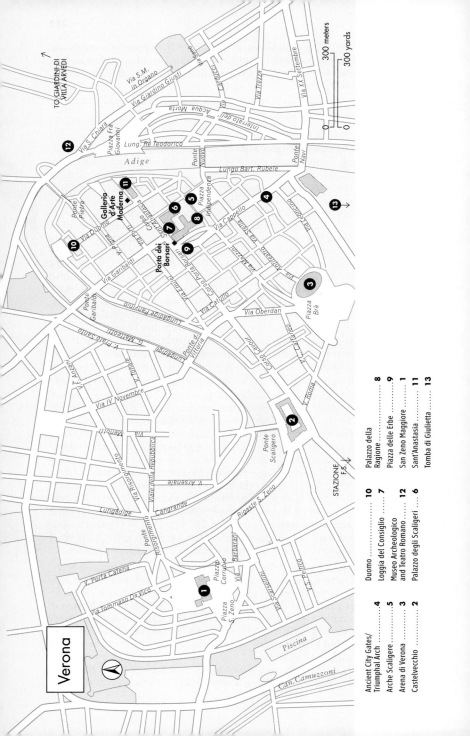

Verona

TO GIARDINI DI
VILA ARVEDI

Via S.M.
in Organo

Via Giardino Giusti

Via S. Chiara

Via Fra
Giovanni

Piazza
Frà
Giovanni

Lung. Re Teodorico

Adige

Ponte
Pietra

Galleria
d'Arte
Moderna

Via Duomo

Via Carucci

Via Trezza

Via XX Settembre

Interrato dell'Acqua Morta

Ponte
Nuovo

Lungo Bart. Rubele

Ponte
Navi

Via S. Alessio

Corso Sant'Anastasia

Piazza
Indipendenza

Via Cappello

Ponte Pietra

Via Pietra

Via Garibaldi

Porta dei
Borsari

Corso Porta Borsari

Via Emilei

Corso Cavour

Via Diaz

Via Mazzini

Via Stella

Via Anfiteatro

Via Leoncino

Piazza
Brà

Via Oberdan

Corso Cavour

V.C. Cattaneo

Via Roma

Ponte
Garibaldi

Lungadige G. Matteotti

Ponte d. Vittoria

Lungadige Panvinio

Via Cattaneo

Corso Porta Nuova

Ponte
Risorgimento

Viale della Repubblica

Cangrande

Lungadige

Via Risorgimento

Via IV Novembre

Via A. Manzoni

V.F. Anzani

Ponte
Scaligero

Via Roma

STAZIONE
F.S.

V. Arsenale

Piazza
Corrubbio

Via Barbaran

V. Barbaran

Piazza
S. Zeno

Rigaste S. Zeno

V.S. Petrico

Regaste Redentore

V. Porta Catena

Via Tommaso Da Vico

Piscina

Can. Camuzzoni

300 meters

300 yards

0

0

Ancient City Gates/
Triumphal Arch 4
Arche Scaligere 5
Arena di Verona 3
Castelvecchio 2

Duomo 10
Loggia del Consiglio 7
Museo Archeologico
and Teatro Romano 12
Palazzo degli Scaligeri 6

Palazzo della
Ragione 8
Piazza delle Erbe 9
San Zeno Maggiore 1
Sant'Anastasia 11
Tomba di Giulietta 13

Adige. ⊠ *Corso Castelvecchio 2* ☎ *045/8062611* ✆ *€6 (free with Chiese Vive or VeronaCard)* ⊗ *Mon. 1:30–7:30, Tues.–Sun. 8:30–7:30; last entry at 6:45.*

Duomo. The present church was begun in the 12th century in the Romanesque style; its later additions are mostly Gothic. On pilasters guarding the main entrance are 12th-century carvings thought to represent Oliver and Roland, two of Charlemagne's knights and heroes of several medieval epic poems. Inside, Titian's *Assumption* (1532) graces the first chapel on the left. ⊠ *Via Duomo* ☎ *045/595627* ⊕ *www.chieseverona. it* ✆ *€2.50 (free with Chiese Vive or VeronaCard)* ⊗ *Mar.–Oct., Mon.– Sat. 10–5:30, Sun. and holidays 1:30–5:30; Nov.–Feb., Mon.–Sat. 10–4, Sun. and holidays 1:30–4. Open at other times for religious purposes.*

Piazza delle Erbe. Frescoed buildings surround this medieval square, where a busy Roman forum once stood. During the week it's still bustling, as vendors sell produce and trinkets, much as they have been doing for generations. Relax at one of the cafés and take in the lively scene.

FodorśChoice
★

San Zeno Maggiore. One of Italy's finest Romanesque churches is filled with treasures. A rose window by the 13th-century sculptor Brioloto represents a wheel of fortune, with six of the spokes formed by statues depicting the rising and falling fortunes of mankind. The 12th-century porch is the work of Maestro Niccolò; it's flanked by marble reliefs by Niccolò and Maestro Guglielmo depicting scenes from the Old and New Testaments and from the legend of Theodoric. The bronze doors date from the 11th and 12th centuries; some were probably imported from Saxony and some are from Veronese workshops. They combine allegorical representations with scenes from the lives of saints. Inside, look for the 12th-century statue of San Zeno to the left of the main altar. In modern times it has been dubbed the "Laughing San Zeno" because of a misinterpretation of its conventional Romanesque grin. A justly famous *Madonna and Saints* triptych by Andrea Mantegna (1431–1506) hangs over the main altar, and a peaceful cloister (1120–38) lies to the left of the nave. The detached bell tower was begun in 1045, before the construction of much of the present church, and finished in 1173. ⊠ *Piazza San Zeno* ☎ *045/592813* ⊕ *www.chieseverona.it* ✆ *€2.50 (free with Chiese Vive or VeronaCard)* ⊗ *Nov.–Feb., Mon.–Sat. 10–1 and 1:30–5, Sun. 12:30–5; Mar.–Oct., Mon.–Sat. 8:30–6, Sun. 12:30–6.*

Sant'Anastasia. Verona's largest church, begun in 1290 but only consecrated in 1471, is a fine example of Gothic brickwork and has a grand doorway with elaborately carved biblical scenes. The main reason for visiting this church, however, is *St. George and the Princess* (dated 1434, but perhaps earlier) by Pisanello (1377–1455). It's above the Pellegrini Chapel off the main altar. As you come in, look also for the *gobbi* (hunchbacks) supporting the holy-water basins. ⊠ *Vicolo Sotto Riva 4* ☎ *045/8004925* ✆ *€2.50 (free with Chiese Vive or VeronaCard)* ⊗ *Nov.–Feb., Mon.–Sat. 10–1 and 1:30–5, Sun. 1–5; Mar.–Oct., Mon.– Sat. 10–6, Sun. 1–6.*

WORTH NOTING

Arche Scaligere. On a little square off the Piazza dei Signori are the fantastically sculpted Gothic tombs of the della Scalas, who ruled Verona during the late Middle Ages. The 19th-century English traveler and critic John Ruskin described the tombs as graceful places where people who have fallen asleep live. The tomb of Cangrande I (1291–1329) hangs over the portal of the adjacent church and is the work of the Maestro di Sant'Anastasia. The tomb of Mastino II, begun in 1345, has an elaborate baldacchino, originally painted and gilded, and is surrounded by an iron grillwork fence and topped by an equestrian statue. The latest and most elaborate tomb is that of Cansignorio (1375), the work principally of Bonino di Campione. The major tombs are all visible from the street. ⊠ *Via Arche Scaligere.*

Loggia del Consiglio. This graceful structure on the north flank of the Piazza dei Signori was finished in 1492 and built to house city council meetings. Although the city was already under Venetian rule, Verona still had a certain degree of autonomy, which was expressed by the splendor of the loggia. Very strangely for a Renaissance building of this quality, its architect remains unknown, but it's the finest surviving example of late-15th-century architecture in Verona. The building is not open to the public, but the exterior is worth a visit. ⊠ *Piazza dei Signori.*

Museo Archeologico and Teatro Romano. The archaeological holdings of this museum in a 15th-century former monastery consist largely of the donated collections of Veronese citizens proud of their city's classical past. You'll find few blockbusters here, but there are some noteworthy pieces (especially among the bronzes), and it is interesting to see what cultured Veronese collected between the 17th and 19th centuries. The museum complex includes the Teatro Romano, Verona's 1st-century AD theater, which is open to visitors. ⊠ *Rigaste del Redentore 2* 🕾 *045/8000360* ⊕ *museoarcheologico.comune.verona.it* 🖭 *€4.50 (free with VeronaCard)* ☉ *Mon. 1:30–7:30, Tues.–Sun. 8:30–7:30; last entry at 6:45.*

Palazzo degli Scaligeri (*Palazzo di Cangrande*). The della Scalas ruled Verona from this stronghold, built at the end of the 13th century by Cangrande I. At that time Verona controlled the mainland Veneto from Treviso and Lombardy to Mantua and Brescia. The portal facing the Piazza dei Signori was added in 1533 by the accomplished Renaissance architect Michele Sanmicheli. You'll have to admire the palazzo from the outside, as it's not open to the public. ⊠ *Piazza dei Signori.*

Palazzo della Ragione. An elegant 15th-century pink marble staircase leads up from the *mercato vecchio* (old market) courtyard to the magistrates' chambers in this 12th-century palace, built at the intersection of the main streets of the ancient Roman city. The renovated interior is now used for occasional exhibitions of art from the Galleria dell'Arte Moderna. You can get the highest view in town from atop the attached 270-foot-high, Romanesque **Torre dei Lamberti.** About 50 years after a lightning strike in 1403 knocked its top off, it was rebuilt and extended to its current height. ⊠ *Piazza dei Signori* 🕾 *045/8032726* 🖭 *Free, Torre dei Lamberti €6 (free with VeronaCard)* ☉ *Torre dei Lamberti* *daily 8:30–7:30 (until 8:30 pm in summer). Palazzo open only for exhibitions.*

Tomba di Giulietta. If you want to believe that Juliet is buried in this old chapel near the river, you'll have to put aside the fact that the structure is a former orphanage and Franciscan monastery. In the crypt there's an open sarcophagus labeled as Juliet's tomb that was fashioned in 1937 for tourist purposes; by conducting civil weddings in the chapel, the city of Verona perpetuates the fantasy that Romeo and Juliet existed and were married here. ✉ *Via del Pontiere 35* ☎ *045/8000361* 🎟 *€4.50 (free with VeronaCard)* ⏲ *Mon. 1:45–7:30, Tues.–Sun. 8:30–7:30; last entry at 6:45.*

WORD OF MOUTH

"I was fortunate enough to see *Aida* in the amphitheater in Verona. It was spectacular, particularly, of course, the triumphant march. *Aida* makes full use of the incredible surroundings. The stone terrace seats can be very, very hot, even in the evening."
—Cathinjoetown

4

WHERE TO EAT

$$ NORTHERN ITALIAN Fodor's Choice ★

🍴 **Antica Osteria al Duomo.** This side-street eatery, lined with old wood paneling and decked out with musical instruments, serves Veronese food to a Veronese crowd; they come for the local wine (€1 to €3 per glass) and to savor excellent versions of local dishes such as *bigoli con sugo di asino* (thick whole-wheat spaghetti with sauce made from donkey meat) and *pastissada con polenta* (horse-meat stew with polenta). Don't be deterred by the unconventional meats—they're tender and delicious, and this is probably the best place in town to sample them. This first-rate home cooking is reasonably priced and served by a helpful, efficient staff. It's popular, so arrive early. Reservations are not taken on weekends. [$] *Average main: €15* ✉ *Via Duomo 7/A* ☎ *045/8004505* ⏲ *Closed Sun. (except in Dec. and during Vinitaly).*

$$$ NORTHERN ITALIAN

🍴 **Dodici Apostoli.** In a city where many high-end restaurants tend toward nouvelle cuisine, this is an exceptional place to enjoy classic dishes made with elegant variations on traditional recipes. Near Piazza delle Erbe, it stands on the foundations of a Roman temple. Specialties include gnocchi *di zucca e ricotta* (with squash and ricotta cheese) and *vitello alla Lessinia* (veal with mushrooms, cheese, and truffles) and a signature *pasta e fagioli* (pasta and bean soup). [$] *Average main: €30* ✉ *Vicolo Corticella San Marco 3* ☎ *045/596999* 🌐 *www.12apostoli.com* ✍ *Reservations essential* ⏲ *Closed Mon., 2 wks in Jan., and 2 wks in June. No dinner Sun.*

$$$$ MODERN ITALIAN Fodor's Choice ★

🍴 **Il Desco.** "*Cucina dell'anima*"—food of the soul—is how Chef Elia Rizzo describes his cuisine. True to Italian culinary tradition, he preserves natural flavors through quick cooking and selective ingredients, but tradition gives way to invention, even daring, in the combination of ingredients in dishes such as duck breast with grappa, grapes, and eggplant puree, and beef cheeks with goose liver and caramelized pears. Some find Rizzo's creative combinations, such as adding truffles to a fish fillet, difficult to fathom. For an extravagant gastronomic adventure, try the multicourse tasting menu (€135 per person, not including wine). Il Desco's interior is elegant if overdone, with tapestries, paintings, and an impressive 16th-century lacunar ceiling. The service, though efficient, is not exactly friendly. [$] *Average main: €45* ✉ *Via Dietro San Sebastiano 7* ☎ *045/595358* 🌐 *www.ristoranteildesco.it* ✍ *Reservations essential* 🕒 *Closed Sun. and Mon. (dinner Mon. in July, Aug., and Dec.), 2 wks in June and during Christmas and New Years.*

$$$ MODERN ITALIAN 🍴 **Ostaria La Fontanina.** Veronese come to this restaurant on a quiet street in one of the oldest sections of town to enjoy a sumptuous meal under vine-covered balconies. The Tapparini family takes great pride in the kitchen's modern variations on traditional dishes. *Risotto al Amarone* is made with Verona's treasured red wine, and there's an excellent baccalà. The more adventurous may want to sample the luscious wild boar confit with savory fruit. The service does not always merit the 10% charge automatically added to the bill. [$] *Average main: €25* ✉ *Portichiette fontanelle S. Stefano 3* ☎ *045/913305* 🌐 *www.ristorantelafontanina.com* ✍ *Reservations essential* 🕒 *Closed Sun., 1 wk in Jan., and 2 wks in Aug. No lunch Mon.*

WHERE TO STAY

Book hotels far in advance if you'll be in town during spring's Vinitaly, usually held in late March or early April, and for opera season. Verona hotels are also very busy during the January, May, and September gold fairs in neighboring Vicenza. Hotels jack up prices considerably at all these times.

$$$$ HOTEL 🏨 **Gabbia d'Oro.** Occupying a historic building off Piazza delle Erbe in the ancient heart of Verona, this hotel is a romantic fantasia of ornamentation, rich fabrics, and period-style furniture. **Pros:** central location; great breakfast; romantic atmosphere. **Cons:** some very small rooms, especially considering the price; small bathrooms; some guests may find the décor overly ornate, even stuffy. [$] *Rooms from: €350* ✉ *Corso Porta Borsari 4/a* ☎ *045/8003060* 🌐 *www.hotelgabbiadoro.it* 🛏 *8 rooms, 19 suites* 🍽 *Breakfast.*

$$$ HOTEL 🏨 **Hotel Accademia.** The exterior columns and arches of this hotel in old Verona hint at what guests discover inside: elegance, gracious service, and comfortable, traditional furnishings. **Pros:** central location; old-world charm. **Cons:** expensive parking; prices increase greatly during summer opera season and trade fairs. [$] *Rooms from: €225* ✉ *Via Scala 12* ☎ *045/596222* 🌐 *www.accademiavr.it* 🛏 *93 rooms* 🍽 *Breakfast.*

$$$$ HOTEL 🏨 **Palazzo Victoria.** Business types and tourists experience tasteful luxury at the Victoria, whose rooms blend traditional and contemporary style. **Pros:** quiet and tasteful rooms; central location near the Piazza delle Erbe; good business center. **Cons:** no views; expensive parking (and rates); staff not particularly helpful. [$] *Rooms from: €306* ✉ *Via Adua 8* ☎ *045/5905664* 🌐 *www.palazzovictoria.com* 🛏 *58 rooms, 13 suites* 🍽 *No meals.*

$ HOTEL 🏨 **Torcolo.** In addition to a central location close to the arena and Piazza Brà, you can count on this budget choice for a warm welcome, helpful service, and pleasant rooms with late-19th-century furniture. **Pros:**

nice rooms; staff gives reliable advice. **Cons:** some street noise; showers but no tubs; pricey parking. $ *Rooms from: €95* ⊠ *Vicolo Listone 3* ☎ *045/8007512* ⊕ *www.hoteltorcolo.it* ⇄ *19 rooms* ⊗ *Closed Christmas, and 2 wks in Jan. and Feb.* ⑩ *No meals.*

NIGHTLIFE AND PERFORMING ARTS

Fodor's Choice
★

Arena di Verona. Milan's La Scala and Parma's Teatro Regio offer performances more likely to attract serious opera fans, but neither offers a greater spectacle than the Arena di Verona. Many Italian opera lovers claim their enthusiasm began when they were taken as children to a production at the arena. During the venue's summer season, from July to September, as many as 16,000 attendees sit on the original stone terraces or in modern cushioned stalls. Most of the operas presented are the big, splashy ones, like *Aïda* or *Turandot,* which demand huge choruses, lots of color and movement, and, if possible, camels, horses, or elephants. Order tickets by phone or through the Arena website: if you book a spot on the cheaper terraces, be sure to take or rent a cushion—four hours on a 2,000-year-old stone bench can be an ordeal. ⊠ *Box office, Via Dietro Anfiteatro 6/b* ☎ *045/8005151* ⊕ *www.arena. it* ⇄ *From €20 (for unnumbered, open seating)* ⊗ *Box office: Sept.–late June, weekdays 9–noon and 3:15–5:45, Sat. 9–noon; June–Aug., performance days 10–9, nonperformance days 10–5:45.*

TREVISO AND THE HILLSIDE TOWNS

North of Venice, rivers and streams flow down from the Dolomites through market towns dotting the foothills. Villa Barbaro, one of Palladio's most imposing country villas is nearby, as are the arcaded streets and romantic canals of undiscovered Treviso and the graceful Venetian Gothic structures of smaller hill towns.

ASOLO

33 km (20½ miles) northwest of Treviso.

Once considered the most romantic and charming of Veneto towns, the hamlet of Asolo has unfortunately lost much of its appeal, now that it's given over completely to tourism and vacation houses, with almost no local population. It does still make a nice stop for lunch after a visit to the Palladian villa at Maser, but try to avoid it on weekends and holidays, when the crowds pour in.

Through the centuries, Veneto aristocrats built elegant villas on the hillside, and in the 19th century Asolo became the idyllic haunt of musicians, poets, and painters. Back then it was one of Italy's most perfectly situated villages, with views across miles of hilly countryside; now it bears some of the scars of modern development.

Asolo hosts a modest antiques market on the second Sunday of every month except July and August.

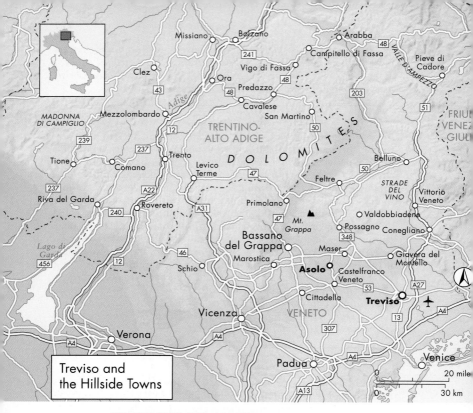

Treviso and
the Hillside Towns

GETTING HERE AND AROUND

There's no train station in Asolo; the closest one is in Montebelluna, 12 km (7½ miles) away. Bus connections are infrequent, and buses are not coordinated with trains, making it about a 2½-hour trip from Venice via public transportation. The best option is to drive.

By car from Treviso take Via Feltrina and continue onto Via Padre Agostino Gemelli (SR348). Follow SR348 about 16 km (10 miles), then turn left on SP667, which you follow for almost 4 km (2½ miles). At the roundabout, take the first exit, Via Monte Grappa (SP284) and follow it for 6½ km (4 miles) to Via Loredan, where you turn right and then left onto Via Bordo Vecchio. Asolo is less than 7 km (4½ miles) away from the Palladian Villa Barbaro at Maser.

VISITOR INFORMATION

Asolo Tourism Office ⊠ *Piazza Maggiore, aka Piazza Garibaldi* ☎ *0423/529046* ⊕ *www.asolo.it* ⊘ *Tues.–Sat. 8:30–12:30, Fri. and Sat. 3:30–6.*

EXPLORING

Brion Family Tomb. One of the major monuments of contemporary Italian architecture, the Brion family tomb was designed and built by the architect Carlo Scarpa (1906–78) between 1970 and 1972. Combining Western rationalism with Eastern spirituality, Scarpa avoids the gloom and bombast of conventional commemorative monuments, creating, in his words, a secluded Eden. ⊠ *SP6, Via Castellan, near village of San Vito, about 7 km (4½ miles) south of Asolo* ⊠ *Free* ☉ *Apr.–Sept., daily 8–7; Oct.–Mar., daily 9–3:30.*

Fodor'sChoice ★ **Museo Canova** (*Gypsoteca*). The most significant cultural monument in the Asolo area is this museum dedicated to the work of the Italian neoclassical sculptor Antonio Canova (1757–1822), whose sculptures are featured in many major European and North American cultural institutions. Set up shortly after the sculptor's death in his hometown, the village of Possagno, the museum houses most of the original plaster casts, models, and drawings made by the artist in preparation for his marble sculptures. In 1957 the Museo Canova was extended by the Italian architect Carlo Scarpa. ⊠ *Via Canova 74, Possagno, 13.5 km (8¼ miles) northwest of Asolo* ☎ *0423/544323* ⊕ *www.museocanova. it* ⊠ *€10* ☉ *Tues.–Sun. 9:30–6.*

Piazza Maggiore. Renaissance palaces and long-established cafés grace this piazza, Asolo's town center.

Museo Civico. In the piazza, the frescoed 15th-century Loggia del Capitano contains the Museo Civico, which displays a collection of eccentric memorabilia—the Italian actress Eleonora Duse's correspondence, the poet Robert Browning's spinet, and portraits of the noble Caterina Cornaro (1454–1510). ⊠ *Piazza Maggiore* ☎ *0423/952313* ⊠ *€5; €6, includes ruins of Caterina Cornaro's castle* ☉ *Weekends 10–7 and by appointment.*

NEED A BREAK? **Caffè Centrale.** While away some idle moments at Caffè Centrale, which has overlooked the fountain in Piazza Maggiore and the Duomo since about 1700. Now it's half café and half gift shop. ⊠ *Via Roma 72* ☎ *0423/952141* ⊕ *www.caffecentrale.com* ☉ *Wed.–Mon., 7 am–midnight* ☉ *Closed Tues.*

Tempio Canoviano. One of the most impressive and historically significant Neoclassical buildings in Italy, the Tempio Canoviano was designed by Canova in 1819 and finished in 1830, incorporating motifs from the rotunda of the Roman Pantheon and the *pronaos* (inner portico) of the Parthenon. The church contains several works by Canova, including his tomb, along with paintings by Luca Giordano, Palma il Giovane, and il Pordenone. ⊠ *Piazza Canova, Possagno, 16 km (10 miles) north of Asolo* ☎ *0423/544323* ⊠ *Free* ☉ *Winter, daily 9–noon and 2–5; summer, daily 9–noon and 3–6.*

Fodor'sChoice ★ **Villa Barbaro.** See the Palladio Country feature in this chapter. ⊠ *Via Cornuda 7, Maser* ☎ *0432/923004* ⊕ *www.villadimaser.it* ⊠ *€7* ☉ *Hrs vary, check website.*

WHERE TO EAT

$$
NORTHERN
ITALIAN
✕ **Al Bacaro.** At this family-style restaurant, you may want take a leap and try a dish with stewed game, tripe, or snails. Less adventurous diners can go for other homey options, such as goulash, polenta with cheese and mushrooms, or one of Bacaro's open-face sandwiches, generously topped with fresh salami, speck, or other cold cuts. Although the restaurant essentially caters only to tourists, as is the case with most

eateries in Asolo, the food here is better than average. $ *Average main: €15* ⊠ *Via Browning 165* ☎ *0423/55150* ⊘ *Closed Wed.*

$$$
NORTHERN
ITALIAN
Fodor'sChoice
★
✕ **Locanda Baggio.** Even if the swarms of tourists and commercialization of Asolo put you off, a lunch or dinner at this family-run restaurant makes a trip to the hillside village worthwhile. This is the best restaurant in Asolo, and the prix-fixe menu is one of the best values in the region. Chef Nino Baggio specializes in elegant versions of traditional cuisine—the rabbit stuffed with sausage, for example, is deboned and served with a crust of grana cheese—and takes pride in his homemade pasta, bread, and desserts. If you are here in November, try one of the dishes incorporating precious white truffles from Alba. $ *Average main: €25* ⊠ *Via Bassane 1* ☎ *0423/529648* ⊕ *www.locandabaggio.it* ⊘ *Closed Mon., and 2 wks in Aug. No lunch Tues.*

WHERE TO STAY

$$$
B&B/INN
▨ **Al Sole.** This elegant pink-washed hotel in a 16th-century building overlooks the main square and has wide views over picturesque Asolo or its leafy hinterland. **Pros:** central location; beautiful views; attentive service; free shuttle service to the surrounding area. **Cons:** rates increase in the high season; standard rooms have less interesting views than more expensive ones. $ *Rooms from: €245* ⊠ *Via Collegio 33* ☎ *0423/951332* ⊕ *www.albergoalsole.com* ⤳ *22 rooms, 1 suite* ⊘ *Generally closed early Jan.–mid-Feb.* ⭘| *Breakfast.*

$
B&B/INN
▨ **Hotel Duse.** A spiral staircase winds its way up this narrow, centrally located building to rooms with a view of the main square. **Pros:** simple but tasteful rooms; central location. **Cons:** some street noise; not as much of a bargain when you add the cost of breakfast and parking; only dial-up Internet. $ *Rooms from: €120* ⊠ *Via Browning 190* ☎ *0423/55241* ⊕ *www.hotelduse.com* ⤳ *14 rooms* ⊘ *Closed 3 wks in Jan. and Feb.* ⭘| *No meals.*

$$$
HOTEL
▨ **Villa Cipriani.** A romantic garden surrounded by gracious country homes is the setting for this luxurious 16th-century villa. **Pros:** incomparable views; truly elegant grounds; good spa services. **Cons:** small bathrooms; furnishings are old but not always tasteful; pricey restaurant; rooms in the annex are very small. $ *Rooms from: €240* ⊠ *Via Canova 298* ☎ *0423/523411* ⊕ *www.villaciprianiasolo.com* ⤳ *31 rooms* ⭘| *Breakfast.*

TREVISO

35 km (22 miles) southeast of Maser, 30 km (19 miles) north of Venice.

Treviso has been dubbed "Little Venice" because of its meandering, moss-bank canals. They can't really compare with Venice's spectacular waterways, but on the whole, Treviso's historic center, with its medieval arcaded streets, has a great deal of charm. Treviso is a fine place to stop for a few hours on the way from Venice to the wine country in the north or to the Palladian villas in the hinterland.

Allied bombing on Good Friday in 1944 destroyed half the city—it was bombed by mistake after a report that Hitler would be in Tarvisio, on the Austrian border, was misread. Despite this, Treviso managed to preserve what remained of its old town's narrow streets while introducing

Traveling the Wine Roads

You'd be hard-pressed to find a more stimulating and varied wine region than northeastern Italy. From the Valpolicella, Bardolino, and Soave produced near Verona to the superlative whites of the Collio region, wines from the Veneto and Friuli–Venezia Giulia earn more Denominazione di Origine Controllata seals for uniqueness and quality than those of any other area of Italy.

You can travel on foot, by car, or by bicycle over hillsides covered with vineyards, each field nurturing subtly different grape varieties. On a casual trip through the countryside you're likely to come across wineries that will welcome you for a visit; for a more organized tour, check local tourist information offices, which have maps of roads, wineries, and vendors. Be advised that Italy has become more stringent about its driving regulations; designated drivers can help avoid the risk of fines, embarrassment, or worse.

One of the most hospitable areas in the Veneto for wine enthusiasts is the stretch of country north of Treviso, where you can follow designated wine roads—tours that blend a beautiful rural setting with the delights of the grape. Authorized wine shops, where you can stop and sample, are marked with a sign showing a triangular arrangement of red and yellow grapes. There are three routes to choose from, and they're manageable enough that you can do them all comfortably over the course of a day or two.

MONTELLO AND ASOLO HILLS
This route provides a good balance of vineyards and nonwine sights. It winds from Nervesa della Battaglia, 18 km

(10 miles) north of Treviso, past two prime destinations in the area, the village of Asolo and the Villa Barbaro at Maser. Asolo produces good prosecco, while Montello, a hill near Nervesa, favors merlot and cabernet. Both areas also yield pinot and chardonnay.

PIAVE RIVER
The circular route follows the Piave River and runs through orchards, woods, and hills. Among the area's gems are the dessert wines Torchiato di Fregona and Refrontolo Passito, both made according to traditional methods.

Raboso del Piave, renowned since Roman times, ages well and complements local dishes such as beans and pasta or goose stuffed with chestnuts. Other reds include merlot and cabernet sauvignon. As an accompaniment to fish, try a Verduzzo del Piave or, for an aperitivo, the warm-yellow Pinot Grigio del Piave.

PROSECCO
This route runs for 47 km (29 miles) between Valdobbiadene and Conegliano, home of Italy's first wine institute, winding between knobby hills covered in grapevines. These hang in festoons on row after row of pergolas to create a thick mantle of green.

Turn off the main route to explore the narrower country lanes, most of which eventually join up. They meander through tiny hamlets and past numerous family wineries where you can taste and buy the wines. Spring is an excellent time to visit, with no fewer than 15 local wine festivals held between March and early June.

4

modernity far more gently than in many other parts of Italy. These days it's one of the wealthiest small cities in the country, with fashionable shops and boutiques at every turn in the busy city center.

GETTING HERE AND AROUND

Treviso is 30 minutes by train from Venice; there are frequent daily departures. By car from Venice, pick up the SS13 in Mestre (Via Terraglio) and follow it all the way to Treviso; the trip takes about 45 minutes.

VISITOR INFORMATION

Treviso Tourism Office ✉ *Palazzo Scotti, Via S. Andrea 3* ☎ *0422/547632* 🌐 *turismo.provincia.treviso.it* 🕒 *Tues.–Fri. 9–1 and 2–6, Mon. and Sat. 9–1.*

EXPLORING

Piazza dei Signori. The center of medieval Treviso, this piazza remains the town's social hub, with outdoor cafés and some impressive public buildings. The most important of these, the Palazzo dei Trecento (1185–1268), was the seat of the city government, composed of the Council of 300, during the Middle Ages. Behind it is a small alley that leads to the *pescheria* (fish market), on an island in one of the small canals that flow through town.

Quartiere Latino. While strolling the city, take in this restored district between Riviera Garibaldi and Piazza Santa Maria Battuti. It's the site of university buildings, upscale apartments, and bustling restaurants and shops. If you walk along the northern part of the historic city wall, you'll look down on the island home of ducks, geese, and goats. Their little farm occupies some of the city's prettiest real estate.

San Nicolò. The most important church in Treviso, this huge Venetian Gothic structure from the early 14th century has an ornate vaulted ceiling and frescoes (circa 1350) of saints by Tommaso da Modena (circa 1325–79) on the columns. The depiction of *St. Agnes* on the north side is particularly interesting. Also worth examining are Tommaso's realistic portraits of 40 Dominican friars, found in the Sala del Capitolo of the seminary next door. They include the earliest-known painting of a subject wearing eyeglasses, an Italian invention (circa 1280–1300). ✉ *Seminario Vescovile, Via San Nicolò* ☎ *0422/548626* 🕒 *Church daily 8–12:30 and 3:30–7; seminary daily 8–6.*

WHERE TO EAT

$$ NORTHERN ITALIAN 🍴 **All'Antico Portico.** This little old brick trattoria on a quiet square in Treviso's historic center is a favorite among locals and tourists. The menu changes daily, but always features well-executed versions of simple local dishes. You might find oversize ravioli with ricotta and Parmesan covered with butter and sage, or a salad of improbably tender *piovra* (octopus), served at room temperature with potatoes, olives, and vegetables. [$] *Average main: €17* ✉ *Piazza Santa Maria Maggiore 18* ☎ *0422/545259* 🌐 *www.anticoportico.it* 🕒 *Closed Tues.*

$$ NORTHERN ITALIAN 🍴 **Beccherie.** The name means butcher shop, and this area behind Treviso's Palazzo Trecento is where people bought and sold meat for centuries. It is only fitting that Beccherie should specialize in *bollito,* a celebrated dish of assorted boiled meats and sauces, which originated in

Piedmont but is now so much a part of Veneto cooking that most Veneti regard it as their own. The varied menu, based on local cuisine, changes according to the season. The owner's mother, Depillo Alba Campeol, invented the famous dessert tiramisù in the 1960s, and the Beccharie still makes it to the original, feather-light recipe. Locals have been keeping this family-owned restaurant busy since 1939. Reservations are recommended for dinner. $ *Average main: €23* ⊠ *Piazza Ancilotto 10* ☎ *0422/540871* ⊘ *Closed Mon., and last 2 wks in July. No dinner Sun.*

$$
✕ **Il Basilisco.** Gastronomically adventurous diners who visit this simple
VENETIAN restaurant will find Veneto cuisine in the *cucina povera* (poor people's food) tradition and discover that, with talent and imagination, tasty dishes can be created from the most humble and unusual ingredients. Start with a savory dish of pasta with rabbit tripe, or *nervetti*, gelatinous veal tendons in a sauce of celery root. Main courses are somewhat more conventional, such as a timbale of local anchovies with a sauce of chicory and sun-dried tomatoes. If all this sounds a little too unusual, there are dishes such as veal liver in a pepper sauce, or a couscous of calamari and vegetables. $ *Average main: €18* ⊠ *Via Bison 34* ☎ *0422/541822* ⊕ *www.ristorantebasilisco.com* ⌂ *Reservations essential* ⊘ *Closed Sun. No lunch Mon. and Sat.*

$
✕ **Osteria Muscoli's.** The bar at this hangout is always busy with locals
WINE BAR popping in for an *ombra* (glass of wine), but there are also tables out on the little island of the *pescheria* (fish market), in the middle of the adjacent canal, where you can sit and enjoy your drink accompanied by a platter of savory delights, possibly with chunks of ham off the bone, a wedge of potato-and-porcini pie, pepper cheese, stuffed pickled tomatoes, or *crostini* (grilled open-face sandwiches) with *sfilacci* (shredded, cured horse meat). ■ TIP➡ **Lunch and dinner are served here, but this is more a place for a savory snack than a meal.** $ *Average main: €12* ⊠ *Via Pescheria 23* ☎ *0422/583390* ▭ *No credit cards* ⊘ *Closed Sun.*

$$
✕ **Osteria Ponte Dante.** Pleasant and simple, this osteria provides a roman-
NORTHERN tic setting at the junction of two canals. The kitchen turns out homestyle
ITALIAN dishes such as *ai porcini e ricotta affumicata* (with porcini mushrooms and smoked mozzarella) and a classic *fritto misto di pesce* (mixed fried fish), all at reasonable prices. $ *Average main: €20* ⊠ *Piazza Garibaldi 6* ☎ *0422/582924* ⊕ *www.locandapontedante.com/osteria* ▭ *No credit cards* ⊘ *Closed Sun.*

$$
✕ **Toni del Spin.** Wood paneled and with a 1930s-style interior, this bus-
VENETIAN tling trattoria oozes old-fashioned character. The wholesome menu, chalked on a hanging wooden board, is based on local Veneto cooking. The "Spin" in the restaurant's name refers to the spine of the baccalà, one of several justly famous specialties (served without the titular spine). In autumn and winter, be sure to try Treviso's hallmark product, radicchio, in risotto or pasta. The chef-owner, Alfredo Sturlese, is also proud of his *sopa coada* (pigeon-and-bread soup). ■ TIP➡ **Reservations are essential, even for lunch, since the word is out that this is the best value in town.** $ *Average main: €16* ⊠ *Via Inferiore 7* ☎ *0422/543829* ⊕ *www.ristorantetonidelspin.com* ⌂ *Reservations essential* ⊘ *Closed 3 wks in July and Aug. No lunch Mon.*

WHERE TO STAY

$$ HOTEL **Carlton Hotel.** Pass the river flowing outside, walk through the lobby, and seek out the huge scenic terrace atop the old city wall—even the parking lot of this comfortable hotel has a view. **Pros:** central location; one of very few hotels in the city center. **Cons:** interior is not always appealing; some rooms need refurbishing. [$] *Rooms from: €140* ✉ *Largo di Porta Altinia 15* ☎ *0422/411661* 🌐 *www.hotelcarlton.it* 🛏 *93 rooms* 🍴 *Breakfast.*

FRIULI–VENEZIA GIULIA

Friuli–Venezia Giulia is perhaps Italy's best-kept secret. It's home to impressive and beautiful medieval artistic monuments—some of which actually predate those in Venice—as well as important frescoes by the Venetian master painter Tiepolo. The atmospheric old Austrian port of Trieste was a major center of literature in the late 19th and early 20th century.

The peripheral location of the Friuli–Venezia Giulia region in Italy's northeastern corner makes it easy to overlook, but in addition to its artistic treasures, its mix of Italian, Slavic, and Central European cultures, evident in places like the medieval city of Udine, make it a fascinating area to explore. It's also got a strong wine tradition: Cividale del Friuli and the Collio wine regions are a short hop away from Udine.

UDINE

94 km (58 miles) northeast of Treviso, 127 km (79 miles) northeast of Venice.

The main reason for devoting some time to Udine is to see works by the last of the great Italian painters, Gianbattista Tiepolo (1696–1770). Distributed in several palaces and churches around town, this is the greatest assembly of his art outside Venice. In fact, Udine calls itself "*la città di Tiepolo.*"

The largest city on the Friuli side of the region, Udine has a provincial, genteel atmosphere and lots of charm. The city sometimes seems completely unaffected by tourism, and things are still done the way they were decades ago. In the medieval and Renaissance historical center of town, you'll find unevenly spaced streets with appealing wine bars and open-air cafés. Friulani are proud of their culture, with many restaurants featuring local cuisine, and street signs and announcements written in both Italian and Friulano (Furlan). Although Friulano is sometimes classified as a dialect, it's really a separate language from Italian.

Commanding a view from the Alpine foothills to the Adriatic Sea, Udine stands on a mound that, according to legend, was erected so Attila the Hun could watch the burning of Aquileia, an important Roman center to the south. Although the legend is unlikely (Attila burned Aquileia about 500 years before the first historical mention of Udine), the view from Udine's castle across the alluvial plane down to the sea is impressive. In the Middle Ages Udine flourished, thanks to its favorable trade location and the right granted by the local patriarch to hold regular markets.

GETTING HERE AND AROUND

There's frequent train service from both Venice and Trieste; the trip takes about two hours from Venice, and a little over an hour from Trieste. By car from Venice, take the SR11 to the E55 and head east. Take the E55 (it eventually becomes the Autostrada Alpe Adria) to SS13 (Viale Venezia) east into Udine. Driving from Trieste, take the SS202 to the E70, which becomes the A4. Turn onto the E55 north, which is the same road you would take coming from Venice. Driving times are 1½ hours from Venice and one hour from Trieste.

VISITOR INFORMATION

The tourist office sells the FVG (Friuli Venezia Giulia) Card, which includes admission to most museums in Udine and other important sites in the region. Its price ranges from €15, for 48 hours, up to €29, for one week.

Udine Tourism Office ⊠ *Piazza I Maggio 7* ☎ *0432/295972* ⊕ *www. turismofvg.it* ⊗ *Mon.–Sat. 9–1 and 2–6, Sun. 9–1.*

EXPLORING

Castello. From its hilltop site, the castle (construction began 1517) has panoramic views extending to Monte Nero (7,360 feet) in neighboring Slovenia. Here Udine's civic museums of art and archaeology are centralized under one roof. Particularly worth seeing is the national and regional art collection in the **Galleria d'Arte Antica,** which has canvases by Venetians Vittore Carpaccio (circa 1460–1525) and Gianbattista Tiepolo, an excellent Caravaggio, and carefully selected works by lesser-known but still interesting Veneto and Friuli artists. ■TIP→ The museum's small collection of drawings includes several by Tiepolo; some find his drawings even more moving than his paintings. ⊠ *Via Lionello 1* ☎ *0432/271591* ☎ *€5 (free with FVG Card)* ⊗ *Oct.–late Apr., Tues.–Sun. 10:30–5; late Apr.–Sept., Tues.–Sun. 10:30–7.*

Duomo. A few steps from the Piazza della Libertà is Udine's 1335 Duomo. Its Cappella del Santissimo has important early frescoes by Tiepolo, and the Cappella della Trinità has a Tiepolo altarpiece. There is also a beautiful late Tiepolo *Resurrection* (1751) in an altar by the sculptor Giuseppi Toretti. Ask the Duomo's attendant to let you into the adjacent **Chiesa della Purita** to see more important late paintings by Tiepolo. ⊠ *Piazza del Duomo 1* ☎ *0432/506830* ☎ *Free* ⊗ *Daily 7–noon and 4–6:45.*

Fodor'sChoice ★ **Palazzo Arcivescovile.** The Palazzo Arcivescovile (also known as Palazzo Patriarcale) contains several rooms of frescoes by the young Gianbattista Tiepolo, painted from 1726 to 1732, which comprise the most important collection of early works by Italy's most brilliant 18th-century painter. The Galleria del Tiepolo (1727) contains superlative Tiepolo frescoes depicting the stories of Abraham, Isaac, and Jacob. The *Judgment of Solomon* (1729) graces the Pink Room. There are also beautiful and important Tiepolo frescoes in the staircase, throne room, and palatine chapel of this palazzo. Even in these early works

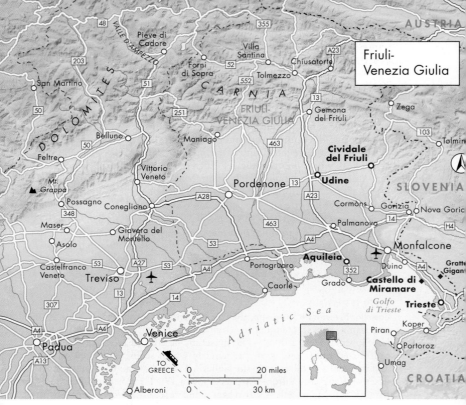

we can see the Venetian master's skill in creating an illusion of depth, not only through linear perspective, but also through subtle gradations in the intensity of color, with the stronger colors coming forward and the paler ones receding into space. Tiepolo was one of the first artists to use this method of representing space and depth, which reflected the scientific discoveries of perception and optics in the 17th century. In the same building, the **Museo Diocesano** features a collection of sculptures from Friuli churches from the 13th through the 18th century. ✉ *Piazza Patriarcato 1* ☎ *0432/25003* ⊕ *www.musdioc-tiepolo.it* 🎫 *€7, includes Museo Diocesano* ⊘ *Wed.–Sun. 10–1 and 3:30–6:30.*

Piazza della Libertà. Udine was conquered by the Venetians in 1420, so there is a distinctly Venetian stamp on the architecture of the historic center, most noticeably here, in the large main square. The Loggia del Leonello, begun in 1428, dominates the square and houses the municipal government. Its similarity to the facade of Venice's Palazzo Ducale (finished in 1424) is clear, but there is no evidence that it is an imitation of that palace. It's more likely a product of the same architectural fashion. Opposite stands the Renaissance Porticato di San Giovanni (1533–35) and the Torre dell'Orologio, a 1527 clock tower with naked *mori* (Moors), who strike the hour on the top.

WHERE TO EAT

$$ FRIULIAN Fodor's Choice ★ 🍴 **Hostaria alla Tavernetta.** One of Udine's most trusted restaurants is steps from the Piazza Duomo. The Hostaria alla Tavernetta, open since 1954, has rustic fireside dining downstairs and smaller, more elegantly decorated rooms upstairs, where there's also a small terrace. On the menu are regional specialties such as *orzotto* (barley prepared like risotto), delicious *cjalzòns* (ravioli stuffed with ricotta, apples, raisins, and spices and topped with smoked ricotta, butter, and cinnamon), and perhaps the most tender suckling pig you have ever eaten. The restaurant offers a reasonably priced prix-fixe menu. The service is pleasant and attentive, and there's a fine selection of Friuli's celebrated wines and grappas. [$] *Average main: €18* ✉ *Via di Prampero 2* ☎ *0432/501066* ⏲ *Closed Sun. and Mon., 2nd wk in Jan., 1 wk in June, 2 wks in mid-Aug.*

$$ FRIULIAN FAMILY 🍴 **Osteria Al Vecchio Stallo.** This former stable bursts with character, its beautiful courtyard shaded by grape arbors. The menu includes a wide choice of traditional Friuli home cooking prepared simply. As an appetizer, try the prized prosciutto from the neighboring village of San Daniele, which some regard even more highly than the famous Parma version. Start with cjalzòns, or the *mignàculis con luagne* (pasta with local sausage), followed by Friuli classics such as *frico con patate* (hash-brown potatoes with Montasio cheese) or goulash with polenta. On Friday there are also fish dishes. There's a great selection of wines by the glass. [$] *Average main: €18* ✉ *Via Viola 7* ☎ *0432/21296* 💳 *No credit cards* ⏲ *Closed Wed. Sept.–June, Sun. in July and Aug., 3 wks in Aug., and Dec. 25–Jan. 7.*

$$$ ITALIAN 🍴 **Vitello d'Oro.** Udine's very elegant landmark restaurant is the one reserved by most local people for special occasions. The big terrace in front is popular for alfresco dining in summer. The menu features both meat and fish but specializes in fish. You might start with an antipasto of assorted raw shellfish, including the impossibly sweet Adriatic *scampi,* followed by the fresh fish of the day. Service is impeccable, as is the Friuli-focused wine list. Perhaps the best way to go is the multicourse tasting menu. [$] *Average main: €30* ✉ *Via Valvason 4* ☎ *0432/508982* 🌐 *www.vitellodoro.com* ✍ *Reservations essential* ⏲ *Closed Wed., and Sun. June–Aug. No lunch Mon.*

WHERE TO STAY

$$ HOTEL 🏨 **Hostaria Hotel Allegria.** The comfortable lounges and guest rooms in this 15th-century building are done with plenty of wood, polished into finely crafted furnishings and wall features, and lighting is designed to dramatic effect. **Pros:** well-appointed rooms; great staff; discounted weekend rates; within easy walking distance to town center. **Cons:** rooms may be too minimalist for some; fee for parking. [$] *Rooms from: €140* ✉ *Via Grazzano 18* ☎ *0432/201116* 🌐 *www.hotelallegria.it* 🛏 *21 rooms* 🍽 *Breakfast.*

$$ HOTEL 🏨 **Hotel Clocchiatti.** You have two choices here: the 19th-century villa, where there are canopy beds and Alpine-style wood ceilings and paneling, and the "Next Wing," with rich colors and spare furnishings in starkly angular rooms. **Pros:** individually decorated rooms; quiet surroundings; swimming pool; excellent breakfast; Wi-Fi. **Cons:** 10-minute drive from town center; small bathrooms; no restaurant; rooms in

more modern annex are more expensive. $ *Rooms from: €130* ✉ *Via Cividale 29* ☎ *0432/505047* ⊕ *www.hotelclocchiatti.it* ⌐27 *rooms* ⑩ *Breakfast.*

CIVIDALE DEL FRIULI

17 km (11 miles) east of Udine, 144 km (89 miles) northeast of Venice.

Cividale is the most important place for taking in the impressive and beautiful art of the Lombards, a Germanic people who entered Italy in 568 and who ruled parts of Italy until the late 8th century. The city was founded in AD 53 by Julius Caesar, then commander of Roman legions in the area. Here you can also find Celtic, Roman, and medieval Jewish ruins alongside Venetian Gothic buildings, including the Palazzo Comunale. Strolling through the part of the city that now occupies the former Gastaldia, the Lombard ducal palace, gives you spectacular views of the medieval city and the river.

GETTING HERE AND AROUND

There's hourly train service from Udine. Since the Udine–Cividale train line isn't part of the Italian national rail system, you have to buy the tickets from the tobacconist or other retailers within the Udine station. You can't buy a ticket through to Cividale from another city.

By car from Udine, take Via Cividale, which turns into SS54; follow SS54 into Cividale.

EXPLORING

Duomo. Cividale's Renaissance Duomo is largely the work of Pietro Lombardo, principal architect of Venice's famous Santa Maria dei Miracoli. The church contains a magnificent 12th-century silver gilt altarpiece. ✉ *Piazza Duomo* ☎ *0432/731144* ⊘ *Daily 7:30–7:30.*

Museo Archeologico. Trace the area's history here and learn about the importance of Cividale and Udine in the period following the collapse of the Roman Empire. The collection includes weapons and jewelry from 6th-century Lombard warriors, who swept through much of what is now Italy. ✉ *Piazza Duomo 13* ☎ *0432/700700* ⊕ *www.cividale.com/citta/museo.asp* ⧉*€4* ⊘ *Mon. 9–2, Tues.–Sun. 8:30–7:30.*

Museo Cristiano e Tesoro del Duomo. Entered via a courtyard to the right of the Duomo, this museum contains two interesting and important monuments of Lombard art: the Altar of Duke Ratchis (737–744) and the Baptistry of Patriarch Callisto (731–776). Both were found under the floor of the present Duomo in the early 20th century. The museum also has two fine paintings by Veronese, one by Pordenone, and a small collection of medieval and Renaissance vestments. ✉ *Via Candotti 1* ☎ *0432/730403* ⧉*€4; €6 combination ticket with Tempietto Longobardo* ⊘ *Wed.–Sun. 10–1 and 3–6.*

Fodor'sChoice ★ **Tempietto Longobardo** (*Lombard Church*). Seeing the beautiful and historically important Tempietto Longobardo from the 8th century is more than enough reason to visit Cividale. Now inside the 16th-century Monastery of Santa Maria in Valle, the Tempietto was originally the chapel of the ducal palace, known as the Gastaldia. The west wall is the best-preserved example of the art and architecture of the Lombards, a Germanic people who entered Italy in 568. It has an archway with an exquisitely rendered vine motif, guarded by an 8th-century procession of female figures, showing the Lombard interpretation of classical forms that resembles the style of the much earlier Byzantine mosaics in Ravenna, which had passed briefly to Lombard rule in 737. This procession of female figures had originally extended to the side walls of the Tempietto, but was destroyed by an earthquake in 1222. The post-Lombard frescoes decorating the vaults and the east wall date from the 13th and 14th centuries, and the fine carved wooden stalls also date from the 14th century. ✉ *Via Monastero Maggiore* ☎ *0432/700867* 🎫 *€4; €6 combination ticket with Museo del Duomo* 🕓 *Oct.–Mar., Mon.–Sat. 10–1 and 2–5, Sun. 10–5; Apr.–Sept., Mon.–Sat. 10–1 and 3–6, Sun. 10–6.*

WHERE TO STAY

$$ B&B/INN 🏨 **La Cjase dai Toscans.** In a central location, this 15th-century palazzo, once home to the Dukes of Tuscany, is now a charming and romantic bed-and-breakfast, with large rooms furnished in antique style. **Pros:** large, well-appointed rooms; high-speed Wi-Fi; good breakfast; nearby parking is free or at moderate cost; for a fee, transportation can be arranged from Udine train station. **Cons:** some noise from the street and the cathedral bells. [$] *Rooms from: €130* ✉ *Corso Mazzini 15/1* ☎ *349/0765288 (cell phone)* 🌐 *www.lacjasedaitoscans.it* 🛏 *4 rooms* 🍴 *No meals.*

AQUILEIA

77 km (48 miles) west of Trieste, 163 km (101 miles) east of Venice.

This sleepy little town is refreshingly free of the tourists that you might expect at such a culturally historic place. In the time of Emperor Augustus, it was Italy's fourth-most-important city (after Rome, Milan, and Capua), as well as the principal northern Adriatic port of Italy and the beginning of Roman routes north. Aquileia's Roman and early Christian remains convey an image of the transition from pagan to Christian Rome.

GETTING HERE AND AROUND

Getting to Aquileia by public transportation is difficult but not impossible. There's frequent train service from Venice and Trieste to Cervignano di Friuli, which is 8 km (5 miles) away from Aquileia by taxi (about €20), and infrequent bus service. (Ask the newsstand attendant or the railroad ticket agent for assistance.) By car from Venice or Trieste, take Autostrada A4 (Venezia–Trieste) to the Palmanova exit and continue 17 km (11 miles) to Aquileia. From Udine, take Autostrada A23 to the Palmanova exit.

VISITOR INFORMATION

Aquileia Tourism Office ✉ *Bus Terminal, Via Iulia Augusta* ☎ *0431/919491* 🕓 *Daily 8:30–noon and 1:30–5:30.*

EXPLORING

Archaeological Site. Roman remains of the forum, houses, cemetery, and port are surrounded by cypresses here. The little stream was once an important waterway extending to Grado. Unfortunately, many of the excavations of Roman Aquileia could not be left exposed because of the extremely high water table under the site and had to be reburied after archaeological studies had been conducted; nevertheless, what remains aboveground, along with the monuments in the archaeological museum, gives an idea of the grandeur of this ancient city. The area is well signposted. ⊠ *Near basilica* ⊕ *www.museoarcheo-aquileia. it* ▭ *Free* ⊙ *Daily 8:15–7.*

Fodor'sChoice ★   **Basilica.** The highlight of this monument is the spectacular 3rd- to 4th-century mosaic covering the entire floor of the basilica and the adjacent crypt, which remains as one of the most beautiful and important of early-Christian monuments. Theodore, the basilica's first bishop, built two parallel basilicas, now the north and the south halls, on the site of a Gnostic chapel in the 4th century. These were joined by a third hall, forming a "U," with the baptismal font in the middle. The complex was rebuilt between 1021 and 1031, and later accumulated the Romanesque portico and the Gothic bell tower, producing the church you see today. The mosaic floor of the present-day basilica is essentially the remains of the floor of Theodore's south hall, while those of the Cripta degli Scavi are those of his north hall, along with the remains of the mosaic floor of a pre-Christian Roman house and warehouse.

The mosaics of the basilica are important not only because of their beauty, but also because they provide a window into Gnostic symbolism and the conflict between Gnosticism and the early-Christian church.

This integration of Gnosticism into a Christian church is particularly interesting, since Gnosticism had already been branded a heresy by influential early Church fathers. In retaining these mosaics, Theodore may have been publicly expressing a leaning toward Gnosticism. Alternatively, the area of the north hall may have been Theodore's private residence, where the retention of Gnostic symbolism may have been more acceptable.

The 4th-century mosaics of the south hall (the present-day nave of the basilica) are somewhat more doctrinally conventional, and represent the story of Jonah as prefiguring the salvation offered by the Church.

Down a flight of steps, the **Cripta degli Affreschi** contains beautiful 12th-century frescoes, among them Saint Peter sending Saint Mark to Aquileia and the beheading of Saints Hermagoras and Fortunatus, to whom the basilica is dedicated. ⊠ *Aquileia* ☎ *0431/91067* ⊕ *www. aquileia.net* ▭ *Basilica free, both crypts €3, campanile €2, €9 for admission to all sites in Aquileia* ⊙ *Basilica: Apr.–Sept., daily 9–7; Mar. and Oct., 9–6; Nov.–Feb., weekdays 9–4:30, weekends 9–5. Campanile: Apr.–Sept., daily 9:30–1:30 and 3:30–6:30; Oct., weekends 9:30–1:30 and 3:30–6:30. Note: The Basilica sometimes has shorter hrs or is closed for a day; phone ahead or check the website.*

Museo Archeologico. A wealth of material from the Roman era includes portrait busts from Republican times, semiprecious gems, amber—containing preserved flies—and gold work, and a fine glass collection. Beautiful pre-Christian mosaics are from the floors of Roman houses and palaces. ⊠ *Via Roma 1* ☎ *0431/91096* ⊕ *www. museoarcheo-aquileia.it* ⊠ *€4, €9 for admission to all sites in Aquileia* ⊗ *Tues.–Sun. 8:30–7:30.*

TRIESTE

71 km (44 miles) southeast of Cividale del Friuli, 163 km (101 miles) east of Venice.

Trieste is Italy's only truly cosmopolitan city. In a country, perhaps even in a continent, where the amalgamation of cultures has frequently proved difficult, Trieste stands out as one of the few authentic melting pots. Not only do Italian, Slavic, and Central European cultures meet here, they actually merge together to create a unique Triestino culture. To discover this culture, visiting Trieste's coffeehouses, local eateries, and piazzas is probably more important than visiting its churches and museums, interesting though they are.

Trieste is built along a fringe of coastline where a rugged karst plateau tumbles abruptly into the beautiful Adriatic. It was the only port of the Austro-Hungarian Empire and, therefore, a major industrial and financial center. In the early years of the 20th century, Trieste and its surroundings also became famous by their association with some of the most important names of Italian literature, such as Italo Svevo, and Irish and German writers. James Joyce drew inspiration from the city's multiethnic population, and Rainer Maria Rilke was inspired by the coast to the west.

The city has lost its importance as a port and a center of finance, but perhaps because of its multicultural nature, at the juncture of Latin, Slavic, and Germanic Europe, it's never fully lost its role as an intellectual center. In recent years the city has become a center for science and technology. The streets hold a mix of monumental Neoclassical and Art Nouveau architecture, built by the Austrians during Trieste's days of glory, granting an air of melancholy stateliness to a city that lives as much in the past as the present.

GETTING HERE AND AROUND

Trains to Trieste depart regularly from Venice, Udine, and other major Italian cities. By car, it's the eastern terminus of the Autostrada Torino–Trieste (E70). Trieste is served by Ronchi dei Ligioneri Airport, which receives flights from major Italian airports and some European cities. The airport is 33 km (20½ miles) from the city; transportation into Trieste is by taxi or Bus No. 51.

VISITOR INFORMATION

Trieste Tourism Office ⊠ *Via dell'Orlogio 1, corner of Piazza dell'Unità d'Italia* ☎ *040/3478312* ⊕ *www.turismofvg.it* ⊗ *Mon.–Sat. 9–6, Sun. 9–1 and 2–6.*

EXPLORING
TOP ATTRACTIONS
Castello di San Giusto. This hilltop castle, built between 1470 and 1630, was constructed on the ruins of the Roman town of Tergeste. Given the excellent view, it's no surprise that 15th-century Venetians turned the castle into a shipping observation point; the structure was further enlarged by Trieste's subsequent rulers, the Habsburgs. The castle also contains the Civic Museum, which has a small collection of furnishings, tapestries, and weaponry. ⊠ *Piazza della Cattedrale 3* ☎ *040/309362* 🖅 *Castle with museums €4* ☉ *Winter, Tues.–Sun. 10–5; summer, Tues.–Sun. 10–6 (castle walls from 9).*

Piazza dell'Unità d'Italia. This imposing square, ringed by grandiose facades, was set out as a plaza open to the sea, like Venice's Piazza San Marco, in the late Middle Ages. It underwent countless changes through the centuries, and its present size and architecture are essentially products of late-19th- and early-20th-century Austria. It was given its current name in 1955, when Trieste was finally given to Italy. On the inland side of the piazza note the facade of the **Palazzo Comunale** (Town Hall), designed by the Triestino architect Giuseppi Bruni in 1875. It was from this building's balcony in 1938 that Mussolini proclaimed the infamous racial laws, depriving Italian Jews of most of their rights. The sidewalk cafés on this vast seaside piazza are popular meeting places in the summer months.

WORTH NOTING
Cattedrale di San Giusto. Dating from the 14th century and occupying the site of an ancient Roman forum, the cathedral contains remnants of at least three previous buildings, the earliest a hall dating from the 5th century. A section of the original floor mosaic still remains, incorporated into the floor of the present church. In the 9th and 11th centuries, two adjacent churches were built—the Church of the Assumption and the Church of San Giusto. The beautiful apse mosaics of these churches, done in the 12th and 13th centuries by a Venetian artist, still remain in the apses of the side aisles of the present church. The mosaics in the main apse date from 1932. In the 14th century the two churches were joined and a Romanesque-Gothic facade was attached, ornamented with fragments of Roman monuments taken from the forum. The jambs of the main doorway are the most conspicuous Roman element. ⊠ *Piazza della Cattedrale 3* ☎ *040/309666* ☉ *Daily 8:30–noon and 4–7.*

Piazza della Borsa. A statue of Habsburg emperor Leopold I looks out over this square, which contains Trieste's original stock exchange, the **Borsa Vecchia** (1805), an attractive neoclassical building now serving as the chamber of commerce. It sits at the end of the Canal Grande, dug in the 18th century by the Austrian empress Maria Theresa as a first step in the expansion of what was then a small fishing village of 7,000 into the port of her empire.

Risiera di San Sabba. In September 1943 the Nazi occupation established Italy's only concentration camp in this rice-processing factory outside of Trieste. In April 1944 a crematorium was put into operation. The Nazis destroyed much of the evidence of their atrocities before their retreat, but a good deal of the horror of the place is still perceptible in the reconstructed museum (1975). The site, an Italian national monument since 1965, receives more than 100,000 visitors per year. It can be reached easily by municipal Bus No. 8 or 10; by car it is off the Autostrada A4, exit Valmaura/Stadio/Cimitero. ✉ *Via Giovanni Palatucci 5* ☎ *040/826202* 🎟 *Free, guided tour €3* ⏲ *Daily 9–7.*

San Silvestro. This small Romanesque gem, dating from the 9th to the 12th century, is the oldest church in Trieste still in use and in approximately its original form. Its interior walls still have some fragmentary remains of Romanesque frescoes. The church was deconsecrated under the secularizing reforms of the Austrian emperor Josef II in 1785 and was later sold to the Swiss Evangelical community; it then became, and is still, the Reformed Evangelical and Waldesian Church of Trieste. ✉ *Piazza San Silvestro 1* ☎ *040/363952* ⏲ *Call for hrs.*

4

OFF THE BEATEN PATH

Castello Di Duino. This 14th-century castle, where in 1912 Rainer Maria Rilke wrote his masterpiece, the *Duino Elegies,* is 12 km (7½ miles) from Trieste. Take Bus No. 44 or 51 from the Trieste train station. The easy path along the seacoast from the castle toward Trieste has gorgeous views that rival the Amalfi Coast and the Cinque Terre. The castle itself, still the property of the Princes of Thurn and Taxis, contains a collection of antique furnishings and an amazing Palladian circular staircase, but the main attractions are the surrounding gardens and the spectacular views. ✉ *Frazione Duino 32, Duino-Ausina* ☎ *040/208120* 🌐 *www.castellodiduino.it* 🎟 *€8* ⏲ *Mid-Mar.–late Mar., Wed.–Mon. 9:30–4; Apr.–Sept., Wed.–Mon. 9:30–5:30; early Oct.–mid-Oct., Wed.–Mon. 9:30–5; mid-Oct.–late Oct., Wed.–Mon. 9:30–4.*

OFF THE BEATEN PATH

Grotta Gigante. More than 300 feet high, 900 feet long, and 200 feet wide, this gigantic cave is filled with spectacular stalactites and stalagmites. The required tour takes 50 minutes; bring a sweater to ward off the year-round chill and be willing (and able) to descend 500 steps and then climb back up. To get here you can take Bus No. 42, which leaves every 30 minutes from the Piazza Oberdan. A more scenic route is to take the tram uphill from Piazza Oberdan to Opicina, where you connect with Bus No. 42. ✉ *10 km (6 miles) north of Trieste* ☎ *040/327312* 🌐 *www.grottagigante.it* 🎟 *€12* ⏲ *Apr.–June, Tues.–Sun. 10–6, July and Aug., daily 10–6; Sept., Tues.–Sun. 10–6; Oct.–Mar., Tues.–Sun. 10–4. Tours leave on the hr.*

WHERE TO EAT

$$$ SEAFOOD

🍴 **Al Bagatto.** At this warm little seafood place near the Piazza Unità, the chef-owner Roberto Marussi personally shepherds your meal from start to finish. The menu includes traditional dishes, among them *baccalà mantecato* (creamed cod with olive oil), and more inventive creations, such as sea bass tartare with fresh ricotta. Roberto's dishes often integrate nouvelle ingredients without overshadowing the freshness of whatever local fish he bought in the market that morning. For a particularly romantic or festive evening, Al Bagatto can organize a private dinner for you and your friends aboard its boat, in the Gulf of Trieste. [$] *Average main: €28* ✉ *Via L. Cadorna 7* ☎ *040/301771* ✍ *Reservations essential* ⏲ *Closed Sun. No lunch.*

$ ✕**Antipastoteca di Mare.** Hidden halfway up the hill to the Castello di
SEAFOOD San Giusto, in what the Triestini call the old city, this informal little restaurant specializes in traditional preparations from the *cucina
povera*—literally the "cooking of the poor," though it has lately become
a culinary movement in which creative flair transforms the humblest
ingredients. The inexpensive fish—bluefish, sardines, mackerel, mussels,
and squid—are accompanied by salad, potatoes, polenta, and house
wine. The consistently tasty and fresh dishes, especially the fish soup
and the *sardoni in savor* (large sardines with raisins, pine nuts, and caramelized onions; *savor* is the Triestino-dialect equivalent of the Venetian
saor), show what a talented chef can do on a limited budget. $ *Average
main: €12* ⊠ *Via della Fornace 1* ☎ *040/309606* ⚓ *Reservations essential* ⊟ *No credit cards* ⊗ *Closed Mon. No dinner Sun.*

$$ ✕**Buffet da Siora Rosa.** Serving delicious and generous portions of tra-
NORTHERN ditional Triestino buffet fare, such as boiled pork and sausages, with
ITALIAN savory sauerkraut—Siora Rosa is a bit more comfortable than many
FAMILY buffets. In addition to ample seating in the simple dining room, there
are tables outside for when the weather is good. The restaurant is fre-
quented mainly by Triestini, including students and faculty from the
nearby university. You may be the only tourist in the place, but the
helpful waitresses generally speak English. $ *Average main: €16* ⊠ *Pi-
azza Hortis 3* ☎ *040/301460* ⊟ *No credit cards* ⊗ *Closed weekends
and holidays.*

$ ✕**Da Pepi.** A Triestino institution, this is the oldest and most esteemed
NORTHERN of the many "buffet" restaurants serving pork and sausages around
ITALIAN town. It and similar holes-in-the-wall (few tables, simple interior) are
Fodor's Choice as much a part of the Triestino scene as the cafés. It specializes in *bol-
★ lito di maiale*, a dish of boiled pork and pork sausages accompanied by
delicately flavored sauerkraut, mustard, and grated horseradish. Unlike
other Italian restaurants, buffets don't close between lunch and dinner,
and draft beer is the drink of choice. $ *Average main: €12* ⊠ *Via Cassa
di Risparmio 3* ☎ *040/366858* ⊗ *Closed Sun., and the last 2 wks in July.*

$$ ✕**Suban.** An easy trip just outside town, this landmark trattoria has
NORTHERN been in business since 1865. Sit by the dining room fire or relax on a
ITALIAN huge terrace and watch the sunset. This is Triestino food with Slovene,
Hungarian, and Austrian accents. Start with *jota carsolina* (a rich soup
of cabbage, potatoes, and beans), and then you might order a roast
joint of veal fragrant with rosemary and thyme, or a tender pork filet
with red and yellow peppers, sausage, and sweet paprika. ■TIP➔ **Portions tend to be small, so if you're hungry, order both a first and second
course, as well as an antipasto.** To get here by public transit take Bus
No. 35 from Piazza Oberdan. $ *Average main: €22* ⊠ *Via Comici 2*
☎ *040/54368* ⚓ *Reservations essential* ⊗ *Closed Tues., 2 wks in early
Jan., and 1st 3 wks of Aug.*

WHERE TO STAY

$$ ⌂ **Duchi d'Aosta.** Each of these rooms on the spacious Piazza Unità
HOTEL d'Italia is beautifully furnished in Venetian Renaissance style, with
Fodor's Choice dark-wood antiques, rich carpets, and plush fabrics. **Pros:** lots of
★ charm paired with modern convenience; great location; attentive staff;
sumptuous breakfast. **Cons:** rooms overlooking the piazza can be very

expensive; restaurant overpriced; late check-in (3 pm, though rooms are often ready sooner); expensive parking. $ *Rooms from: €189* ✉ *Piazza Unità d'Italia 2/1* ☎ *040/7600011* ⊕ *www.grandhotelduchidaosta.com* ⇥ *55 rooms* ⦿ *Breakfast.*

$ ⌂ **Hotel Victoria Trieste.** A modern full-service hotel with updated tradi-
HOTEL   tional décor, the Victoria is centrally located, which is helpful for those on business in Trieste, but it's also within easy reach of city's historic sites. **Pros:** large, pleasant rooms; in-room Wi-Fi; in-room hydromas-sage tubs; sauna; pleasant, helpful staff; reasonable prices. **Cons:** €13 parking fee. $ *Rooms from: €120* ✉ *Alfredo Oriani 2* ☎ *040/362415* ⊕ *www.hotelvictoriatrieste.com* ⇥ *44 rooms* ⦿ *No meals.*

$$ ⌂ **L'Albero Nascosto Hotel Residence.** Rooms on a busy, narrow street in
B&B/INN   the centro storico contain paintings by local artists and antique fur-niture, and most have kitchenettes; they don't have phones, but the owners offer loaner cell phones. **Pros:** very central; spacious and simple yet tasteful rooms. **Cons:** no elevator; no staff on site after 8 pm; street noise can be a problem (if noise-sensitive, ask for a room in the back). $ *Rooms from: €165* ✉ *Via Felice Venezian 18* ☎ *040/300188* ⊕ *www.alberonascosto.it* ⇥ *10 rooms* ⦿ *Breakfast.*

NIGHTLIFE AND PERFORMING ARTS

CAFÉS

Trieste is justly famous for its coffeehouses. The elegant civility of Tri-este plays out in a caffè culture combining the refinement of Vienna with the passion of Italy. In Trieste, as elsewhere in Italy, ask for a café and you'll get a thimbleful of high-octane espresso. Your cappuccino here will come in the Viennese fashion, with a dollop of whipped cream. Many cafés are part of a *torrefazione* (roasting shop), so you can sample a cup and then buy beans to take with you.

Antico Caffè San Marco. Few cafés in Italy can rival Antico Caffè San Marco for its historic and cultured atmosphere. Founded in 1914, it was largely destroyed in World War I and rebuilt in the 1920s, then restored several more times, but some of the original Art Nouveau interior remains. It became a meeting place for local intellectuals and was the haunt of the Triestino writers Italo Svevo and Umberto Saba. It remains open until midnight, and light meals are available. ✉ *Via Battisti 18* ☎ *040/363538* ⊘ *Closed Mon.*

Caffè Degli Specchi. For a great view of the great piazza, you can't do better than this café, whose many mirrors make for engaging people-watching. Originally opened in 1839, it was taken over by the British Navy after World War II, and Triestini were not allowed in unless accompanied by an Englishman. Because of its location, the café, open until 11 pm Thursday though Saturday (until 9 pm on other nights), is heavily frequented by tourists. It's now owned by the Segafredo Zanetti coffee company, and some feel it has lost its local character. ✉ *Piazza dell'Unità d'Italia 7* ☎ *040/365777* ⊕ *www.caffespecchi.it.*

Caffè Tommaseo. Founded in 1830, this classic café is a comfortable place to linger, especially on weekend evenings and at lunchtime (from 11 to 1:30) on Sunday, when there's live music. Although you can still have just a caffè, Tommaseo has evolved into a pastry shop and restaurant, with an extensive menu. It's open nightly until midnight. ✉ *Piazza Tommaseo 4/C* ☎ *040/362666* ⊕ *www.caffetommaseo.it.*

MUSIC

Teatro Verdi. Trieste's main opera house, built under Austrian rule in 1801, is of interest to aficionados of architecture as well as to music lovers. Gian Antonio Selva, the architect of Venice's Teatro La Fenice, designed the interior, and Matteo Pertsch designed the facade. You'll have to attend a performance to view Teatro Verdi's interior; guided tours aren't conducted for individuals. ■ TIP→ **Opera season runs from October through May, with a brief operetta festival in July and August.** ✉ *Piazza Verdi 1* ☎ *040/9869883* ⊕ *www.teatroverdi-trieste.com.*

CASTELLO DI MIRAMARE

7 km (4½ miles) northwest of Trieste.

The 19th-century castle on the Gulf of Trieste is nothing less than a major expression of the culture of the decaying Austrian Habsburg monarchy. Nowhere else—not even in Vienna—can you savor the decadent opulence of the last years of the Empire.

GETTING HERE AND AROUND

Bus No. 36 from Piazza Oberdan in Trieste runs here every half hour.

EXPLORING

FAMILY

Fodor's Choice

★

Miramar. Maximilian of Habsburg, brother of Emperor Franz Josef and the retired commander of the Austrian Navy, built this seafront extravaganza between 1856 and 1860, complete with a throne room under wooden ceiling in the shape of a ship's keel. In keeping with late 19th-century taste, the rooms are generally furnished with elaborate, somewhat ponderous copies of medieval, Renaissance, and French period furniture, and the walls are covered in red damask. Maximilian's retirement was interrupted in 1864, when he became emperor of Mexico at the initiative of Napoléon III. He was executed three years later by a Mexican firing squad. His wife, Charlotte of Belgium, went mad and returned first to Miramar and later to her native country. During the last years of the Habsburg reign, Miramar became one of the favorite residences of Franz Josef's wife, the Empress Elizabeth (Sissi). The castle was later owned by Duke Amadeo of Aosta, who renovated some rooms in the rationalist style and installed modern plumbing in his Art Deco bathroom. Tours in English are available by reservation. Surrounding the castle is a 54-acre park, partly wooded and partly sculpted into attractive gardens. ✉ *Viale Miramare, off SS14* ☎ *040/224143* ⊕ *www. castello-miramare.it* ⌂ *Castle €6, park free* ☉ *Castle: daily 9–7; last entry ½ hr before closing. Park: Apr.–Sept., daily 8–7; Nov.–Feb., daily 8–5; Mar. and Oct., daily 8–6.*

THE DOLOMITES

Trentino–Alto Adige

WELCOME TO THE DOLOMITES

TOP REASONS TO GO

★ **Driving in the Dolomites:** Your rental Fiat will think it's a Ferrari on a gorgeous drive through the heart of the Dolomites.

★ **Hiking:** No matter your fitness level, there's an unforgettable walk in store for you here.

★ **Museo Archeologico dell'Alto Adige, Bolzano:** The impossibly well-preserved body of the iceman Ötzi, the star attraction at this museum, provokes countless questions about what life was like 5,000 years ago.

★ **Trento:** A graceful fusion of Austrian and Italian styles, this breezy, frescoed town is famed for its imposing castle.

1 Trentino. This butterfly-shape province is Italy with a German accent. Its principal city, history-rich Trento, is at the center. To the northwest is Madonna di Campiglio, one of Italy's most fashionable ski resorts. To the north, the cities of Bolzano and Brunico make practical bases for exploring the mountains.

2 Bolzano (Bozen). Alto Adige's capital is the Dolomites' liveliest city. Look for high-gabled houses, wrought-iron signs, and centuries-old wine cellars.

3 Alto Adige. This region was a part of Austria until the end of World War I, and Austrian sensibilities still predominate over Italian. At the spa town of Merano you can soak in hot springs, take the "grape cure," and stroll along lovely walkways. To the southwest, Caldaro has an appealing wine region.

4 The Heart of the Dolomites. The spectacular Sella mountain range and the surrounding Val di Fassa and Val Gardena make up this region. It's distinguished by great views and great mountain sports, in both summer and winter. At the town of Canazei, the cable car 3,000 feet up to the Col Rodella lookout packages the vast panorama perfectly.

AUSTRIA

ALP

Glorenza
Spondigna

SWITZERLAND

38

ORTLES ORTLERGRUPPE

PIEMONTE

VAL DI SOLE

Madonna di Campiglio

Pinzolo

TRENTINO

Tione

Arco

40
41
38
38
42
239
237
240

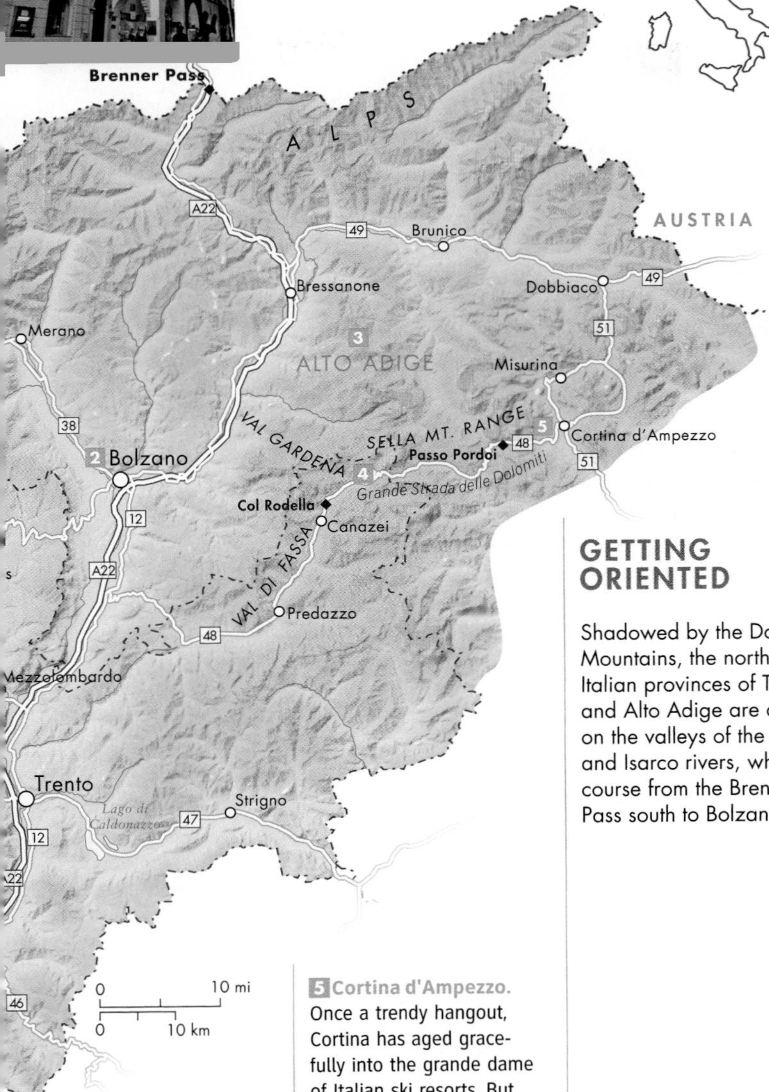

Brenner Pass

A L P S

AUSTRIA

A22

49 Brunico

Bressanone

Dobbiaco 49

51

Merano

ALTO ADIGE

Misurina

38

VAL GARDENA

SELLA MT. RANGE

Cortina d'Ampezzo

2 Bolzano

Passo Pordoi 48

5

Grande Strada delle Dolomiti

51

12

Col Rodella

Canazei

VAL DI FASSA

A22

Predazzo

48

Mezzotombardo

Trento

Strigno

Lago di
Caldonazzo

47

12

22

46

0   10 mi

0   10 km

GETTING ORIENTED

Shadowed by the Dolomite Mountains, the northeast Italian provinces of Trentino and Alto Adige are centered on the valleys of the Adige and Isarco rivers, which course from the Brenner Pass south to Bolzano.

5 Cortina d'Ampezzo.
Once a trendy hangout, Cortina has aged grace-fully into the grande dame of Italian ski resorts. But it's arguably at its best in summer, when there are countless options for hiking and mountain activities.

EATING AND DRINKING WELL IN THE DOLOMITES

Everything in Alto Adige (and, to a lesser extent, Trentino) has more than a tinge of the Teutonic—and the food is no exception. The rich and creamy cuisine here, including fondues, polentas, and barley soups, reflects the Alpine climate and Austrian and Swiss influences.

The quintessential restaurant here is the wood-panel Tirolean *Stube* (pub) serving hearty meat-and-dumpling fare, and there's also a profusion of pastry shops and lively beer halls.

Although the early dining schedule you'll find in Germany or Austria is somewhat tempered here, your options for late-night meals are more limited than they are in places farther south, where *la dolce vita* has a firmer grip.

Thankfully, the coffee is every bit as good as in parts south—just expect to hear "*danke, grazie*" when paying for your cappuccino.

BEST OF THE WURST

Not to be missed are the outdoor wurst carts, even (or perhaps especially) in colder weather. After placing your order you'll get a sheet of wax paper, followed by a dollop of mustard, a Kaiser roll, and your chosen sausage.

You can sometimes make your selection by pointing to whatever picture is most appealing; if not, pass on the familiar-sounding *Frankfurter* and try the local *Meraner*. Carts can reliably be found in Bolzano (try Piazza delle Erbe, or in front of the archaeological museum) and Merano (Piazza del Grano, or along the river).

POLENTA AND DUMPLINGS

Polenta is a staple in the region, in both its creamy and firm varieties, often topped with cheese or mushrooms (or both). Dumplings also appear on many menus; the most distinctive to the region are *canederli* (also known as *Knödel*), *pictured at right,* made from seasoned bread in many variations, and served either in broth or with a sauce.

Other dumplings to look for are the dense *strangolapreti* (literally, "priest-chokers") and *gnocchi di ricotta alla zucca* (ricotta and pumpkin dumplings).

CHEESE

Every isolated mountain valley in the Trentino–Alto Adige seems to make its own variety of cheese, and the local specialty is often simply called *nostrano* (ours).

The best known of the cheeses are the mild Asiago and *fontal* and the more pungent *puzzone di Moena* (literally, "stinkpot"). Try the *schiz*: fresh cheese that's sliced and fried in butter, sometimes with cream added.

PASTRIES AND BAKED GOODS

Bakeries turn out a wide selection of crusty dark rolls and caraway-studded rye breads—maybe not typical Italian bread, but full of flavor. Pastries are reminiscent of what you'd expect to find in Vienna. Apple strudel, *pictured below,* is everywhere, and for good reason: the best apples in Italy are grown

here. There are other exceptional fruits as well, including pears, plums, and grapes that make their way into baked goods.

ALIMENTARI

If you're planning a picnic or getting provisions for a hike, you'll be well served by the fine *alimentari* (food shops) of Trentino and Alto Adige. They stock a bounty of regional specialties, including cheeses, pickles, salami, and smoked meats. These are good places to pick up a sample of *speck tirolese,* the salt-cured, cold-smoked, deboned ham hock usually cut in paper-thin slices, like prosciutto (though proud speck producers often bristle at the comparison). Don't discard the fat—it's considered the best part.

WINE

Though Trentino and Alto Adige aren't as esteemed for their wines as many other Italian regions, they produce a wide variety of crisp, dry, and aromatic whites—Kerner, Müller-Thurgau, and Traminer, to name a few—not surprisingly, more like what you'd expect from German vineyards than Italian. Among the reds, look for *lagrein* and the native *teroldego,* a fruity, spicy variety produced only in the tiny valley north of Trento. The Trento D.O.C. appellation yields a marvelous sparkling wine in a class with Champagne.

Updated by
Lorna Holland
and Dante
Zambrano
Cassella

The Dolomites, the inimitable craggy peaks Le Corbusier called "the most beautiful work of architecture ever seen," are never so arresting as at dusk, when the last rays of sun create a pink hue that languishes into purple—locals call this magnificent transformation the *enrosadira*. You can certainly enjoy this glow from a distance, but the Dolomites are such an appealing year-round destination precisely because of the many ways to get into the mountains themselves. In short order, your perspective—like the peaks around you—will become a rosier hue.

The Dolomites are strange, rocky pinnacles that jut straight up like chimneys: the otherworldly pinnacles that Leonardo depicted in the background of his *Mona Lisa*. In spite of this incredible beauty, the vast, mountainous domain of northeastern Italy has remained relatively undeveloped. Below the peaks, rivers meander through valleys dotted with peaceful villages, while pristine lakes are protected by picture-book castles. In the most secluded Dolomite vales, unique cultures have flourished: the Ladin language, an offshoot of Latin still spoken in the Val Gardena and Val di Fassa, owes its unlikely survival to centuries of topographic isolation.

The more accessible parts of Trentino–Alto Adige, on the other hand, have a history of near-constant intermingling of cultures. The region's Adige and Isarco valleys make up the main access route between Italy and Central Europe, and as a result, the language, cuisine, and architecture are a blend of north and south. The province of Trentino is largely Italian-speaking, but Alto Adige is predominantly Germanic: until World War I the area was Austria's Südtirol. As you move north toward the famed Brenner Pass—through the prosperous valley towns of Rovereto, Trento, and Bolzano—the Teutonic influence is increasingly dominant; by the time you reach Bressanone, it's hard to believe you're in Italy at all.

THE DOLOMITES PLANNER

MAKING THE MOST OF YOUR TIME

For a brief stay, your best choice for a base is vibrant Bolzano, where you can get a sense of the region's contrasts—Italian and German, medieval and modern. After a day or two in town, venture an hour south to history-laden Trento, north to the lovely spa town of Merano, or southwest to Caldaro and its Strada di Vino; all are viable day trips from Bolzano, and Trento and Merano make good places to spend the night as well.

If you have more time, you'll want to get up into the mountains, which are the region's main attraction. The trip on the Grande Strada delle Dolomiti (Great Dolomites Road) through the Heart of the Dolomites from Bolzano to Cortina d'Ampezzo is one of Italy's most spectacular drives. Summer or winter, this is a great destination for mountain sports, with scores of trails for world-class hiking and skiing.

Be sure to look into the Südtirol Museumobil Card when planning your visit. Besides entry to 80 museums, the card allows you free use of the regional train system from Brennero to Trento, and the use of all public buses in Südtirol. The card is available for three days (€23) or seven days (€28). The Museumobil Card can be purchased at train stations, tourist offices, some museums, and hotels. The Brixen Card, free with paid lodging in Bressanone, is also a great value for travelers. It offers free transportation throughout Südtirol (South Tyrol) and Trento, and entrance to more than 78 museums, plus free guided tours and discounts at partner venues. See ⊕ *www.brixencard.info* for a list of participating hotels and bed-and-breakfasts. Detailed information about Vie Ferrate in the eastern Dolomites can be found at ⊕ *www.dolomiti. org*. Capable tour organizers include the **Scuola di Alpinismo** (Mountaineering School) in Madonna di Campiglio (☎ *0465/442634* ⊕ *www. guidealpinecampiglio.it*) and Cortina d'Ampezzo (☎ *0436/868505* ⊕ *www.guidecortina.com*).

GETTING HERE AND AROUND

BUS TRAVEL

Regular bus service connects larger cities to the south (Verona, Venice, and Milan) with valley towns in Trentino–Alto Adige (Rovereto, Trento, Bolzano, and Merano). You'll need to change to less-frequent local buses to reach resorts and smaller villages in the mountains beyond.

If you're equipped with current schedules and don't mind adapting your schedules to theirs, it's possible to visit even the remotest villages by bus. ATVO provides year-round service to Cortina from Venice's Piazzale Roma bus park, while CortinaExpress has a fast winter bus connection to Venice airport and the nearby Mestre train station. DolomitiBus covers the eastern Dolomites, including a number of small towns. SAD/Val Gardena service is available from Bolzano and Bressanone, as well as seasonal SkiBus service. SIT provides further information.

Bus Contacts ATVO ☎ *0421/5944* ⊕ *www.atvo.it.* **CortinaExpress** ☎ *0436/867350* ⊕ *www.cortinaexpress.it.* **DolomitiBus** ☎ *0437/217111* ⊕ *www.dolomitibus.it.* **SAD/Val Gardena** ✉ *Viale della Stazione 1, Ortisei*

☎ *0471/777777* ⊕ *www.valgardena.it/en.* **SIT** (*Servizio Integrato di Trasporto*). ✉ *Alto Adige* ☎ *0471/551155, 0039/056676224* ⊕ *www.sii.bz.it.* **Trentino Trasporti** ☎ *0461/821000* ⊕ *www.ttesercizio.it.*

CAR TRAVEL

Driving is easily the most convenient way to travel in the Dolomites; it can be difficult to reach the ski areas (or any town outside of Rovereto, Trento, Bolzano, and Merano) without a car. Driving is also the most exhilarating way to get around, as you rise from broad valleys into mountains with narrow, winding roads straight out of a sports-car ad. The most important route in the region is the A22, the main north–south highway linking Italy with Central Europe by way of the Brenner Pass. It connects Innsbruck with Bressanone, Bolzano, Trento, and Rovereto, and near Verona joins the A4 autostrada (which runs east–west across northern Italy, from Trieste to Turin). By car, Trento is three hours from Milan and 2½ hours from Venice. Bolzano is another hour's drive to the north, with Munich four hours farther on.

If you're planning a driving tour of the Dolomites, consider flying into Munich. Car rentals are less expensive in Germany, and it's easier to get automatic transmission if that's what you need to drive. (Standard transmission is better, however, for challenging mountain roads.)

Caution is essential (tap your horn in advance of hairpin turns), as are chains in winter, when roads are often covered in snow. Sudden closures are common, especially on high mountain passes, and can occur as early as September and as late as May. Even under the best conditions, expect to negotiate mountain roads at speeds no greater than 50 kph (30 mph).

TRAIN TRAVEL

The rail line following the course of the Isarco and Adige valleys—from Munich and Innsbruck, through the Brenner Pass, and southward past Bressanone, Bolzano, Trento, and Rovereto en route to Verona—is well trafficked, making trains a viable option for travel between these towns. Eurocity trains on the Dortmund–Venice and Munich–Innsbruck–Rome routes stop at these stations, and you can connect with other Italian lines at Verona. Although branch lines from Trento and Bolzano do extend into some of the smaller valleys (including hourly service between Bolzano and Merano), most of the mountain attractions are beyond the reach of trains.

Train Contact Trenitalia ☎ *892021 within Italy* ⊕ *www.trenitalia.com.*

RESTAURANTS

When dining out in the Dolomites, it's evident you are in a part of Italy that was once part of the Austrian Empire. While you can still find traditional Italian pasta and pizza, in this region the tastes blend with Austro-Germanic flare. Sausages, *spätzle* (like pasta but with a different consistency), meats, cheeses, and polenta can be found on nearly every menu—foods that will sustain the body through a long day of skiing or hiking. Most restaurants either raise their own crops and livestock, or have a direct relationship with their farmers and providers.

HOTELS

Classic Dolomite lodging options include restored castles, chalets, and stately 19th-century hotels. The small villages that pepper the Dolomites often have scores of flower-bedecked inns, many of them inexpensive. Hotel information offices at train stations and tourist offices can help if you've arrived without reservations. The Bolzano train station has a 24-hour hotel service, and tourist offices will give you a list of all the hotels in the area, arranged by location, stars, and price. Hotels at ski resorts cater to longer stays at full or half board. Many Italians come to the Dolomites every winter for their Settimana Bianca (White Week), and if you care to join them you should book ski vacations as packages well in advance. Most rural accommodations close from early November to mid- or late December, as well as for a month or two after Easter. The majority of *rifugi* (mountain huts) on hiking trails are operated by the **Club Alpino Italiano** (⊕ *www.cai.it*). Contact information for both CAI-run and private rifugi is available from local tourist offices; most useful are those in Madonna di Campiglio (⊕ *www.campiglio.com*), Cortina d'Ampezzo (⊕ *www.dolomiti.org*), Val di Fassa (⊕ *www.fassa.com*), and Val Gardena (⊕ *www.val-gardena.net*).

Hotel reviews have been shortened. For full information, visit Fodors.com.

WHAT IT COSTS				
	$	**$$**	**$$$**	**$$$$**
RESTAURANTS	under €15	€15–€24	€25–€35	over €35
HOTELS	under €125	€125–€200	€201–€300	over €300

Prices in the dining reviews are the average cost of a main course at dinner, or, if dinner is not served, at lunch. Prices in the reviews are the lowest cost of a standard double room in high season.

TRENTINO

Until the end of World War I, Trentino was Italy's frontier with the Austro-Hungarian Empire, and although this province remains unmistakably Italian, Germanic influences are tangible in all aspects of life here, including architecture, cuisine, culture, and language. Visitors are drawn by historical sites reflecting a strategic position at the intersection of southern and Central Europe: Trento was the headquarters of the Catholic Counter-Reformation. Numerous year-round mountain resorts, including fashionable Madonna di Campiglio, are in the wings of the butterfly-shape region.

TRENTO

51 km (32 miles) south of Bolzano.

Trento is a prosperous, cosmopolitan university town that retains an architectural charm befitting its historical importance. It was here, from 1545 to 1563, that the structure of the Catholic Church was redefined at the Council of Trent. This was the starting point of the Counter-Reformation, which brought half of Europe back to Catholicism. The word *consiglio* (council) appears everywhere in Trento—in hotel, restaurant, and street names, and even on wine labels.

Today the Piazza del Duomo remains splendid, and its enormous medieval palazzo dominates the city landscape in virtually its original form. The 24-hour Trento Card (€20), grants free or reduced admission to all major town sights in Trento and Rovereto, and can be bought at the tourist offices or participating museums. The card can be converted into a three-month card for free, and can also be reloaded as a prepaid transit card with reduced rates. There are a number of other perks, including tours, free public transportation, wine tastings, and the cable car ride to Belvedere di Sardagna.

GETTING HERE AND AROUND

The A22 is the main highway to Trento. From the north, take the Trento Nord exit; from the south, take the Trento Sud exit. There are signs directing you to the city center. Trento is easily accessible from Venice (2½ hours) and Verona (just over an hour), and is only 4½ hours from Munich. The city center is pedestrian-friendly, or you can use the transit options in conjunction with the Trento Card for discounts on the city buses.

VISITOR INFORMATION

Trento Tourism Office. If there is not an English speaker on site, another useful resource is ⊕ *dentrotrento.trentinocultura.net,* which includes virtual maps and a dictionary of phrases. ⊠ *Via Manci 2* ☎ *0461/216000* ⊕ *www.apt.trento.it.*

EXPLORING

TOP ATTRACTIONS

Fodor'sChoice
★
Castello del Buonconsiglio (*Castle of Good Counsel*). The position and size of this stronghold of the prince-bishops made it easier to defend than the Palazzo Pretorio. Look for the evolution of architectural styles: the medieval fortifications of the Castelvecchio section (on the far left) were built in the 13th century; the fancier Renaissance Magno Palazzo section (on the far right) wasn't completed until 300 years later. Part of the Castello now houses the **Museo Provinciale d'Arte,** where permanent and visiting exhibits of art and archaeology hang in frescoed medieval halls or under Renaissance coffered ceilings. The 13th-century **Torre dell'Aquila** (Eagle's Tower) is home to the castle's artistic highlight, a 15th-century *ciclo dei mesi* (cycle of the months). The four-wall fresco is full of charming and detailed scenes of medieval life in both court and countryside. Reservations are required to visit the tower; check the schedule at the ticket office. ⊠ *Via Bernardo Clesio 5* ☎ *0461/233770* ⊕ *www.buonconsiglio.it* ⊑ *€8, Torre dell'Aquila €1 extra* ⊗ *May 5–Oct., Tues.–Sun 10–6; Nov.–late Apr., Tues.–Sun. 9:30–5.*

Palazzo Pretorio. The fortified residence of the prince-bishops, who enjoyed considerable power and autonomy within the medieval hierarchy, was built in the 13th century and situated so as to seem like a wing of the Duomo. The remarkable palazzo has lost none of its original splendor. The crenellations are not merely decorative: the square pattern

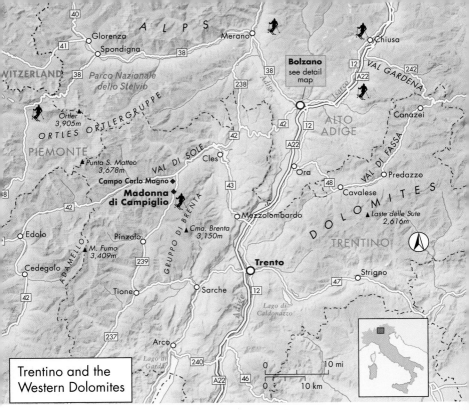

Trentino and the
Western Dolomites

represents ancient allegiance to the Guelphs (the triangular crenellations seen elsewhere in town represent Ghibelline loyalty). The palazzo now houses the **Museo Diocesano Tridentino,** where you can see paintings showing the seating plan of the prelates during the Council of Trent; early-16th-century tapestries by Pieter van Aelst (1502–56), the Belgian artist who carried out Raphael's 15th-century designs for the Vatican tapestries; carved wood altars and statues; and an 11th-century sacramentary, or book of services. These and other precious objects all come from the cathedral's treasury. Accessible through the museum, a subterranean archaeological area reveals the 1st-century Roman Porta Veronensis, which marked the road to Verona. ⊠ *Piazza del Duomo 18* ☏ *0461/234419* ⊕ *www.museodiocesanotridentino.it* 🎟 *€5 (free 1st Sun. of month)* ⊙ *June–Sept., Mon. and Wed.–Fri. 9:30–12:30 and 2:30–6, weekends 10–1 and 2–6; Oct.–May, Mon. and Wed.–Sat. 9:30–12:30 and 2–5:30, Sun. 10–1 and 2–6.*

Tridentum. The ancient Roman city of Tridentum lies beneath much of Trento's city center. Centuries of Adige River flooding buried ruins that only recently have been unearthed on public and private land. Beneath this piazza lies the largest of the archaeological sites, revealing some marvels of Roman technology, such as under-floor home heating and under-street sewers complete with manhole covers. The Romans also used lead pipes for four centuries before recognizing it was hazardous to health. Other excavations you can visit lie beneath the Palazzo Pretoria and the Scrigno del Duomo restaurant. ⊠ *Piazza Cesare Battisti* ☎ *0461/230171* 🎫 *€2.50* ⊙ *June–Sept., Tues.–Sun. 9:30–1 and 2–6; Oct.–May, Tues.–Sun. 9–1 and 2–5:30.*

WORTH NOTING

Belvedere di Sardagna. Take the Funivia Trento–Sardagna cable car up to the Belvedere di Sardagna, a lookout point 1,200 feet above medieval Trento. ■TIP→ **This is open year-round, but can close due to inclement weather.** ⊠ *Ponte San Lorenzo* ☎ *0461/232154* 🎫 *€5 round-trip* ⊙ *Daily 7 am–10:30 pm.*

Duomo. This massive Romanesque church, also known as the Cathedral of San Vigilio, forms the southern edge of the Piazza del Duomo. Locals refer to this square as the city's *salotto* (sitting room), as in fine weather it's always filled with students and residents drinking coffee, sipping an aperitivo, or reading the newspaper. The Baroque **Fontana del Nettuno** presides over it all. When skies are clear, pause here to savor the view of the mountaintops enveloping the city.

Within the Duomo, unusual arcaded stone stairways border the austere nave. Ahead is the *baldacchino* (altar canopy), a copy of Bernini's masterpiece in St. Peter's in Rome. To the left of the altar is a mournful 16th-century crucifix, flanked by the Virgin Mary and John the Apostle. This crucifix, by German artist Sisto Frey, was a focal point of the Council of Trent: each decree agreed on during the two decades of deliberations was solemnly read out in front of it. Stairs on the left side of the altar lead down to the 4th-century Paleo-Christian burial vault. Outside, walk around to the back of the cathedral to see an exquisite display of 14th-century stonemason's art, from the small porch to the intriguing knotted columns on the graceful apse. ⊠ *Piazza del Duomo* ☎ *39/0461231239* ⊙ *Daily 9:45 am–6 pm.*

Guided Tours of Trento. Guided tours of Trento begin from the tourism office. Private tours for groups of 1–25 people for three hours are €132; for 25–50 people tours are €144. ■TIP→ **Tours are not always offered in English; to guarantee an English-speaking guide, call for reservations.** ⊠ *Via Manci 2* ☎ *0461/216000* ⊕ *www.apt.trento.it.*

Santa Maria Maggiore. Many sessions of the Council of Trent met in this Renaissance church. Limited light enters through the simple rose window over the main door, so you have to strain to see the magnificent ceiling, an intricate combination of stucco and frescoes. The church is off the northwest side of the Piazza del Duomo, about 200 yards down Via Cavour. ⊠ *Vicolo Orsoline 1* ☎ *0461/980132* ⊙ *Daily 8–noon and 2–6.*

QUICK BITES

Scrigno del Duomo. More than 30 wines by the glass, accompanied by an excellent selection of local cheeses, are served in an upstairs room with some of the oldest frescoes in town. Salads and regional specialties are also available; the canederli are especially flavorful here. ⊠ *Piazza del Duomo 29* ☎ *0461/220030* ⊕ *www.scrignodelduomo.com.*

Via Belenzani. Locals refer to this street as Trento's outdoor gallery because of the frescoed facades of the hallmark Renaissance palazzi. It's an easy 50-yard walk up the lane behind the church of Santa Maria Maggiore.

WHERE TO EAT

$$$ NORTHERN ITALIAN 🍴 **Al Vò.** Trento's oldest trattoria (it's the descendant of a 14th-century tavern) remains one of its most popular lunch spots. Locals crowd into a simple, modern dining room to enjoy regional specialties such as gnocchi with vegetables, and *baccalà* (salted cod). An impressive (and inexpensive) selection of local wines is available; try the food-friendly red teroldego, made in the valley north of Trento. [$] *Average main: €25* ✉ *Vicolo del Vò 11* ☎ *0461/985374* 🌐 *www.ristorantealvo.it* 🕘 *Closed Sun. No dinner Mon.–Wed. and Sat.*

$$ NORTHERN ITALIAN 🍴 **Antica Birreria Pedavena.** Come here for the beer—a half-dozen varieties are brewed in-house (as evinced by the big vats looming in front of you) and served in a cavernous beer hall. Meals include wursts, meat and cheese platters, pizzas, and huge salads. It's open continuously from 9 am to 12:30 am (until 1 am on Friday and Saturday). Smaller wood-paneled dining rooms and a summer terrace allow for more peaceful dining. [$] *Average main: €19* ✉ *Via Santa Croce 15* ☎ *0461/986255* 🌐 *www.birreriapedavena.com.*

$$ NORTHERN ITALIAN 🍴 **Le Due Spade.** An intimate dining room that started out as a Tirolean tavern around the time of the Council of Trent, this is known for superb cuisine, both traditional and more innovative, adeptly served amid the coziness of wood paneling and an antique stove. The menu, which is updated throughout the year, is divided into mountain and seafood specialties. Not to be missed are *mezzelune di patate* (potato ravioli with cheese and black truffles) and *trancio di orato* (salted seabream baked in a pastry crust). Be sure to save room for the very creative desserts, including pastries created by the chef according to the season. **■ TIP→ Given the restaurant's deserved popularity with locals and the limited seating, reservations are a must.** [$] *Average main: €22* ✉ *Via Rizzi 11* ☎ *0461/234343* 🌐 *www.leduespade.com* ✍ *Reservations essential* 🕘 *Closed Sun. No lunch Mon.*

$$ PIZZA 🍴 **Pizzeria Laste.** Owner Guido Rizzi is a national pizza-making champion; he invented pizza Calabrese, a white pizza with garlic, mozzarella, and red-pepper flakes. Each of his 35 pies—especially the *sedano* (mozzarella, celery root, aged Parmesan cheese, oregano)—is delectable. Save room for desserts like the pizza *dolce,* which is made with bananas, strawberries, kiwi, and caramel. In a pleasant hilltop villa above the city center, the pizzeria is a bit hard to reach, but worth it. [$] *Average main: €18* ✉ *Via delle Laste 63* ☎ *0461/231570* 🌐 *www.pizzerialaste.com* 🕘 *Closed Tues.*

$$ NORTHERN ITALIAN 🍴 **Trattoria Orso Grigio.** The family-run "gray bear," just off the main piazza, serves tasty fare in a congenial atmosphere. Choose from typical regional dishes—look for *rufioi* (homemade ravioli stuffed with savoy cabbage)—served in a bright garden courtyard when the weather is fine. The wine list is mostly regional and pairs well with the menu. [$] *Average main: €22* ✉ *Via degli Orti 19* ☎ *0461/984400* 🌐 *www.orsogrigiotrento.com* 🕘 *Closed Sun.*

WHERE TO STAY

$$ HOTEL **Accademia.** Stylish, contemporary bedrooms with comfortable beds and handsome lithographs occupy an ancient, character-filled house close to Piazza del Duomo. **Pros:** central location; charming outdoor restaurant; range of gluten-free options. **Cons:** some rooms are small; stark décor. [$] *Rooms from: €125* ✉ *Vicolo Colico 4* ☎ *0461/233600* 🌐 *www.accademiahotel.it* 🛏 *35 rooms, 5 suites* ⏲ *Closed late Dec.–mid-Jan.* 🍴 *Breakfast.*

$ B&B/INN **Castel Pergine.** Tucked into a 13th-century castle's labyrinth of stone and brick chambers, prisons, and chapels are sparse, rustic rooms with carved-wood trim, lace curtains, and heavy wooden beds, some canopied. **Pros:** romantic setting; great restaurant. **Cons:** simple accommodations; need a car to get around. [$] *Rooms from: €120* ✉ *Via al Castello 10, Pergine Val Sugana, 12 km (7½ miles) east of Trento* ☎ *0461/531158* 🌐 *www.castelpergine.it* 🛏 *20 rooms (17 with bath)* ⏲ *Closed Nov.–Mar. No lunch Mon.* 🍴 *Multiple meal plans.*

$$ HOTEL **Hotel Garni Aquila d'Oro.** Each room has its own contemporary design, some have saunas and terraces with hot tubs and stunning views, and all enjoy a prime location near Piazza del Duomo. **Pros:** excellent location; friendly service. **Cons:** common areas rather cramped. [$] *Rooms from: €160* ✉ *Via Belenzani 76* ☎ *0461/986282* 🌐 *www.aquiladoro.it* 🛏 *16 rooms* 🍴 *Breakfast.*

$ B&B/INN **Hotel Garni Venezia.** For reasonably priced accommodations, it's hard to beat this *garni* (bed-and-breakfast) right on Piazza Duomo, where six of the simple rooms have wonderful views. **Pros:** great location; friendly environs. **Cons:** piazza can be noisy; not all rooms have private baths or TVs. [$] *Rooms from: €65* ✉ *Via Belenzani, 70, Piazza Duomo 45* ☎ *0461/234559* 🌐 *www.hotelveneziatn.it* 🛏 *43 rooms* 🍴 *Multiple meal plans.*

$$ RESORT **Imperial Grand Hotel Terme.** If you're in the mood for some pampering, choose a grand room with a frescoed ceiling in the graciously restored, golden-yellow palace in the nearby spa town of Levico Terme. **Pros:** beautiful park setting; pleasant indoor pool. **Cons:** standard rooms are small; use of thermal baths costs extra. [$] *Rooms from: €200* ✉ *Via Silva Domini 1, Levico Terme, 20 km (12 miles) east of Trento* ☎ *0461/706104* 🌐 *www.imperialhotel.it* 🛏 *79 rooms* ⏲ *Closed Nov.–Mar.* 🍴 *Some meals.*

NIGHTLIFE AND PERFORMING ARTS

I Suoni delle Dolomiti (*The Sounds of the Dolomites*). This annual series of free concerts is held high in the hills of Trentino in July and August, offering the wonderful experience of enjoying chamber music played in grassy meadows. ☎ *0461/219300* 🌐 *www.isuonidelledolomiti.it.*

SHOPPING

Enoteca di Corso. This atmospheric shop, a bit outside the town center, is laden with local products, including wine and sweets. ✉ *Corso 3 Novembre 64* ☎ *0461/916424.*

La Salumeria Lunelli. This specialty food shop boasts an impressive array of sauces (including one made with bear meat), as well as wines, grappas, and liqueurs. A picnic can be handily assembled from a huge assortment of local salami and cheeses. ⊠ *Via Mazzini 46* ☎ *39/0461238053* ⊕ *www.lunelli.it.*

Panificio Pulin. Whole grain breads and delicate pastries are on offer in this fragrant bakery. ⊠ *Via Cavour 23* ☎ *0461/234544.*

Piazza Alessandro Vittoria. You can pick up meats, cheeses, produce, local truffles, and porcini mushrooms at the small morning market in the square.

EN ROUTE
Traveling west and then north from Trento to Madonna di Campiglio, you zigzag through lovely mountain valleys, past small farming communities such as Tione.

San Vigilio. Outside the small mountain village of Pinzolo (on the SS239), stop at the church of San Vigilio to see the remarkable 16th-century fresco on the exterior south wall. Painted in 1539 by the artist Simone Baschenis, the painting describes the Dance of Death: a macabre parade of 40 sinners from all walks of life (in roughly descending order of worldly importance), each guided to his end by a ghoulish escort. ⊠ *Via San Vigilio, Pinzolo.*

MADONNA DI CAMPIGLIO

80 km (50 miles) northwest of Trento, 100 km (62 miles) southwest of Bolzano.

The winter resort of Madonna di Campiglio vies with Cortina d'Ampezzo as the most fashionable place for Italians to ski and be seen in the Dolomites. Madonna's popularity is well deserved, with 62 lifts connecting more than 150 km (93 miles) of well-groomed ski runs and equally good lodging and trekking facilities. The resort itself is a modest 5,000 feet above sea level, but the downhill runs, summer hiking paths, and mountain-biking trails venture high up into the surrounding peaks (including Pietra Grande at 9,700 feet).

GETTING HERE AND AROUND

By car from Trento, take the SS45 toward Vezzano. After Vezzano, continue to the SS237 until Ragoli, and turn onto the SP 34. Follow the SP 34 for 6 km (4 miles), and turn onto the SS239 for another 23 km (15 miles) until you arrive at Madonna di Campiglio. The more convenient railway station is at Trento; then you can ride the Trentino Trasporti bus for two hours from Trento for €4.50.

VISITOR INFORMATION

Madonna di Campiglio Tourism Office ⊠ *Via Pradalago 4* ☎ *0465/447501* ⊕ *www.campigliodolomiti.it.*

EXPLORING

Campo Carlo Magno. The stunning pass at Campo Carlo Magno (5,500 feet) is 3 km (2 miles) north of Madonna di Campiglio. This is where Charlemagne is said to have stopped in AD 800 on his way to Rome to be crowned emperor. Stop here to glance over the whole of northern Italy. If you continue north, take the descent with caution—in the space of a mile or so, hairpin turns and switchbacks deliver you down more than 2,000 feet.

WHERE TO EAT

$$ NORTHERN ITALIAN

🍴 **Cascina Zeledria.** Although the majority of meals in Madonna are taken in resort hotels, Italians consider an on-mountain dinner like one in this remote, rustic refuge to be an indispensable part of a proper ski week. In winter, you'll be collected on a Sno-Cat and ferried up the slopes (you'll hike up in warmer months). After the 10-minute ride, sit down to grill your own meats and vegetables over stone griddles; the kitchen-prepared mushrooms and polenta are house specialties. **TIP→ You must call in advance to reserve a table and arrange for transportation.** [$] *Average main: €22* ✉ *Località Zeledria* ☎ *0465/440303* 🌐 *www.zeledria.it* ✍ *Reservations essential* 🕓 *Closed May, June, Oct., and Nov.*

$$$ WINE BAR

🍴 **Ferrari Spazio Bollicine Nabucco.** This intimate venue has the feel of a rustic-yet-stylish chalet and is done in a black-and-white color scheme. Guests settle into these pleasant surroundings for an après-ski aperitivo or a light meal, based on local ingredients and paired with sparkling wines from Ferrari, a well-known Trentino vintner. [$] *Average main: €30* ✉ *Piazza Righi B3* ☎ *0465/440756* 🌐 *www.ferraritrento.it.*

WHERE TO STAY

$$ HOTEL

🏨 **Golf Hotel.** You need to make your way north to the Campo Carlo Magno Pass to reach this grand hotel, the former summer residence of Habsburg emperor Franz Josef, replete with verandas, Persian rugs, and bay windows. **Pros:** attractive indoor pool; elegant rooms. **Cons:** long walk into town; popular with business groups. [$] *Rooms from: €140* ✉ *Via Cima Tosa 3* ☎ *0465/441003* 🌐 *www.atahotels.it/golf-campiglio* 🛏 *109 rooms, 13 suites* 🕓 *Closed late Apr.–June and Sept.–early Dec.* 🍽 *Multiple meal plans.*

$$$ HOTEL Fodor's Choice ★

🏨 **Grifone.** At this comfortable lodge with a distinctive wood facade, flower-bedecked balconies catch the sun and contemporary guest rooms and suites have views of the forested slopes. **Pros:** convenient location; charming décor. **Cons:** half board is mandatory; lacks a/c; a bit out of town (but the Spinale cable car is nearby). [$] *Rooms from: €250* ✉ *Via Vallesinella 7* ☎ *0465/442002* 🌐 *www.hotelgrifone.it* 🛏 *38 rooms, 2 suites* 🕓 *Closed mid-Apr.–June and Sept.–Nov.* 🍽 *Some meals.*

$$ HOTEL

🏨 **Hotel Casa del Campo.** This charming Tirolean-style hotel is just yards from the ski slopes and paths for "ski-fondo" (cross-country skiing). **Pros:** fantastic service; great location for outdoor activities; hydromassage showers and tubs. **Cons:** seven-day minimum stay, or 20% service fee for shorter stays in high season. [$] *Rooms from: €190* ✉ *Passo Campo Carlo Magno* ☎ *0465/443130* 🌐 *www.casadelcampo.it* ✍ *Reservations essential* 🛏 *36 rooms* 🍽 *Some meals.*

SPORTS AND THE OUTDOORS

HIKING AND CLIMBING

The Madonna di Campiglio tourism office has maps of a dozen trails leading to waterfalls, lakes, and stupefying views.

Monte Spinale (*Spinale Peak*). The cable car to 6,900-foot-high Monte Spinale offers skiers magnificent views of the Brenta Dolomites in winter. It also runs during peak summer season. ✉ *Off Via Monte Spinale* ☎ *0465/447744* 🎫 *€9 round-trip.*

SKIING

Funivie Madonna di Campiglio. Miles of interconnecting ski runs—some of the best in the Dolomites—are linked by the cable cars and lifts of Funivie Madonna di Campiglio. Advanced skiers will like the extremely difficult terrain found on certain mountain faces, but there are also many intermediate and beginner runs, all accessible from town. There are also plenty of off-piste opportunities. Passes can be purchased at the main *funivia* (cable car) in town, and multiday passes are available. ✉ *Via Presanella 12* ☎ *0465/447744* ⊕ *www.funiviecampiglio.it* ✍ *Passes €41–€47 per day.*

EN ROUTE The route between Madonna di Campiglio and Bormio (2½ hours) takes you through a series of high mountain passes. After Campo Carlo Magno, turn left at Dimaro and continue 37 km (23 miles) west through Passo del Tonale (6,200 feet). At Ponte di Legno, turn north on SS300. You pass the Lago Nero (Black Lake) on your left just before the summit. Continue on to Bormio through the Passo di Gavia (8,600 feet).

THE WESTERN DOLOMITES

The Parco Nazionale dello Stelvio extends through western Trentino and the Altoatesino area of Alto Adige, and even into eastern Lombardia. It's named for the famed Stelvio, Europe's highest road pass and the site of the highest battle fought during World War I.

BOLZANO (BOZEN)

32 km (19 miles) south of Merano, 50 km (31 miles) north of Trento.

Bolzano (Bozen), capital of the autonomous province of Alto Adige, is tucked among craggy peaks in a Dolomite valley 77 km (48 miles) from the Brenner Pass and Austria. Tirolean culture dominates Bolzano's language, food, architecture, and people. It may be hard to remember that you're in Italy when walking the city's colorful cobblestone streets and visiting its lantern-lighted cafés, where you may enjoy sauerkraut and a beer among a lively crowd of blue-eyed German speakers. However, the fine Italian espresso and the boutiques will help remind you where you are. The long, narrow arcades of its Via dei Portici house shops that specialize in Tirolean crafts and clothing, as well as many Italian designers. With castles and steeples topping the landscape, this quiet city at the confluence of the Isarco (Eisack) and Talvera rivers has retained its provincial appeal. Proximity to fabulous skiing and mountain climbing—not to mention the world's oldest preserved human body—make it a worthwhile tourist destination. And its streets are immaculate: residents here have the highest per capita earnings of any city in Italy.

GETTING HERE AND AROUND

By car from Trento, take the A22 for 60 km (37 miles) to Bolzano Sud. The train station is just steps away from Piazza Walther, and has regular service from Italy and Munich (four hours). The SASA bus can help you connect between Bolzano and other parts of the region. There is an airport in Bolzano, but its connections are not as convenient as the larger airports at Venice, Verona, and Munich.

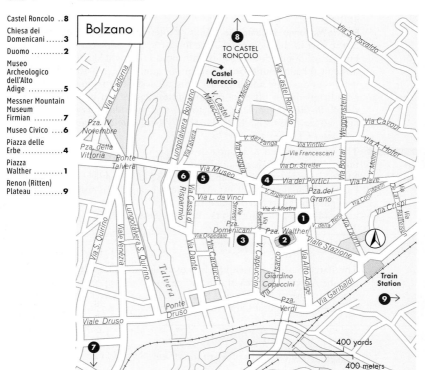

VISITOR INFORMATION

Bolzano Tourism Office ✉ *Piazza Walther 8* ☎ *0471/307000* ⊕ *www. bolzano-bozen.it* ⊙ *Weekdays 9–7, Sat. 9:30–6.*

EXPLORING

TOP ATTRACTIONS

Chiesa dei Domenicani. The 13th-century Dominican Church is renowned as Bolzano's main repository for paintings, especially frescoes. In the adjoining **Cappella di San Giovanni** you can see works from the Giotto school that show the birth of a pre-Renaissance sense of depth and individuality; come prepared with 50-cent coins for the lights. ✉ *Piazza Domenicani* ☎ *0471/973133* ⊙ *Mon.–Sat. 9:30–5, Sun. noon–6.*

Duomo. A lacy spire looks down on the mosaic-like roof tiles of the city's Gothic cathedral, built between the 12th and 14th century. Inside are 14th- and 15th-century frescoes and an intricately carved stone pulpit dating from 1514. Outside, don't miss the **Porta del Vino** (Wine Gate) on the northeast side; decorative carvings of grapes and harvest workers attest to the longstanding importance of wine to this region. ✉ *Piazza della Parrocchia 27* ☎ *0471/978676* ⊙ *Mon.–Sat. 10–noon and 2–5.*

Fodor'sChoice
★

Museo Archeologico dell'Alto Adige. This museum has gained international fame for Ötzi, its 5,300-year-old iceman (discovered in 1991), the world's oldest naturally preserved body. In 1998 Italy acquired it from Austria after it was determined that the body lay 100 yards inside Italian territory. The iceman's leathery remains are displayed in a freezer vault, preserved along with his longbow, ax, and clothing. The rest of the museum relies on models and artifacts from nearby archaeological sites; exhibits are changed out regularly. An English-language audio guide leads you not only through Ötzi's Copper Age, but also into the preceding Mesolithic and Neolithic eras, and the Bronze and Iron ages that followed. In July and August, the museum's supervised play area keeps young children entertained while adults experience the museum. ⊠ *Via Museo 43* ☎ *0471/320100, 0471/320123* ⊕ *www.iceman.it* ⌫ *€9* ⊙ *Jan.–June and Sept.–Nov., Tues.–Sun. 10–6; July, Aug., and Dec., daily 10–6; last entry at 5:30.*

Piazza delle Erbe. A bronze statue of Neptune, which dates to 1745, presides over a bountiful fruits-and-vegetables market in this square. The stalls spill over with colorful displays of local produce; bakeries and grocery stores showcase hot breads, pastries, cheeses, and delicatessen meats—a complete picnic. Try the *speck tirolese* (a thinly sliced smoked ham) and the apple strudel.

Piazza Walther. This pedestrians-only square is Bolzano's heart; in warmer weather it serves as an open-air living room where locals and tourists can be found at all hours sipping a drink (such as a glass of chilled riesling). In the center stands Heinrich Natter's white-marble, neo-Romanesque **Monument to Walther,** built in 1889. The piazza's namesake was the 12th-century German wandering minstrel Walther von der Vogelweide, whose songs lampooned the papacy and praised the Holy Roman Emperor.

WORTH NOTING

Castel Roncolo (*Schloss Runkelstein*). Green hills and farmhouses north of town surround this meticulously kept castle with a red roof. It was built in 1237, destroyed half a century later, and then rebuilt soon thereafter. There's a beautifully preserved cycle of medieval frescoes inside. A tavern in the courtyard serves excellent local food and wines. To get here from Piazza Walther, take the free shuttle (Tuesday through Sunday every half hour 10–5), or Bus No. 12 or 14. It's a 20-minute walk from Piazza delle Erbe: head north along Via Francescani, continue through Piazza Madonna, connecting to Via Castel Roncolo. ⊠ *Via San Antonio 15* ☎ *0471/329808 for castle, 0471/324073 for tavern* ⊕ *www.roncolo. info* ⌫ *€8* ⊙ *Tues.–Sun. 10–5; last entry at 4:30.*

Messner Mountain Museum Firmian. Perched on a peak overlooking Bolzano, 10th-century Castle Sigmundskron is home to one of five Dolomite museums established by Reinhold Messner—the first climber to conquer Everest solo and the first to reach its summit without oxygen. The Tibetan tradition of *kora,* a circular pilgrimage around a sacred site, is the inspiration for this museum, where visitors contemplate the relationship between man and mountain, guided by images and objects Messner collected during his adventures. Guided tours begin every half hour. The museum is 3 km (2 miles) southwest of Bolzano, just off the Appiano exit on the highway to Merano. ⊠ *Sigmundskron Castle 53,*

Sigmundskronerstrasse ☎ *0471/631264* 🌐 *www.messner-mountain-museum.it* 🎫 *€9* 🕒 *Late Mar.–mid-Nov., Fri.–Wed. 10–6; last entry at 5.*

Museo Civico. Bolzano's municipal museum has a rich collection of traditional costumes, wood carvings, and archaeological exhibits. Not all floors are open, but entrance is free while renovations are ongoing. ✉ *Via Cassa di Risparmio 14* ☎ *0471/974625* 🌐 *www.bolzano.net/museocivico.htm* 🎫 *Varies with exhibitions* 🕒 *Tues.–Sun. 10–5.*

Renon (Ritten) Plateau. The earth pyramids of Renon Plateau are a bizarre geological formation where erosion has left a forest of tall, thin, needle-like spires of rock, each topped with a boulder. To get here, take the Soprabolzano cable car (€10) from Via Renon, about 300 yards left of the Bolzano train station. At the top, switch to the electric train (€6) that takes you to the plateau, which is in Collalbo, just above Bolzano. The two rides take about 12 minutes. ✉ *Via Renon, Collalbo* ☎ *0471/356100* 🎫 *€10 round-trip* 🕒 *Daily 7–9.*

WHERE TO EAT

$$ NORTHERN ITALIAN

🍴 **Alexander.** Typical Tirolean dishes are served at this convivial spot. The venison ham and the lamb cutlets *al timo con salsa all'aglio* (with thyme and garlic sauce) are particularly good, but make sure to leave room for the rich chocolate cake. [$] *Average main: €23* ✉ *Via Aosta 37* ☎ *0471/918608* 🌐 *www.ristorantealexander.net* 🕒 *Closed Sat.*

$$ WINE BAR

🍴 **Batzenhausl.** Locals hold animated conversations over glasses of regional wine in a modern take a traditional Stube. Tasty south Tirolean specialties include speck tirolese and *mezzelune casarecce ripiene* (house-made stuffed half-moons of pasta). If you're seeking a quiet meal, ask for a table on the second floor, near the handsome stained-glass windows. **TIP→ This is a good place for a late bite, as food is served until midnight.** [$] *Average main: €23* ✉ *Via Andreas Hofer 30* ☎ *0471/050950* 🌐 *www.batzen.it.*

$$ NORTHERN ITALIAN

🍴 **Cavallino Bianco.** A spacious, comfortable dining room near Via dei Portici is a dependable favorite with residents as well as visitors. A wide selection of Italian and German dishes are served to large tables of families enjoying their meals together. [$] *Average main: €21* ✉ *Via Bottai 6* ☎ *0471/973267* 🌐 *www.weissesroessl.org* 🕒 *Closed Sun. No dinner Sat.*

$$ NORTHERN ITALIAN

🍴 **Hopfen & Co.** Fried white *Würstel* (sausages), sauerkraut, and grilled ribs complement the excellent home-brewed Austrian-style pilsner and wheat beer at this bustling pub-restaurant. There's live music on Thursday night, attracting Bolzano's students and young professionals. [$] *Average main: €18* ✉ *Piazza delle Erbe, Obstplatz 17* ☎ *0471/300788.*

$$ NORTHERN ITALIAN

🍴 **Wirthaus Vögele.** Ask residents of Bolzano where they like to dine out, and odds are good they'll tell you Vögele, one of the area's oldest inns. The classic wood-panel dining room on the ground level is often packed, but don't despair, as the restaurant has two additional floors. The menu features Südtirol standards, including canederli with speck and venison. [$] *Average main: €18* ✉ *Goethestrasse 3* ☎ *0471/973938* 🌐 *www.voegele.it* 🕒 *Closed Sun.*

$$$ NORTHERN ITALIAN

🍴 **Zür Kaiserkron.** Traditional Tirolean opulence and attentive service set the stage for some of the best food in town. Appetizers might include potato blini with salmon caviar, and marinated artichokes with butter

CLOSE UP

Enrosadira and the Dwarf King

The French nobleman and geologist Déodat Guy Silvain Tancrède Gratet de Dolomieu (1750–1801) got his name applied to the Dolomite range after demonstrating that the peaks have a particular composition of stratified calcium magnesium carbonate that generates a rosy evening glow, a spectacle known as *enrosadira*. For those unconvinced that such a phenomenon can be explained by geology alone, Ladin legend offers a compelling alternative.

Laurin, King of the Dwarfs, became infatuated with the daughter of a neighboring (human) king, and captured her with the aid of a magic hood that made him invisible. As he spirited her back to the mountains, the dwarf king was pursued by many knights, who were able to track the kidnapper after spotting his beloved rose garden. Laurin was captured and imprisoned, and when he finally managed to escape and return home, he cast a spell turning the betraying roses into rocks—so they could be seen neither by day nor by night. But Laurin forgot to include dusk in his spell, which is why the Dolomites take on a rosy glow just before nightfall. (This story is the subject of frescoes in the bar of Bolzano's Parkhotel Laurin.)

(not to be missed if available). Main dishes, such as veal with black truffle–and–spinach canederli make use of ingredients from the local valleys. This place is popular with local businesspeople. $ *Average main: €26* ⊠ *Piazza della Mostra 2* ☎ *0471/980214* ⊕ *www.kaiserkron.bz* ⊛ *Reservations essential* ☉ *Closed Sun. and holidays.*

WHERE TO STAY

$$
HOTEL
Fodor's Choice
★
🖳 **Hotel Greif.** Individually designed guest rooms in a centuries-old Bolzano landmark feature clean-line modern furnishings and contemporary art paired with 19th-century paintings and sketches. **Pros:** elegant décor; helpful staff; central location. **Cons:** rooms vary in size; sometimes filled with tour groups. $ *Rooms from: €188* ⊠ *Piazza Walther 1* ☎ *0471/318000* ⊕ *www.greif.it* ⤳ *27 rooms, 6 suites* ⦿⧵ *Breakfast.*

$$$$
HOTEL
🖳 **Luna-Mondschein.** Comfortable, wood-paneled rooms, some with balconies, overlook a garden or the mountains, and all are swathed in the charming ambience of this inn dating to 1798. **Pros:** central location; great buffet breakfast. **Cons:** rooms vary in size; rooms facing garage can be noisy. $ *Rooms from: €304* ⊠ *Via Piave 15* ☎ *0471/975642* ⊕ *www.hotel-luna.it* ⤳ *80 rooms* ⦿⧵ *Multiple meal plans.*

$$
HOTEL
Fodor's Choice
★
🖳 **Parkhotel Laurin.** An exercise in Art Nouveau opulence, presiding over a large park in the middle of town, is one of the best hotels in all of Alto Adige, with art-filled modern guest rooms and handsome public spaces. **Pros:** convenient location; excellent restaurant. **Cons:** rooms facing park can be noisy; can be packed with business groups. $ *Rooms from: €169* ⊠ *Via Laurin 4* ☎ *0471/311000* ⊕ *www.laurin.it* ⤳ *93 rooms, 7 suites* ⦿⧵ *Multiple meal plans.*

$$$
B&B/INN
🖳 **Schloss Korb.** This romantic 13th-century castle with crenellations and a massive tower is perched in a park amid vine-covered hills, viewed through some of the cozy rooms through Romanesque arched windows.

Pros: romantic setting; charming traditional furnishings. **Cons:** not all rooms are in the castle; need a car to get around. $ *Rooms from: €204* ✉ *Via Castel d'Appiano 5, Missiano/Appiano* ☎ *0471/636000* ⊕ *www. schlosskorb.com* 🍴 *35 rooms, 10 suites* ⊙ *Closed Nov.–Mar.* 🍽 *Multiple meal plans.*

ALTO ADIGE

Prosperous valley towns (such as the famed spa center of Merano) and mountain resorts entice those seeking both relaxation and adventure. Alto Adige (Südtirol) was for centuries part of the Austro-Hungarian Empire, only ceded to Italy at the end of World War I. Ethnic differences led to inevitable tensions in the 1960s and again in the '80s, though a large measure of provincial autonomy has, for the most part, kept the lid on nationalist ambitions. Today Germanic and Italian balance harmoniously, as do medieval and modern influences, with ancient castles regularly playing host to contemporary art exhibitions.

MERANO (MERAN)

29 km (18 miles) north of Bolzano, 16 km (10 miles) east of Naturno.

The second-largest town in Alto Adige, Merano (Meran) was once the capital of the Austrian region of Tirol. When the town and surrounding area were ceded to Italy as part of the 1919 Treaty of Versailles, Innsbruck became Tirol's capital. Merano continued to be known as a spa town, attracting European nobility for its therapeutic waters and its "grape cure," which consists simply of eating the grapes grown on the surrounding hillsides. Sheltered by mountains, Merano has an unusually mild climate, with summer temperatures rarely exceeding 80°F (27°C) and winters that usually stay above freezing, despite the skiing that's within easy reach. Along the narrow streets of Merano's old town, houses have little towers and huge wooden doors, and the pointed arches of the Gothic cathedral sit next to Neoclassical and Art Nouveau buildings. Merano serves as a good respite from mountain adventures, or from the bustle of nearby Trento and Bolzano.

GETTING HERE AND AROUND

By car from Bolzano, take the SP165 to the SP117 toward Merano (29 km [18 miles]). There is regular service by Trenitalia to the train station in Merano from all points in Italy.

VISITOR INFORMATION

Merano Tourism Office ✉ *Corso Libertà 45* ☎ *0473/272000* ⊕ *www. meran.eu.*

EXPLORING

TOP ATTRACTIONS

Castel Trauttmansdorff. This Gothic castle was restored in the 19th century and now serves as a museum, celebrating 200 years of tourism in south Tirol. Outside, a sprawling garden has an extensive display of exotic flora organized by country of origin. An English-language audio guide is available for €2.50, and public and private tours are available at additional charge. The castle is about 2 km (1 mile) southeast of town.

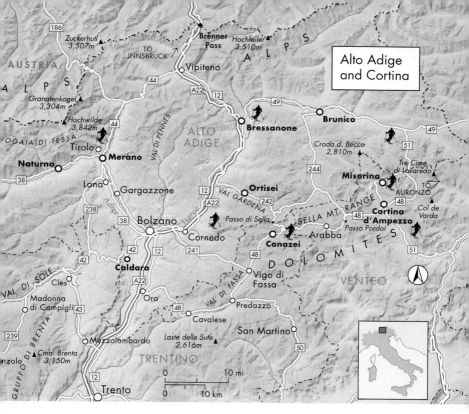

✉ Via Valentino 51a ☎ 0473/235730 ⊕ www.trauttmansdorff.it 💶 €12
🕐 Apr.–Oct., daily 9–7; June–Aug., Fri. 9 am–11 pm; early Nov., daily
9–5; last admission 1 hr early.

Museo Agricolo di Brunnenburg. Overlooking the town atop Mt. Tap-
peinerweg is Castel Fontana, which was the home of poet Ezra Pound
from 1958 to 1964. Still in the Pound family, the castle now houses
the Museo Agricolo di Brunnenburg, devoted to Tirolean country life.
Among its exhibits are a blacksmith's shop and a room with Pound
memorabilia. ✉ Via Castello 17, Brunnenburg ⊹ Take Bus No. 3,
which departs every hr on the hr from Merano to Dorf Tirol (20 mins)
☎ 0473/923533 💶 €5 🕐 Apr.–Oct., Sun.–Thurs. 10–5.

FAMILY **Terme di Merano.** This sprawling spa complex has 25 pools (including a
brine pool with underwater music) and eight saunas (with an indoor
"snow room" available for cooling down). Along with family-friendly
options for bathing, personalized services for grown-ups include traditional cures using local products, such as grape-based applications
and whey baths. An admission charge of about €15 gets you two hours
in thermal baths; €25 is for a full day's use of all baths and saunas.
✉ Piazza Terme 9 ☎ 0473/252000 ⊕ www.termemerano.it 🕐 Daily
9 am–10 pm.

WORTH NOTING

Duomo. The 14th-century Gothic cathedral, with a crenellated facade and an ornate campanile, sits in the heart of the old town. The Capella di Santa Barbara, just behind the Duomo, is an octagonal church containing a 15th-century pietà. **TIP→ Mass is held in German only.** ✉ *Piazza del Duomo* ☎ *0473/230174* 🕒 *Daily 8–6.*

Fodor's Choice ★ **Promenades.** A stroll along one of Merano's well-marked, impossibly pleasant promenades may yield even better relaxation than time in its famous spa. **Passeggiata Tappeiner** (Tappeiner's Promenade) is a 3-km (2-mile) path with panoramic views from the hills north of the Duomo and diverse botanical pleasures along the way. **Passeggiata d'Estate** (Summer Promenade) runs along the shaded south bank of the Passirio River, and the **Passeggiata d'Inverno** (Winter Promenade), on the exposed north bank, provides more warmth and the Wandelhalle—a sunny area decorated with idyllic paintings of surrounding villages. The popular Austrian empress Sissi (Elisabeth of Wittelsbach, 1837–98) put Merano on the map as a spa destination; a trail named in her honor, the **Sentiero di Sissi** (Sissi's Walk), follows a path from Castel Trauttmansdorff to the heart of Merano.

QUICK BITES

Cafe Gilf. You can enjoy a rich hot chocolate or a cold beer above a gurgling waterfall at the northeast edge of the Passeggiata d'Inverno. ✉ *Winterpromenade 51* ☎ *0473/690321* 🕒 *Fri.–Wed. 10–8.*

Cafe Saxifraga. An extensive selection of teas and other beverages can be enjoyed on the patio; the café has an enviable position overlooking Merano and the peaks enveloping the town. ✉ *Via Monte San Zeno 33, Tappeiner Promenade* ☎ *0473/239249* 🌐 *www.saxifraga.it* 🕒 *Closed Nov.–Mar.*

WHERE TO EAT

$$ NORTHERN ITALIAN 🍴 **Haisrainer.** Among the rustic wine taverns lining Via dei Portici, this one is most popular with locals and tourists alike (a menu in English is available). Warm wooden walls provide a comfortable setting for Tirolean and Italian standards: try the *zuppa al vino bianco* (stew with white wine) or the seasonal risottos (with asparagus in spring, or Barolo wine in chillier months). [$] *Average main: €22* ✉ *Via dei Portici 100* ☎ *0473/237944* 🕒 *Closed Sun.*

$$ ITALIAN 🍴 **Sieben.** Young Meraners crowd the bar on the ground floor of this modern bistro, in the town's central arcade. Upstairs, an older crowd enjoys the contemporary cooking and attentive service in the jazz-themed dining room. Sieben occasionally hosts jazz concerts in summer. [$] *Average main: €23* ✉ *Via dei Portici 232* ☎ *0473/210636* 🌐 *www.bistrosieben.it* 🕒 *Closed Sun., and Nov.–Apr.*

$$$ NORTHERN ITALIAN 🍴 **Sissi.** In relaxed, light-filled surroundings just off Via dei Portici, rustic regional dishes are prepared with precision. Menu choices may include gnocchi *di formaggio con salsa all' erba cipollina* (with cheese and chives) and *vitello alle castagne e tartufo nero* (veal with chestnuts and black truffles). **TIP→ "Table 11" is kept for special guests; ask if it is available.** [$] *Average main: €25* ✉ *Via Galilei 44* ☎ *0473/231062* 🌐 *www.andreafenoglio.com* ✍ *Reservations essential* 🕒 *Closed Mon., and 3 wks Feb.–Mar. No lunch Tues.*

$$
NORTHERN
ITALIAN

✕**Vinoteca-Pizzeria Relax.** If you have difficulty choosing from the long list of tasty pizzas here, ask the friendly English-speaking staff for help with the menu. You're unlikely to find a better selection of wine, or a more pleasant environment for sampling it. You can also buy bottles of the locally produced vintage to take home. $ *Average main: €15* ✉ *Via Cavour 31, opposite Palace Hotel* ☎ *0473/236735* ⊕ *www.weine-relax. it* ⊙ *Closed Sun., and 2 wks Feb.–Mar.*

WHERE TO STAY

$$$
HOTEL
Fodor's Choice
★

Castello Labers. Behind the red-tile gables, towers, and turrets of a Tirolean-style castle is a realm of distinctive luxury, where ceiling beams and frescoes are complemented by sumptuous Art Nouveau furnishings. **Pros:** romantic setting on a hilltop; spectacular views; pool and sauna. **Cons:** long walk into town; some bathrooms are small. $ *Rooms from: €280* ✉ *Via Labers 25, 3 km (2 miles) northeast of Merano's center* ☎ *0473/234484* ⊕ *www.labers.it* ⇋ *32 rooms, 1 suite* ⊙ *Closed early Nov.–late Apr.* ⦿ *Multiple meal plans.*

$
HOTEL

Conte di Merano. Steps away from Via dei Portici and open year-round, these simple, comfortable rooms done in pleasing traditional style are an efficient base for exploring the town. **Pros:** central; reasonable rates. **Cons:** basic décor. $ *Rooms from: €110* ✉ *Via delle Corse 78* ☎ *0473/490260* ⊕ *www.grafvonmeran.com* ⇋ *20 rooms* ⦿ *Breakfast.*

$$
RESORT

Meister's Hotel Irma. This goal of this hotel and spa, opened in 1924, is to relax the body and the spirit through a stay in a traditional room, a mini-apartment, or even in the unique treehouse room. **Pros:** great service; spectacular gardens and spa. **Cons:** expensive restaurant and bar. $ *Rooms from: €160* ✉ *Via Belvedere 17* ☎ *0437/212000* ⊕ *www. hotel-irma.com/en/home.html* ⇋ *62 rooms* ⊙ *Closed mid-Jan.–mid-Mar.* ⦿ *Some meals.*

NATURNO (NATURNS)

44 km (27 miles) northwest of Bolzano, 61 km (38 miles) east of Passo dello Stelvio.

As the name suggests, Naturno is a great location for a nature-based vacation; you can access a number of hiking trails to explore the area by foot. City planners have redesigned the town, reducing traffic and making the town more pedestrian friendly. The locals take great pride in their produce; the fresh fruit, wine, and cheeses of this area are alone worth the drive.

GETTING HERE AND AROUND

By car from Bolzano, take the SS42 to the SS38 toward Merano. Naturno is 15 km (9 miles) past Merano. The town is very pedestrian-friendly, so talk to your hotel about where to leave your car, or head straight to a parking garage. Naturno is easily accessible by train from Bolzano or Merano.

VISITOR INFORMATION

Naturno Tourism Office ✉ *Piazza Municipio 1* ☎ *0473/666077* ⊕ *www. naturns.it.*

STUMBLING ON ÖTZI

It was at the Similaun rifugio in September 1991 that a German couple arrived talking of a dead body they'd discovered near a "curious pickax." The couple, underestimating the age of the corpse by about 5,300 years, thought it was a matter for the police. This was to be the world's introduction to Ötzi, the oldest mummy ever found. World-famous mountaineers Reinhold Messner and Hans Kammerlander happened to be passing through the same rifugio during a climbing tour, and a few days later they were on the scene, freeing the iceman from the ice.

Ötzi's remarkable story was under way. You can see him on display, along with his longbow, ax, and clothes, at Bolzano's Museo Archeologico dell'Alto Adige, where he continues to be preserved at freezing temperatures.

EXPLORING

Castel Juval. Since 1983 this 13th-century castle in the hills above the hamlet of Stava has been the home of the south Tirolese climber and polar adventurer Reinhold Messner, the first climber to conquer Everest solo. Part of the castle has been turned into one of five in Messner's chain of Dolomite museums, where guided tours (Italian and German only) are required to view his collection of Tibetan art and masks from around the world. It's a five-minute shuttle ride from Naturno (there's no parking at the castle), or an hour-long hike on many local trails. The walk from where the shuttle lets off to the castle is steep and about ¾ mile. It's paved, but can be a difficult walk. ✉ *Juval 3, Kastelbell* ☎ *0348/4433871, 0471/631264 for shuttle* 🌐 *www.messner-mountain-museum.it* 🎟 *€9* 🕒 *Late Mar.–June and Sept.–early Nov., Thurs.–Tues. 10–4.*

San Procolo (*Prokolus*). The frescoes here are some of the oldest in the German-speaking world, dating from the 8th century. A small, modern museum offers multimedia installations (in Italian or German only) presenting four epochs in the region's history: ancient, medieval, Gothic, and the era of the Great Plague of 1636 (which claimed a quarter of Naturno's population, some of whom are buried in the church's cemetery). There are leaflets and other information in English on request. ✉ *Via San Procolo* ☎ *0473/667312* 🌐 *www.naturns.it/en/prokulus* 🎟 *€2 suggested donation* 🕒 *Mar.–Nov., Tues.–Sun. 10–12:30 and 2:30–5:30; Nov.–Mar., Tues.–Sun. 10–12:30 and 2–5.*

WHERE TO EAT

$$ NORTHERN ITALIAN Fodor's Choice ★

🍴 **Schlosswirt Juval.** Reinhold Messner's restored farmhouse, which is below Castel Juval, holds an old-style restaurant serving Mediterranean standards and traditional local dishes. Not to be missed are the smoked hams and flavorful cheeses provided by the farm outside; they are well paired with the estate's Castel Juval wine. Dinner is often accompanied by live jazz. The walk from the shuttle to the restaurant is not paved, and the flagstone pavers on the hillside could be challenging for some. [$] *Average main: €22* ✉ *Juval 2, Castelbello* ☎ *0473/668056*

⊕ *www.schlosswirtjuval.it* ▭ *No credit cards* ⊘ *Closed Wed. and mid-Dec.–Mar.*

EN
ROUTE

Forst Brewery. The source of the full-flavor beer served throughout the region is the striking Forst Brewery, on the road connecting Naturno and Merano. Tours are possible June to August (daily 2–4), but call ahead for reservations. You can turn up any time of year to sample the product line. In warm weather, cross a covered, flower-lined bridge to reach the delightful beer garden. ⊠ *Via Venosta 8, Lagundo* ☎ *0473/260111* ⊕ *www.forst.it* ⊘ *Daily 10 am–11 pm.*

CALDARO (KALTERN)

15 km (9 miles) south of Bolzano.

A vineyard village with clear views of castles high up on the surrounding mountains represents the centuries of division that forged the unique character of the area. Caldaro architecture is famous for the way it blends Italian Renaissance elements of balance and harmony with the soaring windows and peaked arches of the Germanic Gothic tradition. The church of Santa Caterina, on the main square, is a good example.

GETTING HERE AND AROUND

By car from Bolzano, follow the SS42 south toward Caldaro. This road is famously known as the "Strada del Vino," or "Wine Road"—you will pass several vineyards along the way. If you head straight to the Wine Museum in Caldaro, you can pick up maps and plan a route through the vineyards based on specific tastes.

VISITOR INFORMATION

Caldaro Tourism Office ⊠ *Piazza Mercato 8* ☎ *0471/963169* ⊕ *www.kaltern.com.*

EXPLORING

Fodor'sChoice ★

South Tyrolean Wine Museum. Head here to learn how local wine has historically been made, stored, served, and worshipped, through a series of fun exhibits. You can board the bus in front of the tourist office for a museum tour and wine tasting in the cellar, or call ahead to reserve. ⊠ *Via dell'Oro 1, near main square* ☎ *0471/963168* ⊕ *www.weinmuseum.it* ⊡ *€4, wine tasting €5* ⊘ *Late Mar.–early Nov., Tues.–Sat. 10–5, Sun. 10–noon.*

BRESSANONE (BRIXEN)

42 km (25 miles) northeast of Bolzano.

Bressanone is an important artistic center and was the seat of prince-bishops for centuries. Like their counterparts in Trento, these medieval administrators had the delicate task of serving two masters—the pope (the ultimate spiritual authority) and the Holy Roman Emperor (the civil and military power), who were virtually at war throughout the Middle Ages. Bressanone's prince-bishops became experts at tact and diplomacy.

GETTING HERE AND AROUND

Driving from Bolzano, follow the SS12 northeast 42 km (26 miles) to Bressanone. Trains run from Bolzano, as does SAD Bus No. 350.

VISITOR INFORMATION

Bressanone Tourism Office ✉ *Viale Ratisbona 9* ☎ *0472/836401* 🌐 *www.brixen.org.*

EXPLORING

Abbazia di Novacella. This Augustinian abbey founded in 1142 has been producing wine for at least nine centuries and is most famous for the delicate stone-fruit character of its dry white Sylvaner. You can wander the delightful grounds; note the progression of Romanesque, Gothic, and Baroque building styles. Guided tours of the abbey (in Italian and German) depart daily at 10, 11, 2, 3, and 4, as well as at noon and 1 in summer; from January through March, tours are by reservation only. Guided tours of the gardens and vineyard are also available in season. ✉ *Via Abbazia 1, Varna, 3 km (2 miles) north of Bressanone* ☎ *0472/836189* 🌐 *www.kloster-neustift.it* 🎫 *Guided tours €7, wine tastings €8.50* ⏲ *Grounds Mon.–Sat. 10–7; tasting room Mon.–Sat. 10–7.*

Duomo. The imposing town cathedral was built in the 13th century but acquired a Baroque facade 500 years later; its 14th-century cloister is decorated with medieval frescoes. Guided tours are available from Easter to November 1 Monday through Saturday from 10:30 to 3. ■ TIP→ **Tours are in Italian or German; call ahead for an English guide.** ✉ *Piazza Duomo 1* ☎ *0472/837392* ⏲ *Weekdays 6 am–noon and 3–6 pm, weekends 6–6.*

Museo Diocesano (*Diocesan Museum*). The Bishop's Palace houses an abundance of local medieval art, particularly Gothic wood carvings. The wooden statues and liturgical objects were all collected from the cathedral treasury. During the Christmas season, curators arrange the museum's large collection of antique Nativity scenes; look for the shepherds wearing Tirolean hats. ✉ *Palazzo Vescovile 2* ☎ *0472/830505* 🌐 *www.hofburg.it* 🎫 *€7* ⏲ *Mid-Mar.–Oct. and Nov. 27–Jan. 6, Tues.–Sun. 10–5.*

WHERE TO EAT AND STAY

$$ NORTHERN ITALIAN

🍴 **Fink.** This warm, wood-paneled, upstairs dining room is under the arcades of the pedestrians-only town center. Among the house specialties are *carré di maiale gratinato* (pork chops roasted with cheese and served with cabbage and potatoes) and *castrato alla paesana,* a substantial lamb stew. In addition to hearty Tirolean specialties, there's an affordable daily set menu, as well as homemade pastries. [$] *Average main: €20* ✉ *Via Portici Minori 4* ☎ *0472/834883* 🌐 *www.restaurant-fink.it* ⏲ *Closed Wed. No dinner Tues.*

$$$ HOTEL Fodor's Choice ★

🏨 **Elephant.** At this cozy inn, 450 years old and still one of the region's best, each room is unique and many are filled with antiques and paintings. **Pros:** lovely ambience; good restaurant; lavish breakfast. **Cons:** rooms vary in size; often filled with groups. [$] *Rooms from: €240* ✉ *Via Rio Bianco 4* ☎ *0472/832750* 🌐 *www.hotelelephant.com* 🛏 *44 rooms* 🍽 *Breakfast.*

CLOSE UP

Hiking the Dolomites

In 2009 UNESCO (the United Nations Educational, Scientific, and Cultural Organization) added the Dolomites to its list of natural heritage sites.

The dramatic terrain, inspiring vistas, and impossibly pleasant climate are complemented by excellent facilities for enjoying the mountains.

PICKING A TRAIL

The Dolomites have a well-maintained network of trails for hiking and rock climbing. As long as you're in reasonably good shape, the number of appealing hiking options can be overwhelming. Trails are well marked and designated by grades of difficulty: T for tourist path, H for hiking path, EE for expert hikers, and EEA for equipped expert hikers. On any of these paths you're likely to see carpets of mountain flowers between clutches of dense evergreens, with chamois and roe deer milling about.

If you're just out for a day in the mountains, you can leave the details of your walk open until you're actually on the spot; local tourist offices (especially those in Cortina and Madonna) can help you choose the right route based on trail conditions, weather, and desired exertion level.

TRAVELING THE VIE FERRATE

If you're looking for an adventure somewhere between hiking and climbing, consider a guided trip along the Vie Ferrate (Iron Paths). These routes offer fixed climbing aids (steps, ladders, bridges, safety cables) left by Alpine divisions of the Italian and Austro-Hungarian armies and later converted for recreational use. Previous experience is generally not required, but vertigo-inducing heights do demand a strong stomach.

BEDDING DOWN

One of the pleasures of an overnight adventure in the Dolomites is staying at a *rifugio,* one of the refuges that dot the mountainsides, often in remote locations.

There are hundreds of them, and they range in comfort from spartan to posh. Most fall somewhere in between—they're cozy mountain lodges with dormitory-style accommodations. Pillows and blankets are provided (there's no need to carry a sleeping bag), but you have to supply your own sheet. Bathrooms are usually shared, with cold showers. Reservations are a must, especially in August, although Italian law requires rifugi to accept travelers for the night if there's insufficient time to reach other accommodations before dark.

EATING WELL

Food is as much a draw at rifugi as location. The rustic dishes, such as salami, dumplings, hearty stews, are all excellent—an impressive feat, made all the more remarkable when you consider that supplies often have to arrive by helicopter. Your dinner may cost as much as your bed for the night—about €20 per person—and it's difficult to determine which is the better bargain. Snacks and packed lunches are available for purchase, but many opt to sit down for the midday meal. Multilingual stories are swapped, food and wine shared, and new adventures launched.

5

BRUNICO (BRUNECK)

33 km (20 miles) east of Bressanone, 65 km (40 miles) northwest of Cortina d'Ampezzo.

Brunico's medieval quarter nestles below a 13th-century bishop's castle. In the heart of the Val Pusteria, this quiet and quaint town is divided by the Rienza River, with the old quarter on one side and the modern town on the other.

GETTING HERE AND AROUND

From Bressanone follow the E66 east for 30 km (19 miles) to Brunico. If driving from Cortina d'Ampezzo, take the SR48 over the Passo Falzarego and continue to the SP244 toward Brunico. There are bus (SAD) and train (Trenitalia) connections available at Bolzano.

VISITOR INFORMATION

Brunico Tourism Office ✉ *Piazza Municipio 7* ☎ *0474/555722* 🌐 *www.bruneck.com.*

EXPLORING

Museo Etnografico dell'Alto Adige (*Alto Adige Ethnographic Museum*). A re-creation of a Middle Ages farming village is built around a 300-year-old mansion. The wood-carving displays are especially interesting. ✉ *Herzog-Diet-Strasse 24* ☎ *0474/552087* 🌐 *www.volkskundemuseum.it* 🎫 *€6* 🕒 *Easter–Oct., Tues.–Sat. 10–5, Sun. 2–6; July and Aug., Mon.–Sat. 10–5.*

WHERE TO STAY

$$$$ HOTEL 🏨 **Alpine Wellness Resort Majestic.** Right in front of the Plan de Corones, this is a great base for a skiing or hiking vacation, with bus service to the ski slopes and a spa and pools on site to unwind after a big day out. **Pros:** convenient for skiers and hikers. **Cons:** meal portions are a little small. [$] *Rooms from: €392* ✉ *Via Im Gelande 20* ☎ *0474/410993* 🌐 *www.hotel-majestic.it* 🛏 *60 rooms* 🕒 *Closed Easter–May* 🍴 *Some meals.*

SPORTS AND THE OUTDOORS

SKIING

Alta Badia. The Alta Badia ski area, which includes 53 ski lifts and 130 km (80 miles) of slopes, can be reached by heading 30 km (19 miles) south on SS244 from Brunico. It's cheaper and more Austrian in character than the more famous ski destinations in this region. Groomed trails for cross-country skiing (usually loops marked off by the kilometer) accommodate differing degrees of ability. Inquire at the local tourist office. ☎ *0471/836176 for Corvara* 🌐 *www.altabadia.org.*

THE HEART OF THE DOLOMITES

The area between Bolzano and the mountain resort Cortina d'Ampezzo is dominated by two major valleys, Val di Fassa and Val Gardena. Both share the spectacular panorama of the Sella mountain range, known as the Heart of the Dolomites. Val di Fassa cradles the beginning of the Grande Strada delle Dolomiti (Great Dolomites Road; SS48 and SS241), which runs from Bolzano as far as Cortina. This route, opened in 1909, comprises 110 km (68 miles) of relatively easy grades and smooth driving between the two towns—a slower, more scenic alternative to traveling by way of Brunico and Dobbiaco along SS49. And scenic it is: the road passes into a stark, high-altitude landscape punctuated with needlelike mountain peaks, climbing to 7,346 feet.

In both Val di Fassa and Val Gardena, recreational options are less expensive, though less comprehensive, than in better-known resorts like Cortina. The culture here is firmly Germanic. Val Gardena is freckled with well-equipped, photo-friendly towns with great views overlooked by the oblong Sasso Lungo (Long Rock), which is more than 10,000 feet above sea level. It's also home to the Ladins, descendants of soldiers sent by the Roman emperor Tiberius to conquer the Celtic population of the area in the 1st century AD. Forgotten in the narrow cul-de-sacs of isolated mountain valleys, the Ladins have developed their own folk traditions and speak an ancient dialect that is derived from Latin and similar to the Romansch spoken in some high valleys in Switzerland.

MISURINA

Nestled on the shores of Lake Misurina, among the Dolomites, Misurina's high altitude, low air humidity, and total absence of dust mites and air pollution, has some saying the "Pearl of the Dolomites" has some of the purest air in the world.

The town itself is rather small, but it's a perfect base to explore Lake Misurina and the Tre Cime of Lavaredo. The mountains surrounding are rich in history and artifacts from WWI, as well as earlier empirical wars. Along some of the hikes and *via ferratas* (a mountain path with steel cables and fixed anchors and ladders), you can explore caves and trenches complete with informational placards giving details about troop positions and fighting.

GETTING HERE AND AROUND

From Brunico, drive southeast on the SS49/E66 to Dobbiaco. Turn right onto SS51 and drive for 13 km (8 miles). Turn left onto 48bis in the direction of Auronzo. Arrive at Lago di Misurina in 6 km (4 miles).

VISITOR INFORMATION

Misurina Tourism Office ✉ *Via Monte Piana* ☎ *0435/39016, 0435/99603* ⊕ *www.auronzomisurina.it* ⊘ *Closed in winter months.*

EXPLORING

Tre Cime of Lavaredo. Without a doubt, the "Three Peaks"—Cima Piccola (9,373 feet), Cima Grande (9,839 feet), and Cima Ovest (9,753 feet)—are the symbols for the Dolomite UNESCO World Heritage Site. From the town of Misurina, only two of the three *cime* (peaks) are visible. In order to get up close and personal, drive or take a bus along the dedicated toll road from May through October. Once at the top, follow footpath 101 from Rifugio Auronzo to Forcella Laveredo (easy) for about an hour. There are many other footpaths and *vie ferrate* (protected climbing routes), which allow you to climb the cime and access the base. The *rifugi* (mountain huts) offer hot meals without a reservation, and dorm-style lodging, which is best reserved in advance. ✉ *Parco Naturale Tre Cime, Auronzo di Cadore* ☎ *0435/39002.*

WHERE TO EAT AND STAY

$$ FRIULIAN FAMILY

🍴 **Malga Rin Bianco.** When in the mood for fresh, properly cooked regional food, this *malga* (rustic house) with great mountain views can't be beat. The salami and cheeses are made on-site, and the bar boasts a variety of homemade and commercial grappas, many of which are brewed with local herbs and plants. Try some *capriolo* (mountain goat stew), polenta, *skitz* (grilled cheese that doesn't melt), or fresh, local mushrooms for some authentic flavors. There's a steep climb from the parking lot to the restaurant, so call ahead to arrange for closer parking if you have mobility issues. **TIP→ Because of the remote location, the malga is cash-only.** [$] *Average main: €22* ✉ *Strada Tre Cime* ☎ *0435/39025* 💳 *No credit cards.*

$ HOTEL ALL-INCLUSIVE FAMILY

🏨 **The Grand Hotel Misurina.** On the shores of beautiful Lake Misurina, this grand hotel is but a few kilometers from the renowned winter resort, Cortina d'Ampezzo. **Pros:** located in town center; perfect for large groups; shuttle to ski areas. **Cons:** rooms have simple furnishings; Wi-Fi (fee) in common areas only. [$] *Rooms from: €110* ✉ *Via Monte Piana 21* ☎ *0435/39191* 🌐 *www.grandhotelmisurina.com* 🛏 *87 rooms, 38 apartments* 🍽 *All-inclusive.*

$$ B&B/INN FAMILY

🏨 **Chalet Lago Antorno.** Located in a quiet, panoramic spot, the chalet is an ideal place for anyone looking to explore the mountains or those wanting to relax and unwind in the most beautiful scenery of the Alps. **Pros:** family-run; typical décor and regional flavor. **Cons:** away from town center; not suitable for large groups. [$] *Rooms from: €170* ✉ *Misurina, Auronzo di Cadore* ☎ *0435/39148* 🌐 *www.lagoantorno.it* 🛏 *10 rooms* 🍽 *Some meals.*

SPORTS AND THE OUTDOORS

BIKING

Cycling enthusiasts flock to the Dolomites to take part in the challenges the mountains have to offer. Much of the region is used by Olympic athletes to train, and several important bike races (such as the Giro di Italia) take place in the area. Some of the descents along gravely roads are high adrenalin rushes, while others follow paved roads and bike paths. Great news for cyclers: the Auronzo-Misurina Cycle Track is set to be completed in 2015, providing about 20 miles of bicycle path between the two towns.

SKIING

Two major ski lifts service the area from Misurina and Auronzo. From Misurina take the Col de Varda lift. Auronzo di Cadore is about 30 minutes drive from Misurina, where the Monte Agudo lift goes from Taiarezze (2,952 ft) to Rifugio Monte Agudo (5,160 ft). There are restaurants and maps available at the top. Views from Auronzo differ from Misurina in that all three cime are visible from here.

Col de Varda. This area is an excellent starting point for great hiking and biking excursions, and the views of Lake Misurina, Mt. Cristallo, the Sesto Dolomites, and the Cadini, Sorapiss, and Tofane massifs are breathtaking. To enjoy the views, take the 10-minute chairlift ride, which starts in Misurina at 9,735 feet and finishes at the Col de Varda at 6,909 feet. Rifugio Col de Varda has a bar and restaurant, as well as rooms to rent; it's on Alta Via number 4. ☎ *0435/39041* ⊕ *www. rifugiocoldevarda.it* 🎫 *€11 round-trip* ⊙ *June–Sept., daily 9–5, Dec.– Apr., daily 9–4:30.*

FAMILY **Fun Bob.** The 1.8-mile-long "bob" (think wheeled cart) track starts at the upper station of the Taiarezze-Malon ski lift in Auronzo and follows the same path as the winter ski slopes. The "ride" lasts about 15 minutes and you may hit a maximum speed of 27 mph. Children over 8 are allowed to drive their own car, but those under 7 must ride with an adult. ⊠ *Via Roma 24, Auronzo di Cadore* ☎ *0435/99603* ⊕ *auronzomisurina.it/en/fun-bob-2* 🎫 *€10* ⊙ *June–Sept., daily 10–1 and 2–6.*

CORTINA D'AMPEZZO

The archetypal Dolomite resort, Cortina d'Ampezzo entices those seeking both relaxation and adventure. The town is the western gateway to the Strade Grande delle Dolomiti, and actually crowns the northern Veneto region and an area known as Cadore in the northernmost part of the province of Belluno. Like Alto Adige to the west, Cadore (birthplace to the Venetian Renaissance painter Titian) was on the Alpine front during WWI, and was the scene of many battles that have been commemorated in refuges and museums.

Although its appeal to younger Italians has been eclipsed by the steeper, sleeker Madonna di Campiglio, Cortina remains, for many, Italy's most idyllic incarnation of an Alpine ski town.

GETTING HERE AND AROUND

To drive to Cortina d'Ampezzo from Trento or Bolzano, take the A22 north to Bressanone/Pustertal. Turn right on the SS49/E66, then right on to the SS51 and follow it into Cortina. The Dolomiti Bus provides service to and from Cortina, but it's not very convenient or reliable. The town itself is pedestrian friendly and has local bus service to area ski slopes. Beware of taxis, as the rates are very high, and the fare may begin from the taxi's point of origin, not necessarily where you get in the vehicle.

VISITOR INFORMATION

Cortina d'Ampezzo Tourism Office ⊠ *Piazza Roma 1* ☎ *0436/3231* ⊕ *cortina.dolomiti.org.*

EXPLORING

Surrounded by mountains and dense forests, the "Queen of the Dolomites" is in a lush meadow 4,000 feet above sea level. The town hugs the slopes beside a fast-moving stream, and a public park extends along one bank. Higher in the valley, luxury hotels and the villas of the rich are identifiable by their attempts to hide behind stands of firs and spruces. The bustling center of Cortina d'Ampezzo has little nostalgia, despite its Alpine appearance. The tone is set by shops and cafés as chic as their well-dressed patrons, whose corduroy knickerbockers may well have been tailored by Armani. Unlike neighboring resorts that have a strong Germanic flavor, Cortina d'Ampezzo is unapologetically Italian and distinctly fashionable.

WHERE TO EAT

$$$ NORTHERN ITALIAN

🍴 **Ristorante Lago Pianozes.** This small, family-run establishment is just outside of Cortina beside the picturesque Lago Pianozes. Fabrizio, the owner, is friendly and knowledgeable, not only about his food and wine, but also about the surrounding region. The menu varies according to the seasons, always incorporating local recipies. Reservations are recommended, as seating is limited. [$] *Average main: €28* ✉ *Campo di Sotto Pianozes 1* ☎ *0436/5601* ✍ *Reservations essential.*

$$$ NORTHERN ITALIAN

🍴 **Tavernetta.** These Tirolean-style wood-paneled dining rooms near the Olympic ice-skating rink are a Cortina institution. Join the local clientele in sampling local specialties such as pasta with a *ragù bianco tartuffato* (white truffle sauce), and wild game. [$] *Average main: €25* ✉ *Via Castello 53* ☎ *0436/868102* ⏲ *Closed Tues., and mid-June–mid-July.*

WHERE TO STAY

$$$ HOTEL

🏨 **Corona.** Noted ski instructor Luciano Rimoldi, who has coached such luminaries as Alberto Tomba, runs an inviting Alpine lodge where modern art adorns small but comfortable pine-paneled rooms. **Pros:** cozy atmosphere; friendly staff; quiet location; ski shuttle stops out front. **Cons:** small rooms; outside the town center. [$] *Rooms from: €240* ✉ *Via Val di Sotto 12* ☎ *0436/3251* 🌐 *www.hotelcoronacortina.it* 🛏 *44 rooms* ⏲ *Closed Apr., May, and mid-Sept.–Nov.* 🍽 *Multiple meal plans.*

$$$$ RESORT

🏨 **Cristallo Hotel Spa & Golf.** Winner of Italy's Best Ski Hotel for 2013 and 2014, this luxury grande dame is lauded for its service, spa, and more; the architecture was immortalized in 1963's *The Pink Panther*. **Pros:** the award-winning service, food, and atmosphere speak for themselves. **Cons:** not in town; a car or expensive taxi service is required to reach Cortina. [$] *Rooms from: €525* ✉ *Via R. Menardi 42* ☎ *0436/881111* 🛏 *73 rooms* 🌐 *www.cristallo.it/en/golf* ⏲ *Closed Apr.–June* 🍽 *Multiple meal plans.*

$$$$ HOTEL

🏨 **De la Poste.** Loyal skiers return year after year to this old-school mountain retreat, where each unique room has antiques in characteristic Dolomite style (almost all have wooden balconies) and the main terrace bar is one of Cortina's social centers. **Pros:** professional service; romantic. **Cons:** a bit stuffy; expensive; in a busy neighborhood. [$] *Rooms from: €400* ✉ *Piazza Roma 14* ☎ *0436/4271* 🌐 *www.delaposte.it* 🛏 *68 rooms* ⏲ *Closed Apr.–mid-June and Oct.–mid-Dec.* 🍽 *Breakfast.*

$$$$ RESORT Fodor's Choice ★

🏨 **Miramonti Majestic.** A touch of luxurious formality rather than rustic charm comes through in the imperial Austrian design of this century-old landmark tucked into a magnificent mountain valley. **Pros:** magnificent location; loads of old-world charm in lounges and guest rooms alike; splendid views; great pool and spa. **Cons:** about 1 km (½ mile) outside town center; 3-night minimum stay; sky-high rates. [$] *Rooms from: €775* ✉ *Località Peziè 103* ☎ *0436/4201* 🌐 *www.miramontimajestic.it* 🛏 *122 rooms* ⏲ *Closed Apr.–June and Sept.–mid-Dec.* 🍽 *Breakfast.*

SPORTS AND THE OUTDOORS

HIKING AND CLIMBING

Hiking information is available from the excellent local tourism office.

Gruppo Guide Alpine Cortina Scuola di Alpinismo (*Mountaineering School*). This group organizes climbing trips and trekking adventures. ⊠ *Corso Italia 69/a* ☎ *0436/868505* ⊕ *www.guidecortina.com.*

SKIING

Cortina's long and picturesque ski runs will delight intermediates, but advanced skiers may pine for steeper terrain, which can be found only off-piste. Efficient ski-bus service connects the town with the high-speed chairlifts and gondolas that ascend in all directions from the valley.

Dolomiti Superski pass. The Dolomiti Superski pass provides access to the surrounding Dolomites (€42–€53 per day), with 450 lifts and gondolas serving 1,200 km (750 miles) of trails. Buy one at the ticket office next to the bus station and at other outlets in the Dolomites. ⊠ *Via Marconi 15* ☎ *0471/795397* ⊕ *www.dolomitisuperski.com.*

Faloria gondola. The Faloria gondola runs from the center of town. From the top you can get up to most of the central mountains. ⊠ *Via Ria de Zeta 10* ☎ *0436/2517* ⊕ *www.cortinacube.it* 🎫 *€18 round-trip.*

Monte Cristallo. Some of the most impressive views (and steepest slopes) are on Monte Cristallo, based at Misurina, 15 km (9 miles) northeast of Cortina by car or bus.

Passo Falzarego. The topography of the Passo Falzarego ski area, 16 km (10 miles) east of town, is dramatic. The cable car takes you to one of the highest points in the Dolomites (Rifugio Lagazuoi)—on a clear day, you'll experience some of the best views from here. It's also easy to see why this was such a deadly area for soldiers in WWI. Hiking is uneven in places, and there are vie ferrate that require the use of helmets and flashlights. Other paths that lead to tunnels don't require helmets. ⊕ *www.rifugiolagazuoi.com.*

EN ROUTE At 7,346 feet, **Passo Pordoi** is the highest surface road pass in the Dolomites; keep an eye out for the Marmolada Glacier. It connects Arabba, in Val Cordevole (province of Belluno) with Canazei, in Val di Fossa (province of Trento). Be warned: there are 28 hairpin turns from Passo Pordoi to Canazei, but there are also a few scenic and picnic pull offs along the way. The Pass is home to several hotels and a ski school, as well as some souvenir shops, restaurants, and snack carts. Although the hotels are not glamorous, some offer half-board packages at reasonable prices.

The cable car (May–October €16) takes you to the Sass Pordoi, often called the "Terrace of the Dolomites." At more than 9,100 feet, there are a myriad of hiking trails and vie ferrate with varying degrees of difficulty (and none of which are easy), leading to rifugi and other peaks and passes in the region. Skiing is available year-round, but the most popular winter skiing areas are Belvedere and Sella Ronda; much of the area is part of the Dolomiti Superski package. ■TIP➔ **Even if the road for the pass is closed, many of the cable cars in neighboring valley towns will be running to carry you to various summits.**

5

CANAZEI

60 km (37 miles) west of Cortina d'Ampezzo, 52 km (32 miles) east of Bolzano.

Of the year-round resort towns in the Val di Fassa, Canazei is the most popular. The mountains around this small town are threaded with hiking trails and ski slopes, surrounded by large clutches of conifers.

GETTING HERE AND AROUND

There is bus service from Bolzano and Bressanone (the nearest train stations), but the service is infrequent, and often has interruptions and cancelations. By car from the A22, take the Bolzano Nord exit onto the SS241. Cross the Passo Costalunga into the Val di Fassa. From the town of Vigo, follow signs for Canazei.

VISITOR INFORMATION

Canazei Tourism Office ✉ *Stréda de Pareda 67* ☎ *0462/608811* 🌐 *www.canazei.org.*

EXPLORING

Fodor's Choice ★ **Col Rodella.** An excursion from Campitello di Fassa, about 4 km (2½ miles) west of Canazei, to the vantage point at Col Rodella has unmissable views. A cable car rises some 3,000 feet to a full-circle vista of the Heart of the Dolomites, including the Sasso Lungo and the rest of the Sella range. ✉ *Localita' Ischia 1* ☎ *0462/608811* 🎟 *Cable car €16.50 round-trip* ⏲ *Early Dec.–Easter and mid-June–mid-Oct.*

WHERE TO STAY

$$ HOTEL 🏨 **Alla Rosa.** The view of the imposing Dolomites is the real attraction in rooms that pleasantly blend rustic and contemporary furnishings, so ask for a balcony. **Pros:** in the center of town; great views. **Cons:** half board mandatory in winter high season; busy neighborhood. [$] *Rooms from: €200* ✉ *Strèda del Faure 18* ☎ *0462/601107* 🌐 *www.hotelallarosa.com* 🛏 *49 rooms* 🍴 *Multiple meal plans.*

EN ROUTE **Passo di Sella** (*Sella Pass*). The Passo di Sella can be approached from the SS48, affording some of the most spectacular mountain vistas in Europe before it descends into the Val Gardena. The road continues to Ortisei, passing the smaller resorts of Selva Gardena and Santa Cristina. 🌐 *www.visittrentino.it/it/passo-pordoi-sella.*

ORTISEI (ST. ULRICH)

28 km (17 miles) north of Canazei, 35 km (22 miles) northeast of Bolzano.

Ortisei (St. Ulrich), the jewel in the crown of Val Gardena's resorts, is a hub of activity in both summer and winter; there are hundreds of miles of hiking trails and accessible ski slopes.

For centuries Ortisei has also been famous for the expertise of its woodcarvers, and there are still numerous workshops. Apart from making religious sculptures—particularly the wayside calvaries you come upon everywhere in the Dolomites—Ortisei's carvers were long known for producing wooden dolls, horses, and other toys. As itinerant peddlers, they traveled every spring on foot with their loaded packs as far as Paris, London, and St. Petersburg. Shops in town still sell woodcrafts.

Ortisei has been a mountain-vacation destination since the 1930s. The most famous cable car in the area, the Alpe di Siusi, operates in summer and winter. The largest village in the Val Gardena, Ortisei makes a picturesque and practical base for exploring much of the Heart of the Dolomites.

GETTING HERE AND AROUND

By car from Bolzano, take the SS12 to the SS242 in the direction of Ortisei. From Canazei, follow the SS242 north to Ortisei. Bus service is available on the Val Gardena network from Bolzano and Bressanone.

VISITOR INFORMATION

Ortisei Tourist Office ✉ *Via Rezia 1* ☎ *0471/777600* 🌐 *www.valgardena.it.*

EXPLORING

5

Alpe di Siusi cable car. First opened in 1935, the cable car from Ortisei to Alpe di Siusi climbs more than 6,100 feet to the widest plateau in Europe. There are over 52 km (32 miles) of Alpine pastures lined with summertime hiking trails. In the winter, 20 ski lifts and cross-country trails keep active visitors happy. There is a restaurant at the top of the Mt. Seuc ski lift, or you can pick up a map at the tourist office in Ortisei listing the mountain huts and restaurants that can be reached by foot. Opening days and times depend on the season and daily weather conditions. Check the website or call ahead to avoid disappointment. ✉ *Via Setil 9* ☎ *0471/797897* 🌐 *www.alpedisiusi-seiseralm.com/eng/index.html* 🎫 *€18.90* ⏲ *Varies according to weather.*

Museo della Val Gardena. Fine historic and contemporary examples of local woodworking are on display here. ✉ *Via Rezia 83* ☎ *0471/797554* 🌐 *www.museumgherdeina.it* 🎫 *€7* ⏲ *Dec.–Mar., Tues.–Fri. 10–noon and 2–6; May 15–Oct., weekdays 10–noon and 2–6; July and Aug., Mon.–Sat. 10–noon and 2–6.*

WHERE TO STAY

$$$ HOTEL 🏨 **Hotel Grones.** The attention to detail at this hotel, located just a few minutes' walk from the ski slopes or downtown, makes it a great base for a mountain vacation. **Pros:** friendly staff; quiet location; gluten-free options. **Cons:** it's a slightly uphill walk to town; half board mandatory. [$] *Rooms from: €230* ✉ *110 Stufan St.* ☎ *0471/797040* 🌐 *www.grones.info/en/* 🛏 *23 rooms* ⏲ *Closed Apr., May, and mid-Oct.–early Dec.* 🍴 *Some meals.*

SPORTS AND THE OUTDOORS

SKIING

With almost 600 km (370 miles) of accessible downhill slopes and more than 90 km (56 miles) of cross-country skiing trails, Ortisei is one of the most popular ski resorts in the Dolomites. Prices are good, and facilities are among the most modern in the region. In warmer weather, the slopes surrounding Ortisei are a popular hiking destination, as well as a playground for vehicular mountain adventures: biking, rafting, and paragliding.

Sella Ronda. An immensely popular ski route, the Sella Ronda relies on well-placed chairlifts to connect 26 km (16 miles) of downhill skiing around the colossal Sella massif, passing through several towns along the way. You can ski the loop, which requires intermediate ability and a full day's effort, either clockwise or counterclockwise. Going with a guide is recommended. ⊕ *www.sella-ronda.info.*

Val Gardena Tourism Office. The Val Gardena tourism office can provide detailed information about sports-equipment rental outfits and tour operators. ⊠ *Via Dursan 80C, Santa Cristina* ☎ *0471/777777* ⊕ *www. valgardena.it.*

6

MILAN, LOMBARDY, AND THE LAKES

WELCOME TO MILAN, LOMBARDY, AND THE LAKES

TOP REASONS TO GO

★ **Lake Como, one of the most beautiful lakes in the world:** Ferries crisscross the waters, taking you from picture-book villages to stately villas to Edenic gardens, all backdropped in the distance by the snowcapped Alps.

★ **Leonardo's Last Supper:** Behold one of the world's most famous works of art for yourself.

★ **The sky's no limit:** A funicular ride in Bergamo whisks you up to the magnificent medieval city.

★ **Milan alla Moda:** As you window-shop the afternoon away in Milan's Quadrilatero shopping district, catch a glimpse of fashion's latest trends.

★ **A night at La Scala:** What the Louvre is to art, Milan's La Scala is to the world of opera.

1 **Milan.** The country's center of finance and commerce is constantly looking to the future. Home of the Italian stock exchange, it's also one of the world's fashion capitals and has cultural and artistic treasures that rival those of Florence and Rome.

2 **Bergamo, Pavia, Cremona, and Mantua.** South of Milan are the walled cities where Renaissance dukes built towering palaces and ornate churches. They sit on the Po Plain, one of Italy's wealthiest regions.

3 **Lake Garda.** Italy's largest lake measures 16 km (10 miles) across at its widest point and 50 km (31 miles) from end to end. It's more laid-back than the other lakes, and its waters and shores are a haven for outdoors enthusiasts.

4 **Lake Como.** This relatively narrow lake is probably the country's best-known and most charmingly populated body of water. You can almost always see across to the other side, which lends a great sense of intimacy. Lake Lecco, to the southeast, is actually a branch of Lake Como.

5 **Lake Maggiore.** It may be smaller than Lake Garda and less famous than Lake Como, but Lake Maggiore is impressively picturesque, with the Alps as a backdrop. One of the greatest pleasures here is exploring the lake's islands.

GETTING ORIENTED

In Lombardy, jagged mountains and deep glacial lakes stretch from the Swiss border down to Milan's outskirts, where they meet the flat, fertile plain that extends from the banks of the River Po. Lake Como is north of Milan, while Lake Maggiore is to the northwest and Lake Garda is to the east. Scattered across the plains to the south are the Renaissance city-states of Bergamo, Pavia, Cremona, and Mantua.

6

SWITZERLAND

A L P S

Chiavenna
36

Sondrio   Edolo
38
Morbegno
4
Lago Como
llagio

Lecco   Darfo-Boario   TRENTINO-
LOMBARDY   ALTO-ADIGE
42

342   Gargnano
Bergamo   *Lago d'Iseo*
A4   Gardone Riviera
A4   A4   510
11   Brescia   3
                                Lago Garda
11   235   Sirmione
415
Melegnano   Crema   *Oglio*   VENETO
A1   Lodi   A21
9   2   236
                River
                                Mantua
                10
me Po   Cremona

                River

0   20 mi
0   20 km

EMILIA-
ROMAGNA

EATING WELL IN MILAN, LOMBARDY, AND THE LAKES

Lombardy may well offer Italy's most varied, rich, and refined cuisine. Local cooking is influenced by the neighboring regions of the north; foreign conquerors have left their mark; and today well-traveled Milanese, business visitors, and industrious immigrants are likely to find more authentic ethnic cuisine in Milan than in any other Italian city.

Milan runs counter to many of the established Italian dining customs. A "real" traditional Milanese meal is a rarity; instead, Milan offers a variety of tastes, prices, and times of day, from expense-account elegance in fancy restaurants to abundant *aperitivo*-time nibbles. The city's cosmopolitan nature means trends arrive here first, and things move fast. Meals are not the drawn-out pastime they tend to be elsewhere in Italy. But food is still consistently good—competition among restaurants is fierce and the local clientele is demanding, which means you can be reasonably certain that if a place looks promising, it won't disappoint.

THE COTOLETTA QUESTION

Everyone has an opinion on *cotoletta (photo lower right)*, the breaded veal cutlet known across Italy as *una Milanese*.

It's clearly related to Austria's Wiener schnitzel, but did the Austrians introduce it when they dominated Milan or did they take it home when they left? Should it be with bone or without? Some think it's best with fresh tomato and arugula on top; others find this sacrilege.

Two things unite all camps: the meat must be well beaten until it's thin, and it must never leave a grease spot after it's fried.

REGIONAL SPECIALTIES

Ask an Italian what Lombards eat, and you're likely to hear *cotoletta, càsoeûla,* and *risotto giallo*—all dishes that reinforce Lombardy's status as the crossroads of Italy. *Cotoletta alla Milanese* may very well have Austrian roots. *Càsoeûla* is a cabbage-and-pork stew that resembles French cassoulet, though some say it has Spanish origins. *Risotto giallo* (also known as *Milanese*), *pictured at left,* is colorful and perfumed with exotic saffron. With no tomatoes, olive oil, or pasta, these dishes hardly sound Italian.

BUTTER AND CHEESE

Agricultural traditions and geography mean that animal products are more common here than in southern Italy—and that means butter and cream take olive oil's place. A rare point of agreement about cotoletta is that it's cooked in butter. The first and last steps of risotto-making—toasting the rice and letting it "repose" before serving—use ample amounts of butter. And the second-most-famous name in Italian cheese (after Parmesan) is likely Gorgonzola, named for a town near Milan. The best now comes from Novara.

RISOTTO

Rice is Lombardy's answer to pasta, and the region is the center of Italian (and European) rice production. From Milan's risotto giallo, with its costly

saffron tint, to Mantua's risotto with pumpkin or sausage, there's no end to the variety of rice dishes. Canonical risotto should be *all'onda,* or flow off the spoon like a wave. Keeping with the Italian tradition of nothing wasted, yesterday's risotto is flattened in a pan and fried in butter to produce *riso al salto,* which at its best has a crispy crust and a tender middle.

PANETTONE

Panettone, a tall, fluffy, sweet, yeast bread, is flavored with sweet candied fruit, *pictured below left.* Invented in Milan, it graces nearly every table during the Christmas holiday. It's now so ubiquitous that its price is used as an economic indicator: is it up or down, compared to last year? Consumption begins on December 7, Milan's patron saint's day, and goes until supplies run out at January's end.

WINE

Lombardy isn't one of Italy's most heralded wine regions, but the Valtellina area to the northeast of Milan produces two notable reds from the nebbiolo grape: Valtellina Superiore and the intense dessert wine Sforzato di Valtellina. The Franciacorta region around Brescia makes highly regarded sparkling wines. Lake breezes bring crisp, smooth whites from the shores around Lake Garda.

Updated by
Liz Humphreys

Lombardy is one of Italy's most dynamic regions—offering everything from world-class ski slopes to luxurious summer lake resorts. Milan is the pulse of the nation—commercial, fashionable, and forward-looking. The great Renaissance cities of the Po Plain—Pavia, Cremona, and Mantua—offer the romantic Italian characteristics visitors dream about, embracing their past by preserving national treasures while ever keeping an eye on the present. Topping any list of the region's attractions are the glacial lakes. Above them stand the Alps, which have been praised as the closest thing to paradise by writers throughout the ages, from Virgil to Hemingway.

Millions of travelers have concurred: for sheer beauty, the lakes of northern Italy—Como, Maggiore, Garda, and Orta—have few equals. Along their shores are 18th- and 19th-century villas, exotic formal gardens, sleepy villages, and dozens of Belle Époque–era resorts that were once Europe's most fashionable, and that still retain a powerful allure.

Milan can be disappointingly modern and congested—a little too much like the place you've come to Italy to escape—but its historic buildings and art collections in many ways rival those of Florence and Rome. And if you love to shop, Milan is one of the world's great fashion centers, and offers experiences and goods for every taste, from Corso Buenos Aires, which has a higher ratio of stores per square foot than anywhere else in Europe, to the edgy street style of Corso di Porta Ticinese and upscale Via Montenapoleone, where there's no limit on what you can spend. Milan is home to global fashion giants such as Armani, Prada, Versace, Salvatore Ferragamo, and Ermenegildo Zegna; behind them stands a host of less famous designers who help fill all those fabulous shops.

MILAN, LOMBARDY, AND THE LAKES PLANNER

MAKING THE MOST OF YOUR TIME

Italy's commercial hub isn't usually at the top of the list for visiting tourists, but Milan is the nation's most modern city, with its own sophisticated appeal: its fashionable shops rival those of New York and Paris, its soccer teams are Italy's answer to the Yankees and the Mets, its opera performances set the standard for the world, and its art treasures are well worth the visit.

The biggest draw in the region, though, is the Lake District. Throughout history, the magnificently beautiful lakes of Como, Garda, Maggiore, and Orta have attracted their fair share of well-known faces—from Winston Churchill and Russian royalty to George Clooney and Madonna. Each lake town has its own history and distinct character. If you have limited time, visit the lake you think best suits your style, but if you have time to spare, make the rounds to two or three to get a sense of their contrasts.

GETTING HERE AND AROUND

AIR TRAVEL

The region's main international gateway airport is Aeroporto Malpensa (☎ 02/232323 ⊕ *www.milanomalpensa-airport.com*), 48 km (30 miles) northwest of Milan. Some international and domestic flights also fly into more central Aeroporto Linate (☎ 02/232323 ⊕ *www.milano-linate-airport.com*), 7 km (4 miles) east of Milan, while European low-cost carriers like Ryanair use Aeroporto Milano Bergamo Orio al Serio (☎ 035/326323 ⊕ *www.orioaeroporto.it*), 55 km (34 miles) northeast of Milan and 5 km (3 miles) south of Bergamo.

BOAT TRAVEL

Frequent daily ferry and hydrofoil services link the lakeside towns and villages. Residents take them to get to work and school, while visitors use them for exploring the area. There are also special round-trip excursions, some with (optional) dining service on board.

Navigazione Laghi. Schedules and ticket price are available on the website and are posted at the landing docks. ☎ *800/551801 within Italy* ⊕ *www.navigazionelaghi.it*.

BUS TRAVEL

Bus service isn't the best way to travel between cities here, because trains are faster, cheaper, and more convenient. There's also regular bus service for reaching and traveling between the small towns on the lakes. It's less convenient than going by boat or by car, and it's used primarily by locals (particularly schoolchildren), but sightseers can use it as well. The bus service around Lake Garda serves mostly towns on the western shore.

Arriva Italia. This network of buses runs in Como, Bergamo, and Cremona. ☎ *02/34534110* ⊕ *www.arriva.it*.

Autostradale. Autostradale goes to airports Linate, Malpensa, and Bergamo's Orio al Serio from the central train station, and to Turin from its hub at Lampugnano (red line metro), northwest of Milan's city

6

center. There are also bus services from Milan to resort towns like St. Moritz and Cortina. Reservations are required. ☎ *02/33910794* ⊕ *www.autostradale.it.*

CAR TRAVEL

Getting almost anywhere by car is a snap, as several major highways intersect at Milan, all connected by the *tangenziale,* the city's ring road. The A4 autostrade runs west to Turin and east to Venice; A1 leads south to Bologna, Florence, and Rome; A7 angles southwest down to Genoa. A8 goes northwest toward Lake Maggiore, and A9 north runs past Lake Como and into Switzerland's southernmost tip.

To get around the lakes themselves by car, you have to follow secondary roads. S572 follows the southern and western shores of Lake Garda, SS45b edges the northernmost section of the western shore, and S249 runs along the eastern shore. Around Lake Como, follow S340 along the western shore, S36 on the eastern shore, and S583 on the lower arms. S33 and S34 trace the western shore of Lake Maggiore. Although the roads around the lake can be beautiful, they're full of harrowing twists and turns, making for a slow, challenging drive—often with an Italian speed racer on your tail.

ACI. Your car-rental company should be your first resource if you have a problem while driving in Italy, but it's also good to know that the ACI, the Italian auto club, offers 24-hour roadside assistance (free for members, for a fee for nonmembers). Regularly spaced roadside service phones are available on the autostrade. ☎ *803/116, 800/116800 (international toll-free number)* ⊕ *www.aci.it.*

TRAIN TRAVEL

Milan's majestic Central Station (Milano Centrale), 3 km (2 miles) northwest of the Duomo, has frequent service within the region to Como, Bergamo, Brescia, Sirmione, Pavia, Cremona, and Mantua. There are plenty of signs to help you get around, but its sheer size requires considerable walking and patience, so allow for some extra time here.

For general information on trains and schedules, as well as online ticket purchases, visit the website of the Italian national railway, **FS** (⊕ *www. trenitalia.com*).

Tickets bought without a reservation need to be validated by stamping them in yellow machines on the train platforms. Tickets with reservations don't require validation. When in doubt, validate—it can't hurt.

RESTAURANTS

Prices in the reviews are the average cost of a main course at dinner or, if dinner is not served, at lunch.

HOTELS

Given that this is the wealthiest part of Italy, most hotels here cater to a clientele willing to pay for extra comfort. Outside Milan, many are converted villas with well-landscaped grounds. Most of the famous lake resorts are expensive; many smaller lakeside hotels are more reasonably priced. Local tourism offices throughout the region are an excellent source of information about affordable lodging.

Please note the time for "high season" can vary here—in the lakes it's at the height of summer, not surprisingly, but in Milan it depends on what fairs and exhibitions are being staged. Prices in almost all hotels can go up dramatically during the Furniture Fair in early April. Fashion, travel, and tech fairs also draw big crowds throughout the year, raising prices. In contrast to other cities in Italy, however, you can often find discounts on weekends. The three lakes—Maggiore, Garda, and Como—have little to offer except quiet from November to March, when most gardens, hotels, and restaurants are closed.

Hotel reviews have been shortened. For full information, visit Fodors. com.

WHAT IT COSTS				
	$	$$	$$$	$$$$
RESTAURANTS	under €15	€15–€24	€25–€35	over €35
HOTELS	under €125	€125–€200	€201–€300	over €300

Prices in the dining reviews are the average cost of a main course at dinner, or, if dinner is not served, at lunch. Prices in the reviews are the lowest cost of a standard double room in high season.

MILAN

Milan is Italy's business hub and crucible of chic. Between the Po's rich farms and the industrious mountain valleys, it's long been the country's capital of commerce, finance, fashion, and media. Rome may be bigger and have the political power, but Milan and the affluent north are what really make the country go. It's also Italy's transport hub, with the biggest international airport, the most rail connections, and the best subway system. Leonardo da Vinci's *Last Supper* and other great works of art are here, as well as a spectacular Gothic Duomo, the finest of its kind. Milan even reigns supreme where it really counts (in the minds of many Italians), routinely trouncing the rest of the nation with its two premier soccer teams.

And yet, Milan hasn't won the battle for hearts and minds when it comes to tourism. Most visitors prefer Tuscany's hills and Venice's canals to Milan's hectic efficiency and wealthy indifference, and it's no surprise that in a country of medieval hilltop villages and skilled artisans a city of grand boulevards and global corporations leaves visitors asking the real Italy to please stand up. They're right, of course: Milan is more European than Italian, a new buckle on an old boot, and although its old city can stand cobblestone for cobblestone against the best of them, seekers of Roman ruins and fairy-tale towns may pass. But Milan's secrets reveal themselves slowly to those who look. A side street conceals a garden complete with flamingos (Giardini Invernizzi, on Via dei Cappuccini, just off Corso Venezia), and a renowned 20th-century art collection hides modestly behind an unspectacular facade a block from Corso Buenos Aires (the Casa-Museo Boschi di Stefano). Visitors lured by the world-class shopping will appreciate Milan's European

6

sophistication while discovering unexpected facets of a country they may have only thought they knew.

Virtually every invader in European history—Gaul, Roman, Goth, Lombard, and Frank—as well as a long series of rulers from France, Spain, and Austria, took a turn at ruling the city. After being completely sacked by the Goths in AD 539 and by the Holy Roman Empire under Frederick Barbarossa in 1157, Milan became one of the first independent city-states of the Renaissance. Its heyday of self-rule proved comparatively brief. From 1277 until 1500 it was ruled first by the Visconti and then the Sforza dynasties. These families were known, justly or not, for a peculiarly aristocratic mixture of refinement, classical learning, and cruelty; much of the surviving grandeur of Gothic and Renaissance art and architecture is their doing. Be on the lookout in your wanderings for the Visconti family emblem—a viper, its jaws straining wide, devouring a child.

GETTING HERE AND AROUND

The city center is compact and walkable; trolleys and trams make it even more accessible, and the efficient Metropolitana (subway) and buses provide access to locations farther afield. Driving in Milan is difficult and parking a real pain, so a car is a liability. In addition, drivers within the second ring of streets (the *bastioni*) must pay a daily congestion charge on weekdays between 7:30 am and 7:30 pm (till 6 pm on Thursday). You can pay the charge at tobacconists, Banca Intesa Sanpaolo ATMs, or online at ⊕ *areac.atm-mi.it*; parking meters and parking garages in the area also include it in the cost.

BICYCLE TRAVEL

BikeMI. This innovative sharing system has more than 200 designated spots for picking up or dropping off a bicycle around the city. Weekly and daily rates for tourists are available. Buy your subscription online; the site has a map showing stations and availability. Keep in mind, though, that traffic makes biking in the city risky for inexperienced cyclists, and be careful not to get your tires caught on the tram tracks. ⊕ *www.bikemi.com.*

PUBLIC TRANSPORTATION

A standard public transit ticket costs €1.50 and is valid for a 90-minute trip on a subway, bus, or tram. An all-inclusive subway, bus, and tram pass costs €4.50 for 24 hours or €8.25 for 48 hours. Individual tickets and passes can be purchased from news vendors and tobacconists, and at ticket counters and ticket machines at larger stops. Another option is a *carnet* (€13.80), good for 10 tram or subway rides. Once you have your ticket or pass, either stamp it or insert it into the slots in station turnstiles or on poles inside trolleys and buses. (The electronic tickets won't function if they become bent or demagnetized. If you have a problem, contact a station manager, who can usually issue a new ticket.) Trains run from 6 am to 12:30 am.

ATM (*Azienda Trasporti Milanesi*). Milan's transit authority has information offices at the Duomo, Stazione Cadorna, Stazione Centrale, Garibaldi, Loreto, and Romolo stops. ⊕ *www.atm-mi.it/en.*

Radiobus. From 10 pm to 2 am, Radiobus will pick you up and drop you off anywhere in Milan for €3. Advance booking is recommended, starting at 1 pm for same-day travel. ☎ *02/48034803* ⊕ *www.atm-mi.it/en.*

TAXI TRAVEL

Taxi fares in Milan are higher than in American cities. A short ride can run about €15 during rush hour or during fashion week. Taxis wait at stands marked by an orange "Taxi" sign, or you can call one of the city's taxi companies.

Dispatchers may speak some English; they'll ask for the phone number you're calling from, and they'll tell you the number of your taxi and how long it'll take to arrive. If you're in a restaurant or bar, ask the staff to call a cab for you.

Taxi Contacts Amicotaxi ☎ *02/4000.* **Autonoleggio Pini.** For a nontaxi car service, contact Autonoleggio Pini. Most drivers and reservation staff speak English. ☎ *02/29400555* ⊕ *www.limousinepini.eu.* **Autoradiotaxi** ☎ *02/8585.* **Radiotaxi–Yellow Taxi** ☎ *02/6969.* **Taxiblu** ☎ *02/4040.*

TOURS

City Sightseeing Milano. Open-top double-decker buses provide hop-on, hop-off tours on three routes departing from Piazza Castello. An all-inclusive day pass costs €25. ☎ *02/867131* ⊕ *www.milano.city-sightseeing.it.*

VISITOR INFORMATION

Milan Tourism Office. The tourism office in Piazza Castello is the perfect place to begin your visit. There are excellent maps, booklets with museum descriptions, itineraries on a variety of themes, and a selection of brochures about smaller museums and cultural initiatives. Pick up a copy of the English-language monthly *Hello Milano* (⊕ *www.hellomilano.it*), which has a day-to-day schedule of events and a comprehensive map. The Autostradale bus operator, sightseeing companies, and a few theaters have desks in the tourism office where you can buy tickets.

There is also a location at the central railway station in front of platform 21 and in the Galleria Vittorio Emanuele. ⊠ *Piazza Castello 1, Castello Sforzesco* ☎ *02/77404343* ⊕ *www.visitamilano.it* ⊙ *Weekdays 9–6, Sat. 9–1:30 and 2–6, Sun. 9–1:30 and 2–5.*

EXPLORING

DUOMO

Milan's main streets radiate out from the massive Duomo, a late Gothic cathedral that was started in 1386. Heading north is the handsome Galleria Vittorio Emanuele, an enclosed shopping arcade that opens at one end to the world-famous opera house known as La Scala. Heading northeast from La Scala is Via Manzoni, which leads to the *Quadrilatero della moda,* or fashion district.

Heading northeast from the Duomo is the pedestrians-only street Corso Vittorio Emanuele. Northwest of the Duomo is Via Dante, at the top of which is the imposing outline of the Castello Sforzesco.

TOP ATTRACTIONS

Fodor's Choice ★ **Duomo.** This intricate Gothic structure has been fascinating and exasperating visitors and conquerors alike since it was begun by Galeazzo Visconti III (1351–1402), first duke of Milan, in 1386. Consecrated in the 15th or 16th century, it was not completed until just before the coronation of Napoleon as king of Italy in 1809. Whether you concur with travel writer H.V. Morton's 1964 assessment that the cathedral is "one of the mightiest Gothic buildings ever created," there is no denying that for sheer size and complexity it is unrivaled. It is the second-largest church in the world—the largest being St. Peter's in Rome—and its capacity is estimated to be 40,000. Usually it is empty, though, a sanctuary from the frenetic pace of life outside and the perfect place for solitary contemplation.

The building is adorned with 135 marble spires and 2,245 marble statues. The oldest part is the apse. Its three colossal bays of curving and counter-curving tracery, especially the bay adorning the exterior of the stained-glass windows, should not be missed. At the end of the southern transept down the right aisle lies the **tomb of Gian Giacomo Medici.** The tomb owes some of its design to Michelangelo but was executed by Leone Leoni (1509–90) and is generally considered to be his masterpiece; it dates from the 1560s. Directly ahead is the Duomo's most famous sculpture, the gruesome but anatomically instructive figure of San Bartolomeo (St. Bartholomew), who was flayed alive. As you enter the apse to admire those splendid windows, glance at the sacristy doors to the right and left of the altar. The lunette on the right dates to 1393 and was decorated by Hans von Fernach. The one on the left also dates to the 14th century and is ascribed jointly to Giacomo da Campione and Giovanni dei Grassi. Although air pollution drastically reduces the view on all but the rarest days, the roof is still worth a look: walk out the left (north) transept to the stairs and elevator. As you stand among the forest of marble pinnacles, remember that virtually every inch of this gargantuan edifice, including the roof itself, is decorated with precious white marble dragged from quarries near Lake Maggiore by Duke Visconti's team along a road laid fresh for the purpose and through the newly dredged canals. Audio guides can be rented inside the Duomo from March to December and at Duomo Point in Piazza Duomo (just behind the cathedral) all year long; a ticket allowing you to use your camera inside the cathedral costs €2 (included with audio guide purchase). Exhibits at the **Museo del Duomo** shed light on the cathedral's history and include some of the treasures removed from the exterior for preservation purposes. ✉ *Piazza del Duomo* ☎ *02/72023375* ⊕ *www. duomomilano.it* 🎫 *Stairs to roof €7, elevator €12. Museum €6.* ⊙ *Cathedral daily 7–6:40. Roof: mid-Sept.–mid-May, daily 9–6:30 (last entry at 6); mid-May–mid-Sept., Sun.–Thurs. 9–6:30, Fri. and Sat. 9 am–9:30 pm (last entry at 9). Museum Tues.–Sun. 10–6 (last entry at 4:50).* Ⓜ *Duomo.*

Fodor's Choice ★ **Galleria Vittorio Emanuele.** This spectacular, late-19th-century glass-top, Belle Époque, barrel-vaulted tunnel is essentially one of the planet's earliest and most select shopping malls, with upscale tenants that include Gucci, Tod's, and Louis Vuitton. This is the city's heart, midway between the Duomo and La Scala. It teems with life, inviting people-watching from the tables that spill from the bars and restaurants, where you can enjoy an overpriced coffee. Books, records, clothing, food, pens, pipes, hats, and jewelry are all for sale. Known as Milan's "parlor," the Galleria is often viewed as a barometer of the city's well-being. The historic, if somewhat overpriced and inconsistent, Savini restaurant hosts the beautiful and powerful of the city, just across from McDonald's. Even in poor weather the great glass dome above the octagonal center is a splendid sight. The paintings at the base of the dome represent Europe, Asia, Africa, and America. Those at the entrance arch are devoted to science, industry, art, and agriculture. And the floor mosaics are a vastly underrated source of pleasure, even if they are not to be taken too seriously. Be sure to follow tradition and spin your heels once or twice on the more "delicate" parts of the bull beneath your feet in the northern apse; the Milanese believe it brings good luck. ⊠ *Piazza del Duomo* Ⓜ *Duomo.*

QUICK BITES

Caffè Zucca. One thing has remained constant in the Galleria: the Caffè Zucca, known by the Milanese as Camparino. Its inlaid counter, mosaics, and wrought-iron fixtures have been welcoming tired shoppers since 1867. Enjoy a Campari or Zucca aperitif as well as the entire range of Italian coffees, served either in the Galleria or in an elegant upstairs room where lunch is also available. ⊠ *Galleria Vittorio Emanuele, Duomo* ⊕ *www.caffemiani.it.*

Pinacoteca Ambrosiana. Cardinal Federico Borromeo, one of Milan's native saints, founded this picture gallery in 1618 with the addition of his personal art collection to a bequest of books to Italy's first public library. More recent renovations have reunited the core works of the collection, including such treasures as Caravaggio's *Basket of Fruit* and Raphael's monumental preparatory drawing (known as a "cartoon") for *The School of Athens,* which hangs in the Vatican. In addition to works by Lombard artists are paintings by Botticelli, Luini, Titian, and Jan Brueghel. A wealth of charmingly idiosyncratic items on display include 18th-century scientific instruments and gloves worn by Napoléon at Waterloo. Access to the library, the Biblioteca Ambrosiana, is limited to researchers who apply for entrance tickets. ⊠ *Piazza Pio XI 2, Duomo* ☎ *02/806921* ⊕ *www.ambrosiana.it* ⤢ *€15* ☯ *Tues.–Sun. 10–6; last entrance at 5:15* Ⓜ *Duomo.*

Santa Maria Presso San Satiro. Just a few steps from the Duomo, this architectural gem was first built in 876 and later perfected by Bramante (1444–1514), demonstrating his command of proportion and perspective, keynotes of Renaissance architecture. Bramante tricks the eye with a famous optical illusion that makes a small interior seem extraordinarily spacious and airy, while accommodating a beloved 13th-century fresco. ⊠ *Via Torino 17–19, Duomo* ☎ *02/874683* ☯ *Weekdays 8:30–6, Sat. 3:30–7, Sun. 8:30–12:30 and 3:30–7* Ⓜ *Duomo; Tram 2, 3, 4, 12, 14, 19, 20, 24, or 27.*

6

WORTH NOTING

Battistero Paleocristiano/Baptistry of San Giovanni alle Fonti. More specifically known as the Baptistry of San Giovanni alle Fonti, this 4th-century baptistry is one of two that lie beneath the Duomo. Although opinion remains divided, it is widely believed to be where Ambrose, Milan's first bishop and patron saint, baptized Augustine. Tickets are available at the kiosk inside the cathedral and include a visit to the Duomo's museum. ⊠ *Piazza del Duomo, enter through Duomo* ☎ *02/72022656* ⊕ *www.duomomilano.it* 🎟 *€6* ☾ *Tues.–Sun. 10–6; last ticket sold at 4:50* Ⓜ *Duomo.*

Museo del Novecento. Ascend a Guggenheim-esque spiral walkway to reach the modern art collection at this petite yet jam-packed collection of Italian contemporary art adjacent to the Duomo. The museum highlights 20th-century Italian artists, including a strong showing of Futurist artists such as Boccioni and Severini and sculptures from Marini, along with a smattering of works by other European artists including Picasso, Braque, and Matisse. Admission price increases for special exhibitions, held several times a year. ⊠ *Via Marconi 1, Duomo* ☎ *02/88444061* ⊕ *www.museodelnovecento.org* 🎟 *€5; €10 during special exhibitions* ☾ *Mon. 2:30–7:30, Tues., Wed., Fri., and Sun. 9:30–7:30, Thurs. and Sat. 9:30–10:30* Ⓜ *Duomo.*

Fodor'sChoice ★ **Palazzo Reale.** This elaborately decorated former royal palace close to the Duomo, with painted ceilings and grand staircases, is almost worth a visit in itself, but it also functions as one of Milan's major art exhibition spaces, with a focus on modern artists. Recent exhibits have highlighted works by Chagall, Klimt, Warhol, Pollock, and Kandinsky. Check the website before you visit to see what's on; purchase tickets online in advance to save time in the queues, which are often long and chaotic. ⊠ *Piazza del Duomo 12, Duomo* ☎ *02/0202* ⊕ *www.artpalazzoreale.it* 🎟 *€12 for exhibitions* ☾ *Mon. 2:30–7:30, Tues., Wed., Fri., and Sun. 9:30–7:30, Thurs. and Sat. 9:30–10:30; ticket office closes 1 hr early* Ⓜ *Duomo.*

CASTELLO

Castello Sforzesco. Wandering the grounds of this tranquil castle and park near the center of Milan is a great respite from the often-hectic city, and the interesting museums inside are an added bonus. The castle's crypts and battlements, including a tunnel that emerges well into the Parco Sempione behind, can be visited via private tour from **Ad Artem** (☎ *02/6596937* ⊕ *www.adartem.it*) or **Opera d'Arte** (☎ *02/45487400* ⊕ *www.operadartemilano.it*).

For the serious student of Renaissance military engineering, the Castello must be something of a travesty, so often has it been remodeled or rebuilt since it was begun in 1450 by the *condottiere* (hired mercenary) who founded the city's second dynastic family, Francesco Sforza, fourth duke of Milan. Though today "mercenary" has a pejorative ring, during the Renaissance all Italy's great soldier-heroes were professionals hired by the cities and principalities they served. Of them—and there were thousands—Francesco Sforza (1401–66) is considered one of the greatest, most honest, and most organized. It is said he could remember the names not only of all his men but of their horses as well. His rule signaled the enlightened age of the Renaissance but preceded the next foreign rule by a scant 50 years.

Since the turn of the 20th century, the Castello has been the depository of several city-owned collections of Egyptian and other antiquities, musical instruments, arms and armor, decorative arts and textiles, prints and photographs (on consultation), paintings, and sculpture. Highlights include the **Sala delle Asse,** a frescoed room still sometimes attributed to Leonardo da Vinci (1452–1519), which, at the time of writing, is closed for restoration and scheduled to reopen sometime during 2015. Michelangelo's unfinished *Rondanini Pietà* is believed to be his last work—an astounding achievement for a man nearly 90, and a moving coda to his life. The *pinacoteca* (picture gallery) features 230 paintings from medieval times to the 18th century, including works by Antonello da Messina, Canaletto, Andrea Mantegna, and Bernardo Bellotto. The **Museo dei Mobili** (furniture museum), which traces the development of Italian furniture from the Middle Ages to current design, includes a delightful collection of Renaissance treasure chests made of exotic woods with tiny drawers and miniature architectural details. A single ticket purchased in the office in an inner courtyard admits visitors to these separate installations, which are dispersed around the castle's two immense courtyards. ⊠ *Piazza Castello, Castello* ☎ *02/88463700* ⊕ *www.milanocastello.it* 🎫 *Castle free. Museums €5 (free Tues. 2–5:30, Wed.–Fri. and weekends 4:30–5:30)* ☉ *Castle: Apr.–Oct, daily 7–7; Nov.–Mar., daily 7–6. Museums: Tues.–Sun. 9–5:30; last entry at 5* Ⓜ *Cadorna, Lanza, or Cairoli; Tram 1, 2, 4, 12, 14, or 19; Bus 18, 37, 50, 58, 61, or 94.*

SEMPIONE

Parco Sempione. Originally the gardens and parade grounds of the Castello Sforzesco, this open space was reorganized during the Napoleonic era, when the arena on its northeast side was constructed, and then turned into a park during the building boom at the end of the 19th century. It is still the lungs of the city's fashionable western neighborhoods, and the **Aquarium** still attracts Milan's schoolchildren (⊠ *Viale Gadio 2* ☎ *02/88445392* ⊕ *www.acquariocivicomilano.eu* 🎫 *€5* ☉ *Tues.–Sun. 9–1 and 2–5:30)* The park became a bit of a design showcase in 1933 with the construction of the Triennale.

Fiat Café offers outdoor dining in summer, along with a view of De Chirico's sculpture-filled fountain *Bagni Misteriosi* (Mysterious Baths). ⊠ *Sempione* ☉ *Oct.–Apr., daily 6:30–9; May, daily 6:30–10; June–Sept., daily 6:30–11:30* Ⓜ *Cairoli, Lanza, or Cadorna; Tram 1, 2, 4, 12, 14, 19, or 27; Bus 43, 57, 61, 70, or 94.*

Torre Branca. It is worth visiting Parco Sempione just to see the Torre Branca. Designed by the architect Gio Ponti (1891–1979), who was behind so many of the projects that made Milan the design capital that it is, this steel tower rises 330 feet over the Triennale. Take the elevator to get a nice view of the city, then have a drink at the glitzy Just Cavalli Café (daily; restaurant opens at 7 pm, club opens at 11 pm) at its base. ⊠ *Parco Sempione* ☎ *02/3314120* ⊕ *www.turismo.milano.it*

🖼 €5 ⊙ *Mid-May–mid-Sept., Tues., Thurs., and Fri., 3–7 and 8:30 to midnight, Wed. 10:30–12:30 and 3–7, and 8:30–midnight, weekends 10:30–2 and 2:30–7:30, and 8:30–midnight; mid-Sept.–mid-May, Wed. 10:30–12:30 and 4–6:30, Sat. 10:30–1, 3–6:30, and 8:30–midnight, Sun. 10:30–2 and 2:30–7. Closed during bad weather.* Ⓜ *Cadorna; Tram 1; Bus 61.*

BRERA

To the north of the Duomo lie the winding streets of this elegant neighborhood, once the city's bohemian quarter.

Fodor's Choice
★

Pinacoteca di Brera (*Brera Gallery*). The collection here is star-studded even by Italian standards. The entrance hall (Room I) displays 20th-century sculpture and painting, including Carlo Carrà's (1881–1966) confident, stylish response to the schools of Cubism and Surrealism. The museum has nearly 40 other rooms, arranged in chronological order—so pace yourself.

The somber, moving *Cristo Morto* (Dead Christ) by Mantegna dominates Room VI, with its sparse palette of umber and its foreshortened perspective. Mantegna's shocking, almost surgical precision tells of an all-too-human agony. It's one of Renaissance painting's most quietly wondrous achievements, finding an unsuspected middle ground between the excesses of conventional gore and beauty in representing the Passion's saddest moment.

Room XXIV offers two additional highlights of the gallery. Raphael's (1483–1520) *Sposalizio della Vergine* (Marriage of the Virgin) with its mathematical composition and precise, alternating colors, portrays the betrothal of Mary and Joseph. *La Vergine con il Bambino e Santi* (Madonna with Child and Saints), by Piero della Francesca (1420–92), is an altarpiece commissioned by Federico da Montefeltro (shown kneeling, in full armor, before the Virgin); it was intended for a church to house the duke's tomb. Room XXXVIII houses one of the most romantic paintings in Italian history. *Il Bacio* by Francesco Hayez (1791–1882) depicts a couple from the Middle Ages engaged in a passionate kiss. The painting was meant to portray the patriotic spirit of Italy's Unification and freedom from the Austro-Hungarian empire. ✉ *Via Brera 28, Brera* ☎ *02/72263264* ⊕ *www.brera.beniculturali. it* 🖼 *€10 general admision, €12 during special exhibitions* ⊙ *Tues.– Thurs. and weekends 8:30–7:15, Fri. 8:30–9:15; last admission 35 mins before closing* Ⓜ *Montenapoleone or Lanza; Tram 1, 4, 12, 14, or 27; Bus 61.*

Triennale Design Museum. In addition to honoring Italy's design talent, the Triennale also offers a regular series of exhibitions on design from around the world. A spectacular bridge entrance leads to the permanent collection, an exhibition space, and a stylish café (whose seating is an encyclopedia of design icons). The Triennale also manages the fascinating museum-studio of designer Achille Castiglioni, in nearby Piazza Castello (hour-long guided tours Tuesday to Friday at 10, 11, and noon, Thursday at 6:30, 7:30, and /8:30; €10. Call or email in advance to book a tour; ☎ *02/805–3606* ⊕ *www.achillecastiglioni.it*). ✉ *Via Alemagna 6, Brera* ☎ *02/724341* ⊕ *www.triennaledesignmuseum.it* 🖼 *€10*

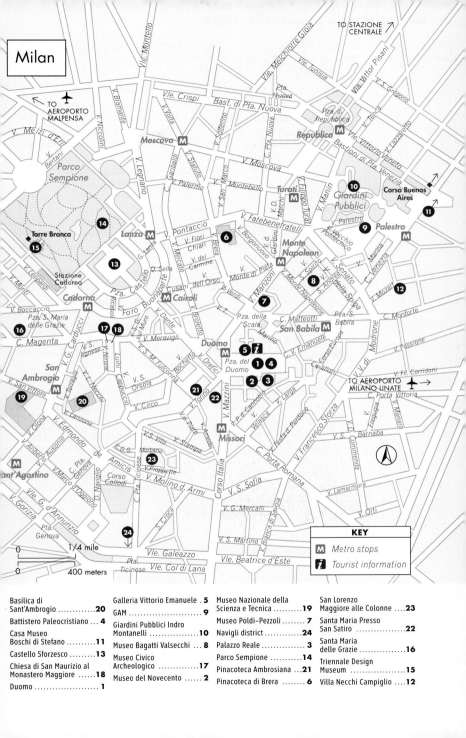

Milan

TO STAZIONE CENTRALE

TO AEROPORTO MALPENSA

Parco Sempione

Torre Branca

Stazione Cadorna

Moscova Ⓜ

Lanza Ⓜ

Cadorna Ⓜ

Pza. S. Maria delle Grazie

San Ambrogio Ⓜ

Sant'Agostino Ⓜ

Pta. Genova

Cairoli Ⓜ

Duomo

Pza. del Duomo

Pza. della Scala

Missori Ⓜ

Turati Ⓜ

Pza. d. Republica

Republica Ⓜ

Giardini Pubblici

Palestro Ⓜ

Corso Buenos Aires

Monte Napoleon

San Babila Ⓜ

TO AEROPORTO MILANO LINATE

KEY

Ⓜ Metro stops

ℹ Tourist information

1/4 mile

400 meters

⊘ *Tues.–Sun. 10:30–8:30, Thurs. 10:30 am–11 pm; last entrance 1 hr before closing* Ⓜ *Cadorna; Bus 61.*

QUADRILATERO

Via Manzoni, which lies northeast of La Scala, leads to Milan's Quadrilatero della moda, or fashion district.

Museo Bagatti Valsecchi. Glimpse the lives of 19th-century Milanese aristocrats with a visit to this lovely historic house-museum, once the home of two brothers, Barons Fausto and Giuseppe Bagatti. Family members inhabited the house until 1974; it opened to the public as a museum in 1984. The house is decorated with the brothers' fascinating collection of 15th- and 16th-century Renaissance art, furnishings, and objects, including armor, musical instruments, and textiles. The detailed audio guide included with admission provides a thorough insight into the history of the artworks and intriguing stories of the family itself. ⊠ *Via Gesu 5, Quadrilatero* ☎ *02/76006132* ⊕ *www. museobagattivalsecchi.org* ⌦ *€9 (€6 on Wed.)* ⊘ *Tues.–Sun. 1–5:45* Ⓜ *Montenapoleone; Tram 1.*

Museo Poldi-Pezzoli. This exceptional museum, opened in 1881, was once a private residence and collection, and contains not only pedigreed paintings but also porcelain, textiles, and a cabinet with scenes from Dante's life. The gem is undoubtedly the *Portrait of a Lady* by Antonio Pollaiuolo (1431–98), one of the city's most prized treasures and the source of the museum's logo. The collection includes masterpieces by Botticelli (1445–1510), Andrea Mantegna (1431–1506), Giovanni Bellini (1430–1516), and Fra Filippo Lippi (1406–69). Private guided tours are available by reservation. ⊠ *Via Manzoni 12, Quadrilatero* ☎ *02/794889* ⊕ *www.museopoldipezzoli.it* ⌦ *€9* ⊘ *Wed.–Mon. 10–6; last entrance at 5:30* Ⓜ *Montenapoleone or Duomo; Tram 1.*

BUENOS AIRES

Casa-Museo Boschi di Stefano (*Boschi di Stefano House and Museum*). To most people, Italian art means Renaissance art. But the 20th century in Italy was also productive, if less well-known as a time of artistic achievement. An apartment on the second floor of a stunning Art Deco building designed by Milan architect Portaluppi houses this collection, which was donated to the city of Milan in 2003 and is a tribute to the enlightened private collectors who replaced popes and nobles as Italian patrons. The walls are lined with the works of postwar greats, such as Fontana, De Chirico, and Morandi. Along with the art, the museum holds distinctive postwar furniture and stunning Murano glass chandeliers. ⊠ *Via Jan 15, Buenos Aires* ☎ *02/20240568* ⊕ *www. fondazioneboschidistefano.it* ⌦ *Free* ⊘ *Tues.–Sun. 10–6; last entry at 5:30* Ⓜ *Lima; Tram 33; Bus 60.*

PALESTRO

GAM: Galleria d'Arte Moderna/Villa Reale. One of the city's most beautiful buildings is an outstanding example of Neoclassical architecture, built between 1790 and 1796 as a residence for a member of the Belgioioso family. It later became known as the Villa Reale (royal) when it was donated to Napoleon, who lived here briefly with Empress Josephine. Its origins as a residence are reflected in the elegance of its proportions and its private garden. The museum provides a unique glimpse of the splendors hiding behind Milan's discreet and often stern facades.

The collection derives from private donations from Milan's hereditary and commercial aristocracies and includes the collection left by prominent painter and sculptor Marino Marini. The immense *Quarto Stato* (*Fourth Estate*) is at the top of the grand staircase. Completed in 1901 by Pellizza da Volpedo, this painting of striking workers is an icon of 20th-century Italian art and labor history, and as such it has been satirized almost as much as the *Mona Lisa.* ⊠ *Via Palestro 16, Palestro* ☎ *02/88445947* ⊕ *www.gam-milano.com* ✉ *€5 (free Wed.–Sun. after 4:30 and Tues. after 2)* ⊗ *Tues.–Sun. 9–5:30; last entry 30 min before closing* Ⓜ *Palestro or Turati; Tram 1 or 2; Bus 94 or 61.*

Villa Necchi Campiglio. In 1932, architect Piero Portaluppi designed this sprawling estate in an Art Deco style, with inspiration coming from the decadent cruise ships of the 1920s. Once owned by the Necchi Campiglio industrial family, the tasteful and elegant home—which sits on one of Milan's most exclusive streets, Via Mozart—is a reminder of the refined, modern culture of the nouveau riche who accrued financial power in Milan during that era. The 2009 film *I Am Love,* directed by Luca Guadagnino and starring Tilda Swinton, was mostly set in Villa Necchi. Tickets can be purchased at the ticket counter on the estate grounds. There is also a well-regarded restaurant-café on the grounds that is open for lunch. ■TIP➡ **Tours of the estate run about every 30 minutes and include English-speaking guides if needed.** ⊠ *Via Mozart 14, Palestro* ☎ *02/76340121* ⊕ *www.casemuseo.it* ✉ *€9* ⊗ *Wed.–Sun. 10–6; last entrance at 5:30* Ⓜ *Palestro, San Babila, or Montenapoleone; Bus 54, 61, or 94.*

SANT'AMBROGIO

If the part of the city to the north of the Duomo is dominated by its shops, Sant'Ambrogio and other parts to the south are known for their works of art. The most famous is *Il Cenacolo*—known in English as *The Last Supper.* If you have time for nothing else, make sure you see this masterpiece. You will need reservations to see this fresco, which is housed in the refectory of Santa Maria delle Grazie. Make these at least three weeks before you depart for Italy, so you can plan the rest of your time in Milan.

TOP ATTRACTIONS

Basilica di Sant'Ambrogio (*Basilica of Saint Ambrose*). Milan's bishop, Saint Ambrose (one of the original Doctors of the Catholic Church), consecrated this church in AD 387. Saint Ambroeus, as he is known in Milanese dialect, is the city's patron saint, and his remains—dressed in elegant religious robes, a miter, and gloves—can be viewed inside a glass case in the crypt below the altar. Until the construction of the more imposing Duomo, this was Milan's most important church. Much restored and reworked over the centuries (the gold-and-gem-encrusted altar dates from the 9th century), Sant'Ambrogio retains its Romanesque characteristics (5th-century mosaics may be seen for €2). The church is often closed for weddings on Saturday. ⊠ *Piazza Sant'Ambrogio 15*

02/86450895 ⊕ www.basilicasantambrogio.it ⊙ Mon.–Sat. 10–noon and 2:30–6, Sun. 3–5 M *Sant'Ambrogio; Bus 50, 58, or 94.*

QUICK BITES

Bar Magenta. Open since 1907, Bar Magenta maintains its old-school charm with its vintage Campari and Moretti beer posters and its quintessential Milanese clientele. The bar overflows at night, when teenagers virtually block the sidewalk and traffic. Beyond coffee at all hours, lunch, and beer, the real attraction is its mix of old and new, working-class, trendy, and aristocratic. ⊠ *Via Carducci 13, at Corso Magenta, Sant'Ambrogio* *02/8053808 ⊕ barmagenta.jimdo.com* M *Sant'Ambrogio or Cadorna.*

Fodor's Choice
★

Santa Maria delle Grazie. Leonardo da Vinci's *The Last Supper,* housed in this church and former Dominican monastery, has had an almost unbelievable history of bad luck and neglect—its near destruction in an American bombing raid in August 1943 was only the latest chapter in a series of misadventures, including, if one 19th-century source is to be believed, being whitewashed over by monks. Well-meant but disastrous attempts at restoration have done little to rectify the problem of the work's placement: it was executed on a wall unusually vulnerable to climatic dampness. Yet Leonardo chose to work slowly and patiently in oil pigments—which demand dry plaster—instead of proceeding hastily on wet plaster according to the conventional fresco technique. After years of restorers patiently shifting from one square centimeter to another, Leonardo's masterpiece is now free of centuries of retouching, grime, and dust. Astonishing clarity and luminosity have been regained.

Despite Leonardo's carefully preserved preparatory sketches, in which the apostles are clearly labeled by name, there still remains some small debate about a few identities in the final arrangement. But there can be no mistaking Judas, small and dark, his hand calmly reaching forward to the bread, isolated from the terrible confusion that has taken the hearts of the others. One critic, Frederick Hartt, offers an elegantly terse explanation for why the composition works: it combines "dramatic confusion" with "mathematical order." Certainly, the amazingly skillful and unobtrusive repetition of threes—in the windows, in the grouping of the figures, and in their placement—adds a mystical aspect to what at first seems simply the perfect observation of spontaneous human gesture.

Reservations are required to view the work. Viewings are in 15-minute, timed slots, and visitors must arrive 15 minutes before their assigned time in order not to lose their place. Reservations can be made by phone or through the website; it is worthwhile to call, as tickets are set aside for phone reservations. Call at least three weeks ahead if you want a Saturday slot, two weeks for a weekday slot. The telephone reservation office is open 8 am to 6:30 pm Monday to Saturday. Operators do speak English, though not fluently, and to reach one you must wait for the Italian introduction to finish and then press "2." However, you can sometimes get tickets from one day to the next. Some city bus tours include a visit in their regular circuit, which may be a good option. Guided tours in English are available for €3.50 and also require a reservation.

The painting was executed in what was the order's refectory, which is now referred to as the **Cenacolo Vinciano.** Take a moment to visit Santa Maria delle Grazie itself. It's a handsome, completely restored church, with a fine dome, which Bramante added along with a cloister about the time that Leonardo was commissioned to paint *The Last Supper.* ✉ *Piazza Santa Maria delle Grazie 2, off Corso Magenta, Sant'Ambrogio* ☎ *02/4987588 for Last Supper info, 02/92800360 for reservations, 02/4676111 for church* ⊕ *www.cenacolovinciano.net, www.grazieop. it* ✆ *Last Supper €6.50, plus €1.50 reservation fee; church free* ☉ *Last Supper Tues.–Sun. 8:15–6:45. Church: weekdays 7–noon and 3–7:30, Sun. 7:30–12:30 and 3:30–9* Ⓜ *Cadorna or Conciliazione; Tram 18.*

WORTH NOTING

Chiesa di San Maurizio al Monastero Maggiore. Next to the Museo Civico Archeologico, you'll find this little gem of a church, constructed starting in 1503 and decorated almost completely with magnificent 16th-century frescoes. The modest exterior belies the treasures inside, including a concealed backroom once used by nuns that includes a fascinating fresco of Noah loading the ark with animals, including two unicorns. ✉ *Corso Magenta 15, Sant'Ambrogio* ☎ *02/20404175* ☉ *Tues.–Sat. 9:30–5:30* Ⓜ *Cadorna or Cairoli; Tram 16 or 27; Bus 50, 58, or 94.*

Museo Civico Archeologico (*Municipal Archaeological Museum*). Appropriately situated in the heart of Roman Milan, this museum housed in a former monastery displays everyday utensils, jewelry, silver plate, and several fine examples of mosaic pavement from Mediolanum, the ancient Roman name for Milan. The museum opens into a garden that is flanked by the square tower of the roman circus and the polygonal Ansperto tower, adorned with frescoes dating to the end of the 13th and 14th centuries, portraying St. Francis and other saints receiving the stigmata. ✉ *Corso Magenta 15, Sant'Ambrogio* ☎ *02/88445208* ⊕ *www.poliarcheo.it* ✆ *€5 (free Tues. after 2 and Wed.–Sun. after 4:30)* ☉ *Tues.–Sun. 9–5:30; last entry at 5* Ⓜ *Cadorna or Cairoli; Tram 16 or 27; Bus 50, 58, or 94.*

FAMILY   **Museo Nazionale della Scienza e Tecnica** (*National Museum of Science and Technology*). This converted cloister is best known for the collection of models based on Leonardo da Vinci's sketches (although these are not captioned in English, the labeling in many other exhibits is bilingual). On the ground level, in the hallway between the courtyards, is a room featuring interactive, moving models of the famous *vita aerea* (aerial screw) and *ala battente* (beating wing), thought to be forerunners of the modern helicopter and airplane, respectively. The museum also houses a varied collection of industrial artifacts including trains, a celebrated Italian-built submarine, and several reconstructed workshops including a watchmaker's, a lute maker's, and an antique pharmacy. Displays also illustrate papermaking and metal founding, which were fundamental to Milan's—and the world's—economic growth. There's a bookshop and a bar. ■ TIP→ **Avoid this museum on weekends. It's a popular spot for families, and there are long lines on those days.** ✉ *Via San Vittore 21, Sant'Ambrogio* ☎ *02/48555558* ⊕ *www.museoscienza.org* ✆ *€10* ☉ *Tues.–Fri. 9:30–5, weekends 9:30–6:30; last entrance 30 mins before closing* Ⓜ *Sant'Ambrogio; Bus 50, 58, or 94.*

6

PORTA VENEZIA

FAMILY   **Giardini Pubblici Indro Montanelli** (*Public Gardens Indro Montanelli*). Giuseppe Piermarini, architect of La Scala, laid out these gardens across Via Palestro from the Villa Reale in 1770. Designed as public pleasure gardens, today they still are popular with families who live in the city center. Generations of Milanese have taken pony rides and gone on the miniature train and merry-go-round. The park also contains a small planetarium and the **Museo Civico di Storia Naturale** (Municipal Natural History Museum). ⊠ *Corso Venezia 55, Porta Venezia* ☎ *02/88463337* ⊕ *www.assodidatticamuseale.it* ⚞ *Gardens free, museum €5 (free Tues. after 2 and Wed.–Sun. after 4:30)* ☉ *Gardens: Nov.–Feb., daily 6:30–8; Mar., Apr., and Oct., daily 6:30–9; May, daily 6:30–10; June–Sept., daily 6:30–11:30. Municipal Natural History Museum: Tues.–Sun. 9–5:30 (last entry at 5)* Ⓜ *Palestro; Tram 9, 29, or 30.*

NAVIGLI

Navigli District. In medieval times, a network of *navigli*, or canals, crisscrossed the city. Almost all have been covered over, but two—Naviglio Grande and Naviglio Pavese—are still navigable. Once a down-at-the-heels neighborhood, the Navigli district has undergone some gentrification over the past 20 years. Humble workshops have been replaced by boutiques, art galleries, cafés, bars, and restaurants, and at night the Navigli serves up a scene about as close as you will get to southern-style Italian street life in Milan. On weekend nights, it is difficult to walk among the youthful crowds thronging the narrow streets along the canals. Check out the antiques fair on the last Sunday of the month from 9 am to 6 pm. ■ TIP→ **During the summer months, be sure to put on some mosquito repellent.** ⊠ *South of Corso Porta Ticinese, Navigli* Ⓜ *Porta Genova; Tram 2, 3, 9, 14, 15, 29, or 30.*

TICINESE

San Lorenzo Maggiore alle Colonne. Sixteen ancient Roman columns line the front of this sanctuary; 4th-century paleo-Christian mosaics survive in the Cappella di Sant'Aquilino (Chapel of Saint Aquilinus). ⊠ *Corso di Porta Ticinese 39, Ticinese* ☎ *02/89404129* ⊕ *www.sanlorenzomaggiore.com* ⚞ *Mosaics €2* ☉ *Mon.–Sat. 7:30–6:45, Sun. 9–7* Ⓜ *Missori.*

WHERE TO EAT

DUOMO

$$$$ ✕ **Cracco.** Tasting menus are a good way to savor many of chef Carlo
MODERN ITALIAN   Cracco's delicate inventions at this crisply elegant restaurant, though an à la carte menu is also available. Specialties include Milanese classics revisited—Cracco's take on saffron risotto and cotoletta should not be missed. Delightful appetizers and desserts vary seasonally, but may include scampi cream with freshwater shrimp, a disk of "caramelized Russian salad," and mango cream with mint gelatin. Ⓢ *Average main: €44* ⊠ *Via Victor Hugo 4, Duomo* ☎ *02/876774* ⊕ *www.ristorantecracco.it* ⚞ *Reservations essential* ☉ *Closed Sun. Sept.–June,*

3 wks in Aug., and last wk in Dec. No lunch Sat. and Mon. Sept.–June. Ⓜ *Duomo.*

$$$
MODERN ITALIAN

✕ **Don Carlos.** One of the few restaurants open after La Scala lets out, Don Carlos, in the Grand Hotel et de Milan, is nothing like its indecisive operatic namesake (whose betrothed was stolen by his father). Flavors are bold, presentation is precise and full of flair, and the service is attentive. The walls are blanketed with sketches of the theater, and the low-key opera recordings are every bit as well chosen as the wine list, setting the perfect stage for discreet business negotiation or, better yet, refined romance. Ⓢ *Average main: €32* ✉ *Grand Hotel et de Milan, Via Manzoni 29, Duomo* ☎ *02/7234640* ⊕ *www.ristorantedoncarlos.it* ⌸ *Reservations essential* ⊘ *No lunch* Ⓜ *Montenapoleone; Tram 1 or 2.*

$$$
ITALIAN

✕ **Giacomo Arengario.** Join the businesspeople, ladies who lunch, and in-the-know tourists at this elegant restaurant with a glorious view of the Duomo atop the Museo del Novecento. To complement the vistas, renowned Milanese restaurateur Giacomo Bulleri offers up a mix of well-prepared seafood, pasta, and meat courses for lunch and dinner. The spaghetti with mussels and clams is studded with fresh seafood, while the sea bass baked in salt is always a winner, and the servers are happy to recommend pairings from the extensive wine list. Just make sure you request seating by the windows when you book, to gaze at some of the best views in town; otherwise, you may be relegated to the viewless back room. Ⓢ *Average main: €30* ✉ *Via Marconi 1, Duomo* ☎ *02/72093814* ⊕ *www.giacomoarengario.com* ⌸ *Reservations essential* Ⓜ *Duomo.*

$
VEGETARIAN

✕ **La Vecchia Latteria.** With only two small dining rooms, this family-owned lunch spot dishes out an impressive amount of vegetarian cuisine. Opened in 1951 by Giorgio's parents, La Vecchia Latteria (The Old Dairy) began life as a breakfast place, but transformed into a vegetarian restaurant when Giorgio's wife Teresa started introducing her Sicilian influence into the kitchen in the 1980s. Nestled on a small street just steps away from the Duomo, it offers an array of freshly prepared, in-season dishes, including *parmigiana di melanzane* (eggplant Parmesan), lasagna with Taleggio cheese, and *scamorza dolce* (sweet cheese made from Italian cows' milk). The menu changes daily; try the mixed plate, which offers a taste of eight different small dishes. To beat the lunch rush, arrive before 1 pm. Between the months of February and July, on Tuesday and Thursday nights, as well as occasional times throughout the year, the restaurant hosts an aperitivo called "Eppi Auar" ("Happy Hour") from 7 to 10 pm with live music and an all-you-can-eat buffet for €9. Ⓢ *Average main: €9* ✉ *6 Via dell'Unione, Duomo* ☎ *02/874401* ⊘ *Closed Sun. No dinner Mon., Wed., Fri., or Sat.* Ⓜ *Duomo or Missori.*

$
ECLECTIC

✕ **Rinascente Food & Restaurants.** The seventh floor of this famous Italian department store is a gourmet food market surrounded by several small restaurants that can be a good option for lunch, an aperitivo overlooking the Duomo, or dinner after a long day of shopping. There are several places to eat, including the popular mozzarella bar Obica, My Sushi, De Santis for "slow food" sandwiches, and the sophisticated Maio restaurant. A terrace overlooking the Duomo is shared by three locations. You'd best get here early—it's popular, and there are often lines at mealtimes. $ *Average main: €10* ⊠ *Piazza del Duomo* ☎ *02/8852471* ⊕ *www.rinascente.it* Ⓜ *Duomo.*

BRERA

$$$
MODERN ITALIAN

✕ **Fioraio Bianchi Caffe.** A French-style bistro in the heart of Milan, Fioraio Bianchi Caffe was opened more than 40 years ago by Raimondo Bianchi, a great lover of flowers. In fact, eating at this restaurant is like dining in the middle of a boutique Parisian flower shop. It's a popular haunt for local glitterati, and despite the French atmosphere, many dishes like chestnut tortiglioni pasta with lamb ragu and chanterelles and Piancenza-style baccala with polentina ensure a classy, inventive Italian meal. Reservations recommended. $ *Average main: €28* ⊠ *Via Montebello 7, Brera* ☎ *02/29014390* ⊕ *www.fioraiobianchicaffe.it* ⊗ *Closed Sun., and 3 wks in Aug.* Ⓜ *Turati.*

QUADRILATERO

$
MODERN ITALIAN

✕ **Chic & Go Milano.** Step into these chic and trendy surroundings for a quick sandwich as exquisite as the fashion found in the nearby shops. Though the lobster panini will run you a cool €14, other top-notch ingredients like Angus tartare, crab, salmon, prosciutto, and mozzarella di bufala are not bad value considering the designer labels that abound in the neighborhood. $ *Average main: €8* ⊠ *Via Montenapoleone 25, Quadrilatero* ☎ *02/782648, 02/43986187* ⊕ *www.chic-and-go.com* Ⓜ *Montenapoleone; Tram 1.*

$$
ITALIAN

✕ **Paper Moon.** This cross between a neighborhood restaurant and a celebrity hangout is hidden behind Via Montenapoleone and thus handy to the restaurant-scarce Quadrilatero. Clients include families from this well-heeled area, professionals, football players, and television stars. What the menu lacks in originality it makes up for in reliable consistency—pizza and cotoletta, to name just two. Like any Italian restaurant, it's not child-friendly in the American sense—no high chairs or children's menu—but children will find food they like. It's open until midnight. $ *Average main: €15* ⊠ *Via Bagutta 1, Quadrilatero* ☎ *02/76022297* ⊕ *www.papermoonmilano.com* ⊗ *Closed Sun., and 1 wk in Aug.* Ⓜ *San Babila.*

CINQUE GIORNATE

$$$
ITALIAN

✕ **Da Giacomo.** The fashion and publishing crowd, as well as international bankers and businesspeople, favor this Tuscan-Ligurian restaurant. The emphasis is on fish; even the warm slice of pizza served while you study the menu has seafood on it. The specialty, *gnocchi Da Giacomo,* has a savory seafood-and-tomato sauce. Service is friendly and efficient; the wine list broad; and the most celebrated dish on the dessert cart is the *bomba Da Giacomo,* a savory mountain of Chantilly cream, mascarpone, and strawberries. With its tile floor and bank of fresh seafood, the place has a refined neighborhood-bistro style. $ *Average main: €25* ⊠ *Via P. Sottocorno 6, entrance in Via Cellini, Cinque Giornate* ☎ *02/76023313* ⊕ *www.giacomoristorante.com* ⌦ *Reservations essential* Ⓜ *Tram 9, 12, 23, or 27; Bus 60 or 73.*

GARIBALDI

$$$
CONTEMPORARY
Fodor'sChoice
★

× **Ceresio 7 Pools & Restaurant.** Book well in advance for one of Milan's most fashionable eateries, where the tables are lacquered red and modern artwork crowds the walls—exactly what you'd expect from the twin brothers Dean and Dan Caten behind the fashion label Dsquared2. The food cred matches the scene, with sophisticated dishes pairing luxe ingredients like Catalan lobster salad with Carmagnola peppers and marinated salmon with foie gras. Creative pastas may include cream of squash ravioli with curry and bufala mozzarella, while elegant meat and seafood mains like wild sea bass with potato, mushrooms, and fennel seeds won't disappoint. When the weather's warm, people-watch while enjoying drinks and aperitivo on the expansive terrace alongside two swimming pools and a fabulous skyline view. $ Average main: €32 ⊠ Via Ceresio 7, Garibaldi ☎ 02/31039221 ⊕ www.ceresio7.com ⌂ Reservations essential Ⓜ Garibaldi; Tram 2, 4, 12, or 14; Bus 37 or 190.

$
NORTHERN
ITALIAN

× **Osteria Vecchi Sapori.** Simple but savory fare and a menu that varies weekly characterize one osteria with two locations run by two brothers, Paolo and Roberto. Specialties include truffle tagliolini, and stuffed pasta, such as Gorgonzola-filled ravioli with walnut sauce, or pear and Parmesan tortelli with a saffron butter sauce. The extensive, meat-rich secondi are paired with creamy polenta *taragna* (made with cornmeal and buckwheat flour) or hand-cut fried potatoes. The dessert menu changes daily, with in-house cakes, sorbetto, and tiramisù reflecting traditional tastes and seasonal availability. $ Average main: €14 ⊠ Via Carmagnola 3, Garibaldi ☎ 02/6686148 ⊕ www.vecchisapori.it ⊗ No lunch weekends Ⓜ Garibaldi, Isola, or Gioia; Tram 2, 4, or 33; Bus 94.

$
PIZZA

× **Pizzeria Fabbrica.** This lively pizzeria has two wood-burning ovens going full-steam every day of the week. Skip the appetizers and go straight to the pizzas, which vary from traditional (*quattro stagioni*) to vegetable-based (with zucchini, spinach, rucola, and more) to in-house specialties like the *tartufona* (with truffle oil). The menu also offers antipasti, pasta like *pici* with fresh pecorino and pepper, and secondi. Save room for a worthy dessert like the *torta caprese al cioccolato* or tiramisù—though after pizza, you might want to share. The Fabbrica is large enough to handle groups; seek out a seat in the garden when the weather's nice. $ Average main: €9 ⊠ Viale Pasubio 2, Garibaldi ☎ 02/6552771 ⊕ www.lafabbricapizzeria.it ⊗ No lunch Sun. Ⓜ Garibaldi.

LORETO

$$
MILANESE

× **Da Abele.** If you love risotto, then make a beeline for this neighborhood trattoria. The superb risotto dishes change with the season, and every day there are three on the menu: one meat, one fish, and one vegetarian. It is tempting to try them all. The setting is relaxed, the service informal, the prices strikingly reasonable. Outside the touristy center of town but quite convenient by subway, this trattoria is invariably packed with locals. $ Average main: €15 ⊠ Via Temperanza 5, Loreto ☎ 02/2613855 ⊕ www.trattoriadaabele.it ⌂ Reservations essential ⊗ Closed Mon., Aug., and Dec. 24–Jan. 3. No lunch Ⓜ Pasteur.

6

PORTA ROMANA

$ ✕ **U Barba.** Simple, fresh, authentic Ligurian specialties (in the Ligurian dialect, its name means "the uncle") will take you back to lazy summer days on the Italian Riviera—even during Milan's wet winter weather. Such classic coastal specialties as *trofie al pesto* (an egg-free pasta served with pesto) and *cozze ripieni* (stuffed mussels), coupled with a basket of warm focaccia, reign supreme in this favorite of Milan's fashion crowd overlooking a lively bocce court. Ⓢ *Average main: €14* ⊠ *Via Pier Candido Decembrio 33, Porta Romana* ☎ *02/45487032* ⊕ *www.ubarba.it* ⟿ *Reservations essential* ⊗ *Closed Mon. No lunch Tues.–Fri.* Ⓜ *Lodi TIBB; Tram 16; Bus 90.*

NORTHERN ITALIAN

PORTA VENEZIA

$$$ ✕ **Joia.** At this haute-cuisine vegetarian haven near Piazza della Repubblica, delicious dishes—all without eggs and many without flour—are artistically prepared by chef Pietro Leemann. Vegetarians, who often get short shrift in Italy, will marvel at the variety of culinary offerings and artistry here. The ever-changing dishes here are presented in unusual formats: tiny glasses of creamed vegetables or ravioli in the shape of a human hand. For the best sampling of the creative foods on offer, try one of the interesting tasting menus: €75 for the five-course Discovery menu, €85 for the eight-course Emphasis on Nature, €110 for the 16-course Zenith, or, for a better deal, the €35 tasting menu at lunch. Ⓢ *Average main: €30* ⊠ *Via Panfilo Castaldi 18, Porta Venezia* ☎ *02/29522124* ⊕ *www.joia.it* ⟿ *Reservations essential* ⊗ *Closed Sun., 3 wks in Aug., and Dec. 24–Jan. 7. No lunch Sat.* Ⓜ *Repubblica or Porta Venezia; Tram 1, 5, 9, or 33.*

VEGETARIAN

$ ✕ **Pizza OK.** Thin-crust pizza is almost the only item on the menu at this family-run pizzeria with four locations, the oldest near Corso Buenos Aires in the Porta Venezia area. The pizza is extra thin and large, and possibilities for toppings seem endless. A good choice for families, this dining experience will be easy on your pocketbook. Other locations are on Via San Siro 9 in Corso Vercelli, Piazza Sempione 8, and Via Chiesa Rossa 109. Ⓢ *Average main: €7* ⊠ *Via Lambro 15, Porta Venezia* ☎ *02/29401272* ⊗ *Closed Aug. 7–20 and Dec. 24–Dec. 26* Ⓜ *Porta Venezia; Tram 5, 23, or 33.*

PIZZA

CAIROLI

$$$$ ✕ **ATMosfera.** Take a ride on Milan's 1930s-era trams, enjoy a tour of the city, and have a romantic dinner at the same time. With many cable cars out of service these days, ATMosfera shows that in Milan, old traditions die hard. Diners can choose between a meat, fish, and vegetarian four-course set menu, which varies throughout the year, and prices also include a bottle of wine, mineral water, and coffee. Dinner lasts about two hours, and visitors are asked to arrive at least 15 minutes prior to the 8 pm departure from Piazza Castello, at the corner of Via Beltrami; there's occasionally a second tram that leaves at 11. Due to limited space, reservations are mandatory through the website, by email, or by phone. Ⓢ *Average main: €70* ⊠ *Piazza Castello, Cairoli* ☎ *02/48607607 for reservations (weekdays 2–7)* ⊕ *atmosfera.atm.it*

MILANESE

⚓ *Reservations essential* ☉ *Closed Jan. 1–16* Ⓜ *Cairoli Castello; Tram 1 or 4; Bus 61.*

WHERE TO STAY

DUOMO

$$$$
HOTEL
🏨 **Grand Hotel et de Milan.** Only blocks from La Scala you'll find everything you hope for in a traditionally elegant European hotel; with ancient tapestries and persimmon velvet enlivening the 19th-century look without sacrificing dignity and luxury. **Pros:** traditional and elegant; great location off Milan's main shopping streets. **Cons:** gilt décor may not suit those who like more modern design; no spa. Ⓢ *Rooms from: €475* ✉ *Via Manzoni 29, Duomo* ☎ *02/723141* ⊕ *www.grandhoteletdemilan. it* ↗ *72 rooms, 23 suites* ⏐◯⏐ *No meals* Ⓜ *Montenapoleone.*

$$
HOTEL
🏨 **Hotel Canada.** Nice wood flooring, comfortable rooms, and contemporary furnishings that maximize space and bring in light all help recommend this conveniently located bargain in pricey Milan. **Pros:** central location; plentiful breakfast buffet; friendly and helpful staff. **Cons:** simple and somewhat dated décor; on busy street, so some rooms can be noisy. Ⓢ *Rooms from: €189* ✉ *Via Santa Sofia 16, Crocetta* ☎ *02/58304844* ⊕ *www.canadahotel.it* ↗ *37 rooms* ⏐◯⏐ *Breakfast* Ⓜ *Crocetta; Tram 3, 15, 16, or 24.*

$$
HOTEL
🏨 **Hotel Gran Duca di York.** These spare but classically elegant and efficient rooms are arranged around a courtyard—four have private terraces—and are very good value for pricey Milan. **Pros:** central; airy; updated and well-decorated rooms. **Cons:** rooms are simple, with many on the small side. Ⓢ *Rooms from: €172* ✉ *Via Moneta 1/a, Duomo* ☎ *02/874863* ⊕ *www.ducadiyork.com* ↗ *33 rooms* ☉ *Closed Aug.* ⏐◯⏐ *Breakfast* Ⓜ *Cordusio or Duomo; Tram 2, 12, 14, 16, or 27.*

$$$
HOTEL
🏨 **Hotel Spadari al Duomo.** The fact that this chic city center inn is owned by an architect's family shows in the details, including custom-designed furniture and paintings by young Milanese artists on rotating display in the stylish guest rooms. **Pros:** good breakfast; central location; attentive staff. **Cons:** no balconies; some rooms on the small side. Ⓢ *Rooms from: €250* ✉ *Via Spadari 11, Duomo* ☎ *02/72002371* ⊕ *www.spadarihotel. com* ↗ *40 rooms, 1 suite* ⏐◯⏐ *Breakfast* Ⓜ *Duomo; Tram 2, 3, 12, 14, 16, 24, or 27.*

$$
HOTEL
🏨 **Hotel Star.** The animal murals here may be a bit off-putting, but the price is extremely reasonable, the staff are helpful, and the rooms are well-equipped and comfortable. **Pros:** central; reasonably priced; breakfast is included. **Cons:** themed décor not to everyone's taste. Ⓢ *Rooms from: €160* ✉ *Via dei Bossi 5, Duomo* ☎ *02/801501* ⊕ *www.hotelstar. it* ↗ *30 rooms* ⏐◯⏐ *Breakfast.*

$$$$
HOTEL
Fodor's Choice
★
🏨 **Park Hyatt Milan.** Extensive use of warm travertine stone and modern art creates a sophisticated yet inviting and tranquil backdrop in these spacious and opulent guest rooms. **Pros:** central; contemporary; refined. **Cons:** not particularly intimate; very expensive. Ⓢ *Rooms from: €590* ✉ *Via Tommaso Grossi 1, Duomo* ☎ *02/88211234* ⊕ *milan.park.hyatt. com* ↗ *81 rooms, 25 suites* Ⓜ *Duomo; Tram 1.*

6

$$$$ HOTEL **UNA Maison Milano.** Inside this faithfully restored palazzo dating from the early 1900s, spaciousness is accentuated with soft white interiors, muted fabrics and marbles, and clean, contemporary lines. **Pros:** the warmth of a residence and the luxury of a design hotel; lovely bathrooms and other modern amenities. **Cons:** breakfast not included; pricey. [$] *Rooms from: €330* ✉ *Via Mazzini 4, Duomo* ☎ *02/85605* 🌐 *www.unamaisonmilano.it* 🛏 *15 rooms, 6 junior suites, 5 suites, 1 penthouse* 🍴 *No meals* [M] *Duomo; Tram 2, 3, 12, 14, 16, 24, or 27.*

'LET'S GO TO THE COLUMNS'

"Andiamo al Le Colonne" in Milanese youthspeak means to meet up at the sober Roman columns in front of the Basilica San Lorenzo Maggiore. Attracted to the Corso di Porta Ticinese by its bars and shops, hipsters spill out on the street to chat and drink. Neighbors may complain about the noise and confusion, but students and nighthawks find it indispensable for socializing at all hours. It's a street—no closing time.

QUADRILATERO

$$$$ HOTEL Fodor's Choice ★ **Armani Hotel Milano.** Located in Milan's fashion district, this minimalist boutique hotel looks like it has been plucked from the pages of a sleek shelter magazine. **Pros:** complimentary minibar (minus alcohol); lovely spa area and 24-hour gym; great location near major shopping streets. **Cons:** exclusive vibe not for everyone; incredibly expensive. [$] *Rooms from: €703* ✉ *Via Manzoni 31, Quadrilatero* ☎ *02/88838888* 🌐 *milan.armanihotels.com* 🛏 *63 rooms, 32 suites* 🍴 *No meals* [M] *Montenapoleone.*

$$$$ HOTEL **Four Seasons.** Built in the 15th century as a convent and surrounding a colonnaded cloister, this sophisticated retreat in the heart of Milan's upscale shopping district certainly exudes a feeling that is anything but urban. **Pros:** quiet, elegant setting that feels removed from noisy central Milan; friendly and helpful staff; wonderful restaurant. **Cons:** rooms feel a little bland; breakfast isn't included in the rate; all this refinement does not come cheap. [$] *Rooms from: €695* ✉ *Via Gesù 6–8, Quadrilatero* ☎ *02/77088* 🌐 *www.fourseasons.com/milan* 🛏 *68 rooms, 50 suites* 🍴 *No meals* [M] *Montenapoleone; Tram 1.*

SANT'AMBROGIO

$$$ HOTEL **Antica Locanda Leonardo.** Half the rooms in this 19th-century building face a courtyard and the others a back garden; many have balconies and one ground-floor room has a private garden with table and chairs. **Pros:** very quiet and homey; breakfast is ample. **Cons:** more like a bed-and-breakfast than a hotel; no minibars. [$] *Rooms from: €230* ✉ *Corso Magenta 78, Sant'Ambrogio* ☎ *02/48014197* 🌐 *www.anticalocandaleonardo.com* 🛏 *16 rooms* ⏲ *Closed 1st wk in Jan. and 3 wks in Aug.* 🍴 *Breakfast* [M] *Conciliazione, Sant'Ambrogio, or Cadorna; Tram 1, 16, 19, or 27.*

REPUBBLICA

$$ HOTEL **Hotel Casa Mia Milan.** Lying on the edge of Milan's Giardini Pubblici (Public Gardens), these simple rooms are easy to reach from the central train station (a few blocks away) and easy on the budget. **Pros:**

very good value; free Wi-Fi. **Cons:** borders a dodgy neighborhood of Milan; up a flight of stairs and no elevator; spartan décor. $ *Rooms from: €159* ✉ *Viale Vittorio Veneto 30, Repubblica* ☎ *02/6575249* ⊕ *www.casamiahotel.it* ↗ *15 rooms* ⦿*Breakfast* Ⓜ *Repubblica; Tram 1, 5, 9, 33.*

$$$$ ⌐ **Hotel Principe di Savoia Milano.** Milan's grande dame has all the trap-
HOTEL   pings of an exquisite traditional luxury hotel: lavish mirrors, drapes, and carpets, limousine services, and the city's largest guest rooms, out-fitted with eclectic fin-de-siècle furnishings. **Pros:** substantial spa–health club; close to Central Station. **Cons:** located in a not-very-central or attractive neighborhood; breakfast and other meals overly expen-sive. $ *Rooms from: €405* ✉ *Piazza della Repubblica 17* ☎ *02/62301* ⊕ *www.hotelprincipedisavoia.com* ↗ *257 rooms, 44 suites* ⦿*No meals* Ⓜ *Repubblica; Tram 1, 9, or 33.*

$$$$ ⌐ **Westin Palace.** Don't be fooled by the functional 1950s-era exterior
HOTEL   of Milan's premier business address: inside, many rooms have been renovated into a contemporary look with soothing gray walls and brown marble bathrooms, while the older rooms are furnished with Empire-style antiques. **Pros:** full-service hotel with extensive services; some freshly renovated rooms in a modern style. **Cons:** lacking in local character; not in the most central or attractive location; extra charge for Wi-Fi. $ *Rooms from: €395* ✉ *Piazza della Repubblica 20* ☎ *02/63361* ⊕ *www.westinpalacemilan.it* ↗ *197 rooms, 30 suites* ⦿*No meals* Ⓜ *Repubblica; Tram 1, 5, 9, or 33.*

TICINESE

$$$$ ⌐ **Hotel Magna Pars Suites Milano.** In the trendy Navigli canals area, this
HOTEL   ultrastylish all-suite boutique hotel in a former perfume factory boasts Italian-designed furniture and paintings from local Brera Academy art-ists; all rooms overlook one of two tranquil central courtyards, ensuring a quiet night's sleep. **Pros:** modern, design-y feel; attentive service; won-derful food at the attached restaurant. **Cons:** spa on the small side; a bit of a trek to central Milan attractions. $ *Rooms from: €379* ✉ *Via For-cella 6, Porta Ticinese* ☎ *02/8338371* ⊕ *www.magnapars-suitesmilano. it* ↗ *39 suites* ⦿*Breakfast* Ⓜ *Porta Genova; Tram 2, 9, or 19.*

$$$$ ⌐ **The Yard.** Knickknacks and memorabilia from sports including golf,
HOTEL   horseback riding, and boxing inspire the room decor in this electic and
Fodor's Choice   extremely hip hotel at the foot of the lively Corso di Porta Ticinese by
★   the Navigli canals—but even if you're not a sports fan, you'll appreci-ate this friendly boutique hotel's contemporary flair. **Pros:** extremely attractive and comfortable; interesting location near many restaurants and bars; ultrafriendly staff. **Cons:** Lacking some of the amenities of large hotels; about a half-hour hike from the Duomo and central Milan attractions. $ *Rooms from: €318* ✉ *Piazza XXIV Maggio 8, Porta Ticinese* ☎ *02/89415901* ⊕ *www.theyardmilano.com* ↗ *14 rooms* ⦿*Breakfast* Ⓜ *Tram 3 or 9.*

NIGHTLIFE AND PERFORMING ARTS

NIGHTLIFE

The *aperitivo,* or prelunch or predinner drink, is available everywhere in Italy, but in Milan it is a big part of life and a must-try. Milan bar owners have enriched the usual nibbles of olives, nuts, and chips with full finger (and often fork) buffets serving cubes of pizza and cheese, fried vegetables, rice salad, sushi, and even pasta, and they've baptized it "Appy Hour"—with the first "h" dropped and the second one pronounced. For the price of a drink (around €8), you can make a meal of hors d'oeuvres (though don't be greedy).

DUOMO

Bar STRAF. This architecturally stimulating but dimly lit atmosphere has such artistic features as recycled fiberglass panels and vintage 1970s furnishings. The music is an eclectic mix of chilling tunes during the daytime, with more upbeat and vibrant tracks pepping it up at night. Located on a quiet side street near the Duomo, STRAF draws a young and lively, if tourist-heavy, crowd. ⊠ *Via San Raffaele 3, Duomo* 🕾 *02/805081* ⊕ *www.straf.it* Ⓜ *Duomo.*

Café Trussardi. Open throughout the day, this is a great place for coffee and bumping into Milan's elite, who are entertained by video art on an enormous plasma screen. ⊠ *Piazza della Scala 5, Duomo* 🕾 *02/80688295* ⊕ *www.trussardi.it* Ⓜ *Tram 1.*

Fodor'sChoice
★
Peck Italian Bar. This foodie paradise near the Duomo with an enormous deli featuring Italian specialty foods also has a bar and restaurant that serves up traditional—and excellent—pastas, pizza slices, olives, toasted nuts, and a good selection of wines by the glass in a refined setting. ⊠ *Via Cesare Cantù 3, Duomo* 🕾 *02/8693017* ⊕ *www.peck.it* ⊘ *Closed Sun.* Ⓜ *Duomo; Tram 2, 12, 14, 16, or 27.*

BRERA

Bulgari Hotel Bar. Having drinks or a light lunch at the Bulgari Hotel Bar lets you step off the asphalt and into one of the city's most impressive, private urban gardens—even indoors you seem to be outside, separated from the elements by a spectacular wall of glass. This is a great place to run into international hotel guests and jet-setting Milanese, and the bar staff mixes up a wide range of traditional and invented drinks—including the Bulgari Cocktail with gin, Aperol, and orange, pineapple, and lime juices. ⊠ *Via Privata Fratelli Gabba 7/b, Brera* 🕾 *02/8058051* ⊕ *www.bulgarihotels.com* Ⓜ *Montenapoleone; Tram 1.*

Jamaica Bar. A traditional hangout for students from the nearby Brera art school, this bar pulses with life on summer nights, when street vendors and fortune-tellers jostle for space alongside the outdoor tables. ⊠ *Via Brera 32, Brera* 🕾 *02/876723* ⊕ *www.jamaicabar.it* Ⓜ *Lanza or Montenapoleone; Tram 1, 2, 4, 12, or 14.*

'N Ombra de Vin. This highly rated enoteca serves wine by the glass and, in addition to the plates of sausage and cheese nibbles, has light food and not-so-light desserts. It's a great place for people-watching on Via San Marco, while indoors offers a more dimly lit, romantic setting. Check out the impressive vaulted basement, where bottled wine and spirits are sold. ✉ *Via S. Marco 2, Brera* ☎ *02/6599650* ⊕ *www. nombradevin.it* Ⓜ *Lanza, Turati, or Montenapoleone; Tram 1, 2, 4, 12, or 14.*

QUADRILATERO

Armani/Lounge. The Lounge at the Armani Hotel Milano has kept Milan abuzz since its opening. A modern architectural marvel, it's got high ceilings, louvered windows, and expansive views of the city's rooftops. It's great for a relaxing after-work tea with friends or a predinner aperitivo. ✉ *Via Manzoni 31, Quadrilatero* ☎ *02/88838888* ⊕ *milan. armanihotels.com* Ⓜ *Montenapoleone; Tram 1.*

GARIBALDI

Blue Note. The first European branch of the famous New York nightclub features regular performances by some of the most famous names in jazz, as well as blues and rock concerts. Dinner is available, and there's a popular jazz brunch on Sunday. It's closed Monday. ✉ *Via Borsieri 37, Garibaldi* ☎ *02/69016888* ⊕ *www.bluenotemilano.com* Ⓜ *Isola; Tram 7, 31, or 33.*

Dry Cocktails & Pizza. The current hotspot for both classic and creative cocktails, this trendy industrial space has a pizza joint in the back if you get hungry. Reservations taken only for the restaurant between 7 and 9:30 pm. ✉ *Via Solferino 33, Garibaldi* ☎ *02/63793414* ⊕ *www. drymilano.it* Ⓜ *Moscova, Turati, or Repubblica; Tram 1, 9, or 33; Bus 37.*

NAVIGLI

Brellin Café. This popular spot in the arty Navigli district has live music. It serves late-night snacks as well as traditional Milanese dishes for lunch and dinner. ✉ *Vicolo dei Lavandai at Alzaia Naviglio Grande, Navigli* ☎ *02/58101351, 02/89402700* ⊕ *www.brellin.it* Ⓜ *Porta Genova; Tram 2 or 9.*

TICINESE

SHU. For a break from the traditional, check out this ultratrendy gleaming interior that looks like a cross between something from *Star Trek* and Cocteau's *Beauty and the Beast.* ✉ *Via Molino delle Armi, Ticinese* ☎ *02/58315720* Ⓜ *Tram 3 or 15; Bus 94.*

PORTA VIGENTINA

Magazzini Generali. What was once an abandoned warehouse is now a fun, futuristic venue for dancing. It also is a popular spot for fashion shows, and its concert schedule attracts well-known international acts. The cover charge includes a drink, and entrance is free on Wednesday. It's usually standing room–only for concerts. ✉ *Via Pietrasanta 16, Porta Vigentina* ☎ *02/5393948* ⊕ *www.magazzinigenerali.it* Ⓜ *Tram 24; Bus 79, 90, or 91.*

CORSO COMO

Tocqueville 13. Regular nightclub fare Thursday through Sunday is embellished with occasional live music, featuring young and emerging talent. ✉ *Via Alexis de Tocqueville 13, Corso Como* ☎ *3939527044* ⊕ *www.tocqueville13.club* ✆ *Closed Mon.–Wed.* Ⓜ *Porta Garibaldi.*

BEYOND THE CITY CENTER

Plastic. Its venerable age notwithstanding (it opened in 1980), this is still one of Milan's most avant-garde and fun clubs, complete with drag-queen shows. The action starts late, even by Italian standards—don't bother going before midnight. They don't take reservations, and there aren't any tables. Entrance on Sunday is free. ⊠ *Via Gargano 15, Beyond City Center* ☎ *02/733996* ☾ *Closed Mon.–Thurs.* Ⓜ *Tram 27; Bus 60, 62, 66, 73, or K511.*

PERFORMING ARTS

For events likely to be of interest to non–Italian speakers, see *Hello Milano* (⊕ *www.hellomilano.it*), a monthly magazine available online and in print at the tourist office in Piazza Duomo; *Easy Milano* (⊕ *www.easymilano.it*); or the *American* (⊕ *www.theamericanmag.com*), which has a thorough cultural calendar. The tourist office publishes the monthly *Milano Mese,* which also includes some listings in English.

MUSIC

Auditorium di Milano. This modern hall, known for its excellent acoustics, is home to the **Orchestra Verdi** and **Choir of Milano,** founded by the Milan-born conductor Richard Chailly. The season, which runs from September to June, includes many top international performers and rotating guest conductors. ⊠ *Largo Gustav Mahler Corso, San Gottardo 39, at Via Torricelli, Conchetta, Castello* ☎ *02/83389401* ⊕ *www.laverdi.org* Ⓜ *Tram 3 or 15, Bus 59 or 91.*

Conservatorio. The two halls belonging to the Conservatorio host some of the leading names in classical music. Series are organized by several organizations, including the venerable chamber music society the **Società del Quartetto** (☎ *02/76005500* ⊕ *www.quartettomilano.it*). ⊠ *Via del Conservatorio 12, Duomo* ☎ *02/762110* ⊕ *www.consmilano.it* Ⓜ *San Babila; Tram 9, 12, 23, or 27; Bus 60 or 73.*

Teatro Dal Verme. Frequent classical music concerts are staged here from October to May. ⊠ *Via San Giovanni sul Muro 2, Castello* ☎ *02/87905* ⊕ *www.dalverme.org* Ⓜ *Cairoli; Tram 1 or 4.*

OPERA

Fodor'sChoice
★

Teatro alla Scala. You need know nothing of opera to sense that La Scala is closer to a cathedral than an auditorium. Hearing opera sung in the magical setting of La Scala is an unparalleled experience. Here, Verdi established his reputation and Maria Callas sang her way into opera lore. It looms as a symbol—both for the performer who dreams of singing here and for the opera buff. Audiences are notoriously demanding and are apt to jeer performers who do not measure up.

If you are lucky enough to be here during the opera season, do whatever is necessary to attend. Tickets go on sale two months before the first performance and are usually sold out the same day. The season runs from December 7, the feast day of Milan patron Saint Ambrose, through June. For tickets, visit the **Biglietteria Centrale** (⊠ *Galleria del Sagrato, Piazza Del Duomo* ☾ *Daily noon–6*), which is in the Duomo subway station. Tickets are also available online or via La Scala's automated booking system (☎ *02/860775*). To pick up tickets for performances—from two hours prior until 15 minutes after the start of a performance—go to the box office at the theater, which is around the corner at Via Filodrammatici 2. Although you might not get seats for the more popular operas with big-name stars, it is worth trying; ballets are easier. There are also 140 tickets available on a first-come, first-served basis starting 2½ hours before the start of each performance at the box office. The theater is closed from the end of July through August and on national and local holidays.

At the **Museo Teatrale alla Scala** you can admire an extensive collection of librettos, paintings of the famous names of Italian opera, posters, costumes, antique instruments, and design sketches for the theater. It is also possible to take a look at the theater itself. Special exhibitions reflect current productions. ⊠ *Piazza della Scala, Largo Ghiringhelli 1, Duomo* ☎ *02/72003744 for theater, 02/88797473 for museum* ⊕ *www. teatroallascala.org* ✉ *Museum €7* ⊙ *Museum daily 9–12:30 and 1:30–5:30; last entry ½ hr prior to closing* Ⓜ *Duomo or Cordusio; Tram 1.*

6

SHOPPING

Milan is the birthplace of many of the world's most celebrated brands and high-ticket retail establishments: Prada, Versace, and Armani all call Milan home. The city has produced some of the industry's biggest talents, and reigns as one of the most important fashion capitals in the world. "Fashion tourists" come from cities like Shanghai, Moscow, and Tokyo to shop here.

Weekly open markets selling fruits and vegetables—and a great deal more—are still a regular sight in Milan. Many also sell clothing and shoes.

DUOMO

Borsalino. The kingpin of milliners, Borsalino has managed to stay trendy since it opened in 1857. ⊠ *Galleria Vittorio Emanuele II 92, Duomo* ☎ *02/89015436* ⊕ *www.borsalino.com* Ⓜ *Duomo; Tram 1.*

Gucci. This Florence-born brand attracts lots of fashion-forward tourists in hot pursuit of its monogrammed bags, shoes, and accessories. ⊠ *Galleria Vittorio Emanuele, Duomo* ☎ *02/8597991* ⊕ *www.gucci. com* Ⓜ *Duomo; Tram 1.*

La Rinascente. The flagship location of this always-bustling and very central department store—adjacent to both the Duomo and the Galleria Vittorio Emanuele—carries a wide range of Italian and international brands, both high-end and casual, for men, women, and children. There's also a fine selection of beauty and home products. ⊠ *Piazza del Duomo* ☎ *02/88521* ⊕ *www.rinascente.it* Ⓜ *Duomo; Tram 1, 2, 12, 14, 16, or 27.*

CLOSE UP

Milan's Furniture Fair

During the Salone del Mobile, Milan's furniture fair, in early April, the city is abuzz—there are showroom openings, cocktail parties, and product launches, and design types dressed in black and wearing hipster glasses fill the sidewalks and bars.

Except for a few free days, the Salone del Mobile is for professionals only, but you can still participate. Newspapers such as *Corriere della Sera* usually run an English supplement, and special design-week freebies list public events around Milan called "Fuorisalone" (⊕ *www.fuorisalone. it*). Major players such as bathroom-and-kitchen specialist Boffi (⊠ *Via Solferino 11*) and Capellini (⊠ *Via Santa Cecilia 4*) launch new products in their stores. But don't visit if you haven't planned ahead. Hotel rooms and restaurant seating are impossible to find. See ⊕ *www.salonemilano.it* for dates.

Trussardi. This family-run label offers sleek, fashion-forward accessories, leather goods, and clothes at its flagship store. ⊠ *Piazza della Scala 5, Duomo* ☏ *02/80688242* ⊕ *www.trussardi.com* Ⓜ *Duomo; Tram 1.*

Versace. Run by flamboyant Donatella Versace and known for its rock-and-roll styling, Versace's first store opened on Via della Spiga in 1978 and its latest flagship is inside the Galleria Vittorio Emanuele II. ⊠ *Galleria Vittorio Emanuele II 33/35, Duomo* ☏ *02/89011479* ⊕ *www. versace.com* Ⓜ *Duomo; Tram 1.*

BRERA

With its narrow streets and outdoor cafés, Brera is one of Milan's most charming neighborhoods. Wander through it to find smaller shops with some appealing offerings from lesser-known names that cater to the well-schooled taste of this upscale area. The densest concentration is along Via Brera, Via Solferino, and Corso Garibaldi.

Mercato di Via S. Marco. The Monday- and Thursday-morning markets here cater to the wealthy residents of the central Brera neighborhood. In addition to food stands where you can get cheese, roast chicken, and dried beans and fruits, there are several clothing and shoe stalls that are important stops for some of Milan's most elegant women. Check out the knitwear at Valentino, about midway down on the street side. ⊠ *Brera* ⊕ *Lanza; Tram 2, 4, 12, or 14.*

QUADRILATERO

The heart of Milan's shopping reputation is the Quadrilatero della Moda district north of the Duomo. Here the world's leading designers compete for shoppers' attention, showing off their ultrastylish clothes in stores that are works of high style themselves. It's difficult to find any bargains, but regardless of whether you're making a purchase, the area is a great place for window-shopping and people-watching.

Armani Megastore. The main Giorgio Armani label, as well as the Armani Collezioni, Armani Casa, Armani Junior, Emporio Armani, Armani Jeans, EA7, and Giorgio Armani beauty brands are all sold under this monumental store's roof. ✉ *Via Manzoni 31, Quadrilatero* ☎ *02/72318600* ⊕ *www.armani.com* Ⓜ *Montenapoleone; Tram 1.*

Fodor's Choice ★ **DMagazine Outlet.** This store boasts some of the best prices in the area for luxury items such as Prada, Gucci, Lanvin, and Cavalli. DMagazine has two other locations on Via Forcella 31 and Via Bigli 4. ✉ *Via Manzoni 44, Quadrilatero* ☎ *02/36514365* ⊕ *www.dmagazine.it* Ⓜ *Montenapoleone; Tram 1.*

Fodor's Choice ★ **Dolce & Gabbana.** This fabulous duo has created an empire based on hot, sultry designs for men and women. While the women's store is on Via della Spiga, you'll find the men's at Corso Venezia 15. ✉ *Via della Spiga 26, Quadrilatero* ☎ *02/76001155* ⊕ *www.dolcegabbana.it* Ⓜ *Montenapoleone; Tram 1.*

Emporio Armani. Giorgio Armani's younger, fashion-forward label is the more affordable, ready-to-wear brand in the Armani galaxy. ✉ *Via Montenapoleone 2, Quadrilatero* ☎ *02/72318600* ⊕ *www.armani.com* Ⓜ *San Babilo.*

Kiton. Neopolitan suitmaker Kiton is known for its high-quality made-in-Italy tailored menswear. This family-run label attracts an international following. ✉ *Via Gesu 11, Quadrilatero* ☎ *02/76390240* ⊕ *www. kiton.it* Ⓜ *Montenapoleone; Tram 1.*

Fay. Part of the Tod's empire, Fay sells women's and men's clothes and accessories at its flagship store, designed by the famed American architect Philip Johnson. ✉ *Via della Spiga 15, Quadrilatero* ☎ *02/76017597* ⊕ *www.fay.it* Ⓜ *Montenapoleone, San Babila, or Palestro; Tram 1.*

Gallo Boutique. Known for their luxe and colorful striped socks, Gallo also carries casual wear and accessories for men, women, and kids. ✉ *Via Manzoni 16, Quadrilatero* ☎ *02783602* ⊕ *www.gallospa.it* Ⓜ *Montenapoleone; Tram 1.*

Gio Moretti. A true luxury destination, Gio Moretti has everything from designer gowns to books on design and architecture. ✉ *Via della Spiga 4, Quadrilatero* ☎ *02/76003186* ⊕ *www.giomoretti.com* Ⓜ *Montenapoleone, San Babila, or Palestro; Tram 1.*

Missoni. Famous for their kaleidoscope-patterned knits, this family-run brand sells whimsical designs for men and women. ✉ *Via Sant'Andrea 2/b, Quadrilatero* ☎ *02/76003555* ⊕ *www.missoni.it* Ⓜ *Montenapoleone or San Babila; Tram 1.*

Miu Miu. Prada's more upbeat, youthful brand has a wide offering of bold-printed women's fashions and accessories. ✉ *Via Sant'Andrea 21, Quadrilatero* ☎ *02/76001799* ⊕ *www.miumiu.com* Ⓜ *Montenapoleone, San Babila, or Palestro; Tram 1.*

Moschino. Known for its bold prints, colors, and appliqués, Moschino is a brand for daring fashionistas. ✉ *Via Sant'Andrea 12, Quadrilatero* ☎ *02/76000832* ⊕ *www.moschino.com* Ⓜ *Montenapoleone, San Babila, or Palestro; Tram 1.*

Prada. Founded in Milan, Prada has several locations throughout the city. Its Via della Spiga location carries upscale accessories and bags coveted by women worldwide. ✉ *Via della Spiga 18, Quadrilatero*

☎ *02/780465* ⊕ *www.prada.com* Ⓜ *Montenapoleone, San Babila, or Palestro; Tram 1.*

Roberto Cavalli. Famous for his wild animal prints, Roberto Cavalli creates sexy designs for men and women. The world's largest Cavalli boutique opened in Milan in February 2014. ✉ *Via Montenapoleone 6, Quadrilatero* ☎ *02/7630771* ⊕ *www.robertocavalli.com* Ⓜ *San Babila.*

Salvatore Ferragamo Donna. This Florence-based brand is a leader in leather goods and accessories, and carries designs for women in this store. ✉ *Via Montenapoleone 3, Quadrilatero* ☎ *02/76000054* ⊕ *www. ferragamo.com* Ⓜ *San Babila.*

Salvatore Ferragamo Uomo. Ferragamo's men's accessories, leather goods, and ties are a staple for Milan's male fashion set. ✉ *Via Montenapoleone 20/4, Quadrilatero* ☎ *02/76006660* ⊕ *www.ferragamo.com* Ⓜ *Montenapoleone; Tram 1.*

Tod's. This leather-good leader sells luxury handbags as well as casual loafers for men and women. It also sells a complete line of men's clothing. ✉ *Via della Spiga 22, Quadrilatero* ☎ *02/76002423* ⊕ *www.tods. com* Ⓜ *Montenapoleone, San Babila, or Palestro; Tram 1.*

Valentino. Even after the departure of its founding father Valentino Garavani, this Roman-based fashion brand still flourishes. ✉ *Via Montenapoleone 20, Quadrilatero* ☎ *02/76006182* ⊕ *www.valentino.com* Ⓜ *Montenapoleone; Tram 1.*

CENTRO DIREZIONALE

Antonioli. Antonioli raises the bar for Milan's top trendsetters. Uniting the most cutting-edge looks of each season, it is perhaps the most fashion-forward concept store in the city. Aside from Italian brands like Valentino, it also stocks a competitive international array of designers like Ann Demeulemeester, Rick Owens, Givenchy, Gareth Pugh, Haider Ackermann, Maison Martin Margiela, and Christopher Kane. ✉ *Via Pasquale Paoli 1, Centro Direzionale* ☎ *02/36566494* ⊕ *www. antonioli.eu* Ⓜ *Porta Genova; Tram 2; Bus 47 or 74.*

PORTA VENEZIA

Milan has several shopping streets that serve nearby residential concentrations. **Corso Buenos Aires** begins in the Porta Venezia area, and runs northeast from the Giardini Pubblici. The wide and busy street is lined with affordable shops. It has the highest concentration of clothing stores in Europe, so be prepared to give up halfway. Avoid Saturday after 3, when it seems the entire city is here looking for bargains.

VIA TORINO

For inexpensive and trendy clothes—for the under-25 set—stroll Via Torino, which begins in Piazza Duomo. Stay away on Saturday afternoon if you don't like crowds.

CORSO COMO

Fodor$Choice ★ **10 Corso Como.** A shrine to Milan's creative fashion sense, 10 Corso Como was founded by the former fashion editor and publisher Carla Sozzani. The clothing and design establishment also includes a garden café, workshop, and gallery. ✉ *Corso Como 10* ☎ *02/29002674* ⊕ *www.10corsocomo.com* Ⓜ *Porta Garibaldi.*

Pasticceria Biffi. This Milan institution opened its doors in 1847, before Italy's Unification, and is the official pastry shop of this traditionally wealthy neighborhood. Have a coffee or a rich hot chocolate in its paneled rooms before facing the crowds in Corso Vercelli. ⊠ *Corso Magenta 87* ☎ *02/48006702* ⊕ *www.biffipasticceria.it.*

SANT'AGOSTINO

Mercato Papiniano. Bargains in apparel—though not designer brands—and household goods can be found at this huge market all day on Saturday and from about 8:30 to 1 on Tuesday. The stalls to look for are at the Piazza Sant'Agostino end of the market. It's very crowded and demanding—watch out for pickpockets. ⊠ *Sant' Agostino* Ⓜ *Sant'Agostino.*

BERGAMO, PAVIA, CREMONA, AND MANTUA

Once proud medieval towns rivaling Milan in power, these centers of industry and commerce still play a key role in Italy's wealthiest, most populous region. Pavia is celebrated for its extraordinarily detailed Carthusian monastery, and Cremona for its incomparable violin-making tradition. Mantua—the most picturesque of the towns—was the home of the fantastically wealthy Gonzaga dynasty for almost 300 years. While Pavia, Cremona, and Mantua are on the low-lying Po Plain, Bergamo is nestled against the foothills of the Alps.

BERGAMO

52 km (32 miles) northeast of Milan.

If you're driving from Milan to Lake Garda, the perfect deviation from your autostrada journey is the lovely medieval town of Bergamo, which is also a wonderful side trip by train from Milan. With direct service from Milan, you'll be whisked from the restless pace of city life to the medieval grandeur of Bergamo Alta in less than an hour.

From behind a set of battered Venetian walls high on an Alpine hilltop, Bergamo majestically surveys the countryside. Behind are the snow-capped Bergamese Alps, and two funiculars connect the modern **Bergamo Bassa** (Lower Bergamo) to the ancient **Bergamo Alta** (Upper Bergamo). Bergamo Bassa's long arteries and ornate piazze speak to its centuries of prosperity, but it's nonetheless overshadowed by Bergamo Alta, whose magnificent architecture has a fairy-tale allure.

GETTING HERE AND AROUND

Bergamo is along the A4 autostrada. By car from Milan, take A51 out of the city to pick up A4; the drive is 52 km (32 miles) and takes about 45 minutes. By train, Bergamo is about one hour from Milan and 1½ hours from Sirmione.

VISITOR INFORMATION

Bergamo Tourism Office ⊠ *Torre del Gombito, Via Gombito 13, Bergamo Alta* ☎ *035/242226* ⊕ *www.turismo.bergamo.it* ☉ *Daily 9–5:30* ⊠ *Viale Papa Giovanni XXIII 57* ☎ *035/210204* ☉ *Daily 9–12:30 and 2–5:30.*

EXPLORING

Accademia Carrara. Bergamo is home to an art collection that's surprisingly rewarding given its size and remote location. Many of the Venetian masters are represented—Mantegna, Bellini, Carpaccio (circa 1460–1525/26), Tiepolo (1727–1804), Francesco Guardi (1712–93), Canaletto (1697–1768)—as well as Botticelli (1445–1510). At the time of this writing, the museum is undergoing remodeling, but a selection of works can be seen at Palazzo della Regione in Piazza Vecchia, Bergamo Alta. ✉ *Bergamo Bassa, Piazza Carrara 82* ☎ *035/270413* 🌐 *www.accademiacarrara.bergamo.it* 🎫 *€5* 🕓 *Palazzo della Regione: June–Sept., Sun. and Tues.–Fri. 10–9, Sat. 10 am–11 pm; Oct.–May, Sun. and Tues.–Fri. 9:30–5:30, Sat. 10–6.*

NEED A BREAK?

Pasticceria Nessi. Save room for dessert while dining in Bergamo, because Pasticceria Nessi serves up the most delightful local treat. *Polenta e osei* is a hand-decorated, fluffy golden mound made with an ever-so-soft sponge cake and filled with maraschino cherries, hazelnut cream, almond paste, and chocolate. ✉ ***Via Gombito 34*** ☎ ***035/247073.***

Cappella Colleoni. Bergamo's **Duomo** and **Battistero** are the most substantial buildings in Piazza Duomo. But the most impressive structure is the Cappella Colleoni, which boasts a kaleidoscope of marble decoration and golden accents. ✉ *Piazza Duomo* ☎ *035/210223 for Duomo, 035/210061 for Cappella* 🕓 *Duomo daily 7:30–noon and 3–6:30. Cappella: Apr.–Oct., Mon.–Sat. 9–1:30 and 2:30–6, Sun. 9–1 and 3–6; Nov.–Mar., Mon.–Sat. 9–12:30 and 2:30–5, Sun. 9–1 and 3–6.*

Torre Civica. The massive 13th-century Torre Civica offers a great view of the two cities. Climb the stairs or take an elevator to the top of the tower, where the bells ring every half hour. ✉ *Piazza Vecchia* ☎ *035/210104* 🎫 *€3* 🕓 *Apr.–Oct., Tues.–Fri. 9:30–6, weekends 9:30–8; Nov.–Mar., Tues.–Fri. 9:30–1 and 2:30–6, weekends 9:30–6.*

WHERE TO EAT

$ NORTHERN ITALIAN

🍴 **Agnello d'Oro.** This 17th-century tavern on Upper Bergamo's main promenade is furnished with wooden booths and a plethora of copper cookware. It has a cozy northern Italian vibe, local clientele, and a variety of bold local wines. Specialties include Bergamo-style risotto and varieties of polenta served with game and mushrooms. Upstairs are several floors of small, simple, but extremely cozy and well-priced guest rooms. [$] *Average main: €14* ✉ *Via Gombito 22, Bergamo Alta* ☎ *035/249883* 🌐 *www.agnellodoro.it* 🕓 *Closed Mon., and Jan. 7–Feb. 5. No dinner Sun.*

$ NORTHERN ITALIAN Fodor's Choice ★

🍴 **Al Donizetti.** Find a table in the back of this central, cheerful restaurant before choosing local cured meats and cheeses to accompany your wine (more than 800 bottles are available, many by the glass). Heartier meals are also available, such as polenta with asiago cheese and smoked ham, but save room for the desserts, which go well with the available dessert wines. [$] *Average main: €13* ✉ *Via Gombito 17/a, Bergamo Alta* ☎ *035/242661* 🌐 *www.donizetti.it.*

$ NORTHERN ITALIAN 🍴 **Da Ornella.** The vaulted ceilings of this popular trattoria on the main street in the upper town are marked with ancient graffiti, created by (patiently) holding candles to the stone overhead. Ornella herself is in the kitchen, turning out the house specialties: polenta taragna cooked with butter and cheese, served with rabbit, chicken, or sliced mushrooms with oil, garlic, and parsley. Ask her to suggest the perfect wine pairing for your meal. [$] *Average main: €14* ✉ *Via Gombito 15, Bergamo Alta* ☎ *035/232736* 🕒 *Closed Thurs.*

$$$ NORTHERN ITALIAN 🍴 **Due Colombe Ristorante Al Borgo Antico.** Lake Iseo, bordering the Franciacorta wine region, is one of the Italian lake region's least-known lakes, yet it's only about an hour's drive from Milan and 20 minutes from Bergamo. Travelers would do well to follow the locals' lead to sample Chef Stefano Cerveni's delightful cooking at his cozy restaurant just south of the lake. The elegant dining area with beamed ceilings and stone walls juxtaposes with the thoroughly modern menu offering a choice of "classic" and "creative" dishes, though all use local ingredients in unexpected ways. You might start with the warm organic chicken salad with dried Monte Isola sardines, jelly green sauce, and chicken popcorn, perhaps followed by the pink duck breast with grape must and foie gras terrine, and ending with the acacia honey parfait with caramelized hazelnuts and local extra virgin olive oil. For a unique experience, let the sommelier choose local Franciacorta wines to pair with your dishes. [$] *Average main: €30* ✉ *Via Foresti 13, Borgonato Cortefranco* ☎ *030/982–8227* 🌐 *www.duecolombe.com* ✍ *Reservations essential* 🕒 *Closed Mon. No dinner Sun.*

$$$ INTERNATIONAL 🍴 **Taverna Colleoni dell'Angelo.** Pierangelo Cornaro is the name behind the Taverna Colleoni, on the Piazza Vecchia right behind the Duomo. He serves imaginative fish, mushroom, and meat dishes, both regional and international, all expertly prepared. [$] *Average main: €28* ✉ *Piazza Vecchia 7, Bergamo Alta* ☎ *035/232596* 🌐 *www.colleonidellangelo.com* 🕒 *Closed Mon.*

WHERE TO STAY

$$$$ HOTEL Fodor's Choice ★ 🏨 **L'Albereta.** Perched in the vineyard-covered hills of Franciacorta—Italy's up-and-coming premium sparking wine region about an hour east of Milan—this charming Relais & Chateaux property features an enormous 150,000-square-foot spa, the perfect antidote to the city's chaos. **Pros:** cozy, calm, and luxurious atmosphere; excellent on-site restaurants; second-to-none spa facilities. **Cons:** rooms quite varied in terms of size and level of renovation; not all rooms have Lake Iseo views. [$] *Rooms from: €320* ✉ *Via Vittorio Emanuele 23, Erbusco* ☎ *030/7760550* 🌐 *www.albereta.it* 🛏 *39 rooms, 18 suites* 🍽 *Breakfast.*

$$$$ HOTEL Fodor's Choice ★ 🏨 **Relais San Lorenzo.** Ideally positioned on the edge of Bergamo Alta, a stone's throw from the old town's delightful shops and restaurants, this ultramodern luxury hotel nods to its historic location by incorporating Roman ruins found during construction into the restaurant and bar. **Pros:** wonderful old town location; top-notch restaurant; quiet and peaceful atmosphere. **Cons:** rooms on the pricey side; parking in the underground garage will run you an extra €35 a day. [$] *Rooms from: €340* ✉ *Piazza Mascheroni 9, Bergamo Alta* ☎ *035/237383* 🌐 *www.*

6

relaisanlorenzo.com ⬐ *23 rooms, 7 suites* ⊘ *Closed 2 wks in Jan.* ⦿ *Breakfast.*

PAVIA

40 km (25 miles) south of Milan.

Pavia was once Milan's chief regional rival. The city dates from at least the Roman era and was the capital of the Lombard kings for two centuries (572–774). It was at one time known as "the city of a hundred towers," but only a few have survived the passing of time. Its prestigious university was founded in 1361 on the site of a 10th-century law school, but it has roots that can be traced to antiquity.

GETTING HERE AND AROUND

By car from Milan, start out on the A7 autostrada and exit onto A53 as you near Pavia; the drive is 40 km (25 miles) and takes about 45 minutes. Pavia is 30–40 minutes by train from Milan and 1½ hours (by slower regional service) from Cremona. The Certosa is 30 minutes by train from several Milan stations.

VISITOR INFORMATION

Pavia Tourism Office ⊠ *Palazzo del Broletto, Piazza della Vittoria 14, Pavia* ☎ *0382/079943* ⊕ *www.comune.pv.it.*

EXPLORING

Castello Visconteo. The town's 14th-century fortress-castle now houses the local **Museo Civico** (Municipal Museum), with a Romanesque and Renaissance sculpture gallery, an archaeological collection, and a large picture gallery displaying works by Correggio, Bellini, Tiepolo, Hayez, Pelizza da Volpedo, and La Foppa, among others. ⊠ *Viale XI Febbraio 35, near Piazza Castello, Pavia* ☎ *0382/399770* ⊕ *www.museicivici. pavia.it* ⬐ *€6* ⊘ *July, Aug., Dec., and Jan., Tues.–Sun. 9–1:30; Feb.– June and Sept.–Nov., Tues.–Sun. 10–5:50; last entry 45 mins before closing.*

Certosa (*Carthusian monastery*). The main draw in Pavia is the Certosa, 9 km (5½ miles) north of the city center. Its elaborate facade shows the same relish for ornamentation as Milan's Duomo. The Certosa's extravagant grandeur was due in part to the plan to have it house the tombs of the family of the first duke of Milan, Galeazzo Visconti III (who died during a plague, at age 49, in 1402). The best marble was used, taken undoubtedly by barge from the quarries of Carrara, roughly 240 km (150 miles) away. Though the floor plan may be Gothic—a cross shape divided into a series of squares—the gorgeous fabric that rises above it is triumphantly Renaissance. On the facade, in the lower frieze, are medallions of Roman emperors and Eastern monarchs; above them are low reliefs of scenes from the life of Christ and from the career of Galeazzo Visconti III.

The first duke was the only Visconti to be interred here, and not until some 75 years after his death, in a tomb designed by Gian Cristoforo Romano. Look for it in the right transept. In the left transept is a more appealing tomb—that of a rather stern middle-aged man and a beautiful young woman. The man is Ludovico il Moro Sforza, seventh duke of Milan, who commissioned Leonardo to paint *The Last Supper.* The woman is Ludovico's wife, Beatrice d'Este (1475–97), one of the most celebrated women of her day, the embodiment of brains, culture, birth, and beauty. Married when he was 40 and she was 16, they had enjoyed six years together when she died while delivering a stillborn child. Ludovico commissioned the sculptor Cristoforo Solari to design a joint tomb for the high altar of Santa Maria delle Grazie in Milan. Originally much larger, the tomb for some years occupied the honored place as planned. Then, for reasons that are still mysterious, the Dominican monks sold the tomb to their Carthusian brothers in Pavia and part of it and its remains were lost. ⊠ *Certosa, Località Monumento 4, 9 km (5½ miles) north of Pavia* ☎ *0382/925613* ⊕ *www.comune. pv.it/certosadipavia* ⊒ *Donations accepted* ☉ *May–Aug., Tues.–Sun. 9–11:30 and 2:30–6; Apr. and Sept., Tues.–Sun. 9–11:30 and 2:30– 5:30; Mar. and Oct., Tues.–Sun. 9–11:30 and 2:30–5; Nov.–Feb., Tues.– Sun. 9–11:30 and 2:30–4:30.*

San Pietro in Ciel d'Oro. This Romanesque masterpiece houses the tomb of Christianity's most celebrated convert, Saint Augustine (354–430), who rests in an intricately carved, Gothic, white marble ark on the high altar. ⊠ *San Pietro in Ciel d'Oro 2, Pavia* ☎ *0382/303036* ⊕ *santagostinopavia.wordpress.com* ☉ *Daily 7–noon and 3–7. Mass Mon.–Sat. at 9 and 6:30; Sun. at 9, 11, and 6:30.*

WHERE TO EAT

$$$

NORTHERN
ITALIAN

✕ **Locanda Vecchia Pavia al Mulino.** In sophisticated Art Nouveau surroundings, you can find creative versions of traditional Lombard cuisine, including risotto *alla certosina* (with sturgeon eggs, frogs' legs, and river shrimp). All seafood dishes are done with similar verve, as are *lasagnette di pasta fresca alla robiola spnaci* (lasagne with fresh soft cheese and spinach), *nocette d'agnello* (noisette of lamb), and veal shank stew. The veranda, open in summer only, has a view of the Certosa monastery, 150 yards away. Ⓢ *Average main: €31* ⊠ *Via al Monumento 5, Certosa* ☎ *0382/925894* ⊕ *www.vecchiapaviaalmulino.it* ⊰ *Reservations essential* ☉ *Apr.–Oct.: closed Mon. and Tues. lunch; Nov.–Mar., closed Mon., no dinner Sun. Closed Aug. and Jan.*

CREMONA

85 km (53 miles) east of Pavia, 100 km (62 miles) southeast of Milan.

Cremona is a classical-music lover's dream. With violin shops on every block along its crooked old streets, it is where the world's best violins are crafted. Andrea Amati (1510–80) invented the modern instrument here in the 16th century. Though cognoscenti continue to revere the Amati name, it was an apprentice of Amati's nephew for whom the fates had reserved wide and lasting fame. In a career that spanned an incredible 68 years, Antonio Stradivari (1644–1737) made more than 1,200 instruments—including violas, cellos, harps, guitars, and mandolins, in addition to his fabled violins. They remain the most coveted, most expensive stringed instruments in the world.

Strolling about this quiet, medium-size city, you can't help noting that violin making continues to flourish. There are, in fact, more than 50

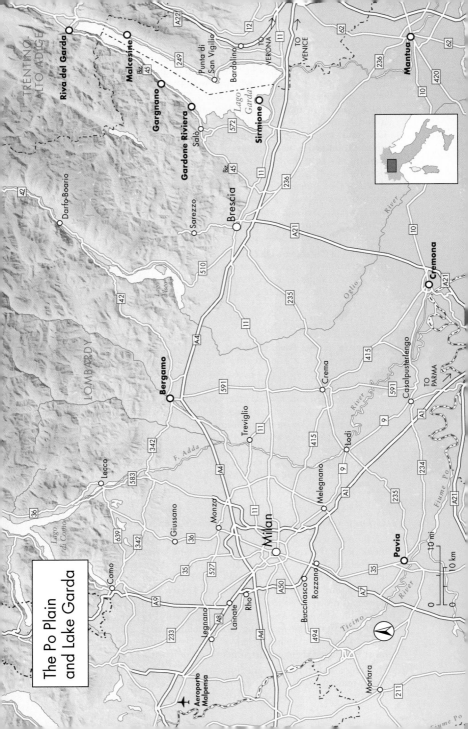

The Po Plain
and Lake Garda

TRENTINO-ALTO ADIGE

LOMBARDY

Riva del Garda
Malcesine
Gargnano
Gardone Riviera
Salò
Sirmione
Punta di San Vigilio
Bardolino
TO VERONA
TO VENICE
Mantua

Lago di Garda

Darfo-Boario
Sarezzo
Brescia
Lago d'Iseo

Cremona
TO PARMA

Bergamo
Lecco
Lago di Como
Como
Giussano
Monza
Treviglio
Crema
Casalpusterlengo
Lodi
Melegnano

Milan
Rho
Lainate
Legnano
Aeroporto Malpensa
Buccinasco
Rozzano
Pavia
Mortara

A22
12
62
249
45
572
Bez.
45
236
420
10
236
42
510
A4
591
11
235
Oglio River
A21
10
415
591
9
A1
234
235
A21
Fiume Po
Ticino River
342
583
36
639
342
35
527
36
11
A4
A8
A9
233
A50
494
A7
35
211
F. Adda

10 mi
10 km
0

liutai (violin makers), many of them graduates of the Scuola Internazionale di Liuteria (International School of Violin Making). You're usually welcome in these ateliers, where traditional craftsmanship reigns supreme, especially if you're contemplating the acquisition of your own instrument; the tourist office can provide addresses.

Cremona's other claim to fame is *torrone* (nougat), which is said to have been created here in honor of the marriage of Bianca Maria Visconti and Francesco Sforza, which took place in October 1441. The new confection, originally prepared by heating almonds, egg whites, and honey over low heat, and shaped and named after the city's tower, was created in symbolic celebration. The annual Festa del Torrone is held in the main piazza on the third Sunday in October.

GETTING HERE AND AROUND

By car from Milan, start out on the A1 autostrada and switch to A21 at Piacenza; the drive is about 100 km (62 miles) and takes about 1½ hours. From Pavia, take SP617 to A21; the trip is 85 km (53 miles) and takes about an hour. By train, Cremona is about an hour from Milan and 1½ hours from Desenzano, near Sirmione on Lake Garda.

VISITOR INFORMATION

Cremona Tourism Office ⊠ *Piazza del Comune 5* ☎ *0372/406391* ⊕ *www. turismocremona.it* ⊗ *Sept.–June, daily 9:30–1 and 2–5; July and Aug., Mon–Sat. 9:30–1 and 2–5, Sun. 9:30–1.*

EXPLORING

TOP ATTRACTIONS

Duomo. Cremona's Romanesque Duomo was consecrated in 1190. It's an impressive structure in a breathtaking piazza, and certainly one of the most beautiful churches in Italy. Here you can find the *Story of the Virgin Mary and the Passion of Christ,* the central fresco of an extraordinary cycle commissioned in 1514 and featuring the work of local artists, including Boccaccio Boccanccino, Giovanni Francesco Bembo, and Altobello Melone. ⊠ *Piazza del Comune* ☎ *0372/495011* ⊕ *www. cattedraledicremona.it* ⊗ *Weekdays 8–noon and 3:30–7.*

Fodor's Choice
★

Museo del Violino. At this lovely and informative museum dedicated to all things violin, even those not already enamored by the instrument will find something to appreciate. Historic violins made in Cremona by masters including Stradivari are presented as works of art; be sure to get the audio guide included with admission to listen to recordings as you stroll. An audio chamber lets you hear more beautiful violin concerts performed by famed artists—and if you're lucky, there will be a live concert going on at the innovative on-site auditorium, where the seats wrap around the stage and musicians for an immersive experience. ⊠ *Palazzo dell'Arte, Piazza Marconi 5* ☎ *0372/801801, 0372/080809 tickets* ⊕ *www.museodelviolino.org* ⊟ *€10* ⊗ *Tues.–Sun. 10–6.*

QUICK
BITES

Pasticceria Dondeo. Prepare to visit the sights of Cremona or wait for the next train at the Pasticceria Dondeo, just to the right of the station. Dating back to 1912, this is one of Cremona's oldest and most beautiful Art Nouveau cafés and pastry shops. The fresh zabaglione and beignets are heaven. ⊠ *Via Alghieri Dante 38* ☎ *0372/21224.*

6

Piazza del Comune. The Duomo, tower, baptistery, and Palazzo Communale (city hall) surround this distinctive and harmonious square: the combination of old brick, rose- and cream-color marble, terra-cotta, and old copper roofs brings Romanesque, Gothic, and Renaissance together with unusual success. ✉ *Piazza del Comune 8.*

WORTH NOTING

No. 1 Piazza Roma. Legendary violin maker Antonio Stradivari lived, worked, and died near the verdant square at No. 1 Piazza Roma (not open to the public). According to local lore, Stradivari kept each instrument in his bedroom for a month before varnishing it, imparting part of his soul before sealing and sending it out into the world. In the center of the park is **Stradivari's grave,** marked by a simple tombstone.

Torrazzo (*Big Tower*). Dominating Piazza del Comune is perhaps the tallest campanile in Italy, visible for a considerable distance across the Po Plain. It's open to visitors, but in winter, hours fluctuate depending on the weather. The tower's astronomical clock is the 1583 original. ✉ *Piazza del Comune* ☎ *0372/495029* 🎫 *€5* 🕓 *Daily 10–12:30 and 2:30–5:40.*

WHERE TO EAT AND STAY

$$ NORTHERN ITALIAN

🍴 **Centrale.** Close to the cathedral, this old-style trattoria is a favorite among locals for traditional regional fare, such as succulent *cotechino* (pork sausage) and *tortelli di zucca* (a small pasta with pumpkin filling), at moderate prices. Centrale prides itself on its *bolliti,* boiled meats like veal tongue and cheek, which are served with *salsa verde* (a sauce of parsely and capers), as well as Cremona's most famous condiment, *mostarda,* a spicy, candied fruit. [$] *Average main: €15* ✉ *Via Pertusio 4* ☎ *0372/28701* 🕓 *Closed Thurs. and July.*

$$ NORTHERN ITALIAN

🍴 **La Sosta.** This traditional *osteria,* which prides itself as being part of the international Slow Food movement, looks to the 16th century for culinary inspiration, following a time-tested recipe for a favored first course, gnocchi *Vecchia Cremona.* The homemade salami is also excellent. To finish off the evening, try the *semifreddo al torrone* (nougat parfait) and a dessert wine. [$] *Average main: €22* ✉ *Via Sicardo 9* ☎ *0372/456656* 🌐 *www.osterialasosta.it* 🕓 *Closed 3 wks in Aug. No dinner Sun.*

$ CAFÉ

🍴 **Pasticceria Duomo.** This portal to the past opened in 1883 and still serves up such handmade local delights as *pan torrone* (a loaf cake made with chunks of nougat) and *torta cremona* (a cake made with almond flour and filled with amarena cherries). A relaxing stop between visiting museums, it's the perfect place to have a cappuccino and relax by the fireplace. [$] *Average main: €10* ✉ *Via Boccaccino, 6* ☎ *0372/22273* 🌐 *www.pasticceriaduomo.it.*

$$ HOTEL

🏨 **Delle Arti Design Hotel.** The name suits the elegant modern interiors and eclectic designer furniture, all geared to solid comfort. **Pros:** affordable, modern, industrial design; friendly staff; lots of amenities; garage nearby. **Cons:** probably too contemporary for those seeking the traditional. [$] *Rooms from: €170* ✉ *Via Bonomelli 8* ☎ *0372/23131* 🌐 *www.dellearti.com* 🛏 *33 rooms, 3 suites* 🕓 *Closed Aug. 5–29 and late Dec.* 🍽 *Breakfast.*

$ 　🖵 **Hotel Impero.** This comfortable, modern hotel is well equipped to sat-
HOTEL isfy both leisure and business travelers, with pleasant, functional rooms, the best of which overlook the piazza. **Pros:** central location; highly professional staff. **Cons:** rooms are a little bland and out of style; can be noisy. $ *Rooms from: €95* ⊠ *Piazza della Pace 21* ☎ *0372/413013* ⊕ *www.hotelimpero.cr.it* ⤴ *53 rooms* 🍽 *Breakfast.*

SHOPPING

Sperlari. Head to this famed shop for a taste of Cremona's famous nougat. Cremona's best *mostarda* (a mustardy condiment made from preserved fruit served with meat and cheese) has also been sold from this handsome shop since 1836; Sperlari and parent company Fieschi have grown into a confectionary empire. Look for the historical product display in the back. The store also sells teas, marmalades, and other Italian delights. ⊠ *Via Solferino 25* ☎ *0372/232346* ⊕ *www.sperlari1836.com.*

MANTUA

192 km (119 miles) southeast of Milan.

Mantua (Mantova in Italian) stands tallest among the ancient walled cities of the Po Plain; it may not be flashy or dramatic, but its beauty is subtle and deep, hiding a rich trove of artistic, architectural, and cultural gems beneath its slightly somber facade. Its fortifications are circled on three sides by the passing Mincio River, which long provided Mantua with protection, fish, and a steady stream of river tolls as it meandered from Lake Garda to join the Po. Although Mantua first came to prominence in Roman times as the home of Virgil, its grand monuments date to the glory years of the Gonzaga dynasty. From 1328 until the Austrian Habsburgs sacked the city in 1708, the dukes and marquesses of the Gonzaga clan reigned over a wealthy independent commune, and the arts thrived in the relative peace of that period. Raphael's star pupil, Andrea Mantegna, who served as court painter for 50 years, was the best-known of a succession of artists and architects who served Mantua through the years, and some of his finest work, including his only surviving fresco cycle, can be seen here. Giulio Romano (circa 1499–1546), Mantegna's apprentice, built his masterpiece, Palazzo Te, on an island in the river. Leon Battista Alberti (1404–72), who designed two impressive churches in Mantua, was widely emulated later in the Renaissance.

GETTING HERE AND AROUND

Mantua is 5 km (3 miles) west of the A22 autostrada. The drive from Milan, following A4 to A22, takes a little more than two hours. The drive from Cremona, along SP10, is 1¼ hours. Most trains arrive in just under two hours from Milan, depending on the type of service, and in about 1½ hours from Desenzano, near Sirmione on Lake Garda, via Verona.

VISITOR INFORMATION

Mantua Tourism Office. Ask about the museums card, which entitles you to visit either five or eight museums for one price. ⊠ *Piazza A. Mantegna 6* ☎ *0376/432432* ⊕ *www.turismo.mantova.it* ⊙ *Weekdays 9–1:30 and 2:30–5, weekends 9–5.*

EXPLORING

Casa di Andrea Mantegna. Serious Mantegna aficionados will want to visit the house the artist designed and built around an intriguing circular courtyard, which is usually open to view. The exterior is interesting for its unusual design, and the interior, with its hidden frescoes, can be seen by appointment or during occasional art exhibitions.

Hours and prices vary depending on the exhibition. ⊠ *Via Acerbi 47* ☎ *0376/360506* ⊕ *www.casadelmantegna.it* ☉ *Tues.–Sun. 10–12:30 and 3–6.*

Palazzo Ducale. The 500-room palace that dominates the Mantua skyline was built for the Gonzaga family, though much of the art within the castle was sold or stolen as the dynasty waned in power and prestige. A glimpse of past grandeur is still possible in the **Camera degli Sposi** (literally, the "Chamber of the Wedded Couple"), where Duke Ludovico and his wife held court. (At the time of this writing, the wedding chamber is undergoing renovations and is completely closed to the public, so check before you go.) Mantegna painted the hall over a nine-year period at the height of his power, finishing at age 44. He made a startling advance in painting by organizing the picture plane in a way that systematically mimics the experience of human vision. The circular trompe-l'oeil around the vaulted ceiling is famous for the many details that attest to Mantegna's greatness: the three-dimensional quality of the seven Caesars (the Gonzagas saw themselves as successors to the Roman emperors and paid homage to classical culture throughout the palazzo); the self-portrait of Mantegna (in purple, on the right side of the western fresco); and the dwarf peering out from behind the dress of Ludovico's wife (on the northern fresco). Only 20 people at a time are allowed in the Camera degli Sposi, and only for 10 minutes at a time. Read about the room before you enter, so that you can spend your time looking up. Reservations are mandatory for Camera degli Sposi, though visitors may take a fast-paced guided tour of the rest of the castle (conducted in Italian; signs in each room provide explanations in English). ⊠ *Piazza Sordello 40* ☎ *041/2411897* ⊕ *www.mantovaducale.beniculturali. it* ⌷ *€6.50, plus €1 for reservation to see Camera degli Sposi (free 1st Sun. of month)* ☉ *Tues.–Thurs. and weekends 8:15–7:15; last entry at 6:20. Fri. 8:15–9:30, last entry at 8:30.*

Palazzo Te. One of the greatest of all Renaissance palaces, built between 1525 and 1535 by Federigo II Gonzaga, is the Mannerist masterpiece of artist-architect Giulio Romano, who created a pavilion where the strict rules of courtly behavior could be relaxed for libertine pastimes. Romano's purposeful breaks with classical tradition are lighthearted and unprecedented. For example, note the "slipping" triglyphs along the upper edge of the inside courtyard. Two highlights are the **Camera di Amore e Psiche** (Room of Cupid and Psyche), which depicts a wedding set among lounging nymphs, frolicking satyrs, and even a camel and an elephant; and the gasp-producing **Camera dei Giganti** (Room of the Giants), which shows Jupiter expelling the Titans from Mount Olympus. The scale of the work is overwhelming; the floor-to-ceiling work completely envelops the viewer. The room's rounded corners, and the river rock covering the original floor, were meant to make it seem cavelike. It is a "whisper chamber" in which words softly uttered in one corner can be heard in the opposite one. Note the graffiti from as far back as the 17th century. At the time of this writing, some of the rooms are closed for renovations. ✉ *Viale Te 13* ☎ *0376/323266* 🌐 *www.palazzote.it* 🎟 *€12* 🕒 *Weekdays 9–6.*

Sant'Andrea. Mantegna's tomb is in the first chapel to the left in the basilica of Sant'Andrea, most of which was built in 1472. The current structure, a masterwork by the architect Alberti, is the third built on this spot to house the relic of the Precious Blood: the crypt holds two reliquaries containing earth believed to be soaked in the blood of Christ, brought to Mantua by Longinus, the soldier who pierced his side. They are displayed only on Good Friday. ✉ *Piazza di Mantegna* ☎ *0376/328504* 🌐 *www.santandreainmantova.it* 🕒 *Daily 8–noon and 3–7.*

WHERE TO EAT

$$$$ NORTHERN ITALIAN

🍴 **Ambasciata.** Heralded by food critics the world over as one of Italy's finest restaurants, Ambasciata (Italian for "embassy") takes elegance and service to new levels. Chef Romano Tamani, who is co-owner with his brother Francesco, makes frequent appearances abroad but is at home in tiny Quistello, 20 km (12 miles) southeast of Mantua. He offers those willing to make the trek (and pay the bill) an ever-changing array of superlative creations, such as *timballo di lasagne verdi con petto di piccione sauté alla crème de Cassis* (green lasagna with breast of pigeon and redcurrant). [$] *Average main: €52* ✉ *Via Martiri di Belfiore 33, Quistello* ☎ *0376/619169* 🌐 *www.ristoranteambasciata.com* ✍ *Reservations essential* 🕒 *Closed Mon., Jan. 1–15, and 2 wks in Aug. No dinner Sun.*

WHERE TO STAY

$$ HOTEL

🏨 **Casa Poli.** Refreshing, minimalist influences, creative touches (like the room number projected onto the hall floor), and attention to detail create a welcoming ambience with contemporary flair. **Pros:** attentive staff; tasteful and modern; families welcome. **Cons:** although convenient, not in the absolute center of the city; some traffic noise in front-facing rooms; no on-site restaurant. [$] *Rooms from: €144* ✉ *Corso Garibaldi 32* ☎ *0376/288170* 🌐 *www.hotelcasapoli.it* 🛏 *34 rooms* 🍽 *Breakfast.*

LAKE GARDA

Lake Garda has had a perennial attraction for travelers and writers alike; even the essayist Michel de Montaigne (1533–92), whose 15 months of travel journals contain not a single other reference to nature, paused to admire the view down the lake from Torbole, which he called "boundless."

Lake Garda is 50 km (31 miles) long, ranges roughly 1 km to 16 km (½ mile to 10 miles) wide, and is as much as 1,135 feet deep. The terrain is flat at the lake's southern base and mountainous at its northern tip. As a consequence, its character varies from stormy inland sea to crystalline Nordic-style fjord. It's the biggest lake in the region and by most accounts the cleanest. If you're driving, take care on the hazardous hairpin turns on the lake road.

GETTING HERE AND AROUND

The town of Sirmione, at the south end of the lake, is 10 km (6 miles) from Desenzano, which has regular train service; it's about an hour and 20 minutes by train from Milan and 25 minutes from Verona. The A4 autostrada passes to the south of the lake, and A22 runs north–south about 10 km (6 miles) from the eastern shore.

SIRMIONE

138 km (86 miles) east of Milan.

Dramatically rising out of Lake Garda is the enchanting town of Sirmione. "*Paene insularum, Sirmio, insularumque ocelle,*" wrote Catullus in a homecoming poem: "It is the jewel of both peninsulas and islands." The forbidding Castello Scaligero stands guard behind the small bridge connecting Sirmione to the mainland; beyond, cobbled streets wind their way through medieval arches past lush gardens, stunning lake views, and gawking crowds. Originally a Roman resort town, Sirmione served under the dukes of Verona and later Venice as Garda's main point of defense. It's now reclaimed its original function, bustling with visitors in summer. Cars aren't allowed into town; parking is available by the tourist office at the entrance.

VISITOR INFORMATION

Sirmione Tourism Office ⊠ *Viale Marconi 6* 📞 *030/916114* ⊕ *www.sirmionebs.it.*

EXPLORING

Bardolino. This small town, one of the most popular summer resorts on the lake, is 32 km (20 miles) north of Sirmione along Lake Garda's eastern shore, at the wider end. It's most famous for its red wine, which is light, dry, and often slightly sparkling; the Cura dell'Uva (Grape Cure Festival), held here in late September–early October, is a great excuse to indulge in the local product. Bardolino has two handsome Romanesque churches, both near the center: **San Severo,** from the 11th century, and **San Zeno,** from the 9th. ⊕ *www.bardolinoweb.it.*

Castello Scaligero. As hereditary rulers of Verona for more than a century before they lost control of the city in 1402, the Della Scala counted Garda among their possessions. It was they who built this lakeside redoubt, along with almost all the other castles on the lake. You can go inside to take in the nice view of the lake from the tower, or you can swim at the nearby beach. ⊠ *Piazza Castello* 📞 *030/916468* 💲 *€4* 🕐 *Tues.–Sun. 8:30–7:30.*

Grotte di Catullo (*Grottoes of Catullus*). Locals will almost certainly tell you that these romantic lakeside ruins were once the site of the villa of

Catullus (87–54 BC), one of the greatest pleasure-seeking poets of all time. Present archaeological wisdom, however, does not concur, and there is some consensus that this was the site of two villas of slightly different periods, dating from about the 1st century AD. But never mind—the view through the cypresses and olive trees is lovely, and even if Catullus didn't have a villa here, he is closely associated with the area and undoubtedly did have a villa nearby. The ruins are at the top of the isthmus and are poorly signposted: walk through the historic center and past the various villas to the top of the spit; the entrance is on the right. Alternately, take one of the frequent tourist trains from town for €1 each way. A small **museum** offers a brief overview of the ruins (on the far wall). ⌂ *Piazzale Orti Manara* ☎ *030/916157* 💶*€6* ⏱ *Apr.–Oct., Tues.–Sat. 8:30–7:30, Sun. 8:30–6:30; Nov.–Feb., Tues.–Sat. 8:30–7:30, Sun. 8:30–1:30; Mar., Tues.–Sat. 8:30–7, Sun. 8:30–2.*

WHERE TO EAT AND STAY

$$$
ITALIAN
✕ **La Rucola.** Next to Sirmione's castle, this elegant, intimate restaurant tucked into three charming rooms has a creative menu, with seafood and meat dishes accompanied by a good choice of wines. At dinner, a tasting menu is available for €100. 💲 *Average main: €30* ⌂ *Via Strentelle 3* ☎ *030/916326* ⊕ *www.ristorantelarucola.it* ⏱ *Closed Thurs., and Jan.–mid-Feb.*

$$
SEAFOOD
✕ **Ristorante Al Pescatore.** Lake fish is the specialty at this simple, popular restaurant in Sirmione's historical center. For a reasonably priced meal, try grilled trout with a bottle of local white wine and settle your meal with a walk in the nearby park. 💲 *Average main: €15* ⌂ *Via Piana 20* ☎ *030/916216* ⊕ *www.ristorantealpescatore.com* ⏱ *Closed Wed., and Dec. 10–25.*

$$$
HOTEL
🛏 **Hotel Sirmione e Promessi Sposi.** Scandinavian slat beds, matching floral draperies and wall coverings, and built-in white furniture impart a homey feel that, along with the luxurious thermal spa, keeps many guests returning year after year. **Pros:** next to the lake; beautiful grounds. **Cons:** not all rooms have lake views; the price of all this beauty is high. 💲 *Rooms from: €227* ⌂ *Piazza Castello 19* ☎ *030/916331, 030/9904922 for booking* ⊕ *www.termedisirmione.com* 🛏 *100 rooms* 🍽 *Multiple meal plans.*

$$$$
HOTEL
🛏 **Palace Hotel Villa Cortine.** This former private villa in a secluded park risks being just plain ostentatious, but it's saved by the sheer luxury of the lakeside setting, the charming décor of the older rooms, and the high professionalism of its staff. **Pros:** an opulent experience; lovely pool area. **Cons:** very expensive; no spa at hotel but thermal baths a short walk away. 💲 *Rooms from: €455* ⌂ *Viale C. Gennari 2* ☎ *030/9905890* ⊕ *www.palacehotelvillacortine.com* 🛏 *47 rooms, 6 suites* ⏱ *Closed mid-Oct.–Mar.* 🍽 *Breakfast.*

MALCESINE

63 km (39 miles) north of Sirmione, 180 km (112 miles) east of Milan.

Malcesine is one of the loveliest areas along the upper eastern shore of Lake Garda. It's principally known as a summer resort, with sailing and windsurfing schools. It tends to be crowded in season, but there are nice walks from the town toward the mountains. Six lifts and more than 11 km (7 miles) of runs of varying degrees of difficulty serve skiers.

VISITOR INFORMATION
Malcesine Tourism Office ⊠ *Via Capitanato 6* ☎ *0456/589902* ⊕ *www. malcesinepiu.org.*

EXPLORING
Castello Scaligero. Dominating the town is a 12th-century castle built by Verona's dynastic della Scala family. ☎ *045/6570333* 🎫 *€6* ⊙ *May–Sept., daily 9:30–8; Oct.–Apr., weekends 11–4.*

Monte Baldo. The futuristic *funivia* (cable car), zipping visitors to the top of Monte Baldo (5,791 feet), is unique because it rotates. After a 10-minute ride, you're high in the Veneto where you can take a stroll and enjoy spectacular views of the lake. You can ride the cable car down or bring along a mountain bike (or even a hang glider) for the descent. ⊠ *Via Navene Vecchia 12* ☎ *045/7400206* ⊕ *www.funiviedelbaldo.it* 🎫 *€20 round-trip* ⊙ *Dec. 22–Mar. 9, daily 8–5; Apr. 5–Oct. 31, daily 8–6:45.*

RIVA DEL GARDA

18 km (11 miles) north of Malcesine, 180 km (112 miles) east of Milan.

Riva del Garda is set on the northern tip of Lake Garda, against a dramatic backdrop of jagged cliffs and miles of beaches. The old city, surrounding a pretty harbor, was built up during the 15th century, when it was a strategic outpost of the Venetian Republic.

VISITOR INFORMATION
Riva del Garda Tourism Office ⊠ *Largo Medaglie d'Oro al Valor Militare 5* ☎ *0464/554444* ⊕ *www.gardatrentino.it.*

EXPLORING
Piazza 3 Novembre. This lakeside plaza, the heart of Riva del Garda, is surrounded by medieval palazzi. Standing in the piazza and looking out onto the lake you can understand why Riva del Garda has become a windsurfing destination: air currents ensure good breezes on even the most sultry midsummer days.

Torre Apponale. Predating the Venetian period by three centuries, this sturdy tower looms above the medieval residences of the main square; its crenellations recall its defensive purpose. You can climb the 165 steps to see the view from the top. ☎ *0464/573869* ⊕ *www.gardatrentino.it* 🎫 *€2* ⊙ *Late Mar.–May and Oct.–early Nov., Tues.–Sun. 10–6; June–Sept., daily 10–6.*

EN ROUTE After passing the town of Limone—where it's said the first lemon trees in Europe were planted—take the fork to the right about 5 km (3 miles) north of Gargnano and head to Tignale. The view from the Madonna di Montecastello church, some 2,000 feet above the lake, is spectacular. Adventurous travelers will want to follow this pretty inland mountain road to Tremosine. Be warned that the road winds its way up the mountain through hairpin turns and blind corners that can test even the most experienced drivers.

WHERE TO EAT AND STAY

$$$
NORTHERN
ITALIAN

✕ **Ristorante Castel Toblino.** A lovely stop for a lakeside drink or a romantic dinner, this 16th-century castle is right on a lake in Sarche, about 20 km (12 miles) north of Riva toward Trento. Dishes highlight seasonal, local ingredients, such as ravioli with duck, marjoram, and black truffle, *canederlotti* (dumplings) with chanterelles and alpine cheese, and venison and porcini mushrooms on rösti. The helpful servers can recommend the perfect Trentino wine to wash it all down. $ *Average main:* €25 ⊠ *Via Caffaro 1, Sarche* ☎ *0461/864036* ⊕ *www.casteltoblino.com* ⊘ *Closed Tues., and Nov.–Feb.*

$$
RESORT
FAMILY

🏨 **Du Lac et du Parc Grand Resort.** Riva's largest resort has elegance befitting its cosmopolitan name, with comfortable, well-appointed rooms, including studio-apartments perfect for families, and personalized service rarely found on Lake Garda since its aristocratic heyday. **Pros:** expansive and lush surroundings with many lodging options; a pampering and indulgent staff. **Cons:** not that cozy; no beach of its own. $ *Rooms from:* €199 ⊠ *Viale Rovereto 44* ☎ *0464/566600* ⊕ *www.dulacetduparc.com* ⤳ *159 rooms, 100 suites* ⊘ *Closed Nov.–Mar.* ❑ *Breakfast.*

$$
HOTEL

🏨 **Hotel Sole.** Comfortable, relatively affordable, and recently refurbished rooms occupy this classic lakeside 15th-century palazzo in the center of town, and those in front have terraces that open to breathtaking views of the lake. **Pros:** prime location on the lake; modern hotel conveniences; comfortable beds. **Cons:** sometimes taken over by tour groups; not for those looking for ultracontemporary design; food gets mixed reviews. $ *Rooms from:* €200 ⊠ *Piazza 3 Novembre 35* ☎ *0464/552686* ⊕ *www.hotelsoleriva.it* ⤳ *77 rooms, 4 suites* ⊘ *Closed Nov.–Dec. 24 and mid-Jan.–mid-Mar.* ❑ *Breakfast.*

$$$$
HOTEL
Fodor'sChoice
★

🏨 **Lido Palace.** The chic-est option in Riva, with ultramodern rooms inside a 19th-century palace, this beautiful hotel right on the lake also includes a high-end spa and the best restaurant in town. **Pros:** friendly service; gorgeous spa and pools; top-notch food. **Cons:** not all rooms have lake views or balconies; pricey. $ *Rooms from:* €425 ⊠ *Viale Carducci 10* ☎ *0464/021899* ⊕ *www.lido-palace.it* ⤳ *28 rooms, 6 junior suites, 8 suites* ⊘ *Closed mid-Jan.–early Mar.* ❑ *Breakfast.*

GARGNANO

30 km (19 miles) south of Riva del Garda, 144 km (89 miles) east of Milan.

This small port town was an important Franciscan center in the 13th century, and now comes alive in the summer months when German tourists, many of whom have villas here, crowd the small pebble beach. An Austrian flotilla bombarded the town in 1866, and some of the houses still bear marks of cannon fire. Mussolini owned two houses in Gargnano: one is now a language school and the other, Villa Feltrinelli, has been restored and reopened as a luxury hotel.

VISITOR INFORMATION

Gargnano Tourism Office ⊠ *Piazza Boldini 2* ☎ *0365/791243* ⊕ *www.gargnanosulgarda.it.*

WHERE TO EAT AND STAY

$$$ NORTHERN ITALIAN 🍴 **La Tortuga.** This rustic trattoria is more sophisticated than it first appears, with an extensive wine cellar and nouvelle-style twists on local dishes. Specialties include *zafferano risotto pistilli, fois gras e aceto balsamico* (saffron risotto with foie gras and balsamic vinegar), *persico con rosmarino* (perch with rosemary), and *capesante scottate su purè di fagoli, olio al rosmarino* (seared scalllops on bean puree with rosemary oil). The *palette di piccoli campioni di lago e di mare* (mixed lake and sea fish) is a worthy introduction to regional delights. [$] *Average main: €30* ✉ *Via XXIV Maggio 5* ☎ *0365/71251* 🌐 *www.ristorantelatortuga.it* ✍ *Reservations essential* 🕓 *Closed Tues., and Nov.–Mar. No lunch Mon.–Sat.*

$ HOTEL 🏨 **Garni Bartabel.** At this cozy inn on the main street of town, rooms are small but attractive, with Venetian-style furnishings and pastel décor, and reasonable prices. **Pros:** very attractive lake views; a bargain for this area. **Cons:** few luxuries; modest furnishings. [$] *Rooms from: €65* ✉ *Via Roma 39* ☎ *0365/71300* 🌐 *www.hotelbartabel.it* 🛏 *10 rooms* 🕓 *Closed Nov.–Mar.* 🍽 *Breakfast.*

$$$$ RESORT 🏨 **Lefay Resort & Spa Lago di Garda.** The first thing you'll notice about this elegant resort in the hills above Gargnano are the stupendous views of the lake and mountains; the second thing will be the 32,000-square-foot spa, where you may just want to stay all day—and some guests do. **Pros:** fabulously relaxing spa; lovely location; delicious breakfast buffet. **Cons:** village of Gargnano is down a steep and twisty road; dining at the property is quite expensive. [$] *Rooms from: €480* ✉ *Via Angelo Feltrinelli 136* ☎ *0365/241899* 🌐 *lagodigarda.lefayresorts.com* 🛏 *90 rooms* 🕓 *Closed Jan.–early Feb.* 🍽 *Breakfast.*

GARDONE RIVIERA

12 km (7 miles) south of Gargnano, 139 km (86 miles) east of Milan.

Now pleasantly faded, this once-fashionable 19th-century resort is best known these days for the hilltop estate of the poet Gabriele d'Annunzio, made as an elaborate memorial to himself. The middle-European appearance of its towers and palaces helps set this lakeside town apart from the rest of Italy. With the Italian Alps in the backdrop and crystalline lake views in the summer, it's a gorgeous, albeit underappreciated, destination.

EXPLORING

Heller Garden. More than 2,000 Alpine, subtropical, and Mediterranean species thrive at the Giardino Botanico Heller. ✉ *Via Roma 2* ☎ *0366/410877* 🌐 *www.hellergarden.com* 🎟 *€10* 🕓 *Mar.–Oct., daily 9–7.*

Il Vittoriale. The estate of the larger-than-life Gabriele d'Annunzio (1863–1938), one of Italy's major modern poets, and later war hero and supporter of Mussolini, is filled with the trappings of conquests in art, love, and war. His eccentric house crammed with quirky memorabilia can only be seen during a 30-minute guided tour, also given in English, and the extensive gardens are definitely worth a stroll, particularly to see the curious full-size war ship's prow. There's also an imposing mausoleum, made of white marble, along with two museums showcasing personal items from d'Annunzio's exploits. ✉ *Via Vittoriale 12* 📞 *0365/296511* 🌐 *www.vittoriale.it* 💰 *€16 for park, d'Annunzio Eroe and d'Annunzio Segreto museums, and guided tour of house; €13 for park and both museums; €8 for park and d'Annunzio Segreto museum.* 🕐 *Grounds: Apr.–Sept., daily 8:30–7; Oct.–Mar., daily 9–4. House and museum: Apr.–Sept., Tues.–Sun. 8:30–6:15; Oct.–Mar., Tues.–Sun. 9–4.*

Salò Market. Four kilometers (2½ miles) south of Gardone Riviera is the enchanting lakeside town of Salò, which history buffs may recognize as the capital of the ill-fated Social Republic, set up in 1943 by the Germans after they liberated Mussolini from the Gran Sasso. Every Saturday morning an enormous market is held in the Piazza dei Martiri della Libertà, with bargains on household goods, clothing, food, and other items. In August or September a lone vendor often sells locally unearthed *tartufi neri* (black truffles) at affordable prices. ✉ *Salò.*

WHERE TO STAY

$$$
HOTEL
Grand Hotel Fasano. Used as a hunting lodge in the 19th century, the Fasano has matured into a seasonal hotel of a high standard, with opulent, old-fashioned rooms and salons and many amenities. **Pros:** exquisitely stylish rooms; relaxing surroundings. **Cons:** not all rooms have lake views; staff can be snooty. 💲 *Rooms from: €270* ✉ *Corso Zanardelli 190* 📞 *0365/290220* 🌐 *www.ghf.it* 🛏 *75 rooms* 🕐 *Closed early Nov.–mid-Apr.* 🍴 *Breakfast.*

$$$
HOTEL
Grand Hotel Gardone. At this majestic 1800s palace surrounded by attractive landscaped gardens, nearly all the rooms have balconies that look out over the water, all bathrooms have been renovated in marble, and the service is top-notch. **Pros:** well-appointed; expansive gardens; lakeside pool. **Cons:** not much to do in the immediate area; no Wi-Fi in guest rooms. 💲 *Rooms from: €255* ✉ *Via Zanardelli 84* 📞 *0365/20261* 🌐 *www.grangardone.it* 🛏 *143 rooms, 25 suites* 🕐 *Closed mid-Oct.–Mar.* 🍴 *Breakfast.*

$$$
HOTEL
Villa Fiordaliso. This pink-and-white lakeside villa is now a fine restaurant, but it also has seven tastefully furnished rooms, some overlooking the lake. **Pros:** combines a movie set–worthy charm with the intimacy of a B&B; elaborate breakfast spread served at any time you want. **Cons:** short on amenities; rooms can be noisy. 💲 *Rooms from: €250* ✉ *Corso Zanardelli 150* 📞 *0365/20158* 🌐 *www.villafiordaliso.it* 🛏 *7 rooms* 🕐 *Closed Nov.–mid-Mar.* 🍴 *Breakfast.*

LAKE COMO

If you're after palatial villas, rose-laden belvederes, hanging wisteria and bougainvillea, lanterns casting a glow over lakeshore restaurants, and majestic Alpine vistas, then Lake Como is for you. Though summer crowds threaten to diminish the lake's dreamy mystery and slightly faded old-money gentility, the allure of this spectacular place endures. Como remains a consummate pairing of natural and man-made beauty. The villa gardens, like so many in Italy, are a union of two landscape traditions: that of Renaissance Italy, which values order, and that of Victorian England, which strives to create the illusion of natural wildness.

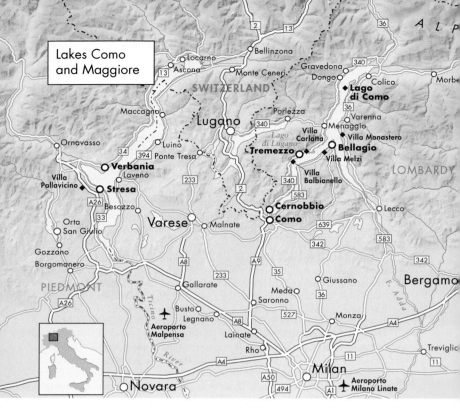

Such gardens are often framed by vast areas of picturesque farmland—fruit trees, olive groves, and vineyards.

Lake Como is some 47 km (30 miles) long north to south and is Europe's deepest lake (almost 1,350 feet). Car ferries and *vaporetti* (water buses) traverse the lake in season, making it easy to get to the other main towns, Cernobbio, Tremezzo, and Varenna. Many travelers head directly to boats waiting to take them to Bellagio and the *centro di lago*, the center region of the lake's three branches, and its most beautiful section. You should not pass by the 2,000-year-old walled city of Como, however, a leading textile center famous for its silks—even if you only linger long enough to see the medieval town center and pretty lakefront. Remember that Lake Como is extremely seasonal: if you go to Bellagio, for example, from November through February, you'll find nothing open—not a bar, restaurant, or shop.

GETTING HERE AND AROUND

Trains run regularly from Milan to the town of Como; the trip takes half an hour from the Central Station and an hour from the Cardorna Station. There's also service to the tiny town of Varenna, just across the lake from Bellagio; the trip from Milan takes 1¼ hours. Como is off the A9 autostrada. To get to the town from Milan, take A8 to A9; the drive takes about an hour. Ferries (mainly pedestrian) run regularly from Como and Varenna to different spots around the lake. For schedules, visit ⊕ *www.navigazionelaghi.it.*

BELLAGIO

30 km (19 miles) northeast of Como, 56 km (35 miles) northwest of Bergamo.

Sometimes called the prettiest town in Europe, Bellagio always seems perfectly adorned, with geraniums ablaze in every window and bougainvillea veiling its staircases, or *montées*. At dusk Bellagio's nightspots—including the wharf, where an orchestra serenades dancers under the stars—beckon you to come and make merry. It's an impossibly enchanting location, one that inspired the French composer Gabriel Fauré to call Bellagio "a diamond contrasting brilliantly with the sapphires of the three lakes in which it is set."

GETTING HERE AND AROUND

Boats can take you from here to Tremezzo, where Napoléon's worst Italian enemy, Count Sommariva, resided at Villa Carlotta; and a bit farther south of Tremezzo, to Villa Balbianello. Check with the tourist office for the hours of the launch to Tremezzo.

VISITOR INFORMATION

Bellagio Tourism Office ⊠ *Piazza Mazzini (Pontile Imbarcadero)* ☎ *031/950204* ⊕ *www.bellagiolakecomo.com.*

EXPLORING

Villa Melzi. The famous gardens of the Villa Melzi were once a favorite picnic spot for Franz Lizst, who advised author Louis de Ronchaud in 1837, "When you write the story of two happy lovers, place them on the shores of Lake Como. I do not know of any land so conspicuously blessed by heaven." The gardens are open to the public, and though you can't get into the 19th-century villa, don't miss the lavish Empirestyle family chapel. The Melzi were Napoléon's greatest allies in Italy (the family has passed down the name "Josephine" to the present day). Guided tours are available with advance booking. ⊠ *Via Melzi d'Eril 8* ☎ *339/4573838* ⊕ *www.giardinidivillamelzi.it* 🎫 *€6.50* ☉ *Late Mar.–late Oct., daily 9:30–6:30.*

Villa Monastero. By ferry from Bellagio it's a quick trip across the lake to Varenna. The principal sight here is the spellbinding garden of the Villa Monastero, which, as its name suggests, was originally a monastery. There's also a house museum where you can admire 18th century furnishings, as well as an international science and convention center. ⊠ *Viale Giovanni Polvani 4, Varenna* ☎ *0341/295450* ⊕ *www.villamonastero.eu* 🎫 *Garden €5, house and garden €8* ☉ *Garden: Mar.–early Nov., daily 9:30–7. House-museum: Mar.–July and Sept.–early*

Nov., weekends 9:30–7; Aug., daily 9:30–7. Last entry 30 mins before closing. Check the website for special Sun. openings in Nov. and Dec.

Villa Serbelloni Garden. This property of the Rockefeller Foundation has celebrated gardens on the site of Pliny the Elder's villa, overlooking Bellagio. There are only two 1½-hour-long guided visits per day, restricted to 30 people each, and in May these tend to be commandeered by group bookings. It's wise to arrive early to sign up. It also closes due to bad weather, so call in advance. ⊠ *Near Palazza della Chiesa* ☏ *031/951555* ⊕ *www.bellagiolakecomo.com* ⤳ *€9* ⊘ *Mid-Mar.–early Nov., Tues.– Sun. at 11 and 3:30; tours gather 15 mins before start.*

WHERE TO EAT AND STAY

$$ ✕ **Ristorante La Punta.** When tourist-heavy Bellagio starts to wear you
ITALIAN down, take respite at this charming restaurant located literally on the town's northern point, with amazing lake views both of Varenna to the north and Tremezzo to the west. It's only about a 10-minute scenic walk from the center of town. As you might expect, the menu is heavy on lake fish, so you'll want to start with the *antipasto di lago* (mixed fish platter) or the *patè di pesce* (fish pâté); for the mains, the baked lasagna and gnocchi with cream and Gorgonzola sauce get rave reviews. Though the dishes aren't innovative, they're fresh and well-prepared, and having that view to gaze at as you dine makes things even better. End the meal off right with the warm chocolate fondant cake. Ⓢ *Average main: €20* ⊠ *Via Eugenio Vitali 19* ☏ *031/951888* ⊕ *www.ristorantelapunta. it* ⌂ *Reservations essential.*

$$ ⊟ **Du Lac.** Most rooms at this comfortable old hotel owned by an Anglo-
HOTEL Italian family have views of the lake and mountains, while the rooftop terrace garden is a perfect spot for drinks or dozing. **Pros:** pleasant in-house restaurant; comfortable; friendly service. **Cons:** décor a little worn around the edges; not all rooms have lake views. Ⓢ *Rooms from: €195* ⊠ *Piazza Mazzini 32* ☏ *031/950320* ⊕ *www.bellagiohoteldulac. com* ⤳ *42 rooms* ⊘ *Closed Nov.–Mar.* ⓘⓞⓘ *Breakfast.*

$$$$ ⊟ **Grand Hotel Villa Serbelloni.** This grand lakeside hotel, designed to
HOTEL cradle nobility in high style, remains a refined haven for the discreetly
Fodor's Choice wealthy. **Pros:** historic lake hotel; great pool and health club; good low-
★ season deals. **Cons:** the luxury does not come cheap. Ⓢ *Rooms from: €462* ⊠ *Via Roma 1* ☏ *031/950216* ⊕ *www.villaserbelloni.com* ⤳ *61 rooms, 20 suites, 13 apartments* ⊘ *Hotel closed early Nov.–early Apr.; apartments closed Jan.* ⓘⓞⓘ *Breakfast.*

$$$$ ⊟ **Hotel Belvedere.** In Italian, belvedere means "beautiful view," and
HOTEL it's an apt name for this enchanting spot where antique furniture and eye-catching rugs complement the modern rooms, many of which have balconies and views of the lake. **Pros:** attention to detail; great views; lovely pool. **Cons:** a climb from the waterfront; need to request a lakeview room in advance. Ⓢ *Rooms from: €327* ⊠ *Via Valassina 31* ☏ *031/950410* ⊕ *www.belvederebellagio.com* ⤳ *56 rooms, 9 suites, 4 studios* ⊘ *Closed Nov.–Apr.* ⓘⓞⓘ *Breakfast.*

$$ ⊟ **Hotel Florence.** Most of the large and comfortable rooms in this villa
HOTEL dating from the 1880s are furnished with interesting antiques and have splendid views of the lake. **Pros:** central location; appealing public spaces. **Cons:** location may feel too central if you're looking to get

away from it all; no a/c in some rooms. $ *Rooms from: €150* ⊠ *Piazza Mazzini 46* ☎ *031/950342* ⊕ *www.hotelflorencebellagio.it* ↻ *30 rooms* ☾ *Closed mid-Oct.–mid-Apr.* ⦿ *Breakfast.*

TREMEZZO

34 km (21 miles) north of Cernobbio, 78 km (48 miles) north of Milan.

The dreamy lakeside town of Tremezzo is close to two outstanding and magical villas, as well as sprawling gardens and one of the lake's grandest hotels.

EXPLORING

Villa Balbianello. The relentlessly picturesque Balbianello may be the most magical house in all of Italy; you probably know it from cameos in the movies *Casino Royale* and *Star Wars Episode II: Attack of the Clones.* It sits on its own little promontory, Il Dosso d'Avedo, around the bend from the tiny fishing village of Ossuccio. The villa is composed of loggias, terraces, and *palazzini* (tiny palaces), all spilling down verdant slopes to the lakeshore, where you'll find an old Franciscan church, a magnificent stone staircase, and a statue of San Carlo Borromeo blessing the waters.

The villa is usually reached by boat from Como and Bellagio, which leaves you at the village of Lenno. From there, marked signs lead you to the villa—it's either accessible by foot via a 20-minute walk or a more challenging 45-minute hike, or there is often private boat service for €7 round-trip, €5 one-way. ⊠ *Il Dosso d'Avedo, Lenno, 5 km (3 miles) southwest of Tremezzo* ☎ *0344/56110* ⊕ *www.visitfai.it/dimore/villadelbalbianello* 🎫 *€13 villa and gardens, with 1-hr guided tour; €7.50 gardens only* ☾ *Mid-Mar.–mid-Nov., Tues. and Thurs.–Sun. 10–6; last entry to gardens at 5:30* Ⓜ *Ferry stop Lenno.*

Villa Carlotta. If you're lucky enough to visit Tremezzo in late spring or early summer, you will find the magnificent Villa Carlotta a riot of color, with more than 14 acres of azaleas and dozens of varieties of rhododendrons in full bloom. The height of the blossoms is late April to early May. The villa was built between 1690 and 1743 for the luxury-loving marquis Giorgio Clerici. The garden's collection is remarkable, particularly considering the difficulties of transporting delicate plants before the age of aircraft. Palms, banana trees, cacti, eucalyptus, a sequoia, orchids, and camellias are among the more than 500 species.

The villa's interior is worth a visit, particularly if you have a taste for the romantic sculptures of Antonio Canova (1757–1822). The best known is his *Cupid and Psyche,* which depicts the lovers locked in an odd but graceful embrace, with the young god above and behind, his wings extended, while Psyche awaits a kiss that will never come. The villa can be reached by boats from Bellagio and Como. ⊠ *Via Regina 2* ☎ *0344/40405* ⊕ *www.villacarlotta.it* 🎫 *€9* ☾ *Late Mar.–mid-Oct., daily 9–7:30; last ticket sold at 6, museum closes at 6:30. Mid-Mar.–late Mar. and mid-Oct.–mid-Nov., daily 10–6; last ticket sold at 5, museum closes at 5:30.*

WHERE TO EAT AND STAY

$$$$ ITALIAN 🍴 **La Locanda dell'Isola.** For a dining experience you won't soon forget, make your way to Sala Comacina (about a 10-minute drive south of Tremezzo) and take a 5-minute speedboat to Lake Como's only island, Isola Comacina. There you'll be treated to the same rustic set menu served at La Locanda since 1947: veggie antipasti; thinly sliced prosciutto and *bresaola* (air-dried beef); grilled salmon trout; fried chicken with salad; Parmesan cheese sliced from an enormous wheel; and oranges or peaches with ice cream for dessert. The finale: brandied coffee set afire with a dramatic flourish while charismatic owner Benvenuto Puricelli regales you with tales of the island's history. The views are phenomenal, the stories are fun, and the food is better than it needs to be. At €70 per person, including wine and water (and no credit cards), it's a little steep but worth the price. Work off your meal afterward by hiking around the tranquil island. [$] *Average main: €70* ✉ *Isola Comacino* ☎ *0344/55083, 0344/56755* 🌐 *comacina.it* ✍ *Reservations essential* 💳 *No credit cards* 🕘 *Closed Tues., and Nov.–Feb.*

$$$$ RESORT Fodor's Choice ★ 🏨 **Grand Hotel Tremezzo.** Creature comforts in this turn-of-the-20th-century building—one of the top grand hotels on the lake—include a lush park, three heated swimming pools (one of them floats on pontoons on the lake), a small private beach, and sumptuous guest rooms where old-world style is accented with modern amenities. **Pros:** lakeside location; beautiful views; gracious service. **Cons:** not well situated if you're looking for shopping or nightlife; very expensive; somewhat busy road between hotel and lake. [$] *Rooms from: €632* ✉ *Via Regina 8* ☎ *0344/42491* 🌐 *www.grandhoteltremezzo.com* 🛏 *77 rooms, 13 suites* 🕘 *Closed mid-Nov.–Feb.* 🍽 *Breakfast.*

$$ B&B/INN 🏨 **Hotel Rusall.** On the hillside above Tremezzo in the middle of a large garden, this hotel has small, comfortably simple rooms that offer quiet, privacy, and the chance to lie by the pool and enjoy a nice view. **Pros:** lovely walks into town and in the countryside; more intimate than grander lake hotels. **Cons:** takes some effort to reach the hillside location; no a/c. [$] *Rooms from: €128* ✉ *Via San Martino 2* ☎ *0344/40408* 🌐 *www.rusallhotel.com* 🛏 *23 rooms* 🕘 *Closed weekdays Nov.–Dec. and all of Jan.–Mar.* 🍽 *Multiple meal plans.*

CERNOBBIO

5 km (3 miles) north of Como, 53 km (34 miles) north of Milan.

The legendary resort of Villa d'Este is reason enough to visit this jewel on the lake, but the town itself is worth a stroll. The place still has a neighborhood feel to it, especially on summer evenings and weekends when the piazza is full of families and couples strolling.

VISITOR INFORMATION

Cernobbio Tourism Office ✉ *Via Regina 23* ☎ *031/349341* 🌐 *www.comune.cernobbio.co.it* 🕘 *Closed Nov.–Apr.*

WHERE TO EAT AND STAY

$$ MODERN ITALIAN 🍴 **Casa Santo Stefano.** The newest addition to Cernobbio's restaurant scene occupies a lovely villa in the hills with chic white-and-wood rooms and wonderful mountain and lake vistas; ask to dine on the terrace

if the weather allows. The food is a modern interpretation of Italian cuisine, with light and fresh seasonal menus that update monthly and may include dishes such as porcini flan with green celery and Parmesan, guinea fowl stuffed with chestnuts, and timbale of sea bream with a salad of spelt and pumpkin. If all that food leaves you sleepy, spend the night in one of their three airy guestrooms that include access to the pool and garden. $ *Average main: €19* ✉ *Via Caronti 7/B* ☎ *031/3347621* ⊕ *www.casasantostefano.it* ⌂ *Reservations essential* ⊗ *Closed Tues. No lunch Mon. and Wed.*

$$
NORTHERN
ITALIAN
✕ **Il Gatto Nero.** A vantage point in the hills above Cernobbio provides a splendid view of the lake at this celebrity favorite. Specialties include *spaghetti alla chitarra con carbonara di fave e pecorino di Pienza* (spaghetti with broad beans and Pecorino cheese), *risotto alla parmigiana con ganassino* (risotto with Parmesan cheese and braised beef), and lake fish. Save room for the warm chocolate torte, with its delicious liquid-chocolate center. Reservations are a good idea. $ *Average main: €22* ✉ *Via Monte Santo 69* ☎ *031/512042* ⊕ *www.ristorantegattonero.com* ⊗ *Closed Mon. No lunch Tues.*

$$$$
HOTEL
Fodor's Choice
★
🏨 **Villa d'Este.** One of the grandest hotels in Italy has long wlecomed Europe's rich and famous, housing them in guest rooms still furnished in the Empire style. **Pros:** fine service; amazing grounds; excellent restaurant. **Cons:** may seem too formal to some; not all rooms feature lake views; all this grandness comes with a hefty price tag. $ *Rooms from: €840* ✉ *Via Regina 40* ☎ *031/3481* ⊕ *www.villadeste.it* 🛏 *152 rooms, 7 suites, 2 private villas* ⊗ *Closed mid-Nov.–1st wk of Mar.* ⦿ *Breakfast.*

COMO

5 km (3 miles) south of Cernobbio, 30 km (19 miles) southwest of Bellagio, 49 km (30 miles) north of Milan.

Como commands the south shore of the lake. In its center, elegant cobblestone pedestrian streets wind their way past parks and bustling cafés. However, it's only partly a resort: the city also has an industrial heritage, deeply rooted in the production of textiles, particularly silk and the silk trade. If you're traveling by car, leave it at the edge of the town center in the well-lighted underground parking facility right on the lake.

VISITOR INFORMATION
Como Tourism Office ✉ *Piazza Cavour 17* ☎ *031/269712* ⊕ *www. lakecomo.com* ⊗ *Mon.–Sat. 9–1 and 2–5.*

EXPLORING
Duomo. The splendid 15th-century Renaissance-Gothic Duomo was begun in 1396. The facade was added in 1455, and the transepts were completed in the mid-18th century. The dome was designed by Filippo Juvara (1678–1736), chief architect of many of the sumptuous palaces of the royal house of Savoy. The facade has statues of two of Como's most famous sons, Pliny the Elder and Pliny the Younger, whose writings are among the most important documents from antiquity. Inside, the works of art include Luini's *Holy Conversation,* a fresco cycle by Morazzone, and the *Marriage of the Virgin Mary* by Ferrari. ✉ *Piazza*

del Duomo ☎ *031/265244* ⊕ *www.cattedraledicomo.it* ⊙ *Mon.–Sat. 7:30–7:30, Sun. 7:30–9:30.*

Museo Didattico della Seta (*Silk Museum*). From silkworm litters to textile finishing machinery, this small but complete collection preserves the history of a manufacturing region that continues to supply almost three-fourths of Europe's silk. The friendly staffers will give you an overview of the museum; they are also happy to provide brochures and information about local retail shops. The location isn't well marked: follow the textile school's driveway around to the low-rise concrete building on the left, and take the shallow ramp down to the entrance. ⊠ *Via Castelnuovo 9* ☎ *031/303180* ⊕ *www.museosetacomo.com* 🎫 *€10* ⊙ *Tues.–Fri. 9–noon and 3–6.*

San Fedele. At the heart of Como's medieval quarter, the city's first cathedral is well worth a peek. The apse walls and ceiling are completely frescoed, as are the ceilings above the altar. ⊠ *Piazza San Fedele* ☎ *031/267295* ⊕ *www.parrocchiasanfedelecomo.it* ⊙ *Daily 8–noon and 3:30–7.*

Sant'Abbondio. If you head into Como's industrial quarter, you will come upon this beautiful church, a gem of Romanesque architecture begun by Benedictine monks in 1013 and consecrated by Pope Urban II in 1095. Inside, the five aisles converge on a presbytery with a semicircular apse decorated with a cycle of 14th-century frescoes by Lombard artists heavily influenced by the Sienese school. To see them, turn right as you enter and put 50¢ in the mechanical box for a few minutes of lighting. In the nave, the cubical capitals are the earliest example of this style in Italy. ⊠ *Via Sant'Abbondio* ☎ *031/304518* ⊕ *www.santabbondio.eu* ⊙ *Daily 8–6; winter daily 8–4:30.*

WHERE TO EAT AND STAY

$$
MODERN ITALIAN
✗ **The Market Place.** This intimate restaurant just outside Como's historic center serves up full-flavored modern Italian food in interesting combinations—and at €37 for a five-course tasting menu, and only €15 more for four wine pairings, it may be the best deal in town. Though the décor is on the sparse side, you'll be spending your time focusing on the well-presented dishes; the young, helpful servers take time to describe each course. The playful seasonal menu may include red shrimp tartare with avocado and fried squid, eggplant ravioli with tomato coulis and Parmesan mousse, or pork loin with roasted pepper cream, spinach, and endive. The place is popular with tourists and locals alike, so make a reservation to ensure you get a table. Ⓢ *Average main: €20* ⊠ *Via Borsieri 21/a* ☎ *031/270712* ⊕ *www.themarketplace.it* 🍴 *Reservations essential* ⊙ *Closed Sun. and Mon.*

$$$
HOTEL
🏨 **Albergo Terminus.** This early-20th-century Art Nouveau landmark commands a panoramic view over Lake Como; inside, the marbled public spaces and old-fashioned guest rooms are done up in floral patterns and furnished with large walnut wardrobes and silk-covered sofas. **Pros:** old-world charm; right on the lake; sauna and gym. **Cons:** limited number of rooms with lake views; décor in some rooms seems dated, with dizzying floral wallpaper. Ⓢ *Rooms from: €230* ⊠ *Lungo*

Lario Trieste 14 ☎ *031/329111* 🌐 *www.albergoterminus.it* 🛏 *50 rooms* 🍴 *Breakfast.*

$$$$ HOTEL 🏨 **CastaDiva Resort & Spa.** If you're looking for an extravagant hotel with a modern feel away from the hustle-and-bustle, this collection of seven 19th-century villas, named for opera singer and former resident Guiditta Pasta, has been brought thoroughly into the 21st-century. **Pros:** lovely, secluded lakeside location; fabulous extensive spa area; knowledgeable staff. **Cons:** a 10- to 15-minute drive to the town of Como; lack of dining options nearby; some may find the décor more over-the-top than refined. [$] *Rooms from: €790* ✉ *Via Caronti 69, Blevio* ☎ *031/32513035* 🌐 *www.castadivaresort.com* 🛏 *73 rooms, 2 private villas* 🕒 *Closed Nov.–mid-Mar.* 🍴 *Breakfast.*

$$ HOTEL Fodor's Choice ★ 🏨 **Posta Design Hotel.** This newly renovated boutique hotel on pedestrian-only Piazza Volta in downtown Como, just a block from the lake, infuses minimalist modern design into a sleek 1931 building designed by Rationalist architect Giuseppe Terragni. **Pros:** central location; comfortable rooms; friendly service. **Cons:** parking at public garage about a five-minute walk away, though you'll get a 20% discount; sparse amenities (no minibars in rooms, no breakfast, no gym). [$] *Rooms from: €189* ✉ *Via Garibaldi 2* ☎ *031/2769011* 🌐 *www.postadesignhotel.com* 🛏 *14 rooms* 🕒 *Closed Dec. 23–early Jan.*

SPORTS AND THE OUTDOORS

Lake Como has lots of ways to stay active and outdoors, from windsurfing at the lake's northern end, to boating, sailing, and Jet Skiing at Como and Cernobbio. The lake is also quite swimmable in summer. For hikers there are lovely paths all around the lake. For an easy trek, take the funicular up to Brunate, and walk along the mountain to the lighthouse for a stunning view of the lake.

LAKE MAGGIORE

Magnificently scenic, Lake Maggiore has a unique geographical position: its mountainous western shore is in Piedmont, its lower eastern shore is in Lombardy, and its northern tip is in Switzerland. The lake stretches nearly 50 km (30 miles) and is up to 5 km (3 miles) wide. The better-known resorts are on the western shore.

GETTING HERE AND AROUND

Trains run regularly from Milan to the town of Stresa on Lake Maggiore; the trip takes 1 to 1½ hours, depending on the type of train. By car from Milan to Stresa, take the A8 autostrada to A8dir, and from A8dir take A26; the drive is about 1¼ hours.

STRESA AND THE ISOLE BORROMEE

80 km (50 miles) northwest of Milan.

One of the better-known resorts on the western shore, Stresa is a tourist town that provided one of the settings for Hemingway's *A Farewell to Arms.* It has capitalized on its central lakeside position, though the

6

luxurious elegance that distinguished its heyday has faded; the grand hotels are still grand, but traffic now encroaches on their parks and gardens.

The best way to escape to yesteryear is to head for the Isole Borromee (Borromean Islands) in Lake Maggiore. Boats to the three islands depart every 15 to 30 minutes from the dock at Stresa's Piazza Marconi, as well as from Piazzale Lido at the northern end of the promenade. There's also a boat from Verbania; check locally for the seasonal schedule. Although you can hire a private boatman, it's cheaper and just as convenient to use the regular service. Make sure you buy a ticket allowing you to visit all the islands—Bella, Dei Pescatori, and Madre. The islands take their name from the Borromeo family, which has owned them since the 12th century.

VISITOR INFORMATION

Stresa Tourism Office ☒ *Piazza Marconi 16* ☎ *0323/31308* ⊕ *www. stresaturismo.it.*

Isole Borromee Information ☎ *0323/30556* ⊕ *www.borromeoturismo.it.*

EXPLORING

Funivia. For amazing views, take the Funivia—a cable car that takes you to heights from which you can see seven lakes: Maggiore, Orta, Mergozzo, Varese, Camabbio, Monate, and Biandronno. Situated between Lakes Maggiore and Orta, it offers tourists 360-degree views of the Po Valley right across to the distant Alpine peaks. At the top, nature and adventure lovers can rent mountain bikes and ride on properly marked paths, while others can just relax at a local restaurant. ☒ *Piazzale Lido 8* ☎ *0323/30295* ⊕ *www.stresa-mottarone.it* ☚ *€19 round-trip in spring and summer. €13.50 round-trip in fall and winter* ⊙ *Apr. 1–Oct. 31, daily 9:30–6; Nov.–mid-Mar., daily 8:10–5:40.*

Isola Bella (*Beautiful Island*). The most famous of the three Isole Borromee (Borromean Islands), and the first that you'll visit, is named after Isabella, whose husband, Carlo III Borromeo (1538–84), built the palace and terraced gardens for her as a wedding present. Before Count Carlo began his project, the island was rocky and almost devoid of vegetation; the soil for the garden had to be transported from the mainland. Wander up the 10 terraces of the gardens, where peacocks roam among the scented shrubs, statues, and fountains, for a splendid view of the lake. Visit the palazzo to see the rooms where famous guests—including Napoléon and Mussolini—stayed in 18th-century splendor. Those three interlocked rings on walls and even streets represent the powerful Borromeo, Visconti, and Sforza families. ☒ *Isola Bella* ☎ *0323/30556* ⊕ *www.isoleborromee.it* ☚ *Garden, palazzo, and painting gallery €15* ⊙ *Late Mar.–late Oct., daily 9–5:30.*

Isola dei Pescatori (*Island of the Fishermen, also known as Isola Superiore*). Stop for a while at the smallest Borromean Island, less than 100 yards wide and only about ½ km (¼ mile) long. It's the perfect place for a seafood lunch before, after, or in between your visit to the other two islands. Of the 10 or so restaurants on this tiny island, the three worth visiting are **Ristorante Unione** (☎ *0323/933798*), **Ristorante Verbano** (☎ *0323/30408*), and **Ristorante Belvedere** (☎ *0323/32292*). The island's little lanes strung with fishing nets and dotted with shrines to the Madonna are the definition of picturesque; little wonder that in high season the village is crowded with postcard stands.

Isola Madre (*Mother Island*). All of this Borromean Island is a botanical garden, with a season that stretches from late March to late October due to the climatic protection of the mighty Alps and the tepid waters of Lago Maggiore. The cacti and palm trees here, so far north and so near the border with Switzerland, are a beautiful surprise. Take time to see the profusion of exotic trees and shrubs running down to the shore in every direction. Two special times to visit are April (for the camellias) and May (for azaleas and rhododendrons). Also on the island is a 16th-century palazzo, where the Borromeo family still lives for part of the year. The palazzo has an antique puppet theater on display, complete with string puppets, prompt books, and elaborate scenery designed by Alessandro Sanquirico, who was a scenographer at La Scala in Milan. ⊠ *Isola Madre* ☎ *0323/30556* ⊕ *www.isoleborromee.it* 🎫 *€12* ☉ *Late Mar.–late Oct., daily 9–5:30.*

Parco della Villa Pallavicino. As you wander around the palms and semitropical shrubs, don't be surprised if you're followed by a peacock or even an ostrich: they're part of the zoological garden and are allowed to roam almost at will. From the top of the hill on which the villa stands you can see the gentle hills of the Lombardy shore of Lake Maggiore and, nearer and to the left, the jewel-like Borromean Islands. In addition to a bar and restaurant, the grounds also have picnic spots. ⊠ *Via Sempione 8* ☎ *0323/31533* ⊕ *www.parcozoopallavicino.it* 🎫 *€9.50* ☉ *Mid-Mar.–late Oct., daily 9–6.*

WHERE TO EAT AND STAY

$$
MODERN ITALIAN
✕ **Trattoria due Piccioni.** In a town with an overabundance of touristy pizza and pasta places, this unassumingly modern family-run bistro raises the bar. While the shabby-chic décor and friendly service entice, the real draw is the short but smart menu, chock-full of thoughtful and inventive twists on Italian cuisine. Start with the little vegetable cakes with warm local cream cheese followed by a house-made pasta such as ravioli with sheep ricotta, hazelnuts, and lemon or gnocchi with a ragout of fish from the lake, or opt for a heartier main like the duck confit with thyme, honey, and braised onions. Just make sure to leave room for the "birramisù," an unusual and delicious take on tiramisù made with stout beer. Ⓢ *Average main: €16* ⊠ *Via P. Tomaso 61* ☎ *0323/934556* ⊕ *www.duepiccioni.it* ☉ *Closed Wed.*

$$$$
HOTEL
Fodor's Choice
★
🛏 **Grand Hotel des Iles Borromees.** This palatial, Liberty-style hotel has catered to a demanding European clientele since 1863, and spacious salons and guest rooms still have lavish furnishings of the turn of the 20th century. **Pros:** the grace and style of a bygone era, with modern amenities; sumptuously decorated rooms, particularly the fabulous Hemingway Suite. **Cons:** very expensive; some staff a little snooty. Ⓢ *Rooms from: €451* ⊠ *Corso Umberto I 67* ☎ *0323/938938* ⊕ *www.borromees.it* 🛏 *179 rooms, 11 suites* ☉ *Closed Dec. and Jan.* ⑩ *Breakfast.*

$ ⛾ **Primavera.** These compact, simply furnished rooms in a 1950s build-
HOTEL   ing hung with flower boxes are a few blocks up from the lake. **Pros:** good
value; convenient location. **Cons:** no lake views; small, plainly furnished
rooms. Ⓢ *Rooms from: €100* ⊠ *Via Cavour 39* ☎ *0323/31286* ⊕ *www.
hotelprimaverastresa.com* ⋙ *37 rooms* ☾ *Closed Jan.* ⛾ *Breakfast.*

VERBANIA

16 km (10 miles) north of Stresa, 95 km (59 miles) northwest of Milan.

The quaint town of Verbania is across the Gulf of Pallanza from its
more touristy neighbor, Stresa. It is known for the Villa Taranto, which
has magnificent botanical gardens. With its majestic gardens and greenery, it is often called the Garden of Lake Maggiore.

EXPLORING

Villa Taranto. The Villa Taranto was acquired in 1931 by Scottish captain
Neil McEachern, who helped make the magnificent gardens here what
they are today, adding terraces, waterfalls, more than 3,000 plant species from all over the world—including 300 varieties of dahlias—and
broad meadows sloping gently to the lake. While the gardens can be
visited, the villa itself is not open to the public. ⊠ *Via Vittorio Veneto
111* ☎ *0323/404555* ⊕ *www.villataranto.it* ▤ *€10* ☾ *Late Mar.–Sept.,
daily 8:30–6:30; Oct.–early Nov., daily 9–4.*

WHERE TO STAY

$ ⛾ **Il Chiostro.** Using space formed from a 17th-century monastery merged
HOTEL   with an adjoining 19th-century textile factory, this hotel offers simple,
functional rooms, some overlooking a lovely garden. **Pros:** friendly
and efficient staff; quiet atmosphere; affordable for the area. **Cons:**
rooms are fairly plain; limited amenities. Ⓢ *Rooms from: €120* ⊠ *Via
Fratelli Cervi 14* ☎ *0323/404077* ⊕ *www.chiostrovb.it* ⋙ *100 rooms*
⛾ *Multiple meal plans.*

$$ ⛾ **Il Sole di Ranco.** For more than 150 years the same family has run this
HOTEL   elegant lakeside inn about an hour's drive from Verbania, where guest
rooms and suites are in two late-19th-century villas surrounded by a
garden perched high on the banks of the lake opposite Stresa. **Pros:**
classic lake setting; tranquil grounds, meticulously maintained. **Cons:**
a bit distant from lake's tourist center (although the hotel offers tours
with private drivers); décor on the old-fashioned side. Ⓢ *Rooms from:
€190* ⊠ *Piazza Venezia 5, Ranco* ☎ *0331/976507* ⊕ *www.ilsolediranco.
it* ⋙ *14 rooms* ☾ *Closed late Dec.–early Feb.* ⛾ *Breakfast.*

PIEDMONT AND
VALLE D'AOSTA

WELCOME TO PIEDMONT AND VALLE D'AOSTA

TOP REASONS TO GO

★ **Sacra di San Michele:** Explore one of the country's most spectacularly situated religious monuments.

★ **Castello Fénis:** This castle transports you back in time to the Middle Ages.

★ **Monte Bianco:** A cable car ride over the snowcapped mountain will take your breath away.

★ **Turin's Museo Egizio:** A surprising treasure— one of the world's richest collections of Egyptian art outside Cairo.

★ **Regal wines:** Some of Italy's most revered reds—led by Barolo, dubbed "the king of wines"—come from the hills of southern Piedmont.

★ **Turin's Galleria Sabauda:** Witness to the regal splendor of the reigning House of Savoy, this museum is famed for its spectacular Old Master collection.

1 Turin. The region's main city isn't just the car capital of Italy and home to the Holy Shroud. Neoclassical piazzas, shops filled with chocolates and chic fashions, and elegant Baroque palazzos have been restored in grand style.

2 The Monferrato and the Langhe. These hills are famous among food and wine connoisseurs. Asti gave the world Asti Spumante, Alba is known for its truffles and mushrooms, and the Langhe hills produce some of Italy's finest wines.

3 Valle d'Aosta. The mountains and valleys of this region cry out to be strolled, climbed, and skied. Here, the highest Alpine peaks—including Monte Bianco (aka Mont Blanc) and the Matterhorn—shelter resorts such as Breuil-Cervinia and Courmayeur and the great nature preserve known as the Gran Paradiso.

4 The Colline and Savoy Palaces. West of Turin, this is a region of medieval castles and fortifications, the highlight of which is the storybook town of Rivoli.

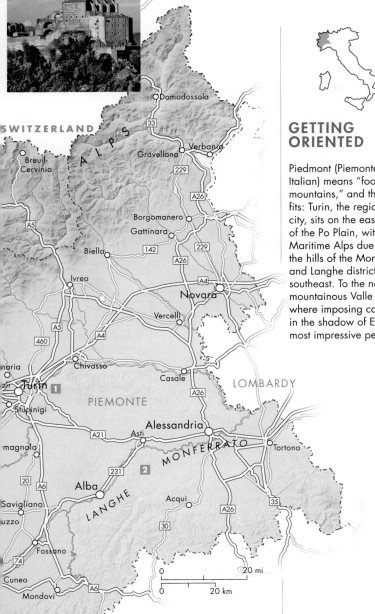

GETTING ORIENTED

Piedmont (Piemonte in Italian) means "foot of the mountains," and the name fits: Turin, the region's major city, sits on the eastern end of the Po Plain, with the Maritime Alps due south and the hills of the Monferrato and Langhe districts to the southeast. To the north is the mountainous Valle d'Aosta, where imposing castles sit in the shadow of Europe's most impressive peaks.

7

Map labels:

SWITZERLAND

Domodossola

Breuil-Cervinia

A L P S

33

Verbania

Gravellona

229

A26

Borgomanero

Gattinara

A5

Biella

142

229

A26

Ivrea

A4

Novara

Vercelli

A5

A4

460

naria

Chivasso

Casale

LOMBARDY

zli

Turin 1

A26

Stupinigi

PIEMONTE

magnola

A21

Asti

Alessandria

Tortona

231

2

MONFERRATO

20

A6

Alba

Acqui

A26

35

Savigliano

LANGHE

30

uzzo

Fossano

74

0   20 mi

Cuneo

A6

0   20 km

Mondovi

28

LIGURIA

EATING AND DRINKING WELL IN PIEDMONT AND VALLE D'AOSTA

In Piedmont and Valle d'Aosta you can find rustic specialties from farmhouse hearths, fine cuisine with a French accent, and everything in between. The Piedmontese take their food and wine very seriously.

There's a significant concentration of upscale restaurants in Piedmont, with refined cuisine designed to showcase the region's fine wines. Wine-oriented menus are prevalent both in cities and in the country, where even simply named trattorias may offer a *menu di degustazione* (a multicourse tasting menu that highlights the chef's specialties) accompanied by wines paired with each dish.

In Turin the ritual of the *aperitivo* (aperitif) has been finely tuned, and most cafés from the early evening onward provide lavish buffets that are included in the price of a cocktail—a respectable substitute for dinner if you're traveling on a limited budget. As a result, restaurants in Turin tend to fill only after 9 pm.

GREAT GRISSINI

Throughout the region, though especially in Turin, you'll find that most meals are accompanied by *grissini* (bread sticks), *pictured above.*

When they are freshly made and hand-rolled, these renditions are a far cry from the thin and dry, plastic-wrapped versions available elsewhere.

Grissini were invented in Turin in the 17th century to ease the digestive problems of little Prince Vittorio Amedeo II (1675–1730). Napoléon called them *petits batons* and was supposedly addicted to them.

TRUFFLES

The *tartufo* (truffle) is a peculiar delicacy—a gnarly clump of fungus that grows wild in forests a few inches underground. It's hunted down using truffle-sniffing dogs. The payoff is a powerful, perfume flavor that makes gourmets swoon, and that they are willing to pay a small fortune for. Though truffles are more abundant farther south in Umbria, the most coveted ones are the *tartufi bianchi* (white truffles), *pictured at right,* from Alba in Piedmont. A thin shaving of truffle often tops pasta dishes; they're also used to flavor soups and other dishes.

POLENTA AND PASTA

The area's best-known dish is probably polenta, creamy cornmeal served with *carbonada* (a meat stew), melted cheese, or wild mushrooms. *Agnolotti*—crescent-shape pasta stuffed with meat filling, *pictured below*—is another specialty, often served with the pan juices of roast veal. *Agnolotti del plin* is a smaller version topped with melted butter and shaved truffles.

CHEESE

In keeping with their northern character, Piedmont and Valle d'Aosta are both known for *fonduta,* a version of fondue made with melted cheese, eggs, and sometimes grated truffles. Fontina and ham also often deck out the ubiquitous

French-style crêpes *alla valdostana,* served casserole-style.

MEAT

The locally raised beef of Piedmont is some of Italy's most highly prized; it's often braised or stewed with the region's hearty red wine. In winter, *bollito misto* (various meats, boiled and served with a rich sauce) shows up on many menus, and *fritto misto,* a combination of fried meats and vegetables, is another specialty.

DESSERTS AND SWEETS

Though desserts here are less sweet than in some other Italian regions, treats like *panna cotta* (a cooked milk custard), *torta di nocciole* (hazelnut torte), and *bonet* (a pudding made with hazelnuts, cocoa, milk, and macaroons) are delights. Turin is renowned for its delicate pastries and fine chocolates, especially for *gianduiotti,* made with hazelnuts.

WINE

Piedmont is one of Italy's most important wine regions, producing full-bodied reds, such as Barolo, Barbaresco, freisa, barbera, and the lighter dolcetto. Asti Spumante, a sweet sparkling wine, comes from the region, while Valle d'Aosta is famous for brandies made from fruits or herbs.

Updated
by Peter
Blackman

Northwest Italy's Piedmont and Valle d'Aosta regions come with a large dose of mountain splendor, bourgeois refinement, culinary achievement, and scenic beauty. Two of Europe's most famous peaks, Monte Bianco (Mont Blanc) and Monte Cervino (the Matterhorn), straddle Valle d'Aosta's borders with France and Switzerland, and the region draws skiers and hikers from all over. You can ascend the mountains by cable car, or, if you're an experienced climber, make a go of it with professional guides. For the less actively inclined, a visit to the mountain museum in Bard might well do the trick.

To the south, the mist-shrouded lowlands skirting the Po River are home to Turin, a city that may not have the artistic treasures of Rome or the cutting-edge style of Milan, but has developed a sense of urban sophistication that makes it a pleasure to visit. The first capital of unified Italy and the fourth-largest city in the country, it was once often overlooked on tourist itineraries as a mere industrial center (FIAT is based here). It was the Winter Olympic Games of 2006 that put Turin on many tourists' map. Still, despite its higher profile, and its many excellent museums, cafés, and restaurants, Turin never feels overrun.

Farther south, vineyards carpet the rolling hills of the Langhe and Monferrato areas, where Barolo, Barbaresco and Asti Spumante wines, some of Italy's finest, are produced. It's here, as well, that the prized white truffle of Alba is found and celebrated during an autumn fair.

Piedmont has the longest border with France of any other region, and the fact of its having been ruled by the French Savoy for centuries is revealed in a Gallic influence in all walks of life—especially in the food and architecture. Turin's mansard roofs and porticoed avenues can make a walk through its streets feel like a stroll down a Parisian boulevard. Food is richer, creamier, and perhaps more refined than many other parts of Italy, and the standard of service, even in simple restaurants, is often very high.

PIEDMONT AND VALLE D'AOSTA PLANNER

MAKING THE MOST OF YOUR TIME

Turin needs at least two or three days to visit properly. If you have extra time, visit one of the magnificent palaces and hunting lodges built by the Savoy family. They surround Turin in the so-called *corona di delizie* (crown of delights) and make for an easy day trip.

Plan on several days to visit the Langhe and Monferrato areas. The towns of Alba and Asti should not be missed, but neither should the smaller wine towns that dot the rolling hills of both regions. You'll need your own car here, but will be rewarded with great views, great food, and great wine. If you're coming here in September and October, when there are festivals in both Alba and Asti, make sure to book your trip well in advance.

Unless you are planning on a skiing or hiking holiday, the Valle d'Aosta requires less time to visit. The emphasis here is on the natural beauty of the mountains, but if you are driving between France and Italy, the region certainly merits a one- or two-night stopover, in either Courmayeur or Aosta; be sure not to miss the Castello di Fénis and the Forte di Bard on your way.

GETTING HERE AND AROUND

BUS TRAVEL

Turin's main bus station is on the corner of Corso Inghilterra and Corso Vittorio Emanuele. There's also a major bus station at Aosta, across the street from the train station.

GTT. Urban buses, trams, and the subway are all operated by this company. ⊠ *Turin* ☎ *800/019152 (toll-free in Italy)* ⊕ *www.comune.torino. it/gtt.*

SADEM. This Turin-based bus line provides service throughout Piedmont and Valle d'Aosta, as well as a regular shuttle service to Caselle, the Turin airport, and to the Malpensa airport outside Milan. Tickets for the airport shuttle can be purchased online. ⊠ *Turin* ☎ *800/801600 (toll-free in Italy)* ⊕ *www.sadem.it.*

SAVDA. This Aosta-based company specializes in mountain service, providing frequent links between Aosta, Turin, and Courmayeur as well as Milan. ⊠ *Aosta* ☎ *0165/367011, 800/170444 (toll-free in Italy)* ⊕ *www.savda.it.*

CAR TRAVEL

Like any mountainous region, the Italian Alps can be tricky to navigate by car. Roads that look like highways on the map can be narrow and twisting, with steep slopes and cliffside drops. Generally, roads are well maintained, but the distance covered by all of those curves tends to take longer than you might expect, so it's best to figure in extra time for getting around. This is especially true in winter, when weather conditions can slow traffic and close roads. Check with local tourist offices or, in

7

a pinch, with the police to make sure roads are passable and safe, and to find out whether you need tire chains for snowy and icy roads.

For travel across the French, Swiss, and Italian borders in Piedmont and Valle d'Aosta, only a few routes are usable year-round: the 12-km (7-mile) Mont Blanc tunnel connecting Chamonix with Courmayeur; the Colle del Gran San Bernardo/Col du Grand St. Bernard (connecting Martigny to Aosta on Swiss highway E27 and Italian highway SS27, with 6 km [4 miles] of tunnel); and the Traforo del Fréjus (between Modane and Susa, with 13 km [8 miles] of tunnel). Other passes become increasingly unreliable between November and April.

TRAIN TRAVEL

Turin is on the main Paris–Rome TGV express line and is also connected with Milan, 90 minutes away on the fast train. The fastest (Frecciarossa) trains cover the 667-km (414-mile) trip to Rome in just over four hours; other trains take between five and seven hours.

Services to the larger cities east of Turin are part of the extensive and reliable train network of the Lombard Plain. West of the region's capital, however, the train services soon peter out in the mountains. Continuing connections by bus serve these valleys; information about train-bus mountain services can be obtained from train stations and tourist information offices, or by contacting FS–Trenitalia, the Italian national train service.

FS–Trenitalia. Italy's national train service. ☎ *892021 (toll-free in Italy), 06/68475475* ⊕ *www.trenitalia.com.*

Italo. The Italian state-run railway's only competition, Italo operates fast and regular train service between many, but not all, of Italy's major cities. ☎ *06/0708* ⊕ *www.italotreno.it.*

RESTAURANTS

In the region's restaurants you'll taste a mountain-city contrast: the hearty peasant cooking served in tiny stone villages and the French-accented delicacies found in the plain are both eminently satisfying.

WHAT IT COSTS			
	$	$$	$$$	$$$$
RESTAURANTS	under €15	€15–€24	€25–€35	over €35
HOTELS	under €125	€125–€200	€201–€300	over €300

Prices in the dining reviews are the average cost of a main course at dinner, or, if dinner is not served, at lunch. Prices in the reviews are the lowest cost of a standard double room in high season.

HOTELS

High standards and opulence are characteristic of Turin's better hotels, and the same is true at the top mountain resorts. Hotels in Turin and other major towns are generally geared to business travelers; make sure to ask whether lower weekend rates or special deals for two- or three-night stays are available.

Summer vacationers and winter skiers keep occupancy rates and prices high at resorts during peak seasons. Many mountain hotels require guests to pay for either half or full board and insist on a stay of several nights; some have off-season rates that can reduce the cost by a full price category. If you're planning to ski, ask about package deals that give you a discount on lift tickets. *For expanded reviews, facilities, and current deals, visit Fodors.com.*

TURIN

Turin—Torino, in Italian—is roughly in the center of Piedmont–Valle d'Aosta and 128 km (80 miles) west of Milan; it's on the Po River, on the edge of the Po Plain, which stretches east all the way to the Adriatic. Turin's flatness and wide, angular, tree-lined boulevards are a far cry from Italian *metropoli* to the south; the region's decidedly northern European bent is quite evident in its nerve center. Apart from its role as northwest Italy's major industrial, cultural, intellectual, and administrative hub, Turin also has a reputation as Italy's capital of black magic and the supernatural. This distinction is enhanced by the presence of Turin's most famous and controversial relic, the Sacra Sindone (Shroud of Turin), still believed by many Catholics to be Christ's burial shroud. (For its part, the Vatican has not taken an official position on its authenticity.)

GETTING HERE AND AROUND

Turin is well served by the Italian *autostrade* (highway) system and can be reached easily by car from all directions: from Milan on the A4 autostrada (2 hours); from Bologna (4 hours) and Florence (5 hours) on the A1 and A21; from Genoa on the A6 autostrada (2 hours).

Bus service to and from other major Italian cities is also plentiful, and Turin can be reached by fast train service from Paris in less than six hours. Fast train service also connects the city with Milan, Genoa, Bologna, Florence, and Rome.

Public boats, operated by Turin's public transport system (☎ *800/019152 or 011/5764733* ⊕ *www.comune.torino.it/gtt*), make for a pleasant way to reach the Borgo Medioevale from the Murazzi dock at the northern end of the Parco del Valentino.

VISITOR INFORMATION

Turin's group and personally guided tours are organized by the city's tourist office. It also provides maps and details about a wide range of thematic self-guided walks through town. The Torino+Piemonte Card, which provides discounts on transportation and museum entrances for two-, three-, five-, or seven-day visits, can be purchased here.

Turin Tourist Information Center ⊠ *Piazza Castello, at Via Garibaldi* ☎ *011/535181* ⊕ *www.turismotorino.org* ☺ *Daily 9–6.*

EXPLORING

DOWNTOWN TURIN

TOP ATTRACTIONS

Duomo di San Giovanni. The most impressive part of Turin's 15th-century cathedral is the shadowy black marble–walled **Cappella della Sacra Sindone** (Chapel of the Holy Shroud), where the famous relic was housed before a fire in 1997. The chapel was designed by the priest and architect Guarino Guarini (1604–83), a genius of the Baroque style who was official engineer and mathematician to the court of Duke Carlo Emanuele II of Savoy. The fire caused severe structural damage, and the chapel is closed indefinitely while restoration work proceeds.

The Sacra Sindone is a 4-yard-long sheet of linen, thought by millions to be the burial shroud of Christ, bearing the light imprint of his crucified body. The shroud first made an appearance around the middle of the 15th century, when it was presented to Ludovico of Savoy in Chambéry. In 1578 it was brought to Turin by another member of the Savoy royal family, Duke Emanuele Filiberto. It was only in the 1990s that the Catholic Church began allowing rigorous scientific study of the shroud. Not surprisingly, the results have been hazy, bolstering both sides of the argument. On one hand, three separate university teams—in Switzerland, Britain, and the United States—have concluded, as a result of carbon-14 dating, that the cloth dates to between 1260 and 1390. On the other hand, they are unable to explain how medieval forgers could have created the shroud's image, which resembles a photographic negative, and how they could have had the knowledge or means to incorporate traces of Roman coins covering the eyelids and endemic Middle Eastern pollen woven into the cloth. Either way, the shroud continues to be revered as a holy relic, exhibited to the public on very rare occasions. At other times, it is preserved in a sealed casket in the left aisle of the cathedral. In lieu of the real thing, a photocopy is on permanent display nearby. ⊠ *Via XX Settembre 87, Centro* ☏ *011/4361540* ⊘ *Weekdays 7–12:30 and 3–7, weekends 8–12:30 and 3–7.*

Galleria Sabauda. Housed in the restored *Manica Nuova* (new wing) of the **Palazzo Reale** the gallery displays some of the most important paintings from the vast collections of the house of Savoy. The collection is particularly rich in Dutch and Flemish paintings: note the *Stigmate di San Francesco* (*St. Francis Receiving the Stigmata*) by Jan Van Eyck (1395–1441), in which the saint receives the marks of Christ's wounds while a companion cringes beside him. Other Dutch masterpieces include paintings by Anthony Van Dyck (1599–1641) and Rembrandt (1606–69). *L'arcangelo Raffaele e Tobiolo* (*Tobias and the Angel*) by Piero del Pollaiuolo (circa 1443–96) is showcased, and other featured Italian artists include Fra Angelico (circa 1400–55), Andrea Mantegna (1431–1506), and Paolo Veronese (1528–88). ⊠ *Via XX Settembre 86, Centro* ☏ *011/5641729* ⊕ *www.galleriasabauda.beniculturali. it/* ▣ *€12, includes the Palazzo Reale, Armeria Reale, and Museo di Antichità* ⊘ *Tues.–Thurs. and weekends 8:30–7:30, Fri. 8:30 am–9:30 pm; ticket sales end 90 mins before closing.*

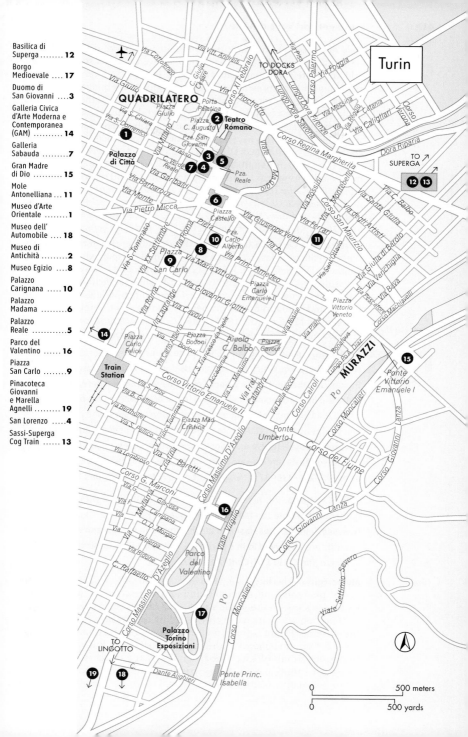

Turin

QUADRILATERO

TO DOCKS
DORA

TO
SUPERGA

Palazzo
di Città

Teatro
Romano

Museo di
Antichità

Pza.
Reale

Piazza
Castello

Piazza
San Carlo

Palazzo
Carignana

Piazza
Carlo
Emanuele I

Piazza
Vittorio
Veneto

MURAZZI

Ponte
Vittorio
Emanuele I

Train
Station

Piazza
Carlo
Felice

Piazza
Bodoni

Aivola
C. Balbo

Piazza
Cavour

Ponte
Umberto I

Piazza Mad.
Cristina

Ponte
Umberto I

Parco
del
Valentino

Palazzo
Torino
Esposizioni

TO
LINGOTTO

Ponte Princ.
Isabella

| 0 | | 500 meters |
| 0 | | 500 yards |

Mole Antonelliana. You can't miss the unusual square dome and thin, elaborate spire of this Turin landmark above the city's rooftops. This odd structure, built between 1863 and 1889, was intended to be a synagogue, but costs escalated and eventually it was bought by the city of Turin. In its time it was the tallest brick structure in the world, and it is still the tallest building in Italy. You can take the crystal elevator to reach the terrace at the top of the dome for an excellent view of the city, the plain, and the Alps beyond. Also worth a visit is the Mole Antonelliana's **Museo Nazionale del Cinema** (National Cinema Museum), which covers more than 34,000 square feet and houses many items of film memorabilia as well as a film library with some 7,000 titles. ⊠ *Via Montebello 20, Centro* ☎ *011/8138560 for museum* ⊕ *www.museocinema. it* ✉ *Museum €10, elevator €7; combination ticket €14* ☉ *Museum: Tues.–Fri. and Sun. 9–8, Sat. 9 am–11 pm. Elevator: Tues.–Fri. and Sun. 10–8, Sat. 10 am–11 pm. Ticket sales end 1 hr before closing.*

Museo d'Arte Orientale. Housed in the magnificently renovated 17th-century Palazzo Mazzonis, this is a beautifully displayed collection of Southeast Asian, Chinese, Japanese, Himalayan, and Islamic art, including sculptures, paintings, and ceramics. Highlights include a towering 13th-century wooden statue of the Japanese temple guardian Kongo Rikishi and a sumptuous assortment of Islamic manuscripts. ⊠ *Via San Domenico 11, Centro* ☎ *011/4436927* ⊕ *www.maotorino.it* ✉ *€10* ☉ *Tues.–Sun. 10–6; ticket sales end 1 hr before closing.*

QUICK BITES

Al Bicerin. A chocolate lover's pilgrimage to Turin inevitably leads to this small coffee shop, which first opened its doors in 1763. Nietzsche, Puccini, Dumas, and the political reformer Cavour have all sipped here, and if you order the house specialty, the *bicerin* (a hot drink with layers of chocolate, coffee, and cream), you'll understand why. Don't be surprised if the friendly and energetic owner, Marité Costa, also tries to tempt you with one of her flavored *zabajoni* (warm eggnogs). Chocolate goodies, including chocolate-flavor pasta, are on sale in the café store. ⊠ *Piazza della Consolata 5, Centro* ☎ *011/4369325* ⊕ *www.bicerin.it* ☉ *Closed Wed., and Aug.*

Caffè San Carlo. This historic coffee shop is usually filled with locals gathered at marble-top tables under a huge crystal chandelier and frescoed ceilings. Breakfast and lunch, afternoon snacks, and evening aperitifs are all served in this particularly elegant Neoclassical setting. ⊠ *Piazza San Carlo 156, Centro* ☎ *011/532586.*

Fodor's Choice ★

Museo Egizio. The Egyptian Museum's superb collection includes statues of pharaohs and mummies and entire frescoes taken from royal tombs—it's one of the world's finest and largest museums of its kind. The striking sculpture gallery, designed by the Oscar-winning production designer Dante Ferretti, is a veritable who's who of ancient Egypt. Look for the magnificent 13th-century BC statue of Ramses II and the fascinating Tomb of Kha. The latter was found intact with furniture, supplies of food and clothing, writing instruments, and a complete set of personal cosmetics and toiletries. Due to be completed in early

2015, an extensive renovation of the museum's older wings should make the museum more resplendent than ever. The museum is housed in the **Palazzo dell'Accademia delle Scienze,** a Baroque tour de force designed by the priest and architect Guarino Guarini. ⊠ *Via Accademia delle Scienze 6, Centro* ☎ *011/5617776* ⊕ *www.museoegizio.it* 🎫 *€7.50* ⊗ *Tues.–Sun. 8:30–7:30; ticket sales end 1 hr before closing.*

Palazzo Madama. In the center of Piazza Castello, this castle was named for the Savoy queen Madama Maria Cristina, who made it her home in the 17th century. The building incorporates the remains of a Roman gate with later-medieval and Renaissance additions, and the monumental Baroque facade and grand entrance staircase were added by Filippo Juvarra (1678–1736). The palace now houses the **Museo Civico d'Arte Antica,** whose collections comprise more than 30,000 items dating from the Middle Ages to the Baroque era. The paintings, sculptures, illuminated manuscripts, and various decorative objects on display illustrate almost 10 centuries of Italian and European artistic production. Works by Jan Van Eyck, Antonella da Messina (circa 1430–79), and Orazio Gentileschi (1563–1639) highlight the collection. ⊠ *Piazza Castello 10, Centro* ☎ *011/4433501* ⊕ *www.palazzomadamatorino.it* 🎫 *Staircase and courtyard free, museum €10* ⊗ *Grand staircase and medieval courtyard: Tues.–Sun. 9–7. Museum: Tues.–Sat. 10–6, Sun. 10–7. Ticket sales end 1 hr before closing.*

Palazzo Reale. This 17th-century palace, a former Savoy royal residence, is an imposing work of brick, stone, and marble that stands on the site of one of Turin's ancient Roman city gates. In contrast to its sober exterior, the two main floors of the palace's interior are swathed in luxurious Rococo trappings, including tapestries, gilt ceilings, and sumptuous 17th- to 19th-century furniture. You also can head down to the basement and the old kitchens to see where food for the last kings of Italy was once dished up. Currently the second floor and the gardens behind the palace are closed for restoration. ⊠ *Piazzetta Reale 1, Centro* ☎ *011/4361455* ⊕ *www.ilpalazzorealeditorino.it* 🎫 *€12, includes Armeria Reale, Galleria Sabauda, and Museo di Antichità* ⊗ *Tues.–Sun. 8:30–7:30.*

Armeria Reale (*Royal Armory*). This wing of the Royal Palace holds one of Europe's most extensive collections of arms and armor. It's a must-see for connoisseurs. ⊠ *Piazza Castello 191, Centro* ☎ *011/543889* 🎫 *€12, includes Palazzo Reale, Galleria Sabauda, and Museo di Anitichità* ⊗ *Tues.–Sun. 8:30–7:30.*

Piazza San Carlo. Surrounded by shops, arcades, fashionable cafés, and elegant Baroque palaces, this is one of the most beautiful squares in Turin. In the center stands a statue of Duke Emanuele Filiberto of Savoy, the victor at the battle of San Quintino, in 1557. The melee heralded the peaceful resurgence of Turin under the Savoy after years of bloody dynastic fighting. The fine bronze statue erected in the 19th century is one of Turin's symbols. At the southern end of the square, framing the continuation of Via Roma, are the twin Baroque churches of San Carlo and Santa Cristina. ⊠ *Piazza San Carlo, Centro.*

San Lorenzo. Architect, priest, and mathematician Guarino Guarini was in his mid-sixties when he began this church in 1668. The masterful use of geometric forms and the theatrical control of light and shadow show him working at his mature and confident best. ■TIP→ Stand in the center of the church and look up into the cupola to appreciate the full effect. ✉ *Via Palazzo di Città 4, Centro* ☎ *011/4361527* ⊕ *www.sanlorenzo.torino.it* ⊙ *Mon.–Sat. 7:30–noon and 4–7, Sun. 9–1 and 3–7:30.*

Baratti e Milano. In the glass-roofed Galleria Subalpina, near Via Po, stands one of Turin's charming old cafés. It's famous for its exquisite chocolates—you might want to buy their *gianduiotti* (hazelnut chocolates) or candied chestnuts to take home to friends. Light lunches are also served. ✉ *Piazza Castello 29, Centro* ☎ *011/4407138* ⊕ *www.barattiemilano.it* ⊙ *Closed Mon.*

Mulassano. This tiny café, decorated with marble and finely carved wood panels, is famous for its *tramezzini* (small triangular sandwiches made with white bread and filled with all sorts of goodies), which they claim to have invented here in the 1920s. Popular with the pre- and post-theater crowd, the café also offers a unique roulette system for clients trying to decide on who pays the bill—ask the cashier for an explanation. ✉ *Piazza Castello 15, Centro* ☎ *011/547990* ⊕ *www.caffemulassano.com.*

WORTH NOTING

Galleria Civica d'Arte Moderna e Contemporanea (GAM). In 1863 Turin was the first Italian city to begin a public collection devoted to contemporary art. Housed in a modern building on the edge of downtown, a permanent display of more than 600 paintings, sculptures, and installation pieces provides an exceptional glimpse of how Italian contemporary art has evolved since the late 1800s. The Futurist, Pop, neo-Dada, and Arte Povera movements are particularly well represented, and the gallery has a fine video and art film collection. ✉ *Via Magenta 31, Centro* ☎ *011/4429518* ⊕ *www.gamtorino.it* ▨ *€10* ⊙ *Tues., Wed., and Fri.–Sun. 10–6, Fri. 10 am–10:30 pm; ticket sales end 1 hr before closing.*

Museo di Antichità. A small but fascinating collection of artifacts found at archaeological sites in and around Turin is displayed here. A spiral ramp winds down through the subterranean museum; and, as in a real archaeological site, the deeper you go the older the objects on display. A life-size silver bust of the Roman Emperor Lucio Vero (AD 161–169) is one of the masterpieces in the collection. ✉ *Via XX Settembre 88, Centro* ☎ *011/5212251* ⊕ *museoarcheologico.piemonte.beniculturali. it* ▨ *€12, includes Galleria Sabauda, Armeria Reale, and Palazzo Reale* ⊙ *Tues.–Sun. 8:30–7:30.*

Palazzo Carignano. Half of this building is the Baroque triumph of Guarino Guarini, the priest and architect who designed many of Turin's most noteworthy buildings. Built between 1679 and 1685, his red-brick palace later played an important role in the creation of the modern-day nation. Vittorio Emanuele II of Savoy (1820–78), the first king of a united Italy, was born here, and, after a 19th-century Neoclassical extension, Italy's first parliament met here between 1860 and 1865. The palace now houses the **Museo del Risorgimento,** a museum honoring the 19th-century movement for Italian unity. ⊠ *Via Accademia delle Scienze 5, Centro* ☎ *011/5621147* ⊕ *www.museorisorgimentotorino.it* 🎫 *€10* ⊘ *Tues.–Sun. 10–6; ticket sales end 1 hr before closing.*

ALONG THE PO

TOP ATTRACTIONS

FAMILY **Borgo Medioevale.** Along the banks of the Po, this complex, built for a General Exhibition in 1884, is a faithful reproduction of a typical Piedmont village in the Middle Ages. Crafts shops, houses, a church, and stores are clustered in the narrow lanes, and in the center of the village is the **Rocca Medioevale,** a medieval castle that's its main attraction. ⊠ *Viale Virgilio 107, San Salvario* ☎ *011/4431701* ⊕ *www. borgomedioevaletorino.it* 🎫 *Village free, Rocca Medioevale €6* ⊘ *Village: Apr.–Oct., daily 9–8; Nov.–Mar., daily 9–7. Rocca Medioevale: Tues.–Sun. 10–6; groups of no more than 30 enter castle every 30 mins. Ticket counter closes at 6:15.*

FAMILY
Fodor's Choice
★
Museo dell'Automobile. No visit to this motor city would be complete without a pilgrimage to see the perfectly preserved Bugattis, Ferraris, and Isotta Fraschinis at this museum. Here you can get an idea of the importance of FIAT—and cars in general—to Turin's economy. There's a collection of antique cars from as early as 1896, and displays show how the city has changed over the years as a result of the auto industry. ⊠ *Corso Unità d'Italia 40, Millefonti* ☎ *011/677666* ⊕ *www. museoauto.it* 🎫 *€8* ⊘ *Mon. 10–2, Tues. 2–7, Wed.–Thurs. and Sun. 10–7, Fri. and Sat. 10–9; last entrance 1 hr before closing.*

Parco del Valentino. This pleasant riverside park is a great place to stroll, bike, or jog. Originally the grounds of a relatively simple hunting lodge, the park owes its present arrangement to Madama Maria Cristina of France, who received the land and lodge as a wedding present after her marriage to Vittorio Amedeo I of Savoy. With memories of 16th-century French châteaux in mind, she began work in 1620 and converted the lodge into a magnificent palace, the **Castello del Valentino.** The building, now home to the University of Turin's Faculty of Architecture, is not open to the public. Next to the palace are the university's botanical gardens, established in 1729, where local and exotic flora can be seen in a hothouse, herbarium, and arboretum. ⊠ *Parco del Valentino, San Salvario* ☎ *011/6705970 for botanical gardens* ⊕ *www.ortobotanico. unito.it* 🎫 *Botanical gardens €5* ⊘ *Botanical gardens: mid-Apr.–mid-Oct., Sat. 3–7, Sun. 10–1 and 3–7.*

Fodor's Choice
★
Pinacoteca Giovanni e Marella Agnelli. This gallery was opened in 2002 by Gianni Agnelli (1921–2003), the head of FIAT and patriarch of one of Italy's most powerful families, just four months before his death. The emphasis here is on quality rather than quantity: 25 works of art from the Agnelli private collection are on permanent display, along with temporary exhibitions. There are four magnificent scenes of Venice by Canaletto (1697–1768); two splendid views of Dresden by Canaletto's nephew, Bernardo Bellotto (1720–80); several works

7

by Manet (1832–83), Renoir (1841–1919), Matisse (1869–1954), and Picasso (1881–1973); and fine examples of the work of Italian futurist painters Balla (1871–1958) and Severini (1883–1966). The gallery is on the top floor of the **Lingotto,** a former FIAT factory that was completely transformed between 1982 and 2002 by architect Renzo Piano. The multilevel complex now holds a shopping mall, several movie theaters, restaurants, two hotels, and an auditorium. ■ TIP→ **Don't miss the beautifully preserved spiral ramps that once took cars up and down the original building.** ✉ *Via Nizza 230, Lingotto* ☎ *011/0062713* 🌐 *www.pinacoteca-agnelli.it* 🎟 *€8, includes admission to the FIAT testing ramp on top of building* 🕒 *Tues.–Sun. 10–7; last entrance at 6:15.*

WORTH NOTING

Basilica di Superga. Visible from miles around, this thoroughly Baroque church was designed by Juvarra in the early 18th century and, since 1731, has been the burial place of kings: no fewer than 58 members of the Savoy family are memorialized in the crypt. ✉ *Strada Basilica di Superga 75, Sassi* ☎ *011/8997456* 🌐 *www.basilicadisuperga.com* 🎟 *Basilica free, crypt €5* 🕒 *Basilica: weekdays 9–noon and 3–5, weekends 9–noon and 3–6. Crypt: Mar.–Oct., daily 9:30–7; Nov.–Feb., daily 9:30–6; last entrance 45 mins before closing.*

Gran Madre di Dio. On the east bank of the Po, this Neoclassical church is modeled after the Pantheon in Rome. It was built between 1827 and 1831 to commemorate the return of the house of Savoy to Turin after the fall of Napoléon's empire. ✉ *Piazza Gran Madre di Dio 4, Borgo Po* ☎ *011/8193572* 🕒 *Mon.–Sat. 7:30–noon and 4:30–7, Sun. 7:30–1 and 3:30–7.*

FAMILY **Sassi-Superga Cog Train.** The 18-minute ride from Sassi up the Superga hill is a real treat on a clear day. The view of the Alps is magnificent at the hilltop **Parco Naturale Collina Torinese,** a tranquil retreat from the bustle of the city. If you feel like a little exercise, you can walk back down to Sassi (about two hours) on one of the well-marked wooded trails that start from the upper station. Other circular trails lead through the park and back to Superga. ✉ *Piazza G. Modena, Sassi* ☎ *800/019152 (toll-free in Italy)* 🌐 *www.comune.torino.it/gtt* 🎟 *Weekdays €4 one-way, weekends €6 one-way* 🕒 *Hourly service Mon. and Wed.–Fri. 9–noon and 2–5, hourly service weekends 9–8; bus service replaces train on Tues.*

WHERE TO EAT

$$$ PIEDMONTESE Fodor's Choice ★

🍴 **Al Garamond.** The well-spaced tables and the ancient brick vaulting in this small, bright space set the stage for traditional meat and seafood dishes served with creative flair. Try the tantalizing *rombo in crosta di patate al barbera* (turbot wrapped in sliced potatoes and baked with barbera wine) or the equally delicious *brasatura della guancetta di vitella su vellutata di cavolfiori* (braised veal cheek with creamed cauliflower). For dessert, the mousse *di liquirizia e salsa di cioccolato bianco* (licorice mousse with white-chocolate sauce) is delightful, even if you don't usually like licorice. The level of service is very high, even by demanding Turin standards. [$] *Average main: €25* ✉ *Via G. Pomba 14,*

Centro ☎ *011/8122781* ⊕ *www.algaramond.it* ⌗ *Reservations essential* ⊘ *Closed Sun., Jan. 1–6, and 3 wks in Aug. No lunch Sat.*

$$$ ✕ **Casa Vicina.** Hidden away in the basement of the Lingotto food empo-
PIEDMONTESE rium, this is one of Turin's top destinations for fine dining. The décor is
Fodor's Choice starkly modern and, without windows, it might seem claustrophobic to
★ some, but the food makes up for everything. Traditional dishes, particu-
larly those from northern Piedmont, are served up with creative style.
Among the antipasti, the *insalata russa con battuta di tonno* (Russian
salad with tuna) is as tasty as it is unusual. The agnolotti *alla Vecchia
Eporedia* are an equally delicious rendition of this commonly found
pasta dish, served with the pan juices of roast veal. Second courses
include the wonderful *filetto di Fassone in crosta di cipolla e senape*
(beef filet in a crust of onions and mustard). The wine list is an encylo-
pedia, with many small but notable wineries included. Ⓢ *Average main:
€30* ⊠ *Via Nizza 224, Lingotto* ☎ *011/19506840* ⊕ *www.casavicina.it*
⌗ *Reservations essential* ⊘ *Closed Sun. and Mon.*

$$ ✕ **Consorzio.** Extremely popular for lunch during the week, this lively
PIEDMONTESE and informal osteria is in Turin's business district. The service is relaxed,
the décor low-key, and the menu highlights organic meats and veg-
etables from the region. The *tortino di verdura* (vegetable flan) and the
gnocchi *con pecorino, pancetta, e fave* (with sheep's cheese, bacon, and
broad beans) make for a light and satisfying meal. There's a good selection of Piedmont wines. Ⓢ *Average main: €16* ⊠ *Via Monte di Pietà 23,
Centro* ☎ *011/2767661* ⊕ *www.ristoranteconsorzio.it* ⌗ *Reservations
essential* ⊘ *Closed Sun. No lunch Sat.*

$$ ✕ **Da Mauro.** This bustling spot in the center of Turin's business district
TUSCAN teems with locals at both lunch and dinner. After a flux of Tuscan
migrants moved to Turin in the sixties, Da Mauro was one of the first
restaurants to cater to their tastes. It's been here ever since. The menu
changes daily and is as long and as varied as one might wish, with both
Tuscan-style seafood and meat courses always present. The tagliatelle
con sugo di anatra (with duck sauce), and the *misto pesce alla livornese*
(Livorno-style fish stew) are both excellent. Service is brisk and effi-
cient—it's not the place to come for a leisurely meal. Ⓢ *Average main:
€15* ⊠ *Via Maria Vittoria 21, Centro* ☎ *011/8170604* ▭ *No credit cards*
⊘ *Closed Mon.*

$$$ ✕ **Del Cambio.** Set in a palace dating to 1757, this is one of Europe's most
PIEDMONTESE beautiful and historic restaurants, with decorative moldings, mirrors,
and hanging lamps that look just as they did when Italian national hero
Cavour dined here more than a century ago. The cuisine draws heavily
on Piedmontese tradition and is paired with fine wines of the region.
Agnolotti pasta *con sugo d'arrosto* (with pan juice of roast veal) is a
recommended first course. The *filetto di vitello gratinato alle spezie con
zucca, cavalfiore, e castagne* (spiced and breaded veal filet with pumpkin, cauliflower and chestnuts) make an admirable main course, if you
happen to be here in the fall. Ⓢ *Average main: €33* ⊠ *Piazza Carignano
2, Centro* ☎ *011/546690* ⊕ *www.delcambio.it* ⌗ *Reservations essential*
⊘ *Closed Mon., and 3 wks in Aug. No dinner Sun.*

$ ✕ **La Dentera.** For a break from the usually elaborate slow-food style of
ITALIAN Piedmont cuisine try one of the 34 different pizzas available from this

7

lively spot near the base of the Sassi–Superga cog train. The chef's pizza specials include the *dentera* (with anchovies, red bell pepper, oil, and garlic) and the *cremagliera* (with Gorgonzola). It's a great spot for a quick bite before or after visiting the Superga Basilica. $\boxed{S}$ *Average main: €8* ⊠ *Corso Casale 321, Sassi* ☎ *011/8987108.*

$ ✕**Pastificio Defilippis.** Famous for freshly made pasta since 1872, this
PIEDMONTESE shop also serves pasta creations to a packed lunch crowd all week long. Some of the favorites include *rigatoni all'arrabbiata* (with a spicy tomato and meat sauce) and *agnolotti di prosciutto e zucchine al burro* (with ham, zucchini, and melted butter). Second courses and desserts are also available, but the pasta is the main event. Meals are served on two floors and outdoor seating is available in the summer, so even if you find it full when you arrive, the wait is never very long. $\boxed{S}$ *Average main: €12* ⊠ *Via Lagrange 39, Centro* ☎ *011/542137* ⊕ *www.pastificiodefilippis. com* 🚫 *No credit cards* ⊗ *No dinner.*

$$ ✕**Porta di Po.** They're vigilant about sticking to Piedmontese special-
PIEDMONTESE ties at this elegant restaurant with minimalist décor. All the seasonal favorites are here, including the delicious *tajarin ai quaranta uova con salsiccia di Bra* (pasta made with 40 eggs and served with sausage), and the *brasato di vitello piemontese al barbera* (veal braised in red wine), which melts in your mouth. Desserts are all traditional, and the limited wine list presents a reasonable collection of regional wines. $\boxed{S}$ *Average main: €22* ⊠ *Piazza Vittorio Veneto 1e, Centro* ☎ *011/8127642* ⊕ *www.portadipo.it* ⊗ *Closed Sun., and 2 wks in Sept.*

$$ ✕**Trattoria Anna.** If you are hankering for something different from
SEAFOOD the usual meat-based Piedmontese cuisine, give this simple, extremely popular, family-run spot a try. They serve only seafood, and they do it well. The *tagliatelle Walter* (pasta with shellfish) and the *grigliata di pesce* (mixed grilled fish) are both excellent. $\boxed{S}$ *Average main: €20* ⊠ *Via Bellezia 20, Centro* ☎ *011/4362134* ⌫ *Reservations essential* ⊗ *Closed Mon., and 2 wks in Aug. No lunch.*

$$$ ✕**Vintage 1997.** The first floor of an elegant townhouse in the center
NORTHERN of Turin makes a fitting location for this sophisticated restaurant. You
ITALIAN might try such specialties as *vitello tonnato alla vecchia maniera* (roast veal with a light tuna sauce made without mayonnaise) or *merluzzo in crosta di erbette con patate e scalogno caramellato* (cod fillet in a crust of herbs served with potatoes and caramelized scallions). For the espe-cially hungry food-lover there's the "Piemunt Plus" menu, a 13-course feast that covers the full range of the restaurant's cuisine. There's an excellent wine list, with regional, national, and international vintages well represented. $\boxed{S}$ *Average main: €30* ⊠ *Piazza Solferino 16/h, Centro* ☎ *011/535948* ⊕ *www.vintage1997.com* ⊗ *Closed Sun., and 3 wks in Aug. No lunch Sat.*

$$$ ✕**Vò.** The two-man team of sommelier Luca Cossu and chef Stefano
PIEDMONTESE Borra have turned this small and intimate restaurant into one of Turin's top eateries. The food is Piedmontese with a definite French twist. You'll find a varied and interesting menu, with two highlights being the tasty risotto *al franciacorta e crescione mantecato al burro bianco* (with spar-kling white wine, watercress, and white butter) and *scaloppa di rombo in crosta di riso nero con farinata alle olive e carciofi* (turbot in a crust

of black rice, olives, and artichoke). **■ TIP→ The two available tasting menus are reasonably priced.** [$] *Average main: €25* ✉ *Via Provana 3, Centro* ☎ *011/8390288* 🌐 *www.ristorantevo.it* ✍ *Reservations essential* ⏲ *Closed Sun. No lunch Sat.*

WHERE TO STAY

The Turin Tourist Information Center provides a booking service for accommodations in the city and throughout the region. Book hotels through them at least 48 hours in advance, B&Bs at least seven days in advance.

$$ HOTEL 🏨 **Genio.** Though they're just steps away from the main train station, these spacious and tastefully decorated rooms are a quiet haven from the bustle of the city. **Pros:** close to the central train station; very friendly service. **Cons:** 15-minute walk to the center of town; area around the hotel is a little seedy. [$] *Rooms from: €170* ✉ *Corso Vittorio Emanuele II 47, Centro* ☎ *011/6505771* 🌐 *www.hotelgenio.it* 🛏 *115 rooms* 🍴 *Breakfast.*

$$ HOTEL 🏨 **Grand Hotel Sitea.** One of the city's finest hotels, the Sitea is in the centro storico and decorated in a warmly classical style; the public areas and guest rooms are elegant, spacious, and comfortable. **Pros:** central location; well-appointed rooms; large bathrooms. **Cons:** the a/c can be noisy; carpets are a little worn. [$] *Rooms from: €160* ✉ *Via Carlo Alberto 35, Centro* ☎ *011/5170171* 🌐 *www.grandhotelsitea.it* 🛏 *119 rooms, 1 suite* 🍴 *Breakfast.*

$$ HOTEL 🏨 **LingottoTech.** Designed by architect Renzo Piano, this luxury hotel is part of the former Lingotto FIAT factory. **Pros:** interesting design and location; good weekend rates sometimes available. **Cons:** outside the city center; many signs of wear and tear. [$] *Rooms from: €160* ✉ *Via Nizza 230, Lingotto* ☎ *011/6642000* 🌐 *www.nh-hotels.it/hotel/nh-torino-lingotto-tech* 🛏 *141 rooms, 1 suite* 🍴 *Breakfast.*

$$$ HOTEL Fodor's Choice ★ 🏨 **Victoria.** Rare style, attention to detail and comfort are the hallmarks of this in-town retreat that's furnished and managed along the lines of a refined English townhouse. **Pros:** tranquil location in the center of town; excellent spa facilities; wonderful breakfast. **Cons:** standard rooms are small; parking nearby can be difficult; no views. [$] *Rooms from: €230* ✉ *Via Nino Costa 4, Centro* ☎ *011/5611909* 🌐 *www.hotelvictoria-torino.com* 🛏 *97 rooms, 9 suites* 🍴 *Breakfast.*

NIGHTLIFE AND PERFORMING ARTS

NIGHTLIFE

Two areas of Turin are enormously popular nightlife destinations: the Quadrilatero, to the north of the city center, and the Murazzi embankment, near the Ponte Vittorio Emanuele I. The center of town is also popular, especially earlier in the evening.

Caffè Elena. This wine bar is a trendy place for an aperitivo (there's an ample free buffet) or for a drink before going clubbing. It's in the large piazza at the end of Via Po. ✉ *Piazza Vittorio Veneto 5, Centro* ☎ *011/8123341.*

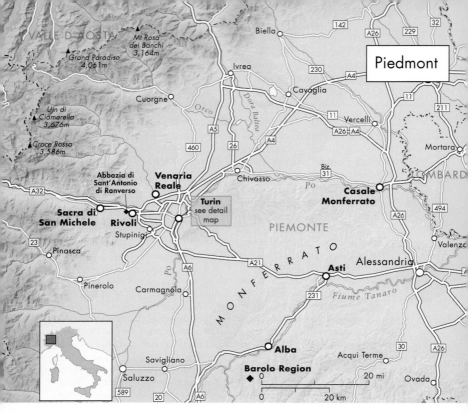

Jammin'. On the Murazzi, near the Ponte Vittorio Emanuele I, this is a popular disco with a varied crowd; there's live music on Friday. ⊠ *Murazzi del Po 17, Centro* ☎ *011/882869* ⊗ *May–Sept., Mon.–Sat. 9 pm–4 am.*

Pastis. The Quadrilatero Romano, which roughly corresponds to the grid pattern of Roman Turin near Piazza della Reppublica, is a hopping area filled with nightclubs and ethnic restaurants. Places open and close with startling frequency here, but Pastis has shown considerable staying power—several local cultural groups hold their meetings in the bar. ⊠ *Piazza Emanuele Filiberto 9b, Centro* ☎ *011/5211085.*

PERFORMING ARTS

MUSIC

Giovanni Agnelli Auditorium. Classical music concerts are held at the theater designed by Renzo Piano in the renovated Lingotto building; internationally famous conductors and orchestras are frequent guests. ⊠ *Via Nizza 280, Lingotto* ☎ *011/6677415* ⊕ *www.lingottomusica.it.*

MITO Settembre Musica Festival. Running for three weeks in September, this popular festival of classical music is held in a variety of venues around town. The program of performances and tickets become available in May each year. ⊠ *Via San Francesco da Paola 3* ☎ *011/4424787* ⊕ *www.mitosettembremusica.it.*

OPERA

Teatro Regio. Premieres at the Teatro Regio, one of Italy's leading opera houses, sell out well in advance. You can buy tickets for most performances at the box office or on the website, where discounts are offered on the day of the performance. The season runs from October through July. ⊠ *Piazza Castello 215, Centro* ☎ *011/8815557* ⊕ *www.teatroregio.torino.it.*

SPORTS AND THE OUTDOORS

BICYCLING

Ufficio Iniziative Ambientali (*Office for Environmental Initiatives*). Turin has about 160 km (100 miles) of bike paths running through the city and its parks. From April to October, bicycles are available for daily rental at stands throughout the city. ⊠ *Via Padova 29, Madonna di Campagna* ☎ *011/4420177* ⊕ *www.comune.torino.it/bici.*

SHOPPING

Many people know that Turin produces more than 75% of Italy's cars, but they're often unaware that it's also a hub for clothing manufacturing. Top-quality boutiques stocking local, national, and international lines are clustered along Via Roma and Via Garibaldi. Piazza San Carlo, Via Po, and Via Maria Vittoria are lined with antiques shops, some of which specialize in 18th-century furniture and domestic items.

CHOCOLATE

The Italian tradition of making chocolate began in Turin during the early 17th century. Chocolate at that time was an aristocratic drink, but in the 19th century a Piedmontese invention made it possible to further refine cocoa to create solid bars and candies.

Peyrano. The most famous of all Turin chocolates is the wedge-shape *gianduiotto*, flavored with hazelnuts and first concocted in 1867. The tradition has been continued at this small, family-run shop, where more than 80 types of chocolates are made. ⊠ *Corso Moncalieri 47, Centro* ☎ *011/6602202* ⊕ *www.ilgiustodelcioccolato.it.*

Stratta. In business since 1836, this famed shop sells confectionery of all kinds—not just the chocolates in the lavish window displays but also fancy cookies, rum-laced fudges, and magnificent cakes. ⊠ *Piazza San Carlo 191, Centro* ☎ *011/547920* ⊕ *www.stratta1836.it.*

MARKETS

Balon Flea Market. Go to this famous market on Saturday morning for bargains on secondhand books, antiques, and clothing. There is good browsing to be had among the stalls, which spill out of Borgo Dora into the surrounding side streets. During the second weekend of every month, the market extends its hours into Sunday, becoming the so-called "Gran" Balon. (Be aware, however, that the market is also famous for its pickpockets.) ⊠ *Borgo Dora, Centro* ☉ *Balon, Sat. 6–5; Gran Balon, Sat. 6–5 and Sun. 8–7.*

Fodor's Choice ★   **Mercato di Porta Palazzo.** For food lovers, people-watchers, or anyone interested in the lively local scene, the immensely popular market in this huge square to the north of town is not to be missed. Outdoors, the keepers of hundreds of vegetable stalls vie with one another to create the most appetizing displays. Indoors, the meat vendors provide an equally tantalizing array of local products, while the fishmongers proudly display the fresh catch of the day. ⊠ *Piazza della Repubblica, Centro* ⊕ *www.scopriportapalazzo.com* ⊙ *Weekdays 7–2, Sat. 7–5:30.*

SPECIALTY FOOD AND DELIS

Borgiattino. Specialty food stores and delicatessens abound in central Turin, but for a truly spectacular array of cheeses and other delicacies, this should be your first stop. ⊠ *Corso Vinzaglio 29, Centro* ☎ *011/5629075.*

Eataly. Now with branches in Milan, Bologna, New York, and Tokyo, this is probably Turin's most famous food emporium. In addition to a food market, food-related bookstore, kitchen equipment retailers, and a wine bar, there are several different food counters and restaurants serving hamburgers, haute cuisine, and lots more in between. ⊠ *Via Nizza 230, Lingotto* ☎ *011/19506801* ⊕ *www.eatalytorino.it.*

THE COLLINE AND SAVOY PALACES

As you head west from Turin into the Colline ("little hills"), castles and medieval fortifications begin to pepper the former dominion of the house of Savoy, and the Alps come into better and better view. In this region lie the storybook medieval town of Rivoli; 12th-century abbeys; and, farther west in the mountains, the ski resort of Sestriere, one of the venues used during the 2006 Winter Olympics.

VENARIA REALE

10 km (6 miles) northwest of Turin.

This immense palace was built in the 16th century as a hunting lodge.

GETTING HERE AND AROUND

Starting in Turin, from the north side of Piazza della Reppublica, take Bus No. 11 to reach Venaria; the trip takes approximately 40 minutes. By car, follow Corso Regina Margherita to the A55 highway. Head north and leave the highway at the Venaria exit, following signs for the Venaria Reale.

EXPLORING

Fodor's Choice ★   **Reggia di Venaria Reale.** Extensive Italianate gardens surround this 16th-century hunting lodge built for Carlo Emanuele II of Savoy. Inside, its Great Gallery is worthy of Versailles. The basements now house a historical exhibition that relates the story of the Savoy. The upper floors are given over to changing exhibitions. A sound-and-light show by the British film director Peter Greenaway enlivens rooms throughout the palace, and a permanent installation of works by the Arte Povera artist Giuseppe Penone can be seen in the gardens outside. ⊠ *Piazza della Reppublica 4, Venaria Reale* ☎ *011/4992333* ⊕ *www.lavenaria.it*

Continued on page 425

ON THE TRAIL OF BAROLO

Picture yourself in the background of a grand medieval mural, and you won't be far off from what you experience driving through the idyllic wooded landscape south of Turin, in Piedmont's Langhe district.

The crests of the graceful hills are dotted with villages, each lorded over by an ancient castle. The gentle slopes of the valleys below are lined with row upon row of Nebbiolo grapes, the choicest of which are used to make Barolo wine. Dubbed "the king of wines and wine of kings" in the 19th century after finding favor with King Carlo Alberto, Barolo still wears the crown, despite stiff competition from all corners of Italy.

Above, Serralunga's castle
Right, bottles of old vintage Barolo

The Langhe district is smaller and surprisingly less visited by food-and-wine enthusiasts than Chianti and the surrounding areas of Tuscany, but it yields similar rewards. The best way to tour the Barolo-producing region is on day trips from the delightful truffle town of Alba—getting around is easy, the country roads are gorgeous, and the wine is fit for a king.

ALL ABOUT BAROLO

The Nebbiolo grapes that go into this famous wine come not just from Barolo proper (the area surrounding the tiny town of Barolo), but also from a small zone that encompasses the hill towns of Novello, Monforte d'Alba, Serralunga d'Alba, Castiglione Falletto, La Morra, and Verduno. All are connected by small but easy-to-navigate roads.

When wine lovers talk about Barolo, they talk about tannins—the quality that makes red wine dry out your mouth. Tannins come from the grape skins; red wine—which gets its color from the skins—has them, white wine doesn't. Tannins can be balanced out by acidity (the quality that makes your mouth water), but they also soften over time. As a good red wine matures, flavors emerge more clearly, achieving a harmonious balance of taste and texture.

A bottle of Barolo is often born so overwhelmingly tannic that many aficionados won't touch the stuff until it has aged 10 or 15 years. But a good Barolo ages beautifully, eventually spawning complex, intermingled tastes of tobacco, roses, and earth. It's not uncommon to see bottles for sale from the 1980s, 1970s, or even earlier.

WHERE TO DRINK IT

The word *enoteca* in Italian can mean a wine store, or a wine bar, or both. The words "wine bar," on the other hand—which are becoming increasingly trendy—mean just that. Either way, these are great places to sample and buy the wines of the Langhe.

BEYOND BAROLO

By no means do the fruits of the Langhe end with Barolo. The region boasts Italy's highest concentration of DOC (denominazione di origine controllata) and DOCG (denominazione di origine controllata e garantita) wines, the two most prestigious categories of appellation in Italy. The other DOCG in the Langhe is Barbaresco, which, like Barolo, is made from the Nebbiolo grape. Barbaresco is not quite as tannic as Barolo, however, and can be drunk younger.
www.enotecadelbarbaresco.it

HOW MUCH DOES IT COST?

The most reasonably priced, but still enjoyable Barolos will cost you €20 to €30. A very good but not top-of-the-line bottle will cost €40 to €60. For a top-of-the-line bottle you may spend anywhere from €80 to €200.

LABELS TO LOOK FOR

Barolo is a strictly controlled denomination, but that doesn't mean all Barolos are equal. Legendary producers include Prunotto, Aldo Conterno, Giacomo Conterno, Bruno Giacosa, Famiglia Anselma, Mascarello, Pio Cesare, and Michele Chiarlo.

✉ €16, includes the Reggia and the gardens ☉ Reggia: Tues.–Fri. 9–5, weekends 9–8; last entrance 1 hr before closing. Gardens: Tues.–Sun. 9–1 hr before sunset.

RIVOLI

16 km (10 miles) west of Venaria, 13 km (8 miles) west of Turin.

The Savoy court was based in Rivoli in the Middle Ages, and the town retains several remnants from that richly dramatic period.

GETTING HERE AND AROUND

GTT buses and trams regularly link central Turin with Rivoli. The journey takes just over one hour.

By car, follow Corso Francia from central Turin all the way to Rivoli. Unless there's a lot of traffic the trip should take a half hour.

EXPLORING

Fodor'sChoice ★ **Museo d'Arte Contemporanea** (*Museum of Contemporary Art*). The Baroque castle of Rivoli now houses a fascinating museum of contemporary art. The building was begun in the 17th century, then redesigned but never finished by Juvarra in the 18th century; it was finally converted into a museum in the late 20th century by the minimalist Turin architect Andrea Bruno. On display are changing international exhibitions and a permanent collection of 20th-century Italian art. To get to Rivoli from downtown Turin, take Metro Line 1 to Fermi and then the shuttle bus service to the museum. See the museum's website for more information. ⊠ Piazzale Mafalda di Savoia ☎ 011/9565222 ⊕ www.castellodirivoli.org ✉ €6.50 ☉ Tues.–Fri. 10–5, weekends 10–7.

SACRA DI SAN MICHELE

20 km (13 miles) west of Abbazia di Sant'Antonio di Ranverso, 43 km (27 miles) west of Turin.

Perhaps best known as inspiration for the setting of Umberto Eco's novel *The Name of the Rose*, this abbey was built on Monte Pirchiriano in the 11th century so it would stand out: it occupies the most prominent location for miles around, hanging over a 3,280-foot bluff. When monks came to enlarge the abbey they had to build part of the structure on supports more than 90 feet high—an engineering feat that was famous in medieval Europe and is still impressive today. By the 12th century this important abbey controlled 176 churches in Italy, France, and Spain; one of the abbeys under its influence was Mont-Saint-Michel, in France. Because of its strategic position, the Abbey of Saint Michael came under frequent attacks over the next five centuries and was eventually abandoned in 1622. It was restored, somewhat heavy-handedly, in the late 19th and early 20th centuries.

GETTING HERE AND AROUND

Unless you want to do a 14-km (9-mile) uphill hike from the town of Avigliana, a car is essential for an excursion here—take the Avigliana Est exit from the Torino–Bardonecchia autostrada (A32).

7

EXPLORING

Sacra di San Michele. To reach the church, you must climb 150 steps, past 12th-century sculptures, from the **Porta dello Zodiaco,** a splendid Romanesque doorway decorated with the signs of the zodiac. On the left side of the interior are 16th-century frescoes representing New Testament themes; on the right are depictions of the founding of the church. In the crypt are some of the oldest parts of the structure, three small 9th- to 12th-century chapels. Note that some sections of the abbey are open only on weekends and, when particularly crowded, visits may be limited to hour-long tours. ■TIP→ **Weather permitting, the views from the walls and terraces surrounding the church are breathtaking.** ✉ *Via Sacra di San Michele 14, Sant'Ambrogio di Torino* ☎ *011/939130* ⊕ *www.sacradisanmichele.com* 🎫 *€5* ⊗ *Mid-Mar.–June and early Oct., Tues.–Fri. 9:30–12:30 and 2:30–6, weekends 9:30–noon and 2:30–6:30; July–Sept., Mon. 9:30–12:30 and 2:30–6, Tues.–Fri. 9:30–12:30 and 3–6, weekends 9:30–noon and 2:40–6; late Oct.–mid-Mar., Tues.–Fri. 9:30–12:30 and 2:30–5, weekends 9:30–noon and 2:30–5:30.*

THE MONFERRATO AND THE LANGHE

Southeast of Turin, in the hilly wooded area around Asti known as the Monferrato, and farther south in a similar area around Alba known as the Langhe, the landscape is a patchwork of vineyards and dark woods, dotted with hill towns and castles. This is wine country, producing some of Italy's most famous reds and sparkling whites. And hidden away in the woods are the secret places where hunters and their dogs unearth the precious, aromatic truffles worth their weight in gold at Alba's truffle fair.

ASTI

60 km (37 miles) southeast of Turin.

Asti is best known outside Italy for its wines—excellent reds as well as the famous sparkling white *spumante.* The town itself has some impressive reminders of the days when its strategic position on trade routes between Turin, Milan, and Genoa gave it broad economic power. In the 12th century Asti began to develop as a republic, at a time when other Italian cities were also flexing their economic and military muscles. It flourished in the following century, when the inhabitants began erecting lofty **towers** (✉ *West end of Corso Vittorio Alfieri*) for its defense. As in Pavia, near Milan, this gave rise to the medieval nickname "city of a hundred towers." In the center of Asti some of these remain, among them the 13th-century **Torre Comentina** and the well-preserved **Torre Troyana,** a tall, slender tower attached to the **Palazzo Troya.** The 18th-century church of **Santa Caterina** has incorporated one of Asti's medieval towers, the **Torre Romana** (itself built on an ancient Roman base), as its bell tower. Corso Vittorio Alfieri is Asti's main thoroughfare, running west–east across the city. This road, known in medieval times as Contrada Maestra, was built by the Romans.

Skiing in Piedmont and Valle d'Aosta

Skiing is the major sport in both Piedmont and Valle d'Aosta. Excellent facilities abound at resort towns such as Courmayeur and Breuil-Cervinia. The so-called Via Lattea (Milky Way)—five skiing areas near Sestriere with 400 km (almost 250 miles) of linked runs and 90 ski lifts—provides practically unlimited skiing. Lift tickets, running around €35 for a day's pass, are a good deal compared to those at major U.S. resorts.

To Italian skiers, a weeklong holiday on the slopes is known as a *settimana* *bianca* (white week). Ski resort hotels in Piedmont and Valle d'Aosta encourage these getaways by offering six- and seven-day packages, and though they're designed with the domestic market in mind, you can get a bargain by taking advantage of the offers. The packages usually, though not always, include half or full board.

You should have your passport with you if you plan a day trip into Switzerland—though odds are you won't be asked to show it.

GETTING HERE AND AROUND

Asti is less than an hour away from Turin by car on the A21. GTT bus service connects the two towns, but isn't direct. Train service to Asti, on the other hand, is frequent and fast.

FESTIVALS

Douja d'Or National Wine Festival. For 10 days in mid-September, Asti is host to a popular wine festival—an opportunity to see Asti and celebrate the product that made it famous. During the course of the festival a competition is held to award "Oscars" to the best wine producers, and stands for wine tastings allow visitors to judge the winners for themselves. Musical events and other activities accompany the festival. Check the festival's website for the schedule of events. ☎ *0141/530357 for tourist office* ⊕ *www.doujador.it.*

Palio di Asti. September is a month of fairs and celebrations in Asti, and this horse race that's run through the streets of town is the highlight. First mentioned in 1275, this annual event has been going strong ever since. After an elaborate procession in period costumes, nine horses and jockeys representing different sections of town vie for the honor of claiming the *palio,* a symbolic flag of victory.

VISITOR INFORMATION

Asti Tourism Office ⊠ *Piazza Alfieri 34* ☎ *0141/530357* ⊕ *www. astiturismo.it.*

EXPLORING

Duomo. Dedicated to the Assumption of the Virgin, the Duomo is an object lesson in Italian Gothic architecture. Built in the early 14th century, it is decorated so as to emphasize geometry and verticality: pointed arches and narrow vaults are completely covered with frescoes that help the eye to soar upward. The porch on the south side of the cathedral facing the square was built in 1470; it represents the Gothic style at its most florid and excessive. ✉ *Piazza Cattedrale 1* ☎ *0141/592924* 🕒 *Daily 9–noon and 3–6.*

San Secondo. This Gothic church is dedicated to Asti's patron saint, believed by some to have been decapitated by the Emperor Hadrian on this very spot. San Secondo is also the patron of the city's favorite folklore and sporting event, the annual Palio di Asti, a colorful medieval-style horse race similar to Siena's. It's held each year on the third Sunday of September in the vast Campo del Palio to the south of the church. ✉ *Piazza San Secondo, south of Corso Vittorio Alfieri* ☎ *0141/530066* 🕒 *Mon.–Sat. 10:45–noon and 3:30–5:30, Sun. 3:30–5:30.*

WHERE TO EAT AND STAY

$$ PIEDMONTESE 🍴 **L'Angolo del Beato.** Regional specialties such as *bagna cauda* (literally "hot bath," a dip for vegetables made with anchovies, garlic, butter, and olive oil) and *tagliolini al ragù di anatra* (pasta with a duck sauce) are the main attractions at this Asti institution, housed in a building that dates to the 12th century. There's also an extensive list of several hundred Piedmont wines. [$] *Average main: €20* ✉ *Vicolo Cavalleri 2* ☎ *0141/531668* 🌐 *www.angolodelbeato.it* 🕒 *Closed Sun., last wk of Dec., 1st wk of Jan., and 3 wks in Aug.*

$ B&B/INN 🏨 **Reale.** Spacious rooms in a 19th-century building on Asti's main square are eclectically decorated, with a mix of contemporary and period furniture. **Pros:** spacious rooms; central location. **Cons:** lobby area is a little worn; rooms facing the main square can be noisy. [$] *Rooms from: €120* ✉ *Piazza Alfieri 6* ☎ *0141/530240* 🌐 *www.hotelristorantereale.it* 🛏 *24 rooms* 🍽 *Breakfast.*

$ HOTEL 🏨 **Relais Sant'Uffizio.** It's surprising to know that this now delightfully peaceful and elegant retreat, with a luxurious spa and swimming pool, surrounded by vineyards and rolling hills, was home to the Inquisition in the 16th century. **Pros:** tranquil and beautiful location; excellent spa and exercise facilities; friendly staff; very good value. **Cons:** 20 km (12 miles) north of Asti and isolated; private transportation required. [$] *Rooms from: €120* ✉ *Strada Sant Uffizio 1, Cioccaro di Penango* ☎ *0141/916292* 🌐 *www.relaissantuffizio.com* 🛏 *39 rooms, 2 suites* 🕒 *Closed Feb.* 🍽 *Breakfast.*

SHOPPING

Tuit. This shop and café on a quiet street just off Piazza Alfieri is a branch of Turin's Eataly food emporium. It's a great place to shop for local and regional food specialties or to enjoy a light meal. Both the *tortino di melanzane di pomodori pachino* (eggplant flan with Sicilian cherry tomatoes) and the risotto *mantecato alla zucca e amaretti* (with butter, pumpkin, and amaretti cookies) are delicious. ✉ *Via Carlo Grandi 3* ☎ *0141/095813* 🌐 *www.tuit.it* 🕒 *Daily 9:30–9:30.*

ALBA

30 km (18 miles) southwest of Asti.

This small town has a gracious atmosphere and a compact core, studded with medieval towers and Gothic buildings. In addition to being a wine center of the region, Alba is known as the "City of the White

Truffle" for the dirty little tubers that can cost as much as €2,200 a pound. For picking out your truffle and having a few wisps shaved on top of your food, expect to shell out an extra €16 or so—which may be worth it, at least once.

GETTING HERE AND AROUND

By car from Turin follow the A6 south to Marene and then take the A33 east. The A33 autostrada connects Asti and Alba. GTT offers frequent bus service between Alba and Turin—the journey takes approximately 1½ hours. There's no direct train service, but you can get to Alba from Turin by making one transfer in Asti, Bra, or Cavallermaggiore; the entire trip takes about 1½ hours.

VISITOR INFORMATION

Alba Tourism Office ✉ *Piazza Risorgimento 2* ☎ *0173/35833* ⊕ *www.langheroero.it.*

FESTIVALS

Fodor'sChoice **Fiera Internazionale del Tartufo Bianco** (*International White Truffle Fair*).
★ From the second Saturday in October to the second Sunday in November, Alba hosts an internationally famous truffle fair, held on weekends. Merchants, chefs, and other aficionados of this pungent yet delicious fungus come from all over the world to buy and to taste white truffles at the height of their season. Though the affair is very commercialized, it still makes Alba a great place to visit in the fall. ■TIP→ **Hotel and restaurant reservations for October and November should be made well in advance.** ✉ *Cortile della Madalena* ☎ *0173/361051* ⊕ *www.fieradeltartufo.org.*

FAMILY **Palio degli Asini.** Alba's hilarious donkey race, a lampoon of Asti's eminently serious horse race, is held on the first Sunday of October. Tickets to watch this competition between Alba's districts, with riders dressed in medieval garb astride their stubborn beasts, can be hard to get; they go on sale at the beginning of July each year. Contact Alba's tourist information office for details. ☎ *0173/35833 for tourist office* ⊕ *www.langheroero.it.*

WHERE TO EAT

$$ ✕ **La Libera.** Modern and subdued, this small spot on a quiet back street
PIEDMONTESE is conducive to slow, relaxed dining. The antipasti include a splendid *piatto della tradizione* (an array of typical Piedmont starters). As a first course, the ravioli *in brodo di cappone* (in a fish broth) is excellent. A variety of tasty meat dishes make up the list of second courses, and there's a superb selection of local cheeses to follow. The wine list is extensive, with over six pages dedicated to Barolo alone. Ⓢ *Average main: €16* ✉ *Via Elvio Pertinace 24a* ☎ *0173/293155* ⊕ *www.lalibera.com* ♥ *Closed Sun., and several wks in Feb. and July. No lunch Mon.*

$$$ ✕ **Locanda del Pilone.** The elegant, formal dining room of the Locanda
PIEDMONTESE del Pilone hotel is one of the best restaurants in the region, serv-
Fodor'sChoice ing refined variations of traditional dishes. The *scamone di fassone,*
★ *topinambur e ricotta* (rump of Fassone veal with Jewish artichoke and cheese) is as delicious as it is unusual. With about 1,200 labels, the wine list is a marvel in itself, and the service is exemplary. Ⓢ *Average*

main: €30 ✉ *Località Madonna di Como 34* ☎ *0173/366616* ⊕ *www.*
locandadelpilone.com ⌂ *Reservations essential.*

$$$
PIEDMONTESE
Fodor'sChoice
★

✕**Massimo Camia.** Chef Massimo Camia's restaurant is in an elegant
and modern space, with views of the Barolo vineyards that surround
the Damilano winery; the service is impeccable and the food is divine.
Try the *guanciale al Barolo* (beef cheek stewed in Barolo wine) or the
faraona croccante in doppia panatura con cipolle caramilate (guinea
fowl in a crumbly crust with caramalized onions); both are mouthwa-
teringly good. Desserts include a *tortino di nocciola con salsa inglese
al Moscato* (hazelnut tart with custard). The restaurant is outside the
town of La Morra, a 20-minute drive to the southwest of Alba. Ⓢ *Av-
erage main: €28* ✉ *Via Alba–Barolo 122, La Morra* ☎ *0173/56355*
⊕ *www.massimocamia.it* ⌂ *Reservations essential* ⊘ *Closed Tues. No
lunch Wed.*

$$
PIEDMONTESE

✕**Osteria Italia.** A short drive from the center of Alba brings you to the
hamlet of San Rocco Seno d'Elvio and this old-style trattoria. The décor
is as simple as the menu, which makes a pleasant change from the more
elaborate restaurants that you often find in the center of the city. This
osteria (really just a "rustic-style" trattoria) is owned by the husband-
and-wife team of Renato and Marina Del Piano, and they run it well.
To start try the *sformato di erbette con fonduta e tartuffo nero* (herb
flan with cheese fondue and black truffles). In truffle season, the *uova
all'occhio di bue con il tartufo bianco d'Alba* (lightly fried eggs with
white truffles) is the *only* way to eat white truffles, they say. Ⓢ *Average
main: €15* ✉ *Frazione San Rocco Seno d'Elvio 5, 5 km (3 miles) southeast of Alba* ☎ *0173/286942* ⊕ *www.osteriaitalia.it* ⊘ *Closed Mon.*

$$
PIEDMONTESE

✕**Vigin Mudest.** Delicious regional specialties are served at this bustling,
family-run restaurant in the center of Alba. There's a sumptuous buf-
fet spread of hot and cold antipasti, and their version of *carne cruda
albese* (beef carpaccio in the style of Alba) is a favorite with the locals
who flock here. All of the pasta (including the thin egg yolk–rich *taja-
rin* traditional to the region) is homemade, and the risotto al Barolo is
particularly tasty. Outdoor seating is available in summer. Ⓢ *Average
main: €18* ✉ *Via Vernazza 11* ☎ *0173/441701* ⊕ *www.viginmudest.it*
⌂ *Reservations essential* ⊘ *Closed Mon.*

$$
WINE BAR

✕**Vincafè.** This excellent enoteca specializes in tastes of Langhe wines,
accompanied by *salumi* (cured meats), cheeses, and other regional products. On the menu, you'll find a whole range of Piedmont specialties:
the *tortino ia funghi porcini con fonduta leggera* (mushroom flan with
a light cheese sauce) and tajarin *al ragù di salsiccia di Bra* (with Bra
sausage sauce) are particularly good. More than 350 wines, as well as
grappas and liqueurs, are on Vincafè's distinguished list. It opens at
noon and food's served until midnight. Ⓢ *Average main: €15* ✉ *Via
Emanuele 12* ☎ *0173/364603* ⊕ *www.vincafe.com.*

WHERE TO STAY

$
B&B/INN

▦ **La Meridiana.** This lovely manor house is on a hill overlooking the
historic center, surrounded by dolcetto and nebbiolo grapevines. **Pros:**
friendly, family atmosphere; in a secluded setting convenient for exploring the Langhe; nice views from the many terraces and balconies. **Cons:**
long walk to nearest restaurants (though some units have kitchens);

no a/c in some rooms. $ *Rooms from: €100* ⌷ *Località Altavilla 9* ☎ *0173/440112* ⊕ *www.villalameridianaalba.it* ↩ *8 rooms, 2 suites* ▭ *No credit cards* ⭕ *Breakfast.*

$$
B&B/INN
⌷ **Locanda del Pilone.** It would be hard to imagine a more command-ing position for these simply but tastefully decorated accommodations above Alba. **Pros:** spectacular location with 360-degree views; excellent restaurant. **Cons:** isolation makes own transportation a must; no a/c. $ *Rooms from: €200* ⌷ *Località Madonna di Como 34* ☎ *0173/366616* ⊕ *www.locandadelpilone.it* ↩ *6 rooms, 2 suites* ⭕ *Breakfast.*

$$
B&B/INN
⌷ **Palazzo Finati.** This carefully restored 19th-century townhouse has charm and character that set it apart from the other, more business-oriented hotels in Alba. **Pros:** quiet location in the center of town; rooms facing the courtyard have terraces; changing exhibitions of contemporary art adorn the walls. **Cons:** staff coverage is limited at night; breakfast room is a bit gloomy. $ *Rooms from: €190* ⌷ *Via Vernazza 8* ☎ *0173/366324* ⊕ *www.palazzofinati.it* ↩ *4 rooms, 5 suites* ☾ *Closed 2 wks in Aug., and Christmas–mid-Jan.* ⭕ *Breakfast.*

THE BAROLO REGION

17 km (11 miles) southwest of Alba, 72 km (45 miles) southeast of Turin.

The Langhe district may not get as much attention as other wine-pro-ducing regions in Italy, but the payoff for visiting can be just as satisfy-ing. Try to schedule a day trip to one or several of the wine estates here.

GETTING HERE AND AROUND
The easiest way to reach Barolo and its wineries is to drive from Alba.

EXPLORING
Famiglia Anselma. Probably best for wine lovers who have at least reached an intermediate level of fandom, this winery is known for its steadfast commitment to producing only Barolo—nothing else—and for its policy of holding wines for several years before release. The winemaker here, Maurizio Anselma, is something of a prodigy in the Barolo world, and he's quite open to visitors. ⌷ *Loc. Castello della Volta, Barolo* ☎ *0173/560511* ⊕ *www.anselma.it.*

Marchesi di Barolo. Right in the town of Barolo, this wine estate makes an easy, if touristy, option for getting to know the local wines. In the estate's user-friendly enoteca you can taste wine, buy thousands of dif-ferent bottles from vintages going way back, and look at display bottles, including an 1859 Barolo. Marchesi di Barolo's *cantine* (wine cellars), at Via Roma 1, are open daily 10:30–5:30. ⌷ *Via Alba 12, Barolo* ☎ *0173/564400* ⊕ *www.marchesibarolo.com.*

Podere Rocche dei Manzoni. A good, accessible example of the new school of local winemaking is this wine estate, about 6 km (4 miles) south of Barolo. The facade of the cantina is like a Roman temple of brick, complete with imposing columns. Rocche dei Manzoni's reds include four Barolos, one dolcetto, one Langhe Rosso, two Langhe D.O.C.s, and two Barbera d'Albas. ⌷ *3 Località Manzini Soprano, Monforte d'Alba* ☎ *0173/78421* ⊕ *www.barolobig.com.*

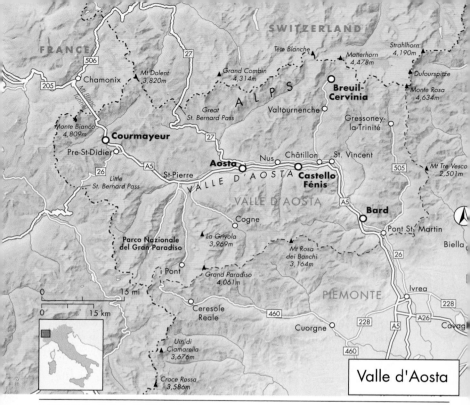

Valle d'Aosta

VALLE D'AOSTA

In Valle d'Aosta, a semiautonomous, bilingual region near the border with France and Switzerland, the unspoiled beauty of the highest peaks in the Alps, the Matterhorn and Monte Bianco, competes with the magnificent scenery of Italy's oldest national park, Gran Paradiso. Luckily, you don't have to choose—the region is small, so you can fit skiing, après-ski, and wild ibex into one memorable trip. The main Aosta Valley, largely on an east–west axis, is hemmed in by high mountains where glaciers have gouged out 14 tributary valleys, six to the north and eight to the south. A car is helpful here, but take care: though distances are relatively short as the crow flies, steep slopes and winding roads add to your mileage and travel time.

Coming up from Turin, beyond Ivrea, the road takes you through steep ravines guarded by brooding, romantic castles. Pont St. Martin, about 18 km (11 miles) north of Ivrea, is the beginning of bilingual (Italian and French) territory.

BARD

65 km (40 miles) north of Turin.

This small medieval town clings to a rocky crag that almost completely blocks the entrance to the Valle d'Aosta from Piedmont. Recognized for its strategic importance since prehistoric times, the location was first fully fortified by the Romans, and then by the Ostrogoths in the 6th century. As befits its military heritage, the village is rather gray and somber, but the magnificent fortress that sits atop it makes a visit well worthwhile.

GETTING HERE AND AROUND

Bard is just off the A5 autostrada that runs north from Turin into the Valle d'Aosta—by car the trip takes about an hour. Train service from Turin is infrequent, but there's regular service to and from Aosta. Traveling to Bard by bus is not a viable option.

EXPLORING

FAMILY
Fodor's Choice
★

Forte di Bard. A few minutes beyond the French-speaking village of Pont St. Martin, you pass through the narrow Gorge de Bard to reach the fortress that has stood guarding the valley entrance for more than eight centuries. In 1800 Napoléon entered Italy through this valley, using the cover of darkness to get his artillery units past the castle unnoticed. Ten years later he remembered this inconvenience and had the fortress destroyed. It was rebuilt in the 19th century and now houses the lavishly multimedia **Museo degli Alpi,** dedicated to the history and culture of the Alps and the Valle d'Aosta region. There's also a fun section for young children that's dedicated to the geology and history of the region. ☎ 0125/833811 ⊕ www.fortedibard.it ⌂ €8 ⊗ Wed.–Fri. 10–6, weekends 10–7; last entrance 1 hr before closing.

EN
ROUTE

Between Bard and the town of Donnas, 5 km (3 miles) south along the S26, you can walk on a short but fascinating section of a 1st-century Roman consular road that passed here on its way to France. Still showing the deeply worn tracks left by the passage of cart and chariot wheels, this section of road includes an archway carved through solid rock (used during the Middle Ages as the city gate of Donnas) and a milestone (XXXVI, to indicate 36 Roman miles from Aosta).

BREUIL-CERVINIA/THE MATTERHORN

50 km (30 miles) north of Bard, 116 km (72 miles) north of Turin.

Sitting in a huge natural basin at the foot of the Matterhorn, this town, once a high Alpine pasture, grew to become one of Europe's most famous ski areas, when a road connecting it to the Valle d'Aosta was completed in 1934. It bustles in the winter and has become a popular spot for hikers in the summer, but it's sleepy for much of the rest of the year.

GETTING HERE AND AROUND

From Aosta take the A5 and then the SR46 (1 hour); from Turin take the A5 and then the SR46 (90 minutes). SADEM has regular bus service from Turin; SAVDA buses travel here from Milan. Breuil-Cervinia isn't on a train line.

VISITOR INFORMATION

Breuil-Cervinia Tourism Office ✉ *Piazzale Funivie* ☎ *0166/944311* 🌐 *www.cervinia.it.*

EXPLORING

Matterhorn (*Monte Cervino in Italian; Mont Cervin in French*). The famous peak straddles the border between Italy and Switzerland, and all sightseeing and skiing facilities are operated jointly. Splendid views of the peak can be seen from **Plateau Rosa** and the **Cresta del Furggen,** both of which can be reached by cable car from the center of Breuil-Cervinia. Although many locals complain that the tourist facilities and condominiums have changed the face of their beloved village, the cable car does give access to climbing and off-trail skiing in ridges that were once inaccessible.

WHERE TO STAY

$$ B&B/INN 🏨 **Cime Bianche.** This calm, quiet mountain lodge offers commanding views of the Matterhorn and surrounding peaks from the balconies of its simply furnished, wood-paneled guest rooms. **Pros:** next to the ski slopes; great restaurant; lovely views. **Cons:** lobby is showing wear; busy during the ski season; location is far from everything but slopes; multiday stays with some meals usually required. [$] *Rooms from: €160* ✉ *Località La Vieille 44, near ski lift* ☎ *0166/949046* 🌐 *www.hotelcimebianche.com* 🛏 *13 rooms* 🕓 *Closed May, June, and Oct. Restaurant closed Mon.* 🍴 *Some meals.*

$$$$ RESORT 🏨 **Hermitage.** The entryway's marble relief of Saint Theodolus reminds you that this was the site of a hermitage, but asceticism has given way to comfort and elegance—a fire is always glowing in the enormous hearth, the dining room is candlelit, the bright bedrooms have balconies, and the suites have antique fireplaces and 18th-century furnishings. **Pros:** superlative staff; refined atmosphere; frequent shuttle service into town and to ski lifts. **Cons:** located 2 km (1 mile) from the town center; half board is mandatory during the winter season; very expensive. [$] *Rooms from: €720* ✉ *Via Piolet 1, Località Chapellette* ☎ *0166/948998* 🌐 *www.hotelhermitage.com* 🛏 *30 rooms, 6 suites* 🕓 *Closed May, June, Sept., and Nov.* 🍴 *Some meals.*

$$$$ B&B/INN 🏨 **Les Neiges d'Antan.** In an evergreen forest at Perrères, just outside Cervinia, this family-run inn is quiet and cozy, with three big fireplaces and a nice view of the Matterhorn. **Pros:** secluded and beautiful setting; excellent restaurant; well-designed spa facilities. **Cons:** 5 km (3 miles) outside Breuil-Cervinia (a car is essential); entrance and lobby areas are showing some wear. [$] *Rooms from: €320* ✉ *Frazione Perrères 10* ☎ *0166/948775* 🌐 *www.lesneigesdantan.it* 🛏 *21 rooms, 3 suites* 🕓 *Closed May and June* 🍴 *Breakfast.*

SPORTS AND THE OUTDOORS

CLIMBING

Serious climbers can make the ascent of the Matterhorn from Breuil-Cervinia after registering with the local mountaineering officials at the tourist office. This ascent is for experienced climbers only. Less demanding hikes follow the lower slopes of the valley of the River Marmore, to the south of town.

Società delle Guide Alpine. The Society's guides are available to accompany you on treks and also lead skiing, canyoneering, and ice-climbing excursions. ⊠ *Strada Villair 2, Courmayeur* ☎ *0165/842064* ⊕ *www.guidecourmayeur.com.*

SKIING

Sixty lifts and a few hundred miles of ski runs ranging from beginner to expert make Breuil-Cervinia one of the best and most popular resort areas in Italy. Because the slopes border a glacier, there's skiing year-round.

CASTELLO FÉNIS

34 km (22 miles) northwest of Bard, 104 km (65 miles) north of Turin.

The tiny town of Fénis owes its origins to the presence of the medieval castle that once provided shelter for the local peasants that lived nearby. Today, the population of the town is less than 2,000, with most either farmers or part of the tourist industry.

GETTING HERE AND AROUND

To reach the castle by car, take the Nus exit from the main A5 autostrada. SAVDA buses provide infrequent service between Aosta and Fénis. The closest train station, in Nus, is a 5-km (3-mile) walk from the castle.

EXPLORING

FAMILY

Fodor's Choice
★

Castello Fénis. The best-preserved medieval fortress in Valle d'Aosta, this many-turreted castle was built in the mid-14th century by Aimone di Challant, a member of a prolific family related to the Savoys. The castle, which used a double ring of walls for its defense, would make a perfect setting for a fairy tale, given its pointed towers, portcullises, and spiral staircases. The 15th-century courtyard surrounded by wooden balconies is elegantly decorated with well-preserved frescoes. Inside you can see the kitchen, with an enormous fireplace that provided central heat in winter; the armory; and the spacious, well-lighted rooms used by the lord and lady of the manor. If you have time to visit only one castle in Valle d'Aosta, this should be it. ⊠ *Frazione Chez Croiset 22, Fénis* ☎ *0165/764263* ⊠ *€5* ⊗ *Apr.–Aug., daily 9–7; Mar. and Sept., daily 10–6; Oct., Wed.–Mon. 10–6; Nov.–Feb., Wed.–Mon. 10–4. Maximum of 25 people allowed to enter every ½ hr.*

AOSTA

12 km (7 miles) west of Castello Fénis, 113 km (70 miles) north of Turin.

Aosta stands at the junction of two of the important trade routes that connect France and Italy, the valleys of the Rhône and the Isère. Its significance as a trading post was recognized by the Romans, who built a garrison here in the 1st century BC, and the present-day layout of the streets is the clearest example you'll find of Roman urban planning in Italy. Well-preserved Roman walls form a perfect rectangle around the center, and the regular pattern of streets reflects its role as a military stronghold. Though its gray-stone buildings and slate roofing give a rather cold feeling to the town, Aosta has recently began to appear on several lists as one of the most livable towns in Italy.

GETTING HERE AND AROUND

Aosta can easily be reached by car or bus from Milan and Turin. The town is off the main A5 autostrada. SAVDA buses regularly travel to and from Milan, Turin, and Chamonix in France. Direct train service (2 hours) is also available from Turin, but a change of trains is required if traveling here from Milan (3 hours).

FESTIVALS

Sant'Orso Fair. On the last weekend of January, the streets of Aosta are brightened by an arts-and-crafts market that brings artisans from all over the Valle d'Aosta. All the traditional techniques are featured: wood carving and sculpture, soapstone work, wrought iron, leather, wool, lace, and household items of all kinds. Food and wine are sold at outdoor stands, and wandering minstrels enliven the whole event. ☎ *0165/235462* ⊕ *www.lovevda.it.*

VISITOR INFORMATION

Aosta Tourism Office ✉ *Piazza Porta Praetoria 3* ☎ *0165/235462* ⊕ *www. lovevda.it.*

EXPLORING

TOP ATTRACTIONS

Arco di Augusto. At the eastern entrance to town, and commanding a fine view over Aosta and the mountains, stands the Arch of Augustus, built in 25 BC to mark Rome's victory over the Celtic Salassi tribe. (The sloping roof was added in 1716 in an attempt to keep rain from seeping between the stones.) ✉ *Piazza Arco d'Augusto.*

Collegiata di Sant'Orso. This church has layers of history literally visible in its architecture. Originally there was a 6th-century chapel on this site founded by the Archdeacon Orso, a local saint. Most of this structure was destroyed or hidden when an 11th-century church was erected over it. This church, in turn, was encrusted with Gothic, and later Baroque, features, resulting in a jigsaw puzzle of styles, that, surprisingly, manage to work together. The 11th-century features are almost untouched in the crypt, and if you go up the stairs on the left from the main church you can see the 11th-century frescoes (ask the sacristan who let you in). These restored frescoes depict the life of Christ and the apostles. Although only the tops are visible, you can see the expressions on the faces of the disciples. Take the outside doorway to the right of the main entrance to see the church's crowning glory, its 12th-century cloister, enclosed by some 40 stone columns with masterfully carved capitals depicting scenes from the Old and New Testaments and the life of Saint Orso. The turrets and spires of Aosta peek out above. ⊠ *Via Sant'Orso 10* ☏ *0165/262026* ⊙ *Daily 9–5:30.*

Duomo. Aosta's cathedral dates to the 10th century, but all that remains from that period are the bell towers. The decoration inside is primarily Gothic, but the main attraction of the cathedral predates that era by 1,000 years: among the many ornate objects housed in the treasury is a carved ivory diptych from AD 406 portraying the Roman Emperor Honorius. ⊠ *Piazza Papa Giovanni XXIII* ☏ *0165/40251* 🖭 *Duomo free, treasury €6* ⊙ *Duomo: Apr.–Sept., Mon.–Sat. 6:30–noon and 3–8, Sun. 7–noon and 3–8; Oct.–Mar., Mon.–Sat. 6:30–noon and 3–7, Sun. 7–noon and 3–7. Treasury: Apr.–Sept., Tues.–Sun. 9–11:30 and 3–5:30; Oct.–Mar., Sun. 3–5:30.*

WORTH NOTING

Teatro Romano. The 72-foot-high ruin of the facade of the Teatro Romano guards the remains of the 1st-century BC amphitheater, which once held 20,000 spectators. Only a bit of the outside wall and seven of the amphitheater's original 60 arches remain. The latter, once incorporated into medieval buildings, are being brought to light by ongoing archaeological excavations. The actual site cannot be visited, but you can get a good view of it from the adjacent Via Baillage. ⊠ *Via Anfiteatro 4.*

WHERE TO EAT

$

NORTHERN
ITALIAN

✕ **Praetoria.** Just outside the Porta Pretoria, this simple and unpretentious restaurant serves hearty local dishes such as *crespelle alla valdostana* (crêpes with ham and cheese) and polenta with a variety of sauces and accompaniments. The pasta is made on the premises, and all of the menu offerings are prepared from traditional recipes. Desserts are as straightforward as the rest, but the *torta de mele Renette in salsa vaniglia* (apple tart with vanilla sauce) is outstanding. Ⓢ *Average main: €13* ⊠ *Via Sant'Anselmo 9* ☏ *0165/44356* ⊕ *www.praetoriaristorante. it* ⊙ *Closed Wed. No dinner Tues.*

$$$

NORTHERN
ITALIAN

✕ **Vecchio Ristoro.** The elegant, intimate spaces of this converted mill are furnished with antiques, and a traditional ceramic stove provides additional warmth in cool weather. The chef-proprietor takes pride in creative versions of regional recipes, including *gnocchetti di castagnesu crema di zucca* (chestnut gnocchi with pumpkin cream) and *quaglietto disossata farcita alle castagne fatta al forno* (roast quail with chestnut stuffing). To finish, you might be tempted by the dark chocolate mousse with a rum cream filling. Ⓢ *Average main: €25* ⊠ *Via Tourneuve 4* ☏ *0165/33238* ⊕ *www.ristorantevecchioristoro.it* ⊙ *Closed Sun., 3 wks in June, and 1 wk in Nov. No lunch Mon.*

WHERE TO STAY

$$

B&B/INN

🛏 **Le Miramonti.** Built on the banks of a branch of the Dora Baltea River, this delightful, small, family-run establishment offers all the woody Alpine interiors, traditional regional furnishings, and other homey comforts needed for a relaxing evening after a strenuous day. **Pros:** friendly, efficient service; excellent location for outdoor sports. **Cons:** isolated location in a small village; the rooms near the river may seem noisy to some. [$] *Rooms from: €180* ✉ *Via Piccolo San Bernardo 3, La Thuile* ☎ *0165/883084* 🌐 *www.lemiramonti.it* 🛏 *35 rooms, 5 suites* ⏲ *Closed May, Oct., and Nov.* 🍴 *Breakfast.*

$$ B&B/INN Fodor's Choice ★ 🏨 **Milleluci.** At this small and inviting family-run hotel overlooking Aosta, bedrooms, some with balconies, are bright and charmingly decorated; all have splendid views of the city and mountains. **Pros:** panoramic views; great spa facilities; cozy and traditionally decorated rooms. **Cons:** 1 km (½ mile) north of town—need a car to get around; no a/c. [$] *Rooms from: €180* ✉ *Località Porossan Roppoz 15* ☎ *0165/235278* 🌐 *www.hotelmilleluci.com* 🛏 *31 rooms* 🍴 *Breakfast.*

COURMAYEUR/MONTE BIANCO

35 km (21 miles) northwest of Aosta, 150 km (93 miles) northwest of Turin.

The main attraction of Courmayeur is a knock-'em-dead view of Europe's tallest peak, Monte Bianco. The celebrities and the wealthy who come here these days are following a tradition that dates back to the late 17th century, when Courmayeur's natural springs first began to attract visitors. The spectacle of the Alps gradually surpassed the springs as the biggest draw: the Alpine letters of the English poet Percy Bysshe Shelley were almost advertisements for the region. Since 1965, when the Mont Blanc tunnel opened, ever-increasing numbers of travelers have passed through the area, and it's now hugely popular with both skiers and hikers during the winter and summer months.

Planners have managed to keep some restrictions on wholesale development within the town, and its angled rooftops and immaculate cobblestone streets maintain a cozy (if slightly prefab) feeling.

GETTING HERE

Courmayeur is on the main A5 autostrada and can easily be reached by car from both Turin and Milan via Aosta. SAVDA buses run regularly from both Turin and Milan. Train service isn't available.

VISITOR INFORMATION

Courmayeur Tourism Office ✉ *Piazzale Monte Bianco 3* ☎ *0165/841612* 🌐 *www.courmayeurmontblanc.it.*

EXPLORING

Monte Bianco (*Mont Blanc*). Monte Bianco's attraction is not so much its shape (much less distinctive than that of the Matterhorn) as its expanse and the vistas from the top. You can reach the summit via a cable car that ascends from La Palud, a small town 4 km (2½ miles) north of Courmayeur. In summer, if you get the inclination, you can then switch cable cars and descend into Chamonix, in France. In winter you can ski parts of the route off-piste. The Funivie La Palud whisks you up first to the Pavillon du Mont Fréty—a starting point for many beautiful hikes—and then to the Rifugio di Torino, before arriving at the viewing platform at **Punta Helbronner** (more than 11,000 feet), which is also the border post with France.

The next stage up—only in summer—is on the **Télépherique de L'Aiguille du Midi,** as you pass into French territory. The trip is particularly impressive: you dangle over a huge glacial snowfield (more than 2,000 feet below) and make your way slowly to the viewing station above Chamonix. It's one of the most dramatic rides in Europe. From this point you're looking down into France, and if you change cable cars at the Aiguille du Midi station you can make your way down to Chamonix itself. The return trip, through the Monte Bianco tunnel, is made by bus. Schedules are unpredictable, depending on weather conditions and demand; contact the Funivie Monte Bianco for information. At this writing, the section of the cable car between Rifugio di Torino and Punta Helbronner is closed for replacement; a new line is due to open in 2015. ⊠ *Frazione La Palud 22* ☎ *0165/89925 in Courmayeur, 0450/532275 in Chamonix* ⊕ *www.montebianco.com* ⊡ *€16 round-trip to Pavillon du Mont Fréty, €38 round-trip to Helbronner, €62 round-trip to Aiguille du Midi, €96 round-trip to Chamonix with return by bus* ⊗ *Closed mid-Oct.–mid-Dec. depending on weather conditions and demand.*

Parco Nazionale del Gran Paradiso. Cogne, 52 km (32 miles) southeast of Courmayeur, is the gateway to this huge park, which was once the domain of King Vittorio Emanuele II (1820–78). Bequeathed to the nation after World War I, it is one of Europe's most rugged and unspoiled wilderness areas, with wildlife and many plant species protected by law. The park is one of the few places in Europe where you can see the *ibex* (a mountain goat with horns up to 3 feet long) and the *chamois* (a small antelope). The park, which is 703 square km (271 square miles), is open free of charge throughout the year; there's an information office in Cogne. ■ TIP→ **Try to visit in May, when spring flowers are in bloom and most of the meadows are clear of snow.** ⊠ *Villaggio Cogne 12* ☎ *0165/749264* ⊕ *www.grand-paradis.it.*

WHERE TO EAT

$$

NORTHERN
ITALIAN

✕ **Cadran Solaire.** The Garin family made over the oldest tavern in Courmayeur to create a warm and inviting restaurant that has a 17th-century stone vault, old wooden floor, and huge stone fireplace. The menu offers seasonal specialties and innovative interpretations of regional dishes: when available, the ravioli *maison* (filled with ricotta cheese flavored with walnuts and bathed with butter and sage) are particularly delicious. The cozy bar is a popular and crowded place for a predinner drink. $ *Average main: €22* ⊠ *Via Roma 122* ☎ *0165/844609* ⌐ *Reservations essential* ⊗ *Closed Tues., and May and Oct.*

$$$$

NORTHERN
ITALIAN

Fodor'sChoice
★

✕ **Maison de Filippo.** Here you'll find country-style home cooking in a mountain house with lots of atmosphere that's furnished with antiques, farm tools, and bric-a-brac of all kinds. There's only a set menu, which includes an abundance of antipasti, a tempting choice of local soups and pasta dishes, and an equally impressive array of traditional secondi, including cheese fondue and an equally hearty *carbonada* (beef stew and polenta). Cheese, dessert, and fresh fruit complete the meal. Don't head here if you are looking for something light to eat, and make sure to reserve in advance—it's one of the most popular restaurants in Valle d'Aosta. $ *Average main: €45* ⊠ *Via Passerin d'Entrèves 8*

☎ *0165/869797* ⚱ *Reservations essential* ⊗ *Closed Tues., and mid-May–June, Oct., and Nov.*

WHERE TO STAY

$$ 🍽 **Croux.** Half the rooms at this bright, comfortable hotel near the
HOTEL town center have balconies, the other half have great views of the
mountains. **Pros:** central location; great views. **Cons:** only half the
rooms have views; on a busy road. $ *Rooms from: €160* ✉ *Via Croux
8* ☎ *0165/846735* ⊕ *www.hotelcroux.it* ⇗ *31 rooms* ⊗ *Closed mid-
Apr.–mid-June, Oct., and Nov.* ⏹ *Breakfast.*

$$$ 🍽 **Royal e Golf.** With wide terraces and wood paneling, this longtime
HOTEL landmark in the center of Courmayeur is the most elegant spot in town,
and the cheery rooms have plenty of amenities. **Pros:** central location
on Courmayeur's main pedestrian street; panoramic views; heated outdoor pool. **Cons:** standard rooms can be small; meal plan required;
expensive; town center can be busy. $ *Rooms from: €245* ✉ *Via Roma
87* ☎ *0165/831611* ⊕ *www.hotelroyalegolf.com* ⇗ *81 rooms, 5 suites*
⊗ *Closed wk after Easter–mid-June and mid-Sept.–Nov.* ⏹ *Breakfast.*

$$$ 🍽 **Villa Novecento.** Run with friendly charm and efficiency, the Novecento
B&B/INN is a peaceful haven in the style of a comfortable mountain lodge, com-
Fodor's Choice plete with a log fire in winter, traditional fabrics, wooden furnishings,
★ and early 19th-century prints. **Pros:** charming and cozy; good restau-
rant; close to town center but away from the hubbub. **Cons:** park-
ing is limited; no a/c. $ *Rooms from: €240* ✉ *Viale Monte Bianco 64*
☎ *0165/843000* ⊕ *www.villanovecento.it* ⇗ *26 rooms* ⏹ *Breakfast.*

THE ITALIAN
RIVIERA

WELCOME TO
THE ITALIAN RIVIERA

TOP REASONS TO GO

★ **Walking the Cinque Terre:** Hike the famous Cinque Terre trails past gravity-defying vineyards, colorful, rock-perched villages, and the deep blue Mediterranean Sea.

★ **Portofino:** See the world through rose-tinted sunglasses at this glamorous little harbor village.

★ **Genoa's historical center and port:** From the palaces of Via Garibaldi to the labyrinthine backstreets of the old city to the world-class aquarium, the city is full of surprising delights.

★ **Giardini Botanici Hanbury:** A spectacular natural setting harbors one of Italy's largest, most exotic botanical gardens.

★ **Pesto:** The basil-rich sauce was invented in Liguria, and it's never been equaled elsewhere.

1 Cinque Terre. Five isolated seaside villages seem removed from the modern world—despite the many hikers who populate the trails between them.

2 Riviera di Levante. East of Genoa, the Riviera of the Rising Sun has tiny bays and inlets, set among dramatic cliffs and mountainsides, making for some of the most beautiful coastline in Italy. The pastel-hue town of Portofino has charmed generations of the rich and famous.

3 Genoa. Birthplace of Christopher Columbus, this city is an urban anomaly among Liguria's charming villages. At its heart is Italy's largest historic district, filled with beautiful architecture.

4 **Riviera di Ponente.**
The Riviera of the Setting
Sun, reaching from the
French border to Genoa, has
protected bays and sandy
beaches. The seaside resorts
of Bordighera and San Remo
share some of the glitter of
their French cousins to the
west.

GETTING ORIENTED

A thin crescent of rugged
and verdant land surrounded
by France, Piedmont,
Tuscany, the Alps, and the
Mediterranean Sea, Liguria
is best known as the Italian
Riviera. Genoa, the region's
largest city and one of Italy's
most important ports, lies
directly in the middle, with
the Riviera di Ponente to the
northwest and the Riviera
di Levante to the southeast.
It's here that the Italians perfected *il dolce far niente*—the
sweet art of idleness.

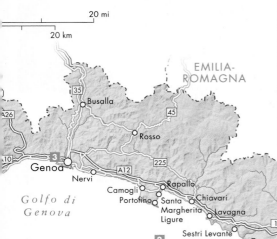

20 mi

20 km

EMILIA-ROMAGNA

Busalla

Rosso

3 Genoa

Nervi

Golfo di Genova

Camogli
Portofino
Santa Margherita Ligure

Rapallo
Chiavari
Lavagna

TUSCANY

2 Sestri Levante

Levanto

Monterosso al Mare
Vernazza
Manarola
Riomaggiore

CINQUE TERRE

1 La Spezia

Sarzana

Lerici

R I V I E R A   D I   L E V A N T E

8

EATING AND DRINKING WELL IN THE ITALIAN RIVIERA

Ligurian cuisine might surprise you. As you'd expect given the long coastline, it employs all sorts of seafood, but its real claim to fame is the exemplary use of vegetables and herbs.

Basil is practically revered in Genoa (the word is derived from the Greek *basileus,* meaning "king"), and the city is considered the birthplace of pesto, the basil-rich pasta sauce. This and other herbs—laurel, fennel, and marjoram—are cultivated, but also grow wild on the sun-kissed hillsides. Naturally, seafood plays a prominent role on the menu, appearing in soups, salads, and pasta dishes. Especially bountiful are anchovies, sea bass, squid, and octopus. Vegetables—particularly artichokes, eggplant, and zucchini—are abundant, usually prepared with liberal amounts of olive oil and garlic.

Like much of Italy, Liguria has a wide range of eating establishments from cafeteria-like *tavole calde* to family-run trattorias to sophisticated *ristoranti*. Lunch is served between 12:30 and 2:30 and dinner between 7:30 and 11. Also popular, especially in Genoa, are *enoteche* (wine bars), which serve simply prepared light meals late into the night.

FABULOUS FOCACCIA

When you're hankering for a snack, turn to bakeries and small eateries serving focaccia *(pictured above)*. The flat bread here is more dense and flavorful than what's sold as focaccia in American restaurants; it's the region's answer to pizza, usually eaten on the go.

It comes simply salted and dribbled with olive oil; flavored with rosemary and olives; covered with cheese or anchovies; and even *ripiena* (filled), usually with cheese or vegetables and herbs. Another local delicacy is *farinata*, a chickpea pancake baked like a pizza.

ANTIPASTI

Seafood antipasti are served in abundance at most Ligurian restaurants. These usually include marinated anchovies from Monterosso, *cozze ripiene* (mussel shells stuffed with minced mussel meat, prosciutto, Parmesan, herbs, and bread crumbs), and *sopressato di polpo* (flattened octopus in olive oil and lemon sauce).

PASTA

Liguria's classic pasta sauce is pesto, made from basil, garlic, olive oil, pine nuts, and hard cheese. It's usually served with *trenette* (similar to spaghetti) or the slightly sweet *testaroli* (a flat pasta made from chestnut flour).

You can also find *pansotti* (triangular pockets of pasta filled with a cheese mixture; *pictured below*), and *trofie* (short pasta twists) with *salsa di noci,* a rich sauce of garlic, walnuts, and cream that, as with pesto, is ideally pounded with a mortar and pestle.

Spaghetti *allo scoglio* has an olive oil, tomato, and white wine–based sauce containing an assortment of local *frutti di mare* (seafood) including shrimp, clams, mussels, and cuttlefish.

FISH AND MEAT

Fish is the best bet for a second course: the classic preparation is a whole grilled or baked whitefish—*branzino* (sea bass) and *orata* (dorado) are good choices— served *alle Ligure* with olives, potatoes,

tomatoes, Ligurian spices, and a drizzle of olive oil. A popular meat dish is *cima alla Genovese,* a veal roll stuffed with a mixture of eggs and vegetables, served as a cold cut.

PANIGACCI

One of the real treats of the region is *panigacci* from the Lunigiana area. Small, terra-cotta dishes known as *testine* are place in a wood-burning oven or fire to heat at the highest of temperatures. Then balls of dough are laid in the dishes and stacked one on top of the other in order to flatten and cook the dough. What emerges is flat, firm, almost pita-like bread. Panigacci is usually served with *stracchino* cheese (similar to cream cheese), pesto or nut sauce, and cold cuts—a delicious, hearty meal.

WINE

Local vineyards produce mostly light and refreshing whites such as Pigato from the Ponente and Vermentino from the Levante, although both light reds and appealing *rosati* (Italy's form of rosé) are on the rise. Rossese di Dolceacqua, from near the French border, is considered the best red wine the region has to offer, but for a more robust accompaniment to meats, opt for the more full-bodied reds of the neighboring Piedmont region. For a post dinner or dessert wine, try the "hard to find the real thing" *sciacchetrà,* made exclusively in the Cinque Terre.

8

Updated by Megan McCaffrey-Guerrera

Nestled between the south of France and the Tuscan border lies the region of Liguria, with verdant and lush mountains to the north and east, and the sapphire blue Mediterranean to the south and west. In between is a land of lush vegetation, medieval hilltop hamlets, panoramic vistas, colorful seaside villages, pristine beaches, and one of Italy's most underrated cities, Genoa.

There is plenty to do—from hiking and biking, to water sports and fishing, to eating (very) well—and plenty to see, including some of Italy's most aesthetically pleasing architecture in Cinque Terre, to just enjoying la dolce vita along its coast, better known as the Italian Riviera.

The Italian Riviera oozes charm and irresistible allure, with many seaside resort towns and colorful villages that stake intermittent claim to the rocky shores of the Ligurian Sea and seem like the long-lost cousins of newer seaside paradises found elsewhere. It has been a haven for artists, writers, celebrities, and royalty since the 1800s, and continues to fascinate visitors throughout the year due to its mild climate. Here the grandest palazzi share space with frescoed, angular *terratettos* (tall, skinny houses). The rustic and elegant, the provincial and chic, the small-town and cosmopolitan all collide here in a sun-drenched blend that defines the Italian side of the Riviera. There are chic resort towns such as San Remo and Portofino, the unique beauty and outdoor adventures of the Cinque Terre, numerous quaint seaside and hilltop villages to explore, plus the history and architectural charm of Genoa. Mellowed by the balmy breezes blowing off the sea, travelers bask in the sun, explore the picturesque fishing villages, and pamper themselves at the resorts that dot this ruggedly beautiful landscape.

THE ITALIAN RIVIERA PLANNER

MAKING THE MOST OF YOUR TIME

Your first decision, particularly given limited time, is between the two Rivieras. The Riviera di Levante, east of Genoa, is more rustic and has a more distinct personality, with the unique Cinque Terre, ritzy Portofino, and the panoramic Gulf of Poets. The Riviera di Ponente, west of Genoa, is a classic European resort experience with many white-sand beaches and more nightlife and accommodation choices—similar to, but not as glamorous as, the French Riviera across the border.

In either case, your second decision is whether to visit Genoa. Despite its rough exterior and (diminishing) reputation as a seamy port town, Genoa's artistic and cultural treasures are significant—you won't find anything remotely comparable elsewhere in the region. Unless your goal is to avoid urban life entirely, consider a night or two in the city.

The Italian Riviera is extremely seasonal. From April to October, the area's bustling with shops, cafés, clubs, and restaurants that stay open late. In high season (Easter and June–August), it can be very crowded and lively. Yet, the rest of the year, the majority of resorts close down, and you'll be hard-pressed to find accommodations or restaurants open.

GETTING HERE AND AROUND

BUS TRAVEL

Generally speaking, buses are a difficult way to come and go in Liguria.

While there are local buses that run between villages along the Riviera Ponente, it's not an extensive network and can be a challenge to navigate.

Volpibus. This firm provides service from the airport in Nice as well as Milan, but there's no bus service between Genoa and other major Italian cities. ☎ 010/561661 ⊕ www.volpibus.com.

ATP. Things run somewhat easier along the Riviera Levante where ATP has regular, regional services. ☎ 0185/373275 ⊕ www.atp-spa.it.

CAR TRAVEL

With the freedom of a car, you could drive from one end of the Riviera to the other on the autostrada in about three hours. Two good roads run parallel to each other along the coast of Liguria. Closer to shore and passing through all the towns and villages is SS1, the Via Aurelia, which was laid out by the ancient Romans and has excellent views at almost every turn but gets crowded in July and August. More direct and higher up than SS1 are autostrade A10, west of Genoa, and A12, to the south—engineering wonders with literally hundreds of long tunnels and towering viaducts. These routes save time on weekends, in summer, and on days when festivals slow traffic in some resorts to a standstill.

TRAIN TRAVEL

Train travel is by far the most convenient mode of transportation throughout the region. It takes 3½ hours for an express train to cover the entire Liguria coast. Local trains take upward of five hours or more to get from one end of the coast to the other, stopping in or near all the towns along the way.

For schedules, check the website of the national railway, **FS** (☎ *892021* ⊕ *www.trenitalia.com*).

HIKING

Walking Liguria's extensive network of trails, and taking in the gorgeous views, is a major outdoor activity and an attraction to the region. The mild climate and laid-back state of mind can lull you into underestimating just how strenuous such walks can be. Wear good shoes, use sunscreen, and carry plenty of water—you'll be glad you did. Trail maps are available from tourist information offices, or upon entry to the Cinque Terre National Park.

On Portofino promontory, the relatively easy walk to the Abbazia di San Fruttuoso is popular, and there's a more challenging hike from Ruta to the top of Monte Portofino. From Genoa, you can take the Zecca–Righi funicular up to Righi and walk along the ring of fortresses that used to defend the city, or ride the Genova–Casella railroad to one of the trailheads near the station stops.

Walking tours can introduce you to lesser-known aspects of the region. For the Cinque Terre and the rest of the Province of La Spezia, the **Cooperativa Arte e Natura** (✉ *Viale Amendola 172, La Spezia* ☎ *0187/739410*) is a good source for English-speaking guides as well as other languages. A full day costs around €210 for groups up to 25 people.

RESTAURANTS

Prices in the dining reviews are the average cost of a main course at dinner, or, if dinner is not served, at lunch.

HOTELS

Liguria's lodging options may be a step behind such resort areas as Positano and Taormina, so reservations for its better accommodations (and for the more limited ones in the Cinque Terre) should be made far in advance. Lodging tends to be pricey in high season, particularly June to August. *For expanded reviews, facilities, and current deals, visit Fodors.com*

WHAT IT COSTS			
$	**$$**	**$$$**	**$$$$**
RESTAURANTS under €15	€15–€24	€25–€35	over €35
HOTELS under €125	€125–€200	€201–€300	over €300

Prices in the reviews are the lowest cost of a standard double room in high season. Prices in the reviews are the average cost of a main course at dinner or, if dinner is not served, at lunch.

CINQUE TERRE

The photogenic, preposterously beautiful Cinque Terre make it the Cinderella of the Italian Riviera. In their rugged simplicity, the five old fishing towns of Monterosso, Vernazza, Corniglia, Manarola, and Riomaggiore seem to mock the caked-on artifice of glitzy neighboring resorts. With a clear blue sea in the foreground, spectacularly multicolor buildings emerge almost seamlessly from cliffs, and rocky mountains rise precipitously to gravity-defying vineyards and dusty olive groves. The five small villages (Cinque Terre literally means "Five Lands") cling to the cliffs along a gorgeous stretch of the Ligurian coast. The geography here prevents expansion or any real technological advancement, and the small towns can't help but retain their enchanting intimacy.

The terrain is so steep that for centuries, footpaths were the only way to get from place to place. These footpaths provide beautiful views of the rocky coast tumbling into the sea, as well as access to secluded beaches and grottoes. Since its designation in 1997 as a UNESCO World Heritage Site, Cinque Terre has become one of Italy's most popular destinations. Despite some lingering damage from the 2011 flash floods, each town has maintained its own distinct charm.

RIOMAGGIORE

17 km (11 miles) northwest of La Spezia, 101 km (60 miles) east of Genoa.

At the eastern end of the Cinque Terre, Riomaggiore is built into a river gorge (thus the name, which means "major river") and is easily accessible from La Spezia by train or car. The landscape is terraced and steep—be prepared for many stairs!—and leads down to a small harbor, protected by large slabs of alabaster and marble that serve as tanning beds for sunbathers, being the site of several outdoor cafés with fine views. According to legend, the settlement of Riomaggiore dates as far back as the 8th century, when Greek religious refugees came here to escape persecution by the Byzantine emperor.

The village is divided into two parts. If you arrive by train, you will have to pass through a tunnel that flanks the train tracks in order to reach the historic side of town. To avoid the crowds and get a great view of the Cinque Terre coast, walk straight uphill as soon as you exit the station. This winding road takes you over the hill to the 14th-century **church of Saint John the Baptist,** toward the medieval town center and the Genovese-style tower houses that dot the village. Follow Via Roma (the Old Town's main street) downhill, pass under the train tracks, and you'll arrive in the charming fishermen's port of the village. Lined with traditional fishing boats and small trattorias, this is a lovely spot for a romantic lunch or dinner. Unfortunately, Riomaggiore doesn't have as much old-world charm as its sister villages; its easy accessibility has brought traffic and more modern construction here than elsewhere in the Cinque Terre.

GETTING HERE AND AROUND

The enormous parking problems presented by these cliff-dwelling villages have been mitigated somewhat by a large, covered parking structure at the La Spezia Centrale station, which costs €1.50 per hour. It's clean and secure (you cannot enter without a ticket code to open the door), and it's open 24/7. This is a good backup solution for those with cars, although others may choose to take a day trip from Pisa or

Lucca and rely on bus and train services. Arrive early (first train to the Cinque Terre is at 10 am) as it can fill up, especially in the high season.

WHERE TO EAT

$$$$ LIGURIAN 🍴 **Dau Cila.** There's wonderful seaside dining on Riomaggiore harbor, with a vast menu of local Ligurian dishes and an extensive wine list. **■ TIP→ On bad-weather days, take advantage of the lovely dining room with vaulted ceilings, built into the rock.** [$] *Average main: €45* ✉ *Via San Giacomo 65* ☎ *0187/760032* ✍ *Reservations essential* ⏲ *Closed Nov.–Mar.*

$$$$ LIGURIAN 🍴 **La Lanterna.** Colorful chalkboards out in front of this small trattoria by the harbor list the day's selection of fresh fish; the set-up might sound modest, but this is arguably the finest restaurant in the Cinque Terre. During the winter, Chef Massimo serves as a teacher at the Culinary Academy in Switzerland, and he always returns with new ideas for his menu. When available, the *cozze ripiene* (stuffed mussels) shouldn't be missed. Other offerings may be a touch exotic, such as stingray with Ligurian herbs and white wine. [$] *Average main: €40* ✉ *Via San Giacomo 10* ☎ *0187/920589* ⏲ *Closed Jan. and 2 wks in Nov.*

MANAROLA

Fodor's Choice ★ *16 km (10 miles) northwest of La Spezia, 117 km (73 miles) southeast of Genoa.*

The enchanting pastel houses of Manarola spill down a steep hill overlooking a spectacular turquoise swimming cove and a bustling harbor. The whole town is built on black rock. Above the town, ancient terraces still protect abundant vineyards and olive trees. This village is the center of wine and olive-oil production in the region, and its streets are lined with shops selling local products.

Surrounded by steep terraced vineyards, Manarola's one road tumbles from the **Chiesa di San Lorenzo** (14th century) high above the village, down to the rocky port below. Since the Cinque Terre wine cooperative is located in **Groppo,** a hamlet overlooking the village (and reachable by foot or by the green Park bus; ask at Park offices for schedules), the vineyards are accessible. If you'd like to snap a shot of the most famous view of the town, you can walk from the port area to the cemetery above. Along the way you'll pass the town's play yard, uncrowded bathrooms, and a tap with clean drinking water.

WHERE TO STAY

$$ HOTEL 🏨 **Ca' d'Andrean.** If you want to stay in one of the less crowded Cinque Terre offerings, this tiny, simple hotel is one of your best options. **Pros:** quiet location; lovely garden. **Cons:** rooms are comfy but basic. [$] *Rooms from: €130* ✉ *Via Discovolo 101* ☎ *0187/920040* 🌐 *www.cadandrean.it* 🛏 *10 rooms* 💳 *No credit cards* ⏲ *Closed mid-Nov.–Mar.* 🍴 *No meals.*

Continued on page 454

HIKING THE CINQUE TERRE

FIVE REMOTE VILLAGES MAKE ONE MUST-SEE DESTINATION

"Charming" and "breath-taking" are adjectives that get a workout when you're traveling in Italy, but it's rare that both apply to a single location. The Cinque Terre is such a place, and this combination of characteristics goes a long way toward explaining its tremendous appeal.

The area is made up of five tiny villages (Cinque Terre literally means "Five Lands") clinging to the cliffs along a gorgeous stretch of the Ligurian coast. The terrain is so steep that for centuries footpaths were the only way to get from place to place. It just so happens that these paths provide beautiful views of the rocky coast tumbling into the sea, as well as access to secluded beaches and grottoes.

Backpackers "discovered" the Cinque Terre in the 1970s, and its popularity has been growing ever since. Despite summer crowds, much of the original appeal is intact. Each town has maintained its own distinct charm, and views from the trails in between are as breathtaking as ever.

Monterosso

Corniglia

Terracing around Cornig

HIKING THE CINQUE TERRE

Monterosso—Vernazza Trail
The most demanding portion of the trail. Often narrow, with significant climbs and descents, particularly near Vernazza. Your labors are rewarded with the Trail No. 2's best views.

Mount Malpertuso ▲

Mount ▲ Castello

Le Stalle

Trail No 8a

Mount Gaginara ▲

38

(Red Trail)

Drignana

Vernazza—Corniglia Trail
Ups and downs interspersed with olive groves and terraced vineyards.

370

Madonna di Soviore

Trail No 1

Santuario del Reggio
1hr

1hr 30min

51

Trail No 8

Trail No 89

Santuario Bernardino
1hr

S. Bernardo
Trail No 8

Trail No 7

3 km/2 mi—1 hr 30 min

Trail No 2 (Blue Trail)
3 km/2 mi—2 hrs

Vernazza

Guvano Beach

del Frate Island

Palma Pt

Molinara Pt

0 _____ 1 mi

0 _____ 1 km

Monterosso al Mare

FERRY TO LEVANTO

Monterosso
The most resort-like of the villages, with the largest beach.

Vernazza
Pretty and visitor-friendly. The best spot for lingering in a café and watching waves crash against the shore.

THE CLASSIC HIKE

Hiking is the most popular way to experience the Cinque Terre, and Trail No. 2, the Sentiero Azzurro (Blue Trail), is the most traveled path. To cover the entire trail is a full day: it's approximately 13 km (8 miles) in length, takes you to all five villages, and requires about five hours, not including stops, to complete. The best approach is to start at the eastern-most town of Riomaggiore and warm up your legs on the easiest segment of the trail. As you work your way west, the hike gets progressively more demanding. Between Corniglia and Manarola take the ferry (which provides its own beautiful views) or the inland train running between the towns instead.

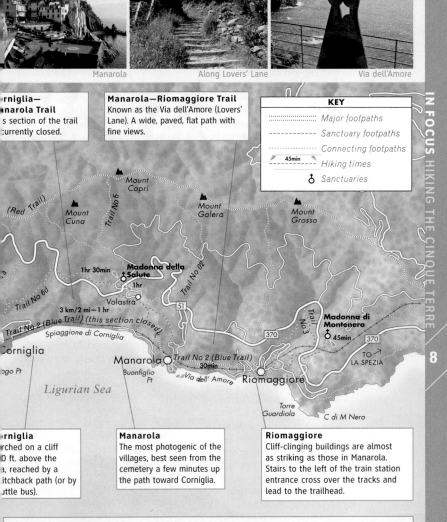

Manarola

Along Lovers' Lane

Via dell'Amore

**rniglia—
anarola Trail**
s section of the trail
currently closed.

Manarola—Riomaggiore Trail
Known as the Via dell'Amore (Lovers'
Lane). A wide, paved, flat path with
fine views.

KEY

:::::::::::::::::	Major footpaths
- - - - - - - -	Sanctuary footpaths
· · · · · · · ·	Connecting footpaths
45min	Hiking times
☖	Sanctuaries

Mount
Capri

(Red Trail)

Mount
Cuna

Trail No 6

Mount
Galera

Mount
Grosso

1hr 30min

Trail No 6d

**Madonna della
☖ Salute**

1hr

Volastra

Trail No 02

3 km/2 mi – 1 hr

Trail No 2 (Blue Trail) (this section closed)

Spiaggione di Corniglia

51

Trail
No 3

**Madonna di
Montenero**

☖ 45min

370

Corniglia

370

TO →
LA SPEZIA

8

Manarola ☖ Trail No 2 (Blue Trail)

ogo Pt

Buonfiglio
Pt

30min

Via dell'Amore

Riomaggiore

Ligurian Sea

Torre
Guardiola

C di M Nero

rniglia
rched on a cliff
0 ft. above the
a, reached by a
itchback path (or by
uttle bus).

Manarola
The most photogenic of the
villages, best seen from the
cemetery a few minutes up
the path toward Corniglia.

Riomaggiore
Cliff-clinging buildings are almost
as striking as those in Manarola.
Stairs to the left of the train station
entrance cross over the tracks and
lead to the trailhead.

BEYOND TRAIL NO.2

Trail No. 2 is just one of a network of
trails crisscrossing the hills. If you're
a dedicated hiker, spend a few nights
and try some of the other routes.
Trail No. 1, the Sentiero Rosso (Red
Trail), climbs from Portovenere (east of
Riomaggiore) and returns to the sea at
Levanto (west of Monterosso al Mare).
To hike its length takes from 9 to 12
hours; the ridge-top trail provides spectacular views from high above the villages, each of which can be reached
via a steep path. Other shorter trails
go from the villages up into the hills,
some leading to religious sanctuaries.
Trail No. 9, for example, starts from
the old section of Monterosso and ends
at the Madonna di Soviore Sanctuary.

CLOSE UP

Hiking the Cinque Terre

Although often described as beautiful, relaxing, and easy, it would be fair to say that the first applies to anywhere in the Cinque Terre, but best to leave the other two for your time after hiking between the villages. Many people do not realize just how demanding parts of these trails can be—it's best to come prepared. We recommend bringing: a Cinque Terre Card and cash (smaller shops, eateries, and the park entrances do not accept credit cards).

When completely open, a hike through the entire region takes about four to five hours plus time for exploring each village and taking a lunch break. It's an all-day, if not two-day trek. We recommend an early start, especially in summer when midday temperatures can rise to 90 degrees. Note that only "Sentiero Azzuro" (Trail No. 2, which includes the famous "Via dell'Amore," or Lover's Lane) requires the Cinque Terre Card. The other 20-plus trails in the area are free. All trails are well marked with a red and white hiking trail sign. The trails from village to village get progressively steeper as you move from south (Riomaggiore) to the north (Monterosso). If you're a day-tripper arriving by car, use the new underground lot at the La Spezia Centrale train station (€1.50/hour in summer) and take the train to Riomaggiore (6–8 minutes) to begin your hiking adventure.

OUR FAVORITES
Other trails to consider include: **Monterosso to Santuario Madonna di Soviore**, a fairly strenuous but rewarding 1½ hours up to a lovely 8th-century sanctuary. There is also a restaurant and a priceless view. **Riomaggiore to Montenero and**

Portovenere is 1 hour up to the sanctuary and another 3 hours on to Portovenere, passing through some gorgeous, less-traveled terrain. **Manarola to Volastra to Corniglia** runs high above the main trail and through vineyards and lesser-known villages. **Monterosso to Levanto** is a good 2½-hour hike, passing over Punta Mesco with glorious views of the Cinque Terre to the south, Corsica to the west, and the Alps to the north.

Each town has something that passes for a beach (usually with lots of pebbles or slabs of terraced rock), but there is only one option for both sand and decent swimming—in Monterosso, just across from the train station. It's equipped with chairs, umbrellas, and snack bars.

PRECAUTIONS
If you're hitting the trails, you'll want to carry water with you, wear sturdy shoes (hiking boots are best), and have a hat and sunscreen handy. Note that the lesser-used trails aren't as well maintained as Trail No. 2. If you're undertaking the full Trail No. 1 hike, bring something to snack on as well as your water bottle. Note, at press time, that the Via dell'Amore and the portion of Trail No. 2 between Manarola and Corniglia are closed indefinitely due to such landslides. ⚠ Check weather reports; especially in late fall and winter, thunderstorms can make shelterless trails slippery and dangerous. Rain in October and November can cause landslides and close the trails.

$$
HOTEL
Fodor's Choice ★

🏨 **La Torretta.** The Cinque Terre's only "boutique" hotel is in a 17th-century tower and sits high on the hill above the rainbow-hue village of Manarola with truly lovely views of the terraced vineyards, colorful village homes, and the Mediterranean sea; inside, décor is chic, sleek, and antiques-bedecked. **Pros:** well-maintained; a cut above most lodging in the Cinque Terre. **Cons:** if the luggage shuttle is not running during its limited hours, it is a steep walk up (and a lot of exercise!) to the hotel. [$] *Rooms from: €200* ✉ *Vico Volto 20* ☎ *0187/920327* 🌐 *www.torrettas.com* 🛏 *4 rooms, 7 suites* 🕒 *Closed Nov.–mid-Mar.* 🍴 *Breakfast.*

CORNIGLIA

Fodor's Choice ★

27 km (17 miles) northwest of La Spezia, 100 km (60 miles) southeast of Genoa.

The buildings, narrow lanes, and stairways of Corniglia are strung together amid vineyards high on the cliffs. On a clear day, views of the entire coastal strip are excellent, from Elba in the south to the Italian Alps in the north. The high perch and lack of harbor make this farming community the most remote and therefore least crowded of the Cinque Terre. In fact, the 365 steps that lead from the train station to the town center dissuade many tourists from making the hike to the village. You can also take the green Park bus, but they run infrequently and are usually packed with tired hikers.

Corniglia is built along one road edged with small shops, bars, gelaterias, and restaurants. Midway along Via Fieschi is the **Largo Taragio,** the main square and heart of the village. Shaded by leafy trees and umbrellas, this is a lovely spot for a midhike gelato break. Here you'll find the 14th-century **Chiesa di San Pietro.** Its rose window of marble imported from Carrara is impressive, particularly considering the work required to get it here!

VERNAZZA

Fodor's Choice ★

27 km (17 miles) northwest of La Spezia, 96 km (59 miles) southeast of Genoa.

With its narrow streets and small squares, Vernazza is arguably the most charming of the five Cinque Terre towns, and therefore, usually the most crowded. Historically, it was the most important of them, since it was the only one fortunate enough to have a natural port and, therefore, became wealthier than its neighbors—as evinced by the elaborate arcades, loggias, and marble work lining Via Roma and Piazza Marconi.

The village's pink, slate-roof houses and colorful squares contrast with the remains of the medieval fort and castle, including two towers, in the Old Town. The Romans first inhabited this rocky spit of land in the 1st century.

Today, Vernazza has a fairly lively social scene. **Piazza Marconi** looks out across Vernazza's small sandy beach to the sea, towards Monterosso. The numerous restaurants and bars crowd their tables and umbrellas on

CLOSE UP

Accessing the Trails of the Cinque Terre

WHEN TO GO
The ideal times to visit the Cinque Terre are September and May, when the weather is mild and the summer tourist season isn't in full swing (between June and August it can be unbearably hot and crowded).

GETTING HERE AND AROUND
The local train on the Genoa–La Spezia line stops at each of the Cinque Terre villages, and runs approximately every 30 minutes. Tickets for each leg of the journey (€1.80–€2) are available at the five train stations. In Corniglia, the only one of the Cinque Terre that isn't at sea level, a shuttle service (€1) is provided for those who don't wish to climb (or descend) 300-plus steps that link the train station with the clifftop town.

Along the Cinque Terre coast two ferry lines operate. From June to September, Golfo Paradiso runs from Genoa and Camogli to Monterosso al Mare and Vernazza. The smaller but more frequent Golfo dei Poeti stops at each village from Lerici (east of Riomaggiore) to Monterosso, with the exception of Corniglia, four times a day. A one-day ticket costs €30.

ADMISSION
Entrance tickets for use of the trails are available at ticket booths located at the start of each section of Trail No. 2, and at information offices in the Levanto, Monterosso, Vernazza, Corniglia, Manarola, Riomaggiore, and La Spezia train stations.

A one-day pass costs €7.50, which includes a trail map and an information leaflet; a two-day pass is €14.50. A one-day Cinque Terre Card costs €12 and a two-day pass is €23. The card combines park entrance fees with unlimited daily use of the regional train between La Spezia, the five villages, and Levanto just north of Monterosso.

FOR MORE INFORMATION
⊕ www.cinqueterre.com; ⊕ www.lecinqueterre.org; ⊕ www.parconazionale-5terre.it; ⊕ www.rebuildmonterosso.com; ⊕ savevernazza.com; ⊕ www.littleparadiso.com (blog); ⊕ lifeinliguria.blogspot.it (blog).

the outskirts of the piazza, creating a patchwork of sights and sounds that form one of the most unique and beautiful places in the world.

EXPLORING

If mass is not going on (there will be a cord blocking the entrance if it is), take a peek into the **church of Saint Margaret of Antioch.** Little changed since its enlargement in the 1600s, this 14th-century edifice has simple interiors but truly breathtaking views toward the sea: a stark contrast to the other, elaborate churches of the Cinque Terre.

On the other side of the piazza, stairs lead to a lookout **fortress and cylindrical watchtower,** built in the 11th century as protection against pirate attacks. For a small fee you can climb to the top of the tower for a spectacular view of the coastline.

WHERE TO EAT AND STAY

$$$$ LIGURIAN 🍴 **Gambero Rosso.** Relax on Vernazza's main square at this fine trattoria looking out at a church. Enjoy such delectable dishes as shrimp salad, vegetable torte, and squid-ink risotto. The creamy pesto, served atop spaghetti, is some of the best in the Cinque Terre. End your meal with Cinque Terre's own *sciacchetrà*, a dessert wine served with semisweet biscotti. Don't drink it out of the glass—dip the biscotti in the wine instead. [$] *Average main: €45* ✉ *Piazza Marconi 7* ☎ *0187/812265* 🌐 *www.ristorantegamberorosso.net* 🕓 *Closed Mon. and Nov.–Mar.*

$$ B&B/INN 🏨 **La Malà.** A cut above other lodging options in the Cinque Terre, these small guest rooms are equipped with flat-screen TVs, air-conditioning, marble showers, comfortable bedding, and have views of the sea or the port, which can also be enjoyed at their most bewitching from the shared terrace literally suspended over the Mediterranean. **Pros:** clean, fresh-feeling rooms; oh, the views. **Cons:** there are some stairs involved; for the price, one should not have to go to a bar for a small continental breakfast. [$] *Rooms from: €160* ✉ *Giovanni Battista 29* ☎ *334/2875718* 🌐 *www.lamala.it* 🛏 *4 rooms* 🕓 *Closed Jan. 10–Mar.* 🍽 *No meals.*

MONTEROSSO AL MARE

Fodor's Choice ★ *32 km (20 miles) northwest of La Spezia, 89 km (55 miles) southeast of Genoa.*

It's the combined draw of beautiful beaches, rugged cliffs, crystal-clear turquoise waters, and plentiful small hotels and restaurants that make Monterosso al Mare into the largest of the Cinque Terre villages (population 1,800) and also the busiest in midsummer.

Monterosso has the most festivals of the five villages, starting with the Lemon Feast on the Saturday preceding Ascension Sunday, followed by the Flower Festival of Corpus Christi, celebrated yearly on the second Sunday after Pentecost. During the afternoon, the streets and alleyways of the historic center are decorated with thousands of colorful flower petals set in beautiful designs that the evening procession passes over. Finally, the Salted Anchovy and Olive Oil Festival takes place each year during the second weekend of September.

EXPLORING

From the train station, heading west, you pass through a tunnel and exit into the *centro storico* (historic center) of the village. Nestled into the wide valley that leads to the sea, Monterosso is built above numerous streams, which have been covered to make up the major streets of the village. Via Buranco, the oldest street in Monterosso, leads out to the most characteristic piazza of the village, Piazza Matteotti (locals pass through here daily to shop at the supermarket and butcher). This piazza also contains the oldest and most typical wineshop in the village, Enoteca da Eliseo—stop here between 6 pm and midnight to share tables with fellow tourists and locals over a bottle of Cinque Terre wine. There's also the **Chiesa di San Francesco,** built in the 12th century, which is an excellent example of the Ligurian Gothic style. Its distinctive black stripes and marble rose window make it one of the most photographed sites in the Cinque Terre.

Fegina, the newer side of the village (and site of the train station), has relatively modern homes ranging from Liberty Style (Art Nouveau) to the early 1970s. At the far eastern end of town, you'll run into a private sailing club sheltered by a vast rock carved with an impressive statue of Neptune. From here, you can reach the challenging trail to Levanto (a great 2½ hour hike). This trail has the added bonus of a five-minute detour to the **ruins of a 14th-century monastery.** The expansive view from this vantage point allowed the monks who were housed here to easily scan the waters for enemy ships that might invade the villages and alert residents to coming danger. Have your camera ready for this Cinerama-like vista.

Though having the most nightlife on the Cinque Terre (thanks to its numerous wine bars and pubs) Monterosso is also the most family-friendly. With its expanse of free and equipped beaches, extensive pedestrian areas, large children's play park, and summer activities, Monterosso is a top spot for kids.

The **local outdoor market** is held on Thursday and attracts crowds of tourists and villagers from along the coast to shop for everything from pots, pans, and underwear to fruits, vegetables, and fish. Often a few stands sell local art and crafts, as well as olive oil and wine.

WHERE TO EAT

$$ WINE BAR 🍴 **Enoteca Internazionale.** Located on the main street in Centro, this wine bar offers a wide variety of vintages, both local and from further afield, plus delicious light fare; its umbrella-covered patio is a perfect spot to recuperate after a day of hiking. The owner, Susanna, is a certified sommelier who's always forthcoming with helpful suggestions on local wines. [$] *Average main: €20* ✉ *Via Roma 62* ☎ *0187/817278* ⏲ *Closed Tues., and Jan.–Mar.*

$$$$ SEAFOOD 🍴 **Miky.** This is arguably the best restaurant in Monterosso, specializing in tasty, fresh seafood dishes including grilled calamari and monkfish ravioli. It has a beautiful little garden in the back, perfect for lunch on a sunny day. The Da Fina family has recently opened a *cantina* just a few doors down, which is a bit more casual. It includes seaside dining and is perfect for those searching for a bit of nightlife. [$] *Average main: €45* ✉ *Via Fegina 104* ☎ *0187/817608* 🌐 *www.ristorantemiky.it* ✍ *Reservations essential* ⏲ *Closed mid-Nov.–mid-Mar.*

$$$$ LIGURIAN Fodor's Choice ★ 🍴 **Ristorante Belforte.** High above the sea in one of Vernazza's remaining stone towers is this unique spot serving delicious Cinque Terre cuisine such as *branzino sotto sale* (sea bass cooked under salt), stuffed mussels, and *insalata di polpo* (octopus salad). The setting is magnificent, so try for an outdoor table. Reservations are a must. [$] *Average main: €45* ✉ *Via Guidoni 42, Vernazza* ☎ *0187/812222* 🌐 *www.ristorantebelforte.it* ✍ *Reservations essential* ⏲ *Closed Tues., and Nov.–Easter.*

WHERE TO STAY

$$ B&B/INN 🏨 **Bellambra B&B.** Modern rooms with charm and comfort in the heart of the old town make this a terrific base for exploring the Cinque Terre. **Pros:** relatively new; spacious rooms and bathrooms; location;

helpful service. **Cons:** can be a bit noisy; no elevator with steep, narrow stairs. $ *Rooms from: €165* ⊠ *Via Roma 64* ☎ *39/3920121912* ⊕ *www.bellambra5terre.com* ⤳ *4 rooms, 1 apartment* ⦿ *Breakfast.*

$$
B&B/INN
Fodor's Choice
★
Il Giardino Incantato. With wood-beam ceilings and stone walls, the stylishly restored and updated rooms in this 16th-century house in the historic center of Monterosso ooze comfort and old-world charm. **Pros:** spacious rooms; gorgeous garden; excellent hosts. **Cons:** no views. $ *Rooms from: €170* ⊠ *Via Mazzini 18* ☎ *0185/818315* ⊕ *www. ilgiardinoincantato.net* ⤳ *3 rooms, 1 junior suite* ⊗ *Closed Nov.–Mar.* ⦿ *Breakfast.*

$$$$
HOTEL
Porto Roca. Far from the madding crowds, the Cinque Terre's only "high-end" hotel is perched on the famous terraced cliffs right over the main beach and magnificent sea, with large balconies to savor all the panoramic views. **Pros:** unobstructed sea views; tranquil location; pool. **Cons:** some of the rooms could use a revamp; back-facing rooms can be a bit dark; expensive for level of comfort offered. $ *Rooms from: €320* ⊠ *Via Corone 1* ☎ *0187/817502* ⊕ *www.portoroca.it* ⤳ *39 rooms, 3 junior suites, 3 apartments* ⊗ *Closed Nov.–Mar.* ⦿ *No meals.*

RIVIERA DI LEVANTE

Stretching east from Lerici to Genoa (and incorporating Cinque Terre) lies the Riviera di Levante (Riviera of the Rising Sun). It has a more raw, unpolished side to it than the Riviera di Ponente, east of Genoa, and its stretches of rugged coastline are dotted with colorful fishing villages. It's also home to one of Europe's well-known playgrounds for the rich and famous, the inlet of Portofino. Around every turn of this area's twisting roads the hills plummet sharply to the sea, forming deep, hidden bays and coves. Beaches on this coast tend to be rocky, backed by spectacular sheer cliffs, yet there are some rather lovely sandy beaches in Lerici, Monterosso, Levanto, and Paraggi near Portofino.

LERICI

106 km (66 miles) southeast of Genoa, 65 km (40 miles) west of Lucca.

Lerici is located in the spectacular Bay of La Spezia, otherwise known as the Gulf of Poets, and is famous for its natural beauty. Near Liguria's border with Tuscany, this picturesque village dates back to medieval times when, under the rule of Pisa, it fought cross-bay battles with Genovese Portovenere, as well as with local pirates. The town is set on a magnificent coastline of gray cliffs jutting down into a crystal-clear sea and surrounded by a national park that is nearly an unframed painting of pine forests, olive trees, and tiny colorful hamlets. The waterfront piazza is filled with trompe-l'oeil frescoed buildings, and seaside cafés line a charming little harbor that holds sailboats and *gozzi,* the typical small fishing boats of the area.

There are several white beaches and bathing establishments dotting the 2-km (1-mile) walk along the bay from the village center to nearby San Terenzo. From the village, you can also reach some beautiful hiking

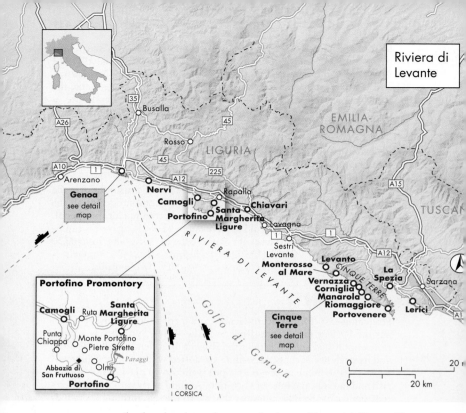

Genoa
see detail
map

Cinque
Terre
see detail
map

trails that head southeast to both seaside and hilltop villages like Fiascherino, Tellaro, and Montemarcello.

GETTING HERE AND AROUND

By car, Lerici is less than a 10-minute drive west from the A12 with plenty of blue signs indicating the way. There's a large pay-parking lot about a 10-minute walk along the seaside promenade from the center. By train, the closest station is either Sarzana (10-minute drive) or La Spezia Centrale (20-minute drive) on the main north–south line between Genoa and Pisa.

VISITOR INFORMATION

Lerici Tourism Office ⊠ *Via Biaggini 6* ☎ *0187/967164* ⊕ *www. aptcinqueterre.sp.it.*

EXPLORING

Castello di Lerici. The promontory is dominated by this 13th-century Pisan castle that now houses a museum of paleontology and offers a suberb position for weddings overlooking the entire Gulf of Poets. ⊠ *Piazza S. Giorgio 1* ☎ *0187/969042* ⊕ *www.castellodilerici.it* ⊡ *€5* ⊗ *Mar. 16–June, Sept.–Oct. 19, and Dec. 26–Jan. 6, Tues.–Sun. 10:30–12:30 and 2:30–5:30; July and Aug., daily 10:30–12:30 and 6:30–midnight; Oct. 20–Dec. 23 and Jan. 7–Mar. 15, Tues.–Fri. 10:30–12:30, weekends 10:30–12:30 and 2:30–5:30.*

WHERE TO EAT

$$$$
ITALIAN

✕ **Bonta Nascoste.** In the local dialect, *bonta nascoste* means "hidden goodness," a reference to the back-alleyway location and consistently delicious dishes, including fresh pasta and local fish. This charming spot also serves a handful of delicious meat choices. There are only eight tables (and a couple more outside in summer), so reserve ahead. $ *Average main: €40* ✉ *Via Cavour 52* ☎ *0187/965500* ⊕ *www.bontanascoste. it* ⚲ *Reservations essential* ☾ *Closed Tues., and 2 wks in Nov. and June.*

$$$
LIGURIAN

✕ **Il Frantoio.** Located in an old olive-oil mill (the enormous wood grinder still sits in the middle of the dining room), this is a no-frills but fine-food restaurant serving excellent antipasti *al mare* and homemade pasta dishes. You can eat very well for a bit less than at most of the touristy spots in town. $ *Average main: €35* ✉ *Via Cavour 19* ☎ *0187/964174* ⚲ *Reservations essential.*

$$$$
LIGURIAN
Fodor's Choice
★

✕ **Miranda.** Perched amid the clustered old houses in seaside Tellaro, 4 km (2½ miles) southeast of Lerici, this small family-run restaurant has become a gourmet's destination because of chef Angelo Cabani's imaginative Ligurian cooking. His seafood menu changes daily, but might include shrimp and lobster salad with fennel, or risotto with asparagus and shrimp. This pretty building also houses a small inn with seven charming and comfortable rooms. $ *Average main: €60* ✉ *Via Fiascherino 92, Tellaro* ☎ *0187/964012* ⊕ *www.miranda1959. com* ☾ *Closed Mon., and 2 wks in Nov. and Jan.*

$$$$
LIGURIAN

✕ **Osteria di Redarca.** Within the pine forest of the Montemarcello National Park, this *osteria* (a simple, informal restaurant) serves some of the best homemade pastas in the area. It also offers a "surf 'n' turf" menu, with abundant cooked-to-perfection fish platters and succulent meat dishes. The location may not be seaside, but the setting and the food are both a treat. $ *Average main: €45* ✉ *Rocchetta Località Redarca 6* ☎ *0187/966140* ☾ *Closed Wed., and 2 wks in Jan.*

WHERE TO STAY

$$
HOTEL

🛏 **Doria Park.** The junior suites have large terraces and Jacuzzi tubs, but any of the sea-view rooms are a real value, and the location, between olive-tree hills and the village center, is the best in Lerici. **Pros:** sea views; comfortable beds; not far from the main piazza and harbor. **Cons:** many stairs, including several sets that can be challenging for people with weak knees or heavy bags. $ *Rooms from: €160* ✉ *Via Doria 2* ☎ *0187/967124* ⊕ *www.doriaparkhotel.it* ⇄ *48 rooms, 5 suites* ¶◯¶ *Breakfast.*

$$
HOTEL
FAMILY

🛏 **Florida.** Extras such as sea-view balconies make this seafront, family-run establishment well worth the euros. **Pros:** beachfront location; bay views; friendly staff. **Cons:** small rooms; beach across the street can be noisy, especially in summer. $ *Rooms from: €125* ✉ *Lungomare Biaggini 35* ☎ *0187/967332* ⊕ *www.hotelflorida.it* ⇄ *40 rooms* ☾ *Closed approx. Dec.–Feb.* ¶◯¶ *Breakfast.*

**EN
ROUTE**
Ten minutes inland from Lerici is the medieval village of **Sarzana,** designed by the military leader Castruccio Castracani, who also designed Lucca. Here, you'll find some of the most authentic and well-restored palazzos in Liguria. Its pedestrians-only cobblestone streets bustling with people, fine boutiques, and packed cafés are perfect for a

8

passeggiata (evening stroll). For three weeks in August it hosts a lively antiques market with great buys and opportunities for people-watching.

LA SPEZIA

11 km (7 miles) northwest of Lerici, 103 km (64 miles) southeast of Genoa.

La Spezia is sometimes thought of as nothing but a large, industrialized naval port en route to the Cinque Terre and Portovenere, but it does possess some charm, and it gives you a look at a less tourist-focused part of the Riviera. Its palm-lined promenade, fertile citrus parks, renovated Liberty-style palazzos, and colorful balcony-lined streets make parts of La Spezia surprisingly beautiful. Monday through Saturday mornings, you can stroll through the fresh fish, produce, and local-cheese stalls at the outdoor market on Piazza Cavour, and on Friday take part in the busy flea market on Via Garibaldi. There's also Porto Mirabello, a newly built tourist port with a pool club, shops, and several restaurants that overlook the fleet of super-yachts.

GETTING HERE AND AROUND

By car, take La Spezia exit off the A12. La Spezia Centrale train station is on the main north–south railway line between Genoa and Pisa.

VISITOR INFORMATION

La Spezia Tourism Office ✉ *Via Mazzini 45* ☎ *0187/770900* 🌐 *turismo-cultura.spezianet.it.*

EXPLORING

Castello di San Giorgio. The remains of this massive 13th-century castle atop a small hill above the modern town now house a small museum dedicated to local archaeology. ✉ *Via XXVII Marzo* ☎ *0187/751142* 🎟 *€5.50* 🕒 *June–Aug., Tues.–Sun. 9:30–12:30 and 5–8; Sept.–May, Tues.–Sun. 9:30–12:30 and 2–5.*

WHERE TO EAT

$ PIZZA 🍴 **La Pia.** Considered an institution, this *farinateria* and pizzeria dates back to 1887. During the lunch hour, you will find a line out the door, while inside—and on the patio in summer—locals munch on *farinata,* or chickpea pancakes (a Ligurian delicacy), and on thick-crust pizzas served hot out of the wood-fired oven. [$] *Average main: €15* ✉ *Via Magenta 12* ☎ *0187/739999* 🌐 *www.lapia.it* ✍ *Reservations not accepted* 🕒 *Closed Wed., and 2 wks in Aug. and Nov.*

PORTOVENERE

12 km (7 miles) south of La Spezia, 114 km (70 miles) southeast of Genoa.

The colorful facades and pedestrians-only *calata* (promenade) make Portovenere the quintessential Ligurian seaside village; it's often referred to as the sixth town of the Cinque Terre, but it has half the crowds. As a UNESCO World Heritage Site, its harbor is lined with tall, thin *terratetto* houses that date from as far back as the 11th century and are connected in a wall-like formation to protect against attacks by the

Pisans and local pirates. Its tiny *carruggi* (alley-like passageways) lead to an array of charming shops, homes, and gardens, and eventually to the village's impressive **Castle Doria,** high on the olive tree–covered hill. To the west, standing guard over the Mediterranean, is the picturesque medieval **Chiesa di San Pietro,** once the site of a temple to Venus (Venere in Italian), from which Portovenere gets its name. Nearby, in a rocky area leading to the sea, is Byron's Cave, a favorite spot that the poet loved to swim out into the sea from.

GETTING HERE AND AROUND

By car from the port city of La Spezia, follow the blue signs for Portovenere. It's about a 20-minute winding drive along the sea through small fishing villages. From La Spezia train station you can hire a taxi for about €30. By bus from Via Garibaldi in La Spezia (a 10-minute walk from the train station) it takes 20 minutes.

VISITOR INFORMATION

Portovenere doesn't have a tourist office; you can get information at the Comune (Town Hall) or at the tourist office in La Spezia Centrale train station.

EXPLORING

Grotto Arpaia. Lord Byron (1788–1824) is said to have written *Childe Harold's Pilgrimage* in Portovenere. Near the entrance to the huge, strange Grotto Arpaia, at the base of the sea-swept cliff, is a plaque recounting the poet's strength and courage as he swam across the gulf to the village of San Terenzo, near Lerici, to visit his friend Shelley (1792–1822).

San Pietro. This 13th-century Gothic church is built on the site of an ancient pagan shrine, on a formidable solid mass of rock above the Grotto Arpaia. With its black-and-white-stripe exterior, it is a landmark recognizable from far out at sea. There's a spectacular view of the Cinque Terre coastline from the front porch of the church. ⊠ *Waterfront promenade* ☉ *Daily 9–6.*

WHERE TO EAT AND STAY

$$
WINE BAR
✕ **Bacicio.** Tucked away on Portovenere's main caruggio, this enoteca and antipasto bar is popular with locals and slowly being discovered by tourists looking for good, local dishes. The owner whips up some wonderful finger food—including *crostini* (grilled bread) with fresh anchovies and smoked herring with spicy orange salsa—and offers a robust list of local wines. He also designed the entire place, right down to the tables and chairs made from anchors and pieces of old boats. Ⓢ *Average main: €20* ⊠ *Via Cappellini 17* ☎ *0187/792054* ⌦ *Reservations not accepted* ▭ *No credit cards* ☉ *Closed Wed., Jan., and Nov.*

$$$$
LIGURIAN
✕ **Le Bocche.** At the end of the Portovenere promontory in the shadow of San Pietro, this is the village's most exclusive restaurant. The menu consists of in-season fish, prepared with a creative touch, such as marinated tuna encrusted with pistachios. The setting is romantic and unique, as you feel almost immersed in the Mediterranean. The dinner menu is quite expensive (as is the lengthy wine list), but there is a light lunch menu at lower prices. Ⓢ *Average main: €55* ⊠ *Calata Doria 102* ☎ *0187/790622* ☉ *Closed Jan.–mid Feb.*

8

$$$$ ✕ **Locanda Lorena.** Across the small bay of Portovenere lies the rug-
LIGURIAN   ged island of Palmaria. There is only one restaurant on the island, and here Iseo (aka Giuseppe), an accomplished chef, does the cooking. Fresh pasta and local fish like *branzino* (sea bass) are headliners at this fun dining spot with lovely views looking back toward Portovenere. To get here, take the restaurant's free riva boat from the Portovenere jetty. Ⓢ *Average main: €50* ✉ *Palmaria Island* ☎ *0187/792370* ⊕ *www. locandalorena.com* ⊙ *Closed Nov.*

$$$ 🏨 **Grand Hotel Portovenere.** This 13th-century Franciscan convent turned
HOTEL   four-star hotel was closed for more than two years, but it has finally received a much-needed facelift and has reopened. **Pros:** excellent location and views. **Cons:** renovations have meant new hefty rates. Ⓢ *Rooms from: €210* ✉ *Via Garibaldi 5* ☎ *0187/777751* ⊕ *www. portoveneregrand.it* ⇱ *44 rooms, 8 suites* ⊙ *Closed Nov.–Mar.* †⊙†*Breakfast.*

$$ 🏨 **Hotel Belvedere.** True to the name, the best rooms in this sunny Lib-
HOTEL   erty-style building face the bay of Portovenere, with lovely views of Palmaria Island and the Gulf of Poets. **Pros:** reasonably priced rooms with water views. **Cons:** parts of the hotel could use a makeover; limited parking. Ⓢ *Rooms from: €170* ✉ *Via G. Garibaldi 26* ☎ *0187/790608* ⊕ *www.belvedereportovenere.it* ⇱ *17 rooms* ⊙ *Closed Nov.–mid-Mar.* †⊙†*Breakfast.*

LEVANTO

8 km (5 miles) northwest of Monterosso al Mare, 60 km (36 miles) southeast of Genoa.

Nestled at the end of a valley of pine forests, olive groves, vineyards, and medieval villages lies this sunny seaside town: an alternative and usually less expensive base to explore the Cinque Terre and the Riviera di Levante.

EXPLORING

There's a long sandy beach and a charming, colorful old quarter with plenty of shops, bars, and restaurants. Levanto has become a haven for not only sun worshippers but also divers, surfers, and hikers (and the path between Levanto and Monterosso, about a 2½-mile hike with free entrance, is breathtakingly beautiful in its own right). It's also an ideal starting point for day trips by train or boat to many interesting places along the Riviera such as Portovenere, Lerici, Tellaro, and Fiascherino heading toward La Spezia; and Portofino, Santa Margherita, Camogli, and Sestri Levante heading toward Genoa.

GETTING HERE AND AROUND

By car, take the Carodanno/Levanto exit off the A12 for 25 minutes to the town center. By train, Levanto is on the main north–south railway, one stop north of Monterosso.

VISITOR INFORMATION

Levanto Tourism Office ✉ *Piazza Mazzini 1* ☎ *0187/808125* ⊕ *www. aptcinqueterre.sp.it.*

WHERE TO STAY

$$ **La Giada del Mesco.** Tastefully decorated and bright guest rooms on
HOTEL   the Punto Mesco headland have unobstructed vistas of the Mediterranean Sea and Riviera coastline. **Pros:** great position; nice pool. **Cons:** shuttle service is not always available; the 3½ km (1½ miles) into town is quite a walk, so you'll need a car. $ *Rooms from: €160* ✉ *Via Mesco 16* ☎ *0187/802674* ⊕ *www.lagiadadelmesco.com* ⤴ *12 rooms* ☾ *Closed mid-Nov.–Feb.* ⦿ *Breakfast.*

CHIAVARI

46 km (29 miles) northwest of Levanto, 38 km (23 miles) southeast of Genoa.

Chiavari is a fishing town (rather than village) of considerable character, with narrow, twisting streets and a good harbor. Chiavari's citizens were intrepid explorers, and many emigrated to South America in the 19th century. The town boomed, thanks to the wealth of the returning voyagers, but Chiavari retains many medieval traces in its buildings.

GETTING HERE AND AROUND

By car, take the Chiavari exit off the A12. The Chiavari train station is located on the main north–south train line between Genoa and Pisa.

VISITOR INFORMATION

Chiavari Tourism Office ✉ *Corso Assaroti 1* ☎ *0185/325216* ⊕ *www. comune.chiavari.ge.it.*

EXPLORING

Museo Archeologico. A worthy collection in the town center displays objects from an 8th-century BC necropolis, or ancient cemetery, excavated nearby. ✉ *Palazzo Costaguta, Via Costaguta 4, Piazza Matteotti* ☎ *0185/320829* ⊕ *www.archeoge.beniculturali.it* ⤴ *Free* ☾ *Tues.–Sat. and 2nd and 4th Sun. of month 9–1:30.*

SANTA MARGHERITA LIGURE

60 km (37 miles) northwest of Levanto, 31 km (19 miles) southeast of Genoa.

A beautiful old resort town favored by well-to-do Italians, Santa Margherita Ligure has everything a Riviera playground should have—with plenty of palm trees and attractive hotels, cafés, and a marina packed with yachts. Some of the older buildings here are still decorated on the outside with the trompe-l'oeil frescoes typical of this part of the Riviera. This is a pleasant, convenient base, which for many represents a perfect balance on the Italian Riviera: more spacious than the Cinque Terre; less glitzy than San Remo; more relaxing than Genoa and environs; and ideally situated for day trips, such as an excursion to Portofino.

GETTING HERE AND AROUND

By car, take the Rapallo exit off the A12 and follow the blue signs, about a 10-minute drive. The Santa Margherita Ligure train station is on the main north–south line between Genoa and Pisa.

8

VISITOR INFORMATION

Santa Margherita Ligure Tourism Office ✉ *Piazza Vittorio Veneto* ☎ *0185/287485* 🌐 *www.smlturismo.it.*

WHERE TO EAT

$$$$ LIGURIAN

🍴 **La Paranza.** From the piles of tiny *bianchetti* (young sardines) in oil and lemon that are part of the antipasto *di mare* (of the sea), to the simple, perfectly grilled whole sole, fresh seafood in every shape and form is the specialty here. Mussels, clams, octopus, salmon, or whatever else is fresh that day is what's on the menu. Locals say this is the town's best restaurant, but if you're looking for a stylish evening out, look elsewhere—La Paranza is about food, not fashion. It's just off Santa Margherita's port. [$] *Average main: €45* ✉ *Via Jacopo Ruffini 46* ☎ *0185/283686* 🌐 *www.laparanzasantamargherita.it* ✍ *Reservations essential* ⏲ *Closed Mon., and Nov.*

$$$$ LIGURIAN Fodor's Choice ★

🍴 **La Stalla dei Frati.** The breathtaking hilltop views of Santa Margherita from this villa-turned-restaurant are worth the harrowing 3-km (2-mile) drive from the port. Cesare Frati, your congenial host, is likely to tempt you with his homemade fettuccine *ai frutti di mare* (with seafood) followed by the *pescato del giorno alla moda ligure* (catch of the day baked Ligurian style, with potatoes, olives, and pine nuts) and a delightfully fresh lemon sorbet to complete the feast. [$] *Average main: €60* ✉ *Via G. Pino 27, Nozarego* ☎ *0185/289447* 🌐 *www.ristorantelastalladeifrati.it* ⏲ *Closed Mon. and Nov.*

$$$$ ECLECTIC

🍴 **Oca Bianca.** The menu breaks away from the local norm—there is no seafood on offer. Meat dishes are the specialty here, and choices may include mouthwatering preparations of lamb from France or New Zealand, steak from Ireland or Brazil, South African ostrich, and Italian pork. Delicious antipasti, an extensive wine list, and the attentive service add to the experience. Dinner is served until 1 am. [$] *Average main: €65* ✉ *Via XXV Aprile 21* ☎ *0185/262631* 🌐 *www.ristoranteocabianca.net* ✍ *Reservations essential* ⏲ *Closed Mon., and Jan. Lunch by reservation only.*

$$$$ LIGURIAN Fodor's Choice ★

🍴 **U' Giancu.** Owner Fausto Oneto is a man of many hats. Though original cartoons cover the walls of his restaurant and a playground is the main feature of the outdoor seating area, he is completely serious about his cooking. Lamb dishes are particularly delicious, his own garden provides the freshest possible vegetables, and the wine list (ask to visit the cantina) is excellent. For those who want to learn the secrets of Ligurian cuisine, Fausto provides lively morning cooking lessons. U' Giancu is 8 km (5 miles) northwest of Santa Margherita Ligure. [$] *Average main: €45* ✉ *Via San Massimo 78, Località San Massimo, Rapallo* ☎ *0185/261212* 🌐 *www.ugiancu.it* ⏲ *Closed Wed., and Nov.*

WHERE TO STAY

$$$ HOTEL

🏨 **Continental.** A stately seaside mansion surrounded by a lush garden shaded by tall palms and pine trees offers stylish accommodations done in a blend of classic furnishings, mostly inspired by the 19th century. **Pros:** lovely location; private beach. **Cons:** rooms in the annex are not as nice as those in the main building; breakfast is unimaginative. [$] *Rooms from: €215* ✉ *Via Pagana 8* ☎ *0185/286512* 🌐 *www.hotel-continental.it* 🛏 *69 rooms, 4 junior suites* 🍽 *Breakfast.*

$$$$ ⛱ **Grand Hotel Miramare.** Classic Riviera elegance prevails at this palatial
RESORT hotel overlooking the bay, where antique furniture and crystal chandeliers fill the high-ceiling rooms. **Pros:** top-notch service; private beach;
well-maintained rooms and marble bathrooms. **Cons:** traffic in summer
from the road in front of the hotel. Ⓢ *Rooms from: €450* ⊠ *Via Milite
Ignoto 30* ☎ *0185/287013* ⊕ *www.grandhotelmiramare.it* ⤴ *75 rooms,
9 suites* ⊗ *Closed Jan. 6–Mar. 18* ⦿ *Breakfast.*

$$ ⛱ **Hotel Jolanda.** They may not have sea views, but stylish, comfortable,
HOTEL and spacious rooms are tastefully decorated, and some have large bal-
conies. **Pros:** reasonable rates in a high-price area. **Cons:** no sea view;
parking is limited and expensive. Ⓢ *Rooms from: €150* ⊠ *Via Luisito
Costa 6* ☎ *0185/287512* ⊕ *www.hoteljolanda.it* ⤴ *47 rooms, 3 suites*
⦿ *Breakfast.*

PORTOFINO

*5 km (3 miles) south of Santa Margherita Ligure, 36 km (22 miles)
east of Genoa.*

One of the most photographed villages along the coast, with a decidedly
romantic and affluent aura, Portofino has long been a popular destina-
tion for the rich and famous. Once an ancient Roman colony and taken
by the Republic of Genoa in 1229, it's also been ruled by the French,
English, Spanish, and Austrians, as well as by marauding bands of 16th-
century pirates. Elite British tourists first flocked to the lush harbor in
the mid-1800s. Some of Europe's wealthiest drop anchor in Portofino
in summer, but they stay out of sight by day, appearing in the evening
after buses and boats have carried off the day-trippers.

There's not actually much to *do* in Portofino other than stroll around
the wee harbor, see the castle, walk to Punta del Capo, browse at the
pricey boutiques, and sip a coffee while people-watching. However,
weaving through picture-perfect cliffside gardens and gazing at yachts
framed by the sapphire Ligurian Sea and the cliffs of Santa Margherita
can make for quite a relaxing afternoon. There are also several tame,
photo-friendly hikes into the hills to nearby villages.

Unless you're traveling on a deluxe budget, you may want to stay in
Camogli or Santa Margherita Ligure rather than at one of Portofino's
few very expensive hotels. Restaurants and cafés are good but also
pricey (don't expect to have a beer here for much under €10).

GETTING HERE AND AROUND

By car, exit at Rapallo off the A12 and follow the blue signs (about a
20-minute drive mostly along the coast). The nearest train station is
Santa Margherita Ligure.

Trying to reach Portofino by bus or car on the single narrow road
can be a nightmare in summer and on holiday weekends. No trains
go directly to Portofino: you must stop at Santa Margherita and take
public Bus No. 82 from there (€1.20). An alternative is to take a boat
from Santa Margherita.

Portofino can also be reached from Santa Margherita on foot: it's about
a 40-minute (very pleasant) walk along the sea.

8

VISITOR INFORMATION

Portofino Tourism Office ✉ *Via Roma 35* ☎ *0185/269024.*

EXPLORING

Abbazia di San Fruttuoso (*Abbey of San Fruttuoso*). A medieval stronghold built by the Benedictines of Monte Cassino protects a minuscule fishing village that can be reached only on foot or by water—a 20-minute boat ride from Portofino and also reachable from Camogli, Santa Margherita Ligure, and Rapallo. The restored abbey is now the property of a national conservation fund (FAI), it occasionally hosts temporary exhibitions and contains the tombs of some illustrious members of the Doria family. Plan on spending a few hours enjoying the abbey and grounds, and perhaps lunching at one of the modest beachfront trattorias nearby (open only in summer). Boatloads of visitors can make this place very crowded very fast; you might appreciate it most off-season. ✉ *15-min boat ride or 2-hr walk northwest of Portofino* ☎ *0185/772703* 🎟 *€5, €7.50 with exhibition* ⏲ *June–Sept. 15, daily 10–5:45; May and Sept. 16–30, daily 10–4:45; Oct.–Mar., Tues.–Sun. 10–3:45. Last entry 1 hr before closing.*

Castello Brown. From the harbor, follow the signs for the climb to Castello Brown—the most worthwhile sight in Portofino—with its medieval relics, impeccable gardens, and sweeping views. The castle was founded in the Middle Ages but restored in the 16th through 18th century. In true Portofino form, it was owned by Genoa's English consul from 1870 until it opened to the public in 1961. ✉ *Above harbor* ☎ *010/2518125* 🌐 *www.castellobrown.com* 🎟 *€3* ⏲ *Apr.–Oct., Wed.–Mon. 10–7; Nov.–Mar., Wed.–Mon. 10–5.*

Paraggi. The only sand beach near Portofino is at Paraggi, a cove on the road between Santa Margherita and Portofino. The bus will stop here on request.

Punta Portofino. Pristine views can be had from the deteriorating *faro* (lighthouse) at Punta Portofino, a 15-minute walk along the point that begins at the southern end of the port. Along the seaside path you can see numerous impressive, sprawling private residences behind high iron gates.

San Giorgio. This small church, sitting on a ridge above Portofino, is said to contain the relics of its namesake, brought back from the Holy Land by the Crusaders. Portofino enthusiastically celebrates Saint George's Day every April 23. ✉ *Above harbor* ☎ *0185/269337* ⏲ *Daily 7–6.*

WHERE TO EAT

$ BAKERY 🍴 **Canale.** If the staggering prices of virtually all of Portofino's restaurants put you off, the long line outside this family-run bakery indicates that you're not alone and that something special is in store. Here all the focaccia genovese is baked on the spot and served fresh from the oven, along with all kinds of sandwiches, pastries, and other refreshments. [$] *Average main: €10* ✉ *Via Roma 30* ☎ *0185/269248* 💳 *No credit cards* ⏲ *Closed Nov.–Feb.*

$$$$ LIGURIAN 🍴 **Ristorante Puny.** If you want to be in the middle of everything, dine well, and don't mind spending a small fortune, this is the place in Portofino! The unforgettable pappardelle *al portofino* delicately blends two classic Ligurian flavors: tomato and pesto. Seafood specialties include

baked fish with bay leaves, potatoes, and olives, as well as the inventive *moscardini al forno* (baked mini-octopus with lemon and rosemary in tomato sauce). $ *Average main: €60* ⊠ *Piazza Martiri dell'Olivetta 4–5, on harbor* ☎ *0185/269037* ⚓ *Reservations essential* ⊙ *Closed Thurs., and Jan. and Feb.*

WHERE TO STAY

$$$$ Eight Hotel Portofino. Immaculate, comfortable, and soothingly
HOTEL designed guest rooms with canopy beds, pastel walls, and ultramodern bathrooms spread across two small 19th-century townhouses on a quiet back street. **Pros:** luxurious accommodations in the middle of the village; secluded garden at the back. **Cons:** some of the lower-level rooms don't receive much light; no sea views. $ *Rooms from: €540* ⊠ *Via Del Fondaco 11* ☎ *0185/26991* ⊕ *www.eighthotels.it* ⇄ *17 rooms, 1 suite* ⊙ *Closed Dec.–Mar.* ⑩ *Breakfast.*

$$$$ Splendido. This 1920s luxury hotel is where the rich and famous come
HOTEL to relax and play on the Italian Riviera. **Pros:** all rooms have garden or sea views; caring staff; lovely gardens. **Cons:** be prepared to spend upward of €100 for a simple lunch for two (it's not just the rooms that are pricey). $ *Rooms from: €1200* ⊠ *Salita Baratta 16* ☎ *0185/267802* ⊕ *www.hotelsplendido.com* ⇄ *69 rooms, 39 suites* ⊙ *Closed mid-Nov.–late Mar.* ⑩ *Some meals.*

SPORTS AND THE OUTDOORS

HIKING

If you have the stamina, you can hike to the Abbazia di San Fruttuoso from Portofino. It's a steep climb at first, and the walk takes about 2½ hours one way. If you're extremely ambitious and want to make a day of it, you can hike another 2½ hours all the way to Camogli. Much more modest hikes from Portofino include a one-hour uphill walk to Cappella delle Gave, a bit inland in the hills, from where you can continue downhill to Santa Margherita Ligure (another 1½ hours) and a gently undulating paved trail leading to the beach at Paraggi (½ hour). Finally, there's a 2½-hour hike from Portofino that heads farther inland to Ruta, through Olmi and Pietre Strette. The trails are well marked and maps are available at the tourist information offices in Rapallo, Santa Margherita Ligure, Portofino, and Camogli.

CAMOGLI

15 km (9 miles) northwest of Portofino, 20 km (12 miles) east of Genoa.

Camogli, at the edge of the large promontory and nature reserve known as the Portofino Peninsula, has always been a town of sailors. By the 19th century it was leasing its ships throughout the continent. Today multicolor houses, remarkably deceptive trompe-l'oeil frescoes, and a massive 17th-century seawall mark this appealing harbor community, which is perhaps as beautiful as Portofino but without the glamour. When exploring on foot, don't miss the second, more antiquated harbor, which is reached through a narrow archway at the northern end of the first one.

8

GETTING HERE AND AROUND

By car, exit the A12 at Recco and follow the blue signs. There are several pay-parking lots near the village center. Camogli is on the main north–south railway line between Genoa and La Spezia.

VISITOR INFORMATION

Camogli Tourism Office ✉ *Via XX Settembre 33/R* ☎ *0185/771066* 🌐 *www.prolococamogli.it.*

OFF THE BEATEN PATH

Ruta. The footpaths that leave from Ruta, 4 km (2½ miles) east of Camogli, thread through rugged terrain and contain a multitude of plant species. Weary hikers are sustained by stunning views of the Riviera di Levante from various vantage points along the way.

WHERE TO EAT AND STAY

$$$$ SEAFOOD

🍴 **Vento Ariel.** This small, friendly restaurant serves some of the best seafood in town. Dine on the shaded terrace in summer and watch the bustling activity in the nearby port. Only the freshest seafood is served; try the spaghetti *alle vongole* (with clams) or the mixed grilled fish. [$] *Average main: €40* ✉ *Calata Porto* ☎ *0185/771080* 🌐 *www.ventoariel.it* 🕒 *Closed Wed., 1st half of Dec., and Jan.*

$$$ HOTEL

🏨 **Cenobio dei Dogi.** Perched majestically a step above Camogli, many of the rooms in the former summer palace of Genoa's doges have expansive balconies with commanding vistas of Camogli's cozy port. **Pros:** location and setting are wonderful; lovely pool and gardens; private beach. **Cons:** crowds make it seem overbooked in summer; décor is a bit old-fashioned. [$] *Rooms from: €220* ✉ *Via Nicolò Cuneo 34* ☎ *0185/7241* 🌐 *www.cenobio.it* 🛏 *103 rooms, 5 suites* 🍽 *Breakfast.*

$$$ B&B/INN

🏨 **Villa Rosmarino.** A beautiful Ligurian villa in the beautiful hills just above Camogli offers chic, contemporary, and comfortable accommodations, along with well-manicured gardens and a welcoming pool. **Pros:** large beds; well-equipped bathrooms; total sense of relaxation. **Cons:** rooms are small and may not have enough amenities for everyone's taste. [$] *Rooms from: €220* ✉ *Via Figari 38* ☎ *0185/771580* 🌐 *www.villarosmarino.com* 🛏 *6 rooms* 🍽 *Breakfast.*

NIGHTLIFE AND THE ARTS

Sagra del Pesce. The highlight of the festival of San Fortunato is held on the second Sunday of May each year. It's a crowded, colorful, and free-to-the-public feast of freshly caught fish, cooked outside at the port in a frying pan 12 feet wide.

GENOA

Genoa (Genova in Italian) was the birthplace of Christopher Columbus, but the city's proud history predates that explorer by hundreds of years. Genoa was already an important trading station by the 3rd century BC, when the Romans conquered Liguria. The Middle Ages and the Renaissance saw it rise to become a jumping-off place for the Crusaders, a commercial center of tremendous wealth and prestige, and a strategic bone of international contention. A network of fortresses defending the city connected by a wall second only in length to the Great Wall of China was constructed in the hills above, and Genoa's bankers, merchants, and princes adorned the city with palaces, churches, and impressive art collections.

Crammed into a thin crescent of land between sea and mountains, Genoa expanded up rather than out, taking on the form of a multilayer wedding cake, with churches, streets, and entire residential neighborhoods built on others' rooftops. Public elevators and funiculars are as common as buses and trains.

But with its impressive palaces and museums, the largest medieval city center in Europe, and an elaborate network of ancient hilltop fortresses, Genoa may be just the dose of culture you're looking for. Europe's biggest boat show, the annual Salone Nautico Internazionale, is held here. Fine restaurants are abundant, and classical dance and music are richly represented. The Teatro Carlo Felice is the local opera venue, and it's where the internationally renowned annual Niccolò Paganini Violin Contest takes place.

GETTING HERE AND AROUND

By car, take the Genoa Ovest exit off the A12 and take the upper bridge (*sopralevata*) to the second exit, Genova Centro–Piazza Corvetto. But be forewarned: driving in Genoa is harrowing and best avoided whenever possible. If you want to see the city on a day trip, go by train; regular train service operates from Genoa's two stations. If you're staying in the city, park in a garage or by valet and go by foot and taxi throughout your stay.

The best way by far to get around Genoa is on foot, with the occasional assistance of public transportation. Many of the more interesting districts are either entirely closed to traffic, have roads so narrow that no car could fit, or are, even at the best of times, blocked by gridlock. Although it might seem a daunting task, exploring the city is made simple by its geography. The historical center of Genoa occupies a relatively narrow strip of land running between the mountains and the sea. You can easily visit the most important monuments in one or two days. The main bus station in Genoa is at Piazza Principe. Local buses, operated by the municipal transport company AMT, serve the steep valleys that run to some of the towns along the western coast. Tickets may be bought at local bus stations or at newsstands. (You must have a ticket before you board.) AMT also operates the funicular railways and the elevators that service the steeper sections of the city.

Transportation Contacts AMT. ✉ *Piazza Acquaverde* ☎ 010/5582414 ⊕ *www. amt.genova.it.* **Stazione Brignole.** Departures from Stazione Brignole go to points east and south. All the coastal resorts are on this line. ✉ *Piazza Giuseppe Verdi, Foce* ☎ 010/892021. **Stazione Principe.** Departures from Stazione Principe travel to points west. ✉ *Piazza del Principe, San Teodoro.*

VISITOR INFORMATION

Genoa Tourism Offices—main office ✉ *Via Garibaldi, 12r, Maddalena* ☎ *010/5572903* ⊕ *www.genova-turismo.it* ☉ *Daily 9 am–6:20 pm* ✉ *Largo Pertini 13* ☎ *010/8606122.*

EXPLORING

THE MEDIEVAL CORE AND POINTS ABOVE

The medieval center of Genoa, threaded with tiny streets flanked by 11th-century portals, is roughly the area between the port and Piazza de Ferrari. This mazelike pedestrian zone is officially called the Caruggi District, but the Genovese, in their matter-of-fact way, simply refer to the area as the place of the *vicoli* (alleys). In this warren of narrow, cobbled streets extending north from Piazza Caricamento, the city's oldest churches sit among tiny shops selling antique furniture, coffee, cheese, rifles, wine, gilt picture frames, camping gear, and even live fish. The 500-year-old apartment buildings lean so precariously that penthouse balconies nearly touch those across the street, blocking what little sunlight would have shown down onto the cobblestones. Wealthy Genovese built their homes in this quarter in the 16th century, and prosperous guilds, such as the goldsmiths for whom Vico degli Indoratori and Via degli Orefici were named, set up shop here.

TOP ATTRACTIONS

Cimitero Monumentale di Staglieno. One of the most famous of Genovese landmarks is this bizarrely beautiful cemetery; its fanciful marble and bronze sculptures sprawl haphazardly across a hillside on the outskirts of town. A pantheon holds indoor tombs and some remarkable works like an 1878 *Eve* by Villa. Don't miss Rovelli's 1896 **Tomba Raggio,** which shoots Gothic spires out of the hillside forest. The cemetery began operation in 1851 and has been lauded by such visitors as Mark Twain and Evelyn Waugh. It covers a good deal of ground (allow at least half a day to explore). Take Bus No. 12, 13, or 14 from the Stazione Genova Brignole, Bus No. 34 or 48 from Stazione Principe, or a taxi. ⌧ *Piazzale Resasco, Piazza Manin* ☎ *010/870184* ⌦ *Free* ⌚ *Daily 7:30 am–4:30 pm.*

Galleria Nazionale. Housed in the richly adorned **Palazzo Spinola** north of Piazza Soziglia, this beautiful museum contains masterpieces by Luca Giordano and Guido Reni. The *Ecce Homo,* by Antonello da Messina, is a hauntingly beautiful painting, of historical interest because it was the Sicilian da Messina who first brought Flemish oil paints and techniques to Italy from his sojourns in the Low Countries. ⌧ *Piazza Pellicceria 1, Maddalena* ☎ *010/2705300* ⊕ *www.visitgenoa.it* ⌦ *€4* ⌚ *Tues.–Sat. 8:30–7:30, Sun. 1:30–7:30.*

Palazzo Bianco. It's difficult to miss the splendid white facade of this town palace as you walk down Via Garibaldi, once one of Genoa's most important streets. The building houses a fine collection of 17th-century art, with the Spanish and Flemish schools well represented. ⌧ *Via Garibaldi 11, Maddalena* ☎ *010/2759185* ⌦ *€12, includes Palazzo Rosso and Palazzo Doria Tursi* ⌚ *Tues.–Fri. 9–7, weekends 10–7.*

Fodor's Choice ★ **Palazzo Reale.** Lavish rococo rooms provide sumptuous display space for paintings, sculptures, tapestries, and Asian ceramics. The 17th-century palace—also known as the Palazzo Balbi Durazzo—was built by the Balbi family, enormously wealthy Genovese merchants. Its regal pretensions were not lost on the Savoy, who bought the palace and turned it into a royal residence in the early 19th century. The gallery of mirrors and the ballroom on the upper floor are particularly decadent. Look for works by Sir Anthony Van Dyck, who lived in Genoa for six years, beginning in 1621, and painted many portraits of the Genovese nobility. The formal gardens, which you can visit for €1, provide a welcome respite from the bustle of the city beyond the palace walls, as well as great views of the harbor. ✉ *Via Balbi 10, Pré* ☎ *010/2710236* ⊕ *www. palazzorealegenova.it* 🎫 *€4, €6.50 with Galleria Nazionale* ☉ *Tues. and Wed. 9–1:30, Thurs.–Sun. 9–7.*

Palazzo Rosso. This 17th-century Baroque palace was named for the red stone used in its construction. It now contains, apart from a number of lavishly frescoed suites, works by Titian, Veronese, Reni, and Van Dyck. ✉ *Via Garibaldi 18, Maddalena* ☎ *010/2759185* ⊕ *www.visitgenoa.it* 🎫 *€12, includes Palazzo Bianco and Palazzo Doria Tursi* ☉ *Tues.–Fri. 9–7, weekends 10–7.*

Zecca–Righi funicular. A seven-stop commuter funicular begins at Piazza della Nunziata and ends at a high lookout on the fortified gates in the 17th-century city walls. Ringed around the circumference of the city are a number of huge fortresses; this gate was part of the city's system of defenses. From Righi you can undertake scenic all-day hikes from one fortress to the next. ✉ *Piazza della Nunziata, Pré* ☎ *010/5582414* ⊕ *www.amt.genova.it* 🎫 *€2, €4.50 for 24-hr Genovapass* ☉ *Daily 6 am–11:45 pm.*

WORTH NOTING

Castelletto. To reach this charming neighborhood high above the city center, you take one of Genoa's handy municipal elevators that whisk you skyward from Piazza Portello, at the end of Galleria Garibaldi, for a good view of the old city. ✉ *Piazza Portello, Castelletto* 🎫 *€1.40* ☉ *Daily 6:40 am–midnight.*

FAMILY **Granarolo Funicular.** Take a cog railway up the steeply rising terrain to another part of the city's fortified walls. It takes 15 minutes to hoist you from Stazione Principe, on Piazza Acquaverde, to **Porta Granarolo,** 1,000 feet above, where the sweeping view gives you a sense of Genoa's size. The funicular departs about every half hour. ✉ *Piazza del Principe, San Teodoro* ☎ *010/5582414* ⊕ *www.amt.genova.it* 🎫 *€2* ☉ *Daily 6 am–11:45 pm.*

Loggia dei Mercanti. This merchants' row dating to the 16th century is lined with shops selling local foods and gifts, as well as raincoats, rubber boots, and fishing line. ✉ *Piazza Banchi, Maddalena.*

Museo d'Arte Orientale Chiossone. One of Europe's most noteworthy collections of Japanese, Chinese, and Thai objects is housed in galleries in the Villetta di Negro park on the hillside above Piazza Portello. There's also a fine view of the city from the museum's terrace. ✉ *Piazzale Mazzini 4, Maddalena* ☎ *010/542285* ⊕ *www.museidigenova.it/ spip.php?rubrique263* 🎫 *€5* ☉ *Tues.–Fri. 9–7, weekends 10–7.*

Palazzo dell'Università. Built in the 1630s as a Jesuit college, this has been Genoa's university since 1803. The exterior is unassuming, but climb the stairway flanked by lions to visit the handsome courtyard, with its portico of double Doric columns. ✉ *Via Balbi 5, Pré* ☎ *010/2099523* ⊕ *www.unige.it.*

8

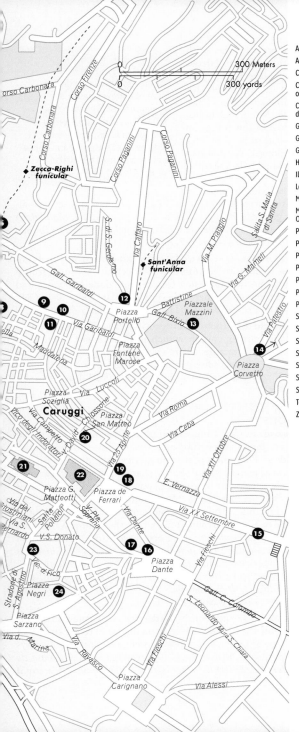

Palazzo Doria Tursi. In the 16th century, wealthy resident Nicolò Grimaldi had a palace built of pink stone quarried in the region. It's been reincarnated as Genoa's Palazzo Municipale (Municipal Building), and so most of the goings-on inside are the stuff of local politics and quickie weddings. You can visit the richly decorated **Sala Paganini**, where the famous Guarnerius violin that belonged to Niccolò Paganini

(1782–1840) is displayed, along with the gardens that connect the palace with the neighboring Palazzo Bianco. ⊠ *Via Garibaldi 9, Maddalena* ☎ *010/5572193* ⊕ *www.visitgenoa.it* ⛭ *€12, includes Palazzo Bianco and Palazzo Rosso* ⊙ *Tues.–Fri. 9–7, weekends 10–7.*

San Siro. Genoa's oldest church was the city's cathedral from the 4th to the 9th century. Rebuilt in the 16th and 17th centuries, it now feels a bit like a haunted house—imposing frescoes line dank hallways, and chandeliers hold crooked candles flickering in the darkness. ⊠ *Via San Siro, Maddalena* ☎ *010/2461674* ⊙ *Daily 8–noon and 3–7.*

Santissima Annunziata del Vastato. Exuberantly frescoed vaults decorate the 16th- to 17th-century church, which is an excellent example of Genovese Baroque architecture. There's a 40-minute guided tour each Sunday at 11:30 (minimum of five people). ⊠ *Piazza della Nunziata, Pré* ☎ *010/2465525* ⊙ *Weekdays 7:30 am–8 pm, Sat. 7:30–1 and 3–8:30, Sun. 8–1 and 3–8.*

SOUTHERN DISTRICTS AND THE AQUARIUM
TOP ATTRACTIONS

FAMILY **Acquario di Genova.** Europe's biggest aquarium, second in the world only to Osaka's in Japan, is the third-most-visited museum in Italy and a must for children. Fifty tanks of marine species, including sea turtles, dolphins, seals, eels, penguins, and sharks, share space with educational displays and re-creations of marine ecosystems, including a tank of coral from the Red Sea. An entire "Aquarium Village" has been created, which also includes a biosphere, hummingbird forest, and interactive submarine exhibit. If arriving by car, take the Genova Ovest exit from the autostrada. ⊠ *Ponte Spinola, Porto Vecchio* ☎ *0101/2345678* ⊕ *www.acquario.ge.it* ⛭ *€24; Aquarium Village tickets €48, includes entrance to all attractions* ⊙ *Mar.–June, Sept., and Oct., weekdays 9–8, weekends 8:30 am–9 pm; July and Aug., daily 8:30 am–10:30 pm; Nov.–Feb., weekdays 9:30–9, weekends 9:30–8. Entry permitted every ½ hr; last entry 2 hrs before closing.*

Galata Museo del Mare. Devoted entirely to the city's seafaring history, this museum is probably the best way (at least on dry land) to get an idea of the changing shape of Genoa's busy port. Foremost among the displays is a full-size replica of a 17th-century Genovese galleon. ⊠ *Calata de Mari 1, Ponte dei Mille* ☎ *010/2345655* ⊕ *www.galatamuseodelmare.it*

⌂ €12 ⏱ *Mar.–Oct., daily 10–7:30; Nov.–Feb., Tues.–Fri. 10–6, weekends 10–7:30. Last entry 1 hr before closing.*

The Harbor. A boat tour gives you a good perspective on the layout of the harbor, which dates to Roman times. The Genoa inlet, the largest along the Italian Riviera, was also used by the Phoenicians and Greeks as a harbor and a staging area from which they could penetrate inland to form settlements and to trade. The port is guarded by the Diga Foranea, a striking wall 5 km-long (3 mile-long) long built into the ocean. The **Lanterna,** a lighthouse more than 360 feet tall, was built in 1544; it's one of Italy's oldest lighthouses and a traditional emblem of Genoa.

Consorzio Liguria Viamare. Boat tours of the harbor, operated by the Consorzio Liguria Viamare, launch from the aquarium pier and last about an hour. The tours include a visit to the breakwater outside the harbor, the Bacino delle Grazie, and the Molo Vecchio (Old Port). There are also daily excursions down the coast as far as the Cinque Terre and Portovenere. ⌂ *Via Sottoripa 7/8, Porto Vecchio* ☎ *010/265712* ⊕ *www.liguriaviamare.it* ⌂ *Port tour €6, tours to Cinque Terre from €33* ⏱ *Daily; departure times vary.*

Palazzo Ducale. This palace was built in the 16th century over a medieval hall, and its facade was rebuilt in the late 18th century and later restored. It now houses temporary exhibitions and a restaurant-bar serving fusion cuisine. Reservations are necessary to visit the dungeons and tower. Guided tours (€5) of the palace, its prison tower, and its exhibitions are available. ⌂ *Piazza Matteotti 9, Portoria* ☎ *010/5574004* ⊕ *www.palazzoducale.genova.it* ⌂ *Free, except specific exhibits at various admission* ⏱ *Daily 9–7.*

San Lorenzo. Contrasting black slate and white marble, so common in Liguria, embellishes the cathedral at the heart of medieval Genoa, inside and out. Consecrated in 1118, the church honors Saint Lawrence, who passed through the city on his way to Rome in the 3rd century. For hundreds of years the building was used for religious and state purposes such as civic elections. Note the 13th-century Gothic portal, the fascinating twisted barbershop columns, and the 15th- to 17th-century frescoes inside. The last campanile dates from the early 16th century. The **Museo del Tesoro di San Lorenzo** (San Lorenzo Treasury Museum) housed inside has some stunning pieces from medieval goldsmiths and silversmiths, for which medieval Genoa was renowned. ⌂ *Piazza San Lorenzo, Molo* ☎ *010/2471831* ⌂ *Cathedral free, museum €4.50* ⏱ *Cathedral daily 8–noon and 3–7; museum Mon.–Sat. 9–noon and 3–6, and 1st Sun. of month 3–6.*

Sant'Agostino. This 13th-century Gothic church was damaged during World War II, but still has a fine campanile and two well-preserved cloisters that house an excellent museum displaying pieces of medieval architecture and fresco paintings. Highlights of the collection are the enigmatic fragments of a tomb sculpture by Giovanni Pisano (circa 1250–1315). ⌂ *Piazza Sarzano 35/R, Molo* ☎ *010/2511263* ⊕ *www.visitgenova.it* ⌂ *€4* ⏱ *Tues.–Fri. 9–7, weekends 10–7.*

8

CLOSE UP

The Art of the Pesto Pestle

You may have known Genoa primarily for its salami or its brash explorer, but the city's most direct effect on your life away from Italy may be through its cultivation of one of the world's best pasta sauces. The sublime blend of basil, extra-virgin olive oil, garlic, pine nuts, and grated pecorino and Parmigiano-Reggiano cheeses that forms *pesto alla Genovese* is one of Italy's crowning culinary achievements, a concoction that Italian food guru Marcella Hazan has called "the most seductive of all sauces for pasta." Ligurian pesto is served only over spaghetti, gnocchi, lasagna, or—most authentically—*trenette* (a flat, spaghetti-like pasta) or *trofie* (short, doughy pasta twists), and

then typically mixed with boiled potatoes and green beans. Pesto is also occasionally used to flavor minestrone.

The small-leaf basil grown in the region's sunny seaside hills is considered by many to be the best in the world, and pesto sauce was invented primarily as a showcase for that singular flavor. The simplicity and rawness of pesto is one of its virtues, as cooking (or even heating) basil ruins its delicate flavor. In fact, pesto aficionados refuse even to subject the basil leaves to an electric blender; Genovese (and other) foodies insist that true pesto can be made only with mortar and pestle.

Santa Maria di Castello. One of Genoa's most significant religious buildings, an early Christian church, was rebuilt in the 12th century and finally completed in 1513. You can visit the adjacent cloisters and see the fine artwork contained in the museum. Hours vary according to religious services. ⊠ *Salita di Santa Maria di Castello 15, Molo* ☎ *010/25495225* ⊕ *www.santamariadicastello.it* ☜ *Free* ☾ *Daily 9:30–noon and 3:30–6:30.*

WORTH NOTING

Accademia delle Belle Arti. Founded in 1751, the city's famous art school houses a collection of paintings from the 16th to the 19th century. Genovese artists of the Baroque period are particularly well represented. ⊠ *Largo Pertini 4, Portoria* ☎ *010/506131* ⊕ *www.accademialigustica.it* ☜ *€5* ☾ *Tues.–Fri. 2:30–6:30.*

Childhood home of Christopher Columbus. The ivy-covered remains of this fabled medieval house stand in the gardens below the Porta Soprana. A small and rather disappointing collection of objects and reproductions relating to the life and travels of Columbus are on display inside. ⊠ *Piazza Dante, Molo* ☎ *010/2516714* ⊕ *www.associazioneportasoprana.it* ☜ *€5* ☾ *Weekends and holidays 10–6, other days by reservation.*

FAMILY   **Il Bigo.** This spiderlike white structure, designed by world-renowned architect Renzo Piano, was erected in 1992 to celebrate the Columbus quincentenary. You can take its **Ascensore Panoramico Bigo** (Bigo Panoramic Elevator) up 650 feet for a 360-degree view of the harbor, city, and sea. In winter there's an ice-skating rink next to the elevator, in an area covered by sail-like awnings. ⊠ *Ponte Spinola, Porto*

Vecchio ☎ 010/2485711 skating rink 🎟 Elevator €4, skating rink €8 🕒 Elevator: Jan. 7–Feb. and Nov.–Dec. 25, weekends 10–5; Mar.–May, Sept., and Oct., Mon. 2–6, Tues.–Sun. 10–6; June–Aug., Mon. 4–11 pm, Tues.–Sun. 10 am–11 pm; Dec. 26–Jan. 6, daily 10–5. Skating rink: Nov. or Dec.–Mar., weekdays 8 am–9:30 pm, Sat. 10 am–2 am, Sun. 10 am–midnight.

Mercato Orientale. In the old cloister of a church along Via XX Settembre, this bustling produce, fish, and meat market is a wonderful sensory overload. Get a glimpse of colorful everyday Genovese life watching the merchants and buyers haggle over prices. ✉ *Via XX Settembre, Portoria* 🌐 *www.mercatoorientale.org* 🕒 *Mon.–Sat. 7–1 and 3:30–7:30.*

Porta Soprana. A striking 12th-century twin-tower structure, this medieval gateway stands on the spot where a road from ancient Rome entered the city. It is just steps uphill from Columbus's boyhood home, and legend has it that the explorer's father was employed here as a gatekeeper. ✉ *Piazza Dante, Molo.*

San Donato. Although somewhat marred by 19th- and 20th-century restorations, the 12th-century San Donato—with its original portal and octagonal campanile—is a fine example of Genovese Romanesque architecture. Inside, an altarpiece by the Flemish artist Joos Van Cleve (circa 1485–1540) depicts the Adoration of the Magi. ✉ *Piazza San Donato, Portoria* ☎ *010/2468869* 🕒 *Mon.–Sat. 8–noon and 3–7, Sun. 9–12:30 and 3–7.*

San Matteo. This typically Genovese black-and-white-stripe church dates from the 12th century; its crypt contains the tomb of Andrea Doria (1466–1560), the Genovese admiral who maintained the independence of his native city. The well-preserved Piazza San Matteo was, for 500 years, the seat of the Doria family, which ruled Genoa and much of Liguria from the 16th to the 18th century. The square is bounded by 13th- to 15th-century houses decorated with portals and loggias. ✉ *Piazza San Matteo, Maddalena* ☎ *010/2474361* 🕒 *Mon.–Sat. 8–noon and 4–7, Sun. 9:30–10:30 and 4–5.*

Teatro Carlo Felice. The World War II–ravaged opera house in Genoa's modern center, Piazza de Ferrari, was rebuilt and reopened in 1991 to host the fine Genovese opera company; its massive tower has been the subject of much criticism. Lavish productions of old favorites and occasional world premieres are staged from October to May. ✉ *Passo Eugenio Montale 4, Piazza de Ferrari, Portoria* ☎ *010/53811* 🌐 *www.carlofelice.it.*

8

WHERE TO EAT

$$$$ LIGURIAN 🍴 **Antica Osteria del Bai.** Elegance, romance, and delicious food are to be found at this cliffside institution overlooking the sea in a nice suburb of the city. A seaside theme pervades the art and menu, which might include black gnocchi with lobster sauce or ravioli ai frutti di mare. [$] *Average main: €65* ✉ *Via Quarto 16, Quarto* ☎ *010/387478* 🌐 *www.osteriadelbai.it* 👔 *Jacket and tie required* 🕒 *Closed Mon., Jan. 10–20, and Aug. 1–20.*

$$$ LIGURIAN 🍴 **Bakari.** Hip styling and ambient lighting hint at this eatery's creative, even daring, takes on Ligurian classics. Sure bets are the spinach-and-cheese gnocchi, any of several carpaccios, and the delicate beef dishes. Reserve ahead, request a table on the more imaginative ground floor, or just stop by for an aperitivo, live music, and people-watching. [$] *Average main: €35* ✉ *Vico del Fieno 16/R, northwest of Piazza San Matteo, Maddalena* ☎ *010/2476170* 🌐 *bakariristorante.wix.com/bakari* 🕒 *Closed Sun. No lunch Sat.*

$$$$ WINE BAR 🍴 **Enoteca Sola.** Menus are chosen specifically to complement wines at Pino Sola's airy, casually elegant enoteca in the heart of the modern town. The short menu emphasizes seafood and varies daily but might include stuffed artichokes or baked stockfish. The real draw, though, is the wine list, which includes some of the winners of the prestigious Italian Tre Bicchieri (Three Glasses) Award, denoting only the very best. [$] *Average main: €45* ✉ *Via C. Barabino 120/R, Foce* ☎ *010/594513* 🌐 *www.enotecaristorantesola.com* 🕒 *Closed Sun., and 2 wks in Aug.*

$$ LIGURIAN 🍴 **Il Genovese.** Roberto Panizza's cute trattoria has some of the city's best and least expensive Ligurian dishes. The setting is casual and comfortable, and the staff friendly and knowledgeable about the region's delicacies featured on the always-interesting menu. Some of Liguria's best pesto is served here—by the man who runs the annual Pesto World Championship. [$] *Average main: €24* ✉ *Via Galata 35r, Brignole* ☎ *010/8692937* 🕒 *Mon.–Sat. noon–2:30 and 7–10:30.*

$$$$ ITALIAN 🍴 **Maxela.** Beef is king in these charming surroundings, where meals were first served in 1790. The owners have retained most of its original design, including wood benches and slabs of marble for tables. Daily specials are listed on chalkboards, or you can just walk up to the butcher counter and pick your cut of choice. They also have a very reasonable "fix priced" lunch menu (under €20 per person) with abundant choices. [$] *Average main: €45* ✉ *Vico Inferiore del Ferro 9/R, Maddalena* ☎ *010/2474209* 🌐 *www.maxela.it* 🕒 *Closed Sun.*

$$ LIGURIAN 🍴 **Trattoria Ugo.** This unassuming trattoria is full of old-world Genovese charm and delicious dishes. Popular among locals for the homemade pastas and cima all Genovese, the menu changes daily and consists of only a few choices, all at relatively inexpensive prices. [$] *Average main: €20* ✉ *Via dei Gustiniani 86, Maddalena* ☎ *010/2469302* 🕒 *Closed Sun. and Mon.*

WHERE TO STAY

$ HOTEL 🏨 **Agnello d'Oro.** Here you'll find comfortable, clean, and inexpensive lodging with friendly service next to the historical center. **Pros:** free Wi-Fi; 100 yards from Stazione Principe; near the Palazzo Reale. **Cons:** few amenities. [$] *Rooms from: €85* ✉ *Vico delle Monachette 6, Pré* ☎ *010/2462084* 🌐 *www.hotelagnellodoro.it* 🛏 *17 rooms* 🍽 *Breakfast.*

$$ HOTEL 🏨 **Best Western City.** A bland apartment-building exterior gives way to a polished lobby and light, modern rooms, many with spectacular views, in the heart of the city. **Pros:** generous breakfast; location can't be beat; great views from upper floors. **Cons:** regular rooms are small. [$] *Rooms*

from: €127 ✉ *Via San Sebastiano 6, Portoria* ☎ *010/584707* 🌐 *www.bwcityhotel-ge.it* 🛏 *64 rooms, 3 suites* 🍴 *Breakfast.*

$ HOTEL 🏨 **Best Western Metropoli.** Rooms and bathrooms are bright and spacious at this welcoming inn on the border of the historic district and Via Garibaldi. **Pros:** guest rooms and bathrooms are large; great rooms for families. **Cons:** parking lot is a bit of a hike; can be confusing to find if you are driving. [$] *Rooms from: €110* ✉ *Piazza Fontane Marose, Portoria* ☎ *010/2468888* 🌐 *www.bestwestern.it* 🛏 *48 rooms* 🍴 *Breakfast.*

$$ HOTEL 🏨 **Bristol Palace.** One of Europe's gracious 19th-century grand hotels carefully guards its reputation for courtesy, service, and elegance, with spacious, high-ceiling, handsomely furnished guest rooms and lovely public spaces. **Pros:** new outdoor dining terrace is lovely; in the heart of the shopping district. **Cons:** busy street outside can sometimes be noisy. [$] *Rooms from: €180* ✉ *Via XX Settembre 35, Portoria* ☎ *010/592541* 🌐 *www.hotelbristolpalace.com* 🛏 *128 rooms, 5 suites* 🍴 *Breakfast.*

$$ HOTEL 🏨 **Melia Bentley Genova.** Bright and sleekly decorated guest rooms and the in-house "Genovese-gourmet" restaurant frequented by celebrities and soccer players bring a lot of glamour to the city. **Pros:** top-of-the-line style and amenities at a good price. **Cons:** it's a bit of a walk to the port and centro. [$] *Rooms from: €175* ✉ *Via Corsica 4, Carignano* ☎ *010/5315111* 🌐 *www.melia-hotels.com* 🛏 *85 rooms, 14 suites* 🍴 *Breakfast.*

SHOPPING

Liguria is famous for its fine laces, silver-and-gold filigree work, and ceramics. Also look for bargains in velvet, macramé, olivewood, and marble. Genoa is the best spot to find all these specialties. In the heart of the medieval quarter, Via Soziglia is lined with shops selling handicrafts and tempting foods. Via XX Settembre and Via Roma are famous for their exclusive shops. High-end shops line Via Luccoli. The best shopping area for trendy-but-inexpensive Italian clothing is near San Siro, on Via San Luca.

CLOTHING AND LEATHER GOODS

Pescetto. Look for designer clothes, perfumes, and fancy gifts at Pescetto. ✉ *Via Scurreria 8, Molo* ☎ *010/2473433.*

JEWELRY

Codevilla. The well-established Codevilla is one of the best jewelers in the city. They sell top-of-the-line watches but also custom jewelry. ✉ *Via Roma 83/85r* ☎ *010/2472567.*

WINES

Vinoteca Sola. Here you can purchase the best Ligurian wines and have them shipped home. You can even buy futures for vintages to come. ✉ *Piazza Colombo 13–15/R, near Stazione Brignole, Foce* ☎ *010/594513* 🌐 *www.vinotecasola.it.*

8

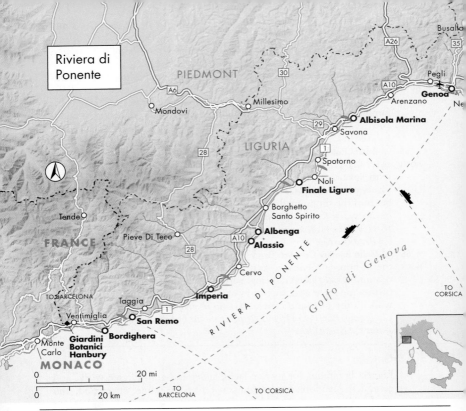

PIEDMONT

Busalla

A26

35

Mondovi

Millesimo

30

A6

A10

Pegli

Genoa

Arenzano

Ne

Albisola Marina

29

Savona

LIGURIA

28

Spotorno

1

Noli

Finale Ligure

Borghetto
Santo Spirito

Tende

Pieve Di Teco

Albenga

A10

Alassio

28

FRANCE

Cervo

Imperia

RIVIERA DI PONENTE

Golfo di Genova

TO
CORSICA

Taggia

1

TO BARCELONA

Ventimiglia

San Remo

Monte
Carlo

Giardini
Botanici
Hanbury

Bordighera

MONACO

0   20 mi

0   20 km

TO
BARCELONA

TO CORSICA

NERVI: A SIDE TRIP FROM GENOA

11 km (7 miles) east of Genoa.

The identity of this stately late-19th-century resort, famous for its
1½-km-long (1-mile-long) seaside **Passeggiata Anita Garibaldi**, its palm-
lined roads, and its 300 acres of parks rich in orange trees, is given away
only by the sign on the sleepy train station. Although Nervi is technically part of the city, its peace and quiet are as different from Genoa's
hustle and bustle as its clear blue water is from Genoa's crowded port.
From the centrally located train station, walk east along the seaside
promenade to reach the beaches, a cliff-side restaurant, and the 2,000
varieties of rose in the public **Parco Villa Grimaldi**, all the while enjoying one of the most breathtaking views on the Riviera. Nervi, and the
road between it and Genoa, is known for their nightlife in summer.

GETTING HERE

By car, exit the A12 at Genova Nervi and follow the "Centro" signs.
The Nervi train station is on the main north–south line, and you can
also take the commuter trains from Genova Principe and Brignole. It
can also be reached on Bus No. 15 from Genoa's Piazza Cavour.

WHERE TO EAT AND STAY

$$ **Romantik Hotel Villa Pagoda.**
HOTEL A 19th-century merchant's mansion
Fodor'sChoice modeled after a Chinese temple has
★ a private park, access to the famed clifftop walk, and magnificent ocean views; request a tower room for the best vantage point. **Pros:** lovely guest and common rooms; everything has a touch of class. **Cons:** nearby train can be softly heard. $ *Rooms from: €148* ✉ *Via Capolungo 15* ☎ *010/3726161* ⊕ *www.villapagoda.it* ↗ *13 rooms, 4 suites* ⊗ *Closed Nov.–Mar.* ⑪ *Breakfast.*

RIVIERA DI PONENTE

The Riviera di Ponente (Riviera of the Setting Sun) covers the narrow strip of northwest Liguria from Genoa to the French border. The sapphire Mediterranean Sea to one side and the verdant foothills of the Alps on the other allow for temperate weather and a long growing season—which it is why it's also called "Riviera dei Fiori" (Riviera of the Flowers). Once filled with charming seaside villages, elegant homes, and sophisticated visitors, this area now struggles to maintain a balance between its natural beauty and development. Highly populated resort areas and some overly industrialized areas are jammed into the thin stretch of white-sand and pebble beaches. But, there are still several worthwhile villages along the sea and hinterland. While its sister, the Riviera di Levante, may retain more of its natural beauty, the Ponente remains a popular retreat for visitors looking for sunshine, nightlife, and relaxation.

8

ALBISOLA MARINA

43 km (27 miles) west of Genoa.

GETTING HERE AND AROUND

By car, take the Albisola exit off the A10 and follow the signs for the Albisola marina center. Albisola is on the main railway line between Genoa and France.

EXPLORING

Lungomare degli Artisti. Albisola Marina has a centuries-old tradition of ceramics making. Numerous shops here sell the distinctive wares, and a whole sidewalk, Lungomare degli Artisti, which runs along the beachfront, has been transformed by the colorful ceramic works of well-known artists.

SHOPPING

Ceramiche San Giorgio. Producing ceramics since the 17th century, Ceramiche San Giorgio is known for both classic and modern designs. ✉ *Corso Matteotti 5* ☎ *019/482747* ⊕ *www.ceramichesangiorgio.com.*

FINALE LIGURE

30 km (19 miles) southwest of Albisola Marina, 72 km (44 miles) southwest of Genoa.

Lovely Finale Ligure is actually made up of three small villages: Finalmarina, Finalpia, and Finalborgo, and makes a wonderful base for exploring the Ponente. The former two have fine sandy beaches and a mix of traditional and modern resort amenities. Finalborgo, less than 1 km (½ mile) inland, is an attractive medieval walled village with nice shops and restaurants. Just above, is a hauntingly preserved medieval settlement, planned to a rigid blueprint, with 15th-century walls. The surrounding countryside is pierced by deep, narrow valleys and caves; the limestone outcroppings provide the warm pinkish stone found in many buildings in Genoa. Rare reptiles lurk among the exotic flora.

GETTING HERE AND AROUND

By car, take the Finale Ligure exit off the A10 and follow the "Centro" signs. Finale Ligure is on the main train line between Genoa and France.

VISITOR INFORMATION

Finale Ligure Tourism Office ✉ *Via San Pietro 14* ☎ *019/681019* ⏲ *Closed Sun.*

OFF THE BEATEN PATH

Noli. Just 9 km (5½ miles) northeast of Finale Ligure, the ruins of a castle loom benevolently over the tiny medieval gem of Noli. It's hard to imagine that this charming seaside village was—like Genoa, Venice, Pisa, and Amalfi—a prosperous maritime republic in the Middle Ages. Let yourself get lost among its labyrinth cobblestone streets filled with shops and cafés or enjoy a day in the sun on its lovely stretch of beach. If you don't have a car, get a bus for Noli at Spotorno, where local trains stop.

WHERE TO EAT AND STAY

$$$$ LIGURIAN

🍴 **Ai Torchi.** You could easily become a homemade-pesto snob at this restored 5th-century olive-oil-mill-turned-chic-restaurant in the historical center of Finalborgo. The high prices are justified by excellent inventive seafood and meat dishes and by the lovely setting. [$] *Average main: €60* ✉ *Via dell'Annunziata 12, Finalborgo* ☎ *019/690531* ⏲ *Closed Jan. 6–30, and Tues. Sept.–July.*

$$ B&B/INN

🏨 **Ca de' Tobia.** This lovely guesthouse conisists of five rooms and a suite on the seafront promenade of Noli and are stylishly done with wood floors, splashes of bright colors, and modern décor. **Pros:** ultrachic; full of modern amenities. **Cons:** right on the main road through town, so there is some street noise. [$] *Rooms from: €150* ✉ *Via Aurelia 35, Noli* ☎ *0197/485845* 🌐 *www.cadetobia.it* 🛏 *5 rooms, 1 suite* 🍽 *Breakfast.*

$$ HOTEL Fodor's Choice ★

🏨 **Hotel San Pietro Palace.** Originally built in the 17th century, this patial building has been elegantly restored and now houses a classy four-star hotel. **Pros:** decent on-site restaurant; very nice accommodations; great sea views. **Cons:** cental location leads to some noice from the promenade as well as early morning trash trucks; parking is off-site and expensive. [$] *Rooms from: €200* ✉ *Via San Pietro 9* ☎ *019/6049156* 🌐 *www.hotelsanpietropalace.it* 🛏 *28 rooms, 3 suites* 🍽 *Breakfast.*

$$$ **HOTEL** **FAMILY** **Punta Est.** An old villa with a newer wing is perched on a fragrant hillside just above the white-sand beaches, making this a wonderful retreat from the crowds down at the water's edge. **Pros:** nice pool and charming garden areas. **Cons:** some rooms are a bit outdated. [$] *Rooms from: €225* ✉ *Via Aurelia 1* ☎ *019/600611* 🌐 *www.puntaest.com* 🛏 *36 rooms and 3 suites* 🕓 *Closed mid-Oct.–mid-Apr.* 🍴 *Breakfast.*

ALBENGA

20 km (12 miles) southwest of Finale Ligure, 90 km (55 miles) southwest of Genoa.

Albenga has a medieval core, with narrow streets laid out by the ancient Romans. A network of alleys is punctuated by centuries-old towers surrounding the 18th-century Romanesque cathedral, with a late-14th-century campanile and a baptistery dating to the 5th century. It's a nice place to take an afternoon stroll and explore its many quaint shops and cafés.

GETTING HERE AND AROUND

By car, take the Albenga exit off the A10 and follow the "Centro" signs. Albenga is on the main train line between Genoa and France.

VISITOR INFORMATION

Albenga Tourism Office ✉ *Viale Martiri della Libertà* ☎ *0182/558444* 🌐 *www.visitriviera.it* 🕓 *Mon.–Sat. 9–12:30 and 3–7:30; Sun. in summer.*

EXPLORING

OFF THE BEATEN PATH

Bardineto. For a look at some of the Riviera's mountain scenery, make an excursion by car to this attractive village in the middle of an area rich in mushrooms, chestnuts, and raspberries, as well as local cheeses. A ruined castle stands above the village. From Borghetto Santo Spirito (between Albenga and Finale Ligure), drive inland 25 km (15 miles). ✉ *Via Roascio 5, Bardineto.*

8

ALASSIO

100 km (62 miles) southwest of Genoa.

Although Alassio is no longer a sleepy fishing village, the centro still possesses some old-world charm, colorful buildings, a great beachfront promenade, and white-sand beaches. Spend the day soaking up some sun, grab a seafood lunch or pizza along the boardwalk, and then finish off with a passeggiata and shopping on its caruggi.

GETTING HERE AND AROUND

By car, take the Albenga exit off the A10 and follow the blue signs for Alassio. Alassio is on the main train line between Genoa and France.

VISITOR INFORMATION

Alassio Tourism Office ✉ *Via Mazzini* ☎ *0182/6477027* 🌐 *www.comune.alassio.sv.it.*

IMPERIA

12 km (7 miles) west of Cervo, 116 km (71 miles) southwest of Genoa.

Imperia actually consists of two towns: Porto Maurizio, a medieval town built on a promontory, and Oneglia, now an industrial center for oil refining and pharmaceuticals. Porto Maurizio has a virtually intact medieval center, an intricate spiral of narrow streets and stone portals, and some imposing 17th- and 18th-century palaces. There's little of interest in modern Oneglia, except for a visit to the olive-oil museum.

GETTING HERE AND AROUND

By car, take the Imperia Est exit off the A10 and follow the signs for "Centro" or "Porto Maurizio." Both Imperia and Porto Maurizio are on the main rail line between Genoa and France.

VISITOR INFORMATION

Imperia Tourism Office ⊠ *Piazza Dante 4, Oneglia* ☎ *0183/2744982* ⊕ *www.visitrivieradeifiori.it.*

EXPLORING

Museo dell'Olivo. Imperia is king when it comes to olive oil, and the story of the olive is the theme of this small museum. Displays of the history of the olive tree, farm implements, presses, and utensils show how olive oil has been made in many countries throughout history. A multilanguage audio guide is available for €4. ⊠ *Via Garessio 11/13* ☎ *0183/295762* ⊕ *www.museodellolivo.com* 🖅 *€5* 🕑 *Mon.–Sat. 9–12:30 and 3–6:30.*

WHERE TO STAY

$$
B&B/INN

🏨 **Relais San Damian.** All the rooms are suites at this charming inn, set among the olive trees high above Porto Maurizio and the Mediterranean Sea. **Pros:** large suites and plenty of outdoor space; gorgeous pool area. **Cons:** limited amenities (no TVs or phones). $ *Rooms from: €150* ⊠ *Strada Vasia 47* ☎ *0183/280309* ⊕ *www.san-damian.com* 🛌 *9 suites* 🕑 *Closed Nov.–Feb.* 🍽 *Breakfast.*

SAN REMO

50 km (31 miles) southwest of Cervo, 146 km (90 miles) southwest of Genoa.

Once the crown jewel of the Riviera di Ponente, San Remo is still the area's largest resort, lined with polished hotels, exotic gardens, and seaside promenades. Renowned for its VIPs, glittering casino, annual music festival, and romantic setting, San Remo maintains remnants of its glamorous past from the late 19th century to World War II, but it also suffers from the same epidemic of overbuilding that has changed so much of the Ponente for the worse. Still, it continues to be a lively town, even in the off-season.

The Mercato dei Fiori, Italy's most important wholesale flower market, is held here in a market hall between Piazza Colombo and Corso Garibaldi, though it's open to dealers only. More than 20,000 tons of carnations, roses, mimosa flowers, and innumerable other kinds of cut flowers are dispatched from here each year. As the center of northern Italy's flower-growing industry, the town is surrounded by hills where verdant terraces are now blanketed with plastic to form immense greenhouses.

GETTING HERE AND AROUND

By car, take the San Remo exit off the A10 and follow the "Centro" signs. San Remo is on the main train line between Genoa and France.

VISITOR INFORMATION

San Remo Tourism Office ✉ *Palazzo Riviera, Largo Nuvoloni 1* ☎ *0184/59059* 🕒 *Mon.–Sat. 8–7, Sun. 9–1.*

EXPLORING

Cristo Salvatore, Santa Caterina d'Alessandria, e San Serafino di Sarov. This onion-dome Russian Orthodox church testifies to a long Russian presence on the Italian Riviera. Russian empress Maria Alexandrovna, wife of Czar Alexander I, built a summer house here, and in winter San Remo was a popular destination for other royal Romanovs. The church was consecrated in 1913. ✉ *Via Nuvoloni 2* ☎ *0184/531807* 🎟 *€1 donation* 🕒 *Daily 9:30–12:30 and 3–6:30.*

La Pigna (*The Pinecone*). San Remo's "old city" climbs upward to Piazza Castello, which offers a splendid view of the town and sea below. Some lovely old palazzi and squares have been restored, and the neighborhood gives you a sense of what it is was like to live in San Remo in centuries gone by.

San Remo Casinò. In addition to gaming, this lovely Art Nouveau landmark offers a restaurant, a nightclub, and a theater that hosts concerts and the annual San Remo Music Festival. There is free admission, but if you want to try your luck at the gaming tables, bets begin at €10. **TIP→ Dress is elegant, with jacket and tie requested at the French gaming tables.** ✉ *Corso Inglesi 18* ☎ *0184/5951* 🌐 *www.casinosanremo.it* 🕒 *Slot machines: Sun.–Thurs. 10 am–2:30 am, Fri. and Sat., 10 am–3:30 am. Tables: Sun.–Thurs. 2:30 pm–2:30 am, Fri. and Sat. 3 pm–3:30 am.*

OFF THE BEATEN PATH

Bussana Vecchia. In the hills where flowers are cultivated for export, this self-consciously picturesque former ghost town is a flourishing artists' colony. The town was largely destroyed by an earthquake in 1877, when the inhabitants packed up and left en masse. For almost a century the houses, church, and crumbling bell tower were empty shells, overgrown by weeds and wildflowers. Since the 1960s painters, sculptors, artisans, and bric-a-brac dealers have restored the dwellings as houses and studios. ✉ *8 km (5 miles) east of San Remo.*

WHERE TO EAT AND STAY

$$$ LIGURIAN

🍴 **Nuovo Piccolo Mondo.** Old wooden chairs dating to the 1920s, when the place opened, evoke the homey charm of this small, family-run trattoria. A faithful clientele keeps the kitchen busy, so get here early to grab a table and order Ligurian specialties such as *sciancui* (a roughly cut flat pasta with a mixture of beans, tomatoes, zucchini, and pesto) and *polpo e patate* (stewed octopus with potatoes). [$] *Average main: €30* ✉ *Via Piave 7* ☎ *0184/509012* 🕒 *Closed Sun.*

$$$ LIGURIAN

🍴 **Taverna al 29.** At the entrance of the old town is this intimate and comfortable dining establishment run by a husband (host) and wife (chef). The tavern's cuisine is linked to the Ligurian territory with old recipes revisited with creativity yet authenitcity. They also serve a good variety of gluten-free dishes. [$] *Average main: €35* ✉ *Piazza Cassini 5* ☎ *0184/570034* ✍ *Reservations essential* ⏲ *Mon.–Sat. 7:30–11 pm.*

$$ HOTEL 🏨 **Paradiso.** Bright, well-equipped rooms face a quiet palm-fringed garden and pool or the sea; some enjoy sea views from nice-size balconies. **Pros:** friendly service; nice pool; free loungers and umbrellas at nearby beach. **Cons:** a steep walk up some stairs and a hill from town. [$] *Rooms from: €170* ✉ *Via Roccasterone 12* ☎ *0184/571211* 🌐 *www.paradisohotel.it* 🛏 *41 rooms* 🍴 *Breakfast.*

$$$ HOTEL 🏨 **Royal.** This is arguably Liguria's second-most-luxurious resort after the Splendido in Portofino: each room is beautifully decorated differently, all have modern amenities, and most have views of the sea. **Pros:** the glamour of yesteryear with all the expected high-end amenities; reasonable prices given the surroundings. **Cons:** on-site meals and beverages are expensive. [$] *Rooms from: €285* ✉ *Corso Imperatrice 80* ☎ *0184/5391* 🌐 *www.royalhotelsanremo.com* 🛏 *114 rooms, 13 suites* ⏲ *Closed Nov.–mid-Feb.* 🍴 *Breakfast.*

BORDIGHERA

12 km (7 miles) west of San Remo, 155 km (96 miles) southwest of Genoa.

Bordighera sits as an attractive seaside resort with panoramas from Genoa (on a clear day) to Monte Carlo. A large English colony, attracted by the mild climate, settled here in the second half of the 19th century and is still very much in evidence today; you regularly find people taking afternoon tea in the cafés, and streets are named after Queen Victoria and Shakespeare. This was the first town in Europe to grow date palms, and its citizens still have the exclusive right to provide the Vatican with palm fronds for Easter celebrations.

Thanks partly to its many year-round English residents, Bordighera doesn't close down entirely in the off-season like some Riviera resorts, but rather serves as a quiet winter haven for all ages. With plenty of hotels and restaurants and a lovely seafront promenade, Bordighera makes a good base for exploring the region and is quieter and less commercial than San Remo.

GETTING HERE AND AROUND

By car, take the Bordighera exit off the A10 and follow the signs for "Centro," about a 10-minute drive. Bordighera is on the main railway line between Genoa and France.

VISITOR INFORMATION

Bordighera Tourism Office ✉ *Via Vittorio Emanuele 172/174* ☎ *0184/262322* 🌐 *www.bordighera.it* ⏲ *Mon.–Sat. 9:30–12:30 and 3–6, Sun. 10–12:30.*

EXPLORING

Lungomare Argentina. Running parallel to the ocean, Lungomare Argentina is a pleasant promenade, 1½ km (1 mile) long, which begins at the western end of the town and provides good views westward to the French Côte d'Azur.

WHERE TO EAT AND STAY

$$$

SEAFOOD

✕**Agua.** This beachfront dining establishment has changed name and owners several times, but it continues to have some of the best food in town with a fantastic setting. The brother team running it has some very inventive and delicious dishes on their menu including calamari sauteed with strips of artichoke and seared tuna on a bed of radicchio. The wine list is extensive and ventures well into the nearby border of France with select bottles of rosé. $ *Average main: €35* ✉ *Lungomare Aregntina 3* ☎ *018/4262108* ⌛ *Reservations essential* ⊘ *Closed Mon., and Jan. 9–Feb.*

$$$$

LIGURIAN

Fodor'sChoice

★

✕**Magiargè.** A mix of great charm and great food make this small osteria in the historic center an absolute dining delight. Dishes are Ligurian with a creative twist, such as the *stoccafisso sopra panizza* (salt cod served over a chickpea polenta) and *fritteline di bianchetti* (small frittatas made with tiny white fish). The selection of local wines is excellent. $ *Average main: €40* ✉ *Via della Loggia 6* ☎ *329/8005050* ⊕ *www.magiarge.it* ⌛ *Reservations essential* ⊘ *Closed Thurs.*

$$

HOTEL

🏨**Hotel Piccolo Lido.** Sea-view rooms at this quaint little spot along the promenade have nice little balconies, and there's a terrace perfect for enjoying the sunset and vistas of France. **Pros:** a good value; nice views. **Cons:** few amenities. $ *Rooms from: €140* ✉ *Lungomare Argentina 2* ☎ *0184/261297* ⊕ *www.hotelpiccololido.it* ⇗ *33 rooms* ⦿*Breakfast.*

$$

HOTEL

🏨**Hotel Villa Elisa.** On a street filled with beautiful old villas, this Victorian-era former residence has a relaxed and friendly atmosphere, beautiful gardens, and well-equipped rooms at reasonable prices. **Pros:** helpful staff; a good value; pool and garden make this a good choice for children. **Cons:** only partial views in sea-view rooms; limited parking; covered parking costs extra. $ *Rooms from: €140* ✉ *Via Romana 70* ☎ *0184/261313* ⊕ *www.villaelisa.com* ⇗ *33 rooms, 2 suites, 1 apt for up to 6 people* ⊘ *Closed Nov.–mid-Feb.* ⦿*Breakfast.*

EN
ROUTE

From Bordighera, travel west to Ventimiglia, then take a provincial road swinging 10 km (6 miles) up the Nervi River valley to a sweetly named medieval town, **Dolceacqua** (its name translates as Sweetwater), with a ruined castle. Liguria's best-known red wine is the local Rossese di Dolceacqua. A further 6 km (4 miles) along the road sits Pigna, a fascinating medieval village built in concentric circles on its hilltop.

GIARDINI BOTANICI HANBURY

10 km (6 miles) west of Bordighera.

GETTING HERE AND AROUND

Take the SS1 along the coast west from Bordighera, through the town of Ventimiglia, and toward the French border. The gardens are about 1 km (½ mile) beyond the tunnel.

EXPLORING

Fodor'sChoice **Giardini Botanici Hanbury.** Mortola Inferiore, only 2 km (1 mile) from the
★ French border, is the site of the world-famous Giardini Botanici Hanbury (Hanbury Botanical Gardens), one of the largest and most beautiful in Italy. Planned and planted in 1867 by a wealthy English merchant, Sir Thomas Hanbury, and his botanist brother, Daniel, the terraced gardens contain species from five continents, including many palms and succulents. There are panoramic views of the sea from the gardens. ✉ *Corso Montecarlo 43, Località Mortola Inferiore* ☎ *0184/229507* ⊕ *www.giardinihanbury.com* 🖅 *€7.50 July–Mar. 19, €9 Mar. 20–June* ☉ *Mar.–mid-June, daily 9:30–6; mid-June–mid-Sept., daily 9:30–7; mid-Sept.–mid-Oct., daily 9:30–6; mid-Oct.–Feb., Tues.–Sun. 9:30–6. Last entry 1 hr before closing.*

OFF THE
BEATEN
PATH
Balzi Rossi. Prehistoric humans left traces of their lives and magic rites in the Balzi Rossi (Red Rocks), caves carved in the sheer rock. You can visit the caves and a small museum displaying some of the objects found there. ✉ *Via Balzi Rosso 9, 2 km (1 mile) west of Giardini Botanici Hanbury* ☎ *0184/38113* 🖅 *€2* ☉ *Daily 8:30–7:30.*

9

EMILIA–ROMAGNA

WELCOME TO EMILIA–ROMAGNA

TOP REASONS TO GO

★ **The signature food of Emilia:** This region's food—prosciutto crudo, Parmigiano-Reggiano, balsamic vinegar, and above all, pasta—makes the trip to Italy worthwhile.

★ **Mosaics that take your breath away:** The intricate tiles in Ravenna's Mausoleo di Galla Placidia, in brilliantly well-preserved colors, depict vivid portraits and pastoral scenes.

★ **Arguably Europe's oldest wine bar:** Nicholas Copernicus tippled here while studying at Ferrara's university in the early 1500s; Osteria al Brindisi, in the centro storico, has been pouring wine since 1435.

★ **The nightlife of Bologna:** This red-roof city has had a lively student culture since the university—Europe's oldest—was founded in the late 11th century.

★ **The medieval castles of San Marino:** Its three castles dramatically perch on a rock more than 3,000 feet above the flat landscape of Romagna.

1 **Emilia.** A landscape of medieval castles and crumbling farmhouses begins just east of Milan, in the western half of Emilia-Romagna. Here you'll find the delicious delights of **Parma,** with its buttery prosciutto, famous cheese, and dazzling palaces. Next along the road, continuing east, comes **Reggio Emilia,** of Parmigiano-Reggiano fame, then Modena, the city of balsamic vinegar.

2 **Bologna.** Emilia's principal cultural and intellectual center is famed for its arcaded sidewalks, grandiose medieval towers, and sublime restaurants.

3 Ferrara. This prosperous, tidy city north of Bologna has a rich medieval past and its own distinctive cuisine.

4 Romagna. The eastern half of Emilia-Romagna begins east of Bologna, where spa towns extend north and south of the Via Emilia and the A1 autostrada, and runs to the Adriatic. **San Marino,** south of Rimini, is an anomaly in every way. As its own tiny republic, it hangs implausibly on a cliff above the Romagna plain.

5 Ravenna. The main attractions of this well-preserved Romagna city are its memorable mosaics—glittering treasures left from Byzantine rule.

GETTING ORIENTED

Emilia-Romagna owes its beginnings to the Romans, who built the Via Emilia in 187 BC. Today the road bisects the flat, foggy region, paralleling the Autostrada del Sole (A1), making it easy to drive straight through. Bologna is in the middle of everything, with Piacenza, Parma, and Modena to the northwest, and the Adriatic to the southeast. Ferrara and Ravenna are the only detours—they're north of Via Emilia.

VENETO

Fiume Po River

Ferrara **3** *Po di Volano*

Modena

A13

16

A1

✈ Bologna **2**

Mare Adriatico

9

Ravenna **5**

Imola

Faenza A14

avullo

A1

64 Vado

Forlì ✈ 9

Cesenatico

Cesena

TUSCANY

67 *R O M A G N A* **4**

Rimini

71

72 SAN MARINO

San Marino ✪

0 —— 20 mi
0 —— 20 km

THE MARCHES

EATING AND DRINKING WELL IN EMILIA-ROMAGNA

Italians rarely agree about anything, but many concede that some of the country's finest foods originated in Emilia-Romagna. Tortellini, fettuccine, Parmesan cheese, prosciutto crudo, and balsamic vinegar are just a few of the Italian delicacies born here.

One of the beauties of Emilia-Romagna is that its exceptional food can be had without breaking the bank. Many trattorias serve up classic dishes, mastered over the centuries, at reasonable prices. Cutting-edge restaurants and wine bars are often more expensive; their inventive menus are full of *fantasia*—reinterpretations of the classics. For the budget-conscious, Bologna, a university town, has great places for cheap eats.

Between meals, you can sustain yourself with the region's famous sandwich, the *piadina*. It's made with pitalike thin bread, usually filled with prosciutto or mortadella, cheese, and vegetables; then put under the grill and served hot, with the cheese oozing at the sides. These addictive sandwiches can be savored at sit-down places or ordered to go.

THE REAL RAGÙ

Emilia-Romagna's signature dish is *tagliatelle al ragù* (flat noodles with meat sauce), known as "spaghetti Bolognese" most everywhere else. This *primo* (first course) is on every menu, and no two versions are the same. The sauce starts in a sauté pan with finely diced carrots, onions, and celery. Purists add nothing but minced beef, but some use *guanciale* (pork cheek), sausage, veal, or chicken. Regular ministrations of broth are added, and sometimes wine, milk, or cream. After a couple of hours of cooking, the ragù is ready to be joined with pasta and Parmigiano-Reggiano and brought to the table.

PORK PRODUCTS

It's not just mortadella and cured pork products like prosciutto and *culatello* that Emilia-Romagnans go crazy for—they're wild about the whole hog.

You'll frequently find cotechino and zampone, both *secondi* (second courses), on menus. *Cotechino, photo below,* is a savory, thick, fresh sausage served with lentils on New Year's Eve (the combination is said to augur well for the new year) and with mashed potatoes year-round. *Zampone,* a stuffed pig's foot, is redolent of garlic and deliciously fatty.

BOLLITO MISTO

The name means "mixed boil," and they do it exceptionally well in this part of Italy. According to Emilia-Romagnans, it was invented here, though other northern Italians, especially from Milan and the Piedmont, might argue this point. Chicken, beef, tongue, and zampone are tossed into a stockpot and boiled; they're then removed from the broth and served with a fragrant *salsa verde* (green sauce), made green by parsley and spiced with anchovies, garlic, and capers. This simple yet rich dish is usually served with mashed potatoes on the side, and savvy diners will mix some of the piquant salsa verde into the potatoes as well.

STUFFED PASTA

Among the many Emilian variations on stuffed pasta, *tortellini (pictured at left),*

are the smallest. *Tortelli (photo upper right)* and *cappellacci* are larger pasta "pillows," about the size of a brussels sprout, but with the same basic form as tortellini. They're often filled with pumpkin or spinach and cheese.

Tortelloni are, in theory, even bigger, although their sizes vary. Stuffed pastas are generally served simply, with melted butter, sage, and—what else?—Parmigiano-Reggiano cheese or, in the case of tortellini, *in brodo* (in beef, chicken, or capon broth or a combination of any of them), which brings out the subtle richness of the filling.

WINES

Emilia-Romagna's wines accompany the region's fine food rather than vying with it for accolades. The best-known is *lambrusco,* a sparkling red produced on the Po Plain that has some admirers and many detractors. It's praised for its tartness and condemned for the same; it does, however, pair brilliantly with the local fare. The region's best wines include Sangiovese di Romagna (somewhat similar to Chianti), from the Romagnan hills, and barbera, from the Colli Piacetini and Apennine foothills. Castelluccio, Bonzara, Zerbina, Leone Conti, and Tre Monti are among the region's top producers—keep an eye out for them.

Updated
by Patricia
Rucidlo

Gourmets the world over claim that Emilia-Romagna's greatest contribution to humankind has been gastronomic. Birthplace of fettuccine, tortellini, lasagna, prosciutto, and Parmigiano-Reggiano cheese, the region has a spectacular culinary tradition. But there are many reasons to come here aside from the desire to be well fed: Parma's Correggio paintings, Giuseppe Verdi's villa at Sant'Agata, the medieval splendor of Bologna's palaces, Ferrara's medieval alley, the rolling hills of the Romagna countryside, and, perhaps foremost, the Byzantine beauty of mosaic-rich Ravenna—glittering as brightly today as it did 1,500 years ago.

As you travel through Emilia, the western half of the region, you'll encounter the sprawling plants of Italy's industrial food giants, like Barilla and Fini, standing side by side with the fading villas and farmhouses that have long punctuated the flat, fertile land of the Po Plain. Bologna, the principal city of Emilia, is a busy cultural and, increasingly, business center, less visited but in many ways just as engaging as the country's more famous tourist destinations—particularly given its acknowledged position as the leading city of Italian cuisine. The rest of the region follows suit: eating is an essential part of any Emilian experience.

The area's history is laden with culinary legends, such as how the original tortellino was modeled on the shape of Venus's navel and the original *tagliolini* (long, thin egg pasta) was served at the wedding banquet of Annibale Bentivoglio and Lucrezia d'Este—a marriage uniting two of the noblest families in the region. You'll need to stay focused just to make sure you try all the basics: Parma's famed prosciutto and Parmigiano-Reggiano cheese, Modena's balsamic vinegar, the ragù whose poor imitations are known worldwide as "Bolognese"—and, of course, the best pasta in the world.

EMILIA-ROMAGNA PLANNER

MAKING THE MOST OF YOUR TIME

Plan on spending at least two days in Bologna, the region's cultural and historical capital. You shouldn't miss Parma, with its stunning food and graceful public spaces. Also plan on visiting Ferrara, a misty, mysterious medieval city. If you have time, go to Ravenna for its memorable Byzantine mosaics and Modena for its harmonious architecture and famous balsamic vinegar.

If you have only a few days in the region, it's virtually impossible to do all five of those cities justice. If you're a dedicated gourmand (or *buona forchetta*, as Italians say), move from Bologna west along the Via Emilia (SS9) to Modena and Parma. If you're more interested in architecture, art, and history, choose the eastern route, heading north on the A13 to Ferrara and then southeast on the SS16 to Ravenna.

If you have more time, you won't have to make such tough choices. You can start in Milan, go east, and finish on the Adriatic—or vice versa.

GETTING HERE AND AROUND

CAR TRAVEL

A car is particularly useful for visiting the spa towns of Romagna, which aren't well connected by train. Historic centers are off-limits to cars, but they're also quite walkable, so you may just want to park your car and get around on foot once you arrive.

Entering Emilia-Romagna by car is as easy as it gets. Coming in from the northwest on the Autostrada del Sole (A1), you'll first hit Piacenza, a mere 45-minute drive southeast of Milan. On the other side of the region, Venice is about an hour from Ferrara by car on the A13.

Bologna is on the autostrada, so driving between cities is a breeze, though take special care if you're coming from Florence, as the road is winding and the drivers speed. The Via Emilia (SS9), one of the oldest roads in the world, runs through the heart of the region. Although less scenic, the A1 toll highway, which runs parallel to the Via Emilia from Bologna, can get you where you're going about twice as fast. From Bologna, the A13 runs north to Ferrara, and the A14 takes you east to Ravenna. Much of the historic center of Bologna is closed off to cars daily from 7 am to 8 pm.

TRAIN TRAVEL

When it comes to public transportation in the region, trains are better than buses—they're fairly efficient, quite frequent, and most stations aren't too far from the center of town. The railroad track follows the Via Emilia (SS9). In Emilia it generally takes from 30 to 45 minutes to get from one major city to the next. To reach Ferrara or Ravenna, you typically have to change to a local train at Bologna. Ferrara is a half hour north of Bologna on the train, and Ravenna is just over an hour.

9

Bologna is an important rail hub for northern Italy and has frequent, fast service to Milan, Florence, Rome, and Venice. The routes from Bologna to the south usually go through Florence, about 40 minutes away on a high-speed train. The high-speed train service Alta Velocità cuts the time from Milan to Bologna to only one hour. On the northeastern edge of the region, Venice is 1½ hours east of Ferrara by train. Check the website of the state railway, the **Ferrovie dello Stato** (*FS* ⊕ *www.trenitalia.com*), for information, or stop in a travel agency, as many sell train tickets (without a markup) and agents often speak English. **Italo** (⊕ *www.italotreno.it*), a privately owned high-speed train line, competes with the state-sponsored service. Italo's Turin–Salerno line makes stops in Bologna, Florence, Rome, Naples, and Salerno; the Venice–Napoli line stops in Padova, Bologna, Florence, and Rome. Some of these also stop at secondary stations.

RESTAURANTS

Prices in the dining reviews are the average cost of a main course at dinner, or, if dinner is not served, at lunch.

HOTELS

Emilia-Romagna has a reputation for demonstrating a level of efficiency uncommon in most of Italy. Even the smallest hotels are usually well run, with high standards of quality and service. Bologna is very much a businessperson's city, and many hotels here cater to the business traveler, but there are smaller, more intimate hotels as well. It's smart to book in advance—the region hosts many fairs and conventions that can fill up hotels even during low season. *Hotel reviews have been shortened. For full information, visit Fodors.com.*

WHAT IT COSTS			
$	$$	$$$	$$$$
RESTAURANTS under €15	€15–€24	€25–€35	over €35
HOTELS under €125	€125–€200	€201–€300	over €300

Prices in the dining reviews are the average cost of a main course at dinner, or, if dinner is not served, at lunch. Prices in the reviews are the lowest cost of a standard double room in high season.

EMILIA

The Via Emilia runs through Emilia's heart in a straight shot from medieval Piacenza, 67 km (42 miles) southeast of Milan, through Bologna, and ultimately to Romagna and the Adriatic Coast. On the way you encounter many of Italy's cultural riches—from the culinary and artistic treasures of Parma to the birthplace and home of Giuseppe Verdi. Take time to veer into the countryside, with its ramshackle farmhouses and 800-year-old abbeys; to stop for a taste of prosciutto; and to detour north to the mist-shrouded tangle of streets that make up Ferrara's old Jewish ghetto.

EMILIA-ROMAGNA THROUGH THE AGES

Ancient History. Emilia-Romagna owes its beginnings to a road. In 187 BC the Romans built the Via Aemilia—a long road running northwest from the Adriatic port of Rimini to the central garrison town of Piacenza—and it was along this central spine that the primary towns of the region developed.

Despite the unifying factor of what came to be known as the Via Emilia, this section of Italy has had a fragmented history. Its eastern part, roughly the area from Faenza to the coast (known as Romagna), looked first to the Byzantine east and then to Rome for art, political power, and, some say, national character. The western part, from Bologna to Piacenza (Emilia), looked more to the north with its practice of self-government and dissent.

Bologna was founded by the Etruscans and eventually came under the influence of the Roman Empire. The Romans established a garrison here, renaming the old Etruscan settlement Bononia. It was after the fall of Rome that the region began its fragmentation. Romagna, centered in Ravenna, was ruled from Constantinople. Ravenna eventually became the capital of the empire in the west in the 5th century, passing to papal control in the 8th century.

Even today, the city is still filled with reminders of two centuries of Byzantine rule.

Family Ties. The other cities of the region, from the Middle Ages on, became the fiefdoms of important noble families—the Este in Ferrara and Modena, the Pallavicini in Piacenza, and the Bentivoglio in Bologna. Today all these cities bear the marks of their noble patrons. When in the 16th century the papacy managed to exert its power over the entire area, some of these cities were divided among the papal families—hence the stamp of the Farnese family on Parma and Piacenza.

A Leftward Tilt. Bologna and Emilia-Romagna have established a robust tradition of rebellion and dissent. The Italian socialist movement was born in the region, as was Benito Mussolini. In keeping with the political climate of his home state, he was a firebrand socialist during the early part of his career. Despite having Mussolini as a native son, Emilia-Romagna didn't take to Fascism: it was here that the anti-Fascist resistance was born, and during World War II the region suffered terribly at the hands of the Fascists and the Nazis.

PIACENZA

67 km (42 miles) southeast of Milan, 150 km (93 miles) northwest of Bologna.

Piacenza has always been associated with industry and commerce. Its position on the Po River has made it an important inland port since the earliest times; the Etruscans, and then the Romans, had thriving settlements here. As you approach the city today you could be forgiven for thinking that it holds little of interest. Piacenza is surrounded by ugly industrial suburbs (with particularly unlovely concrete factories and a power station), but if you forge ahead you'll discover a preserved medieval center and an unusually clean city. Its prosperity is evident in the great shopping to be had along Corso Vittorio Emanuele II.

GETTING HERE AND AROUND

Regional trains run often from Milan to Piacenza and take a little more than an hour; Eurostar service cuts the travel time in half, and Alta Velocità trains make it from Milan to Bologna in an hour. The Intercity from Bologna to Piacenza takes about 1½ hours and closer to two hours on regional trains. Both have frequent service. Piacenza is easily accessible by car via the A1, either from Milan or from Bologna. If you're coming from Milan, take the Piacenza Nord exit; from Bologna, the Piacenza Est exit.

VISITOR INFORMATION

Piacenza Tourism Office ✉ *Piazza Cavalli 7* ☎ *0523/329324* ⊕ *www.comune.piacenza.it.*

EXPLORING

Duomo. Attached like a sinister balcony to the bell tower of Piacenza's 12th-century Duomo is a *gabbia* (iron cage), where miscreants were incarcerated naked and subjected to the scorn of the crowd in the marketplace below. Inside the cathedral, less evocative but equally impressive medieval stonework decorates the pillars and the crypt, and there are extravagant frescoes in the dome of the cupola begun by Morazzone (1573–1626). Guercino (1591–1666) completed them upon Morazzone's death. The Duomo can be reached by following Via XX Settembre from Piazza dei Cavalli. ✉ *Piazza Duomo* ☎ *0523/335154* ☉ *Daily 7:30–noon and 4–7.*

Musei di Palazzo Farnese. The city-owned museum of Piacenzan art and antiquities is housed in the vast **Palazzo Farnese.** The ruling family had commissioned a monumental palace, but construction, begun in 1558, was never completed as planned. The highlight of the museum's eclectic collection is the tiny 2nd-century BC Etruscan *Fegato di Piacenza,* a bronze tablet shaped like a *fegato* (liver), marked with the symbols of the gods of good and ill fortune. By comparing this master "liver" with one taken from the body of a freshly slaughtered sacrifice, priests predicted the future. The collection also contains Botticelli's beautiful *Madonna and Child with St. John the Baptist.* Because it's under glass, you have the rare opportunity of getting very close to the piece to admire the artist's brushwork. Reserve ahead for free 1½-hour guided tours. ✉ *Piazza Cittadella 29* ☎ *0523/492661* ⊕ *www.palazzofarnese.piacenza.it* 🎫 *€6* ☉ *Museum: Tues.–Thurs. 9–1, Fri. and Sat. 9–1 and 3–6, Sun. 9:30–1 and 3–6.*

Piazza dei Cavalli (*Square of the Horses*). The hub of the city is the Piazza dei Cavalli. The flamboyant equestrian statues from which the piazza takes its name are depictions of Ranuccio Farnese (1569–1622) and, on the left, his father, Alessandro (1545–92). The latter was a beloved ruler, enlightened and fair; Ranuccio, his successor, less so. Both statues are the work of Francesco Mochi, a master Baroque sculptor. Dominating the square is the massive 13th-century **Palazzo Pubblico,** also known as "Il Gotico." This two-tone, marble-and-brick, turreted and crenellated building was the seat of town government before Piacenza fell under the iron fists of the ruling Pallavicini and Farnese families.

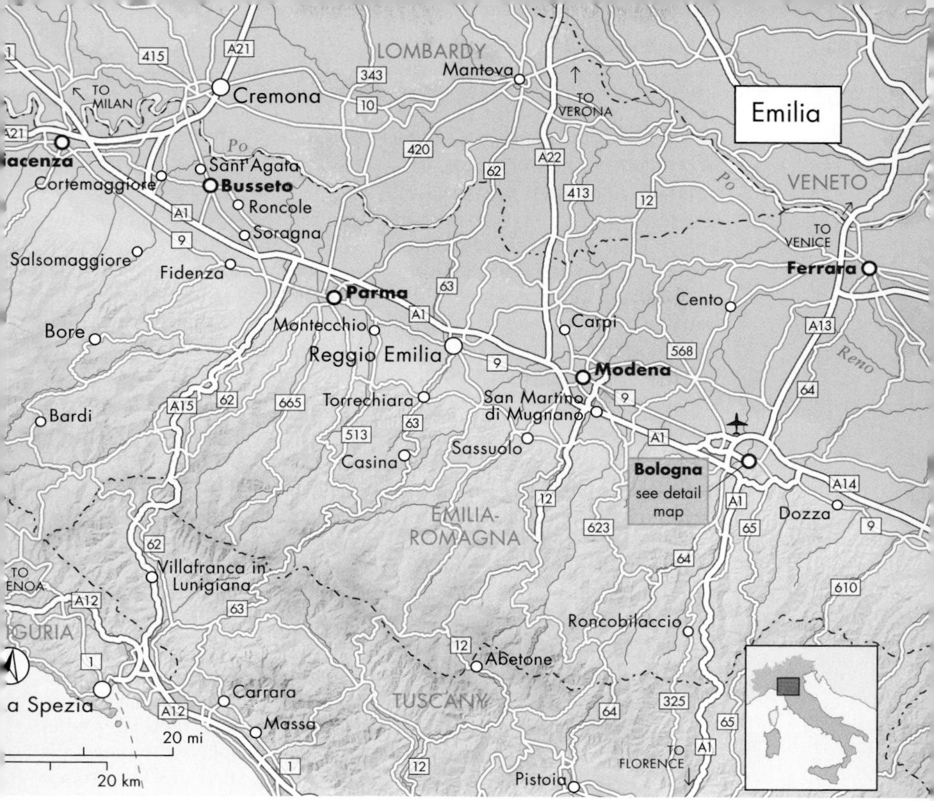

WHERE TO EAT

$$$ MODERN ITALIAN Fodor's Choice ★ 🍴 **Antica Osteria del Teatro.** A simple 15th-century palazzo on a square in the center of town gives no hint to what awaits inside. Warm ochre-sponged walls adorned with contemporary prints provide the backdrop for some serious food. Presiding over this jewel for some 30 years, chef Filippo Chiappini Dattilo has pursued his twin passions, Italian cuisine and French technique. The local specialty, *culatello,* is served with exquisite *porcini sott'olio* (mushrooms in olive oil). Another traditional dish, *pisarei e faso* (Piacentinian for pasta fagioli), is livened up with shrimp and squid. The colorful risotto *mantecato con granchio reale* (risotto with crab) arrives redolent of mandarin, with which it has been generously seasoned. Excellent service and an equally excellent wine list make dining here a true pleasure. [$] *Average main: €30* ✉ *Via Verdi 16* ☎ *0523/323777* 🌐 *www.anticaosteriadelteatro.it* ✍ *Reservations essential* ⏲ *Closed Sun. and Mon., Jan. 1–10, and Aug. 1–25.*

BUSSETO

30 km (19 miles) southeast of Piacenza, 25 km (16 miles) southeast of Cremona in Lombardy.

GETTING HERE AND AROUND

If you're coming by car from Parma, drive along the A1/E35 and follow signs for the A15 in the direction of Milan/La Spezia. Choose the exit in the direction of Fidenza/Salsomaggiore Terme, following signs to the SP12, which connects to the SS9W. At Fidenza, take the SS588 heading north, which will take you into Busseto. If you're without a car, you'll have to take a bus from Parma, as there's no train service.

VISITOR INFORMATION

Busseto Tourism Office ⊠ *Piazza G. Verdi 10* ☎ *0524/92487* ⊕ *www.bussetolive.com.*

EXPLORING

Teatro Verdi. In the center of Busseto is the lovely Teatro Verdi, dedicated, as you might expect, to the works of the hamlet's famous son. Guided tours (in both English and Italian) of the well-preserved, ornate, 19th century–style theater are offered every half hour. Check with the Busseto tourist office for the performance schedule. ⊠ *Piazza G. Verdi 10* ☎ *0524/92487* ⚏ *Tours €4* ⊗ *Tours: Nov.–Feb., 9:30–1 and 2:30–5; Mar.–Oct., Tues.–Sun. 9:30–1 and 3–6.*

Villa Pallavicino. Busseto's main claim to fame is its native son, master composer Giuseppe Verdi (1813–1901). The 15th-century Villa Pallavicino is where Verdi worked and lived with his mistress (and later wife) Giuseppina Strepponi. Recently renovated, it displays the maestro's piano, scores, composition books, and walking sticks. ⊠ *Via Provesi 35* ☎ *0524/931002* ⊕ *www.museogiuseppeverdi.it* ⚏ *€9* ⊗ *Mar.–Oct., Tues.–Sun. 10–6:30; Nov., Tues.–Sun. 10–5:30; Dec.–Feb., weekends 10–5:30, Tues.–Fri. by reservation only.*

Villa Sant'Agata. For Verdi lovers, Villa Sant'Agata (also known as Villa Verdi) is a veritable shrine. It's the grand country home Verdi built for himself in 1849—and the place where some of his greatest works were composed. Visits are by tour only, and you have to reserve a few days in advance by phone or online. ⊠ *Via Verdi 22, Sant'Agata Villanova sull'Arda, 4 km (2½ miles) north of Busseto on SS588, toward Cremona* ☎ *0523/830000* ⊕ *www.villaverdi.org* ⚏ *Tours €9* ⊗ *Tours: mid-Jan.–Feb., Sat. and holidays 8:30–11:45 and 2:30–5:30; Mar.–mid-Apr. and mid-June–Aug., Tues.–Sun. 9:30–11:45 and 2:30–6:15; mid-Apr.–mid-June and Sept.–Oct., Tues.–Sun. 9:30–6:15.*

PARMA

40 km (25 miles) southeast of Busseto, 97 km (60 miles) northwest of Bologna.

Parma stands on the banks of a tributary of the Po River. Despite damage during World War II, much of the stately historic center seems untouched by modern times. This is a prosperous city, and it shows in its well-dressed residents, clean streets, and immaculate piazzas.

Bursting with gustatory delights, Parma draws crowds for its sublime cured pork product, *prosciutto crudo di Parma* (known locally simply as "prosciutto crudo"). The pale-yellow Parmigiano-Reggiano cheese produced here and in nearby Reggio Emilia is the original—and best—of a class known around the world as "Parmesan."

Almost every major European power has had a hand in ruling Parma at one time or another. The Romans founded the city—then little more than a garrison on the Via Emilia—after which a succession of feudal lords held sway. In the 16th century came the ever-conniving Farnese family, which died out in 1731 on the death of Antonio Farnese. It then went to the Spanish, and fell into French hands in 1796. In 1805 Marie-Louise (better known to the Parmigiani as Maria Luigia), the wife of Napoléon, took command of the city. She was a much-beloved figure in her adopted town until her death in 1847.

GETTING HERE AND AROUND

Train service, via Eurostar, Intercity, and Regionale trains, runs frequently from Milan and Bologna. It takes a little over an hour from Milan and slightly less than an hour from Bologna. By car, Parma is just off the A1 autostrada, halfway between Bologna and Piacenza.

VISITOR INFORMATION

Parma Tourism Office ⊠ *Piazza Garibaldi 1* ☎ *0521/218889* ⊕ *www.turismo.comune.parma.it.*

EXPLORING

TOP ATTRACTIONS

Battistero (*Baptistery*). Baptisms still happen (one Saturday and one Sunday during the month) in this baptistery, which has a simple pink-stone Romanesque exterior and an uplifting Gothic interior. The doors are richly decorated with figures, animals, and flowers, and inside, the building is adorned with stucco figures (probably carved by Antelami) showing the months and seasons. Early 14th-century frescoes depicting scenes from the life of Christ grace the walls. ⊠ *Piazza del Duomo* ⌂ *€6* ⊗ *Daily 9–12:30 and 3–6:30.*

Fodor's Choice
★

Camera di San Paolo. This was the reception room for the erudite abbess Giovanna da Piacenza. In 1519 she hired Correggio to provide its decoration. Mythological scenes depict glorious frescoes of the *Triumphs of the Goddess Diana*, the *Three Graces*, and the *Three Fates*. ⊠ *Via Melloni 15, off Strada Garibaldi near Piazza Pilotta* ☎ *0521/233309* ⌂ *€2* ⊗ *Tues.–Sun. 8:30–2.*

Duomo. The magnificent 12th-century cathedral has two vigilant stone lions standing guard beside the main door. The arch of the entrance is decorated with a delicate frieze of figures representing the months of the year, a motif repeated inside the baptistery. Some of the church's original artwork still survives, notably the simple yet evocative *Descent from the Cross,* a carving in the right transept by Benedetto Antelami (active 1178–1230), whose masterwork is this cathedral's baptistery. It's an odd juxtaposition to turn from his austere work to the exuberant fresco in the dome, the *Assumption of the Virgin* by Antonio Allegri, better known to us as Correggio (1494–1534). The fresco is best viewed when the sun is strong, as this building is not particularly well lighted. ✉ *Piazza del Duomo* ☎ *0521/235886* ⊙ *Daily 7:30–12:30 and 3–7.*

Musei del Cibo (*Food Museums*). Three museums outside Parma showcase the city and the region's most famous foods. The Musei del Cibo, as they're collectively known, offer tastings, a bit of history, and a tour through the process of making these specialties. None is more than a 20-minute drive or taxi ride from the city. It's a good idea to call before making the trek, though, as opening hours are limited. ⊕ *www. museidelcibo.it.*

Museo del Parmigiano Reggiano. The trademark crumbly cheese is the focus of this museum. ✉ *Corte Castellazzi, Via Volta 5, Soragna, 32 km (20 miles) northwest of Parma* ☎ *0524/596129* 🎫 *€5* ⊙ *Mar.–early Dec., weekends 10–1 and 3–6, weekdays by reservation only; Dec.– Feb., by reservation only.*

Museo del Pomodoro. It's hard to imagine what Italian cuisine would be like without the New World tomato. This museum explains all the mysteries. ✉ *Strada Giarola 11, Corte di Giarola, Collecchio* ☎ *0521/228152* ⊕ *www.museidelcibo.it* 🎫 *€4* ⊙ *Mar. 1–Dec. 8, weekends 10–6, weekdays by reservation only.*

Museo del Prosciutto di Parma. Visit this museum for an in-depth look at Italy's most famous cured pork product. ✉ *Via Bocchialini, Langhirano* ☎ *0521/864324* 🎫 *€4* ⊙ *Mar.–Dec., weekends 10–6, by reservation only.*

Museo del Salame. This museum is all about cured meats. ✉ *Castello di Felino, 23 km (14 miles) southwest of Parma* ☎ *0521/431809* 🎫 *€4* ⊙ *Mar.–Dec., weekends 10–1 and 3–6, by reservation only.*

Piazza del Duomo. This spacious cobblestone piazza contains the cathedral and the Battistero, plus the Palazzo del Vescovado (Bishop's Palace). Behind the Duomo is the Baroque church of San Giovanni.

Fodor's Choice
★
Teatro Farnese/Galleria Nazionale. To enter the gallery, you pass through the magnificent Baroque Teatro Farnese, built in 1617–18. Made entirely of wood, it was largely destroyed in a 1944 Allied bombing, but it's been flawlessly restored. Masterpieces by Correggio, Parmigianino, Leonardo da Vinci (1452–1519), El Greco (1541–1614), and Bronzino (1503–72) hang at the little-visited Galleria Nazionale. The museum is housed on the piano nobile of the massive and somewhat forbidding **Palazzo della Pilotta,** which was constructed on the riverbank in 1618. The palazzo takes its name from the game *pilotta*, a sort of handball played within the palace precincts in the 17th century. The building also suffered much damage in a May 1944 Allied bombing, and has been greatly restored. ✉ *Piazza della Pilotta* ⊕ *www.gallerianazionaleparma. it* 🎫 *€6* ⊙ *Tues.–Sat. 8:30–6:30, Sun. 8:30–1:30.*

WORTH NOTING

Piazza Garibaldi. This is the heart of Parma, where people gather to pass the time of day, start their *passeggiata* (evening stroll), or simply hang out. Strada Cavour, leading off the piazza, is Parma's prime shopping street: it's also crammed with wine bars teeming with locals. This square and nearby Piazza del Duomo make up one of the loveliest historic centers in Italy. So it's a perfect place to stop for a snack or light lunch.

San Giovanni Evangelista. Beyond the elaborate Baroque facade of San Giovanni Evangelista, the Renaissance interior reveals several works by Correggio: *St. John the Evangelist* (in the lunette above the door in the left transept) is considered among his finest. Also in this church (in the second and fourth chapels on the left) are works by Parmigianino, a contemporary of Correggio's. Once seen, Parmigianino's long-necked Madonnas are never forgotten. ✉ *Piazzale San Giovanni 1, Piazza del Duomo* ☎ *0521/235311* 🕓 *Daily 8–noon and 3–5:45.*

Santa Maria della Steccata. Dating from the 16th century, this delightful church has one of Parma's most recognizable domes. In the dome's large arch there's a wonderful decorative fresco by Francesco Mazzola, better known as Parmigianino (1503–40). He took so long to complete it that his patrons briefly imprisoned him for breach of contract. ✉ *Piazza Steccata 9, off Via Dante near Piazza Garibaldi* ☎ *0521/234937* 🌐 *www.santuari.it/steccata* 🕓 *Daily 9–noon and 3–6.*

WHERE TO EAT

$ WINE BAR 🍴 **Enoteca Antica Osteria Fontana.** Gregarious locals patronize this old-school *enoteca* (wine bar). The interior may be minimal, with yellow walls and wooden tables, but the wine list and sandwich menu are substantial. You can feast on *tartines* (little bread squares with creative toppings) or chow down on a grilled panini—the seemingly endless options for the latter include *coppa* (a cured pork product), pancetta, and Gorgonzola. Low prices draw Parma's twentysomethings (and everyone else), with customers often spilling onto the street, wine glasses in hand. There's an enormous selection of wine bottles to go, so you can avoid the madding crowd with takeout. [$] *Average main: €5* ✉ *Strada Farini 24/a, near Piazza Garibaldi* ☎ *0521/286037* ✍ *Reservations not accepted* 🕓 *Closed Sun. and Mon.*

$ EMILIAN 🍴 **La Filoma.** If you want to try Parmesan specialties without breaking the bank, this is the place to go. The dining room evokes the turn of two centuries ago with its high ceilings and damask drapes, though an element of kitsch prevails. The food shines, from the classic *anolini in brodo di manzo e cappone* (a local variation on tortellini in broth) to the exquisite guinea fowl stuffed with prosciutto and Parmigiano. Vegetarian options include a fragrant and tasty *flan di porcini al salsa di Parmigiano* (a mushroom flan with a delicate parmigiano sauce). [$] *Average main: €14* ✉ *Borgo XX Marzo 15* ☎ *0521/2061811* 🌐 *www.lafiloma.it* ✍ *Reservations essential* 🕓 *Closed Tues., and weekends July and Aug. No lunch Wed.*

$$ EMILIAN Fodor's Choice ★ 🍴 **Parizzi Ristorante.** Chef-owner Marco Parizzi is the third-generation cook in this elegant restaurant, which evolved from his grandfather's *salumeria* (delicatessen) into a restaurant serving Parmesan classics and contemporary cuisine. The *Piatti Tipici* (list of typical dishes) offers an *anolini in brodo di gallina e manzo* (stuffed pasta in meat broth), redolent with hints of nutmeg, that shouldn't be missed. Contemporary creations are tasty flights of fancy: *petto di anatra caramellato,* for one, beautifully pairs the decidedly non-Italian Jerusalem artichoke with caramelized duck breast served with a very Italian type of chicory. There are two tasting menus—"Terra" (earth) and "Mare" (sea)—and a well-priced wine list, culled by Marco's wife Cristina, with contemporary wines and

a section of "Rarità" collected by the two elder Parizzi. $ *Average main: €24* ⊠ *Strada Repubblica 71* ☎ *0521/285952* ⊕ *www.ristoranteparizzi.it* ⌒ *Reservations essential* ⊘ *Closed Mon., Aug., and Jan. 8–15.*

$

EMILIAN

Fodor'sChoice

★

✕**Tabarro.** Genial proprietor Diego Sorba jettisoned his academic career (he has a PhD in Irish literature) to follow his true calling: wine and food. His little wine bar on one of Parma's main drags has a couple of keg tables outside, a few stools on the ground floor, and a communal table upstairs. The simple food, based largely on porcine products—equine as well; people in this part of the world like to eat horse—is delicious, but it is meant mainly to pair with and accentuate the fine wines on offer. There are plenty of seriously good Italian wines to choose from, and there are also a fair number of French wines. The place is convivial, lively, and full of locals. $ *Average main: €12* ⊠ *Strada Farini 5/b* ☎ *3452/995013* ⊕ *www.tabarro.net* ⊘ *Closed Sun.*

$

EMILIAN

✕**TCafe.** The beauty of TCafe is that it does just about everything: the festivities begin with breakfast and end with evening aperitivi. Locals flock to this place, which once housed the aristocratic dalla Rosa Prati's art collection, to catch up on gossip, read the papers, and have lunch. That meal includes local specialties (among them plates of mortadella and culatello), a soup of the day, sandwiches, and tasty salads such as *petto d'anatra affumicato con misticanza e vinaigrette all'arancia* (smoked–duck breast salad with mixed greens and an orange vinaigrette). The lengthy wine list includes something for all tastes, as does the equally extensive list of artisanal beers. $ *Average main: €10* ⊠ *Strada, del Duomo 7* ☎ *0521/386429* ⊕ *www.temporarypalazzo.it.*

WHERE TO STAY

$$

HOTEL

Fodor'sChoice

★

🛏 **Palazzo dalla Rosa Prati.** Vittorio dalla Rosa Prati has converted part of his family's 15th-century palace on Piazza del Duomo into luxurious, self-catering accommodations, and those with connecting rooms are ideal for families. **Pros:** the hotel has an opera box at Teatro Regio that guests may reserve; Penhaligon's bath products; room service of continental breakfast included in the price. **Cons:** staff leave at 10 pm; parking can sometimes be a problem. $ *Rooms from: €185* ⊠ *Strada al Duomo 7* ☎ *0521/386429* ⊕ *www.palazzodallarosaprati.it* ↻ *7 rooms, 11 apartments* ⦿ *Breakfast.*

$

B&B/INN

🛏 **Parizzi Suites and Studio.** A 17th-century palace has been refurbished with 21st-century amenities to provide a lovely place to rest one's head. **Pros:** central location; great staff; breakfast served in rooms. **Cons:** staff not always at desk. $ *Rooms from: €100* ⊠ *Strada della Republica 71* ☎ *0521/207032* ⊕ *www.parizzisuite.it* ↻ *13 suites* ⦿ *Breakfast.*

MODENA

56 km (35 miles) southeast of Parma, 38 km (24 miles) northwest of Bologna.

Modena is famous for local products: Maserati, Ferrari, and opera star Luciano Pavarotti, born near here and buried in his family plot in Montale Rangone in 2007. However, it's Modena's heavenly scented balsamic vinegar, aged up to 40 years, that's probably its greatest achievement. The town has become another Emilian food mecca, with terrific restaurants and *salumerie* (delicatessens) at every turn. Though extensive modern industrial sprawl surrounds the city, the small historic center is filled with narrow medieval streets, pleasant piazzas, and typical Emilian architecture.

GETTING HERE AND AROUND
Modena, on the Bologna–Milan line, is easily accessible by train, and it's an easy walk from the station to the centro storico. The Intercity connection from Florence takes about 90 minutes. By car, Modena is just off the A1 autostrada.

VISITOR INFORMATION
Modena Tourism Office ⊠ *Piazza Grande, Via Scudari 8* ☎ *059/2032660* ⊕ *www.visitmodena.org.*

EXPLORING

Consorzio Produttori Aceto Balsamico Tradizionale di Modena. Connoisseurs of balsamic vinegar can arrange visits to local producers through the Consorzio. It's best to contact the organization via its website to set things up. ⊠ *Strada Vaciglio Sud 1085/1* ☎ *059/395633* ⊕ *www. balsamico.it* ⊐ *Free* ☉ *By appointment.*

Duomo. The 12th-century Romanesque cathedral was begun by the architect Lanfredo in 1099 and consecrated in 1184. Medieval sculptures depicting scenes from Genesis adorn the facade, but walk around to the Piazza Grande side as well to see the building's marvelous arcading. It's a rare example of a cathedral having more than one principal view. The interior, completely clad in brick, imparts a sober and beautiful feel. An elaborate gallery has scenes of the Passion of Christ carved by Anselmo da Campione and his assistants circa 1160–80. The tomb of San Geminiano is in the crypt. The white-marble bell tower is known as **La Torre Ghirlandina** (the Little Garland Tower) because of its distinctive weather vane. ⊠ *Piazza Grande* ☎ *059/216078* ⊕ *www. duomodimodena.it* ☉ *Daily 6:30–12:30 and 3:30–7.*

Galleria Ferrari. This museum has become a pilgrimage site for auto enthusiasts. It takes you through the illustrious history of Ferrari, from early 1951 models to the present—the legendary F50 and cars driven by Michael Schumacher in Formula One victories being highlights. You can also take a look at the glamorous life of founder Enzo Ferrari (a re-creation of his office is on site), and a glance into the production process. ⊠ *Via Dino Ferrari, Maranello, 17 km (11 miles) south of Modena* ☎ *0536/943204* ⊕ *www.museoferrari.com* ⊐ *€15* ☉ *Oct.–Apr., daily 9:30–6; May–Nov., daily 9:30–7.*

WHERE TO EAT

$ ✕ **Aldina.** On the second floor of a building across from the covered
EMILIAN market, steps from the Piazza Grande, this simple, typical trattoria is in the very nerve center of the city. Here you'll find exemplary preparations of the region's crown jewels: tortellini in brodo, tagliatelle al ragù, and roast meats. Wash it down with lambrusco, as locals have for ages, and save room for the *zuppa inglese* (layered sponge cake with custard), which is terrific. The kitchen also turns out dishes with *fantasia*, putting a contemporary twist on classics. $ *Average main: €10* ⊠ *Via Albinelli*

9

40 ☎ 059/236106 💳 No credit cards 🕓 Closed Sun., and July and Aug. No dinner Mon.–Thurs.

$ EMILIAN 🍴 **Ermes.** Ebullient host Ermes Rinaldi greets you as you walk in and seats you wherever he happens to have room—no matter that you might be put with people you don't know. It's part of the fun, as this quasi-communal style of lunching encourages conviviality. In the kitchen, Bruna, Ermes's wife, turns out splendid versions of *cucina casalinga modenesi* (home cooking, Modena style). Ermes recites the short list of primi and secondi, which change daily and arrive promptly. The accompanying wine is local, simple, and inexpensive: most stick to lambrusco. So it's no wonder this place is favored by everyone from suits to construction workers to students. [$] *Average main: €8* ✉ *Via Ganaceto 89–91* ☎ *059/238065* 💳 *No credit cards* 🕓 *Closed Sun. No dinner.*

$$$ EMILIAN Fodor's Choice ★ 🍴 **Hosteria Giusti.** In the back room of the Salumeria Giusti, established in 1605 and reportedly the world's oldest deli, you'll find four tables in a room tastefully done with antique furnishings. You'll also find some of the best food in Emilia Romagna—perfectly executed takes on traditional dishes. The *gnocco fritto* (fried dough) with *salumi* (cured meats) arrives as little clouds of lightly fried dough, topped with pancetta, or prosciutto, among other things. The anolini in brodo might feature the most fragrant broth in the world—inhale the aroma before tucking in. If you're tempted by too many things, half-portions may be available. Just leave room for dessert, especially *La Tassina*: served in a little espresso cup, it bursts with chocolate, anise, and egg. The wine list is divine, as is the staff. Reserve well ahead. [$] *Average main: €27* ✉ *Vicolo Squallore 46* ☎ *059/222533* 🌐 *www.hosteriagiusti.it* ✍ *Reservations essential* 🕓 *Closed Sun. and Mon. and Dec.–Jan. 10. No dinner.*

$ ECLECTIC 🍴 **Mon Café.** Locals swarm to this café, which does just about everything, and does it well. It opens at 7 in the morning, and offers tasty breakfast pastries; it closes late at night, and offers nightcaps. In between, lunch is served, as is dinner. Though Italian dishes are on the menu, the *fantasia* part of the menu is more fun. Tapas are served in two portions; the *petto di pollo dorato con carciofi* (lightly breaded and sautéed chicken breast with artichokes) is served in a zesty yogurt dressing and whets the appetite. You might want to follow it with *spaghettini con bocconcini di coda di rospo* (thin noodles with monkfish medallions), and conclude with the delicious *salame di cioccolato* (it looks like salami but is, in fact, made wholly of chocolate and served with a crème anglaise). The place comprises two rooms, showcasing temporary art series on their elephant-color walls. The wine list is winning, as is the service. [$] *Average main: €12* ✉ *Corso, Canalchiaro 128* ☎ *059/223257* 🌐 *www.mon-cafe.it* 🕓 *Closed Mon.*

$$$$ EMILIAN Fodor's Choice ★ 🍴 **Osteria Francescana.** Chef/proprietor Massimo Bottura says he learned about food from under his grandmother's table. He's done stints with Adria and Ducasse, takes inspiration from music and literature, and pours all these influences into creating some of the most memorable food in all of Italy while remaining true to his Modenese roots. The restaurant contains only 11 tables. Colors are muted, and service is superior. Though it's possible to order à la carte, most everyone opts for one of the three tasting menus—Tradizioni, Classici, and Sensazioni

Continued on page 514

EMILIA
ONE TASTE AT A TIME

4 towns, dozens of foods, and a mouthful of flavors you'll never forget

Imagine biting into the silkiest prosciutto in the world or the most delectable homemade tortellini you've ever tasted. In Emilia, Italy's most famous food region, you'll discover simple tastes that exceed all expectations. Beginning in Parma and moving eastward to Bologna, you'll find the epicenters of such world-renowned culinary treats as *prosciutto crudo*, Parmigiano-Reggiano, *aceto balsamico*, and tortellini. The secret to this region is not the discovery of new and exotic delicacies, but rather the rediscovery of foods you thought you already knew—in much better versions than you've ever tasted before.

TASTE 1 | PROSCIUTTO CRUDO

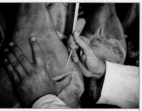
Quality testing

From Piacenza to the Adriatic, ham is the king of meats in Emilia-Romagna, but nowhere is this truer than in **Parma**.

Parma is the world's capital of *prosciutto crudo*, raw cured ham (*crudo* for short). Ask for *crudo di Parma* to signal its local provenance; many other regions also make their own crudo.

CRUDO LANGUAGE

It's easy to get confused with the terminology. Crudo is the product that Americans simply call "prosciutto" or the Brits might call "Parma ham." *Prosciutto* in Italian, however, is a more general term that means any kind of ham, including *prosciutto cotto*, or simply *cotto*, which means "cooked ham." Cotto is an excellent product and frequent pizza topping that's closer to (but much better than) what Americans would put in a deli sandwich.

Greasing the ham

Crudo is traditionally eaten in one of three ways: in a dry sandwich (*panino*); by itself as an appetizer, often with shaved butter on top; or as part of an appetizer or snack platter of assorted *salumi* (cured meats).

WHAT TO LOOK FOR

For the best crudo di Parma, look for slices, always cut to order, that are razor thin and have a light, rosy red color (not dark red). Don't be shy about going into a simple *salumeria* (a purveyor of cured meats) and ordering crudo by the pound. You can enjoy it straight out of the package on a park bench—and why not?

Fire branding

BEST SPOT FOR A SAMPLE

You can't go wrong with any of Parma's famed salumerie, but **Salumeria Garibaldi** is one of the town's oldest and most reliable. You'll find not only spectacular prosciutto crudo, but also delectable cheeses, wines, porcini mushrooms, and more.

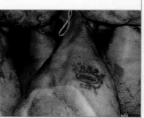
Quality trademark

LEARN MORE

For more information on crudo di Parma, contact the **Consorzio del Prosciutto di Parma** through the tourist office, or stop by the famous store, La Prosciutteria.

TASTE 2 | PARMIGIANO-REGGIANO

From Parma, it's only a half-hour trip east to **Reggio Emilia**, the birthplace of the crumbly and renowned Parmigiano-Reggiano cheese. Reggio (not to be confused with Reggio di Calabria in the south) is a charming little Emilian town that has been the center of production for this legendary cheese for more than 70 years.

SAY CHEESE
Grana is the generic Italian term for hard, aged, full-flavored cheese that can be grated. Certain varieties of Pecorino Romano, for example, or Grana Padano, also fall under this term, but Parmigiano-Reggiano, aged for as long as four years, is the foremost example.

NOT JUST FOR GRATING
In Italy, Parmigiano-Reggiano is not only grated onto pasta, but also often served by itself in chunks, either as an appetizer—perhaps accompanied by local salumi (cured meats)—or even for dessert, when it might be drizzled with honey or Modena's balsamic vinegar.

MEET THE MAKERS
If you're a cheese enthusiast, you shouldn't miss the chance to take a free two-hour guided tour of a Parmigiano-Reggiano–producing farm. You'll witness the entire process and get to meet the cheesemakers. Tours can be arranged by contacting the **Consorzio del Formaggio Parmigiano-Reggiano** in Reggio Emilia at least 20 days in advance. (Ask specifically for an English-language tour if that's what you want.)

BEST SPOT FOR A SAMPLE
The production of Parmigiano-Reggiano is heavily controlled by the Consorzio del Formaggio, so you can buy the cheese at any store or supermarket in the region and be virtually guaranteed equal quality and price. For a more distinctive shopping experience, however, try buying Parmigiano-Reggiano at the street market on Reggio's central square. The market takes place on Tuesday and Friday from 8 AM to 1 PM year-round. You can pick up a small piece to eat while you're in Italy, or have larger pieces shrink-wrapped to take home.

Warming milk in copper cauldrons

Breaking up the curds

Placing cheese in molds

Aging cheese wheels

Parmigiano-Reggiano

TASTE 3 | ACETO BALSAMICO DI MODENA

Tasting tradizionale vinegar

Modena is home to *Aceto Balsamico Tradizionale di Modena*, a kind of balsamic vinegar unparalleled anywhere else on Earth. The balsamic vinegar you've probably tried—even the pricier versions sold at specialty stores—may be good on salads, but it bears only a fleeting resemblance to the real thing.

HOW IS IT MADE?

The *tradizionale* vinegar that passes strict government standards is made with Trebbiano grape must, which is cooked over an open fire, reduced, and fermented from 12 to 25 or more years in a series of specially made wooden casks. As the vinegar becomes more concentrated, so much liquid evaporates that it takes more than 6 gallons of must to produce one quart of vinegar 12 years later. The result is an intense and syrupy concoction best enjoyed sparingly on grilled meats, strawberries, or Parmigiano-Reggiano cheese. The vinegar has such a complexity of flavor that some even drink it as an after-dinner liqueur.

Wooden casks for fermenting

BEST SPOT FOR A SAMPLE

The **Consorzio Produttori Aceto Balsamico Tradizionale di Modena** offers tours and tastings by reservation only. The main objective of the consortium is to monitor the quality of the authentic balsamic vinegar, made by only a few licensed restaurants and small producers.

The consortium also limits production, keeping prices sky high. Expect to pay €60 for a 100-ml (3.4 oz) bottle of tradizionale, which is generally aged 12 to 15 years, or €90 and up for the older tradizionale extra vecchio variety, which is aged 25 years.

But perhaps the best place to sample this vinegar, in its various stages and permutations, is in situ—that is, in any one of Modena's remarkable restaurants. You can have a simple trattoria meal at Ermes, whose recipes rely heavily on that liquid gold. Or you can splurge at Osteria Francescana, where three-starred Michelin chef Massimo Bottura works miracles with local ingredients.

OTHER TASTES OF EMILIA

❑ **Cotechino**: a sausage made from pork and lard, a specialty of Modena

❑ **Culatello de Zibello**: raw cured ham produced along the banks of the Po River, and cured and aged for more than 11 months

❑ **Mortadella**: soft, smoked sausage made with beef, pork, cubes of pork fat, and seasonings, a specialty of Bologna

❑ **Ragù**: a sauce made from minced pork and beef, simmered in milk, onions, carrots, and tomatoes

❑ **Salama da sugo**: salty, oily sausage aged and then cooked, a specialty of Ferrara

❑ **Tortelli and cappellacci**: pasta pillows with the same basic form as tortellini, but stuffed with cheese and vegetables

TASTE 4 | TORTELLINI

The venerable city of **Bologna** is called "the Fat" for a reason: this is the birthplace of tortellini, not to mention other specialties such as mortadella and ragù. Despite the city's new reputation for chic nightclubs and flashy boutiques, much of the food remains as it ever was.

You'll find the many Emilian variations on stuffed pasta all over the region, but they're perhaps at their best in Bologna, especially the native tortellini.

INSPIRED BY THE GODS
According to one legend, tortellini was inspired by the navel of Venus, goddess of love. As the story goes, Venus and some other gods stopped at a local inn for the night. A nosy chef went to their room to catch a glimpse of Venus. Peering through the keyhole, he saw her lying only partially covered on the bed. He was so inspired after seeing her perfect navel that he created a stuffed pasta, tortellini, in its image.

Stretching the dough

ON THE MENU
Tortellini is usually filled with beef (sometimes cheese), and is served two ways: *asciutta* is "dry," meaning it is served with a sauce such as ragù, or perhaps just with butter and Parmigiano. *Tortellini in brodo* is immersed in a lovely, savory beef broth.

Adding the filling

Tortellini alla panna contains a meat filling and is sauced with cream. Aficionados, however, argue frequently about what to stuff into these little bundles, and probably no two cooks do it the same. Some purists insist that only beef will do; others mix it up with sausages, mortadella, spices, and cheese (usually Parmigiano).

Shaping each piece

BEST SPOT TO BUY
Don't miss **Tamburini**, Bologna's best specialty food shop, where aromas of Emilia-Romagna's famous specialties waft out through the room and into the streets.

Tortellini di Bologna

(Traditional, Classic, and Sensational). One signature dish is *5 stagionature di Parmigiano Reggiano* (five versions of Parmesan in various stages, served in five different textures and temperatures). Bottura's *tortellini alla crema* is light, delicate, and perhaps the definitive version of this dish. 💲 *Average main: €110* ✉ *Via Stella 22* ☎ *059/223912* ⊕ *www.osteriafrancescana.it* ⌂ *Reservations essential* ⊙ *Closed Sun. No lunch Sat.*

WHERE TO STAY

$$
B&B/INN
Fodor's Choice
★

Quarto Piano. Proprietors Antonio di Resta and Alessandro Bertoni have combined their impeccable sense of style and love of things French to produce a lovely little bed-and-breakfast located just a few steps away from the Duomo. **Pros:** intimate (just two rooms); lovely bath products; fluffy towels. **Cons:** only two rooms—it books up quickly. 💲 *Rooms from: €140* ✉ *Via Bonacorsa 27* ☎ *059/8755487* ⊕ *www. bbquartopiano.it* ➵ *2 rooms* ⊙ *Closed Aug.* ❍ *Breakfast.*

BOLOGNA

Bologna, a city rich with cultural jewels, has long been one of the best-kept secrets in northern Italy. Tourists in the know can bask in the shadow of its leaning medieval towers and devour the city's wonderful food.

The charm of the centro storico, with its red-arcaded passageways and sidewalks, can be attributed to wise city counselors who, at the beginning of the 13th century, decreed that roads couldn't be built without *portici* (porticoes). Were these counselors to return to town eight centuries later, they'd marvel at how little has changed.

Bologna, with a population of about 373,000, has a university-town vibe—and it feels young and lively in a way that many other Italian cities don't. It also feels full of Italians in a way that many other towns, thronged with tourists, don't. Bolognesi come out at aperitivo time, and you might be struck by the fact that it's not just youngsters who are out doing the passeggiata, or having a glass of wine with *affettati misti* (mixed cured meats).

From as early as the Middle Ages the town was known as "Bologna the Fat" for the agricultural prosperity that resulted in a well-fed population. In the 21st century Bolognese food remains, arguably, the best in Italy. With its sublime cuisine, lively spirit, and largely undiscovered art, Bologna is a memorable destination.

GETTING HERE AND AROUND

Frequent train service from Florence to Bologna makes getting here easy. The *Italo* and *Frecciarossa* and *Frecciaargento* (high-speed trains) run several times an hour and take just under 40 minutes. If you're driving from Florence, take the A1, exiting onto the A14, and then get on the RA1 to Uscita 7–Bologna Centrale. The trip takes about an hour. From Milan, take the A1, exiting to the A14 as you near the city; from there, take the A13 and exit at Bologna; then follow the RA1 to Uscita 7–Bologna Centrale. The trip takes just under three hours.

VISITOR INFORMATION

Bologna Tourism Offices ✉ *Aeroporto di Bologna* ☎ *051/6472113* ⊕ *www.bolognawelcome.it* ✉ *Piazza Maggiore 1* ☎ *051/239660* ⊕ *www.bolognawelcome.it.*

EXPLORING

Piazza Maggiore and the adjacent Piazza del Nettuno are the historic centers of the city. Arranged around these two squares are the imposing Basilica di San Petronio, the massive Palazzo Comunale, the Palazzo del Podestà, the Palazzo Re Enzo, and the Fontana del Nettuno—one of the most visually harmonious groupings of public buildings in the country. From here, sights that aren't on one of the piazzas are but a short walk away, along delightful narrow cobblestone streets or under the ubiquitous arcades that double as municipal umbrellas. Take at least a full day to explore Bologna; it's compact and lends itself to easy exploration, but there's plenty to see.

TOP ATTRACTIONS

Basilica di San Petronio. Construction on this vast cathedral began in 1390; and the work, as you can see, still isn't finished more than 600 years later. The wings of the transept are missing and the facade is only partially decorated, lacking most of the marble that was intended to adorn it. The main doorway was carved in 1425 by the great Sienese master Jacopo della Quercia. Above the center of the door is a Madonna and Child flanked by saints Ambrose and Petronius, the city's patrons. Michelangelo, Giulio Romano, and Andrea Palladio (among others), submitted designs for the facade, which were all eventually rejected.

The interior of the basilica is huge. The Bolognesi had planned an even bigger church—you can see the columns erected to support the larger version outside the east end—but had to tone down construction when the university seat was established next door in 1561. The **Museo di San Petronio** contains models showing how it was originally supposed to look. The most important art in the church is in the fourth chapel on the left: these frescoes by Giovanni da Modena date 1410–15. ✉ *Piazza Maggiore* ☎ *051/22544* 🎫 *Free* ☉ *Church: daily 7:45–1 and 3–6. Museum: weekdays 9:30–12:30 and 3–5:30, Sat. 9:30–12:30 and 3–4:30, Sun. 3–5:30.*

Fontana del Nettuno. Sculptor Giambologna's elaborate 1563–66 Baroque fountain and monument to Neptune occupying Piazza Nettuno has been aptly nicknamed "Il Gigante" (The Giant). Its exuberantly sensual mermaids and undraped God of the sea drew fire when it was constructed, but not enough, apparently, to dissuade the populace from using the fountain as a public washing stall for centuries. ✉ *Piazza del Nettuno, next to Palazzo Re Enzo.*

Le Due Torri. Two landmark towers, mentioned by Dante in *The Inferno*, stand side by side in the compact Piazza di Porta Ravegnana. Once every family of importance had a tower as a symbol of prestige and power—and as a potential fortress. Now only 60 remain out of more than 200 that once presided over the city. **Torre Garisenda** (from the late 11th century), which tilts 10 feet off perpendicular, was shortened to 165 feet in the 1300s and is now closed to visitors. **Torre degli**

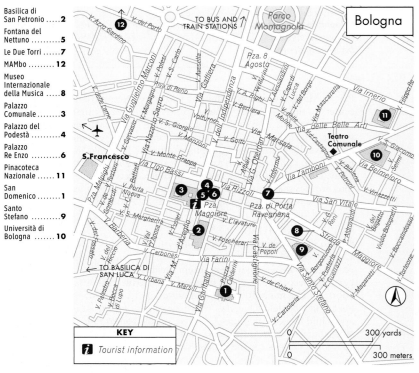

Asinelli (circa 1109) is 320 feet tall and leans 7½ feet. If you're up to a serious physical challenge—and not claustrophobic—you may want to climb its 500 narrow wooden steps to get the view over Bologna. ⊠ *Piazza di Porta Ravegnana, east of Piazza Maggiore* 🎫 *€3* ⏱ *Torre degli Asinelli daily 9–5.*

FAMILY

Fodor's Choice ★

Santo Stefano. This splendid and unusual basilica contains between four and seven connected churches (authorities differ). A 4th-century temple dedicated to Isis originally occupied this site, but much of what you see was erected between the 10th and 12th centuries. The oldest existing building is **Santi Vitale e Agricola,** parts of which date from the 5th century. The exquisite beehive-shape San Sepolcro contains a Nativity scene much loved by Bologna's children, who come at Christmastime to pay their respects to the Christ child. Just outside the church, which probably dates from the 5th century (with later alterations), is the **Cortile di Pilato** (Pilate's Courtyard), named for the basin in the center. Despite the fact that the basin was probably crafted around the 8th century, legend has it that Pontius Pilate washed his hands in it after condemning Christ. Also in the building are a museum displaying various medieval religious works and its shop, which sells honey, shampoos, and jams made by the monks. ⊠ *Via Santo Stefano 24, Piazza Santo Stefano, University area* ☎ *051/223256* ⏱ *Daily 9–noon and 3:30–6.*

Università di Bologna. Take a stroll through the streets of the university area: a jumble of buildings, some dating as far back as the 15th century and most to the 17th and 18th. The neighborhood, as befits a college town, is full of bookshops, coffee bars, and inexpensive restaurants. Though not particularly distinguished, they're characteristic of student life in the city. Try eating at the *mensa universitaria* (cafeteria) if you want to strike up a conversation with local students (most speak English). Political slogans and sentiments are scrawled on walls all around the university and tend to be ferociously leftist, sometimes juvenile, and often entertaining. Among the university museums, the most interesting is the **Museo di Palazzo Poggi,** which displays scientific instruments plus paleontological, botanical, and university-related artifacts. ⊠ *Via Zamboni 33, University area* ☎ *051/2099610* ⊕ *www.museopalazzopoggi.unibo.it* ⌸ *€3* ☾ *Museum: Tues.–Fri. 10–1 and 2–4, weekends 10:30–1:30 and 2:30–5:30.*

WORTH NOTING

MAMbo. The name of this museum stands for Museo d'Arte Moderna di Bologna, or Bologna's Museum of Modern Art. It houses a permanent collection of modern art (defined as post–World War II until five minutes ago) and stages a revolving series of temporary exhibitions by cutting-edge artists. All of this is set within a remarkable space: you might have a hard time telling that the sleek minimalist structure was built in 1915 as the Forno del Pane, a large bakery that made bread for city residents. A bookshop and a restaurant complete the complex, the latter offering Sunday brunch and delicious aperitivi. ⊠ *Via Don Minzoni 14* ☎ *051/6496611* ⊕ *www.mambo-bologna.org* ⌸ *€6* ☾ *Tues., Wed., and Fri. noon–6, Thurs. and weekends noon–8.*

Museo Internazionale e Biblioteca della Musica di Bologna. The music museum in the spectacular Palazzo Aldini Sanguinetti, with its 17th- and 18th-century frescoes, offers among its exhibits a 1606 harpsichord and a collection of beautiful music manuscripts dating from the 1500s. ⊠ *Strada Maggiore 34, University area* ☎ *051/2757720* ⊕ *www.museomusicabologna. it* ⌸ *Free* ☾ *Oct.–July, Tues.–Fri. 9:30–4, weekends 10–6:30.*

Palazzo Comunale. A mélange of building styles and constant modifications characterize this huge palace dating from the 13th to 15th century. When Bologna was an independent city-state, this was the seat of government—a function it still serves today. Over the door is a statue of Bologna-born Pope Gregory XIII (reigned 1572–85), most famous for reorganizing the calendar. There are good views from the upper stories of the palace. The first-floor **Sala Rossa** (Red Room) is open on advance request and during some exhibitions, and the **Sala del Consiglio Comunale** (City Council Hall) is open to the public for a few hours in the late morning. The old stock exchange, part of the Palazzo Comunale, which you enter from Piazza Nettuno, has been turned into a library. Dubbed the **Sala Borsa** (⊕ *www.bibliotecasalaborsa.it*), it has an impressive interior courtyard. Within the palazzo are two museums. The **Collezioni Comunali d'Arte** exhibits paintings from the Middle Ages as well as some Renaissance works by Luca Signorelli (circa 1445–1523) and Tintoretto (1518–94). The **Museo Giorgio Morandi** is dedicated to the 20th-century still-life artist Giorgio Morandi. Underground caves and the foundations of the old cathedral can be visited by appointment made through the tourist office. ⌧ *Piazza Maggiore 6* ☎ *051/2194400 Palazzo/Sala Borsa* 🎫 *€5, except during special art exhibitions* ⊙ *Sala del Consiglio Comunale: Tues.–Sat. 10–1. Sala Borsa: Tues.–Fri. 10–8, Sat. 10–7.*

Palazzo del Podestà. This classic Renaissance palace facing the Basilica di San Petronio was erected in 1484, and attached to it is the soaring **Torre dell'Arengo.** The bells in the tower have rung whenever the city has celebrated, mourned, or called its citizens to arms. ⌧ *Piazza del Nettuno* ⊙ *During exhibitions only.*

Palazzo Re Enzo. Built in 1244, this palace became home to King Enzo of Sardinia, who was imprisoned here in 1249 after he was captured during the fierce battle of Fossalta. He died here 23 years later. The palace has other macabre associations as well: common criminals received last rites in the tiny courtyard chapel before being executed in Piazza Maggiore. The courtyard is worth peeking into, but the palace merely houses government offices. ⌧ *Piazza Re Enzo, Piazza Maggiore area* ☎ *051/637 5111* ⊙ *During exhibitions only.*

Pinacoteca Nazionale. Bologna's principal art gallery contains many works by the immortals of Italian painting. Its prize possession is the *Ecstasy of St. Cecilia* by Raphael (1483–1520). There's also a beautiful polyptych by Giotto (1267–1337), as well as *Madonna and Child with Saints Margaret, Jerome, and Petronio* by Parmigianino (1503–1540): note the rapt eye contact between St. Margaret and the Christ Child. ⌧ *Via delle Belle Arti 56, University area* ☎ *051/4209411* ⊕ *www. pinacotecabologna.beniculturali.it* 🎫 *€4* ⊙ *Tues.–Sun. 9–7.*

San Domenico. The tomb of St. Dominic, who died here in 1221, is called the **Arca di San Domenico,** and is found in this church in the sixth chapel on the right. Many artists participated in its decoration, notably Niccolò di Bari, who was so proud of his 15th-century contribution that he changed his name to Niccolò dell'Arca to recall this famous work. The young Michelangelo (1475–1564) carved the angel on the right. In the right transept of the church is a tablet marking the last resting place of hapless King Enzo, the Sardinian ruler imprisoned in the Palazzo Re Enzo. The attached museum contains religious relics. ⌧ *Piazza San Domenico 13, off Via Garibaldi, south of Piazza Maggiore* ☎ *051/6400411* ⊕ *www.conventosandomenico.org* ⊙ *Church: daily 8–12:30 and 3:30–6:30. Museum: weekdays 10–noon and 3:30–6, Sat. 9:30–noon and 3:30–5:30, Sun. 3:30–5:30.*

WHERE TO EAT

. $$
EMILIAN
Fodor'sChoice
★

✕ **Da Cesari.** Just off Piazza Maggiore, this one-room restaurant has white tablecloths, dark-wood paneling, and wine bottle–lined walls. Host Paolino Cesari has been presiding over his eatery since 1955, and he and his staff go out of their way to make you feel at home. The food's terrific—if you love pork products, try anything on the menu with *mora romagnola.* Paolino has direct contact with the people who raise this breed that nearly became extinct (he calls it "my pig"). The highly flavorful meat makes divine salame, among other things. All the usual Bolognese classics are here, as well as—in fall and winter—an inspired *scaloppa all Petroniano* (veal cutlet with prosciutto and fontina) that comes smothered in white truffles. [$] *Average main: €15* ✉ *Via de' Carbonesi 8, south of Piazza Maggiore* ☎ *051/237710* 🌐 *www.da-cesari.it* ✍ *Reservations essential* ⏲ *Closed Sun., Aug., and 1 wk in Jan.*

$$ EMILIAN 🍴 **Da Gianni a la Vecia Bulagna.** Locals simply call it "da Gianni," and they fill these two unadorned rooms at lunch and dinner. Though the interior is plain and unremarkable, it doesn't much matter—this place is all about food. The usual starters such as a tasty tortellini in brodo are on hand, as are daily specials such as gnocchi made with pumpkin, then sauced with melted cheese. *Bollito misto* (mixed meats boiled in a rich broth) is a fine option here, and the *cotechino con purè di patate* (a deliciously oily sausage with mashed potatoes) is elevated to sublimity by the accompanying salsa verde. [$] *Average main: €16* ✉ *Via Clavature 18, Piazza Maggiore area* ☎ *051/229434* ✍ *Reservations essential* ⏲ *Closed Mon. No dinner Sun.*

$ ITALIAN 🍴 **Divinis.** Bottles lining the walls on both floors of this spot are a testimony to its commitment to serving fine wines, whether by the glass or by the bottle. The wine list runs to 102 pages—and terrific food accompanies the wines. Cheese and cured meat plates are on offer, as are superlative soups, salads, and secondi on a menu that changes frequently. Special events, such as wine tastings and tango dancing, happen throughout the week. Divinis's continuous opening hours, a rarity in Italy, are an added plus. You could have a coffee at 11 am or a glass of wine well after midnight. [$] *Average main: €12* ✉ *Via Battibecco 4/c, Piazza Maggiore* ☎ *051/2961502* 🌐 *www.divinis.it* ✍ *Reservations essential* ⏲ *Closed Sun.*

$ MODERN EUROPEAN 🍴 **Marco Fadiga Bistrot.** If you're looking for terrific food and something out of the ordinary—an Italian restaurant that also serves non-Italian food—dine at this French-styled *bistrot*: a warren of brilliantly colored rooms lit by chandelier. Chef Marco Fadiga has spent much time in England and France, and their culinary influences show. What's on offer each night is written on a blackboard, which is brought to the table. You can have marvelous raw oysters, as well as the *plateau* (a very un-Italian assortment of raw things from the sea). Traditionalists will thrill to his tortellini in brodo, and adventurous sorts might like the *tartare di orata* (sea bream tartare) served with fresh and candied fruit. [$] *Average main: €14* ✉ *Via Rialto 23/c, Piazza Maggiore area* ☎ *051/220118* 🌐 *www.marcofadigabistrot.it* ✍ *Reservations essential* ⏲ *Closed Sun. and Mon. No lunch.*

$ WINE BAR Fodor's Choice ★ 🍴 **Tamburini.** Two small rooms inside plus kegs and bar stools outside make up this lively, packed little spot. At lunchtime, office workers swarm to the "bistrot self service" for remarkably tasty primi and secondi. After lunch, Tamburini becomes a wine bar with a vast array of selections by the glass and the bottle. The overwhelming plate of *affettati misti* is crammed with top-quality local ham products and succulent cheeses (including, sometimes, a goat Brie). An adjacent *salumeria* offers many wonderful things to take away. [$] *Average main: €10* ✉ *Via Drapperie 1, Piazza Maggiore area* ☎ *051/234726* ⏲ *No dinner.*

$ EMILIAN 🍴 **Trattoria del Rosso.** Although its interior—glaring yellow walls and the oddly placed ceramic plate—is nothing to write home about, this trattoria pulls in the locals. A mostly young crowd chows down on basic

9

regional fare at rock-bottom prices. Nimble staff bearing multiple plates sashay neatly between the closely spaced tables delivering such standards as *crescentine con salumi e squacquerone* (deep-fried flour puffs with cured meats and soft cheese) and tortellini in brodo. It is the kind of place where there's always a line of hungry people outside waiting to get in, but where the waiters don't glare at you if you only order a plate of pasta: another reason, perhaps, why it's a favorite of university students. $ *Average main: €9* ⊠ *Via Augusto Righi 30, University area* ☎ *051/236730* ⊕ *www.trattoriadelrosso.com* ☾ *Closed Thurs.*

$ ✕ **Trattoria di Via Serra.** The only disadvantage of this trattoria is that it's
EMILIAN   not in the centro storico. A plus, however, is that it's minutes away from the train station, which makes a detour here while in transit well worth it—and even when you're not. Much care has been taken with the décor: the rooms, overseen by host Flavio, are small and intimate, and the walls are of wood painted a creamy whitish gray. Even more care has been taken with the menu. The chef, Tommaso, deftly turns out Bolognese classics as well as dishes with great *fantasia*. His *tosone fresco avvolta nella pancetta* is basically spun sugar, though his medium is Parmesan, with unsmoked bacon and greens. Save room for dessert. $ *Average main: €13* ⊠ *Via Serra 9B, beyond the City Center* ☎ *051/3612330* ⚛ *Reservations essential* ☾ *Closed Mon. No lunch Tues.–Thurs.*

WHERE TO STAY

$ ⊞ **Albergo Centrale.** A stone's throw from Piazza Maggiore, this place
HOTEL   that started out as a pensione in 1875 has been brought firmly into the 21st century and offers the winning combination of comfort, affordability, and some family-size rooms. **Pros:** very good value; excellent location. **Cons:** might be too plain for some tastes; street-facing rooms can get some noise. $ *Rooms from: €89* ⊠ *Via della Zecca 2, Piazza Maggiore* ☎ *051/225114* ⊕ *www.albergocentralebologna.it* ⤳ *31 rooms (26 with bath)* ❍| *Breakfast.*

$$ ⊞ **Art Hotel Novecento.** This swank place, inspired by the 1930s Viennese
HOTEL   Secession movement, is in a serene cul-de-sac just minutes from Piazza
Fodor's Choice   Maggiore. **Pros:** spacious single rooms ideal for solo travelers; friendly,
★   capable concierge service; sumptuous buffet breakfast. **Cons:** some standard doubles are small; might be too trendy for some. $ *Rooms from: €140* ⊠ *Piazza Galileo 4/3, Piazza Maggiore area* ☎ *051/7457311* ⊕ *www.bolognarthotels.it/novecento* ⤳ *24 rooms, 1 suite* ❍| *Breakfast.*

$ ⊞ **Art Hotel Orologio.** The location of this stylish and welcoming hotel
HOTEL   can't be beat: it's right around the corner from Piazza Maggiore on a
Fodor's Choice   quiet side street. **Pros:** central location; family-friendly rooms; welcomes
★   all animals. **Cons:** some steps to elevator; pet-friendly environment may not appeal to allergy sufferers. $ *Rooms from: €120* ⊠ *Via IV Novembre 10, Piazza Maggiore area* ☎ *051/7457411* ⊕ *www.bolognarthotels. it/orologio* ⤳ *26 rooms, 6 suites, 1 apartment* ❍| *Breakfast.*

NIGHTLIFE AND PERFORMING ARTS

NIGHTLIFE

As a university town, Bologna has long been known for its busy nightlife. As early as 1300 it was said to have 150 taverns. Most of the city's current 200-plus pubs and bars are frequented by Italian students, young adults, and international students, with the university district forming the hub. In addition to the university area, the pedestrian zone on Via del Pratello, lined with plenty of bars, has a hopping nightlife scene; as does Via delle Moline, which promises cutting-edge cafés and bars. A more upscale, low-key evening experience can be had at one of Bologna's many wine bars, where the food is often substantial enough to constitute dinner.

BARS

Bar Calice. A year-round indoor-outdoor operation (with heat lamps), this bar is extremely popular with thirtysomethings, sometimes pushing baby carriages. Its large menu includes raw oysters. ☒ *Via Clavature 13/a, at Via Marchesana, Piazza Maggiore area* ☎ *051/6569296.*

Fodor'sChoice **Nu Bar Lounge.** This high-energy place draws a cocktail-loving crowd
★ that enjoys fun drinks such as "I'm Too Sexy for This Place," a combination of vodka, triple sec, apple juice, and lemon. ☒ *Via de' Musei 6, off Buca San Petronio, Piazza Maggiore area* ☎ *051/222532* ⊕ *www. nu-lounge.com.*

Osteria del Sole. Though "osteria" in an establishment's name suggests that food will be served, such is not the case here. This place is all about drinking wine; the entrance has warnings posted, such as "He who doesn't drink will please stay outside" and "Dogs who don't drink are forbidden to come in." It's been around since 1465, and locals pack in, bearing food from outside to accompany the wine. ☒ *Vicolo Ranocchi 1/d, Piazza Maggiore* ☎ *347/9680171* ⊕ *www.osteriadelsole.it.*

CAFÉS

Zanarini. Chic Bolognesi congregate at this bar that serves coffee in the morning and swank aperitivi in the evening. Tasty sandwiches and pastries are also available. ☒ *Piazza Galvani 1* ☎ *051/2750041.*

MUSIC VENUES

Cantina Bentivoglio. With live music staged every evening, Cantina Bentivoglio is one of Bologna's most appealing nightspots. You can enjoy light and more substantial meals here as well. ☒ *Via Mascarella 4/b, University area* ☎ *051/265416* ⊕ *www.cantinabentivoglio.it.*

Osteria Buca delle Campane. In a 13th-century building, this underground tavern has good, inexpensive food and the after-dinner scene is popular with locals, including students, who come to listen to live music. The kitchen stays open until long past midnight. Reservations are strongly advised. ☒ *Via Benedetto XIV 4/a, University area* ☎ *051/220918* ⊕ *www.bucadellecampane.it.*

PERFORMING ARTS

MUSIC AND OPERA

Teatro Comunale. This 18th-century theater presents concerts by Italian and international orchestras throughout the year, but the highly acclaimed opera performances from November through May are the main attraction. Reserve seats for them well in advance. ✉ *Largo Respighi 1, University area* ☎ *051/529958* ⊕ *www.tcbo.it* ⊙ *Ticket office Tues.–Sat. 10–2.*

SHOPPING

CLOTHING

Castel Guelfo Outlet City. If you don't feel like paying Galleria Cavour prices, this mall is about 20 minutes outside Bologna on the A14 auto-strada toward Imola (take the Castel San Pietro Terme exit; 980 feet after the tollbooth, turn right onto Via San Carlo). It includes about 50 discounted stores, some from top designers such as Ferré. ✉ *Via del Commercio 20/a, Loc. Poggio Piccolo, Castel Guelfo* ☎ *0542/670765* ⊕ *www.thestyleoutlets.it* ⊙ *Closed Mon. morning.*

Galleria Cavour. One of the most upscale malls in Italy, the Galleria houses many of the fashion giants, including Gucci, Versace, and jew-eler-watchmaker Bulgari. ✉ *Via Luigi Carlo Farini, south of Piazza Maggiore* ⊕ *www.galleriacavour.net.*

WINE AND FOOD

Bologna is a good place to buy wine. Several shops have a bewilder-ingly large selection—to go straight to the top, ask the managers which wines have won the prestigious Tre Bicchieri (Three Glasses) award from Gambero Rosso's wine bible, *Vini d'Italia.*

Eataly. At this lively shop with an attached bookstore you can grab a bite to eat or have a glass of wine while stocking up on high-quality olive oil, vinegar, cured meats, and artisanal pasta. On the top floor, you have a full-fledged trattoria meal, but what you can't have is anything decaffeinated: it's considered "chemical." ✉ *Via degli Orafici 19, Piazza Maggiore area* ☎ *051/0952820* ⊕ *www.eataly.it.*

Enoteca Italiana. Consistently recognized as one of the best wine stores in the country, Enoteca Italiana lives up to its reputation with shelves lined with excellent selections from all over Italy at reasonable prices. The delicious sandwiches, served with wines by the glass, make a great light lunch. ✉ *Via Marsala 2/b, north of Piazza Maggiore* ☎ *051/235989* ⊕ *www.enotecaitaliana.it.*

La Baita. Fresh tagliolini, tortellini, and other Bolognese pasta delicacies are sold here, along with sublime food to take away. The cheese counter is laden with superlative local specimens. ✉ *Via Pescherie Vecchia 3/a, Piazza Maggiore area* ☎ *051/223940.*

Le Dolcezze. If you favor sweets, head to Le Dolcezze, a top local *pastic-ceria* (pastry shop). Its cakes are excellent and the *panettone* (a sweet bread produced only around Christmas) is considered by some to be the best in town. ✉ *Via Murri 121, Piazza Maggiore area* ☎ *051/444582.*

Majani. Classy Majani has been producing chocolate since 1796. Its staying power may be attributed to high-quality candies that are as nice to look at as they are to eat. ✉ *Via de'Carbonesi 5, Piazza Maggiore area* ☎ *051/234302* ⊕ *www.majani.com.*

Mercato delle Erbe. This food market that's more than a century old bustles year-round. ⊠ *Via Ugo Bassi 25, Piazza Maggiore area* ☎ *051/230186* ⊕ *www.mercatodelleerbe.it* ☉ *Mon.–Wed. and Fri. 7–1:15 and 5–7:30 (4:30–7:30 Oct.–Mar.), Thurs. and Sat. 7–1:15.*

Fodor's Choice ★ **Mercato di Mezzo.** Formerly a fruit and vegetable market, the Mercato has morphed into a food hall. Various stalls offer the best that Bologna has to offer, and the Bolognesi are gobbling it up. Order from whatever place strikes your fancy, and sit anywhere there's room. ⊠ *Via Peschiere Vecchie, Piazza Maggiore area.*

Paolo Atti & Figli. This place has been producing some of Bologna's finest pastas, cakes, and other delicacies for more than 130 years. ⊠ *Via Caprarie 7, Piazza Maggiore area* ☎ *051/220425* ⊕ *www.paoloatti.com.*

Fodor's Choice ★ **Roccati.** Sculptural works of chocolate, as well as basic bonbons and simpler sweets, have been crafted here since 1909. ⊠ *Via Clavature 17/a, Piazza Maggiore area* ☎ *051/261964* ⊕ *www.roccaticioccolato.com.*

Scaramagli. Friendly owners run this midsize, down-to-earth wine store. ⊠ *Strada Maggiore 31/d, University area* ☎ *051/227132* ⊕ *www.scaramagli.it.*

FERRARA

47 km (29 miles) northeast of Bologna, 74 km (46 miles) northwest of Ravenna.

When the legendary Ferrarese filmmaker Michelangelo Antonioni called his beloved hometown "a city that you can see only partly, while the rest disappears to be imagined," perhaps he was referring to the low-lying mist that rolls in off the Adriatic each winter and shrouds Ferrara's winding knot of medieval alleyways, turreted palaces, and ancient wine bars—once inhabited by the likes of Copernicus—in a ghostly fog. But perhaps Antonioni was also suggesting that Ferrara's striking beauty often conceals a dark and tortured past.

Today you're likely to be charmed by Ferrara's prosperous air and meticulous cleanliness, its excellent restaurants and chic bars (for coffee and any other liquid refreshment), and its lively wine-bar scene. You'll find aficionados gathering outside any of the wine bars near the Duomo even on the foggiest of weeknights. Though Ferrara is a UNESCO World Heritage Site, the city draws amazingly few tourists—which only adds to its appeal.

■ TIP→ **If you plan to explore the city fully, consider buying a Card Musei ("Museum Card," also known as "My Ferrara Tourist Card"). Two days cost €10, three days €12, and six days €18). Purchase the card at the Palazzo dei Diamanti or any of Ferrara's museums; it grants admission to every museum, palace, and castle in town. The first Monday of the month is free at many museums.**

GETTING HERE AND AROUND

Train service is frequent from Bologna (usually three trains per hour) and takes either a half hour or 45 minutes, depending on which train type you take. It's 37 minutes from Florence to Bologna, and then about a half hour from Bologna to Ferrara. The walk from the station is easy, takes about 20 minutes, and is not particularly interesting. You can take either Bus No. 1 or No. 9 from the station to the center; buy your ticket at the news agent inside the station and remember to stamp your ticket upon boarding the bus. If you're driving from Bologna, take the RA1 out of town, then the A13 in the direction of Padova, exiting at Ferrara Nord. Follow the SP19 directly into the center of town. The trip should take about 45 minutes.

VISITOR INFORMATION

Ferrara Tourism Office ✉ *Castello Estense, Piazza Castello* ☎ *0532/299303* ⊕ *www.ferrarainfo.com.*

EXPLORING

TOP ATTRACTIONS

Fodor'sChoice
★

Castello Estense. The former seat of Este power, this massive castle dominates the center of town. The building was a suitable symbol for the ruling family: cold and menacing on the outside, lavishly decorated within. The public rooms are grand, but deep in the bowels of the castle are chilling dungeons where enemies of the state were held in wretched conditions—a function these quarters served as recently as 1943, when anti-Fascist prisoners were detained there. In particular, the **Prisons of Don Giulio, Ugo,** and **Parisina** have some fascinating features, like 15th-century graffiti protesting the imprisonment of lovers Ugo and Parisina, who were beheaded in 1425 because Ugo's father, Niccolò III, didn't like the fact that his son was cavorting with Niccolò's wife.

The castle was established as a fortress in 1385, but work on its luxurious ducal quarters continued into the 16th century. Representative of Este grandeur are the **Sala dei Giochi,** extravagantly painted with athletic scenes, and the **Sala dell'Aurora,** decorated to show the times of the day. The terraces of the castle and the hanging garden—once reserved for the private use of the duchesses—have fine views of the town and the surrounding countryside. You can cross the castle's moat, traverse its drawbridge, and wander through many of its arcaded passages at any time. ✉ *Piazza Castello* ☎ *0532/299233* ⊕ *www.castelloestense.it* 🎫 *€8 (€12 during special exhibitions)* ☉ *Tues.–Sun. 9:30–5:30; ticket office closes at 4:45.*

Duomo. The magnificent Gothic cathedral, a few steps from the Castello Estense, has a three-tier facade of slender arches and beautiful sculptures over the central door. Work began in 1135 and took more than 100 years to complete. The interior was completely remodeled in the 17th century. ✉ *Piazza Cattedrale* ☎ *0532/207449* ☉ *Mon.–Sat. 7:30–noon and 3–6:30, Sun. 7:30–12:30 and 3:30–7:30.*

Palazzo dei Diamanti (*Palace of Diamonds*). Named for the 12,600 small, pink-and-white marble pyramids (or "diamonds") that stud its facade, this building was designed to be viewed in perspective—both faces at once—from diagonally across the street. Work began in the 1490s and finished around 1504. Today the palazzo contains the **Pinacoteca Nazionale,** an extensive art gallery that also hosts temporary exhibits. ⊠ *Corso Ercole I d'Este 19–21* ☎ *0532/244949* ⊕ *www. palazzodiamanti.it* ⛁ *€10* ⊗ *Daily 9–7.*

Fodor's Choice
★ **Palazzo Schifanoia.** The oldest, most characteristic area of Ferrara is south of the Duomo, stretching between the Corso Giovecca and the city's ramparts. Here various members of the Este family built pleasure palaces, the best-known of which is the Palazzo Schifanoia (*schifanoia* means "carefree" or, literally, "fleeing boredom"). Begun in the late 14th century, the palace was remodeled between 1464 and 1469. The lavish interior is well worth visiting—particularly the **Salone dei Mesi,** which contains an extravagant series of frescoes showing the months of the year and their mythological attributes. Since a 2013 earthquake, only the Salone and the adjacent **Ala degli Stucchi** have remained open to the public. ⊠ *Via Scandiana 23* ☎ *0532/64178* ⊕ *www.artecultura. fe.it* ⛁ *€3* ⊗ *Tues.–Sun. 9:30–6; call ahead to confirm.*

Via delle Volte. One of the best-preserved medieval streets in Europe, the Via delle Volte clearly evokes Ferrara's past. The series of ancient *volte* (arches) along the narrow cobblestone alley once joined the merchants' houses on the south side of the street to their warehouses on the north side. The street ran parallel to the banks of the Po River, which was home to Ferrara's busy port.

WORTH NOTING

Casa Romei. This ranks among Ferrara's loveliest Renaissance palaces. Built by the wealthy banker Giovanni Romei (1402–83), it's a vast structure with a graceful courtyard. Mid-15th-century frescoes decorate rooms on the ground floor; the *piano nobile* (main floor) contains detached frescoes from local churches as well as lesser-known Renaissance sculptures. The Sala delle Sibelle has a very large 15th-century fireplace and beautiful wood-coffered ceilings. ⊠ *Via Savonarola 30* ☎ *0532/234130 for tickets, 0532/234100 for info* ⊕ *www. soprintendenzaravenna.beniculturali.it* ⛁ *€3 (free 1st Sun. of month)* ⊗ *Sun.–Wed. 8:30–2, Thurs.–Sat., 2–7:30.*

Museo della Cattedrale. Some of the original decorations of the town's main church, the former church, and cloister of San Romano, reside in the Museo della Cattedrale, which is across the piazza from the Duomo. Inside you'll find 22 codices commissioned between 1477 and 1535; early-13th-century sculpture by the Maestro dei Mesi; a mammoth oil on canvas by Cosmé Tura from 1469; and an exquisite Jacopo della Quercia, the *Madonna della Melograno.* Though this last work dates from 1403 to 1408, the playful expression on the Christ child seems very 21st century. ⊠ *Via San Romano 1* ☎ *0532/761299* ⊕ *www. artecultura.fe.it* ⛁ *€6* ⊗ *Tues.–Sun. 9:30–1 and 3–6.*

9

WHERE TO EAT

$
EMILIAN
✕ **Enoteca Enotria.** This little two-room enoteca opened in 1986 in the old Jewish section of town and since then has been pouring significant French and other wines. The first room has just a counter where the wine is poured, a couple of stools, and a table; two more tables in the other room, lined with wine bottles, complete the space. Locals come for the

wine, but also for the simple but good food—plates of *affettati misti* (cured meats) and cheeses—to pair with the wines. Enotria opens at 8:30 in the morning, closes at 2, and reopens in the late afternoon, making it a wonderful quick stop before the usual lunch and dinner opening hours (12:30 pm and 7 pm). $ *Average main: €11* ⊠ *Via Saraceno 39/A–41* ☎ *0532/209166* ⊕ *www.enotecaenotria.it* ⊗ *Closed Mon.*

$$$
MODERN ITALIAN

✕ **Il Don Giovanni.** Just down the street from Castello Estense, this warm and inviting restaurant consists of a handful of tables inside a 17th-century palace. Chef Pier Luigi Di Diego and partner Marco Merighi pay strict attention to what's seasonal. Here tortellini are stuffed with guinea fowl and sauced with *zabaione* (custard), Parmesan, and pro-sciutto *croccante* (fried prosciutto). Equally inventive is the delicate *tegame di pernice rossa ai frutti di bosco* (partridge in a fruit sauce), which delights the palate. Next door, the same proprietors run the less expensive but more crowded **La Borsa.** The trendy wine bar has excellent cured meats, cheeses, lovely primi and secondi, and a fantastic by-the-glass wine list. ■TIP→ **The wine bar is open for lunch and dinner, the restaurant for dinner only.** $ *Average main: €29* ⊠ *Corso Ercole I d'Este 1* ☎ *0532/243363* ⊕ *www.ildongiovanni.com* ⌖ *Reservations essential* ⊗ *Closed Mon. No lunch.*

$
EMILIAN

✕ **il Sorpasso.** Named after 1962 cult movie *Il Sorpasso*, this restaurant serves terrific, honestly priced food. The interior's unassuming: white walls lined with movie posters, and white floors. No matter—the fine cooking and the sourcing of local ingredients whenever possible help this trattoria surpass many others. Start with the *crema d'aglio di Voghiera* (a silky garlic soup, a local recipe) and then segue to a Ferrarese classic such as *cappellaci di zucca* (pasta stuffed with pumpkin). Or indulge in the *fave e puntarelle* (fava beans and chicory) served both raw and cooked in two different versions. For a break from Italian cuisine, try the teriyaki. All of this can be gloriously washed down with local wines by the glass, or bottles from everywhere. $ *Average main: €11* ⊠ *Via Saraceno 118* ☎ *0532/790289* ⊕ *www.trattoriailsorpasso.it* ⌖ *Reservations essential* ⊗ *Closed Tues. No lunch Sat.*

$$
EMILIAN

✕ **L'Oca Giuliva.** Food, service, and ambience harmonize blissfully at this casual but elegant restaurant inside a 12th-century building. Patrons enter through a tiny wine bar, some pausing for glass of wine before proceeding into the restaurant. The chef shows a deft hand with area specialties and shines with the fish dishes: his *scampo saltato su una crema di fave e cime di rape* (a sweet crustacean, quickly sautéed, with a fava-bean puree with cooked bitter greens) shifts the palate into gear. Dishes such as the *gnocchi al cacao con ragù di cervo* (cocoa potato gnocchi with a venison sauce) show his more fanciful side. If the chestnut ice cream happens to be on the menu, don't miss it. A terrific cheese plate complements the amazing wines poured here. $ *Average main: €17* ⊠ *Via Boccanale di Santo Stefano 38* ☎ *0532/207628* ⊕ *www. ristorantelocagiuliva.it* ⊗ *Closed Mon. No lunch Tues.*

$
WINE BAR
Fodor's Choice
★

✕ **Osteria al Brindisi.** Ferrara is a city of wine bars, beginning with this one—allegedly Europe's oldest—which opened in 1435. Copernicus drank here while a student in the late 1400s, and the place still has a somewhat undergraduate aura. Most of the staff and clientele are twentysomethings. Perfectly dusty wine bottles line the walls, and there are wooden booths in another small room for those who want to eat while they drink. The young staff pour well-selected wines by the glass, and offer three different sauces (butter and sage, tomato, or ragù) with the *cappellacci di zucca* (pasta stuffed with butternut squash). Those in search of lighter fare might enjoy any of the salads or the grilled vegetable plate with melted pecorino. [$] *Average main: €8* ✉ *Via degli Adelardi 11* ☎ *0532/209142* 🌐 *www.albrindisi.net.*

$$ EMILIAN Fodor's Choice ★ 🍴 **Quel Fantastico Giovedì.** Locals and other cognoscenti frequent this sleek eatery just minutes away from the Piazza del Duomo. Two small rooms—one white, the other with red accents—have linen tablecloths and jazz playing softly in the background. Chef Gabriele Romagnoli uses prime local ingredients to create gustatory taste sensations on a menu that changes daily. His *sformatino di patate* (potato flan) resembles a French gratin, but he sauces it with *salamina e Parmigiano* (that deliciously unctuous pork product made into a smooth sauce with the help of Parmesan cheese), thus rendering it deliciously Ferrarese. Fish figures prominently among his dishes. The restaurant's tasting menu is well priced, its wine list divine, and the service, led by hands-on, gregarious proprietor Mara Farinelli, is always top-notch. [$] *Average main: €16* ✉ *Via Castelnuovo 9* ☎ *0532/760570* ✍ *Reservations essential* ⏲ *Closed Wed. No lunch Tues.*

$ EMILIAN 🍴 **Trattoria Centrale.** Pasta constantly being produced from scratch is the big draw here. Order a plate of *cappellaci di zucca alla ferrarese* (pumpkin-stuffed pasta with a hearty meat ragù) and, depending on where you sit, you might actually witness your pasta being rolled out, stuffed, and sauced. Centrale is an unassuming place, with white walls, white linens, and an ebullient owner-host. Servings tend to be huge, though mercifully the *salamina in sugo*—a delicious local specialty of salame atop creamy mashed potatoes—comes in smaller portions. [$] *Average main: €14* ✉ *Via Boccaleone 8* ☎ *0532/470940* ✍ *Reservations essential* ⏲ *Closed Sun.*

WHERE TO STAY

$ HOTEL 🏨 **Hotel Annunziata.** Brightly colored fittings enliven the white-walled, hardwood-floor guest rooms—think minimalism with a splash—at this hotel on a quiet little piazza near the forbiddingly majestic Castello Estense. **Pros:** perfect location (you can't get much more central); stellar staff; terrific buffet breakfast. **Cons:** it books up quickly. [$] *Rooms from: €114* ✉ *Piazza, Repubblica 5* ☎ *0532/201111* 🌐 *www.annunziata.it* 🛏 *27 rooms* 🍽 *Breakfast.*

$ B&B/INN Fodor's Choice ★ 🏨 **Locanda Borgonuovo.** In the early 18th century this lodging began life as a convent (later suppressed by Napoleon), but now it's a delightful city-center bed-and-breakfast, popular with performers at the city's Teatro Comunale. **Pros:** phenomenal breakfast featuring local foods and terrific cakes made in-house; bicyles can be borrowed for free. **Cons:** steep stairs to reception area and rooms; must reserve far in advance. [$] *Rooms from: €90* ✉ *Via Cairoli 29* ☎ *0532/211100* 🌐 *www.borgonuovo.com* 🛏 *4 rooms, 2 apartments* 🍽 *Breakfast.*

ROMAGNA

Anywhere in Emilia-Romagna, the story goes, a weary, lost traveler will be invited into a family's home and offered a drink. But the Romagnesi claim that he'll be served water in Emilia and wine in Romagna. The hilly, mostly rural, and largely undiscovered Romagna region has crumbling farmhouses dotting rolling hills, smoking chimneys, early Christian churches, and rowdy local bars dishing out rounds and rounds of *piadine* (a pitalike thin bread filled with meat, cheese, vegetables, or any combination thereof, and then quickly grilled). Ravenna, the site of shimmering Byzantine mosaics, dominates the region.

Heading southeast from Bologna, Via Emilia (SS9) and the parallel A14 autostrada lead to the town of Faenza. From here, go north to the Adriatic Coast on the SS71 to reach Ravenna. Alternatively, the slower SS16 cuts a northwest–southeast swath through Romagna.

IMOLA

42 km (26 miles) southeast of Bologna.

Affluent Imola, with its wide and stately avenues, lies on the border between Emilia and Romagna. It was populated as early as the Bronze Age, came under Roman rule, and was eventually annexed to the Papal States in 1504. Imola is best known for its Formula One auto-racing tradition: the San Marino Grand Prix has been held here every spring since 1981. Auto-racing as a serious sport in Imola dates to 1953, when, with the support of Enzo Ferrari, the racetrack just outside the city center was inaugurated. However, unless you happen to pop into town in mid-April for the race, you'll more likely find yourself in Imola shopping for its well-known ceramics or sampling the cuisine at the town's world-famous restaurant, San Domenico.

GETTING HERE AND AROUND

Local trains from Bologna run often and take a little under a half hour. If you're driving from Bologna, take the RA1 to the A14 (following signs for Ancona). Take the exit for Imola. If you're coming from Milan, you can catch the Eurostar to Bologna, and then transfer to the local train. Travel time from Milan to Bologna is a little over an hour.

VISITOR INFORMATION

Imola Tourism Office ⌂ *Arcade of the City Center 135* ☏ *0542/602111* ⊕ *www.visitareimola.it.*

WHERE TO EAT

$$$$
MODERN ITALIAN
Fodor's Choice
★

✕ **San Domenico.** Year after year this restaurant defends its position as one of Italy's most refined culinary destinations, and heads of state, celebrities, and those with bottomless pocketbooks venture here to savor the fare. The majestic appointments complement chef Valentino Marcattili's wondrous creations, like his memorable *uovo in raviolo San Domenico,* in which a large raviolo is stuffed with a raw egg yolk—which miraculously cooks only a little, then spills out and mixes with Parmesan cheese, *burro di malga* (butter from an Alpine dairy farm), and sensational white truffles. The wine list impresses with more than 3,000

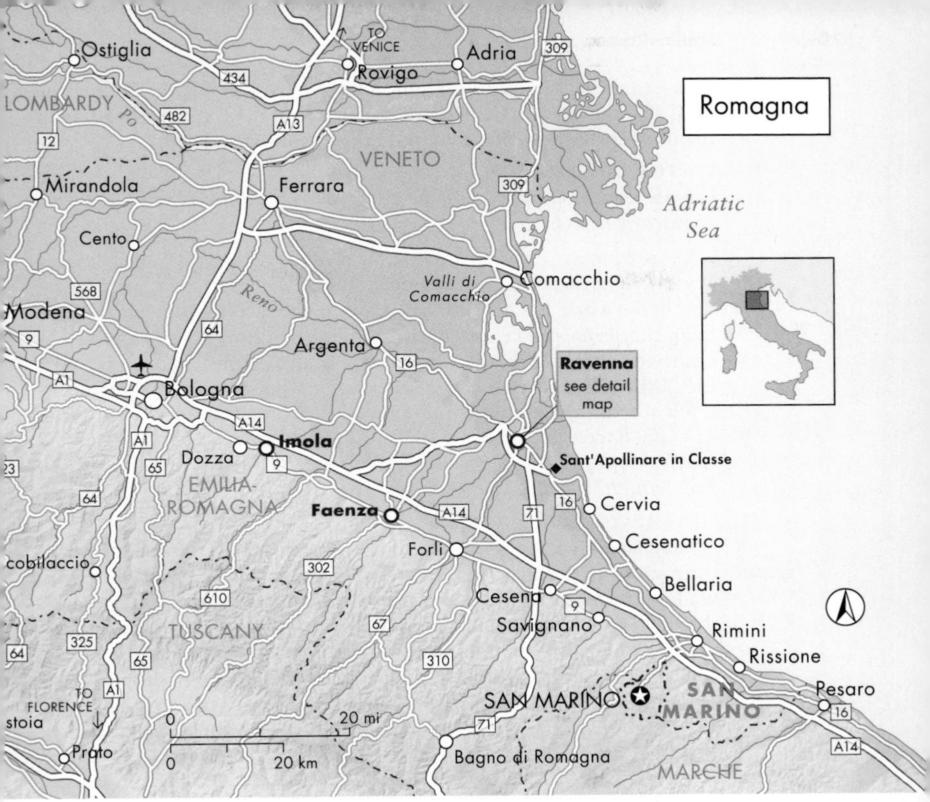

choices. ■ **TIP→ In summer the restaurant opens for lunch on weekends and Monday.** [$] *Average main: €60* ✉ *Via G. Sacchi 1* ☎ *0542/29000* 🌐 *www.sandomenico.it* ✍ *Reservations essential* ⏲ *Closed Mon., 1 wk in Jan., and 1 wk in Aug. No dinner Sun.; no lunch.*

FAENZA

49 km (30 miles) southeast of Bologna.

In the Middle Ages Faenza was the crossroads between Emilia-Romagna and Tuscany, and the 15th century saw many Florentine artists working in town. In 1509, when the Papal States took control, Faenza became something of a backwater town. It did, however, continue its 12th-century tradition of making top-quality ceramics. In the 16th century local artists created a color called *bianchi di Faenza* ("Faenza white"), which was widely imitated and wildly desired all over Europe. The Frenchified *faience,* referring to the color and technique, soon entered the lexicon, where it remains to this day. In the central **Piazza del Popolo,** dozens of shops sell the native ceramic wares.

GETTING HERE AND AROUND

Trains run frequently from Bologna to Faenza, making the trip in about a half hour. There's also sporadic service from Florence, a beautiful two-hour ride. The walk to the centro storico, though easy, isn't especially interesting. By car it takes about an hour from Bologna. Follow the SP253 to the RA1, at which point pick up on the A14/E45 heading in the direction of Ancona. Exit and take the SP8 into Faenza.

VISITOR INFORMATION

Faenza Tourism Office ✉ *Voltore Molinella 2* ☎ *0546/25231* 🌐 *www.prolocofaenza.it.*

EXPLORING

Museo Internazionale delle Ceramiche. One of the largest ceramics museums in the world has a well-labeled, well-lighted collection, with objects from the Renaissance among its highlights. Though the emphasis is clearly on local work, the rest of Italy is also represented. Don't miss the 20th- and 21st-century galleries, which prove that decorative arts often surpass their utile limitations and become genuinely sculptural. ✉ *Viale Baccarini 19* ☎ *0546/697311* 🌐 *www.micfaenza.org* 🎟 *€8* 🕒 *Apr.–Sept., Tues.–Sun. 10–7; Oct.–Mar., Tues.–Thurs. 10–1:30, Fri.–Sun. 9:30–5:30.*

WHERE TO EAT

$ EMILIAN 🍴 **Marianaza.** A large open-hearth fireplace dominates this simple trattoria, and wonderful aromas of grilled meats and garlic greet you as you walk in. Marianaza, like the town of Faenza itself, successfully blends the best of Emilian-Romagnan and Tuscan cuisine: the extraordinary primi are mostly tortellini-based, and the secondi rely heavily on the grill. Luana at the grill and Natasha overseeing the floor provide a grandiose duet of seamless harmony to their almost-always full house; keep in mind that in Italy a woman at the grill is a rare sight indeed. [$] *Average main: €10* ✉ *Via Torricelli 21* ☎ *0546/681461.*

RIMINI

52 km (32 miles) southeast of Ravenna, 121 km (75 miles) southeast of Bologna.

Rimini is one of the most popular summer resorts on the Adriatic Coast and one of the most popular in Italy. July and August are the most crowded, packed with people who don't mind crammed beaches and not-terribly-blue water. In the off-season (October through March), Rimini is a cold, windy fishing port with few places open. Any time of year, one of Rimini's least touristy areas is the port; rambling down the **Via Sinistra del Porto** or **Via Destra del Porto** past all the fishing boats, you're far from the crush of sunbathers.

The town stands at the junction of two great Roman consular roads, the Via Emilia and the Via Flaminia. In Roman times it was an important port, making it a strategic and commercial center. From the 13th century onward, Rimini was controlled by the Malatesta family, an unpredictable clan capable of grand gestures and savage deeds.

GETTING HERE

Trains run hourly from Ravenna to Rimini and take about an hour. By car from Ravenna, take the SS16/E55, then follow the SS3bis/E45/E55 in the direction of Roma/Ancona. Follow directions for Ancona Nord, then follow signs for Ancona. Take the A14/E55 to the Rimini

Nord exit, then the SP136 to the SS16, and follow signs for the center of town. Alternatively, take the coastal road, SS16, which hugs the shoreline much of the way, passing through Cervia. Although its length of 52 km (32 miles) is not great, this scenic route is naturally slower (beware of fog in winter). The coast north of Rimini is lined with dozens of small resort towns, but only one really has any charm—the seaport of Cesenatico; the others are mini-Riminis, and in summer the narrow road is hopelessly clogged with traffic.

There's frequent train service (usually four trains per hour) from Bologna to Rimini. It takes between an hour and an hour and a half, depending upon what type of train you choose. By car from Bologna, take the SP253 out of town, pick up the RA1, and then enter the A14 heading toward Ancona. Get off at the Rimini Nord exit, follow the SP136 to the SS16 to the center of town.

VISITOR INFORMATION

Rimini tourism office ⊠ *Train station, Piazzale Cesare Battisti* ☎ *0541/ 51331* ⊕ *www.riminiturismo.it.*

EXPLORING

Arco d'Augusto. Rimini's oldest monument is the Arco d'Augusto, now stranded in the middle of a square just inside the city ramparts. It was erected in 27 BC, making it the oldest surviving ancient Roman arch. ⊠ *Largo Giulio Cesare.*

Tempio Malatestiano. The Malatesta constructed the Tempio Malatestiano, also called the Basilica Cattedrale, with a masterful facade by Leon Battista Alberti (1404–72). Inside, the chapel to the right of the high altar contains a wonderful (if faded) fresco by Piero della Francesca (1420–92) depicting Sigismondo Malatesta kneeling before a saint. The two greyhounds in the right corner are significantly less faded than the rest. ⊠ *Via IV Novembre 35* ☎ *0541/51130* ⊕ *www.diocesi.rimini.it* ☞ *Free* ⊙ *Mon.–Sat. 8–12:30 and 3:30–6:30, Sun. 9–1.*

WHERE TO EAT AND STAY

$

EMILIAN

✕ **La Marianna.** If on foot, you'll likely approach this trattoria via the Ponte di Tiberio, a bridge from the 1st century AD named after the ruling Roman emperor. La Marianna is all about fish, and aside from vegetable side dishes and dessert; there's little on the menu that wasn't recently swimming (or lurking) in the sea. Locals flock here, and with good reason—the food is excellent, and the prices are reasonable. $ *Average main: €14* ⊠ *Via Tiberio 19* ☎ *0541/22530* ⊕ *www. trattorialamarianna.it* ⌂ *Reservations essential.*

$$$$

HOTEL

FAMILY

Grand Hotel. This 1908 extravaganza, made famous by Federico Fellini in his film *Amarcord,* is grander than ever. **Pros:** sumptuous buffet breakfast that starts early (7 am) and ends late (11 am); the American Bar; beach across the street; programs for children in summer. **Cons:** not in the center of town; some rooms more fabulous than others. $ *Rooms from: €425* ⊠ *Parco Federico Fellini* ☎ *0541/56000* ⊕ *www. grandhotelrimini.com* ⇥ *163 rooms, 4 suites* ⊚ *Breakfast.*

9

SAN MARINO

90 km (56 miles) southeast of Faenza, 139 km (86 miles) southeast of Bologna.

The world's smallest and oldest republic, as San Marino dubs itself, is surrounded entirely by Italy. It consists of three ancient castles perched on sheer cliffs rising implausibly out of the flatlands of Romagna, and a tangled knot of cobblestone streets below that are lined with tourist boutiques, cheesy hotels and restaurants, and gun shops. The 1½-hour drive from Faenza is justified, however, by the sweeping views from the castle of the countryside. The 3,300-foot-plus precipices will make jaws drop and acrophobes quiver.

Visiting San Marino in winter—off-season—increases the appeal of the experience, as tourist establishments shut down and you more or less have the castles to yourself. In August every inch of walkway on the rock is mobbed with sightseers. Don't worry about changing money, showing passports, and the like (although the tourist office at Contrada del Collegio will stamp your passport for €2.50). San Marino is, for all practical purposes, Italy—except, that is, for its majestic perch, its gun laws, and its reported 99% national voter turnout rate.

GETTING HERE AND AROUND

To get to San Marino by car, take highway SS72 west from Rimini. From Borgo Maggiore, at the base of the rock, a cable car will whisk you up to the town. Alternatively, you can drive up the winding road; public parking is available. There is a regular bus service to and from Rimini, with service sometime every hour throughout the year (less frequent service on Sunday); a one-way ticket from Rimini to San Marino costs €4.50. The trip takes about 45 minutes.

VISITOR INFORMATION

State Board of Tourism ✉ *Contrada Omagnano 20* ☎ *0549/882914* ⊕ *www.visitsanmarino.com.*

EXPLORING

Piazza della Libertà. A must-see is the Piazza della Libertà, where the Palazzo Pubblico is guarded by soldiers in green uniforms. As you'll notice by peering into the shops along the old town's winding streets, the republic is famous for crossbows and other items (think fireworks or firearms) that are illegal almost everywhere else.

Tre Castelli. San Marino's headline attractions are its Tre Castelli—medieval architectural wonders that appear on every coat of arms in the city. Starting in the center of town, walk a few hundred yards past the trinket shops, along a paved clifftop ridge, from the 10th-century **Rocca della Guaita** to the 13th-century **Rocca della Cesta** (containing a museum of ancient weapons that's worthwhile mostly for the views from its terraces and turrets), and finally to the 14th-century **Rocca Montale** (closed to the public), the most remote of the castles.

Every step of the way affords spectacular views of Romagna and the Adriatic—it's said that on a clear day you can see Croatia. The walk makes for a good day's exercise, but is by no means arduous. Even if you arrive after visiting hours, it's supremely rewarding. ☎ *0549/991369*

⊕ *www.museidistato.sm* ✍ *Il Torre Guaita and il Torre Cesta €4* ⏱ *Mid-Sept.–mid-June, daily 9–5; mid-June–mid-Sept., daily 8–8.*

RAVENNA

76 km (47 miles) east of Bologna, 93 km (58 miles) southeast of Ferrara.

A small, quiet, well-heeled city, Ravenna has brick palaces, cobblestone streets, magnificent monuments, and spectacular Byzantine mosaics. The high point in its civic history occurred in the 5th century, when Pope Honorious moved his court here from Rome. Gothic kings Odoacer and Theodoric ruled the city until it was conquered by the Byzantines in AD 540. Ravenna later fell under the sway of Venice, and then, inevitably, the Papal States.

Because Ravenna spent much of its past looking east, its greatest art treasures show that Byzantine influence. Churches and tombs with the most unassuming exteriors contain within them walls covered with sumptuous mosaics. These beautifully preserved Byzantine mosaics put great emphasis on nature, which you can see in the delicate rendering of sky, earth, and animals. Outside Ravenna, the town of Classe hides even more mosaic gems.

GETTING HERE AND AROUND

By car from Bologna, take the SP253 to the RA1, and then follow signs for the A14/E45 in the direction of Ancona. From here, follow signs for Ravenna, taking the A14dir Ancona–Milano–Ravenna exit. Follow signs for the SS16/E55 to the center of Ravenna. From Ferrara the drive is more convoluted, but also more interesting. Take the SS16 to the RA8 in the direction of Porto Garibaldi taking the Roma/Ravenna exit. Follow the SS309/E55 to the SS309dir/E55, taking the SS253 Bologna/Ancona exit. Follow the SS16/E55 into the center of Ravenna.

VISITOR INFORMATION

Ravenna Tourism Office ✉ *Via Salara 8* ☎ *0544/35404* ⊕ *www.turismo.ra.it.*

EXPLORING

A combination ticket (available at ticket offices of all included sights) admits you to four of Ravenna's important monuments: the Mausoleo di Galla Placidia, the Basilica di San Vitale, the Battistero Neoniano, and Sant'Apollinare Nuovo. Start out early in the morning to avoid lines (reservations are necessary for the Mausoleo and Basilica in May and June). A half day should suffice to walk the town; allow a half hour for the Mausoleo and the Basilica.

TOP ATTRACTIONS

Fodor's Choice ★ **Basilica di San Vitale.** The octagonal church of San Vitale was built in AD 547, after the Byzantines conquered the city, and its interior shows a strong Byzantine influence. The area behind the altar contains the most famous works, depicting Emperor Justinian and his retinue on one wall, and his wife, Empress Theodora, with her retinue, on the opposite one. Notice how the mosaics seamlessly wrap around the columns and

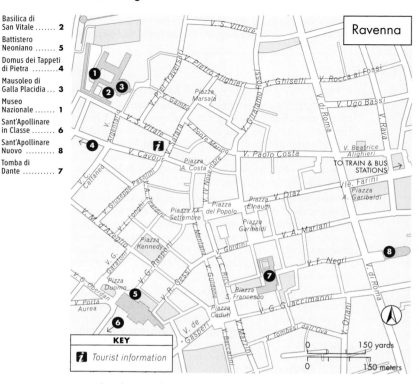

KEY

🛈 *Tourist information*

curved arches on the upper sides of the altar area. ✉ *Via San Vitale, off Via Salara* ☎ *0544/541688 for reservations* ⊕ *www.ravennamosaici.it* 🎫 *Combination ticket €9.50 mid-June–Feb., €11.50 Mar.–mid-June (includes all diocesan monuments)* ⏱ *Nov.–Feb., daily 9:30–4:45; Mar. and Oct., daily 9–5:15; Apr.–Sept., daily 9–6:45. Last entry 15 mins before closing* ☞ *Reservations recommended Mar.–mid-June.*

Fodor's Choice
★
Battistero Neoniano. Next door to Ravenna's 18th-century cathedral, the baptistery has one of the town's most important mosaics. It dates to the beginning of the 5th century AD, with work continuing through the century. In keeping with the building's role, the great mosaic in the dome shows the baptism of Christ, and beneath are the Apostles. The lowest register of mosaics contains Christian symbols, the Throne of God, and the Cross. Note the naked figure kneeling next to Christ—he is the personification of the River Jordan. ✉ *Via Battistero* ☎ *0544/541688 for reservations, 800/303999 (toll-free) for info* ⊕ *www.ravennamosaici. it* 🎫 *Combination ticket €9.50 mid-June–Feb., €11.50 Mar.–mid-June (includes all diocesan monuments)* ⏱ *Nov.–Feb., daily 10–4:45; Mar. and Oct., daily 9:30–5:15; Apr.–Sept., daily 9–6:45. Last entry 15 mins before closing.*

Fodor's Choice
★
Mausoleo di Galla Placidia. The little tomb and the great church stand side by side, but the tomb predates the Basilica di San Vitale by at least 100

years. These two adjacent sights are decorated with the best-known, most elaborate mosaics in Ravenna. Galla Placidia was the sister of the Roman emperor Honorius, who moved the imperial capital to Ravenna in AD 402. She is said to have been beautiful and strong-willed, and to have taken an active part in the governing of the crumbling empire. This mausoleum, constructed in the mid-5th century, is her memorial.

Viewed from the outside, it's a small, unassuming red-brick building: the exterior's seeming poverty of charm only serves to enhance by contrast the richness of the interior mosaics, in deep midnight blue and glittering gold. The tiny central dome is decorated with symbols of Christ, the evangelists, and striking gold stars. Over the door is a depiction of the Good Shepherd. Eight of the Apostles are represented in groups of two on the four inner walls of the dome; the other four appear singly on the walls of the two transepts. Notice the small doves at their feet, drinking from the water of faith. Also in the tiny transepts are some delightful pairs of deer (representing souls), drinking from the fountain of resurrection. There are three sarcophagi in the tomb, none of which are believed to contain the remains of Galla Placidia. She died in Rome in AD 450, and there's no record of her body's having been transported back to the place where she wished to lie.

■ TIP→ Reservations are required for the Mausoleo from March through mid-June. ⊠ *Via San Vitale, off Via Salara* ☎ *0544/541688 for reservations* ⊕ *www.ravennamosaici.it* 🎟 *Combination ticket €9.50 mid-June–Feb., €11.50 Mar.–mid-June (includes all diocesan monuments)* ☉ *Nov.–Feb., daily 9:30–4:45; Mar. and Oct., daily 9–5:15; Apr.–Sept., daily 9–6:45. Last entry 15 mins before closing.*

Fodor's Choice ★ **Sant'Apollinare Nuovo.** The mosaics displayed in this church date from the early 6th century, making them slightly older than those in San Vitale. Since the left side of the church was reserved for women, it's only fitting that the mosaics on that wall depict 22 virgins offering crowns to the Virgin Mary. On the right wall are 26 men carrying the crowns of martyrdom. They approach Christ, surrounded by angels. ⊠ *Via Roma, at Via Guaccimanni* ☎ *0544/219518, 0544/541688 for reservations* ⊕ *www.ravennamosaici.it* 🎟 *Combination ticket €9.50 mid-June–Feb., €11.50 Mar.–mid-June (includes all diocesan monuments)* ☉ *Nov.–Feb., daily 10–4:45; Mar. and Oct., daily 9:30–5:15; Apr.–Sept., daily 9–6:45. Last entry 15 mins before closing.*

WORTH NOTING

Domus dei Tappeti di Pietra (*Ancient Home of the Stone Carpets*). This archaeological site was uncovered in 1993 during digging for an underground parking garage near the 18th-century church of Santa Eufemia. Ten feet below ground level lie the remains of a Byzantine palace dating from the 5th and 6th centuries AD. Its beautiful and well-preserved network of floor mosaics displays elaborately designed patterns, creating the effect of luxurious carpets. ⊠ *Via Barbiani, enter through Sant'Eufemia* ☎ *0544/32512* ⊕ *www.domusdeitappetidipietra.it* 🎟 *€4* ☉ *July and Aug., daily 10–6 and 8:30–10:30; Mar.–June, Sept., and Oct., daily 10–6:30; Nov.–Feb., Tues.–Fri. 10–5, weekends 10–6.*

Museo Nazionale (*National Museum of Ravenna*). Next to the Church of San Vitale and housed in a former Benedictine monastery, the museum contains artifacts from ancient Rome, Byzantine fabrics and carvings, and pieces of early Christian art. The collection is well displayed and artfully lighted. In the first cloister are marvelous Roman tomb slabs from excavations nearby; upstairs, you can see a reconstructed 18th-century pharmacy. ✉ *Via Fiandrini* ☎ *0544/543711* 🎫 *€5* 🕓 *Tues.–Sun. 8:30–7:30.*

Sant'Apollinare in Classe. This church about 5 km (3 miles) southeast of Ravenna is landlocked now, but when it was built it stood in the center of the busy shipping port known to the ancient Romans as Classis. The arch above and the area around the high altar are rich with mosaics. Those on the arch, older than the ones behind it, are considered superior. They show Christ in Judgment and the 12 lambs of Christianity leaving the cities of Jerusalem and Bethlehem. In the apse is the figure of Sant'Apollinare himself, a bishop of Ravenna, and above him is a magnificent Transfiguration against blazing green grass, animals in odd perspective, and flowers. ✉ *Via Romea Sud 224, off SS71, Classe* ☎ *0544/473569* 🎫 *€5* 🕓 *Daily 8:30–7.*

Tomba di Dante. The tomb of Dante is in a small Neoclassical building next door to the large church of St. Francis. Exiled from his native Florence, the author of *The Divine Comedy* died here in 1321. The Florentines have been trying to reclaim their famous son for hundreds of years, but the Ravennans refuse to give him up, arguing that since Florence did not welcome Dante in life it does not deserve him in death. Perhaps as penance, every September the Florentine government sends olive oil that's used to fuel the light hanging in the chapel's center. ✉ *Via Dante Alighieri 4 and 9* 🎫 *Free* 🕓 *Nov.–Mar., daily 10–4; Apr.–Oct., daily 10–6.*

WHERE TO EAT AND STAY

$$ EMILIAN 🍴 **Bella Venezia.** Pale yellow walls, crisp white tablecloths, and warm light provide the backdrop for some seriously good regional food. The menu offers local specialties, but also gives a major nod to Venice—Ravenna's conqueror of long ago. The flavorful and delicate *cappelletti romagnoli* (stuffed pasta in broth) is a lovely starter. Follow up with *cotoletta alla Bisanzio* (a fried veal cutlet topped with cherry tomatoes and arugula), a house specialty. Desserts are made daily on the premises; save room for the killer tiramisù. [$] *Average main: €15* ✉ *Via IV Novembre 16* ☎ *0544/212746* 🌐 *www.bellavenezia.it* 🕓 *Closed Sun., and 3 wks in Dec. and Jan.*

$ EMILIAN 🍴 **Ca' de' Ven.** Some may quibble with the notion that the exiled Dante ever set foot in the two structures that house this restaurant, but Lord Byron irrefutably did. The buildings, joined by a glass-ceiling courtyard, securely date to the 15th century. The setting itself is reason enough to come; that the food is so good makes a visit here all the more satisfying. At lunchtime Ca' de' Ven teems with locals tucking in to piadine, stuffed or topped with various ingredients, and the grilled dishes—among them *tagliata di pollo* (sliced chicken breast tossed with arugula and set atop exquisitely roasted potatoes)—are among the highlights. [$] *Average main: €13* ✉ *Via Corrado Ricci 24* ☎ *0544/30163* 🌐 *www.cadeven.it* ✍ *Reservations essential.*

$ EMILIAN 🍴 **I Battibecchi.** Simple, honest food doesn't get any tastier than what's served at this tiny venue (there are about 20 seats) with an even tinier kitchen. Nicoletta Molducci, chef and owner, takes pride in turning out terrific regional dishes. The short menu provides the usual local specialties such as cappelletti romagnoli or al ragù, supplemented by an ever-changing list of daily specials. The *polpettini al lesso* (little meatballs) in a lively tomato sauce with peas and pancetta is one of many winning dishes that might be on offer. Attentive service and a fine wine list make having a meal here a true pleasure. [$] *Average main: €14* ✉ *Via della Tesoreria Vecchia 16* ☎ *0544/219536* 🌐 *www.osteriadeibattibecchi.it.*

$$ EMILIAN Fodor's Choice ★ 🍴 **Osteria del Tempo Perso.** A couple of jazz-, rock-, and food-loving friends joined forces to open this smart little restaurant in the centro storico. The interior's warm, terra-cotta-sponged walls give off an orange glow, and wine bottles line the walls, interspersed with photographs of musical greats. The classics are cooked well here, with the local specialty, cappelletti, prepared three different ways—sauced with butter, with a meat ragù, or in broth. But the kitchen also produces contemporary fare. The *gamberi croccanti con riso venere e vellutata di zucca*—shrimp so lightly fried you'd hardly know it, served with wild rice and pumpkin puree—is an absolute winner. The carefully culled wine list includes many local wines, and the service is stellar. [$] *Average main: €18* ✉ *Via Gamba 12* ☎ *0544/215393* 🌐 *www.osteriadeltempoperso.it* ⏲ *No lunch weekdays and July and Aug.*

$$ HOTEL 🏨 **Albergo Cappello.** In operation since the late 19th century and restored a century later, this charming place reflects a Venetian influence, with many Murano chandeliers hanging in the high-ceiling, wood-coffered public rooms. **Pros:** good location; accommodating staff; good restaurant. **Cons:** only seven rooms. [$] *Rooms from: €139* ✉ *Via IV Novembre 41* ☎ *0544/219876* 🌐 *www.albergocappello.it* 🛏 *2 rooms, 5 suites* 🍽 *No meals.*

NIGHTLIFE AND PERFORMING ARTS

Mosaics by Night. On Friday night from June to August, the Byzantine mosaic masterpieces in town are illuminated. The event is also held on certain Tuesdays. To check, call the tourist office, which offers guided tours.

Ravenna Festival. Orchestras from all over the world perform in city churches and theaters during this music festival that takes place in June and July. 🌐 *www.ravennafestival.org.*

CENTRAL ITALY

WHAT'S WHERE

1 Florence. It's hard to think of a place that's more closely linked to one specific historical period than Florence. In the 15th century the city was at the center of an artistic revolution, later labeled the Renaissance, which changed the way people saw the world. Five hundred years later the Renaissance remains the reason people visit Florence—the abundance of treasures is mind-boggling. Present-day Florentines have a somewhat uneasy relationship with their city's past; the never-ending stream of tourists is something they seem to tolerate more often than embrace. Still, they pride themselves on living well, and that means you'll find exceptional restaurants and first-rate shopping to go with all that amazing art.

2 Tuscany. Nature outdid herself in Tuscany, the central Italian region that has Florence as its principal city. Descriptions and photographs can't do the landscape justice—the hills, draped with woods, vineyards, and olive groves, may not have the drama of mountain peaks or waves crashing on the shore, yet there's an undeniable magic about them. Aside from Florence, Tuscany has several midsize cities that are well worth visiting, but the

greatest appeal lies in the smaller towns, often perched on hilltops and not significantly altered since the Middle Ages. Despite its popularity with fellow travelers, Tuscany remains a place you can escape to.

3 Umbria and the Marches. This region is closer to the Apennines than Tuscany is, so the landscape is wilder, the valleys deeper, and the mountains higher. The greater isolation of Umbria's towns and, until the unification of Italy, their association with the Papal States, may have encouraged the development of a keen sense of spirituality. Several of Italy's major saints are from the region, including St. Benedict of Norcia, St. Rita of Cascia, St. Chiara of Assisi, and most famously St. Francis of Assisi. There's no city with the size or significance of Florence, but a number of the smaller towns, particularly Assisi, Perugia, Spoleto, and Orvieto, have lots to hold your interest. Umbria's Roman past is much in evidence—expect to see Roman villas, aqueducts, and temples. To the east, in the Marches, the main draw is Urbino, where the Ducal Palace reveals more about the Renaissance than a shelf of art history books.

PLANNER

When to Go

Throughout Tuscany and Umbria, the best times to visit are spring and fall. Days are warm, nights are cool, and though there are still tourists, the crowds are smaller. In the countryside the scenery is gorgeous, with abundant greenery and flowers in spring, and burnished leaves in autumn.

July and August are the most popular times to visit. Note, though, that the heat is often oppressive and mosquitoes are prevalent. Try to start your days early and visit major sights first to beat the crowds and the midday sun. For relief from the heat, head to the mountains of the Garfagnana, where hiking is spectacular, or hit the beach at resort towns such as Forte dei Marmi and Viareggio, along the Maremma coast, on the island of Elba, or on the long, flat stretches of sandy beach on the east coast of the Marches.

November through March you might wonder who invented the term "sunny Italy." The panoramas are still beautiful, even with overcast skies, frequent rain, and occasional snow. In winter Florence benefits from shorter museum lines and less competition for restaurant tables. Outside the cities, though, many hotels and restaurants close for the season.

On the Calendar: Events and Festivals

Several major events mark the calendar in Tuscany and Umbria, drawing attendees from around the world.

For the two weeks leading up to Lent, the town of Viareggio along the coast of northwest Tuscany is given over to the sometimes-bawdy revelry of **Carnevale.** The festivities are second only to Venice's in size and lavishness.

Twice a year, on July 2 and August 16, Siena goes medieval with the **Palio,** a bareback horse race around its main square.

However, Palio is not a mere competition—it's a celebration of tradition and culture dating back 1,000 years.

For two weeks in late June and early July, stars from the worlds of classical music and the performing arts make their way to the Umbrian hill town of Spoleto to take part in the **Festival dei Due Mondi.** Opera fans crowd the outdoor **Puccini Festival** held in July and August at Torre del Lago, while Florence's **Maggio Musicale,** which extends through most of the year, attracts an international audience for performances of opera, classical music, and ballet.

While the big events are impressive, the calendar also overflows with smaller traditional *sagre* (festivals or fairs). You'll find them in towns of every size, January through December, with names like **Sagra del Cinghiale** (Wild Boar Festival), **Sagra della Castagna** (Chestnut Festival), and **Festa del Fungo** (Mushroom Festival). There's the **Befanate** (celebrating Italy's witchlike Santa equivalent, Befena) in Grosseto during Epiphany, the **Teatro Povero** (a folk theater production) in Monticchiello in July, and, throughout southern Tuscany on the night of April 30, the **Canta il Maggio** (Songs for Spring) are performed. Some of the most beautiful festivals are the *infiore* (flower petal decorations) that color the streets of many towns at Corpus Domini (the ninth Sunday after Easter)—Spello's infiorata is particularly splendid.

Sagre are fun, and there's often delicious traditionally prepared food to be had. You can check with the local or regional tourist information offices for the dates and times of any sagre that happen to coincide with your visit.

Getting Here

Most flights to Tuscany originating in the United States stop either in Rome, London, Paris, or Frankfurt, and then connect to Florence's small **Aeroporto A. Vespucci** (commonly called **Peretola**), or to Pisa's **Aeroporto Galileo Galilei**. The only exception at this writing is Delta's direct flight from New York (JFK) to Pisa, which operates only during the summer peak season.

Alternatively, it's an hour by train or an hour and a half by car to reach the lovely town of Orvieto from Rome's **Aeroporto Leonardo da Vinci** (commonly called **Fiumicino**). Another option is to fly to Milan and pick up a connecting flight to Pisa, Florence, Perugia, or Ancona in the Marches.

Biking and Hiking

In spring, summer, and fall, bicyclists pedaling up and down Tuscany's hills are as much a part of the landscape as the cypress trees. Many are on weeklong organized tours, but it's also possible to rent bikes for jaunts in the countryside or to join afternoon or daylong rides.

Hiking is a simpler matter: all you need is a pair of sturdy shoes. The tourist information offices in most towns can direct you on walks ranging from an hour to a full day in duration. You can also sign on for more elaborate guided tours.

Italy by Design (⊠ *Via delle Lame 52, Florence* ☎ *055/6532381* ⊕ *www.italybydesign.info*) provides city walks in Florence with expert guides, and made-to-measure hiking and driving vacations throughout Italy. The Salerno-based **Genius Loci** (⊠ *Via Rotondo 5, Salerno* ☎ *089/791896* ⊕ *www.genius-loci.it*) offers guided and self-guided biking and walking tours for the budget-conscious throughout Italy. **Italian Connection**

(⊠ *894 Weeks Landing Rd., Cape May, NJ* ☎ *0932/231816* in Italy ⊕ *www.italian-connection.com*) conducts high-end walking and culinary trips throughout Italy.

Driving in Italy

When you hit the road, don't be surprised to encounter tailgating and high-risk passing. Your best response is to take the same safety-first approach you use at home. On the plus side, Italy's roads are usually well maintained (though *strade regionali*, local roads, often are not). Note that wearing a seat belt and having your lights on at all times are required by law.

TYPICAL TRAVEL TIMES		
	HOURS BY CAR	HOURS BY TRAIN
Florence–Rome	3 hrs	1 hr 35 mins
Florence–Venice	3 hrs 30 mins	2 hrs 5 mins
Florence–Bologna	1 hr 30 mins	40 mins
Florence–Pisa	1 hr 30 mins	1 hr 5 mins
Florence–Perugia	1 hr 45 mins	2 hrs 15 mins
Siena–Perugia	1 hr 30 mins	3 hrs
Perugia–Assisi	30 mins	20 mins
Perugia–Orvieto	1 hr 15 mins	1 hr 45 mins
Assisi–Rome	2 hrs 15 mins	2 hrs 10 mins
Orvieto–Rome	1 hr 30 mins	1 hr 10 mins

CENTRAL ITALY TOP ATTRACTIONS

Galleria degli Uffizi, Florence

(A) Florence has many museums, but the Uffizi is king. Walking its halls is like stepping into an art history textbook, except here you're looking at the genuine article—masterpieces by Leonardo, Michelangelo, Raphael, Botticelli, Caravaggio, and dozens of other luminaries. When planning your visit, make a point to reserve a ticket in advance. (⇨ *Chapter 10.)*

Duomo, Florence

(B) The Cathedral of Santa Maria del Fiore, commonly known as the Duomo, is Florence's most distinctive landmark, sitting at the very heart of the city and towering over the neighboring rooftops. Its massive dome is one of the world's great engineering masterpieces. For an up-close look, you can climb the 463 steps to the top—then gaze out at the city beneath you. (⇨ *Chapter 10.)*

Leaning Tower, Pisa

(C) This tower may be too famous for its own good (it's one of Italy's most popular tourist attractions), but there's something undeniably appealing about its perilous tilt, and climbing to the top is a kick. The square on which it sits, known as the Piazza dei Miracoli, has a majestic beauty that no quantity of tourists can diminish. (⇨ *Chapter 11.)*

Piazza del Campo, Siena

(D) The sloping, fan-shape square in the heart of Siena is one of the best places in Italy to engage in the distinctly Italian activity of hanging out and people-watching. The flanking Palazzo Pubblico and Torre del Mangia are first-rate sights. (⇨ *Chapter 11.)*

San Gimignano, Central Tuscany

(E) This classic Tuscan hill town has been dubbed a "medieval Manhattan" because of its numerous towers, built by noble families of the time, each striving

to outdo its neighbors. The streets fill with tour groups during the day, but if you stick around until sunset, the crowds diminish, and you see the town at its most beautiful. (⇨ *Chapter 11.*)

Abbazia di Sant'Antimo, Southern Tuscany

In a peaceful valley, surrounded by gently rolling hills, olive trees, and thick oak woods, Sant'Antimo is one of Italy's most beautifully situated abbeys—and a great off-the-beaten-path destination. Stick around for mass, and you'll hear the halls resound with Gregorian chant. (⇨ *Chapter 11.*)

Palazzo Ducale, Urbino, the Marches

(F) East of Umbria in the Marches region, Urbino is a college town in the Italian style—meaning its small but prestigious university dates to the 15th century. The highlight here is the Palazzo Ducale, a palace that exemplifies the Renaissance ideals of grace and harmony. (⇨ *Chapter 12.*)

Basilica di San Francesco, Assisi

(G) The basilica, built to honor St. Francis, consists of two great churches: one Romanesque, fittingly solemn with its low ceilings and guttering candles; the other Gothic, with soaring arches and stained-glass windows (the first in Italy). They're both filled with some of Europe's finest frescoes. (⇨ *Chapter 12.*)

Duomo, Orvieto

(H) The facade of Orvieto's monumental Duomo contains a bas-relief masterpiece depicting the stories of the Creation and the Last Judgment (with the horrors of hell shown in striking detail). Inside, there's more glorious gore in the right transept, frescoed with Luca Signorelli's *Stories of the Antichrist and the Last Judgment*. (⇨ *Chapter 12.*)

TOP EXPERIENCES

The View from Florence's Piazzale Michelangelo

One of the best ways to introduce yourself to Florence is by walking up to this square on the hill south of the Arno. From here you can take in the whole city, and much of the surrounding countryside, in one spectacular vista. To extend the experience, linger at one of the outdoor cafés, and for the finest view of all, time your visit to correspond with sunset.

Strolling the Ramparts of Lucca

Lucca, 80 km (50 miles) west of Florence, isn't situated on a hilltop in the way commonly associated with Tuscan towns, and it doesn't have quite the abundance of art treasures that you find in Siena or Pisa (to say nothing of Florence). Yet for many visitors Lucca is a favorite Tuscan destination, and the source of its appeal has everything to do with its ramparts.

These hulking barricades have surrounded the city center since the 17th century; built as a source of security, they now are part of an elevated, oval park, complete with walkways, picnic areas, grass, and trees. The citizens of Lucca spend much of their spare time here, strolling, biking, and lounging, oblivious to the novelty of their situation but clearly happy with it.

Wine Tasting in Chianti

The gorgeous hills of the Chianti region, between Florence and Siena, produce exceptional wines, and they never taste better than when sampled on their home turf. Many Chianti vineyards are visitor-friendly, but the logistics of a visit are different from what you may have experienced in other wine regions.

If you just drop in, you're likely to get a tasting, but for a tour you usually need to make an appointment several days ahead of time. The upside is that your tour may end up being a half day of full immersion—including extended conversation with the winemakers and even a meal.

Hiking in the Footsteps of St. Francis

Umbria, which bills itself as "Italy's Green Heart," is fantastic hiking country. Among the many options are two with a Franciscan twist. From the town of Cannara, 16 km (10 miles) south of Assisi, an easy half-hour walk leads to the fields of Pian d'Arca, where St. Francis delivered his sermon to the birds.

For a slightly more demanding walk, you can follow the saint's path from Assisi to the Eremo delle Carceri (Hermitage of Prisons), where Francis and his followers went to "imprison" themselves in prayer, and from here you may continue along the trails that crisscross Monte Subasio.

Sampling Umbrian Truffles

The truffle (*tartufo* in Italian) is a peculiar delicacy; a gnarly clump of fungus that grows wild in the forest a few inches underground, is hunted down by specially trained truffle-sniffing dogs (or sometimes pigs), and can sell for a small fortune. The payoff is a powerful, aromatic flavor that makes food lovers swoon. Umbria is one of Italy's richest black truffle–hunting grounds, and in many of the region's restaurants you'll encounter truffle-infused dishes or be offered a shaving of truffle over your pasta. Indulge yourself at least once—it's an experience you won't forget.

CENTRAL ITALY TODAY

Preserving Artistic Heritage

Work continues on the expansion of Florence's Museo dell'Opera del Duomo. Though most of the museum has been closed while the renovation takes place, Lorenzo Ghiberti's *Doors of Paradise* and Michelangelo's *Pietà* are still on display. Almost €24 million have been invested in the project, which will incorporate the old building and the structure of a nearby 18th-century theater. It is likely that the latter occupies the site where Michelangelo carved the *David* at the beginning of the 16th century. In addition, the 28 panels of Ghiberti's north doors of the Baptistery have been replaced by copies while the originals are restored. The cleaned panels will be displayed in the new museum. Andrea Pisano's south doors are also due to receive the same treatment. During early work on the foundations of the new building, excavations unearthed a brick model of the dome of Florence's Duomo—it's quite possibly an early prototype used by architect Filippo Brunelleschi to test his new building technique. It will most likely be on display in the new museum as well. Expansion, and new displays also mark the future of the Uffizi Gallery, making second and third visits a must over the next several years— even if you think you've seen it all before.

Reconciling Antiquity and Modernity

Storms of controversy still surround the construction of Florence's new high-speed train line, with a proposed tunnel underneath the city being the main bone of contention. Though due to restart work during 2015, the tunneling machine has sat silent for more than two years while concerns over the vibrations it causes were voiced and a legal case against some of the developers of the project went to court. With typical Tuscan irony, the machine has been dubbed the "Mona Lisa," quite possibly because Leonardo da Vinci is thought to have worked on the painting for 14 years. The project also involves the ultramodern redesign (drawn up in now distant 2003) of Florence's second train station, Campo di Marte, by British architect Sir Norman Foster, which, by the time the station is finished—work has hardly begun—may not be so ultramodern as once planned.

Cooking with New Ingredients

It has long been known, and documented since the 13th century, that the hills of central Tuscany, Umbria and the Marches provide the ideal soil and climatic conditions for growing the type of crocus from which saffron is harvested. Traditionally used only for medicinal purposes and the dyeing of textiles, *zafferano* (saffron) never appears in central Italian traditional cooking. The newly formed Associazione dello Zafferano Italiano (Italian Saffron Association), headquartered just outside Florence, hopes to popularize the use of saffron in local cuisine by promoting the quality of the local product and its culinary uses. Next time you visit, don't be surprised to find the spice, the most expensive by weight in the world, labeled "Product of Central Italy" and lending flavor to a wide variety of newly invented dishes.

Uncovering Its Origins

A recent study, using bone samples from burial sites, has shown that Etruscan DNA is identical to that of some contemporary inhabitants of Volterra and the Casentino, a mountain region to the east of Florence. So don't be surprised if you spot a face that might resemble someone who lived 2,500 years ago!

A GREAT ITINERARY

Day 1: Florence

If you're coming in on an international flight, you'll probably settle in Florence in time for an afternoon stroll or siesta (depending on your jet-lag strategy) before dinner.

Logistics: On your flight in, read through the restaurant listings in this guide and begin anticipating the first dinner of your trip. Look for a place near your hotel, and when you arrive, reserve a table (or have your concierge do it for you).

Making a meal the focus of your first day is a great way to ease into Italian life. Note that Sunday and Monday are favorite closing days for many Florence restaurants, and Monday sees most important museums closed.

Day 2: Florence

Begin your morning at the **Uffizi Gallery** (reserve your ticket in advance). The extensive collection will occupy much of your morning. Next, take in the neighboring **Piazza della Signoria,** one of Florence's impressive squares, then head a few blocks north to the **Duomo.** There, check out Ghiberti's famous bronze doors on the **Battistero** (they're high-quality copies; the originals are in the Museo dell'Opera del Duomo), and work up an appetite by climbing the 463 steps to the cupola of Brunelleschi's splendid cathedral dome, atop which you'll experience a memorable view.

Spend the afternoon relaxing, shopping, and wandering Florence's medieval streets; or, if you're up for more of a journey, head out to **Fiesole** to experience the ancient amphitheater and beautiful views of the Tuscan countryside.

Day 3: Florence

Keep the energy level up for your second full day in Florence, sticking with art and architecture for the morning, trying to see most of the following: Michelangelo's *David* at the **Galleria dell'Accademia,** the **Medici Chapels,** the **Palazzo Pitti** and **Boboli Gardens,** and the churches of **Santa Maria Novella** and **Santa Croce.**

If it's a clear day, spend the afternoon on a trip to **Piazzale Michelangelo,** high on a hill, for sweeping views of idyllic Florentine countryside. Given all the walking you've been doing, this would be a good night to recharge by trying the famed *bistecca alla fiorentina* (a grilled T-bone steak with olive oil).

Logistics: You can get up to the Piazzale Michelangelo by taxi or by taking Bus No. 12 or 13 from the Lungarno. Otherwise, do your best to get around on foot; Florence is a brilliant city for walking.

Day 4: San Gimignano

Now that you've been appropriately introduced to the bewildering splendor of Renaissance Italy, it's time for a change of pace—and time for a rental car, which will enable you to see the back roads of Tuscany and Umbria. After breakfast, head on out. On a beautiful day the lazy drive from Florence to **San Gimignano,** past vineyards and typical Tuscan landscapes, is truly spectacular.

The first thing that will hit you when you arrive at the hill town of San Gimignano will be its multiple towers. The medieval skyscrapers of Italy once occupied the role now played by Ferraris or Hummers: they were public displays of wealth and family power. After finding your way to a hotel in the old town, set out on foot and check out the city's turrets and alleyways, doing your best to get away from the trinket

shops. Later, enjoy a leisurely dinner with the light but delicious local white wine, Vernaccia di San Gimignano.

Logistics: Some hotels might be able to coordinate with some rental-car agencies so that your car can be brought to your hotel for you. The historic center of Florence is closed to nonresidents' cars (including rentals). You can drive out of the center, but must give your license plate number to your hotel if you drive in—there's a heavy fine otherwise.

Once you navigate your way out of Florence (no easy task), San Gimignano is only 57 km (35 miles) to the southwest, so it's an easy drive; you could even take a detour on the SR222 (Strada Chianti-giana), stop at one of the Chianti wine towns, and visit a winery along the way.

Day 5: Siena

In the morning, set out for nearby **Siena,** which is known worldwide for its Palio, a festival that culminates in an elaborate horse-race competition among the 17 *contrade* (medieval neighborhoods) of the city. Because of the enormous influx of tourists, especially in summer, Siena isn't everyone's cup of tea, but it's still one of Tuscany's most impressive sights.

However many tourists you have to bump elbows with, it's hard not to be blown away by the city's precious medieval streets and memorable fan-shape **Piazza del Campo.**

Not to be missed while in town are the spectacular **Duomo,** the **Battistero,** and the **Spedale di Santa Maria della Scala,** an old hospital and hostel that now contains an underground archaeological museum.

Logistics: It's a short and pleasant drive from San Gimignano to Siena, but once there, parking can be a challenge. Look for the *stadio* (soccer stadium), where there's a parking lot that often has space. Try to avoid arriving in Siena on Wednesday morning—the town's weekly market is in full swing, and the traffic and parking can be nightmarish.

Day 6: Arezzo/Cortona

Get an early start, because there's a lot to see today. From Siena you'll first head to **Arezzo,** home to the **Basilica di San Francesco,** which contains important frescoes by Piero della Francesca. Check out the **Piazza Grande** along with its beautiful Romanesque church, **Pieve di Santa Maria.**

Try to do all of this before lunch, after which you'll head straight to **Cortona.** If Arezzo didn't capture your imagination, Cortona, whose origins date to the 5th century BC, will. Olive trees and vineyards give way to a medieval hill town

with views over ridiculously idyllic Tuscan countryside and Lake Trasimeno. Cortona is a town for walking and relaxing, not sightseeing, so enjoy yourself, wandering through the **Piazza della Repubblica** and **Piazza Signorelli,** and perhaps doing a bit of shopping.

Logistics: Siena to Arezzo is 63 km (39 miles) on the E78. From Arezzo to Cortona, it's 30 km (18 miles)—take S71.

Day 7: Assisi

Today you'll cross over into Umbria, a region just as beautiful as Tuscany but still less trodden. Yet another impossibly beautiful hill town, **Assisi,** is the home of St. Francis and host to the many religious pilgrims that come to venerate his legacy. A visit here is the most treasured memory of many a traveler's visit to Italy.

Upon arriving and checking into your lodging, head straight for the **Basilica di San Francesco,** which displays the tomb of St. Francis and unbelievable frescoes. From here take Via San Francesco to **Piazza del Commune** and see the **Tempio di Minerva** before a break for lunch. After lunch, see **San Rufino,** the town cathedral, and then go back through the piazza to Corso Mazzini and see **Santa Chiara.** If you're a true Franciscan, you could instead devote the afternoon to heading out 16 km (10 miles) to **Cannara,** where St. Francis delivered his sermon to the birds.

Logistics: From Cortona, take the S71 to the A1 autostrada toward Perugia. After about 40 km (24 miles), take the Assisi exit (E45), and it's another 14 km (8 miles).

Day 8: Spoleto

This morning will take you from a small Umbrian hill town to a slightly bigger one: **Spoleto,** a walled city that's home to a world-renowned arts festival each summer. But Spoleto's own renown rivals that of its festival. Its **Duomo** is wonderful. Its fortress, **La Rocca,** is impressive. And the **Ponte delle Torri,** a 14th-century bridge that separates Spoleto from Monteluco, is a marvelous sight, traversing a gorge 260 feet below and built on the foundations of a Roman aqueduct.

See all these during the day, stopping for a light lunch of a *panino* (sandwich) or salad, saving your appetite for a serious last dinner in Italy: Umbrian cuisine is excellent everywhere, but Spoleto is a memorable culinary destination. Do your best to sample black truffles, a proud product of the region; they're delicious on pasta or meat.

Logistics: One school of thought would be to time your visit to Spoleto's world-renowned arts festival that runs from mid-June through mid-July. Another would be to do anything you can to avoid it. It all depends on your taste for big festivals and big crowds.

The trip from Assisi to Spoleto is a lovely 47-km (29-mile) drive (S75 to the S3) that should take you less than an hour, a little longer if you plan a stop in the charming town of Spello on the way.

Day 9: Spoleto/Departure

It's a fair distance from Spoleto to the Florence airport, your point of departure. Depending on your comfort level with driving in Italy, allow at least 2½ hours to get there.

FLORENCE

10

WELCOME TO FLORENCE

TOP REASONS TO GO

★ **Galleria degli Uffizi:** Italian Renaissance art doesn't get much better than this vast collection bequeathed to the city by the last Medici, Anna Maria Luisa.

★ **Brunelleschi's Dome:** His work of engineering genius is the city's undisputed centerpiece.

★ **Michelangelo's *David*:** One look and you'll know why this is one of the Western world's most famous sculptures.

★ **The view from Piazzale Michelangelo:** From this perch you have the city laid out before you. The colors at sunset heighten the experience.

★ **Piazza Santa Croce:** After you've had your fill of Renaissance masterpieces, hang out here and watch the world go by.

1 Around the Duomo. Here you're in the heart of Florence. Among the numerous highlights are the city's greatest museum (the Uffizi) and arguably its most impressive square (Piazza della Signoria).

2 San Lorenzo. The blocks from the basilica of San Lorenzo to the Galleria dell'Accademia bear the imprints of the Medici and of Michelangelo, culminating in the latter's masterful *David*. Just to the north, the former convent of San Marco is an oasis of artistic treasures decorated with ethereal frescoes.

3 Santa Maria Novella. This part of town includes the train station, 16th-century palaces, and the city's swankest shopping street, Via Tornabuoni.

4 Santa Croce. The district centers on its namesake basilica, which is filled with the tombs of Renaissance (and other) luminaries. The area is also known for its leather shops.

5 The Oltrarno. Across the Arno you encounter the massive Palazzo Pitti and narrow streets of the Santo Spirito, filled with artisans' workshops and antiques stores. A climb to Piazzale Michelangelo gives you a spectacular view of the city.

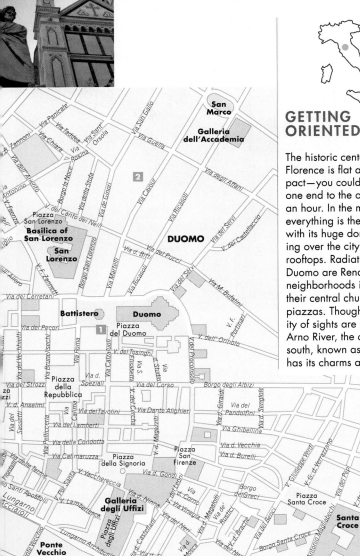

GETTING ORIENTED

The historic center of Florence is flat and compact—you could walk from one end to the other in half an hour. In the middle of everything is the Duomo, with its huge dome towering over the city's terra-cotta rooftops. Radiating from the Duomo are Renaissance-era neighborhoods identified by their central churches and piazzas. Though the majority of sights are north of the Arno River, the area to the south, known as the Oltrarno, has its charms as well.

10

EATING AND DRINKING WELL IN FLORENCE

In Florence simply prepared meats, grilled or roasted, are the culinary stars, usually paired with seasonal vegetables like artichokes or porcini. Bistecca's big here, but there's plenty more that tastes great on the grill, too.

Traditionalists go for their gustatory pleasures in trattorie and osterie, places where decor is unimportant and place mats are mere paper. Culinary innovation has come slowly in this town, though some cutting-edge restaurants have been appearing, usually with young chefs who've worked outside Italy, and are eager to reinterpret Tuscan classics while incorporating decidedly non-Tuscan ingredients. By American standards, Florentines eat late: 1:30 or 2 is typical for lunch and 9 is considered about right for dinner. Consuming a primo, secondo, and dolce is largely a thing of the past. For lunch, many Florentines simply grab a panino and a glass of wine at a bar. Those opting for a simple trattoria lunch often order a plate of pasta and dessert.

STALE AND STELLAR

Florence lacks signature pasta dishes, perhaps because it has raised frugality with bread to a culinary craft. Stale bread is the basis for three classic Florentine primi: pappa al pomodoro, ribollita, and panzanella. *Pappa* is made with tomatoes and stale bread. *Ribollita* is a vegetable soup fortified with *cavolo nero* (called Tuscan kale in the United States), cannellini beans, and thickened with bread. *Panzanella*, a summer dish, is reconstituted Tuscan bread combined with tomatoes, cucumber, and basil. They all are enhanced with fragrant Tuscan olive oil.

A CLASSIC ANTIPASTO: *CROSTINI DI FEGATINI*

This beloved dish consists of a chicken-liver spread, served warm or at room temperature, on toasted, garlic-rubbed bread. It can be served smooth, like a pâté, or in a chunkier, more rustic version. It's made by sautéing chicken livers with finely diced carrot and onion, enlivened with the addition of wine, broth, or Marsala reductions, and mashed anchovies and capers.

A CLASSIC SECONDO: *BISTECCA FIORENTINA*

The town's culinary pride and joy is a thick slab of beef, resembling a T-bone steak, from large white oxen called Chianina. The meat's slapped on the grill and served incredibly rare, sometimes with a pinch of salt.

It's always seared on both sides, and just barely cooked inside (experts say 5 minutes per side, and then 15 minutes with the bone sitting perpendicularly on the grill). To ask for it more well-done is to incur disdain; if you can't eat it this way, do please order something else.

A CLASSIC CONTORNO: CANNELLINI BEANS

Simply boiled, they provide the perfect accompaniment to bistecca. The small white beans are best when they go straight from the garden into the pot. They should be anointed with a generous dose of Tuscan olive oil; the

combination is oddly felicitous, and it goes a long way toward explaining why Tuscans are referred to as "*mangiafagioli*" ("bean eaters") by other Italians.

A CLASSIC DOLCE: *BISCOTTI DI PRATO*

These are sometimes the only dessert on offer (if you find yourself in such a restaurant, you'll know you're in a really, truly Florentine eatery) and are more or less an afterthought to the glories that have preceded them. "Biscotti" means twice-cooked (or, in this case, twice-baked). They are hard almond cookies that soften considerably when dipped languidly into *vin santo* ("holy wine"), a sweet dessert wine, or into a simple *caffè*.

A CLASSIC WINE: CHIANTI CLASSICO

This blend from the region just south of Florence relies mainly on the local, hardy sangiovese grape; it's aged for at least one year before hitting the market. (*Riserve* are aged at least an additional six months.)

Chianti is usually the libation of choice for Florentines, and it pairs magnificently with grilled foods and seasonal vegetables. Traditionalists opt for the younger, fruitier (and usually less expensive) versions often served in straw flasks. You can sample Chianti Classico all over town, and buy it in local *salumerie, enoteche,* and supermarkets.

10

Updated by Patricia Rucidlo

Why visit Florence, the city that shook up the Western world in the Middle Ages and gifted it with what would later be called the Renaissance? There are many reasons: its biggest draw is its unsurpassable art, from the sensuousness of Botticelli's nudes to the muscularity, masculinity, and virtual perfection of Michelangelo's *David*. Also to see firsthand Brunelleschi's engineering and architectural genius, from the powerful cupola crowning the cathedral to his fledgling Ospedale degli Innocenti (arguably the first Renaissance building in Italy).

Visitors have been captivated by this city along the Arno for centuries, and it has always been high on the list of places to visit on the Grand Tour. For centuries it has captured the imaginations of travelers in search of rooms with views and phenomenal art. Florence's is a subtle beauty—its staid palaces built in local stone are not showy, even though they are very large. A walk along the Arno offers views that don't quit and haven't much changed in 700 years. Navigating Piazza della Signoria and other major squares, always packed with tourists, requires patience. There's a reason why everyone wants to be here. Florence's *centro storico* (historic center) is little changed since Lorenzo de'Medici roamed its streets; outside the center, where most of the city's residents live, is less picturesque, but full of Florentines (they tend not to hang out in the historic center if they can help it).

When the sun sets over the Arno and, as Mark Twain described it, "overwhelms Florence with tides of color that make all the sharp lines dim and faint and turn the solid city to a city of dreams," it's hard not to fall under the city's spell.

FLORENCE PLANNER

MAKING THE MOST OF YOUR TIME

With some planning, you can see Florence's most famous sights in a couple of days. Start off at the city's most awe-inspiring architectural wonder, the **Duomo**, climbing to the top of the dome if you have the stamina (and are not claustrophobic: it gets a little tight going up and coming back down). On the same piazza, check out Ghiberti's bronze doors at the **Battistero.** (They're actually high-quality copies; the Museo dell'Opera del Duomo has the originals.) Set aside the afternoon for the **Galleria degli Uffizi,** making sure to reserve tickets in advance.

On Day 2, visit Michelangelo's *David* in the **Galleria dell'Accademia** (reserve tickets here, too). Linger in **Piazza della Signoria**, Florence's main civic square, where a copy of *David* stands in the spot the original occupied for centuries, then head east a couple of blocks to **Santa Croce,** the city's most artistically rich church. Double back and walk across Florence's landmark bridge, the **Ponte Vecchio.**

Do all that, and you'll have seen some great art, but you've just scratched the surface. If you have more time, put the **Bargello,** the **Museo di San Marco,** and the **Cappelle Medicee** at the top of your list. When you're ready for an art break, stroll through the **Boboli Gardens** or explore Florence's lively shopping scene, from the food stalls of the **Mercato Centrale** to the chic boutiques of the **Via Tornabuoni.**

HOURS

Florence's sights keep tricky hours. Some are closed Wednesday, some Monday, some every other Monday. Quite a few shut their doors each day (or on most days) by 2 in the afternoon. Things get even more confusing on weekends. Make it a general rule to check the hours closely for any place you're planning to visit; if it's someplace you have your heart set on seeing, it's worthwhile to call to confirm.

Here's a selection of major sights that might not be open when you'd expect. And be aware that, as always, hours can and do change.

The **Accademia** and the **Uffizi** are both closed Monday.

The **Battistero** is open from 11 until 7, Monday through Saturday, and Sunday from 8:30 to 2.

The **Bargello** closes at 1:50 pm, and is closed entirely on alternating Sundays and Mondays. However, it's often open much later during high season and when there's a special exhibition on.

The **Cappelle Medicee** are closed alternating Sundays and Mondays (those Sundays and Mondays when the Bargello is open).

The **Duomo** closes at 4 on Thursday (as opposed to 5 other weekdays and 4:45 on Saturday; from July to September it also stays open until 5 on Thursday). Sunday it's open only from 1:30 to 4:45; the dome of the Duomo is closed Sunday.

Museo di San Marco closes at 1:50 weekdays but stays open until 7 weekends—except for alternating Sundays and Mondays, when it's closed entirely.

Palazzo Medici-Riccardi is closed Wednesday.

10

RESERVATIONS

At most times of day you'll see a line of people snaking around the Uffizi. They're waiting to buy tickets, and you don't want to be one of them. Instead, call ahead for a reservation (☎ 055/294883; reservationists speak English). You'll be given a reservation number and a time of admission—the sooner you call, the more time slots you'll have to choose from. Go to the museum's reservation door at the appointed hour, give the clerk your number, pick up your ticket, and go inside. You'll pay €4 for this privilege, but it's money well spent. You can also book tickets online through the website ⊕ *www.polomuseale.firenze.it*; the booking process takes some patience, but it works.

Use the same reservation service to book tickets for the Galleria dell'Accademia, where lines rival those of the Uffizi. (Reservations can also be made for the Palazzo Pitti, the Bargello, and several other sights, but they usually aren't needed—although lately, in summer, lines can be long at Palazzo Pitti.) An alternative strategy is to check with your hotel: many will handle reservations.

At this writing, a decision had been made to allow free entry to all state-run museums (the Uffizi, Accademia, Bargello, San Marco, Cappelle Medicee, and others) on the first Sunday of the month. Reservations are not accepted then, and you'd do best to either visit the museum on Saturday or first thing on Tuesday morning.

GETTING HERE AND AROUND

AIR TRAVEL

Aeroporto A. Vespucci. Florence's small Aeroporto A. Vespucci, commonly called **Peretola**, is just outside of town, and receives flights from Milan, Rome, London, and Paris. ⊠ *10 km (6 miles) northwest of Florence* ☎ *055/30615* ⊕ *www.aeroporto.firenze.it.*

To get into the city center from the airport by car, take the A11 autostrada. A SITA bus will take you directly from the airport to the center of town. Tickets can be purchased on the bus.

Aeroporto Galileo Galilei. Pisa's Aeroporto Galileo Galilei is the closest landing point with significant international service, including a few direct flights from New York each week on Delta. Sadly, the flight is seasonal and shuts down when it's cold outside. It's a straight shot down the SS67 to Florence. A train service, which used to connect Pisa's airport station with Santa Maria Novella, has as of press time been temporarily suspended. It's easy to take the shuttle bus to the train station at Pisa Centrale, and then go on to Florence Santa Maria Novella. ⊠ *12 km (7 miles) south of Pisa and 80 km (50 miles) west of Florence* ☎ *050/849300* ⊕ *www.pisa-airport.com.*

BUS TRAVEL

Florence's flat, compact city center is made for walking, but when your feet get weary you can use the efficient bus system, which includes small electric buses making the rounds in the center. Buses also climb to Piazzale Michelangelo and San Miniato south of the Arno.

Maps and timetables for local bus service are available for a small fee at the ATAF (Azienda Trasporti Area Fiorentina) booth next to the train station, or for free at visitor information offices. Tickets must be bought in advance from tobacco shops, newsstands, automatic ticket machines near main stops, or ATAF booths. The ticket must be canceled in the small validation machine immediately upon boarding.

You have several ticket options, all valid for one or more rides on all lines. A €1.20 ticket is good for one hour from the time it is first canceled. A multiple ticket—four tickets, each valid for 70 minutes—costs €4.50. A 24-hour tourist ticket costs €5. Two-, three-, and seven-day passes are also available.

Long-distance buses provide inexpensive service between Florence and other cities in Italy and Europe. **Lazzi Eurolines** (⊠ *Via Mercadante 2* ☎ *055/363041* ⊕ *www.lazzi.it*) and **SITA** (⊠ *Via Santa Caterina da Siena 17/r* ☎ *055/47821* ⊕ *www.sitabus.it*) are the major lines.

CAR TRAVEL

Florence is connected to the north and south of Italy by the Autostrada del Sole (A1). It takes about 1½ hours of driving on scenic roads to get to Bologna (although heavy truck traffic over the Apennines often makes for slower going), about 3 hours to Rome, and 3 to 3½ hours to Milan. The Tyrrhenian Coast is an hour west on the A11.

An automobile in Florence is a major liability. If your itinerary includes parts of Italy where you'll want a car (such as Tuscany), pick the vehicle up on your way out of town.

TAXI TRAVEL

Taxis usually wait at stands throughout the city (in front of the train station and in Piazza della Repubblica, for example), or you can call for one (☎ *055/4390 or 055/4242*). The meter starts at €3.30 from any taxi stand; if you call Radio Dispatch (that means that a taxi comes to pick you up wherever you are), it starts at €5.40. Extra charges apply at night, on Sunday, for radio dispatch, and for luggage. Women out on the town after midnight seeking taxis are entitled to a 10% discount on the fare; you must, however, request it.

TRAIN TRAVEL

Florence is on the principal Italian train route between most European capitals and Rome, and within Italy it is served frequently from Milan, Venice, and Rome by high speed Eurostar trains. Avoid trains that stop only at the Campo di Marte or Rifredi station, which are not convenient to the city center.

Stazione Centrale di Santa Maria Novella. Florence's main train station is in the center of town. ☎ *892021* ⊕ *www.trenitalia.com.*

VISITOR INFORMATION

The Florence tourist office, known as the **APT** (☎ *055/290832* ⊕ *www. firenzeturismo.it*), has branches next to the Palazzo Medici-Riccardi, across the street from Stazione di Santa Maria Novella (the main train station), and at the Bigallo, in Piazza del Duomo. The offices are generally open from 9 in the morning until 7 in the evening. The multilingual staff will give you directions and the latest on happenings in the city. It's particularly worth a stop if you're interested in finding out about performing-arts events. The APT website provides information in both Italian and English.

10

EXPLORING

AROUND THE DUOMO

The heart of Florence, stretching from the Piazza del Duomo south to the Arno, is as dense with artistic treasures as any place in the world. Its churches, medieval towers, Renaissance palaces, and world-class museums and galleries contain some of the most outstanding achievements of Western art.

Much of the centro storico is closed to automobile traffic, but you still must dodge mopeds, cyclists, and masses of fellow tourists as you walk the narrow streets, especially in the area bounded by the Duomo, Piazza della Signoria, Galleria degli Uffizi, and Ponte Vecchio. Via dei Calzaiuoli, between Piazza del Duomo and Piazza della Signoria, is the city's favorite passeggiata.

TOP ATTRACTIONS

Bargello. This building started out as the headquarters for the Capitano del Popolo (captain of the people) during the Middle Ages, and was later used as a prison. The exterior served as a "most wanted" billboard: effigies of notorious criminals and Medici enemies were painted on its walls. Today it houses the **Museo Nazionale,** home to what is probably the finest collection of Renaissance sculpture in Italy. The concentration of masterworks by Michelangelo (1475–1564), Donatello (circa 1386–1466), and Benvenuto Cellini (1500–71) is remarkable; the works are distributed among an eclectic collection of arms, ceramics, and miniature bronzes, among other things. For Renaissance art lovers, the Bargello is to sculpture what the Uffizi is to painting.

✉ *Via del Proconsolo 4, Bargello* ☎ *055/294883* ⊕ *www.polomuseale. firenze.it* ⌦ *€4* ⊙ *Daily 8:15–1:50; closed 2nd and 4th Mon. of month.*

Battistero (*Baptistery*). The octagonal Baptistery is one of the supreme monuments of the Italian Romanesque style and one of Florence's oldest structures. Local legend has it that it was once a Roman temple dedicated to Mars (it wasn't), and modern excavations suggest that its foundations date from the 1st century AD. The round Romanesque arches on the exterior date from the 11th century, and the interior dome mosaics from the beginning of the mid-13th century are justly renowned, but—glittering beauties though they are—they could never outshine the building's famed bronze Renaissance doors decorated with panels crafted by Lorenzo Ghiberti. These doors—or at least copies of them—on which Ghiberti worked most of his adult life (1403–52) are on the north and east sides of the Baptistery, and the Gothic panels on the south door were designed by Andrea Pisano (circa 1290–1348) in 1330. Ghiberti's original doors were removed to protect them from the effects of pollution and acid rain and have been beautifully restored; at this writing, the museum was closed and expected to reopen sometime in late 2015. Ghiberti's north doors depict scenes from the life of Christ; his later east doors (dating from 1425–52), facing the Duomo facade, render scenes from the Old Testament. Both merit close examination, for they are very

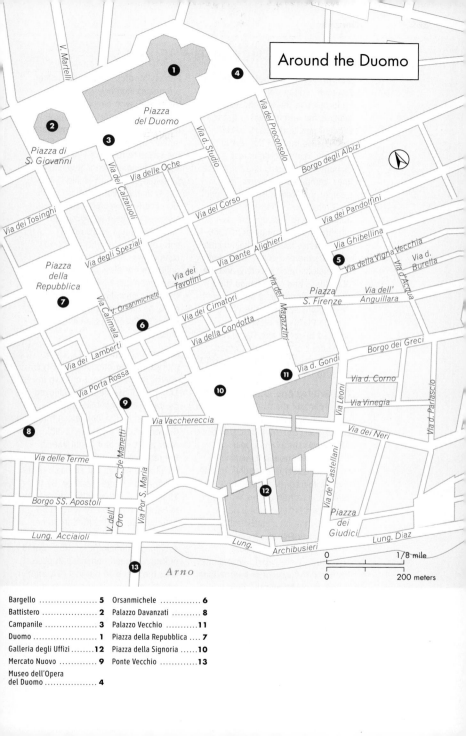

Around the Duomo

FLORENCE THROUGH THE AGES

Guelph versus Ghibelline. Though Florence can lay claim to a modest importance in the ancient world, it didn't come into its own until the Middle Ages. In the early 1200s the city, like most of the rest of Italy, was rent by civic unrest. Two factions, the Guelphs and the Ghibellines, competed for power. The Guelphs supported the papacy, and the Ghibellines supported the Holy Roman Empire. Bloody battles—most notably one at Montaperti in 1260—tore Florence and other Italian cities apart. By the end of the 13th century the Guelphs ruled securely, and the Ghibellines had been vanquished. This didn't end civic strife, however: the Guelphs split into the Whites and the Blacks for reasons still debated by historians. Dante Alighieri, author of *The Divine Comedy*, was banished from Florence in 1301 because he was a White.

The Guilded Age. Local merchants had organized themselves into guilds by sometime beginning in the 12th century. In 1250, they proclaimed themselves the *primo popolo* (literally, "first people"), making a landmark attempt at republican rule. Though the episode lasted only 10 years, it constituted a breakthrough in Western history. Such a daring stance by the merchant class was a byproduct of Florence's emergence as an economic powerhouse. Florentines were papal bankers; they instituted the system of international letters of credit; and the gold florin became the international standard of currency. With this economic strength came a building boom. Sculptors such as Donatello and Ghiberti decorated them; painters such as Giotto and Botticelli frescoed their walls.

Mighty Medici. Though ostensibly a republic, Florence was blessed (or cursed) with one very powerful family, the Medici, who came to prominence in the 1430s and were initially the de facto rulers and then the absolute rulers of Florence for several hundred years. It was under patriarch Cosimo il Vecchio (1389–1464) that the Medici's position in Florence was securely established. Florence's golden age occurred during the reign of his grandson Lorenzo de' Medici (1449–92). Lorenzo was not only an astute politician but also a highly educated man and a great patron of the arts. Called "il Magnifico" (the Magnificent), he gathered around him poets, artists, philosophers, architects, and musicians.

Lorenzo's son Piero (1471–1503) proved inept at handling the city's affairs. He was run out of town in 1494, and Florence briefly enjoyed its status as a republic while dominated by the Dominican friar Girolamo Savonarola (1452–98). After a decade of internal unrest, the republic fell and the Medici were recalled to power, but Florence never regained its former prestige. By the 1530s most of the major artistic talent had left the city—Michelangelo, for one, had settled in Rome. The now mostly ineffectual Medici, eventually attaining the title of grand dukes, remained nominally in power until the line died out in 1737, after which time Florence passed from the Austrians to the French and back again until the unification of Italy (1865–70), when it briefly became the capital under King Vittorio Emanuele II.

different in style and illustrate the artistic changes that marked the beginning of the Renaissance.

As a footnote to Ghiberti's panels, one small detail of the larger east doors is worth a special look. To the lower left of the Jacob and Esau panel, Ghiberti placed a tiny self-portrait bust. From either side, the portrait is extremely appealing—Ghiberti looks like everyone's favorite uncle—but the bust

is carefully placed so that you can make direct eye contact with the tiny head from a single spot. When that contact is made, the impression of intelligent life—of *modern* intelligent life—is astonishing. It's no wonder that these doors received one of the most famous compliments in the history of art from an artist known to be notoriously stingy with praise: Michelangelo declared them so beautiful that they could serve as the Gates of Paradise. ☒ *Piazza del Duomo* ☎ *055/2302885* ⊕ *www. operaduomo.firenze.it* ☒ *€10* ☉ *Mon.–Sat. 11:15–7, Sun. 8:30–2, 1st Sat. of month 8:30–2.*

Fodor'sChoice ★ **Duomo.** *(See the highlighted listing in this chapter.)* ☒ *Piazza del Duomo* ☎ *055/2302885* ⊕ *www.operaduomo.firenze.it* ☒ *Church free; combination ticket €10, includes Baptistery, Crypt, Museo, Campanile, cupola* ☉ *Duomo only: May and Oct., Thurs.–Sat. 10–4:45, Sun. 1:30–4:45; July–Sept., Sat. 10–4:45, Sun. 1:30–4:45; Jan.–Apr., Nov., and Dec., Thurs. 10–4:30, Sat. 10–4:45, Sun. 1:30–4:45. Crypt: Mon.–Wed. and Fri. 10–5, Thurs. 10–4:30, Sat. 10–4:45. Cupola: weekdays 8:30–7, Sat. 8:30–5:40.*

Fodor'sChoice ★ **Galleria degli Uffizi.** The venerable Uffizi Gallery occupies two floors of the U-shaped **Palazzo degli Uffizi,** designed by Giorgio Vasari (1511–74) in 1560 to hold the *uffizi* (administrative offices) of the Medici grand duke Cosimo I (1519–74). Later, the Medici installed their art collections here, creating what was Europe's first modern museum, open to the public (at first only by request) since 1591.

Among the highlights are Paolo Uccello's *Battle of San Romano,* its brutal chaos of lances one of the finest visual metaphors for warfare ever captured in paint (in returned from a glorious restoration in the summer of 2012); the *Madonna and Child with Two Angels,* by Fra Filippo Lippi (1406–69), in which the impudent eye contact established by the angel would have been unthinkable prior to the Renaissance; the *Birth of Venus* and *Primavera* by Sandro Botticelli (1445–1510), the goddess of the former seeming to float on air and the fairy-tale charm of the latter exhibiting the painter's idiosyncratic genius at its zenith; the portraits of the Renaissance duke Federico da Montefeltro and his wife Battista Sforza, by Piero della Francesca (circa 1420–92); the *Madonna of the Goldfinch* by Raphael (1483–1520), and check out the brilliant blues that decorate the sky, as well as the eye contact between mother and child, both clearly anticipating the painful future; Michelangelo's *Doni Tondo*; the *Venus*

10

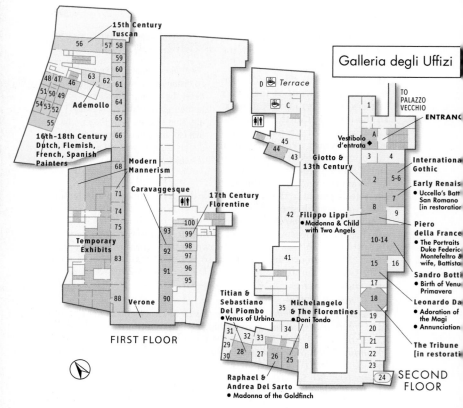

Galleria degli Uffizi

15th Century Tuscan

56 57 58
59
60
48 47 46 63 62 61
51 50 49 64
54 53 52 65
55 66
Ademollo

16th–18th Century Dutch, Flemish, French, Spanish Painters

68 **Modern Mannerism**

Caravaggesque

71
74
75
Temporary Exhibits
83

17th Century Florentine

100
93 99
92 98
97
91 96
95
90

88 **Verone**

FIRST FLOOR

D 🍴 **Terrace**
🍴 C
🚻

45
44
43 **Giotto & 13th Century**

Titian & Sebastiano Del Piombo
● Venus of Urbino

42 **Filippo Lippi**
● Madonna & Child with Two Angels

41

35 **Michelangelo & The Florentines**
● Doni Tondo

31
29 32 33 34
30 28 27 26 25
B

Raphael & Andrea Del Sarto
● Madonna of the Goldfinch

TO PALAZZO VECCHIO

1 **ENTRANC**

Vestibolo d'entrata ◆ A

3 4 **Internationa Gothic**

2 5-6

7 **Early Renais**
● Uccello's Batt San Romano [in restoratior]

8 9

Piero della France
● The Portraits Duke Federic Montefeltro & wife, Battista

10-14

15 16 **Sandro Botti**
● Birth of Venu Primavera

17

18 **Leonardo Da**
● Adoration of the Magi
19 ● Annunciation

20

21 **The Tribune** [in restorati]

22

23

24 **SECOND FLOOR**

of Urbino by Titian (circa 1488/90–1576); and the splendid *Bacchus* by Caravaggio (circa 1571/72–1610). In the last two works, the approaches to myth and sexuality are diametrically opposed (to put it mildly). Don't forget to see the Caravaggios, which you'll pass through during the exiting process. In summer 2012, many new rooms were opened (complementing the blue rooms housing non-Italian art from the year before) and, at press time, rooms were continuing to be added. This means that getting out of the museum takes even longer. Don't think you've missed the Raphaels, which used to live in the room next door to Michelangelo's stunning panel painting; they are now practically the last thing you'll see before leaving, so remember to save some stamina in order to truly appreciate their splendor. And don't think you've missed the Michelangelo, as in winter 2013 it was moved from Sala 25 to Sala 35. At this writing, and at last count, the Uffizi numbered 102 rooms, many of which were empty, awaiting more recent, non-Italian Renaissance additions.

Late in the afternoon is the least crowded time to visit. For a €4 fee, advance tickets can be reserved by phone, online, or, once in Florence, at the Uffizi reservation booth (✉ *Consorzio ITA, Piazza Pitti 1* ☎ *055/294883*) at least one day in advance of your visit. Keep the confirmation number and take it with you to the door at the museum marked "Reservations." In the past, you were ushered in almost immediately. But overbooking (especially in high season) has led to long lines and long waits even with a reservation, but you may pay by credit card. Taking photographs in the Uffizi has been legal since summer 2014, and has contributed to making what ought to be a sublime museumgoing experience more of a day at the zoo. When there's a special exhibit on, which is often, the base ticket price goes up to €12.50. ✉ *Piazzale degli Uffizi 6, Piazza della Signoria* ☎ *055/23885* ⊕ *www.uffizi.firenze.it; reservations www.polomuseale.firenze.it* 🎫 *€10, €12.50 during special exhibitions; reservation fee €4* ⊙ *Tues.–Sun. 8:15–6:50.*

Piazza della Signoria. This is by far the most striking square in Florence. It was here, in 1497, that the famous "bonfire of the vanities" took place, when the fanatical friar Savonarola induced his followers to hurl their worldly goods into the flames; it was also here, a year later, that he was hanged as a heretic and, ironically, burned. A plaque in the piazza pavement marks the exact spot of his execution.

10

The statues in the square and in the 14th-century **Loggia dei Lanzi** on the south side vary in quality. Cellini's famous bronze *Perseus* holding the severed head of Medusa is certainly the most important sculpture in the loggia. Other works here include *The Rape of the Sabine Women* and *Hercules and the Centaur,* both late-16th-century works by Giambologna (1529–1608), and in the back, a row of sober matrons dating from Roman times.

Ponte Vecchio (*Old Bridge*). This charmingly simple bridge was built in 1345 to replace an earlier bridge swept away by flood. Its shops first housed butchers, then grocers, blacksmiths, and other merchants. But in 1593 the Medici grand duke Ferdinand I (1549–1609), whose private corridor linking the Medici palace (Palazzo Pitti) with the Medici offices (the Uffizi) crossed the bridge atop the shops, decided that all

Continued on page 571

THE DUOMO
FLORENCE'S BIGGEST MASTERPIECE

For all its monumental art and architecture, Florence has one undisputed centerpiece: the Cathedral of Santa Maria del Fiore, better known as the Duomo. Its cupola dominates the skyline, presiding over the city's rooftops like a red hen over her brood. Little wonder that when Florentines feel homesick, they say they have *"nostalgia del cupolone."*

The Duomo's construction began in 1296, following the design of Arnolfo da Cambio, Florence's greatest architect of the time. By modern standards, construction was slow and haphazard—it continued through the 14th and into the 15th century, with some dozen architects having a hand in the project.

In 1366 Neri di Fioravante created a model for the hugely ambitious cupola: it was to be the largest dome in the world, surpassing Rome's Pantheon. But when the time finally came to build the dome in 1418, no one was sure how—or even if—it could be done. Florence was faced with a 143-ft hole in the roof of its cathedral, and one of the greatest challenges in the history of architecture.

Fortunately, local genius Filippo Brunelleschi was just the man for the job. Brunelleschi won the 1418 competition to design the dome, and for the next 18 years he oversaw its construction. The enormity of his achievement can hardly be overstated. Working on such a large scale (the dome weighs 37,000 tons and uses 4 million bricks) required him to invent hoists and cranes that were engineering marvels. A "dome within a dome" design and a novel herringbone bricklaying pattern were just two of the innovations used to establish structural integrity. Perhaps most remarkably, he executed the construction without a supporting wooden framework, which had previously been thought indispensable.

Brunelleschi designed the lantern atop the dome, but he died soon after its first stone was laid in 1446; it wouldn't be completed until 1461. Another 400 years passed before the Duomo received its façade, a 19th-century neo-Gothic creation.

DUOMO TIMELINE

1296 Work begins, following design by Arnolfo di Cambio.

1302 Arnolfo dies; work continues, with sporadic interruptions.

1331 Management of construction taken over by the Wool Merchants guild.

1334 Giotto appointed project overseer, designs campanile.

1337 Giotto dies; Andrea Pisano takes leadership role.

1348 The Black Plague; all work ceases.

1366 Vaulting on nave completed; Neri di Fioravante makes model for dome.

1417 Drum for dome completed.

1418 Competition is held to design the dome.

1420 Brunelleschi begins work on the dome.

1436 Dome completed.

1446 Construction of lantern begins; Brunelleschi dies.

1461 Antonio Manetti, a student of Brunelleschi, completes lantern.

1469 Gilt copper ball and cross added by Verrocchio.

1587 Original façade is torn down by Medici court.

1871 Emilio de Fabris wins competition to design new façade.

1887 Façade completed.

WHAT TO LOOK FOR INSIDE THE DUOMO

The interior of the Duomo is a fine example of Florentine Gothic with a beautiful marble floor, but the space feels strangely barren—a result of its great size and the fact that some of the best art has been moved to the nearby **Museo dell'Opera del Duomo.**

Notable among the works that remain are two towering equestrian frescoes of famous mercenaries: *Niccolò da Tolentino* (1456), by Andrea del Castagno, and *Sir John Hawkwood* (1436), by Paolo Uccello. There's also fine terra-cotta work by Luca della Robbia. Ghiberti,

Brunelleschi's great rival, is responsible for much of the stained glass, as well as a reliquary urn with gorgeous reliefs. A vast fresco of the Last Judgment, painted by Vasari and Zuccari, covers the dome's interior. Brunelleschi had wanted mosaics to go there; it's a pity he didn't get his wish.

In the crypt beneath the cathedral, you can explore excavations of a Roman wall and mosaic fragments from the late sixth century; entry is near the first pier on the right. On the way down you pass Brunelleschi's modest tomb.

1. Entrance; stained glass by Ghiberti
2. Fresco of Niccolò da Tolentino by Andrea del Castagno
3. Fresco of John Hawkwood by Paolo Uccello
4. *Dante and the Divine Comedy* by Domenico di Michelino
5. Lunette: *Ascension* by Luca della Robbia
6. Above altar: two angels by Luca della Robbia. Below the altar: reliquary of St. Zenobius by Ghiberti.
7. Lunette: *Resurrection* by Luca della Robbia
8. Entrance to dome
9. Bust of Brunelleschi by Buggiano
10. Stairs to crypt
11. Campanile

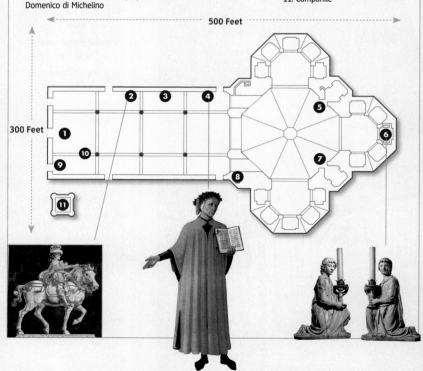

500 Feet

300 Feet

MAKING THE CLIMB

Climbing the 463 steps to the top of the dome is not for the faint of heart—or for the claustrophobic—but those who do it will be awarded a smashing view of Florence ❶. Keep in mind that the way up is also the way down, which means that while you're huffing and puffing in the ascent, people very close to you in a narrow staircase are making their way down ❷.

300 Feet

75 Feet

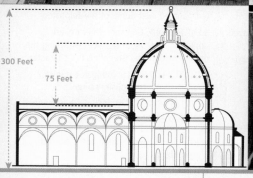

DUOMO BASICS

• Even first thing in the morning during high season (May through September), a line is likely to have formed to climb the dome. Expect an hour wait.

• For an alternative to the dome, consider climbing the less trafficked campanile, which gives you a view from on high of the dome itself.

• Dress code essentials: covered shoulders, no short shorts, and hats off upon entering.

THE CRYPT

The crypt is worth a visit: computer modeling allows visitors to see its ancient Roman fabric and subsequent rebuilding. A transparent plastic model shows exactly what the earlier church looked like.

BRUNELLESCHI vs. GHIBERTI
The Rivalry of Two Renaissance Geniuses

In Renaissance Florence, painters, sculptors, and architects competed for major commissions, with the winner earning the right to undertake a project that might occupy him (and keep him paid) for a decade or more. Stakes were high, and the resulting rivalries fierce—none more so than that between Filippo Brunelleschi and Lorenzo Ghiberti.

The two first clashed in 1401, for the commission to create the bronze doors of the Baptistery. When Ghiberti won, Brunelleschi took it hard, fleeing to Rome, where he would remain for 15 years. Their rematch came in 1418, over the design of the Duomo's cupola, with Brunelleschi triumphant. For the remainder of their lives, the two would miss no opportunity to belittle each other's work.

FILIPPO BRUNELLESCHI (1377–1446)

MASTERPIECE: The dome of Santa Maria del Fiore.

BEST FRIENDS: Donatello, whom he stayed with in Rome after losing the Baptistery doors competition; the Medici family, who rescued him from bankruptcy.

SIGNATURE TRAITS: Paranoid, secretive, bad tempered, practical joker, inept businessman.

SAVVIEST POLITICAL MOVE: Feigned sickness and left for Rome after his dome plans were publicly criticized by Ghiberti, who was second-in-command. The project proved too much for Ghiberti to manage on his own, and Brunelleschi returned triumphant.

MOST EMBARRASSING MOMENT: In 1434 he was imprisoned for two weeks for failure to pay a small guild fee. The humiliation might have been orchestrated by Ghiberti.

OTHER CAREER: Shipbuilder. He built a huge vessel, *Il Badalone*, to transport marble for the dome up the Arno. It sank on its first voyage.

INSPIRED: The dome of St. Peter's in Rome.

LORENZO GHIBERTI (1378–1455)

MASTERPIECE: *The Gates of Paradise*, the ten-paneled east doors of the Baptistery.

BEST FRIEND: Giovanni da Prato, an underling who wrote diatribes attacking the dome's design and Brunelleschi's character.

SIGNATURE TRAITS: Instigator, egoist, know-it-all, shrewd businessman.

SAVVIEST POLITICAL MOVE: During the Baptistery doors competition, he had an open studio and welcomed opinions on his work, while Brunelleschi labored behind closed doors.

OTHER CAREER: Collector of classical artifacts, historian.

INSPIRED: *The Gates of Hell* by Auguste Rodin.

The Gates of Paradise detail

this plebeian commerce under his feet was unseemly. So he threw out the butchers and blacksmiths and installed 41 goldsmiths and eight jewelers. The bridge has been devoted solely to these two trades ever since.

The **Corridoio Vasariano** (⊠ *Piazzale degli Uffizi 6, Piazza della Signoria* 🕾 *055/23885 or 055/294883*), the private Medici elevated passageway, was built by Vasari in 1565. Though the ostensible reason for its construction was one of security, it was more likely designed so that the Medici family wouldn't have to walk amid

the commoners. The corridor is notoriously fickle with its operating hours; at this writing, it is temporarily open but only to groups. It can sometimes be visited by prior arrangement. Call for the most up-to-date details. Take a moment to study the Ponte Santa Trinita, the next bridge downriver, from either the bridge or the corridor. It was designed by Bartolomeo Ammannati in 1567 (probably from sketches by Michelangelo), blown up by the retreating Germans during World War II, and painstakingly reconstructed after the war. The view from the Ponte Santa Trinita is beautiful, which might explain why so many young lovers seem to hang out there.

WORTH NOTING

Campanile. The Gothic bell tower designed by Giotto (circa 1266–1337) is a soaring structure of multicolor marble originally decorated with sculptures by Donatello and reliefs by Giotto, Andrea Pisano, and others (which are now in the Museo dell'Opera del Duomo). A climb of 414 steps rewards you with a close-up of Brunelleschi's cupola on the Duomo next door and a sweeping view of the city. ⊠ *Piazza del Duomo* 🕾 *055/2302885* ⊕ *www.operaduomo.firenze.it* 🎫 *€10* ☉ *Daily 8:30–7:30.*

FAMILY **Mercato Nuovo** (*New Market*). The open-air loggia, built in 1551, teems with souvenir stands, but the real attraction is a copy of Pietro Tacca's bronze *Porcellino* (which translates as "little pig" despite the fact the animal is, in fact, a wild boar). The *Porcellino* is Florence's equivalent of the Trevi Fountain: put a coin in his mouth, and if it falls through the grate below (according to one interpretation), it means you'll return to Florence someday. What you're seeing is a copy of a copy: Tacca's original version, in the Museo Bardini, is actually a copy of an ancient Greek work. ⊠ *Corner of Via Por Santa Maria and Via Porta Rossa, Piazza della Repubblica* ☉ *Market Tues.–Sat. 8–7, Mon. 1–7.*

Museo dell'Opera del Duomo (*Cathedral Museum*). At this writing, the museum was undergoing some serious expansion, and the results will be splendid when work is completed in October 2015. The

10

museum will double in size, and the piazza will be reconstructed, thereby allowing visitors to experience the old facade, torn down in the 1580s, along with the three original baptistery doors (north, south, and east). ⊠ *Piazza del Duomo 9* 🕾 *055/2302885* ⊕ *www. operaduomo.firenze.it* 🎫 *€10* ⏱ *Mon.–Sat. 9–7:30, Sun. 9–1:45.*

Orsanmichele. This multipurpose structure began as an 8th-century oratory and then in 1290 was turned into an open-air loggia for selling grain. Destroyed by fire in 1304, it was rebuilt as a loggia-market. Between 1367 and 1380 the arcades were closed and two stories were added above; finally, at century's end it was turned into a church. Inside is a beautifully detailed 14th-century Gothic tabernacle by Andrea Orcagna (1308–68). The exterior niches contain sculptures (all copies) dating from the early 1400s to the early 1600s by Donatello and Verrocchio (1435–88), among others, which were paid for by the guilds. ⊠ *Via dei Calzaiuoli, Piazza della Repubblica* 🕾 *055/284944* ⏱ *Museum Mon. 10–5.*

Palazzo Davanzati. The prestigious Davanzati family owned this 14th-century palace in one of Florence's swankiest medieval neighborhoods. The place is a delight, as you can wander through the surprisingly light-filled courtyard, and climb the steep stairs to the *piano nobile* (there's also an elevator), where the family did most of its living. The beautiful **Sala dei Pappagalli** (Parrot Room) is adorned with trompe-l'oeil tapestries and gaily painted birds. ⊠ *Piazza Davanzati 13, Piazza della Repubblica* 🕾 *055/2388610* ⊕ *www.polomuseale.firenze.it* 🎫 *€2* ⏱ *Daily 8:15–1:50. Closed 1st, 3rd, and 5th Sun. and 2nd and 4th Mon. of month.*

Palazzo Vecchio (*Old Palace*). Florence's forbidding, fortresslike city hall was begun in 1299, presumably designed by Arnolfo di Cambio, and its massive bulk and towering campanile dominate Piazza della Signoria. It was built as a meeting place for the guildsmen governing the city at the time; today it is still City Hall.

The main attraction is on the second floor: two adjoining rooms that supply one of the most startling contrasts in Florence. The first is the opulently vast **Sala dei Cinquecento** (Room of the Five Hundred), named for the 500-member Great Council, the people's assembly established after the death of Lorenzo the Magnificent, that met here. Giorgio Vasari and others decorated the room, around 1563–65, with gargantuan frescoes celebrating Florentine history; depictions of battles with nearby cities predominate.

In comparison, the little **Studiolo,** just off the Sala dei Cinquecento's entrance, was a private room meant for the duke and those whom he invited in. Here's where the melancholy Francesco I (1541–87), son of Cosimo I, stored his priceless treasures and conducted scientific experiments. Designed by Vasari, it was decorated by him, Giambologna, and many others.

Spectacular 360-degree views may be had from the battlements (only 77 steps) and from the tower (223 more). ✉ *Piazza della Signoria* 📞 *055/2768465* 🌐 *museicivicifiorentini.comune.fi.it* 🎫 *Museo €10, Torre €10; Museo and Torre €14* 🕐 *Mon.–Wed. and Fri.–Sun. 9–7, Thurs. 9–2.*

Piazza della Repubblica. The square marks the site of the ancient forum that was the core of the original Roman settlement. While the street plan around the piazza still reflects the carefully plotted Roman military encampment, the Mercato Vecchio (Old Market), which had been here since the Middle Ages, was demolished and the current piazza was constructed between 1885 and 1895 as a Neoclassical showpiece. The piazza is lined with outdoor cafés, affording ample opportunity for people-watching.

SAN LORENZO

A sculptor, painter, architect, and poet, Florentine native son Michelangelo was a consummate genius, and some of his finest creations remain in his hometown. The Biblioteca Medicea Laurenziana is perhaps his most fanciful work of architecture. A key to understanding Michelangelo's genius can be found in the magnificent Cappelle Medicee, where both his sculptural and architectural prowess can be clearly seen. Planned frescoes were never completed, sadly, for they would have shown in one space the artistic triple threat that he certainly was. The towering yet graceful *David,* perhaps his most famous work, resides in the Galleria dell'Accademia.

After visiting San Lorenzo, resist the temptation to explore the market that surrounds the church: the market is open until 7 pm, while the churches and museums you may want to visit are not. Come back to the market later, after other sites have closed. Note that the Museo di San Marco closes at 1:50 on weekdays.

TOP ATTRACTIONS

Cappelle Medicee (*Medici Chapels*). This magnificent complex includes the **Cappella dei Principi,** the Medici chapel and mausoleum that was begun in 1605 and kept marble workers busy for several hundred years, and the **Sagrestia Nuova** (New Sacristy), designed by Michelangelo and so called to distinguish it from Brunelleschi's Sagrestia Vecchia (Old Sacristy) in San Lorenzo.

Michelangelo received the commission for the Sagrestia Nuova in 1520 from Cardinal Giulio de' Medici (1478–1534), who later became Pope Clement VII. The cardinal wanted a new burial chapel for his cousins Giuliano, Duke of Nemours (1478–1534), and Lorenzo, Duke of Urbino (1492–1519), and he also wanted to honor his father, also named Giuliano, and his uncle, Lorenzo il Magnifico. The result was a tour de force of architecture and sculpture. Architecturally, Michelangelo was as original and inventive here as ever, but it is, quite properly, the powerfully sculpted tombs that dominate the room. The scheme is allegorical: on the tomb on the right are figures representing Day and Night, and on the tomb to the left are figures representing Dawn and Dusk; above them are idealized sculptures of the two men, usually interpreted

10

to represent the active life and the contemplative life. But the allegorical meanings are secondary; what is most important is the intense presence of the sculptural figures and the force with which they hit the viewer. Ticket prices jump to €9 when special exhibitions are on—which is frequently. ✉ *Piazza di Madonna degli Aldobrandini, San Lorenzo* ☎ *055/294883 for reservations* ⊕ *www.cappellemedicee.it* 🎫 *€6 (€8 during special exhibits)* ☉ *Daily 8:15–1:50. Closed 1st, 3rd, and 5th Mon. and 2nd and 4th Sun. of month.*

FAMILY **Galleria dell'Accademia** (*Accademia Gallery*). The collection of Florentine paintings, dating from the 13th to the 18th centuries, is largely unremarkable, but the sculptures by Michelangelo are worth the price of admission. The unfinished *Slaves,* fighting their way out of their marble prisons, were meant for the tomb of Michelangelo's overly demanding patron Pope Julius II (1443–1513). But the focal point is the original *David,* moved here from Piazza della Signoria in 1873. *David* was commissioned in 1501 by the Opera del Duomo (Cathedral Works Committee), which gave the 26-year-old sculptor a leftover block of marble that had been ruined forty years earlier by two other sculptors. Michelangelo's success with the block was so dramatic that the city showered him with honors, and the Opera del Duomo voted to build him a house and a studio in which to live and work.

Today, *David* is beset not by Goliath but by tourists, and seeing the statue at all—much less really studying it—can be a trial. Save yourself a long wait in line by reserving tickets in advance. A Plexiglas barrier surrounds the sculpture, following a 1991 attack on it by a hammer-wielding self-proclaimed art anarchist who, luckily, inflicted only a few minor nicks on the toes. The statue is not quite what it seems. It is so poised and graceful and alert—so miraculously alive—that it is often considered the definitive sculptural embodiment of High Renaissance perfection.

The work was originally commissioned to adorn the exterior of the Duomo and was intended to be seen from a distance and on high. Michelangelo knew exactly what he was doing, calculating that the perspective of the viewer would be such that, in order for the statue to appear proportioned, the upper body, head, and arms would have to be bigger, as they are farther away from the viewer. But he also did it to express and embody, as powerfully as possible in a single figure, an entire biblical story. David's hands *are* big, but so was Goliath, and these are the hands that slew him. Music lovers might want to check out the **Museo degli Instrumenti Musicali** contained within the Accademia; its Stradivarius is the main attraction. ✉ *Via Ricasoli 60, San Marco* ☎ *055/294883 for reservations, 055/2388609 for gallery* ⊕ *www.gallerieaccademia.org* 🎫 *€11; €4 reservation fee* ☉ *Tues.–Sun. 8:15–6:50.*

CLOSE UP

Florence's Trial by Fire

One of the most striking figures of Renaissance Florence was Girolamo Savonarola, a Dominican friar who, for a moment, captured the spiritual conscience of the city. In 1491 he became prior of the convent of San Marco, where he adopted a life of austerity and delivered sermons condemning Florence's excesses and the immorality of his fellow clergy. Following the death of Lorenzo de' Medici in 1492, Savonarola was instrumental in the re-formation of the republic of Florence, ruled by a representative council with Christ enthroned as monarch. In one of his most memorable acts he urged Florentines to toss worldly possessions—from sumptuous dresses to Botticelli paintings—onto a "bonfire of the vanities" in Piazza della Signoria. Savonarola's antagonism toward church hierarchy led to his undoing: he was excommunicated in 1497, and the following year was hanged and burned on charges of heresy. Today, at the Museo di San Marco, you can visit Savonarola's cell.

Fodor's Choice ★ **Mercato Centrale.** Some of the food at this huge, two-story market hall is remarkably exotic. The ground floor contains meat and cheese stalls, as well as some very good bars that have *panini* (sandwiches). In June 2014, a second-floor food hall opened, eerily reminiscent of food halls everwhere. The quality of the food served, however, more than makes up for this. ⊠ *Piazza del Mercato Centrale, San Lorenzo* ⊕ *www. mercatocentrale.it* ⊗ *Market Mon.–Sat. 7–2; food hall daily 10–midnight.*

Museo di San Marco. A Dominican convent adjacent to the church of San Marco now houses this museum, which contains many stunning works by Fra Angelico (circa 1400–55), the Dominican friar famous for his piety as well as for his painting. When the friars' cells were restructured between 1439 and 1444, he decorated many of them with frescoes meant to spur religious contemplation. His unostentatious and direct paintings exalt the simple beauties of the contemplative life. Fra Angelico's works are everywhere, from the friars' cells to the superb panel paintings on view in the museum. Don't miss the famous *Annunciation*, on the upper floor, and the works in the gallery off the cloister as you enter. Here you can see his beautiful *Last Judgment*; as usual, the tortures of the damned are far more inventive and interesting than the pleasures of the redeemed. ⊠ *Piazza San Marco 1* ☎ *055/2388608* ⊕ *www.polomuseale.firenze.it/en/musei/index.php?m=sanmarco* 💶 *€4* ⊗ *Weekdays 8:15–1:50, weekends 8:15–6:50. Closed 1st, 3rd, and 5th Sun., and 2nd and 4th Mon. of month.*

San Lorenzo. Brunelleschi designed this great basilica in the 15th century but never lived to see it finished. Note the dark marble lines on the floor, whose geometry underscores the "new" use of perspective. The **Sagrestia Vecchia** (Old Sacristy), at the end of the left transept, is the Renaissance at its purest; the roundels are by Donatello. ⊠ *Piazza San Lorenzo, San Lorenzo* 💶 *€2.50* ☎ *No phone* ⊗ *Nov.–Feb., Mon.–Sat. 10–5; Mar.–Oct., Mon.–Sat. 10–5, Sun. 1:30–5.*

10

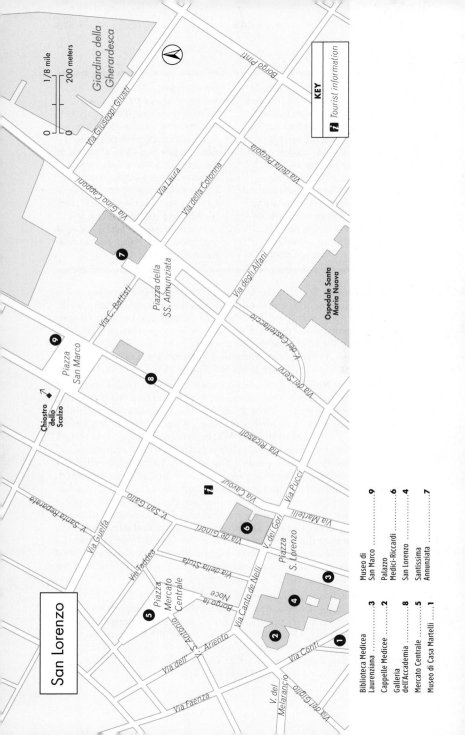

San Lorenzo

Biblioteca Medicea
Laurenziana **3**
Cappelle Medicee **2**
Galleria
dell'Accademia **8**
Mercato Centrale **5**
Museo di Casa Martelli **1**

Museo di
San Marco **9**
Palazzo
Medici-Riccardi **6**
San Lorenzo **4**
Santissima
Annunziata **7**

KEY

𝐢 *Tourist information*

Giardino della
Gherardesca

1/8 mile

200 meters

WORTH NOTING

Biblioteca Medicea Laurenziana (*Laurentian Library*). Michelangelo the architect was every bit as original as Michelangelo the sculptor. Unlike Brunelleschi (the architect of the Spedale degli Innocenti), however, he wasn't obsessed with proportion and perfect geometry. He was interested in experimentation and invention and in the expression of a personal vision that was at times highly idiosyncratic.

It was never more idiosyncratic than in the Biblioteca Medicea Laurenziana, begun in 1524 and finished in 1568 by Bartolomeo Ammannati. Its famous **vestibolo,** a strangely shaped anteroom, has had scholars scratching their heads for centuries. In a space more than two stories high, why did Michelangelo limit his use of columns and pilasters to the upper two-thirds of the wall? Why didn't he rest them on strong pedestals instead of on huge, decorative curlicue scrolls, which rob them all of visual support? Why did he recess them into the wall, which makes them look weaker still? The architectural elements here do not stand firm and strong and tall, as inside San Lorenzo, next door; instead, they seem to be pressed into the wall as if into putty, giving the room a soft, rubbery look that is one of the strangest effects ever achieved by 16th-century architecture.

The anteroom's staircase (best viewed straight-on), which emerges from the library with the visual force of an unstoppable lava flow, has been exempted from the criticism, however. In its highly sculptural conception and execution, it is quite simply one of the most original and fluid staircases in the world. ⊠ *Piazza San Lorenzo 9, entrance to left of San Lorenzo* ☎ *055/210760* ⊕ *www.bml.firenze.sbn.it* ✎ *Special exhibitions €3* ☉ *Sun.–Fri. 9–1.*

Museo di Casa Martelli. The wealthy Martelli family, long associated with the all-powerful Medici, lived, from the 16th century, in this palace on a quiet street near the basilica of San Lorenzo. The last Martelli died in 1986, and in October 2009 the *casa-museo* (house-museum) opened to the public. It's the only nonreconstructed example of such a house in all of Florence, and for that reason alone it's worth a visit. The family collected art, and while most of the stuff is B-list, a couple of gems by Beccafumi, Salvatore Rosa, and Piero di Cosimo adorn the walls. Reservations are essential, and you will be shown the glories of this place by well-informed, English-speaking guides. ⊠ *Via Zanetti 8, San Lorenzo* ☎ *055/290383* ⊕ *www.uffizi.firenze.it* ✎ *€3* ☉ *Guided tours Thurs. 2–7, Fri. 2–5, weekends 9–2.*

Palazzo Medici-Riccardi. The main attraction of this palace, begun in 1444 by Michelozzo for Cosimo de' Medici, is the interior chapel, the so-called **Cappella dei Magi** on the piano nobile. Painted on its walls is Benozzo Gozzoli's famous *Procession of the Magi,* finished in 1460 and celebrating both the birth of Christ and the greatness of the Medici family. Entering the chapel is like walking into the middle of a magnificently illustrated children's storybook, and this beauty makes it one of the most enjoyable rooms in the city. Do note that officially only eight visitors are allowed in at a time for a maximum of seven minutes; sometimes, however, guards are lenient. ⊠ *Via Cavour 1, San Lorenzo* ☎ *055/2760340* ⊕ *www.palazzo-medici.it* ✎ *€7* ☉ *Thurs.–Tues. 9–7.*

10

Santissima Annunziata. Dating from the mid-13th century, this church was restructured in 1447 by Michelozzo, who gave it an uncommon (and lovely) entrance cloister with frescoes by Andrea del Sarto (1486–1530), Pontormo (1494–1556), and Rosso Fiorentino (1494–1540). The interior is a rarity for Florence: an overwhelming example of the Baroque. But it's not really a fair example, because it's merely 17th-century Baroque decoration applied willy-nilly to an earlier structure—exactly the sort of violent remodeling exercise that has given the Baroque a bad name. The **Cappella dell'Annunziata,** immediately inside the entrance to the left, illustrates the point. The lower half, with its stately Corinthian columns and carved frieze bearing the Medici arms, was commissioned by Piero de' Medici in 1447; the upper half, with its erupting curves and impish sculpted cherubs, was added 200 years later. ✉ *Piazza di Santissima Annunziata, San Lorenzo* ☎ *055/266186* ⏰ *Daily 7–12:30 and 4–6:30.*

SANTA MARIA NOVELLA

Piazza Santa Maria Novella, near the train station, suffered from a degree of squalor until a restoration several years in the making and completed in spring 2009, gave it a boost. It's now a gorgeous, pedestrian-only square, with grass (laced with roses) and plenty of places to sit and rest your feet. The streets in and around the piazza have their share of architectural treasures, including some of Florence's most tasteful palaces. Between Santa Maria Novella and the Arno is Via Tornabuoni, Florence's finest shopping street.

TOP ATTRACTIONS

Museo Stibbert. Federico Stibbert (1838–1906), born in Florence to an Italian mother and an English father, liked to collect things. Over a lifetime of doing so, he amassed some 50,000 objects. This museum, which was also his home, displays many of them. He had a fascination with medieval armor and also collected costumes, particularly Uzbek costumes, which are exhibited in a room called the Moresque Hall. These are mingled with an extensive collection of swords, guns, and other devices whose sole function was to kill people. The paintings, most of which date from the 15th century, are largely second-rate. The house itself is an interesting amalgam of neo-Gothic, Renaissance, and English eccentric. To get here, take Bus No. 4 (across the street from the station at Santa Maria Novella) and get off at the stop marked "Fabbroni 4." Then follow signs to the museum. ✉ *Via Federico Stibbert 26* ☎ *055/475520* ⊕ *www.museostibbert.it* 🎟 *€8* ⏰ *Mon.–Wed. 10–2, Fri.–Sun. 10–6. Entry every ½ hr.*

Santa Maria Novella. The facade of this church looks distinctly clumsy by later Renaissance standards, and with good reason: it is an architectural hybrid. The lower half was completed mostly in the 14th century; its pointed-arch niches and decorative marble patterns reflect the Gothic style of the day. About 100 years later (around 1456), architect Leon Battista Alberti was called in to complete the job.

The architecture of the interior is, like that of the Duomo, a dignified but somber example of Florentine Gothic. Exploration is essential, however,

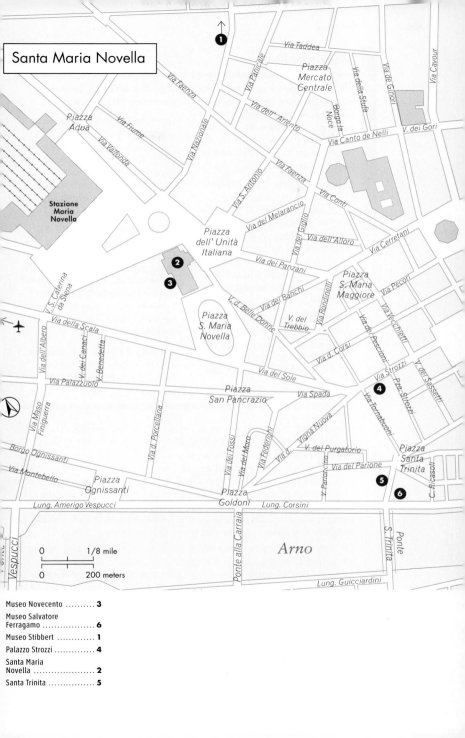

Santa Maria Novella

Meet the Medici

The Medici were the dominant family of Renaissance Florence, wielding political power and financing some of the world's greatest art. You'll see their names at every turn around the city. These are some of the clan's more notable members:

Cosimo il Vecchio (1389–1464), incredibly wealthy banker to the popes, was the first in the family line to act as de facto ruler of Florence. He was a great patron of the arts and architecture; he was the moving force behind the creation of the family palace and the restoration and refurbishment of the Dominican complex of San Marco.

Lorenzo il Magnifico (1449–92), grandson of Cosimo il Vecchio, presided over a Florence largely at peace with her neighbors. A collector of cameos, a writer of sonnets, and lover of ancient texts, he was the preeminent Renaissance man.

Leo X (1475–1521), also known as Giovanni de' Medici, became the first Medici pope, helping extend the family power base to include Rome and the Papal States. His reign was characterized by a host of problems, the biggest one being a former Augustinian friar named Martin Luther.

Catherine de' Medici (1519–89) was married by her great uncle Pope Clement VII to Henry of Valois, who later became Henry II of France. Wife of one king and mother of three, she was the first Medici to marry into European royalty. Lorenzo il Magnifico, her great-grandfather, would have been thrilled.

Cosimo I (1537–74), the first grand duke of Tuscany, should not be confused with his ancestor Cosimo il Vecchio.

because the church's store of art treasures is remarkable. Highlights include the 14th-century stained-glass rose window depicting the *Coronation of the Virgin* (above the central entrance); the Cappella Filippo Strozzi (to the right of the altar), containing late-15th-century frescoes and stained glass by Filippino Lippi; the *cappella maggiore* (the area around the high altar), displaying frescoes by Ghirlandaio; and the Cappella Gondi (to the left of the altar), containing Filippo Brunelleschi's famous wood crucifix, carved around 1410 and said to have so stunned the great Donatello when he first saw it that he dropped a basket of eggs.

Of special interest for its great historical importance and beauty is Masaccio's *Trinity,* on the left-hand wall, almost halfway down the nave. Painted around 1426–27 (at the same time he was working on his frescoes in Santa Maria del Carmine), it unequivocally announced the arrival of the Renaissance. The realism of the figure of Christ was revolutionary in itself, but what was probably even more startling to contemporary Florentines was the barrel vault in the background. The mathematical rules for employing single-point perspective in painting had just been discovered (probably by Brunelleschi), and this was one of the first works of art to employ them with utterly convincing success.

In the the first cloister is a faded and damaged fresco cycle by Paolo Uccello depicting tales from Genesis, with a dramatic vision of the

Deluge (at this writing, in restoration). Earlier and better-preserved frescoes painted in 1348–55 by Andrea da Firenze are in the chapter house, or the **Cappellone degli Spagnoli** (Spanish Chapel), off the cloister. ⊠ *Piazza Santa Maria Novella 19* ☎ *055/210113, 055/282187 museo* ⊕ *www.museicivicifiorentini.it* 🎫 *€5* ⊗ *Mon.–Thurs. 9–5:30, Fri. 11–5:30, Sat. 9–5, Sun. noon–5 (1–5 Oct.–June).*

Santa Trinita. Started in the 11th century by Vallombrosian monks and originally Romanesque in style, the church underwent a Gothic remodeling during the 14th century. (Remains of the Romanesque construction are visible on the interior front wall.) The major works are the fresco cycle and altarpiece in the Cappella Sassetti, the second to the high altar's right, painted by Ghirlandaio between 1480 and 1485. His work here possesses such graceful decorative appeal as well as a proud depiction of his native city (most of the cityscapes show 15th-century Florence in all her glory). The wall frescoes illustrate scenes from the life of St. Francis, and the altarpiece, depicting the *Adoration of the Shepherds,* veritably glows. ⊠ *Piazza Santa Trinita, Santa Maria Novella* ☎ *055/216912* ⊗ *Mon.–Sat. 8–noon and 4–6, Sun. 8–11.*

WORTH NOTING

Museo Novecento. It began life as a 13th-century Franciscan hostel offering shelter to tired pilgrims. It later became a convalescent home, and in the late 18th century it was a school for poor girls. Now the former Ospedale di San Paolo houses a museum devoted to Italian art of the 20th century. Admittedly, most of these artists are not exactly household names, but the museum is so beautifully done that it's worth a visit. The second floor contains works by artists from the second half of the century; start on the third floor, and go directly to the collection of Alberto della Ragione, a naval engineer determined to be on the cutting edge of art collecting. ⊠ *Piazza Santa Maria Novella 10* ☎ *055/286 132* ⊕ *www.museonovecento.it.*

Museo Salvatore Ferragamo. If there's such a thing as a temple for footwear, this is it. The shoes in this dramatically displayed collection were designed by Salvatore Ferragamo (1898–1960) beginning in the early 20th century. Born in southern Italy, the late master jump-started his career in Hollywood by creating shoes for the likes of Mary Pickford and Rudolph Valentino. He then returned to Florence and set up shop in the 13th-century Palazzo Spini Ferroni. The collection includes about 16,000 shoes, and those on display are frequently rotated. Special exhibitions are also mounted here and are well worth visiting—past shows have been devoted to Audrey Hepburn, Greta Garbo, and Marilyn Monroe. ⊠ *Via dei Tornabuoni 2, Santa Maria Novella* ☎ *055/3561* ⊕ *www.museoferragamo.it* 🎫 *€6* ⊗ *Wed.–Mon. 10–6.*

Palazzo Strozzi. The Strozzi family built this imposing palazzo in an attempt to outshine the nearby Palazzo Medici. Based on a model by Giuliano da Sangallo (circa 1452–1516) dating from around 1489 and executed between 1489 and 1504 under il Cronaca (1457–1508) and Benedetto da Maiaino (1442–97), it was inspired by Michelozzo's earlier Palazzo Medici-Riccardi. The palazzo's exterior is simple, severe, and massive: it's a testament to the wealth of a patrician, 15th-century Florentine

10

family. The interior courtyard, entered from the rear of the palazzo, is another matter altogether. It is here that the classical vocabulary—columns, capitals, pilasters, arches, and cornices—is given uninhibited and powerful expression. The palazzo frequently hosts blockbuster art shows. ✉ *Via Tornabuoni, Piazza della Repubblica, Santa Maria Novella* ☎ *055/2776461* ⊕ *www.palazzostrozzi.org* 🎫 *Free* 🕐 *Daily 10–7.*

SANTA CROCE

The Santa Croce quarter, on the southeast fringe of the historic center, was built up in the Middle Ages outside the second set of medieval city walls. The centerpiece of the neighborhood was (and is) the basilica of Santa Croce, which could hold great numbers of worshipers; the vast piazza could accommodate any overflow and also served as a fairground and, allegedly since the middle of the 16th century, as a playing field for no-holds-barred soccer games. A center of leatherworking since the Middle Ages, the neighborhood is still packed with leatherworkers and leather shops.

TOP ATTRACTIONS

Piazza Santa Croce. Originally outside the city's 12th-century walls, this piazza grew with the Franciscans, who used the large square for public preaching. During the Renaissance it was used for *giostre* (jousts), including one sponsored by Lorenzo de' Medici. "Bonfires of the vanities" occurred here, as well as soccer matches in the 16th century. Lined with many palazzi dating from the 15th and 16th centuries, the square remains one of Florence's loveliest piazze and is a great place to people-watch.

Fodor'sChoice ★ **Santa Croce.** Like the Duomo, this church is Gothic, but, also like the Duomo, its facade actually dates to the 19th century. As a burial place, the church probably contains more skeletons of Renaissance celebrities than any other in Italy. The tomb of Michelangelo is on the right at the front of the basilica; he is said to have chosen this spot so that the first thing he would see on Judgment Day, when the graves of the dead fly open, would be Brunelleschi's dome through Santa Croce's open doors. The tomb of Galileo Galilei (1564–1642) is on the left wall; he was not granted a Christian burial until 100 years after his death because of his controversial contention that Earth was not the center of the universe. The tomb of Niccolò Machiavelli (1469–1527), the political theoretician whose brutally pragmatic philosophy so influenced the Medici, is halfway down the nave on the right. The grave of Lorenzo Ghiberti, creator of the Baptistery doors, is halfway down the nave on the left. Composer Gioacchino Rossini (1792–1868) is buried at the end of the nave on the right. The monument to Dante Alighieri (1265–1321), the greatest Italian poet, is a memorial rather than a tomb (he is buried in Ravenna); it's on the right wall near the tomb of Michelangelo.

The collection of art within the complex is by far the most important of any church in Florence. The most famous works are probably the Giotto frescoes in the two chapels immediately to the right of the high altar. They illustrate scenes from the lives of St. John the Evangelist and St. John the Baptist (in the right-hand chapel) and scenes from the life of St. Francis (in the left-hand chapel). Time has not been kind to these

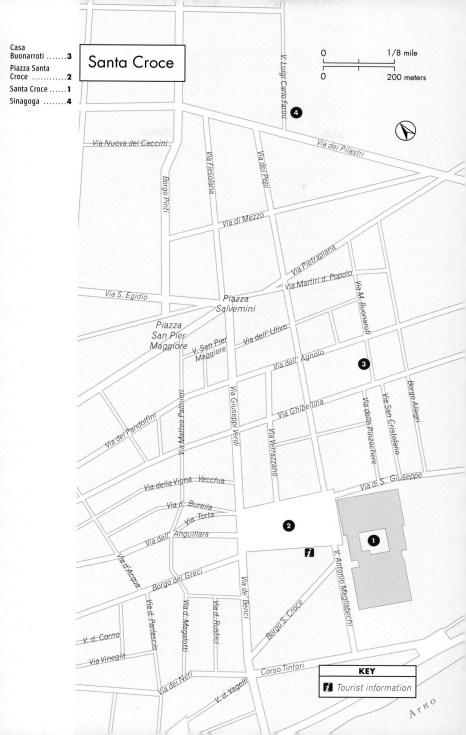

Santa Croce

0   1/8 mile

0   200 meters

❹

Via Nuova dei Caccini

V. Luigi Carlo Farini

Via dei Pilastri

Borgo Pinti

Via Fiesolana

Via dei Pepi

Via di Mezzo

Via Pietrapiana

Via S. Egidio

Via Martiri d. Popolo

Piazza Salvemini

Via M. Buonaroti

Piazza San Pier Maggiore

V. San Pier Maggiore

Via dell' Ulivo

Via dell' Agnolo

❸

Via Matteo Palmieri

Via Giuseppi Verdi

Via Verrazzano

Via Ghibellina

Via delle Pinzochere

Via San Cristofano

Borgo Allegri

Via dei Pandolfini

Via della Vigna Vecchia

Via di S. Giuseppe

Via d. Buretta

Via Torta

Via dell' Anguillara

❷

𝑖

❶

Via d'Acqua

Borgo dei Greci

Via de' Benci

V. Antonio Magliabechi

V. d. Corno

V. d. Partascio

Via d. Magalotti

Via d. Rustici

Borgo S. Croce

Via Vinegia

Via dei Neri

V. d. Vagelli

Corso Tintori

Arno

KEY
𝑖 *Tourist information*

frescoes; through the centuries, wall tombs were placed in the middle of them, they were whitewashed and plastered over, and in the 19th century they suffered a clumsy restoration. But the realism with which Giotto imbued painting can still be seen. He did not paint beautifully stylized religious icons, as the Byzantine style that preceded him prescribed; he instead painted drama—St. Francis surrounded by grieving friars at the very moment of his death. This was a radical shift in emphasis: before Giotto, painting's role was to symbolize the attributes of God; after him, it was to imitate life. His work is indeed primitive compared with later painting, but in the early 14th century it caused a sensation that was not equaled for another 100 years. He was, for his time, the equal of both Masaccio and Michelangelo.

Among the church's other highlights are Donatello's *Annunciation,* a moving expression of surprise (on the right wall, two thirds of the way down the nave); 14th-century frescoes by Taddeo Gaddi (circa 1300–66) illustrating scenes from the life of the Virgin Mary, clearly showing the influence of Giotto (in the chapel at the end of the right transept); and Donatello's *Crucifix,* criticized by Brunelleschi for making Christ look like a peasant (in the chapel at the end of the left transept). Outside the church proper, in the **Museo dell'Opera di Santa Croce** off the cloister, is the 13th-century *Triumphal Cross* by Cimabue (circa 1240–1302), badly damaged by the flood of 1966. A model of architectural geometry, the Cappella Pazzi, at the end of the cloister, is the work of Brunelleschi. ⊠ *Piazza Santa Croce 16* ☏ *055/2466105* ⊕ *www.santacroceopera.it* ✉ *€6 combined admission to church and museum; €8.50 combined ticket with Casa Buonarroti* ☉ *Mon.–Sat. 9:30–5:30, Sun. 1–5.*

Sinagoga. Jews were well settled in Florence by the end of the 14th century, but by 1570 they were required to live within the large "ghetto," at the north side of today's Piazza della Repubblica, by decree of Cosimo I, who had cut a deal with Pope Pius V (1504–72): in exchange for ghettoizing the Jews, he would receive the title Grand Duke of Tuscany.

Construction of the modern Moorish-style synagogue began in 1874 as a bequest of David Levi, who wished to endow a synagogue "worthy of the city." The gilded doors of the Moorish ark, which fronts the pulpit and is flanked by extravagant candelabra, are decorated with symbols of the ancient Temple of Jerusalem and bear bayonet marks from vandals. The synagogue was used as a garage by the Nazis, who failed to inflict much damage in spite of an attempt to blow up the place with dynamite. Only the columns on the left side were destroyed, and even then, the Women's Balcony above did not collapse. Note the Star of David in black and yellow marble inlay on the floor. The original capitals can be seen in the garden.

Some of the oldest and most beautiful Jewish ritual artifacts in all of Europe are displayed upstairs in the small **Museo Ebraico.** ⊠ *Via Farini 4* ☏ *055/2346654* ✉ *Synagogue and museum €6.50* ☉ *Apr.–Sept., Sun.–Thurs. 10–6, Fri. 10–2; Oct.–Mar., Sun.–Thurs. 10–4:45, Fri. 10–2. Guided tours (in English) at 10:30, 11:30, 12:30, 1:30, and 2:30 (no tour Fri. at 2:30).*

WORTH NOTING

Casa Buonarroti. If you are really enjoying walking in the footsteps of the great genius, you may want to complete the picture by visiting the Buonarroti family home. Michelangelo lived here from 1516 to 1525, and later gave it to his nephew, whose son, called Michelangelo il Giovane (Michelangelo the Younger) turned it into a gallery dedicated to his great-uncle. The artist's descendants filled it with art treasures, some by Michelangelo himself. Two early marble works—the *Madonna of the Steps* and the *Battle of the Centaurs*—show the boy genius at work. ⊠ *Via Ghibellina 70* ☎ *055/241752* ⊕ *www.casabuonarroti.it* ✆ *€6.50; €8.50 combined ticket with basilica of Santa Croce* ⊘ *Fri.–Wed. 9:30–2.*

THE OLTRARNO

A walk through the Oltrarno (literally "the other side of the Arno") takes in two very different aspects of Florence: the splendor of the Medici, manifest in the riches of the mammoth Palazzo Pitti and the gracious Giardino di Boboli; and the charm of the Oltrarno, a slightly gentrified but still fiercely proud working-class neighborhood with artisans' and antiques shops.

Farther east across the Arno, a series of ramps and stairs climb to Piazzale Michelangelo, where the city lies before you in all its glory (skip this trip if it's a hazy day). More stairs (behind La Loggia restaurant) lead to the church of San Miniato al Monte. You can avoid the long walk by taking Bus No. 12 or 13 at the west end of Ponte alle Grazie and getting off at Piazzale Michelangelo; you still have to climb the monumental stairs to and from San Miniato, but you can then take the bus from Piazzale Michelangelo back to the center of town. If you decide to take a bus, remember to buy your ticket before you board.

TOP ATTRACTIONS

Fodor'sChoice ★ **Giardino Bardini.** Garden lovers, those who crave a view, and those who enjoy a nice hike should visit this lovely villa and garden, whose history spans centuries. The villa had a walled garden as early as the 14th century; the "Grand Stairs"—a zigzag ascent well worth scaling—has been around since the 16th. The garden is filled with irises, roses, and heirloom flowers, and includes a Japanese garden and statuary. A very pretty walk (all for the same admission ticket) takes you through the Giardino di Boboli and past the Forte Belvedere to the upper entrance to the giardino. ⊠ *Via de'Bardini, San Niccolò* ☎ *005/294883* ✆ *€10, combined ticket with Galleria del Costume, Giardino di Boboli, Museo degli Argenti, Museo delle Porcellane* ⊘ *Nov.–Feb., daily 8:15–4:30; Mar., daily 8:15–5:30; Apr., May, Sept., and Oct., daily 8:15–6:30; June–Aug., daily 8:15–7:30. Closed 1st and last Mon. of month.*

Giardino di Boboli (*Boboli Gardens*). The main entrance to these landscaped gardens is on the right side of the courtyard of **Palazzo Pitti.** The gardens began to take shape in 1549, when the Pitti family sold the palazzo to Eleanor of Toledo, wife of the Medici grand duke Cosimo I. Niccolò Tribolo (1500–50) laid out the first landscaping plans, and after his death, Ammannati, Giambologna, Bernardo Buontalenti (circa 1536–1608), and Giulio (1571–1635) and Alfonso Parigi (1606–56), among

10

others, continued his work. Italian landscaping is less formal than French, but still full of sweeping drama. A copy of the famous *Morgante*, Cosimo I's favorite dwarf astride a particularly unhappy tortoise, is near the exit. Sculpted by Valerio Cioli (circa 1529–99), the work seems to illustrate the perils of culinary overindulgence. A visit here can be disappointing, because the gardens are somewhat underplanted and under-cared for, but it's still a great walk with some terrific views. ⊠ *Enter through Palazzo Pitti* 🕾 *055/294883* ⊕ *www.polomuseale.firenze.it* 🎟€10, combined ticket with Museo degli Argenti, Museo delle Porcellane, Villa Bardini, and Giardino Bardini* ⏱ *Nov.–Feb., daily 8:15–4:30; Mar., daily 8:15–5:30; Apr., May, Sept., and Oct., daily 8:15–6:30; June–Aug., daily 8:15–7:30. Closed 1st and last Mon. of month.*

Palazzo Pitti. This enormous palace is one of Florence's largest architectural set pieces. The original palazzo, built for the Pitti family around 1460, comprised only the main entrance and the three windows on either side. In 1549 the property was sold to the Medici, and Bartolomeo Ammannati was called in to make substantial additions. Although he apparently operated on the principle that more is better, he succeeded only in producing proof that more is just that: more.

Today the palace houses several museums: The **Museo degli Argenti** displays a vast collection of Medici treasures, including exquisite antique vases belonging to Lorenzo the Magnificent. The **Galleria del Costume** showcases fashions from the past 300 years. The **Galleria d'Arte Moderna** holds a collection of 19th- and 20th-century paintings, mostly Tuscan. Most famous of the Pitti galleries is the **Galleria Palatina,** which contains a broad collection of paintings from the 15th to 17th centuries. The price of admission to the Galleria Palatina also allows you to explore the former **Appartamenti Reali,** containing furnishings from a remodeling done in the 19th century. ⊠ *Piazza Pitti* 🕾 *055/210323* ⊕ *www.polomuseale.firenze.it* 🎟€13 combined ticket for Galleria Palatina and Galleria d'Arte Moderna; €13 combined ticket for Galleria del Costume, Giardino Bardini, Giardino di Boboli, Museo degli Argenti, and Museo Porcellane* ⏱ *Tues.–Sun. 8:15–6:50.*

FAMILY **Piazzale Michelangelo.** From this lookout you have a marvelous view of Florence and the hills around it, rivaling the vista from the Forte di Belvedere. A copy of Michelangelo's *David* overlooks outdoor cafés packed with tourists during the day and with Florentines in the evening. In May the **Giardino dell'Iris** (Iris Garden) off the piazza is abloom with more than 2,500 varieties of the flower. The **Giardino delle Rose** (Rose Garden) on the terraces below the piazza is also in full bloom in May and June.

San Miniato al Monte. This church, like the Baptistery, is a fine example of Romanesque architecture and is one of the oldest churches in Florence, dating to the 11th century. A 12th-century mosaic topped by a gilt bronze eagle, emblem of San Miniato's sponsors, the Calimala (cloth merchants' guild), crowns the lovely green-and-white marble facade. Inside are a 13th-century inlaid-marble floor and apse mosaic. Artist Spinello Aretino (1350–1410) covered the walls of the **Sagrestia** with frescoes depicting scenes from the life of St. Benedict. The **Cappella del Cardinale del Portogallo** (Chapel of the Portuguese Cardinal) is one of the richest

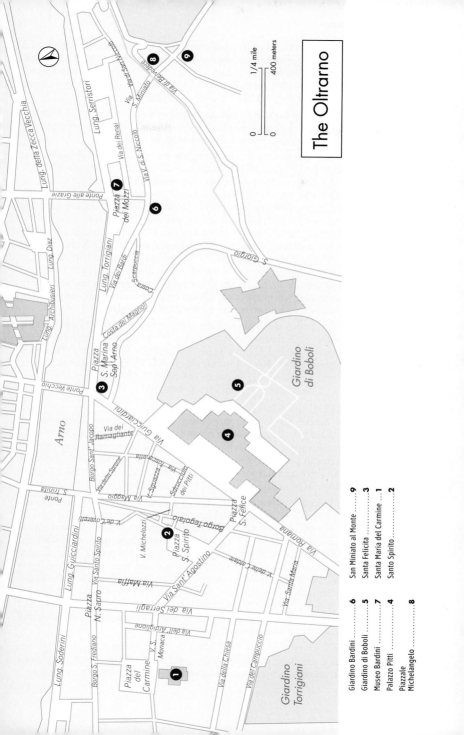

The Oltrarno

0   1/4 mile
0   400 meters

15th-century Renaissance works in Florence. It contains the tomb of a young Portuguese cardinal, Prince James of Lusitania, who died in Florence in 1459. Its glorious ceiling is by Luca della Robbia, and the sculpted tomb by Antonio Rossellino (1427–79). ⊠ *Viale Galileo Galilei, Piazzale Michelangelo* ☎ *055/2342731* ⊙ *Daily 8–12:30 and 3–5:15.*

Santa Maria del Carmine. The **Cappella Brancacci,** at the end of the right transept of this church, houses a masterpiece of Renaissance painting: a fresco cycle that changed the course of Western art.

Masaccio collaborated with Masolino on several of the frescoes, but his style predomintates in the *Tribute Money,* on the upper-left wall; *St. Peter Baptizing,* on the upper altar wall; the *Distribution of Goods,* on the lower altar wall; and the *Expulsion of Adam and Eve,* on the chapel's upper-left entrance pier. If you look closely at the last painting and compare it with some of the chapel's other works, you should see a pronounced difference. The figures of Adam and Eve possess a startling presence primarily thanks to the dramatic way in which their bodies seem to reflect light. Masaccio here shaded his figures consistently, so as to suggest a single, strong source of light within the world of the painting but outside its frame. In so doing, he succeeded in imitating with paint the real-world effect of light on mass, and he thereby imparted to his figures a sculptural reality unprecedented in his day.

Reservations to see the chapel are mandatory, but can be booked on the same day. Your time inside is limited to 15 minutes—a frustration that's only partly mitigated by a highly informative 40-minute DVD about the history of the chapel you can watch either before or after your visit. ⊠ *Piazza del Carmine, Santo Spirito* ☎ *055/2768224 for reservations* ▤ *€6* ⊙ *Mon. and Wed.–Sat. 10–5, Sun. 1–5.*

WORTH NOTING

Museo Bardini. The 19th-century collector and antiquarian Stefano Bardini turned his palace into his own private museum. Upon his death, the collection was turned over to the state and includes an interesting assortment of Etruscan pieces, sculpture, paintings, and furniture, mostly from the Renaissance and Baroque eras. ⊠ *Piazza de' Mozzi 1* ☎ *055/2342427* ⊕ *museicivicifiorentini.comune.fi.it* ▤ *€6* ⊙ *Thurs.–Mon. 11–5.*

Santa Felicita. This late Baroque church (its facade was remodeled between 1736 and 1739) contains the Mannerist Jacopo Pontormo's *Deposition,* the centerpiece of the Cappella Capponi (executed 1525–28) and a masterpiece of 16th-century Florentine art. The remote figures, which transcend the realm of Renaissance classical form, are portrayed in tangled shapes and intense pastel colors (well preserved because of the low lights in the church), in a space and depth that defy reality. Note, too, the exquisitely frescoed *Annunciation,* also by Pontormo, at a right angle to the *Deposition.* The granite column in the piazza was erected in 1381 and marks a Christian cemetery. ⊠ *Piazza Santa Felicita, off Via Guicciardini* ⊙ *Mon.–Sat. 9–noon and 3–6, Sun. 9–1.*

Santo Spirito. The plain, unfinished facade gives nothing away, but the interior, although it appears chilly compared with later churches, is one of the most important examples of Renaissance architecture in Italy.

Continued on page 595

Michelangelo. Leonardo da Vinci. Raphael. This heady triumvirate of the Italian Renaissance is synonymous with artistic genius. Yet they are only three of the remarkable cast of characters whose work defines the Renaissance, that extraordinary flourishing of art and culture in Italy, especially in Florence, as the Middle Ages drew to a close. The artists were visionaries, who redefined painting, sculpture, architecture, and even what it means to be an artist.

WHO'S WHO IN RENAISSANCE ART

THE PIONEER. In the mid-14th century, a few artists began to move away the flat, two-dimensional painting of the Middle Ages. **Giotto**, who painted seemingly three-dimensional figures who show emotion, had a major impact on the artists of the next century.

THE GROUNDBREAKERS. The generations of **Brunelleschi** and **Botticelli** took center stage in the 15th century. **Ghiberti, Masaccio, Donatello, Uccello, Fra Angelico**, and **Filippo Lippi** were other major players. Part of the Renaissance (or "re-birth") was a renewed interest in classical sources—the texts, monuments, and sculpture of Ancient Greece and Rome. Perspective and the illusion of three-dimensional space in painting was another discovery of this era, known as the Early Renaissance. Suddenly the art appearing on the walls looked real, or more realistic than it used to.

Roman ruins were not the only thing to inspire these artists. There was an incredible exchange of ideas going on. In Santa Maria del Carmine, Filippo Lippi was inspired by the work of Masaccio, who in turn was a friend of Brunelleschi. Young artists also learned from the masters via the apprentice system. Ghiberti's workshop (*bottega* in Italian) included, at one time or another, Donatello, Masaccio, and Uccello. Botticelli was apprenticed to Filippo Lippi.

THE BIG THREE. The mathematical rationality and precision of 15th-century art gave way to what is known as the High Renaissance. **Leonardo, Michelangelo**, and **Raphael** were much more concerned with portraying the body in all its glory and with achieving harmony and grandeur in their work. Oil paint, used infrequently up until this time, became more widely employed: as a result, Leonardo's colors are deeper, more sensual, more alive. For one brief period, all three were in Florence at the same time. Michelangelo and Leonardo surely knew one another, as they were simultaneously working on frescoes (never completed) inside Palazzo Vecchio.

When Michelangelo left Florence for Rome in 1508, he began the slow drain of artistic exodus from Florence, which never really recovered her previous glory.

 10

A RENAISSANCE TIMELINE

IN THE WORLD

Black Death in Europe kills one third of the population, 1347-50.

Joan of Arc burned at the stake, 1431.

IN FLORENCE

Founding of the Medici bank, 1397.

Medici family made official papal bankers.

1434, Cosimo il Vecchio becomes de facto ruler of Florence. The Medici family will dominate the city until 1494.

Dante, a native of Florence, writes *The Divine Comedy*, 1302-21.

1300

1400

IN ART

EARLY RENAISSANCE

Masaccio and Masolino fresco San Maria del Carmine, 1424-28.

GIOTTO (ca. 1267-1337)

Giotto fresoes in Santa Croce, 1320-25.

BRUNELLESCHI (1377-1446)

LORENZO GHIBERTI (ca. 1381-1455)

DONATELLO (ca. 1386-1466)

PAOLO UCCELLO (1397-1475)

FRA ANGELICO (ca. 1400-1455)

MASACCIO (1401-1428)

FILIPPO LIPPI (ca. 1406-1469

1334, 67-year-old Giotto is appointed chief architect of Santa Maria del Fiore, Florence's Duomo (below). He begins to work on the Campanile, which will be completed in 1359, after his death.

Donatello sculpts his bronze *David*, c 1440.

Fra Angelico frescoes friars' cells in San Marco 1438-45.

Uccello's *Sir John Hawkwood*, ca. 1436.

Ghiberti wins the competition for the Baptistery doors (above) in Florence, 1401.

Brunelleschi wins the competition for the Duom cupola (right), 1418.

Gutenberg Bible
is printed, 1455.

Columbus discovers
America, 1492.

Martin Luther posts his 95 theses on
the door at Wittenberg, kicking off the
Protestant Reformation, 1517.

Constantinople falls
to the Turks, 1453.

Machiavelli's *Prince*
appears, 1513.

Copernicus proves that
the earth is not the center
of the universe, 1530-43.

Lorenzo "il Magnifico"
(right), the Medici
patron of the arts, rules
in Florence, 1449-92.

Two Medici popes Leo X
(1513-21) and Clement
VII (1523-34) in Rome.

Catherine de'Medici
becomes Queen of
France, 1547.

1450   **1500**   **1550**

HIGH RENAISSANCE   MANNERISM

10

Fra Filippo Lippi's
*Madonna and
Child*, ca. 1452.

1508, Raphael begins
work on the chambers
in the Vatican, Rome.

Giorgio Vasari
publishes his first
edition of *Lives
of the Artists*,
1550.

1504, Michela[...]
David is pu[...]
display in P[...]
della Signo[...]
where it re[...]
until 1873.

Botticelli paints the
Birth of Venus, ca.
1482.

Michelangelo
begins to fresco
the Sistine Chapel
ceiling, 1508.

BOTTICELLI (ca. 1444-1510)

LEONARDO DA VINCI (1452-1519)

RAPHAEL (1483-

MICHELANGELO (1475-

Leonardo paints *The Last Supper* in Milan,
1495-98.

Giotto's *Nativity*   Donatello's *St. John the Baptist*   Ghiberti's *Gates of Paradise*

GIOTTO (CA. 1267-1337)

Painter/architect from a small town north of Florence.

He unequivocally set Italian painting on the course that led to the triumphs of the Renaissance masters. Unlike the rather flat, two-dimensional forms found in then prevailing Byzantine art, Giotto's figures have a fresh, life-like quality. The people in his paintings have bulk, and they show emotion, which you can see on their faces and in their gestures. This was something new in the late Middle Ages. Without Giotto, there wouldn't have been a Raphael.

In Florence: **Santa Croce; Uffizi; Campanile; Santa Maria Novella**
Elsewhere in Italy: **Scrovegni Chapel, Padua; Vatican Museums, Rome**

FILIPPO BRUNELLESCHI (1377-1446)

Architect/engineer from Florence.

If Brunelleschi had beaten Ghiberti in the Baptistery doors competition in Florence, the city's Duomo most likely would not have the striking appearance and authority that it has today. After his loss, he sulked off to Rome, where he studied the ancient Roman structures first-hand. Brunelleschi figured out how to vault the Duomo's dome, a structure unprecedented in its colossal size and great height. His Ospedale degli Innocenti employs classical elements in the creation of a stunning, new architectural statement; it is the first truly Renaissance structure.

In Florence: **Duomo; Ospedale degli Innocenti; San Lorenzo; Santo Spirito; Baptistery Doors Competition Entry, Bargello; Santa Croce**

LORENZO GHIBERTI (CA. 1381-1455)

Sculptor from Florence.

Ghiberti won a competition—besting his chief rival, Brunelleschi—to cast the gilded bronze North Doors of the Baptistery in Florence. These doors, and the East Doors that he subsequently executed, took up the next 50 years of his life. He created intricately worked figures that are more true-to-life than any since antiquity, and he was one of the first Renaissance sculptors to work in bronze. Ghiberti taught the next generation of artists; Donatello, Uccello, and Masaccio all passed through his studio.

In Florence: **Door Copies, Baptistery; Original Doors, Museo dell'Opera del Duomo; Baptistry Door Competition Entry, Bargello; Orsanmichele**

DONATELLO (CA. 1386-1466)

Sculptor from Florence.

Donatello was an innovator who, like his good friend Brunelleschi, spent most of his long life in Florence. Consumed with the science of optics, he used light and shadow to create the effects of nearness and distance. He made an essentially flat slab look like a three-dimensional scene. His bronze is probably the first free-standing male nude since antiquity. Not only technically brilliant, his work is also emotionally resonant; few sculptors are as expressive.

In Florence: *David*, **Bargello;** *St. Mark*, **Orsanmichele; Palazzo Vecchio; Museo dell'Opera del Duomo; San Lorenzo; Santa Croce**
Elsewhere in Italy: **Padua; Prato; Venice**

Fra Angelico's *The Deposition*

Masaccio's *Trinity*

Filippo Lippi's *Madonna and Child*

10

PAOLO UCCELLO (1397-1475)
Painter from Florence.
Renaissance chronicler Vasari once observed that had Uccello not been so obsessed with the mathematical problems posed by perspective, he would have been a very good painter. The struggle to master single-point perspective and to render motion in two dimensions is nowhere more apparent than in his battle scenes. His first major commission in Florence was the gargantuan fresco of the English mercenary Sir John Hawkwood (the Italians called him Giovanni Acuto) in Florence's Duomo.
In Florence: *Sir John Hawkwood*, Duomo; *Battle of San Romano*, Uffizi; Santa Maria Novella
Elsewhere in Italy: Urbino, Prato

FRA ANGELICO (CA. 1400-1455)
Painter from a small town north of Florence.
A Dominican friar, who eventually made his way to the convent of San Marco, Fra Angelico and his assistants painted frescoes for aid in prayer and meditation. He was known for his piety; Vasari wrote that Fra Angelico could never paint a crucifix without a tear running down his face. Perhaps no other painter so successfully translated the mysteries of faith and the sacred into painting. And yet his figures emote, his command of perspective is superb, and his use of color startles even today.
In Florence: Museo di San Marco; Uffizi
Elsewhere in Italy: Vatican Museums, Rome; Fiesole; Cortona; Perugia; Orvieto

MASACCIO (1401-1428)
Painter from San Giovanni Valdarno, southeast of Florence.
Masaccio and Masolino, a frequent collaborator, worked most famously together at Santa Maria del Carmine. Their frescoes of the life of St. Peter use light to mold figures in the painting by imitating the way light falls on figures in real life. Masaccio also pioneered the use of single-point perspective, masterfully rendered in his. His friend Brunelleschi probably introduced him to the technique, yet another step forward in rendering things the way the eye sees them. Masaccio died young and under mysterious circumstances.
In Florence: Santa Maria del Carmine; *Trinity*, Santa Maria Novella

FILIPPO LIPPI (CA. 1406-1469)
Painter from Prato.
At a young age, Filippo Lippi entered the friary of Santa Maria del Carmine, where he was highly influenced by Masaccio and Masolino's frescoes. His religious vows appear to have made less of an impact; his affair with a young nun produced a son, Filippino (Little Philip, who later apprenticed with Botticelli), and a daughter. His religious paintings often have a playful, humorous note; some of his angels are downright impish and look directly out at the viewer. Lippi links the earlier painters of the 15th century with those who follow; Botticelli apprenticed with him.
In Florence: Uffizi; Palazzo Medici Riccardi; San Lorenzo; Palazzo Pitti
Elsewhere in Italy: Prato

Botticelli's *Primavera*

Leonardo's *Portrait of a Young Woman*

Raphael's *Madonna on the Meadow*

BOTTICELLI (CA. 1444–1510)

Painter from Florence.
Botticelli's work is characterized by stunning, elongated blondes, cherubic angels (something he undoubtedly learned from his time with Filippo Lippi), and tender Christs. Though he did many religious paintings, he also painted monumental, nonreligious panels—his *Birth of Venus* and *Primavera* being the two most famous of these. A brief sojourn took him to Rome, where he and a number of other artists frescoed the Sistine Chapel walls.

In Florence: **Birth of Venus, Primavera, Uffizi; Palazzo Pitti**
Elsewhere in Italy: **Vatican Museums, Rome**

LEONARDO DA VINCI (1452–1519)

Painter/sculptor/engineer from Anchiano, a small town outside Vinci.
Leonardo never lingered long in any place; his restless nature and his international reputation led to commissions throughout Italy, and took him to Milan, Vigevano, Pavia, Rome, and, ultimately, France. Though he is most famous for his mysterious *Mona Lisa* (at the Louvre in Paris), he painted other penetrating, psychological portraits in addition to his scientific experiments: his design for a flying machine (never built) predates Kitty Hawk by nearly 500 years. The greatest collection of Leonardo's work in Italy can be seen on one wall in the Uffizi.

In Florence: **Adoration of the Magi, Uffizi**
Elsewhere in Italy: **Last Supper, Santa Maria delle Grazie, Milan**

RAPHAEL (1483–1520)

Painter/architect from Urbino.
Raphael spent only four highly productive years of his short life in Florence, where he turned out made-to-order panel paintings of the Madonna and Child for a hungry public; he also executed a number of portraits of Florentine aristocrats. Perhaps no other artist had such a fine command of line and color, and could render it, seemingly effortlessly, in paint. His painting acquired new authority after he came up against Michelangelo toiling away on the Sistine ceiling. Raphael worked nearly next door in the Vatican, where his figures take on an epic, Michelangelesque scale.

In Florence: **Uffizi; Palazzo Pitti**
Elsewhere in Italy: **Vatican Museums, Rome**

MICHELANGELO (1475–1564)

Painter/sculptor/architect from Caprese.
Although Florentine and proud of it (he famously signed his St. Peter's *Pietà* to avoid confusion about where he was from), he spent most of his 89 years outside his native city. He painted and sculpted the male body on an epic scale and glorified it while doing so. Though he complained throughout the proceedings that he was really a sculptor, Michelangelo's Sistine Chapel ceiling is arguably the greatest fresco cycle ever painted (and the massive figures owe no small debt to Giotto).

In Florence: **David, Galleria dell'Accademia; Uffizi; Casa Buonarroti; Bargello**
Elsewhere in Italy: **St. Peter's Basilica, Vatican Museums, and Piazza del Campidoglio in Rome**

The interior is one of a pair designed in Florence by Filippo Brunelleschi in the early decades of the 15th century (the other is San Lorenzo). It was here that Brunelleschi supplied definitive solutions to the two major problems of interior Renaissance church design: how to build a cross-shape interior using classical architectural elements borrowed from antiquity and how to reflect in that interior the order and regularity that Renaissance scientists (among them Brunelleschi himself) were at the time discovering in the natural world around them.

Brunelleschi's solution to the first problem was brilliantly simple: turn a Greek temple inside out. While ancient Greek temples were walled buildings surrounded by classical colonnades, Brunelleschi's churches were classical arcades surrounded by walls. This brilliant architectural idea overthrew the previous era's religious taboo against pagan architecture once and for all, triumphantly claiming that architecture for Christian use.

Brunelleschi's solution to the second problem—making the entire interior orderly and regular—was mathematically precise: he designed the ground plan of the church so that all its parts were proportionally related. The transepts and nave have exactly the same width; the side aisles are precisely half as wide as the nave; the little chapels off the side aisles are exactly half as deep as the side aisles; the chancel and transepts are exactly one-eighth the depth of the nave; and so on, with dizzying exactitude. For Brunelleschi, such a design technique was a matter of passionate conviction. Like most theoreticians of his day, he believed that mathematical regularity and aesthetic beauty were flip sides of the same coin, that one was not possible without the other.

In the refectory, adjacent to the church, you can see Andrea Orcagna's highly damaged fresco of the Crucifixion. ⊠ *Piazza Santo Spirito* ☎ *055/210030* ✆ *Church free, refectory €3* ✆ *Church Mon.–Sat. 10–12:30 and 4–5:30, Sun. 4–5:30; refectory Sat.–Mon. 10–4*

WHERE TO EAT

Florence's popularity with tourists means that, unfortunately, there's a higher percentage of mediocre restaurants here than you'll find in most Italian towns (Venice, perhaps, might win the prize). Some restaurant owners cut corners and let standards slip, knowing that a customer today is unlikely to return tomorrow, regardless of the quality of the meal. So, if you're looking to eat well, it pays to do some research, starting with the recommendations here. Dining hours start at around 1 for lunch and 8 for dinner. Many of Florence's restaurants are small, so reservations are a must.

Cafés in Italy serve not only coffee concoctions and pastries but also sweets, drinks, and panini, and some have hot pasta and lunch dishes. They usually open from early in the morning to late at night (depending upon the time of year); some are closed on Sunday.

	WHAT IT COSTS			
	$	$$	$$$	$$$$
AT DINNER	under €15	€15–€24	€25–€35	over €35

Restaurant prices are the average cost of a main course at dinner or, if dinner is not served, at lunch.

Use the coordinate (⊕ B2) at the end of each listing to locate a site on the Where to Eat and Stay in Florence map.

AROUND THE DUOMO

$ ITALIAN 🍴 **Coquinarius.** This rustically elegant space, which has served many purposes over the past 600 years, offers some of the tastiest food in town at great prices. It's the perfect place to come if you aren't sure what you're hungry for, as they offer a little bit of everything: salad lovers will have a hard time choosing from among the lengthy list (the Scozzese, with poached chicken, avocado, and bacon, is a winner); those with a yen for pasta will face agonizing choices (the ravioli with pecorino and pears is particularly good). A revolving list of *piatti unici* (single dishes that can be ordered on their own, usually served only at lunch) can also whet your appetite, as well as terrific cheese and cured meat plates. The well-culled wine list has lots of great wines by the glass, and even more by the bottle. [$] *Average main: €10* ✉ *Via delle Oche 15/r, Around the Duomo* ☎ *055/2302153* 🌐 *www.coquinarius.it* ✍ *Reservations essential* ⊕ *E3.*

$ ITALIAN 🍴 **Gelateria Edoardo.** It's the latest, hottest gelateria on the block in part because the *gelati* is certified organic, and because it's right next to the Duomo. Their daring *sorbetto al Chianti Colli Fiorentini* (Chianti ice cream) is new, original, tasty, and contains 4% alcohol. [$] *Average main: €2* ✉ *Piazza del Duomo 45/r* ☎ *055/281 055* 🌐 *www.edoardobio.it* ⊕ *F3.*

$ ITALIAN Fodor's Choice ★ 🍴 **Grom.** A stone's throw from the Duomo, this is one of the best gelaterias in town. Flavors change frequently according to the season, so expect a fragrant *gelato di cannella* (cinnamon ice cream) in winter and lively fresh fruit flavors in summer. Though the original Grom hails from Turin (and there's a Grom in New York City), this is still probably the best gelato in town. [$] *Average main: €5* ✉ *Via del Campanile, Around the Duomo* ☎ *055/216158* 🌐 *www.grom.it* 💳 *No credit cards* ⊕ *E3.*

$ ITALIAN Fodor's Choice ★ 🍴 **'ino.** Serving arguably the best panini in town, proprietor Alessandro sources only the very best ingredients. Located right behind the Uffizi, 'ino is a perfect place to grab a tasty sandwich and glass of wine before forging on to the next museum. [$] *Average main: €8* ✉ *Via dei Georgofili 3/r–7/r, Piazza della Signoria, Around the Duomo* ☎ *055/219208* ⊕ *E4.*

$$$ ITALIAN 🍴 **Pegna.** Looking for some cheddar cheese to pile in your panino? Pegna has been selling both Italian and non-Italian food since 1860. It's closed Saturday afternoon in July and August, Wednesday afternoon September through June, and Sunday year-round. [$] *Average main: €25* ✉ *Via dello Studio 8, Around the Duomo* ☎ *055/282701* 🌐 *www.pegnafirenze.com* ⊕ *F3.*

SAN LORENZO

$ ✕ **Baroni.** The cheese collection at Baroni may be the most comprehensive
INTERNATIONAL   in Florence. They also have high-quality truffle products, vinegars, and
other delicacies. $ *Average main: €10 ⊠ Mercato Centrale, enter at Via
Signa, San Lorenzo* ☎ *055/289576* ⊕ *www.baronialimentari.it* ✛ *D1.*

$ ✕ **da Nerbone.** This *tavola calda* in the middle of the covered Mercato
TUSCAN   Centrale has been serving up food to Florentines who like their tripe
Fodor's Choice   since 1872. Tasty primi and secondi are available every day, but cogno-
★   scenti come for the *panino con il lampredotto* (tripe sandwich). Less
adventurous sorts might want to sample the *bollito* (boiled beef sandwich). Ask that the bread be *bagnato* (briefly dipped in the tripe cooking liquid), and have both the salsa verde and *salsa piccante* (a spicy
cayenne sauce) slathered on top. And go early, as they inevitably sell out
of them. $ *Average main: €13 ⊠ Mercato San Lorenzo* ☎ *055/219949*
▤ *No credit cards* ☉ *Closed Sun. No dinner* ✛ *D1.*

$ ✕ **da Sergio.** In 2015, this little eatery celebrated its centenary, and with
TUSCAN   good reason. It's been in the capable hands of the Gozzi family, who
Fodor's Choice   have ensured continuity and stuck to Tuscan tradition. The food's ter-
★   rific, eminently affordable, and just across the way from the basilica
of San Lorenzo, which means that you can imbibe well-prepared food
while marveling at the Brunelleschi and Michelangelo you've just seen.
The menu is short, and changes daily. Their *lombatina alla griglia* (a
grilled veal T-bone steak) is almost always on, and meat eaters should
not miss it. Pastas are equally terrific. Dessert, in true Florentine fashion is usually limited to biscotti with vin santo. $ *Average main: €9*
⊠ *Piazza San Lorenzo 8/r* ☉ *Closed Sun. No dinner* ✛ *E2*

$ ✕ **Gelateria Carabe.** Specializing in things Sicilian, this shop is known for
ITALIAN   its tart and flavorful *granità* (granular flavored ices), made only in the
summer, which are great thirst-quenchers. $ *Average main: €3 ⊠ Via
Ricasoli 60/r, San Marco* ☎ *055/289476* ⊕ *www.parcocarabe.it* ▤ *No
credit cards* ✛ *F1.*

$ ✕ **il Desco.** This tiny boîte, with a mere handful of tables, is an oasis in
TUSCAN   an area which is pretty much a culinary wasteland. It's owned by the
Bargiacchi family, who are proprietors of the lovely hotel Guelfo Bianco
just next door. Their organic farm in the Tuscan countryside provides
much of what is on the frequently changing menu. The menu plays to
all tastes—classic Tuscan dishes such as *peposo* (a hearty, black pepper–
filled beef stew) can be found, as well as vegetarian. Even vegans have
options: the seitan in *salsa fredda di ceci ai capperi e rosmarino* (seitan
in a room-temperature pureed chickpea sauce flavored with capers and
rosemary) is a winner. The wine list is well thought out, and artisanal
beer is also on the menu. $ *Average main: €13 ⊠ Via Cavour 55/r, San
Lorenzo* ☎ *055/288 330* ⊕ *www.ildescofirenze.it* ✛ *F1.*

$$ ✕ **Mario.** Florentines flock to this narrow family-run trattoria near San
TUSCAN   Lorenzo to feast on Tuscan favorites served at simple tables under a
Fodor's Choice   wooden ceiling dating from 1536. A distinct cafeteria feel and genuine
★   Florentine hospitality prevail: you'll be seated wherever there's room,
which often means with strangers. Yes, there's a bit of extra oil in most
dishes, which imparts calories as well as taste, but aren't you on vaca-
tion in Italy? Worth the splurge is *riso al ragù* (rice with ground beef

10

and tomatoes). [$] *Average main: €20* ✉ *Via Rosina 2/r, corner of Piazza del Mercato Centrale, San Lorenzo* ☎ *055/218550* ✍ *Reservations not accepted* ⏲ *Closed Sun. and Aug. No dinner* ✥ *E1.*

$$ ITALIAN Fodor's Choice ★ 🍴 **Perini.** It's possible to break the bank here, as this might be the best salumeria in Florence. Perini sells prosciutto, mixed meats, sauces for pasta, and a wide assortment of antipasti. [$] *Average main: €20* ✉ *Mercato Centrale, enter at Via dell'Aretino, San Lorenzo* ☎ *055/2398306* ⏲ *Closed Sun.* ✥ *E1.*

$$ TUSCAN Fodor's Choice ★ 🍴 **Taverna del Bronzino.** Want to have a sophisticated meal in a 16th-century Renaissance artist's studio? The former studio of Santi di Tito, a student of Bronzino's, has simple, formal décor, with white tablecloths and place settings. The classic, elegantly presented Tuscan food is superb, and the solid, affordable wine list rounds out the menu—Stefano, the sommelier, really knows his stuff. Desserts shine at this place, so remember to save room, and conclude with a limoncello or mirtillo postprandial drink. Both are made in-house, and provide a perfect conclusion to the meal. Outstanding service makes a meal here heavenly. Reservations are advised, especially for eating at the wine cellar's only table. [$] *Average main: €22* ✉ *Via delle Ruote 25/r, San Marco* ☎ *055/495220* ✍ *Reservations essential* ⏲ *Closed Sun., and 3 wks in Aug.* ✥ *G1.*

SANTA MARIA NOVELLA

$$$$ TUSCAN 🍴 **Buca Lapi.** The Antinori family started selling wine from their palace's basement in the 15th century. Six hundred years later, this *buca* (hole) is a lively, subterranean restaurant filled with Florentine aristocrats chowing down on what might be the best (and most expensive) bistecca fiorentina in town. The classical Tuscan menu has the usual suspects: *crostino di cavolo nero* (black cabbage on toasted garlic bread), along with ribollita and pappa al pomodoro. You might want to cut directly to the chase, however, and order the bistecca, an immense slab of Chianina beef impeccably grilled on the outside, just barely warmed on the inside. (If you're not into rare meat, order something else from the grill.) Roast potatoes and cannellini beans make perfect accompaniments. [$] *Average main: €35* ✉ *Via del Trebbio 1, Santa Maria Novella* ☎ *055/213768* 🌐 *www.bucalapi.com* ✍ *Reservations essential* ✥ *D3.*

$$$ TUSCAN 🍴 **Cantinetta Antinori.** After a morning of shopping on Via Tornabuoni, stop for lunch in this 15th-century palazzo in the company of Florentine ladies (and men) who come to see and be seen over lunch. The panache of the food matches that of the clientele: expect treats such as *tramezzino con pane di campagna al tartufo* (country pâté with truffles served on bread) and the *insalata di gamberoni e gamberetti con carciofi freschi* (crayfish and prawn salad with shaved raw artichokes). [$] *Average main: €27* ✉ *Piazza Antinori 3, Santa Maria Novella* ☎ *055/292234* ⏲ *Closed weekends, 20 days in Aug., and Dec. 25–Jan. 6* ✥ *D3.*

$$ TUSCAN 🍴 **Il Latini.** It may be the noisiest, most crowded trattoria in Florence, but it's also one of the most fun. The genial host, Torello ("little bull") Latini, presides over four big dining rooms, and somehow it feels as if you're dining in his home. Ample portions of ribollita prepare the palate for the hearty meat dishes that follow. Florentines and tourists alike

tuck into the *agnello fritto* (fried lamb) with aplomb. Their *lombatina* (a grilled veal chop) might be the best in town. Even with a reservation, there's always a wait. $ *Average main: €15* ⊠ *Via dei Palchetti 6/r, Santa Maria Novella* ☎ *055/210916* ⊘ *Closed Mon., and 15 days at Christmas* ✛ *C3*.

$
TUSCAN
✕ **Mangiafoco.** It's got brightly colored purple and orange walls, and a warren of small rooms; it also has a large room along with a counter that sells terrific take-away options. The menu changes daily, reflecting both what's in season and the whims of the chef. The wine list is long, and there are a large number of wines offered by the glass. You can tuck into a plate of *fettucine ragù toscana e carciofi* (flat noodes with a meat sauce and artichokes) or opt for any number of their *taglieri* (mixed meat and cheese plates). The latter are served with various gelatins, made from such delicacies as Chianti, vin santo, and balsamic vinegar. They are justifiably proud of their desserts, made in-house. You can also just drop in for a glass of wine, perch on one of their steps, and watch the world go by. $ *Average main: €12* ⊠ *Borgo Santi Apostoli 26/r, Santa Maria Novella* ☎ *055/2658170* ⊕ *www.mangiafoco.com* ⊘ *Closed Sun.* ✛ *D4*.

$
ITALIAN
✕ **Shake.** If you're on your way to the train station, or arriving from the train station, this little juice bar at Piazza Santa Maria Novella provides a perfect place for a rest stop. They serve tasty croissants and panini all day, and make wraps, salads, and sandwiches at lunch (all of which are available to go as they are handily packed). There's also ice cream and, of course, their juices. The "Shake" smoothie, comprising avocado, apple, banana, and yogurt, provides a great way to start the day. $ *Average main: €5* ⊠ *Via degli Avelli 2/r, Santa Maria Novella* ☎ *055/295310* ✛ *D2*.

$$
TUSCAN
Fodor's Choice
★
✕ **Trattoria Sostanza (il Troia).** Since opening its doors in 1869, this trattoria has been serving top-notch, unpretentious food to Florentines who like their bistecca fiorentina very large and very rare. A single room with white tiles on the wall and paper mats on the tables provides the setting for delicious meals. Along with fine Tuscan classics, they have two signature dishes: the *tortino di carciofi* (artichoke tart) and the *pollo al burro* (chicken with butter). The latter is an amazing surprise, a succulent chicken breast cooked very quickly and served as soon as it leaves the grill. Leave room for dessert, as their *torta alla Meringa* (a semifrozen dessert flecked with chocolate and topped with meringue) is scrumptious. $ *Average main: €15* ⊠ *Via della Porcellana 25, Santa Maria Novella* ☎ *055/212691* ⌫ *Reservations essential* ▭ *No credit cards* ✛ *B3*.

$
ITALIAN
✕ **vincanto.** It opens at 11 am, and closes at midnight: this is a rarity in Florentine dining. They do a little bit of everything here, including fine pastas (don't miss the *ignudi*), salads, and pizzas. You can come here for an American-style breakfast, or simply a cup of coffee, or a glass of wine. Because the kitchen stays open from opening to closing, if you're hankering at 4 pm for a chicken burger with curried fried onions, or a pizza laden with Italian pork products, you're in luck. And all of this can be enjoyed with a splendid view of Piazza Santa Maria Novella. $ *Average main: €12* ⊠ *Piazza Santa Maria Novella 23/r* ☎ *055/2679300* ⊕ *www.ristorantevincanto.com* ✛ *C2*.

10

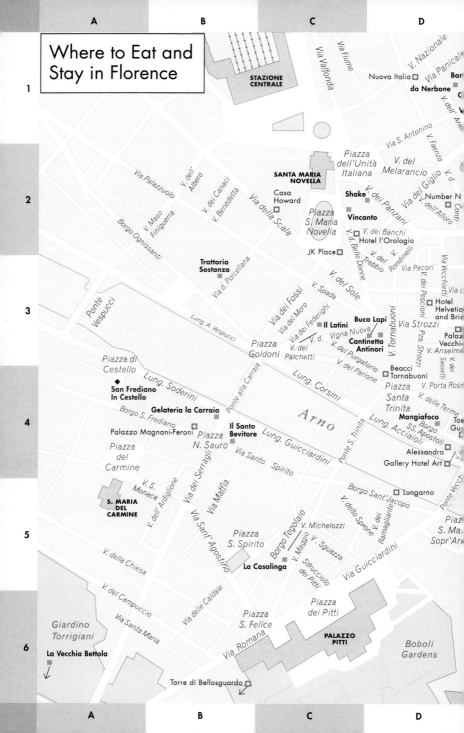

Where to Eat and Stay in Florence

A   **B**   **C**   **D**

STAZIONE CENTRALE

Via Flume
Via Vallonda
Via Nazionale
V. Panical
Nuova Italia
Bar
da Nerbone
V. dell' Ariel

Via S. Antonino
V. Faenza
Piazza dell'Unità Italiana
V. del Melarancio
V. del Giglio
V. d.

SANTA MARIA NOVELLA
Shake
V. dei Panzani
Number N
Conti
V. dell'Alloro
Casa Howard
Vincanto
Via dell' Albero
Via Palazzuolo
V. dei Canaci
V. Maso finiguerra
v. Benedetta
Via della Scala
Piazza S. Maria Novella
V. dei Banchi
Hotel l'Orologio
V.
V. d. Belle Donne
V. del Trebbio
V. Rondinelli
Via Pecori
Via Vecchietti
Via c

Borgo Ognissanti
JK Place

Trattoria Sostanza
Via d. Porcellana

V. del Sole
Hotel Helvetic and Bris

Ponte Vespucci
Lung. A. Vespucci
Via d. Fossi
V. Spada
V. del Moro
Il Latini
Buca Lapi
V. d. Vigna Nuova
Cantinetta Antinori
V. dei Purgatorio
V. Tornabuoni
V. dei Pescioni
Pza. Strozzi
Via Strozzi
Palaz Vecchi
V. Anselmi
V. dei Sassetti

Piazza di Cestello
Piazza Goldoni
Via dei Federighi
V. dei Palchetti
V. del Parione
Beacci Tornabuoni
Piazza Santa Trinita
V. Porta Ross
V. delle Terme

Lung. Soderini
San Frediano In Cestello
Ponte alla Carraia
Lung. Corsini
Arno
Mangiafoco
SS. Apostoli
Borgo
To
Gu

Gelateria la Carraia
Borgo S. Frediano
Il Santo Bevitore
Ponte S. Trinita
Lung. Acciaioli
Alessandra
Gallery Hotel Art
Ponte Vecc

Palazzo Magnani-Feroni
Piazza N. Sauro
Via Santo Spirito
Lung. Guicciardini
Borgo Sant'Jacopo
Lungarno
Piazza del Carmine
V. S. Monaca
V. dell' Ardiglione
Via dei Serragli
Via Maffia
Via Sant'Agostino
V. dello Sprone
V. dei Ramagliante
Piaz S. Ma Sopr'Ar

S. MARIA DEL CARMINE
Piazza S. Spirito
Borgo Tegolaio
V. Michelozzi
V. Maggio
v. Sguazza
V. Guicciardini

V. della Chiesa
La Casalinga
Sdrucciolo dei Pitti
Piazza dei Pitti

V. del Campuccio
Via delle Caldaie
Via Santa Maria
Piazza S. Felice
Via Romana
PALAZZO PITTI
Boboli Gardens

Giardino Torrigiani
La Vecchia Bettola
Torre di Bellosguardo

A   **B**   **C**   **D**

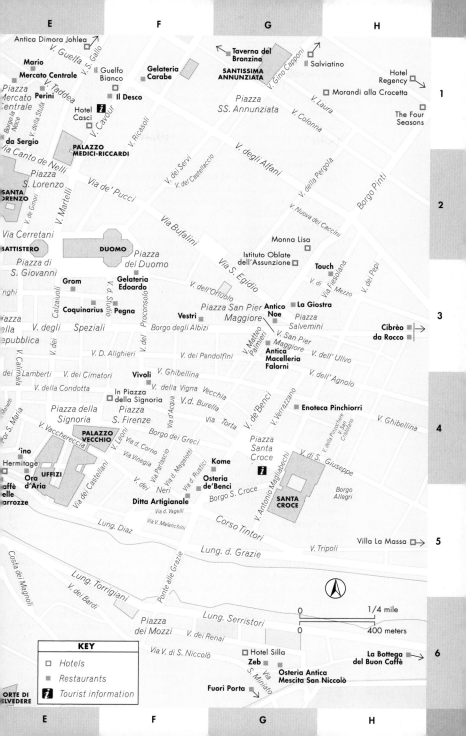

SANTA CROCE

$ TUSCAN Fodor's Choice ★ 🍴 **Antica Macelleria Falorni.** The Falorni family has been in the butcher business since 1806 in Greve in Chianti, and mercifully decided to open a small trattoria in Florence's centro storico. Two small rooms in a medieval tower seat about 25 people. This is Tuscan food served at its absolute best. They do steak tartare five different ways, serve sandwiches featuring their delicious cured pork products, various crostini, and cutting boards (comprising meat and cheeses). You could also sample *Le Ricette della Nonna Beppa* (Grandma Beppa's Recipes), which include a fragrant *il lesso in salsa verde* (various boiled meats served with salsa verde and pickled onions). It's open from noon to midnight—a rarity in Florence. [$] *Average main: €9* ✉ *via Matteo Palmieri 35/37r, Santa Croce* ☎ *055/245430* 🌐 *www.falorni.it* ✥ *G3.*

$ TUSCAN 🍴 **Antico Noe.** If Florence had diners (it doesn't), this would be the best diner in town. The short menu at the one-room eatery relies heavily on seasonal ingredients picked up daily at the market. Though the secondi are good, it's the antipasti and primi that really shine. The menu really comes alive during truffle and artichoke season (don't miss the grilled artichokes if they're on the menu). Locals rave about the tagliatelle *ai porcini* (with mushrooms); the fried eggs liberally laced with truffle might be the greatest truffle bargain in town. Ask for the menu in Italian, as the English version is much more limited. The short wine list has some great bargains, and note that if you opt to order bistecca, you'll jump to a higher price category. [$] *Average main: €10* ✉ *Volta di San Piero 6/r, Santa Croce* ☎ *055/2340838* ⊙ *Closed Sun., and 2 wks in Aug.* ✥ *G3.*

$$$$ TUSCAN Fodor's Choice ★ 🍴 **Cibrèo.** The food at this upscale trattoria is fantastic, from the creamy crostini di fegatini to the melt-in-your-mouth desserts. Many Florentines hail this as the city's best restaurant, and Fodor's readers tend to agree—though some take issue with the prices and complain of long waits for a table (even with a reservation). If you thought you'd never try tripe—let alone like it—this is the place to lay any doubts to rest: the *trippa in insalata* (cold tripe salad) with parsley and garlic is an epiphany. The food is traditionally Tuscan, impeccably served by a staff that's multilingual—a good thing, because there are no written menus. [$] *Average main: €40* ✉ *Via A. del Verrocchio 8/r, Santa Croce* ☎ *055/2341100* ✍ *Reservations essential* ⊙ *Closed Sun. and Mon., and July 25–Sept. 5* ✥ *H3.*

$$ TUSCAN 🍴 **Cibrèo Trattoria.** This intimate little trattoria, known to locals as Cibreino, shares its kitchen with the famed Florentine culinary institution from which it gets its name. They share the same menu, too, though Cibreino's is much shorter. Start with *il gelatina di pomodoro* (tomato gelatin) liberally laced with basil, garlic, and a pinch of hot pepper, and then sample the justifiably renowned *passato in zucca gialla* (puréed yellow-pepper soup) before moving on to any of the succulent second courses. Save room for dessert, as the pastry chef has a deft hand with chocolate tarts. To avoid sometimes agonizingly long waits, come early (7 pm) or late (after 9:30). [$] *Average main: €15* ✉ *Via dei Macci 118, Santa Croce* ☎ *055/2341100* ✍ *Reservations not accepted* ▭ *No credit cards* ⊙ *Closed Sun. and Mon., and July 25–Sept. 5* ✥ *H3.*

$ TUSCAN 🍴 **da Rocco.** At one of Florence's biggest markets you can grab lunch to go, or you could cram yourself into one of the booths and pour from the straw-cloaked flask (wine here is *da consumo,* which means they charge you for how much you drink). Food is abundant, Tuscan, and fast; locals pack in. The ample menu changes daily (nine secondi are the norm), and the prices are great. $ *Average main: €5* ✉ *Mercato Sant'Ambrogio, Piazza Ghiberti, Santa Croce* ⚓ *Reservations not accepted* ▭ *No credit cards* ⊘ *Closed Sun. No dinner* ✛ *H3.*

$

ITALIAN

✕ **Ditta Artigianale.** Seattle has finally come to Florence, and coffee fans couldn't be happier. This place is always crowded with mostly young folk lingering over non-Italian cups of coffee. Light lunch and brunch are also on offer, and in between there's a steady supply of cakes, cookies, and croissants. Cocktail hour brings on the "Tapas" part of their menu. It opens at 8 in the morning, and stays open every night until at least 10 pm. $ *Average main: €8* ✉ *Via de'Neri 32, Santa Croce* ☎ *055/2741541* ▭ *No credit cards* ✛ *F5.*

$$$$

ITALIAN

✕ **Enoteca Pinchiorri.** A sumptuous Renaissance palace with high, frescoed ceilings and bouquets in silver vases provides the backdrop for this restaurant, one of the most expensive in Italy. Some consider it one of the best, and others consider it a non-Italian rip-off, as the kitchen is presided over by a Frenchwoman with sophisticated, yet internationalist, leanings. Prices are high (think €80 for a plate of spaghetti) and portions are small; the vast holdings of the wine cellar (undoubtedly the best in Florence), as well as stellar service, dull the pain, however, when the bill is presented. $ *Average main: €75* ✉ *Via Ghibellina 87, Santa Croce* ☎ *055/242777* ⊕ *www.enotecapinchiorri.com* ⚓ *Reservations essential* ⌂ *Jacket required* ⊘ *Closed Sun. and Mon., and Aug. No lunch* ✛ *G4.*

$$

JAPANESE

✕ **Kome.** If you're looking for a break from the ubiquitous ribollita, stop in at this eatery, which may be the only Japanese restaurant in the world to be housed in a 15th-century Renaissance palazzo. High, vaulted arches frame the Kaiten sushi conveyor belt. It's Japanese food cafeteria-style: selections, priced according to plate color, make their way around a bar, where diners pick whatever they find appealing. Those seeking a more substantial meal head to the second floor, where Japanese barbecue is prepared at your table. The minimalist basement provides a subtle but dramatic backdrop for a well-prepared cocktail. $ *Average main: €20* ✉ *Via de' Benci 41/r, Santa Croce* ☎ *055/2008009* ⊕ *www.komefirenze. it* ✛ *G4.*

$$$

ITALIAN

✕ **La Giostra.** This clubby spot, whose name means "carousel" in Italian, was created by the late Prince Dimitri Kunz d'Asburgo Lorena, and is now expertly run by his handsome twin sons. In perfect English they will describe favorite dishes, such as the *taglierini con tartufo bianco,* a decadently rich pasta with white truffles. The constantly changing menu has terrific vegetarian and vegan options, and any meal that does not include truffles is significantly less expensive than those that do. For dessert, this might be the only show in town with a sublime tiramisù *and* a wonderfully gooey Sacher torte. $ *Average main: €25* ✉ *Borgo Pinti 12/r, Santa Croce* ☎ *055/241341* ⊕ *www.ristorantelagiostra.com* ⚓ *Reservations essential* ⊘ *No lunch weekends* ✛ *G3.*

$$

ITALIAN

Fodor'sChoice

★

✕ **Osteria de'Benci.** A few minutes from Santa Croce, this charming osteria serves some of the most eclectic food in Florence. Try the spaghetti *degli eretici* (in tomato sauce with fresh herbs). The grilled meats are justifiably famous; the *carbonata* is a succulent piece of grilled beef served

10

rare. Weekly specials complement what's happening in the market, and all of the food pairs beautifully with their wine list, which is heavy on things Tuscan. When it's warm, you can dine outside with a view of the 13th-century tower belonging to the prestigious Alberti family. [$] *Average main: €15* ✉ *Via de' Benci 11–13/r, Santa Croce* ☎ *055/2344923* ✍ *Reservations essential* ⏲ *Closed 2 wks in Aug.* ⊕ *F5.*

$$ MODERN ITALIAN 🍴 **Touch.** It's called "Touch," because it's the first restaurant in Florence to feature iPad menus. Redone here is the classic *bollito* (mixed meats served with sauces); the meats are combined, encased with a raviolo covering, and graced with an egg sauce. Then there's the Tuscan club sandwich featuring not turkey, but fegatini. Any fears of eating raw egg in the classic Roman *carbonara* may be assuaged by watching the egg cook, briefly, tableside. Desserts are as creative as what comes before. [$] *Average main: €20* ✉ *Via Fiesolana 18/r, Santa Croce* ☎ *055/2466150* 🌐 *www.touchflorence.com* ✍ *Reservations essential* ⏲ *No lunch* ⊕ *H3.*

$ ITALIAN 🍴 **Vestri.** This shop is devoted to chocolate in all its guises. The small but sublime selection of chocolate-based gelati includes one with hot peppers. [$] *Average main: €3* ✉ *Borgo Albizi 11/r, Santa Croce* ☎ *055/2340374* 🌐 *www.vestri.it* ▭ *No credit cards* ⊕ *F3.*

THE OLTRARNO

$ WINE BAR 🍴 **Fuori Porta.** One of the oldest and best wine bars in Florence, this place serves cured meats and cheeses, as well as daily specials such as the sublime spaghetti *al curry.* Crostini and crostoni—grilled breads topped with a mélange of cheeses and meats—are the house specialties; the *verdure sott'olio* (vegetables with oil) are divine. If the *torta caprese* is on the menu, don't miss it: it's a chocolate bomb with almonds, perhaps the best brownie in Florence. The lengthy wine list offers great wines by the glass, and terrific bottles from all over Italy and beyond. All this can be enjoyed at rustic wooden tables, and outdoors when weather allows. [$] *Average main: €10* ✉ *Via Monte alle Croci 10/r, San Niccolò* ☎ *055/2342483* ⊕ *G6.*

$ ITALIAN 🍴 **Gelateria la Carraia.** Though it's a bit of a haul to get here (it's at the foot of Ponte Carraia, two bridges down from the Ponte Vecchio), you'll be well-rewarded for doing so. They do standard flavors, and then creative ones such as *limone con biscotti* (lemon sorbet biscuits), and they do both of these very well. [$] *Average main: €3* ✉ *Piazza Nazario Sauro 2, Santo Spirito* ☎ *055/280695* 🌐 *www.lacarraiagroup.eu* ▭ *No credit cards* ⊕ *B4.*

$$ TUSCAN 🍴 **Il Santo Bevitore.** Florentines and other lovers of good food flock to "The Holy Drinker" for tasty, well-priced dishes. Unpretentious white walls, dark-wood furniture, and paper placemats make up the simple décor; start with the exceptional verdure sott'olio or the terrina di fegatini before sampling any of the divine pastas, such as the fragrant spaghetti with shrimp sauce. Count yourself lucky if the extraordinary potato gratin, served in compact triangular wedges, is on the menu. The extensive wine list is well priced, and the well-informed staff is happy to explain it. [$] *Average main: €16* ✉ *Via Santo Spirito 64/66r, Santo Spirito* ☎ *055/211264* ⏲ *No lunch Sun.* ⊕ *B4.*

$$$ ✕ **La Bottega del Buon Caffè.** It translates to "The Shop of Good Coffee,"
MODERN ITALIAN which may be the biggest understatement in the Florentine dining scene. The restaurant has an organic farm in the Tuscan countryside, and most of the fruit, vegetables, herbs, and honey on the menu is sourced from there. À la carte possibilities include *code ai scampi scottate, crudo di gamberi rosso su crema di zucchine biologiche e salsa all'arancia* (two different kinds of shrimp—one cooked, one raw—on a creamy organic zucchini and orange sauce) and terrific pastas. Either of two tasting menus, however, might be the way to go. Service is attentive and unobtrusive, making a meal here memorable. $ *Average main: €27* ⊠ *Lungarno Benvenuto Cellini 69/r, Oltrarno* ☎ *055/5535677* ⊕ *www.borgointhecity. com/en/la-bottegadel-buon-caffe* ⌲ *Reservations essential* ✛ *H6.*

$ ✕ **La Casalinga.** *Casalinga* means "housewife," and this place has the
TUSCAN nostalgic charm of a 1950s kitchen with Tuscan comfort food to match. If you eat ribollita anywhere in Florence, eat it here—it couldn't be more authentic. Mediocre paintings clutter the semipaneled walls, tables are set close together, and the place is usually jammed. The menu is long, portions are plentiful, and service is prompt and friendly. For dessert, the lemon sorbet perfectly caps off the meal. $ *Average main: €13* ⊠ *Via Michelozzi 9/r, Santo Spirito* ☎ *055/218624* ⊘ *Closed Sun., 1 wk at Christmas, and 3 wks in Aug.* ✛ *C5.*

$$ ✕ **La Vecchia Bettola.** The name doesn't exactly mean "old dive," but
TUSCAN it comes pretty close. This lively trattoria has been around only since 1979, but it feels as if it's been a whole lot longer. Tile floors and simple wood tables and chairs provide the interior decoration, such as it is. The recipes come from "wise grandmothers" and celebrate Tuscan food in its glorious simplicity. Here prosciutto is sliced with a knife, portions of grilled meat are tender and ample, service is friendly, and the wine list is well priced and good. This place is worth a taxi ride, even though it's just outside the centro storico. $ *Average main: €16* ⊠ *Viale Vasco Pratolini, Oltrarno* ☎ *055/224158* ⊘ *Closed Sun. and Mon.* ✛ *A6.*

$ ✕ **Zeb.** The food is incredibly tasty at this well-priced *alimentari* (deli-
TUSCAN catessen). Zeb stands for *zuppa* e *bollito* (soup and boiled things), and nothing here disappoints. This is home-style Tuscan cuisine at its very best, served in unpretentious, intimate surroundings: there's only room for about 15 guests. In the kitchen are Giuseppina and Alberto, her son. They staunchly insist on cooking what's best that day; which means the menu changes daily, reflecting the season's best offerings. $ *Average main: €9* ⊠ *Via San Miniato 2, Oltrarno* ☎ *055/2342864* ⊕ *www. zebgastronomia.com* ✛ *G6.*

10

WHERE TO STAY

Florence is equipped with hotels for all budgets; for instance, you can find both budget and luxury hotels in the centro storico and along the Arno. Florence has so many famous landmarks that it's not hard to find lodging with a panoramic view. The equivalent of the genteel *pensioni* of yesteryear can still be found, though they are now officially classified as hotels. Generally small and intimate, they often have a quaint appeal that usually doesn't preclude modern plumbing.

Florence's importance not only as a tourist city but also as a convention center and the site of the Pitti fashion collections guarantees a variety of accommodations. The high demand also means that, except in winter, reservations are a must.

If you find yourself in Florence with no reservations, go to **Consorzio ITA** (✉ *Stazione Centrale, Santa Maria Novella* ☎ *055/282893*). You must go there in person to make a booking.

WHAT IT COSTS

	$	$$	$$$	$$$$
FOR TWO PEOPLE	under €125	€125–€200	€201–€300	over €300

Exact prices listed are for a standard double room in high season.

Use the coordinate (✥ B2) at the end of each listing to locate a site on the Where to Eat and Stay in Florence map. Hotel reviews have been condensed for this book.

AROUND THE DUOMO

$$ HOTEL
🏨 **Hermitage.** All rooms here are decorated with lively wallpaper, and some have views of Palazzo Vecchio and others of the Arno. **Pros:** views; friendly, English-speaking staff; enviable position a stone's throw from the Ponte Vecchio. **Cons:** short flight of stairs to reach elevator. [$] *Rooms from: €198* ✉ *Vicolo Marzio 1, Piazza della Signoria, Around the Duomo* ☎ *055/287216* 🌐 *www.hermitagehotel.com* 🛏 *27 rooms, 1 suite* 🍴 *Breakfast* ✥ *E4.*

$$$$ HOTEL
🏨 **Hotel Helvetia and Bristol.** From the cozy yet sophisticated lobby with its stone columns to the guest rooms decorated with prints, you might feel as if you're a guest in a sophisticated manor house. **Pros:** central location; superb staff. **Cons:** rooms facing the street get some noise. [$] *Rooms from: €396* ✉ *Via dei Pescioni 2, Piazza della Repubblica, Around the Duomo* ☎ *055/26651* 🌐 *www.niquesahotels.com* 🛏 *54 rooms, 13 suites* 🍴 *No meals* ✥ *D3.*

$$$ B&B/INN
Fodor's Choice ★
🏨 **In Piazza della Signoria.** A cozy feeling permeates these charming rooms, all of which are uniquely decorated and lovingly furnished; some have damask curtains, others fanciful frescoes in the bathroom. **Pros:** marvelous staff; tasty breakfast with a view of Piazza della Signoria. **Cons:** short flight of stairs to reach elevator. [$] *Rooms from: €250* ✉ *Via dei Magazzini 2, near Piazza della Signoria, Around the Duomo* ☎ *055/2399546* 🌐 *www.inpiazzadellasignoria.com* 🛏 *10 rooms, 3 apartments* 🍴 *Breakfast* ✥ *F4.*

$$$$ HOTEL
🏨 **Palazzo Vecchietti.** If you're looking for a swank setting, and the possibility of staying in for a meal (each room has a tiny kitchenette), look no further than this hotel which, while thoroughly modern, dates to the 15th century. **Pros:** fireplace; central location; courtyard. **Cons:** expensive. [$] *Rooms from: €430* ✉ *Via, degli Strozzi 4, Around the Duomo* ☎ *055/230–2802* 🛏 *12 rooms, 2 apartments* 🕒 *www.palazzovecchietti.it* 🍴 *Breakfast* ✥ *D3.*

SAN LORENZO

$$ B&B/INN Fodor's Choice ★ **Antica Dimora Johlea.** Lively color runs rampant on the top floor of this 19th-century palazzo, with a charming flower-filled rooftop terrace where you can sip a glass of wine while taking in a view of Brunelleschi's cupola. **Pros:** great staff; cheerful rooms; honor bar. **Cons:** staff go home at 7; narrow staircase to get to roof terrace; steps to breakfast room. [$] *Rooms from: €130 ✉ Via San Gallo 80, San Marco ☎ 055/4633292 🌐 www.johanna.it 🛏 6 rooms 💳 No credit cards 🍴 Breakfast ✣ E1.*

$$$ HOTEL **Firenze Number Nine.** Those wanting an elegant hotel with a walk-in gym in the centro storico should look no further. **Pros:** location (couldn't be more central); great staff; walk-in gym and spa; sumptuous breakfast. **Cons:** location (lots of street noise). [$] *Rooms from: €219 ✉ Via del Conti 9/31r, San Lorenzo ☎ 055/293777 🌐 www.firenzenumbernine.com 🛏 25 rooms, 19 suites ✣ D2.*

$$ HOTEL **Hotel Casci.** In this refurbished 14th-century palace, the home of Giacchino Rossini in 1851–55, the friendly Lombardi family run a hotel with spotless, functional rooms. **Pros:** helpful staff; good option for families; English-language DVD collection with good selections for kids. **Cons:** bit of a college-dorm atmosphere; small elevator. [$] *Rooms from: €150 ✉ Via Cavour 13, San Marco ☎ 055/211686 🌐 www.hotelcasci.com 🛏 25 rooms 🍴 Breakfast ✣ E1.*

$$ HOTEL **Il Guelfo Bianco.** The 15th-century building has all modern conveniences, but Renaissance charm still shines in the high-ceiling rooms. **Pros:** stellar multilingual staff. **Cons:** rooms facing the street can be noisy. [$] *Rooms from: €181 ✉ Via Cavour 29, San Marco ☎ 055/288330 🌐 www.ilguelfobianco.it 🛏 40 rooms 🍴 Breakfast ✣ F1.*

SANTA MARIA NOVELLA

$$ B&B/INN **Alessandra.** An aura of grandeur pervades these clean, ample rooms a block from the Ponte Vecchio. **Pros:** several rooms have views of the Arno; the spacious suite is a bargain; tiny terrace allows for solitude while sipping a glass of wine. **Cons:** stairs to elevator; two rooms do not have en-suite baths. [$] *Rooms from: €150 ✉ Borgo Santi Apostoli 17, Santa Maria Novella ☎ 055/283438 🌐 www.hotelalessandra.com 🛏 26 rooms, 1 suite, 1 apartment ⏱ Closed Dec. 10–26 🍴 Breakfast ✣ D4.*

$$$ HOTEL **Beacci Tornabuoni.** Florentine pensioni don't get any classier than this: old-fashioned style, enough modern comfort to keep you happy, all in a 14th-century palazzo. **Pros:** multilingual staff; flower-filled terrace. **Cons:** hall noise can sometimes be a problem. [$] *Rooms from: €219 ✉ Via Tornabuoni 3, Santa Maria Novella ☎ 055/212645 🌐 www.tornabuonihotels.com 🛏 37 rooms, 16 suites 🍴 Breakfast ✣ D4.*

$ B&B/INN **Casa Howard.** This unassuming little inn has no two rooms alike, and an aura of eclectic funk pervades: one room takes its inspiration from Japan; still others are geared to families; others have access to a garden. **Pros:** great location near the basilica of Santa Maria Novella; good vibe. **Cons:** very limited concierge service; staff goes home in the early evening. [$] *Rooms from: €123 ✉ Via della Scala 18, near Piazza Santa Maria Novella ☎ 06/69924555 🌐 www.casahoward.it 🛏 13 rooms 🍴 Breakfast ✣ C2.*

$$$ HOTEL **Gallery Hotel Art.** High design resides at this art showcase near the Ponte Vecchio, where sleek, uncluttered rooms are dressed mostly in neutrals, and luxe touches, such as leather headboards and kimono robes, abound. **Pros:** cool atmosphere; beautiful people; miso soup on the breakfast menu; the in-house Fusion Bar, which pours delightful cocktails. **Cons:** sometimes elevator is slow; too cool for some. [$] *Rooms from: €280* ✉ *Vicolo dell'Oro 5, Santa Maria Novella* ☎ *055/27263* 🌐 *www.lungarnohotels.com* 🛏 *65 rooms, 9 suites* 🍴 *Breakfast* ✥ *D4.*

$$$ HOTEL **Hotel L'Orologio.** The owner of this quietly understated, elegant hotel has a real passion for watches, which is why he chose to name his hotel after them (and why you will see them in many places). **Pros:** location; great staff; stunning breakfast room; fantastic in-house bar. **Cons:** some folks think it too close to the train station. [$] *Rooms from: €250* ✉ *Piazza Santa Maria Novella 24* ☎ *055/277 380* 🌐 *www.whythebesthotels.com* 🛏 *44 rooms, 8 suites* 🍴 *Breakfast* ✥ *C2.*

$$$$ HOTEL Fodor's Choice ★ **JK Place.** Hard to spot from the street, these sumptuous appointments provide all the comforts of a luxe home away from home—expect soothing earth tones in guest rooms, free minibars, crisp linens, and a room service menu with organic dishes. **Pros:** private, intimate feel; stellar staff; free minibar; organic meal choices. **Cons:** breakfast at a shared table (which can be easily gotten around with room service). [$] *Rooms from: €450* ✉ *Piazza Santa Maria Novella 7* ☎ *055/2645181* 🌐 *www.jkplace.com* 🛏 *14 doubles, 6 suites* 🍴 *Breakfast* ✥ *C2.*

$ HOTEL **Nuova Italia.** The genial English-speaking Viti family oversee these clean and simple rooms near the train station and well within walking distance of the sights. **Pros:** reasonable rates; close to everything. **Cons:** no elevator. [$] *Rooms from: €109* ✉ *Via Faenza 26, Santa Maria Novella* ☎ *055/268430* 🌐 *www.hotel-nuovaitalia.com* 🛏 *20 rooms* ⏲ *Closed Dec. 8–Dec. 26* 🍴 *Breakfast* ✥ *D1.*

$$ B&B/INN **Torre Guelfa.** If you want a taste of medieval Florence, try one of these character-filled guest rooms—some with canopied beds, some with balconies—housed in a 13th-century tower. **Pros:** rooftop terrace with tremendous views; wonderful staff; some family-friendly triple and quadruple rooms. **Cons:** 72 steps to get to the terrace. [$] *Rooms from: €190* ✉ *Borgo Santi Apostoli 8, Santa Maria Novella* ☎ *055/2396338* 🌐 *www.hoteltorreguelfa.com* 🛏 *28 rooms, 3 suites* 🍴 *Breakfast* ✥ *D4.*

SANTA CROCE

$$$$ HOTEL **The Four Seasons.** Seven years of restoration have turned this 15th-century palazzo in Florence's center into a luxury hotel where no two guest rooms are alike; many have original 17th-century frescoes, some face the garden, others quiet interior courtyards. **Pros:** a unique "city meets country" experience; the marvelous garden. **Cons:** for this price, breakfast really should be included; some feel it's a little too removed from the centro storico. [$] *Rooms from: €675* ✉ *Borgo Pinti 99e, Santa Croce* ☎ *055/26261* 🌐 *www.fourseasons.com/florence* 🛏 *117 rooms* 🍴 *No meals* ✥ *H1.*

$$$$ HOTEL **Hotel Regency.** Rooms dressed in richly colored fabrics and antique-style furniture remain faithful to the premises' 19th-century origins as a private mansion. **Pros:** faces one of the few green parks in the center

of Florence. **Cons:** a small flight of stairs to get to reception. Ⓢ *Rooms from: €313* ✉ *Piazza d'Azeglio 3, Santa Croce* ☎ *055/245247* ⊕ *www.regency-hotel.com* ⤳ *30 rooms, 4 suites* ⦶ *Breakfast* ✚ *H1.*

$
B&B/INN

▦ **Istituto Oblate dell'Assunzione.** Seven nuns run this convent, minutes from the Duomo, with spotlessly clean, simple rooms; some have views of the cupola, and others look out onto a carefully tended garden where you are welcome to relax. **Pros:** bargain price; great location; quiet rooms; garden. **Cons:** curfew; no credit cards. Ⓢ *Rooms from: €40* ✉ *Borgo Pinti 15, Santa Croce* ☎ *055/2480582* ⊕ *www.sanctuarybbfirenze.com* ⤳ *28 rooms (22 with bath)* ▤ *No credit cards* ✚ *G3.*

$$
HOTEL
Fodor'sChoice
★

▦ **Monna Lisa.** Though some rooms are small, they are tasteful, and best of all, housed in a 15th-century palazzo that retains some of its wood-coffered ceilings from the 1500s, as well as its original staircase. **Pros:** lavish buffet breakfast; cheerful staff; garden. **Cons:** rooms in annex are less charming than those in palazzo; street noise in some rooms. Ⓢ *Rooms from: €199* ✉ *Borgo Pinti 27, Santa Croce* ☎ *055/2479751* ⊕ *www.monnalisa.it* ⤳ *45 rooms* ⦶ *Breakfast* ✚ *G2.*

$$
B&B/INN
Fodor'sChoice
★

▦ **Morandi alla Crocetta.** You're made to feel like privileged friends of the family at this charming and distinguished residence, furnished comfortably in the classic style of a gracious Florentine home. **Pros:** interesting, offbeat location near the sights; terrific staff; great value. **Cons:** two flights of stairs to reach reception and rooms. Ⓢ *Rooms from: €150* ✉ *Via Laura 50, Santissima Annunziata* ☎ *055/2344747* ⊕ *www.hotelmorandi.it* ⤳ *10 rooms* ⦶ *Breakfast* ✚ *H1.*

THE OLTRARNO

$
HOTEL

▦ **Hotel Silla.** Rooms in this 15th-century palazzo, entered through a courtyard lined with potted plants and sculpture-filled niches, are simply furnished, with papered walls; some have views of the Arno, others have stuccoed ceilings. **Pros:** one Fodor's reader raves, "It's in the middle of everything except the crowds." **Cons:** some readers complain of street noise and too-small rooms. Ⓢ *Rooms from: €120* ✉ *Via de' Renai 5, San Niccolò* ☎ *055/2342888* ⊕ *www.hotelsilla.it* ⤳ *35 rooms* ⦶ *Breakfast* ✚ *G6.*

$$$$
HOTEL

▦ **Palazzo Magnani-Feroni.** The perfect place to play the part of a Florentine aristocrat is here at this 16th-century palazzo, which despite its massive halls and sweeping staircase could almost feel like home. **Pros:** 24-hour room service; billiards room; generous buffet breakfast including prosecco; terrific staff. **Cons:** a few steps up to the elevator; many steps up to the rooftop terrace. Ⓢ *Rooms from: €650* ✉ *Borgo San Frediano 5, Oltrarno* ☎ *055/2399544* ⊕ *www.florencepalace.it* ⤳ *12 suites* ⦶ *Breakfast* ✚ *B4.*

10

BEYOND THE CITY CENTER

$$$$
HOTEL
Fodor'sChoice
★

▦ **Il Salviatino.** The dramatic approach (via a curving private drive lined with cypresses) to this 14th-century villa sets the tone: it's all uphill from there, from the welcome glass of prosecco in the hall to the remarkable rooms. **Pros:** great views; attentive staff; startlingly original breakfast; views; not in town. **Cons:** not in town; some hall noise. Ⓢ *Rooms from:*

€680 ☒ *Via del Salviatino 21* ☎ *055/904111* ⊕ *www.salviatino.com* ⤳ *23 rooms, 22 suites* ⦿| *Breakfast* ⊹ *G1.*

$$
B&B/INN
FAMILY
Fodor'sChoice
★

⌂ **Torre di Bellosguardo.** *Bellosguardo* means "beautiful view"; given the view of Florence you get here, the name is fitting. **Pros:** great for escaping heat of the city in summer; a villa experience with the city just minutes away. **Cons:** a car is a necessity; breakfast is not included during high season. $ *Rooms from: €200* ☒ *Via Roti Michelozzi 2* ☎ *055/2298145* ⊕ *www.torrebellosguardo.com* ⤳ *9 rooms, 7 suites* ⊹ *B6.*

$$$$
HOTEL
Fodor'sChoice
★

⌂ **Villa La Massa.** In this tall and imposing villa, 15 minutes out of town, public rooms are outfitted in Renaissance style, and guest rooms have high ceilings, plush carpeting, and deep bathtubs. **Pros:** pleasing mix of city and country life; sumptuous buffet breakfast; views of the Tuscan hills; the restaurant; phenomenal staff. **Cons:** not open year-round. $ *Rooms from: €490* ☒ *Via della Massa 24, Candeli* ☎ *055/62611* ⊕ *www.villalamassa.com* ⤳ *19 rooms, 18 suites* ⊙ *Closed Dec.–Mar.* ⦿| *Breakfast* ⊹ *H5.*

NIGHTLIFE AND PERFORMING ARTS

NIGHTLIFE

Florentines are rather proud of their nightlife options. Most bars now have some sort of happy hour, which usually lasts for many hours and often has snacks that can substitute for a light dinner. (Check, though, that the buffet is free or comes with the price of a drink.) Clubs typically don't open until very late in the evening, and don't get crowded until 1 or 2 in the morning.

BARS

Kitsch. Choose from indoor or outdoor seating and take advantage of the great list of wines by the glass. At aperitivo, €10 will buy you a truly tasty cocktail and give you access to the tremendous buffet; it's so good, you won't need dinner afterward—in fact, they call it "Apericena." That means, roughly, "drink and dinner." ☒ *Via San Gallo 22/r, San Marco* ☎ *328/9039289* ⊕ *www.kitschfirenze.com.*

Sant'Ambrogio Caffè. Come here in the summer for outdoor seating with a view of an 11th-century church (Sant'Ambrogio) directly across the street. Come here when it's not for perfectly mixed drinks and a lively atmosphere filled with (mostly) locals. ☒ *Piazza Sant'Ambrogio 7–8/r, Santa Croce* ☎ *055/2477277* ⊕ *www.caffesantambrogio.it.*

Zoe. Though it's called a "*caffetteria,*" and coffee is served (as well as terrific salads and burgers at lunchtime), Zoe's fine cocktails are the real draw for elegant youngish Florentines who come here to see and be seen. Here's people-watching at its very best. ☒ *Via de' Renai 13/r, San Niccolò* ☎ *055/243111* ⊕ *www.zoebar.it.*

CAFÉS

Cafés in Italy serve not only coffee concoctions and pastries but also drinks; some also serve light and inexpensive lunches. They open early in the morning and usually close around 8 pm.

$$ ITALIAN
🍴 **Caffè Giacosa.** This café opens early in the morning for coffee, serves tasty light lunches, and makes excellent cocktails in the evening. [$] *Average main: €15* ✉ *Via della Spada 10/r, Santa Maria Novella* ☎ *055/2776328* 🌐 *www.caffegiacosa.it.*

$$ ITALIAN Fodor's Choice ★
🍴 **Procacci.** At this classy Florentine institution dating to 1885, try one of the panini tartufati and swish it down with a glass of prosecco. It's closed Sunday. [$] *Average main: €15* ✉ *Via Tornabuoni 64/r, Santa Maria Novella* ☎ *055/211656* 🌐 *www.procacci.at* 🕒 *Closed Sun.*

$$ ITALIAN Fodor's Choice ★
🍴 **Rivoire.** One of the best spots in Florence for people-watching offers stellar service, light snacks, and terrific aperitivi. It's been around since the 1860s, and has been famous for its hot and cold chocolate (with or without cream) for more than a century. Though the food is mostly good (it's not a bad place for a light, but expensive, lunch), it's best to stick to drinks (both alcoholic and non-) and their terrific cakes, pies, and pastries. [$] *Average main: €15* ✉ *Via Vacchereccia 4/r* ☎ *055/214412* 🌐 *www.rivoire.it.*

WINE BARS

Casa del Vino. Come here for creative panini, such as *sgrombri e carciofini sott'olio* (mackerel and marinated baby artichokes), and an ever-changing list of significant wines by the glass. They also have a well-stocked collection of bottles to go. ✉ *Via dell'Ariento 16/r, San Lorenzo* ☎ *055/215609.*

Fodor's Choice ★
Il Santino. Though it has only four tables and four small stools at an equally small bar, Il Santino is blessed with a big wine list and superior cheeses, cured meats, and other delicacies to match. ✉ *Via Santo Spirito 60/r, Santo Spirito* ☎ *055/2302820.*

Fodor's Choice ★
Le Volpi e l'Uva. Le Volpi e l'Uva, off Piazza Santa Trinita, is an oenophile's dream: the waiters pour significant wines by the glass and serve equally impressive cheeses and little sandwiches to go with them. ✉ *Piazza de' Rossi 1, Palazzo Pitti* ☎ *055/2398132.*

PERFORMING ARTS

10

MUSIC

Accademia Bartolomeo Cristofori. Also known as the Amici del Fortepiano (Friends of the Fortepiano), the Accademia Bartolomeo Cristofori sponsors fortepiano concerts throughout the year. ✉ *Via di Camaldoli 7/r, Santo Spirito* ☎ *055/221646* 🌐 *www.accademiacristofori.it.*

Amici della Musica. This organization sponsors classical and contemporary concerts at the **Teatro della Pergola** (✉ *Box office, Via Alamanni 39, Lungarno North* ☎ *055/210804* 🌐 *www.teatrodellapergola.com*). ✉ *Via Pier Capponi 41* 🌐 *www.amicimusica.fi.it.*

Maggio Musicale Fiorentino. After some delay due to funding issues, a new music hall opened in spring 2014; the area is called the **Parco della Musica** (Music Park), and was designed by Paolo Desideri and associates. Three concert halls (two indoor, one outdoor) are planned, and only one has been completed. Maggio Musicale has taken up residence there, and continues to hold forth at the **Teatro Comunale** (✉ *Corso Italia 16, Lungarno North* ☎ *055/287222* 🌐 *www.maggiofiorentino.*

com). Within Italy you can purchase tickets from late April through July directly at the box office or by phone at ☎ *055/2779309*. You can also buy them online. ✉ *Via Alamanni 39* ☎ *055/210804* ⊕ *www. maggiofiorentino.it.*

Orchestra da Camera Fiorentina. This orchestra performs various concerts of classical music throughout the year at Orsanmichele, the grain-market-turned-church. ✉ *Via Monferrato 2* ☎ *055/783374* ⊕ *www.orcafi.it.*

Orchestra della Toscana. The concert season of the Orchestra della Toscana runs from November to June. ✉ *Via Ghibellina 101, Santa Croce* ☎ *055/2340710* ⊕ *www.orchestradellatoscana.it.*

SHOPPING

Window-shopping in Florence is like visiting an enormous contemporary-art gallery. Many of today's greatest Italian artists are fashion designers, and most keep shops in Florence. Discerning shoppers may find bargains in the street markets. ⚠ **Do not buy any knockoff goods from any of the hawkers plying their fake Prada (or any other high-end designer) on the streets. It's illegal, and fines are astronomical if the police happen to catch you. (You pay the fine, not the vendor.)**

Shops are generally open 9 to 1 and 3:30 to 7:30, and are closed Sunday and Monday mornings most of the year. Summer (June to September) hours are usually 9 to 1 and 4 to 8, and some shops close Saturday afternoon instead of Monday morning. When looking for addresses, you'll see two color-coded numbering systems on each street. The red numbers are commercial addresses and are indicated, for example, as "31/r." The blue or black numbers are residential addresses. Most shops take major credit cards and ship purchases, but because of possible delays it's wise to take your purchases with you.

SHOPPING DISTRICTS

Florence's most fashionable shops are concentrated in the center of town. The fanciest designer shops are mainly on **Via Tornabuoni** and **Via della Vigna Nuova.** The city's largest concentrations of antiques shops are on **Borgo Ognissanti** and the Oltrarno's **Via Maggio.** The **Ponte Vecchio** houses reputable but very expensive jewelry shops, as it has since the 16th century. The area near **Santa Croce** is the heart of the leather merchants' district.

AROUND THE DUOMO

CLOTHING

Fodor's Choice
★
Bernardo. Come here for men's trousers, cashmere sweaters, and shirts with details like mother-of-pearl buttons. ✉ *Via Porta Rossa 87/r, Piazza della Repubblica* ☎ *055/283333.*

Cabó. Missoni knitwear is the main draw at Cabó. ✉ *Via Porta Rossa 77–79/r, Piazza della Repubblica* ☎ *055/215774.*

Diesel. Trendy Diesel started in Vicenza; its gear is on the "must have" list of many a self-respecting Italian teen. ⊠ *Via dei Lamberti 13/r* 🕾 *055/2399963* ⊕ *www.diesel.com.*

Patrizia Pepe. The Florentine designer has body-conscious clothes perfect for all ages, especially for women with a tiny streak of rebelliousness. Women who are not size zero—or close to it—need not apply. ⊠ *Via Strozzi 11/19r, Around the Duomo* 🕾 *055/2302518* ⊕ *www. patriziapepe.com.*

MARKETS
Mercato dei Fiori. Every Thursday morning from September through June the covered loggia in Piazza della Repubblica hosts a Mercato dei Fiori; it's awash in a lively riot of plants, flowers, and difficult-to-find herbs. ⊠ *Piazza della Repubblica.*

Mercato del Porcellino. If you're looking for cheery, inexpensive trinkets to take home, you might want to stop and roam through the stalls under the loggia of the Mercato del Porcellino. ⊠ *Via Por Santa Maria at Via Porta Rossa, Piazza della Repubblica.*

SHOES AND LEATHER ACCESSORIES
Furla. Internationally renowned Furla makes beautiful leather bags, shoes, and wallets in up-to-the-minute designs. ⊠ *Via Calzaiuoli 47/r, Piazza della Repubblica* 🕾 *055/2382883* ⊕ *www.furla.com.*

SAN LORENZO

JEWELRY AND ACCESSORIES
Penko. Renaissance goldsmiths provide the inspiration for this dazzling jewelry with a contemporary feel. ⊠ *Via F. Zannetti 14/16r, Around the Duomo* 🕾 *055/211661* ⊕ *www.paolopenko.com.*

MARKETS
Mercato Centrale. This huge indoor food market offers a staggering selection of all things edible. ⊠ *Piazza del Mercato Centrale, San Lorenzo.*

Mercato di San Lorenzo. The clothing and leather-goods stalls of the Mercato di San Lorenzo in the streets next to the church of San Lorenzo have bargains for shoppers on a budget. Do please remember that you get what you pay for.

10

SANTA MARIA NOVELLA

BOOKS AND PAPER
Alberto Cozzi. You'll find an extensive line of Florentine papers and paper products here. The artisans in the shop rebind and restore books and works on paper. Their hours are tricky, so it's best to call first before stopping by. ⊠ *Via del Parione 35/r, Santa Maria Novella* 🕾 *055/294968.*

Pineider. Though it has shops throughout the world, Pineider started out in Florence and still does all its printing here. Stationery and business cards are the mainstay, but the stores also sell fine leather desk accessories as well as a less stuffy, more lighthearted line of products.

✉ *Piazza Rucellai, Santa Maria Novella to the Arno* ☎ *055/284655* ⊕ *www.pineider.com.*

CLOTHING

Emilio Pucci. The aristocratic Marchese di Barsento, Emilio Pucci, became an international name in the late 1950s when the stretch ski clothes he designed for himself caught on with the "dolce vita" crowd—his pseudopsychedelic prints and "palazzo pajamas" became all the rage. ✉ *Via Tornabuoni 20–22/r, Santa Maria Novella* ☎ *055/2658082* ⊕ *www. emiliopucci.com.*

Principe. This Florentine institution sells casual clothes for men, women, and children at far-from-casual prices. It also has a great housewares department. ✉ *Via del Sole 2, Santa Maria Novella* ☎ *055/292764* ⊕ *www.principedifirenze.com.*

Spazio A. For cutting-edge fashion, these fun and funky window displays merit a stop. The shop carries such well-known designers as Alberta Ferretti and Moschino, as well as lesser-known Italian, English, and French designers. ✉ *Via Porta Rossa 109–115/r, Piazza della Repubblica* ☎ *055/212995.*

FRAGRANCES

Antica Officina del Farmacista Dr. Vranjes. Dr. Vranjes elevates aromatherapy to an art form, with scents for the body and for the house. ✉ *Via della Spada 9* ☎ *055/288796* ⊕ *www.drvranjes.it.*

Fodor's Choice ★ **Officina Profumo Farmaceutica di Santa Maria Novella.** The essence of a Florentine holiday is captured in the sachets of this Art Nouveau emporium of herbal cosmetics and soaps made following centuries-old recipes created by friars. It celebrated its 400th birthday in 2012. ✉ *Via della Scala 16, Santa Maria Novella* ☎ *055/216276* ⊕ *www.smnovella.it.*

JEWELRY

Fodor's Choice ★ **Angela Caputi.** Angela Caputi wows Florentine cognoscenti with her highly creative, often outsize plastic jewelry. A small, but equally creative, collection of women's clothing made of fine fabrics is also on offer. ✉ *Borgo Santi Apostoli 44/46* ☎ *055/292993* ⊕ *www.angelacaputi.com.*

Carlo Piccini. Still in operation after several generations, this Florentine institution sells antique jewelry and makes pieces to order; you can also get old jewelry reset here. ✉ *Ponte Vecchio 31/r* ☎ *055/292030* ⊕ *www.carlopiccini.com.*

Cassetti. This jeweler combines precious and semiprecious stones and metals in contemporary settings. ✉ *Ponte Vecchio 54/r* ☎ *055/2396028* ⊕ *www.cassetti.it.*

Gatto Bianco. This contemporary jeweler has breathtakingly beautiful pieces worked in semiprecious and precious stones. ✉ *Borgo Santi Apostoli 12/r, Santa Maria Novella* ☎ *055/282989* ⊕ *www. gattobiancogioielli.com.*

Tiffany. One of Florence's oldest jewelers has supplied Italian (and other) royalty with finely crafted gems for centuries. Its selection of antique-looking classics has been updated with a selection of contemporary silver. ✉ *Via Tornabuoni 25/r, Santa Maria Novella* ☎ *055/215506* ⊕ *www.tiffany.it.*

LINENS AND FABRICS

Fodor's Choice ★ **Loretta Caponi.** Synonymous with Florentine embroidery, the luxury lace, linens, and lingerie have earned the eponymous signora worldwide renown. There's also beautiful (and expensive) clothing for children. ✉ *Piazza Antinori 4/r, Santa Maria Novella* ☎ *055/213668.*

SHOES AND LEATHER ACCESSORIES

Casadei. The ultimate fine leathers are crafted into classic shapes, winding up as women's shoes and bags. ✉ *Via Tornabuoni 74/r, Santa Maria Novella* ☎ *055/287240* ⊕ *www.casadei.com.*

Cellerini. In a city where it seems just about everybody wears an expensive leather jacket, Cellerini is an institution. ✉ *Via del Sole 37/r, Santa Maria Novella* ☎ *055/282533* ⊕ *www.cellerini.it.*

Ferragamo. This classy institution, in a 13th-century palazzo, displays designer clothing and accessories, though elegant footwear still underlies the Ferragamo success. ✉ *Via Tornabuoni 2/r, Santa Maria Novella* ☎ *055/292123* ⊕ *www.ferragamo.com.*

Giotti. You'll find a full line of leather goods, including clothing, here. ✉ *Piazza Ognissanti 3–4/r, Lungarno North* ☎ *055/294265* ⊕ *www. giotti.com.*

SANTA CROCE

MARKETS

Mercato di Sant'Ambrogio. It's possible to strike gold at this lively market, where clothing stalls abut the fruit and vegetables. ✉ *Piazza Ghiberti, off Via dei Macci, Santa Croce.*

Piazza dei Ciompi flea market. You can find bargains here Monday through Saturday and on the last Sunday of the month. ✉ *Sant'Ambrogio, Santa Croce.*

SHOES AND LEATHER ACCESSORIES

Fodor's Choice ★ **Scuola del Cuoio.** A consortium of leatherworkers plies its trade at La Scuola del Cuoio (Leather School), in the former dormitory of the convent of Santa Croce; high-quality, fairly priced jackets, belts, and purses are sold here. ✉ *Piazza Santa Croce 16* ☎ *055/2445334* ⊕ *www. scuoladelcuoio.com.*

OLTRARNO

BOOKS AND PAPER

Giulio Giannini e Figlio. One of Florence's oldest paper-goods stores is *the* place to buy the marbleized stock, which comes in many shapes and sizes, from flat sheets to boxes and even pencils. ✉ *Piazza Pitti 37/r, Oltrarno* ☎ *055/212621* ⊕ *www.giuliogiannini.it.*

Fodor's Choice ★ **Il Torchio.** Photograph albums, frames, diaries, and other objects dressed in handmade paper are high-quality, and the prices lower than usual. ✉ *Via dei Bardi 17, San Niccolò* ☎ *055/2342862* ⊕ *www. legatoriailtorchio.com.*

10

CLOTHING

Maçel. Browse collections by lesser-known Italian designers, many of whom use the same factories as the "A list," at this women's clothing shop. ✉ *Via Guicciardini 128/r, Palazzo Pitti* ☎ *055/287355.*

Madova. Complete your winter wardrobe with a pair of high-quality leather gloves, available in a rainbow of colors and a choice of linings (silk, cashmere, and unlined). ✉ *Via Guicciardini 1/r, Palazzo Pitti* ☎ *055/2396526* ⊕ *www.madova.com.*

FRAGRANCES

Lorenzo Villoresi. Proprietor Lorenzo Villoresi makes one-of-a-kind fragrances, which he develops after a consultation. Such personalized attention does not come cheap. ✉ *Via de'Bardi 14, Oltrarno* ☎ *055/2341187* ⊕ *www.lorenzovilloresi.it.*

MARKETS

Santo Spirito flea market. The second Sunday of every month brings the Santo Spirito flea market. On the third Sunday of the month, vendors at the Fierucola organic fest sell such delectables as honeys, jams, spice mixes, and fresh vegetables.

OUTLETS

For bargains on Italian designer clothing, you need to leave the city.

Barberino Designer Outlet. Prada, Pollini, Missoni, and Bruno Magli, among others, are all found at Barberino Designer Outlet. To get here, take the A1 to the Barberino di Mugello exit, and follow signs to the mall. ✉ *Via Meucci snc* ☎ *055/842161* ⊕ *www.mcarthurglen.com.*

Mall. One-stop bargain shopping awaits at this collection of stores selling goods by such names as Bottega Veneta, Giorgio Armani, Loro Piana, Sergio Rossi, and Yves St. Laurent. ✉ *Via Europa 8* ☎ *055/8657775* ⊕ *www.themall.it.*

Prada Outlet. Cognoscenti drive 45 minutes (or take the train to Montevarchi, and then a taxi) to find a bargain here. ✉ *Levanella Spacceo, Estrada Statale 69, Montevarchi* ☎ *055/9196528* ⊕ *www.prada.com.*

FIESOLE: A SIDE TRIP FROM FLORENCE

A half-day excursion to Fiesole, in the hills 8 km (5 miles) above Florence, gives you a pleasant respite from museums and a wonderful view of the city. From here the view of the Duomo gives you a new appreciation for what the Renaissance accomplished. Fiesole began life as an ancient Etruscan and later a Roman village that held some power until it succumbed to barbarian invasions. Eventually it gave up its independence in exchange for Florence's protection. The medieval cathedral, ancient Roman amphitheater, and lovely old villas behind garden walls are clustered on a series of hilltops. A walk around Fiesole can take from one to two or three hours, depending on how far you stroll from the main piazza.

GETTING HERE AND AROUND

The trip from Florence by car takes 20 to 30 minutes. Drive to Piazza Liberta and cross the Ponte Rosso heading in the direction of the SS65/SR65. Turn right on to Via Salviati and continue on to Via Roccettini. Make a left turn to Via Vecchia Fiesolana, which will take you directly to the center of town. There are several possible routes for the two-hour walk from central Florence to Fiesole. One route begins in a residential area of Florence called Salviatino (Via Barbacane, near Piazza Edison, on the No. 7 bus route), and after a short time, offers peeks over garden walls of beautiful villas, as well as the view over your shoulder at the panorama of Florence in the valley. ⚠ **If you opt for the bus, do remember that the No. 7 is one of the most highly pickpocketed bus routes.**

VISITOR INFORMATION

Fiesole tourism office ⊠ *Via Portigiani 3* ☎ *055/5961323* ⊕ *www.fiesoleforyou.it.*

EXPLORING

Anfiteatro Romano (*Roman Amphitheater*). The beautifully preserved 2,000-seat Anfiteatro Romano, near the Duomo, dates from the 1st century BC and is still used for summer concerts. To the right of the amphitheater are the remains of the **Terme Romani** (Roman Baths), where you can see the gymnasium, hot and cold baths, and rectangular chamber where the water was heated. A beautifully designed **Museo Archeologico,** its facade evoking an ancient Roman temple, is built amid the ruins and contains objects dating from as early as 2000 BC. The nearby **Museo Bandini** is filled with the private collection of Canon Angelo Maria Bandini (1726–1803); he fancied 13th- to 15th-century Florentine paintings, terra-cotta pieces, and wood sculpture, which he later bequeathed to the Diocese of Fiesole. ⊠ *Via Portigiani 1* ☎ *055/5961293* ⊕ *www.museidifiesole.it* 🎫 *€12, includes access to archaeological park and museums* 🕐 *Nov.–Feb., Wed.–Mon. 10–2; Mar. and Oct., daily 10–6; Apr.–Sept., daily 9–5.*

Badia Fiesolana. From the church of San Domenico, it's a five-minute walk northwest to the Badia Fiesolana, which was Fiesole's original cathedral. Dating to the 11th century, it was first the home of the Camaldolese monks. Thanks to Cosimo il Vecchio, the complex was substantially restructured. The facade, never completed owing to Cosimo's death, contains elements of its original Romanesque decoration. The attached convent once housed Cosimo's valued manuscripts. Its mid-15th-century cloister is well worth a look. ⊠ *Via della Badia dei Roccettini 11* ⊕ *www.iue.it* 🕐 *Weekdays 9–6, Sat. 9:30–12:30.*

Duomo. A stark medieval interior yields many masterpieces. In the raised presbytery, the **Cappella Salutati** was frescoed by 15th-century artist Cosimo Rosselli, but it was his contemporary, sculptor Mino da Fiesole (1430–84), who put the town on the artistic map. The Madonna on the altarpiece and the tomb of Bishop Salutati are fine examples of the artist's work. ⊠ *Piazza Mino da Fiesole* ☎ *055/59400* 🕐 *Nov.–Mar., daily 7:30–noon and 2–5; Apr.–Oct., daily 7:30–noon and 3–6.*

10

San Domenico. If you really want to stretch your legs, walk 4 km (2½ miles) toward the center of Florence along Via Vecchia Fiesolana, a narrow lane in use since Etruscan times, to the church of San Domenico. Sheltered in the church is the *Madonna and Child with Saints* by Fra Angelico, who was a Dominican friar here. ⌧ *Piazza San Domenico, off Via Giuseppe Mantellini* ☎ *055/59230* ⌚ *Mon.–Sat. 8–noon.*

San Francesco. This lovely hilltop church has a good view of Florence and the plain below from its terrace and benches. Off the little cloister is a small, eclectic museum containing, among other things, two Egyptian mummies. Halfway up the hill you'll see sloping steps to the right; they lead to a fragrant wooded park with trails that loop out and back to the church.

WHERE TO EAT

$$ ✕ **La Reggia degli Etruschi.** If you want a breath of fresh air—literally—this
ITALIAN lovely little eatery is worth a detour. Stamina is necessary to get here, as it's on a steep hill on the way up to the church of San Francesco. The rewards on arrival, in the form of inventive reworkings of Tuscan classics, are well worth it. The *mezzaluna di pera a pecorino* (little half moon pasta stuffed with pear and pecorino) is sauced with Roquefort and poppy seeds. Slivers of papaya—a rare commodity on restaurant menus in these parts—anoint the tasty *carpaccio di tonno affumicato* (smoked tuna carpaccio). The wine list and the attentive service help make this a terrific place to have a meal. When it's warm, you can sit on the little terrace outside. Ⓢ *Average main: €19* ⌧ *Via San Francesco* ☎ *055/59385* ⊕ *www.lareggiadeglietruschi.com.*

WHERE TO STAY

$$ ⛺ **Villa Aurora.** The attractive, simply furnished hotel on the main piazza
HOTEL takes advantage of its hilltop spot, with beautiful views from many of the rooms, some of which are on two levels with wood-beam ceilings and balconies. **Pros:** some rooms have pretty views; air quality better than in Florence. **Cons:** no elevator; steps to breakfast room. Ⓢ *Rooms from: €149* ⌧ *Piazza Mino da Fiesole 39* ☎ *055/59363* ⊕ *www.villaaurorafiesole.com* ⤴ *23 rooms, 2 suites* ⓘⓞⓘ *Breakfast.*

$$$$ ⛺ **Villa San Michele.** The cypress-lined driveway provides an elegant
HOTEL preamble to this incredibly gorgeous (and very expensive) hotel nestled in the hills of Fiesole. **Pros:** exceptional convent conversion. **Cons:** money must be no object. Ⓢ *Rooms from: €667* ⌧ *Via Doccia 4* ☎ *055/5678200* ⊕ *www.villasanmichele.com* ⤴ *21 rooms, 24 suites* ⌚ *Closed Nov.–Easter.*

NIGHTLIFE AND THE ARTS

Estate Fiesolana. From June through August, Estate Fiesolana, a festival of theater, music, dance, and film, takes place in Fiesole's churches and in the Roman amphitheater—demonstrating that the ancient Romans knew a thing or two about acoustics. ⌧ *Teatro Romano* ☎ *055/5961323* ⊕ *www.comune.fiesole.fi.it.*

TUSCANY

WELCOME TO TUSCANY

TOP REASONS TO GO

★ **Piazza del Campo, Siena:** Sip a cappuccino or enjoy some gelato as you take in this spectacular shell-shape piazza.

★ **Piero della Francesca's True Cross frescoes, Arezzo:** If your Holy Grail is great Renaissance art, seek out these 12 enigmatic scenes in Arezzo's Basilica di San Francesco.

★ **San Gimignano:** Grab a spot at sunset on the steps of the Collegiata as flocks of swallows swoop in and out of the famous medieval towers.

★ **Wine tasting in Chianti:** Sample the fruits of the region's gorgeous vineyards, either at the wineries themselves or in the wine bars found in the towns.

★ **Leaning Tower of Pisa:** It may be touristy, but it's still a whole lot of fun to climb to the top and admire the view.

1 Lucca. This laid-back yet elegant town is surrounded by tree-bedecked 16th-century ramparts that are now a delightful promenade.

2 Pisa. Thanks to an engineering mistake, the name Pisa is recognized the world over. The Leaning Tower, the Battistero, the Camposanto, and the cathedral make an impressive foursome on the Piazza del Duomo.

3 Chianti. The heart of Italy's most famous wine region is dotted with appealing towns. The largest, **Greve,** comes alive with a bustling local market in its town square every Saturday, while **Radda** sits on a hilltop in classic Tuscan style, ringed by a 14th-century walkway. Cutting through the region is the **Strada Chiantigiana,** one of Italy's great drives.

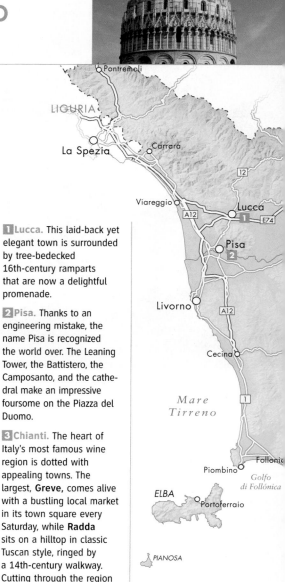

4 Hill Towns Southwest of Florence. The search for the best tiny hill town always leads to **San Gimignano,** known as the "medieval Manhattan" for its 13th-century stone towers. Farther west, Etruscan artifacts and Roman ruins are highlights of **Volterra,** set in a rugged moonscape of a valley.

5 Siena. Throughout the Middle Ages Siena competed with Florence for regional supremacy. Today it remains one of Italy's most enchanting medieval towns, with an exceptional Gothic cathedral and a main square, Il Campo, that has an almost magical charm.

6 Arezzo and Cortona. These two towns south of Chianti are rewarding side trips. **Arezzo** is best known for its sublime frescoes by Piero della Francesca. **Cortona** sits high above the perfectly flat Valdichiana, offering great views of beautiful countryside.

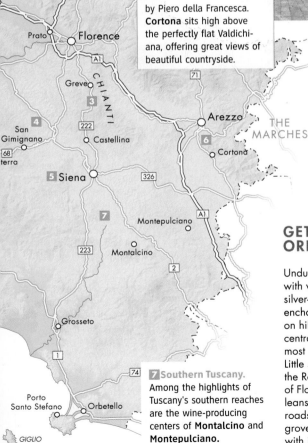

Pistoia

A1

Prato

Florence

A1

Greve

CHIANTI

3

4
San
Gimignano

222

O Castellina

68
terra

5 Siena

326

Arezzo

6

O Cortona

THE
MARCHES

7

Montepulciano

A1

223

Montalcino

2

Grosseto

1

74

Porto
Santo Stefano

Orbetello

GIGLIO

7 Southern Tuscany. Among the highlights of Tuscany's southern reaches are the wine-producing centers of **Montalcino** and **Montepulciano.**

GETTING ORIENTED

Undulating hills blanketed with vineyards, groves of silver-green olive trees, and enchanting towns perched on hilltops are the essence of central Tuscany, one of Italy's most beautiful landscapes. Little seems changed since the Renaissance: to the west of Florence, Pisa's tower still leans; to the south, Chianti's roads wind through cypress groves, taking you to Siena, with its captivating piazza.

EATING AND DRINKING WELL IN TUSCANY

The influence of the ancient Etruscans—who favored the use of fresh herbs—is still felt in Tuscan cuisine three millennia later. Simple and earthy, Tuscan food celebrates the seasons with fresh vegetable dishes, wonderful bread-based soups, and meats perfumed with sage, rosemary, and thyme.

Throughout Tuscany there are excellent upscale restaurants that serve elaborate dishes, but to get a real taste of the flavors of the region, head for the family-run trattorias found in every town. The service and setting are often basic, but the food can be memorable.

Few places serve lighter fare at midday, so expect substantial meals at lunch and dinner, especially in out-of-the-way towns. Dining hours are fairly standard: lunch between 12:30 and 2, dinner between 7:30 and 10.

HOLD THE SALT

Tuscan bread is famous for what it's missing: it's made without salt. That's because it's intended to pick up seasoning from the food it accompanies; it's not meant to be eaten alone or dipped in a bowl of oil (which is a custom developed by American restaurants—it's not standard practice in Italian ones).

That doesn't mean Tuscans don't like to start a meal with bread, but usually it's prepared in some way. It can be grilled and drizzled with olive oil (*fettunta*), covered with chicken liver spread (*crostino nero*), or toasted, rubbed with garlic, and topped with tomatoes (*bruschetta*).

11

AFFETTATI MISTI

The name, roughly translated, means "mixed cold cuts," pictured left, and it's something Tuscans do exceptionally well. A platter of cured meats, served as an antipasto, is sure to include *prosciutto crudo* (ham, cut paper-thin) and *salame* (dry sausage, prepared in dozens of ways—some spicy, some sweet). The most distinctly Tuscan affettati are made from *cinta senese* (a once nearly extinct pig found only in the heart of the region) and *cinghiale* (wild boar, which roam all over central Italy). You can eat these delicious slices unadorned or layered on a piece of bread.

PASTA

Restaurants throughout Tuscany serve dishes similar to those in Florence, but they also have their own local specialties. Many recipes are from the *nonna* (grandmother) of the restaurant's owner, handed down over time but never written down.

Look in particular for pasta creations made with *pici* (a long, thick, hand-rolled spaghetti), *pictured below*. *Pappardelle* (a long, ribbonlike pasta noodle, *pictured upper right*) is frequently paired with sauces made with game, such as *lepre* (hare) or cinghiale. In the northwest, a specialty of Lucca is *tordelli di carne al ragù* (meat-stuffed pasta with a meat sauce).

MEAT

Bistecca fiorentina (a thick T-bone steak, grilled rare) is the classic meat dish of Tuscany, but there are other specialties as well. Many menus will include *tagliata di manzo* (thinly sliced, roasted beef, drizzled with olive oil), *arista di maiale* (roast pork with sage and rosemary), and *salsiccia e fagioli* (pork sausage and beans). In the southern part of the region, don't be surprised to find *piccione* (pigeon), which can be roasted, stuffed, or baked.

WINE

Grape cultivation here also dates from Etruscan times, and vineyards are abundant, particularly in Chianti. The resulting medium-body red wine is a staple on most tables; however, you can select from a multitude of other varieties, including such reds as Brunello di Montalcino and Vino Nobile di Montepulciano and such whites as vermentino and vernaccia.

Super Tuscans (a fanciful name given to a group of wines by American journalists) now command attention as some of the best produced in Italy; they have great depth and complexity. The dessert wine *vin santo* is made throughout the region, and is often sipped with *biscotti* (twice-baked almond cookies), perfect for dunking.

Updated
by Peter
Blackman

Midway down the Italian peninsula, Tuscany (Toscana in Italian) is distinguished by rolling hills, snowcapped mountains, dramatic cypress trees, and miles of coastline on the Tyrrhenian Sea—which all adds up to gorgeous views at practically every turn. The beauty of the landscape proves a perfect foil for the region's abundance of superlative art and architecture. It also produces some of Italy's finest wines and olive oils. The combination of unforgettable art, sumptuous landscapes, and eminently drinkable wines that pair beautifully with its simple food makes a trip to Tuscany something beyond special.

Many of Tuscany's cities and towns have retained the same fundamental character over the past 500 years. Civic rivalries that led to bloody battles centuries ago have given way to soccer rivalries. Renaissance pomp lives on in the celebration of local feast days and centuries-old traditions such as the Palio in Siena and the Giostra del Saracino (Joust of the Saracen) in Arezzo. Often, present-day Tuscans look as though they might have served as models for paintings produced hundreds of years ago. In many ways, the Renaissance still lives on in Tuscany.

TUSCANY PLANNER

MAKING THE MOST OF YOUR TIME

Tuscany isn't the place for a jam-packed itinerary. One of the greatest pleasures here is indulging in rustic hedonism, marked by long lunches and show-stopping sunsets. Whether by car, by bike, or on foot, you'll want to get out into the glorious landscape, but it's smart to keep your plans modest. Set a church or a hill town or an out-of-the-way restaurant as your destination, knowing that half the pleasure is in getting there—admiring as you go the stately palaces, the tidy geometry of row upon row of grapevines, the fields vibrant with red poppies, sunflowers, and yellow broom.

You'll need to devise a strategy for seeing the sights. Take Siena: this beautiful, art-filled town simply can't be missed; it's compact enough that you can see the major sights on a day trip, and that's exactly what most people do. Spend the night, though, and you'll get to see the town breathe a sigh and relax on the day-trippers' departure. In Pisa, the famous tower and rest of the Camposanto are not only worth seeing but a must-see, a highlight of any trip to Italy. But nearby Lucca must not be overlooked either. In fact, this walled town has greater charms than Pisa does, making it a better choice for an overnight, so you should come up with a plan that takes in both places.

GETTING HERE AND AROUND

BUS TRAVEL

Buses are a reliable but time-consuming means of getting around the region because they tend to stop in every town. Trains are a better option in virtually every respect when you're headed to Pisa, Lucca, Arezzo, and other cities with good rail service. But for most smaller towns, buses are the only option. Be aware that making arrangements for bus travel, particularly for a non-Italian speaker, can be a test of patience.

CPT. This agency provides infrequent bus service between Volterra and Colle di Val d'Elsa, and also connects Volterra with the nearest train station in Saline. ⊠ *Pisa* ☎ *050/884111, 199/120150 toll-free in Italy* ⊕ *www.cpt.pisa.it.*

Lazzi. This bus service connects Florence, Pisa, Lucca, Pescia, Pistoia, and Montecatini. ☎ *0573/1937900* ⊕ *www.lazzi.it.*

SENA. The company provides a regular service between Siena and Rome, which takes approximately three hours. ☎ *0861/1991900* ⊕ *www.sena.it.*

SITA. From Florence, these buses serve Siena (a one-hour) and numerous towns in the Chianti region. ⊠ *Siena* ☎ *0577/204328, 800/373760 toll-free in Italy.*

Tra-In. This bus company covers much of the territory south of Florence as well as the province of Siena. ⊠ *Strada Statale 73, Località Due Ponti, Siena* ☎ *0577/204111, 800/922984 toll-free in Italy* ⊕ *www. trainspa.it.*

CAR TRAVEL

Driving is the only way (other than hiking or biking) to reach many of Tuscany's small towns and vineyards. The cities west of Florence are easily accessed by the A11, which leads to Lucca and then to the sea. The A1 takes you south from Florence to Arezzo and Chiusi (where you turn off for Montepulciano). Florence and Siena are connected by a *superstrada* and also the scenic Via Cassia (SR2) and even more panoramic Strada Chiantigiana (SR222), both of which thread through Chianti, skirting rolling hills and vineyards. The hill towns north and west of Siena lie along superstrade and winding local roads—all are well marked, but still you should arm yourself with a good map.

TRAIN TRAVEL

Trains on Italy's main north–south rail line stop in Florence as well as Prato, Arezzo, and Chiusi. Another major line connects Florence with Pisa, and the coastal line between Rome and Genoa passes through Pisa as well. There's regular, nearly hourly service from Florence to Lucca, and several trips a day between Florence and Siena. Siena's train station is 2 km (1 mile) north of the *centro storico* (historic center), but cabs and city buses are readily available.

For other parts of Tuscany—Chianti, Montalcino, and Montepulciano, for example—you're better off traveling by bus or by car. Train stations, when they exist, are far from the historic centers (usually in the valleys below hill towns), and service is infrequent.

Ferrovie dello Stato. You can check timetables on the website of the Italian state railway system and can also get information and tickets at most travel agencies. ☎ *892021 toll-free in Italy* ⊕ *www.trenitalia.com.*

RESTAURANTS

Prices in the reviews are the average cost of a main course at dinner or, if dinner is not served, at lunch.

HOTELS

A visit to Tuscany is a trip into the country. There are plenty of good hotels in the larger towns, but the classic experience is to stay in one of the rural accommodations—often converted private homes, sometimes working farms or vineyards (known as *agriturismi*).

Though it's tempting to think you can stumble upon a little out-of-the-way hotel at the end of the day, you're better off not testing your luck. Make reservations before you go. If you don't have a reservation, you may be able to get help finding a room from the local tourist office.

Hotel reviews have been shortened. For full information, visit Fodors. com.

WHAT IT COSTS			
$	**$$**	**$$$**	**$$$$**
RESTAURANTS under €15	€15–€24	€25–€35	over €35
HOTELS under €125	€125–€200	€201–€300	over €300

Prices in the dining reviews are the average cost of a main course at dinner, or, if dinner is not served, at lunch. Prices in the reviews are the lowest cost of a standard double room in high season.

VISITOR INFORMATION

Many towns in Tuscany have tourist information offices, which can be useful resources for trip-planning advice (and sometimes maps). Such offices are typically open from 8:30 to 1 and 3:30 to 6 or 7; those in smaller towns are usually closed Saturday afternoon and Sunday, and often shut down entirely from early November through Easter.

The tourist information office in Greve is an excellent source for general information about the Chianti wine region and its hilltop towns. In Siena, the centrally located tourist office in Piazza del Campo has information about Siena and its province. Both offices book hotel rooms for a nominal fee. Offices in smaller towns can also be a good place to check if you need last-minute accommodations.

LUCCA

Ramparts built in the 16th and 17th centuries enclose a charming fortress town filled with churches (99 of them), terra-cotta–roof buildings, and narrow cobblestone streets, along which locals maneuver bikes to do their daily shopping. Here Caesar, Pompey, and Crassus agreed to rule Rome as a triumvi-

> **WORD OF MOUTH**
>
> "For history and charm the small walled city of Lucca is, I think, absolutely magical. The food in Lucca also eclipses most all of Tuscany too!" —hanabilly

rate in 56 BC; Lucca was later the first Tuscan town to accept Christianity. The town still has a mind of its own, and when most of Tuscany was voting Communist as a matter of course, Lucca's citizens rarely followed suit. The famous composer Giacomo Puccini (1858–1924) was born here; he is celebrated during the summer Opera Theater and Music Festival of Lucca. The ramparts circling the centro storico are the perfect place to stroll, cycle, or just admire the view.

GETTING HERE AND AROUND

You can reach Lucca easily by train from Florence; the centro storico is a short walk from the station. If you're driving, take the A11/E76.

VISITOR INFORMATION

Lucca Tourism Office ⊠ *Piazza Santa Maria* ☎ *0583/91991* ⊕ *www.luccaturismo.it.*

EXPLORING

Traffic (including motorbikes) is restricted in the walled historic center of Lucca. Walking is the best, most enjoyable way to get around. Or you can rent a bicycle; getting around on bike is easy, as the center is quite flat.

TOP ATTRACTIONS

Duomo. The blind arches on the cathedral's facade are a fine example of the rigorously ordered Pisan Romanesque style, in this case happily enlivened by an extremely varied collection of small, carved columns. Take a closer look at the decoration of the facade and that of the portico below; they make this one of the most entertaining church exteriors in Tuscany. The Gothic interior contains a moving Byzantine crucifix—called the Volto Santo, or Holy Face—brought here, according to legend, in the 8th century (though it probably dates from between the 11th and early 13th centuries). The masterpiece of the Sienese sculptor Jacopo della Quercia (circa 1371–1438) is the marble *Tomb of Ilaria del Carretto* (1407–08). ⊠ *Piazza San Martino* ☎ *0583/490530* ⊕ *www.museocattedralelucca.it* ⊑ *Church free, tomb €3* ⊙ *Duomo: Nov. 3–Mar. 14, weekdays 9:30–4:45, Sat. 9:30–6:45, Sun. 9:30–10:45* *and noon–5; Mar. 15–Nov. 2, weekdays 9:30–5:45, Sat. 9–6:45, Sun. 9:30–10:45 and 11:30–6.*

Passeggiata delle Mura. Any time of day when the weather is nice, you can find the citizens of Lucca cycling, jogging, strolling, or kicking a soccer ball in this green, beautiful, and very large park—neither inside nor outside the city but rather right atop and around the ring of ramparts that defines Lucca. Sunlight streams through two rows of tall plane trees to dapple the *passeggiata delle mura* (walk on the walls), which is 4.2 km (2½ miles) in length. Ten bulwarks are topped with lawns, many with picnic tables and some with play equipment for children. Be aware at all times of where the edge is—there are no railings, and the drop to the ground outside the city is a precipitous 40 feet. ⊕ *www.lemuradilucca.it.*

QUICK BITES

Gelateria Veneta. Gelateria Veneta makes outstanding gelato, sorbet, and ices (some sugar-free). They prepare their confections three times a day, using the same recipes with which the Brothers Arnoldo opened the place in 1927. The pièces de résistance are frozen fruits stuffed with creamy filling: don't miss the apricot sorbet–filled apricot. Note that they close up shop in October and reopen around Easter. ⊠ *Via V. Veneto 74* ☎ *0583/467037* ⊕ *www.gelateriaveneta.net.*

Piazza dell'Anfiteatro Romano. Here's where the ancient Roman amphitheater once stood; some of the medieval buildings built over the amphitheater retain its original oval shape and brick arches.

San Frediano. A 14th-century mosaic decorates the facade of this church just steps from the Anfiteatro. Inside are works by Jacopo della Quercia (circa 1371–1438) and Matteo Civitali (1436–1501), as well as the lace-clad mummy of Saint Zita (circa 1218–78), the patron saint of household servants. ⊠ *Piazza San Frediano* ☎ *No phone* ☺ *Mon.–Sat. 8:30–noon and 3–5, Sun. 10:30–5.*

San Michele in Foro. The facade here is even more fanciful than that of the Duomo. Its upper levels have nothing but air behind them (after the front of the church was built, there were no funds to raise the nave), and the winged Archangel Michael, who stands at the very top, seems precariously poised for flight. The facade, heavily restored in the 19th century, displays busts of such 19th-century Italian patriots as Garibaldi and Cavour. Check out the superb Filippino Lippi (1457/58–1504) panel painting of Saints Jerome, Sebastian, Rocco, and Helen in the right transept. ⊠ *Piazza San Michele* ☺ *Nov.–Mar., daily 9–noon and 3–5; Apr.–Oct., daily 9–noon and 3–6.*

FAMILY   **Torre Guinigi.** The tower of the medieval Palazzo Guinigi contains one of the city's most curious sights: a grove of ilex trees has grown at the top of the tower, and their roots have pushed their way into the room below. From the top you have a magnificent view of the city and the surrounding countryside. (Only the tower is open to the public, not the palazzo.) ⊠ *Via Sant'Andrea* ☎ *0583/583086* ⊕ *www.lemuradilucca.it* ⊠ *€4* ☺ *Nov.–Feb., daily 9:30–4:30; Mar. and Oct., daily 9:30–5:30; Apr.–Sept., daily 9:30–7:30.*

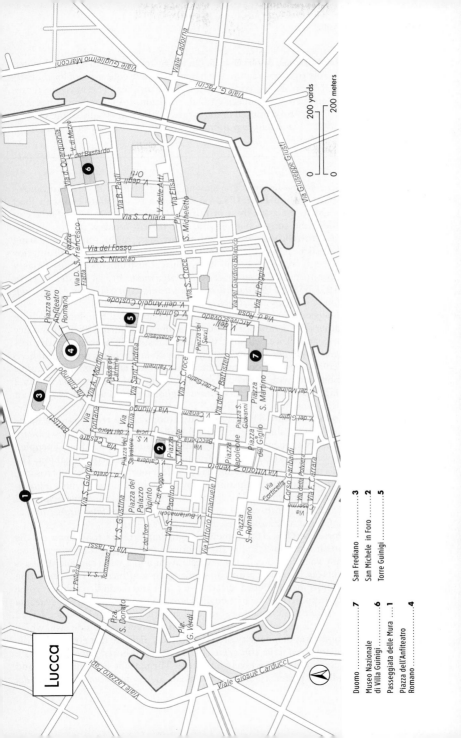

Lucca

Duomo **7**
Museo Nazionale
di Villa Guinigi **6**
Passeggiata delle Mura **1**
Piazza dell'Anfiteatro
Romano **4**

San Frediano **3**
San Michele in Foro **2**
Torre Guinigi **5**

WORTH NOTING

Museo Nazionale di Villa Guinigi. On the eastern end of the historic center, this sadly overlooked museum has an extensive collection of local Etruscan, Roman, Romanesque, and Renaissance art. The museum represents an overview of Lucca's artistic traditions from Etruscan times until the 17th century, housed in the former 15th-century villa of the Guinigi family. ⊠ *Via della Quarquonia 4* ☏ *0583/496033* 🎫 *€4* ⏱ *Tues.–Sat. 9–7, Sun. 9–2.*

WHERE TO EAT

$$
TUSCAN
Fodor's Choice
★

✕**Buca di Sant'Antonio.** The staying power of Buca di Sant'Antonio— it's been around since 1782—is the result of superlative Tuscan food brought to the table by waitstaff who doesn't miss a beat. The menu includes the simple but blissful, like *tortelli lucchesi al sugo* (meat-stuffed tortelli sauced with a fragrant meat ragù), and more daring dishes such as roast *capretto* (kid) with herbs. A white-wall interior hung with copper pots and brass musical instruments creates a classy but comfortable dining space. Ⓢ *Average main: €15* ⊠ *Via della Cervia 3* ☏ *0583/55881* ⊕ *www.bucadisantantonio.com* ⏱ *Closed Mon., 1 wk in Jan., and 1 wk in July. No dinner Sun.*

$$$
TUSCAN

✕**Il Giglio.** This place for all seasons, with a big fireplace for chilly weather and an outdoor terrace in summer, has quiet, late-19th-century charm and classic cuisine. If mushrooms are in season, try the *tacchoni con funghi,* a homemade pasta with mushrooms and a local herb called *nepitella.* A local favorite during winter is the *coniglio con olive* (rabbit stew with olives). Ⓢ *Average main: €34* ⊠ *Piazza del Giglio 2* ☏ *0583/494508* ⊕ *www.ristorantegiglio.com* ⏱ *Closed Wed., and 15 days in Nov. No dinner Tues.*

$
ITALIAN

✕**La Pecora Nera.** This lively, gaily colored little trattoria (the name means "black sheep") with a high-vaulted ceiling is staffed by *giovani disabili* (both mentally challenged and learning-disabled young people), who wait tables under the supervision of a nondisabled companion. The food's terrific, from the homemade tordelli lucchesi to the tasty crostata. Great care is taken with sourcing, when possible, local organic ingredients, and such care translates into a lovely meal. Ⓢ *Average main: €12* ⊠ *Piazza San Francesco 4* ☏ *0583/469738* ⊕ *www.lapecoraneralucca. it* ⏱ *Closed Mon. and Tues. No lunch Wed.–Fri.*

$$
ITALIAN

✕**Port Ellen Clan.** This somewhat odd name refers to a town on the Scottish island of Islay, in the Hebrides, where the proprietor and his family vacation. It calls itself a restaurant and a wine bar, and it also is a whiskey bar serving up fine single malts and blends. The interesting and short menu offers a selection of primi and secondi, as well as some tasty antipasti like the *panino di magro di lesso con salsa verde e tazzina di consommé* (a boiled beef sandwich with a herby green sauce served with a little cup of consommé). All secondi come with a side dish, which is somewhat of a novelty on Italian menus. Eclectic desserts such as the *pera cotta nel wine con gelato* (pears poached in red wine served with ice cream) provide a lovely final note. The place is small, intimate, and candle-lit: perfect for a romantic meal. Ⓢ *Average main: €17* ⊠ *Via del*

Fosso 120 ☎ *0583/493952* 🌐 *www.portellenclan.com* ✍ *Reservations essential* ⏲ *Closed Mon. and Tues. No lunch Wed.–Fri.*

$ ITALIAN 🍴 **Trattoria da Leo.** A few short turns away from the facade of San Michele, this noisy, informal, traditional trattoria delivers *cucina alla casalinga* (home cooking) in the best sense. Try the typical minestra di farro to start or just go straight to secondi piatti; in addition to the usual roast meats, there's excellent chicken with olives and a good cold dish of boiled meats served with a sauce of parsley and pine nuts. Save some room for a dessert, such as the rich, sweet, fig-and-walnut torte or the lemon sorbet brilliantly dotted with bits of sage, which tastes almost like mint—indescribably delicious. So, too, is the chestnut ice cream. [$] *Average main: €9* ✉ *Via Tegrimi 1, at corner of Via degli Asili* ☎ *0583/492236* 🌐 *www.trattoriadaleo.it* 💳 *No credit cards* ⏲ *Closed Sun. Nov.–Mar. No lunch Sun.*

WHERE TO STAY

$ HOTEL 🏨 **Albergo San Martino.** The brocade bedspreads are fresh and crisp, the proprietor friendly, the breakfast, served in a cheerful apricot room, more than ample. **Pros:** comfortable beds; great breakfast (extra). **Cons:** parking is difficult; surroundings are pleasant and stylish though not luxurious. [$] *Rooms from: €110* ✉ *Via della Dogana 9* ☎ *0583/469181* 🌐 *www.albergosanmartino.it* 🛏 *6 rooms, 2 suites* 🍽 *No meals.*

$$ HOTEL 🏨 **Hotel Ilaria.** The former stables of the Villa Bottini have been transformed into a modern hotel with stylish rooms done in a warm wood veneer with blue-and-white fittings. **Pros:** one Fodor's reader sums it up as a "nice, modern small hotel"; free bicycles. **Cons:** though in the city center, it's a little removed from main attractions. [$] *Rooms from: €138* ✉ *Via del Fosso 26* ☎ *0583/47615* 🌐 *www.hotelilaria.com* 🛏 *36 rooms, 5 suites* 🍽 *Breakfast.*

$$ HOTEL 🏨 **Palazzo Alexander.** The building, which dates to the 12th century, has been restructured to create the ease common to Lucchesi nobility: timbered ceilings, warm yellow walls, and brocaded chairs adorn the public rooms, and guest rooms have high ceilings and that same glorious damask. **Pros:** intimate feel; gracious staff; bacon and eggs included in the buffet breakfast; a short walk from San Michele in Foro. **Cons:** some Fodor's readers complain of too-thin walls. [$] *Rooms from: €200* ✉ *Via S. Giustina 48* ☎ *0583/583571* 🌐 *www.palazzoalexander.it* 🛏 *9 rooms, 3 suites, 1 apartment* 🍽 *Breakfast.*

$ HOTEL 🏨 **Piccolo Hotel Puccini.** Steps away from the busy square and church of San Michele, this little hotel is quiet and calm—and a great deal. **Pros:** cheery, English-speaking staff. **Cons:** breakfast costs extra; some rooms are on the dark side. [$] *Rooms from: €98* ✉ *Via di Poggio 9* ☎ *0583/55421* 🌐 *www.hotelpuccini.com* 🛏 *14 rooms* 🍽 *No meals.*

SPORTS AND THE OUTDOORS

A good way to spend the afternoon is to go biking around the large path atop the city's ramparts. There are two good spots right next to each other where you can rent bikes. The prices are about the same (about €12.50 for the day and €2.50 per hour for city bikes) and they are centrally located, just beside the town wall.

Poli Antonio Biciclette. This is the best option for bicycle rental on the east side of town. ✉ *Piazza Santa Maria 42, Lucca East* ☎ *0583/493787* ⊕ *www.biciclettepoli.com.*

SHOPPING

Lucca's justly famed olive oils are available throughout the city (and exported around the world). Look for those made by Fattoria di Fubbiano and Fattoria Fabbri—two of the best.

Antica Bottega di Prospero. Stop by this shop for top-quality local products, including farro, dried porcini mushrooms, olive oil, and wine. ✉ *Via San Lucia 13.*

Caniparoli. Chocolate lovers will be pleased with the selection of artisanal chocolates. This artisanal shop is so serious about their sweets that they do not make them from June to August, because of the heat. ✉ *Via San Paolino 96* ☎ *0583/53456.*

PISA

If you can get beyond the kitsch of the stalls hawking cheap souvenirs around the Leaning Tower, you'll find that Pisa has much to offer. Its treasures aren't as abundant as those of Florence, to which it is inevitably compared, but the cathedral-baptistery-tower complex of Piazza del Duomo, known collectively as the Piazza dei Miracoli (Square of Miracles), is among the most dramatic settings in Italy.

Pisa may have been inhabited as early as the Bronze Age. It was certainly populated by the Etruscans and, in turn, became part of the Roman Empire. In the early Middle Ages it flourished as an economic powerhouse; along with Amalfi, Genoa, and Venice, it was one of the four maritime republics. The city's economic and political power ebbed in the early 15th century as it fell under Florence's domination, though it enjoyed a brief resurgence under Cosimo I in the mid-16th century. Pisa sustained heavy damage during World War II, but the Duomo and Tower were spared, along with some other grand Romanesque structures.

GETTING HERE AND AROUND

Pisa is an easy hour's train ride from Florence. By car it's a straight shot on the Firenze-Pisa-Livorno (Fi-Pi-Li) autostrada. The Pisa–Lucca train runs frequently and takes about 30 minutes.

VISITOR INFORMATION

Pisa Tourism Office ✉ *Piazza Vittorio Emanuele II 16* ☎ *050/42291* ⊕ *www.pisaunicaterra.it.*

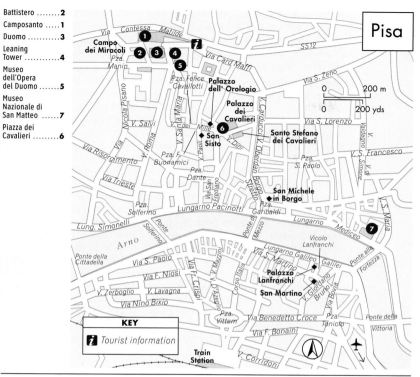

EXPLORING

Pisa, like many Italian cities, is best explored on foot, and most of what you'll want to see is within walking distance. The views along the Arno River are particularly grand and shouldn't be missed—there's a feeling of spaciousness that isn't found along the Arno in Florence.

As you set out, note that there are various combination-ticket options for sights on the Piazza del Duomo.

TOP ATTRACTIONS

Battistero. This lovely Gothic baptistery, which stands across from the Duomo's facade, is best known for the pulpit carved by Nicola Pisano (circa 1220–84; father of Giovanni Pisano) in 1260. Every half hour, an employee will dramatically close the doors, then intone and chant, thereby demonstrating how remarkable the acoustics are in the place. ⊠ *Piazza del Duomo* ☎ *050/835011* ⊕ *www.opapisa.it* ⬛*€5, discounts available if bought in combination with tickets for other monuments* ⊙ *Nov.–Feb., daily 10–5; Mar., daily 9–6; Apr.–Sept., daily 8–8; Oct., daily 9–7.*

Duomo. Pisa's cathedral brilliantly utilizes the horizontal marble-stripe motif (borrowed from Moorish architecture) that became common to Tuscan cathedrals. It is famous for the Romanesque panels on the transept door facing the tower that depict scenes from the life of Christ. The beautifully carved 14th-century pulpit is by Giovanni Pisano (son of Nicola). ⊠ *Piazza del Duomo* ☎ *050/835011* ⊕ *www.opapisa.it* 🎫 *€5* ⊙ *Nov.–Feb., daily 10–12:45 and 2–5; Mar., daily 10–6; Apr.–Sept., daily 10–8; Oct., daily 10–7.*

Fodor's Choice
★
Leaning Tower (Torre Pendente). Legend holds that Galileo conducted an experiment on the nature of gravity by dropping metal balls from the top of the 187-foot-high Leaning Tower of Pisa. Historians, however, say this legend has no basis in fact—which isn't quite to say that it's false. Work on this tower, built as a *campanile* (bell tower) for the Duomo, started in 1173: the lopsided settling began when construction reached the third story. The tower's architects attempted to compensate through such methods as making the remaining floors slightly taller on the leaning side, but the extra weight only made the problem worse. The settling continued, and by the late 20th century it had accelerated to such a point that many feared the tower would simply topple over, despite all efforts to prop it up. The structure has since been firmly anchored to the earth. The final phase to restore the tower to its original tilt of 300 years ago was launched in early 2000 and finished two years later. The last phase removed some 100 tons of earth from beneath the foundation. Reservations, which are essential, can be made online or by calling the Museo dell'Opera del Duomo; it's also possible to arrive at the ticket office and book for the same day. Note that children under eight years of age are not allowed to climb. ⊠ *Piazza del Duomo* ☎ *050/835011* ⊕ *www.opapisa.it* 🎫 *€18* ⊙ *Dec. and Jan., daily 10–5; Nov. and Feb., daily 9:40–5:40; Mar., daily 9–6; Apr.–Sept., daily 8:30–8; Oct., daily 9–7.*

WORTH NOTING

Camposanto. According to legend, the cemetery—a walled structure on the western side of the Piazza dei Miracoli—is filled with earth that returning Crusaders brought back from the Holy Land. Contained within are numerous frescoes, notably *The Drunkenness of Noah*, by Renaissance artist Benozzo Gozzoli (1422–97), presently under restoration; and the disturbing *Triumph of Death* (14th century; artist uncertain), whose subject matter shows what was on people's minds in a century that saw the ravages of the Black Death. ⊠ *Piazza del Duomo* ☎ *050/835011* ⊕ *www.opapisa.it* 🎫 *€5, discounts available if bought in combination with tickets for other monuments* ⊙ *Nov.–Feb., daily 10–5; Mar., daily 9–6; Apr.–Sept., daily 8:30–8; Oct., daily 9–7.*

Museo dell'Opera del Duomo. At the southeast corner of the sprawling Piazza dei Miracoli, this museum holds a wealth of medieval sculptures and the ancient Roman sarcophagi that inspired Nicola Pisano's figures. ⊠ *Piazza del Duomo* ☎ *050/835011* ⊕ *www.opapisa.it* 🎫 *€5, discounts available if bought in combination with tickets for other monuments* ⊙ *Nov.–Feb., daily 10–5; Mar., daily 9–6; Apr.–Sept., daily 8:30–8; Oct., daily 9–7.*

Museo Nazionale di San Matteo. On the north bank of the Arno, this museum contains some beautiful examples of local Romanesque and

Gothic art. ✉ *Piazza Matteo in Soarta 1* ☎ *050/541865* 🎫 *€5* 🕒 *Tues.–Sat. 9–7, holidays 9–2.*

Piazza dei Cavalieri. The piazza, with its fine Renaissance **Palazzo dei Cavalieri, Palazzo dell'Orologio,** and **Chiesa di Santo Stefano dei Cavalieri,** was laid out by Giorgio Vasari in about 1560. The square was the seat of the Ordine dei Cavalieri di San Stefano (Order of the Knights of St. Stephen), a military and religious institution meant to defend the coast from possible invasion by the Turks. Also in this square is the prestigious **Scuola Normale Superiore,** founded by Napoléon in 1810 on the French model. Here graduate students pursue doctorates in literature, philosophy, mathematics, and science. In front of the school is a large statue of Ferdinando I de' Medici dating from 1596. On the extreme left is the tower where the hapless Ugolino della Gherardesca (died 1289) was imprisoned with his two sons and two grandsons—legend holds that he ate them. Dante immortalized him in Canto XXXIII of his *Inferno*. Duck into the **Church of Santo Stefano** (if you're lucky enough to find it open) and check out Bronzino's splendid *Nativity of Christ* (1564–65). ✉ *Piazza dei Cavalieri.*

WHERE TO EAT

$$ TUSCAN Fodor's Choice ★

🍴 **Beny.** Apricot walls hung with etchings of Pisa make this small, single-room restaurant warmly romantic. Husband and wife Damiano and Sandra Lazzerini have been running the place for two decades, and it shows in their obvious enthusiasm while talking about the menu and daily specials (which often astound). Fish is a specialty here: the *ripieno di polpa di pesce a pan grattato con salsa di seppie e pomodoro* (fish-stuffed ravioli with tomato-octopus sauce) delights. Seasonal ingredients are key throughout the menu; Sandra works wonders with *tartufi estivi* (summer truffles), artichokes, and the fresh catch of the day. [$] *Average main: €22* ✉ *Piazza Gambacorti 22* ☎ *050/25067* 🕒 *Closed Sun., and 2 wks in mid-Aug. No lunch Sat.*

$ ITALIAN

🍴 **Osteria dei Cavalieri.** This charming white-wall restaurant, a few steps from Piazza dei Cavalieri, is reason enough to come to Pisa. They can do it all here—serve up exquisitely grilled fish dishes, please vegetarians, and prepare tagliata for meat lovers. Three set menus—from the sea, garden, and earth—are available, or you can order à la carte. For dinner there's an early seating (around 7:30) and a later one (around 9); opt for the later one if you want time to linger over your meal. [$] *Average main: €14* ✉ *Via San Frediano 16* ☎ *050/580858* 🌐 *www.osteriacavalieri.pisa.it* ✍ *Reservations essential* 🕒 *Closed Sun., 2 wks in Aug., and Dec. 29–Jan. 7. No lunch Sat.*

$ ITALIAN

🍴 **Trattoria la Faggiola.** It's only seconds away from the Leaning Tower, which probably explains the "No Pizza" sign written in big, bold letters on the blackboard outside. Inside, another blackboard lists two or three primi and secondi. The amiable Carlo Silvestrini presides over this little eatery, and he cares if you don't clean your plate. That's not a problem though, because everything's good, from the *pasta pasticciata con speck e carciofi* (oven-baked penne with cured ham and artichokes) to the finishing touch of *castagnaccio con crema di ricotta* (a chestnut flan topped with ricotta cream). $ *Average main: €9* ✉ *Via della Faggiola 1* ☎ *050/556179* ⚏ *Reservations essential* ═ *No credit cards.*

WHERE TO STAY

$$$ ⊞ **Hotel Relais dell'Orologio.** What used to be a private family palace is
HOTEL   now an intimate hideaway where 18th-century antiques fill the rooms
and public spaces and some rooms have stenciled walls and wood-
beam ceilings. **Pros:** location—in the center of town, but on a quiet
side street. **Cons:** breakfast costs extra; a bit pricey. $ *Rooms from:*
€300 ✉ *Via della Faggiola 12/14, off Campo dei Miracoli, Santa Maria*
☎ *050/830361* ⊕ *www.hotelrelaisorologio.com* ⇱ *16 rooms, 5 suites*
⦿ *No meals.*

$ ⊞ **Royal Victoria.** In a pleasant palazzo facing the Arno, a 10-minute
HOTEL   walk from the Campo dei Miracoli, room styles range from the 1800s,
complete with frescoes, to the 1920s; the most charming are in the
old tower. **Pros:** friendly staff; lovely views of the Arno from many
rooms. **Cons:** rooms vary significantly in size; all are a little worn.
$ *Rooms from: €110* ✉ *Lungarno Pacinotti 12* ☎ *050/940111* ⊕ *www.*
royalvictoria.it ⇱ *48 rooms (40 with bath)* ⦿ *Breakfast.*

CHIANTI

This is the heartland: both sides of the Strada Chiantigiana (SR222) are
embraced by glorious panoramic views of vineyards, olive groves, and
castle towers. Traveling south from Florence, you first reach the aptly
named one-street town of Strada in Chianti. Farther south, the number
of vineyards on either side of the road dramatically increases—as do
the signs inviting you in for free tastings of wine. Beyond Strada lies
Greve in Chianti, completely surrounded by wineries and filled with
wine shops. There's art to be had as well: Passignano, west of Greve,
has an abbey that shelters a 15th-century *Last Supper* by Domenico
and Davide Ghirlandaio. Farther still, along the Strada Chiantigiana,
are Panzano and Castellina in Chianti, both hill towns. It's from near
Panzano and Castellina that branch roads head to the other main towns
of eastern Chianti: Radda in Chianti, Gaiole in Chianti, and Castelnuovo Berardenga.

The Strada Chiantigiana gets crowded during the high season, but no
one is in a hurry. The slow pace gives you time to soak up the beautiful scenery.

GREVE IN CHIANTI

27 km (17 miles) south of Florence, 40 km (25 miles) northeast of
Colle Val d'Elsa.

If there is a capital of Chianti, it is Greve, a friendly market town with
no shortage of cafés, enoteche, and crafts shops lining its streets.

11

GETTING HERE AND AROUND

Driving from Florence or Siena, Greve is easily reached via the Strada Chiantigiana (SR222). SITA buses travel frequently between Florence and Greve. Tra-In and SITA buses connect Siena and Greve, but a direct trip is virtually impossible. There is no train service.

VISITOR INFORMATION

Greve in Chianti Tourism Office ✉ *Piazza Matteotti 8/11* ☎ *055/8546299.*

EXPLORING

Montefioralle. A tiny hilltop hamlet, about 2 km (1 mile) west of Greve in Chianti, Montefioralle is the ancestral home of Amerigo Vespucci (1454–1512), the mapmaker, navigator, and explorer who named America. (His niece Simonetta may have been the inspiration for Sandro Botticelli's *Birth of Venus,* painted sometime in the 1480s.)

Piazza Matteotti. Greve's gently sloping and asymmetrical central piazza is surrounded by an attractive arcade with shops of all kinds. In the center stands a statue of the discoverer of New York harbor, Giovanni da Verrazano (circa 1480–1527). ■TIP➔ **Check out the lively market held here on Saturday morning.**

WHERE TO EAT

$
TUSCAN
✕ **Da Padellina.** Locals don't flock to this restaurant on the outskirts of Strada in Chianti for the art on the walls—some of it questionable, most of it kitsch—but for the bistecca fiorentina. As big as a breadboard and served rare, one of these justly renowned steaks is enough to feed a family of four, with doggy bags willingly provided if required! First courses are typical and desserts are standard, but the wine list is a varied and extensive surprise. Outdoor seating on the upstairs terrace provides great views of the surrounding countryside. Ⓢ *Average main: €15* ✉ *Via Corso del Popolo 54, Località Strada in Chianti, 10 km (6 miles) north of Greve* ☎ *055/858388* ⊕ *www.ristorantedapadellina. com* ⊘ *Closed Tues.*

$
TUSCAN
✕ **Enoteca Fuoripiazza.** Detour off Greve's flower-strewn main square for food that relies heavily on local ingredients (like cheese and salami produced nearby). The lengthy wine list provides a bewildering array of choices to pair with affettati misti or one of their primi—the *pici* (a thick, short noodle) is deftly prepared here. All the dishes are made with great care and outdoor seating makes summer dining particularly pleasant. Ⓢ *Average main: €12* ✉ *Via I Maggio 2* ☎ *055/8546313* ⊕ *www. enotecafuoripiazza.it* ⊘ *Closed Mon.*

$$$
ITALIAN
✕ **Osteria di Passignano.** In an ancient wine cellar owned by the Antinori family (who also happen to own much of what you see in these parts) is a sophisticated restaurant ably run by chef Marcello Crini and his attentive staff. The menu changes seasonally; traditional Tuscan cuisine is given a delightful twist through the use of unexpected herbs. When porcini mushrooms are in season, a particularly tantalizing treat is the *filetto di vitello in panura di funghi secchi e noci al sedano rapa e porcini* (veal sirloin in a crust of dried mushrooms, walnuts, celeriac, and fresh porcini). The extensive wine list includes local vintages as well as numerous international labels. Day-long cooking courses are also available. Ⓢ *Average main: €35* ✉ *Via di Passignano 33, Passignano*

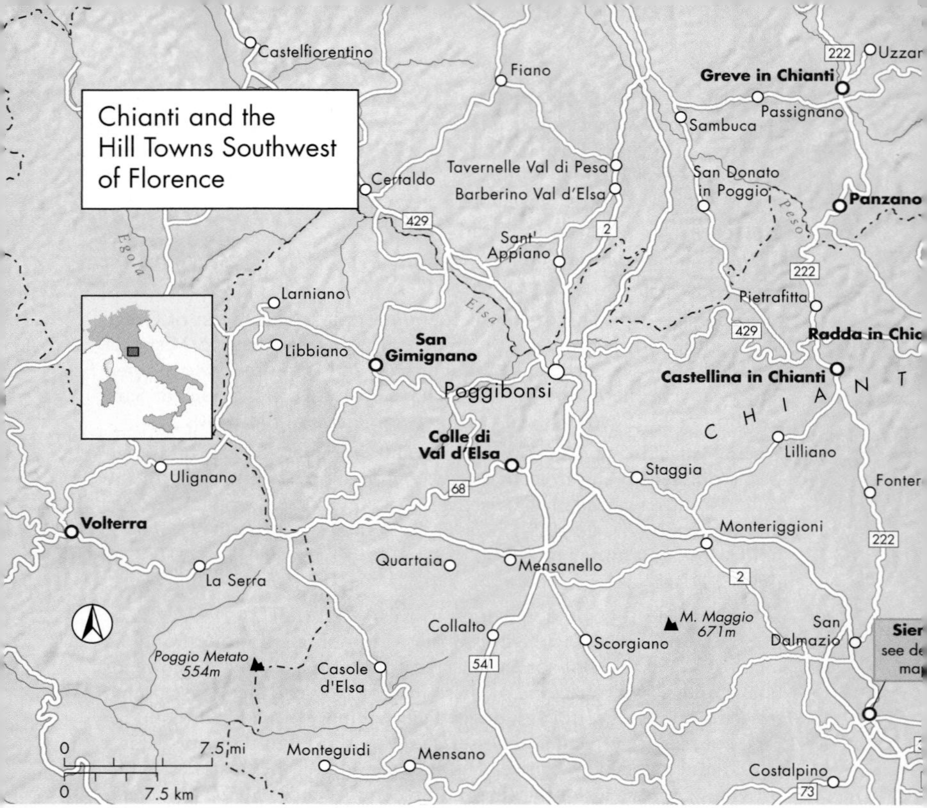
Chianti and the Hill Towns Southwest of Florence
Castelfiorentino
Fiano
Greve in Chianti
222
Uzzan
Passignano
Sambuca
Tavernelle Val di Pesa
Barberino Val d'Elsa
San Donato in Poggio
Pesa
Panzano
Certaldo
429
2
Sant' Appiano
Egola
222
Pietrafitta
Larniano
Elsa
429
Radda in Chia
San Gimignano
Libbiano
Castellina in Chianti
Poggibonsi
CHIANT
Colle di Val d'Elsa
Lilliano
Ulignano
Staggia
Fonter
68
Volterra
Monteriggioni
222
Quartaia
Mensanello
La Serra
2
M. Maggio 671m
Collalto
Scorgiano
San Dalmazio
Poggio Metato 554m
541
Casole d'Elsa
0
7.5 mi
Monteguidi
Mensano
Costalpino
0
7.5 km
73

☎ *055/8071278* 🌐 *www.osteriadipassignano.com* 🕒 *Closed Sun., 3 wks in Jan., and 1 wk in Aug.*

$$$ TUSCAN 🍴 **Ristoro di Lamole.** Although off the beaten path up a winding road lined with olive trees and vineyards, this place is worth the effort to find. The view from the outdoor terrace is divine, as is the simple, exquisitely prepared Tuscan cuisine. Start with the bruschetta drizzled with olive oil or the sublime *verdure sott'olio* (marinated vegetables) before moving on to any of the fine secondi. The kitchen has a way with *coniglio* (rabbit)—don't pass it up if it's on the menu. [$] *Average main: €35* ✉ *Via di Lamole 6, Località Lamole in Chianti* ☎ *055/8547050* 🌐 *www.ristorodilamole.it* 🕒 *Closed Wed. and Nov.–Apr.*

$$$ TUSCAN 🍴 **Ristoro L'Antica Scuderia.** Across the street from the abbey and run by the same family for more than 30 years, this once-simple eatery in the erstwhile monks' stables has undergone a complete face-lift. The interior is decorated along modern-elegant lines, and the menu, while thoroughly based on traditional cuisine, is filled with creative interpretations. The *taglierini al tartuffo* (pasta with truffles) is delicious, the *tagliata al ginepro* (grilled sliced beef with juniper berries) is excellent, and the wine list superb. Pizza is also available, but only at dinner time. Shaded, outdoor seating on the restaurant's stepped terrace provides a pleasant setting for dinner on a warm summer's evening. [$] *Average*

main: €25 ✉ Via di Passignano 17, Passignano ☎ 055/80716233 🌐 www.ristorolanticascuderia.it ⏲ Closed Tues.

WHERE TO STAY

$ B&B/INN **Albergo del Chianti.** Simply but pleasantly decorated bedrooms with plain modern cabinets and wardrobes and wrought-iron beds have views of the town square or out over the tile rooftops toward the surrounding hills. **Pros:** central location; best value in Greve. **Cons:** rooms facing the piazza can be noisy; small bathrooms. [$] *Rooms from: €100 ✉ Piazza Matteotti 86 ☎ 055/853763 🌐 www.albergodelchianti.it 🛏 16 rooms ⏲ Closed Jan. 🍴 Breakfast.*

$$$ B&B/INN Fodor's Choice ★ **Villa Bordoni.** David and Catherine Gardner, Scottish expats, have transformed a ramshackle 16th-century villa into a stunning little retreat where no two rooms are alike—all have stenciled walls; some have four-poster beds, others small mezzanines. **Pros:** splendidly isolated in the hills above Greve; beautiful décor; wonderful hosts. **Cons:** on a long and bumpy dirt road; need a car to get around. [$] *Rooms from: €245 ✉ Via San Cresci 31/32, Località Mezzuola ☎ 055/8546230 🌐 www.villabordoni.com 🛏 8 rooms, 3 suites ⏲ Closed 3 wks in Jan. and Feb. 🍴 Breakfast.*

$$ B&B/INN Fodor's Choice ★ **Villa Il Poggiale.** Renaissance gardens, beautiful rooms with high ceilings and elegant furnishings, a panoramic pool, and expert staff are just a few of the things that make a stay at this 16th-century villa memorable. **Pros:** beautiful gardens and panoramic setting; elegant historical building; exceptionally professional staff. **Cons:** a little isolated, making private transportation necessary; some rooms face a country road and may be noisy during the day. [$] *Rooms from: €160 ✉ Via Empolese 69, San Casciano Val di Pesa, 20 km (12 miles) northwest of Greve ☎ 055/828311 🌐 www.villailpoggiale.it 🛏 20 rooms, 4 suites ⏲ Closed Jan. and Feb. 🍴 Breakfast.*

SHOPPING

Enoteca del Gallo Nero. This is one of the best-stocked enoteche in the whole Chianti region, with a wide selection of labels. *✉ Piazzetta S. Croce 8 ☎ 055/853297.*

PANZANO

7 km (4½ miles) south of Greve, 36 km (22 miles) south of Florence.

The magnificent views of the valleys of the Pesa and Greve rivers easily make Panzano one of the prettiest stops in Chianti. The triangular Piazza Bucciarelli is the heart of the new town. A short stroll along Via Giovanni da Verrazzano brings you up to the old town, Panzano Alto, which is still partly surrounded by medieval walls, but the town's 13th-century castle is now almost completely absorbed by later buildings (its central tower is now a private home).

GETTING HERE AND AROUND

From Florence or Siena, Panzano is easily reached by car along the Strada Chiantigiana (SR222). SITA buses travel frequently between Florence and Panzano. From Siena, the journey by bus is extremely difficult because SITA and Tra-In do not coordinate their schedules. Train service is not available.

EXPLORING

San Leolino. Ancient even by Chianti standards, this hilltop church probably dates to the 10th century, but was completely rebuilt in the Romanesque style sometime in the 13th century. It has a 14th-century cloister worth seeing. The 16th-century terra-cotta tabernacles are attributed to Giovanni della Robbia, and there's also a remarkable triptych (attributed to the Master of Panzano) that was executed sometime in the mid-14th century. Open days and hours are unpredictable; check with the tourist office in Greve in Chianti for the latest. ⊠ *Località San Leolino, 3 km (2 miles) south of Panzano* ☎ *055/8546299.*

WHERE TO EAT AND STAY

$
INTERNATIONAL

✕**Dario Doc.** Local butcher and restaurateur, Dario Cecchini, has extended his empire of meat to include this space located directly above his butcher's shop. Here, you'll find only three items on the menu: the "Mac Dario," a half-pound burger in a crisp crumb crust served with roast potatoes and onions; the "Super Dario," the former with salad and beans added; and the "Welcome," four different dishes of beef and pork served with fresh garden vegetables. All are a nice change from the more standard options found at restaurants throughout Chianti. Outdoor seating is available in summer, but get here early—it's enormously popular. Enter from the public parking area behind the restaurant. $ *Average main: €15* ⊠ *Via XX Luglio 11* ☎ *055/852176* ⊕ *www.dariocecchini.com* ⚠ *Reservations not accepted* ☉ *Closed Sun.*

$$$
TUSCAN

✕**Solociccia.** "Abandon all hope, ye who enter here," announces the menu, "you're in the hands of a butcher." Indeed you are, for this restaurant is the creation of Dario Cecchini, Panzano's local merchant of meat. Served at communal tables, there are three set meals to choose from, all of which highlight meat dishes chosen at Dario's discretion. All are accompanied by seasonal vegetables, white beans with olive oil, focaccia, and a ¼ liter of wine. Though Cecchini emphasizes that steak is never on the menu, this lively, crowded place is definitely not for vegetarians. The entrance is on Via XX Luglio. $ *Average main: €30* ⊠ *Via Chiantigiana 5* ☎ *055/852727* ⊕ *www.solociccia.it* ⚠ *Reservations essential* ☉ *Closed Mon.–Wed. No dinner Sun.*

$$$
B&B/INN
Fodor's Choice
★

▥**Villa Le Barone.** Once the home of the Viviani della Robbia family, this 16th-century villa in a grove of ancient cypress trees retains many aspects of a private country dwelling, complete with homey guest quarters. **Pros:** beautiful location; wonderful restaurant; great base for exploring the region. **Cons:** rooms vary in size; 15-minute walk to nearest town. $ *Rooms from: €250* ⊠ *Via San Leolino 19* ☎ *055/852621* ⊕ *www.villalebarone.com* ⇆ *28 rooms* ☉ *Closed Nov.–Easter* ⏉ *Breakfast.*

RADDA IN CHIANTI

26 km (15 miles) south of Panzano, 55 km (34 miles) south of Florence.

Radda in Chianti sits on a ridge stretching between the Val di Pesa and Val d'Arbia. It is easily reached by following the SR429 from Castellina.

Continued on page 646

GRAPE ESCAPES
THE PLEASURES OF TUSCAN WINE

The vineyards stretching across the landscape
of Tuscany may look like cinematic backdrops,
but in fact they're working farms, and they
produce some of Italy's best wines. No matter
whether you're a wine novice or a connoisseur,
there's great pleasure to be had from exploring this
lush terrain, visiting the vineyards, and uncorking a bottle
for yourself.

GETTING TO KNOW TUSCAN WINE

Most of the wine produced in Tuscany is red (though there are some notable whites as well), and most Tuscan reds are made primarily from one type of grape, sangiovese. That doesn't mean, however, that all wines here are the same. God (in this case Bacchus) is in the details: differences in climate, soil, and methods of production result in wines with several distinct personalities.

Chianti

Chianti is the most famous name in Tuscan wine, but what exactly the name means is a little tricky. It once identified wines produced in the region extending from just south of Florence to just north of Siena. In the mid-20th century, the official Chianti zone was expanded to include a large portion of central Tuscany. That area is divided into eight subregions. **Chianti Classico** is the name given to the original zone, which makes up 17,000 of the 42,000 acres of Chianti-producing vineyards.

Classico wines, which bear the *gallo nero* (black rooster) logo on their labels, are the most highly regarded Chiantis (with **Rùfina** running second), but that doesn't mean Classicos are always superior. All Chiantis are strictly regulated (they must be a minimum 75% to 80% sangiovese, with other varieties blended in to add nuance), and they share a strong, woodsy character that's well suited to Tuscan food. It's a good strategy to drink the local product—**Colli Senesi Chianti** when in Siena, for example. The most noticeable, and costly, difference comes when a Chianti is from *riserva* (reserve) stock, meaning it's been aged for at least two years.

WINE REGIONS OF CENTRAL TUSCANY

DOC & DOCG The designations "DOC" and "DOCG"—Denominazione di Origine Controllata (e Garantita)—mean a wine comes from an established region and adheres to rigorous standards of production. Ironically, the esteemed Super Tuscans are labeled *vini da tavola* (table wines), the least prestigious designation, because they don't use traditional grape blends.

Brunello di Montalcino

The area surrounding the hill town of Montalcino, to the south of Siena, is drier and warmer than the Chianti regions, and it produces the most powerful of the sangiovese-based wines. Regulations stipulate that Brunello di Montalcino be made entirely from sangiovese grapes (no blending) and aged at least four years. **Rosso di Montalcino** is a younger, less complex, less expensive Brunello.

The Super Tuscans

Beginning in the 1970s, some winemakers, chafing at the regulations imposed on established Tuscan wine varieties, began blending and aging wines in innovative ways. Thus were born the so-called Super Tuscans. These pricey, French oak–aged wines are admired for their high quality, led by such star performers as **Sassicaia**, from the Maremma region, and **Tignanello**, produced at the Tenuta Marchesi Antinori near Badia a Passignano. Purists, however, lament the loss of local identity resulting from the Super Tuscans' use of nonnative grape varieties such as cabernet sauvignon and merlot.

Vino Nobile di Montepulciano

East of Montalcino is Montepulciano, the town at the heart of the third, and smallest, of Tuscany's top wine districts.

Blending regulations aren't as strict for Vino Nobile as for Chianti and Brunello, and as a result it has a wider range of characteristics. Broadly speaking, though, Vino Nobile is a cross between Chianti and Brunello—less acidic than the former and softer than the latter. It also has a less pricey sibling, **Rosso di Montepulciano.**

The Whites

Most whites from Tuscany are made from **trebbiano** grapes, which produce a wine that's light and refreshing but not particularly aromatic or flavorful—it may hit the spot on a hot afternoon, but it doesn't excite connoisseurs.

Golden-hewed **Vernaccia di San Gimignano** is a local variety with more limited production but greater personality—it's the star of Tuscan whites. Winemakers have also brought chardonnay and sauvignon grapes to the region, resulting in wines that, like some Super Tuscans, are pleasant to drink but short on local character.

TOURING & TASTING IN TUSCAN WINE COUNTRY

Strade del Vino di Toscana

Tuscany has visitor-friendly wineries, but the way you go about visiting is a bit different here from what it is in California or France. Many wineries welcome drop-ins for a tasting, but for a tour you usually need to make an appointment a few days in advance. There are several approaches you can take, depending on how much time you have and how serious you are about wine:

PLAN 1: FULL IMMERSION. Make an appointment to tour one of the top wineries (see our recommendations on the next page), and you'll get the complete experience: half a day of strolling through vineyards, talking grape varieties, and tasting wine, often accompanied by food. Groups are small; in spring and fall, it may be just you and the winemaker. The cost is usually €10 to €20 per person, but can go up to €40 if a meal is included. Remember to specify a tour in English.

PLAN 2: SEMI-ORGANIZED. If you want to spend a few hours going from vineyard to vineyard, make your first stop one of the local tourist information offices—they're great resources for maps, tasting itineraries, and personalized advice about where to visit. The offices in **Greve**, **Montalcino**, and **Montepulciano** are the best equipped. **Enoteche** (for more about them, turn the page) can also be good places to pick up tips about where to go for tastings.

PLAN 3: SPONTANEOUS. Along Tuscany's country roads you'll see signs for wineries offering **vendita diretta** (direct sales) and **degustazioni** (tastings). For a taste of the local product with some atmosphere thrown in, a spontaneous visit is a perfectly viable approach. You may wind up in a simple shop or an elaborate tasting room; either way, there's a fair chance you'll sample something good. Expect a small fee for a three-glass tasting.

THE PICK OF THE VINEYARDS

Within the Chianti Classico region, these wineries should be at the top of your to-visit list, whether you're dropping in for a taste or making a full tour. (Tours require reservations unless otherwise indicated.)

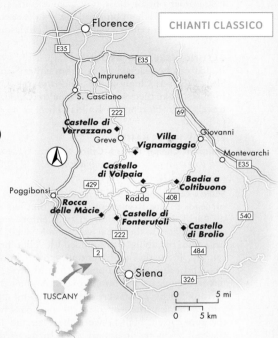

CHIANTI CLASSICO

Florence

E35

E35

Impruneta

S. Casciano

222

69

Castello di Verrazzano ◆

Greve

Villa Vignamaggio

Giovanni

Montevarchi

E35

Castello di Volpaia

Badia a Coltibuono

Poggibonsi

429

Radda

408

Rocca delle Màcie ◆

Castello di Fonterutoli

540

222

Castello di Brolio

2

484

Siena

326

TUSCANY

0   5 mi

0   5 km

Badia a Coltibuono
(✉ Gaiole in Chianti
☎ 0577/749498
⊕ www.coltibuono.
com). Along with an extensive prelunch tour and tasting, there are shorter afternoon tours, no reservation required, starting on the hour from 2 to 5. (See "Radda in Chianti" in this chapter.)

Castello di Fonterutoli
(✉ Castellina in Chianti
☎ 0577/741385 ⊕ www.
fonterutoli.it). Hour-long tours include a walk through the neighboring village.

Castello di Volpaia
(✉ Radda in Chianti
☎ 0577/738066 ⊕ www.
volpaia.com). The tour here includes a visit to the olive oil press and a tour of the town.

Castello di Verrazzano
(✉ Via S. Martino in Valle 12, Greve in Chianti
☎ 055/854243 ⊕ www.
verrazzano.com). Tours here take you down to the cellars, through the gardens, and into the woods in search of wild boar.

Villa Vignamaggio (✉ Via Petriolo 5, Greve in Chianti
☎ 055/854661 ⊕ www.
vignamaggio.com). Along with a wine tour, you can spend the night at this villa where Mona Lisa is believed to have been born. (See "Where to Stay" under "Greve in Chianti" in this chapter.)

Rocca delle Màcie
(✉ Località Le Màcie 45, Castellina in Chianti
☎ 0577/732236
⊕ www.rocca
dellemacie.com).
A full lunch or dinner can be incorporated into your tasting here.

Castello di Brolio
(✉ Gaiole in Chianti
☎ 0577/730220
⊕ www.ricasoli.it).
One of Tuscany's most impressive castles also has a centuries-old winemaking tradition. (See "Radda in Chianti" in this chapter.)

REMEMBER

Always have a designated driver when you're touring and tasting. Vineyards are usually located off narrow, curving roads. Full sobriety is a must behind the wheel.

It's another one of those tiny villages with steep streets for strolling; follow the signs that point you toward the *camminamento medioevale,* a covered 14th-century walkway that circles part of the city inside the walls.

GETTING HERE AND AROUND

Radda can be reached by car from either Siena or Florence along the SR222 (Strada Chiantigiana), and from the A1 autostrada. Three Tra-In buses make their way from Siena to Radda. One morning SITA bus travels from Florence to Radda. There is no train service convenient to Radda.

VISITOR INFORMATION

Radda in Chianti Tourism Office ✉ *Piazza Castello 6* ☎ *0577/738494* ⊕ *www.comune.radda-in-chianti.si.it.*

EXPLORING

Badia a Coltibuono (*Abbey of the Good Harvest*). North of Gaiole a turn-off leads to this Romanesque abbey that has been owned by Lorenza de' Medici's family for more than a century and a half (the family isn't closely related to the Renaissance-era Medici). Wine has been produced here since the abbey was founded by Vallombrosan monks in the 11th century. Today the family continues the tradition, making Chianti Classico and other wines, along with cold-pressed olive oil and various flavored vinegars and floral honeys. A small church with campanile is surrounded by 2,000 acres of oak, fir, and chestnut woods threaded with walking paths—open to all—that pass two small lakes. Though the abbey itself, built between the 11th and 18th centuries, serves as the family's home, parts are open for tours (in English, German, or Italian). Visit the jasmine-draped main courtyard, the inner cloister with its antique well, the musty old cellars, and the Renaissance-style garden redolent of lavender, lemons, and roses. In the shop, **L'Osteria,** you can taste wine and honey, as well as pick up other items like home-made beeswax hand lotion in little ceramic dishes. The Badia is closed on public holidays. ✉ *Località Badia a Coltibuono, 4 km (2½ miles) north of Gaiole in Chianti* ☎ *0577/74481 for tours* ⊕ *www.coltibuono. com* 🎫 *Abbey €6* ☉ *Tours: Apr.–Oct., daily at 2:30, 3:30, and 4:30. Shop: Apr.–Oct., daily 9–7; Nov. and Dec., Tues.–Sun. 9–6; Jan.–Mar., by request.*

Fodor'sChoice ★ **Castello di Brolio.** If you have time for only one castle in Tuscany, this is it. At the end of the 12th century, when Florence conquered southern Chianti, Brolio became Florence's southernmost outpost, and it was often said, "When Brolio growls, all Siena trembles." Brolio was built about AD 1000 and owned by the monks of the Badia Fiorentina; the "new" owners, the Ricasoli family, have been in possession since 1141. Bettino Ricasoli (1809–80), the so-called "Iron Baron," was one of the founders of modern Italy, and is said to have invented the original formula for Chianti wine. Brolio, one of Chianti's best-known labels, is still justifiably famous. Its cellars may be toured by appointment. The grounds are worth visiting, even though the 19th-century manor house is not open to the public. A small museum, where the Ricasoli Collection is housed in a 12th-century tower, displays objects that relate the long history of the family and the origins of Chianti wine. There are two apartments here available for rent by the week. ✉ *Località Brolio, 2 km (1 mile) southeast of Gaiole in Chianti* ☎ *0577/730280* 🌐 *www.ricasoli.it* 🎟 *€5 gardens, €8 gardens and museum, €10 guided tours* 🕒 *Apr.–Oct., daily 10–7; ticket sales until 6.*

Palazzo del Podestà. Radda's town hall (aka Palazzo Comunale), in the middle of town, was built in the second half of the 14th century and has served the same function ever since. Fifty-one coats of arms (the largest is the Medici's) are embedded in the facade, representing the past governors of the town, but unless you have official business, the building is closed to the public. ✉ *Piazza Ferrucci 1.*

WHERE TO EAT AND STAY

$ TUSCAN Fodor's Choice ★ 🍴 **Osteria Le Panzanelle.** Silvia Bonechi's experience in the kitchen—with the help of a few precious recipes handed down from her grandmother—is one of the reasons for the success of this small restaurant. The other is the front-room hospitality of Nada Michelassi. These two *panzanelle* (women from Panzano) serve a short menu of tasty and authentic dishes at what the locals refer to as *il prezzo giusto* (the right price). Both the *pappa al pomodoro* (tomato soup) and the *peposo* (peppery beef stew) are exceptional. Whether you are eating inside or under large umbrellas on the terrace near a tiny stream, the experience is always congenial. "The best food we had in Tuscany," writes one Fodors.com user. Reservations are essential in July and August. [$] *Average main: €15* ✉ *Località Lucarelli 29, 8 km (5 miles) northwest of Radda on the road to Panzano* ☎ *0577/733511* 🌐 *www.osteria.lepanzanelle.it* 🕒 *Closed Mon., and Jan. and Feb.*

$ B&B/INN 🏨 **La Bottega di Giovannino.** This is a fantastic place for the budget-conscious traveler, as rooms are immaculate and most have stunning views of the surrounding hills. **Pros:** great location in the center of town; close to restaurants and shops; super value. **Cons:** some rooms are small; some bathrooms are down the hall; basic décor. [$] *Rooms from: €70* ✉ *Via Roma 6–8* ☎ *0577/738056* 🌐 *www.labottegadigiovannino.it* 🛏 *9 rooms, 1 apartment* 🍽 *No meals.*

$$ HOTEL 🏨 **Palazzo San Niccolò.** The wood-beam ceilings, terra-cotta floors, and some of the original frescoes of a 19th-century town palace remain, but the marble bathrooms have all been updated, some with Jacuzzi tubs. **Pros:** central location; friendly service. **Cons:** some rooms face a main street; room sizes vary. [$] *Rooms from: €140* ✉ *Via Roma 16* ☎ *0577/735666* 🌐 *www.hotelsanniccolo.com* 🛏 *17 rooms, 1 suite* 🕒 *Closed Nov.–Mar.* 🍽 *Breakfast.*

$$ B&B/INN 🏨 **Relais Fattoria Vignale.** A refined and comfortable country house offers numerous sitting rooms with terra-cotta floors and attractive stonework and wood-beam ceilings in guest rooms filled with simple wooden furnishings and handwoven rugs. **Pros:** intimate public spaces; excellent restaurant; helpful and friendly staff; nice grounds and pool. **Cons:** north-facing rooms blocked by tall cypress trees; single rooms are small; annex across a busy road. [$] *Rooms from: €185* ✉ *Via Pianigiani 9* ☎ *0577/738300 for hotel, 0577/738094 for restaurant* 🌐 *www.vignale.it* 🛏 *42 rooms, 5 suites* 🕒 *Closed Nov.–Mar. 15* 🍽 *Breakfast.*

CASTELLINA IN CHIANTI

14 km (8 miles) west of Radda, 59 km (35 miles) south of Florence.

Castellina in Chianti—or simply Castellina—is on a ridge above three valleys: the Val di Pesa, Val d'Arbia, and Val d'Elsa. No matter what direction you turn, the panorama is bucolic. The strong 15th-century medieval walls give a hint of the history of this village, which was an outpost during the continuing wars between Florence and Siena. In the main square, the Piazza del Comune, there's a 15th-century palace and a 15th-century fort constructed around a 13th-century tower. It now serves as the town hall.

GETTING HERE AND AROUND

As with all the towns along the Strada Chiantigiana (SR222), Castellina is an easy drive from either Siena or Florence. From Siena, Castellina is well served by the local Tra-In bus company. However, only one bus a day travels here from Florence. The closest train station is at Castellina Scalo, some 15 km (9 miles) away.

VISITOR INFORMATION

Castellina in Chianti Tourism Office ⊠ *Via Ferruccio 40* ☎ *0577/741392* ⊕ *www.turismo.comune.castellina.si.it.*

WHERE TO EAT AND STAY

$$$
TUSCAN

✕ **Albergaccio.** The fact that the dining room can seat only 35 guests makes a meal here an intimate experience. The ever-changing menu mixes traditional and creative dishes. In late September and October *zuppa di funghi e castagne* (mushroom and chestnut soup) is a treat; grilled meats and seafood are on the list throughout the year. There's also an excellent wine list. When the weather is warm, make sure you dine on the terrace. $ *Average main: €25* ⊠ *Via Fiorentina 63* ☎ *0577/741042* ⊕ *www.albergacciocast.com* ⌂ *Reservations essential* ▬ *No credit cards* ⊙ *Closed Sun. No lunch Wed. and Thurs.*

$$
TUSCAN

✕ **Ristorante Le Tre Porte.** Grilled meat dishes are the specialty at this popular restaurant, with a bistecca fiorentina (served very rare) taking pride of place. Paired with grilled fresh porcini mushrooms when in season (spring and fall), it's a particularly heady dish. The panoramic terrace is a good choice for dining in summer. Inside, the upper floor offers an unmistakably Tuscan setting, while the downstairs is more modern and intimate. Reservations are essential in July and August. $ *Average main: €20* ⊠ *Via Trento e Trieste 4* ☎ *0577/741163* ⊕ *www. ristoranteinchianti.com* ⊙ *Closed Tues.*

$$
TUSCAN

✕ **Sotto Le Volte.** As the name suggests, you'll find this small restaurant under the arches of Castellina's medieval walkway. The restaurant has vaulted ceilings, which make for a particularly romantic setting. The menu is short and eminently Tuscan, with typical soups and pasta dishes. The *costolette di agnello alle erbe* (herbed lamb chops) are especially tasty. $ *Average main: €20* ⊠ *Via delle Volte 14–16* ☎ *0577/056530* ⊕ *www.ristorantesottolevolte.it* ▬ *No credit cards* ⊙ *Closed Wed.*

$
B&B/INN
Fodor's Choice
★

🏛 **Palazzo Squarcialupi.** In this lovely 15th-century palace, rooms are spacious, with high ceilings, tile floors, and 18th-century furnishings, and many have views of the valley below. **Pros:** great location in town center; elegant public spaces; nice spa, pool, and grounds. **Cons:** on a street with no car access; across from a busy restaurant. $ *Rooms from: €120* ✉ *Via Ferruccio 22* ☎ *0577/741186* ⊕ *www.palazzosquarcialupi. com* ⇆ *17 rooms* ☾ *Closed Nov.–Mar.* ⦿ *Breakfast.*

HILL TOWNS SOUTHWEST OF FLORENCE

Submit to the draw of Tuscany's enchanting fortified cities that crown the hills west of Siena, many dating to the Etruscan period. San Gimignano, known as the "medieval Manhattan" because of its forest of stout medieval towers built by rival families, is the most heavily visited. This onetime Roman outpost, with its tilted cobbled streets and ancient buildings, can make the days of Guelph-Ghibelline conflicts palpable. Rising from a series of bleak gullied hills and valleys, Volterra has always been popular for its minerals and stones, particularly alabaster, which was used by the Etruscans for many implements. Examples are now displayed in the exceptional (and exceptionally large) Museo Etrusco Guarnacci.

VOLTERRA

75 km (47 miles) southwest of Florence.

As you approach the town through bleak, rugged terrain, you can see that not all Tuscan hill towns rise above rolling green fields. Volterra stands mightily over Le Balze, a stunning series of gullied hills and valleys formed by erosion that has slowly eaten away at the foundation of the town—now it's about half the size that it was during its Etruscan glory days 25 centuries ago. The town began as one of the 12 most important Etruscan cities that formed the Etruscan League, and excavations in the 18th century revealed a bounty of relics, which are on exhibit at the impressively overstocked Museo Etrusco Guarnacci. The Romans and later the Florentines laid siege to the town to secure its supply of minerals and stones, salt, alum, and alabaster. It's the latter for which the town is best known today, and you'll find carved and colored handicrafts made of alabaster in many of the shops around town.

GETTING HERE AND AROUND

By car, the best route from San Gimignano follows the SP1 south to Castel San Gimignano and then the SS68 all the way to Volterra. Coming from the west, take the SS1, a coastal road to Cecina, then follow the SS68 to Volterra. Either way, there's a long, winding climb at the end of your trip. Traveling to Volterra by bus or train is complicated; avoid it if possible, especially if you have lots of luggage. From Florence or Siena, the journey is best made by bus and involves a change in Colle di Val d'Elsa. From Rome or Pisa, it is best to take the train to Cecina and then take a bus to Volterra or a train to the Volterra-Saline station. The latter is 10 km (6 miles) from town.

VISITOR INFORMATION

Volterra Tourism Office ✉ *Piazza dei Priori 20* ☎ *0588/87257* ⊕ *www. volterratur.it.*

EXPLORING

Duomo. Behind the textbook 13th-century Pisan–Romanesque facade is proof that Volterra counted for something during the Renaissance, when many important Tuscan artists came to decorate the church. Three-dimensional stucco portraits of local saints are on the gold, red, and blue ceiling (1580) designed by Francesco Capriani, including Saint Linus, the successor to Saint Peter as pope and claimed by the Volterrans to have been born here. The highlight of the Duomo is the brightly painted 13th-century wooden life-size *Deposition* in the chapel of the same name. The unusual **Cappella dell'Addolorata** (Chapel of the Grieved) has two terra-cotta Nativity scenes; the depiction of the arrival of the Magi has a background fresco by Benozzo Gozzoli. The 16th-century pulpit in the middle of the nave is lined with fine 14th-century sculpted panels, attributed to a member of the Pisano family. Across from the Duomo in the center of the piazza is the **Battistero,** with stripes that match the Duomo. Evidently this baptistery got a lot of use, as the small marble baptismal font carved by Andrea Sansovino in 1502 was moved to the wall to the right of the entrance in the mid-18th century to make room for a much larger one. ⊠ *Piazza San Giovanni* 🕾 *0588/88524* ⏱ *Daily 9:30–noon and 3:30–6:30.*

Fodor's Choice
★
Museo Etrusco Guarnacci. An extraordinarily large and unique collection of Etruscan relics is made all the more interesting by clear explanations in English. The bulk of the collection is comprised of roughly 700 carved funerary urns: the oldest, dating from the 7th century BC, were made from tufa (volcanic rock); a handful are made of terra-cotta; and the vast majority—from the 3rd to 1st century BC—are from alabaster. The urns are grouped by subject and, taken together, form a fascinating testimony about Etruscan life and death. Some illustrate domestic scenes, others the funeral procession of the deceased. Greek gods and mythology, adopted by the Etruscans, also figure prominently. The sculpted figures on many of the covers may have been made in the image of the deceased, reclining and often holding the cup of life overturned. Particularly well known is Gli Sposi (Husband and Wife), a haunting, elderly duo in terra-cotta. The Ombra della Sera (Evening Shadow)—an enigmatic bronze statue of an elongated, pencil-thin male nude—highlights the collection. Also on display are Attic vases, bucchero ceramics, jewelry, and household items. ⊠ *Via Don Minzoni 15* 🕾 *0588/86347* 💶 *€14, includes the Pinacoteca and Teatro Romano* ⏱ *Mid-Mar.–Oct., daily 10:30–5:30; Nov.–mid-Mar., daily 10–4:30.*

Pinacoteca. One of Volterra's best-looking Renaissance buildings contains an impressive collection of Tuscan paintings arranged chronologically on two floors. Head straight for Room 12, with Luca Signorelli's (circa 1445–1523) *Madonna and Child with Saints* and Rosso Fiorentino's *Deposition.* Though painted just 30 years apart, they serve to illustrate the shift in style from the early-16th-century Renaissance ideals to full-blown Mannerism: the balance of Signorelli's composition becomes purposefully skewed in Fiorentino's painting, where the colors go from vivid but realistic to emotively bright. Other important paintings in the small museum include Ghirlandaio's *Apotheosis of Christ with Saints* and a polyptych of the *Madonna and Saints* by Taddeo di

Bartolo, which once hung in the Palazzo dei Priori. ✉ *Via dei Sarti 1* ☎ *0588/87580* 🎟 *€14, includes the Museo Etrusco Guarnacci and the Teatro Romano* 🕒 *Mid-Mar.–Oct., daily 10:30–5:30; Nov.–mid-Mar., daily 10–4:30.*

Porta all'Arco Etrusco. Even if a good portion of the arch was rebuilt by the Romans, three dark and weather-beaten 4th-century BC heads (thought to represent Etruscan gods) still face outward to greet those who enter here. A plaque on the outer wall recalls the efforts of the locals who saved the arch from destruction by filling it with stones during the German withdrawal at the end of World War II. ✉ *Via Porta all'Arco.*

Teatro Romano. Just outside the walls past Porta Fiorentina are the ruins of the 1st-century BC Roman theater, one of the best-preserved in Italy, with adjacent remains of the Roman *terme* (baths). You can enjoy an excellent bird's-eye view of the theater from Via Lungo le Mura. ✉ *Viale Francesco Ferrucci* 🎟 *€3.50; €14, includes the Museo Guarnacci and the Pinacoteca* 🕒 *Mid.-Mar.–Oct., daily 10:30–3:30; Nov.–mid-Mar., 10–4.*

WHERE TO EAT AND STAY

$ TUSCAN 🍴 **Da Badò.** This is the best place in town to eat traditional food elbow-to-elbow with the locals. Da Badò is family-run, with Lucia in the kitchen and her sons Giacomo and Michele waiting tables. Lucia likes to concentrate on just a few dishes, so it won't take long to decide between the standards, all prepared with a sure hand: *zuppa alla volterrana* (a soup made with vegetables and bread), *pappardelle alla lepre* (wide fettuccine with rabbit sauce), and a stew of either rabbit or wild boar. A slice of homemade almond tart is a must. [$] *Average main: €12* ✉ *Borgo San Lazzaro 9* ☎ *0588/86477* 🌐 *www.trattoriadabado.com* 🕒 *Closed Wed.*

$$ TUSCAN 🍴 **Il Sacco Fiorentino.** Start with the *antipasti del Sacco Fiorentino,* a medley of sautéed chicken liver, porcini mushrooms, and polenta drizzled with balsamic vinegar. The meal just gets better when you move on to the *tagliatelle del Sacco Fiorentino,* a riot of curried spaghetti with chicken and roasted red peppers. The wine list is a marvel, as it's long and very well priced. White walls, tile floors, and red tablecloths create an understated tone that is unremarkable, but once the food starts arriving, it's easy to forgive the lack of decoration. [$] *Average main: €16* ✉ *Piazza XX Settembre 18* ☎ *0588/88537* 🕒 *Closed Wed.*

$ B&B/INN 🏨 **Etruria.** The rooms are modest and there's no elevator, but the central location, the ample buffet breakfast, and the modest rates make this a good choice for those on a budget. **Pros:** great central location; friendly staff; tranquil garden with rooftop views. **Cons:** some rooms can be noisy during the day; no a/c. [$] *Rooms from: €99* ✉ *Via Matteotti 32* ☎ *0588/87377* 🌐 *www.albergoetruria.it* 🛏 *21 rooms* 🍽 *Breakfast.*

$ HOTEL 🏨 **San Lino.** Within the town's medieval walls, this convent-turned-hotel has wood-beam ceilings, graceful archways, and terra-cotta floors, with nice contemporary furnishings and ironwork in the rooms. **Pros:** steps away from center of town; friendly and helpful staff; convenient parking. **Cons:** rooms facing the street can be noisy; breakfast is adequate, but nothing to write home about. $ *Rooms from: €100* ✉ *Via San Lino 26* ☎ *0588/85250* ⊕ *www.hotelsanlino.com* ⇆ *43 rooms* ⊘ *Closed Nov. and Jan.–Feb.* ❑| *Breakfast.*

SAN GIMIGNANO

27 km (17 miles) east of Volterra, 54 km (34 miles) southwest of Florence.

Fodor'sChoice
★

When you're on a hilltop surrounded by soaring medieval towers silhouetted against the sky, it's difficult not to fall under the spell of San Gimignano. Its tall walls and narrow streets are typical of Tuscan hill towns, but it's the medieval "skyscrapers" that set the town apart from its neighbors. Today 14 towers remain, but at the height of the Guelph–Ghibelline conflict there was a forest of more than 70, and it was possible to cross the town by rooftop rather than by road. The towers were built partly for defensive purposes—they were a safe refuge and useful for pouring boiling oil on attacking enemies—and partly for bolstering the egos of their owners, who competed with deadly seriousness to build the highest tower in town.

Today San Gimignano isn't much more than a gentrified walled city, touristy but still very much worth exploring because, despite the profusion of cheesy souvenir shops lining the main drag, there's some serious Renaissance art to be seen here. Tour groups arrive early and clog the wine-tasting rooms—San Gimignano is famous for its light white vernaccia—and art galleries for much of the day, but most sights stay open through late afternoon, when all the tour groups have long since departed.

San Gimignano is particularly beautiful in the early morning. Take time to walk up to the *rocca* (castle), at the highest point of town. Here you can enjoy 360-degree views of the surrounding countryside. Apart from when it's used for summer outdoor film festivals, it's always open.

GETTING HERE AND AROUND

You can reach San Gimignano by car from the Florence–Siena Superstrada. Exit at Poggibonsi Nord and follow signs for San Gimignano. Although it involves changing buses in Poggibonsi, getting to San Gimignano by bus from Florence is a relatively straightforward affair. SITA operates the service between Siena or Florence and Poggibonsi. From Siena, Tra-In offers direct service to San Gimignano several times daily. You cannot reach San Gimignano by train.

VISITOR INFORMATION

San Gimignano Tourism Office ✉ *Piazza Duomo 1* ☎ *0577/940008* ⊕ *www.sangimignano.com.*

EXPLORING

Fodor'sChoice
★

Collegiata. The town's main church is not officially the Duomo per se, because San Gimignano has no bishop. But behind the simple facade of the Romanesque Collegiata lies a treasure trove of fine frescoes, covering nearly every part of the interior. Bartolo di Fredi's 14th-century fresco cycle of Old Testament scenes extends along one wall. Their distinctly medieval feel, with misshapen bodies, buckets of spurting blood, and lack of perspective, contrasts with the much more reserved scenes from the *Life of Christ* (attributed to 14th-century artist Lippo Memmi), painted on the opposite wall just 14 years later. Taddeo di Bartolo's otherworldly *Last Judgment* (late 14th century), with its distorted and suffering nudes, reveals the great influence of Dante's horrifying imagery in *The Inferno* and was surely an inspira-

tion for later painters. Proof that the town had more than one protector, Benozzo Gozzoli's arrow-riddled *St. Sebastian* was commissioned in gratitude after the locals prayed to the saint for relief from plague. The Renaissance **Cappella di Santa Fina** is decorated with a fresco cycle by Domenico Ghirlandaio illustrating the life of Saint Fina. A small girl who suffered from a terminal disease, Fina repented for her sins—among them having accepted an orange from a boy—and in penance lived out the rest of her short life on a wooden board, tormented by rats. The scenes depict the arrival of Saint Gregory, who appeared to assure her that death was near; the flowers that miraculously grew from the wooden plank; and the miracles that accompanied her funeral, including the healing of her nurse's paralyzed hand and the restoration of a blind choirboy's vision. ✉ *Piazza Pecori 1–2* ☎ *0577/940316* 💻 *€4; €6, includes the Museo d'Arte Sacra* ⏰ *Apr.–Oct., weekdays 10–7:30, Sat. 10–5:30, Sun. 12:30–7:30; Nov. 1–15, Dec. 1–Jan. 15, and Feb. and Mar., Mon.–Sat. 10–5, Sun. 12:30–5. Closed Nov. 16–30 and Jan. 16–31.*

Museo Civico. The impressive civic museum occupies what was the "new" Palazzo del Popolo; the Torre Grossa is adjacent. Dante visited San Gimignano for only one day as a Guelph ambassador from Florence to ask the locals to join the Florentines in supporting the pope—just long enough to get the main council chamber, which now holds a 14th-century *Maestà* by Lippo Memmi, named after him. Off the stairway is a small room containing the racy frescoes by Memmo di Filippuccio (active 1288–1324), depicting the courtship, shared bath, and wedding of a young, androgynous-looking couple. That the space could have been a private room for the commune's chief magistrate may have something to do with the work's highly charged eroticism.

Upstairs, paintings by famous Renaissance artists Pinturicchio (*Madonna Enthroned*), and Benozzo Gozzoli (*Madonna and Child*), and two large *tondi* (circular paintings) by Filippino Lippi (circa 1457–1504) attest to the importance and wealth of San Gimignano. Also worth seeing are Taddeo di Bartolo's *Life of San Gimignano*, with the saint holding a model of the town as it once appeared; Lorenzo di Niccolò's gruesome martyrdom scene in the *Life of St. Bartholomew* (1401); and scenes from the *Life of St. Fina* on a tabernacle that was designed to hold her head. Admission includes the steep climb to the top of the Torre Grossa, which on a clear day has spectacular views.

✉ *Piazza Duomo 2* ☎ *0577/990312* 🎫 *€6* ⏱ *Apr.–Sept., daily 9:30–7; Oct.–Mar., daily 11–5:30.*

Sant'Agostino. Make a beeline for Benozzo Gozzoli's superlative 15th-century fresco cycle depicting scenes from the life of Saint Augustine. The saint's work was essential to the early development of church doctrine. As thoroughly discussed in his autobiographical *Confessions* (an acute dialogue with God), Augustine, like many saints, sinned considerably in his youth before finding God. But unlike the lives of other saints, where the story continues through a litany of deprivations, penitence, and often martyrdom, Augustine's life and work focused on philosophy and the reconciliation of faith and thought. Benozzo's 17 scenes on the choir wall depict Augustine as a man who traveled and taught extensively in the 4th and 5th centuries. The 15th-century altarpiece by Piero del Pollaiolo (1443–96) depicts *The Coronation of the Virgin* and the various protectors of the city. On your way out of Sant'Agostino, stop in at the **Cappella di San Bartolo,** with a sumptuously elaborate tomb by Benedetto da Maiano (1442–97). ✉ *Piazza Sant'Agostino 10* ☎ *0577/907012* 🎫 *Free* ⏱ *Apr.–Oct., daily 10–noon and 3–7; Nov. and Dec., daily 10–noon and 3–6; Jan.–Mar., Mon. 4–7, Tues.–Sun. 10–noon and 3–6.*

WHERE TO EAT

$
TUSCAN
✕ **Enoteca Gustavo.** There's no shortage of places to try Vernaccia di San Gimignano, the justifiably famous white wine with which San Gimignano would be singularly associated—if it weren't for all those towers. At this wine bar, run by energetic Maristella Becucci, you can buy a glass of Vernaccia di San Gimignano and sit down with a cheese plate or with one of the fine crostini. 🍴 *Average main: €8* ✉ *Via San Matteo 29* ☎ *0577/940057.*

$$
ITALIAN
✕ **Osteria del Carcere.** Though it calls itself an *osteria* (a tavern), this place much more resembles a wine bar, with a bill of fare that includes several different types of pâtés and a short list of seasonal soups and salads. The sampler of goat cheeses, which can be paired with local wines, should not be missed. Operatic arias play softly in the background, and service is courteous. 🍴 *Average main: €15* ✉ *Via del Castello 13* ☎ *0577/941905* 🚫 *No credit cards* ⏱ *Closed Wed., and early Jan.–Mar. No lunch Thurs.*

WHERE TO STAY

$$$
HOTEL
🏨 **La Collegiata.** After serving as a Franciscan convent and then the residence of the noble Strozzi family, the Collegiata has been converted into a fine hotel, with no expense spared in the process. **Pros:** gorgeous views from terrace; elegant rooms in main building. **Cons:** long walk into town; service can be impersonal; some rooms are dimly lit. 🍴 *Rooms from: €210* ✉ *Località Strada 27, 1 km (½ mile) north of San Gimignano town center* ☎ *0577/943201* ⊕ *www.lacollegiata.it* 🛏 *20 rooms, 1 suite* ⏱ *Closed Nov.–Mar.* 🍴 *Breakfast.*

$
B&B/INN
🏨 **Pescille.** A rambling farmhouse has been transformed into a handsome hotel with understated contemporary furniture in the bedrooms and country-classic motifs such as farm implements hanging on the walls in the bar. **Pros:** splendid views; quiet atmosphere; 10-minute walk

to town. **Cons:** furnishings a bit austere; there's an elevator for luggage but not for guests. $ *Rooms from: €100* ⊠ *Località Pescille, 4 km (2½ mi) south of San Gimignano* ☎ *0577/940186* ⊕ *www.pescille.it* ⤳ *38 rooms, 12 suites* ⊘ *Closed Nov.–Mar.* ⦿◐ *Breakfast.*

$$ **⊞ Torraccia di Chiusi.** A perfect retreat for families, this tranquil hilltop
B&B/INN *agriturismo* (farm stay) offers simple, comfortably decorated accommodations on extensive grounds 5 km (3 miles) from the hubbub of San Gimignano. **Pros:** tranquil haven close to San Gimignano; great walking possibilities; family-run hospitality; delightful countryside views. **Cons:** 30 minutes from the nearest town on a windy gravel road; need a car to get here. $ *Rooms from: €140* ⊠ *Località Montauto* ☎ *0577/941972* ⊕ *www.torracciadichiusi.it* ⤳ *8 rooms, 3 apartments* ⦿◐ *Breakfast.*

COLLE DI VAL D'ELSA

15 km (9 miles) southeast of San Gimignano, 51 km (32 miles) south of Florence.

Most people pass through on their way to and from popular tourist destinations Volterra and San Gimignano—a shame, since Colle di Val d'Elsa has a lot to offer. It's another town on the Via Francigena that benefited from trade along the pilgrimage route to Rome. Colle got an extra boost in the late 16th century when it was given a bishopric, probably related to an increase in trade when nearby San Gimignano was cut off from the well-traveled road. The town is arranged on two levels, and from the 12th century onward the flat lower portion was given over to a flourishing papermaking industry; today the area is mostly modern, and efforts have shifted toward the production of fine glass and crystal.

GETTING HERE AND AROUND
You can reach Colle di Val d'Elsa by car on either the SR2 from Siena or the Florence–Siena Superstrada. Bus service to and from Siena and Florence is frequent.

VISITOR INFORMATION
Colle di Val d'Elsa Tourism Office ⊠ *Via del Castello 33/b* ☎ *0577/922791.*

EXPLORING
Make your way from the newer lower town (Colle Bassa) to the prettier, upper part of town (Colle Alta). The best views of the valley are to be had from Viale della Rimembranza, the road that loops around the western end of town, past the church of San Francesco. The early-16th-century Porta Nuova was inserted into the preexisting medieval walls, just as several handsome Renaissance palazzos were placed into the medieval neighborhood to create what is now called the Borgo. The Via Campana, the main road, passes through the facade of the surreal Palazzo Campana, an otherwise unfinished building that serves as a door connecting the two parts of the upper town. Via delle Volte, named for the vaulted arches that cover it, leads straight to Piazza del Duomo. There is a convenient parking lot off the SS68, with stairs leading up the hill. Buses arrive at Piazza Arnolfo, named after the town's favorite son, Arnolfo di Cambio (circa 1245–1302), the early-Renaissance architect who designed Florence's Duomo and Palazzo Vecchio (but sadly nothing here).

WHERE TO EAT AND STAY

$$$$ MODERN ITALIAN Fodor's Choice ★ 🍴 **Ristorante Arnolfo.** Food lovers should not miss Arnolfo, one of Tuscany's most highly regarded restaurants. Chef Gaetano Trovato sets high standards of creativity; his dishes daringly ride the line between innovation and tradition, almost always with spectacular results. The menu changes frequently but you are always sure to find fish and lots of fresh vegetables in the summer. You're in for a treat if the specials include *branzino, caviale di arringa, e zucca caramellata, in vino rosso* (sea bass cooked in red wine with herring caviar and caramelized pumpkin). [$] *Average main: €60* ✉ *Via XX Settembre 52* ☎ *0577/920549* 🌐 *www.arnolfo.com* ✍ *Reservations essential* ⏲ *Closed Tues. and Wed., last wks in Jan. and Feb., and last wk in Aug.*

$$ B&B/INN 🏨 **Palazzo San Lorenzo.** A 17th-century palace in the historic center of Colle boasts rooms that exude warmth and comfort, with light-color wooden floors, soothingly tinted fabrics, and large windows. **Pros:** central location; spotless; extremely well maintained. **Cons:** caters to business groups; some of the public spaces feel rather sterile. [$] *Rooms from: €125* ✉ *Via Gracco del Secco 113* ☎ *0577/923675* 🌐 *www.palazzosanlorenzo.it* 🛏 *43 rooms, 6 suites, 6 apartments* 🍽 *Breakfast.*

SIENA

With its narrow streets and steep alleys, a Gothic Duomo, a bounty of early Renaissance art, and the glorious Palazzo Pubblico overlooking its magnificent Campo, Siena is often described as Italy's best-preserved medieval city. It is also remarkably modern: many shops sell clothes by up-and-coming designers. Make a point of catching the passeggiata, when locals throng the Via di Città, Banchi di Sopra, and Banchi di Sotto, the city's three main streets.

Victory over Florence in 1260 at Montaperti marked the beginning of Siena's golden age. During the following decades Siena erected its greatest buildings (including the Duomo); established a model city government presided over by the Council of Nine; and became a great art, textile, and trade center. Siena succumbed to Florentine rule in the mid-16th century, when a yearlong siege virtually eliminated the native population. Ironically, it was precisely this decline that, along with Sienese pride, prevented further development, to which we owe the city's marvelous medieval condition today.

Although much looks as it did in the early 14th century, Siena is no museum. Walk through the streets and you can see that the medieval *contrade,* the 17 neighborhoods into which the city has been historically divided, are a vibrant part of modern life. You may see symbols of the contrade—Tartuca (turtle), Oca (goose), Istrice (porcupine), Torre (tower)—emblazoned on banners and engraved on building walls. The Sienese still strongly identify themselves with the contrada where they were born and raised; loyalty and rivalry run deep. At no time is this more visible than during the centuries-old Palio, a twice-yearly horse race held in the Piazza del Campo, but you need not visit then to come to know the rich culture of Siena, evident at every step.

GETTING HERE AND AROUND

From Florence, the quickest way to Siena is via the Florence–Siena Superstrada. Otherwise, take the Via Cassia (SR2), for a scenic route. Coming from Rome, leave the A1 at Valdichiana, and follow the Siena–Bettole Superstrada. SITA provides excellent bus service between Florence and Siena. Because buses are direct and speedy, they are preferable to the train, which sometimes involves a change in Empoli.

If you come by car, you're better off leaving it in one of the parking lots around the perimeter of town. Driving is difficult or impossible in most parts of the city center. Practically unchanged since medieval times, Siena is laid out in a "Y" over the slopes of several hills, dividing the city into *terzi* (thirds).

Tra-In. City buses run frequently within and around Siena, including the centro storico. Tickets cost €1.30 and must be bought in advance at tobacconists or newsstands. Routes are marked with signposts. ☎ *0577/204111* ⊕ *www.trainspa.it.*

TIMING

It's a joy to walk in Siena—hills notwithstanding—as it's a rare opportunity to stroll through a medieval city rather than just a town. (There is quite a lot to explore, in contrast to tiny hill towns that can be crossed in minutes.) The walk can be done in as little as a day, with minimal stops at the sights. But stay longer and take time to tour the churches and museums, and to enjoy the streetscapes themselves. Many of the sites have reduced hours Sunday afternoon and Monday.

VISITOR INFORMATION

Siena Tourism Office ⊠ *Piazza del Campo 56* ☎ *0577/280551* ⊕ *www.terresiena.it.*

EXPLORING

TOP ATTRACTIONS

Fodor'sChoice ★ **Cripta.** After it had lain unseen for possibly 700 years, a crypt was rediscovered under the grand *pavimento* (floor) of the Duomo during routine excavation work and was opened to the public in 2003. An unknown master executed the breathtaking frescoes here sometime between 1270 and 1280; they retain their original colors and pack an emotional punch even with sporadic damage. The *Deposition/Lamentation* gives strong evidence that the Sienese school could paint emotion just as well as the Florentine school—and did it some 20 years before Giotto. Guided tours in English take place more or less every half hour and are limited to no more than 35 persons. ⊠ *Scale di San Giovanni, to right of cathedral, Città* ☎ *0577/286300* ⊕ *www.operaduomo.siena.it* 🎫 *€6; €12 combined ticket, includes the Duomo, Battistero, and Museo dell'Opera Metropolitana* ☉ *Mar.–May, Sept., and Oct., daily 9:30–7; June–Aug., daily 9:30–8; Nov.–Feb., daily 10–5.*

Fodor'sChoice ★ **Duomo.** Siena's cathedral is beyond question one of the finest Gothic churches in Italy. The multicolor marbles and painted decoration are typical of the Italian approach to Gothic architecture—lighter and much less austere than the French. The amazingly detailed facade has few

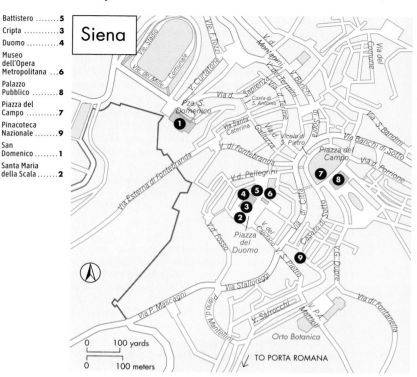

rivals in the region, although it's quite similar to the Duomo in Orvieto. It was completed in two brief phases at the end of the 13th and 14th centuries. The statues and decorative works were designed by Nicola Pisano and his son Giovanni, although most of what we see today are copies, the originals having been removed to the nearby Museo dell'Opera Metropolitana. The gold mosaics are 18th-century restorations. The Campanile (no entry) is among central Italy's finest, the number of windows increasing with each level, a beautiful and ingenious way of reducing the weight of the structure as it climbs to the heavens.

The Duomo's interior, with its black-and-white striping throughout and finely coffered and gilded dome, is simply striking. Step in and look back up at Duccio's (circa 1255–1319) panels of stained glass that fill the circular window. Finished in 1288, it's the oldest example of stained glass in Italy. The Duomo is most famous for its unique and magnificent inlaid-marble floors, which took almost 200 years to complete; more than 40 artists contributed to the work, made up of 56 separate compositions depicting biblical scenes, allegories, religious symbols, and civic emblems. The floors are covered for most of the year for conservation purposes, but are unveiled during September and October. The Duomo's carousel pulpit, also much appreciated, was carved by Nicola Pisano (circa 1220–84) around 1265; the *Life of Christ* is depicted on the rostrum frieze. In striking contrast to all the Gothic decoration in the nave are the magnificent Renaissance frescoes in the **Biblioteca Piccolomini,** off the left aisle. Painted by Pinturicchio (circa 1454–1513) and completed in 1509, they depict events from the life of native son Aeneas Sylvius Piccolomini (1405–64), who became Pope Pius II in 1458. The frescoes are in excellent condition, and have a freshness rarely seen in work so old.

The Duomo is grand, but the medieval Sienese people had even bigger plans. They wanted to enlarge the building by using the existing church as a transept for a new church, with a new nave running toward the southeast, to make what would be the largest church in the world. But only the side wall and part of the new facade were completed when the Black Death struck in 1348, decimating Siena's population. The city fell into decline, funds dried up, and the plans were never carried out. (The dream of building the biggest church was actually doomed to failure from the start—subsequent attempts to get the project going revealed that the foundation was insufficient to bear the weight of the proposed structure.) The beginnings of the new nave, extending from the right side of the Duomo, were left unfinished, perhaps as a testament to unfulfilled dreams, and ultimately enclosed to house the adjacent **Museo dell'Opera Metropolitana.** The **Cripta** was discovered during routine preservation work on the church and has been opened to the public. ✉ *Piazza del Duomo, Città* ☎ *0577/286300* 💶 *€4 Nov.–Aug.; €7 Sept. and Oct.; €12 combined ticket includes the Cripta, Battistero, and Museo dell'Opera Metropolitana* ⊗ *Mar.–May, Mon.–Sat. 10:30– 7:30, Sun. 1:30–5:30; June–Aug., Mon.–Sat. 10:30–8, Sun. 1:30–6:30; Sept. and Oct., daily 10:30–7:30, Nov.–Feb., Mon.–Sat. 10:30–6:30, Sun. 1:30–5:30.*

Palazzo Pubblico. *(See the highlighted listing in this chapter)* ✉ *Piazza del Campo 1, Città* ☎ *0577/292232* 💶 *Museum €9, tower €10* ⊗ *Museum: Nov.–mid-Mar., daily 10–6; mid-Mar.–Oct., daily 10–7; ticket sales end ½ hr before closing. Tower: Nov.–mid-Mar., daily 10–4; mid-Mar.–Oct., daily 10–7; ticket sales end 45 mins before closing.*

Fodor's Choice ★ **Piazza del Campo.** If you are in town for the Palio horse race, held every July 2 and August 16, contact the tourist office to find out about ticket availability, or ask your hotel if it can procure you a seat. Reserved seating in the stands is sold out months in advance of the races. The entire area in the center is free and unreserved, but you need to show up early in order to get a prime spot against the barriers. ✉ *Città.*

WORTH NOTING

Battistero. The Duomo's 14th-century Gothic Baptistery was built to prop up the apse of the cathedral. There are frescoes throughout, but the highlight is a large bronze 15th-century baptismal font designed by Jacopo della Quercia (1374–1438). It's adorned with bas-reliefs by various artists, including two by Renaissance masters: the *Baptism of Christ* by Lorenzo Ghiberti (1378–1455) and the *Feast of Herod* by Donatello. ✉ *Piazza San Giovanni, Città* ☎ *0577/286300* ⊕ *www.operaduomo. siena.it* 💶 *€4; €12 combination ticket, includes the Cripta, Duomo, and Museo dell'Opera del Duomo* ⊗ *Mar.–May, Mon.–Sat. 10:30–7:30,*

Continued on page 664

Climbing the 400 narrow steps of the **Torre del Mangia** rewards you with unparalleled views of Siena's rooftops and the countryside beyond.

The **Palazzo Pubblico,** Siena's town hall since the 14th century.

Something about the fan-shaped, sloping design of **Il Campo** encourages people to s and relax (except durin the Palio, when they stand and scream). The communal atmosphere here is unlike that of a other Italian piazza.

PIAZZA DEL CAMPO

Fodor's Choice ★

The fan-shaped **Piazza del Campo,** known simply as il Campo (The Field), is one of the finest squares in Italy. Constructed toward the end of the 12th century on a market area unclaimed by any contrada, it's still the heart of town. The bricks of the Campo are patterned in nine different sections—representing each member of the medieval Government of Nine. At the top of the Campo is a copy of the **Fonte Gaia,** decorated in the early 15th century by Siena's greatest sculptor, Jacopo della Quercia, with 13 sculpted reliefs of biblical events and virtues. Those lining the rectangular fountain are 19th-century copies; the originals are in the Spedale di Santa Maria della Scala. On Palio horse race days (July 2 and August 16), the Campo and all its surrounding buildings are packed with cheering, frenzied locals and tourists craning their necks to take it all in.

The Gothic **Palazzo Pubblico,** the focal point of the Piazza del Campo, has served as Siena's town hall since the 1300s. It now also contains the **Museo Civico,** with walls covered in early Renaissance frescoes. The nine governors of Siena once met in the Sala della Pace, famous for Ambrogio Lorenzetti's frescoes called *Allegories of Good and Bad Government,* painted in the late 1330s to demonstrate the dangers of tyranny. The good government side depicts utopia, showing first the virtuous ruling council surrounded by angels and then scenes of a perfectly running city and countryside. Conversely, the bad government fresco tells a tale straight out of Dante. The evil ruler and his advisers have horns and fondle strange animals, and the town scene depicts the seven mortal sins in action. Interestingly, the bad government fresco is severely damaged, and the good government fresco is in terrific condition. The **Torre del Mangia,** the palazzo's famous bell tower, is named after one of its first bell ringers, Giovanni di Duccio (called Mangiaguadagni, or earnings eater). The climb up to the top is long and steep, but the view makes it worth every step. *For opening hours and prices, see the Exploring section.*

THE PALIO

The three laps around a makeshift racetrack in Piazza del Campo are over in less than two minutes, but the spirit of Siena's Palio— a horse race held every July 2 and August 16—lives all year long.

The Palio is contested between Siena's contrade, the 17 neighborhoods that have divided the city since the Middle Ages. Loyalties are fiercely felt. At any time of year you'll see on the streets contrada symbols—Tartuca (turtle), Oca (goose), Istrice (porcupine), Torre (tower)—emblazoned on banners and engraved on building walls. At Palio time, simmering rivalries come to a boil.

It's been that way since at least August 16, 1310, the date of the first recorded running of the Palio. At that time, and for centuries to follow, the race went through the streets of the city. The additional July 2 running was instituted in 1649; soon thereafter the location was moved to the Campo and the current system for selecting the race entrants established. Ten of the contrade are chosen at random to run in the July Palio. The August race is then contested between the 7 contrade left out in July, plus 3 of the 10 July participants, again chosen at random. Although the races are in theory of equal importance, Sienese will tell you that it's better to win the second and have bragging rights for the rest of the year.

The race itself has a raw and arbitrary character—it's no Kentucky Derby. There's barely room for the 10 horses on the makeshift Campo course, so falls and collisions are inevitable. Horses are chosen at random three days before the race, and jockeys (who ride bareback) are mercenaries hired from surrounding towns. Almost no tactic is considered too underhanded. Bribery, secret plots, and betrayal are commonplace—so much so that the word for "jockey," *fantino*, has come to mean "untrustworthy" in Siena. There have been incidents of drugging (the horses) and kidnapping (the jockeys); only sabotaging a horse's reins remains taboo.

Above: The tension of the starting line. Top left: The frenzy of the race. Bottom left: A solemn flag bearer follows in the footsteps of his ancestors.

AQUILA	BRUCO	CHIOCCIOLA

MEDIEVAL CONTRADE

Festivities kick off three days prior to the Palio, with the selection and blessing of the horses, trial runs, ceremonial banquets, betting, and late-night celebrations. Residents don their contrada's colors and march through the streets in medieval costumes. The Campo is transformed into a racetrack lined with a thick layer of sand. On race day, each horse is brought to the church of the contrada for which it will run, where it's blessed and told, "Go little horse and return a winner." The Campo fills through the afternoon, with spectators crowding into every available space until bells ring and the piazza is sealed off. Processions of flag wavers in traditional dress march to the beat of tambourines and drums and the roar of the crowds. The *palio* itself—a banner for which the race is named, dedicated to the Virgin Mary—makes an appearance, followed by the horses and their jockeys.

The race begins when one horse, chosen to ride up from behind the rest of the field, crosses the starting line. There are always false starts, adding to the frenzied mood. Once underway, the race is over in a matter of minutes. The victorious rider is carried off through the streets of the winning contrada (where in the past tradition dictated he was entitled to the local girl of his choice), while winning and losing sides use television replay to analyze the race from every possible angle. The winning contrada will celebrate into the night, at long tables piled high with food and drink. The champion horse is guest of honor.

CIVETTA	DRAGO
GIRAFFA	ISTRICE
LEOCORNO	LUPA
NICCHIO	OCA
ONDA	PANTERA
SELVA	TARTUCA
TORRE	VALDIMONTONE

Sun. 1:30–5:30; June–Aug., Mon.–Sat. 10:30–8, Sun. 1:30–6:30; Sept. and Oct., daily 10:30–7:30; Nov.–Feb., Mon.–Sat. 10:30–6:30, Sun. 1:30–5:30.

WORD OF MOUTH

"The one thing I'd do in Siena—short of attending the Palio—is stay overnight. All the tourists leave and it's very dark and medieval. It feels like you've time-traveled back 500 years." —Mimar

Fodor's Choice ★ **Museo dell'Opera Metropolitana.** Part of the unfinished nave of what was to have been a new cathedral, the museum contains the Duomo's treasury and some of the original decoration from its facade and interior. The first room on the ground floor displays weather-beaten 13th-century sculptures by Giovanni Pisano (circa 1245–1318) that were brought inside for protection and replaced by copies, as was a tondo of the *Madonna and Child* (now attributed to Donatello) that once hung on the door to the south transept. The masterpiece is unquestionably Duccio's *Maestà,* one side with 26 panels depicting episodes from the Passion, the other side with a *Madonna and Child Enthroned.* Painted between 1308 and 1311 as the altarpiece for the Duomo (where it remained until 1505), its realistic elements, such as the lively depiction of the Christ child and the treatment of interior space, proved an enormous influence on later painters. The second floor is divided between the **treasury,** with a crucifix by Giovanni Pisano and several statues and busts of biblical characters and classical philosophers, and **La Sala della Madonna degli Occhi Grossi** (the Room of the Madonna with the Big Eyes), named after the namesake painting it displays by the Maestro di Tressa, who painted in the early 13th century. The work originally decorated the Duomo's high altar, before being displaced by Duccio's *Maestà.* There is a fine view from the tower inside the museum. ✉ *Piazza del Duomo 8, Città* ☎ *0577/286300* 🌐 *www.operaduomo.siena.it* 🎫 *€7; €12 combination ticket, includes the Cripta, Duomo, and Battistero* ⏲ *Mar.–May, Mon.–Sat. 10:30–7:30, Sun. 1:30–5:30; June–Aug., Mon.–Sat. 10:30–8, Sun. 1:30–6:30; Sept. and Oct., daily 10:30–7:30; Nov.–Feb., Mon.–Sat. 10:30–6:30, Sun. 1:30–5:30.*

Pinacoteca Nazionale. The superb collection of five centuries of local painting in Siena's national picture gallery can easily convince you that the Renaissance was by no means just a Florentine thing—Siena was arguably just as important a center of art and innovation as its rival to the north, especially in the mid-13th century. Accordingly, the most interesting section of the collection, chronologically arranged, has several important "firsts." Room 1 contains a painting of the *Stories of the True Cross* (1215) by the so-called Master of Tressa, the earliest identified work by a painter of the Sienese school, and is followed in Room 2 by late-13th-century artist Guido da Siena's *Stories from the Life of Christ,* one of the first paintings ever made on canvas (earlier painters used wood panels). Rooms 3 and 4 are dedicated to Duccio, a student of Cimabue (circa 1240–1302) and considered to be the last of the proto-Renaissance painters. Ambrogio Lorenzetti's landscapes in Room 8 are the first truly secular paintings in Western art. Among later works in the rooms on the floor above, keep an eye out for the preparatory sketches used by Domenico Beccafumi (1486–1551) for the 35 etched marble panels he made for the floor of the Duomo. ⊠ *Via San Pietro 29, Città* ☎ *0577/286143* ⊕ *www.pinacotecanazionale.siena. it* ⌨ *€4* ⊘ *Tues.–Sat. 8:15–7:15, Sun. and Mon. 9–1; last entrance ½ hr before closing.*

San Domenico. Although the Duomo is celebrated as a triumph of 13th-century Gothic architecture, this church, built at about the same time, turned out to be an oversize, hulking brick box that never merited a finishing coat in marble, let alone a graceful facade. Named for the founder of the Dominican order, the church is now more closely associated with Saint Catherine of Siena. Just to the right of the entrance is the chapel in which she received the stigmata. On the wall is the only known contemporary portrait of the saint, made in the late 14th century by Andrea Vanni (circa 1332–1414). Farther down is the famous **Cappella di Santa Caterina,** the church's official shrine. Catherine, or bits and pieces of her, was literally spread all over the country—a foot is in Venice, most of her body is in Rome, and only her head (kept in a reliquary on the chapel's altar) and her right thumb are here. She was revered throughout the country long before she was officially named a patron saint of Italy in 1939. On either side of the chapel are well-known frescoes by Sodoma (aka Giovanni Antonio Bazzi, 1477–1549) of *St. Catherine in Ecstasy.* Don't miss the view of the Duomo and town center from the apse-side terrace. ⊠ *Piazza San Domenico, Camollìa* ☎ *0577/280893* ⊕ *www.basilicacateriniana.com* ⊘ *Mar.–Oct., daily 7–6:30; Nov.–Feb., daily 9–6.*

Fodor'sChoice
★
Santa Maria della Scala. For more than 1,000 years, this complex across from the Duomo was home to Siena's hospital, but now it serves as a museum to display some terrific frescoes and other Sienese Renaissance treasures. Restored 15th-century frescoes in the Sala del Pellegrinaio (once the emergency room) tell the history of the hospital, which was created to give refuge to passing pilgrims and to those in need, and to distribute charity to the poor. Incorporated into the complex is the church of the Santissima Annunziata, with a celebrated *Risen Christ* by Vecchietta (aka Lorenzo di Pietro, circa 1412–80). Down in the dark Cappella di Santa Caterina della Notte is where Saint Catherine went to pray at night. The subterranean archaeological museum contained within the *ospedale* (hospital) is worth seeing even if you're not particularly taken with Etruscan objects: the interior design is sheer brilliance—it's beautifully lighted, eerily quiet, and an oasis of cool on hot summer days. The displays—including the *bucchero* (dark, reddish clay) ceramics, Roman coins, and tomb furnishings—are clearly marked and can serve as a good introduction to the history of regional excavations. Don't miss della Quercia's original sculpted reliefs from the Fonte Gaia. Although the fountain has been faithfully copied for the Campo, there's something incomparably beautiful about the real thing. ⊠ *Piazza del Duomo 1, Città* ☎ *0577/534511* ⊕ *www.santamariadellascala.com* ⌨ *€6* ⊘ *Mid-Mar.–mid-Oct., daily 10:30–6:30; mid-Oct.–mid-Mar., Thurs.–Mon. 10:30–4; ticket office closes 1 hr before closing.*

WHERE TO EAT

$$$
TUSCAN
Fodor's Choice
★

X **Le Logge.** Bright flowers provide a dash of color at this classic Tuscan dining room, and stenciled designs on the ceilings add some whimsy. The wooden cupboards (now filled with wine bottles) lining the walls recall its past as a turn-of-the-19th-century grocery store. The menu, with four or five primi and secondi, changes regularly, but almost always includes their classic *malfatti all'osteria* (ricotta and spinach dumplings in a cream sauce). Desserts such as *coni con mousse al cioccolato e gelato allo zafferano* (two diminutive ice-cream cones with chocolate mousse and saffron ice cream) provide an inventive ending to the meal. When not vying for one of the outdoor tables, make sure to ask for one in the main downstairs room. $ *Average main: €25* ⊠ *Via del Porrione 33, San Martino* ☎ *0577/48013* ⊕ *www.osterialelogge.it* ⌂ *Reservations essential* ⊘ *Closed Sun., and 3 wks in Jan.*

$
TUSCAN

X **Osteria Il Grattacielo.** Wiped out from too much sightseeing? Consider a meal at this hole-in-the-wall restaurant where locals congregate for a simple lunch over a glass of wine. There's a collection of verdure sott'olio, a wide selection of affettati misti, and various types of frittatas. All of this can be washed down with the cheap, yet eminently drinkable, house red. A couple of bench tables provide outdoor seating in summer. Don't be put off by the absence of a written menu. All the food is displayed at the counter, so you can point if you need to. $ *Average main: €10* ⊠ *Via Pontani 8, Camollia* ☎ *0577/289326* ⌂ *Reservations not accepted* ▭ *No credit cards* ⊘ *Closed Sun.*

$
TUSCAN

X **Trattoria Papei.** The menu hasn't changed for years, and why should it? The pici *al cardinale* (with a duck and bacon sauce) is wonderful, and all the other typically Sienese dishes are equally delicious. Grilled meats are the true speciality; the *bistecca di vitello* (grilled veal steak) is melt-in-your-mouth wonderful. Tucked away behind the Palazzo Pubblico in a square that serves as a parking lot for most of the day, the restaurant's location isn't great, but the food is. Thanks to portable heaters, there is outdoor seating all year-round. $ *Average main: €14* ⊠ *Piazza del Mercato 6, Città* ☎ *0577/280894* ⊘ *Closed Mon.*

WHERE TO STAY

$
B&B/INN

⌂ **Antica Torre.** The cordial Landolfo family has carefully evoked a private home with their eight guest rooms inside a restored 16th-century tower. **Pros:** near the town center; charming atmosphere. **Cons:** narrow stairway up to the rooms; low ceilings; cramped bathrooms. $ *Rooms from: €100* ⊠ *Via Fieravecchia 7, San Martino* ☎ *0577/222255* ⊕ *www.anticatorresiena.it* ⤴ *8 rooms* ⦿ *Breakfast.*

$$
B&B/INN

⌂ **Hotel Santa Caterina.** Manager Lorenza Capannelli and her fine staff are welcoming, hospitable, enthusiastic, and go out of their way to ensure a fine stay in rooms where dark, straight-lined wood furniture stands next to beds with floral spreads. **Pros:** friendly staff; a short walk to center of town; breakfast in the garden. **Cons:** on a busy intersection; outside city walls. $ *Rooms from: €160* ⊠ *Via Piccolomini 7, San Martino* ☎ *0577/221105* ⊕ *www.hscsiena.it* ⤴ *22 rooms* ⦿ *Breakfast.*

$$ B&B/INN **Palazzo Fani Mignanelli.** You'll find all the trimmings of an old-style town palace in this quiet haven where rooms with a view over the rooftops of Siena are decorated with period antiques. **Pros:** peaceful retreat; excellent location for exploring town. **Cons:** on the third floor of an otherwise run-down building; some stairs; basic breakfast. [$] *Rooms from: €150* ✉ *Banchi di Sopra 15, Città* ☎ *0577/283566* 🌐 *www.residenzadepoca.it* 🛏 *11 rooms* 🍴 *Breakfast.*

$$ HOTEL Fodor's Choice ★ **Palazzo Ravizza.** This romantic palazzo exudes a sense of genteel shabbiness, and lovely guest rooms have high ceilings, antique furnishings, and bathrooms decorated with hand-painted tiles. **Pros:** 10-minute walk to the center of town; pleasant garden with a view beyond the city walls; professional staff. **Cons:** not all rooms have views; some rooms are a little cramped. [$] *Rooms from: €180* ✉ *Pian dei Mantellini 34, Città* ☎ *0577/280462* 🌐 *www.palazzoravizza.it* 🛏 *38 rooms, 4 suites* 🍴 *Breakfast.*

SHOPPING

Enoteca Italiana. Italy's only state-sponsored enoteca has a vast selection of wines from all parts of the country. Housed in the fortress that the Florentines built to dominate Siena after they conquered the town in 1555, it's a must for any lover of Italian wines. ✉ *Fortezza Medicea 1, Camollìa* ☎ *0577/228832* ⏲ *Mon.–Sat., noon–1 am.*

AREZZO AND CORTONA

The hill towns of Arezzo and Cortona are the main attractions of eastern Tuscany; despite their appeal, this part of the region gets less tourist traffic than its neighbors to the west. You'll truly escape the crowds if you venture north to the Casentino, which is backwoods Tuscany—tiny towns and abbeys are sprinkled through beautiful forestland, some of which is set aside as a national park.

AREZZO

63 km (39 miles) northeast of Siena, 81 km (50 miles) southeast of Florence.

Arezzo is best known for the magnificent Piero della Francesca frescoes in the church of San Francesco. It's also the birthplace of the poet Petrarch (1304–74), the Renaissance artist and art historian Giorgio Vasari, and Guido d'Arezzo (aka Guido Monaco), the inventor of contemporary musical notation. Arezzo dates from pre-Etruscan times, when around 1000 BC the first settlers erected a cluster of huts. Arezzo thrived as an Etruscan capital from the 7th to the 4th century BC, and was one of the most important cities in the Etruscans' anti-Roman 12-city federation, resisting Rome's rule to the last.

The city eventually fell and in turn flourished under the Romans. In 1248 Guglielmino degli Ubertini, a member of the powerful Ghibelline family, was elected bishop of Arezzo. This sent the city headlong into the enduring conflict between the Ghibellines (pro-emperor) and the

Guelphs (pro-pope). In 1289 Florentine Guelphs defeated Arezzo in a famous battle at Campaldino. Among the Florentine soldiers was Dante Alighieri (1265–1321), who often referred to Arezzo in his *Divine Comedy*. Guelph–Ghibelline wars continued to plague Arezzo until the end of the 14th century, when Arezzo lost its independence to Florence.

GETTING HERE AND AROUND

Arezzo is easily reached by car from the A1 autostrada, the main highway running between Florence and Rome. Direct trains connect Arezzo with Rome (2½ hours) and Florence (1 hour). Direct bus service is available from Florence, but not from Rome.

VISITOR INFORMATION

Arezzo Tourism Office ⊠ *Giovanni Paolo II* ☎ *0575/1822770* ⊕ *www.arezzoturismo.it.*

EXPLORING

Fodor's Choice ★ **Basilica di San Francesco.** The famous Piero della Francesca frescoes depicting the *Legend of the True Cross* (1452–66) were executed on the three walls of the Capella Bacci, the main apse of this 14th-century church. What Sir Kenneth Clark called "the most perfect morning light in all Renaissance painting" may be seen in the lowest section of the right wall, where the troops of Emperor Maxentius flee before the sign of the cross. The rest of the church is decorated with 14th-, 15th- and 16th-century frescoes of mixed quality. Reservations are recommended June through September. ⊠ *Piazza San Francesco 2* ☎ *0575/352727* ⊕ *www.pierodellafrancesca.it* ☜ *€8* ☉ *Weekdays 9–6:30, Sat. 9–5:30, Sun. 1–5:30.*

Duomo. Arezzo's medieval cathedral at the top of the hill contains an eye-level fresco of a tender *Maria Maddalena* by Piero della Francesca (1420–92); look for it in the north aisle next to the large marble tomb near the organ. Construction of the Duomo began in 1278, but twice came to a halt, and the church wasn't completed until 1510. The ceiling decorations and the stained-glass windows date to the 16th century. The facade, designed by Arezzo's Dante Viviani, was added later (1901–14). ⊠ *Piazza del Duomo 1* ☎ *0575/23991* ☉ *Daily 7–12:30 and 3–6:30.*

NEED A BREAK?

Caffè dei Costanti. Outdoor seating on Arezzo's main pedestrian square and a tasty range of chef's salads (named after the waitresses that serve here) make this a very pleasant spot for a light lunch during a tour of town. In continuous operation since 1886, it's the oldest café in Arezzo, and the charming old-world interior served as backdrop to scenes in Roberto Benigni's 1997 film, *Life is Beautiful.* If you're here in the early evening, Caffè dei Costanti serves up an ample buffet of snacks to accompany your

predinner aperitivo. ✉ *Piazza San Francesco 19* ☎ *0575/1824075* 🌐 *www.caffedeicostanti.it.*

Piazza Grande. With its irregular shape and sloping brick pavement, framed by buildings of assorted centuries, Arezzo's central piazza echoes Siena's Piazza del Campo. Though not quite so magnificent, it's lively enough during the outdoor antiques fair the first weekend of the month and when the **Giostra del Saracino** (Saracen Joust), featuring medieval costumes and competition, is held here on the third Saturday of June and on the first Sunday of September.

Fodor's Choice ★ **Santa Maria della Pieve** (*Church of Saint Mary of the Parish*). The curving, tiered apse on Piazza Grande belongs to a fine Romanesque church that was originally an Early-Christian structure, which had been constructed over the remains of a Roman temple. The church was rebuilt in Romanesque style in the 12th century. The splendid facade dates from the early 13th century, but includes granite Roman columns. A magnificent polyptych, depicting the Madonna and child with four saints, by Pietro Lorenzetti (circa 1290–1348), embellishes the high altar. ✉ *Corso Italia 7* ☎ *0575/22629* ⏲ *May–Sept., daily 8–7; Oct.–Apr., daily 8–noon and 3–6.*

WHERE TO EAT AND STAY

$$ SEAFOOD 🍴 **I Tre Bicchieri.** Chef Luigi Casotti hails from Amalfi and this shows through in his fine adaptations of dishes more commonly served near the Bay of Naples. The *raviolone farcito con gamberi rossi di Sicilia e tonno* (a large raviolo stuffed with Sicilian prawns and tuna served with a sauce of tomatoes, capers, and olives) and the *filetto di branzino in panuria di erbe* (breaded fillet of sea bass) are particularly delicious. [$] *Average main: €15* ✉ *Piazzetta Sopra i Ponti 3–5* ☎ *0575/26557* 🌐 *www.ristoranteitrebicchieri.com.*

$ ITALIAN 🍴 **La Torre di Gnicche.** Wine lovers shouldn't miss this wine bar–eatery, just off Piazza Grande, with more than 700 labels on the list. Seasonal dishes of traditional fare, such as *acquacotta del casentino* (porcini mushroom soup) and *baccalà in umido* (salt-cod stew), are served in the simply decorated, vaulted dining room. You can accompany your meal with one, or more, of the almost 30 wines that are available by the glass. Limited outdoor seating is available in warm weather. [$] *Average main: €14* ✉ *Piaggia San Martino 8* ☎ *0575/352035* 🌐 *www.latorredignicche.it* ⏲ *Closed Wed., Jan., and 2 wks in July.*

$$ HOTEL 🏨 **Castello di Gargonza.** Enchantment reigns at this tiny 13th-century countryside hamlet, part of the fiefdom of the aristocratic Florentine Guicciardini and reinvented by the modern Count Roberto Guicciardini as an agriturismo. **Pros:** romantic, one-of-a-kind accommodation in a medieval castle; peaceful, isolated setting. **Cons:** standard rooms are extremely basic; a little out of the way for exploring the region; private transportation is a necessity. [$] *Rooms from: €160* ✉ *Località Gargonza, Monte San Savino, off SR73, 28 km (17 miles) southwest of Arezzo* ☎ *0575/847021* 🌐 *www.gargonza.it* 🛏 *37 rooms, 8 apartments* ⏲ *Closed last 3 wks in Jan. and Feb.* 🍴 *Breakfast.*

$$$$ HOTEL Fodor's Choice ★ 🏨 **Il Borro.** The location has been described as "heaven on earth," and a stay at Salvatore Ferragamo's estate is sure to bring similar descriptions

Arezzo, Cortona, and Southern Tuscany

to mind. **Pros:** superlative service; great location for exploring eastern Tuscany; unique setting and atmosphere. **Cons:** off the beaten track, making private transport a must; not all suites have country views; ultramodern spa facility seems out of place. $ *Rooms from: €320* ⌂ *Località Il Borro, outside village of San Giustino Valdarno, 20 km (12 miles) northwest of Arezzo* ☎ *055/977053* ⊕ *www.ilborro.com* ⇄ *16 suites, 3 villas, 7 farmhouses, 4 apartments* ⦶ *Breakfast.*

SHOPPING

Ever since Etruscan goldsmiths set up their shops here more than 2,000 years ago, Arezzo has been famous for its jewelry. Today the town lays claim to being one of the world's capitals of jewelry design and manufacture, and you can find an impressive display of big-time baubles in the town center's shops.

Arezzo is also famous, at least in Italy, for its antiques dealers. The first weekend of every month, between 8:30 and 5:30, a popular and colorful flea market selling antiques and not-so-antique items takes place in the town's main square, **Piazza Grande,** and in the streets and parks nearby.

CORTONA

29 km (18 miles) south of Arezzo, 79 km (44 miles) east of Siena, 117 km (73 miles) southeast of Florence.

Brought into the limelight by Frances Mayes's book *Under the Tuscan Sun* and a subsequent movie, Cortona is no longer the destination of just a few specialist art historians and those seeking reprieve from busier tourist venues. The main street, Via Nazionale, is now lined with souvenir shops and fills with crowds during summer. Though the main sights of Cortona make braving the bustling center worthwhile, much of the town's charm lies in its maze of quiet backstreets. It's here that you will see laundry hanging from windows, find children playing, and catch the smell of simmering pasta sauce. Wander off the beaten track and you won't be disappointed.

GETTING HERE AND AROUND

Cortona is easily reached by car from the A1 autostrada: take the Valdichiana exit toward Perugia, then follow signs for Cortona. Regular bus service, provided by Etruria Mobilità, is available between Arezzo and Cortona (one hour). Train service to Cortona is made inconvenient by the location of the train station, in the valley 3 km (2 miles) steeply below the town itself. From there, you have to rely on bus or taxi service to get up to Cortona.

VISITOR INFORMATION

Cortona Tourism Office ⌂ *Piazza Signorelli 9* ☎ *0575/637223* ⊕ *arezzo. intoscana.it.*

EXPLORING

Museo Diocesano. Housed in part of the original cathedral structure, this nine-room museum houses an impressive number of large, splendid paintings by native son Luca Signorelli (1445–1523), as well as a beautiful *Annunciation* by Fra Angelico (1387/1400–55), which is a delightful surprise in this small town. The former oratory of the Compagnia del

Gesù, reached by descending the 1633 staircase opposite the Duomo, is part of the museum. The church was built between 1498 and 1505 and restructured by Giorgio Vasari in 1543. Frescoes depicting sacrifices from the Old Testament by Doceno (1508–56), based on designs by Vasari, line the walls. ⊠ *Piazza Duomo 1* ☎ *0575/62830* ⌸ *€5* ⊗ *Apr.–Oct., daily 10–7; Nov.–Mar., Tues.–Sun. 10–5.*

Santa Maria al Calcinaio. Legend has it that the image of the Madonna appeared on a wall of a medieval *calcinaio* (lime pit used for curing leather), the site on which the church was then built between 1485 and 1513. The linear gray-and-white interior recalls Florence's Duomo. Sienese architect Francesco di Giorgio (1439–1502) most likely designed the sanctuary: the church is a terrific example of Renaissance architectural principles. ⊠ *Località Il Calcinaio 227, 3 km (2 miles) southeast of Cortona's center* ☎ *0575/604830* ⊗ *Mon.–Sat. 3:30–6, Sun. 10 am–12:30.*

WHERE TO EAT AND STAY

$$ ✕ **Osteria del Teatro.** Photographs from theatrical productions spanning
TUSCAN many years line the walls of this tavern off Cortona's large Piazza del Teatro. The food is simply delicious—try the *filetto al lardo di colonnata e prugne* (beef cooked with bacon and prunes). Service is warm and friendly. Ⓢ *Average main: €18* ⊠ *Via Maffei 2* ☎ *0575/630556* ⊕ *www.osteria-del-teatro.it* ⊗ *Closed Wed., and 2 wks in Nov. and in Feb.*

$ ⌂ **Hotel San Michele.** Cortona might tempt you to step back in time and
HOTEL stay there awhile, and the spacious, beamed, richly furnished rooms in a 15th-century palazzo in the center of town provide the perfect hideaway. **Pros:** lovely surroundings in perfect hill-town location; character-filled rooms; excellent service, including valet parking. **Cons:** limited views from some rooms; some street noise. Ⓢ *Rooms from: €120* ⊠ *Via Guelfa 15* ☎ *0575/604348* ⊕ *www.hotelsanmichele.net* ⇱ *42 rooms* ⦿| *Breakfast.*

$$$ ⌂ **Il Falconiere.** Accommodation options here include rooms in an 18th-
B&B/INN century villa, suites in the *chiesetta* (chapel, or little church), or for more seclusion, Le Vigne del Falco suites at the far end of the property. **Pros:** attractive setting in the valley beneath Cortona; excellent service; elegant but relaxed. **Cons:** a car is a must; some find rooms in main villa a little noisy; a bit fancy for the environs. Ⓢ *Rooms from: €300* ⊠ *Località San Martino 370, 3 km (1½ mile) north of Cortona* ☎ *0575/612679* ⊕ *www.ilfalconiere.com* ⇱ *13 rooms, 7 suites* ⊗ *Hotel closed last 3 wks in Jan.–mid-Feb.* ⦿| *Breakfast.*

SOUTHERN TUSCANY

Southeast of Siena, not far from the Umbrian border, the towns of Montepulciano, Montalcino, and Pienza are Tuscan classics—perched on hills, constructed during the Middle Ages and the Renaissance, and saturated with fine wine. Venture farther south and you encounter Tuscany with a rougher edge: the Maremma region is populated by cowboys, and a good portion of the landscape remains wild. But you won't forget you're in Italy here; the wine is still excellent, and some locals store their supply in Etruscan tombs.

WINE ON THE WEB

A good place for an overview of Tuscan wine country is ⊕ *www. terreditoscana.regione.toscana.it.* (Click on "Le Strade del Vino"; the page that opens next will give you the option of choosing an English-language version.) This site shows 14 *strade del vino* (wine roads) that have been mapped out by consortiums representing major wine districts (unfortunately, Chianti Classico isn't included), along with recommended itineraries. You'll also find links to the consortium Web sites, where you can dig up more detailed information on touring. The Vino Nobli di Montepulciano site is ⊕ *www.consorziovinonobile.it,* the Chianti Classico consortium's site is ⊕ *www.chianticlassico.com,* and Brunello di Montalcino is ⊕ *www. consorziobrunellodimontalcino.it.* (All have English versions.)

MONTEPULCIANO

65 km (40 miles) southeast of Siena.

Perched on a hilltop, Montepulciano is made up of a pyramid of red-brick buildings set within a circle of cypress trees. At an altitude of almost 2,000 feet, it is cool in summer and chilled in winter by biting winds sweeping down its spiraling streets. The town has an unusually harmonious look, the result of the work of three architects: Antonio da Sangallo "il Vecchio" (circa 1455–1534), Vignola (1507–73), and Michelozzo (1396–1472). The group endowed it with fine palaces and churches in an attempt to impose Renaissance architectural ideals on an ancient Tuscan hill town.

GETTING HERE

From Rome or Florence, take the Chiusi–Chianciano exit from the A1 (Autostrada del Sole). From Siena, take the SR2 south to San Quirico and then the SP146 to Montepulciano. Tra-In offers bus service from Siena to Montepulciano several times a day. Montepulciano's train station is in Montepulciano Stazione, 10 km (6 miles) away.

VISITOR INFORMATION

Montepulciano Tourism Office ⊠ *Piazza Don Minzoni 1* ☎ *0578/757341* ⊕ *www.prolocomontepulciano.it.*

EXPLORING

Duomo. On the Piazza Grande the unfinished facade of Montepulciano's cathedral doesn't measure up to the beauty of its neighboring palaces. On the inside, however, its Renaissance roots shine through. The high altar has a splendid triptych painted in 1401 by Taddeo di Bartolo (circa 1362–1422), and you can see fragments of the tomb of Bartolomeo Aragazzi, secretary to Pope Martin V, which was sculpted by Michelozzo between 1427 and 1436. ⊠ *Piazza Grande* ☎ *0578/757341* ☉ *Daily 9–12:30 and 3–6.*

Piazza Grande. Filled with handsome buildings, this large square on the heights of the old historic town is Montepulciano's pièce de résistance.

Fodor'sChoice   **San Biagio.** Designed by Antonio da Sangallo il Vecchio, and considered
★   his masterpiece, this church sits on the hillside below the town walls and is a model of High Renaissance architectural perfection. Inside the church is a painting of the Madonna that, according to legend, was the only thing remaining in an abandoned church that two young girls entered on April 23, 1518. The girls saw the eyes of the Madonna moving, and that same afternoon so did a farmer and a cow, who knelt down in front of the painting. In 1963 the image was proclaimed the "Madonna del Buon Viaggio" (Madonna of the Good Journey), the protector of tourists in Italy. ⊠ *Via di San Biagio* ☎ *0578/757164* ⊙ *Daily 9–12:30 and 3:30–7:30.*

WHERE TO EAT

$$$ ✕ **La Grotta.** You might be tempted to pass right by the innocuous
TUSCAN   entrance across the street from San Biagio, but you'd miss some fan-
Fodor'sChoice   tastic food. Try the *pici fatti a mano con ragù di anatra e lenticchie*
★   (homemade noodles with duck sauce and lentils) or *carrè di agnello alle erbe aromatiche con verdure al forno* (rack of lamb with herbs and baked vegetables). Wash it down with the local wine, which just happens to be one of Italy's finest: Vino Nobile di Montepulciano. The desserts, such as an extravagantly rich triple-chocolate flan, are prepared with particular flair. $ *Average main: €25* ⊠ *Via di San Biagio 15* ☎ *0578/757479* ⊕ *www.lagrottamontepulciano.it* ⊙ *Closed Wed., and Jan.–mid-Mar.*

$ ✕ **Osteria del Conte.** As high in Montepulciano as you can get, just behind
TUSCAN   the Duomo, this small and intimate restaurant is expertly run by the
Fodor'sChoice   mother and son team of Lorena and Paolo Brachi. Passionate about the
★   food they prepare, both have a flair for the region's traditional dishes— the pici *all'aglione* (with garlic sauce) and the *filetto ai funghi porcini* (steak with porcini mushrooms) are mouthwateringly good. The wine list, though limited in range, presents a decent selection of wines from both Montepulciano and Montalcino. For a change from the usual Tuscan meat dishes, fresh fish is served on Friday. Outdoor seating is limited. $ *Average main: €12* ⊠ *Via di San Donato 19* ☎ *0578/756062* ⊕ *www.osteriadelconte.it* ⊙ *Closed Wed.*

WHERE TO STAY

$$$$ ▦ **Podere Dionora.** At this secluded and serene country inn, earth-tone
B&B/INN   fabrics complement antiques in the individually decorated rooms, all of
Fodor'sChoice   which have functioning fireplaces. **Pros:** secluded setting; great views;
★   attentive service. **Cons:** long walk to the nearest town; need a car to get around. $ *Rooms from: €330* ⊠ *Via Vicinale di Poggiano 9, 3 km (2 miles) east of Montepulciano town center* ☎ *0578/717496* ⊕ *www. dionora.it* ⊃ *6 rooms* ⊙ *Closed mid-Dec.–mid-Feb.* ❍| *Breakfast.*

$$$ ▦ **Relais San Bruno.** Alberto Pavoncelli converted his family's summer
B&B/INN   home, just minutes from the town center, into a splendid inn where
Fodor'sChoice   well-appointed rooms are have expansive views. **Pros:** king-size beds in
★   most rooms; functioning fireplaces; relaxed but attentive service. **Cons:** cottages can be chilly; need a car to get around. $ *Rooms from: €250* ⊠ *Via di Pescaia 5/7* ☎ *0578/716222* ⊕ *www.sanbrunorelais.com* ⊃ *7 rooms, 2 suites, 1 cottage* ❍| *Breakfast.*

$$ **San Biagio.** A five-minute walk from the church of the same name,
B&B/INN this family-run inn makes a great base for exploring Montepulciano and
the surrounding countryside. **Pros:** heated indoor pool; family-friendly
atmosphere. **Cons:** some rooms face a busy road; lots of tour groups.
$ *Rooms from: €135 ⊠ Via San Bartolomeo 2 ☎ 0578/717233 ⊕ www.
albergosanbiagio.it ⌐ 27 rooms ⵌⵗ Breakfast.*

SHOPPING

La Dolce Vita. An elegantly restored monastery is home to this excellent
enoteca in the upper part of Montepulciano, which has a wide selec-
tion of wines by the glass, as well as bottles for sale. ⊠ *Via di Voltaia
del Corso 80/82 ☎ 0578/757872.*

PIENZA

*14 km (9 miles) west of Montepulciano, 52 km (32 miles) southeast
of Siena.*

Pienza owes its appearance to Pope Pius II (1405–64), who had grand
plans to transform his hometown of Corsignano (its former name) into
a compact model Renaissance town. The architect entrusted with the
transformation was Bernardo Rossellino (1409–64), a protégé of the
great Renaissance architectural theorist Leon Battista Alberti (1404–
72). His mandate was to create a cathedral, a papal palace, and a
town hall that adhered to the pope's humanistic principles. Gothic and
Renaissance styles were fused, and the buildings were decorated with
Sienese paintings. The net result was a project that expressed Renais-
sance ideals of art, architecture, and civilized good living in a single
scheme: it stands as an exquisite example of the architectural canons
that Alberti formulated in the early Renaissance and that were utilized
by later architects, including Michelangelo, in designing many of Italy's
finest buildings and piazzas. Today the cool nobility of Pienza's center
seems almost surreal in this otherwise unpretentious village, renowned
for its smooth sheep's-milk pecorino cheese.

GETTING HERE AND AROUND

From Siena, drive south along the SR2 to San Quirico d'Orcia and then
take the SP146. The trip should take just over an hour. Tra-In shuttles
passengers between Siena and Pienza. There is no train service.

VISITOR INFORMATION

Pienza Tourism Office ⊠ *Piazza Dante 18 ☎ 0578/749071 ⊕ www.pienza.
info.*

EXPLORING

Duomo. This 15th-century cathedral was built by the architect Rossellino
under the influence of Alberti. The travertine facade is divided in three
parts, with Renaissance arches under the pope's coat of arms encircled
by a wreath of fruit. Inside, the cathedral is simple but richly decorated
with Sienese paintings. The building's perfection didn't last long—the
first cracks appeared immediately after the building was completed, and
its foundations have shifted slightly ever since, as rain has eroded the
hillside behind. You can see this effect if you look closely at the base of

the first column as you enter the church and compare it with the last. ✉ *Piazza Pio II* ☎ *0578/749071* ⏲ *Daily 10–1 and 3–7.*

Palazzo Piccolomini. In 1459 Pius II commissioned Rossellino to design the perfect palazzo for his papal court. The architect took Florence's Palazzo Rucellai by Alberti as a model and designed this 100-room palace. Three sides of the building fit perfectly into the urban plan around it, while the fourth, looking over the valley, has a lovely loggia uniting it with the gardens in back. Guided tours departing every 30 minutes take you to visit the papal apartments, including a beautiful library, the Sala delle Armi (with an impressive weapons collection), and the music room, with its extravagant wooden ceiling forming four letter Ps: Pope, Pius, Piccolomini, and Pienza. The last tour departs 30 minutes before closing. ✉ *Piazza Pio II* ☎ *0578/748392* 🌐 *www.palazzopiccolominipienza.it* 🎟 *€7* ⏲ *Mid-Mar.–mid-Oct., Tues.–Sun. 10–6:30; mid-Oct.–mid-Mar., Tues.–Sun. 10–4:30. Last entrance 30 mins before closing.*

WHERE TO EAT AND STAY

$$ TUSCAN 🍴 **La Chiocciola.** Take the few minutes to walk from the old town for typical Pienza fare, including homemade pici with hare or wild-boar sauce. The restaurant's version of *formaggio in forno* (baked cheese) with assorted accompaniments such as fresh porcini mushrooms is reason enough to venture here. [$] *Average main: €15* ✉ *Via Mencatelli 2* ☎ *0578/748683* 🌐 *www.trattorialachiocciola.it* ⏲ *Closed Wed.s and 2 wks in Feb.*

$ TUSCAN 🍴 **Osteria Sette di Vino.** Tasty dishes based on the region's cheeses are the specialty at this simple and inexpensive osteria on a quiet, pleasant square in the center of Pienza. Try versions of pici or the starter of radicchio baked quickly to brown the edges. The local pecorino cheese appears often on the menu—the pecorino *grigliata con pancetta* (grilled with cured bacon) is divine. Can't decide? Try the pecorino tasting menu. [$] *Average main: €10* ✉ *Piazza di Spagna 1* ☎ *0578/749092* 💳 *No credit cards* ⏲ *Closed Wed., July 1–15, and Nov.*

$ B&B/INN Fodor's Choice ★ 🏨 **Agriturismo Cerreto.** Built a short distance from Pienza in the 18th and 19th centuries, this grouping of farm buildings is now done in traditional Tuscan décor with terra-cotta flooring, wood beams, wrought-iron bed frames, and heavy oak furniture. **Pros:** peaceful country setting; great for families and small groups; good base for exploring the Val d'Orcia. **Cons:** private transportation a must; closest restaurants and town 5 km (3 miles) away. [$] *Rooms from: €110* ✉ *Strada Provinciale per Sant'Anna in Camprena, 5 km (3 miles) north of Pienza* ☎ *0578/749121* 🌐 *www.agriturismocerreto.com* 🛏 *9 rooms* 🍽 *Breakfast.*

MONTALCINO

23 km (14 miles) west of Pienza, 41 km (25 miles) south of Siena.

Tiny Montalcino, with its commanding view from high on a hill, can claim an Etruscan past. It saw a fair number of travelers, as it was directly on the road from Siena to Rome. During the early Middle Ages it enjoyed a brief period of autonomy before falling into the orbit of

Siena in 1201. Now Montalcino's greatest claim to fame is its production of Brunello di Montalcino, one of Italy's most esteemed red wines. Driving up to the town, you pass by sangiovese vineyards, whose grapes are used to make the Brunello wine. You can sample the excellent but expensive red in wine cellars in town, or visit a nearby winery, such as Fattoria dei Barbi, for a guided tour and tasting—but it's always best to call ahead for reservations.

> ## ENOTECHE: WINE SHOPS
>
> The word *enoteca* in Italian can mean "wine store," "wine bar," or both. In any event, *enoteche* (the plural, pronounced "ay-no-*tek*-ay") are excellent places to sample and buy Tuscan wines, and they're also good sources of information about local wineries.

GETTING HERE AND AROUND

By car, follow the SR2 south from Siena, then follow the SP45 to Montalcino. Several Tra-In buses travel between Siena and Montalcino daily, making a tightly scheduled day trip possible. No direct train service is available.

VISITOR INFORMATION

Montalcino Tourism Office ☒ *Costa del Municipio 1* ☏ *0577/849331* ⊕ *www.prolocomontalcino.com.*

EXPLORING

La Fortezza. Providing refuge for the last remnants of the Sienese army during the Florentine conquest of 1555, the battlements of this 14th-century fortress are still in excellent condition. Climb up the narrow, spiral steps for the 360-degree view of most of southern Tuscany. An enoteca for tasting wines is on site. ☒ *Piazzale Fortezza* ☏ *0577/849211* 🎫 *€3* ☺ *Nov.–Mar., Tues.–Sun. 9–6; Apr.–Oct., daily 9–8.*

Museo Civico e Diocesano d'Arte Sacra. This fine museum is housed in a building that once belonged to 13th-century Augustinian monks. The ticket booth is in the glorious refurbished cloister, and the sacred art collection, gathered from churches throughout the region, is displayed on two floors in former monastic quarters. Though the art here might be called "B-list," a fine altarpiece by Bartolo di Fredi (circa 1330–1410), the *Coronation of the Virgin*, makes dazzling use of gold. In addition, there's a striking 12th-century crucifix that originally adorned the high altar of the church of Sant'Antimo. Also on hand are many wood sculptures, a typical medium in these parts during the Renaissance. ☒ *Via Ricasoli 31* ☏ *0577/846014* 🎫 *€8* ☺ *Sept.–Nov., Tues.–Sun. 10–1 and 2–5:40; Apr.–Oct., Tues.–Sun. 10–1 and 2–5:50.*

WHERE TO EAT AND STAY

$$
WINE BAR
Fodor'sChoice
★

✕ **Enoteca Osteria Osticcio.** Tullio and Francesca Scrivano have beautifully remodeled this restaurant and wine shop. Upon entering, you descend a staircase to a tasting room filled with rustic wooden tables. Adjacent is a small dining area with a splendid view of the hills far below, and outside is a lovely little terrace perfect for sampling Brunello di Montalcino when the weather is warm. The menu is light and pairs nicely with the wines, which are the main draw. The *acciughe sotto pesto* (anchovies with pesto) is a particularly fine treat. $ *Average main: €18* ✉ *Via Matteotti 23* ☎ *0577/848271* ⊕ *www.osticcio.it* ⊗ *Closed Sun.*

$$$$ ⊞ **Castiglion del Bosco.** This estate, one of the largest still in private hands
HOTEL in Tuscany, was purchased by Massimo Ferragamo at the beginning of
Fodor'sChoice this century and meticulously converted into a second-to-none resort
★ that incorporates a medieval *borgo* (village) and surrounding farm-houses. **Pros:** extremely secluded; exclusive and tranquil location; top-notch service; breathtaking scenery. **Cons:** well off the beaten track; the nearest town is 12 km (7½ miles) away; private transportation required. $ *Rooms from: €570* ✉ *Località Castiglion del Bosco* ☎ *0577/1913111* ⊕ *www.castigliondelbosco.com* ⇥ *23 suites, 10 villas* ❍| *Breakfast.*

$ ⊞ **La Crociona.** A quiet and serene family-owned farm in the middle
B&B/INN of a small vineyard with glorious views houses guests in lovely apart-ments that can sleep up to five people. **Pros:** peaceful location; great for families; friendly atmosphere. **Cons:** no a/c; need a car to get around. $ *Rooms from: €120* ✉ *Località La Croce 15* ☎ *0577/848007* ⊕ *www. lacrociona.com* ⇥ *7 apartments* ❍| *No meals.*

ABBAZIA DI SANT'ANTIMO

10 km (6 miles) south of Montalcino, 51 km (32 miles) south of Siena.

GETTING HERE AND AROUND

The Abbazia di Sant'Antimo, nestled below the town of Castelnuovo dell'Abate, is a 15-minute drive from Montalcino. Tra-In bus service is extremely limited, and the abbey cannot be reached by train.

EXPLORING

Fodor'sChoice   **Abbazia di Sant'Antimo.** It's well worth going out of your way to visit
★ this 12th-century Romanesque abbey, as it's a gem of pale stone in the silvery green of an olive grove. The exterior and interior sculp-ture is outstanding, particularly the nave capitals, a combination of French, Lombard, and even Spanish influences. The sacristy (seldom open) forms part of the primitive Carolingian church (founded in AD 781), its entrance flanked by 9th-century pilasters. The small vaulted crypt dates from the same period. Above the nave runs a *matroneum* (women's gallery), an unusual feature once used to separate the congre-gation. Equally unusual is the ambulatory, for which the three radiating chapels were almost certainly copied from a French model. ■ **TIP→ Stay to hear the canonical hours celebrated in Gregorian chant.** On the road that leads up toward Castelnuovo dell'Abate is a small shop that sells souvenirs and has washrooms. A 2½-hour hiking trail (signed as "#2") leads to the abbey from Montalcino. Starting near Montalcino's small cemetery, the trail heads south through woods, along a ridge road to the tiny hamlet of Villa a Tolli, and then downhill to Sant'Antimo. ✉ *Castel-nuovo dell'Abate* ☎ *0577/835659* ⊕ *www.antimo.it* ⊗ *Sept.–June, daily 5:45 am–9 pm; July and Aug., daily 5:45 am–9:30 pm.*

UMBRIA AND THE MARCHES

WELCOME TO UMBRIA AND THE MARCHES

TOP REASONS TO GO

★ **Palazzo Ducale, Urbino:** A visit here reveals more about the ideals of the Renaissance than a shelf of history books could.

★ **Assisi, shrine to Saint Francis:** Recharge your soul in this rose-color hill town with a visit to the gentle saint's majestic basilica, adorned with great frescoes.

★ **Spoleto, Umbria's musical Mecca:** Crowds may descend and prices ascend here during summer's Festival dei Due Mondi, but Spoleto's hushed charm enchants year-round.

★ **Tantalizing truffles:** Are Umbria's celebrated "black diamonds" coveted for their pungent flavor, their rarity, or their power in the realm of romance?

★ **Orvieto's Duomo:** Arresting visions of heaven and hell on the facade and brilliant frescoes within make this Gothic cathedral a dazzler.

1 Perugia. Umbria's largest town is easily reached from Rome, Siena, or Florence. Home to some of Perugino's great frescoes and a hilltop *centro storico* (historic center), it's also favored by chocolate lovers, who celebrate their passion at October's Eurochocolate Festival.

2 Assisi. The city of Saint Francis is a major pilgrimage site, crowned by one of Italy's greatest churches. Despite the throngs of visitors, it still maintains its medieval hill-town character.

3 Northern Umbria. The quiet towns lying around Perugia include Deruta, which produces exceptional ceramics. A trip through the rugged terrain of northeast Umbria takes you to Gubbio, where from the Piazza della Signoria you can admire magnificent views of the countryside below.

4 Spoleto. Though it's known to the world for its annual performing-arts festival, Spoleto offers much more than Puccini in its Piazza del Duomo. There are Filippo Lippi frescoes in the cathedral, a massive castle towering over the town, and a bridge across the neighboring valley that's an engineering marvel.

12

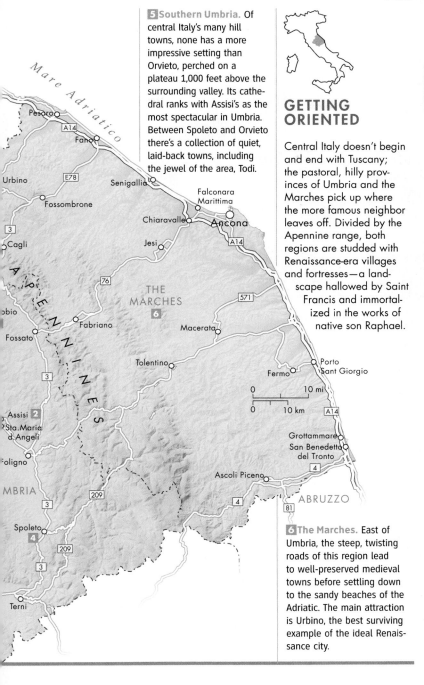

5 **Southern Umbria.** Of central Italy's many hill towns, none has a more impressive setting than Orvieto, perched on a plateau 1,000 feet above the surrounding valley. Its cathedral ranks with Assisi's as the most spectacular in Umbria. Between Spoleto and Orvieto there's a collection of quiet, laid-back towns, including the jewel of the area, Todi.

GETTING ORIENTED

Central Italy doesn't begin and end with Tuscany; the pastoral, hilly provinces of Umbria and the Marches pick up where the more famous neighbor leaves off. Divided by the Apennine range, both regions are studded with Renaissance-era villages and fortresses—a landscape hallowed by Saint Francis and immortalized in the works of native son Raphael.

6 **The Marches.** East of Umbria, the steep, twisting roads of this region lead to well-preserved medieval towns before settling down to the sandy beaches of the Adriatic. The main attraction is Urbino, the best surviving example of the ideal Renaissance city.

EATING AND DRINKING WELL IN UMBRIA AND THE MARCHES

Central Italy is mountainous, and its food is hearty and straightforward, with a stick-to-the-ribs quality that sees hardworking farmers and artisans through a long day's work and helps them make the steep climb home at night.

In restaurants here, as in much of Italy, you're rewarded for seeking out local cuisine, and you'll often find better and cheaper food if you're willing to stray a few hundred yards from the main sights. Spoleto is noted for its good food and service, probably a result of high expectations from the international arts crowd. For gourmets, however, it's hard to beat Spello, which has both excellent restaurants and first-rate wine merchants.

A rule of thumb for eating well throughout Umbria is to order what's in season; the trick is to stroll through local markets to see what's for sale. A number of restaurants in the region offer *degustazione* (tasting) menus, which give you a chance to try different local specialties without breaking the bank.

TASTY TRUFFLES

More truffles are found in Umbria than anywhere else in Italy. Spoleto and Norcia are prime territory for the *tartufo nero* (reddish-black interior and fine white veins), *pictured below right*, prized for its extravagant flavor and intense aroma.

The mild summer truffle, *scorzone estivo* (black outside and beige inside), is in season May through December. The *scorzone autunnale* (burnt brown color and visible veins inside) is found October through December. Truffles can be shaved into omelets or over pasta, pounded into sauces, or chopped and mixed with oil.

12

LENTILS AND SOUPS

The town of Castelluccio di Norcia is particularly known for its lentils and its *farro* (an ancient grain used by the Romans, similar to wheat), and a variety of beans used in soups. Throughout Umbria, look for *imbrecciata*, a soup of beans and grains, delicately flavored with local herbs. Other ingredients that find their way into thick Umbrian soups are wild beet, sorrel, mushrooms, spelt, chickpeas, and the elusive, fragrant saffron, grown in nearby Cascia.

OLIVE OIL

Nearly everywhere you look in Umbria, olive trees grace the hillsides. The soil of the Apennines allows the olives to ripen slowly, guaranteeing low acidity, a cardinal virtue of fine oil. Look for restaurants that proudly display their own oil, often a sign that they care about their food.

Umbria's finest oil is found in Trevi, where the local product is intensely green and fruity. You can sample it in the town's wine bars, which often do double duty, offering olive-oil tastings.

PORK PRODUCTS

Much of traditional Umbrian cuisine revolves around pork. It can be cooked in wood-fire stoves, sometimes basted with a rich sauce made from innards and red wine. The roasted pork known as *porchetta (pictured at left)* is grilled

on a spit and flavored with fennel and herbs, leaving a crisp outer sheen.

The art of pork processing has been handed down through generations in Norcia, so much so that charcuterie producers throughout Italy are often known as *norcini*. Don't miss *prosciutto di Norcia*, which is aged for two years.

WINE

Sagrantino grapes are the star in Umbria's most notable red wines. For centuries they've been used in sagrantino *passito*, a semisweet wine made by leaving the grapes to dry for a period after picking in order to intensify their sugar content. In recent decades, sagrantino *secco* (dry) has occupied the front stage. Both passito and secco have a deep red-ruby color, with a full body and rich flavor.

In the past few years the phenomenon of the *enoteca* (wine shop and wine bar) has taken off, making it easier to arrange wine tastings. Many also let you sample different olive oils on toasted bread, known as *bruschetta*. Some wine information centers, such as La Strada del Sagrantino in the town of Montefalco, will help set up appointments for tastings.

Updated
by Jonathan
Willcocks

Birthplace of saints and home to some of the country's greatest artistic treasures, central Italy is a collection of misty green valleys and picture-perfect hill towns laden with centuries of history. Umbria and the Marches are the Italian countryside as you've imagined it: verdant farmland, steep hillsides topped with medieval fortresses, and winding country roads. No single town here has the extravagant wealth of art and architecture of Florence, Rome, or Venice, but this works in your favor: small jewels of towns feel knowable, not overwhelming.

And the cultural cupboard is far from bare. Orvieto's cathedral and Assisi's basilica are two of the most important sights in Italy, while Perugia, Todi, Gubbio, and Spoleto are rich in art and architecture.

East of Umbria, the Marches (Le Marche to Italians) stretch between the Apennines and the Adriatic Sea. It's a region of great turreted castles on high peaks defending passes and roads—a testament to the centuries of battle that have taken place here. Rising majestically in Urbino is a splendid palace, built by Federico da Montefeltro, where the humanistic ideals of the Renaissance came to their fullest flower, while the town of Ascoli Piceno can lay claim to one of the most beautiful squares in Italy. Virtually every small town in the region has a castle, church, or museum worth a visit—but even without them, you'd still be compelled to stop for the interesting streets, panoramic views, and natural beauty.

UMBRIA AND THE MARCHES PLANNER

MAKING THE MOST OF YOUR TIME

Umbria is a nicely compact collection of character-rich hill towns; you can settle in one, then explore the others, as well as the countryside and forest in between, on day trips.

12

Perugia, Umbria's largest and most lively city, is a logical choice for your base, particularly if you're arriving from the north. If you want something a little quieter, virtually any other town in the region will suit your purposes; even Assisi, which overflows with bus tours during the day, is delightfully quiet in the evening and early morning. Spoleto and Orvieto are the most developed towns to the south, but they're still of modest proportions.

If you have the time to venture farther afield, consider trips to Gubbio, northeast of Perugia, and Urbino, in the Marches. Both are worth the time it takes to reach them, and both make for pleasant overnight stays. In southern Umbria, Valnerina and the Piano Grande are out-of-the-way spots with the region's best hiking.

FESTIVALS

Eurochocolate Festival. If you've got a sweet tooth and are visiting in fall, book up early and head to Perugia for the Eurochocolate Festival. This is one of the biggest chocolate festivals in the world, with a million visitors, and is held in the third week of October. ⊕ *www.eurochocolate.com.*

Festival dei Due Mondi. Each summer Umbria hosts one of Italy's biggest arts festivals: Spoleto's Festival dei Due Mondi, the Festival of the Two Worlds. Starting out as a classical music festival, it has now evolved into one of Italy's brightest gatherings of arts aficionados. Running from late June through early July, it features modern and classical music, theater, dance, and opera. Increasingly there are also a number of small cinema producers and their films. ⊕ *www.festivaldispoleto.com.*

Umbria Jazz Festival. Perugia is hopping for 10 days in July, when more than a million people flock to see famous names in contemporary music perform at the Umbria Jazz Festival. In recent years the stars have included B.B. King, Wynton Marsalis, Sting, Eric Clapton, and Elton John. ⊕ *www.umbriajazz.com.*

If you want to attend any of these events, you should make arrangements in advance. And if you don't want to attend, you should plan to avoid the cities during festival time, when hotel rooms and restaurant tables are at a premium. A similar caveat applies for Assisi during religious festivals at Christmas, Easter, the feast of Saint Francis (October 4), and Calendimaggio (May 1), when pilgrims arrive en masse.

GETTING HERE AND AROUND

BUS TRAVEL

Perugia's bus station is in Piazza Partigiani, which you can reach by taking the escalators from the town center.

Bucci. Connections between Rome, Spoleto, and the Marches are provided by this bus company. ☎ *0721/32401* ⊕ *www.autolineebucci.com.*

Sulga Line. Perugia is served by the Sulga Line, which has daily departures to Rome's Stazione Tiburtina, Fiumicino airport in Rome and to Florence's Piazza Adua. ☎ *800/099661* ⊕ *www.sulga.it.*

Local bus service between all the major and minor towns of Umbria is good. Some of the routes in rural areas are designed to serve as many places as possible and are therefore quite roundabout and slow.

Schedules change often, so consult with local tourist offices before setting out.

CAR TRAVEL

On the western edge of the region is the Umbrian section of the Autostrada del Sole (A1), Italy's principal north–south highway. It links Florence and Rome with Orvieto and passes near Todi and Terni. The S3 intersects with the A1 and leads on to Assisi and Urbino. The Adriatica Superstrada (A14) runs north–south along the coast, linking the Marches to Bologna and Venice.

The steep hills and deep valleys that make Umbria and the Marches so idyllic also make for challenging driving. Fortunately, the area has an excellent, modern road network, but be prepared for tortuous mountain roads if your explorations take you off the beaten track. Central Umbria is served by a major highway, the S75bis, which passes along the shore of Lake Trasimeno and ends in Perugia. Assisi is served by the modern highway S75; the S75 connects to the S3 and S3bis, which cover the heart of the region. Major inland routes connect coastal A14 to large towns in the Marches, but inland secondary roads in mountain areas can be winding and narrow. Always carry a good map, a flashlight, and a cell phone in case of a breakdown.

TRAIN TRAVEL

Several direct daily trains run by the Italian state railway, **Ferrovia dello Stato** (*FS* ☎ *892021 toll-free in Italy* ⊕ *www.trenitalia.com*), link Florence and Rome with Perugia and Assisi, and local service to the same area is available from Terontola (on the Rome–Florence line) and from Foligno (on the Rome–Ancona line). Intercity trains between Rome and Florence make stops in Orvieto, and the main Rome–Ancona line passes through Narni, Terni, Spoleto, and Foligno.

Within Umbria, a small, privately owned railway operated by **Ferrovia Centrale Umbra** (☎ *075/57540*) runs from Città di Castello in the north to Terni in the south via Perugia. Note: train service isn't available to either Gubbio or Urbino.

RESTAURANTS

Prices in the reviews are the average cost of a main course at dinner or, if dinner is not served, at lunch.

HOTELS

Virtually every older town, no matter how small, has some kind of hotel. A trend, particularly around Gubbio, Orvieto, and Todi, is to convert old villas, farms, and monasteries into first-class hotels. The natural splendor of the countryside more than compensates for the distance from town—provided you have a car. Hotels in town tend to be simpler than their country cousins, with a few notable exceptions in Spoleto, Gubbio, and Perugia.

Hotel reviews have been condensed. For full information, visit Fodors. com.

WHAT IT COSTS				
	$	**$$**	**$$$**	**$$$$**
RESTAURANTS	under €15	€15–€24	€25–€35	over €35
HOTELS	under €125	€125–€200	€201–€300	over €300

Prices in the dining reviews are the average cost of a main course at dinner, or, if dinner is not served, at lunch. Prices in the reviews are the lowest cost of a standard double room in high season.

VISITOR INFORMATION

Umbria Regional Tourism Office. Umbria's regional tourism office is in Perugia. The staff are well informed about the area and can give you a wide selection of leaflets and maps to assist you during your trip. It's open daily 9–7. ✉ *Piazza Matteotti 18, Perugia* ☎ *075/5736458* ⊕ *www.regioneumbria.eu.*

PERUGIA

Perugia is a majestic, handsome, wealthy city, and with its trendy boutiques, refined cafés, and grandiose architecture, it doesn't try to hide its affluence. A student population of more than 30,000 means that the city is abuzz with activity throughout the year. Umbria Jazz, one of the region's most important music festivals, attracts music lovers from around the world every July, and Eurochocolate, the international chocolate festival, is an irresistible draw each October for anyone with a sweet tooth.

GETTING HERE

The best approach to the city is by train. The area around the station doesn't attest to the rest of Perugia's elegance, but buses running from the station to Piazza d'Italia, the heart of the old town, are frequent. If you're in a hurry, take the *minimetro,* a one-line subway, to Stazione della Cupa. The metro station is on the left as you come out of the station.

If you're driving to Perugia and your hotel doesn't have parking facilities, leave your car in one of the lots close to the center. Electronic displays indicate the location of lots and the number of spaces free. If you park in the Piazza Partigiani, take the escalators that pass through the fascinating subterranean excavations of the Roman foundations of the city and lead to the town center.

EXPLORING

Thanks to Perugia's hilltop position, the medieval city remains almost completely intact. It's the best-preserved hill town of its size, and few other places in Italy better illustrate the model of the self-contained city-state that so shaped the course of Italian history.

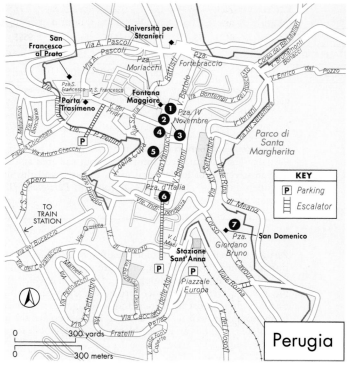

TOP ATTRACTIONS

Collegio del Cambio (*Bankers' Guild Hall*). These elaborate rooms, on the ground floor of the **Palazzo dei Priori,** served as the meeting hall and chapel of the guild of bankers and moneychangers. Most of the frescoes were completed by the most important Perugian painter of the Renaissance, Pietro Vannucci, better known as Perugino (circa 1450–1523). He included a remarkably honest self-portrait on one of the pilasters. The iconography includes common religious themes, such as the Nativity and the Transfiguration seen on the end walls. On the left wall are female figures representing the virtues, and beneath them are the heroes and sages of antiquity. On the right wall are figures presumed to have been painted in part by Perugino's most famous pupil, Raphael. (His hand, experts say, is most apparent in the figure of Fortitude.) The *cappella* (chapel) of San Giovanni Battista has frescoes painted by Giannicola di Paolo, another student of Perugino's. ⊠ *Corso Vannucci 25* ☎ *075/5728599* 💶 *€4.50, includes Collegio della Mercanzia* 🕓 *Mon.–Sat. 9–12:30 and 2:30–5:30, Sun. 9–1.*

Corso Vannucci. A string of elegantly connected *palazzi* (palaces) expresses the artistic nature of this city center, the heart of which is concentrated along Corso Vannucci. Stately and broad, this pedestrians-only street runs from Piazza Italia to Piazza IV Novembre. Along the way, the entrances to many of Perugia's side streets might tempt you to wander off and explore. But don't stray too far as evening falls, when Corso Vannucci fills with Perugians out for their evening *passeggiata,* a pleasant predinner stroll that may include a pause for an aperitivo at one of the many bars that line the street.

Fodor's Choice ★ **Galleria Nazionale dell'Umbria.** The region's most comprehensive art gallery is housed on the fourth floor of the **Palazzo dei Priori.** Enhanced by skillfully lit displays and computers that allow you to focus on the works' details and background information, the collection includes work by native artists—most notably Pintoricchio (1454–1513) and Perugino—and others of the Umbrian and Tuscan schools, among them Gentile da Fabriano (1370–1427), Duccio (circa 1255–1318), Fra Angelico (1387–1455), Fiorenzo di Lorenzo (1445–1525), and Piero della Francesca (1420–92). In addition to paintings, the gallery has frescoes, sculptures, and some superb examples of crucifixes from the 13th and 14th centuries. Some rooms are dedicated to Perugia itself, showing how the medieval city evolved. ☒ *Corso Vannucci 19, Piazza IV Novembre* ☏ *075/58668410* ⊕ *www.artiumbria.beniculturali.it* 🎫 *€6.50* ☉ *Tues.–Sun. 8:30–7:30; last admission ½ hr before closing.*

Palazzo dei Priori (*Palace of Priors*). A series of elegant connected buildings, the palazzo serves as Perugia's city hall and houses three of the city's museums. The buildings string along Corso Vannucci and wrap around the Piazza IV Novembre, where the original entrance is located. The steps here lead to the **Sala dei Notari** (Notaries' Hall). Other entrances lead to the **Galleria Nazionale dell'Umbria,** the **Collegio del Cambio,** and the **Collegio della Mercanzia.** The Sala dei Notari, which dates back to the 13th century and was the original meeting place of the town merchants, had become the seat of the notaries by the second half of the 15th century. Wood beams and an interesting array of frescoes attributed to Maestro di Farneto embellish the room. Coats of arms and crests line the back and right lateral walls; you can spot some famous figures from Aesop's *Fables* on the left wall. The palazzo facade is adorned with symbols of Perugia's pride and past power: the griffin is the city symbol, and the lion denotes Perugia's allegiance to the Guelph (or papal) cause. ☒ *Piazza IV Novembre 25* 🎫 *Free* ☉ *Tues.–Sun. 9–1 and 3–7.*

Rocca Paolina. A labyrinth of little streets, alleys, and arches, this underground city was originally part of a fortress built at the behest of Pope Paul III between 1540 and 1543 to confirm papal dominion over the city. Parts of it were destroyed after the end of papal rule, but much still remains. Begin your visit by taking the escalators that descend through the subterranean ruins from Piazza Italia down to Via Masi. In the summer this is the coolest place in the city. ☒ *Piazza Italia* 🎫 *€3* ☉ *Tues.–Sun. 10–1:30 and 2:30–6.*

WORTH NOTING

Duomo. Severe yet mystical, the Cathedral of San Lorenzo is most famous for being the home of the wedding ring of the Virgin Mary, stolen by the Perugians in 1488 from the nearby town of Chiusi. The ring, kept high up in a red-curtained vault in the chapel immediately to the left of the

UMBRIA THROUGH THE AGES

The earliest inhabitants of Umbria, the Umbri, were thought by the Romans to be the most ancient inhabitants of Italy. Little is known about them; with the coming of Etruscan culture the tribe fled into the mountains in the eastern portion of the region. The Etruscans, who founded some of the great cities of Umbria, were in turn supplanted by the Romans. Unlike Tuscany and other regions of central Italy, Umbria had few powerful medieval families to exert control over the cities in the Middle Ages—its proximity to Rome ensured that it would always be more or less under papal domination.

In the center of the country, Umbria has for much of its history been a battlefield where armies from north and south clashed. Hannibal destroyed a Roman army on the shores of Lake Trasimeno, and the bloody course of the interminable Guelph–Ghibelline conflict of the Middle Ages was played out here. Dante considered Umbria the most violent place in Italy. Trophies of war still decorate the Palazzo dei Priori in Perugia, and the little town of Gubbio continues a warlike rivalry begun in the Middle Ages—every year it challenges the Tuscan town of Sansepolcro to a crossbow tournament. Today the bowmen shoot at targets, but neither side has forgotten that 500 years ago they were shooting at each other.

In spite of—or perhaps because of—this bloodshed, Umbria has produced more than its share of Christian saints. The most famous is Saint Francis, the decidedly pacifist saint whose life shaped the Church of his time. His great shrine at Assisi is visited by hundreds of thousands of pilgrims each year. Saint Clare, his devoted follower, was Umbria-born, as were Saint Benedict, Saint Rita of Cascia, and the patron saint of lovers, Saint Valentine.

entrance, is stored under lock—15 locks, to be precise—and key most of the year. It's shown to the public on July 30 (the day it was brought to Perugia) and the second-to-last Sunday in January (Mary's wedding anniversary). The cathedral itself dates from the Middle Ages, and has many additions from the 15th and 16th centuries. The most visually interesting element is the altar to the Madonna of Grace; an elegant fresco on a column at the right of the entrance of the altar depicts *La Madonna delle Grazie* and is surrounded by prayer benches decorated with handwritten notes to the Holy Mother. Around the column are small amulets—symbols of gratitude from those whose prayers were answered. There are also elaborately carved choir stalls, executed by Giovanni Battista Bastone in 1520. The altarpiece (1484), an early masterpiece by Luca Signorelli (circa 1441–1523), shows the Madonna with Saint John the Baptist, Saint Onophrius, and Saint Lawrence. Sections of the church may be closed to visitors during religious services.

The **Museo Capitolare** displays a large array of precious objects associated with the cathedral, including vestments, vessels, and manuscripts. Outside the Duomo is the elaborate **Fontana Maggiore,** which dates from 1278. It's adorned with zodiac figures and symbols of the seven arts. ⊠ *Piazza IV Novembre* ☎ *075/5723832* ▭ *Museum €3.50*

⏲ Duomo: Mon.–Sat. 8–12:30 and 4–6, Sun. 8–noon and 4–6:30. Museum: Tues.–Sun. 9–5; last admission ½ hr before closing.

Museo Archeologico Nazionale. An excellent collection of Etruscan artifacts from throughout the region sheds light on Perugia as a flourishing Etruscan city long before it fell under Roman domination in 310 BC. Little else remains of Perugia's mysterious ancestors, although the Arco di Augusto, in Piazza Fortebraccio, the northern entrance to the city, is of Etruscan origin. ✉ *Piazza G. Bruno 10* ☎ *075/5727141* 🌐 *www.archeopg.arti.beniculturali.it* 🎟 *€4* ⏲ *Mon. 10–7:30, Tues.–Sun. 8:30–7:30.*

> **WORD OF MOUTH**
>
> "Two things you must not fail to do in Perugia are to (a) join the evening walk on the Corso Vannucci beginning at about 5 pm and (b) take the escalators that go up and down and through the historic city walls. Also: Hang out as often as you dare at Sandri's, one of Italy's most marvelous cafe/pastry shops, on the Corso Vannucci." —nessundorma

12

WHERE TO EAT

$$ UMBRIAN 🍴 **Antica Trattoria San Lorenzo.** Brick vaults are not the only distinguishing feature of this small, popular eatery next to the Duomo, as both the food and the service are outstanding. Particular attention is paid to adapting traditional Umbrian cuisine to the modern palate. There's also a nice variety of seafood dishes on the menu. The *trenette alla farina di noce con pesce di mare* (flat noodles made with walnut flour topped with fresh fish) is a real treat. [$] *Average main: €17* ✉ *Piazza Danti 19-A* ☎ *075/5721956* 🌐 *www.anticatrattoriasanlorenzo.com* ⏲ *Closed Sun.*

$$ UMBRIAN 🍴 **Dal Mi' Cocco.** A great favorite with Perugia's university students, it is fun, crowded, and inexpensive. You may find yourself seated at a long table with other diners, but some language help from your neighbors could come in handy—the menu is in pure Perugian dialect. The fixed-price meals change with the season, and each day of the week brings some new creation *dal cocco* (from the "coconut," or head) of the chef. [$] *Average main: €15* ✉ *Corso Garibaldi 12* ☎ *075/5732511* ✍ *Reservations essential* 💳 *No credit cards* ⏲ *Closed late July–mid-Aug.*

$$ ITALIAN 🍴 **La Rosetta.** The dining room of the hotel of the same name is a peaceful, elegant spot. In winter you dine inside under medieval vaults; in summer, in the cool courtyard. The food is simple but reliable, and flawlessly executed. The restaurant caters to travelers seeking to get away from the bustle of central Perugia. [$] *Average main: €17* ✉ *Piazza d'Italia 19* ☎ *075/5720841* ✍ *Reservations essential.*

$$ UMBRIAN 🍴 **La Taverna.** Medieval steps lead to a rustic two-story space where wine bottles and artful clutter decorate the walls. Good choices from the regional menu include *caramelle al gorgonzola* (pasta rolls filled with red cabbage and mozzarella and topped with a Gorgonzola sauce) and grilled meat dishes, such as the *medaglioni di vitello al tartuffo* (grilled veal with truffles). [$] *Average main: €18* ✉ *Via delle Streghe 8, off Corso Vannucci* ☎ *075/5724128* ⏲ *Daily.*

WHERE TO STAY

$$ HOTEL **Castello dell'Oscano.** A splendid neo-Gothic castle, a late 19th-century villa, and a converted farmhouse hidden in the tranquil hills north of Perugia offer a wide range of accommodations. **Pros:** quiet elegance; fine gardens; Umbrian wine list. **Cons:** distant from Perugia; not easy to find. [$] *Rooms from: €200* ✉ *Strada della Forcella 37, Cenerente* ☎ *075/584371* 🌐 *www.oscano.com* 🛏 *24 rooms, 8 suites, 13 apartments* 🍴 *Breakfast.*

$ HOTEL **Hotel Fortuna.** The elegant décor in the large rooms, some with balconies, complements the frescoes, which date from the 1700s. **Pros:** central but quiet; cozy, friendly atmosphere; elevator. **Cons:** some small rooms; no restaurant. [$] *Rooms from: €120* ✉ *Via Bonazzi 19, Corso Vannucci* ☎ *075/5722845* 🌐 *www.hotelfortunaperugia.com* 🛏 *51 rooms* 🍴 *Breakfast.*

$$ HOTEL **Locanda della Posta.** Renovations have left the lobby and other public areas rather bland, but the rooms in this converted 18th-century palazzo are soothingly decorated in muted colors. **Pros:** some fine views; central position. **Cons:** some street noise; some small rooms; no restaurant. [$] *Rooms from: €150* ✉ *Corso Vannucci 97* ☎ *075/5728925* 🛏 *38 rooms, 1 suite* 🍴 *Breakfast.*

$$ HOTEL **Posta dei Donini.** Beguilingly comfortable guest rooms are set on lovely grounds, where gardeners go quietly about their business. **Pros:** plush atmosphere; a quiet and private getaway. **Cons:** outside Perugia; uninteresting village. [$] *Rooms from: €150* ✉ *Via Deruta 43, San Martino in Campo* ☎ *075/609132* 🌐 *www.postadonini.it* 🛏 *33 rooms* 🍴 *No meals.*

$$ HOTEL **Tre Vaselle.** Rooms spread throughout four stone buildings are spacious and graced with floors of typical red-clay Tuscan tiles. **Pros:** perfect for visiting Torgiano wine area and Deruta; friendly staff; nice pool. **Cons:** somewhat far from Perugia; in center of uninspiring village. [$] *Rooms from: €150* ✉ *Via Garibaldi 48, Torgiano* ☎ *075/9880447* 🌐 *www.3vaselle.it* 🛏 *47 rooms* 🍴 *No meals.*

NIGHTLIFE AND THE ARTS

With its large student population, the city has plenty to offer in the way of bars and clubs. The best ones are around the city center, off Corso Vannucci. *Viva Perugia* is a good source of information about nightlife; this monthly, sold at newsstands, has a section in English.

MUSIC FESTIVALS

Sagra Musicale Umbra. Held from mid-August to mid-September, the Sagra Musicale Umbra celebrates sacred music. ☎ *338/8668820* 🌐 *www.perugiamusicaclassica.com.*

SHOPPING

Take a stroll down any of Perugia's main streets, including Corso Vannucci, Via dei Priori, Via Oberdan, and Via Sant'Ercolano, and you'll see many well-known designer boutiques and specialty shops.

The most typical thing to buy in Perugia is some Perugina chocolate, which you can find almost anywhere. The best-known chocolates made by Perugina are the chocolate-and-hazelnut-filled nibbles called *baci* (literally, "kisses"). They're wrapped in silver paper that includes a sliver of paper, like the fortune in a fortune cookie, with multilingual romantic sentiments or sayings.

ASSISI

The small town of Assisi is one of the Christian world's most important pilgrimage sites and home of the Basilica di San Francesco—built to honor Saint Francis (1182–1226) and erected in swift order after his death. The peace and serenity of the town is a welcome respite after the hustle and bustle of some of Italy's major cities.

Like most other towns in the region, Assisi began as an Umbri settlement in the 7th century BC and was conquered by the Romans 400 years later. The town was Christianized by Saint Rufino, its patron saint, in the 3rd century, but it's the spirit of Saint Francis, a patron saint of Italy and founder of the Franciscan monastic order, that's felt throughout its narrow medieval streets. The famous 13th-century basilica was decorated by the greatest artists of the period.

GETTING HERE

Assisi lies on the Terontola–Foligno rail line, with almost hourly connections to Perugia and direct trains to Rome and Florence several times a day. The Stazione Centrale is 4 km (2½ miles) from town, with a bus service about every half hour. Assisi is easily reached from the A1 autostrada (Rome–Florence) and the S75b highway. The walled town is closed to traffic, so cars must be left in the parking lots at Porta San Pietro, near Porta Nuova, or beneath Piazza Matteotti. Pay your parking fee at the *cassa* (ticket booth) before you return to your car to get a ticket to insert in the machine that will allow you to exit. It's a short but sometimes steep walk into the center of town; frequent minibuses make the rounds for weary pilgrims (buy tickets from a newsstand or tobacco shop near where you park your car).

VISITOR INFORMATION

Assisi Tourism Office ✉ *Piazza del Commune 22* ☎ *075/8138680* ⊕ *www.regioneumbria.eu.*

EXPLORING

Assisi is pristinely medieval in architecture and appearance, owing in large part to relative neglect from the 16th century until 1926, when the celebration of the 700th anniversary of Saint Francis's death brought more than 2 million visitors. Since then, pilgrims have flocked here in droves, and today several million arrive each year to pay homage. But not even the constant flood of visitors to this town of just 3,000 residents can spoil the singular beauty of this significant religious center, the home of some of the Western tradition's most important works of art. The hill on which Assisi sits rises dramatically from the flat plain, and

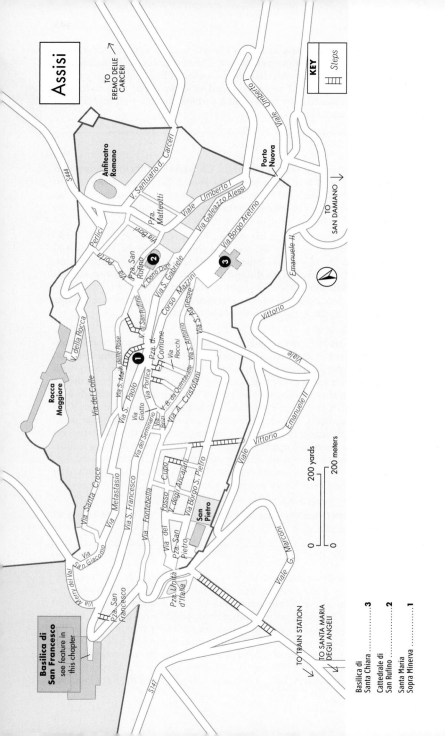

Assisi

Basilica di San Francesco
see feature in this chapter

Rocca Maggiore

Anfiteatro Romano

TO EREMO DELLE CARCERI

Porto Nuova

TO SAN DAMIANO

San Pietro

TO SANTA MARIA DEGLI ANGELI

TO TRAIN STATION

KEY

Sleps

0   200 yards
0   200 meters

Basilica di
Santa Chiara **3**

Cattedrale di
San Rufino **2**

Santa Maria
Sopra Minerva **1**

S444

S444

Via G. Giacomo
Via Merry del Val
Via Santa Croce
Via Metastasio
Via S. Francesco
Via S. Croce
Via del Colle
V. della Rocca
Via S. Maria delle Rose
Via S. Paolo
Via del Seminario
Via Giotto
Via Frati
Via Portica
Via Fontebella
Via del
Fosso
Cupo
V. degli Ancajani
Via Borgo S. Pietro
Pza. San Pietro
Pza. Unità d'Italia
Via A. Cristofani
V. B. tta Quintavalle
Via Rocchi
Pza. del Comune
Via S. Rufino
Via S. Antonio
Via S. Agnese
Corso Mazzini
Via S. Gabriele
V. Dono Doni
Pza. San Rufino
Via Bovi
Pza. Matteotti
V. Santuario d. Carceri
Perlici
Porta Perlici
Via Umberto I
Viale Umberto I
Via Galeazzo Alessi
Via Borgo Aretino
Viale Vittorio Emanuele II
Viale Vittorio Emanuele-II
Viale Umberto I
Viale G. Marconi
Pza. San Francesco

the town is dominated by a medieval castle at the very top.

Even though Assisi is sometimes besieged by busloads of sightseers who clamor to visit the famous basilica, it's difficult not to be charmed by the tranquillity of the town and its medieval architecture. Once you've seen the basilica, stroll through the town's narrow winding streets to see beautiful vistas of the nearby hills and valleys peeking through openings between the buildings.

TOP ATTRACTIONS

Basilica di San Fransisco. *See the highlighted feature in this chapter.* ⊠ *Piazza di San Francesco* ☎ *075/819001* ☉ *Lower Church: Easter–Oct., Mon.–Sat. 6 am–6:45 pm, Sun. 6:30 am–7:15 pm; Nov.–Easter, daily 6:30–6. Upper Church: Easter–Oct., Mon.–Sat. 8:30–6:45, Sun. 8:30–7:15; Nov.–Easter, daily 8:30–6.*

Basilica di Santa Chiara. The lovely, wide piazza in front of this church is reason enough to visit. The red-and-white-stripe facade frames the piazza's panoramic view over the Umbrian plains. Santa Chiara is dedicated to Saint Clare, one of the earliest and most fervent of Saint Francis's followers and the founder of the order of the Poor Ladies—or Poor Clares—which was based on the Franciscan monastic order. The church contains Clare's body, and in the **Cappella del Crocifisso** (on the right) is the cross that spoke to Saint Francis. A heavily veiled nun of the Poor Clares order is usually stationed before the cross in adoration of the image. ⊠ *Piazza Santa Chiara* ☎ *075/812282* ☉ *Nov.–mid-Mar., daily 7–noon and 2–6; mid-Mar.–Oct., daily 7–noon and 2–7.*

Cattedrale di San Rufino. Saint Francis and Saint Clare were among those baptized in Assisi's Cattedrale, which was the principal church in town until the 12th century. The baptismal font has since been redecorated, but it's possible to see the crypt of Saint Rufino, the bishop who brought Christianity to Assisi, and who was martyred on August 11, 238 (or 236, by some accounts). Admission to the crypt includes the small **Museo Capitolare**, with its detached frescoes and artifacts. ⊠ *Piazza San Rufino* ☎ *075/812712* ⊕ *www.assisimuseodiocesano.com* ▨ *Crypt and Museo Capitolare €3* ☉ *Cathedral: daily 7:30–noon and 2–6. Crypt and museum: mid-Mar.–mid-Oct., daily 10–1 and 3–6; mid-Oct.–mid-Mar., daily 10–1 and 2:30–6.*

WORTH NOTING

Santa Maria Sopra Minerva. Dating from the time of the Emperor Augustus (27 BC–AD 14), this structure was originally dedicated to the Roman goddess of wisdom, in later times used as a monastery and prison before being converted into a church in the 16th century. The expectations raised by the perfect classical facade are not met by the interior, which was subjected to a thorough Baroque transformation in the 17th century. ⊠ *Piazza del Comune* ☎ *075/812268* ☉ *Daily 7–7.*

OFF THE BEATEN PATH

Eremo delle Carceri. About 4 km (2½ miles) east of Assisi is a monastery set in a dense wood against Monte Subasio. The "Hermitage of Prisons" was the place where Saint Francis and his followers went to "imprison" themselves in prayer. The only site in Assisi that remains essentially unchanged since Saint Francis's time, the church and monastery are the kinds of tranquil places that Saint Francis would have appreciated. The walk out from town is very pleasant, and many trails lead from here across the wooded hillside of Monte Subasio (now a protected forest), with beautiful vistas across the Umbrian countryside. True to their Franciscan heritage, the friars here are entirely dependent on alms from visitors. ✉ *Via Santuario delle Carceri, 4 km (2½ miles) east of Assisi* ☎ *075/812301* 🎟 *Donations accepted* 🕒 *Nov.–Mar., daily 9–6; Apr.–Oct., daily 9–5:30.*

WHERE TO EAT

Assisi isn't a late-night town, so don't plan on any midnight snacks. What you can count on is the ubiquitous *stringozzi* (thick spaghetti), as well as the local specialty *piccione all'assisana* (roasted pigeon with olives and liver). The locals eat *torta al testo* (a dense flatbread, often stuffed with vegetables or cheese) with their meals.

$$ UMBRIAN

🍴 **Buca di San Francesco.** In summer, dine in a cool green garden; in winter, under the low brick arches of the cozy cellars. The unique settings and the first-rate fare make this central restaurant Assisi's busiest. Try homemade spaghetti *alla buca,* served with a roasted mushroom sauce. [$] *Average main: €18* ✉ *Via Eugenio Brizi 1* ☎ *075/812204* 🕒 *Closed Mon., and 10 days in late July.*

$$ UMBRIAN Fodor's Choice ★

🍴 **La Pallotta.** At this homey, family-run trattoria with a crackling fireplace and stone walls, the women do the cooking and the men serve the food. Try the stringozzi *alla pallotta* (with a pesto of olives and mushrooms). Connected to the restaurant is an inn whose eight rooms have firm beds and some views across the rooftops of town. [$] *Average main: €18* ✉ *Vicolo della Volta Pinta 3* ☎ *075/812649* 🌐 *www.hotelpallotta.it* 🕒 *Closed Tues., and 2 wks in Jan. or Feb.*

$$ UMBRIAN

🍴 **Osteria Piazzetta dell'Erba.** Hip service and sophisticated presentations attract locals, who enjoy a wide selection of appetizers, including smoked goose breast, and four or five types of pasta, plus various salads and a good selection of torta al testo. For dessert, try the homemade biscuits, which you dunk in sweet wine. The owners carefully select wine at local vineyards, buy it in bulk, and then bottle it themselves, resulting in high quality and reasonable prices. Outdoor seating is available. [$] *Average main: €16* ✉ *Via San Gabriele dell'Addolorata 15a* ☎ *075/815352* 🕒 *Closed Mon., and a few wks in Jan. or Feb.*

$$ UMBRIAN

🍴 **San Francesco.** An excellent view of the Basilica di San Francesco from the covered terrace is just one reason to enjoy the best restaurant in town, where creative Umbrian dishes are made with aromatic locally grown herbs. The seasonal menu might include gnocchi topped with a sauce of wild herbs and *oca stufata di finocchio selvaggio* (goose stuffed with wild fennel). Appetizers and desserts are especially good. [$] *Average main: €20* ✉ *Via di San Francesco 52* ☎ *075/812329* 🕒 *Closed Wed., and July 15–30.*

Continued on page 700

ASSISI'S BASILICA DI SAN FRANCESCO

The legacy of St. Francis, founder of the Franciscan monastic order, pervades Assisi. Each year the town hosts several million pilgrims, but the steady flow of visitors does nothing to diminish the singular beauty of one of Italy's most important religious centers. The pilgrims' ultimate destination is the massive Basilica di San Francesco, which sits halfway up Assisi's hill, supported by graceful arches.

The basilica is not one church but two. The Romanesque **Lower Church** came first; construction began in 1228, just two years after St. Francis's death, and was completed within a few years. The low ceilings and candlelit interior make an appropriately solemn setting for St. Francis's tomb, found in the crypt below the main altar. The Gothic **Upper Church**, built only half a century later, sits on top of the lower one, and is strikingly different, with soaring arches and tall stained-glass windows (the first in Italy). Inside, both churches are covered floor to ceiling with some of Europe's finest frescoes: the Lower Church is dim and full of candlelit shadows, and the Upper Church is bright and airy.

VISITING THE BASILICA

THE LOWER CHURCH

The most evocative way to experience the basilica is to begin with the dark Lower Church. As you enter, give your eyes a moment to adjust. Keep in mind that the artists at work here were conscious of the shadowy environment—they knew this was how their frescoes would be seen.

In the first chapel to the left, a superb fresco cycle by Simone Martini depicts scenes from the life of St. Martin. As you approach the main altar, the vaulting above you is decorated with the *Three Virtues of St. Francis* (poverty, chastity, and obedience) and *St. Francis's Triumph*, frescoes attributed to Giotto's followers. In the transept to your left, Pietro Lorenzetti's *Madonna and Child with St. Francis and St. John* sparkles when the sun hits it. Notice Mary's thumb; legend has it Jesus is asking which saint to bless, and Mary is pointing to Francis. Across the way in the right transept, Cimabue's *Madonna Enthroned Among Angels and St. Francis* is a famous portrait of the saint. Surrounding the portrait are painted scenes from the childhood of Christ, done by the assistants of Giotto.

Nearby is a painting of the crucifixion attributed to Giotto himself.

You reach the crypt via stairs midway along the nave—on the crypt's altar, a stone coffin holds the saint's body. Steps up from the transepts lead to the cloister, where there's a gift shop, and the treasury, which contains holy objects.

THE UPPER CHURCH

The St. Francis fresco cycle is the highlight of the Upper Church. (See facing page.) Also worth special note is the 16th-century choir, with its remarkably delicate inlaid wood. When a 1997 earthquake rocked the basilica, the St. Francis cycle sustained little damage, but portions of the ceiling above the entrance and altar collapsed, reducing their frescoes (attributed to Cimabue and Giotto) to rubble. The painstaking restoration is ongoing.
⚠ The dress code is strictly enforced—no bare shoulders or bare knees.

FRANCIS, ITALY'S PATRON SAINT

PREGANDO ASPETTERO CHE TORNI

St. Francis was born in Assisi in 1181, the son of a noblewoman and a well-to-do merchant. His troubled youth included a year in prison. He planned a military career, but after a long illness Francis heard the voice of God, renounced his father's wealth, and began a life of austerity. His mystical embrace of poverty, asceticism, and the beauty of man and nature struck a responsive chord in the medieval mind; he quickly attracted a vast number of followers. Francis was the first saint to receive the stigmata (wounds in his hands, feet, and side corresponding to those of Christ on the cross). He died on October 4, 1226, in the Porziuncola, the secluded chapel in the woods where he had first preached the virtue of poverty to his disciples. St. Francis was declared patron saint of Italy in 1939, and today the Franciscans make up the largest of the Catholic orders.

THE UPPER CHURCH'S ST. FRANCIS FRESCO CYCLE

The 28 frescoes in the Upper Church depicting the life of St. Francis are the most admired works in the entire basilica. They're also the subject of one of art history's biggest controversies. For centuries they thought to be by Giotto (1267-1337), the great early Renaissance innovator, but inconsistencies in style, both within this series and in comparison to later Giotto works, have thrown their origin into question. Some scholars now say Giotto was the brains behind the cycle, but that assistants helped with the execution; others claim he couldn't have been involved at all.

Two things are certain. First, the style is revolutionary—which argues for Giotto's in-

volvement. The tangible weight of the figures, the emotion they show, and the use of perspective all look familiar to modern eyes, but in the art of the time there was nothing like it. Second, these images have played a major part in shaping how the world sees St. Francis. In that respect, who painted them hardly matters.

Starting in the transept, the frescoes circle the church, showing events in the saint's life (and afterlife). Some of the best are grouped near the church's entrance—look for the nativity at Greccio, the miracle of the spring, the death of the knight at Celano, and, most famously, the sermon to the birds.

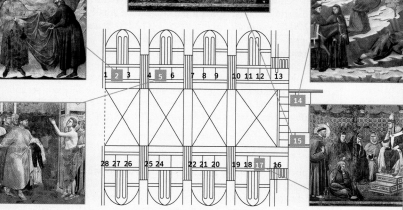

The St. Francis fresco cycle
1. Homage of a simple man
2. Giving cloak to a poor man
3. Dream of the palace
4. Hearing the voice of God
5. Rejection of worldly goods
6. Dream of Innocent III
7. Confirmation of the rules
8. Vision of flaming chariot
9. Vision of celestial thrones
10. Chasing devils from Arezzo
11. Before the sultan
12. Ecstasy of St. Francis
13. Nativity at Greccio
14. Miracle of the spring
15. Sermon to the birds
16. Death of knight at Celano
17. Preaching to Honorius III
18. Apparition at Arles
19. Receiving the stigmata
20. Death of St. Francis
21. Apparition before Bishop Guido and Fra Agostino
22. Verification of the stigmata
23. Mourning of St. Clare
24. Canonization
25. Apparition before Gregory IX
26. Healing of a devotee
27. Confession of a woman
28. Repentant heretic freed

WHERE TO STAY

Reservations are essential at Assisi's hotels between Easter and October and over Christmas. Latecomers are often forced to stay in the modern town of Santa Maria degli Angeli, 8 km (5 miles) away. As a last-minute option, you can always inquire at restaurants to see if they're renting out rooms.

Until the early 1980s, pilgrim hostels outnumbered ordinary hotels in Assisi, and they present an intriguing and economical alternative to conventional lodgings. They're usually called *conventi* or *ostelli* ("convents" or "hostels") because they're run by convents, churches, or other Catholic organizations. Rooms are spartan but peaceful. Check with the tourist office for a list.

$$ **Castello di Petrata.** Wood beams and sections of exposed medieval
HOTEL   stonework add a lot of character to this fortress built in the 14th
Fodor's Choice   century, while comfortable couches turn each individually decorated
★   room into a delightful retreat. **Pros:** great views of town and countryside; medieval character; pool. **Cons:** slightly isolated; far from Assisi town center. $ *Rooms from: €140* ⊠ *Via Petrata 25, Località Petrata* ☎ *075/815451* ⊕ *www.castellopetrata.it* ⤳ *16 rooms, 7 suites* ⊗ *Closed Jan.–Mar.* ⓘ *Breakfast.*

$ **Hotel Umbra.** Rooms on the upper floors of this charming 16th-century
HOTEL   townhouse near Piazza del Comune look out over the Assisi rooftops to the valley below, as does a sunny terrace. **Pros:** friendly welcome; pleasant small garden. **Cons:** difficult parking; some small rooms. $ *Rooms from: €100* ⊠ *Via degli Archi 6* ☎ *075/812240* ⊕ *www.hotelumbra.it* ⤳ *25 rooms* ⊗ *Closed Dec. and Jan.* ⓘ *Breakfast.*

$$ **San Francesco.** Rooms and facilities range from simple to dreary,
HOTEL   but you can't beat the location—the roof terrace and some of the rooms look out onto the basilica. **Pros:** excellent location; great views and breakfast. **Cons:** simple rooms; sometimes noisy in peak season. $ *Rooms from: €130* ⊠ *Via San Francesco 48* ☎ *075/812281* ⊕ *www.hotelsanfrancescoassisi.it* ⤳ *44 rooms* ⓘ *Breakfast.*

NORTHERN UMBRIA

To the north of Perugia, placid, walled Gubbio watches over green countryside, true to its nickname, "City of Silence"—except for the fast and furious festivals in May, as lively today as when they began more than 800 years ago. To the south, along the Tiber River valley, are the towns of Deruta and Torgiano, best known for their hand-painted ceramics and wine—as locals say, go to Deruta to buy a pitcher and to Torgiano to fill it.

GUBBIO

35 km (22 miles) southeast of Città di Castello, 39 km (24 miles) northeast of Perugia, 92 km (57 miles) east of Arezzo.

There's something otherworldly about this jewel of a medieval town tucked away in a mountainous corner of Umbria. Even at the height of

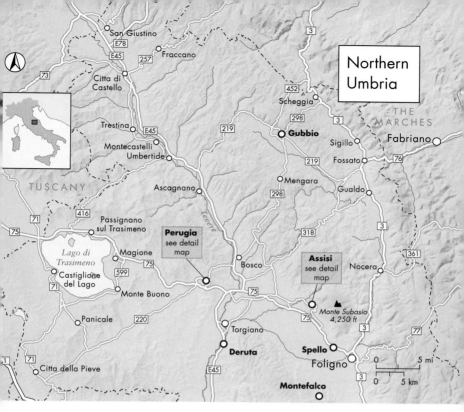

summer, the cool serenity and quiet of Gubbio's streets remain intact. The town is perched on the slopes of Monte Ingino, meaning the streets are dramatically steep. Gubbio's relatively isolated position has kept it free of hordes of high-season visitors, and most of the year the city lives up to its Italian nickname, "La Città del Silenzio" (City of Silence). Parking in the central Piazza dei Quaranta Martiri—named for 40 hostages murdered by the Nazis in 1944—is easy and secure, and it's wise to leave your car in the piazza and explore the narrow streets on foot.

At Christmas, kitsch is king. From December 7 to January 10, colored lights are strung down the mountainside in a shape resembling an evergreen, the world's largest Christmas tree.

GETTING HERE

The closest train station is Fossato di Vico, about 20 km (12 miles) from Gubbio. Ten daily buses connect the train station with the city, a 30-minute trip. If you're driving from Perugia, take the SS298, which rises steeply up toward the Gubbio hills. The trip will take you one hour. There are also 10 buses a day that leave from Perugia's Piazza Partigiani, the main Perugia bus terminal.

VISITOR INFORMATION

Gubbio Tourism Office ✉ *Via della Repubblica 15* ☎ *075/9220693.*

EXPLORING

Basilica di Sant'Ubaldo. Gubbio's famous *ceri*—three 16-foot-tall pillars crowned with statues of Saints Ubaldo, George, and Anthony—are housed in this basilica atop Monte Ingino. The pillars are transported to the Palazzo dei Consoli on the first Sunday of May, in preparation for the Festa dei Ceri, one of central Italy's most spectacular festivals. ⊠ *Monte Ingino* ☎ *075/9273872* ⊗ *Daily 8:30–noon and 4–7.*

Duomo. On a narrow street on the highest tier of the town, the Duomo dates to the 13th century, with some Baroque additions—in particular, a lavishly decorated bishop's chapel. ⊠ *Via Ducale* ⊗ *Daily 8–1 and 3–7.*

Funicular. For a bracing ride to the top of Monte Ingino, hop on the funicular that climbs the hillside just outside the city walls at the eastern end of town. It's definitely not for those who suffer from vertigo. ⊠ *Follow Corso Garibaldi or Via XX Settembre to end* ⊕ *www. funiviagubbio.it* ☎ *€4, €5 round-trip* ⊗ *Sept.–June, daily 10–1:15 and 2:30–5; July and Aug., daily 9–7.*

Palazzo dei Consoli. Gubbio's striking Piazza Grande is dominated by this medieval palazzo, attributed to a local architect known as Gattapone, who is still much admired by today's residents (though some scholars have suggested that the palazzo was in fact the work of another architect, Angelo da Orvieto). In the Middle Ages, the Parliament of Gubbio assembled in the palace, which has become a symbol of the town and now houses a museum with a collection famous chiefly for the Tavole Eugubine. These seven bronze tablets are written in the ancient Umbrian language, employing Etruscan and Latin characters, and provide the best key to understanding this obscure tongue. Also in the museum is a fascinating miscellany of rare coins and earthenware pots. A lofty loggia provides exhilarating views over Gubbio's roofscape and beyond. For a few days at the beginning of May, the palace also displays the famous *ceri,* the ceremonial wooden pillars at the center of Gubbio's annual festivities. ⊠ *Piazza Grande* ☎ *075/9274298* ⊕ *www.comune. gubbio.pg.it* ☎ *€5* ⊗ *Apr.–Oct., daily 10–1 and 3–6; Nov.–Mar., daily 10–1 and 2:30–5:30.*

Palazzo Ducale. This scaled-down copy of the Palazzo Ducale in Urbino (Gubbio was once the possession of that city's ruling family, the Montefeltro) contains a small museum and a courtyard. Some of the public rooms offer magnificent views. ⊠ *Via Ducale* ☎ *075/9275872* ☎ *€5* ⊗ *Tues.–Sun. 8:30–7:30.*

WHERE TO EAT AND STAY

$$

UMBRIAN

✕ **Grotta dell'Angelo.** The rustic trattoria sits in the lower part of the old town near the main square. The menu features simple local specialties, including *capocollo* (a type of salami), stringozzi, and lasagna *tartufata* (with truffles). The few outdoor tables are in high demand in

12

the summer. The restaurant also offers a few small, basically furnished guest rooms, which should be booked in advance. $ *Average main: €18* ⊠ *Via Gioia 47* ☎ *075/9271747* ⌂ *Reservations essential* ⊙ *Closed Tues. and Jan. 7–Feb. 7.*

$$
UMBRIAN
Fodor'sChoice
★

✕ **Taverna del Lupo.** One of the city's most famous taverns gets hectic on weekends and during the high season. Lasagne made in the Gubbian fashion, with ham and truffles, is an unusual indulgence, and the *suprema di faraono* (guinea fowl in a delicately spiced sauce) is a specialty. The restaurant has two fine wine cellars and an extensive wine list. Save room for the excellent desserts. $ *Average main: €24* ⊠ *Via Ansidei 21* ☎ *075/9274368* ⊙ *Closed Mon. Oct.–June.*

$$
UMBRIAN

✕ **Ulisse e Letizia.** A stone-and-wood structure from the 1300s (once an important ceramics factory) is the setting for flavorful seasonal menus. The creative fare might include tagliatelle *al tartuffo* (in a truffle sauce), *gnochetti al finocchio selvatico* (potato dumplings with wild fennel), and *raviolini di faro con asparagi* (tiny ravioli with spelt and asparagus). $ *Average main: €20* ⊠ *Via Mastro Giorgio 2* ☎ *075/9221970* ⊙ *Closed Mon.*

$$
HOTEL

☖ **Hotel Bosone Palace.** A former palace is now home to an elegant hotel, where elaborate frescoes grace the ceilings of the two enormous suites and delightful breakfast room. **Pros:** friendly welcome; excellent location. **Cons:** some noise in tourist season; simple lobby. $ *Rooms from: €130* ⊠ *Via XX Settembre 22* ☎ *075/9220688* ⊕ *www.hotelbosone.com* ⇄ *28 rooms, 2 suites* ⊙ *Closed 3 wks in Jan.* ⚏ *Breakfast.*

DERUTA

7 km (4½ miles) south of Torgiano, 19 km (11 miles) southeast of Perugia.

This 14th-century medieval hill town is most famous for its ceramics. A drive through the countryside to visit the ceramics workshops is a good way to spend a morning, but be sure to stop in the town itself.

GETTING HERE AND AROUND

From Perugia follow the directions for Rome and the E45 highway; Deruta has its own exits. There are also trains from the smaller Sant'Anna train station in Perugia. Take the train in the direction of Terni, and get off at Deruta.

VISITOR INFORMATION

Deruta Tourism Office ⊠ *Piazza dei Consoli 4* ☎ *075/9711559* ⊕ *www. regioneumbria.eu.*

EXPLORING

Museo Regionale della Ceramica (*Regional Ceramics Museum*). It's only fitting that Deruta is home to an impressive ceramics museum, part of which extends into the adjacent 14th-century former convent of San Francesco. The museum tells the history of ceramics, with panels (in Italian and English) explaining artistic techniques and production processes, and also holds the country's largest collection of Italian ceramics—nearly 8,000 pieces are on display. The most notable are the Renaissance vessels using the *lustro* technique, which originated in Arab and Middle Eastern cultures some 500 years before coming into use in Italy in the late 1400s. Lustro, as the name sounds, gives the ceramics a rich finish, which is accomplished with the use of crushed precious materials such as gold and silver. ✉ *Largo San Francesco* ☎ *075/9711000* ⊕ *www.comunederuta.gov.it/cultura-e-territorio/ museo-regionale-della-ceramica* 🎫 *€5, includes admission to Pinoteca Comunale* ⊗ *Wed.–Sun. 10:30–1 and 2:30–5.*

SHOPPING

Deruta is home to more than 70 ceramics shops. They offer a range of ceramics, including extra pieces from commissions for well-known British and North American tableware manufacturers. If you ask, most owners will take you to see where they actually throw, bake, and paint their wares. A drive along Via Tiberina Nord takes you past one shop after another.

SPELLO

12 km (7 miles) southeast of Assisi, 33 km (21 miles) north of Spoleto.

Spello is a gastronomic paradise, especially compared to Assisi. Only a few minutes from Assisi by car or train, this hilltop town at the edge of Monte Subasio makes an excellent strategic and culinary base for exploring nearby towns. Its hotels are well appointed and its restaurants serve some of the best cuisine and wines in the region—sophisticated in variety and excellent in quality. Spello's art scene includes first-rate frescoes by Pinturicchio and Perugino and contemporary artists who can be observed at work in studios around town. If antiquity is your passion, the town also has some intriguing Roman ruins. And the warm, rosy-beige tones of the local *pietra rossa* stone on the buildings brighten even cloudy days.

GETTING HERE AND AROUND

Spello is an easy half-hour drive from Perugia. From the E45 highway, take the exit toward Assisi and Foligno. Merge onto the SS75 and take the Spello exit. There are also regular trains on the Perugia–Assisi line. Spello is 1 km (½ mile) from the train station, and buses run every 30 minutes for Porta Consolare. From Porta Consolare continue up the steep main street that begins as Via Consolare and changes names several times as it crosses the little town, following the original Roman road. As it curves around, notice the winding medieval alleyways to the right and the more uniform Roman-era blocks to the left.

VISITOR INFORMATION

Spello Tourism Office ✉ *Piazza Matteotti 3* ☎ *0742/301009* ⊕ *www. prospello.it* ⊗ *Daily 9:30–12:30 and 3:30–5:30.*

EXPLORING

Santa Maria Maggiore. The two great Umbrian artists hold sway in this 16th century basilica. Pinturicchio's vivid frescoes in the Cappella Baglioni (1501) are striking for their rich colors, finely dressed figures, and complex symbolism. Among Pinturicchio's finest works are the *Nativity, Christ Among the Doctors* (on the far left side is a portrait of Troilo Baglioni, the prior who commissioned the work), and the *Annunciation* (look for Pinturicchio's self-portrait in the Virgin's room).

The artist painted them after he had already won great acclaim for his work in the Palazzi Vaticani in Rome for Borgia Pope Alexander VI. Two pillars on either side of the apse are decorated with frescoes by Perugino (circa 1450–1523). ✉ *Piazza Matteotti 18* ☎ *0742/301792* 🌐 *www.smariamaggiore.com* 🕓 *Daily 9–12:30 and 3–6:30.*

WHERE TO EAT AND STAY

$$ UMBRIAN Fodor's Choice ★

🍴 **Il Molino.** A former mill is one of the region's best restaurants. Appetizers are varied, and often highlight foods found only here, like the *risina*, a tiny white bean. The meat is first-rate, either elaborately prepared or grilled and topped with a signature sauce, and for any dish, the type of olive oil and the names of the local farmers who grew the produce are noted on the menu. Service is attentive and the wine list has plenty of local and Italian options, including the pungent Sagrantino di Montefalco and fresh Orvieto whites. Outside seating lets you soak up the passing street scene; inside is a series of impressive 14th-century arches. [$] *Average main: €22* ✉ *Piazza Matteotti 6/7* ☎ *0742/301021* 🕓 *Closed Tues.*

$$ HOTEL

🏨 **Hotel Palazzo Bocci.** Lovely sitting areas, a reading room, bucolic ceiling and wall frescoes, and a garden terrace all add quiet and elegant charm to this 14th-century building, where several rooms have valley views. **Pros:** central location; splendid views of the valley from public areas and some rooms. **Cons:** noisy in summer months; not all rooms have views. [$] *Rooms from: €150* ✉ *Via Cavour 17* ☎ *0742/301021* 🌐 *www.palazzobocci.com* 🛏 *23 rooms* 🍽 *Breakfast.*

$ HOTEL

🏨 **La Bastiglia.** Polished wood planks and handwoven rugs have replaced the rustic flooring of a former grain mill, and comfortable sitting rooms and cozy bedrooms are filled with a mix of antique and modern pieces. **Pros:** lovely terrace restaurant; cozy rooms; fine views from top-floor rooms, some with terraces. **Cons:** some shared balconies; breakfast is underwhelming; no elevator and plenty of steps, so pack light. [$] *Rooms from: €120* ✉ *Via Salnitraria 15* ☎ *0742/651277* 🌐 *www.labastiglia.com* 🛏 *31 rooms, 2 suites* 🕓 *Closed early Jan.–early Feb.* 🍽 *Breakfast.*

MONTEFALCO

6 km (4 miles) southeast of Bevagna, 34 km (21 miles) south of Assisi.

Nicknamed the "balcony over Umbria" for its high vantage point over the valley that runs from Perugia to Spoleto, Montefalco began as an important Roman settlement situated on the Via Flaminia. The town owes its current name—which means "Falcon's Mount"—to Emperor Frederick II (1194–1250). Obviously a greater fan of falconry than Roman architecture, he destroyed the ancient town, which was then called Coccorone, in 1249, and built in its place what would later become Montefalco. Aside from a few fragments incorporated in a private house just off Borgo Garibaldi, no traces remain of the old Roman center. However, Montefalco has more than its fair share of interesting art and architecture and is well worth the drive up the hill.

GETTING HERE AND AROUND

If you're driving from Perugia, take the E45 toward Rome. Take the Foligno exit, then merge onto the SP445 and follow it into Montefalco. The drive takes around 50 minutes. The nearest train station is in Foligno, about 7 km (4½ miles) away. From there you can take a taxi or a bus into Montefalco.

VISITOR INFORMATION

La Strada del Sagrantino ✉ *Piazza del Comune 17* ☎ *0742/378490* 🌐 *www.stradadelsagrantino.it.*

WHERE TO EAT AND STAY

Montefalco is a good stop for sustenance: here you need go no farther than the main square to find a restaurant or bar with a hot meal, and most establishments, both simple and sophisticated, offer a splendid combination of history and small-town hospitality.

$$ WINE BAR

🍴 **L'Alchemista.** "The Alchemist" is an apt name, as the chef's transformations are indeed magical. Try the *fiore molle della Valnerina,* baked saffron cheese, bacon, and zucchini—served only here. In summer, cold dishes to try are *panzanella* (vegetable salad mixed with bread) or the barley salad tossed with vegetables. The *farro* (spelt) soup made with sagrantino wine is a local specialty. The desserts are delicious: all are made on the premises and not too sweet. [$] *Average main: €15* ✉ *Piazza del Comune 14* ☎ *0742/378558* ⏲ *Closed Tues., and Jan.–Mar.*

$$ HOTEL Fodor's Choice ★

🏨 **Villa Pambuffetti.** If you want to be pampered in the refined atmosphere of a private villa, this is the spot, with the warmth of a fireplace in the winter, a pool to cool you down in summer, and cozy reading nooks and guest rooms year-round. **Pros:** peaceful gardens; refined furnishings; excellent dining room. **Cons:** outside the town center; can get crowded on weekends. [$] *Rooms from: €190* ✉ *Viale della Vittoria 20* ☎ *0742/379417* 🌐 *www.villapambuffetti.it* 🛏 *15 rooms, 3 suites* 🍽 *Breakfast.*

SPOLETO

For most of the year, Spoleto is one more in a pleasant succession of sleepy hill towns, resting regally atop a mountain. But for three weeks every summer the town shifts into high gear for a turn in the international spotlight during the Festival dei Due Mondi (Festival of Two Worlds), an extravaganza of theater, opera, music, painting, and sculpture. As the world's top artists vie for honors, throngs of art aficionados vie for hotel rooms. If you plan to spend the night in Spoleto during the festival, make sure you have confirmed reservations, or you may find yourself scrambling at sunset.

Spoleto has plenty to lure you during the rest of the year as well: the final frescoes of Filippo Lippi, beautiful piazzas and streets with Roman and medieval attractions, and superb natural surroundings with rolling hills and a dramatic gorge. Spoleto makes a good base for exploring all of southern Umbria, as Assisi, Orvieto, and the towns in between are all within easy reach.

The Sagrantino Story

Sagrantino grapes have been used for the production of red wine for centuries. The wine began centuries ago as sagrantino *passito,* a semisweet version in which the grapes are left to dry for a period after picking to intensify the sugar content. One theory traces the origin of sagrantino back to ancient Rome in the works of Pliny the Elder, the author of *Natural History,* who referred to the "Itriola" grape, which some researchers think may be sagrantino. Others believe that in medieval times Franciscan friars returned from Asia Minor with the grape. ("Sagrantino" perhaps derives from *sacramenti,* the religious ceremony in which the wine was used.)

The passito is still produced today, and is preferred by some. But the big change in sagrantino wine production came in the past decades, when sagrantino *secco* (dry) came onto the market. Both passito and secco have a deep ruby-red color that tends toward garnet highlights, with a full body and rich flavor.

For the dry wines, producers not to be missed are Terre di Capitani, Antonelli, Perticaia, and Caprai. Try those labels for the passito as well, in addition to Ruggeri and Scacciadiavoli. Terre di Capitani is complex and has vegetable and mineral tones that join tastes of wild berries, cherries, and chocolate—this winemaker pampers his grapes and it shows. Antonelli is elegant, refined, and rich. The Ruggeri passito is one of the best, so don't be put off by its homespun label. Caprai is bold and rich in taste, and has the largest market share, including a high percentage exported to the United States. Perticaia has a full, rounded taste.

Some wineries are small and not equipped to receive visitors. At La Strada del Sagrantino in Montefalco's main square, you can pick up a map of the wine route and set up appointments, book accommodations, and then visit local enoteche. At the enoteca, ask the sommelier to guide you to some smaller producers you'll have difficulty finding elsewhere.

Salute!

GETTING HERE AND AROUND

Spoleto is an hour's drive from Perugia. From the E45 highway, take the exit toward Assisi and Foligno, then merge onto the SS75 until you reach the Foligno Est exit. Merge onto the SS3, which leads to Spoleto. There are regular trains on the Perugia–Foligno line. From the train station it's a 15-minute uphill walk to the center, so you'll probably want to take a taxi.

Parking options inside the walls include Piazza Campello (just below the Rocca) on the southeast end, Via del Trivio to the north, and Piazza San Domenico on the west end. You can also park at Piazza della Vittoria farther north, just outside the walls. There are also several well-marked lots near the train station. If you arrive by train, you can walk 1 km (½ mile) from the station to the entrance to the lower town. Regular bus connections are every 15–30 minutes. You can also use the *trenino,* as locals call the shuttle service, from the train station to

Piazza della Libertà, near the upper part of the old town, where you'll find the tourist office.

VISITOR INFORMATION

Spoleto Tourism Office ⊠ *Piazza della Libertà 7* ☎ *0743/218620* ⊕ *www. regioneumbria.eu.*

EXPLORING

The walled city is set on a slanting hillside, with the most interesting sections clustered toward the upper portion. Like most other towns with narrow, winding streets, Spoleto is best explored on foot. Bear in mind that much of the city is on a steep slope, so there are lots of stairs and steep inclines. The well-worn stones can be slippery even when dry; wear rubber-sole shoes for good traction. Several pedestrian walkways cut across Corso Mazzini, which zigzags up the hill. A €12 combination ticket purchased at the tourist office allows you entry to all the town's museums and galleries.

TOP ATTRACTIONS

Duomo. The 12th-century Romanesque facade received a Renaissance facelift with the addition of a loggia in a rosy pink stone, creating a stunning contrast in styles. One of the finest cathedrals in the region is lighted by eight rose windows that are especially dazzling in the late afternoon sun. The original floor tiles date from an earlier church that was destroyed by Frederick I (circa 1123–90).

Above the church's entrance is Bernini's bust of Pope Urban VIII (1568–1644), who had the church redecorated in 17th-century Baroque. Fortunately he didn't touch the 15th-century frescoes painted in the apse by Fra Filippo Lippi (circa 1406–69) between 1466 and 1469. These immaculately restored masterpieces—the *Annunciation, Nativity,* and *Dormition*—tell the story of the life of the Virgin. The *Coronation of the Virgin,* adorning the half dome, is the literal and figurative high point. Portraits of Lippi and his assistants are on the right side of the central panel. The Florentine artist priest, "whose colors expressed God's voice" (the words inscribed on his tomb), died shortly after completing the work. His tomb, which you can see in the right transept (note the artist's brushes and tools), was designed by his son, Filippino Lippi (circa 1457–1504).

Another fresco cycle, including work by Pinturicchio, is in the Cappella Eroli, off the right aisle. Note the grotesques in the ornamentation, then very much in vogue with the rediscovery of ancient Roman paintings. The bounty of Umbria is displayed in vivid colors in the abundance of leaves, fruits, and vegetables that adorn the center seams of the cross vault. In the left nave, not far from the entrance, is the well-restored 12th-century crucifix by Alberto Sozio, the earliest known example of this kind of work, with a painting on parchment attached to a wood cross. To the right of the presbytery is the Cappella della Santissima Icona (Chapel of the Most Holy Icon), which contains a small Byzantine painting of a Madonna given to the town by Frederick Barbarossa as a peace offering in 1185, following his destruction of the cathedral

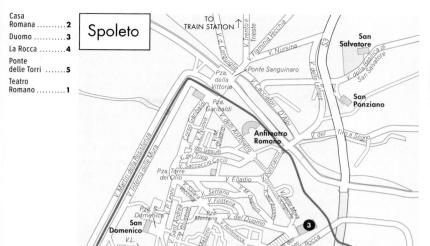

and town three decades earlier. ✉ *Piazza del Duomo* ☎ *0743/231063* ⊙ *Apr.–Oct., daily 8:30–12:30 and 3:30–6; Nov.–Mar., daily 8:30–12:30 and 3:30–5.*

Ponte delle Torri (*Bridge of the Towers*). Standing massive and graceful through the deep gorge that separates Spoleto from Monteluco, this 14th-century bridge is one of Umbria's most photographed monuments, and justifiably so. Built over the foundations of a Roman-era aqueduct, it soars 262 feet above the forested gorge—higher than the dome of St. Peter's in Rome. Sweeping views over the valley and a pleasant sense of vertigo make a walk across the bridge a must, particularly on a starry night. ✉ *Via del Ponte.*

WORTH NOTING

Casa Romana. Spoleto became a Roman colony in the 3rd century BC, but the best excavated remains date from the 1st century AD. Best preserved among them is the Casa Romana. According to an inscription, it belonged to Vespasia Polla, the mother of Emperor Vespasian (one of the builders of the Colosseum and perhaps better known by the Romans for taxing them to install public toilets, later called "Vespasians"). The rooms, arranged around a large central atrium built over an *impluvium* (rain cistern), are decorated with black-and-white geometric mosaics.

✉ *Palazzo del Municipio, Via Visiale 9* ☎ *0743/234250* ⊕ *www. spoletocard.it* 🎟 *€3; €6 combination ticket, includes Pinacoteca Comunale and Galleria d'Arte Moderna* ⊗ *Wed.–Mon. 11–7.*

La Rocca Albornoziana. Built in the mid-14th century for Cardinal Egidio Albornoz, this massive fortress served as a seat for the local pontifical governors, a tangible sign of the restoration of the Church's power in the area when the pope was ruling from Avignon. Several popes spent time here, and one of them, Alexander VI, in 1499 sent his capable teenage daughter Lucrezia Borgia (1480–1519) to serve as governor for three months. The Gubbio-born architect Gattapone (14th century) used the ruins of a Roman acropolis as a foundation and took materials from many Roman-era sites, including the Teatro Romano. La Rocca's plan is long and rectangular, with six towers and two grand courtyards, an upper loggia, and inside some grand reception rooms. In the largest tower, Torre Maestà, you can visit an apartment with some interesting frescoes. A small shuttle bus gives you that last boost up the hill from the ticket booth to the entrance of the fortress. If you phone in advance, you may be able to secure an English-speaking guide. ✉ *Piazza Campello* ☎ *0743/224952* ⊕ *www.spoletocard.it* 🎟 *€7.50* ⊗ *Daily 9:30–7:30* ⊗ *Mon. closes at 8; last admission 45 mins. before closing.*

Teatro Romano. The Romans who colonized the city in 241 BC constructed this small theater in the 1st century AD; for centuries afterward it was used as a quarry for building materials. The most intact portion is the hallway that passes under the *cavea* (stands). The rest was heavily restored in the early 1950s and serves as a venue for Spoleto's Festival dei Due Mondi. The theater was the site of a gruesome episode in Spoleto's history: during the medieval struggle between Guelph (papal) and Ghibelline (imperial) forces, Spoleto took the side of the Holy Roman Emperor. Afterward, 400 Guelph supporters were massacred in the theater, their bodies burned in an enormous pyre. In the end, the Guelphs were triumphant, and Spoleto was incorporated into the states of the Church in 1354.

Through a door in the west portico of the adjoining building is the **Museo Archeologico,** with assorted artifacts found in excavations primarily around Spoleto and Norcia. The collection contains Bronze Age and Iron Age artifacts from Umbrian and pre-Roman eras. Another section contains black-glaze vases from the Hellenistic period excavated from the necropolis of Saint Scolastica in Norcia. The highlight is the stone tablet inscribed on both sides with the Lex Spoletina (Spoleto Law). Dating from 315 BC, this legal document prohibited the desecration of the woods on the slopes of nearby Monteluco. ✉ *Piazza della Libertà* ☎ *0743/223277* ⊕ *www.spoletocard.it* 🎟 *€4* ⊗ *Daily 8:30–7:30.*

WHERE TO EAT

$$ UMBRIAN 🍴 **Apollinare.** Low wooden ceilings and flickering candlelight make this monastery from the 10th and 11th centuries Spoleto's most romantic spot. The kitchen serves sophisticated, innovative variations on local dishes. Sauces of cherry tomatoes, mint, and a touch of red pepper, or of porcini mushrooms, top the long, slender strangozzi. The *caramella* (light puff-pastry cylinders filled with local cheese and served with a creamy Parmesan sauce) is popular. In warm weather you can dine under a canopy on the piazza across from the Museo Archeologico. [$] *Average main: €20* ✉ *Via Sant'Agata 14* ☎ *0743/223256* ⏲ *Closed Tues.*

$$ UMBRIAN 🍴 **Il Tartufo.** As the name indicates, dishes prepared with truffles are the specialty here—don't miss the risotto al tartufo. Incorporating the ruins of a Roman villa, the surroundings are rustic on the ground floor and more modern upstairs. In summer, tables appear outdoors and the traditional fare is spiced up to appeal to the cosmopolitan crowd attending (or performing in) the Festival dei Due Mondi. [$] *Average main: €21* ✉ *Piazza Garibaldi 24* ☎ *0743/40236* ✍ *Reservations essential* ⏲ *Closed Mon., and last 2 wks in July. No dinner Sun.*

$$ UMBRIAN 🍴 **Osteria del Trivio.** Everything is made on the premises and the menu changes daily, depending on what's in season. Dishes might include stuffed artichokes, pasta with local mushrooms, or chicken with artichokes. For dessert, try the homemade biscotti, made for dunking in sweet wine. There's a printed menu, but the owner can explain the dishes in a number of languages. [$] *Average main: €19* ✉ *Via del Trivio 16* ☎ *0743/44349* ⏲ *Closed Tues., and 3 wks in Jan.*

$$ UMBRIAN 🍴 **Ristorante Panciolle.** A small garden filled with lemon trees in the heart of Spoleto's medieval quarter provides one of the most appealing settings you could wish for. Dishes change throughout the year, and may include pastas served with asparagus or mushrooms, as well as grilled meats. More expensive dishes prepared with fresh truffles are also available in season. [$] *Average main: €18* ✉ *Via Duomo 3/5* ☎ *0743/45677* ✍ *Reservations essential* ⏲ *Closed Wed.*

WHERE TO STAY

$$ HOTEL 🏨 **Cavaliere Palace Hotel.** A sense of old-world comfort pervades the 17th-century home of an influential cardinal, and many rooms retain their sumptuous frescoed ceilings. **Pros:** quiet elegance; central position. **Cons:** finding parking can be a problem; crowded in summer. [$] *Rooms from: €180* ✉ *Corso Garibaldi 49* ☎ *0743/220350* 🌐 *www.spoletocavalierepalace.com* 🛏 *29 rooms, 2 suites* 🍽 *Breakfast.*

$ HOTEL 🏨 **Hotel Clitunno.** Cozy guest rooms and intimate public rooms, some with timbered ceilings, give the sense of a traditional Umbrian home—albeit one with a good restaurant. **Pros:** friendly staff; good restaurant. **Cons:** difficult to find a parking space; some small rooms. [$] *Rooms from: €80* ✉ *Piazza Sordini 6* ☎ *0743/223340* 🌐 *www.hotelclitunno.com* 🛏 *45 rooms* 🍽 *Breakfast.*

CLOSE UP

A Taste of Truffles

Umbria is rich with truffles—more are found here than anywhere else in Italy—and those not consumed fresh are processed into pastes or flavored oils. The primary truffle areas are around the tiny town of Norcia, which holds a truffle festival every February, and near Spoleto, where signs warn against unlicensed truffle hunting at the base of the Ponte delle Torri.

Although grown locally, the rare delicacy can cost a small fortune, up to $200 for a quarter pound—fortunately, a little goes a long way. At such a price there's great competition among the nearly 10,000 registered truffle hunters in the province, who use specially trained dogs to sniff them out among the roots of several types of trees, including oak and ilex. Despite a few incidents involving inferior tubers imported from China, you can be reasonably assured that the truffle shaved onto your pasta has been unearthed locally. Don't pass up the opportunity to try this delectable treat. The intense aroma of a dish perfumed with truffles is unmistakable and the flavor memorable.

$$ HOTEL Fodor's Choice ★

Hotel San Luca. Hand-painted friezes decorate the walls of the spacious guest rooms, and elegant comfort is the gracenote throughout—you can sip afternoon tea in oversize armchairs by the fireplace, or take a walk in the sweet-smelling rose garden. **Pros:** very helpful staff; peaceful location. **Cons:** outside the town center; a long walk to the main sights. *Rooms from: €150* ✉ *Via Interna delle Mura 19* ☎ *0743/223399* 🌐 *www.hotelsanluca.com* *33 rooms, 2 suites* *Breakfast.*

SOUTHERN UMBRIA

Narni and Todi are pleasant medieval hill towns. The former stands over a steep gorge, its Roman pedigree evident in dark alleyways and winding streets; the latter is a fairy-tale village with incomparable views and one of Italy's most perfect piazzas. Nearby, Orvieto, built on a tufa mount, produces one of Italy's favorite white wines and has one of the country's greatest cathedrals and most compelling fresco cycles.

TODI

34 km (22 miles) south of Perugia, 34 km (22 miles) east of Orvieto.

As you stand on Piazza del Popolo, looking out onto the Tiber Valley below, it's easy to see why Todi is often described as Umbria's prettiest hill town. Legend has it that the town was founded by the Umbri, who followed an eagle who had stolen a tablecloth. They liked this lofty perch so much that they settled here for good. The eagle is now perched on the insignia of the medieval palaces in the main piazza.

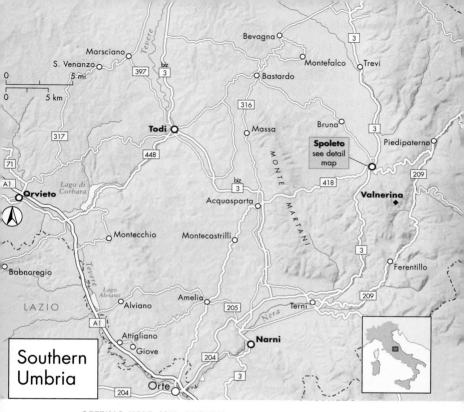

Southern
Umbria

GETTING HERE AND AROUND

Todi is best reached by car, as the town's two train stations are way down the hill and connected to the center by infrequent bus service. From Perugia, follow the E45 toward Rome. Take the Todi/Orvieto exit, then follow the SS79bis into Todi. The drive takes around 40 minutes.

VISITOR INFORMATION

Todi Tourism Office ✉ *Piazza del Popolo 38–39* ☎ *075/8942526* ⊕ *www. regioneumbria.eu.*

EXPLORING

Duomo. One end of the Piazza del Popolo is dominated by this 12th-century Romanesque-Gothic masterpiece, built over the site of a Roman temple. The simple facade is enlivened by a finely carved rose window. Look up at that window as you step inside and you'll notice its peculiarity: each "petal" of the rose has a cherub's face in the stained glass. Also take a close look at the capitals of the double columns with pilasters: perched between the acanthus leaves are charming medieval sculptures of saints—Peter with his keys, George and the dragon, and so on. You can see the rich brown tones of the wooden choir near the altar, but unless you have binoculars or request special permission in advance, you can't get close enough to see all the exquisite detail in this Renaissance masterpiece of woodworking (1521–30). The severe solid mass of the Duomo is mirrored by the Palazzo dei Priori (1595–97) across the way. ✉ *Piazza del Popolo* ☎ *075/8943041* ☉ *Daily 8–1 and 3–6.*

Piazza del Popolo. Built above the Roman Forum, Piazza del Popolo is Todi's high point, a model of spatial harmony with stunning views onto the surrounding countryside. In the best medieval tradition, the square was conceived to house both the temporal and the spiritual centers of power.

WHERE TO EAT AND STAY

$$ ✕ **Ristorante Umbria.** Todi's most popular restaurant for more than four
UMBRIAN   decades is reliable for its sturdy country food and the wonderful view from the terrace. Because it has only 16 tables outside, make sure you reserve ahead. In winter, try legume soup, homemade pasta with truffles, or *palombaccio alla ghiotta* (roasted squab). Steaks, accompanied by a rich dark-brown wine sauce, are good as well. $ *Average main: €18* ✉ *Via San Bonaventura 13* ☎ *075/8942737* ☉ *Closed Tues.*

$ ⌂ **San Lorenzo 3.** Surrounded by antique furniture, paintings, and period
HOTEL   knickknacks, you will be as charmed by a sense of being in the 19th century as you are by the magnificent views over valleys and hills. **Pros:** old-world atmosphere; excellent central location. **Cons:** few modern amenities; basic furnishings; some shared bathrooms. $ *Rooms from: €110* ✉ *Via San Lorenzo 3* ☎ *075/8944555* ⊕ *www.sanlorenzo3.it* ↗ *6 rooms (3 with bath)* ▤ *No credit cards* ☉ *Closed Jan. and Feb.* ⋈ *Breakfast.*

ORVIETO

30 km (19 miles) southwest of Todi, 81 km (51 miles) west of Spoleto.

Carved out of an enormous plateau of volcanic rock high above a green valley, Orvieto has natural defenses that made the high walls seen in many Umbrian towns unnecessary. The Etruscans were the first to settle here, digging a honeycombed network of more than 1,200 wells and storage caves out of the soft stone. The Romans attacked, sacked, and destroyed the city in 283 BC; since then, it has grown up out of the rock into an enchanting maze of alleys and squares. Orvieto was solidly Guelph in the Middle Ages, and for several hundred years popes sought refuge in the city—at times needing protection from their enemies, at times seeking respite from the summer heat of Rome.

When painting his frescoes inside the Duomo, Luca Signorelli asked that part of his contract be paid in Orvietan wine, and he was neither the first nor the last to appreciate the region's popular white. In past times, the caves carved underneath the town were used to ferment the trebbiano grapes used in making Orvieto Classico; now, local wine production has moved out to more traditional vineyards, but you can still while away the afternoon in tastings at any number of shops in town.

GETTING HERE AND AROUND

Orvieto is well connected by train to Rome, Florence, and Perugia. It's also adjacent to the A1 autostrada that runs between Florence and Rome. Parking areas in the upper town tend to be crowded. A better idea is to follow the signs for the Porta Orvetiana parking lot, then take the funicular that carries people up the hill.

VISITOR INFORMATION

A Carta Orvieto Unica (single ticket) is expensive but a great deal if you want to visit everything. For €18 you get admission to the three major sights in town—Cappella di San Brizio (at the Duomo), Museo Archeologico Claudio Faina, and Orvieto Underground—along with entry to the Torre del Moro with views of Orvieto, plus a combination bus-funicular pass or five hours of free parking.

> ### WORD OF MOUTH
>
> "Orvieto makes a nice day or overnight stop. Lots of great shoe shops. The nearby hilltop village of Civita makes a great side trip— you have to park your vehicle and walk across a suspension bridge to get there, but when you arrive, you'll find a quaint and cute village." —DOCK

Orvieto Tourism Office ✉ *Piazza del Duomo 24* ☏ *0763/341772* ⊕ *www.regioneumbria.eu.*

EXPLORING

Fodor's Choice ★

Duomo. Orvieto's stunning cathedral was built to commemorate the Miracle at Bolsena. In 1263 a young priest who questioned the miracle of transubstantiation (in which the Communion bread and wine become the flesh and blood of Christ) was saying mass at nearby Lago di Bolsena. His doubts were put to rest, however, when a wafer he had just blessed suddenly started to drip blood, staining the linen covering the altar. The cloth and the host were taken to the pope, who proclaimed a miracle and a year later provided for a new religious holiday—the Feast of Corpus Domini. Thirty years later, construction began on the Duomo in Orvieto to celebrate the miracle and house the stained altar cloth.

It's thought that Arnolfo di Cambio (circa 1245–1302), the famous builder of the Duomo in Florence, was given the initial commission, but the project was soon taken over by Lorenzo Maitani (circa 1275–1330), who consolidated the structure and designed the monumental facade. Maitani also made the bas-relief panels between the doorways, which graphically tell the story of the Creation (on the left) and the Last Judgment (on the right). The lower registers, now protected by Plexiglas, succeed in conveying the horrors of hell as few other works of art manage to do, an effect made all the more powerful by the worn gray marble. Above, gold mosaics are framed by finely detailed Gothic decoration.

Inside, the cathedral is rather vast and empty; the major works are in the transepts. To the left is the **Cappella del Corporale,** where the square linen cloth (*corporale*) is kept in a golden reliquary that's modeled on the cathedral and inlaid with enamel scenes of the miracle. The cloth is removed for public viewing on Easter and on Corpus Domini (the ninth Sunday after Easter). In the right transept is the **Cappella di San Brizio,** or Cappella Nuova. In this chapel is one of Italy's greatest fresco cycles, notable for its influence on Michelangelo's *Last Judgment,* as well as for the extraordinary beauty of the figuration. In these works, a few by Fra Angelico and the majority by Luca Signorelli, the damned fall to hell, demons breathe fire and blood, and Christians are martyred. Some scenes are heavily influenced by the imagery in Dante's (1265–1321)

Divine Comedy. ✉ *Piazza del Duomo* ☎ *0763/342477* 🎫 *Cappella di San Brizio €3* ⊗ *Mar.–Oct., daily 9:30–6:30; Nov.–Feb., daily 9:30–1 and 2:30–5.*

Museo Archeologico Claudio Faina. This superb private collection, beautifully arranged and presented, goes far beyond the usual museum offerings of a scattering of local remains. The collection is particularly rich in Greek- and Etruscan-era pottery, from large Attic amphorae (6th–4th century BC) to Attic black- and red-figure pieces to Etruscan *bucchero* (dark-reddish clay) vases. Other interesting pieces in the collection include a 6th-century sarcophagus and a substantial display of Roman-era coins. ✉ *Piazza del Duomo 29* ☎ *0763/341511* ⊕ *www.museofaina. it* 🎫 *€4* ⊗ *Apr.–Sept., daily 9:30–6; Oct.–Mar., Tues.–Sun. 10–5.*

Orvieto Underground. More than just about any other town, Orvieto has grown from its own foundations. The Etruscans, the Romans, and those who followed dug into the tufa (the same soft volcanic rock from which catacombs were made) to create more than 1,000 separate cisterns, caves, secret passages, storage areas, and production areas for wine and olive oil. Much of the tufa removed was used as building blocks for the city that exists today, and some was partly ground into *pozzolana,* which was made into mortar. You can see the labyrinth of dugout chambers beneath the city on the **Orvieto Underground tour** (✉ *Orvieto tourism office, Piazza del Duomo 24*), run daily at 11, 12:15, 4, and 5:15. Admission for the hour-long English tour is €6. ☎ *0763/341772 for tourism office* ⊕ *www.orvietounderground.it.*

Pozzo della Cava. If you're short on time but want a quick look at the cisterns and caves beneath the city, head for the Pozzo della Cava, an Etruscan well for spring water. ✉ *Via della Cava 28* ☎ *0763/342373* 🎫 *€3* ⊗ *Tues.–Fri. 9–8.*

WHERE TO EAT AND STAY

The streets around the Duomo are lined with all types of bars and restaurants where you can eat simple or elaborate food and try wines by the glass.

$$

UMBRIAN

Fodor's Choice
★

✕ **Il Giglio D'Oro.** A great view of the Duomo is coupled with superb food. Eggplant is transformed into an elegant custard with black truffles in the *sformatino di melenzane con vellutata al tartuffo nero.* Pastas, like *ombrichelli al pesto umbro,* are traditional, but perhaps with a new twist like fresh coriander leaves instead of the usual basil. Lamb roasted in a crust of bread is delicately seasoned with a tomato cream sauce. The wine cellar includes some rare vintages. ⓢ *Average main: €19* ✉ *Piazza Duomo 8* ☎ *0763/341903* ⊗ *Closed Wed.*

$$

UMBRIAN

✕ **Le Grotte del Funaro.** Dine inside tufa caves under central Orvieto, where the two windows afford splendid views of the hilly countryside. The traditional Umbrian food is reliably good, with simple grilled meats and vegetables and pizzas. Oddly, though, the food is outclassed by the extensive wine list, with top local and Italian labels and quite a few rare vintages. ⓢ *Average main: €18* ✉ *Via Ripa Serancia 41* ☎ *0763/343276* 🍽 *Reservations essential* ⊗ *Closed 1 wk in July.*

$$

UMBRIAN

✕ **Trattoria La Grotta.** Franco, the owner, has been in this location for more than 20 years and has attracted a steady American clientele

Hiking the Umbrian Hills

Magnificent scenery makes the heart of Italy excellent walking, hiking, and mountaineering country. In Umbria, the area around Spoleto is particularly good; several pleasant, easy, and well-signed trails begin at the far end of the Ponte alle Torri bridge over Monteluco. From Cannara, an easy half-hour walk leads to the fields of Pian d'Arca, the site of Saint Francis's sermon to the birds. For slightly more arduous walks, you can follow the saint's path, uphill from Assisi to the Eremo delle Carceri, and then continue along the trails that crisscross Monte Subasio. At 4,250 feet, the Subasio's treeless summit affords views of Assisi, Perugia, far-off Gubbio, and the distant mountain ranges of Abruzzo.

For even more challenging hiking, the northern reaches of the Valnerina are exceptional; the mountains around Norcia should not be missed. Throughout Umbria and the Marches, you'll find that most recognized walking and hiking trails are marked with the distinctive red-and-white blazes of the Club Alpino Italiano. Tourist offices are a good source for walking and climbing itineraries to suit all ages and levels of ability, while bookstores, *tabacchi* (tobacconists), and *edicole* (newsstands) often have maps and hiking guides that detail the best routes in their area. Depending on the length and location of your walk, it can be important that you have comfortable walking shoes or boots, appropriate attire, and plenty of water to drink.

without losing his local following—or his touch with homemade pasta, perhaps with a duck or wild-boar sauce. Roast lamb, veal, and pork are all good, and the desserts are homemade. Franco knows the local wines well and has a carefully selected list, including some from smaller but still excellent wineries, so ask about them. $\boxed{\$}$ *Average main: €19* ⊠ *Via Luca Signorelli 5* ☎ *0763/341348* ⊘ *Closed Tues.*

\$\$
HOTEL 🏨 **Hotel Palazzo Piccolomini.** This 16th-century family palazzo has been beautifully restored, with inviting public spaces and handsome guest quarters where contemporary surroundings are accented with old beams, vaulted ceilings, and other distinctive touches. **Pros:** peaceful atmosphere; efficient staff; good location. **Cons:** slightly overpriced. $\boxed{\$}$ *Rooms from: €154* ⊠ *Piazza Ranieri 36* ☎ *0763/341743* ⊕ *www.palazzopiccolomini.it* ⤙ *28 rooms, 3 suites* ⦿ *Breakfast.*

NARNI

13 km (8 miles) southwest of Terni, 46 km (29 miles) southeast of Orvieto.

Once a bustling and important town at a major crossroads on the Via Flaminia, Narni is now a quiet backwater with only the occasional tourist invading its hilltop streets. Modern development is kept out of sight in the new town of Narni Scalo, below. This means that you'll find the older neighborhood safely preserved behind, and in the case of Narni's subterranean Roman ruins, beneath, the town's sturdy walls.

GETTING HERE AND AROUND

From Perugia, take the E45 highway toward Rome. Merge onto the SS675, then take the exit to San Gemini and follow signs for Narni Scalo. The drive takes around 1½ hours. There are also regular trains from Perugia.

VISITOR INFORMATION

Terni Tourism Office. Stop here for information about Narni and a number of other smaller towns. ✉ *Via Cassian Bon 4, Terni* ☎ *0744/423047* 🌐 *www.regioneumbria.eu.*

EXPLORING

Roman Aqueduct. You can take a unique tour of Narni's underground Roman aqueduct—the only one open to the public in all of Italy—but it's not for the claustrophobic. Contact Narni Sotterranea at least ten days ahead to book a visit. ✉ *Narni Sotterranea, Via San Bernardo 12* ☎ *0744/722292* 🌐 *www.narnisotterranea.it* 🎟 *€20* 🕒 *Apr.–Oct., by appointment.*

WHERE TO EAT

$$ UMBRIAN 🍴 **Il Cavallino.** Run by the third generation of the Bussetti family, this trattoria is south of Narni on the Via Flaminia. The most dependable menu selections are the grilled meats. Rabbit roasted with rosemary and sage and juicy grilled T-bone steaks are house favorites; in winter, phone ahead to request the wild pigeon. The wine list has a limited selection of dependable local varieties. [$] *Average main: €15* ✉ *Via Flaminia Romana 220, 3 km (2 miles) south of town center* ☎ *0744/761020* 🕒 *Closed Tues., and Dec. 20–26.*

VALNERINA

Terni is 13 km (8 miles) northeast of Narni, 27 km (17 miles) southeast of Spoleto.

The Valnerina (the valley of the River Nera, to the east of Spoleto) is the most beautiful of central Italy's many well-kept secrets. The twisting roads that serve the rugged landscape are poor, but the drive is well worth the effort for its forgotten medieval villages and dramatic mountain scenery.

GETTING HERE AND AROUND

You can head into the area from Terni on the S209, or on the SP395bis north of Spoleto, which links the Via Flaminia (S3) with the middle reaches of the Nera Valley through a tunnel.

EXPLORING

Cascata delle Marmore. The road east of Terni (SS Valnerina) leads 10 km (6 miles) to the Cascata delle Marmore (Waterfalls of Marmore), which, at 541 feet, are the highest in Europe. A canal was dug by the Romans in the 3rd century BC to prevent flooding in the nearby agricultural plains. Nowadays the waters are often diverted to provide hydroelectric power for Terni, reducing the roaring falls to an unimpressive trickle, so check with the information office at the falls (there's a timetable on their website in English) or with Terni's tourist office before heading here. On summer evenings, when the falls are in full spate, the cascading water is floodlit to striking effect. The falls are usually at their most energetic at midday and at around 4 pm. This is a good place for hiking, except in December and January, when most trails may be closed. ⊠ *SP79, 10 km (6 miles) east of Terni* ☎ *0744/62982* ⊕ *www.marmorefalls.it* ⊠ *€9* ⊙ *May, weekends noon–1 and 4–5; June–Aug., daily 11–10; mid-Mar.– Apr. and Sept., weekends noon–9; Jan.–mid-Mar., weekends noon–4.*

Norcia. The birthplace of Saint Benedict, Norcia is best known for its Umbrian pork and truffles. Norcia exports truffles to France and hosts a truffle festival, the **Sagra del Tartufo,** every February. The surrounding mountains provide spectacular hiking. ⊠ *67 km (42 miles) northeast of Terni.*

Piano Grande. A mountain plain 25 km (15 miles) to the northeast of the valley, Piano Grande is a hang glider's paradise and a wonderful place for a picnic or to fly a kite. It's also nationally famous for the quality of the lentils grown here, which are a traditional part of every Italian New Year's feast.

THE MARCHES

An excursion from Umbria into the Marches region allows you to see a part of Italy rarely visited by foreigners. Not as wealthy as Tuscany or Umbria, the Marches has a diverse landscape of mountains and beaches, and marvelous views. Like that of neighbors to the west, the patchwork of rolling hills of Le Marche (as it's known in Italian) is stitched with grapevines and olive trees, bearing luscious wine and olive oil.

Traveling here isn't as easy as in Umbria or Tuscany. Beyond the narrow coastal plain and away from major towns, the roads are steep and twisting. An efficient bus service connects the coastal town of Pesaro to Urbino. Train travel in the region is slow, however, and stops are limited—although you can reach Ascoli Piceno by rail.

URBINO

75 km (47 miles) north of Gubbio, 116 km (72 miles) northeast of Perugia, 230 km (143 miles) east of Florence.

Majestic Urbino, atop a steep hill with a skyline of towers and domes, is something of a surprise to come upon. Although quite remote, it was once a center of learning and culture almost without rival in Western Europe. The town looks much as it did in the glory days of the 15th century: a cluster of warm brick and pale stone buildings, all topped with russet-color tile roofs. The focal point is the immense and beautiful Palazzo Ducale.

The city is home to the small but prestigious Università di Urbino— one of the oldest in the world—and the streets are usually filled with students. Urbino is very much a college town, with the usual array of bookshops, bars, and coffeehouses. In summer the Italian student population is replaced by foreigners who come to study Italian language and arts at several prestigious private fine-arts academies.

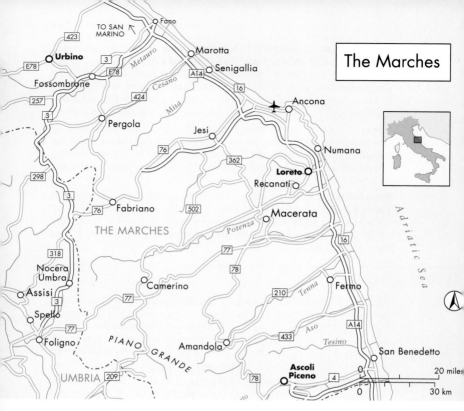

The Marches

TO SAN MARINO
Fano
Urbino
Fossombrone
Marotta
Senigallia
Metauro
Cesano
Pergola
Misa
Ancona
Jesi
Numana
Loreto
Recanati
Fabriano
Macerata
THE MARCHES
Potenza
Nocera Umbra
Assisi
Camerino
Fermo
Spello
Tenna
Foligno
PIANO GRANDE
Amandola
Aso
San Benedetto
Tesino
UMBRIA
Ascoli Piceno
Adriatic Sea

20 miles
30 km

Urbino's fame rests on the reputation of three of its native sons: Duke Federico da Montefeltro (1422–82), the enlightened warrior-patron who built the Palazzo Ducale; Raffaello Sanzio (1483–1520), or Raphael, one of the most influential painters in history and an embodiment of the spirit of the Renaissance; and the architect Donato Bramante (1444–1514), who translated the philosophy of the Renaissance into buildings of grace and beauty. Unfortunately there's little work by either Bramante or Raphael in the city, but the duke's influence can still be felt strongly.

GETTING HERE AND AROUND

Take the SS3bis from Perugia, and follow the directions for Gubbio and Cesena. Exit at Umbertide and take the SS219, then the SS452, and at Calmazzo, the SS73bis to Urbino.

VISITOR INFORMATION

Urbino Tourism Office ⊠ *Piazza de Rinascimento 1* ☎ *0722/2613* ⊕ *www. turismo.pesarourbino.it/en.html.*

EXPLORING

Casa Natale di Raffaello (*House of Raphael*). This is the house in which the painter was born and where he took his first steps in painting, under the direction of his artist father. There's some debate about the fresco of the Madonna here; some say it's by Raphael, whereas others attribute it to his father—with Raphael's mother and the young painter himself standing in as models for the Madonna and Child. ⊠ *Via Raffaello 57* ☎ *0722/320105* ⊑ *€3.50* ⊘ *Apr.–Nov., Mon.–Sat. 9–7, Sun. 10–1; Oct.–Mar., Mon.–Sat. 9–2, Sun. 10–1.*

Fodor's Choice ★ **Palazzo Ducale** (*Ducal Palace*). The Palazzo Ducale holds a place of honor in the city. If the Renaissance was, ideally, a celebration of the nobility of man and his works, of the light and purity of the soul, then there's no other place in Italy—the birthplace of the Renaissance—where these tenets are better illustrated. From the moment you enter the peaceful courtyard, you know you're in a place of grace and beauty, the harmony of the building reflecting the high ideals of the time. Today the palace houses the **Galleria Nazionale delle Marche** (National Museum of the Marches), with a superb collection of paintings, sculpture, and other objets d'art. Some works were originally the possessions of the Montefeltro family; others were brought here from churches and palaces throughout the region. Masterworks in the collection include Paolo Uccello's *Profanation of the Host,* Titian's *Resurrection* and *Last Supper,* and Piero della Francesca's *Madonna of Senigallia.* But the gallery's highlight is Piero's enigmatic work long known as *The Flagellation of Christ.* Much has been written about this painting, and few experts agree on its meaning. Legend had it that the figures in the foreground represent a murdered member of the Montefeltro family (the barefoot young man) and his two killers. However, Sir John Pope-Hennessy—the preeminent scholar of Italian Renaissance art—argues that they represent the arcane subject of the vision of Saint Lawrence. Academic debates notwithstanding, the experts agree that the work is one of the painter's masterpieces. Piero himself thought so: it's one of the few works he signed (on the lowest step supporting the throne). ⊠ *Piazza Duca Federico* ☎ *0722/322625* ⊕ *www.galleriaborghese.it* ⊑ *€5* ⊘ *Mon. 8:30–2, Tues.–Sun. 8:30–7:15; ticket office closes at 6.*

WHERE TO EAT AND STAY

$
ITALIAN
✕ **Angolo Divino.** At this osteria in the center of Urbino, tradition reigns supreme: the menu is written in local dialect, flanked by Italian and English translations. Dishes range from the deliciously simple spaghetti *col pane grattugiato* (with bread crumbs) to the temptingly rich *filetto al tartufo* (beef filet with truffles). $ *Average main: €14* ⊠ *Via S. Andrea 14* ☎ *0722/327559* ⊘ *Closed Mon., and mid-Oct.–mid-Nov. No dinner Sun.*

$$
ITALIAN
✕ **La Vecchia Fornarina.** Locals often crowd this small, two-room trattoria near the Piazza della Repubblica. The specialty is meaty country fare, such as *coniglio* (rabbit) and *vitello alle noci* (veal cooked with walnuts) or *ai porcini* (with mushrooms). There's also a good selection of pasta dishes. $ *Average main: €15* ⊠ *Via Mazzini 14* ☎ *0722/320007* ⌣ *Reservations essential.*

$$
HOTEL
🏨 **Hotel Bonconte.** Pleasant rooms just inside the city walls and close to the Palazzo Ducale are decorated with a smattering of antiques, and those in front have views of the valley below Urbino. **Pros:** some nice views; away from the bustle. **Cons:** an uphill walk to town center; service can be sleepy. $ *Rooms from: €160* ⊠ *Via delle Mura 28* ☎ *0722/2463* ⊕ *www.viphotels.it* ⇥ *23 rooms, 2 suites* ⦿ *No meals.*

12

LORETO

31 km (19 miles) south of Ancona, 118 km (73 miles) southeast of Urbino.

There's a strong Renaissance feel about this hilltop town, which is home to one of the most important religious sites in Europe, the Santuario della Santa Casa (House of the Virgin Mary). Bramante and Sansovino gave the church its Renaissance look, although many other artists helped create its special atmosphere. Today the town revolves around the religious calendar; if you can be here on December 10, you will witness the Feast of the Translation of the Holy House, when huge bonfires are lighted to celebrate the miraculous arrival of the house in 1294.

GETTING HERE AND AROUND

If you're driving from Perugia, take the SS318 and then the SS76 highway to Fabriano and then on to Chiaravalle, where it merges with the A14 autostrada. The drive takes around 2½ hours. Trains also go to Loreto, but the station is about a mile outside the town center. Regular buses leave from the station to the center.

VISITOR INFORMATION

Loreto Tourism Office ⊠ *Via Solari 3* ☎ *071/970276* ⊕ *www.turismo. marche.it.*

EXPLORING

Basilica della Santa Casa. Loreto is famous for one of the best-loved shrines in the world, that of the **Santuario della Santa Casa** (House of the Virgin Mary), within the Basilica della Santa Casa. Legend has it that angels moved the house from Nazareth, where the Virgin Mary was living at the time of the Annunciation, to this hilltop in 1295. The reason for this sudden and divinely inspired move was that Nazareth had fallen into the hands of Muslim invaders, whom the angelic hosts viewed as unsuitable keepers of this important shrine. Excavations made at the behest of the Catholic Church have shown that the house did once stand elsewhere and was brought to the hilltop—by either crusaders or a family named Angeli—around the time the angels (*angeli*) are said to have done the job.

The house itself consists of three rough stone walls contained within an elaborate marble tabernacle. Built around this centerpiece is the giant Basilica della Santa Casa, which dominates the town. Millions of visitors come to the site every year (particularly at Easter and on the December 10 Feast of the Holy House), and the little town of Loreto can become uncomfortably crowded with pilgrims. Many great Italian architects, including Bramante, Antonio da Sangallo the Younger (1483–1546), Giuliano da Sangallo (circa 1445–1516), and Sansovino (1467–1529), contributed to the design of the basilica. It was begun in the Gothic style in 1468 and continued in Renaissance style through the late Renaissance. The bell tower is by Luigi Vanvitelli (1700–73). Inside the church are a great many mediocre 19th- and 20th-century paintings, but also some fine works by Renaissance masters such as Luca Signorelli and Melozzo da Forlì (1438–94).

If you're a nervous air traveler, you can take comfort in the fact that the Holy Virgin of Loreto is the patron saint of air travelers and that Pope John Paul II composed a prayer for a safe flight—available here in a half-dozen languages. ⊠ *Piazza della Madonna* ☎ *071/970276* ⊕ *www. santuarioloreto.it* ⊘ *Apr.–Sept., daily 6:30 am–8 pm; Oct.–Mar., daily 6:30 am–7 pm. Santuario closed daily 12:30–2:30.*

12

ASCOLI PICENO

88 km (55 miles) south of Loreto, 105 km (65 miles) south of Ancona.

Ascoli Piceno sits in a valley ringed by steep hills and cut by the Tronto River. In Roman times it was one of central Italy's best-known market towns, and today, with almost 60,000 residents, it's a major fruit and olive producer, making it one of the most important towns in the region. Despite growth during the Middle Ages and at other times, the streets in the town center continue to reflect the grid pattern of the ancient Roman city. You'll even find the word *rua*, from the Latin *ruga*, used for "street" instead of the Italian *via*. Now largely closed to traffic, the city center is great to explore on foot.

GETTING HERE AND AROUND

From Perugia take the SS75 to Foligno, then merge onto the SS3 to Norcia. From here take the SS4 to Ascoli Piceno. There are also trains, but the journey would be quite long, taking you from Perugia to Ancona before changing for Ascoli Piceno.

VISITOR INFORMATION

Ascoli Piceno Tourism Office ⊠ *Piazza Aringo 7* ☎ *0736/253045* ⊕ *www. turismo.marche.it.*

EXPLORING

Piazza del Popolo. The heart of the town is the majestic Piazza del Popolo, dominated by the Gothic church of **San Francesco** and the **Palazzo del Popolo**, a 13th-century town hall that contains a graceful Renaissance courtyard. The square functions as the living room of the entire city and at dusk each evening is packed with people strolling and exchanging news and gossip—the sweetly antiquated ritual called the *passeggiata*, performed all over the country.

WHERE TO STAY

$ **Il Pennile.** A modern, family-run hotel in a quiet residential area out-
HOTEL   side the old city center is pleasantly set amid a grove of olive trees. **Pros:** peaceful; a good budget option. **Cons:** distance from town center; basic rooms. Ⓢ *Rooms from: €70* ⊠ *Via G. Spalvieri* ☎ *0736/41645* ⊕ *www. hotelpennile.it* ⤳ *33 rooms* ⏐⊙⏐ *Breakfast.*

SOUTHERN ITALY

WHAT'S WHERE

1 Naples and Campania.
Campania is the gateway to southern Italy—and as far south as many travelers get. The region's happy combination of spectacular geology and rich cultural heritage makes it a wildly popular place to unwind. Dream away two magical weeks on the pint-size islands of Capri and Ischia and the fabled resorts—Positano, Amalfi, Ravello—of the Amalfi Coast. Or explore the past at the archaeological ruins of Pompeii, Herculaneum, and Paestum. Naples, a chaotic metropolis, is arguably Italy's most fun and operatic city.

2 The Southern Peninsula.
The southernmost regions of the peninsula—Puglia, Basilicata, and Calabria—are known for their laid-back medieval villages, shimmering seas, and varied landscapes. The coastline of Puglia, along the heel of Italy's boot, is popular with beachgoers, but for the most part you're off the beaten path here, with all the pleasures and challenges that entails. The most distinctive attractions are the *Sassi* (cave dwellings in the Basilicata village of Matera) and *trulli* (mysterious conical-roof dwellings found in abundance in Puglia's Valle d'Itria). Both are UNESCO World Heritage Sites.

GARGANO
PENINSULA

Foggia

Adriatic Sea

Bari

Alberobello
Matera
Brindisi
PUGLIA
Potenza
Lecce
BASILICATA
Taranto
Aliano
2
Gallipoli

Maratea

*Gulf of
Taranto*

Diamante

Rende Cosenza

CALABRIA
Crotone

Pizzo
Catanzaro
Tropea

Stilo
Bagnara
Calabria
Milazzo
Locri
Messina Reggio

Taormina

Ionian Sea

Siracusa

| 0 | | 50 mi |
| 0 | | 50 km |

SARDINIA
SICILY

3 **Sicily.** Baroque church–hopping could be a sport in the cacophonous streets of Palermo and seafaring Siracusa. The breezes are sultry, and everyday life is without pretense, as witnessed in the workaday stalls of the fish markets in ports all along the Tyrrhenian and Ionian coasts, bursting with tuna, swordfish, and sardines. Greek ruins stand sentinel in Agrigento's Valley of the Temples, blanketed in almond, oleander, and juniper blossoms.

SOUTHERN ITALY PLANNER

Speaking the Language

Here, as in much of Italy, when locals talk among themselves, they often revert to a dialect unintelligible to the student of textbook Italian. Each region has a dialect of its own; Neapolitan, Sicilian, Salentinu (spoken in the tip of the heel) and Barese (around Bari) are distinctive enough to be considered separate languages.

Nowadays pretty much everyone speaks standard Italian as well, so you can still benefit from whatever knowledge you have of the language. English-speakers aren't as prevalent as in points north, but this is the land of creative gesticulation and other improvised nonverbal communication. Chances are, you'll be able to get your message across.

Getting Here

Aeroporto Capodichino (NAP), 8 km (5 miles) outside Naples, serves the Campania region. It handles domestic and international flights, including several flights daily between Naples and Rome (55 minutes).

The three main airports of the deep south are at Bari and Brindisi in Puglia and at Lamezia Terme in Calabria. All three have regular flights to and from Rome and Milan. In addition, Reggio di Calabria's airport has flights to and from Rome.

Sicily can be reached from all major international cities on flights connecting through Rome, Milan, or Naples. Planes to Palermo land at **Aeroporto Falcone-Borsellino** in Punta Raisi, 32 km (19 miles) west of town. Catania's **Aeroporto Fontanarossa**, 5 km (3 miles) south of the city center, is the main airport on Sicily's eastern side

There are direct trains from Rome to Palermo, Catania, and Siracusa, as well as an overnight train from Milan. The Rome–Palermo and Rome–Siracusa trips take around 12 hours. After Naples, the run is mostly along the coast, so try to book a window seat on the right if you're not on an overnight train. At Villa San Giovanni, in Calabria, the train is separated and loaded onto a ferryboat to cross the strait to Messina. Direct trains run from Milan, Rome, and Bologna to Bari and Lecce.

TYPICAL TRAVEL TIMES		
	HOURS BY CAR	HOURS BY TRAIN
Naples–Rome	2 hrs 30 mins	1 hr 10 mins
Bari–Lecce	2 hrs	1 hr 45 mins
Naples–Matera	4 hrs	6 hrs
Naples–Cosenza	4 hrs 15 mins	4 hrs
Naples–Messina	7 hrs 15 mins	5 hrs 30 mins
Messina–Palermo	2 hrs 45 mins	3 hrs
Messina–Siracusa	2 hrs	2 hrs 45 mins
Siracusa–Palermo	3 hrs	4 hrs 15mins
Palermo–Agrigento	2 hrs 45 mins	2 hrs 5 mins

When to Go

Spring: In April, May, and early June southern Italy is at its best. The weather is generally pleasant, and the fields are in full bloom. Easter is a busy time for most tourist destinations—if you're traveling then, you should have lodging reserved well ahead of time. By May the seawater is warm enough for swimming by American standards, but you can often have the beach to yourself, as Italians shy away until at least June.

Summer: Temperatures can be torrid in summer, making it a less than ideal time for a visit to the south. In Campania, Naples can feel like an inferno, the archaeological sites swarm with visitors, and the islands and Amalfi Coast resorts are similarly overrun. Even the otherwise perfect villages of the interior are too dazzlingly white for easy comfort from July to early September. If you seek a beach, whether on the mainland or in Sicily, keep in mind that during August all of Italy flock to the shores. Even relatively isolated resorts can be overrun.

Fall: Visit the south from late September through early November and you can find gentle, warm weather and acres of beach space; swimming temperatures last through October. Watch the clock, however, as the days do get shorter. At most archaeological sites you're rounded up two hours before sunset—but by then most crowds have departed, so late afternoon is still an optimum time to see Pompeii, Herculaneum, or Agrigento in peace and quiet.

Winter: Early winter is relatively mild—bougainvillea and other floral displays can bloom through Christmas—but, particularly later in the season, cold fronts can arrive and stay for days. In resort destinations many hotels, restaurants, and other tourist facilities close down from November until around Easter. Elsewhere, you need to reserve rooms well in advance between Christmas and Epiphany (January 6) and during local festivals (such as Agrigento's celebration of the almond in February or the Carnevale in Acireale and Sciacca).

On the Calendar

These are some of the top seasonal events in southern Italy:

From December through June, the **stagione operistica** (opera season) is underway at Teatro San Carlo in Naples.

In early Spring in Agrigento's Valley of the Temples, **Sagra del Mandorlo in Fiore** (Almond Blossom Festival ⊕ *www. sagradelmandorlo.net*) is a week of folk music and dancing, with participants from many countries.

The **Settimana Santa** (Holy Week), culminating with Easter, features parades and outdoor events in every city and most small towns. Sorrento, Trapani, Cagliari and many towns in Puglia (⊕ *www. settimanasantainpuglia.it*) have noteworthy festivities.

Twice a year—on September 19 and the first Sunday in May—Naples celebrates the **Feast of San Gennaro.** In the Duomo, worshippers anxiously await the miraculous liquefaction of a remnant of the saint's blood, after which there's a ceremonial parade.

Maggio dei Monumenti is a cultural initiative in Naples lasting the entire month of May. Special exhibits, palaces, private collections, and churches are open to the public for free or at a discount.

SOUTHERN ITALY TOP ATTRACTIONS

Underground Naples

(A) Below the chaos of Naples is Napoli Sotterranea, a netherworld of ancient Greek quarries and aqueducts, Roman streets, and World War II bomb shelters. Parts have been cleaned up and made accessible to the public.

The Ruins around Vesuvius

(B) This may be the closest you'll ever get to time travel. Thanks to Vesuvius's blowing its top in AD 79, the towns round its base were carpeted in fallout and preserved for posterity. Allow a good half day to look around bustling Pompeii or the more compact, less busy, and better preserved Herculaneum. For the best Roman frescoes, head to the Villa Oplontis between the two ancient cities.

The Amalfi Coast

(C) One moment you're gazing out at a luxury sailing craft, the next you're dodging mules on precipitous footpaths.

"Comforts of the 21st century in a medieval setting" just about sums up the remarkable Amalfi Coast.

Matera's Sassi

You can see why Matera is a favorite with filmmakers shooting biblical scenes. You get that "time warp" feeling, especially in early morning or at night among the Sassi, with buildings seemingly gouged out of the limestone cliffs.

Lecce

(D) With its much-feted Baroque facades and extensive Roman remains in the city center, Lecce has a legitimate claim to being Puglia's fairest city. As an added bonus, nearby are a largely undeveloped coastline and the magical walled town of Otranto.

Bronzi di Riace, Reggio di Calabria

(E) Few bronze statues have survived intact from the ancient Greek world. The presence of not one but two larger-than-life bronzes, restored to almost perfect condition, is reason enough to trek to Reggio di Calabria, on the eastern side of the Strait of Messina.

Mt. Etna

(F) You can take the single-gauge railway around its foothills, splurge on an SUV experience near the summit, or just stroll across old lava fields on its northern flank. Alternatively, go down into the gorge of Alcantara and see what happens when lava flow meets mountain spring water.

Imperial Roman Villa, Piazza Armerina

(G) "Villa" doesn't begin to describe this opulent palace from the latter years of the Roman Empire. The stunning mosaics that fill every room are perhaps the best preserved and certainly the most extensive of the ancient Roman Empire.

Duomo, Siracusa

(H) Few buildings encapsulate history better than the Duomo of Siracusa. The cathedral started life as a temple dedicated to the goddess Athena sometime in the early 5th century BC, as one glance at the majestic fluted columns inside confirms.

Sardinia's Beaches

The 20 km (12½ mile) stretch of the Costa Smeralda, on the island's northeast is an oasis of lush Mediterranean maquis enclosing white sandy beaches with crystal-clear water. One of Europe's most expensive locations, it attracts the jet set in summer, but the crowds disperse and deals can be found outside high season. Further north, the pristine beauty of the Maddalena Archipelago led UNESCO to declare it a World Heritage Site.

TOP EXPERIENCES

Edenic Gardens

"What nature gives you makes you rich," they say in Campania. One look at Capri's perfectly tonsured palm trees, Sorrento's frangipani, and Amalfi's lemon trees laden with fruit, and you'll know what they mean.

So it is not surprising to learn that one of the major joys of this region is the abundance of spectacular gardens. Many of the most celebrated were created by English "green thumbs," such as the Romantic, exotic Eden created by Lord Grimthorpe at his Villa Cimbrone or the even larger horticultural extravaganza laid out by Sir Frances Neville Reid at the spectacular Villa Rufolo, both located in Ravello. From La Mortella in Forio, Ischia, to the Orto Botanico in Naples to the Villa San Michele in Capri, Campania's gardens are *incomparabili*.

Pasticceria Siciliana

Cannolo, setteveli, cartoccio, cassata, and diminutive *cassatina*: it sounds like the list of characters from an opera, but these ricotta-filled delights can be found in any self-respecting *pasticceria* (pastry shop) on the island of Sicily. The top performers cluster around Palermo and Catania: Massaro and Cappello, both a short walk from Palermo's Porta Nuova, have been delighting palates for more than a century, while Savia's pedigree in Catania stretches even farther back. The secret lies in the freshness and simplicity of the ricotta made from the whey of ultrafresh sheep or goat's milk, and, depending on the recipe, studded with chocolate chips, liqueur, or candied fruit.

Fiery Landscapes

Volcanoes have long fascinated people on the move. The ancient Greeks—among the first sailors around the central Mediterranean—explained away Etna as the place where the god Hephaestus had his workshop. Millennia later, northern European visitors to Naples in the 18th and 19th centuries would climb the erupting Vesuvius or cross the steaming craters of the Campi Flegrei west of the city. Farther south, in the Aeolian Islands northeast of Sicily, Stromboli performs a lightshow about every 20 minutes, ejecting incandescent cinder, lapilli, and lava bombs high into the air. To add to the fascination, several of the Aeolian Islands rise sheer out of the Mediterranean, and beaches are black with volcanic fallout. Though stripped of their mythology by generations of geologists and deprived by local authorities of even a frisson of risk, Italy's volcanoes are still terrifically appealing.

The Great Summer Performances

Exploiting its Mediterranean climate and atmospheric venues, southern Italy lays on an impressive range of cultural events in the summer. The ancient theaters of Segesta, Siracusa, and Taormina in Sicily are used for anything from Greek plays to pop concerts, while in Campania the Greek temples at Paestum serve as a scenic backdrop for opera and symphonic music. The 18th-century villas near Herculaneum at the foot of Vesuvius have also joined the musical act in recent years. With time (and money), visit Capri for a sunset concert at Villa San Michele. For the most gorgeous setting, head to Ravello. Here, at the Villa Rufolo, the Ravello Music Festival (☎ *089/858422* ⊕ *www.ravellofestival.com*) takes place, on a breathtaking terrace set over a Cinerama vista of the bluer-than-blue Bay of Salerno.

SOUTHERN ITALY TODAY

Upping the Tempo

Every year in late August upwards of 150,000 revellers gather in Melpignano, a tiny town south of Lecce, for La Notte del Taranta (⊕ *www.lanottedellataranta. it*). The climax of a month-long festival throughout the province, it celebrates Puglia's popular folk dance, *la taranta*, or *la pizzica*, showcasing a thriving southern Italian tradition.

Every region in the Mezzogiorno claims its own variant of the Tarantella, and you will often come across impromptu sessions as you explore the area. *La pizzica* has its origins around Salento. Accompanied by accordions and *zampogna* (bagpipes), it generally begins mid-tempo with a large goatskin tambourine keeping the beat, then speeds up to a frenetic rhythm. Swaying dancers face each other, intensely reenacting the dance's supposed origins—an attempt to sweat out the venom of a spider bite.

For a taste, check out Stewart Copeland's (drummer of the Police) *La Notte Della Taranta,* a live recording of his 2003 performance at the festival. Fans of the dance include Willem Dafoe, who invited a band to play at his wedding in Otranto, and it is rumored Justin Timberlake and Jessica Biel's Puglian wedding culminated in a lively *pizzica*.

Ensuring Nature Ever Flourishes

While the north has developed relatively rapidly in the past 50 years, the entrepreneurial spirit in the south struggles to make good. Despite a pool of relatively cheap, willing labor, foreign investment across the entire south is merely one-tenth of that going to Lombardy alone. The discrepancy can be attributed in large part to the stifling presence of organized crime. Each major region has its own criminal association: in Naples, it's the Camorra. The system creates add-on costs at many levels, especially in retail.

It's not all bad news though: southern Italy's remarkable cultural and natural heritage is its major asset. UNESCO lists 15 World Heritage Sites in southern Italy alone, while the last decade has seen the creation of several national parks, marine parks, and regional nature preserves. Environmental and cultural associations have mushroomed as locals increasingly perceive the importance of preserving across the generations. In general, the small average farm size in the south has helped preserve a pleasing mosaic of habitats in the interior.

Somewhere for Pilgrims and Pleasure Seekers

Tourism is on the rise in Puglia and Basilicata, while Campania (traditionally the biggest tourist region) continues to pull in the crowds. Sicily still attracts nature lovers and adventure seekers who cycle or hike its rugged terrain, and Calabria remains largely a beach-holiday destination crowded only from mid-July through August. Religious tourism accounts for large numbers of visitors throughout the year; just as many visitors pay their respects to the Madonna di Pompei sanctuary as others do to the archaeological site up the road. In almost every village in southern Italy you're likely to see the bearded statue of Capuchin priest Padre Pio.

A GREAT ITINERARY

Day 1: Naples

Fly into Naples's **Aeroporto Capodichino**, a scant 8 km (5 miles) from the city. Naples is rough around the edges and may be a bit jarring if you're a first-time visitor, but it's classic Italy, and most visitors end up falling in love with the city's alluring palazzi and spectacular pizza.

First things first, though: recharge with a nap and, after that, a good caffè—Naples has some of the world's best. Revive in time for an evening stroll down Naples's wonderful shopping street, Via Toledo, to Piazza Plebescito, before dinner and bed.

Logistics: Under no circumstances should you rent a car for Naples. Take a taxi from the airport—it's not far, or overly expensive—and you should face few logistical obstacles on your first day in Italy.

Day 2: Naples

Start the day at the **Museo Archaeologico Nazionale**, budgeting at least two hours for the collection. Then take **Via Santa Maria di Costantinopoli** and grab a caffè at one of the outdoor cafés in Piazza Bellini. From here, head down Via dei Tribunali for a pizza at **I Decumani** or **Di Matteo**. Continue along Tribunali, crossing Via Duomo (taking in a visit to the city's cathedral) to see Caravaggio's *The Seven Works of Mercy* at **Pio Monte della Misericordia**. Descend Via Duomo and turn right onto Spaccanapoli, turning off behind Piazza San Domenico for a brief stop at the **Cappella Sansevero** for a look at the pinnacle of Masonic sculpture. Continue along Spaccanapoli to Piazza del Gesù and the churches of **Il Gesù Nuovo** and **Santa Chiara**, then walk downhill, and turn left to follow Via Monteoliveto and Via Medina to the port and the **Castel Nuovo**, and on past the **Teatro San Carlo** to the enormous **Palazzo Reale**. Walk 15

minutes south to the **Castel dell'Ovo** in the **Santa Lucia waterfront area**, one of Naples's most charming neighborhoods. Then it's back up to Via Caracciolo and the Villa Comunale, before heading back to your hotel for a short rest before dinner and perhaps a night out at one of Naples's lively bars or clubs.

Logistics: This entire day is easily done on foot.

Day 3: Pompeii/Sorrento

After breakfast, pack your luggage and head from Naples to **Pompeii**, one of the true archaeological gems of Europe. If it's summer, be prepared for an onslaught of sweltering heat as you make your way through the incredibly preserved ruins of a city that was devastated by the whims of **Mt. Vesuvius** nearly 2,000 years ago. You'll see the houses of noblemen and merchants, brothels, political graffiti, and more. From Pompeii, it's on to **Sorrento**, your first taste of the wonderful peninsula that marks the beginning of the fabled Amalfi Coast. Sorrento is touristy, but it may well be the Italian city of your imagination: cliffhanging, cobblestone-paved, and graced with an infinite variety of fishing ports and coastal views. There, have a relaxing dinner of fish and white wine before calling it a day.

Logistics: Naples to Pompeii by car is all about the A3: a short 24 km (15 miles) brings you to this archaeological gem. From Pompeii it's a short ride back on the A3 until the exit for Sorrento; from the exit, you'll take the SS145 to reach Sorrento. Most people choose the easier option of the Circumvesuviana, a twice-hourly train to Sorrento, stopping at Pompeii's Villa dei Misteri.

Day 4: Positano/Ravello

Your stay in Sorrento will be short, as there's much of the **Amalfi Coast** still to see: **Positano,** your next stop, is a must. It's one of the most visited towns in Italy for good reason: its blue-green seas, stairs "as steep as ladders," and white Moorish-style houses make for a truly memorable setting. Walk, gaze, and eat (lunch), before heading on to the less traveled, even loftier town of **Ravello,** your Amalfi Coast dream come true, an aerie that's "closer to the sky than the sea." Don't miss the **Duomo, Villa Rufolo,** or **Villa Cimbrone** before settling in for a dinner in the sky.

Logistics: Sorrento to Positano is a 30-km (19-mile) jaunt, but the winding roads will draw it out for the better part of an hour—a scenic hour. From Positano, Ravello is another slow 18 km (11 miles) to the east, perched high above the rest of the world. The SITA bus is your best option; motorists should be prepared to use low gears if driving a stick shift (as they almost surely will be).

Day 5: Matera

Those with a car will have a bit of a drive to get to Basilicata from the Amalfi Coast; leaving Campania and entering Basilicata is generally a lonely experience. Little-traveled roads, wild hills, and distant farms are the hallmarks of this province, which produces deep, dark aglianico wines and has perfected the art of peasant food. You'll spend a while in your car to make it to **Matera,** a beautiful, ancient city full of Paleolithic **Sassi** (cave-like dwellings hewn out of rock)—but it's worth it. Spend the afternoon exploring the Sassi, then enjoy a relaxing dinner at one of Matera's excellent restaurants.

Logistics: It's a long haul from your starting point, Ravello, to Matera—if using public transportation you may find it easier to return first to Naples—but the effort is worth it, as Basilicata's landscape is so pretty. Once in Matera, if staying in the Sassi, motorists should get extra-detailed driving and parking instructions from the hotel beforehand—navigating through thousand-year-old alleyways can be challenging.

Day 6: Lecce

This drive will take a good 2½ hours, so get an early start. Those without a car should return to Bari, then take the train south. The Baroque city of **Lecce** will mark your introduction to Puglia, the heel of Italy's boot. It's one of Italy's best-kept secrets, as you'll soon find out upon checking out the spectacular church of **Santa Croce,** the ornate Duomo, and the

harmonious **Piazza Sant'Oronzo.** The shopping is great, the food is great, and the evening *passeggiata* (stroll) is great. Don't miss the opportunity, if you wind up at a bar or café in the evening, to chat with Lecce's friendly residents—unfazed by tourism, the welcoming Leccesi represent southern Italians at their best.

Logistics: It's not far from Matera to Lecce as the crow flies, but the trip is more involved than you might think; patience is required. The best route is via Taranto—don't make the mistake of going up through Bari.

Day 7: Bari

The trip from Lecce to **Bari** is a short one. Check into your hotel and spend the morning and afternoon wandering through Bari's *centro storico* (historic center). The wide-open doors of the town's humble houses and apartments, with bickering families and grandmothers drying their pasta in the afternoon sun, will give you a taste of the true flavor of Italy's deep south. Don't miss Bari's castle and the walk around the ridge of the ancient city walls, with views of wide-open sea at every turn. Finish the day with a good fish dinner, and celebrate your last night in Italy by checking out one of the city's multitude of lively bars—Bari boasts some of southern Italy's most hopping nightlife.

Logistics: This is one of your most straightforward, if not quickest, connections: a direct train or the coastal S16 for 154 km (95 miles) until you hit Bari. The road is a two-lane highway, though, so don't be surprised if the trip takes two hours or more. If you get tired, beautiful Ostuni (dubbed the "*città bianca*," or the "white city") is a perfect hilltop pit stop halfway there.

Day 8: Bari/Departure

Bad news: this is your wake-up-and-leave day. Bari's Aeroporto Palese is small but quite serviceable. Exploit its absence of crowds and easy access and use it as a portal to your next destination. Connections through Rome or Milan are more frequent than you might think. Plan on leaving with southern Italy firmly established in your heart as the best place to see the Italy that once was—and be thankful that you were able to see it while it's still like this.

Logistics: Bari hotels offer easy airport transfers; take advantage of them. There are also regular public-transportation connections between the central train station and the airport. Return your rental car at the Bari airport; you won't have to arrive at the airport more than an hour or so before your flight.

NAPLES AND
CAMPANIA

WELCOME TO NAPLES AND CAMPANIA

TOP REASONS TO GO

★ **Naples, Italy's most operatic city:** Walk through the energy, chaos, and beauty that is Spaccanapoli, the city's historic district, and you'll create an unforgettable memory.

★ **Exploring Pompeii:** The excavated ruins of Pompeii offer a unique, occasionally spooky glimpse into everyday life—and sudden death—in Roman times.

★ **"The Living Room of the World":** Pose oh-so-casually with the beautiful people on La Piazzetta, the central crossroads of Capri—a stage-set square that always seems ready for a gala performance.

★ **Ravishing Ravello:** High above the famously blue Bay of Salerno, this place is a contender for the title of "most beautiful village in the world."

★ **A world made of stairs:** Built like a vertical amphitheater, Positano may very well be the world's most photographed fishing village. The town's only job is to look enchanting—and it does that very well.

1 Naples. Italy's third-largest city can seduce you one moment and exasperate you the next: it's lush, chaotic, friendly, scary, amusing, confounding, and very beautiful.

2 Herculaneum, Vesuvius, and Pompeii. Two towns show you through their excavated ruins how ancient Romans lived the good life—until, one day in AD 79, Mt. Vesuvius buried them in volcanic ash and lava.

3 Ischia and Procida. Though they lack Capri's glitz, these two sister islands in the Bay of Naples share a laid-back charm.

4 Capri. The rocky island mixes natural beauty and *dolce vita* glamour.

5 Sorrento and the Sorrentine Peninsula. Perched over the Bay of Naples with an incomparable view of Mt. Vesuvius, this Belle Époque resort town is sheer delight.

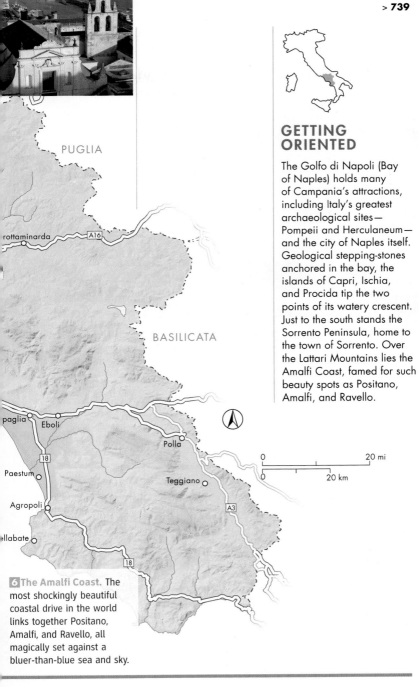

GETTING ORIENTED

The Golfo di Napoli (Bay of Naples) holds many of Campania's attractions, including Italy's greatest archaeological sites— Pompeii and Herculaneum— and the city of Naples itself. Geological stepping-stones anchored in the bay, the islands of Capri, Ischia, and Procida tip the two points of its watery crescent. Just to the south stands the Sorrento Peninsula, home to the town of Sorrento. Over the Lattari Mountains lies the Amalfi Coast, famed for such beauty spots as Positano, Amalfi, and Ravello.

PUGLIA

rottaminarda   A16

BASILICATA

paglia   Eboli
                        Polla
        18
Paestum
                    Teggiano
Agropoli
                              A3
llabate

        18

0   20 mi
0   20 km

6 The Amalfi Coast. The most shockingly beautiful coastal drive in the world links together Positano, Amalfi, and Ravello, all magically set against a bluer-than-blue sea and sky.

EATING AND DRINKING WELL IN NAPLES AND CAMPANIA

Think of Neapolitan food and you conjure up images of pasta, pizza, and tomatoes. The stereotype barely scratches the surface of what's available in Naples—to say nothing of the rest of Campania, where the cuisine reflects an enormously diverse landscape.

The region is known for its enclaves of gastronomy, notable among them the tip of the Sorrentine Peninsula. You may well come across *cucina povera*, a cuisine inspired by Campania's *contadino* (peasant) roots, with all the ingredients sourced from a nearby garden. Expect to see roadside stalls selling stellar local produce, including *annurca* apples (near Benevento), giant lemons (Amalfi Coast), roasted chestnuts (especially near Avellino), and watermelons (the plains around Salerno). Try to get to one of the local *sagre* village feasts celebrating a *prodotto tipico* (local specialty), which could be anything from snails to wild boar to cherries to (commonly) wine.

A TIPPING TIP

Neapolitans are easily recognized in bars elsewhere in Italy by the tip they leave on the counter when ordering. This habit does not necessarily ensure better service in bars in Naples, notorious for their fairly offhand staff, but you do blend in better with the locals.

In restaurants, a service charge is often included (alternatively 5%–10% is reasonable). In pizzerias, tips are given less often unless you've splurged on side dishes or sweets, or have had particularly good service.

PIZZA

Naples is the undisputed homeland of pizza, and you'll usually encounter it here in two classic forms: *margherita* and *marinara*. Given the larger-than-your-plate portions of standard pizzas some choose to ask for a *mignon* (kids' portion), or even share, divided between two plates. Take-away outlets in most town centers sell pizza by the slice, along with the usual range of fried *arancini* (rice balls) and *crocchè di patate* (potato fritters).

COFFEE

Given the same basic ingredients—coffee grounds, water, a machine—what makes *caffè* taste so much better in Naples than elsewhere remains a mystery. If you find the end product too strong, ask to have it with a dash of milk (caffè *macchiato*) or a little diluted (caffè *lungo*). Many bars serve with sugar already added, so if you want it without, request *senza zucchero* or *amaro*.

BUFFALO CHEESE

Long feted for the melt-in-your-mouth mozzarella cheese *(pictured at right)* made from its milk, the river buffalo—related to the Asian water buffalo—is also the source of other culinary delights. Throughout the region, look for buffalo ricotta and mascarpone, as well as buffalo *provola* and *scamorza,* which may be lightly smoked (resulting in a golden crust). Caserta has more

mature *nero di bufala* (aged like sheep's cheese), while around Salerno you'll find smoked *caciocavallo* cheese as well as *carne di bufala* (buffalo meat), which can be braised to perfection.

THE ORAL TRADITION

Locals in Campania like to bypass the restaurant menu and ask what the staff recommend. Take this approach and you'll often wind up with a daily special or the house specialty. Though you're unlikely to get multilingual staff outside the larger hotels and main tourist areas, the person you talk to will spare no effort to get the message across.

WINE

Wine in Campania has an ancient pedigree. Some say fancifully that Campania's undisputed king of reds, the *aglianico,* got its name from the word "Hellenic"; and *fiano,* the primary white grape, closely resembles the Roman variety *apianus*. Horace, the Latin poet, extolled the virtues of drinking wine from Campania. A century later, Pliny the Elder was harsher in his judgment: wine from Pompeii would give you a hangover until noon the next day, and Sorrento wine tasted of vinegar.

In recent decades though, Campania has gained respect for its boutique reds. Due to the rugged landscape, small farms, and limited mechanization, prices can be relatively high, but the quality is high as well.

Updated
by Fergal
Kavanagh

A region of evocative names—Capri, Sorrento, Pompeii, Positano, Amalfi—Campania conjures up visions of cliff-shaded, sapphire-hue coves, sun-dappled waters, and mighty ruins. More travelers visit this corner than any other in Southern Italy, and it's no wonder.

Home to Vesuvius, the area's unique geology is responsible for Campania's photogenic landscape. A spectacular coastline stretches out along a deep blue sea, punctuated by rocky islands.

Through the ages, the area's temperate climate, warm sea, fertile soil, and natural beauty have attracted Greek colonists, then Roman emperors—who called the region "Campania Felix," "the happy land"—and later Saracen raiders and Spanish invaders. The result has been a rich and varied history, reflected in everything from architecture to mythology. The highlights span millennia: the near-intact Roman towns of Pompeii and Herculaneum, the Greek temples in Paestum, the Norman and Baroque churches in Naples, the white-dome fisherman's houses of Positano, the "dolce vita" resorts of Capri. Campania piles them all onto one mammoth must-see sandwich.

The region's complex identity is most intensely felt in its major metropolis, Naples. Exasperating both critics and defenders, Napoli is lush, chaotic, scary, funny, confounding, intoxicating, and very beautiful. Few who visit remain ambivalent. You needn't participate in the mad whirl of the city, however. The best pastime in Campania is simply finding a spot with a stunning view and indulging in *"il dolce far niente"* ("the sweetness of doing nothing").

NAPLES AND CAMPANIA PLANNER

MAKING THE MOST OF YOUR TIME

In Campania there are three primary travel experiences: Naples, with its restless exuberance; the resorts (Capri, Sorrento, the Amalfi Coast), dedicated to leisure and indulgence; and the archaeological sites (Pompeii, Herculaneum, Paestum), where the ancient world is frozen in time.

Each is wonderful in its own way. If you have a week, you can get a good taste of all three. With less time, you're better off choosing between them rather than stretching yourself thin.

Pompeii, being a day trip, is the simplest to plan for. To get a feel for Naples, you should give it a couple of days at a minimum. The train station makes a harsh first impression (a recent overhaul softens the blow), but the city grows on you as you take in the sights and interact with the locals.

That said, many people bypass Naples and head right for the resorts. These places are all about relaxing—you'll miss the point if you're in a rush. Though Sorrento isn't as spectacular as Positano or Capri, it makes a good base because of its central location.

DISCOUNTS AND DEALS

A big boon for museum lovers, The **Campania Artecard** pass offers free or discounted admission to more than 80 museums and monuments over a three- or seven-consecutive-day period for the city or the whole region, plus discounted services ranging from audio guides to theater tickets and parking.

The benefits depend on the pass: Naples (three days; €21), including three sights and a fourth at up to 50% off, plus transportation; Campania region (three days; €32), including Pompeii and other Bay of Naples sights and Ravello and Paestum, two sights included and a third at up to 50% off, plus transportation; Campania region, seven days (€34), five sights included and a sixth for up to 50% off, no transportation. In addition, there are generous youth discounts. As sites and discounts are frequently updated, check ⊕ *www.campaniartecard.it* for the latest details. Cards are available at all major participating museums and archaeological sites, at main city hotels, as well as at the airport and train station.

GETTING HERE AND AROUND

BOAT TRAVEL

Several companies offer a variety of fast craft and passenger and car ferries connecting the islands of Capri, Ischia, and Procida with Naples and Pozzuoli year-round. Hydrofoils and other fast craft leave from Naples's Molo Beverello, adjacent to Piazza Municipio, with some departures in high season also from Mergellina, about 1½ km (1 mile) west of Piazza Municipio. Slower car ferries leave from the berths at Calata Porta di Massa, a 10-minute walk, or 3-minute shuttle bus ride, east of Molo Beverello.

Information on departures is published every day in the local paper, *Il Mattino*. Alternatively, ask at the tourist office or at the port, or contact these companies directly. Always double-check schedules in stormy weather.

Contacts Alilauro ☎ 081/4972222 ⊕ www.alilauro.it. **Caremar** ☎ 081/5513882 ⊕ www.caremar.it. **Navigazione Libera del Golfo** (NLG). ☎ 081/5520763 ⊕ www.navlib.it. **SNAV** ☎ 081/4285555 ⊕ www.snav.it.

BUS TRAVEL

Within Campania there's an extensive network of local buses, although finding information about it can be trying.

SITA buses. SITA buses bound for Salerno leave every 30 minutes between 6 am and 9 pm, Monday through Saturday, from its terminal in the port near the Stazione Marittima. There are also four departures from the airport. There are no services on Sunday. SITA buses also serve the Amalfi Coast, connecting Sorrento with Salerno. ☎ *089/405145* ⊕ *www.sitasudtrasporti.it.*

CAR TRAVEL

You can get along fine without a car in Campania, and there are plenty of reasons not to have one. Much of Naples is pedestrianized, meaning motorized arteries are often bottlenecked; you can't bring a car to Capri (except in winter, when everything's closed); and parking in the towns of the Amalfi Coast is hard to come by and expensive.

Italy's main north–south route, the A1 (aka the Autostrada del Sole), connects Rome with Naples and Campania. In good traffic the drive to Naples takes a little more than two hours. The A3 autostrada, a somewhat perilous continuation of the A1, runs south from Naples through Campania and into Calabria. Herculaneum (Ercolano) and Pompeii (Pompei) both have marked exits off the A3. For Vesuvius, take the Portici Ercolano exit. For the Sorrento Peninsula and the Amalfi Coast, exit at Castellammare di Stabia. To get to Paestum, take the A3 to the Battipaglia exit, and follow the road to Capaccio Scalo–Paestum. Roads on the Sorrento Peninsula and Amalfi Coast are narrow and twisting, but they have outstanding views.

If you come to Naples by car, find a garage, agree on the rate, and leave it there for the duration of your stay. (If you park on the street, you run the risk of theft.)

Contacts Garage Cava ⊠ *Via Mergellina 6, Naples* ☎ *081/660023* ⊙ *24 hrs.* **Grilli** ⊠ *Hotel Ramada, Via Ferraris 40, near Stazione Centrale, Naples* ☎ *081/264344* ⊙ *6 am–midnight.* **Turistico.** Turistico also rents out electric bicycles. ⊠ *Via de Gasperi 14, near port, Naples* ☎ *081/5525442* ⊙ *6:30 am–midnight.*

TAXI TRAVEL

When taking a taxi in Naples, make sure that the meter is switched on at the start of your trip. Trips around the city are unlikely to cost less than €6 or more than €20. Set fares for various destinations within the city should be displayed in the taxi—for instance, in accordance with the new taxi tariff, you should pay €7 for travel between the centro storico and Stazione Centrale. You need to establish this before the trip begins. Extra charges for things like baggage and night service should also be displayed. For trips outside the city, negotiate your fare before getting in. Watch out for overcharging at three locations: the airport, the railway station, and the hydrofoil marina. And in peak summer weeks, don't forget that many cabs in Naples have no air-conditioning—which the metro and some city buses do have—so you can practically bake if caught in one during a half-hour traffic jam.

TRAIN TRAVEL

There are up to three trains every hour between Rome and Naples. Both the Alta Velocità Freccia Rossa and Italo trains (the fastest types of train service) make the trip in a little more than an hour, with the Intercity taking two. All trains to Naples stop at the newly refurbished Stazione Centrale.

The efficient (though run-down) suburban Circumvesuviana runs from Naples's Porta Nolana and stops at Stazione Centrale before continuing to Herculaneum, Pompeii, and Sorrento. Travel time between Naples and Sorrento on the Circumvesuviana line is about 75 minutes.

For ticketing purposes, the region is divided into travel zones by distance from Naples. A ticket for Herculaneum costs €2, to Pompeii €2.60, and Sorrento €3.60. If you're traveling from Naples to anywhere else in Campania, be sure to ask for a *biglietto integrato*. It's slightly more expensive than the direct ticket (about €1 more), but there will be no need to buy a separate ticket for your subway, tram, or bus ride to the train station as the biglietto integrato covers the whole journey.

Contacts Circumvesuviana ⊕ *www.eavsrl.it.* **Stazione Centrale** ✉ *Piazza Garibaldi, Naples* ☎ *892021* ⊕ *www.trenitalia.com, www.italotreno.it.*

PUBLIC TRANSIT IN NAPLES

Naples's rather old Metropolitana (subway system, also called Linea 2), provides fairly frequent service and can be the fastest way to get across the traffic-clogged city.

The other, continually expanding, urban subway system, Metropolitana Collinare (or Linea 1), links the hill area of the Vomero and beyond with Stazione Centrale, the National Archaeological Museum, and Via Toledo. Many of the stations along Linea 1 are also mini–art galleries. Trains on both lines run from around 6 am until around 10:30 pm, with services on Linea 1 often running until 2 am on summer weekends.

For standard public transit—including the subways, buses, and funiculars—a Ticket Integrato Campania costs €1.50 and is valid for 90 minutes as far as Pozzuoli to the west and Portici to the east; €4.50 buys a *biglietto giornaliero,* good for the whole day.

Bus travel has become viable over the last few years, especially with the introduction of larger buses on regular routes. Electronic signs display wait times at many stops.

RESTAURANTS

Prices in the reviews are the average cost of a main course at dinner or, if dinner is not served, at lunch.

HOTELS

Most parts of Campania have accommodations in all price categories, but they tend to fill up in high season, so reserve well in advance. In summer, on the coast and the islands, hotels that serve meals often require you to take half board.

Hotel reviews have been shortened. For full information, visit Fodors. com.

WHAT IT COSTS				
	$	$$	$$$	$$$$
RESTAURANTS	under €15	€15–€24	€25–€35	over €35
HOTELS	under €125	€125–€200	€201–€300	over €300

Prices in the dining reviews are the average cost of a main course at dinner, or, if dinner is not served, at lunch. Prices in the reviews are the lowest cost of a standard double room in high season.

TOURS

City Sightseeing. Close to the port, beside the main entrance to Castel Nuovo, is the terminal for double-decker buses belonging to City Sightseeing. For €22 you can take up to four different excursions, giving you reasonable coverage of the downtown sights and outlying attractions like the Museo di Capodimonte. ⊠ *Piazza Municipio, Naples* ☎ *081/5517279* ⊕ *www.napoli.city-sightseeing.it.*

NAPLES

A huge zest for living and crowded conditions in the shadow of Vesuvius make Naples the most vibrant city in Italy—a steaming, bubbling minestrone in which each block is a small village, every street the setting for a Punch-and-Judy show, and everything seems to be a backdrop for an opera not yet composed.

It's said that northern Italians vacation here to remind themselves of the time when Italy was *molto Italiana*—*really* Italian. In this respect, Naples—Napoli in Italian—doesn't disappoint: Neapolitan rainbows of laundry wave in the wind over alleyways open-windowed with friendliness, mothers caress children, men break out into impromptu arias at sidewalk cafés, and street scenes offer Fellini-esque slices of life. Everywhere contrasting elements of faded gilt and romance, rust and calamity, grandeur and squalor form a pageant of pure *Italianità*—Italy at its most Italian.

Much of Naples' architectural inheritance is on display in the Spaccanapoli district, where the Piazza Gesù Nuovo and the surrounding blocks are a showplace for the city's most beloved churches. Compared to most other great metropolises of the world, Naples has little tourist infrastructure, forcing you to become a native very quickly, as you'll find out if you spend some time wandering through the narrow, gridlike streets of the centro storico.

VISITOR INFORMATION

Azienda Autonoma di Soggiorno Cura e Turismo di Napoli. With an additional office in Piazza del Gesù, this helpful info point distributes maps and the useful magazine *Qui Napoli*. ⊠ *Via San Carlo, 9, Piazza del Plebiscito* ☎ *081/402394* ⊕ *www.inaples.it.*

CAMPANIA THROUGH THE AGES

Ancient History. Lying on Mediterranean trade routes plied by several pre-Hellenic civilizations, Campania was settled by the ancient Greeks from approximately 800 BC onward. Here myth and legend blend with historical fact. The town of Herculaneum is said—rather improbably—to have been established by Hercules himself; and Naples in ancient times was called Parthenope, the name attributed to one of the sirens who preyed on hapless sailors in antiquity.

Thanks to archaeological research, some of the layers of myth have been stripped away to reveal a pattern of occupation and settlement well before Rome became established. Greek civilization flourished for hundreds of years all along this coastline, but there was nothing in the way of centralized government until centuries later when the Roman Republic, uniting all Italy for the first time, absorbed the Greek colonies with little opposition. Generally, the peace of Campania was undisturbed during these centuries of Roman rule.

Foreign Influences. Naples and Campania, like Italy in general, decayed along with the Roman Empire and collapsed into the abyss of the Middle Ages. Naples itself regained some importance under the rule of the Angevins in the latter part of the 13th century and continued its progress in the 1440s under Aragonese rule. The nobles who served under the Spanish viceroys in the 16th and 17th centuries enjoyed their pleasures, even as Spain milked the area for taxes.

After a short Austrian occupation, Naples became the capital of the Kingdom of the Two Sicilies, which the Bourbon kings established in 1738. Their rule was generally benevolent as far as Campania was concerned, and their support of papal authority in Rome was important in the development of the country as a whole. Their rule was important artistically, too, contributing to the architecture of the region, and attracting great musicians, artists, and writers who were drawn by the easy life at court. Finally, Giuseppe Garibaldi launched his famous expedition, and in 1860 Naples was united with the rest of Italy.

Modern Times. Things were relatively tranquil through the years that followed—with visitors thronging to Capri, Sorrento, Amalfi, and, of course, Naples—until World War II. Allied bombings did considerable damage in and around Naples. At the fall of the Fascist government, the sorely tried Neapolitans rose up against Nazi occupation troops and in four days of street fighting drove them out of the city. A monument was raised to the *scugnizzo* (the typical Neapolitan street urchin), celebrating the youngsters who participated in the battle. With the end of the war, artists, tourists, writers, and other lovers of beauty returned to the Campania region.

As time passed, some parts gained increased attention from knowing visitors, while others lost the cachet they once had. Years of misgovernment have left their mark, yet the region's cultural and natural heritage is finally being revalued as local authorities and inhabitants recognize the importance the area's largest industry—tourism.

13

EXPLORING

TOLEDO

Naples's setting on what is possibly the most beautiful bay in the world has long been a boon for its inhabitants—the expansive harbor has always brought great mercantile wealth to the city—and, intermittently, a curse. Throughout history, a "who's who" of Greek, Roman, Norman, Spanish, and French despots have quarreled over this gateway to Campania. The monuments they created remain prominent features of the city center: one of the most magnificent opera houses in Europe, a palace that rivals Versailles, an impregnable *castello* (castle), a majestic church modeled on Rome's Pantheon, and a 19th-century shopping galleria.

TOP ATTRACTIONS

Castel Nuovo. Known to locals as Maschio Angioino, in reference to its Angevin builders, this imposing castle is now used more for marital than military purposes—a portion of it serves as a government registry office. A white four-tiered triumphal entrance arch, ordered by Alfonso of Aragon after he entered the city in 1443 to seize power from the increasingly beleaguered Angevin Giovanna II, upstages the building's looming Angevin stonework. At the arch's top, as if justifying Alfonso's claim to the throne, the Archangel Gabriel slays a demon.

Across the courtyard within the castle is the **Sala Grande,** also known as the Sala dei Baroni, which has a stunning vaulted ceiling 92 feet high. In 1486 local barons hatched a plot against Alfonso's son, King Ferrante, who reacted by inviting them to this hall for a wedding banquet, which promptly turned into a mass arrest. (Ferrante is also said to have kept a crocodile in the castle as his pet executioner.) You can also visit the **Sala dell'Armeria,** where a glass floor reveals recent excavations of Roman baths from the Augustan period. To one side are giant photographs of three Roman ships, wood amazingly intact, unearthed during recent digging of the nearby metro station and now in Pisa for restoration. In the next room on the left, the **Cappella Palatina,** look on the frescoed walls for Nicolo di Tomaso's painting of Robert Anjou, one of the first realistic portraits ever. Of the famous Giotto pictures described by Petrarch remain only a few tiny fragments.

The castle's first floor holds a small gallery that includes a beautiful early Renaissance Adoration of the Magi by Marco Cardisco, with the roles of the three Magi played by the three Aragonese kings: Ferrante I, Ferrante II, and Charles V. ✉ *Piazza Municipio, Toledo* ☎ *081/7957722* 💶*€6* 🕐 *Mon.–Sat. 9–6* Ⓜ *Toledo, Piazza Municipio.*

Galleria Umberto. Across from the Teatro San Carlo towers the imposing entrance to the glass-capped, Neoclassical Galleria Umberto, a late-19th-century shopping arcade where you can sit at one of several cafés and watch the vivacious Neapolitans as they go about their business. ✉ *Via San Carlo, near Piazza Plebiscito* Ⓜ *Toledo, Piazza Municipio.*

Fodor's Choice ★ **Palazzo Reale.** A leading Naples showpiece created as an expression of Bourbon power and values, the Palazzo Reale dates to 1600. Renovated and redecorated by successive rulers—and once lorded over by a dim-witted king who liked to shoot his hunting guns at the birds in his tapestries—it is filled with salons designed in the most lavish 18th-century Neapolitan style. The Spanish viceroys originally commissioned the palace, ordering the Swiss architect Domenico Fontana to build a suitable new residence for King Philip III, should he chance to visit Naples. He died in 1621 before ever doing so. The palace saw its greatest moment of splendor in the 18th century, when Charles III of Bourbon became the first permanent resident; the flamboyant Naples-born architect Luigi Vanvitelli redesigned the facade, and Ferdinando Fuga, under Ferdinand IV, created the **Royal Apartments,** sumptuously furnished and full of precious paintings, tapestries, porcelains, and other objets d'art.

To access these 30 rooms, climb the monumental *Scalone d'Onore* (Staircase). On the right is the **Court Theater,** built by Fuga for Charles III and his private opera company. Damaged during World War II, it was restored in the 1950s; note the resplendent royal box. Antechambers lead to Room VI, the **Throne Room,** the ponderous titular object dating to sometime after 1850.

Decoration picks up in the **Ambassadors' Room,** with choice Gobelin tapestries gracing the light-green walls. The ceiling painting honoring Spanish military victories is by local artist Belisario Corenzio (1610–20). Room IX was the bedroom of Charles's queen, Maria Amalia. The brilliantly gold private oratory has beautiful paintings by Francesco Liani (1760).

The **Great Captain's Room** has ceiling frescoes by Battistello Caracciolo (1610–16); all velvet, fire, and smoke, they reveal the influence of Caravaggio's visit to the city. A jolly series by Federico Zuccari depicts 12 proverbs. More majestic still is Titian's portrait (circa 1543) of Pier Luigi Farnese.

Room XIII was **Joachim Murat's writing room** when he was king of Naples; brought with him from France, some of the furniture is courtesy of Adam Weisweiler, cabinetmaker to Marie Antoinette. Room XVIII is notable for Guercino's depiction of Joseph's dream. The huge Room XXII, painted in green and gold with kitschy faux tapestries, is known as the **Hercules Hall,** because it once housed the *Farnese Hercules,* an epic sculpture of the mythological Greek hero. Pride of place now goes to the Sèvres porcelain.

The **Palatine Chapel,** redone by Gaetano Genovese in the 1830s, is gussied up with an excess of gold, although it has a stunning Technicolor marble intarsia altar from the previous chapel (Dionisio Lazzari, 1678). Also here is a Nativity scene with pieces sculpted by Giuseppe Sammartino and others. Pleasant 19th-century landscapes grace the next few rooms; then there is Queen Maria Carolina's Ferris wheel–like reading lectern (once enabling her to do a 19th-century reader's version of channel surfing). Speaking of reading, another wing holds the **Biblioteca Nazionale Vittorio Emanuele III.** Starting out as Farnese bits and pieces, it was enriched with the papyri from Herculaneum found in 1752 and opened to the public in 1804. The sumptuous rooms can still be viewed, and there's a tasteful garden that looks onto Castel Nuovo.

✉ *Piazza Plebiscito, Toledo* ☎ *081/5808111, 848/800288 for schools and guided tours* ⊕ *www.palazzorealenapoli.it* 🎫 *€4, includes audio guide* ⊙ *Thurs.–Tues. 9–8* Ⓜ *Toledo, Piazza Municipio.*

Palazzo Zevallos. Tucked inside this beautifully restored palazzo (until recently a bank) is a small museum that's worth seeking out. Enter through Cosimo Fanzago's gargoyled doorway and climb to the second floor. The first room to the left holds the star attraction, Caravaggio's last work, *The Martyrdom of Saint Ursula.* The saint here is, for dramatic effect, deprived of her usual retinue of a thousand followers. On the left, a face of pure spite, is the king of the Huns, who has just shot Ursula with an arrow after his proposal of marriage has been rejected. The museum has recently expanded to include some of the city's finest 17th and 18th century paintings, part of the Banca Intesa Sanpaolo's collection. ✉ *Via Toledo 185, Toledo* ☎ *800/454229* ⊕ *www.gallerieditalia.com/en/palazzi/palazzo-zevallos-stigliano* 🎫 *€5* ⊙ *Tues.–Fri. and Sun. 10–6, Sat. 10–8* Ⓜ *Toledo.*

Gran Caffè Gambrinus. The most famous coffeehouse in town, founded in 1850, sits across from the Palazzo Reale. Though its glory days as an intellectual salon are well in the past, the rooms inside, with mirrored walls and gilded ceilings, make this an essential stop. It was here that Oscar Wilde, down on his luck, would, for the price of a cup of tea, amaze Anglophone visitors with his still-intact wit. Visiting the café, one feels like a Grand Tourist come lately, with the added bonuses of reasonable prices and well-groomed waitstaff. Disappointingly, it's not the best coffee in town. ✉ *Via Chiaia 1–2, near Piazza Plebiscito* ☎ *081/417582* ⊕ *www.grancaffegambrinus.com* Ⓜ *Toledo, Piazza Municipio.*

Fodor'sChoice
★

Sant'Anna dei Lombardi. Long favored by the Aragonese kings, this church, simple and rather anonymous from the outside, houses some of the most important ensembles of Renaissance sculpture in southern Italy. Begun with the adjacent convent of the Olivetani and its four cloisters in 1411, it was given a Baroque makeover in the mid-17th century by Gennaro Sacco. This, however, is no longer so visible, because the bombs of 1943 led to a restoration favoring the original *quattrocento* (15th-century) lines. The wonderful coffered wooden ceiling adds a bit of pomp. Inside the porch is the tomb of Domenico Fontana, one of the major architects of the late 16th century, who died in Naples after beginning the Palazzo Reale.

On either side of the original entrance door are two fine Renaissance tombs. The one on the left as you face the door belongs to the Ligorio family (whose descendant Pirro designed the Villa d'Este in Tivoli) and is a work by Giovanni da Nola (1524). The tomb on the right is a masterpiece by Giuseppe Santacroce (1532) done for the del Pozzo family. To the left of the Ligorio Altar (the corner chapel on the immediate right as you face the altar) is the Mastrogiudice Chapel, whose altar contains precious reliefs of the *Annunciation* and *Scenes from the Life of Jesus* (1489) by Benedetto da Maiano, a great name in Tuscan sculpture. On the other side of the entrance is the Piccolomini Chapel, with a *Crucifixion* by Giulio Mazzoni (circa 1550), a refined marble altar (circa 1475), a funerary monument to Maria d'Aragona by another prominent Florentine sculptor, Antonello Rossellino (circa 1475), and on the right, a rather sweet fresco of the Annunciation by an anonymous follower of Piero della Francesca.

The true surprises of the church are to the right of the altar, in the presbytery and adjoining rooms. The chapel just to the right of the main altar, belonging to the Orefice family, is richly decorated in pre-Baroque (1596–98) polychrome marbles and frescoes by Luis Rodriguez; from here you continue on through the Oratory of the Holy Sepulchre, with the tomb of Antonio D'Alessandro and his wife, to reach the church's showpiece: a potently realistic life-size group of eight terra-cotta figures by Guido Mazzoni (1492), which make up a Pietà; the faces are said to be modeled from people at the Aragonese court. Toward the rear of the church is the Cappella dell'Assunta, with a fun painting in its corner of a monk by Michelangelo's student Giorgio Vasari, and the lovely Sacrestia Vecchia (Old Sacristy), adorned with one of the most successful decorative ensembles Vasari ever painted (1544) and breathtaking wood-inlay stalls by Fra' Giovanni da Verona and assistants (1506–10) with views of famous buildings. ⊠ *Piazza Monteoliveto 15, Toledo* ☎ *081/5513333* ⊙ *Mon.–Sat. 10–1 and 2–4, Sun. 9–1* Ⓜ *Dante, Toledo.*

Teatro San Carlo. La Scala in Milan is the famous one, but San Carlo is more beautiful, and Naples is, after all, the most operatic of cities. The Neoclassical structure, designed by Antonio Niccolini, was built in a mere nine months after an 1816 fire destroyed the original. Many operas were composed for the house, including Donizetti's *Lucia di Lammermoor* and Rossini's *La Donna del Lago*. In the theater, nearly 200 boxes are arranged on six levels, and the 1,115-square-meter (12,000-square-foot) stage permits productions with horses, camels, and elephants, and even has a backdrop that can be raised to reveal the Palazzo Reale Gardens. Above the rich red-and-gold auditorium is a ceiling fresco by Giuseppe Cammarano representing Apollo presenting poets to Athena. Performance standards are among Europe's highest— even the great Enrico Caruso was hissed here. If you're not attending an opera, you can still see the splendid theater on a 30-minute guided tour. Perhaps your experience will mirror that of the French author Stendhal, who wrote, "The first impression one gets is of being suddenly transported to the palace of an oriental emperor. There is nothing in Europe to compare with it, or even give the faintest idea of what it is like." ■TIP→ **English-language tours, which take place daily except on holidays, can be booked in advance on the theater's website.** ⊠ *Via San Carlo 101–103, Toledo* ☎ *081/5534565 Mon.–Sat., 081/7972468 Sun.* ⊕ *www.teatrosancarlo.it* 🎫 *Tour €6* ⊙ *Tours: Mar.–Dec., Mon.– Sat. on the half hr 10:30–12:30 and 2:30–4:30, Sun. on the half hr 10:30–12:30; Jan. and Feb. mornings only* Ⓜ *Toledo, Piazza Municipio.*

WORTH NOTING

Piazza Plebiscito (*People's Square*). After spending time as a parking lot, this square was restored in 1994 to one of Napoli Nobilissima's most majestic spaces, with a Doric semicircle of columns resembling Saint Peter's Square in Rome. The piazza was erected in the early 1800s

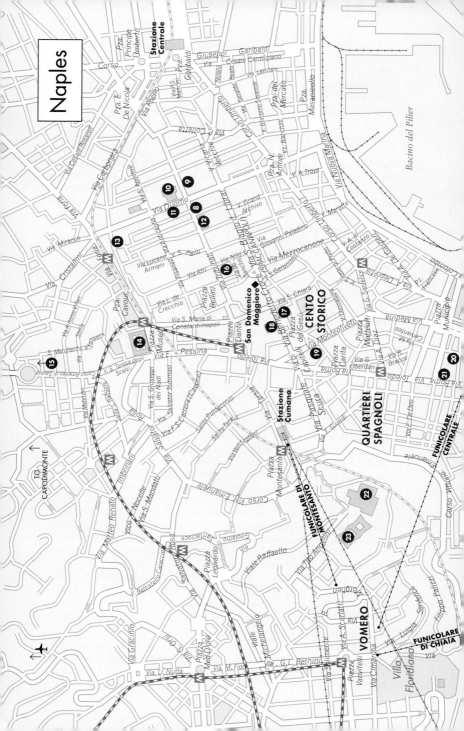

13

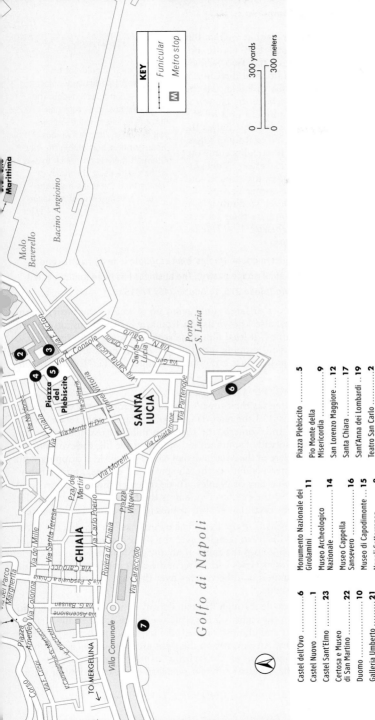

KEY

- Funicular
- **M** Metro stop

0   300 yards
0   300 meters

Golfo di Napoli

Bacino Angioino

Molo Beverello

Marittima

Porto S. Lucia

SANTA LUCIA

Piazza del Plebiscito

CHIAIA

Villa Comunale

TO MERGELLINA

Pza. dei Martiri

Piazza Vittoria

under the Napoleonic regime, but after the regime fell, Ferdinand, the new King of the Two Sicilies, ordered the addition of the Church of San Francesco di Paola. On the left as you approach the church is a statue of Ferdinand and on the right one of his father, Charles III, both of them clad in Roman togas. Around dusk, floodlights come on, creating a magical effect. A delightful sea breeze airs the square, and on Sunday one corner becomes an improvised soccer stadium where local youths emulate their heroes. ⊠ *Piazza Plebiscito* Ⓜ *Toledo, Piazza Municipio.*

QUICK BITES

Pintauro. This just might be Naples' best *sfogliate* (a tasty ricotta- and semolina-filled shell-shape pastry). The business has been family-owned since 1785. ⊠ *Via Toledo 275, Toledo* ☎ *348/7781645.*

Via Toledo. Sooner or later you'll wind up at one of the busiest commercial arteries, also known as Via Roma, which is thankfully closed to through traffic—at least along the stretch leading from the Palazzo Reale. Don't avoid dipping into this parade of shops and coffee bars where plump pastries are temptingly arranged. ⊠ *Via Toledo, Toledo* Ⓜ *Toledo.*

THE VOMERO TO THE LUNGOMARE

Neapolitans often say their town's glories are vertical—the white *guglia* (religious obelisk) of the historic quarter, the eight-story tenements of Spaccanapoli, and Vomero, the towering hill that overlooks the city center. A rich spread of southern Italian amplitude fills the eye from the balcony belvedere of the Museo di San Martino: hillsides dripping with luxuriant greenery, countless church spires and domes, and far below the intensely blue Bay of Naples. To tie together the lower parts and upper reaches of the city, everyone uses the *funicolare*—the funicular system that runs on three separate routes up and down the Vomero.

Castel dell'Ovo (*Castle of the Egg*). The oldest castle in Naples, the 12th-century Castel dell'Ovo dangles over the Porto Santa Lucia on a thin promontory. Built atop the ruins of an ancient Roman villa, the castle these days shares its views with some of the city's top hotels. Its gigantic rooms, rock tunnels, and belvederes over the bay are among Naples's most striking sights.

You enter the castle through its main entrance, past its forbidding trio of cannons. On the right is a large picture of the castle in the Renaissance. Turn left and glimpse through the battlements the sleepy Borgo Marinaro below. An elevator on the right ascends to the castle top, or you can also continue along the walkway overlooking the ramparts. The roof's Sala della Terrazze offers a postcard-come-true view of Capri.

This is a peaceful spot for strolling and enjoying the views, all the more so now that the Lungomare outside is a pedestrians-only area.

As for the castle's name, the poet Virgil is supposed have hidden inside it an egg that had protective powers as long as it remained intact. The belief was taken so seriously that to quell the people's panic after Naples suffered an earthquake, an invasion, and a plague in quick succession, its monarch felt compelled to produce an intact egg, solemnly declaring it to be the Virgilian original. ⊠ *Santa Lucia waterfront, Via Eldorado 3, off Via Partenope* 🕾 *081/7956180* 🎫 *Free* ☉ *Mon.–Sat. 8–6:45, Sun. 8–1:45.*

Castel Sant'Elmo. Perched on the Vomero, this massive castle is almost the size of a small town. Built by the Angevins in the 14th century to dominate the port and the old city, it was remodeled by the Spanish in 1537. The parapets, configured in the form of a six-point star, provide fabulous views. The whole bay lies on one side; on another, the city spreads out like a map, its every dome and turret clearly visible; and to the east is slumbering Vesuvius. Once a major military outpost, the castle these days hosts occasional cultural events. Its prison, the Carcere alto di Castel Sant'Elmo, is the site of the **Museo del Novecento Napoli,** which traces Naples's 20th-century artistic output, from the futurist period through the 1980s. ⊠ *Largo San Martino, Vomero* 🕾 *081/848800288* ⊕ *www.polomusealenapoli.beniculturali.it* 🎫 *€5* ☉ *Wed.–Mon. 8:30–7:30; museum 8:30–6* Ⓜ *Vanvitelli.*

Fodor'sChoice ★   **Certosa e Museo di San Martino.** Atop a rocky promontory with a fabulous view of the entire city and majestic salons that would please any monarch, the Certosa di San Martino is a monastery that seems more like a palace. In fact, by the 18th century Ferdinand IV was threatening to halt the religious order's government subsidy, so sumptuous was this *certosa,* or charter house, which had been started in 1325. Although the Angevin heritage can be seen in the pointed arches and cross-vaulted ceiling of the **Certosa Church,** over the years its dour Gothic was traded in for varicolored Neapolitan Baroque.

The sacristy leads into the **Cappella del Tesoro,** with Luca Giordano's ceiling fresco of Judith holding aloft Holofernes's head and the painting by Il Ribera (the *Pietà* over the altar is one of his masterpieces). The polychrome marble work of the architect and sculptor Cosimo Fanzago (1591–1678) is at its finest here, and he displays a gamut of sculptural skills in the **Chiostro Grande** (Great Cloister). Fanzago's ceremonial portals at each corner of the cloister are among the most spectacular of all Baroque creations, aswirl with Michelangelo-esque ornament.

The **Quarto del Priore** (Prior's Quarters), the residence of the only monk allowed contact with the outside world, is an extravaganza of salons filled with frescoes, majolica-tile floors, and paintings, plus extensive gardens where scenic *pergolati* (roofed balconies) overlook the bay.

Entering from the Quarto del Priore side, you come upon two splendid gilded coaches and then the **"Vessels of the King"** naval museum, with a 20-meter (65-foot) boat occupying a whole room. Beyond lie two rooms with Early Renaissance masterpieces; subsequent rooms hold works by later artists, including the tireless Luca Giordano. Past the library, with its heavenly majolica-tile floor, comes the **Sezione Prese-piale,** the world's greatest collection of Christmas cribs. Pride of place goes to the *Presepe (Nativity)* of Michele Cucineniello. Equally amazing in its own way is a crib inside an eggshell. ⊠ *Piazzale San Martino 5, Vomero* ☎ *081/2294589* ⊕ *www.polomusealenapoli.beniculturali. it* 🎟€6 ☉ *Thurs.–Tues. 9–7:30; ticket office closes at 6:30. Christmas crèches Thurs.–Mon.; some rooms occasionally closed for lack of staffing* Ⓜ *Vanvitelli.*

Fodor's Choice
★

Lungomare (*Seafront*). The first thing mayor Luigi de Magistris did after his 2011 election was to banish traffic from the sea front. Strolling, skating, or biking along Via Caracciolo and Via Partenope with Capri, Mt. Vesuvius, and the Castel dell'Ovo in your sights is truly the quintessential Italian experience. ⊠ *Via Caracciolo* Ⓜ *Mergellina.*

SPACCANAPOLI

To get the essence of Naples, you need to discover Spaccanapoli, the unforgettable neighborhood that is the heart of old Naples. This is the Naples of peeling facades and enough waving laundry to suggest a parade; of small alleyways fragrant with freshly laid flowers at the many shrines to the Blessed Virgin. Here, where the cheapest pizzerias in town feed the locals like kings, the full raucous street carnival of Neapolitan popular culture is punctuated with improbable oases of spiritual calm.

TOP ATTRACTIONS

Duomo. Though the cathedral was established in the 1200s, the building you see was erected a century later and has since undergone radical changes—especially during the Baroque period. Inside, 110 ancient columns salvaged from pagan buildings are set into the piers that support the 350-year-old wooden ceiling. Off the left aisle you step down into the 4th-century church of **Santa Restituta,** which was incorporated into the cathedral. Though Santa Restituta was redecorated in the late 1600s in the prevalent Baroque style, the mosaics in the **Battistero** (Baptistery) are claimed to be the oldest in the Western world.

On the right aisle of the cathedral, in the **Cappella del Tesoro di San Gennaro,** multicolor marbles and frescoes honor Saint Januarius, the miracle-working patron saint of Naples, whose altar and relics are encased in silver. Three times a year—on September 19 (his feast day); on the Saturday preceding the first Sunday in May, which commemorates the transfer of his relics to Naples; and on December 16—his dried blood, contained in two sealed vials, is believed to liquefy during rites in his honor; the rare occasions on which it does not liquefy portend ill, as in 1980, the year of the Irpinia earthquake. The most spectacular painting on display is Ribera's *San Gennaro in the Furnace* (1647), depicting the saint emerging unscathed from the furnace while his persecutors scatter in disarray. These days large numbers of devout Neapolitans offer up prayers in his memory. The **Museo del Tesoro di San Gennaro** houses a rich collection of treasures associated with the saint. Paintings by Solimena and Luca Giordano hang alongside statues, busts, candelabras, and tabernacles in gold, silver, and marble by Cosimo Fanzago and other 18th-century Baroque masters. ⊠ *Via Duomo 149, Spaccanapoli* ☎ *081/449097 for Duomo, 081/294980* *for Museo ⊕ www.museosangennaro.it ✉ Cathedral €5, Battistero €2 ⊙ Cathedral daily 9–6; Battistero weekdays 8:30–12:30 and 3:30–6:30, holidays 8:30–1 and 3:30–6:30; Capella di San Gennaro weekdays 8:30–1 and 3:30–7:30, Sun. 8:30–1 and 4:30–6:30.*

QUICK BITES

Scaturchio. While you're exploring the old part of town, take a break at Scaturchio. Although the coffee is top-of-the-line and the ice cream and pastries are quite good—including the specialty, the *ministeriale*, a pert chocolate cake whipped with rum-cream filling—it's the atmosphere that counts here. In the heart of Spaccanapoli, it's where nuns, punks, businesspeople, and housewives come to share the good things they all have in common. ✉ *Piazza San Domenico Maggiore 19, Spaccanapoli* ☎ *081/5516944* ⊕ *www.scaturchio.it* ⊙ *Daily 7:30 am–8:30 pm* Ⓜ *Università.*

13

Gesù Nuovo. A stunning architectural contrast to the plain Romanesque frontage of the nearby Santa Chiara, the oddly faceted stone facade of this elaborate Baroque church dates to the late 16th century. Originally a palace, the building was seized by Pedro of Toledo in 1547 and donated to the Jesuits on the condition the facade remain intact. Recent research has revealed that the symbols on the stones on the front are Aramaic musical notes that produce a 45-minute concerto. Behind the entrance is Francesco Solimena's action-packed *Helidorus' Eviction from the Temple*. The bulk of the interior decoration took more than 40 years and was completed only in the 18th century. You can find the familiar Baroque sculptors (Naccherino, Finelli) and painters. The gracious *Visitation* above the altar in the second chapel on the right is by Massimo Stanzione, who also contributed the fine frescoes in the main nave: they're in the presbytery (behind and around the main altar).

Don't miss the votive chapel dedicated to the surgeon and university teacher Saint Giuseppe Moscato, along with a re-creation of his studio. ✉ *Piazza Gesù Nuovo, Spaccanapoli* ☎ *081/5578111* ⊙ *Daily 7–12:30 and 4–7:30* Ⓜ *Dante.*

Fodor'sChoice
★

Museo Cappella Sansevero (*Sansevero Chapel Museum*). The dazzling funerary chapel of the Sangro di Sansevero princes combines noble swagger, overwhelming color, and a touch of the macabre—which is to say, it expresses Naples perfectly. The chapel was begun in 1590 by Prince Giovan Francesco di Sangro to fulfill a vow to the Virgin if he were cured of a dire illness. The seventh Sangro di Sansevero prince, Raimondo, had the building modified in the mid-18th century and is generally credited for its current Baroque styling, whose noteworthy elements include the splendid marble-inlay floor. A larger-than-life figure, Prince Raimondo was popularly believed to have signed a pact with the devil allowing him to plumb nature's secrets. He commissioned the young sculptor Giuseppe Sammartino to create numerous works, including the chapel's centerpiece: the remarkable *Veiled Christ,* which has a seemingly transparent marble veil some say was produced using a chemical formula provided by the prince. ■TIP→ If you have the stomach for it, take a look in the crypt, where some of the anatomical experiments conducted by the prince are gruesomely displayed. ✉ *Via Francesco de Sanctis 19, off Vicolo Domenico Maggiore, Spaccanapoli* ☎ *081/5518470* ⊕ *www.museosansevero.it* 🎟 *€7 (€5 with Campania Artecard)* ⊙ *Mon. and Wed.–Sat. 9:30–6:10, Sun. 9–1:40* Ⓜ *Dante.*

FAMILY

Fodor'sChoice
★

Napoli Sotterranea (*Underground Naples*). Fascinating two-hour tours of a portion of Naples's fabled underground city provide an initiation into the complex layering of history in the city center. Efforts to dramatize the experience—amphorae lowered on ropes to draw water from cisterns, candles distributed to negotiate narrow passages as in pre-electric days, objects shifted to reveal secret passages—combined with excellent guiding in English make this particularly exciting for children.

After a descent into "Naples's stomach" (food storehouses), the first stop is an amphitheater where Nero famously performed three times. During one of his performances, an earthquake struck and—so Suetonius relates—the emperor forbade the 6,000 spectators to leave. The rumbling, he insisted, was only the gods applauding his performance. Across a small street above, another descent delivers you to a section of a 400-km (249-mile) system of quarries and aqueducts used from Greek times until the 1845 cholera epidemic. In 1942 a section was reopened to provide air-raid shelter big enough to sleep 3,000 people. A further descent takes you to a Greco-Roman quarry. Finally, prepare for a highly claustrophobic 1-km (½-mile) walk with only a candle to light your way.

At the end of the aqueduct you come to first a Greek and then a much larger Roman cistern. Near the entrance is the War Museum, which displays uniforms, armed transportation vehicles, and weapons from World War II. A room at the end of the tour contains examples of that most Neapolitan of art forms, *la presepe* (the crib). ■ TIP→ **Be prepared on the underground tour to go up and down many steps and handle a few narrow corridors. Temperatures in summer will be much lower below than at street level, so bundle up.** ✉ *Piazza San Gaetano 68, along Via dei Tribunali, Spaccanapoli* ☎ *081/296944* ⊕ *www. napolisotterranea.org* 🎟 *€10* ⊙ *Tours every 2 hrs daily 10–6* Ⓜ *Piazza Cavour.*

Fodor'sChoice
★

Pio Monte della Misericordia. One of Spaccanapoli's defining sites, this octagonal church was built around the corner from the Duomo for a charitable institution seven noblemen founded in 1601. The institution's aim was to carry out acts of Christian charity: feeding the hungry, clothing the poor, nursing the sick, sheltering pilgrims, visiting prisoners, ransoming Christian slaves, and burying the indigent dead—acts immortalized in the history of art by Caravaggio's famous altarpiece depicting the *Sette Opere della Misericordia* (*Seven Acts of Mercy*). In this haunting work the artist has brought the Virgin, borne atop the shoulders of two angels, down into the streets of Spaccanapoli (scholars have suggested a couple of plausible locations) populated by figures in whose spontaneous and passionate movements the people could see themselves. The original church was considered too small and was destroyed in 1658 to make way for a new church that was designed by Antonio Picchiatti and built between 1658 and 1672. Pride of place is given to the great Caravaggio above the altar, but there are other important Baroque-era paintings on view here. Some hang in the church—among them seven other works of mercy depicted individually by Caravaggio acolytes—while other works, including a wonderful self-portrait by Luca Giordano, are in the adjoining *pinacoteca* (picture gallery). ⊠ *Via Tribunali 253, Spaccanapoli* ☎ *081/446973* ⊕ *www. piomontedellamisericordia.it* ⌂ *€7, includes audio guide* ☉ *Thurs.– Tues. 9–2* Ⓜ *Piazza Cavour (in construction: Duomo).*

WORTH NOTING

Monumento Nazionale dei Girolamini. "I Girolamini" is another name for the Oratorians, followers of St. Philip Neri, to whom this splendid church is dedicated. The church is part of a larger complex managed as the Monumento Nazionale dei Girolamini. The Florentine architect Giovanni Antonio Dosio designed I Girolamini, which was erected between 1592 and 1619; the dome and facade were rebuilt (circa 1780) in the most elegant Neoclassical style after a design by Ferdinando Fuga. Inside the entrance wall is Luca Giordano's grandiose fresco (1684) of Christ chasing the money-changers from the temple. The intricate carved-wood ceiling, damaged by Allied bombs in 1943, has now been restored to its original magnificence.

The Oratorians also built the **Casa dei Padri dell'Oratorio** (House of the Oratorio Fathers). Step through its gate to see the two cloisters designed by Dosio and other Florentine architects around 1600. The gallery in this section contains 16th- and 17th-century paintings by Ribera and other Baroque masters. One of Europe's most gloriously decorated 18th-century libraries, the **Biblioteca dei Girolamini** (Girolamini Library), was closed at time of writing, but it helped make this an intellectual nexus during the Renaissance and Baroque periods. ■TIP→ **The ticket office is on Via Duomo, behind the church.** ⊠ *Via Duomo 142, Spaccanapoli* ☎ *081/2294571* ⊕ *www.polomusealenapoli.beniculturali. it* ⌂ *€5* ☉ *Mon., Thurs., and Fri. 8:30–7, weekends 8:30–2* Ⓜ *Piazza Cavour.*

San Lorenzo Maggiore. One of the grandest medieval churches of the Decumano Maggiore, San Lorenzo features a very unmedieval facade of 18th-century splendor. Due to the effects and threats of earthquakes, the church was reinforced and reshaped along Baroque lines in the 17th and 18th centuries. Begun by Robert d'Anjou in 1265 on the site of a 6th-century church, this structure has a single, barnlike nave that reflects the Franciscans' desire for simple spaces with enough room to preach to large crowds. A grandiose triumphal arch announces the transept, and the main altar (1530) is the sculptor Giovanni da Nola's masterpiece; notice the fascinating historical views of Naples in the reliefs.

The apse, designed by an unknown French architect of great caliber, is pure French Angevin in style, complete with an ambulatory of nine side chapels that is covered by a magnificent web of cross arches. The church's most important monument is found here: the tomb of Catherine of Austria (circa 1323), by Tino da Camaino, among the first sculptors to introduce the Gothic style into Italy. The left transept contains the 14th-century funerary monument of Carlo di Durazzo and yet another

Cosimo Fanzago masterpiece, the **Cappellone di Sant'Antonio.** Outside the 17th-century cloister is the entrance to the **Greek and Roman** *scavi,* or excavations, under San Lorenzo. Near the area of the forum, these digs have revealed streets, markets, and workshops of another age.

Next door to the church is the **Museo dell'Opera di San Lorenzo,** installed in the 16th-century palazzo around the *torre campanaria* (bell tower). In Room 1, ancient remains from the Greek agora beneath combine with modern maps to provide a fascinating impression of import and export trends in the 4th century BC. The museum also contains ceramics dug up from the Svevian period, many pieces from the early Middle Ages, large tracts of mosaics from the 6th-century basilica, and helpful models of how the ancient Roman forum and nearby buildings must have looked. A multimedia facility has recently been added to do justice to a place that exists in several historical dimensions. ⊠ *Via dei Tribunali 316, Spaccanapoli* ☎ *081/2110860* ⊕ *www. sanlorenzomaggiore.na.it, www.laneapolissotterrata.it* 🖾 *Excavations and museum €9* ⊗ *Museum: Mon.–Sat. 9:30–5:30, Sun. 9:30–1:30. Church: daily 8–1 and 5:30–7; closed to sightseers during services* Ⓜ *Cavour, Dante.*

Santa Chiara. Offering a stark and telling contrast to the opulence of the nearby Gesù Nuovo, Santa Chiara is the leading Angevin Gothic monument in Naples. The fashionable house of worship for 14th-century nobility and a favorite Angevin church from the start, the church of St. Clare was intended to be a great dynastic monument by Robert d'Anjou. His second wife, Sancia di Majorca, added the adjoining convent for the Poor Clares to a monastery of the Franciscan Minors so she could vicariously satisfy a lifelong desire for the cloistered seclusion of a convent. This was the first time the two sexes were combined in a single complex. Built in a Provençal Gothic style between 1310 and 1328 (probably by Guglielmo Primario) and consecrated in 1340, the church had its aspect radically altered, as did so many others, in the Baroque period. A six-day fire started by Allied bombs on August 4, 1943, put an end to all that, as well as to what might have been left of the important cycle of frescoes by Giotto and his Neapolitan workshop. The church's most important tomb towers behind the altar. Sculpted by Giovanni and Pacio Bertini of Florence (1343–45), it is, fittingly, the tomb of the founding king: the great Robert d'Anjou, known as "the Wise." Nearby are the tombs of Carlo, duke of Calabria, and his wife, Marie de Valois, both by Tino da Camaino.

Around the left side of the church is the **Chiostro delle Clarisse,** the most famous cloister in Naples. Complemented by citrus trees, the benches and octagonal columns comprise a light-handed masterpiece of painted majolica designed by Domenico Antonio Vaccaro, with a delightful profusion of landscapes and light yellow and green floral motifs realized by Donato and Giuseppe Massa and their studio (1742). ⊠ *Piazza Gesù Nuovo, Spaccanapoli* ☎ *081/5516673* ⊕ *www. monasterodisantachiara.eu* 🖾 *Museum and cloister €6* ⊗ *Church daily 7:30–1 and 4:30–8, museum and cloister Mon.–Sat. 9:30–5:30, Sun. 10–2:30* Ⓜ *Dante, Università.*

MUSEO ARCHEOLOGICO NAZIONALE
TO CAPODIMONTE

Madre (*Museum of Contemporary Art Donnaregina*). With 8,000 square meters (86,111 square feet) of exhibition space, a host of young and helpful attendants, and regular late-night events, the Madre is one of the most visited museums in Naples. Most of the artworks on the first floor were installed in situ by their creators, but the second-floor gallery exhibits works by both international and Italian contemporary artists. The museum also hosts temporary shows by major international artists. ⊠ *Via Settembrini 79, San Lorenzo* ☎ *081/19313016* ⊕ *www. madrenapoli.it/en* 🎫 *€7 (free on Mon.)* ⊙ *Mon. and Wed.–Sat. 10–7:30, Sun. 10–8* Ⓜ *Piazza Cavour.*

Fodor'sChoice
★

Museo Archeologico Nazionale (*National Museum of Archaeology*). Also known as MANN, this legendary museum has experienced something of a rebirth in recent years. Its unrivaled collections include world-renowned archaeological finds that put most other museums to shame, from some of the best mosaics and paintings from Pompeii and Herculaneum to the legendary Farnese collection of ancient sculpture. The core "masterpiece" collection is almost always open to visitors but other rooms are subject to staffing shortages and sometimes close on a rotating basis. Some of the "newer" rooms, covering archaeological discoveries in the Greco-Roman settlements and necropolises in and around Naples, have helpful informational panels in English. A fascinating, free display of the finds unearthed during digs for the Naples metro has been set up in the Museo station, close to the museum's entrance. ⊠ *Piazza Museo 19, Spaccanapoli* ☎ *081/4422149, 081/4422111* ⊕ *cir. campania.beniculturali.it/museoarcheologiconazionale* 🎫 *€8* ⊙ *Wed.– Mon. 9–7:30* Ⓜ *Museo.*

Museo di Capodimonte. The grandiose 18th-century, Neoclassical Bourbon royal palace houses fine and decorative art. Capodimonte's greatest treasure is the excellent collection of paintings well displayed in the **Galleria Nazionale,** on the palace's first and second floors. Aside from the artworks, part of the royal apartments still has a complement of beautiful antique furniture (most of it on the splashy scale so dear to the Bourbons), and a staggering range of porcelain and majolica from the various royal residences. Most rooms have fairly comprehensive information cards in English, whereas the audio guide is overly selective and somewhat quirky. The main galleries on the first floor are devoted to work from the 13th to the 18th century, including many pieces by Dutch and Spanish masters. On the second floor look for stunning paintings by Simone Martini (circa 1284–1344), Titian (1488/90–1576), and Caravaggio (1573–1610). The palace is in the vast Bosco di Capodimonte (Capodimonte Park), which served as the royal hunting preserve and later as the site of the Capodimonte porcelain works. ⊠ *Via Miano 2, Porta Piccola, Via Capodimonte, Capodimonte* ☎ *081/7499111, 081/7499109* ⊕ *www.polomusealenapoli. beniculturali.it* 🎫 *€7.50 (€6.50 after 2 pm)* ⊙ *Thurs.–Tues. 8:30–7:30; ticket office closes at 6:30.*

13

WHERE TO EAT

CHIAIA

$$
SOUTHERN
ITALIAN

✕ **Amici Miei.** Favored by meat eaters who can't abide another bite of sea bass, this small, dark, and cozy den is known for dishes such as tender carpaccio with fresh artichoke hearts. There are also excellent pasta selections, including orecchiette with chickpeas or *alla barese* (with chewy green turnips), or that extravaganza, the *carnevale lasagne,* an especially rich concoction that sustains revelers in the build-up before Lent. Everyone finishes with a slice of chocolate-hazelnut *torta caprese.* $ *Average main: €16* ⊠ *Via Monte di Dio 78, Chiaia* ☎ *081/7646063* ⊕ *www.ristoranteamicimiei.com* ⌂ *Reservations essential* ☾ *Closed Mon., and June–Aug. No dinner Sun* Ⓜ *Amedeo.*

$$$
NEAPOLITAN
Fodor'sChoice
★

✕ **Da Dora.** Despite its location up an unpromising-looking *vicolo* (alley) off the Riviera di Chiaia, this small restaurant has achieved cult status for its seafood platters. It's remarkable what owner-chef Giovanni can produce in his tiny kitchen. Start with linguine *alla Dora,* laden with local seafood and fresh tomatoes, and perhaps follow up with grilled *pezzogna* (blue-spotted bream). Like many restaurants on the seafront, Dora has its own guitarist on busy nights, who is often robustly accompanied by the kitchen staff. $ *Average main: €25* ⊠ *Via Fernando Palasciano 30, Chiaia* ☎ *081/680519* ⌂ *Reservations essential* ☾ *No dinner Sun.* Ⓜ *Amedeo.*

$
ITALIAN

✕ **L'Ebbrezza di Noè.** A simple enoteca by day and, in a way, more of a place to sip drinks and snack than to have a full meal, L'Ebbrezza has a dining area in the back that fills up in the evening. Owner Luca's enthusiasm for what he does is quite moving—as you sample a recommendation you can sense that he hopes you like it as much as he does. The attention paid to the quality of the wine carries over to the food. Here you can taste *paccheri* (large pasta) stuffed with eggplant *parmigiana,* or one of the fantastic soups. Other highlights include rare cheeses, among them the Sicilian *ragusano di razza modicana* and the local *caciocavallo podolico,* and the daily selection of hot dishes. $ *Average main: €12* ⊠ *Vico Vetriera a Chiaia 8b/9, Chiaia* ☎ *081/400104* ⊕ *www. lebbrezzadinoe.com* ☾ *Closed Mon., and Aug. No lunch* Ⓜ *Amedeo.*

$$
NEAPOLITAN

✕ **Umberto.** Run by the Di Porzio family since 1916, Umberto is one of the city's classic restaurants. It combines the classiness of its neighborhood, Chiaia, and the friendliness one finds in other parts of Naples. Try the *tubettoni "d' 'o treddeta"* ("three-finger" pasta with octopus, tomato, olives and capers); it bears the nickname of the original Umberto, who happened to be short a few digits. Owner Massimo and sisters Lorella and Roberta (Umberto's grandchildren) are all wine experts and oversee a fantastic cellar. Note that Umberto is also one of the city's few restaurants catering to diners with a gluten allergy, as well as to vegetarians. $ *Average main: €15* ⊠ *Via Alabardieri 30–31, Chiaia* ☎ *081/418555* ⊕ *www.umberto.it* ☾ *No lunch Mon.* Ⓜ *Amedeo.*

PIAZZA GARIBALDI

$
PIZZA

✕ **Da Michele.** You may recognize Da Michele from the movie *Eat, Pray, Love,* but for more than 140 years before Julia Roberts arrived, this place was a culinary reference point. Despite offering only two types of pizza—*marinara* (with tomato, garlic, and oregano) and *margherita* (with tomato, mozzarella, and basil)—plus a small selection of drinks, it still manages to attract long lines. The prices have something to do with it. But the pizza itself suffers no rivals, so even customers waiting in line are good-humored: the boisterous, joyous atmosphere wafts out with the smell of yeast and wood smoke onto the street. ■ TIP→ **Get a number at the door, and then hang outside until it's called.** [$] *Average main: €5* ✉ *Via Sersale 1/3, off Corso Umberto between Piazza Garibaldi and Piazza Nicola Amore, Piazza Garibaldi* ☎ *081/5539204* 🌐 *www.damichele.net* 💳 *No credit cards* 🕒 *Closed 2 wks in Aug. and Sun. June–Nov.* [M] *Garibaldi.*

13

$ NEAPOLITAN 🍴 **Mimì alla Ferrovia.** Patrons of this Neapolitan institution have included the filmmaker Federico Fellini and that truely Neapolitan comic genius and aristocrat, Totò. Mimì cheerfully lives up to its history, serving fine versions of everything from pasta *e fagioli* (with beans) to the sea bass *al presidente,* baked in a pastry crust and enjoyed by any number of visiting Italian presidents. The owner's son Salvatore is the chef, working wonders in the kitchen. This is not so much a "see and be seen" place as common ground for the famous and the unknown to mingle, feast, and be of good cheer. ■ TIP→ **Given the fairly seedy neighborhood, travel here and back by taxi, especially at night.** [$] *Average main: €13* ✉ *Via A. D'Aragona 19/21, Piazza Garibaldi* ☎ *081/5538525* 🌐 *www.mimiallaferrovia.com* 🕒 *Closed Sun. Jan.–Nov., and last wk in Aug.* [M] *Garibaldi.*

POSILLIPO

$$$ NEAPOLITAN Fodor's Choice ★ 🍴 **Trattoria da Cicciotto.** Chic and charming Da Cicciotto corrals more than a few members of the city's fashionable set—if you dine here, there's a fair chance you'll find a Neapolitan count or off-duty film star enjoying this jewel. A tiny stone terrace overlooks a pleasant anchorage, centered on an antique column, with seats and canopy exquisitely upholstered in blue-and-white matching-but-mixing fabrics. You can appreciate the outdoor setting at either lunch or dinner, and don't even bother with a menu—just start digging into the sublime antipasti and go with the waiter's suggestions. ■ TIP→ **Cicciotto sits at the end of the same long winding road that leads to the famed 'A Fenestella restaurant and shoreline, so phone for the restaurant's free shuttle service if starting out from the city center.** [$] *Average main: €25* ✉ *Calata del Ponticello a Marechiaro 32, Posillipo* ☎ *081/5751165* 🌐 *www.trattoriadacicciotto.it* ✍ *Reservations essential.*

SANTA LUCIA

$$$$ ITALIAN 🍴 **La Terrazza.** The Hotel Excelsior's Terrazza restaurant attracts visiting A-list stars with its marble floorings and brown-leather furnishings (all aimed at highlighting the silver cutlery). The à la carte menu fuses Italian regional culinary styles—try the rhombus fish fillet *al cartoccio* (baked and served in a transparent paper) with potatoes and black olives from Gaeta. Dress up, and expect to be impressed. [$] *Average main: €40* ✉ *Hotel Excelsior, Via Partenope 48, Santa Lucia* ☎ *081/7640111* 🌐 *www.laterrazzaexcelsior.com* 🕒 *Closed Sun.*

Continued on page 766

PIZZA NAPLES STYLE: The Classic Margherita

Locally grown San Marzano tomatoes are a must.

The best pizza should come out with cheese bubbling and be ever-so-slightly charred around its edges.

Only buffalo-milk mozzarella or fior di latte cheese should be used.

The dough must be made from the right kind of durum wheat flour and be left to rise for at least six hours.

Be prepared: ranging from the size of a plate to that of a Hummer wheel, Neapolitan pizza is different from anything you might find elsewhere in Italy—not to mention what's served up at American pizza chains. The "purest" form is the marinara, topped with only tomatoes, garlic, oregano, and olive oil.

OTHER FAVORITES ARE . . .

- **CAPRICCIOSA** (the "capricious"), made with whatever the chef has on hand.

- **SICILIANA** with mozzarella and eggplant.

- **DIAVOLA** with spicy salami.

- **QUATTRO STAGIONI** ("four seasons"), made with produce from each one.

- **SALSICCIA E FRIARIELLI** with sausage and a broccoli-like vegetable.

A PIZZA FIT FOR A QUEEN

During the patriotic fervor following Italian unification in the late 19th century, a Neapolitan chef decided to celebrate the arrival in the city of the new Italian queen Margherita by designing a pizza in her—and the country's—honor. He took red tomatoes, white mozzarella cheese, and a few leaves of fresh green basil—reflecting the three colors of the Italian flag—and gave birth to the modern pizza industry.

Margherita of Savoy

ONLY THE BEST

An association of Neapolitan pizza chefs has standardized the ingredients and methods that have to be used to make pizza certified DOC (*denominazione d'origine controllata*) or STG (*specialità tradizionale garantita*). See the illustration on the opposite page for the basic requirements.

Buffalo-milk mozzarella

FIRED UP!

The Neapolitan pizza must be made in a traditional wood-burning oven. Chunks of beech or maple are stacked up against the sides of the huge, tiled ovens, then shoved onto the slate base of the oven, where they burn quickly at high temperatures. If you visit Pompeii, you will see how similar the old Roman bread-baking ovens are to the modern pizza oven. The *pizzaiolo* (pizza chef) then uses a long wooden paddle to put the pizza into the oven, where it cooks quickly.

A pizzaiolo at work

PIZZERIE

Hundreds of restaurants specialize in pizza in Naples, and the best of these make pizza and nothing else. As befits the original fast food, *pizzerie* tend to be simple, fairly basic places, with limited menu choices, and quick, occasionally brusque service.

Typical pizzeria in Naples

THE REAL THING

Naples takes its contribution to world cuisine seriously. The Associazione Verace Pizza Napoletana (www.pizzanapoletana.org) was founded in 1984 in order to share expertise, maintain quality levels, and provide courses for aspiring pizza chefs and pizza lovers. The group also organizes the annual Pizzafest—three days in September dedicated to the consumption of pizza, when *maestri* from all over the region get together and cook off.

Simple, fresh toppings

SPACCANAPOLI

$
PIZZA

✕ **Gino Sorbillo.** There are three restaurants called Sorbillo along Via dei Tribunali; this is the one with the crowds waiting outside. Order the same thing the locals come for: a basic Neapolitan pizza (try the unique pizza al pesto or the stunningly simple marinara—just tomatoes and oregano). They're cooked to perfection by the third generation of pie makers who run the place. The pizzas are enormous, flopping over the edge of the plate onto the white marble tabletops. $ *Average main: €8* ✉ *Via dei Tribunali 32, Spaccanapoli* ☎ *081/446643* ⊕ *www.sorbillo. it* ⊙ *Closed Sun. Jan.–Nov., and 3 wks in Aug.* Ⓜ *Dante.*

$
PIZZA

✕ **I Decumani.** Every pizzeria along Via dei Tribunali is worth the long wait (all the good ones are jammed packed) but none more so than the Decumani, thanks to the superlative *pizzaioli* (pizza makers)—say hello to Gianni and Enzo for us—at work here. They turn out a wide array of pizzas and do them all to perfection. If you aren't on a diet, try the *frittura* and you'll be pleasantly surprised with this mix of Neapolitan-style tempura: zucchini, eggplants, rice-balls, and many other delicacies. $ *Average main: €7* ✉ *Via dei Tribunali 58, Spaccanapoli* ☎ *081/5571309* ⊙ *Closed Mon. Jan.–Nov.* Ⓜ *Cavour, Dante.*

$$$$
NEAPOLITAN

✕ **Palazzo Petrucci.** In a 17th-century mansion facing the grand Piazza San Domenico Maggiore, Palazzo Petrucci doesn't lack for dramatic dining options—under the vaulted ceiling of the former stables, in the gallery where a glass partition reveals the kitchen, or in the cozy room overlooking the piazza. Fortify yourself with a complimentary glass of prosecco before agonizing between the à la carte offerings and the menu degustazione (€60). A popular starter is mille-feuille of local mozzarella with raw prawns and vegetable sauce. The *paccheri all'impiedi* (large tube pasta served standing on end) in a rich ricotta-and-meat sauce is an interesting twist on an old regional favorite. The interior is elegantly minimal; the culinary delights are anything but. They also have a gourmet pizzeria next door. $ *Average main: €60* ✉ *Piazza San Domenico Maggiore 4, Spaccanapoli* ☎ *081/5524068* ⊕ *www.palazzopetrucci.it* ✍ *Reservations essential* ⊙ *Closed 2 wks in Aug. No lunch Mon.; no dinner Sun.* Ⓜ *Dante.*

TOLEDO

$
NEAPOLITAN
Fodor'sChoice
★

✕ **Trattoria San Ferdinando.** This cheerful trattoria seems to be run for the sheer pleasure of it. Try the excellent fish or the traditional (but cooked with a lighter, modern touch) pasta dishes, especially those with *verdura* (fresh leaf vegetables) or with potatoes and smoked mozzarella (*pasta e patate con la provola*). Close to Teatro San Carlo and aptly decorated with playbills and theatrical memorabilia, both ancient and modern, this is an excellent place to stop after a visit to the opera. ■TIP→ **Look for the entrance almost immediately on the right as you go up Via Nardones from Piazza Trieste e Trento—ring the bell outside to be let in.** $ *Average main: €15* ✉ *Via Nardones 117, Toledo* ☎ *081/421964* ⊙ *Closed Sun. and Mon., and last 3 wks of Aug. No dinner Sat. and Tues.* Ⓜ *Toledo/Municipio.*

Folk Songs à la Carte

If you want to hear *canzoni napole-tane*—the fabled Neapolitan folk songs—performed live, you can try to catch top city troupes, such as the Cantori di Posillipo and I Virtuosi di San Martino, at venues like the Teatro Trianon. An easier alternative is to head for one of the more traditional restaurants (such as Mimì alla Ferrovia), where most every night you can expect your meal to be interrupted by a *posteggiatore*. These singers aren't employed by the restaurants, but they're encouraged to come in, swan around the tables with a battered old guitar, and belt out classics such as "Santa Lucia," "O' Surdato Innamurate," "Torna a Surriento," and, inevitably, "Funiculi Funiculà."

These songs are the most famous of a vast repertoire that found international fame with the mass exodus of southern Italians to the United States in the early 20th century. "Funiculi Funiculà" was written by Peppino

Turco and Luigi Denza in 1880 to herald the new funicular railway up Vesuvius. "O Sole Mio," by Giovanni Capurro and Eduardo di Capua, has often been mistakenly taken for the Italian national anthem. "Torna a Surriento" was composed by Ernesto di Curtis in 1903 to help remind the current Italian prime minister how wonderful he thought Sorrento was (and how many government subsidies he had promised the township).

Interest in this genre has been rekindled, both locally and internationally, by John Turturro's 2010 film *Passione*, which explores the current and historical music scene. Note that singers are more than happy to do requests, even inserting the name of your *innamorato* or *innamorata* into the song. When they've finished they'll stand discreetly by your table. Give them a few euros and you'll have friends for life (or at least for the night).

13

WHERE TO STAY

PIAZZA GARIBALDI

$$
HOTEL
Fodor's Choice
★

MGallery Palazzo Caracciolo. Built in the 1200s, this one-time home of Murat, King of Naples, offers royal treatment within walking distance of the train station and centro storico. **Pros:** a tranquil respite; great value. **Cons:** not an ideal area for evening strolls; some evening events mean loud music until late. **$** *Rooms from: €130 ⊠ Via Carbonara 112, Piazza Garibaldi ☎ 081/0160111 ⊕ www.mgallery.com ⌂ 139 rooms* ⦿ *Breakfast* Ⓜ *Stazione, Cavour.*

TOLEDO

$
HOTEL

Palazzo Turchini. Just a few minutes' walk from the Castel Nuovo, Palazzo Turchini is one of the centro storico's more attractive smaller hotels. **Pros:** good location for the port; more intimate than neighboring business hotels; breakfast is included. **Cons:** close to a busy traffic hub. **$** *Rooms from: €120 ⊠ Via Medina 21, Toledo ☎ 081/5510606 ⊕ www.palazzoturchini.it ⌂ 27 rooms* ⦿ *Breakfast* Ⓜ *Municipio.*

$$
HOTEL

Renaissance Naples Hotel Mediterraneo. A modern, efficient business hotel, the Mediterraneo is within walking distance of both the Teatro San Carlo and Spaccanapoli. **Pros:** convenient to the port; attractive rooftop breakfast terrace. **Cons:** restaurant's food is mediocre. $ *Rooms from: €180* ✉ *Via Nuova Ponte di Tappia 25, Toledo* ☎ *081/7970001* ⊕ *www.mediterraneonapoli.com* ⤳ *256 rooms* �🍽 *Breakfast* Ⓜ *Toledo* ✛ *E4.*

SPACCANAPOLI

$$
HOTEL
Fodor's Choice
★

🏨 **Costantinopoli 104.** An oasis of what Italians call "*stile liberty*" (Art Nouveau), with impressive stained-glass fittings and striking artwork, this serene, elegant hotel is well placed for touring the Museo Archeologico Nazionale and Spaccanapoli. **Pros:** pool (a rarity in Neapolitan hotels) and garden; pleasant service. **Cons:** buildings surround the pool; hotel can be difficult to find (look for the sign that reads "Villa Spinelli," the place's former name). $ *Rooms from: €180* ✉ *Via Costantinopoli 104, Spaccanapoli* ☎ *081/5571035* ⊕ *www.costantinopoli104.com* ⤳ *19 rooms* �🍽 *Breakfast* Ⓜ *Museo.*

$$
HOTEL
Fodor's Choice
★

🏨 **Hotel Palazzo Decumani.** This contemporary upscale hotel near transportation links and Spaccanapoli's major sights occupies an early-20th-century palazzo. **Pros:** residents-only lounge-bar; large rooms and bathrooms; soundproofed windows. **Cons:** can be hard to find—follow signs from Corso Umberto. $ *Rooms from: €140* ✉ *Piazzetta Giustino Fortunato 8, Spaccanapoli* ☎ *081/4201379* ⊕ *www.palazzodecumani. com* ⤳ *28 rooms* �🍽 *Breakfast* Ⓜ *Duomo.*

CHIAIA

$$
HOTEL

🏨 **Chiaja Hotel de Charme.** No views here, but this 18th-century palazzo has a great location and its apartments, all on the first floor, have plenty of atmosphere. **Pros:** near Piazza del Plebiscito and the Royal Palace; on bustling pedestrians-only street. **Cons:** no views in a town with some great ones; even with a/c, some rooms get hot in summer; difficult to reach by car. $ *Rooms from: €139* ✉ *Via Chiaia 216, Chiaia* ☎ *081/415555* ⊕ *www.hotelchiaia.it* ⤳ *33 rooms* �🍽 *Breakfast* Ⓜ *Toledo.*

$$$
HOTEL

🏨 **Grand Hotel Parker's.** Midway up the Vomero hill, with fine views of the bay and distant Capri, this landmark hotel, first opened in 1870, continues to serve up a supremely elegant dose of old-style atmosphere to visiting VIPs, ranging from rock stars to Russian leaders. **Pros:** excellent restaurant; fabulous views. **Cons:** a long walk from the funicular; a very long walk or taxi ride from city center and seafront; not quite as grand as it once was. $ *Rooms from: €300* ✉ *Corso Vittorio Emanuele 135, Vomero* ☎ *081/7612474* ⊕ *www.grandhotelparkers.it* ⤳ *73 rooms, 9 suites* �🍽 *Breakfast* Ⓜ *Amedeo.*

$$
HOTEL
Fodor's Choice
★

🏨 **Hotel Palazzo Alabardieri.** Just off the chic Piazza dei Martiri, this is the most fashionable choice among the city's smaller luxury hotels—for some, there is simply no other hotel in Naples. **Pros:** impressive public salons; central yet quiet location; polite, pleasant staff. **Cons:** no sea view; difficult to reach by car. $ *Rooms from: €145* ✉ *Via Alabardieri 38, Chiaia* ☎ *081/415278* ⊕ *www.palazzoalabardieri.it* ⤳ *39 rooms* �🍽 *Breakfast* Ⓜ *Amedeo.*

$$
HOTEL

🏨 **Pinto-Storey Hotel.** The name juxtaposes a 19th-century Englishman who fell in love with Naples with a certain Signora Pinto; together they went on to establish this hotel that overflows with warmth and charm.

Pros: safe neighborhood; near public transit; option of not using a/c for an €8-per-night discount; courteous reception; traditional Anglophile atmosphere. **Cons:** not close to major sights; only a few rooms have views; can be hard to find (look for the large diagonal wooden door and press the 4th-floor buzzer). $ *Rooms from: €130* ⊠ *Via G. Martucci 72, Chiaia* ☎ *081/681260* ⊕ *www.pintostorey.it* ⤺ *16 rooms* ⏆ *No meals* Ⓜ *Amedeo.*

SANTA LUCIA

$$$

HOTEL

Fodor's Choice

★

Grand Hotel Vesuvio. You'd never guess from the modern exterior that this is the oldest of Naples's great seaside hotels—the place where Enrico Caruso died, Oscar Wilde dallied with lover Lord Alfred Douglas, and Bill Clinton charmed the waitresses. **Pros:** luxurious atmosphere; historic setting; directly opposite Borgo Marinaro; traffic-free Lungomare is just outside. **Cons:** spa and pool cost extra; reception staff can be snooty; not all rooms have great views. $ *Rooms from: €230* ⊠ *Via Partenope 45, Santa Lucia* ☎ *081/7640044* ⊕ *www.vesuvio.it* ⤺ *149 rooms, 21 suites* ⏆ *Breakfast.*

$$$

HOTEL

Hotel Santa Lucia. Neapolitan enchantment can be yours if you stay at this luxurious, quietly understated hotel that overlooks the port immortalized in the song "Santa Lucia." **Pros:** great views from most rooms; proximity to the port is convenient for trips to the islands; bikes for hire at €5 an hour. **Cons:** rooms disappointingly boxy. $ *Rooms from: €220* ⊠ *Via Partenope 46, Santa Lucia* ☎ *081/7640666* ⊕ *www.santalucia.it* ⤺ *95 rooms* ⏆ *Breakfast.*

$

HOTEL

Transatlantico Napoli. Perhaps enjoying Naples's most enchanting setting, at the edge of Borgo Marinaro's toy-size harbor, in the shadow of the Castel dell'Ovo, this modestly priced hotel also sits at the top of most travelers' "dream lodgings" list. **Pros:** fabulous location; gentle prices. **Cons:** rather cheap and ugly furniture. $ *Rooms from: €120* ⊠ *Via Luculliana 15, Santa Lucia* ☎ *081/7648842* ⊕ *www. transatlanticonapoli.com* ⤺ *8 rooms* ⏆ *Breakfast.*

NIGHTLIFE AND PERFORMING ARTS

NIGHTLIFE

Bars and clubs are found in many areas around Naples. The sophisticated crowd heads to Posillipo and the Vomero, Via Partenope along the seafront, and the Chiaia area (between Piazza dei Martiri and Via dei Mille). A more bohemian contingent makes for the centro storico and the area around Piazza Bellini. The scene is relatively relaxed—you might even be able to sit down at a proper table. Keep in mind that clubs, and their clientele, can change rapidly, so do some investigating before you hit the town.

Caffè Intramoenia. The granddaddy of all the bars in Piazza Bellini was set up as a bookstore in the late 1980s and still has its own small publishing house with a variety of attractive titles. Seats in the heated veranda are at a premium in winter, though many customers sit outside year-round. ⊠ *Piazza Bellini 70, Spaccanapoli* ☎ *081/290988* ⊕ *www.intramoenia. it* Ⓜ *Dante/Museo/Cavour.*

Enoteca Belledonne. Between 8 and 9 in the evening it seems as though the whole upscale Chiaia neighborhood has descended into the tiny space for an aperitivo. The small tables and low stools are notably uncomfortable, but the cozy atmosphere and the pleasure of being surrounded by glass-front cabinets full of wine bottles with beautiful labels more than makes up for it. Excellent local wines are available by the glass at great prices. ⊠ *Vico Belledonne a Chiaia 18, Chiaia* ☎ *081/403162* ⊕ *www. enotecabelledonne.com* Ⓜ *Amedeo.*

L'ebbrezza di Noè. A particularly quiet and refined option in Chiaia is L'ebbrezza di Noè, which is both a stand-up bar and a sit-down eatery. ⊠ *Vico Vetriera a Chaia 9, Chiaia* ☎ *081/400104* ⊕ *www. lebbrezzadinoe.com* Ⓜ *Amedeo.*

OPERA

Teatro San Carlo. Opera is serious business in Naples—not in terms of the music so much as the costumes, the stage design, the players, and the politics. What's happening on stage can be secondary to the news of who's there, who they're with, and what they're wearing. Given the circumstances, it's hardly surprising that the city's famous San Carlo Company doesn't offer a particularly innovative repertoire. Nonetheless, the company's performances are usually of very a high quality—and if they're not in form, the audience lets them know it. Performances take place in the historic Teatro San Carlo, the luxury liner of opera houses in southern Italy. In 2008 the concert hall underwent a massive renovation, with everything from the seats to the gold inlay on the ceiling frescoes replaced, and the statue of the mermaid Parthenope (missing since 1969) restored to its place on the building's facade. ⊠ *Via San Carlo 101–103, Piazza Municipio* ☎ *081/7972412 for box office, 081/7972331* ⊕ *www.teatrosancarlo.it* Ⓜ *Municipio.*

SHOPPING

Leather goods, jewelry, and cameos are some of the best items to buy in Campania. In Naples you can generally find good deals on handbags, shoes, and clothing. Most boutiques and department stores are open Monday 4:30–8 and Tuesday–Saturday 9:15–1 and 4:30–8. The larger chains now open on Sunday, too.

SHOPPING DISTRICTS

Most of the luxury shops in Naples are along a crescent that descends the Via Toledo to Piazza Trieste e Trento and then continues along Via Chiaia to Via Filangieri and on to Piazza Amedeo, as well as continuing south toward Piazza dei Martiri and the Riviera di Chiaia. The charming shops specializing in Presepi (Christmas crèches) are in Spaccanapoli, on the Via San Gregorio Armeno. Via San Sebastiano, close to the Conservatory, is the kingdom of musical instruments.

CHIAIA

Marinella. Count the British royal family among the customers of this shop that has been selling old-fashioned made-to-measure ties for more than 100 years. ⊠ *Via Riviera di Chiaia 287/a, Chiaia* ☎ *081/2451182* ⊕ *www.marinellanapoli.it* Ⓜ *Amedeo.*

Tramontano. Since 1865 this place has been crafting fine leather luggage, bags, belts, and wallets. ✉ *Via Chiaia 142, Chiaia* ☎ *081/414837* ⊕ *www.tramontano.it* Ⓜ *Amedeo.*

SPACCANAPOLI

Ferrigno. Shops selling Nativity scenes cluster along the Via San Gregorio Armeno in Spaccanapoli, and they're all worth a glance—the most famous is Ferrigno. Maestro Giuseppe Ferrigno died in 2008, but the family business continues, still faithfully using 18th-century techniques. ✉ *Via San Gregorio Armeno 10, Spaccanapoli* ☎ *081/5523148* ⊕ *www. arteferrigno.it* Ⓜ *Duomo.*

FAMILY **Ospedale delle Bambole.** This tiny storefront operation with a laboratory is a world-famous "hospital" for dolls. In business since 1850, it's a wonderful place to take kids *and* their injured toys. ✉ *Via San Biagio dei Librai 81, Spaccanapoli* ☎ *081/203067* ⊕ *www.ospedaledellebambole. com* 🕐 *Weekdays 10–4, Sat. 10–2* Ⓜ *Duomo.*

HERCULANEUM, VESUVIUS, AND POMPEII

Volcanic ash and mud preserved the Roman towns of Herculaneum and Pompeii almost exactly as they were on the day Mt. Vesuvius erupted in AD 79, leaving them not just archaeological ruins but museums of daily life in the ancient world. The two cities and the volcano that buried them can be visited from either Naples or Sorrento, thanks to the Circumvesuviana, the suburban railroad that provides fast, frequent, and economical service.

HERCULANEUM

10 km (6 miles) southeast of Naples.

GETTING HERE AND AROUND

To get to Herculaneum by car, take the A3 Naples–Salerno autostrada and exit at Ercolano. Follow signs for the "*Scavi*" (excavations). The Circumvesuviana railway connects Herculaneum to Naples, Portici, Torre del Greco, Torre Annunziata, Pompeii, and Sorrento.

EXPLORING

Fodor'sChoice **Herculaneum Ruins.** Lying more than 50 feet below the present-day
★ town of Ercolano, the ruins of Herculaneum are set among the acres of greenhouses that make this area one of Europe's principal flower-growing centers. In AD 79 the gigantic eruption of Vesuvius, which also destroyed Pompeii, buried the town under a tide of volcanic mud. The semiliquid mass seeped into the crevices and niches of every building, covering household objects, enveloping textiles and wood—and sealing all in a compact, airtight tomb. Excavation began in 1738 under King Charles of Bourbon, using the technique of underground tunnels. Digging was interrupted but recommenced in 1828, continuing into the following century. Today, less than half of Herculaneum has been excavated. With contemporary Ercolano and the unlovely Resina Quarter sitting on top of the site, progress is limited. From the ramp leading down to Herculaneum's well-preserved edifices, you get a good overall

Bay of Naples

Parco Regionale del Partenio

Monteforte
Nola
Palma
Casavatore
Marano di Nápoli
Qualiano
Marina di Lago di Pátria
Marina di Varcature
Cumae
Pozzuoli
Sollatara
Baia
Bacoli
Miseno
Capo Miseno
Pomigliano
Somma
S Anastasia
Cércola
Volla
Cásoria
Casavatore
Miano
Capodimonte
Agnano Terme
Mergellina
Marechiaro

Naples see detail map

Golfo di Pozzuoli
Isola di Nisida
Golfo di Napoli

Procida
Procida Porto
Isola di Prócida
Punta Solchiaro

Ischia
Ischia Porto
Lacco Ameno
Punta Cornacchia
Forio
Spiaggia di Citara
Sant' Angelo
Punta Sant'Angelo
Isola d'Ischia

S Giuseppe
Ottaviano
Cércola

Vesuvius
Parco del Vesuvio
Terzigno

Oplontis

Torre del Greco
Herculaneum
Pórtici
Torre del Greco
Boscoreale
Boscotrecase
Torre Annunziata

Pompeii see detail map

Sarno
Pagani
Nocera
S Antônio
Gragnana
Castellammare di Stábia

Circumvesuviana Rail Line

Vico Equense
Marina di Equa
Piano di Sorrento
Meta
Sorrento
Alimuri
Marina di Puolo
Marina di Stábia
Massa Lubrense
Términi
Metrano
Sant Agata sui Dué Golfi
Punta Campanella

SORRENTINE PENINSULA

Cetara
Maiori
Amalfi
Ravello
Praiano
Positano

THE AMALFI COAST

Bocca Piccola

Marina Grande
Capri
Marina Piccola
Isola di Capri
Grotta Azzurra
Punta dell'Arcera
Anacapri

Capri see detail map

Sorrento & Amalfi Coast see detail map

Golfo di Napoli

Tyrrhenian Sea

10 mi
10 km
0

Pompeii Prep

Pompeii, impressive under any circumstances, really comes alive if you do some homework before seeing it in person.

First, read up—there are piles of good books on the subject, including these engaging, jargon-free histories: *Pompeii: The Day a City Died* by Robert Etienne, *Pompeii: Public and Private Life* by Paul Zanker, and *The Lost World of Pompeii* by Colin Amery.

For accurate historical information woven into the pages of a thriller, pick up *Pompeii: A Novel* by Robert Harris.

Second, be sure to visit the Museo Archeologico Nazionale (MANN) in Naples, where most of the finest art from Pompeii now resides. The museum is a remarkable treasure trove—and a rewarding place to visit, even if Pompeii isn't in your plans.

13

view of the site, as well as an idea of the amount of volcanic debris that had to be removed to bring it to light.

About 5,000 people lived in Herculaneum when it was destroyed, many of them fishermen, craftsmen, and artists. Though Herculaneum had only one third the population of Pompeii and has been only partially excavated, what has been found is generally better preserved. In some cases you can even see the original wooden beams, staircases, and furniture. Unfortunately, at the time of writing, the **Villa dei Papiri** (Villa of the Papyri) is closed to the public. The subject of this excavation in a corner of the site was built by Julius Caesar's father-in-law (with a replica built by Paul Getti in Malibu almost 2,000 years later). The building is named for the 1,800 carbonized papyrus scrolls dug up here in the 18th century, leading scholars to believe that this may have been a study center or library. You can view full-color virtual reproductions in the nearby MAV museum. Also worth special attention are the carbonized remains within the **Casa del Tramezzo di Legno** (House of the Wooden Partition).

Be sure to stock up on refreshments beforehand, as there is no food concession at the archaeological site. At the entrance, pick up a map showing the gridlike layout of the dig, which is divided into numbered blocks, or *insulae*. Splurge on an audio guide (€6.50 for one, €10 for two), and then head down the tunnel to start the tour at the old shoreline. Most of the houses are open and offer a representative cross-section of domestic, commercial, and civic buildings can be seen. Decorations are especially delicate in the **Casa di Nettuno ed Anfitrite** (House of Neptune and Amphitrite), named for the subjects of a still-bright mosaic on the wall of the *nymphaeum* (a recessed grotto with a fountain). North of this house is the **Casa del Bel Cortile** (House of the Beautiful Courtyard). Both the **Casa dei Cervi** (House of the Stags) and the **Terme Suburbane** (Suburban Baths) are closed for restoration. As an alternative, you can head to the House of the Ship, which contains a small Roman vessel whose wood and equipment has survived very much intact. ■ TIP➜ At the entrance you can pick up a copy of "Pianta degli

Scavi Archeologici di Ercolano," the excellent free pamphlet and map about the site that's as good as most of the guides you must pay for. ⊠ *Corso Resina 6, Ercolano* ☎ *081/8575347* ⊕ *www.pompeiisites.org* 💰 *€11 for Herculaneum only; €20 for biglietto cumulativo, includes 5 sites (Pompeii, Herculaneum, Boscoreale, Oplontis, and Stabiae) valid for 3 days* ⊗ *Nov.–Mar., daily 8:30–5, last entrance at 3:30; Apr.–Oct., daily 8:30–7:30, ticket office closes at 6.*

FAMILY

Fodor'sChoice

★

Museo Archeologico Virtuale (MAV). Dazzling "virtual" versions of Herculaneum's streets and squares, computerized re-creations of the House of the Faun, even a "multi-D" simulation of Vesuvius erupting: Herculaneum's 1st-century-meets-the-21st-century museum extravaganza has it all. After stopping at the ticket office for the headset audio tour (€3), you descend, as in an excavation, to a floor below. Passing ancient faces that have now been given a name, the "*percorso*" path inserts you inside a re-creation of Herculaneum's first dig. You'll experience Herculaneum's Villa dei Papiri before and—even more dramatically—during the eruption, courtesy of special effects; enter "the burning cloud" of AD 79 (actually vaporized water); then emerge, virtually speaking, inside Pompeii's House of the Faun, which can be seen both as it is and as it was for two centuries BC. The next re-creation—complete with rippling grass and moving cart and oxen—is again Villa dei Papiri. Then comes a stellar pre- and postflooding view of Baia's "Nymphaeum," the now-displaced statues arrayed as they were in the days of Emperor Claudius, who commissioned them.

Visitors here are invited to take a front-row seat for *Day and Night in the Forum of Pompeii,* with soldiers, litter-bearing slaves, and toga-clad figures moving spectrally to complete the spell; or to make a vicarious visit to the Lupanari brothels, their various pleasures illustrated in virtual and graphic frescoes along the walls. There are holograms of jewelry of the earthquake fugitives and a touch-and-browse section of the Villa dei Papiri's scrolls, too. Recent installations include, beside a wooden model of Herculaneum's theater, its virtual re-creation. It was here that a local farmer, while digging a well, first came across what proved to be not merely a single building, but a whole town. The farmer reputedly removed some statues; here their virtual equivalents stand in their niches by daylight as an actor learns his lines. A dove flies skyward, and then, with nightfall, the torches ignite. Equally fascinating are the virtual baths, where the mysteries of Roman plumbing come alive before your eyes. For an extra €4 and the most spectacular of all, is the Sensurround film of Vesuvius erupting. The words of Pliny the Elder provide a timeless commentary while the floor vibrates before your feet. "Wisdom begins in wonder," said Socrates, and this museum nobly proves the ancient philosopher correct. ⊠ *Via IV Novembre 44, Ercolano* ☎ *081/19806511* ⊕ *www.museomav.it* 💰 *€11.50; €7.50 museum only, €5 eruption simulation only* ⊗ *Tues.–Sun. 9:30–5.*

Continued on page 782

ANCIENT POMPEII
TOMB OF A CIVILIZATION

The site of Pompeii, petrified memorial to Vesuvius's eruption on the morning of August 24, AD 79, is the largest, most accessible, and probably most famous of excavations anywhere.

A busy commercial center with a population of 10,000–20,000, ancient Pompeii covered about 160 acres on the seaward end of the fertile Sarno Plain. Today Pompeii is choked with both the dust of 25 centuries and more than 2 million visitors every year; only by escaping the hordes and lingering along its silent streets can you truly fall under the site's spell. On a quiet backstreet, all you need is a little imagination to sense the shadows palpably filling the dark corners, to hear the ancient pipe's falsetto and the tinny clash of cymbals, to envision a rain of rose petals gently covering a Roman senator's dinner guests. Come in the late afternoon when the site is nearly deserted and you will understand that the true pleasure of Pompeii is not in the seeing but in the feeling.

A FUNNY THING HAPPENS ON THE WAY TO THE FORUM

as you walk through Pompeii. Covered with dust and decay as it is, the city seems to come alive. Perhaps it's the familiar signs of life observed along the ancient streets: bakeries with large ovens just like those for making pizzas, tracks of cart wheels cut into the road surface, graffiti etched onto the plastered surfaces of street walls. Coming upon a *thermopolium* (snack bar), you imagine natives calling out, "Let's move on to the am-phitheater." But a glance up at Vesuvius, still brooding over the scene like an enormous headstone, reminds you that these folks—whether

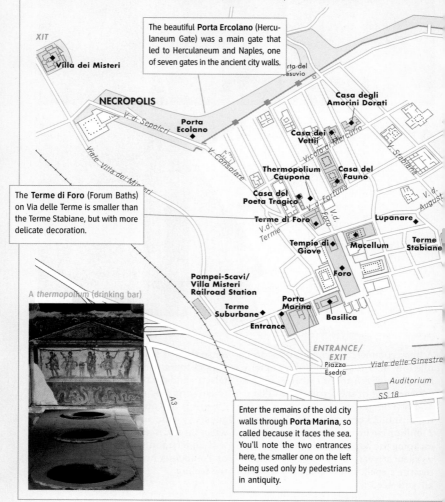

The beautiful **Porta Ercolano** (Herculaneum Gate) was a main gate that led to Herculaneum and Naples, one of seven gates in the ancient city walls.

The **Terme di Foro** (Forum Baths) on Via delle Terme is smaller than the Terme Stabiane, but with more delicate decoration.

A *thermopolium* (drinking bar)

Enter the remains of the old city walls through **Porta Marina**, so called because it faces the sea. You'll note the two entrances here, the smaller one on the left being used only by pedestrians in antiquity.

XIT
Villa dei Misteri
Porta del Vesuvio
NECROPOLIS
V. d. Sepolcri
Porta Ecolano
Viale Villa dei Misteri
V. Consolare
Casa degli Amorini Dorati
Casa dei Vettii
Vicolo di Mercurio
V. Stabiana
Thermopolium Caupona
Casa del Fauno
Casa del Poeta Tragico
V. d. Fortuna
V. d. Foro
Terme di Foro
Lupanare
V. d. Terme
Tempio di Giove
Macellum
Terme Stabiane
Pompei-Scavi/ Villa Misteri Railroad Station
Foro
Terme Suburbane
Porta Marina
Entrance
Basilica
ENTRANCE/ EXIT
Piazza Esedra
Viale delle Ginestre
Auditorium
SS 18
A3
V. d. August

Pompeii's cemetery, or Necropolis

imagined in your head or actually wearing a mantle of lava dust—have not taken a breath for centuries. The town was laid out in a grid pattern, with two main intersecting streets. The wealthiest took a whole block for themselves; those less fortunate built a house and rented out the front rooms, facing the street, as shops. There were good numbers of *tabernae* (taverns) and *thermopolia* on almost every corner, and frequent shows at the amphitheater.

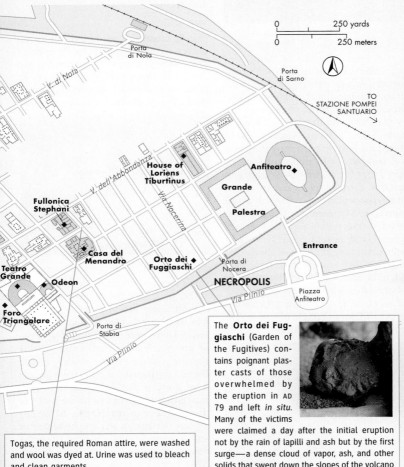

The **Orto dei Fuggiaschi** (Garden of the Fugitives) contains poignant plaster casts of those overwhelmed by the eruption in AD 79 and left *in situ*. Many of the victims were claimed a day after the initial eruption not by the rain of lapilli and ash but by the first surge—a dense cloud of vapor, ash, and other solids that swept down the slopes of the volcano like a boiling avalanche at 40–50 miles per hour.

Togas, the required Roman attire, were washed and wool was dyed at. Urine was used to bleach and clean garments.

PUBLIC LIFE IN ANCIENT POMPEII

Forum

THE CITY CENTER

As you enter the ruins at Porta Marina, make your way uphill to the **Foro** (Forum), which served as Pompeii's cultural, political, and religious center. You can still see some of the two stories of colonnades that used to line the square. Like the ancient Greek *agora* in Athens, the Forum was a busy shopping area, complete with public officials to apply proper standards of weights and measures. Fronted by an elegant three-column portico on the eastern side of the forum is the **Macellum**, the covered meat and fish market dating to the 2nd century BC; here vendors sold goods from their reserved spots in the central market. It was also in the Forum that elections were held, politicians let rhetoric fly, speeches and official announcements were made, and worshippers crowded around the **Tempio di Giove** (Temple of Jupiter), at the northern end of the forum.

Basilica

On the southwestern corner is the **Basilica**, the city's law court and the economic center. These rectangular aisled halls were the model for early Christian churches, which had a nave (central aisle) and two side aisles separated by rows of columns. Standing in the Basilica, you can recognize the continuity between Roman and Christian architecture.

THE GAMES

The **Anfiteatro** (Amphitheater) was the ultimate in entertainment for Pompeians and offered a gamut of experiences, but essentially this was for gladiators rather than wild animals. By Roman standards, Pompeii's amphitheater was quite

Amphitheater

small (seating 20,000). Built in about 80 BC, making it the oldest permanent amphitheater in the Roman world, it was oval and divided into four seating areas. There were two main entrances—at the north and south ends—and a narrow passage on the west called the Porta Libitinensis, through which the dead were probably dragged out. A wall painting found in a house near the theater (now in the Naples Museum) depicts the riot in the amphitheater in AD 59 when several citizens from the nearby town of Nocera were killed. After Nocerian appeals to Nero, shows were suspended for three years.

BATHS AND BROTHELS

Fresco of Pyramus and Thisbe in the House of Loreius Tiburtinus

In its day, Pompeii was celebrated as the Côte d'Azur, the seaside Brighton, the Fire Island of the ancient Roman empire. Evidence of a Sybaritic bent is everywhere—in the town's grandest villas, in its baths, and especially in its rowdiest *lupanaria* (brothels), murals still reveal a worship of hedonism. Satyrs, bacchantes, hermaphrodites, and acrobatic couples are pictured indulging in hanky-panky.

The first buildings to the left past the ticket turnstiles are the **Terme Suburbane** (Suburban Baths), built—by all accounts without permission—right up against the city walls. The baths have eyebrow-raising frescoes in the *apodyterium* (changing room) that strongly suggest that more than just bathing and massaging went on here.

On the walls of **Lupanare** (brothel) are scenes of erotic games in which clients could engage. The **Terme Stabiane** (Stabian Baths) had underground furnaces, the heat from which circulated beneath the floor, rose through flues in the walls, and escaped through chimneys. The water temperature could be set for cold, lukewarm, or hot. Bathers took a lukewarm bath to prepare themselves for the hot room. A tepid bath came next, and then a plunge into cold water to tone up the skin. A vigorous massage with oil was followed by rest, reading, horseplay, and conversation.

Thanks to those deep layers of pyroclastic deposits from Vesuvius that protected the site from natural wear and tear over the centuries, graffiti found in Pompeii provide unique insights into the sort of things that the locals found important 2,000 years ago. A good many were personal and lend a human dimension to the disaster that not even the sights can equal.

At the baths: "What is the use of having a Venus if she's made of marble?"

At the entrance to the front lavatory at a private house: "May I always and everywhere be as potent with women as I was here."

On the Viale ai Teatri: "A copper pot went missing from my shop. Anyone who returns it to me will be given 65 bronze coins."

In the Basilica: "A small problem gets larger if you ignore it."

PRIVATE LIFE IN ANCIENT POMPEII

The facades of houses in Pompeii were relatively plain and seldom hinted at the care and attention lavished on the private rooms within. When visitors arrived they passed the shops and entered an open peristyle, from which the occupants received air, sunlight, and rainwater, the latter caught by the *impluvium*, a rectangular-shaped receptacle under the sloped roof. In the back was a receiving room, the *tablinum*, and behind was an-

House of Paquius Proculus

other open area, the atrium. Life revolved around this uncovered inner courtyard, with rows of columns and perhaps a garden with a fountain. Only good friends ever saw this part of the house, which was surrounded by *cubicula* (bedrooms) and the *triclinium* (dining area). Interior floors and walls usually were covered with colorful marble tiles, mosaics, and frescoes.

Several homes were captured in various states by the eruption of Vesuvius, each representing a different slice of Pompeiian life.

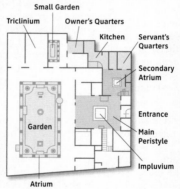

Small Garden
Triclinium
Owner's Quarters
Kitchen
Servant's Quarters
Secondary Atrium
Entrance
Garden
Main Peristyle
Impluvium
Atrium

The **Casa del Fauno** (House of the Faun) displayed wonderful mosaics, now at the Museo Archeologico Nazionale in Naples. The **Casa del Poeta Tragico** (House of the Tragic Poet) is a typical middle-class house. On the floor is a mosaic of a chained dog and the inscription *cave canem* ("Beware of the dog"). The **Casa degli Amorini Dorati** (House of the Gilded Cupids) is an elegant, well-preserved home with original marble decorations in the garden. Many paintings and mosaics were executed at **Casa del Menandro** (House of Menander), a patrician's villa named for a fresco of the Greek playwright. Two blocks beyond the Stabian Baths you'll notice on the left the current digs at the **Casa dei Casti Amanti** (House of the Chaste Lovers). A team of plasterers and painters were at work here when Vesuvius erupted, redecorating one of the rooms and patching up the cracks in the bread oven near the entrance—possibly caused by tremors a matter of days before.

The **House of the Vettii** is the best example of a house owned by wealthy *mercatores* (merchants). It contains vivid murals—a magnificent *pinacoteca* (picture gallery) within the very heart of Pompeii. The scenes here—except for those in the two wings off the atrium—were all painted after the earthquake of AD 62. Once inside, cast an admiring glance at the delicate frieze around the wall of the *triclinium* (on the right of the peristyle garden as you enter from the atrium), depicting cupids engaged in various activities, such as selling oils and perfumes, working as goldsmiths and metalworkers, acting as wine merchants, or performing in chariot races. Another of the main attractions in the Casa dei Vettii is the small cubicle beyond the kitchen area (to the right of the atrium) with its faded erotic frescoes now protected by Perspex screens.

UNLOCKING THE VILLA DEI MISTERI

Villa dei Misteri

There is no more astounding, magnificently memorable evidence of Pompeii's devotion to the pleasures of the flesh than the frescoes on view at the **Villa dei Misteri** (Villa of the Mysteries), a palatial abode 400 yards outside the city gates, northwest of Porta Ercolano. Unearthed in 1909, this villa had more than 60 rooms painted with frescoes; the finest are in the *triclinium*. Painted in the most glowing Pompeiian reds and oranges, the panels relate the saga of a young bride (Ariadne) and her initiation into the mysteries of the cult of Dionysus, who was a god imported to Italy from Greece and then given the Latin name of Bacchus. The god of wine and debauchery also represented the triumph of the irrational—of all those mysterious forces that no official state religion could fully suppress.

Pompeii's best frescoes, painted in glowing reds and oranges, retain an amazing vibrancy.

The Villa of the Mysteries frescoes were painted circa 50 BC, most art historians believe, and represent the peak of the Second Style of Pompeiian wall painting. The triclinium frescoes are thought to have been painted by a local artist, although the theme may well have been copied from an earlier cycle of paintings from the Hellenistic period. In all there are 10 scenes, depicting children and matrons, musicians and satyrs, phalluses and gods. There are no inscriptions (such as are found on Greek vases), and after 2,000 years historians remain puzzled by many aspects of the triclinium cycle. Scholars endlessly debate the meaning of these frescoes, but anyone can tell they are the most beautiful paintings left to us by antiquity. In several ways, the eruption of Vesuvius was a blessing in disguise, for without it, these masterworks of art would have perished long ago.

PLANNING YOUR DAY IN POMPEII

The only restaurant inside the site is both overpriced and busy, so it makes sense to bring along water and snacks. If you come so equipped, there are some shady, underused picnic tables outside the Porta di Nola, to the northeast of the site.

Making the most of your time

Visiting Pompeii does have its frustrating aspects: many buildings are blocked off by locked gates, and enormous group tours tend to clog up more popular attractions. But the site is so big that it's easy to lose yourself amid the quiet side streets. To really see the site, you'll need four or five hours.

Three buildings within Pompeii—Terme Suburbane, Casa del Menandro, and Casa degli Amorini Dorati—are open for restricted viewing. Reservations must be made on-line at ⊕ www.arethusa.net, where you can find information on hours.

Tours

To get the most out of Pompeii, rent an audio guide (€6.50 for one, €10 for two; you'll need to leave ID) and opt for one of the three itineraries (2 hours, 4 hours, or 6 hours). If hiring a guide, make sure the guide is registered for an English tour and standing inside the gate; agree beforehand on the length of the tour and the price, and prepare yourself for soundbites of English mixed with dollops of hearsay.

Modern Pompeii

Caught between the hammer and anvil of cultural and religious tourism, the modern town of Pompei (to use the modern-day Italian spelling, not the ancient Latin) is now endeavoring to polish up its act. In attempts to ease congestion and improve air quality at street level, parts of the town have been pedestrianized and parking restrictions tightened. Several hotels have filled the sizable niche in the market for excellent deals at affordable prices. As for recommendable restaurants, if you deviate from the archaeological site and make for the center of town, you will be spoiled for choice.

If you like Pompeii

If you intend to visit other archaeological sites nearby during your trip, you should buy the *biglietto cumulativo*, a combination ticket with access to four area sites (Herculaneum, Pompeii, Oplontis, Boscoreale). It costs €20 and is valid for three days. Unlike many archaeological sites in the Mediterranean region, those around Naples are almost all well served by public transport; ask about transportation options at the helpful Porta Marina information kiosk.

POMPEII

22 km (14 miles) southeast of Naples, 17 km (10.5 miles) southeast of Herculaneum.

GETTING HERE AND AROUND

Pompeii has two central Circumvesuviana stations served by two separate train lines. The Naples–Sorrento train stops at "Pompei Scavi–Villa dei Misteri," 100 yards from the Porta Marina Superiore ticket office of the archaeological site, while the Naples–Poggiomarino train stops at Pompei Santuario—more convenient for the entrance to the amphi-theater and the modern town center—where you'll find the Santuario della Madonna del Rosario, and hotels and restaurants. A third FS (Fer-rovie dello Stato) train station south of the town center is only really convenient if arriving from Salerno or Rome.

If, like many visitors every year do, you take the wrong train from Naples (stopping at the other station "Pompei"), all is not lost. There's another entrance to the excavations at the far end of the site, just a seven-minute walk to the Amphitheater.

To get to Pompeii by car, take the A3 Napoli–Salerno autostrada to the "Pompei" exit and follow signs for the nearby "Scavi." There are numerous guarded car parks near the Porta Marina, Piazza Essedra, and Anfiteatro entrances where you can leave your vehicle for a fee.

EXPLORING

Fodor'sChoice ★ **Pompeii.** *See the highlighted feature in this chapter.* ⊠ *Pompeii* ☎ *081/8575347* ⊕ *www.pompeiisites.org* 💶 *€11 for 1 full day; €20 for 3 days, includes entrance to Herculaneum, Oplontis, Stabia, and 1 other site* ⊙ *Apr.–Oct., daily 8:30–7:30, last admission at 6; Nov.–Mar., daily 8:30–5, last admission at 3:30* Ⓜ *Pompei–Villa dei Misteri*

VESUVIUS

8 km (5 miles) northeast of Herculaneum, 16 km (10 miles) east of Naples.

GETTING HERE AND AROUND

To arrive by car, take the A3 Napoli–Salerno autostrada exit "Torre del Greco" and follow Via E. De Nicola from the tollbooth and follow signs for the Parco Nazionale del Vesuvio.

Vesuvio Express. Based at Ercolano Circumvesuviana train station, runs minibuses to the parking lot and the starting point of the path up to the cone's summit (€10 round-trip). There are also services from Pompeii. ☎ *081/7393666* ⊕ *www.vesuvioexpress.info.*

EXPLORING

Mt. Vesuvius. Although its destructive powers are undoubtedly dimin-ished, Vesuvius's threat of an eruption is ever present. Seen from the other side of the Bay of Naples, Vesuvius appears to have two peaks: on the northern side is the steep face of Monte Somma, possibly part of the original crater wall in AD 79; to the south is the present-day cone of Vesuvius, which has actually formed within the ancient crater. The AD 79 cone would have been considerably higher, perhaps peak-ing at more than 6,000 feet. The upper slopes bear the visible scars left by 19th- and 20th-century eruptions, the most striking being the lava flow from 1944 lying to the left (north side) of the approach road from Ercolano on the way up.

As you tour the cities that felt that wrath, you may be overwhelmed by the urge to explore the volcano itself, and it's well worth the trip. The view, when the air is clear, is magnificent, with the curve of the coast and the tiny white houses among the orange and lemon blossoms. When the summit becomes lost in mist, though, you'll be lucky to see your

13

hand in front of your face. If you notice the summit clearing—it tends to be clearer in the afternoon—head for it. If possible, see Vesuvius after you've toured the ruins of buried Herculaneum to better appreciate the magnitude of the volcano's power. Admission to the crater includes a compulsory guide, usually a young geologist who speaks a smattering of English. At the bottom you'll be offered a stout walking stick (a small tip is appreciated when you return it). ■TIP→ **The climb can be tiring if you're not used to steep hikes. Because of the volcanic stone you should wear athletic shoes, not sandals.** ☎ *081/7775720* 🖅 *€8* ⊙ *Daily 9 am–2 hrs before sunset.*

OPLONTIS (TORRE ANNUNZIATA)

20 km (12 miles) southeast of Naples, 5 km (3 miles) west of Pompeii.

Fodor's Choice
★

Surrounded by the fairly drab 1960s urban landscape of Torre Annunziata, Oplontis justifies its reputation as one of the more mysterious archaeological sites to be unearthed in the 20th century. The villa complex has been imaginatively ascribed—from a mere inscription on an amphora—to Nero's second wife, Poppaea Sabina. Her family was well known among the landed gentry of neighboring Pompeii, although, after a kick in the stomach from her emperor husband, she died some 15 years before the villa was overwhelmed by the eruption of 79.

GETTING HERE AND AROUND

By car, take the A3 Napoli–Salerno autostrada to the "Torre Annunziata" exit. Follow Via Veneto west, then turn left onto Via Sepolcri for the excavations. By train, take the Circumvesuviana railway to Torre Annunziata, the town's modern name (€2.90 from Naples).

ISCHIA AND PROCIDA

Though Capri gets star billing among the islands that line the Bay of Naples, Ischia and Procida also have their own lower-key appeal. Once entirely dependent on its thermal springs, Ischia is now the archaeological front-runner in the bay, thanks to the noted museum in Lacco Ameno. Procida has opened up to tourism, with some newer, smaller hotels remaining open throughout the year, and it has started to capitalize on its chief natural asset, the unspoiled isle of Vivara. Ischia was the setting for much of *The Talented Mr. Ripley* (1999), starring Matt Damon and Gwyneth Paltrow, while Procida's pastel colors will be familiar to anyone who has seen the widely acclaimed Italian film, *Il Postino* (1994).

ISCHIA

45 mins by hydrofoil, 90 mins by car ferry from Naples, 60 mins by ferry from Pozzuoli.

Although Capri leaves you breathless with its charm and beauty, Ischia (pronounced "EES-kee-ah," with the stress on the first syllable), also called the Isola Verde (Green Island)—not, as is often believed, because of its lush vegetation, but for its typical green tuff rock—takes time to cast its spell. In fact, an overnight stay is definitely not long enough for the island to get into your blood. Here you have to look harder for signs of antiquity, the traffic can be reminiscent of Naples (albeit on a good day) and the island displays all the hallmarks of rapid, uncontrolled urbanization. Ischia does have its jewels, though. There are the wine-making villages beneath the lush volcanic slopes of Monte Epomeo, and, unlike Capri, the island enjoys a life of its own that survives when the tourists head home.

Ischia is volcanic in origin. From its hidden reservoir of seething molten matter come the thermal springs said to cure whatever ails you. Today the island's main industry, tourism, revolves around the more than 100 thermal baths; most of them are attached to hotels.

A good 35-km (22-mile) road makes a circuit of the island; the ride takes most of a day, if you stop along the way to enjoy the views and perhaps have lunch. You can also book a boat tour around it at the booths in various ports along the coast; there's a one-hour stop at Sant'Angelo. The information office is at the harbor. You may drive on Ischia year-round, and you'll find plenty of taxis.

GETTING HERE AND AROUND

Ischia is well connected with the mainland in all seasons. The last boats leave for Naples and Pozzuoli at about 8 pm (though in the very high season there is a midnight sailing), and you should allow plenty of time for getting to the port and buying a ticket. Ischia has three ports—Ischia Porto, Casamicciola, and Forio (hydrofoils only)—so you should choose your ferry or hydrofoil according to your destination. Non-Italians can bring cars to the island relatively freely.

Ischia's bus network reaches all the major sites and beaches on one of its 18 lines. The principal lines are CD and CS, circling the island in clockwise and counterclockwise directions—in the summer months runs continue until after midnight. The main bus terminus is in Ischia Porto at the start of Via Cosca, where buses run by the company EAV (☎ 081/19800119) radiate out around the island. There are also convenient *fermate* (stops) at the two main beaches—Citara and Maronti—with timetables displayed at the terminus. Tickets cost €1.90 for 90 minutes, €6 for 24 hours; note that conditions can get hot and crowded at peak beachgoing times.

VISITOR INFORMATION

Azienda Autonoma di Cura, Soggiorno e Turismo. The information office is housed in the historic municipal bath building. It is also the information point for Procida. ☒ *Via Iasolino 7, Ischia Porto* ☎ *081/5074231* ⊕ *www.infoischiaprocida.it* ☾ *Mon.–Sat. 9–2 and 3–8.*

EXPLORING

Forio. The far-western and southern coasts of Ischia are more rugged and attractive. Forio, at the extreme west, has a waterfront church and is a good spot for lunch or dinner.

Giardini Poseidon Terme (*Poseidon Gardens Spa*). These sybaritic hot pools are on Citara Beach, south of Forio. You can sit like a Roman senator on a stone chair recessed in the rock and let the hot water cascade over you—all very campy, and fun. ☒ *Via Giovanni Mazzella 87*

☎ *081/9087111* 🌐 *www.giardiniposeidonterme.com* 🎟 €32 *for 1 day* 🕒 *Apr.–Oct., daily 9–7.*

Ischia Ponte. Most of the hotels are along the beach in the part of town called Ischia Ponte, which gets its name from the *ponte* (bridge) built by Alfonso of Aragon in 1438 to link the picturesque castle on a small islet offshore with the town and port. For a while, the castle was the home of Vittoria Colonna, poetess, granddaughter of Renaissance Duke Federico da Montefeltro (1422–82), and platonic soul mate of Michelangelo, with whom she carried on a lengthy correspondence. You'll find a typical resort atmosphere: countless cafés, shops, and restaurants, and a 1-km (½-mile) stretch of fine-sand beach.

Ischia Porto. This is the island's largest town and the usual point of debarkation. It's no workaday port, however, but rather a lively resort with plenty of hotels, the island's best shopping area, and low, flat-roof houses on terraced hillsides overlooking the water. Its narrow streets and villas and gardens are framed by pines.

Monte Epomeo. The inland town of Fontana is the base for excursions to the top of this long-dormant volcano that dominates the island landscape. You can reach its 2,585-foot peak in less than 1½ hours of relatively easy walking.

Sant'Angelo. On the southern coast, this is a charming village with a narrow path leading to its promontory; the road doesn't reach all the way into town, so it's free of traffic. It's a five-minute boat ride from the beach of Maronti, at the foot of the cliffs.

WHERE TO EAT

$ SOUTHERN ITALIAN

🍴 **O' Padrone Dò Mare.** A gorgeous seaside location, just off the pedestrian stretch, this is the ideal place to enjoy fresh fish—the name "owner of the sea" says it all. An institution on the island, now in its seventh decade, locals and visitors crowd the terrace which shares the view with the Regina Isabella hotel. Franco, the *padrone,* is justifiably proud of his shellfish-filled spaghetti *misto mare.* [$] *Average main: €12* ✉ *Corso A. Rizzoli, Lacco Ameno* ☎ *081/900244* 🕒 *Closed Nov.–Mar.*

$$ SOUTHERN ITALIAN

🍴 **Ristorante Cocò.** This inviting restaurant with its outside terrace sits on the causeway linking the Aragonese castle to the rest of Ischia and is renowned for its fresh fish, which is highly prized by the Ischitani. Try the linguine *ai calamaretti* (with squid). [$] *Average main: €24* ✉ *Via Aragonese 1, Ischia Ponte* ☎ *081/981823* 🌐 *www.ristorantecocoischia.com* 🕒 *Closed Jan. and Feb.*

$$$ SOUTHERN ITALIAN

Fodor's Choice ★

🍴 **Umberto a Mare.** This iconic eatery has occupied the space below the Santuario del Soccorso since 1936, when the original Umberto began to grill the local catch on the seafront. Grandson Umberto now presides over the kitchen, conjuring up gourmet dishes such as *crudo di ricciola marinata* (marinated raw Mediterranean amber jack) and *paccheri dolcemare*, a sweet pasta dish with squid, sultanas, pine nuts, and a touch of cinnamon. The setting is divine, with a terrace overlooking the Bay of Citara and the green tuff *scogli innamorati* (lovers' rocks). [$] *Average main: €25* ✉ *Via Soccorso 2, Forio* ☎ *081/997171* 🌐 *www.umbertoamare.it* 🕒 *Closed Nov.–Mar.*

WHERE TO STAY

$$
HOTEL
Fodor'sChoice
★

□ **Albergo Il Monastero.** The Castello Aragonese, on its own island, is the unrivaled location for this unique hotel, where a peaceful ambience and simple but comfortable rooms overlooking the Mediterranean far below add to the fairy-tale impression, and the friendly management adds to the magic. **Pros:** stunning views; how often do you get to stay in a castle? **Cons:** a long way from the entrance to your room; some consider it too far from the town's action. $ *Rooms from: €135* ⊠ *Castello Aragonese 3, Ischia Ponte* ☎ *081/992435* ⊕ *www.albergoilmonastero.it* ⤴ *22 rooms, 1 suite* ☾ *Closed Nov.–Mar.* ⏀| *Breakfast.*

$$$$
HOTEL
Fodor'sChoice
★

□ **Mezzatorre Resort & Spa.** Far from the madding, sunburned crowds that swamp Ischia, this luxurious getaway sits in splendid isolation on the extreme promontory of Punta Cornacchia. **Pros:** tranquil retreat; wonderful views; shuttle provided from Lacco Ameno. **Cons:** very isolated. $ *Rooms from: €450* ⊠ *Via Mezzatorre 23, Forio d'Ischia* ☎ *081/986111* ⊕ *www.mezzatorre.it* ⤴ *57 rooms* ☾ *Closed Nov.–Apr.* ⏀| *Breakfast.*

$
HOTEL

□ **Villa Antonio.** With a superlative panoramic view over the Bay of Cartaromana, with the Castello Aragonese posing front and center, the Antonio offers a quiet haven five minutes from the crowds. **Pros:** attractive price; lovely seaside location. **Cons:** many steps to negotiate before elevator; guest rooms' small windows don't do justice to the view. $ *Rooms from: €90* ⊠ *Via S. Giuseppe della Croce, Ischia Ponte* ☎ *081/982660* ⊕ *www.villantonio.it* ⤴ *18 rooms* ▤ *No credit cards* ☾ *Closed Nov.–mid-Mar.* ⏀| *Breakfast.*

PROCIDA

35 mins by hydrofoil, 1 hr by car ferry from Naples.

Lying barely 3 km (2 miles) from the mainland and 10 km (6 miles) from the nearest port (Pozzuoli), Procida is an island of enormous contrasts. It's the most densely populated island in Europe—just more than 10,000 people crammed into less than 3½ square km (2 square miles)—and yet there are oases like Marina Corricella and Vivara, which seem to have been bypassed by modern civilization. The inhabitants of the island—the *Procidani*—have an almost symbiotic relationship with the Mediterranean: many join the merchant navy, others either fish or ferry vacationers around local waters. And yet land traffic here can be more intense than on any other island in the Bay of Naples.

GETTING HERE AND AROUND

Procida's ferry timetable caters to the many daily commuters who live on the island and work in Naples or Pozzuoli. The most frequent—and cheapest—connections are from the Port of Pozzuoli. After stopping at Procida's main port, Marina Grande (also called Sancio Cattolico), many ferries and hydrofoils continue on to Ischia, for which Procida is considered a halfway house.

13

EXPLORING

Corricella. This sleepy fishing village, used as the setting for the waterfront scenes in the Oscar-winning film *Il Postino,* has been relatively immune to life in the limelight. Apart from the opening of an extra restaurant and bar, there have been few changes. This is the type of place where even those with failing grades in art class feel like reaching for a paintbrush to record the delicate pink and yellow facades. The **Graziella** bar at the far end of the seafront offers the island's famous lemons squeezed over crushed ice to make an excellent granita.

WHERE TO EAT

$$ SOUTHERN ITALIAN 🍴 **La Conchiglia.** A meal here on the Chiaia beach really offers an appreciation of the magic of Procida. Coricella is a picture-postcard on your left and Capri twinkles in the distance beyond the lapping waves. The seafood is divinely fresh and the pasta dishes usually soul-warming. Access here is either on foot down the steps from Via Pizzaco or by the orange boat every two hours from the Corricella harborfront—phone owner Gianni for times (it's free for diners). [$] *Average main: €16* ✉ *Via Pizzaco 10, Procida* ☎ *081/8967602* 🌐 *www.laconchigliaristorante.com* 🕒 *Closed mid-Nov.–Mar.*

CAPRI

Still Italy's most glamorous seaside getaway, this craggy, whale-shape island has an epic beauty: cliffs that are the very embodiment of time, bougainvillea-shaded pathways overlooking the sea, trees seemingly hewn out of rock by the Greeks. Capri has always been a stage that mere mortals could share with the Beautiful People: often an eclectic potpourri of duchesses who have left their dukes at home, fading French film actresses, pretenders to obscure thrones, waspish couturiers, and sleek supermodels.

Today, Capri's siren song continues to seduce thousands of visitors. On summer days the port and *piazzetta* are often crammed, so if you can visit in spring or fall, do so. Yet even the crowds are not enough to destroy Capri's very special charm. The town itself is a Moorish stage set of sparkling white houses, tiny squares, and narrow medieval alleyways hung with flowers, while its hillsides are spectacular settings for luxurious seaside villas. Even in the height of summer, you can enjoy a degree of privacy on one of the many paved paths that have been mapped out through species-rich Mediterranean maquis, winding around the island hundreds of feet above the sea.

GETTING HERE AND AROUND

Capri is well connected with the mainland in all seasons, though there are more sailings between April and October. However, you can't return to Naples after the last sailing (11 pm in high season, often 8 pm or even earlier in low season). Hydrofoils, Seacats, and similar vessels leave from Molo Beverello (below Piazza Municipio) in Naples, while far less frequent car ferries leave from Calata Porta di Massa, 1,000 yards to the east. There's also service to and from Sorrento's

Marina Piccola. Much of Capri is pedestrianized, and a car is a great hindrance, not a help.

Several ferry and hydrofoil companies ply the waters of the Bay of Naples, making frequent trips to Capri. Schedules change from season to season; the most reliable source for departure times is *Il Mattino*, Naples's daily newspaper. There's little to be gained—sometimes nothing—from buying a round-trip ticket, which will just tie you down to the return schedule of one line. Book in advance in spring and summer for a Sunday return to the mainland.

13

VISITOR INFORMATION

Azienda Autonoma di Cura, Soggiorno e Turismo. The tourist office's excellent website has an English-language version. ⊠ *Banchina del Porto, Marina Grande* ☎ *081/8370634* ⊕ *www.capritourism.com* ☺ *High season: Mon.–Sat. 9:30–1:30 and 3:30–45, Sun. 9–3. Winter: Mon.–Sat. 9:30–2:30* ⊠ *Via G. Orlandi 59, Anacapri* ☎ *081/8371524* ⊠ *Piazza Umberto I, Capri Town* ☎ *081/8370686.*

EXPLORING

TOP ATTRACTIONS

Fodor's Choice ★ **Certosa di San Giacomo.** One of the true highlights of historic Capri and a base for the island's arts, this grand, palatial complex is between the Castiglione and Tuoro hills, and was for centuries a Carthusian monastery dedicated to St. James.

You enter the complex via a grandly imposing entryway, which leads to the Biblioteca Comunale Popolare Luigi Bladier (public library—Capri's only free Internet point) and the spacious church of San Giacomo (built in 1690, reopened after renovations in 2010). After admiring the church's Baroque frescoes, follow the signpost down toward the Parco, which leads down an avenue flanked by pittosporum and magnolia toward the magnificent monastery gardens and some welcome benches with stunning views. Take heed of the signs reminding you to watch your step, as the ground is uneven in places. Beyond a covered road lies the Chiostro Grande (Large Cloister), originally the site of the monks' cells and now the home of a high school, and nearby is the 15th-century Chiostro Piccolo (Small Cloister)—both often the venues for summertime open-air concerts. The Quarto del Priore hosts art exhibitions from international artists, but the showstopper here is the Museo Diefenbach, comprising a collection of restored large canvases by influential German painter K. W. Diefenbach, who visited Capri in 1900 and stayed until his death in 1913. ⊠ *Via Certosa* ☎ *081/8376218* ⊕ *www.polomusealenapoli.beniculturali.it* ⊠ *€4* ☺ *Tues.–Sun. 9–2, summer also 5–8.*

Fodor's Choice ★ **Grotta Azzurra.** Only when the Grotta Azzurra was "discovered" in 1826 by the Polish poet August Kopisch and Swiss artist Ernest Fries, did Capri become a tourist haven. The watery cave's blue beauty became a symbol of the revolt from reason and the return to nature that marked the Romantic era, and it soon became a required stop on the Grand Tour. In reality, the grotto had long been a local landmark. During the

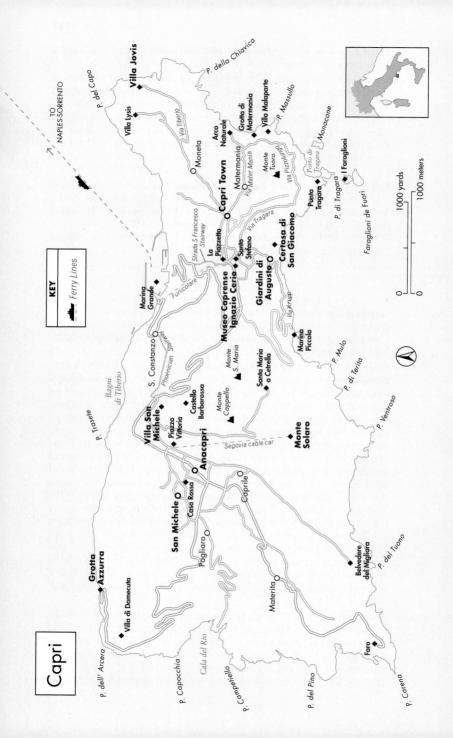

Capri

KEY
◼ Ferry Lines

TO
NAPLES-SORRENTO

P. della Chiavica

Villa Jovis

Villa Lysis

P. del Capo

Via Tiberio

Moneta

Arco Naturale

Grotta di Matermania

Villa Malaparte

P. Massullo

Capri Town

Matermania

Via Mater Mania

Monte Tuoro

Via Pizzolungo

Porto de Tragara

Monacone

Punta Tragara

I Faraglioni

P. di Tragara

Marina Grande

Strada S Francesco Stairway

La Piazzetta

Museo Caprense Ignazio Cerio

Santo Stefano

Via Tragara

Certosa di San Giacomo

Giardini di Augusto

Faraglioni de Fuori

Funicolare

S. Constanzo

Phoenician Stairway

Monte S. Maria

Santa Maria a Cetrella

Via Krupp

Marina Piccola

P. Mulo

Bagni di Tiberio

P. Trasele

Villa San Michele

Piazza Vittoria

Castello Barbarossa

Monte Cappello

P. di Terita

Anacapri

Segovia cable car

Monte Solaro

P. Ventroso

San Michele

Casa Rossa

Caprile

Pagliaro

Materita

Belvedere del Migliara

P. del Tuono

Grotta Azzurra

Villa di Damecuta

P. dell' Arcera

P. Capocchia

Cala del Rio

Campetiello

P.

Faro

P. del Pino

P. Carena

1000 yards

1000 meters

Roman era—as testified by the extensive remains, primarily below sea level, and several large statues now at the Certosa di San Giacomo—it had been the elegant, mosaic-decorated nymphaeum of the adjoining villa of Gradola. The water's extraordinary sapphire color is caused by a hidden opening in the rock that refracts the light. At highest illumination the very air inside seems tinted blue.

The Grotta Azzurra can be reached from Marina Grande or from the small embarkation point below Anacapri on the northwest side of the island, accessible by bus from Anacapri. You board one boat to get to the grotto, then transfer to a smaller boat that takes you inside. If there's a backup of boats waiting to get in, you'll be given precious little time to enjoy the gorgeous color of the water and its silvery reflections. *€26 from Marina Grande, €12.50 by rowboat from Grotta Azzurra near Anacapri ⊙ 9–1 hr before sunset; closed if sea is even minimally rough.*

Fodor's Choice
★

Villa San Michele. From Anacapri's Piazza Vittoria, picturesque Via Capodimonte leads to Villa San Michele, the charming former home of Swedish doctor and philanthropist Axel Munthe (1857–1949). At the ancient entranceway to Anacapri at the top of the Scala Fenicia, the villa is set around Roman-style courtyards, marble walkways, and atria. Rooms display the doctor's varied collections, which range from bric-a-brac to antiquities. Medieval choir stalls, Renaissance lecterns, and gilded statues of saints are all part of the setting, with some rooms preserving the doctor's personal memorabilia. A spectacular pergola path overlooking the entire Bay of Naples leads from the villa to the famous Sphinx Parapet, where an ancient Egyptian sphinx looks out toward Sorrento: you cannot see its face—on purpose. It is said that if you touch the sphinx's hindquarters with your left hand while making a wish, it will come true. The parapet is connected to the little Chapel of San Michele, on the grounds of one of Tiberius's villas.

Besides hosting summer concerts, the Axel Munthe Foundation has an ecomuseum that fittingly reflects Munthe's fondness for animals. Here you can learn about various bird species—accompanied by their songs—found on Capri. ⊠ *Viale Axel Munthe 34, Anacapri* ☎ *081/8371401* ⊕ *www.villasanmichele.eu* *€7 ⊙ Nov.–Feb., daily 9–3:30; Mar., daily 9–4:30; Apr. and Oct., daily 9–5; May–Sept., daily 9–6.*

WORTH NOTING

Anacapri. A tortuous road leads up to Anacapri, the island's "second city," about 3 km (2 miles) from Capri Town. To get here you can take a bus either from Via Roma in Capri Town or from Marina Grande (both €1.80), or a taxi (about €30 one-way; agree on the fare before starting out). Crowds are thick down Via Capodimonte leading to Villa San Michele and around Piazza Vittoria, the square where you catch the chairlift to the top of Monte Solaro. Via Vinestrale leads to the noted **Le Boffe quarter,** centered on the Piazza Ficacciate. Le Boffe owes its name to the distinctive domestic architecture prevalent here, which uses vaults and sculpted groins instead of crossbeams. Elsewhere, Anacapri is quietly appealing. It's a good starting point for walks, such as the 80-minute round-trip journey to the **Migliara Belvedere,** on the island's southern coast.

Capri Town. On arrival at the port, pick up the excellent map of the island (€1) at the tourist office. You may have to wait for the funicular railway (€1.80 one-way) to Capri Town, some 450 feet above the harbor. So this might be the time to splurge on an open-top taxi—it could save you an hour in line. From the upper station, walk out into Piazza Umberto I, better known as "the Piazzetta," the island's social hub.

Giardini di Augusto (*Gardens of Augustus*). From the terraces of this beautiful public garden, you can see the village of Marina Piccola below—restaurants, cabanas, and swimming platforms huddle among the shoals—and admire the steep, winding Via Krupp, actually a staircase cut into the rock. Friedrich Krupp, the German arms manufacturer, loved Capri and became one of the island's most generous benefactors. If you find the path too challenging you can reach the beach by taking a bus from the Via Roma terminus down to Marina Piccola. ⊠ *Via Matteotti, beyond monastery of San Giacomo* 🎫 *€1* ⊙ *Summer, daily 9–7:30; winter, daily 9–5:30.*

Monte Solaro. An impressive limestone formation and the highest point on Capri (1,932 feet), Monte Solaro affords gasp-inducing views toward the bays of both Naples and Salerno. A 12-minute chairlift ride will take you right to the top (refreshments available at the bar), where you can launch out on a number of scenic trails on the western side of the island. Picnickers should note that even in summer it can get windy at this height, and there are few trees to provide shade or refuge. ⊠ *Piazza Vittoria, Anacapri* ☎ *081/8371428* 🎫 *€7.50 one-way, €10 round-trip* ⊙ *Daily 9:30–5. Closed Jan. 7– Feb. 7 and in adverse weather.*

San Michele. In the heart of Anacapri, the octagonal Baroque church of San Michele, finished in 1719, is best known for its exquisite majolica pavement designed by Solimena and executed by the *mastro-riggiolaro* (master tiler) Chiaiese from Abruzzo. A walkway skirts the depiction of Adam and a duly contrite Eve being expelled from the Garden of Eden, but you can get a fine overview from the organ loft, reached by a winding staircase near the ticket booth (a privileged perch you have to pay for). ⊠ *Piazza San Nicola, Anacapri* ☎ *081/8372396* ⊕ *www. chiesa-san-michele.com* 🎫 *€2* ⊙ *Apr.–Oct., daily 9–6:45; Nov. and Mar., daily 10–2.*

Villa di Damecuta. One of the best excursions from Anacapri is to the ruins of the Roman Villa di Damecuta. Sited strategically on a ridge with views sweeping across the Bay of Naples toward Procida and Ischia, the villa would have had its main access point at the landing stage right by the Blue Grotto at Gradola. Like Villa Jovis to the east, Villa di Damecuta was extensively plundered over the centuries prior to its proper excavation in 1937. Below the medieval tower (Torre Damecuta) there are two rooms (*domus* and *cubiculum*) that are thought to have been Tiberius's secret summer refuge. Affinities with Villa Jovis may be seen in the *ambulatio* (walkway) complete with seats and a stunning backdrop. To reach Villa Damecuta, get the bus from Anacapri to Grotta Azzurra and ask the driver to let you off at the proper stop. Alternatively, you can walk from the center of Anacapri down the bus route (about 30 minutes, no sidewalks), or try your luck in the network of virtually traffic-free little alleyways running parallel to the main road. ✉ *Via A. Maiuri* 🎫 *Free* ⏲ *Daily 9–1 hr before sunset.*

Villa Jovis. Named in honor of the ancient Roman god Jupiter, or Jove, the villa of the emperor Tiberius is riveted to the towering Rocca di Capri like an eagle's nest overlooking the strait separating Capri from Punta Campanella, the tip of the Sorrentine peninsula.

Capri in Roman times was the site of 12 spacious villas, but Villa Jovis is both the best preserved and must have been the largest, occupying nearly 23,000 square feet. The entrance to the site lies just beyond the *pharos* (lighthouse), built under Tiberius and used until the 17th century to warn ships away from the narrows between Capri and the mainland. Pick up a site map at the ticket office—it gives a useful breakdown of the various areas of the villa to be visited. A walk around the perimeter of the site gives an idea of the overall layout of the palatial residence, which in places rose to five stories in height. From here descend some steps and then a ramp to the *ambulatio* (walkway), which offers additional spectacular views and plenty of shade, as well as a *triclinium* (dining room) halfway along. The center of the site is a complex devoted to cisterns. Unlike in Pompeii, there was no aqueduct up here to provide fresh running water, so the cisterns next to the bath complex were of prime importance. From La Piazzetta allow 45 minutes each way for the walk alone. ✉ *Via A. Maiuri* ☎ *081/8374549* 🎫 *€2* ⏲ *Daily 9–1; closed 1st 2 Tues. and last 2 Sun. of month.*

13

WHERE TO EAT

$$ SOUTHERN ITALIAN

🍴 **Al Grottino.** This small and friendly family-run restaurant, which is in a 14th-century building handy to the Piazzetta, has arched ceilings and lots of atmosphere; autographed photos of famous customers cover the walls. House specialties are *scialatielli ai fiori di zucchine e gambaretti* (homemade pasta with zucchini flowers and shrimps) and *coccette* (pasta with mussels and clams), but the owner delights in taking his guests through the menu of regional dishes. **TIP→ The restaurant also serves gluten-free dishes.** [$] *Average main: €16* ✉ *Via Longano 27, Capri Town* ☎ *081/8370584* 🌐 *www.ristorantealgrottino.net* ⏲ *Closed Nov.–mid-Mar.*

$$$ SOUTHERN ITALIAN

🍴 **Aurora.** Though often frequented by celebrities—whose photographs adorn the walls inside and out—this restaurant offers courtesy and *simpatia* irrespective of your star power. The oldest restaurant on the island, now in its third generation, it has a sleekly minimalist interior, but if you want to see and be seen, book a table outside on one of Capri's chic-est thoroughfares. The cognoscenti start by sharing a pizza *all'Acqua*: a thin crust, with mozzarella and a sprinkling of *peperoncino* (chili). Also try the *gnocchetti al pesto con fagiolini croccanti e pinoli* (dumplings with pesto, beans and pine nuts)—but leave room for the homemade sweets. Often open until 2 am, the Aurora Bar across the way serves aperitivi and light meals. [$] *Average main: €25* ✉ *Via Fuorlovado 18/22, Capri Town* ☎ *081/8370181* 🌐 *www.auroracapri.com* ⏲ *Closed Jan.–mid-Mar.*

$ NEAPOLITAN

🍴 **Barbarossa.** Don't let the shabby staircase deter you, as it leads to the covered terrace of this ristorante-pizzeria overlooking Piazza Vittoria, with panoramic views of the Barbarossa castle on the hill as well as the sea. The no-frills ambience belies the quality of the *cucina*: besides pizza, they specialize in local dishes—be sure to try the risotto *con gamberi a limone* (shrimp with lemon). $ *Average main: €14* ⊠ *Piazza Vittoria 1, Anacapri* ☏ *081/8371483* ⊕ *www.caprirestaurant.it.*

$$$

SOUTHERN
ITALIAN

Fodor's Choice
★

✕ **Da Gelsomina.** Amid its own terraced vineyards with inspiring views to the island of Ischia and beyond, this is much more than just a well-reputed restaurant. Specialties include *pollo a mattone* (chicken grilled on bricks) and locally caught rabbit. It has an immaculately kept swimming pool, which is open to the public for a small fee—a buffet is served as you lounge here. Close to one of the island's finer walks as well as the Philosophy Park, it's an excellent base for a whole day or longer. There's also a five-room *pensione,* with a free transfer service from Anacapri center, by request. $ *Average main: €35* ⊠ *Via Migliara 72, Anacapri* ☏ *081/8371499* ⊕ *www.dagelsomina.com* ⊗ *Closed Jan.–Feb. and Tues. in winter. No dinner in winter.*

$$$$

SOUTHERN
ITALIAN

✕ **La Canzone del Mare.** Although it's not primarily a restaurant, luncheon in the covered pavilion of this legendary bathing lido of the Marina Piccola is Capri at its most picture-perfect. The set menus change every year, but a favorite main dish is paccheri *con gamberi e peperoncini verdi* (with shrimp and green peppers). With two seawater pools, a rocky beach, and the Faraglioni in the distance, the setting is as stellar as ever. You need to pay a fee (€20 for a sunbed, €30 with umbrella) to actually use the bathing *stabilimento* (club), but why not make a day of it? There are five suites available, too, in case a day is not enough. Boats also depart from here for Da Luigi, the lido-restaurant at the base of the Farigloni. $ *Average main: €55* ⊠ *Via Marina Piccola 93, Capri Town* ☏ *081/8370104* ⊕ *www.lacanzonedelmare.com* ⊗ *Closed Oct.–Mar. No dinner.*

$$

SOUTHERN
ITALIAN

Fodor's Choice
★

✕ **La Capannina.** For decades one of Capri's most celebrity-haunted restaurants, La Capannina is near the busy social hub of the Piazzetta, and the discreet flower-decked covered veranda is ideal for dining by candlelight. Specialties, aside from an authentic Capri wine—under the house label—are ravioli *capresi* and linguine *con lo scorfano* (with scorpionfish), squid stuffed with caciotta cheese and marjoram, and an exquisite "Pezzogna" (sea bream cooked whole and topped with a layer of potatoes). The wine cellar is open for perusal, and their nearby gourmet store ships worldwide. The small late-night bar across the side alleyway is under the same ownership. $ *Average main: €20* ⊠ *Via Le Botteghe 12b, Capri Town* ☏ *081/8370732* ⊕ *www.capanninacapri.com* ⊗ *Closed Nov.–mid-Mar., and Wed. in Mar. and Oct.*

$$$

SOUTHERN
ITALIAN

✕ **La Fontelina.** Given its position right on the water's edge, seafood is almost de rigueur here, but for a slightly different starter, try the *polpette di melanzane* (eggplant fritters); then dip into the vegetable buffet. The house sangria is a highly recommendable, blissful mix of white wine and fresh fruit. La Fontelina also functions as a lido, with steps and ladders into fathoms-deep blue water, and this location—accessible by boat from Marina Piccola or on foot from Punta Tragara (10 minutes)—makes it a good place to spend a delightfully comatose day. ■ TIP→ Only lunch is served, and reservations are recommended during high season. $ *Average main: €25* ✉ *Via Faraglioni 2, Capri Town* ☎ *081/8370845* ⏱ *Closed mid-Oct.–Easter. No dinner.*

$$$
SOUTHERN
ITALIAN

✕ **Le Grottelle.** This extremely informal trattoria enjoys a distinctive setting: it's built up against limestone rocks not far from the Arco Naturale, with the kitchen in a cave at the back. Whether you stumble over it (and are lucky enough to get a table) or make it your destination after an island hike, Le Grottelle will prove memorable, thanks to that ambience and sea views encompassing the Amalfi Coast's Li Galli islands. The menu includes ravioli and local rabbit, but go for the seafood, with linguine *con gamberetti e rucola* (with shrimp and arugula) being one of the more interesting specialties. $ *Average main: €25* ✉ *Via Arco Naturale 13, Capri Town* ☎ *081/8375719* ⏱ *Closed Nov.–mid-Mar.*

13

WHERE TO STAY

$$$$
HOTEL
Fodor's Choice
★

🏨 **Caesar Augustus.** A continuing favorite of the Hollywood set, this landmark has long been considered a Caprese paradise thanks to its breathtaking perch atop an Anacapri cliff. **Pros:** possibly the most glamorous place on earth; summer concerts on site. **Cons:** a bit far from the action for some; noisy road. $ *Rooms from: €550* ✉ *Via G. Orlandi 4, Anacapri* ☎ *081/8373395, 081/8371421 for reservations* ⊕ *www.caesar-augustus.com* ⚏ *55 rooms* ⏱ *Closed Nov.–mid-Apr.* �ⓘ *Breakfast.*

$$$$
RESORT
Fodor's Choice
★

🏨 **Capri Palace Hotel & Spa.** This Anacapri icon has grown both physically and conceptually over the years, amassing a noted art collection, launching a fashion and home line (including a line of Capritouch shoes, custom made for each client), and working with some of Italy's top names on unique design touches. **Pros:** noted art collection; stunning (and sometimes surprising) design; postcard views; award-winning spa and dining; five-star service. **Cons:** all that glam comes at a price; some may find the quiet Anacapri location removed from the action (and water). $ *Rooms from: €360* ✉ *Via Capodimonte, 14, Anacapri* ☎ *081/9780111* ⊕ *www.capripalace.com* ⚏ *65 rooms, 13 suites* ⏱ *Closed mid-Oct.–mid-Apr.* �ⓘ *Breakfast.*

$$$$
HOTEL
Fodor's Choice
★

🏨 **Capri Tiberio Palace.** Offering comfort, style, luxury, and sigh-inducing views since the 19th century, this hotel is just short walk from the Piazzetta—near the action, but not quite in the thick of it. **Pros:** friendly staff; pure luxury. **Cons:** no port-to-door guest shuttle. $ *Rooms from: €500* ✉ *Via Croce 11–15, Capri Town* ☎ *081/9787111* ⊕ *www. capritiberiopalace.com* ⚏ *46 room, 17 suites* ⏱ *Closed mid-Oct.–mid-Apr.* ⓘ *Breakfast.*

$$$$
HOTEL
Fodor's Choice
★

🏨 **J. K. Place.** As the most supremely stylish and glamorous hotel in southern Italy, occupying an 1876 villa above Marina Grande harbor, this almost makes other accommodations on Capri seem dowdy and dull. **Pros:** exquisite pool; very close to chic Tiberio beach; free shuttle to town. **Cons:** expensive (only for high rollers); pool visible from main road. $ *Rooms from: €900* ✉ *Via Provinciale Marina Grande 225* ☎ *081/8384001* ⊕ *www.jkcapri.com* ⚏ *22 rooms* ⏱ *Closed mid-Oct.–mid-Apr.* ⓘ *Breakfast.*

$$
HOTEL

🏨 **La Tosca.** Although it's hard to find in the warren of side streets in Capri Town, La Tosca is worth all the trouble. **Pros:** simple unadorned charm; pleasant owner; free Wi-Fi throughout hotel. **Cons:** a 10-minute walk to the Piazzetta; not all rooms have good views. $ *Rooms from: €150 ⊠ Via Birago 5, Capri Town ☎ 081/8370989 ⊕ www.latoscahotel. com ⌷ 10 rooms ☉ Closed Nov.–Feb. ⦿ Breakfast.*

$$$$
HOTEL
Fodor's Choice
★

⌷ **Punta Tragara.** The most beautiful hotel on Capri—originally a private villa designed by Le Corbusier and site of a secret wartime meeting between Churchill and Eisenhower—was opened in the 1970s by Count Manfredi. **Pros:** a taste of the good life; the entire staff seem to have graduated from the finest finishing schools. **Cons:** a 10-minute walk from the center; some find the style dated (although others find that a plus). $ *Rooms from: €570 ⊠ Via Tragara 57, Capri Town ☎ 081/8370844 ⊕ www.hoteltragara.com ⌷ 27 rooms, 11 junior suites, 6 suites ☉ Closed mid-Oct.–mid-Apr. ⦿ Breakfast.*

$$$$
HOTEL
Fodor's Choice
★

⌷ **Quisisana.** Some say there are three villages on Capri: Capri Town, Anacapri, and this celebrated landmark hotel, which looms large in the island's mythology, drawing "didn't-I-meet-you-in-Saint-Tropez?" guests who wouldn't *dream* of staying anywhere else. **Pros:** luxe atmosphere on a large scale. **Cons:** not for all pockets; convention-size and far from cozy. $ *Rooms from: €360 ⊠ Via Camerelle 2, Capri Town ☎ 081/8370788 ⊕ www.quisisana.com ⌷ 132 rooms, 15 suites ☉ Closed Nov.–mid-Mar. ⦿ Breakfast.*

$$
B&B/INN

⌷ **Villa Krupp.** Occupying a beautiful house overlooking the idyllic Gardens of Augustus, this historic hostelry was once the home of Maxim Gorky, whose guests included Lenin. **Pros:** direct access to the Gardens of Augustus; stunning views. **Cons:** a lot of steps to be negotiated; rooms are simple. $ *Rooms from: €140 ⊠ Viale Matteotti 12, Capri Town ☎ 081/8370362 ⊕ www.villakrupp.com ⌷ 12 rooms ☉ Closed Nov.–Mar. ⦿ Breakfast.*

$$$
HOTEL

⌷ **Villa Sarah.** Few hotels offer such a quintessentially Caprese spirit as this; located in one of the island's most pleasant residential quarters, you'll feel like a guest in a private villa. **Pros:** gorgeous pool; lush gardens. **Cons:** a long and steep climb from the Piazzetta; some rooms are small. $ *Rooms from: €220 ⊠ Via Tiberio 3/a, Capri Town ☎ 081/8377817 ⊕ www.villasarah.it ⌷ 19 rooms ☉ Closed Nov.–Mar. ⦿ Breakfast.*

SORRENTO AND THE SORRENTINE PENINSULA

As the hub for a whole banquet of must-see sites—Pompeii and Naples to the north, Capri to the west, and the Amalfi Coast to the south—the beautiful, Belle Époque resort town of Sorrento is unequaled. The rest of the Sorrentine Peninsula, with plains and limestone outcroppings, watchtowers and Roman ruins, groves and beaches, monasteries and villages, winding paths leading to isolated coves and panoramic views of the bays of both Naples and Salerno, remains relatively undiscovered.

SORRENTO

50 km (31 miles) south of Naples.

Winding along a cliff above a small beach and two harbors, the town is split in two by a narrow ravine formed by a former mountain stream. To

Sorrento and Amalfi Coast

the east, dozens of hotels line busy Via Correale along the cliff—many
have "grand" in their names, and some indeed still are. To the west,
however, is the historic sector, which still enchants. It's a relatively flat
area, with winding, stone-paved lanes bordered by balconied buildings,
some joined by medieval stone arches. The central piazza is named
after the poet Torquato Tasso, born here in 1544. This part of town
is a delightful place to walk through, especially in the mild evenings,
when people are out and about and everything is open. Craftspeople
are often at work in their stalls and shops, and are happy to let you
watch—in fact, that's the point. Music spots and bars cluster in the side
streets near Piazza Tasso.

GETTING HERE AND AROUND

From downtown Naples, take a Circumvesuviana train from Stazione Centrale (Piazza Garibaldi) or a hydrofoil from Molo Beverello. If
you're coming directly from the airport in Naples, pick up a direct bus
to Sorrento. By car, take the A3 Naples–Salerno autostrada, exiting at
Castellammare, and then following signs for Penisola Sorrentina, then
for Sorrento.

VISITOR INFORMATION

Azienda Autonoma di Soggiorno Sorrento-Sant'Agnello. Besides dispensing a wealth of information, the tourist office also has a useful booking service for hotels, B&Bs, and vacation apartments throughout the peninsula. ⊠ *Via L. De Maio 35* ☎ *081/8074033* ⊕ *www.sorrentotourism. com* ⊙ *Winter, weekdays 8:30–4:15; summer, Mon.–Sat. 9–7, Sun. 9–1.*

EXPLORING

Convento di San Francesco. Near the Villa Comunale gardens and sharing its view over the Bay of Naples, the convent is celebrated for its 12th-century cloister. Filled with greenery and flowers, the Moorish-style cloister has interlaced pointed arches of tufa, alternating with octagonal columns topped by elegant capitals, supporting smaller arches. The combination makes a suitably evocative setting for summer concerts and theatrical presentations. The church portal is particularly impressive, with the 16th-century door (moved from a church across the road in 1947) featuring *intarsia* (inlaid) work. The interior's 17th-century decoration includes an altarpiece, by a student of Francesco Solimena, depicting St. Francis receiving the stigmata. The convent is now an art school, where students' works are often exhibited. ⊠ *Piazza San Francesco* ☎ *081/8781269* 🎟 *Free* ⊙ *Daily 8–1:30 and 3:30–8.*

Marina Grande. Via Marina Grande turns into a pedestrian lane, then a stairway leading to Sorrento's only real beach at Marina Grande, where fishermen pull up their boats and some good seafood restaurants are found. A frequent bus also descends to the beach; tickets are sold at the *tabacchi* (tobacconist).

Museo Correale di Terranova. In an 18th-century villa with a lovely garden, on land given to the patrician Correale family by Queen Joan of Anjou in 1428, this museum is a highlight of Sorrento and a must for connoisseurs of the *seicento* (Italian 17th century). It has an eclectic private collection amassed by the count of Terranova and his brother—one of the finest devoted to Neapolitan paintings, decorative arts, and porcelains. Magnificent 18th- and 19th-century inlaid tables by Giuseppe Gargiulo, Capodimonte porcelains, and Rococo portrait miniatures are reminders of the age when pleasure and delight were everything. Also on view are regional Greek and Roman archaeological finds, medieval marble work, glasswork, old-master paintings, 17th-century majolicas—even the poet Tasso's death mask. The building itself is fairly charmless, with few period rooms, but the garden offers an allée of palm trees, citrus groves, floral nurseries, and an esplanade with a panoramic view of the Sorrento coast. ⊠ *Via Correale 50* ☎ *081/8781846* ⊕ *www.museocorreale.it* 🎟 *€8* ⊙ *Apr.–Oct., Tues.–Sat. 9:30–6:30; Nov.–Mar., Tues.–Sun. 9:30–1:30.*

Sedile Dominova. Enchanting showpiece of the Largo Dominova—the little square that is the heart of Sorrento's historic quarter—the Sedile Dominova is a picturesque open loggia with expansive arches, balustrades, and a green-and-yellow-tile cupola, originally constructed in the 16th century. The open-air structure is frescoed with 18th-century trompe-l'oeil columns and the family coats of arms, which once belonged to the *sedile* (seat), the town council where nobles met to discuss civic problems as early as the Angevin period. Today Sorrentines still like to congregate around the umbrella-topped tables near the tiny square. ✉ *Largo Dominova, at Via San Cesareo and Via P. R. Giuliani* 🎫 *Free* 🕓 *Daily 9–1 and 4–8.*

Villa Comunale. The largest public park in Sorrento sits on a clifftop overlooking the entire Bay of Naples. It offers benches, flowers, palms, and people-watching, plus a seamless vista that stretches from Capri to Vesuvius. From here steps lead down to Sorrento's main harbor, the Marina Piccola. ✉ *Adjoining church of San Francesco.*

Capo di Sorrento and the Bagno della Regina Giovanna. Just 2 km (1 mile) west of Sorrento, turn right off Statale 145 toward the sea, and then park and walk a few minutes through citrus and olive groves to get to Capo di Sorrento, the craggy tip of the cape, with the most interesting ancient ruins in the area. They were identified by the Latin poet Publius Papinius Statius as the ancient Roman villa of historian Pollio Felix, patron of the great authors Virgil and Horace. Next to the ruins is Bagno della Regina Giovanna (Queen Joan's Bath). A cleft in the rocks allows the sea to channel through an archway into a clear, natural pool, with the water turning iridescent blue, green, and violet as the sunlight changes angles. The easiest way to see all this is to rent a boat at Sorrento; afterward, sailing westward will bring you to the fishermen's haven of Marina di Puolo, where you can lunch on the fresh catch at a modest restaurant.

WHERE TO EAT

$$ SOUTHERN ITALIAN

🍴 **Da Emilia.** Near the Marina Grande, and not the most visually prepossessing place in Sorrento, this spot has rickety wooden tables and red-checker tablecloths, a refreshing change from the town's (occasionally pretentious) elegance. Go for a plate of honest spaghetti with clams, wash it down with a carafe of the slightly acidic white wine, and watch the fishermen mending their nets. [$] *Average main: €18* ✉ *Via Marina Grande 62* ☎ *081/8072720* 🕓 *Closed Tues., and Nov.–Feb.*

$$$$ SOUTHERN ITALIAN Fodor's Choice ★

🍴 **Don Alfonso 1890.** The late R. W. Apple Jr., the *New York Times*'s famous traveling epicure, once declared Don Alfonso the best restaurant in Italy, and it remains a gastronomic giant. The restaurant, a sort of southern Italian Chez Panisse (a pioneer in upscale farm-to-table cuisine) grows all its own produce on a small farm nearby. The operation is a family affair, with mama (Livia) in the dining room and papa (former chef Alfonso Iaccarrino) these days tending to the organic farm plot. And now their sons have moved into the business—one as head chef, the other maître d'. The menu reflects this generational shift, with classic dishes listed beside more edgy inventions. Delicate cheese ravioli topped with a ragù of homegrown tomatoes, might give way to more contemporary fare like fried lobster nuggets or sea urchin ice cream with rose *fettuccine.* [$] *Average main: €40* ✉ *Corso Sant'Agata 13, Sant'Agata sui Due Golfi* ☎ *081/8780026* 🌐 *www.donalfonso.com* 🕓 *Closed Mon., Tues. in Apr., May, and Oct., and Nov.–Mar. No lunch Tues. June–Sept.*

$$ SOUTHERN ITALIAN Fodor's Choice ★

🍴 **Ristorante 'o Parrucchiano La Favorita.** This restaurant is in a sprawling, multilevel, high-ceiling greenhouse and orchard, with tables and chairs set amid enough tropical greenery to fill a Victorian conservatory. The effect is enchantingly 19th century. Opened in 1868 by an ex-priest ('*o Parrucchiano* means "the priest's place" in the local dialect), La Favorita continues to serve classic Sorrentine cuisine. The shrimp baked in lemon leaves, cannelloni, homemade Sorrentine pasta, chocolate and hazelnut cake, and lemon profiteroles are all excellent, but they can't compete with the unique interior. [$] *Average main: €15* ✉ *Corso Italia 71* ☎ *081/8781321* 🌐 *www.parrucchiano.com* ⏲ *Closed Wed. mid-Nov.–mid-Mar.*

$$$$ SOUTHERN ITALIAN Fodor's Choice ★ 🍴 **Ristorante Museo Caruso.** Sorrentine favorites, including *acquerello* (a fresh-fish appetizer) and ravioli with crab and zucchini sauce, are tweaked creatively here. The staff are warm and helpful, the singer on the sound system is the long-departed "fourth tenor" himself, and the operatic memorabilia (including posters and old photos of Caruso) is viewed in a flattering blush-pink light. This elegant restaurant deserves its longtime popularity. It is open from noon to midnight and has five-course tasting menus from €50. ■ TIP→ **Its less expensive sister restaurant La Basilica, just down the road, serves similarly sumptuous fare.** [$] *Average main: €40* ✉ *Via Sant'Antonino 12* ☎ *081/8073156* 🌐 *www.ristorantemuseocaruso.com.*

WHERE TO STAY

$$$$ HOTEL Fodor's Choice ★ 🏨 **Bellevue Syrene.** This luxurious retreat, magnificently set on a bluff high over the Bay of Naples, is one of Italy's most legendary hotels. **Pros:** impeccable design elements; elegant common areas; half board available. **Cons:** very expensive; parking is €25 a day. [$] *Rooms from: €450* ✉ *Piazza della Vittoria 5* ☎ *081/8781024* 🌐 *www.bellevue.it* 🛏 *49 rooms* ⏲ *Closed Jan.–Mar.* 🍽 *Some meals.*

$$$ HOTEL Fodor's Choice ★ 🏨 **Don Alfonso 1890.** Long renowned as Campania's best eatery, Don Alfonso 1890 also offers one of the region's top hotels and from the moment you enter the gates and step on the rustic-paved path that runs between the fabled restaurant and the 19th century lodge, the Iaccarino family strives to make this stay the highlight of your trip. **Pros:** a slice of heaven; the best food in Southern Italy. **Cons:** rather far from Sorrento; not for all pockets. [$] *Rooms from: €280* ✉ *Corso Sant'Agata 13* ☎ *081/8780026* 🌐 *www.donalfonso.com* 🛏 *8 rooms* ⏲ *Closed Nov.–Apr.* 🍽 *Breakfast.*

$$$$ HOTEL Fodor's Choice ★ 🏨 **Excelsior Vittoria.** Overlooking the Bay of Naples, this luxurious Belle Époque dream has been in the same family since 1834; the public salons are virtual museums, with Victorian love seats and *stile liberty* ornamentation. **Pros:** beyond the protected gates you're in the heart of town; gardens buffer city noise. **Cons:** not all rooms have sea views; some rooms are rather small; front desk can be cold. [$] *Rooms from: €350* ✉ *Piazza Tasso 34* ☎ *081/8071044, 800/980053 in Italy only* 🌐 *www.exvitt.it* 🛏 *92 rooms* 🍽 *Breakfast.*

$$$ HOTEL 🏨 **Grand Hotel La Favorita.** Sorrento is rightly known for gorgeous and sumptuous hotels, but the traditional choices have had to make room for this glamorous newcomer—a striking beauty that can hold its own against some great hotel names. **Pros:** central location; beautiful terrace; idyllic garden. **Cons:** no views from the guest rooms. [$] *Rooms from: €260* ✉ *Via Torquato Tasso 61* ☎ *081/8782031* 🌐 *www.hotellafavorita.com* 🛏 *80 rooms, 5 suites* ⏲ *Closed Nov. and Jan.–Mar.* 🍽 *Breakfast.*

$$ ~~ 🖥 **Settimo Cielo.** Even if your wallet won't allow a stay at one of Sor-
HOTEL rento's grand hotels, you can still find lodgings overlooking the water,
Fodor'sChoice and this hotel on the road to Capo Sorrento is an excellent choice for
★ budget travelers. **Pros:** plenty of parking; excellent views. **Cons:** no-frills
décor; long walk along busy road into Sorrento. $ *Rooms from: €140*
✉ *Via Capo 27* ☎ *081/8781012* ⊕ *www.hotelsettimocielo.com* ⤳ *20*
rooms ⦿*Breakfast.*

THE AMALFI COAST   13

One of the most gorgeous places on the planet, this corner of the Cam-
pania region tantalizes, almost unbearably, the visitor who can stay but
a day or two. Poets and millionaires have long journeyed here to see
and sense its legendary sights: perfect, precariously perched Positano;
Amalfi, a shimmering medieval city; romantic mountain-high Ravello;
and ancient Paestum, with its three legendary Greek temples. Today,
the coast's scenic sorcery makes this a top destination, drawing inter-
national visitors, who agree with UNESCO's 1997 decision to make
this a World Heritage Site.

By the late 19th century, tourism had blossomed, giving rise to the
creation of the two-lane Amalfi Drive, which has come to be called
the "Divina Costiera." A thousand or so gorgeous vistas appear along
these almost 40 km (25 miles), stretching from just outside Sorrento
to Vietri, coursing over deep ravines and bays of turquoise-to-sapphire
water, spreading past tunnels and timeless villages.

The justly famed jewels along this coastal necklace are Positano, Amalfi,
and Ravello, but today's traveler will find the satellite baguettes—
including Conca dei Marini, Furore, Atrani, Scala, and Cetara—just
as sparkling. The top towns along the Amalfi Drive may fill up in high
season with tour buses, but in the countryside not much seems to have
changed since the Middle Ages: mountains are still terraced and farmed
for citrus, olives, wine, and dairy; and the sea is dotted with the gentle
reds, whites, and blues of fishermen's boats. Vertiginously high villages,
dominated by the spires of *chiese* (churches), are crammed with houses
on, into, above, and below hillsides to the bay; crossed by mule paths;
and navigated by flights of steps called *scalinatelle* often leading to out-
looks and belvederes that take your breath away—in more ways
than one. Songs have been composed about these serpentine stone steps, and
they may come to haunt your dreams as well; some *costieri* (natives of
the coast) count them one by one to get to sleep.

POSITANO

14 km (9 miles) east of Sorrento, 57 km (34 miles) south of Naples.

When John Steinbeck visited Positano in 1953, he wrote that it was
difficult to consider tourism an industry, because "there are not enough
[tourists]." Alas, there are more than enough now. What Steinbeck
wrote, however, still applies: "Positano bites deep. It is a dream place
that isn't quite real when you are there and becomes beckoningly real
after you have gone."

The most photographed fishing village in the world, this fabled locale is home to some 4,000 *Positanesi,* who are joined daily by hordes arriving from Capri, Sorrento, and Amalfi, eager to celebrate the fact that Positano is, impossibly, there. Its arcaded, cubist buildings, set in tiers up the mountainside, reflect the sky in dawn-color walls: rose, peach, purple, some tinted the ivory of sunrise's drifting clouds. In fact, the colors on these Saracen-inspired dwellings may have originally served to help returning fishermen spot their own digs in an instant.

With the coming of the steamship in the mid-19th century, some three-fourths of the town's 8,000 citizens emigrated to America—mostly to New York—and it eventually regressed into a backwater fishing village. That is, until artists and intellectuals, and then travelers, rediscovered its prodigious charms in the 20th century, especially after World War II; Picasso, Stravinsky, Diaghilev, Olivier, Steinbeck, Klee—even Lenin—were just a few of this town's talented fans. Lemons, grapes, olives, fish, resort gear, and, of course, tourism keep it going, but despite its shimmery sophistication and overwrought popularity, Positano's chief export remains its most precious commodity: beauty.

GETTING HERE AND AROUND

SITA buses leave from the Circumvesuviana train station in Sorrento. Buses also run from Naples and, in summer, Rome. There is a ferry from Sorrento in the summer months.

A word of advice: Wear comfortable walking shoes and be sure your back and legs are strong enough to negotiate those picturesque, but daunting and ladderlike *scalinatelle.* In the center of town, where no buses can go, you're on your own from Piazza dei Mulini. To begin your explorations, make a left turn onto the boutique-flanked Via dei Mulini and head down to the Palazzo Murat, Santa Maria Assunta, and the beach—one of the most charming walks of the coast.

VISITOR INFORMATION

Azienda Autonoma Soggiorno e Turismo ⊠ *Via Regina Giovanna 13* ☎ *089/875067* ⊕ *www.aziendaturismopositano.it* ☉ *Oct.–May, Mon.–Sat. 8:30–4:30; June–Sept., Mon.–Sat. 8:30–7, plus Sun. morning.*

EXPLORING

Palazzo Murat. Past a bevy of resort boutiques, head to Via dei Mulini to view the prettiest garden in Positano: the 18th-century courtyard of the Palazzo Murat, named for Joachim Murat, who sensibly chose the palazzo as his summer residence. This was where Murat, designated by his brother-in-law Napoléon as King of Naples in 1808, came to forget the demands of power and lead the simple life. Since Murat was a Continental style setter, it couldn't be *too* simple; he built this grand abode (now a hotel) near the church of Santa Maria Assunta, just steps from the main beach. Work is progressing to allow visits to the underground Roman villa. ⊠ *Via dei Mulini 23* ☎ *089/875177* ⊕ *www. palazzomurat.it.*

Santa Maria Assunta. The Chiesa Madre, or parish church, of Santa Maria Assunta, lies just south of the Palazzo Murat, its green-and-yellow majolica dome topped by a perky cupola visible from just about anywhere in town. Built on the site of the former Benedictine abbey of

13

Saint Vito, the 13th-century Romanesque structure was almost completely rebuilt in 1700. The last piece of the ancient mosaic floor can be seen under glass behind the altar. Note the carved wooden Christ, a masterpiece of devotional religious art, with its bathetic face and bloodied knees, on view before the altar. At the altar is a Byzantine 13th-century painting on wood of Madonna with Child, known popularly as "the Black Virgin," carried to the beach every August 15 to celebrate the Feast of the Assumption. Legend claims that the painting was once stolen by Saracen pirates, who, fleeing in a raging storm, heard from a voice on high saying, "*Posa, posa*" ("Put it down, put it down"). When they placed the image on the beach near the church, the storm calmed, as did the Saracens. Embedded over the doorway of the church's bell tower, set across the tiny piazza, is a medieval bas-relief of fishes, a fox, and a pistrice (the mythical half-dragon, half-dog sea monster). This is one of the few relics of the medieval abbey of Saint Vito. The Oratorio houses historic statues from the Sacristy; renovations to the Crypt have unearthed 1st-century Roman columns. ⊠ *Piazza Flavio Gioia* ☎ *089/875480* ☉ *Church: daily 8–noon; summer, daily 8–noon and 4–9.*

Spiaggia Grande. The walkway from the Piazza Flavio Gioia leads down to the Spiaggia Grande, or main beach, bordered by an esplanade and some of Positano's best restaurants. Surrounded by the spectacular amphitheater of houses and villas that leapfrog up the hillsides of Monte Commune and Monte Sant'Angelo, this remains one of the most picturesque beaches in the world. Although it faces stiff competition from Spiaggia di Fornillo, which is a far bigger and whiter strand of sand, the Spiaggia Grande wins the beauty contest hands-down. **Amenities:** food and drink; lifeguards; showers; toilets; water sports. **Best for:** snorkeling; swimming.

Fodor's Choice
★

Via Positanesi d'America. Just before the ferry ticket booths to the right of Spiaggia Grande, a tiny road that is the loveliest seaside walkway on the entire coast, rises up and borders the cliffs leading to the Spiaggia di Fornillo. The road is named for the town's large number of 19th-century emigrants to the United States—Positano virtually survived during World War II thanks to the money and packages their descendants sent back home. Halfway up the path lies the Torre Trasìta (Trasìta Tower), the most distinctive of Positano's three coastline defense towers. Now a residence occasionally available for summer rental, the tower was used to spot pirate raids. As you continue along the Via Positanesi d'America, you'll pass a tiny inlet and an emerald cove before Spiaggia di Fornillo comes into view.

WHERE TO EAT

$$

SOUTHERN
ITALIAN

✕ **Da Adolfo.** On a little beach where pirates used to build and launch boats, this laid-back trattoria has long been a favorite Positano landmark. The pirates are long gone, but their descendants now operate the free ferry to and from Positano (every half-hour in the morning)—look for the boat with the red fish on the mast named for the restaurant—or make the steep descent from the main coastal road at Laurito. Sit under a straw canopy on the wooden terrace to enjoy *totani con patate* (squid and potatoes with garlic and oil); then sip white wine with peaches until sundown. Some diners even swim over, so bathing suits are fine. ■TIP➔ **Da Adolfo gets busy, so ask your hotel to book a table for you—personal reservations are often not honored.** $ *Average main: €15* ⊠ *Spiaggia di Laurito, Via Laurito 40* ☎ *089/875022* ⊕ *www.daadolfo.com* ⊘ *Closed Oct.–Apr.*

$$

SOUTHERN
ITALIAN

✕ **La Pergola.** Occupying a prime location near dead center on Spiaggia Grande, this arbor-covered seating area offers a fabulous (and festive, due to the happy crowds) beachside setting. Often confused with the equally good Buca di Bacco upstairs, it was a dance club until the 1970s. Seafood, unsurprisingly, is the main fare—be sure to try the *scialatielli ai frutti di mare* (fresh pasta with shell fish) or sea bass in *acqua pazza* (poached in a herb broth). Pizza and chicken breast with fries are also on the menu and there's self-service counter, helpful for those on a budget or heading out to the beach. ■TIP➔ **La Pergola stays open until 1 am, giving you time to digest before trying the homemade dolci and ice cream, prepared around the corner at Via della Taranta 6.** $ *Average main: €22* ⊠ *Via del Brigantino 35* ☎ *089/811461* ⊕ *www. bucapositano.it* ⊘ *Closed Jan. and Feb.*

$$

SOUTHERN
ITALIAN
Fodor's Choice
★

✕ **Lo Guarracino.** In a supremely romantic setting, this partly arbor-covered aerie is about the most idyllic place to enjoy lemon pasta and a glass of vino as you watch the yachts come and go. Set a few steps above Positano's prettiest seaside path, the terrace vista takes in the cliffs, the sea, Li Galli islands, Spiaggia del Fornillo, and Torre Clavel. The super-charming backroom arbor, beneath thick, twining vines, where tables are covered in cloths that match the tint of the bay, is *the* place to sit. Fine fish specialties are top delights on the menu. The day's catch is often cooked, with potatoes, in the wood-fired pizza oven, which gives it a distinct flavor. $ *Average main: €20* ⊠ *Via Positanesi d'America 12* ☎ *089/875794* ⊘ *Closed Jan.–Mar.*

$$

SOUTHERN
ITALIAN

✕ **Next2.** Wrought-iron gates open from the main thoroughfare of Via Pasitea into Next2's outdoor dining area, which has a stunning view over Positano. The décor is invitingly simple yet sophisticated, with white tablecloths and comfortable lounge chairs. The two owners are passionate about fine cuisine, particularly seafood—try the pan-seared *bonito* (local tuna) with spinach and sweet-and-sour onions—and they'll walk you through the menu and wine list. $ *Average main: €22* ⊠ *Via Pasitea 242* ☎ *089/8123516* ⊕ *www.next2.it* ⏦ *Reservations essential.*

WHERE TO STAY

$$$$

HOTEL
Fodor's Choice
★

🏨 **Hotel Eden Roc.** The closest hotel to the Sponda bus stop, this family-run luxury property provides spectacular views and service. **Pros:** huge rooms; magical views. **Cons:** on the main road (take care as you exit the hotel); a bit of a climb from the town center. $ *Rooms from: €345* ⊠ *Via G.Marconi 110* ☎ *089/875844* ⊕ *www.edenroc.it* ⏦ *25 suites* ⊘ *Closed Dec.–Feb.* ⏦ *Some meals.*

$$

HOTEL
Fodor's Choice
★

🏨 **La Fenice.** This tiny unpretentious hotel on the outskirts of Positano beckons with bougainvillea-laden views, castaway cottages, and a turquoise seawater pool—all perched over a private beach. **Pros:** paradise; 250 steps to private beach. **Cons:** a 10-minute walk to town. $ *Rooms from: €155* ⊠ *Via G. Marconi 4* ☎ *089/875513* ⊕ *www. lafenicepositano.com* ⏦ *14 rooms* ▤ *No credit cards* ⏦ *Breakfast.*

$$$$
HOTEL
Fodor'sChoice
★

Le Sirenuse. As legendary as its namesake sirens, this 18th-century palazzo has long set the standard for luxury in Italian hotels. **Pros:** unrivaled views; many rooms have whirlpool tubs; close to the bus stop. **Cons:** a bit of a climb from the town center; lower-priced rooms are small. $ *Rooms from: €460* ⊠ *Via Cristoforo Colombo 30* ☎ *089/875066* ⊕ *www.sirenuse.it* 🛏 *59 rooms* ⦿*Breakfast.*

$$$
HOTEL
Fodor'sChoice
★

Palazzo Murat. A perfectly central location above the beachside church of Santa Maria Assunta—and an even more perfect entrance through a bougainvillea-draped patio and garden—help make the Murat a top lodging contender. **Pros:** once a regal residence; stunning surroundings. **Cons:** only five rooms have seaside views; constant stream of curious day-trippers. $ *Rooms from: €270* ⊠ *Via dei Mulini 23* ☎ *089/875177* ⊕ *www.palazzomurat.it* 🛏 *31 rooms* ⊗ *Closed Nov.–Mar.* ⦿*Breakfast.*

NIGHTLIFE

L'Africana. This is the premier nightclub on the Amalfi Coast, built into a fantastic grotto above the sea. ⊠ *Vettica Maggiore, Praiano, 10 km (6 miles) east of Positano on coast road* ☎ *089/874858* ⊕ *www.africanafamousclub.com.*

CONCA DEI MARINI

13 km (8 miles) east of Positano, 29 km (18 miles) east of Sorrento.

EXPLORING

FAMILY **Grotta dello Smeraldo** (*Emerald Grotto*). The tacky road sign and squadron of tour buses may put you off, but this cavern is worth a stop. The karstic cave was originally part of the shore, but the lowest end sank into the sea. Intense greenish light filters into the water from an arch below sea level and is reflected off the cavern walls. You visit the Grotta dello Smeraldo, which is filled with huge stalactites and stalagmites, on a large rowboat. Don't let the boatman's constant spiel detract from the 20-minute experience—just tune out and enjoy the sparkles, shapes, and Harry Winston–esque color. You can take an elevator from the coast road down to the grotto, or in the summer you can drive to Amalfi and arrive by boat (€10, excluding the grotto's admission fee). Companies in Positano, Amalfi, and elsewhere along the coast provide service. ■TIP→ **The light at the grotto is best from noon to 3 pm.** ⊠ *Beyond Punta Acquafetente by boat, or off Amalfi Dr.* ☎ *089/831535* 🎟 *€5* ⊗ *Apr.–mid-Oct., daily 9–4; mid-Oct.–Mar., daily 9–3. Closed in adverse weather.*

WHERE TO STAY

$$$$
HOTEL
Fodor'sChoice
★

Monastero Santa Rosa. Set in a 17th-century monastery perched on the dramatic cliffs above the Amalfi Coast (a UNESCO World Heritage Site), this exquisite boutique resort is destined to become one of Italy's most exclusive retreats. **Pros:** true heritage in a UNESCO site; the friendliest staff on the coast. **Cons:** some rooms are small (monks' cells were not that big!); luxury comes at a price. $ *Rooms from: €600* ⊠ *Via Roma 2* ☎ *089/8321199* ⊕ *www.monasterosantarosa.com* 🛏 *12 rooms, 8 suites* ⊗ *Closed Nov.–mid-Apr.* ⦿*Breakfast.*

AMALFI

18 km (11 miles) southeast of Positano, 35 km (22 miles) east of Sorrento.

At first glance, it's hard to imagine that this resort destination, set in a verdant valley of the Lattari Mountains, with its cream-color and pastel-hue buildings tightly packing a gorge on the Bay of Salerno, was in the 11th and 12th centuries the seat of the Amalfi Maritime Republic, one of the world's great naval powers, and a sturdy rival of Genoa and Pisa for control of the Mediterranean. The harbor, which once launched the greatest fleet in Italy, now bobs with ferries and blue-and-white fishing boats. The main street, lined with leather shops and pasticcerie, has replaced a raging mountain torrent, and terraced hills where *banditti* (bandits) once roamed now flaunt the green and gold of lemon groves. Bearing testimony to its great trade with Tunis, Tripoli, and Algiers, Amalfi remains honeycombed with Arab-Sicilian cloisters and covered passages. In a way Amalfi has become great again, showing off its medieval glory days with sea pageants, convents-turned-hotels, ancient paper mills, covered streets, and its mosquelike cathedral.

GETTING HERE AND AROUND

From April to October the optimal way to get to Amalfi is by ferry from Salerno. SitaSud buses run from Naples and Sorrento throughout the year. By car, take the Statale 163 (Amalfitana) from outside Sorrento or Salerno, or take the Angri exit on the A3 autostrada and cross the mountainous Valico di Chiunsi

VISITOR INFORMATION

Amalfi Tourism Office ✉ *Corso delle Repubbliche Marinare 27* ☎ *089/871107* ⊕ *www.amalfitouristoffice.it.*

EXPLORING

Fodor's Choice ★ **Duomo di Sant' Andrea.** Complicated, grand, delicate, and dominating, the 9th-century Amalfi cathedral has been remodeled over the years with Romanesque, Byzantine, Gothic, and Baroque elements, but retains a predominantly Arab-Norman style. Cross and crescent seem to be wed here: the campanile, spliced with Saracen colors and the intricate tile work of High Barbery, looks like a minaret wearing a Scheherazadian turban, the facade conjures up a striped burnoose, and its **Chiostro del Paradiso** (Paradise Cloister) is an Arab-Sicilian spectacular. Built around 1266 as a burial ground for Amalfi's elite, the cloister, the first stop on a tour of the cathedral, is one of southern Italy's architectural treasures. Its flower-and-palm-filled quadrangle has a series of exceptionally delicate intertwining arches on slender double columns.

The chapel at the back of the cloister leads into the earlier (9th century) **basilica.** Romanesque in style, the structure has a nave, two aisles, and a high, deep apse. Note the 14th-century crucifixion scene by a student of Giotto. This section has now been transformed into a museum, housing sarcophagi, sculpture, Neapolitan goldsmiths' artwork, and other treasures from the cathedral complex. Steps from the basilica lead down into the **Cripta di Sant'Andrea** (Crypt of Saint Andrew). The cathedral above was built in the 13th century to house the saint's bones, which

Amalfi's Luscious Lemons

Lemons as big as oranges (and oranges as big as grapefruits) are cultivated on the seemingly endless net-covered pergolas of the Amalfi Coast. From linguine with lemon at trattorias to lemon soufflés at fancy restaurants, the yellow citrus is everywhere—and all parts are used, as can be seen from the delicious habit of baking raisins, figs, or pieces of cheese wrapped in lemon leaves, bound up with thin red thread.

Not only are lemons a main component of meals and drinks, they're also offered as a remedy for everything from flu to bunions. But the most renowned end product is that local digestif known as *limoncello*, which captures in a bottle the color, fragrance, and taste of those tart-sweet lemons. Drink it cold in a tiny, frosty glass or after a shot of hot espresso—a golden memory quenched with each sip.

13

came from Constantinople and supposedly exuded a miraculous liquid believers call the "manna of Saint Andrew." ⊠ *Piazza del Duomo* ☎ *089/871324* ⊕ *www.diocesiamalficava.it* 🎫 *€3* ⊙ *Apr.–Sept., daily 9–7; Nov.–Jan. 6 and Mar., daily 10–3.*

FAMILY **Valle dei Mulini** (*Valley of the Mills*). Uphill from town, this was for centuries Amalfi's center for papermaking, an ancient trade learned from the Arabs, who learned it from the Chinese. Beginning in the 12th century, former flour mills were converted to produce paper made from cotton and linen. In 1211 Frederick II of Sicily prohibited this lighter, more readable paper for use in the preparation of official documents, favoring traditional sheepskin parchment. But by 1811 more than a dozen mills here, with more along the coast, were humming. Natural waterpower ensured that the handmade paper was cost-effective. Flooding in 1954, however, closed most of the mills for good, and many have been converted into private housing. The **Museo della Carta** (Museum of Paper) opened in 1971 in a 15th-century mill: paper samples, tools of the trade, old machinery, and the audiovisual presentation are all enlightening. You can also participate in a paper-making laboratory. ⊠ *Via delle Cartiere 23* ☎ *089/8304561* ⊕ *www.museodellacarta.it* 🎫 *€4, includes guided tour; laboratory €7* ⊙ *Mar.–Oct., daily 10–6:30; Nov.–Feb., Tues.–Sun. 10–2:30.*

WHERE TO EAT

$$ ✕ **Al Teatro.** Once a children's theater, this informal and charming white-
SOUTHERN stucco restaurant in the medieval quarter is 50 steps above the main
ITALIAN drag. A house specialty is grilled squid and calamari with mint sauce, reflecting its position—suspended between sea and mountains. Try also the *scialatielli al Teatro*, with tomatoes and eggplant. ▪TIP➔ **The pizzas from the wood-fired oven are terrific.** 💲 *Average main: €15* ⊠ *Via E. Marini 19* ☎ *089/872473* ⊙ *Closed Wed., and Jan.–mid-Feb.*

$ ✕ **Il Tari.** Locals highly recommend this little ristorante a few min-
SOUTHERN utes' walk north of the Duomo. Named after the ancient coin of the
ITALIAN Amalfi Republic, the restaurant occupies a former stable whose space has altered little outwardly since those equine days, though the white

walls, appealing local art, crisp tablecloths, large panoramic photos, and tile floors make it cozy enough. Winning dishes on the vast menu include the wood oven–baked thin-crust pizza and the *scialatielli alla Saracena* (long spaghetti-style pasta laden with tasty treats from the sea). ■ TIP→ **The prix-fixe options (from €20 to €40) are a great deal.** *$ Average main: €12 ✉ Via P. Capuano 9–11 ☎ 089/871832 🌐 www.amalfiristorantetari.it ⏲ Closed Tues.*

$$$$ | SOUTHERN ITALIAN | Fodor's Choice ★

🍴 **La Caravella.** No wonder this is considered the most romantic restaurant in Amalfi, with lace-covered tables, *ciuccio* (donkey) ceramics, tall candles, and fresh floral bouquets in salons graced with frescoes and marble floors. Opened in 1959, it became the first in Southern Italy to earn a Michelin star in 1966, and once drew a gilded guest list that included such fans as Andy Warhol and Federico Fellini. The menu maintains dishes favored 50 years ago: picture slices of fish grilled in lemon leaves marinated with an almond and wild fennel sauce. ■ TIP→ **A tasting menu is available, but don't miss the antipasti.** *$ Average main: €40 ✉ Via Matteo Camera 12, near Arsenale ☎ 089/871029 🌐 www.ristorantelacaravella.it ✍ Reservations essential ⏲ Closed Tues. mid-Sept.–mid-July. No lunch Mon.–Tues. mid-June–mid-Sept.*

WHERE TO STAY

$ | HOTEL

🏨 **Albergo Sant'Andrea.** Occupying one of the top spots in town this tiny, family-run pensione is just across from the magnificent steps leading to Amalfi's cathedral. **Pros:** on the main square; divine views of the Duomo; friendly staff. **Cons:** steep flight of steps to entrance; very simple rooms. *$ Rooms from: €100 ✉ Piazza del Duomo ☎ 089/871145 🌐 www.albergosantandrea.it 🛏 8 rooms ⏲ Closed Nov.–Mar. 🍽 No meals.*

$$$$ | HOTEL | Fodor's Choice ★

🏨 **Grand Hotel Convento di Amalfi.** This fabled medieval monastery was lauded by such guests as Longfellow and Wagner, and though recent modernization has sacrificed some of its historic charm, it remains an iconic destination. **Pros:** a slice of paradise; iconic Amalfi. **Cons:** traditionalists will miss its old-world charm; a 10-minute walk to town. *$ Rooms from: €420 ✉ Via Annunziatella 46 ☎ 089/8736711 🌐 www.ghconventodiamalfi.com 🛏 36 rooms, 17 suites ⏲ Closed Nov.–Mar. 🍽 Breakfast.*

RAVELLO

Fodor's Choice ★

5 km (3 miles) northeast of Amalfi, 40 km (25 miles) east of Sorrento.

Positano may focus on pleasure, and Amalfi on history, but cool, serene Ravello revels in refinement. Thrust over Statale 163 and the Bay of Salerno on a mountain buttress, below forests of chestnut and ash, above terraced lemon groves and vineyards, it early on beckoned the affluent with its island-in-the-sky views and secluded defensive positioning. Gardens out of the *Arabian Nights,* pastel palazzos, tucked-away piazzas with medieval fountains, architecture ranging from Romano-Byzantine to Norman-Saracen, and those sweeping blue-water, blue-sky vistas have inspired a panoply of large personalities. Today, many visitors flock here to discover this paradisiacal place, some to enjoy the town's celebrated music festival, others just to stroll through the hillside streets to gape at the bluer-than-blue panoramas of sea and sky.

GETTING HERE AND AROUND

Buses from Amalfi make the 20-minute trip along white-knuckle roads. From Naples, take the A3 Naples–Salerno autostrada; then exit at Angri and follow signs for Ravello. The journey takes about 75 minutes. Save yourself the trouble of driving by hiring a car and driver.

VISITOR INFORMATION

Azienda Autonoma Soggiorno e Turismo ⊠ *Via Roma 18b* ☎ *089/857096* ⊕ *www.ravellotime.it* ☾ *Nov.–Mar., daily 9:30–5; Apr.–Oct., daily 9:30–7.*

13

EXPLORING

Fodor's Choice
★

Auditorium Niemeyer. Crowning Via della Repubblica and the hillside, which overlooks the spectacular Bay of Salerno, Auditorium Niemeyer is a startling piece of modernist architecture. Designed with a dramatically curved, all-white roof by the Brazilian architect Oscar Niemeyer (creator of Brasília), it was conceived as an alternative indoor venue for concerts, including those of the famed town music festival, and is now also used as a cinema. The subject of much controversy since its first conception back in 2000, it raised the wrath of some locals who denounced such an ambitious modernist building in medieval Ravello. They need not have worried. The result, inaugurated in 2010, is a design masterpiece—a huge, overhanging canopied roof suspended over a 400-seat concert area, with a giant eye-shape window allowing spectators to contemplate the extraordinary bay vista during performances. The terrace's "lounge bar" complements the experience. ⊠ *Via della Repubblica* ⊕ *www.cinemaravello.it.*

Duomo. Ravello's first bishop, Orso Papiro, founded this cathedral, dedicated to San Pantaleone, in 1086. Rebuilt in the 12th and 17th centuries, it retains traces of medieval frescoes in the transept, an original mullioned window, a marble portal, and a three-story 13th-century bell tower playfully interwoven with mullioned windows and arches. The 12th-century bronze door has 54 embossed panels depicting Christ's life, and saints, prophets, plants, and animals, all narrating biblical lore. Ancient columns divide the nave's three aisles, and treasures include sarcophagi from Roman times and paintings by the southern Renaissance artist Andrea da Salerno. Most impressive are the two medieval pulpits: the earlier one (on your left as you face the altar), used for reading the Epistles, is inset with a mosaic scene of Jonah and the whale, symbolizing death and redemption. The more famous one opposite, used for reading the Gospels, was commissioned by Nicola Rufolo in 1272 and created by Niccolò di Bartolomeo da Foggia. It seems almost Tuscan in style, with exquisite mosaic work and bas-reliefs and six twisting columns sitting on lion pedestals. An eagle grandly tops the inlaid marble lectern.

A chapel to the left of the apse is dedicated to San Pantaleone, a physician beheaded in the 3rd century in Nicomedia. Every July 27 devout believers gather in hope of witnessing a miracle (similar to that of San Gennaro in Naples), in which the saint's blood, collected in a vial and set out on an inlaid marble altar, appears to liquefy and come to a boil. In the crypt is the **Museo del Duomo,** which displays treasures from about the 13th century, during the reign of Frederick II of Sicily. ⊠ *Piazza del Duomo* ☎ *089/858311* ⊕ *www.chiesaravello.com* 🎫 *€3* ⊗ *Daily 9–7 (noon–5:30, access church through museum, to right of steps).*

Fodor'sChoice **Villa Cimbrone.** To the west of Ravello's main square, a somewhat hilly ★ 15-minute walk along Via San Francesco brings you to Ravello's show-stopper, the Villa Cimbrone, whose dazzling gardens perch 1,500 feet above the sea. The ultimate aerie, this medieval-style fantasy was created in 1905 by England's Lord Grimthorpe and made world-famous in the 1930s when Greta Garbo found sanctuary from the press here. The Gothic *castello-palazzo* sits amid idyllic gardens that are divided by the grand Alleé of Immensity, leading in turn to the literal high point of any trip to the Amalfi Coast—the **Belvedere dell'Infinità** (Belvedere of Infinity). This grand stone parapet, adorned with amusing stone busts, overlooks the entire Bay of Salerno and frames a panorama the late writer Gore Vidal, a longtime Ravello resident, described as the most beautiful in the world. The name Cimbrone derives from the rocky ridge on which the villa stands, first colonized by the ancient Romans and hailed as Cimbronium back then. The villa itself is now a five-star hotel. ⊠ *Via Santa Chiara 26* ☎ *089/857459* ⊕ *www.villacimbrone.it* 🎫 *€7* ⊗ *Daily 9–½ hr before sunset.*

Fodor'sChoice **Villa Rufolo.** Directly off Ravello's main piazza is the Villa Rufolo, home ★ to some of the most spectacular gardens in Italy, many of which stunningly frame a Cinerama vista of the Bay of Salerno, often called the "bluest view in the world." If the master storyteller Boccaccio is to be believed, the villa was built in the 13th century by Landolfo Rufolo, whose immense fortune stemmed from trade with the Moors and the Saracens. Norman and Arab architecture mingle in a welter of color-filled gardens so lush the composer Richard Wagner used them as inspiration for Klingsor's Garden, the home of the Flower Maidens, in his opera *Parsifal.* Beyond the Arab-Sicilian cloister and the Norman tower lie the two terrace gardens. The lower one, the "Wagner Terrace," is often the site for Ravello Music Festival concerts, with the orchestra perched on a precarious-looking platform constructed over the precipice. Sir Francis Nevile Reid, a Scotsman, acquired the villa in 1851 and hired Michele Ruggiero, head of the excavations at Pompeii, to restore the villa to its full splendor and replant the gardens with rare cycads, cordylines, and palms. Highlights of the house are its Moorish cloister—an Arabic-Sicilian delight with interlacing lancet arcs and polychromatic palmette decoration—and the 14th-century Torre Maggiore, the so-called Klingsor's Tower, renamed in honor of Richard Wagner's landmark 1880 visit. ⊠ *Piazza Duomo* ☎ *089/857621* ⊕ *www. villarufolo.it* 🎫 *€5, extra charge for concerts* ⊗ *Daily 9–9 (closes early for concert rehearsals); winter, daily 9–5.*

WHERE TO EAT

$ SOUTHERN ITALIAN Fodor's Choice ★ 🍴 **Cumpa' Cosimo.** Lustier-looking than most Ravello spots, Cumpa' Cosimo is run devotedly by Netta Bottone, who tours the tables to ensure her clients are content. Her family has owned this cantina for more than 75 of its 300-plus years, and she has been cooking under the arched ceiling for more than 60 of them. You can't miss with any of the classic Ravellian dishes. A favorite (share it—it's huge) is a *misto* of whatever homemade pasta inspires her, served with a fresh, fragrant pesto. Meats, from Netta's own butcher shop next door, are generally excellent and local wines ease it all down gently. The *funghi porcini* mushroom starter is delicious and the house cheesecake or homemade gelato provide a luscious ending. [$] *Average main: €13* ✉ *Via Roma 46* ☎ *089/857156* ⏲ *Sometimes closed Mon. in winter.*

$ PIZZA 🍴 **Ristorante Pizzeria Vittoria.** Just south of the Duomo, this is a good place for a return to reality and an informal bite. Vittoria's thin-crust pizza with loads of fresh toppings is the star attraction, and locals praise it *molto*—it was a favorite of Gore Vidal. But also try the pasta, maybe fusilli with tomatoes, zucchini, and mozzarella. Vittoria is pretty, too, with arches and tile floors. All this adds up to crowds, so try to arrive on the early side. [$] *Average main: €12* ✉ *Via dei Rufolo 3* ☎ *089/857947* 🌐 *www.ristorantepizzeriavittoria.it* ⏲ *Closed Nov.–Mar., except Christmas.*

WHERE TO STAY

$$$ HOTEL Fodor's Choice ★ 🏨 **Hotel Palumbo.** This is the real deal—the only great hotel left in Ravello that's still a monument to the Grand Tour sensibility that first put the town on the map. **Pros:** impossibly romantic; wonderful coastal retreat; incredible Bay of Salerno views. **Cons:** with all this finery it can be difficult to relax; restaurant closed from November to March. [$] *Rooms from: €245* ✉ *Via San Giovanni del Toro 16* ☎ *089/857244* 🌐 *www.hotelpalumbo.it* 🛏 *10 rooms, 7 suites* 🍽 *Some meals.*

$$ HOTEL 🏨 **Hotel Parsifal.** In 1288 this diminutive property overlooking the coastline housed an order of Augustinian friars; today the intact cloister hosts travelers intent on enjoying themselves mightily. **Pros:** staying in a convent in Ravello; charming manager and his family dote on Americans. **Cons:** slightly removed from town; tiny rooms. [$] *Rooms from: €130* ✉ *Viale Gioacchino d'Anna 5* ☎ *089/857144* 🌐 *www.hotelparsifal.com* 🛏 *17 rooms* 🍽 *All meals.*

$$$$ HOTEL Fodor's Choice ★ 🏨 **Hotel Villa Cimbrone.** Suspended over the azure sea and set amid legendary rose-filled gardens, this Gothic-style castle was once home to Lord Grimthorpe and a hideaway of Greta Garbo. **Pros:** gorgeous pool and grounds; stay where Garbo chose to "be alone." **Cons:** a longish hike from town center (porters can help with luggage); daily arrival of respectful day-trippers. [$] *Rooms from: €530* ✉ *Via Santa Chiara 26* ☎ *089/857459* 🌐 *www.villacimbrone.com* 🛏 *19 rooms* ⏲ *Closed Nov.–Mar.* 🍽 *Breakfast.*

$ HOTEL 🏨 **Villa Amore.** A 10-minute walk from the Piazza del Duomo, this charmingly secluded hotel with a garden is family-run and shares the same exhilarating view of the Bay of Salerno as Ravello's most expensive hotels. **Pros:** wonderful views; inexpensive alternative to its illustrious neighbors. **Cons:** away from the main drag; basic rooms. [$] *Rooms* *from: €100* ⊠ *Via dei Fusco 5* ☎ *089/857135* ⊕ *www.villaamore.it* ↩ *10 rooms* ⏁ *Breakfast.*

PAESTUM

99 km (62 miles) southeast of Naples.

GETTING HERE AND AROUND

By car, take the A3 autostrada south from Salerno, take the Battipaglia exit to SS18. Exit at Capaccio Scala. You can also take a CSTP or SCAT bus (departs hourly) or an FS train from Salerno. The archaeological site is a 10-minute walk from the station.

VISITOR INFORMATION

Paestum Tourism Office ⊠ *Via Magna Grecia 887* ☎ *0828/811016* ⊕ *www. infopaestum.it* ⊗ *Daily 9–1 and 2–4.*

EXPLORING

Fodor's Choice ★

Greek Temples. One of Italy's most majestic sights lies on the edge of a flat coastal plain: the remarkably preserved Greek temples of Paestum. This is the site of the ancient city of Poseidonia, founded by Greek colonists probably in the 6th century BC. When the Romans took it over in 273 BC, they Latinized the name to Paestum and changed the layout of the settlement, adding an amphitheater and a forum. Much of the archaeological material found on the site is displayed in the well-labeled **Museo Nazionale**, and several rooms are devoted to the unique tomb paintings—rare examples of Greek and pre-Roman pictorial art—discovered in the area.

At the northern end of the site opposite the ticket barrier is the **Tempio di Cerere** (Temple of Ceres). Built in about 500 BC, it is thought to have been originally dedicated to the goddess Athena. Follow the road south past the **Foro Romano** (Roman Forum) to the **Tempio di Nettuno** (Temple of Poseidon), a showstopping Doric edifice with 36 fluted columns and an entablature (the area above the capitals) that rivals those of the finest temples in Greece. Beyond is the so-called **Basilica.** The oldest of Paestum's standing structures, it dates from the early 6th century BC. The name is an 18th-century misnomer, though, since it was, in fact, a temple to Hera, the wife of Zeus. ■ TIP→ **Try to see the temples in the late afternoon, when the light enhances the deep gold of the limestone and tourists have left them almost deserted.** ⊠ *Via Magna Grecia* ☎ *0828/811023 for museum, 0828/722654 for ticket office* ⊞ *Site and museum €7 (€10 during special exhibitions); €6 museum only (after site closes)* ⊗ *Excavations daily 8:45–2 hrs before sunset; museum daily 8:30–6:45; museum closed 1st and 3rd Mon. of month.*

WHERE TO STAY

$

B&B/INN

Azienda Agrituristica Seliano. This agriturismo-with-a-difference, about 3 km (2 miles) from Greek temples, consists of a cluster of 19th-century baronial buildings. **Pros:** a great taste of a working farm; a banquet every evening; transfers available from the station. **Cons:** confusing to find; not for non–dog fans. ⓢ *Rooms from: €70* ⊠ *Via Seliano, about 1 km (½ mile) down dirt track west off main road from Capaccio Scalo to Paestum* ☎ *0828/723634* ⊕ *www.agriturismoseliano.it* ↩ *14 rooms* ⊗ *Closed Nov.–Mar., will open for bookings* ⏁ *All meals.*

PUGLIA, BASILICATA, AND CALABRIA

WELCOME TO PUGLIA, BASILICATA, AND CALABRIA

TOP REASONS TO GO

★ **A wander through Sassi:** The simple Basilicata town of Matera is endowed with one of the most unusual landscapes in Europe: a complex network of ancient cave dwellings partially hewn from rock, some of which now house chic bars and restaurants.

★ **A trip to peasant-food heaven:** Dine on Puglia's famous purée of fava beans with chicory and olive oil in a humble country restaurant.

★ **Lecce and its Baroque splendors:** The beautiful, friendly city of Lecce might be known for its peculiar brand of fanciful Baroque architecture, but it's not yet famous enough to have lost its Pugliese charm.

★ **The trulli of the Valle d'Itria:** Strange, conical houses—many of them still in use—dot the rolling countryside of Puglia, centering around Alberobello, a town still composed almost entirely of these *trulli*. They must be seen to be believed.

1 **Bari and the Adriatic Coast.** Puglia's biggest city is a lively, quirky, and sometimes seedy port on the Adriatic Coast. It's also home to the region's principal airport.

2 **The Trulli District.** Named for its mysterious conical houses, the Trulli District is centered on the town of Alberobello.

3 **The Salento Peninsula.** The ports of Puglia include casbahlike fishing villages such as Gallipoli and the gritty shipping centers of Taranto and Brindisi. Italy's heel finally smooths out and terminates in a region of Puglia known as Salento, home to Lecce, famous for its ornate Baroque architecture.

4 **Basilicata.** One of Italy's least visited and most secluded regions is the place to find Matera, whose cave dwellings make the city feel like a Nativity scene.

5 **Calabria.** The region that makes up Italy's "toe" is a land of dusty hill towns, rows of olive trees, and spicy food. Cosenza mixes turn-of-the-20th-century cafés with Fascist-era architecture, and Tropea is an enticing seaside getaway.

6 **The Gargano Promonitory.** The spur of Italy's boot has the pretty whitewashed towns of Vieste and Peschici. It's a popular spot for Italian holidaymakers during July and August.

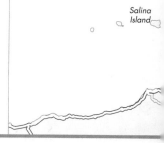

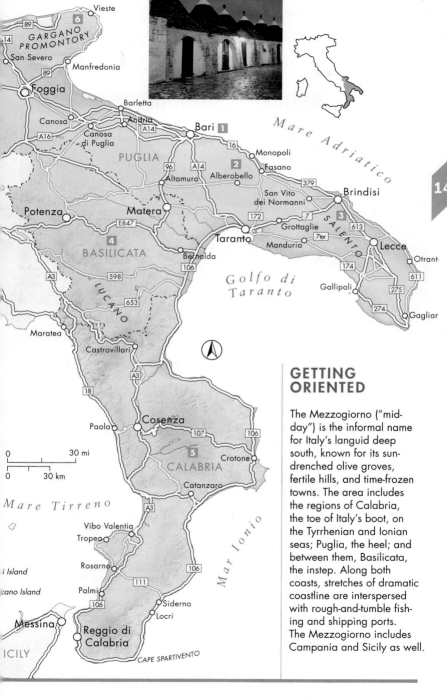

Vieste

6

89

GARGANO
PROMONTORY

14

San Severo

89

Manfredonia

Foggia

Barletta

Canosa

Andria

Bari **1**

A16

Canosa
di Puglia

A14

16

Monopoli

PUGLIA

96

A14

2

Fasano

Altamura

Alberobello

379

San Vito
dei Normanni

Brindisi

Potenza

Matera

172

3

Grottaglie

613

Lecce

7

7ter

BASILICATA

4

Taranto

Manduria

Otrant·

A3

598

Bernalda

106

174

611

LUCANO

653

Golfo di
Taranto

Gallipoli

275

274

Gagliar

Maratea

Castrovillari

A3

18

Cosenza

Paola

107

106

5

Crotone

30 mi

CALABRIA

30 km

Catanzaro

Mare Tirreno

A3

Vibo Valentia

Mar Ionio

Tropea

Rosarno

106

i Island

·ano Island

Palmi

111

Siderno

106

Locri

Messina

Reggio di
Calabria

ICILY

CAPE SPARTIVENTO

Mare Adriatico

14

GETTING
ORIENTED

The Mezzogiorno ("mid-day") is the informal name for Italy's languid deep south, known for its sun-drenched olive groves, fertile hills, and time-frozen towns. The area includes the regions of Calabria, the toe of Italy's boot, on the Tyrrhenian and Ionian seas; Puglia, the heel; and between them, Basilicata, the instep. Along both coasts, stretches of dramatic coastline are interspersed with rough-and-tumble fishing and shipping ports. The Mezzogiorno includes Campania and Sicily as well.

EATING AND DRINKING WELL IN PUGLIA, BASILICATA, AND CALABRIA

The Mediterranean diet was born here. The traditional cuisine reflects its peasant origins, with hearty homemade pasta, thick bean soups, and grilled meat and fish. A defining principle of Italian cooking is to take excellent ingredients and prepare them simply. That philosophy reaches its purest expression here.

The best—and cheapest—meals are often found at family-run trattorias (often with a sign above the door proclaiming, "*cucina casereccio*" [home cooking]). Dishes will be strictly seasonal, so don't expect an extensive menu. However, these bare-bones places manage to create flavors rivaling those of any highbrow restaurant. Assent to the waiter's suggestions and leave yourself in the hands of the chef (who will most likely be his wife or mother).

More upscale establishments turn local ingredients into deliciously inventive dishes. Many such restaurants are set in breathtaking locations, yet prices remain relative bargains compared to similar places farther north.

FABULOUS FAVA

Puré di fave e cicorielle, a purée of fava beans topped with sautéed chicory, is unique to Puglia and Basilicata.

The simple recipe has been prepared here for centuries and continues to be a staple of the local diet. The dried favas are soaked overnight, cooked with potatoes, seasoned with salt and olive oil, and served warm with wild green chicory, often with a sprinkling of ground *peperoncino* (chili pepper). Mix it together before eating, and wash it down with a glass of primitivo or aglianico.

MEAT

As well as its excellent beef, Basilicata is known for its *salsicce lucane* (sausages), seasoned with salt, cayenne pepper, and fennel seeds. Enormous grills are a feature of many of the region's restaurants, infusing the dining area with the aroma of freshly cooked meat. Adventurous eaters in Puglia should look for *turcinieddhri* (a blend of lamb's innards) and *pezzetti di cavallo* (braised horse meat).

PASTA

Puglia is the home of orecchiette, *pictured at right,* with *cime di rapa* (broccoli rabe) and olive oil, a melodious dish that's wondrous in its simplicity. Try also *cavatelli* (rolled-up orecchiette) and *strascenate* (rectangles of pasta with one rough side and one smooth side).

PEPPERS

If you like it hot, Calabria is the place for you. The region is known for its use of hot little peppers that can range from a mild sprinkling in tomato sauce to the tongue-scorching *nduja* paste. The local cured meats, such as *sopressata* (dried spicy salami), and *salsiccia piccante* (hot sausage), *pictured at left,* often sold by street vendors on a roll with peppers, onions, french fries and mayonnaise, are all spiced with peperoncino. Don't forget to try the delicious sweet red onions of Tropea, exclusive to the region.

SEAFOOD

With so much coastline, seafood is an essential element of southern Italian cuisine. Fish can be grilled (*alla griglia*), baked (*al forno*), roasted (*arrosto*), or steamed (*in umido*). Among the highlights are delicate *orata* (sea bream), *pictured below, branzino* (sea bass), *gamberi rossi* (sweet red shrimp), and calamari. Puglia is the home of *cozze pelose* (a kind of mussel), and Calabria's version of sushi is freshly caught sea urchins, considered a delicacy—and an aphrodisiac!

WINES

Puglia produces around 17% of Italy's wine, more than is produced in the whole of Australia. In the past, most of it was *vino sfuso* (jug wine), but over the past 15 years, producers have been concentrating on quality—with impressive results. The ancient *primitivo* grape (an ancestor of California's zinfandel) yields strong, heady wines like Primitivo di Manduria. The *negroamaro* grape is transformed into palatable *rosati* (rosés), as well as the robust Salice Salentino. Pair a dessert with the sweet red Aleatico di Puglia or Moscato di Trani.

In Basilicata, producers use the *aglianico* grape variety to outstanding effect in the prestigious Aglianico del Vulture. In Calabria, they've worked wonders with the *gaglioppo* variety.

Updated by
Margaret
Stenhouse

Venture off the traffic-filled highways and explore the countryside of Italy's boot, made up of the three separate regions—Puglia, Basilicata, and Calabria—each one with its own character. This is Italy's deep south, where whitewashed buildings stand silently over three turquoise seas, castles guard medieval alleyways, and grandmothers dry their handmade orecchiette, the most Puglian of pastas, in the midafternoon heat.

At every turn, these three regions boast dramatic scenery. Geographical divides have preserved an astonishing cultural and linguistic diversity that's unequaled elsewhere on the Italian mainland. Southern Italians are extremely proud of their home towns and will be glad to direct you to some forgotten local chapel in an olive grove, an unmarked monument, or an obscure work of art. The Greek city-states of Magna Graecia (Greater Greece) once ruled here, and ancient names, such as Lucania, are still commonly used. It's here also that you'll find long-isolated hill communities where Albanian and Greek are still spoken by the descendants of 16th-century refugees from the Balkans.

One of southern Italy's most popular vacation destinations is the Gargano Promontory, where safe, sandy shores and secluded coves are nestled between whitewashed coastal towns and craggy limestone cliffs. You'll also find many beautiful stretches of sandy beaches along the coast of the Salento peninsula and the Mediterranean shoreline of Calabria and Basilicata. There are cultural gems everywhere, including Valle d'Itria's fairy-tale *trulli* (curious conical structures, some dating from the 15th century), Matera's *Sassi* (a network of ancient dwellings carved out of rock), and the Baroque churches in the town of Lecce, the jewel of the south. Beyond the cities, seaside resorts, and the few major sights, there's a sparsely populated, sunbaked countryside where road signs are rare and expanses of silvery olive trees, vineyards of primitivo and aglianico, and giant prickly pear cacti fight their way through the rocky soil in defiance of the relentless summer heat.

PUGLIA, BASILICATA, AND CALABRIA PLANNER

MAKING THE MOST OF YOUR TIME

If your priority is relaxing on the beach, plan on a few days at a sea-side resort in one of the Gargano Promontory's fishing villages, such as Peschici, Rodi Garganico, and Vieste, and perhaps a further stay at one of the Calabrian coastal resorts, such as Diamante or Tropea, or Maratea in Basilicata.

Otherwise, choose a base like Polignano a Mare or Trani, especially if you land or dock in Bari. Take day trips out to the Valle d'Itria, or to the remarkable octagonal Castel del Monte. Then head east along the Adriatic route (SS16), stopping to see the idyllic hilltop Ostuni before continuing on to Lecce, where you'll want to spend at least two to three nights exploring the city's Baroque wonders and taking a day trip down to Otranto and Gallipoli.

Next, take regional roads and Via Appia (SS7) to reach Matera, whose Sassi cave dwellings are a southern Italian highlight; allow at least two nights here. Then it's back out to the SS106 to Calabria, along the coast dotted with ancient Greek settlements, as far as Tropea. At this point, cut inland on the SS107 across the Sila Massif, stopping at the hill resort of Camigliatello or carrying on to the more vibrant lowland Cosenza. Reggio Calabria is worthwhile just to see the celebrated Riace bronzes.

GETTING AROUND

BUS TRAVEL

Direct, if not always frequent, connections operate between most destinations within Calabria, Puglia, and Basilicata. In many cases, bus service is the backup when problems with train service arise. Matera is linked with Bari by frequent Ferrovie Appulo Lucane trains and buses and with Taranto by SITA bus. In Calabria various companies make the north–south run with stops along both coasts. Ferrovie della Calabria operates many of the local routes.

Contacts **Ferrovie Appulo Lucane.** This service links Matera to Altamura in Puglia (for connections to Bari) and to Ferrandina (for connections by bus to Potenza). ☎ 199/811811 ⊕ www.fal-srl.it. **Ferrovie della Calabria** ☎ 0961/896111, 328/2391123 ⊕ www.ferroviedellacalabria.it. **SITA** ☎ 0835/385007, 080/5790111, 0971/506811 ⊕ www.sitasudtrasporti.it.

CAR TRAVEL

Though roads are generally good in the south, and major cities are linked by fast *autostrade,* or four-lane highways, driving here is a major test of navigation skills. While you can bypass many cities by using the ring roads around them, getting into the center of many cities can be complicated, with mazes of one-way streets, pedestrianized zones, and limited parking facilities. The more upmarket hotels have garage facilities or valet parking at guests' disposal. Phone your hotel for advice and instructions when you are entering city outskirts. Seemingly under eternal construction, the toll-free (from Salerno) A3 Napoli–Reggio Calabria autostrada links Naples to the south, with major exits at Sicignano (for the interior of Basilicata and Matera), Cosenza (the Sila Massif and Crotone), and Pizzo (for Tropea). Parts of the A3 in northern Calabria cross uplands more than 3,000 feet high, so snow chains may be required during winter months. In the summer and during holiday weekends this is the main north–south route for Italy's sun seekers, so factor in plenty of time for delays and avoid peak travel times. Take the SS18 for coastal destinations—or for a better view—on the Tyrrhenian side, and likewise the SS106 (which is uncongested and fast) for the Ionian. Given speed detectors and driver-tracking technology, it's best to stick to speed limits: you may become unpopular with the drivers behind you, but you'll be spared an unwelcome ticket when you get home.

If you're squeamish about getting lost, don't plan on night driving in the countryside—roads can be confusing without the aid of landmarks or large towns, and GPS is far from infallible. Bari, Brindisi, and Reggio Calabria are notorious for car thefts and break-ins. In these cities, don't leave valuables in the car, and find a guarded parking space if possible.

TRAIN TRAVEL
Trenitalia trains run to Calabria, either following the Ionian Coast as far as Reggio Calabria or swerving inland to Cosenza and the Tyrrhenian Coast.

Ferrovie Appulo-Lucane. This service links Matera to Altamura in Puglia (for connections to Bari) and to Ferrandina (for connections to Potenza). ☎ 199/811811 ⊕ www.fal-srl.it.

Ferrovie Sud-Est. The private Ferrovie Sud-Est connects Martina Franca with Bari, Lecce and Taranto, and the fishing port of Gallipoli. ☎ 080/5462111 in Bari, 0832/668111 in Lecce, 8000/79090 ⊕ www.fseonline.it.

Trenitalia. Within Puglia, the Italian national railroad links Bari to Brindisi, Lecce, and Taranto, but smaller destinations can often be reached only by completing the trip by bus. ☎ 199/892021, 800/892021 ⊕ www.trenitalia.com.

RESTAURANTS
Prices in the dining reviews are the average cost of a main course at dinner, or, if dinner is not served, at lunch.

HOTELS
Hotels in the region range from grand, upscale establishments to small and stylish bijou inns to family-run rural *agriturismi* (country hostelries, often part of farms) that compensate for a lack of amenities with their famous southern hospitality. *Fattorie* and *masserie* (small farms and grander farm estates) offering accommodation are listed at local tourist offices.

In beach areas such as the Gargano Promontory and Salento, campgrounds and bungalow lodgings are ubiquitous and popular with families and budget travelers. Note that many seaside hotels open up just for the summer season, when they often require several-day stays with full or half board. And do remember that in a region like this—blazingly hot in summer and chilly in winter—air-conditioning and central heating can be important.

Hotel reviews have been shortened. For full information, visit Fodors. com.

WHAT IT COSTS				
	$	**$$**	**$$$**	**$$$$**
RESTAURANTS	under €15	€15–€24	€25–€35	over €35
HOTELS	under €125	€125–€200	€201–€300	over €300

Prices in the dining reviews are the average cost of a main course at dinner, or, if dinner is not served, at lunch. Prices in the reviews are the lowest cost of a standard double room in high season.

14

BARI AND THE ADRIATIC COAST

The coast of Puglia has a strong flavor of the Norman presence in the south, embodied in the distinctive Apulian-Romanesque churches, the most atmospheric being in Trani. The busy commercial port of Bari offers architectural nuggets in its compact, labyrinthine old quarter abutting the sea, while Polignano a Mare combines accessibility to the major centers with the charm of a medieval town. For a unique excursion, drive inland to the imposing Castel del Monte, an enigmatic 13th-century octagon.

BARI

260 km (162 miles) southeast of Naples, 450 km (281 miles) southeast of Rome.

The biggest city in the region, Bari is a major port and a transit point for travelers catching ferries across the Adriatic to Greece, Croatia, and Albania. It's also a cosmopolitan city with one of the most interesting historic centers in the region. In recent years, it has become a major center of pilgrimage for Russian Orthodox visitors, due to its connection with St. Nicholas, the patron saint of Russia, as well as of Bari. The old quarter of the city, around the Basilica and the harbor Castle, is a lively maze of whitewashed alleyways buzzing with bars, cafés, restaurants, and crafts shops. Most of the modern town is set out in a logical 19th-century grid, following the designs of Joachim Murat (1767–1815), Napoléon's brother-in-law and King of the Two Sicilies. The heart is **Piazza della Libertà,** where old and young gather in the evenings to stroll up and down and see and be seen.

GETTING HERE AND AROUND

By car, take the Bari-Nord exit from the A14 autostrada. Bari's train station is a hub for Puglia-bound trains. Alitalia and Ryanair fly to Bari Airport from Rome and Milan.

VISITOR INFORMATION

Bari Tourism Office ✉ *Piazza Moro 33/a* ☎ *080/9909341, 080/5242361* ⊕ *www.viaggiareinpuglia.it.*

PUGLIA, PAST AND PRESENT

Puglia has long been inhabited, conquered, and visited. On sea voyages to their colonies and trading posts in the west, the ancient Greeks invariably headed for Puglia first—it was the shortest crossing—before filtering southward into Sicily and westward to the Tyrrhenian coast. In turn, the Romans—often bound in the opposite direction—were quick to recognize the strategic importance of the peninsula. Later centuries were to see a procession of other empires raiding or colonizing Puglia: Byzantines, Saracens, Normans, Swabians, Turks, and Spaniards all swept through, each group leaving their mark. Romanesque churches and the powerful castles built by 13th-century Holy Roman Emperor Frederick II (who also served as king of Sicily and Jerusalem) are among the most impressive of the buildings in the region. Frederick II, dubbed "Stupor Mundi" (Wonder of the World) for his wide-ranging interests in literature, science, mathematics, and nature, was one of the foremost personalities of the Middle Ages.

Recent years have brought a huge economic revival after the decades of neglect following World War II. Having benefited from EU funding, state incentive programs, and subsidies for irrigation, Puglia is now Italy's top regional producer of wine, with most of the rest of the land devoted to olives, citrus fruits, and vegetables. The main ports of Bari, Brindisi, and Taranto are thriving centers, though there remain serious problems of unemployment and poverty. However, the much-publicized arrival of thousands of asylum seekers from Eastern Europe and beyond has not significantly destabilized these cities, as had been feared, and the economic and political refugees have dispersed throughout Italy. Today, despite several years of regionwide *recessione*, an air of prosperity still wafts through the streets of Lecce, Trani, and smaller towns like Otranto and Peschici.

EXPLORING

Fodor's Choice ★ **Basilica di San Nicola.** The 11th-century Basilica di San Nicola, overlooking the sea in the *città vecchia,* houses the bones of Saint Nicholas, the inspiration for Santa Claus. His relics were stolen from Myra, in present-day Turkey, by a band of sailors from Bari and are now buried in the crypt. Because Saint Nicholas is also the patron saint of Russia, the church draws both Roman Catholic and Russian Orthodox pilgrims; souvenir shops in the area display miniatures of the Western saint and his Eastern counterpart side by side. ⊠ *Piazza San Nicola* ☎ *080/5737111* ⊕ *www.basilicasannicola.it* ⊗ *Mon.–Sat. 7 am–8:30 pm, Sun. 7 am–10 pm.*

Castello Svevo. Looming over Bari's cathedral is the huge Castello Svevo. The current building dates from the time of Holy Roman Emperor Frederick II (1194–1250), who rebuilt an existing Norman-Byzantine castle to his own exacting specifications. Designed more for power than beauty, it looks out beyond the cathedral to the small Porto Vecchio (Old Port). Inside, a haphazard collection of medieval Puglian art is frequently enlivened by changing exhibitions featuring local, national, and international artists. ✉ *Piazza Federico II di Svevia* ☎ *080/5286210* 🌐 *www.sbap-ba.beniculturali.it* 🎫 *€3* 🕘 *Thurs.–Tues. 8:30–7.*

Cattedrale di San Sabino. Bari's 12th-century cathedral is the seat of the local bishop and was the scene of many significant political marriages between important families in the Middle Ages. The cathedral is dedicated to San Sabino, a 6th-century bishop who apparently lived to be 105. The architecture reflects the Romanesque style favored by the Normans of that period. Visit the crypt with its ornate columns, polychrome marble altar, and silver-and-gold icon of Maria Santissima di Costantinopoli, also known as the Vergine Odegitria, patron of Bari along with San Nicola. ✉ *Piazza dell'Odegitria* ☎ *080/5210605* 🌐 *www.arcidiocesibaribitonto.it* 🕘 *Daily 8:30–7.*

Via Sparano. By day, you can lose yourself in the maze of white alleyways in Bari Vecchia, the old town stretching along the harbor, now humming with restaurants, cafés, and crafts shops. Residents leave their doors wide open so you catch a glimpse into the daily routine of southern Italy—matrons hand-rolling pasta with their grandchildren home from school for the midday meal, and handymen busy patching up centuries-old arches and doorways. Back in the new town, join the evening *passeggiata* (stroll) on pedestrians-only Via Sparano, then, when night falls, saunter amid the outdoor bars and restaurants in Piazza Mercantile, past Piazza Ferrarese at the end of Corso Vittorio Emanuele.

WHERE TO EAT AND STAY

$$$$ SEAFOOD 🍴 **Ristorante al Pescatore.** In the lively heart of the old town, opposite the castle and just around the corner from the cathedral, stands one of Bari's best seafood restaurants. In summer the fish is grilled outdoors, so you can enjoy the delicious aroma as you sit amid a cheerful clamor of quaffing and dining. Try the house specialty of *crudo di mare,* a platter of mixed local seafood, accompanied by a crisp salad and a carafe of uplifting Pugliese wine. Reservations are essential in July and August. [$] *Average main: €25* ✉ *Piazza Federico II di Svevia 6/8* ☎ *080/5237039.*

$$ HOTEL 🏨 **Palace Hotel.** This downtown landmark is steps away from Corso Vittorio Emanuele in the New City, but is also extremely convenient to the medieval center. **Pros:** convenient location. **Cons:** a little old-fashioned; often very busy. [$] *Rooms from: €170* ✉ *Via Lombardi 13* ☎ *080/5216551* 🌐 *www.palacehotelbari.com* 🛏 *160 rooms, 18 suites* 🍽 *Breakfast.*

TRANI

43 km (27 miles) northwest of Bari.

Trani has a harbor filled with fishing boats and a quaint old town with polished cobblestone streets and medieval churches. The town is also justly famous for its sweet dessert wine, Moscato di Trani. It's smaller than the other ports along this coast.

GETTING HERE AND AROUND

By car, take the Trani exit from the A14 autostrada. Frequent trains run from Bari.

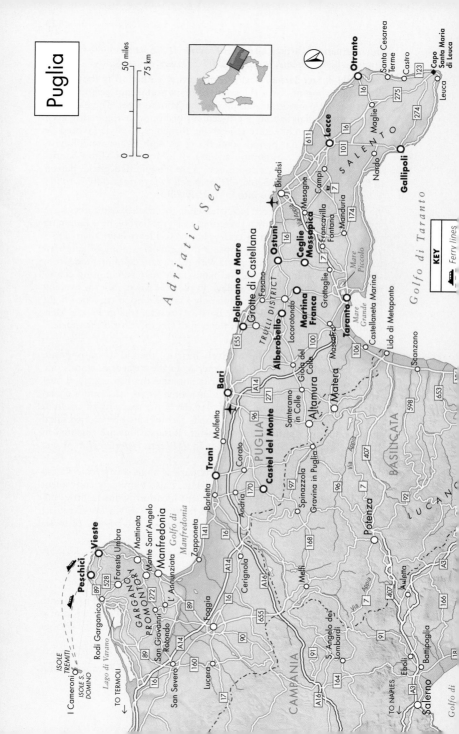

Puglia

50 miles
75 km

KEY
Ferry lines

Adriatic Sea

Otranto
Santa Cesarea Terme
Castro
123
Capo Santa Maria di Leuca
Leuca
275
274
16
Maglie
Nardò
SALENTO
611
Lecce
101
16
Gallipoli
Brindisi
Mesagne
Campi
7
Ostuni
Ceglie Messapica
Francavilla Fontana
7
Manduria
174
Grottaglie
Mare Piccolo
Polignano a Mare
Grotte di Castellana
Fasano
TRULLI DISTRICT
Alberobello
Locorotondo
Martina Franca
100
Taranto
Mare Grande
Castellaneta Marina
Lido di Metaponto
Stanzano
E55
Golfo di Taranto
Bari
A14
271
Gioia del Colle
Massafra
106
Molfetta
Santeramo in Colle
Altamura
Matera
Corato
PUGLIA
Castel del Monte
96
Trani
170
Andria
97
Spinazzola
Gravina in Puglia
96
7
Via Appia
407
BASILICATA
598
653
Barletta
141
Zapponeta
16
Cerignola
A14
A16
Melfi
168
Potenza
7
92
LUCANO
Vieste
Peschici
89
528
Foresta Umbra
Mattinata
Monte Sant'Angelo
Manfredonia
GARGANO PROMONTORY
272
L'Annunziata
San Giovanni Rotondo
Golfo di Manfredonia
89
Foggia
16
A14
655
S. Angelo dei Lombardi
91
Rodi Garganico
Lago di Varano
89
16
San Severo
Lucera
160
90
17
164
91
CAMPANIA
A16
Auletta
407
166
A3
91
92
Eboli
Battipaglia
Salerno
18
Golfo di
TO NAPLES

ISOLE TREMITI
I Cameroni
ISOLE S. DOMINO
TO TERMOLI

TO NAPLES

VISITOR INFORMATION

Trani Tourism Office ✉ *Piazza Trieste 10* ☎ *0883/588830* ⊕ *www. viaggiareinpuglia.it* ⊗ *Weekdays 9–1.*

EXPLORING

Castello. One of Federico II's most imposing fortresses, Trani Castle guarded the Adriatic sea route throughout the Middle Ages. It was the scene of several royal weddings of the Swabian and Anjou houses, as well as the place of imprisonment for life of Siffridina, Countess of Caserta, who had supported the losing Swabian dynasty against Charles I of Anjou. In the early 20th century it became a state prison and remained so until 1974. It now contains a museum. ✉ *Piazza Manfredi 16* ☎ *0883/506603* ⊕ *www.castelloditrani.beniculturali.it* 🎫 *€3* ⊗ *Daily 8–7:30.*

Cattedrale. The stunning, pinkish-white, 11th-century cathedral, considered one of the finest in Puglia, is built on a spit of land jutting into the sea. Dedicated to Saint Nicholas the Pilgrim, it was a favorite place of prayer for crusaders embarking for war in the Holy Land. Its lofty bell tower can be visited by request at the nearby Museo Diocesiano. The climb is worth it for the view. ✉ *Piazza del Duomo* ☎ *0883/582470* 🎫 *Free; bell tower €5* ⊗ *Daily 9–12:15 and 3:30–6:30.*

Via Sinagoga (*Synagogue Street*). In the 12th century, one of the largest Jewish communities in southern Italy flourished here, and on Via Sinagoga two of the four synagogues still stand. The 13th-century **Scolanova** has been reconverted to a synagogue after a long period as a Christian church, while the former **Santa Anna** now houses a museum of Trani's Jewish history.

WHERE TO STAY

$
HOTEL
🏨 **Hotel Trani.** This centrally located hotel has rooms that are pleasant, and it's efficiently and courteously run. **Pros:** close to the train station; within walking distance of the old town; off-street parking at low prices. **Cons:** rooms are a bit outdated. 💲 *Rooms from: €86* ✉ *Corso Imbriani 137* ☎ *0883/588010* ⊕ *www.hoteltrani.it* 🛏 *46 rooms* 🍽 *Breakfast.*

$$
HOTEL
🏨 **La Regia.** This small hotel-restaurant occupies the 17th-century Palazzo Filisio and is superbly positioned in front of the Duomo, in a quiet piazza by the sea. **Pros:** great restaurant; hospitable staff; most rooms have sea views. **Cons:** no parking outside hotel; area can be very busy on weekends. 💲 *Rooms from: €150* ✉ *Piazza Mons. Addazzi 2* ☎ *0883/584444* ⊕ *www.hotelregia.it* 🛏 *10 rooms* 🍽 *Breakfast.*

POLIGNANO A MARE

35 km (22 miles) southeast of Bari, 14 km (9 miles) north of Castellana.

With a well-preserved, whitewashed old town perched on limestone cliffs overlooking the Adriatic, Polignano a Mare makes an atmospheric base for exploring the surrounding area.

It leapt to fame in 2013, when the cast of the popular soap *Beautiful* descended to film some scenes on the Scalinata di Grottone, where there is also a statue of the town's most famous son, Domenico Modugno, author of the song "Volare."

GETTING HERE AND AROUND

From Bari, take the Polignano exit from the SS16. Frequent trains run from Bari.

WHERE TO STAY

$$ HOTEL Fodor's Choice ★ **Grotta Palazzese.** Carved out of a cliff opening onto the Adriatic, the Grotta Palazzese inhabits a stunning group of rocks and grottoes that have wowed onlookers for ages. **Pros:** romantic (albeit overpriced) restaurant; great location. **Cons:** a long climb down to the sea. [$] *Rooms from: €200* ✉ *Via Narciso 59* ☎ *080/4240677* 🌐 *www.grottapalazzese.it* 🛏 *18 rooms, 2 suites* 🕐 *Hotel closed late Oct.–late Apr. Restaurant also open in winter Dec.–Mar.* 🍴 *Breakfast.*

CASTEL DEL MONTE

56 km (35 miles) southwest of Bari.

The isolated Norman Castel del Monte dominates the surrounding countryside from the top of a 1,775-foot-high hill. The nearest town is Andria, 17 km (12 miles) away. Andria is largely modern with chaotic traffic—it's best avoided by taking the ring road around it.

GETTING HERE AND AROUND

Take the Andria-Barletta exit from the A14 autostrada, then follow the SS170d to Castel del Monte. From April through October there's minibus service from Piazza Bersaglieri d'Italia in Andria.

VISITOR INFORMATION

Castel del Monte Tourism Office ✉ *Via Vespucci 114, Andria* ☎ *0883/592283* 🌐 *www.proloco.andria.ba.it* 🕐 *Mon.–Sat. 10–12:30 and 5–8.*

EXPLORING

Fodor's Choice ★ **Castel del Monte.** Crowning an isolated hill 1,778 feet above sea level in the heart of the Alta Murgia national park, this enigmatic octagonal fortress, built by Frederick II in the first half of the 13th century, has puzzled historians and researchers for centuries. The rooms are arranged in a seemingly illogical sequence through eight towers around a central courtyard. Recent interpretations suggest it was an elaborate cultural center conceived by Frederick to study the various scientific disciplines of both the Western and the Arabic worlds. Umberto Eco used it as his inspiration for the riddles in *The Name of the Rose.* It's worth hiring the services of one of the authorized tour guides here to get a deeper insight into the mysteries of this unique monument. Note that if coming by car between April and September you have to park in designated areas about a mile away, and then take a shuttle bus. ✉ *On signposted minor road, 18 km (11 miles) south of Andria* ☎ *0883/569997, 0883/592283 for tour reservations* 🌐 *www.casteldelmonte.beniculturali.it* 🎫 *€5* 🕐 *Apr.–Sept., daily 9–7.30; Oct.–Mar., daily 10:30–6:30. Last entrance ½ hr before closing.*

WHERE TO EAT

$ SOUTHERN ITALIAN ✕ **Taverna Sforza Castel Del Monte.** The Taverna Sforza has been catering to visitors to the isolated Castel del Monte since 1910. Lying at the foot of the hill just below the castle, it has a garden for alfresco dining in summer and a cheery hostelry-type interior with an open fire in winter. Specialties include *maccheroni all'origano, zuppa di fagioli* (borlotti bean soup), and *pollo rosolato al burro* (chicken grilled in butter) served with vegetables from the Taverna's own garden. The restaurant also acts as a cafeteria, wine cellar, and bookshop, and organizes cooking classes of regional dishes in summer. $ *Average main: €12* ⊠ *Castel del Monte SS170, Andria* ☎ *0883/569996* ⊕ *www.tavernasforza.it.*

THE GARGANO PROMONTORY

Forming the spur of Italy's boot, the Gargano Promontory (Promontorio del Gargano) is a striking contrast to the Adriatic's flatter coastline. This is a land of whitewashed coastal towns, wide sandy beaches interspersed with secluded coves, and craggy limestone cliffs topped by deep-green pine and scrubby Mediterranean *maquis* (underbrush). Not surprisingly, it pulls in the crowds in July and August, driving up the prices considerably. Camping is almost always an option, as plentiful and pretty campgrounds dot the Gargano's curvy, cliff-hugging roads. The beaches and the Foresta Umbra national park are great places for kids to let off steam.

14

VIESTE

93 km (58 miles) northeast of Foggia, 179 km (111 miles) northwest of Bari.

This large, whitewashed town jutting off the tip of the spur of Italy's boot is an attractive place to wander around. Though curvy mountain roads render it slightly less accessible from the autostrade and mainline rail stations than, say, Peschici and Mattinata, the range of accommodations (including camping) makes it a useful base for exploring Gargano. The resort attracts legions of tourists in summer, some bound for the Isole Tremiti, a tiny archipelago connected to Vieste by regular ferries.

GETTING HERE AND AROUND

If you're driving from Foggia, take the winding SS89. Regular buses leave from Foggia's train station.

WHERE TO EAT AND STAY

$ ✕ **La Teresina.** At this family-run trattoria at the entrance to Viestre's SOUTHERN centro storico, Nicola and Libera Palumbo serve homey Pugliese dishes ITALIAN such as bean soup with *cavatelle*, the classic orecchiette cima di rape, and a substantial fish soup, made with the best catch of the day. The dining room walls and ceiling are covered with an array of traditional pottery plates, jugs, and amphorae from the nearby ceramic town of Grottaglia. In summer, you can eat outside in the small adjoining courtyard. $ *Average main: €12* ⊠ *Via Cesare Battisti 55* ☎ *0884/701773.*

$ ▦ **Palace Hotel Vieste.** Converted from a 17th-century aristocratic resi-HOTEL dence, the Palace Hotel is next to the Vieste fishing harbor and is a short walk from the historic center. **Pros:** convenient location; pleasant staff. **Cons:** only the suites have balconies; some rooms look onto the surrounding back streets. $ *Rooms from: €110* ⊠ *Via Santa Maria di Merino* ☎ *0884/701218* ⊕ *www.palacehotelvieste.it* ⇥ *39 rooms, 9 suites* ⏹ *Breakfast.*

PESCHICI

22 km (14 miles) northwest of Vieste, 199 km (124 miles) northwest of Bari.

Peschici is a pleasant resort on Gargano's north shore, a cascade of whitewashed houses and streets with a beautiful view over a sweeping cove. Some surrounding areas are particularly popular with campers from northern Europe. Development has not wreaked too much havoc on the town: the mazelike center retains its characteristic low houses topped with little Byzantine cupolas.

GETTING HERE

From Foggia, take the winding S89 road. Regular buses leave from Foggia's train station. Seasonal ferry service leaves from the Trémiti archipelago between June and September.

THE TRULLI DISTRICT

The inland area to the southeast of Bari is one of Italy's oddest enclaves, mostly flat terrain given over to olive cultivation and interspersed with the idiosyncratic habitations that have lent their names to the district. Looking like igloos constructed out of pure stone, the beehive-shape trulli have origins that hark to the 15th century and maybe further. The trulli, found nowhere else in the world, are built of local limestone, without mortar, and with a hole in the top for escaping smoke. Some are painted with mystical or religious symbols, some are isolated, and others are joined together with common roofs. Legends of varying credibility surround the trulli—for example, that they were originally built so that residents could quickly take apart their homes when the tax collectors came by. The center of Trulli Country is Alberobello in the enchanting Valle d'Itria: it has the greatest concentration of buildings. You'll spot them all over this region, some in the middle of desolate fields, and many in disrepair, but always adding a quirky charm to the landscape.

ALBEROBELLO

59 km (37 miles) southeast of Bari, 45 km (28 miles) north of Taranto.

A well-established international tourist destination, Alberobello's amalgamation of more than 1,000 trulli huddled together along steep, narrow streets is a unique and striking phenomenon that has been designated a UNESCO World Heritage Site. As one of the most popular destinations in Puglia, Alberobello has spawned some excellent restaurants (and some not-so-excellent trinket shops).

GETTING HERE AND AROUND

By car, take the Monopoli exit from the SS16, follow the SP237 to Putignano, then SS172 to Alberobello. Trains run hourly from Bari.

VISITOR INFORMATION

Alberobello Tourism Office ⊠ *Via Monte Nero 3* ☎ *080/4322822* ⊕ *www.viaggiareinpuglia.it* ☉ *Summer, daily 9–1 and 4–8.*

EXPLORING

Alberobello–Martina Franca road. The trulli in Alberobello itself are impressive, but the most beautiful concentration of conical trulli is along a stretch of about 15 km (9 miles) on the SS172 Alberobello–Martina Franca road that runs through the tranquil Valle D'Itria. Stop to visit some of the wine farms and oil-pressing mills, surrounded by vast groves of ancient gnarled olive trees. Many here operate on an open-door policy and welcome visitors.

Trullo Sovrano. Alberobello's largest trullo, the 18th-century Trullo Sovrano, is up the hill through the trulli zone (head up Corso Vittorio Emanuele past the obelisk and the basilica). Although this house originally belonged to a wealthy family, it has been furnished in the traditional style of the trullo dwellings to give visitors an insight into living conditions in these unique beehive constructions. Guided tours are included in the entrance price. ✉ *Piazza Sacramento 10* 🌐 *www.alberobellonline.it* 🎟 *€1.50* 🕒 *Daily 10–1:30 and 3:30–7:30.*

WHERE TO EAT AND STAY

$$$ SOUTHERN ITALIAN

🍴 **Il Poeta Contadino.** This is really two establishments under the same management, standing side by side on the main road leading into Alberobello from the SS172. The more upmarket **Poeta Contadino** specializes in regional cooking with a creative twist, while the **Osteria del Poeta** offers traditional dishes at budget prices. The refined, understated dining room of the Poeta Contadino ("Peasant Poet") features candles casting shadows on the ancient stone walls. Dishes might include *triglie con vinaigrette alla menta* (red mullet with a mint vinaigrette) or *filetto di maiale in crosta di erbe con salsa agrodolce* (herb-crusted pork fillet with a sweet-and-sour sauce). In season, try anything with white truffles. [$] *Average main: €25* ✉ *Via Indipendenza 21–27* ☎ *080/4321917* 🌐 *www.ilpoetacontadino.it* ✍ *Reservations essential* 🕒 *Closed Jan.*

$$$ SOUTHERN ITALIAN Fodor's Choice ★

🍴 **L'Aratro.** This welcoming rustic restaurant set inside adjoining trulli has dark-wood beams, whitewashed walls, and an outdoor patio for summer dining. The *antipasti misti* could stand as a meal in itself, but leave room for country-style dishes using lamb and veal. Among the seasonal specialties are *cavatellucci di terra madre* (tomatoes, onions, and *capocollo*—a cured meat—on a bed of fava beans) and roast lamb with *lampasciuni* (a type of wild onion). This is a certified Slow Food restaurant, serving traditional meals using local produce. [$] *Average main: €25* ✉ *Via Monte San Michele 25–29* ☎ *080/4322789* 🌐 *www.ristorantearatro.it* ✍ *Reservations essential.*

$$$ HOTEL

🏨 **Le Alcove.** If you are of a romantic bent, you will welcome this chance to stay in a proper trullo, one of these unusual, conical, whitewashed dwellings for which Alberobello is famous. **Pros:** centrally located near the Trullo Sovrano; quaint, unusual accommodation. **Cons:** rooms are rather small and some have narrow metal staircases leading to the upper area; a few rooms are not in the main building but across the road. [$] *Rooms from: €270* ✉ *Piazza Ferdinando IV 7* ☎ *080/4323754* 🌐 *www.lealcove.it* 🛏 *9 suites* 🍽 *Breakfast.*

OSTUNI

50 km (30 miles) west of Brindisi, 85 km (53 miles) southeast of Bari.

This sun-bleached medieval town lies on three hills not far from the coast. From a distance, Ostuni is a jumble of blazingly white houses and churches spilling over a hilltop and overlooking the sea. Don't be surprised if you hear a lot of English and German spoken in the cobbled streets. The White City, as it is called, has cast its spell on a large number of British and German nationals, who have bought second homes here. That doesn't mean that the town has lost its natural native flavor. Religious festivals, fairs, and colorful traditional events are held as always with the same enthusiasm and fervor.

GETTING HERE AND AROUND

By car, take the Ostuni exit from the SS16. Trenitalia (Italy's national railway) runs frequent trains from Bari. The station, however, is 3 miles (5 km) from the town—there is an almost-hourly local bus service.

VISITOR INFORMATION

Ostuni Tourism Office ✉ *Corso Mazzini 6* ☎ *0831/307219.*

EXPLORING

Ostuni Old Town. Known as "the White City" because of its dazzling white buildings and cobbled streets, Ostuni commands stupendous views out over the coast and the surrounding plain. Its unpolluted sea and clean beaches have earned it international "Blue Flag" recognition ever since 2008. The surrounding countryside contains a number of interesting 17th- and18th-century *masserie* (fortified farms), many of which are now converted into *agriturismi* (farmhouse B&Bs). 🌐 *www.viaggiareinpuglia.it.*

Piazza Libertà. The city's main square divides the new town to the west and the old town to the east. The triangular piazza contains the town symbol: the towering Guglio di Sant'Oronzo (the Spire of Saint Oronzo), the patron saint of Ostuni, in whose honor an elaborate festival is held every year in late August. 🌐 *www.viaggiareinpuglia.it.*

WHERE TO EAT AND STAY

$$ SOUTHERN ITALIAN 🍴 **Osteria del Tempo Perso.** Buried in the side streets of the old town, this laid-back restaurant occupies an actual cave, where ancient rough-hewn stone walls contrast with the elegant table settings; a second room has a plethora of intriguing objects adorning white walls. Service is friendly, and dishes focus on local cuisine, such as delectable eggplant Parmesan, *raganari ai funghi carboncelli* (special local pasta with fresh mushrooms) and fava-bean soup. For dessert enjoy the quaintly named *sporcamuso* (literally "dirty face"), a delicate pastry and cream concoction. [$] *Average main: €16* ✉ *Via G. Tanzarella Vitale 47* ☎ *0831/304819* 🌐 *www.osteriadeltempoperso.com* ⏲ *Closed Mon.*

$$ HOTEL 🏨 **Relais Sant'Egidio, Ostuni.** Nestled in the valley just below Ostuni and surrounded by venerable olive trees, the Relais Sant'Egidio is a stylish adaptation of a 16th-century building. **Pros:** pleasant and modern environment with touches of old-world charm. **Cons:** outside the city walls and short walk uphill to the old center of Ostuni. [$] *Rooms from: €190* ✉ *Via Giosuè Pinto 48/50* ☎ *0831/1985171* 🌐 *www.santeligiorelais.it* 🛏 *22 rooms* 🍽 *No meals.*

CEGLIE MESSAPICA

11 km (7 miles) southwest of Ostuni, 18 km (11 miles) southwest of Martina Franca.

With its 14th-century Piazza Vecchia, tattered Baroque balconies, and lordly medieval castles, the little whitewashed town of Ceglie Messapica is a jewel and the epitome of everyone's notion of the sleepy southern Italian town. Situated at the center of the triangle formed by Taranto, Brindisi, and Fasano, the town was once the military capital of the region, and often defended itself against invasions from the Taranto city-state, which wanted to clear a route to the Adriatic. Nowadays, Ceglie Messapica is a gourmet capital, with a surprising number of excellent restaurants.

GETTING HERE AND AROUND

By car, take the Ostuni exit from the SS16, and follow SP22 to Ceglie Messapica. Ferrovie del Sud-Est runs frequent trains from Bari.

VISITOR INFORMATION

Ceglie Messapica Tourism Office ✉ *Via G. Elia 16, Ceglie Messapica* ☎ *0831/371003* 🌐 *www.viaggiareinpuglia.it/hp/en.*

WHERE TO EAT

$$ SOUTHERN ITALIAN Fodor's Choice ★

🍴 **Al Fornello Da Ricci.** Any respectable culinary tour of Puglia must pass through this elegant dining room in the whitewashed town of Ceglie Messapica. The distinguished kitchen sends out a long succession of antipasti, all of them inspired by ancient Pugliese traditions—meats, cheeses, perhaps fried zucchini flowers stuffed with fresh goat's milk ricotta. Afterwards you can try goat's milk ice cream with mixed berries. [$] *Average main: €18* ✉ *Contrada Montevicoli* ☎ *0831/377104* ✍ *Reservations essential* 🕒 *Closed Tues. No lunch Oct.–Apr.*

$$ SOUTHERN ITALIAN

🍴 **Cibus.** Amid the vaulted stone archways of this simple but highy acclaimed *osteria* (tavernlike restaurant) in the old city sit rows of bottles and books devoted to the worship of food and wine. It's no wonder, then, that the food is so good: after an *antipasto del territorio* (sampling of local meats, cheeses, and other delights) you could try stuffed eggplant or a selection of roast meats. To finish off, there are some unusual desserts. Ask owner Angelo Silibello to show you his impressive cheese larder carved out of the stone walls, where he personally controls the maturing process, or his wine cellar, stocked with the best of Pugliese and Italian wines. [$] *Average main: €16* ✉ *Via Chianche di Scarano* ☎ *0831/388980* 🌐 *www.ristorantecibus.it* 🕒 *Closed Tues., and last wk in June–1st wk in July.*

MARTINA FRANCA

29 km (18 miles) west of Ostuni, 36 km (22 miles) north of Taranto.

Martina Franca is a beguiling town with a dazzling mixture of medieval and Baroque architecture in the light-color local stone. Ornate balconies hang above the twisting, narrow streets, with little alleys leading off into the hills. Martina Franca was developed as a military stronghold in the 14th century, when a surrounding wall with 24 towers was built, but now all that remains of the wall are the four gates that had once been the only entrances to the town. Each July, the town holds the Valle D'Itria music festival (🌐 *www.festivaldellavalleditria.it*).

GETTING HERE AND AROUND

By car, take the Fasano exit from the SS16, then follow the SS172. The Ferrovie Sud-Est runs frequent trains from Bari and Taranto.

VISITOR INFORMATION

Martina Franca Tourism Office ✉ *Piazza XX Settembre 3* ☎ *080/4805702* 🌐 *www.viaggiareinpuglia.it*.

WHERE TO EAT

$ SOUTHERN ITALIAN 🍴 **Ristorante Sagittario.** Just outside the historical center, in Martina Franca's new town, this restaurant is a favorite with locals. The homemade pastas and pizzas are delicious, but it's the excellent grilled meats and the porcini mushroom dishes that keep people coming back for more. The atmosphere is warm and convivial but it can be noisy and crowded, as it is so popular with Italian families and groups, especially as the prices offer excellent value for money. [$] *Average main: €12* ✉ *Via Quarto 15* ☎ *080/4858982*.

WORD OF MOUTH

"We fell in love with Puglia. The Adriatic is so beautiful, the people so friendly (and curious, as there aren't a lot of Americans that travel there), and it is unspoiled. It has a very different 'look' than other parts of Italy we have seen because they have been invaded so many times. The people are taller and more angular, and while I have never been to Greece, it is a bit of what I imagine Greece would be like." —travel52

THE SALENTO PENINSULA

This far south, the mountains run out of steam and the land is uniformly flat. The monotony of endless olive trees is redeemed by the region's most dramatic coastline, with sandstone cliffs falling fast toward the sea. Here you can find a handful of small, alluring fishing towns, such as Otranto and Gallipoli. Taranto and Brindisi don't quite fit this description: both are big ports, where historical importance is obscured by heavy industry. Nonetheless, Taranto has its archaeological museum, and Brindisi, an important ferry jumping-off point, marks the end of the Via Appia (the "Queen of Roads" built by the Romans). Farther south, Salento (the Salentine Peninsula) is the local name for the part of Puglia that forms the end of the heel. Lecce is an unexpected oasis of grace and sophistication, and its swirling architecture will melt even the most uncompromising critic of the Baroque.

TARANTO

100 km (62 miles) southeast of Bari, 40 km (25 miles) south of Martina Franca.

Taranto (the stress is on the first syllable) was an important port even in Greek times, and it's still Italy's largest naval base. It lies toward the back of the instep of the boot on the broad Mare Grande bay, which is connected to a small internal Mare Piccolo basin by two narrow channels, one artificial and one natural. The old town is a series of palazzi in varying states of decay and narrow cobblestone streets on an island between the larger and smaller bodies of water, linked by causeways; the modern city stretches inward along the mainland. Circumnavigating the city can be quite tricky, with a confusing series of flyovers and junctions. Take it as slowly as you can and follow the signs for the *centro storico* (city center) where the main sights are situated.

GETTING HERE AND AROUND

By car, the A14 autostrada takes you almost directly to Taranto. Trenitalia runs frequent trains from Bari and Brindisi.

VISITOR INFORMATION

Taranto Tourism Office ⊠ *Castello Aragonese* ☎ *334/2844098* ⊕ *www.viaggiareinpuglia.it* ⊙ *Summer, daily 9:30 am–10 pm; winter, Mon.–Sat. 9:30–3, Sun. 10–1.*

EXPLORING

Museo Nazionale. After a long labor of restructuring, Taranto's National Archaeological Museum ("the MarTa") has reopened in its former seat, the historic premises of the ex-monastery of San Pasquale. The museum dates from 1887 and its collection of Greek and Roman antiquities is considered to be one of the most important in Italy. Many artifacts were discovered in the vicinity, testifying to the city's centuries-old importance as a port. Admire the rich cache of tomb goods, including magnificent gold jewelry, polychrome terra-cottas, objects in ivory and bone, and rare colored glass. A display of Jewish, Christian, and Muslim funeral epitaphs, dating between the 4th and 11th centuries, demonstrate the peaceful coexistence of the three religions in this multicultural Mediterranean hub from the Byzantine era to the Middle Ages. ⊠ *Via Cavour 10* ☎ *099/4532112* ⊕ *www.museotaranto.org* ☑ *€6.50* ⊙ *Daily 8:30–7:30; last entrance at 7.*

San Domenico. Taranto's most important monument is the ancient church and monastery of San Domenico in the heart of the centro storico. Situated on the narrow strip of land that divides Taranto's two bays, Mare Piccolo and Mare Grande, the present church dates from the mid-14th century, and was once used by the Templars during the Middle Ages. It has origins that go back to the Byzantine period and, before that, to Magna Grecia. Enjoy a quiet stroll under the colonnaded corridors of the peaceful old cloister. ⊠ *Via Duomo 33* ☎ *099/4707733* ☑ *Free* ⊙ *Daily 9–noon and 6:30–7.*

LECCE

Fodor'sChoice ★ *40 km (25 miles) southeast of Brindisi, 87 km (54 miles) east of Taranto.*

Lecce is the crown jewel of the Mezzogiorno. The city is called "the Florence of the south," but that term doesn't do justice to Lecce's uniqueness in the Italian landscape. Though its pretty boutiques, lively bars, bustling streets, laid-back student cafés, and evening passeggiata draw comparisons to the cultural capitals of the north, Lecce's impossibly intricate Baroque architecture and its hyperanimated crowds are distinctively southern. The city is a cosmopolitan oasis two steps from the idyllic Otranto–Brindisi coastline and a hop from the olive-grove countryside of Puglia. Relatively undiscovered by foreign tourists, Lecce exudes an optimism and youthful joie de vivre unparalleled in any other Baroque showcase.

Summer is a great time to visit. In July courtyards and piazzas throughout the city are the settings for dramatic productions. Autumn has its charms as well. A Baroque music festival is held in churches throughout the city in September and October.

GETTING HERE AND AROUND

By car from Bari, take the main toll-free coast road via Brindisi and continue along the SS613 to Lecce. Frequent trains run along the coast from Bari and beyond. The closest airport is in Brindisi.

VISITOR INFORMATION

Lecce Tourism Office ⊠ *Corso Vittorio Emanuele 16* ☎ *0832/682985* ⊕ *www.ilecce.it* ⊗ *Daily 9–6.*

EXPLORING

Duomo. Lecce's magnificent Duomo of Santa Maria Assunta never fails to take visitors by surprise. The sheer theatricality of its position, dominating a vast open square concealed in a maze of pedestrianized alleyways, embodies the very spirit of Baroque architecture. The aim was to stun the faithful with a vision of opulence and power; even today it leaves viewers openmouthed, especially at night when the entire piazza is illuminated like a stage set. The 17th-century church, constructed in rose-tinged local stone, is flanked by the ornate Bishops' Palace, the seminary, and the 236-foot-high bell tower, which dominates the Old City skyline. ⊠ *Piazza del Duomo, off Corso Vittorio Emanuele* ☎ *0832/332699* ⊕ *www.cattedraledilecce.it* ⊗ *Daily 8:30–12:30 and 4–7.*

Piazza Sant'Oronzo. This is the hub of Lecce's social life in the heart of the maze of pedestrianized alleyways lined with cafés, little restaurants, and crafts shops. Named after Oronzo, the city's patron saint, who crowns a Roman column that once marked the end of the Via Appia Antica, the piazza is also occupied by another city symbol, the somewhat odd-looking 17th-century Sedile, formerly the town hall but now an art and exhibition center. The piazza revolves round the sunken hemicycle of the old **Anfiteatro Romano,** where the rows of seats are clearly visible.

Fodor's Choice
★

Santa Croce. Although Lecce was founded before the time of the ancient Greeks, it's often associated with the term *Barocco leccese,* the result of a citywide impulse in the 17th century to redo the town in an exuberant fashion. But this was Baroque with a difference. Such architecture is often heavy and monumental, but here it took on a lighter, more fanciful air, and the church of Santa Croce is a fine example, along with the adjoining **Palazzo della Prefettura.** The facade is a riot of sculptures of saints, angels, leaves, vines, and columns, all in local, glowing, honey-color stone, creating an overall lighthearted effect. ⊠ *Via Umberto I 3* ☎ *0832/241957* ⊕ *www.basilicasantacroce.eu* ⊗ *Daily 9–noon and 5–7.*

WHERE TO EAT

$$
SOUTHERN
ITALIAN

✕ **Alle Due Corti.** Renowned local culinary expert Rosalba De Carlo runs this traditional trattoria, where the long tradition and culture of Salentine cuisine is treated with both respect and originality. The menu is printed in the Leccese dialect; the adventurous can try country dishes like *pezzetti te cavallu* (spicy horse meat in tomato sauce) or *turcineddhi* (roasted baby goat entrails)—a crisp, fully flavored delight. The white-wall interior is stark, but character comes from the red-and-white checked tablecloths and the gregarious local families and groups of friends that inevitably fill the place. [$] *Average main: €16* ✉ *Corte dei Giugni 1* ☎ *0832/242223* 🌐 *www.alleduecorti.com* 🕒 *Closed Sun., and Jan.*

$$ SOUTHERN ITALIAN 🍴 **Corte dei Pandolfi.** Here you can choose from a vast list of Salento's best wines and feast on an unparalleled spread of artisanal *salumi* (cured meats) and local cheeses, accompanied by delicious local honey and *mostarda* (preserved fruit). Traditional *primi* (first courses) and *secondi* (second courses) are also served, as well as vegetarian specialties, with the menu changing with the season's fresh produce—fresh fish is a staple in the summer months. The location is in the pedestrianized centro storico in a little piazza beside the Museo del Teatro Romano, just a few yards away from the Duomo. [$] *Average main: €18* ✉ *Piazzetta Orsini* ☎ *0832/332309* 🌐 *www.cortedeipandolfi.com* 🕒 *Closed Nov. and mid-Dec.*

$ SOUTHERN ITALIAN 🍴 **Le Zie.** This tiny unpretentious trattoria is a great favorite with the local families and it is often crowded. Though situated in the modern city off a busy thoroughfare, it can be quite hard to locate. The food is exclusively Pugliese home cooking and the menu changes daily. Some specialties of the house include *tajeddra con cozze* (a special kind of pasta with mussels) or *polipo in teglia* (stewed octopus), as well as the ubiquitous rustic *purè di fave e cicoria* (bean purée with wild chicory). This is strictly a place for those who want to experience no-frills genuine local color. [$] *Average main: €12* ✉ *Via Costadura 19* ☎ *0832/245178* 🌐 *www.lezie.it* 🕒 *Closed Mon., 1 wk at Easter, last wk in Aug.–1st wk in Sept. No dinner Sun.*

WHERE TO STAY

$$ HOTEL Fodor's Choice ★ 🏨 **Patria Palace.** It's a happy coincidence that the best hotel in Lecce happens to be in one of the best possible locations: right in front of the monumental Santa Croce Basilica, the crown jewel of Lecce Baroque. **Pros:** luxurious rooms; ideal location. **Cons:** a few rooms overlook the back streets. [$] *Rooms from: €150* ✉ *Piazzetta Riccardi 13* ☎ *0832/245111* 🌐 *www.patriapalacelecce.com* 🛏 *63 rooms, 4 suites* 🍽 *Breakfast.*

$$$ HOTEL 🏨 **President.** Rub elbows with visiting dignitaries at this business hotel and conference center near Piazza Mazzini. **Pros:** comfortable rooms; convenient location; low-season bargains. **Cons:** more for business than pleasure; a bit dated. [$] *Rooms from: €220* ✉ *Via Salandra 6* ☎ *0832/456111* 🌐 *www.hotelpresidentlecce.it* 🛏 *144 rooms, 6 suites* 🍽 *Breakfast.*

$$ HOTEL 🏨 **Risorgimento Resort Lecce.** Despite the fact that this elegant hotel in the heart of the centro storico of Lecce has been a landmark in town since 1880, it is bang in the 21st century, with a clean modern décor and vibrant modern color schemes. **Pros:** convenient location; highly professional staff. **Cons:** smart, international-style business hotel without much local atmosphere. [$] *Rooms from: €150* ✉ *Via Augustus Imperatore 19* ☎ *0832/246311* 🌐 *www.risorgimentoresort.it* 🛏 *41 rooms, 6 suites* 🍽 *Breakfast.*

14

OTRANTO

36 km (22 miles) southeast of Lecce, 188 km (117 miles) southeast of Bari.

In one of the first great Gothic novels, Horace Walpole's 1764 *The Castle of Otranto,* the English writer immortalized this city and its mysterious medieval fortress. Otranto (the stress is on the first syllable) has had more than its share of dark thrills. As the easternmost point in Italy—and therefore closest to the Balkan Peninsula—it's often borne the brunt of foreign invasions, including the massacre of 800 citizens by the Moors in 1480 because they refused to give up their faith. From here, you can see across the sea to Albania on a clear day. If you are a fan of the Neolithic, you will be interested in the Grotta dei Cervi, a few miles down the coast. The walls of the cave are covered with hundreds of prehistoric images, painted with red ochre and black bat guano.

GETTING HERE AND AROUND

By car from Lecce, take the southbound SS16 and exit at Maglie. To follow the coast, take the SS53 from Lecce, then follow SS611 south. There's regular train service from Lecce on Ferrovie del Sud-Est.

VISITOR INFORMATION

Otranto Tourism Office ⌧ *Via del Porto* ☎ *0836/801436* ⊕ *www.comune.otranto.le.it* ⊗ *Summer, daily 9–8; Nov.–Mar., Thurs. 9–1 and 3–6.*

EXPLORING

Castello Aragonese. The massive Aragonese Castle is considered a masterpiece of 16th-century military architecture. Rebuilt by the Spanish viceroy Don Pedro di Toledo in 1535 after it was badly damaged in the siege of Otranto (1480) when the invading Turkish armies destroyed the city, its impressive walls and bastions dominate the port and seashore. ⌧ *Piazza Castello* ☎ *0836/801436* 🖭 *€5 (€6 during a special exhibition)* ⊗ *Summer, daily 10 am–midnight; winter, daily 10–6.*

Cattedrale. The best sight in Otranto is the Cattedrale, Santa Maria Annunziata, consecrated in 1088. The 12th-century Pantaleone mosaic, which covers the entire length of the nave, the sanctuary, and apse, depicts scenes from the Old Testament along with traditional medieval chivalric tales and animals, set alongside a Tree of Life. The walls behind the main altar are lined with glass cases containing the skulls and tibias of the 800 martyrs of Otranto, slain by the Ottomans after the siege of 1480 because they refused to renounce their faith. ⌧ *Piazza Basilica* ☎ *0836/801436* ⊕ *www.comune.otranto.le.it* ⊗ *Daily 9–noon and 3–6; summer, daily 8–noon and 3–7.*

WHERE TO STAY

$$$

HOTEL

Corte di Nettuno. From the wrought-iron gates in the shape of waves, to the statue of the sea god Neptune greeting you at the entrance, a nautical theme prevails throughout the Corte di Nettuno. **Pros:** good location near the marina and sights. **Cons:** some people may find the sea theme a bit overdone. 🖆 *Rooms from: €210* ⌧ *Via Madonna del Passo* ☎ *0836/801832* ⊕ *www.cortedinettuno.it* 🛏 *28 rooms* ⊗ *Closed Nov.–Mar.* ⚏ *Breakfast.*

$$ B&B/INN Fodor's Choice ★ **Masseria Montelauro.** Beautifully restored, with stylish designer interiors, this interesting 19th-century former *masseria* (traditional farmhouse for communal living) is an oasis of comfort just a short drive from lovely Otranto. **Pros:** interesting building; lovely interior; friendly, helpful service; great food. **Cons:** car is absolutely necessary; food is pricey. [$] *Rooms from: €180* ✉ *S.P. Otranto–Uggiano, Località Montelauro* ☎ *0836/806203* 🌐 *www.masseriamontelauro.it* 🛏 *26 rooms, 3 suites* 🕑 *Closed Nov.–Apr.* 🍴 *Breakfast.*

GALLIPOLI

37 km (23 miles) south of Lecce, 190 km (118 miles) southeast of Bari.

The fishing port of Gallipoli, on the eastern tip of the Golfo di Taranto, is divided between a new town, on the mainland, and a beautiful fortified town, across a 17th-century bridge, crowded onto its own small island in the gulf. The Greeks called it Kallipolis ("the fair city"), the Romans Anxa. Like the infamous Turkish town of the same name on the Dardanelles, the Italian Gallipoli occupies a strategic location and thus was repeatedly attacked through the centuries—by the Normans in 1071, the Venetians in 1484, and the British in 1809. Today life in Gallipoli revolves around its fishing trade. Fishing boats in primary colors breeze in and out of the bay during the day, and Gallipoli's fish market, below the bridge, throbs with activity all morning.

GETTING HERE AND AROUND

From Lecce, take the SS101. From Taranto, follow the coastal SS174. Frequent trains run from Lecce.

VISITOR INFORMATION

Gallipoli Tourism Office ✉ *Via Kennedy* ☎ *0833/263007* 🌐 *www.prolocogallipoli.it* 🕑 *Summer, daily 8–1 and 4–9; winter, Mon.–Sat. 9–1 and 3:30–7:30.*

EXPLORING

FAMILY **Beaches.** Ample swimming and clean, fine sand make Gallipoli's beaches a good choice for families. The 5-km (3-mile) expanse of sand sweeping south from town has both public and private beaches, the latter equipped with changing rooms, sun beds, and umbrellas. Water-sports equipment can be bought or rented at the waterfront shops in town.

Castello Aragonese. The massive bulk of Gallipoli's castle guards the entrance to the island of the old city, which is linked to the new town by a bridge. Rising out of the sea, the present fortress, dating from the 17th to 18th centuries, is built on the foundations of an earlier Byzantine citadel. It has four towers, and a separate fifth one, known as the Rivellino, where open-air shows are held in summer. ✉ *Gallipoli* 🌐 *www.castellogallipoli.it* 🎫 *€5* 🕑 *Summer, daily 10 am–midnight; winter, daily 10–10.*

Duomo. In the center of the old city, Gallipoli's Duomo is a notable Baroque cathedral from the late 17th century. Built in local limestone, the ornate facade is matched by an equally elaborate interior with columns and altars in fine polychrome marble and paintings by leading local Gallipoli and Neapolitan *maestri* of the time. Particularly interesting are the stone carvings that depict episodes from the city's history. ✉ *Via Antonietta de Pace* ☎ *0833/263007* 🌐 *www.cattedralegallipoli.it* 🕒 *Daily 9–8.*

La Purità. A fine example of *gallipolino* Baroque, the 17th-century Church of Santa Maria della Purità stands at the end of the old town overlooking the famed Purità beach. It contains a wealth of works of art, including the painting at the high altar by Luca Giordano, intricately carved wooden choir stalls, and a 19th-century majolica pavement. ✉ *Riviera Nazario Sauro* ☎ *0833/261699.*

WHERE TO EAT AND STAY

$$$ SEAFOOD 🍴 **Marechiaro.** For more than a century, this historic seafood restaurant in the shadow of Gallipoli's Aragonese Castle has been serving diners. Built on wooden piles, it seems to float like a ship anchored in the bay by the bridge that connects Gallipoli new town with the island that contains the old *borgo*. Its flower-filled terrace has outdoor tables in summer. In winter, eat inside and enjoy the same view through the panoramic windows. Try the renowned *zuppa di pesce alla gallipolina* (a stew of fish, local red shrimp, clams, and mussels) and the local gamberoni. To finish up, you can enjoy the melt-in-your-mouth homemade profiteroles. [$] *Average main: €30* ✉ *Lungomare Marconi* ☎ *0833/266143.*

$$$ HOTEL 🏨 **Relais Corte Palmieri.** An 18th-century aristocratic house in the center of Gallipoli's *borgo antico* (old town) and a short distance from the Purità beach, the Relais Corte Palmieri has been tastefully renovated to modern standards, while preserving its characteristic frescoes and mosaics. **Pros:** quiet elegance right in the heart of the historic center. **Cons:** difficult to get to with own transportation. [$] *Rooms from: €250* ✉ *Corte Palmieri 3* ☎ *0833/266814* 🌐 *www.relaiscortepalmieri.it* 🛏 *20 rooms* 🕒 *Closed late Oct.–late Mar.* 🍽 *Breakfast.*

BASILICATA

Occupying the instep of Italy's boot, Basilicata formed part of Magna Graecia, the loose collection of colonies founded along the coast of southern Italy whose wealth and military prowess rivaled those of the city-states of Greece itself. More recently it was made famous by Carlo Levi (1902–75) in his *Christ Stopped at Eboli*, a book that underscored the poverty of the region. (The title comes from a local saying that implied that progress had stopped at Eboli, some 60 miles to the west, near the coast, and that Bascilicata had "been bypassed by Christianity, by morality, by history itself—that they have somehow been excluded from the full human experience.")

Basilicata is no longer desolate, as it draws travelers in search of bucolic settings, great food, and archaeological treasures. The city of Matera, the region's true highlight, is built on the side of an impressive ravine that's honeycombed with Sassi, some of them still occupied, forming a separate enclave that contrasts vividly with the attractive Baroque town above.

MATERA

62 km (39 miles) south of Bari.

Matera, the town of the unique Sassi, is one of the most intriguing places in southern Italy. The so-called "New Town," full of elegant Baroque churches, palazzi, and broad piazzas—filled to bursting during the evening passeggiata, is perched on the verge of a steep gully crowded with the cave dwellings of the past, now converted into hotels, restaurants and private homes. Many of the ancient rock churches can be visited. This is a particularly good time to visit as Matera has been elected European Cultural Capital for 2019 and already preparations are underway, with all kinds of initiatives and programs being launched.

14

GETTING HERE AND AROUND

From Bari, take the SS96 to Altamura, then the SS99 to Matera. Roughly one train per hour (Ferrovie Appulo Lucane) leaves Bari Centrale for Matera.

VISITOR INFORMATION

Info Point Matera (Tourism Office) ⊠ *Via Ridola 67* ☎ *0835/311655* ⊙ *Summer, daily 10–7; winter, daily 10–1 and 3–6.*

EXPLORING

Duomo. Matera's cathedral was built in the late 13th century and occupies a prominent position between the two Sassi. It has a pungent Apulian-Romanesque flavor; inside, there's a recovered fresco (probably painted in the 14th century) showing scenes from the Last Judgment. On the Duomo's facade the figures of Saints Peter and Paul stand on either side of a sculpture of Matera's patron, the Madonna della Bruna. At the time of writing, the Duomo was closed for a long-term restoration. ⊠ *Piazza del Duomo* ☎ *0835/311655.*

Museo Archaeologico Nazionale Domenico Ridola. Named after a local 19th-century medical doctor, Domenico Ridola, who investigated archaeological sites in the surrounding area, the museum highlights his excavations of the remains of Paleolithic and Neolithic settlements, as well as a richly endowed 4th-century BC tomb. Ridola's finds are on view in the museum, which is housed in the former monastery of Santa Chiara. The collection includes an extensive selection of prehistoric and classical finds, notably Bronze Age implements and beautifully decorated red-figure pottery from Magna Grecia. ⊠ *Via Ridola 24* ☎ *0835/310058* ⊕ *www.basilicata.beniculturali.it* ☞ *€2.50* ⊙ *Mon. 2–8, Tues.–Sun. 9–8.*

San Giovanni Battista. Considered a jewel of medieval architecture, the 13th-century Romanesque church of San Giovanni Battista was restored to its pre-Baroque simplicity in 1926. The elaborately carved portal is a riot of entwining stone vines, flowers, leaves, human figures, and allegorical creatures. Inside, the three naves are flanked by columns crowned with capitals, each one decorated with symbolic animal forms and other images. No two are alike. ⊠ *Via San Biagio* ⊙ *Mon. 2–8, Tues.–Sun. 9–8.*

Fodor'sChoice
★

Sassi. Matera's Sassi are rock-hewn dwellings piled chaotically atop one another, strewn across the sides of a steep ravine. Some date from

Paleolithic times, when they were truly just caves. In the years that followed, the grottoes were slowly adapted as houses only slightly more modern, with their exterior walls closed off and canals regulating rainwater and sewage. Until relatively recently, these troglodytic abodes presented a Dante-esque vision of squalor and poverty, which is graphically described in Carlo Levi's 1945 memoir, *Christ Stopped at Eboli*. In the 1960s, however most of them were emptied of their inhabitants, who were largely consigned to the ugly apartment blocks seen on the way into town. Today, having been designated a UNESCO World Heritage Site, the area has been cleaned up and is gradually being populated once again—and even gentrified, as evidenced by the bars and restaurants that have moved in. The wide Strada Panoramica leads you safely through this desolate region, which still retains its eerie atmosphere and panoramic views.

14

There are two areas of Sassi, the **Sasso Caveoso** and the **Sasso Barisano,** and both can be seen from vantage points in the upper town. Follow the Strada Panoramica down into the Sassi and feel free to ramble among the strange structures, which, in the words of H.V. Morton in his *A Traveller in Southern Italy,* "resemble the work of termites rather than of man." There are more than 100 *chiese rupestri,* or rock-hewn churches, some of which have medieval frescoes, three of which are open to the public. The most spectacular is **Santa Maria de Idris,** right on the edge of the Sasso Caveoso, near the ravine. Guided tours of the town and Sassi area are recommended and can be arranged through the tourist office.

WHERE TO EAT

$$ ✕ **Il Terrazzino.** Perched on a terrace overlooking the famous Sassi canyon, you can sit outside in summer enjoying the unique view. The restaurant proper is in a cavern carved out of the cliff side. Ask to see the spectacular three-level wine cellar. The menu is strictly Basilicata, with specialties like *foglie di ulivo* (olive leaves with various fillings), wonderful fresh ricotta, *grano e ceci* (cheese and chickpea soup), and *pignata* (lamb stew with potatoes, onions, tomatoes, and other seasonal vegetables). The restaurant also serves pizzas in the evenings. $ *Average main:* €16 ⊠ *Vico S. Giuseppe 7* ☎ *0835/334119* ⊕ *www.ilterrazzino. org* ☙ *Tues.*

SOUTHERN
ITALIAN

$$ ✕ **Le Botteghe.** A pleasingly restored building down in the depths of the Sassi, with rough white walls and arched ceilings, contains this stylish restaurant. One standout on the menu is the charcoal-grilled steak, especially selected by a local butcher and cooked wonderfully rare—this is one of the finest pieces of meat in the region. It's best washed down with local Aglianico del Vulture. Solid renditions of local pasta and vegetarian dishes are also available. There's outdoor seating in summer in the little piazza just off Via dei Fiorentini. $ *Average main:* €15 ⊠ *Piazza San Pietro Barisano 22* ☎ *0835/344072* ⊕ *www.lebotteghematera.it* ☙ *No dinner Tues.–Fri.*

SOUTHERN
ITALIAN

WHERE TO STAY

$$$ HOTEL Fodor's Choice ★ **Hotel Sant'Angelo.** What better way to get close to Matera's trogloditic Sassi than to stay in a hotel that actually incorporates some of the caves as highly upgraded guest rooms. **Pros:** unrivaled views; atmospheric rooms. **Cons:** no elevator and many steps to climb. *$ Rooms from: €220 ✉ Piazza San Pietro Caveoso ☎ 0835/314010 🌐 www.hotelsantangelosassi.it 🛏 7 rooms 12 suites 🍴 Breakfast.*

$ HOTEL **I Sassi.** Opened in 1996, I Sassi claims to be Matera's first "grotto hotel," with rooms inside a succession of caves that overlook the huddle of rooftops, descending flights of stone stairs, and the valley floor of Sasso Barisano. **Pros:** good value; good location. **Cons:** bathrooms small and basic; no parking, but there are garage facilities nearby. *$ Rooms from: €90 ✉ Via San Giovanni Vecchio 89 ☎ 0835/331009 🌐 www.hotelsassi.it 🛏 33 rooms, 2 suites 🍴 Breakfast.*

$$ HOTEL Fodor's Choice ★ **Locanda di San Martino.** Situated at the bottom of the Sassi ravine on the Via Fiorentini (which allows limited car access), the Locanda offers a more upmarket form of cave dwelling, with all modern comforts, including an elevator to whisk you up the cliffside to your room. **Pros:** convenient location if you come by car; comfortable rooms; no traffic noise. **Cons:** rooms are reached via outdoor walkway; limited parking nearby. *$ Rooms from: €130 ✉ Via Fiorentini 71 ☎ 0835/256600 🌐 www.locandadisanmartino.it 🛏 33 rooms, 5 suites 🍴 Breakfast.*

$$$$ HOTEL Fodor's Choice ★ **Palazzo Margherita.** This is Francis Ford Coppola's "Xanadu"—a large and luxurious palazzo in the town of his ancestors and now, thanks to the guiding hand of French designer Jacques Grange, Basilicata's top lodging. **Pros:** professional, courteous staff; a garden pool; spacious rooms with lots of high-tech gadgetry. **Cons:** very expensive; private transport needed; not much to do in Bernalda. *$ Rooms from: €1200 ✉ Corso Umberto 64, a 40-min drive south of Matera ✣ Take SS7 out of Matera heading for Potenza and then join SS407 for Metaponto and Taranto. Look for turnoff to Bernalda after 25 km (16 miles) ☎ 0835/549060 🌐 www.palazzomargherita.com 🛏 9 rooms, 7 suites 🍴 Breakfast.*

$$ HOTEL **Palazzo Viceconte.** If cave dwelling is not your style, an elegant former aristocratic residence in the Duomo piazza will certainly appeal. **Pros:** good location with easy walking to almost all the main sights; on a quiet square; courteous staff. **Cons:** rooms vary considerably; in high season; no parking at the hotel. *$ Rooms from: €150 ✉ Via San Potito 7 ☎ 0835/330699 🌐 www.palazzoviceconte.it 🛏 14 rooms, 2 suites 🍴 Breakfast.*

MARATEA

217 km (135 miles) south of Naples.

When encountering Maratea for the first time, you can be forgiven for thinking you've somehow arrived at the French Riviera. The high, twisty road comes complete with glimpses of a turquoise sea below and is divided by the craggy rocks into various separate localities—Maratea, Maratea Porto, Marina di Maratea, Fiumicello, and Cersuta. Maratea is the name given to this cluster of towns, as well as to the main inland village, a tumble of cobblestone streets where the ruins of a much older settlement (Maratea Antica) can be seen. At the summit of the hill stands the gigantic Cristo Redentore, a massive statue of Christ reminiscent of the one in Rio de Janeiro. There's no shortage of secluded sandy strips in between the rocky headlands, which can get crowded in August. A summer minibus service connects all the different points once or twice an hour.

GETTING HERE AND AROUND

By car, take the Lagonegro exit from the A3 autostrada and continue along the SS585. Intercity and regional trains from Reggio Calabria and Naples stop at Maratea. In the summer months there's a bus linking the train station to the upper town 4 km (2½ miles) away.

VISITOR INFORMATION

Maratea Tourism Office ✉ *Piazza Vitolo 1* ☎ *0973/874111* 🌐 *www.basilicataturistica.com.*

14

WHERE TO EAT AND STAY

$$ SOUTHERN ITALIAN 🍴 **Da Cesare.** With an open kitchen so you can watch the chef and a veranda overlooking the azure waters of the Golfo di Policastro, there's always something to see at this family-run seafood restaurant. Even better, it serves some of the freshest catches in town. Specialties of the house include risotto with cuttlefish ink, grilled squid and *grigliata mista* (mixed grilled fish and seafood). [$] *Average main: €20* ✉ *Strada Statale 18, Località Cersuta, about 5 km (3 miles) north of Maratea and 3 km (2 miles) south of Acquafredda* ☎ *0973/871840* 🕒 *Closed Thurs. Nov.–Mar.*

$$$ HOTEL 🏨 **Villa Cheta Elite.** Immersed in Mediterranean greenery with glorious sea views, this elegant and historic villa is in the seaside village of Acquafredda, just north of Maratea. **Pros:** surrounded by lush vegetation; beautiful views of the coast and mountains; lovely Art Nouveau building. **Cons:** on a busy road; no pool; steps to climb. [$] *Rooms from: €240* ✉ *Via Timpone 46, Località Acquafredda* ☎ *0973/878134* 🌐 *www.villacheta.it* 🛏 *23 rooms* 🕒 *Closed Nov.–Apr.* 🍽 *Breakfast.*

CALABRIA

Italy's southernmost mainland region may still be poorer than the rest of the country, but it also claims more than its share of fantastic scenery and great beaches. The accent here is on the landscape, the sea, and the constantly changing dialogue between the two. Don't expect much in the way of big-city sophistication in this least trodden of regions, but instead remain open to the simple pleasures to be found—the country food, the friendliness, the disarming hospitality of the people. Aside from coast and culture, there are also some destinations worth going out of your way for, from the vividly colored murals of Diamante to the hiking trails of the Pollino and Sila national parks.

The drive on the southbound A3 autostrada alone is a breathtaking experience, the more so as you approach Sicily, whose image grows tantalizingly nearer as the road wraps around the coastline once challenged by Odysseus. The road seems to have been under reconstruction since his time, with little sign of completion.

DIAMANTE

51 km (32 miles) south of Maratea, 225 km (140 miles) south of Naples.

One of the most fashionable of the string of small resorts lining Calabria's north Tyrrhenian Coast, Diamante makes a good stop for its whitewashed maze of narrow alleys, brightly adorned with a startling variety of large-scale murals. The work of local and international artists, the murals—which range from cartoons to poems to serious portraits, and from beautiful to downright ugly—give a sense of wandering through a huge, open-air art gallery. Flanking the broad, palm-lined seaside promenade are sparkling beaches to the north and south.

GETTING HERE AND AROUND

Driving from Maratea, take the SS18; from Cosenza, take the SS107 to Paola, then the SS18. Regional trains leave from Naples four times a day, with regular service from Paola.

VISITOR INFORMATION

Diamante Tourist Office ✉ *Via Benedetto Croce 26, Diamante* ☎ *0985/81130* 🌐 *www.prolocodiamante.it* 🕒 *Daily 9–1 and 5–7.*

WHERE TO STAY

$$$ HOTEL 🏨 **Grand Hotel San Michele.** A survivor from a vanishing age, the San Michele occupies a Belle Époque–style villa atop a cliff near the village of Cetraro, 20 km (12 miles) south of Diamante on the SS18. **Pros:** lovely views; nice gardens; comfortable accommodations. **Cons:** a bit pricey. [$] *Rooms from: €220* ✉ *Località Bosco 8/9, Cetraro* ☎ *0982/91012* 🌐 *www.sanmichele.it* 🛏 *78 rooms, 6 suites, 22 residences* 🕒 *Closed Nov.–Easter* 🍴 *Breakfast.*

CASTROVILLARI

68 km (43 miles) east of Diamante, 75 km (48 miles) north of Cosenza.

Accent the first "i" when you pronounce the name of this provincial Calabrian city, notable for its Aragonese castle, synagogue, and 16th-century San Giuliano church. It's also a great jumping-off point for the Albanian-speaking village of Cìvita, and Pollino, Italy's biggest national park, farther afield. Castrovillari's world-class restaurant-inn, La Locanda di Alia, has made the city something of a gastronomical destination.

GETTING HERE AND AROUND

By car, take the A3 autostrada and exit at Frascineto-Castrovillari. Ferrovie della Calabria runs buses from Cosenza, but service is irregular.

WHERE TO EAT

$$$ MODERN ITALIAN Fodor's Choice ★ ✕ **La Locanda di Alia.** This stately inn and restaurant is halfway between the Ionian coast and the National Pollino Park, so it is hardly surprising that chef Gaetano Alia's bill of fare presents the best of both these worlds. The menu offers the freshest of local produce, prepared with an imaginative twist. Try the Piatto del Buon Ricordo, with pork meat from black pigs, dressed with honey and peperoncino, or sword fish with a pear and onion compote and wash it down with your pick of wine from the Locanda cellar. If you like it so much you want to

stay, more than a dozen guest rooms are available. Surrounded by a lush garden, with swimming pool, they're decorated in bright colors with frescoes by local artists. $ *Average main: €25* ⊠ *Via Vietticelli 55* ☎ *0981/46370* ⊕ *www.alia.it* ⌣ *Reservations essential* ⊘ *No dinner Sun.*

COSENZA

75 km (48 miles) south of Diamante, 185 km (115 miles) north of Reggio Calabria.

Cosenza has a steep, stair-filled centro storico that truly hails from another age. Wrought-iron balconies overlook narrow alleyways with old-fashioned storefronts and bars that have barely been touched by centuries of development. Flung haphazardly—and beautifully—across the top and side of a steep hill ringed by mountains, and watched over by a great, crumbling medieval castle, Cosenza also provides the best gateway for the Sila, whose steep walls rear up to the town's eastern side. Though Cosenza's outskirts are largely modern and ugly, culinary gems and picturesque views await in the rolling farmland nearby and the mountains to the east.

GETTING HERE AND AROUND

By car, take the Cosenza exit from the A3 autostrada. By train, change at Paola on the main Rome–Reggio Calabria line. Regional trains run from Naples. Ferrovie della Calabria runs buses from Spezzano della Sila, Castrovillari, and Camigliatello.

EXPLORING

Castello Svevo. Crowning the Pancrazio hill above the old city, with views across to the Sila mountains, Castello Normanno-Svevo is largely in ruins, having suffered successive earthquakes and a lightning strike that ignited gunpowder stored within. The origins are lost to memory. It may have been built by the Byzantines or the Saracens. For a time it was the residence of the Arab Califf Saati Cayti before he was ousted by the Normans. The castle takes its name from the great Swabian emperor Frederick II (1194–1250), who added two octagonal towers. The castle is at present under restoration and not open to the public. ⊠ *Colle Pancrazio* ⊕ *www.cosenzaturismo.it.*

Duomo. Cosenza's original Duomo, probably built in the middle of the 11th century, was destroyed by an earthquake in 1184. A new cathedral was consecrated in the presence of Emperor Frederick II in 1222. After many Baroque additions, later alterations have restored some of the Provençal Gothic style. Inside, look for the lovely monument to Isabella of Aragon, who died after falling from her horse en route to France in 1271. ⊠ *Piazza del Duomo 1* ☎ *0984/77864* ⊕ *www. cattedraledicosenza.it* ⊘ *Summer, daily 8–noon and 4:30–8; winter, daily 8–noon and 4–7.*

Piazza XV Marzo. Cosenza's noblest square, Piazza XV Marzo (commonly called Piazza della Prefettura), houses government buildings as well as the elegant **Teatro Rendano.** From the square, the **Villa**

Comunale (public garden) provides plenty of shaded benches for a rest. ✉ *Piazza XV Marzo* ☎ *0984/8131* 🌐 *www.comune.cosenza.it.*

WHERE TO EAT AND STAY

$$$ SEAFOOD 🍴 **Hippocampus.** If you are a fish lover, this is the place for you. The Ippocampus is well known in Cosenza for its excellent fresh fish and seafood. The antipasti are a generous mix of seasonal catches and may include specialties like baby squid steamed in tomato sauce, octopus, and spicy clams. Follow up with a plate of spaghetti with prawns, clams, and chilies, or grilled swordfish or tuna steak seasoned with Tropea onions. Then clear your palate with a refreshing homemade sorbet. [$] *Average main: €25* ✉ *Via Piave 33* ☎ *0984/22103* ⏲ *Closed Mon. No dinner Sun.*

$ HOTEL 🏨 **Royal Hotel.** The Royal Hotel is modern and aims to attract a primarily business clientele. **Pros:** close to pedestrian-only shopping area; free parking. **Cons:** 15-minute walk from Cosenza's main attractions in the centro storico. [$] *Rooms from: €70* ✉ *Via delle Medaglie d'Oro 1* ☎ *0984/412165* 🌐 *www.hotelroyalsas.it* 🛏 *30 rooms, 4 suites* 🍽 *Breakfast.*

RENDE

13 km (8 miles) northwest of Cosenza.

Rende is a pleasing stop on the way to or from Cosenza. Leave your car in the parking lot at the base of a long and bizarre series of escalators and staircases, which will whisk you off to this pristine hilltop town, whose winding cobblestone streets and turrets preside over idyllic countryside views.

GETTING HERE AND AROUND

By car, take the A3 autostrada and exit at Cosenza-Rende. Local buses make the trip from nearby Cosenza.

WHERE TO EAT

$$ SOUTHERN ITALIAN 🍴 **La Trattoria di Vincenzo.** This cheerful, family-run hostelry a few miles outside Cosenza, in the hamlet of Castiglione Cosentino, offers an authentic Calabrian experience. The dining room is decked with brightly checked tablecloths and curtains and the menu specializes in typical home-cooked dishes using local seasonal ingredients. Beef is from the area and truffles and wild mushrooms are from the surrounding woods. A specialty of the house is the tasty *gnocchi con fonduta di formaggi silani.*(cheese from the Sila mountains). [$] *Average main: €15* ✉ *Via Ponte Crate 1, Castiglione Cosentino* ☎ *0984/401828* 🌐 *www.latrattoriadivincenzo.it* ⏲ *Closed Sun.*

CAMIGLIATELLO

30 km (19 miles) east of Cosenza.

Lined with chalets, Camigliatello is one of the Sila Massif's major resort towns. Most of the Sila isn't mountainous at all; it is, rather, an extensive, sparsely populated plateau with areas of thick forest. Unfortunately, there's been considerable deforestation. However, since 1968, when the area was designated a national park called Parco Nazionale della Sila, strict rules have limited the felling of timber, and forests are now regenerating. There are well-marked trails through pine and beech woods, and ample opportunities for horseback riding. Fall and winter see droves of locals hunting mushrooms and gathering chestnuts, while ski slopes near Camigliatello draw crowds.

GETTING HERE AND AROUND

By car, take the Cosenza Nord exit from the A3, then follow the SS107.

VISITOR INFORMATION

Camigliatello Tourism Office ✉ *Via Roma 5* ☎ *0984/578159* 🌐 *www.camigliatellosilano.eu* ⏲ *Daily 9:30–6:30* ⏲ *Nov.–Easter.*

EXPLORING

La Fossiata. A couple of miles east of town, Lago Cecita makes a good starting point for exploring La Fossiata, a lovely wooded conservation area within the park. The forestry commission office in nearby Cupone can provide maps and arrange guides. ✉ *Cupone Frazione, Spezzano della Sila* ☎ *0984/537109 tourist office* 🌐 *www.parcosila.it.*

WHERE TO STAY

$ HOTEL FAMILY 🏨 **Tasso.** On the edge of Camigliatello, less than 1 km (½ mile) from the ski slopes, this hotel is in a peaceful, picturesque location. **Pros:** beautiful surroundings; lively. **Cons:** dated architecture. [$] *Rooms from: €80* ✉ *Via degli Impianti Sportivi, Spezzano della Sila* ☎ *0984/578113* 🌐 *www.hoteltasso.it* 🛏 *82 rooms* ⏲ *Late Sept.–late June, weekends only* 🍴 *Breakfast.*

CROTONE

105 km (65 miles) east of Cosenza, 150 km (94 miles) northeast of Locri.

One of the most important Magna Graecia colonies in Italy, Crotone was a major cultural center in the 5th century BC, when it was the home of thinkers like philosopher and mathematician Pythagoras. Sadly, modern development has eclipsed much of its former beauty, but it preserves something of an old-town feel, with its imposing 16th-century castle and an archaeological museum of some importance. Its coastal waters, stretching to Capo Rizzuto, make up Italy's biggest protected marine area; and the island Castle Le Castella, 15 km (9 miles) from Crotone, is a vision out of a fairy tale.

GETTING HERE AND AROUND

By car, take the Cosenza Nord exit from the A3 autostrada, then follow the SS107. There are regular trains from Sibari.

VISITOR INFORMATION

Crotone Tourism Office ✉ *Corso Vittorio Emanuele 12* ☎ *0962/921857* 🌐 *www.turiscalabria.it.*

EXPLORING

Museo Archeologico Nazionale. Constructed to house the treasures found at the Sanctuary of Hera Lacinia, as well as many antiquities recovered from the surrounding seabed, the museum is situated in the heart of the old city of Crotone, close to the seafront castle. The most precious part of the collection is the so-called Treasure of Hera, with the goddess's finely wrought gold diadem and belt pendant. You can also see the rare 5th-century BC bronze *askos* (container for oil) in the form of a mermaid, illegally exported to the United States and subsequently recovered by the Italian government from the Getty Museum in California. ⊠ *Via Risorgimento 121* ☎ *0962/23082* ⊕ *www.archeocalabra. beniculturali.it* 🎫 *€2* ⊘ *Daily 9–8.*

Fodor's Choice   **Santuario di Hera Lacinia.** The Sanctuary of Hera Lacinia was once one
★   of the most important shrines of Magna Graecia. Only one column still remains standing, but the site (known as Capo Colonna because of that single pillar) occupies a stunning position on a promontory 11 km (7 miles) south of the town of Crotone. Here, you can see the outlines of the buildings of the vast sanctuary and visit the small museum, which contains finds from recent excavations in the area, as well as archaeological remains recovered from the sea. The sanctuary dates from the 7th century BC when Achaeans from the Greek Peloponnese founded a colony at Crotone. ⊠ *Via per Capo Colonna* ☎ *0962/934814* ⊕ *www. archeocalabra.beniculturali.it* 🎫 *Free* ⊘ *Sanctuary daily 9–7. Museum: July and Aug., Tues.–Sun. 9–7; Sept.–June, Tues.–Sun. 9–1 and 3:30–7*

WHERE TO STAY

$$ ⌂ **Hotel Helios.** The Helios is in a quiet part of town, it's open year-
HOTEL   round, and it's handily located on the coast road to Capo Colonna. **Pros:** bright, airy rooms; efficient courteous staff; on bus route into town. **Cons:** uninspiring architecture; skimpy breakfasts. $ *Rooms from: €125* ⊠ *Viale Magna Grecia Trav.Via Makalla 2* ☎ *0962/901291* ⊕ *www.helioshotels.it* ⇦ *42 rooms* ⦿*Breakfast.*

TROPEA

120 km (75 miles) south of Cosenza, 107 km (66 miles) north of Reggio Calabria.

Ringed by cliffs and wonderful sandy beaches, the Tropea Promontory is still just beginning to be discovered by foreign tourists. The main town of Tropea, its old palazzi built in simple golden stone, easily wins the contest for prettiest town on Calabria's Tyrrhenian coast. On a clear day the seaward views from the waterfront promenade take in Stromboli's cone and at least four of the other Aeolians. You can visit the islands by motorboats that depart daily in summer. Accommodations are good, and beach addicts won't be disappointed by the choice of magnificent sandy bays within easy reach. The beach beside Santa Maria dell'Isola is said to be one of the most beautiful in the Mediterranean, but there are other fine beaches south at Capo Vaticano and north at Briatico.

GETTING HERE AND AROUND
By car, exit the A3 autostrada at Pizzo and follow the southbound SP6/SS522. Eleven trains depart daily from Lamezia Terme.

VISITOR INFORMATION
Tropea Tourism Office ⊠ *Piazza Ercole 19-23* ☎ *0963/61475* ⊕ *www. prolocotropea.eu.*

EXPLORING

Cattedrale. In Tropea's harmonious warren of lanes, seek out the old Norman Cattedrale, whose main altar contains the locally revered icon of the Madonna di Romania, protectress of the city. Also of interest is the imposing 14th-century "Black Crucifix" in one of the side chapels. It's worth popping into the adjoining **Museo Diocesano**, which contains both an archaeological section and a collection of sacred art, including the life-size statue of Santa Domenica in solid silver, dating from 1738. ⊠ *Largo Duomo* ☎ *0963/61034* ☉ *Summer, daily 10–12:30 and 6:30–10; Apr., May, Sept., and Oct., daily 9:30–12:30 and 5–8.*

Santa Maria dell'Isola. The sanctuary of Santa Maria dell'Isola is the symbol of Tropea, and it is easy to see why. Perched high on a rocky promontory and accessible only by a winding flight of stone steps cut into the cliffside, it dominates the view over the sea from Piazza Ercole, the main town square. Believed to date from the 4th century AD, it has been rebuilt many times and took its present form in the 18th century after it was damaged by an earthquake. Reopened in August 2014 after nine years restoration, it is now accessible to visitors. The beach below the rock has been classed among the ten most beautiful beaches in Italy. ⊠ *Lungomare A Sorrentino* ☎ *0963/61034* ⊕ *www.prolocotropea.eu.*

WHERE TO EAT AND STAY

$$
SOUTHERN
ITALIAN
✕ **Pimm's.** Since its glory days in the 1960s, this basement restaurant in Tropea's historic center has offered the town's top dining experience. Seafood is the best choice, with such specialties as pasta with sea urchins, smoked swordfish, and prawns served on a bed of red Tropea onions or gnocchi filled with tiny clams and creamed pistachio nuts. The splendid sea views from the rear windows are a surprising—and substantial—reason to head here. There are also five rooms for overnight guests. $ *Average main: €18* ⊠ *Corso Vittorio Emanuele 2* ☎ *0963/666105* ⊕ *www.villapimms.it* ☉ *Closed Mon.*

$$
HOTEL
Villa Antica. In a fin-de-siècle villa just a stone's throw from Tropea's main square, Piazza Vittorio Veneto, this hotel is within walking distance (downhill) from the train station. **Pros:** open all year; attentive staff; good location. **Cons:** some rooms need renovation; noise from street; no parking available at the hotel. $ *Rooms from: €150* ⊠ *Via Ruffo di Calabria 37* ☎ *0963/607176* ⊕ *www.villaanticatropea.it* ⤳ *28 rooms* ☉ *Breakfast.*

REGGIO CALABRIA

115 km (71 miles) south of Tropea, 499 km (311 miles) south of Naples.

Reggio Calabria, on the tip of Italy's toe, was laid low by the same catastrophic earthquake that struck Messina in 1908. This raw city is one of Italy's busiest ports, where you can find every type of container ship and smokestack. Hydrofoils for Sicily depart from here; vehicle-carrying ferries depart from Villa San Giovanni, 13 km (8 miles) north.

GETTING HERE AND AROUND

The A3 autostrada runs directly to Reggio Calabria. Eight trains depart from Naples and Rome daily. There are daily flights from Rome, Milan, Turin, and Venice.

VISITOR INFORMATION

Reggio Calabria Tourism Office ✉ *Via Roma 3, Reggio Calabria* ☎ *0965/21171.*

EXPLORING

Museo Nazionale della Magna Grecia. In Reggio, one of southern Italy's most important archaeological museums has been waiting for years for the return of its prize exhibit, the statues known as the **Bronzi di Riace,** which were discovered by an amateur deep-sea diver off Calabria's Ionian Coast in 1972. After a lengthy but necessary conservation operation, the 5th century BC bronzes of two Greek warriors, thought to be the work of either Pheidias or Polykleitos, have now returned to take pride of place in their special temperature-controlled room, complete with new earthquake-resistant bases. Visitors are allowed to view the bronzes in groups of 20, every 20 minutes. The visit includes a video illustrating the various phases of restoration. ✉ *Piazza De Nava 26* ☎ *0965/898272* 🌐 *www.archeocalabria.beniculturali.it* 🎟 *€5* ⏲ *Daily 9–8.*

WHERE TO STAY

$$ HOTEL 🏨 **E'Hotel.** On the seafront beside the Lido Comunale, this sleek modern hotel has great views and one of the best locations in town. **Pros:** great location; unbeatable views; luxurious rooms; garage facilities. **Cons:** can be busy during conferences. [$] *Rooms from: €150* ✉ *Via Giunchi 6, Reggio Calabria* ☎ *0965/893000* 🌐 *www.ehotelreggiocalabria.it* 🛏 *44 rooms, 4 suites* 🍴 *Breakfast.*

STILO

50 km (31 miles) north of Locri, 138 km (86 miles) northeast of Reggio Calabria.

Grandly positioned on the side of the rugged Monte Consolino, the village of Stilo is known for being the birthplace and home of the philosopher Tommaso Campanella (1568–1639), whose magnum opus was the socialistic *La Città del Sole* (*The City of the Sun,* 1602)—for which he spent 26 years as a prisoner of the Spanish Inquisition.

GETTING HERE AND AROUND

From Reggio Calabria, follow the Ionian coastal SS106 and exit at Stilo. Regular trains run from Lamezia Terme.

15

SICILY

Visit Fodors.com for advice, updates, and bookings

WELCOME TO SICILY

TOP REASONS TO GO

★ **Taormina—Sicily's most beautiful resort:** The view of the sea and Mt. Etna from its jagged cactus-covered cliffs is as close to perfection as a panorama can get.

★ **A walk on Siracusa's Ortygia Island:** Classical ruins rub elbows with faded seaside palaces and fish markets in Sicily's most striking port city, where the Duomo is literally built atop an ancient Greek temple.

★ **Palermo's palaces, churches, and crypts:** Virtually every great European empire ruled Sicily's strategically positioned capital at some point, and it shows most of all in the diverse architecture, from Roman to Byzantine to Arab-Norman.

★ **Valley of the Temples, Agrigento:** This stunning set of ruins is proudly perched above the sea in a grove full of almond trees; not even in Athens will you find Greek temples this finely preserved.

1 The Ionian Coast. For many, the Ionian Coast is all about touristy Taormina, spectacularly poised on a cliff near Mt. Etna, but don't overlook lively Catania, Sicily's modern nerve center.

2 Siracusa. This was one of the great powers of the classical world. Today, full of fresh fish and remarkable ruins, it's content to be one of Italy's most charming cities.

3 The Interior. In hill towns such as Enna and Ragusa, the interior of Sicily exhibits a slower pace of life than the frenetic coastal cities. Piazza Armerina features the Villa Casale and its ancient Roman mosaics.

4 Agrigento and Western Sicily. Following the island's northern edge west of Palermo, this coast meanders past Monreale and its mosaics, Segesta

with its temple, and the fairy-tale town of Erice. Greek ruins stand sentinel in Agrigento at the Valley of the Temples, blanketed in almond blossoms. Nearly as impressive is Selinunte, rising above rubble and overlooking the sea.

Palermo
Monreale
Bagheria
Trapani
Erice
Termini
Imerese
Segesta
Alcamo
A29
624
115
4
Marsala
A29
Castelvetrano
189
Mazara
del Vallo
Sciacca
115
Canicattì
Mare
Agrigento
Mediterráneo
115

Stromboli

Panarea

Filicudi   Salina

Alicudi   AEOLIAN ISLANDS   Lipari

7

Vulcano

Mare Tirreno

Milazzo

Villa San Giovanni

Capo d'Orlando

Messina

Barcellona Pozzo di Gotto

Reggio di Calabria

efalù

6

TYRRHENIAN COAST

A20

Randazzo

116

120

Mare Ionio

Taormina

Mt. Etna 3,323m

A18   **1**

Adrano

284

Acireale

Paterno

9

A19

3

Enna

Catania

Caltanissetta

Piazza Armerina

417

Lentini

Caltagirone

194

Augusta

626

2 Siracusa

cata   Gela

115

Vittoria

124

Ragusa

Modica

Noto

Pachino

15

5 Palermo.
Sicily's capital and one of Italy's most hectic cities, Palermo conceals notes of extraordinary beauty amid the uncontained chaos of fish markets and impossible traffic.

6 The Tyrrhenian Coast.
Filled with summer beach-goers, the Tyrrhenian Coast also has several quaint villages, including Cefalù, with its famous cathedral.

7 The Aeolian Islands.
You may know these tranquil windswept islands from the *Odyssey*, and some of them seem to have changed little since Homer's time.

GETTING ORIENTED

This splendid island was known to the ancients as Trinacria for its three corners. At the northeastern corner is Messina, connected by car and train ferry to the mainland. The eastern edge of Sicily is its Ionian Coast, which continues south to Catania, Siracusa, and the island's southeastern corner. Sicily's northern edge is the Tyrrhenian Coast, which includes Palermo and extends out to the island's third (western) corner.

EATING AND DRINKING WELL IN SICILY

Sicilian cuisine is one of the oldest in existence, with records of cooking competitions dating to 600 BC. Food in Sicily today reflects the island's unique cultural mix, imaginatively combining fish, fruits, vegetables, and nuts with Italian pastas and Arab and North African elements—couscous is a staple in Palermo.

It's hard to eat badly here. From the lowliest of trattorias to the most highfalutin' ristorante, you'll find the classic dishes that have been the staples of the family dinner table for years—basically pasta and seafood. A more sophisticated place may introduce a few adventurous items onto the menu, but the main difference between the cheapest and the most expensive restaurants will be the level of service and the accoutrements: in more formal ones you'll find greater attention to detail and a more respectful atmosphere, while less pretentious trattorias tend to be family-run affairs, often without even a menu to guide you. However, in this most gregarious of regions in the most convivial of countries, you can expect a lively dining experience wherever you choose to eat.

SICILIAN MARKETS

Sicily's natural fecundity is evident wherever you look, from the prickly pears sprouting on roadsides to the slopes of vineyards and citrus groves covering the inland to the ranks of fishing boats moored in every harbor.

You can come face-to-face with this bounty in the clamorous street markets of Palermo, *pictured above*, and Catania. Here, you'll encounter teetering piles of olives and oranges, enticing displays of cheeses and meats, plus pastries and sweets of every description. The effect is heady and sensuous. Immerse yourself in the hustle and bustle of the Sicilian souk, and you'll emerge enriched.

WINES

Sicilian wines are up-and-coming; they're also among Italy's best bargains. The earthy *nero d'avola* grape bolsters many of Sicily's traditionally sunny, expansive reds, and it's often softened with fruity, bright *frappato* to make Sicily's only DOCG wine, Cerasuolo di Vittoria. Red wines from around Mt. Etna that use the grapes *nerello mascalese* and *nerello cappuccio* are also gaining renown. Sicily produces crisp white varieties, too, such as *carricante, catarratto bianco, inzolia,* and *grillo* that marry delightfully with the island's seafood. When it comes to sweet accompaniments, the small island of Pantelleria produces the smooth dessert wines Zibibbo and Passito.

DELICIOUS FISH

Pasta *con le sarde,* an emblematic dish that goes back to the Saracen conquerors, with fresh sardines *(pictured at right)*, olive oil, raisins, pine nuts, and wild fennel, gets a different treatment at every restaurant. Grilled *tonno* (tuna) and *orata* (dorado) are coastal staples, while delicate *ricci* (sea urchins) are a specialty. King, however, is *pesce spada* (swordfish), best enjoyed *marinato* (marinated), *affumicato* (smoked), or as the traditional *involtini di pesce spada* (roulades).

LOCAL SPECIALTIES

Many ingredients and recipes are unique to particular Sicilian towns and regions. In Catania, for example, you'll be offered *caserecci alla Norma* (a short pasta with a sauce of tomato, eggplant, ricotta, and basil), named after an opera by Bellini (a Catania native). The *mandorla* (bitter almond), the pride of Agrigento, plays into everything from risotto *alle mandorle* (with almonds, butter, Grana cheese, and parsley) to incomparable almond *granita*—an absolute must in summer. Pistachios produced around Bronte, on the lower slopes of Etna, go into pasta sauces as well as ice cream and granita, while capers from the Aeolian Islands add zest to salads and fish sauces.

SNACKS

Two favorite Sicilian snacks are *arancini* ("little oranges"—rice croquettes with a cheese or meat filling; *pictured below*), and *panelle* (seasoned chickpea flour boiled to a paste, cooled, sliced, and fried), normally bought from street vendors or offered as an appetizer at restaurants. Other tidbits to look out for include special foods associated with festivals, often pastries and sweets, such as the ominously named *ossa dei morti* ("dead men's bones," rolled almond cookies). But the most eye-catching of all are the *frutta martorana* (also known as *pasta reale*)—sweet marzipan confections shaped to resemble fruits.

Updated by
Liz Humphreys

The island of Sicily has an abundance of history. Some of the world's best-preserved Byzantine mosaics stand adjacent to magnificent Greek temples and Roman amphitheaters, awe-inspiring Romanesque cathedrals, and over-the-top Baroque flights of fancy. Add in the spectacular sight of lava-strewn Mt. Etna plus Sicily's unique cuisine—mingling Arab and Greek spices, Spanish and French techniques, and some of the world's finest seafood, all accompanied by big, fruity wines—and you can understand why visitors continue to be drawn here, and often find it hard to leave.

Sicily has beckoned seafaring wanderers since the trials of Odysseus were first sung in Homer's *Odyssey*—perhaps the world's first travel guide. Strategically poised between Europe and Africa, this mystical land of three corners and a fiery volcano once hosted two of the most enlightened capitals of the West—one Greek, in Siracusa, and one Arab-Norman, in Palermo. Sicily has been a melting pot of every great civilization on the Mediterranean: Greek and Roman; then Arab and Norman; and finally French, Spanish, and Italian. The invaders through the ages weren't just attracted by the strategic location, however; they recognized a paradise in Sicily's deep blue skies and temperate climate, its lush vegetation, and rich marine life—all of which prevail to this day.

In modern times, the traditional graciousness and nobility of the Sicilian people have survived side by side with the destructive influences of the Mafia under Sicily's semiautonomous government. Alongside some of the most exquisite architecture in the world lie the shabby, half-built results of some of the worst speculation imaginable. In recent years coastal Sicily, like much of the Mediterranean Coast, has experienced a surge in condominium development and tourism. The island has emerged as something of an international travel hot spot, drawing increasing numbers of visitors. Astronomical prices in northern Italy have contributed to the boom in Sicily, where tourism doesn't seem to be leveling off as it has elsewhere in the country. Brits and Germans flock in ever-growing numbers to Agrigento and Siracusa, and in high season Japanese tour groups seem to outnumber the locals in Taormina. And yet, in Sicily's windswept heartland—a region that tourists have barely begun to explore—vineyards, olive groves, and lovingly kept dirt roads leading to family farmhouses still tie Sicilians to the land and to tradition, forming a happy connectedness that can't be defined by economic measures.

SICILY PLANNER

MAKING THE MOST OF YOUR TIME

You should plan a visit to Sicily around Palermo, Taormina, Siracusa, and Agrigento, four don't-miss destinations. The best way to see them all is to travel in a circle. Start your circuit in the northeast in Taormina, worth at least a night or two. If you have time, stay also in Catania, a lively, fascinating city that's often overlooked. From there, connect to the Catania–Ragusa toll-free *autostrada* (four-lane highway) and head toward the spectacular ancient Greek port of Siracusa, which merits at least two nights.

Next, backtrack north on the same highway, and take the A19 autostrada toward Palermo. Piazza Armerina's impressive mosaics and Enna, a sleepy mountaintop city, are worthwhile stops in the interior. Take the SS640 to the Greek temples of Agrigento. Stay here for a night before driving west along the coastal SS115, checking out Selinunte's ruins before reaching magical Erice, a good base for one night. You're now near some of Sicily's best beaches at San Vito Lo Capo.

Take the A19 to Palermo, the chaotic and wonderful capital city, to wrap up your Sicilian experience. Give yourself at least two days here—ideally, four or five. Or, if it's the warm season, consider heading east toward Messina and sailing to one of the lovely Aeolian Islands for a few days of leisure.

GETTING HERE AND AROUND

BUS TRAVEL

Air-conditioned coaches connect major and minor cities and are often faster and more convenient than local trains—still single-track on many stretches—but also slightly more expensive. Various companies serve the different routes. SAIS runs frequently between Palermo and Catania, Messina, Siracusa, and other cities, in each case arriving at and departing from near the train stations.

Contacts Cuffaro. Services run from outside the Palermo train station to Agrigento. ☎ 091/6161510 ⊕ www.cuffaro.info. **Interbus/Etna Trasporti.** These companies operate between Catania, Caltagirone, Piazza Armerina, Taormina, Messina, and Siracusa. ☎ 091/342525 ⊕ www.interbus.it. **SAIS.** This bus service runs between Catania, Messina, Palermo, Piazza Armerina, Caltagirone, Gela, Caltanisetta, and Enna. ☎ 800/211020 (toll-free), 199/244141 from mobiles ⊕ www.saisautolinee.it.

15

CAR TRAVEL

This is the ideal way to explore Sicily. Modern highways circle and bisect the island, making all main cities easily reachable. The A20 auto-strada connects Messina and Palermo; Messina and Catania are linked by the A18; running through the interior, from Catania to west of Cefalù, is the A19; threading west from Palermo, the A29 runs to Tra-pani and the airport, with a leg stretching down to Mazara del Vallo. The south side of the island is less well served, though stretches of the SS115 east of Agrigento are relatively fast and traffic-free.

You'll likely hear stories about the dangers of driving in Sicily. In the big cities—especially Palermo, Catania, and Messina—streets are a honk-ing mess, with lane markings and stop signs taken as mere suggestions; you can avoid the chaos by driving through at off-peak times or on weekends. However, once outside the urban areas and resort towns, the highways and regional state roads are a driving enthusiast's dream—they're winding, sparsely populated, well maintained, and around most bends there's a striking new view. Obviously, don't leave valuables in your car, and make sure baggage is stowed out of sight—in some cities it may be wise to keep the doors locked while in traffic. If leaving the car overnight, splurge on a garage.

TRAIN TRAVEL

There are direct express trains from Rome to Palermo, Catania, and Siracusa. The Rome–Palermo and Rome–Siracusa trips take at least 10 hours. After Naples, the run is mostly along the coast, so try to book a window seat on the right if you're not on an overnight train. At Villa San Giovanni, in Calabria, the train is separated and loaded onto a fer-ryboat to cross the strait to Messina—kids will love it!

Within Sicily, main lines connect Messina, Taormina, Siracusa, and Palermo. Secondary lines are generally very slow and unreliable. The Messina–Palermo run, along the northern coast, is especially scenic. For schedules, check the website of the Italian state railway.

Contact FS ☎ *892021 within Italy only* ⊕ *www.trenitalia.com.*

RESTAURANTS

Prices in the dining reviews are the average cost of a main course at dinner, or, if dinner is not served, at lunch.

HOTELS

The high-quality hotels tend to be limited to the major cities and resorts of Palermo, Catania, Taormina, Siracusa, and Agrigento, along with the odd beach resort.

However, there's recently been an explosion in the development of *agri-turismo* lodgings (rural bed-and-breakfasts), many of them quite basic but others providing the same facilities found in hotels. These country houses also offer all-inclusive, inexpensive, full-board plans that can make for some of Sicily's most memorable meals.

Hotel reviews have been shortened. For full information, visit Fodors. com.

WHAT IT COSTS				
	$	$$	$$$	$$$$
RESTAURANTS	under €15	€15–€24	€25–€35	over €35
HOTELS	under €125	€125–€200	€201–€300	over €300

Prices in the dining reviews are the average cost of a main course at dinner, or, if dinner is not served, at lunch. Prices in the reviews are the lowest cost of a standard double room in high season.

THE IONIAN COAST

On the northern stretch of Sicily's eastern coast, Messina commands an unparalleled position across the Ionian Sea from Calabria, the mountainous tip of mainland Italy's boot. Halfway down the coast, Catania has the vivacity of Palermo, if not the artistic wealth; the city makes a good base for exploring lofty Mt. Etna, as does Taormina.

15

MESSINA

8 km (5 miles) by ferry from Villa San Giovanni, 94 km (59 miles) northeast of Catania, 237 km (149 miles) east of Palermo.

Messina's ancient history lists a series of disasters, but the city nevertheless managed to develop a fine university and a thriving cultural environment. At 5:20 am on December 28, 1908, Messina changed from a flourishing metropolis of 120,000 to a heap of rubble, shaken to pieces by an earthquake that turned into a tidal wave: 80,000 people died as a result and the city was almost completely leveled. As you approach by ferry, you won't notice any outward indication of the disaster, except for the modern countenance of a 3,000-year-old city. The somewhat flat look is a precaution of seismic planning: tall buildings aren't permitted.

GETTING HERE AND AROUND

Frequent hydrofoils and ferries carry passengers and trains across the Straits of Messina from Villa San Giovanni, from just below the train station. There are also regular departures for foot passengers from Reggio Calabria.

VISITOR INFORMATION

Messina Tourism Office ⊠ *Via dei Mille 270* ☎ *090/2935292* ⊕ *www.regione.sicilia.it/turismo.*

EXPLORING

Duomo. The reconstruction of Messina's Norman and Romanesque Duomo, originally built by the Norman king Roger II and consecrated in 1197, has retained much of the original plan—including a handsome crown of Norman battlements, an enormous apse, and a splendid wood-beam ceiling. The adjoining bell tower contains one of the largest and most complex mechanical clocks in the world: constructed in 1933, it has a host of gilded automatons (a roaring lion among them) that spring into action every day at the stroke of noon. ⊠ *Piazza del Duomo* ☎ *090/774895* ⊕ *www.diocesimessina.it* ☉ *Daily 9–1 and 4–7, closed during services.*

Eastern Sicily and the Aeolian Islands

TO NAPLES

TO NAPLES

TO TROPEA

Stromboli

AEOLIAN ISLANDS

Panarea

Alicudi   Filicudi

Salina

Lipari

Vulcano

Tyrrhenian Sea

Golfo di Milazzo

Milazzo

Villa San Giovanni

Messina

CAPO D'ORLANDO

St Agata di Militello

Patti

Reggio di Calabria

Cefalù

TYRRHENIAN COAST

Caldura

113

A20

113

116

113

A20

185

114

106

Pizzo Carbonara

Randazzo

Castelmola

Taormina

117

120

120

Bronte

Giardini-Naxos

Riposto

Nicosia

121

Mt. Etna

Giarre

A19

Adrano

Nicolosi

Acireale

Biancavilla

Enna

192

Paterno

Aci Castello

Aci Trezza

Caltanisetta

A19

Catania

Golfo di Catania

191

Casale

Piazza Armerina

417

288

385

Agnone

E45

626

117b

Mazzarino

Palagonia

194

Caltagirone

124

Lentini

Augusta

Vizzini

Euryalus

A18

Gela

194

Palazzolo Acreide

124

Ionian Sea

115

Vittoria

Ragusa

Siracusa
see detail map

Comiso

Modica

Noto

115

Avola

19

Golfo di Gela

Golfo di Noto

E45

TO MALTA

Pachino

CAPO PASSERO

0   20 r

0   20 km

WHERE TO EAT AND STAY

$ ✕ **Al Padrino.** The jovial owner of this stripped-down trattoria keeps
SICILIAN everything running smoothly. Meat and fish dishes are served with equal
verve in the white-wall dining room. Start with antipasti like eggplant
stuffed with ricotta; then move on to supremely Sicilian dishes such
as pasta with chickpeas or *polpette di alalunga* (albacore croquettes).
Ⓢ *Average main: €12* ✉ *Via Santa Cecilia 56* ☎ *090/2921000* ⊘ *Closed
Sun., and Aug.*

TAORMINA

43 km (27 miles) southwest of Messina.

Fodor's Choice
★
The medieval cliffside town of Taormina is overrun with tourists, yet its
natural beauty is still hard to dispute. The view of the sea and Mt. Etna
from its jagged cactus-covered cliffs is as close to perfection as a panorama can get—especially on clear days, when the snowcapped volcano's white puffs of smoke rise against the blue sky. Writers have extolled
Taormina's beauty almost since it was founded in the 6th century BC by
Greeks from nearby Naxos; Goethe and D. H. Lawrence were among
its well-known enthusiasts. The town's boutique-lined main streets get
old pretty quickly, but the many hiking paths that wind through the
beautiful hills surrounding Taormina promise a timeless alternative. A
trip up to stunning Castelmola (whether on foot or by car) should also
be on your itinerary.

15

GETTING HERE AND AROUND

Buses from Messina or Catania arrive near the center of Taormina,
while trains from these towns pull in at the station at the bottom of
the hill. Local buses bring you the rest of the way. A cable car takes
passengers up the hill from a parking lot about 2 km (1 mile) north of
the train station.

VISITOR INFORMATION

Taormina Tourism Office ✉ *Piazza Vittorio Emanuele 7* ☎ *0942/23243*
⊕ *www.comune.taormina.me.it.*

FESTIVALS

Taormina Film Festival. This famous festival takes place in June.
☎ *0942/21142* ⊕ *www.taorminafilmfest.it.*

EXPLORING

TOP ATTRACTIONS

Fodor's Choice
★
Villa Comunale. Stroll down Via Bagnoli Croce from the main Corso
Umberto to the Villa Comunale. Also known as the Parco Duca di
Cesarò, the lovely public gardens were designed by Florence Treve-
lyan Cacciola, a Scottish lady "invited" to leave England following a
romantic liaison with the future Edward VII (1841–1910). Arriving in
Taormina in 1889, she married a local professor and devoted herself to
the gardens, filling them with native Mediterranean and exotic plants,
ornamental pavilions (known as the beehives), and fountains. Stop by
the panoramic bar, which has stunning views. ✉ *Via Bagnoli Croce*
⊘ *Daily 9 am–1 hr before sunset.*

WORTH NOTING

Castello Saraceno. An unrelenting 20-minute walk up the Via Crucis footpath takes you to the church of the Madonna della Rocca, hollowed out of the limestone rock. Above it towers the medieval Castello Saraceno. Though the gate to the castle has been locked for decades, it's worth the climb just for the panoramic views. ⊠ *Monte Tauro.*

Funivia. Taormina Mare is accessible by a *funivia,* or suspended cable car, that glides past incredible views on its way down. It departs every 15 minutes. In June, July, and August, the normal hours are extended until midnight or later. ⊠ *Via L. Pirandello, down hill from town center toward bus station* ☎ *0942/681493* 📧 *€3 one-way* ⏱ *Apr.–Oct., daily 7:45 am–1 am; Nov.–Mar., daily 7:45 am–8 pm.*

Palazzo Corvaja. Many of Taormina's 14th- and 15th-century palaces have been carefully preserved. Especially beautiful is the Palazzo Corvaja, with characteristic black-lava and white-limestone inlays. Today it houses the tourist office and the **Museo di Arte e Tradizioni Popolari,** which has a collection of Sicilian puppets and folk art, carts, and crèches. ⊠ *Largo Santa Caterina* ☎ *0942/610274* 📧 *Museum €2.60* ⏱ *Museum Tues.–Sun. 10–1.*

Taormina Mare. Below the main city of Taormina is Taormina Mare, where summertime beachgoers jostle for space on a pebble beach against the scenic backdrop of the aptly named island of Isolabella. The first section of beach is mainly reserved for expensive resorts, but the far end, next to Isolabella, has a large free area. The "beautiful island" was once a private residence, but is now a nature reserve which can be visited for a small fee.

Teatro Greco. The Greeks put a premium on finding impressive locations to stage their dramas, such as Taormina's hillside Teatro Greco. Beyond the columns you can see the town's rooftops spilling down the hillside, the arc of the coastline, and Mount Etna in the distance. The theater was built during the 3rd century BC and rebuilt by the Romans during the 2nd century AD. Its acoustics are exceptional: even today a stage whisper can be heard in the last rows. In summer Taormina hosts an arts festival of music and dance events and a film festival; many performances are held in the Teatro Greco. ⊠ *Via Teatro Greco* ☎ *0942/23220* ⊕ *www.taorminafestival.org* 📧 *€8* ⏱ *Daily 9–1 hr before sunset.*

QUICK BITES

Bam Bar. For some of Taormina's best granita, with changing flavors depending on the season, try Bam Bar. It's so popular that it's likely you'll have to queue, but it's worth it. It's closed on Monday. ⊠ *Via di Giovanni 45* ☎ *0942/24355.*

Pasticceria Etna. No marzipan devotee should leave Taormina without trying one of the almond sweets—maybe in the guise of the ubiquitous *fico d'India* (prickly pear) or in more unusual frutta martorana varieties—at Pasticceria Etna. A block of almond paste makes a good souvenir—you can bring it home to make an almond latte or granita. ⊠ *Corso Umberto 112* ☎ *0942/24735* ⊕ *www.pasticceriaetna.com.*

WHERE TO EAT

$ SICILIAN 🍴 **Bella Blu.** If you fancy a meal with a view but don't want to spend a lot, it would be hard to do much better than to come here for the decent €20 three-course prix-fixe meal. Seafood and pizza are the specialties; try the spaghetti with fresh clams and mussels or the pizza *alla Norma* (with ricotta, eggplant, and tomatoes). You can also opt for the €9 pizza and drink menu. Through giant picture windows you can watch the gondola fly up and down from the beach, with the coastline in the distance. Families will especially enjoy the casual, convivial atmosphere and friendly service. [$] *Average main: €11* ✉ *Via Pirandello 28* ☎ *0942/24239* 🌐 *www.bellablutaormina.com* 🕒 *Closed Jan.–Mar.*

$$$ SICILIAN 🍴 **La Giara.** This restaurant, named after a giant vase unearthed under the bar, is famous for being one of Taormina's oldest restaurants. The food's not bad, either. The kitchen blends upscale modern techniques with the simple flavors of traditional cuisine. It specializes in everything fish: one spectacular dish is the fish *cartoccio* (wrapped in paper and baked). You can also extend your evening at the popular, if touristy, piano bar, or at the dance club that operates here on Saturday night (and every night in August). There's a terrace with stunning views, too. [$] *Average main: €26* ✉ *Vico La Floresta 1* ☎ *0942/23360* 🌐 *www.lagiara-taormina.com* 🕒 *Closed mid-Nov.–mid-Mar. No lunch.*

$$ SEAFOOD 🍴 **La Piazzetta.** Sheltered from the city's hustle and bustle, this elegant little eatery exudes a mood of relaxed sophistication. Classic dishes such as risotto *ai frutti di mare* (with seafood) are competently prepared, the grilled fish is extremely fresh, and the service is informal and friendly. The modest room has simple white walls—you're not paying for a view. [$] *Average main: €19* ✉ *Vico Francesco Paladini, off Corso Umberto* ☎ *0942/626317* 🌐 *www.ristorantelapiazzettataormina.it* 🕒 *Closed Nov. and 2 wks in Feb. No lunch Mon.–Thurs. June–Sept.*

$ SEAFOOD 🍴 **L'Arco dei Cappuccini.** Just off Via Costantino Patricio, by the far side of the Cappuccini arch of the name, lies this diminutive restaurant. Outdoor seating and an upstairs kitchen help make room for a few extra tables—a necessity, as locals are well aware that neither the price nor the quality is equaled elsewhere in town. Indulge in the veal cutlet with Etna mushrooms, pasta con le sarde, or a simple slice of grilled *pesce spada* (swordfish). Reservations are usually essential for more than two people. [$] *Average main: €8* ✉ *Via Cappuccini 5A, off Via Costantino Patricio* ☎ *0942/24893* 🕒 *Closed Wed., and Feb.*

$ PIZZA 🍴 **Vecchia Taormina.** Warm, inviting, and unassuming, Taormina's best pizzeria produces deliciously seared crusts topped with fresh, well-balanced ingredients. Try the pizza alla Norma—here, in the province of Messina, it's made with ricotta *al forno* (cooked ricotta), while in the province of Catania, it's made with ricotta *salata* (uncooked, salted ricotta). The restaurant also offers fresh fish in summer, and there's a good list of Sicilian wines. Choose between small tables on either of two levels or on the terrace. [$] *Average main: €11* ✉ *Vico Ebrei 3* ☎ *0942/625589* 🕒 *Closed Wed., and Jan. and Feb.*

15

WHERE TO STAY

$$$$ HOTEL Fodor's Choice ★ **Grand Hotel Timeo.** On a princely perch overlooking the town, the Greek theater, and the bay, this truly grand hotel wears a graceful patina that suggests *la dolce vita.* **Pros:** feeling of indulgence; central location; quiet setting. **Cons:** very expensive; some rooms are small; nonsoundproofed rooms can be an issue. [$] *Rooms from: €580* ✉ *Via Teatro Greco 59* ☎ *0942/6270200* 🌐 *www.grandhoteltimeo.com* 🛏 *70 rooms, 13 suites* 🕒 *Closed Nov.–Mar.* 🍴 *Breakfast.*

$$$ HOTEL **Hotel Metropole Taormina.** One of the only boutique hotels in Taormina, the trendy Metropole boasts one of the most prime locations in town, with the main shopping street of Corso Umberto on one side and views of the sea on the other. **Pros:** free Wi-Fi throughout hotel; lovely spa and public areas; amazing views. **Cons:** bathrooms can be small and dark; expensive overall, with high prices particularly in the bar. [$] *Rooms from: €295* ✉ *Corso Umberto 154* ☎ *0942/681330* 🌐 *www.hotelmetropoletaormina.it* 🛏 *8 rooms, 15 suites* 🕒 *Closed Jan.–Mar.* 🍴 *Breakfast.*

$$ HOTEL **Hotel Villa Paradiso.** On the edge of the old quarter, overlooking the lovely public gardens and facing the sea, this hotel is not as well known as some of its neighbors, despite its 100-year history. **Pros:** friendly service; good value; great rooftop views; wonderful beach. **Cons:** only three free parking spaces (with paid parking close by); not all rooms have views. [$] *Rooms from: €200* ✉ *Via Roma 2* ☎ *0942/23921* 🌐 *www.hotelvillaparadisotaormina.com* 🛏 *37 rooms* 🍴 *Breakfast.*

$$$$ HOTEL Fodor's Choice ★ **San Domenico Palace.** Sweeping views of the castle, the sea, and Mt. Etna from this converted 15th-century Dominican monastery linger in your mind, along with equally memorable levels of luxury and wonderful food in the hotel's highly lauded restaurant, Principe Cerami (open April–October). **Pros:** stellar restaurant; attentive service; quiet and restful. **Cons:** expensive; dull corridors; some small rooms. [$] *Rooms from: €313* ✉ *Piazza San Domenico 5* ☎ *0942/613111* 🌐 *www.san-domenico-palace.com* 🛏 *90 rooms, 15 suites* 🕒 *Closed early Jan.–mid-Mar.* 🍴 *Breakfast.*

$$ HOTEL **Villa Ducale.** The former summer residence of a local aristocrat has been converted into a luxurious hotel where each room has a balcony with a view. **Pros:** away from the hubbub; camera-ready views. **Cons:** A 10- to 15-minute walk to the center of Taormina; the restaurant menu can be limited. [$] *Rooms from: €189* ✉ *Via Leonardo da Vinci 60* ☎ *0942/28153* 🌐 *www.villaducale.com* 🛏 *9 rooms, 8 suites* 🕒 *Closed Dec.–Feb.* 🍴 *Breakfast.*

$$ HOTEL **Villa Fiorita.** Near the historic center and the cable-car station, this converted private house has excellent north-coast views from nearly every room. **Pros:** good rates; pretty rooms. **Cons:** service can be slack; you have to climb 65 steps to get to the elevator. [$] *Rooms from: €125* ✉ *Via L. Pirandello 39* ☎ *0942/24122* 🌐 *www.villafioritahotel.com* 🛏 *24 rooms, 1 suite* 🕒 *Closed Nov.–Mar.* 🍴 *Breakfast.*

NIGHTLIFE AND PERFORMING ARTS

Taoarte. The Teatro Greco and the Palazzo dei Congressi, near the entrance to the theater, are the main venues for the summer festival dubbed Taoarte, held each year between June and August. Performances encompass classical music, ballet, and theater. ☎ *0942/21142* ⊕ *www.taormina-arte.com.*

Teatro dei Due Mari. This company stages Greek tragedy at the Teatro Greco, usually from mid-May to mid-June. ✉ *Via Teatro Greco* ☎ *0941/240912* ⊕ *www.teatrodeiduemari.net.*

EN ROUTE The 50-km (30-mile) stretch of road between Taormina and Messina is flanked by lush vegetation and seascapes. Inlets are punctuated by gigantic, oddly shaped rocks.

CASTELMOLA

5 km (3 miles) west of Taormina.

Although many believe that Taormina has the most spectacular views, tiny Castelmola, floating 1,800 feet above sea level, takes the word "scenic" to a whole new level—literally. Along the cobblestone streets within the ancient walls, the 360-degree panoramas of mountain, sea, and sky are so ubiquitous that you almost get used to them (but not quite). Collect yourself with a sip of the sweet almond wine (best served cold) made in the local bars, or with lunch at one of the humble pizzerias or panino shops.

A 10-minute drive on a winding but well-paved road leads from Taormina to Castelmola; you must park in one of the public lots below the village and walk up to the center, only a few minutes away. On a nice day, hikers are in for a treat if they make the trip on foot from Taormina rather than drive. It's a serious uphill climb, but the 1½-km (¾-mile) path offers breathtaking views, which compensate for the somewhat poor maintenance of the path itself. You'll begin at Porta Catania in Taormina, with a walk along Via Apollo Arcageta past the Chiesa di San Francesco di Paola on the left. The Strada Comunale della Chiusa then leads past Piazza Andromaco, revealing good views of the jagged promontory of Cocolanazzo di Mola to the north. Allow around an hour for the ascent, a half hour for the descent. There's another, slightly longer (2-km [1-mile]) path that heads up from Porta Messina past the Roman aqueduct, Convento dei Cappuccini, and the northeastern side of Monte Tauro. You could take one up and the other down. In any case, avoid the midday sun, wear comfortable shoes, and carry plenty of water with you.

GETTING HERE AND AROUND

Regular buses bound for Castelmola leave from two locations in Taormina: the bus station on Via Pirandello and Piazza San Pancrazio.

EXPLORING

Fodor'sChoice
★
Castello Normanno. The best place to savor Castelmola's views is from the castle ruins, reached by a set of steep staircases rising out of the town center. In all of Sicily there may be no spot more scenic than atop Castello Normanno: you can gaze upon two coastlines, smoking Mount Etna, and the town spilling down the mountainside. Come during daylight hours to take full advantage of the vista.

WHERE TO EAT AND STAY

$ SICILIAN 🍴 **Il Vicolo.** Along a side street, this is one of the simpler dining choices in town, and also one of the better ones. It might not have the views you'll find elsewhere, but a pleasant rustic ambience plus a great selection of handmade pasta and, in the evening, *forno a legna* (wood-fired) pizzas make up for that shortcoming. (In winter, pizzas are served weekends only.) The friendly staff serve the food in a pleasing little room. [$] *Average main: €12* ✉ *Via Pio IX 26* ☎ *0942/28481* 🌐 *www.trattoriailvicolo.com* 🕒 *Closed Tues. Sept.–June, and 2 wks late Jan.–early Feb.*

$ HOTEL 🏨 **Villa Sonia.** Many of the rooms at this well-situated hotel in Castelmola have private terraces with gorgeous grab-the-camera views of Etna. **Pros:** far from the madding crowds; on-site sauna and pool. **Cons:** some accommodations are far from the main building; not much to do in the evening. [$] *Rooms from: €90* ✉ *Via Porta Mola 9* ☎ *0942/28082* 🌐 *www.hotelvillasonia.com* 🛏 *39 rooms, 3 suites* 🕒 *Closed Nov.–Dec. 20 and Jan. 8–Mar. 15* 🍽 *Breakfast.*

NIGHTLIFE

Bar San Giorgio. This place has lorded over Castelmola's town square since 1907. The interior of the bar is filled with knickknacks that tell a fascinating history of the tiny town. Try the *vino de mandorle* (almond wine) from a recipe produced by the original owner more than a century ago. ✉ *Piazza Sant'Antonino* ☎ *0942/28228* 🌐 *www.barsangiorgio.com.*

Bar Turrisi. Truly one of the most unusual places to have a drink in all of Italy, this famous bar has cozy nooks and crannies on three levels—all decked out with phallic images of every size, shape, and color imaginable, from bathroom wall murals inspired by the brothels of ancient Greece to giant wooden carvings honoring Dionysus. The roof terrace has extraordinary views of Taormina and the coast. A limited selection of hearty pasta dishes are served inside. ✉ *Piazza del Duomo 19* ☎ *0942/28181* 🌐 *www.turrisibar.it.*

MT. ETNA

64 km (40 miles) southwest of Taormina, 30 km (19 miles) north of Catania.

The first time you see Mt. Etna, whether she's trailing clouds of smoke or emitting fiery streaks of lava, is certain to be unforgettable. The best-known symbol of Sicily and one of the world's major active volcanoes, Etna is the largest and highest volcano in Europe—the cone of the crater rises 10,902 feet above sea level. Though you'll get wonderful vantage points of Etna from Taormina, Castelmola, and Catania in particular, it also makes a rewarding day trip to see the mountain up close with a hike or climb; you can find routes suitable to every fitness level.

GETTING HERE AND AROUND

Reaching the lower slopes of Mt. Etna is easy, either by driving yourself or taking a bus from Catania. Getting to the more interesting higher levels requires taking one of the stout four-wheel-drive minibuses that leave from Piano Provenzana on the north side and Rifugio Sapienza on the south side. A cable car from Rifugio Sapienza takes you part of the way.

VISITOR INFORMATION

Funivia dell'Etna ⊠ *Rifugio Sapienza* 🕾 *095/914141, 095/914142* ⊕ *www.funiviaetna.com* ⌨*€30* ⏱ *Apr.–Nov. 9–5:30; Dec.–Mar. 9–3:30.*

Nicolosi Tourism Office ⊠ *Piazza Vittorio Emanuele 32/33, Nicolosi* 🕾 *095/914488.*

EXPLORING

Circumetnea. Instead of climbing up Mt. Etna, you can circle it on the Circumetnea, which runs near the volcano's base. The private railroad almost circles the volcano, running 114 km (71 miles) between Catania and Riposto—the towns are just 30 km (19 miles) apart by the coast road. The line is small, slow, and single-track, but has some dramatic vistas of the volcano and goes through lava fields. The one-way trip takes about 3½ hours, with departures every 90 minutes or so. After you've made the trip, you can get back to where you started from on the much quicker, but less scenic, conventional state rail service between Riposto and Catania. ⊠ *Via Caronda 352, Catania* 🕾 *095/541111* ⊕ *www.circumetnea.it* ⌨*€7.25 one-way* ⏱ *Mon.–Sat. 6 am–3 pm (leaving Catania).*

Club Alpino Italiano. A great resource for Mt. Etna climbing and hiking guides. If you have some experience and don't like a lot of hand-holding, these are the guides for you. ⊠ *Via Messina 593/a, Catania* 🕾 *095/7153515* ✎ *giorgiopace@katamail.com* ⊕ *www.caicatania.it.*

Gruppo Guide Etna Nord. If you're a novice climber, call this company to arrange for a guide. Their service is a little more personalized—and expensive—than others. Reserve ahead. ⊠ *Piazza Attilio Castrogiovanni 19, Linguaglossa* 🕾 *095/7774502, 348/0125167* ⊕ *www.guidetnanord.com.*

Fodor'sChoice
★

Mt. Etna. Plato sailed in just to catch a glimpse in 387 BC; in the 9th century AD the oldest gelato of all was shaved off its snowy slopes; and in the 21st century the volcano still claims annual headlines. Etna has erupted a dozen times in the past 30 or so years, most spectacularly in 1971, 1983, 2001, 2002, and 2005. There were also a pair of medium-size eruptions in 2008, one in 2009, and fairly constant eruptive activity during the summer of 2011, winter of 2013, and summer of 2014. Travel in the proximity of the crater depends on Mt. Etna's temperament, but you can walk up and down the enormous lava dunes and wander over its moonlike surface of dead craters. The rings of vegetation change markedly as you rise, with vineyards and pine trees gradually giving way to growths of broom and lichen. ⊠ *Parco del Etna.*

OFF THE BEATEN PATH

The villages that surround Mt. Etna offer much more than pretty views of the smoldering giant. They're charming and full of character in their own right, and make good bases for visiting nearby cities such as Catania, Acireale, and Taormina. **Zafferana Etnea** is famous for its orange-blossom honey; **Nicolosi,** at nearly 3,000 feet, is known as La Porta dell'Etna (The Door to Etna); **Trecastagni** (The Three Chestnut Trees) has one of Sicily's most beautiful Renaissance churches; **Randazzo,** the largest of the surrounding towns, is the site of a popular Sunday-morning

15

wood, textile, and metalwork market; and **Bronte** is Italy's center of pistachio cultivation. The bars there offer various pistachio delicacies such as nougat, *colomba* (Easter sponge cake), panettone, and ice cream.

WHERE TO STAY

$ HOTEL 🏨 **Hotel Villa Paradiso dell'Etna.** A painstaking renovation has returned this 1920s villa to its former elegance, complete with mementos of its illustrious past, and there are breathtaking views of Mt. Etna. **Pros:** beautiful furnishings; delightful gardens; low-season bargains. **Cons:** difficult to find; not much to do in the area; food gets mixed reviews. [$] *Rooms from: €120* ✉ *Via per Viagrande 37, San Giovanni La Punta, 10 km (6 miles) northeast of Catania (exit A18 ME-CT toward San Gregorio, or A19 PA-CT toward Paesi Etnei)* ☎ *095/7512409* 🌐 *www.paradisoetna.it* 🛏 *29 rooms, 4 suites* 🍴 *Breakfast.*

ACIREALE

40 km (25 miles) south of Taormina, 16 km (10 miles) north of Catania.

Acireale sits amid a clutter of rocky pinnacles and lush lemon groves. The craggy coast is known as the Riviera dei Ciclopi, after the legend narrated in the *Odyssey* in which the blinded Cyclops Polyphemus hurled boulders at the retreating Ulysses, thus creating spires of rock, or *faraglioni* (pillars of rock rising dramatically out of the sea). Tourism has barely taken off here, so it's a good destination if you feel the need to put some distance between yourself and the busloads of tourists in Taormina. And though the beaches are rocky, there's good swimming here, too.

The Carnival celebrations, held the two weeks before Lent, are considered the best in Sicily. The streets are jammed with thousands of revelers. Acireale is an easy day trip from Catania.

GETTING HERE AND AROUND

Buses arrive frequently from Taormina and Catania. Acireale is on the main coastal train route, though the station is a long walk south of the center. Local buses pass every 20 minutes or so.

VISITOR INFORMATION

Acireale Tourism Office ✉ *Via Oreste Scionti 15* ☎ *095/891999* 🌐 *www.acirealeturismo.it.*

EXPLORING

Belvedere di Santa Caterina. Lord Byron (1788–1824) visited the Belvedere di Santa Caterina to look out over the Ionian Sea during his Italian wanderings. The viewing point is south of the old town, near the Terme di Acireale, off SS114.

Duomo. With its cupola and twin turrets, Acireale's Duomo is an extravagant Baroque construction dating to the 17th century. In the chapel to the right of the altar, look for the 17th-century silver statue of Santa Venera (patron saint of Acireale) made by Mario D'Angelo, and the early-18th-century frescoes by Antonio Filocamo. ✉ *Piazza del Duomo* ☎ *095/601797* 🌐 *www.diocesiacireale.it* 🕒 *Daily 8–noon and 4–8.*

CLOSE UP

Sweet Sicily

Sicily is famous for its desserts, none more so than the wonderful cannoli (*cannolo* is the singular), whose delicate pastry shell and just-sweet-enough ricotta filling barely resemble their foreign impostors. They come in all sizes, from pinkie-size bites to holiday cannoli the size of a coffee table. Even your everyday bar will display a window piled high with dozens of varieties of ricotta-based desserts, including delicious fried balls of dough. The traditional cake of Sicily is the *cassata siciliana,* a rich, chilled sponge cake with sheep's-milk ricotta and candied fruit. Often brightly colored, it's the most popular dessert at many Sicilian restaurants, and you shouldn't miss it. From behind bakery windows and glass cases beam tiny marzipan sweets fashioned into brightly colored apples, cherries, and even hamburgers and prosciutto.

If it's summer, do as the locals do and dip your morning brioche—the best in Italy—into a cup of brilliantly refreshing coffee- or almond-flavored granita. The world's first ice cream is said to have been made by the Romans from the snow on the slopes of Mt. Etna. Top-quality gelato is also prevalent throughout the island.

15

QUICK BITES

El Dorado. Delicious ice creams—and the *granita di mandorla* (almond granita), available in summer—invite a firsthand acquaintance. It's closed on Thursday. ✉ ***Corso Umberto 5*** ☎ ***095/601464.***

Villa Belvedere. Begin your visit to Acireale with a stroll down to the public gardens, Villa Belvedere, at the end of the main Corso Umberto. A recent facelift has cleaned up the park and restored the statues within it. It promises superb coastal views. ✉ *Corso Umberto.*

WHERE TO EAT

$$$ SEAFOOD 🍴 **La Grotta.** A dining room within a cave, with part of the cave wall exposed, is a feature of this rustic trattoria above the harbor of Santa Maria La Scala. Try the *insalata di mare* (a selection of delicately boiled fish served with lemon and olive oil), pasta with clams or cuttlefish ink, or fish grilled over charcoal. Chef Rosario Strano's menu is small, but there isn't a dud among the selections. [$] *Average main: €30* ✉ *Via Scalo Grande 46* ☎ *095/7648153* 🌐 *www.trattorialagrotta.com* 🕒 *Closed Tues., and mid-Oct.–mid-Nov.*

NIGHTLIFE AND PERFORMING ARTS

FAMILY **Teatro dell'Opera dei Pupi.** Although it has died out in most other parts of the island, the puppet-theater tradition carries on in Acireale. The Teatro dell'Opera dei Pupi has a puppet exhibit and puppet shows by request—call to make a reservation. ✉ *Via Alessi 11* ☎ *095/606272* 🌐 *www.teatropupimacri.it.*

SHOPPING

Acireale is renowned in Sicily for its marzipan, made into fruit shapes and delicious cookies available at many pasticcerie around town.

Pasticceria Castorina. A unique creation here is the "nucatole," a large cookie made with heaping quantities of chocolate, Nutella, nuts, and other wholesome ingredients. ✉ *Corso Savoia 109* ☎ *095/601547.*

EN ROUTE
Aci Castello and Aci Trezza. These two gems on the coastline between Acireale and Catania—the Riviera dei Ciclopi (Cyclops Riviera)—fill with city dwellers in the summer months, but even in colder weather their beauty is hard to fault. Heading south from Acireale on the *litoranea* (coastal) road, you'll first reach Aci Trezza, said to be the land of the one-eyed Cyclops in Homer's *Odyssey.* Less developed than Aci Trezza, Aci Castello has the imposing Castello Normanno (Norman Castle), which sits right on the water. The castle was built in the 11th century with volcanic rock from Mount Etna—the same rock that forms the coastal cliffs.

Trattoria da Federico. It should be easy to satisfy your literal (rather than literary) hunger at Aci Trezza's Trattoria da Federico, which specializes in ultrafresh seafood and also lays out a sprawling antipasto buffet featuring delectable marinated anchovies and eggplant parmigiana. ✉ *Via Provinciale 115, Aci Trezza* ☎ *095/276364* ⊕ *www. trattoriadafederico.it* ⊘ *Closed Mon.*

CATANIA

16 km (10 miles) south of Acireale, 94 km (59 miles) south of Messina, 60 km (37 miles) north of Siracusa.

The chief wonder of Catania, Sicily's second city, is that it's there at all. Its successive populations were deported by one Greek tyrant, sold into slavery by another, and driven out by the Carthaginians. Every time the city got back on its feet it was struck by a new calamity: plague decimated the population in the Middle Ages, a mile-wide stream of lava from Mt. Etna swallowed part of it in 1669, and 25 years later a disastrous earthquake forced the Catanesi to begin again.

Today Catania is completing yet another resurrection—this time from crime, filth, and urban decay. Although the city remains loud and full of traffic, signs of gentrification are everywhere. The elimination of vehicles from the Piazza del Duomo and the main artery of Via Etnea, and the scrubbing of many of the historic buildings have added to its newfound charm. Home to what is arguably Sicily's best university, Catania is full of exuberant youth, and it shows in the chic *osterie* (taverns) that serve wine, the designer bistros, and the trendy ethnic boutiques that have popped up all over town. Even more impressive is the vibrant cultural life.

GETTING HERE AND AROUND
Catania is well connected by bus and train with Messina, Taormina, Siracusa, Enna, and Palermo. The airport of Fontanarossa serves as a transportation hub for the eastern side of the island. From here you can get buses to most major destinations without going into the city center.

VISITOR INFORMATION
Catania Tourism Office ✉ *Via Vittorio Emanuele 172* ☎ *800/841042, 095/7425573* ⊕ *www.comune.catania.it/la-citta/turismo.*

EXPLORING

TOP ATTRACTIONS

Cattedrale di Sant'Agata (Duomo). The Giovanni Vaccarini–designed facade of the cathedral dominates the Piazza del Duomo; composer Vincenzo Bellini is buried inside. Also of note are the three apses of lava that survive from the original Norman structure and a fresco from 1675 in the sacristy that portrays Catania's submission to Etna's attack. Underneath the Cathedral are the ruins of Greco-Roman baths: guided tours of the museum and baths are available with a reservation. ⊠ *Piazza del Duomo, bottom end of Via Etnea* 🕾 *095/320044* ⊕ *www.cattedralecatania.it* 🖻 *Museum €7, baths €5; combined ticket €10* ⊙ *Museum/baths: weekdays 9–2, Sat. 9–1, Sun. by appointment only. Cathedral: daily, outside of services.*

Centro Storico. Black lava stone from Etna, combined with largely Baroque architecture, give Catania's historic center a very distinctive feel. Look out for elephants! Not real ones, of course, but symbols and carvings abound; the main one to see is "u Liotru," guarding the city from his viewpoint on top of the fountain in the middle of the cathedral square. After Catania's destruction by lava and earthquake at the end of the 17th century, the city was rebuilt and "u Liotru" placed outside the cathedral as a kind of talisman. Also of note in the center are Castello Ursino, which is now a museum, the Greco-Roman theater next to the Piazza del Duomo, and the Roman amphitheater in Piazza Stesicoro.

Piazza del Duomo. Shining from a 21st-century renovation, this piazza, which is closed to traffic, has at its heart an elephant carved out of lava, balancing an Egyptian obelisk. This is the city's informal mascot, called "u Liotru" in Sicilian dialect. The square also marks the entrance to Catania's famous *pescheria* (fish market) and is one of the few points in the city where you can see the River Amenano aboveground. Another point of interest is Via Garibaldi, which runs from Piazza del Duomo up toward the impressively huge Porta Garibaldi, a black-and-white triumphal arch built in 1768 to commemorate the marriage of Ferdinando I.

Via Etnea. Lined with cafés and stores selling high-street jewelry, clothing, and shoes, this street is host to one of Sicily's most enthusiastic *passeggiate* (early-evening strolls), in which Catanese of all ages take part. It is closed to automobile traffic until 10 pm during the week and all day on weekends.

WORTH NOTING

Agorà Youth Hostel. An underground river, the Amenano, flows through much of Catania. You can glimpse it at the Fontana dell'Amenano, but the best place to experience the river is at the bar-restaurant of the Agorà Youth Hostel. Here you can sit at an underground table as swirls of water rush by. If you're not there when the bar is open, someone at the reception desk can let you in. Apart from the underground river, the bar area aboveground is a lively, fun area to hang out on a Monday evening, when many other places are closed. ⊠ *Piazza Currò 6* 🕾 *095/7233010* ⊕ *www.agorahostel.com.*

Festa di Sant'Agata. Each February 3–5, the Festa di Sant'Agata honors Catania's patron saint with one of Italy's biggest religious festivals. The saint herself was first tortured, then killed, when she spurned a Roman suitor in favor of keeping her religious purity. Since then, the Catanese have honored her memory by pulling her relics through the streets of Catania on an enormous silver-encrusted carriage. The entire festival is enormously affecting, even for nonbelievers, and is not to be missed by February visitors.

Museo Belliniano. Catania's greatest native son was the composer Vincenzo Bellini (1801–35), whose operas have thrilled audiences since their premieres in Naples and Milan. His home, now the Museo Belliniano, preserves memorabilia of the man and his work. ⊠ *Piazza San Francesco D'Assisi 3* ☏ *095/7150535* ⌦ *€5* ⊙ *Mon.–Sat. 9–7, Sun. 9–1.*

QUICK BITES

Pasticceria Savia. The lively Pasticceria Savia makes superlative arancini with *ragù* (a slow-cooked, tomato-based meat sauce). Or you could choose cannoli or other snacks to munch on while you rest. It's closed Monday. ⊠ *Via Etnea 302–304 and Via Umberto 2, near Villa Bellini* ☏ *095/322335* ⊕ *www.savia.it.*

WHERE TO EAT AND STAY

$$$
SEAFOOD

✕**Ambasciata del Mare.** When a seafood restaurant sits next door to a fish market, it bodes well for the food's freshness. Choose swordfish or *gamberoni* (large shrimp) from a display case in the front of the restaurant; then enjoy it simply grilled with oil and lemon. This basic, bright, and cozy place couldn't be friendlier or more easily accessed—it's right on the corner of Piazza del Duomo by the fountain. Book early. Ⓢ *Average main: €35* ⊠ *Piazza del Duomo 6/7* ☏ *095/341003* ⊕ *www.ambasciatadelmare.it* ⌂ *Reservations essential.*

$
CAFÉ

Caffè del Duomo. Sample the hustle and bustle of Catania at Caffè del Duomo, which has handmade cookies and cakes and a great local atmosphere. Take a seat outside in the piazza and order one of the excellent cannoli to eat with your coffee as you watch the world go by. ⊠ *Piazza Duomo 11–13* ☏ *095/7150556.*

$$$
SICILIAN

✕**La Siciliana.** Brothers Salvo and Vito La Rosa serve memorable seafood and meat dishes, exquisite homemade desserts, and a choice of more than 220 wines. The restaurant specializes in the ancient dish *ripiddu nivicatu* (risotto with cuttlefish ink and fresh ricotta cheese), as well as *sarde a beccafico* (stuffed sardines) and calamari *ripieni alla griglia* (stuffed and grilled squid). A meal at this fine eatery more than justifies the short taxi ride 3 km (2 miles) north of the city center. Ⓢ *Average main: €30* ⊠ *Viale Marco Polo 52a* ☏ *095/376400* ⊕ *www.lasiciliana.it* ⊙ *Closed Mon. No dinner Sun.*

$$
SEAFOOD
Fodor's Choice
★

✕**Osteria Antica Marina.** Just steps from Catania's famous fish market, this bustling osteria makes a perfect stop for ultrafresh seafood, surrounded by an energetic mix of locals and in-the-know tourists. You'd do well to follow their lead and start with the seafood antipasti, a rotating selection of whatever's freshest that day. Antica Marina's famed for its linguine with sea urchin, but you also can't go wrong with spaghetti with mussels and algae or ricotta panzotti in squid ink; just save room for the freshly grilled whole fish. If you can't choose, opt for one of the good-value prix-fixe menus (€25–€65). There's no wine list, but the efficient servers will be happy to recommend a suitable pairing. $ *Average main: €20* ⊠ *Via Pardo 29* ☎ *095/348197* ⊕ *www.anticamarina. it* ⊗ *Closed Wed.*

$

HOTEL

Fodor's Choice

★

🖳 **Una Hotel Palace.** For welcoming service and great views of Etna, this centrally located hotel overlooking Catania's main shopping street can't be beat; you can even take your breakfast on the rooftop terrace (for an extra €10) to enjoy the scenery first thing. **Pros:** amazing views; bountiful breakfast buffet; eager-to-please staff. **Cons:** parking only off-site (fee); some noisy rooms; no free Wi-Fi in classic rooms. $ *Rooms from: €103* ⊠ *Via Etnea 218* ☎ *095/2505111 (international number)* ⊕ *www.unahotels.it/en/una_hotel_palace/catania_hotels.htm* ⇴ *80 rooms, 14 suites.*

NIGHTLIFE AND PERFORMING ARTS

Teatro Massimo Bellini. The opera season at the Teatro Massimo Bellini, October to June, attracts top singers and productions to the birthplace of the great composer Vincenzo Bellini. Guided tours (€6) of the theater's lavish interior, built in 1890, run from Tuesday to Saturday between 9:30 am and noon when theater business permits; call first to ensure you can get a tour. Enter by the box office on Piazza Bellini. ⊠ *Via Perrotta 12* ☎ *095/7150921 for info, 095/7306111 for box office* ⊕ *www.teatromassimobellini.it* ⊗ *Box office: Tues.–Sat. 10–3 and 1 hr before performances.*

SHOPPING

Catania is justly famous for its candies and bar snacks.

I Dolci di Nonna Vincenza. The selection of almond-based delights here may be small, but everything is fresh and phenomenally good. Ask for boxes of mixed cookies by weight, and enjoy the grab-bag selection at your leisure later. International shipping is available. Other stores can be found on Via G. d'Annunzio 216/218, and at Catania airport. ⊠ *Palazzo Biscari, Piazza San Placido 7* ☎ *095/7151844* ⊕ *www. dolcinonnavincenza.it.* ⊠ *Aeroporto Fontanarossa* ☎ *095/7234522 for departures-area location, 095/349388 for arrivals-area location*

Outdoor Fish and Food Market. Beginning behind the Fontana Amenano at the corner of Piazza del Duomo and spreading westwards between Via Garibaldi and Via Transito, this is one of Italy's most memorable markets. It's a feast for the senses, with thousands of just-caught fish (some still wriggling), endless varieties of meats, ricotta, and fresh produce, plus a symphony of vendor shouts to fill the ears. Open Monday through Saturday, the market is at its best in the early morning and finishes up around lunchtime.

SIRACUSA

Siracusa, known to English speakers as Syracuse, is a wonder to behold. One of the great ancient capitals of Western civilization, the city was founded in 734 BC by Greek colonists from Corinth and soon grew to rival, and even surpass, Athens in splendor and power. It became the largest, wealthiest city-state in the West and a bulwark of Greek civilization. Although Siracusa lived under tyranny, rulers such as Dionysius filled their courts with Greeks of the highest cultural stature—among them the playwrights Aeschylus and Euripides, and the philosopher Plato. The Athenians, who didn't welcome Siracusa's rise, set out to conquer Sicily, but the natives outsmarted them in what was one of the greatest military campaigns in ancient history (413 BC). The city continued to prosper until it was conquered two centuries later by the Romans.

Present-day Siracusa still has some of the finest examples of Baroque art and architecture; dramatic Greek and Roman ruins; and a Duomo that's the stuff of legend—a microcosm of the city's entire history in one building. The modern city also has a wonderful, lively, Baroque old town worthy of extensive exploration, as well as pleasant piazzas, outdoor cafés and bars, and a wide assortment of excellent seafood. There are essentially two areas to explore in Siracusa: the Parco Archeologico (Archaeological Zone), on the mainland; and the island of Ortygia, the ancient city first inhabited by the Greeks, which juts out into the Ionian Sea and is connected to the mainland by two small bridges. Ortygia is becoming increasingly popular with tourists, and is starting to lose its old-fashioned charm in favor of modern boutiques.

Siracusa's old nucleus of Ortygia, a compact area, is a pleasure to amble around without getting unduly tired. In contrast, mainland Siracusa is a grid of wider avenues. At the northern end of Corso Gelone, above Viale Paolo Orsi, the orderly grid gives way to the ancient quarter of Neapolis, where the sprawling Parco Archeologico is accessible from Viale Teracati (an extension of Corso Gelone). East of Viale Teracati, about a 10-minute walk from the Parco Archeologico, the district of Tyche holds the archaeological museum and the church and catacombs of San Giovanni, both off Viale Teocrito (drive or take a taxi or city bus from Ortygia). Coming from the train station, it's a 15-minute trudge to Ortygia along Via Francesco Crispi and Corso Umberto. If you're not up for that, take one of the free electric buses leaving every 10 minutes from the bus station around the corner.

GETTING HERE AND AROUND

On the main train line from Messina and Catania, Siracusa is also linked to Catania by frequent buses.

VISITOR INFORMATION

Siracusa Tourism Office ⊠ *Via Roma 31, Ortygia* ☎ *800/055500* ⊕ *www.provincia.siracusa.it.*

WHEN TO GO

Santa Lucia alla Badia. The feast of the city's patron, Santa Lucia, is held on December 13 and 20 at Santa Lucia alla Badia. A splendid silver statue of the saint is carried from the church to the Duomo: a torchlight procession and band music accompany the bearers, while local families watch from their balconies. ⊠ *Piazza del Duomo, near Catacombs of San Giovanni, Ortygia.*

EXPLORING

ARCHAEOLOGICAL ZONE

TOP ATTRACTIONS

Fodor's Choice ★ **Parco Archeologico.** Siracusa is most famous for its dramatic set of Greek and Roman ruins. Though the various ruins can be visited separately, see them all, along with the Museo Archeologico. If the park is closed, go up Viale G. Rizzo from Viale Teracati to the belvedere overlooking the ruins, which are floodlit at night.

Before the park's ticket booth is the gigantic **Ara di Ierone** (Altar of Hieron), which was once used by the Greeks for spectacular sacrifices involving hundreds of animals. The first attraction in the park is the **Latomia del Paradiso** (Quarry of Paradise), a lush tropical garden full of palm and citrus trees. This series of quarries served as prisons for the defeated Athenians, who were enslaved; the quarries once rang with the sound of their chisels and hammers. At one end is the famous **Orecchio di Dionisio** (Ear of Dionysius), with an ear-shape entrance and unusual acoustics inside, as you'll hear if you clap your hands. The legend is that Dionysius used to listen in at the top of the quarry to hear what the slaves were plotting below.

The **Teatro Greco** is the chief monument in the Archaeological Park. Indeed it's one of Sicily's greatest classical sites and the most complete Greek theater surviving from antiquity. Climb to the top of the seating area (which could accommodate 15,000) for a fine view: all the seats converge upon a single point—the stage—which has the natural scenery and the sky as its background. Hewn out of the hillside rock in the 5th century BC, the theater saw the premieres of the plays of Aeschylus. Greek tragedies are still performed here every year in May and June. Above and behind the theater runs the Via dei Sepulcri, in which streams of running water flow through a series of Greek sepulchres.

The well-preserved and striking **Anfiteatro Romano** (Roman Amphitheater) reveals much about the differences between the Greek and Roman personalities. Where drama in the Greek theater was a kind of religious ritual, the Roman amphitheater emphasized the spectacle of combative sports and the circus. This arena is one of the largest of its kind and was built around the 2nd century AD. The corridor where gladiators and beasts entered the ring is still intact, and the seats (some of which still bear the occupants' names) were hauled in and constructed on the site from huge slabs of limestone. ⊠ *Viale Teocrito, entrance on Via Agnello* ☎ *0931/66206* 💶 *€10; combination ticket €13.50, includes Museo Archeologico* 🕐 *9–1 hr before sunset (holidays 9–1 pm); last entrance 1 hr before closing.*

QUICK BITES **Leonardi.** On your way to the Archaeological Park, stop in at this bar-cum-pasticceria for some great Sicilian cakes and ice cream. It's popular with locals, so you may have to line up for your cakes during holiday times. It's closed Wednesday. ⊠ *Viale Teocrito 123, Archaeological Zone* ☎ *0931/61411* ⊕ *www.pasticcerialeonardi.com.*

15

WORTH NOTING

Catacomba di San Giovanni. Not far from the Parco Archeologico, off Viale Teocrito, the catacombs below the church of San Giovanni are one of the earliest-known Christian sites in the city. Inside the crypt of San Marciano is an altar where Saint Paul preached on his way through Sicily to Rome. The frescoes in this small chapel are mostly bright and fresh, though some dating from the 4th century AD show their age. ⊠ *Piazza San Giovanni, Tyche* ☎ *0931/64694* ⌐ *€8* ⊘ *Daily 9:30–12:30 and 2:30–5:30 (may be extended in summer); evening visits are also organized. Closed Mon. in winter.*

Museo Archeologico. The impressive collection of Siracusa's splendid archaeological museum is organized by region around a central atrium and ranges from Neolithic pottery to fine Greek statues and vases. Compare the Landolina Venus—a headless goddess of love who rises out of the sea in measured modesty (a 1st-century AD Roman copy of the Greek original)—with the much earlier (300 BC) elegant Greek statue of Hercules in Section C. Of a completely different style is a marvelous fanged Gorgon, its tongue sticking out, that once adorned the cornice of the Temple of Athena to ward off evildoers. ⊠ *Viale Teocrito 66, Tyche* ☎ *0931/489511* ⊕ *www.regione.sicilia.it/beniculturali/museopaoloorsi* ⌐ *€8; combination ticket €13.50, includes Parco Archeologico* ⊘ *Tues.–Sat. 9–6, Sun. 9–1; last entry 1 hr before closing.*

ORTYGIA

TOP ATTRACTIONS

Fodor's Choice
★

Duomo. Siracusa's Duomo is an archive of island history: the bottommost excavations have unearthed remnants of Sicily's distant past, when the Siculi inhabitants worshipped their deities here. During the 5th century BC (the same time as Agrigento's Temple of Concord was built), the Greeks erected a temple to Athena over it, and in the 7th century Siracusa's first Christian cathedral was built on top of the Greek structure. The massive columns of the original Greek temple were incorporated into the present structure and are clearly visible, embedded in the exterior wall along Via Minerva. The Greek columns were also used to dramatic advantage inside, where on one side they form chapels connected by elegant wrought-iron gates. The Baroque facade, added in the 18th century, displays a harmonious rhythm of concaves and convexes. In front, the piazza is encircled by pink and white oleanders and elegant buildings ornamented with filigree grillwork. ⊠ *Piazza del Duomo, Ortygia* ☎ *0931/65328* ⌐ *€2* ⊘ *Apr.–Oct., daily 8–7:45; Nov.–Mar., daily 8–7.*

Fonte Aretusa. A freshwater spring, the Fountain of Arethusa, sits next to the sea, studded with Egyptian papyrus that's reportedly natural. This anomaly is explained by a Greek legend that tells how the nymph Arethusa was changed into a fountain by the goddess Artemis (Diana) when she tried to escape the advances of the river god Alpheus. She fled from Greece, into the sea, with Alpheus in close pursuit, and emerged in Sicily at this spring. It's said if you throw a cup into the Alpheus River in Greece it will emerge here at this fountain, which is home to a few tired ducks and some faded carp—but no cups. If you want to stand right by the fountain, you need to gain admission through the aquarium;

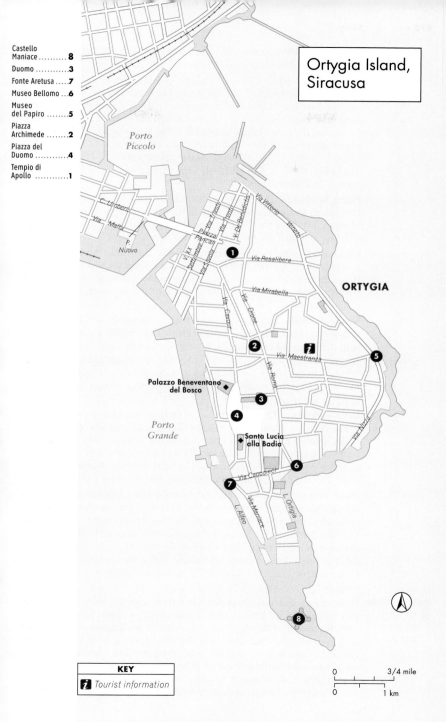

Ortygia Island, Siracusa

Porto Piccolo

Porto Grande

ORTYGIA

Palazzo Beneventano
del Bosco ◆

Santa Lucia
alla Badia ◆

KEY

i *Tourist information*

0   3/4 mile

0   1 km

otherwise, look down on it from Largo Aretusa. ⊠ *Off promenade along harbor, Ortygia.*

Museo del Papiro. Housed in the 16th-century ex-convent of Sant'Agostino, the small but intriguing Papyrus Museum uses informative exhibits and videos to demonstrate how papyri are prepared from reeds and then painted—an ancient tradition in the city. Siracusa, it seems, has the only climate outside the Nile Valley in which the papyrus plant—from which the word "paper" comes—thrives. ⊠ *Via Nizza 14, Ortygia* ☎ *0931/22100* ⊕ *www.museodelpapiro.it* ✉ *€4* ⊘ *May–Sept., Tues.–Sat. 9:15–7, Sun. 9:15–2; Oct.–Apr., Tues.–Sun. 9:15–2. Last entry 1 hr before closing.*

Piazza Archimede. The center of this piazza has a Baroque fountain, the Fontana di Diana, festooned with fainting sea nymphs and dancing jets of water. Look for the Chiaramonte-style **Palazzo Montalto,** an arched-window gem just off the piazza on Via Montalto. ⊠ *Ortygia.*

Fodor'sChoice
★
Piazza del Duomo. In the heart of Ortygia, this ranks as one of Italy's most beautiful piazzas. Its elongated space is lined with Sicilian Baroque treasures and outdoor cafés, in addition to the imposing Duomo. Check with the tourist office for guided tours of the underground tunnels. ⊠ *Ortygia.*

Tempio di Apollo. Scattered through the piazza just across the bridge to Ortygia are the ruins of a temple dedicated to Apollo, a model of which is in the Museo Archeologico. In fact, little of this noble Doric temple remains except for some crumbled walls and shattered columns; the window in the south wall belongs to a Norman church that was built much later on the same spot. ⊠ *Piazza Pancali, Ortygia.*

WORTH NOTING

Castello Maniace. The southern tip of Ortygia island is occupied by this castle built by Frederick II (1194–1250), until recently an army barracks, from which there are fine sea views. Though the castle itself is under restoration until at least October 2015, you can still visit the grounds and admire the vistas. ⊠ *Via del Castello Maniace, Ortygia* ☎ *0931/4508211* ⊘ *Tues.–Fri. 9–1, Sat. 9–5:30, Sun. 9–1.*

Museo Bellomo. Siracusa's principal museum of art is inside a lovely Catalan Gothic palazzo with mullioned windows and an elegant exterior staircase. Among the paintings is the *Annunciation* by 15th-century maestro Antonello da Messina, restored to its original brilliance. There are also exhibits of Sicilian nativity figures, silver, furniture, ceramics, and religious vestments. ⊠ *Palazzo Bellomo, Via Capodieci 14/16, Ortygia* ☎ *0931/69511* ✉ *€8* ⊘ *Tues.–Sat. 9–7, Sun. 9–1; last entry 30 mins before closing.*

OFF THE BEATEN PATH

If Siracusa's Baroque beauties whet your appetite for that over-the-top style, head 32 km (19 miles) southwest to Noto. Lying about 40 minutes away on the A18—and connected to Siracusa by both train and bus—the city is doable as a day trip. Having been decimated by an earthquake in 1693 and rebuilt in the prevailing fashion of the day, Noto has remarkable architectural integrity. A prime example of design from the island's Baroque heyday, it presents a pleasing ensemble of honey-color buildings, strikingly uniform in style but never dull. The domed Cattedrale di San Niccolò (divine in more ways than one) is an undisputed highlight of the extraordinary Baroque architecture for which the town is world famous. The recently restored Palazzo Nicolaci, which offers a rare insight into the lifestyle of social climbers in the 18th century, is another must-see. But simply walking the pedestrianized main street qualifies as an aesthetic experience. When you need a break from the architectural eye candy, indulge in an edible sweet (and a restorative coffee or granita) at a wondrous cake shop, the Caffè Sicilia, located at Corso Vittorio Emanuele 125.

WHERE TO EAT

$$
PIZZA

✕ **Archimede.** Considered the best pizzeria in Ortygia, this place offers pizzas with classical names. Witness the Polifema, with sliced tomatoes, mozzarella, speck, and corn; or the Teocrite, topped with fresh tomato, mozzarella, garlic, onion, and basil. For those who can't face the full-size offerings, minipizzas are also available (albeit at the same price). The calzone *del ciclope* (literally, "of the Cyclops") is stuffed with tomato, mozzarella, ham, and egg. One of the good selection of bottled beers makes a perfect accompaniment. $ *Average main: €15 ✉ Via Gemmellaro 8, Ortygia* ☎ *0931/69701* ⊕ *www.trattoriaarchimede.it* ⊗ *Closed Sun.*

$$
SICILIAN
Fodor's Choice
★

✕ **Don Camillo.** A gracious series of delicately arched rooms, lined with wine bottles and sepia-tone images of Old Siracusa, overflows with locals in the know. Preparations bring together fresh seafood and inspired creativity: taste, for instance, the sublime spaghetti *delle Sirene* (with sea urchin and shrimp in butter) or gamberoni prepared unexpectedly (and wonderfully) in pork fat. The wine list is, in a word, extraordinary. $ *Average main: €20 ✉ Via Maestranza 96, Ortygia* ☎ *0931/67133* ⊕ *www.ristorantedoncamillosiracusa.it* ⊗ *Closed Sun., 2 wks in Jan., and 2 wks in July.*

$$
MODERN ITALIAN

✕ **Oinos.** This restaurant–wine bar's ambitious food represents the most modern face of Siracusa. The dining rooms are stark but inviting, carefully balancing style consciousness with restrained refinement. Surrender to the sensational antipasto *sformatino di patate, cavolo capuccio, scamorza e braduro*, a molded potato tart with cabbage and rich, creamy cheeses. In season, special dishes spotlight white truffles from Alba priced by the gram (as is customary) and worth every penny. $ *Average main: €20 ✉ Via della Giudecca 69/75, Ortygia* ☎ *0931/464900* ⊕ *www.oinosrestaurant.it* ⊗ *Closed Mon., Jan., and Feb. No dinner Sun. in winter.*

$$
SICILIAN

✕ **Taverna Sveva.** At this casual tavern conveniently located in the streets right behind the Castello Maniace, you can sit back and enjoy both land-based and seafood dishes. The surroundings are studiously minimalist (no tablecloths, leather mats) and dishes are served on hand-painted ceramic ware. A major plus is that you can order half portions of several pasta dishes. For your secondo, try the unusual *pesce in crosta di patate* (grilled fish in a potato crust), but leave space for the special tiramisu *agli agrumi* (with citrus fruit). $ *Average main: €15 ✉ Piazza Federico di Svevia 1, Ortygia* ☎ *0931/24663* ⊗ *Closed Jan., and Wed. Sept. 15–June. No lunch June–Sept.*

15

WHERE TO STAY

$ HOTEL Fodor's Choice ★ **Domus Mariae.** On Ortygia's eastern shore, this hotel, in an unusual twist, is owned by Ursuline nuns, who help to make the mood placid and peaceful—but the elegant accommodations are far from monastic. **Pros:** nice breakfast; gorgeous sea views; enthusiastic staff. **Cons:** stairs to climb; not much street parking near the hotel. [$] *Rooms from: €82* ✉ *Via Vittorio Veneto 76, Ortygia* ☎ *0931/24854* 🌐 *www.domusmariaebenessere.com* 🛏 *12 rooms* 🍴 *Breakfast.*

$$ HOTEL **Grand Hotel Ortigia.** An elegant though somewhat old-fashioned design prevails at this venerable institution, which has enjoyed a prime position on the Porto Grande at the base of Ortygia since 1890. **Pros:** wonderful views from the restaurant; attentive service; convenient location. **Cons:** back rooms have no view; small bathrooms; Wi-Fi weak in some rooms. [$] *Rooms from: €164* ✉ *Viale Mazzini 12, Ortygia* ☎ *0931/464600* 🌐 *www.grandhotelortigia.it* 🛏 *41 rooms, 17 suites* 🍴 *Breakfast.*

$$ HOTEL **Grand Hotel Villa Politi.** European royalty, Winston Churchill, and other VIPs have frequented the grand 18th-century Villa Politi; freshly renovated and now equipped with modern luxuries, it still retains its charm and elegance with Rococo furnishings. **Pros:** excellent service; free parking in the hotel lot; expansive outdoor pool. **Cons:** a fair distance from the sights of Ortygia; not many restaurants in the neighborhood. [$] *Rooms from: €169* ✉ *Via M. Politi 2, Archaeological Zone* ☎ *0931/412121* 🌐 *www.villapoliti.com* 🛏 *98 rooms, 2 suites* 🍴 *Breakfast.*

$ B&B/INN **Hotel Aurora.** In a pretty, old palazzo, this bare-bones inn caters mostly to backpackers and those who have the stamina to brave the four-story climb. **Pros:** good value; full of character. **Cons:** breakfast is not always served on the premises; some rooms are poorly furnished; lots of stairs to climb. [$] *Rooms from: €60* ✉ *Via Maestranza 111, Ortygia* ☎ *0931/69475* 🛏 *8 rooms (5 with bath)* 🍴 *Breakfast.*

$$ HOTEL **Mercure Siracusa Prometeo.** Offering excellent an value, the Mercure occupies a glass-fronted building along the busy Viale Teracati and, like most other hotels in the same chain, it's a slick operation with first-rate facilities. **Pros:** a two-minute walk from the archaeological site of Neapolis; swimming pool on the roof; good parking facilities. **Cons:** chain hotel with little character; a long way from the island of Ortygia; €10 charge for breakfast. [$] *Rooms from: €140* ✉ *Viale Teracati 20, Tyche* ☎ *0931/464646* 🌐 *www.hotelmercuresiracusa.com* 🛏 *93 rooms.*

PERFORMING ARTS

Teatro Greco (*Greek Theater*). From mid-May to late June, Siracusa's Teatro Greco stages performances of classical tragedy and comedy. Tickets run €36 to €67, with a small discount if you buy the ticket in person. ✉ *Teatro Greco, Archaeological Zone* ☎ *0931/487200, 800/542644 toll-free in Italy* 🌐 *www.indafondazione.org.*

THE INTERIOR

Sicily's interior is for the most part untrammeled, though the Imperial Roman Villa at Casale, outside Piazza Armerina, gives precious evidence of a bygone epoch. Don't miss the windy mountaintop city of Enna, dubbed "the Navel of Sicily," or Caltagirone, a renowned ceramics center. If you're a wine lover, there are many wineries that can be visited by appointment in and around the Iblea region.

RAGUSA

90 km (56 miles) southwest of Siracusa.

Ragusa and Modica are the two chief cities in Sicily's smallest and sleepiest province, and the centers of a region known as Iblea. The dry, rocky, gentle countryside filled with canyons and grassy knolls is a unique landscape in Sicily. Iblea's trademark drystone walls divide swaths of land in a manner reminiscent of the high English countryside—but summers are decidedly Sicilian, with dry heat so intense that life grinds to a standstill for several hours each day. This remote province hums along to its own tune, clinging to local customs, cuisines, and traditions in aloof disregard even of the rest of Sicily. Ragusa, a modern city with a beautiful historic core, is known for some great local red wines and its wonderful cheese—a creamy, doughy, flavorful version of *caciocavallo,* made by hand every step of the way.

15

GETTING HERE AND AROUND

Trains and buses leave from Siracusa four or five times daily.

VISITOR INFORMATION

Ragusa Tourism Office ✉ *Piazza San Giovanni* ☎ *0932/684780* 🌐 *www.comune.ragusa.it.*

EXPLORING

Basilica di San Giorgio. Designed by Rosario Gagliardi in 1738, this is a fine example of Sicilian Baroque. 🕒 *Mar.–Oct., Wed.–Mon. 10–12:30 and 4–7; Nov.–Feb., Wed.–Mon. 10–12:30 and 4–6.*

Ibla. The lovely historic center of Ragusa, known as Ibla, was completely rebuilt after the devastating earthquake of 1693. A tumble of buildings perched on a hilltop and suspended between a deep ravine and a sloping valley, its tiny squares and narrow lanes make for pleasant meandering.

WHERE TO EAT

$$ SICILIAN 🍴 **Locanda Gulfi.** On the grounds of the expansive Gulfi winery, which produces well-regarded organic wines, you'll find a unique place for a sophisticated lunch or dinner, with sweeping views of the Chiaramonte hills and vineyards (about a half-hour drive north of Ragusa). The modern room features hand-blown chandeliers and a design-focused black-and-red color scheme; in warmer months, enjoy your meal on the lovely terrace. The chef skillfully uses local ingredients to prepare Sicilian dishes with a twist; for instance, you might find sardines fried in a cornmeal crust or pumpkin ravioli with Sicilian black truffle. You can, of course, pair everything with Gulfi wines and, if you overindulge, there's a small country inn on the premises to spend the night. [$] *Average main:*

€21 ⊠ C. da Patria, Chiaramonte Gulfi ☎ 0932/928081 for reservations, 0932/921654 for winery ⊕ www.locandagulfi.it ⚛ Reservations essential ⊙ Closed Mon. No dinner Sun.

CALTAGIRONE

66 km (41 miles) northwest of Ragusa.

Built over three hills, this charming Baroque town is a center of Sicily's ceramics industry. Here you can find majolica balustrades, tile-decorated windowsills, and the monumental Scala Santa Maria del Monte.

GETTING HERE AND AROUND

Buses and trains from Catania stop in the lower town, which is a pleasant stroll from the center. Caltagirone is also well connected by local buses and taxis. Connections with Ragusa, Enna, and Piazza Armerina are less frequent.

VISITOR INFORMATION

Caltagirone Tourism Office ⊠ *Galleria Luigi Sturzo, Piazza Municipio 10* ☎ *0933/41365* ⊕ *www.comune.caltagirone.ct.it.*

EXPLORING

Museo della Ceramica. Caltagirone was declared a UNESCO World Heritage Site for its ceramics as well as for its numerous Baroque churches. Though you may find the museum in a bit of disarray, you will see one of Sicily's most extensive pottery collections, ranging from neolithic finds to red-figure ware from 5th century BC Athens and 18th-century terra-cotta nativity figures, on display here. ⊠ *Via Roma, inside Giardini Pubblici* ☎ *0933/58418, 0933/58423* 🎫 *€4 ⊙ Tues.–Sun. 9–6:30.*

Scala Santa Maria del Monte. Exactly 142 individually decorated tile steps lead up to the neglected Santa Maria del Monte church. On July 24 (the feast of San Giacomo, the city's patron saint) and again on August 15 (the feast of the Assumption) this staircase is illuminated with candles that form a tapestry design. Months of work go into preparing the 4,000 *coppi,* or cylinders of colored paper, that hold oil lamps—then, at 9:30 pm on the nights of July 24, July 25, August 14, and August 15, a squad of hundreds of youngsters (tourists are welcome to participate) spring into action to light the lamps, so that the staircase flares up all at once. ⊠ *Begins at Piazza Municipio.*

PIAZZA ARMERINA

30 km (18 miles) northwest of Caltagirone.

A quick look around the fanciful town of Piazza Armerina is rewarding—it has a provincial warmth, and the crumbling yellow-stone architecture with Sicily's trademark bulbous balconies creates quite an effect. The greatest draw, however, lies just down the road.

GETTING HERE AND AROUND

Piazza Armerina is linked to Caltagirone, Catania, Enna, and Palermo by regular buses. There's no train station.

VISITOR INFORMATION

Piazza Armerina Tourism Office ✉ *Via Generale Muscará 47/A* ☎ *0935/680201* 🌐 *www.comune.piazzaarmerina.en.it.*

EXPLORING

Fodor's Choice ★ **Imperial Roman Villa.** The exceptionally well-preserved Imperial Roman Villa is thought to have been a hunting lodge of the emperor Maximian (3rd–4th century AD). The excavations were not begun until 1950, and most of the wall decorations and vaulting have been lost. However, some of the best mosaics of the Roman world cover more than 12,000 square feet under a shelter that hints at the layout of the original buildings. The mosaics were probably made by North African artisans; they're similar to those in the Tunis Bardo Museum, in Tunisia. The entrance was through a triumphal arch that led into an atrium surrounded by a portico of columns, after which the *thermae,* or bathhouse, is reached. It's colorfully decorated with mosaic nymphs, a Neptune, and slaves massaging bathers. The peristyle leads to the main villa, where in the Salone del Circo you look down on recently restored mosaics illustrating scenes from the Circus Maximus in Rome. A theme running through many of the mosaics, especially the long hall flanking the whole of one side of the peristyle courtyard, is the capturing and shipping of wild animals, which may have been a major source of the master's wealth. Yet the most famous mosaic is the floor depicting 10 girls wearing the ancient equivalent of bikinis, going through what looks like a fairly rigorous set of training exercises. ✉ *SP15, Contrada Casale, 4 km (2½ miles) southwest of Piazza Armerina* ☎ *0935/680036* 🌐 *www.villaromanadelcasale.it* 🎫 *€10 (free 1st Sun. of every month)* 🕒 *Apr.–Oct., daily 9–7; Nov.–Mar., daily 9–5. Last entrance 1 hr before closing. July and Aug., Fri.–Sun. 9–11:30 pm (last entrance at 11 pm).*

WHERE TO EAT

$$ MODERN ITALIAN Fodor's Choice ★ 🍴 **Al Fogher.** A beacon of culinary light shines in Sicily's interior, a region generally filled with good, but basic, places to eat. Ambitious—and successful—dishes here combine traditional ingredients with the creative flair of chef Angelo Treno. Try the borlotti bean soup with angel-hair pasta, mussels, and prawns, or the salt cod cooked in lavender and lemongrass with cauliflower and black olives. The wine list includes nearly 500 labels, and there's even a water list featuring more than a dozen kinds of mineral water. The dining room is unassuming and elegant; in cold weather, you can cozy up to the fireplaces, but the terrace is the place to be in summer. From town, follow Viale Ciancio and Viale Gaeta about 1 km (½ mile) north of Piazza Cascino. [$] *Average main: €18* ✉ *Contrada Bellia, near SS117bis, Aidone exit* ☎ *0935/684123* 🕒 *Closed Mon. No dinner Sun.*

ENNA

33 km (20 miles) northwest of Piazza Armerina, 136 km (85 miles) southeast of Palermo.

Deep in Sicily's interior, the fortress city of Enna (altitude 2,844 feet) commands exceptional views of the surrounding rolling plains, and, in the distance, Mt. Etna. It's the highest provincial capital in Italy and,

15

thanks to its central location, is nicknamed the "Navel of Sicily." Virtually unknown by tourists and relatively untouched by industrialization, this sleepy town charms and prospers in a distinctly old-fashioned, Sicilian way. Enna makes a good stopover for the night or just for lunch, as it's right along the autostrada between Palermo and Catania (and thus Siracusa).

GETTING HERE AND AROUND

Just off the A19 autostrada, Enna is easily accessible by car. With the train station 5 km (3 miles) below the upper town, the most practical public transportation is by bus from Palermo or Catania.

VISITOR INFORMATION

Enna Tourism Office ⊠ *Piazza Napoleone Colaianni 6* ☏ *0935/500875* ⊕ *www.provincia.enna.it.*

EXPLORING

Castello di Lombardia. The narrow, winding streets of Enna are dominated at one end by the impressive cliff-hanging Castello di Lombardia, built by Frederick II, and easily visible as you approach town. Inside the castle, you can climb up the tower for great views from the dead center of the island—on a very clear day, you can see to all three coasts. Immediately to the south you see Lake Pergusa (dried out in late summer), now almost swallowed by Enna's sprawling suburbs and the race-track around its perimeter. According to Greek mythology, this was where Persephone was abducted by Hades. While a prisoner in his underworld realm she ate six pomegranate seeds, and was therefore doomed to spend half of each year there. For the ancients, she emerged at springtime, triggering a display of wild flowers that can still be admired all over Sicily. ⊠ *Piazza di Castello di Lombardia* 🎟 *Free* 🕐 *Daily 9–1 hr before sunset.*

Piazza Vittorio Emanuele. In town, head straight for Via Roma, which leads to Piazza Vittorio Emanuele—the center of Enna's shopping scene and evening passeggiata. The attached **Piazza Crispi,** dominated by the shell of the grand old Hotel Belvedere, affords breathtaking panoramas of the hillside and smoking Etna looming in the distance. The bronze fountain in the middle of the piazza is a reproduction of Gian Lorenzo Bernini's famous 17th-century sculpture *The Rape of Persephone,* a depiction of Hades abducting Persephone.

Rocca di Cerere (*Rock of Demeter*). The Greek cult of Demeter, goddess of the harvest, was said to have centered on Enna. It's not hard to see why its adherents would have worshipped at the Rocca di Cerere, protruding out on one end of town next to the Castello di Lombardia. The spot enjoys spectacular views of the expansive countryside and windswept Sicilian interior.

Torre di Federico II. This mysterious octagonal tower—of unknown purpose—stands above the lower part of town. It has been celebrated for millennia as marking the exact geometric center of the island—thus the tower's, and city's, nickname, "Umbilicus Siciliae" (Navel of Sicily). The interior is not open to the public, but the surrounding park is.

WHERE TO EAT AND STAY

$
SICILIAN ✕ **Centrale.** Housed in an old palazzo, this casual place has served meals since 1889. One entire wall is covered with a vast mirror, the others are adorned with Sicilian pottery, and an outdoor terrace soothes diners in summer. The seasonal menu includes local preparations such as *coppole di cacchio* (peppers stuffed with spaghetti, potato, and basil), grilled pork chops, and a 15th-century specialty called *controfiletto all'annese*—a veal filet with onions, artichokes, pig jowl, and white wine. Choose from a decent selection of Sicilian wines to accompany your meal. $ *Average main: €13* ✉ *Piazza VI Dicembre 9* ☎ *0935/500963* ⊕ *www.ristorantecentrale.net* ☾ *No lunch Sat. in winter.*

$
HOTEL 🏨 **Hotel Sicilia.** Sicily's interior has few decent accommodations, and of Enna's two hotels, this one has more character. **Pros:** central location; friendly staff; good breakfast. **Cons:** a bit dated; some rooms can be noisy. $ *Rooms from: €75* ✉ *Piazza Napoleone Colajanni 7* ☎ *0935/500850* ⊕ *www.hotelsiciliaenna.it* ⤴ *60 rooms* ⭘⭗ *Breakfast.*

15

AGRIGENTO AND WESTERN SICILY

The crowning glory of western Sicily is the concentration of Greek temples at Agrigento, on a height between the modern city and the sea. The mark of ancient Greek culture also lingers in the cluster of ruined cliffside temples at Selinunte and at the splendidly isolated site of Segesta. Traces of the North African culture that for centuries exerted a strong influence on this end of the island are tangible in the coastal town of Marsala. In contrast, the cobblestone streets of hilltop Erice retain a strong medieval complexion, giving the quiet town the air of a last outpost on the edge of the Mediterranean. On the northern coast, not far outside Palermo, Monreale's cathedral glitters with mosaics that are among the finest in Italy.

AGRIGENTO

95 km (59 miles) southwest of Enna.

Agrigento owes its fame almost exclusively to its ancient Greek temples—though it was also the birthplace of playwright Luigi Pirandello (1867–1936).

GETTING HERE AND AROUND

Driving from Enna, take the A19 autostrada 35 km (21 miles) southwest to Caltanissetta; then follow the SS640 to Agrigento. Motorists can also access the town easily via the coastal SS115 and, from Palermo, by the SS189. Buses and trains run from Enna, Palermo, and Catania; both bus and train stations are centrally located.

VISITOR INFORMATION

Agrigento Tourism Office ✉ *Via Empedocle 73* ☎ *0922/20391.*

WHEN TO GO

Festa delle Mandorle (*Almond Blossom Festival*). During the first half of February, when most of the almond trees are in blossom, Agrigento hosts a Festa delle Mandorle, with international folk dances, a costumed parade, and the sale of marzipan and other sweets made from almonds.

Continued on page 890

VALLE DEI TEMPLI

Built on a broad open field that slopes gently to the sun-simmered Mediterranean, Akragas (ancient Agrigento's Greek name) was a showpiece of temples erected to flaunt a victory over Carthage. Despite a later sack by the Carthaginians, mishandling by the Romans, and neglect by the Christians and Muslims, the eight or so monuments in the Valle dei Templi (a UNESCO World Heritage Site) are considered to be, along with the Acropolis in Athens, the finest Greek ruins in all the world.

 TIMING TIP

The temples are at their very best in May, when the weather is warm but the summer tourist crowds haven't yet arrived.

Whether you first come upon the Valle dei Templi in the early morning light, or bathed by golden floodlights at night, it's easy to see why Akragas was celebrated by the Greek poet Pindar as "the most beautiful city built by mortal men."

MAKING THE MOST OF YOUR VISIT

GETTING AROUND
Though getting to, from, and around the dusty ruins of the Valle dei Templi is no great hassle, this important archaeological zone deserves several hours. The site, which opens at 8:30 AM, is divided into western and eastern sections. For instant aesthetic gratification, walk through the eastern zone; for a more comprehensive tour, start way out at the western end and work your way back uphill.

The temples are a bit spread out, but the valley is all completely walkable and generally toured on foot. However, note that there is only one hotel (Villa Athena) that is close enough to walk to the ruins, so you will most likely have to drive to reach the site; parking is at the entrance to the temple area.

WHAT TO BRING
It's a good idea to pack your own snacks and drinks. There are two snack shops with limited selections within the site, and the handful of high-priced bars around the site cater to tourists.

In summer the site can get extremely hot, so wear light clothing, a hat, and sun protection if possible.

A BRIEF HISTORY OF AGRIGENTO

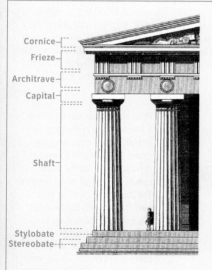

Cornice · Frieze · Architrave · Capital · Shaft · Stylobate · Stereobate

KEY DATES	
750 BC	Greek city-states begin to colonize Sicily and southern Italy.
734 BC	Neighboring Siracusa founded.
582 BC	Akragas settled. The city grows wealthy through trade with Carthage, just across the Mediterranean.
ca. 450 BC—350 BC	Temples at Akragas erected over a period of about 100 years to celebrate the city's prosperity.
413 BC	Battle of Siracusa vs. Athens.
406 BC	Fire from Carthaginian attack destroys much of Akragas. Despite this and future attacks, the city and its temples survive through the Roman era, the Middle Ages, and into the modern age.

The natural defenses of ancient Akragas depended on its secure and quite lovely position between two rivers on a floodplain a short distance from the sea. In Agrigento you will be treated to what many experts consider the world's best-preserved remains of classical Greece. All of the temples in the Valle dei Templi are examples of Doric architecture, the earliest and simplest of the Greek architectural orders (the others are Ionic and Corinthian). Some retain capitals in addition to their columns, while others are reduced to nothing more than fragments of stylobate.

THE TEMPLES

TEMPIO DI ERCOLE

The eight pillars of the **Temple of Hercules**, down the hill from the Temple of Concord, make up Agrigento's oldest temple complex (dating from the 6th century BC), dedicated to the favorite god of the often-warring citizens of Akragas. Partially reconstructed in 1922, it reveals the remains of a large Doric temple that originally had 38 columns. Like all the area temples, it faces east. The nearby Museo Archeologico Regionale contains some of the marble warrior figures that once decorated the temple's pediment.

Tempio di Ercole

TEMPIO DELLA CONCORDIA

The beautiful **Temple of Concord** is perhaps *the* best-preserved Greek temple in existence. The structure dates from about 430 BC, and owes its exceptional state of preservation to the fact that it was converted into a Christian church in the 6th century and was extensively restored in the 18th century. Thirty-two Doric columns surround its large interior, and everything but the roof and treasury are still standing. For preservation, this temple is blocked off to the public, but you can still get close enough to appreciate how well it's withstood the past 2,400 years.

TEMPIO DI GIUNONE

The **Temple of Juno**, east on the Via Sacra from the Temple of Concord, commands an exquisite view of the valley, especially at sunset. It's similar to but smaller than the Concordia and dates from about 450 BC. Traces of a fire that probably occurred during the Carthaginian attack in 406 BC,

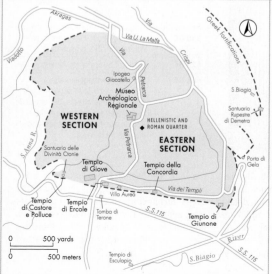

Valle dei Templi was declared a UNESCO World Heritage Site in 1997. Wear good walking shoes if you decide to explore the entire site, as the route covers an area of about 2 miles. The main path running east past the temples is paved and can accommodate wheelchairs, although the separate pathways up to the temples themselves can be rocky and uneven, so watch your footing.

which destroyed the ancient town, can be seen on the walls of the cellar. Thirty of the original 34 columns still stand, of which 16 have retained their capitals.

TEMPIO DI GIOVE

Though never completed, the **Temple of Jupiter** was considered the eighth wonder of the world. With a length of more than 330 feet, it was once the biggest of the Akragas temples and one of the largest temples in the Greek world. The temple was probably built in gratitude for victory over Carthage and was constructed by prisoners captured in that war. Basically Doric in style, it did not have the usual colonnade of freestanding columns but rather a series of half columns attached to a solid wall. This design is unique among known Doric temples—alas, only the stereobate was left behind. Inside the excavation you can see a cast (not the original) of one of the 38 colossal Atlas-like figures, or telamones, that supported the temple's massive roof.

Tempio di Giove

TEMPIO DI CASTORE E POLLUCE

The **Temple of Castor and Pollux** is a troublesome reconstruction of a 5th-century BC temple. It was pieced together by some enthusiastic if misguided 19th-century romantics who, in 1836, haphazardly put together elements from diverse buildings. Ironically, the four gently crumbling columns supporting part of an entablature of the temple have become emblematic of Agrigento.

OTHER SITES OF INTEREST

To the left of the Temple of Concord is a Paleochristian **necropolis**. Early Christian tombs were both cut into the rock and dug into underground catacombs.

Right opposite the Temple of Castor and Pollux, facing north, the **Santuario delle Divinità Ctonie** (Sanctuary of the Chthonic Divinities) has cultic altars and eight small temples dedicated to Demeter, Persephone, and other Underworld deities. In the vicinity are two columns of a temple dedicated to Hephaestus (Vulcan).

At the end of Via dei Templi, where it turns left and becomes Via Petrarca, stands the **Museo Archeologico Regionale**. An impressive collection of antiquities from the site includes vases, votives, everyday objects,

weapons, statues (including one of the surviving original telamones from the Temple of Jupiter), and models of the temples.

The **Hellenistic and Roman Quarter**, across the road from the archaeological museum, consists of four parallel streets, running north–south, that have been uncovered, along with the foundations of some houses from the Roman settlement (2nd century BC). Some of these streets still have their original mosaic pavements, and the complex system of sidewalks and gutters is easy to make out—reminding you that the ancient world wasn't all temples and togas.

EXPLORING

Monastero di Santo Spirito. There are a few other things to do and see in the area. Along the coast, around 12 km (7 miles) to the west of Agrigento near the town of Realmonte, you can view the Scala dei Turchi (Stairs of the Turks), which are natural white cliffs eroded into unusual shapes. By visiting the beaches closest to the temples, near the town of San Leone, you can sunbathe beside the locals. If, instead, you head up the hill from the Valle dei Templi to the modern city you'll have the opportunity to try a local treat or stay at an inexpensive lodging. Need another reason to go there? Just ring the doorbell at the **Monastero di Santo Spirito** and try the *kus-kus* (sweet cake), made of pistachio nuts, almonds, and chocolate, that the nuns prepare. (It's always best to phone ahead to make sure they'll have it.) The cloisters and courtyard of the church are open to the public. ⊠ *Salita di Santo Spirito, off Via Porcello* ☎ *0922/20664* ⊕ *www.monasterosantospiritoag.org* ☉ *Church daily 9–noon and 3–5; call in advance to confirm visit.*

Fodor's Choice
★

Valle dei Templi. *See the featured listing in this chapter.* ⊠ *Zona Archeologica, Via dei Templi* ☎ *0922/621620, 0922/621657* ⊕ *www.parcodeitempli.net* ⎘ *Site €10, with museum €13.50. One ticket covers all temples* ☉ *Daily 8:30–7; last entry 30 mins before closing. Mid-July–mid-Sept., also weekdays 8 pm–10 pm, weekends 8 pm–11 pm. Museum: Tues.–Sat. 9–7, Sun. and Mon. 9–1.*

WHERE TO EAT AND STAY

$
SICILIAN
Fodor's Choice
★

✕ **Il Re di Girgenti.** You wouldn't expect to find an ultramodern, even hip, place to dine within a few minutes' drive of Agrigento's ancient temples, yet Il Re di Girgenti offers up pleasing versions of Sicilian classics in a trendy, country-chic atmosphere (think funky black-and-white tile floors mixed with shelves lined with old-fashioned crockery) popular with young locals. You'll want to join them by starting with the terrific antipasti plate before moving on to rich spaghetti *con ricci* (with sea urchin) and the expertly cooked fillet of sea bass with a pistachio crust. The thoughtful wine list offers good prices on both local wines and those from throughout Sicily. Weather permitting, be sure to dine on the terrace for outstanding temple views. Ⓢ *Average main: €14* ⊠ *Via Panoramica dei Templi 51* ☎ *0922/401388* ⊕ *www.ilredigirgenti.it* ☉ *Closed Tues.*

$$
SICILIAN

✕ **Trattoria dei Templi.** Along a road on the way up to Agrigento proper from the temple area, this family-run vaulted restaurant serves up some tasty traditional food. The menu includes five different homemade pastas each day as well as plenty of fresh fish dishes, all prepared with Sicilian flair. The antipasti, such as the carpaccio of *cernia* (grouper), are exceptional, and the ample wine list has many Sicilian choices. The best bet is to ask for the advice of brothers Giuseppe and Simone, the owners and chief orchestrators in the restaurant. Reservations are recommended in the high season. Ⓢ *Average main: €15* ⊠ *Via Panoramica dei Templi 15* ☎ *0922/403110* ⊕ *www.trattoriadeitempli.com* ☉ *Closed Sun.*

$$
HOTEL

⚏ **Foresteria Baglio della Luna.** Fiery sunsets and moonlight cast a glow over the ancient tower at the center of this farmhouse-hotel complex, in the valley below the temples. **Pros:** quiet location; serene environment.

Cons: hotel could use a refresh; difficult to reach from the temples and the city (buses run hourly); service can be slipshod. Ⓢ *Rooms from: €130* ✉ *Via Serafino Amabile Guastella 1, Contrada Maddalusa* ☎ *0922/511061* ⊕ *www.bagliodellaluna.com* ➷ *21 rooms, 2 suites* ⊘ *Closed Dec.–Mar.* ⦿ *Multiple meal plans.*

$$$$
HOTEL
Fodor's Choice
★

▦ **Villa Athena.** The 18th-century Villa Athena, freshly updated into a sleek, luxurious place to stay, complete with gorgeous manicured gardens and swimming pool, holds a privileged position directly overlooking the Temple of Concordia, a 10-minute walk away—an amazing sight both during the day and when it's lighted at night. **Pros:** perfect location to see the Valle dei Templi; phenomenal temple views; plenty of free parking. **Cons:** expensive; service a bit detached; lack of information on local attractions. Ⓢ *Rooms from: €310* ✉ *Via Passeggiata Archeologica 33* ☎ *0922/596288* ⊕ *www.hotelvillaathena.it* ➷ *21 rooms, 6 suites* ⦿ *Breakfast.*

SELINUNTE

15

100 km (62 miles) northwest of Agrigento, 114 km (71 miles) south of Palermo.

Numerous Greek temple ruins perch on a plateau overlooking an expanse of the Mediterranean at Selinunte (or Selinus). Selinunte is named after a local variety of wild parsley (*Apium graveolens* or *petroselinum*) that in spring grows in profusion among the ruined columns and overturned capitals. Although there are a few places to stay right around Selinunte, many people see it as an easy—and richly rewarding—stopover along the road to or from Agrigento. It takes only an hour or two to see.

GETTING HERE AND AROUND

You can get here by bus or car via the town of Castelvetrano, 11 km (7 miles) north, which is itself accessible from Palermo by car on the A29 autostrada, as well as by bus and train.

VISITOR INFORMATION

Selinunte Tourism Office ✉ *Via Giovanni Caboto, Marinella Selinunte* ☎ *0924/46251.*

EXPLORING

Fodor's Choice
★

Greek Temple Ruins. Selinunte was one of the most superb colonies of ancient Greece. Founded in the 7th century BC, the city became the rich and prosperous rival of Segesta, which in 409 BC turned to the Carthaginians for help. The Carthaginians, in turn, sent an army to destroy the city. The temples were demolished, the city was razed, and 16,000 of Selinunte's inhabitants were slaughtered. The remains of Selinunte are in many ways unchanged from the day of its sacking—burn marks still scar the Greek columns, and much of the site still lies in rubble at its exact position of collapse. The original complex held seven temples scattered over two sites separated by a harbor. Of the seven, only one (reconstructed in 1958) is whole. ■ TIP→ **This is a large archaeological site, so you might make use of the private navetta (shuttle) to save a bit of walking. Alternatively, if you have a car, you can visit the first temples close to the ticket office on foot and then drive westward to**

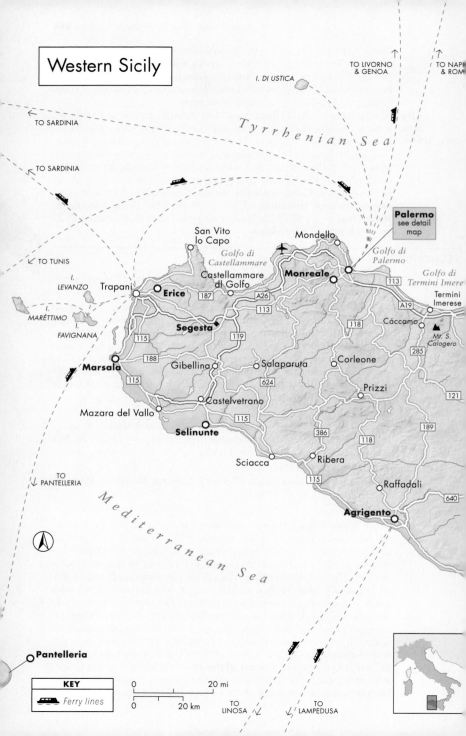

the farther site. Be prepared to show your ticket at various stages. ✉ *SS115, Marinella Selinunte, 13 km (8 miles) southeast of Castelvetrano* ☎ *0924/46277* 🎫 *€6* 🕒 *Daily 9–4.*

WHERE TO EAT

$$ SICILIAN 🍴 **Lido Zabbara.** Known to the locals as "Da Yoyo"—the owner is constantly getting up and down to attend to his customers—this is really no more than a glorified salad bar right on the beach at Selinunte. Pick up a plate and serve yourself from the various delicacies laid out on the center spread; a lunch buffet costs €12, while dinner (Friday and Saturday only) is €20. Wine comes by the carafe and is surprisingly drinkable. As an added plus there are sun beds and umbrellas at reasonable prices if you want to unwind before the next archaeological bonanza. [$] *Average main: €20* ✉ *Via Pigafetta, Marinella Selinunte* ☎ *0924/46194* 💳 *No credit cards* 🕒 *Closed Nov.–Mar. No dinner Sun.–Thurs.*

MARSALA

88 km (55 miles) northwest of Selinunte.

Marsala is readily associated with the world-famous, richly colored fortified wine named after it, and your main reason for stopping will likely be to visit some of the many wineries in the area. But the quiet seaside town, together with the nearby island of Mozia, were also once the main Carthaginian bases in Sicily: from them Carthage fought for supremacy over the island against Greece and Rome. In 1773 a British merchant named John Woodhouse happened upon the town and discovered that the wine here was as good as the port the British had long imported from Portugal. Two other wine merchants, Whitaker and Ingram, rushed in, and by 1800 Marsala was exporting its wine all over the British Empire.

GETTING HERE AND AROUND

Buses and trains from Palermo, Trapani, and Castelvetrano stop in Marsala. Drivers can take the coastal SS115.

VISITOR INFORMATION

Marsala Tourism Office ✉ *Via XI Maggio 100* ☎ *0923/714097* 🌐 *www.comune.marsala.tp.it.*

EXPLORING

Donnafugata Winery. One of Sicily's foremost wine producers, the 160-year-old Donnafugata Winery is open for tours of its *cantina* (wine cellar); reservations are required, and may be placed online or by phone. It's an interesting look at the wine-making process in Sicily, and it ends with a tasting of several whites and reds and a chance to buy. Don't miss the delicious, full-bodied red Mille e Una Notte, and the famous Ben Ryè Passito di Pantelleria, a sweet dessert wine made from dried grapes. ✉ *Via Sebastiano Lipari 18* ☎ *0923/724245, 0923/724263* 🌐 *www.donnafugata.it* 🎫 *Tastings range from €12 (visit and tasting 4 wines) to €30 (visit and tasting 4 wines paired with 4 Mediterranean dishes)* 🕒 *Tours and tastings (by appt. only) Mon. at 11, Tues.–Sat. at 11, 1, 4, and 5:30. Shop: Mon.–Sat. 10–1 and 3–6:30.*

Museo Archeologico Baglio Anselmi. A sense of Marsala's past as a Carthaginian stronghold is captured by the well-preserved Punic warship displayed in the town's Museo Archeologico Baglio Anselmi, along with some of the amphorae and other artifacts recovered from the wreck. The vessel, which was probably sunk during the great sea battle that ended the First Punic War in 241 BC, was dredged up from the mud near the Egadi Islands in the 1970s. There's also a good display of maritime and archaeological finds. ⊠ *Via Lungomare Boéo 2* ☎ *0923/952535* 🖅 *€4* ⊙ *Daily 9–6:30; ticket office closes ½ hr before closing.*

ERICE

45 km (28 miles) northeast of Marsala, 15 km (9 miles) northeast of Trapani.

Perched 2,450 feet above sea level, Erice is an enchanting medieval mountaintop aerie of palaces, fountains, and cobblestone streets. Shaped like an equilateral triangle, the town was the ancient landmark Eryx, dedicated to Aphrodite (Venus). When the Normans arrived they built a castle on Monte San Giuliano, where today there's a lovely public park with benches and belvederes offering striking views of Trapani, the Egadi Islands offshore, and, on a *very* clear day, Cape Bon and the Tunisian coast. Because of Erice's elevation, clouds conceal much of the view for most of winter. Sturdy shoes (for the cobblestones) and something warm to wear are recommended.

GETTING HERE AND AROUND

Make your approach via Trapani, which is on the A29 autostrada and well connected by bus and train with Marsala and Palermo. Mid-March to early January a funivia runs from the outskirts of Trapani to Erice Monday 1–8, Tuesday to Friday 8:10–8, Saturday 9–9, and Sunday 10–8. Going by car or bus from Trapani takes around 40 minutes.

VISITOR INFORMATION

Erice Tourism Office ⊠ *Palazzo Municipale, Piazza Loggia 3* ☎ *0923/869388, 0923/869173.*

EXPLORING

Capo San Vito. The cape has a long sandy beach on a promontory overlooking a bay in the Gulf of Castellammare. The town here, San Vito Lo Capo, is famous for its North African couscous, made with fish instead of meat. In late September it hosts the five-day **Cous Cous Fest,** a serious international couscous competition and festival with live music and plenty of free tastings. San Vito is also one of the bases for exploring the **Riserva dello Zingaro:** this nature reserve—one of the few stretches of coastline in Sicily which is not built-up—is at its best in late spring, when both wildflowers and birds are plentiful. ⊠ *Capo San Vito, 40 km (25 miles) north of Erice.*

WHERE TO EAT AND STAY

$
SICILIAN

✕ **Monte San Giuliano.** At this traditional restaurant near the main piazza, you can sit out on the tree-lined patio or in the white-walled dining room and munch on free *panelle* (chickpea fritters), which are delicate and judiciously seasoned. Follow them up with citrusy *sarde a beccafico* (sardines, arranged in the shape of a bird) and exemplary ravioli in cuttlefish ink. Or order the seafood couscous—it's served with a bowl of fish broth on the side so you can add as much as you wish. A charming touch: all dishes are served tableside, spooned directly from the cooking pots to your plate by the friendly waitstaff. Be sure to peruse the extensive wine list, which offers interesting choices and good values from local wineries. $ *Average main: €12* ✉ *Vicolo San Rocco 7* ☎ *0923/869595* ⊕ *www.montesangiuliano.it* ☾ *Closed Mon., 2 wks in mid-Jan., and 1st 2 wks in Nov.*

$
HOTEL
🏨 **Hotel Elimo.** Like the town of Erice itself, the Hotel Elimo is old-fashioned and yet full of charm; eccentric knickknacks and artwork fill the lobby, and the 21 homey rooms are all different, many boasting terraces with views of either the cobblestone streets or the valleys below (when they're not shrouded by clouds). **Pros:** convenient location; lots of character; helpful staff. **Cons:** some rooms feel a bit musty; small bathrooms. $ *Rooms from: €84* ✉ *Via Vittorio Emanuele 75* ☎ *0923/869377* ⊕ *www.hotelelimo.it* ⤳ *19 rooms, 2 suites* ☾ *Closed Jan. and Feb.* ⑩ *Breakfast.*

$
HOTEL
🏨 **Moderno.** This delightful hotel has a creaky old feel to it, but that's part of the charm—the lobby area, scattered with books, magazines, and knickknacks, calls to mind your aunt's living room. **Pros:** central location; great rooftop terrace. **Cons:** very modest rooms; street-facing rooms can be noisy. $ *Rooms from: €94* ✉ *Via Vittorio Emanuele 67* ☎ *0923/869300* ⊕ *www.hotelmodernoerice.it* ⤳ *40 rooms* ⑩ *Breakfast.*

SHOPPING

Antica Pasticceria del Convento. Here, Maria Grammatico's sister sells similar delectable treats. The shop is open from March through November. ✉ *Via Guarnotti 1* ☎ *0923/869777* ⊕ *www. anticapasticceriadelconvento.it.*

Pasticceria Grammatico. Fans of Sicilian sweets make a beeline for this place, run by Maria Grammatico, a former nun who gained international fame with *Bitter Almonds,* her life story cowritten with Mary Taylor Simeti. Her almond-paste creations are works of art, molded into striking shapes, including dolls and animals. There are a few tables and a tiny balcony with wonderful views. ✉ *Via Vittorio Emanuele 14* ☎ *0923/869390* ⊕ *www.mariagrammatico.it.*

SEGESTA

35 km (22 miles) east of Erice, 85 km (53 miles) southwest of Palermo.

Segesta is the site of one of Sicily's most impressive temples, constructed on the side of a windswept barren hill overlooking a valley of giant fennel. Virtually intact today, the temple is considered by some to be finer in its proportions and setting than any other Doric temple left standing.

15

GETTING HERE AND AROUND

Three or four daily buses travel from Trapani to Segesta. About as many trains from Palermo and Trapani stop at the Segesta-Tempio station, a 20-minute uphill walk from Segesta. The site is easily reached via the A29 autostrada.

EXPLORING

Fodor'sChoice ★ **Tempio Dorico** (*Doric Temple*). Segesta's imposing temple was actually started in the 5th century BC by the Elymian people, who may have

been refugees from Troy. At the very least, evidence—they often sided with the Carthaginians, for example—indicates that they were non-Greeks. However, the style is in many ways Greek. The temple was never finished; the walls and roof never materialized, and the columns were never fluted. Wear comfortable shoes, as you need to park your car in the lot at the bottom of the hill and walk about five minutes up to the temple.

If you're up for a longer hike, a little more than 1 km (½ mile) away near the top of the hill are the remains of a fine **theater** with impressive views, especially at sunset, of the plains and the Bay of Castellammare. (There's also a shuttle bus that leaves every 30 minutes, €1.50 round-trip.) Concerts and plays are staged here in summer. ⊠ *Calatafimi-Segesta* ☎ *0924/952356* 🎫 *€6* ⊙ *Apr.–early Oct., daily 8:30–7; early Oct.–late Oct., daily 8:30–6; late Oct.–Feb., daily 9–5; Mar., daily 9–6. Last entry 1 hr before closing.*

MONREALE

59 km (37 miles) northeast of Segesta, 10 km (6 miles) southwest of Palermo.

Only a short drive from Palermo, the sleepy town of Monreale is well worth the effort just to see the spectacular gold mosaics inside the Duomo. Try to arrive early in the morning or later in the afternoon to avoid the tour-bus hordes.

GETTING HERE AND AROUND

You can reach Monreale on the frequent buses that depart from Palermo's Piazza dell'Indipendenza. From Palermo, drivers can follow Corso Calatafimi west, though the going can be slow.

EXPLORING

Cloister. The lovely cloister of the abbey adjacent to the Duomo was built at the same time as the church but enlarged in the 14th century. The beautiful enclosure is surrounded by 216 intricately carved double columns, every other one decorated in a unique glass mosaic pattern. Afterward, don't forget to walk behind the cloister to the belvedere, with stunning panoramic views over the Conca d'Oro (Golden Conch) valley toward Palermo. ✉ *Piazza del Duomo* ☎ *091/6404403* 🎟 €6 🕓 *Daily 9–7; last entry ½ hr before closing.*

Fodor's Choice ★ **Duomo.** Monreale's splendid cathedral is lavishly decorated with mosaics depicting events from the Old and New Testaments. After the Norman conquest of Sicily the new princes showcased their ambitions through monumental building projects. William II (1154–89) built the church complex with a cloister and palace between 1174 and 1185, employing Byzantine craftsmen. The result was a glorious fusion of Eastern and Western influences, widely regarded as the finest example of Norman architecture in Sicily.

The major attraction is the 68,220 square feet of glittering gold mosaics decorating the cathedral interior. *Christ Pantocrator* dominates the apse area; the nave contains narratives of the Creation; and scenes from the life of Christ adorn the walls of the aisles and the transept. The painted wooden ceiling dates from 1816–37. The roof commands a great view (a reward for climbing 172 stairs).

Bonnano Pisano's bronze doors, completed in 1186, depict 42 biblical scenes and are considered among the most important of medieval artifacts. Barisano da Trani's 42 panels on the north door, dating from 1179, present saints and evangelists. ✉ *Piazza del Duomo* ☎ *091/6404413, 327/3510886* 🌐 *www.cattedralemonreale.it* 🕓 *Mon.–Sat. 8:30–12:45 and 2:30–5, Sun. 8–10 and 2:30–5:30.*

WHERE TO EAT

$$ SICILIAN 🍴 **La Botte 1962.** It's worth the short drive or inexpensive taxi from Monreale to reach this restaurant, which is famous for well-prepared local specialties. Dine alfresco on seafood dishes such as *bavette don Carmelo,* a narrow version of tagliatelle with a sauce of swordfish, squid, shrimp, and pine nuts. Other regular favorites include *involtini alla siciliana* (meat roulades stuffed with salami and cheese); set menus (a good value) are also available, and local wines make a tasty accompaniment. The restaurant is open for Friday and Saturday dinner and Sunday lunch, or for reservations of at least 15 people. [$] *Average main: €18* ✉ *Contrada Lenzitti 20, SS186 Km 10* ☎ *091/414051, 338/4383962* 🌐 *www.mauriziocascino.it* ✍ *Reservations essential* 🕓 *Closed Mon.–Thurs. (except by reservation and for Thurs. dinner in July), and Aug.–early Sept. No lunch Fri. and Sat.; no dinner Sun.*

PALERMO

Once the intellectual capital of southern Europe, Palermo has always been at the crossroads of civilization. Favorably situated on a crescent bay at the foot of Monte Pellegrino, it's attracted almost every culture touching the Mediterranean world. To Palermo's credit, it's absorbed these diverse cultures into a unique personality that's at once Arab and Christian, Byzantine and Roman, Norman and Italian. The city's heritage encompasses all of Sicily's varied ages, but its distinctive aspect is its Arab-Norman identity, an improbable marriage that, mixed in with Byzantine and Jewish elements, created some resplendent works of art. These are most notable in the churches, from small jewels such as

San Giovanni degli Eremiti to larger-scale works such as the cathedral. No less noteworthy than the architecture is Palermo's chaotic vitality, on display at some of Italy's most vibrant outdoor markets, public squares, street bazaars, and food vendors, and, above all, in its grand, discordant symphony of motorists, motorcyclists, and pedestrians that triumphantly climaxes in the new town center each evening with Italy's most spectacular passeggiata.

GETTING HERE AND AROUND

Palermo is well connected by road and rail; its airport links it to other cities in Italy, as well as around Europe.

VISITOR INFORMATION

Palermo Tourism Office ⊠ *Via Principe di Belmonte 92* ☎ *091/585172* ⊕ *www.provincia.palermo.it/turismo* ✉ *Aeroporto di Palermo* ☎ *091/591698* ⊕ *www.palermotourism.com.*

EXPLORING

Sicily's capital is a multilayered, vigorous metropolis with a strong historical profile; approach it with an open mind. You're likely to encounter some frustrating instances of inefficiency and, depending on the season, stifling heat. If you have a car, park it in a garage as soon as you can, and don't take it out until you're ready to depart.

Palermo is easily explored on foot, but you may choose to spend a morning taking a bus tour to help you get oriented. The Quattro Canti, or Four Corners, is the hub that separates the four sections of the old city: La Kalsa (the old Arab section) to the southeast, Albergheria to the southwest, Capo to the northwest, and Vucciria to the northeast. Each of these is a tumult of activity during the day, though at night the narrow alleys empty out and are best avoided in favor of the more animated avenues of the new city north of Teatro Massimo. Sights to see by day are scattered along three major streets: Corso Vittorio Emanuele, Via Maqueda, and Via Roma. The tourist information office in Piazza Belmonte will give you a map and a valuable handout that lists opening and closing times, which sometimes change with the seasons.

TOP ATTRACTIONS

Cattedrale. This church is a lesson in Palermitano eclecticism—originally Norman (1182), then Catalan Gothic (14th to 15th century), then fitted out with a Baroque and Neoclassical interior (18th century). Its turrets, towers, dome, and arches come together in the kind of meeting of diverse elements that King Roger II (1095–1154), whose tomb is inside along with that of Frederick II, fostered during his reign. The back of the apse is gracefully decorated with interlacing Arab arches inlaid with limestone and black volcanic tufa. It's possible to visit the cathedral's roof for some fabulous city views for a €5 fee from Monday to Saturday every half hour 10–4:30, or with a night visit on scheduled Saturdays between April and October. ⊠ *Corso Vittorio Emanuele, Capo* ☎ *091/334373* ⊕ *www.cattedrale.palermo.it* 🖾 *Free. €3 for treasury, crypt, and tombs, €5 for roof visit; €7 for treasury, crypt, royal tombs, and roof visit* ☉ *Cathedral: Mar.–Oct., daily 9–5:30; Nov.–Feb., daily*

Palermo

15

9:30–1. Treasury, crypt, and royal tombs: weekdays 9:30–1:30 and 2:30–5:30. Roof night visits: Apr.–Oct., certain Sat. 9 pm–midnight (last entrance at 11:30 pm); check website for exact dates.

Fodors Choice
★

La Martorana (*Santa Maria dell'Ammiraglio*). Distinguished by an elegant Norman campanile, this church was erected in 1143 but had its interior altered considerably during the Baroque period. High along the western wall, however, is some of the oldest and best-preserved mosaic artwork of the Norman period. Near the entrance is an interesting mosaic of King Roger II being crowned by Christ. In it Roger is dressed in a bejeweled Byzantine stole, reflecting the Norman court's penchant for all things Byzantine. Archangels along the ceiling wear the same stole wrapped around their shoulders and arms. The much plainer San Cataldo is next door. ⊠ *Piazza Bellini 3, Quattro Canti* ☎ 091/6161692 🔟 *€2* ☾ *Mon.–Sat. 9:30–1 and 3:30–5:30, Sun. 9–10:30.*

Museo Archeologico Regionale Salinas (*Salinas Regional Museum of Archaeology*). Especially interesting pieces in this small but excellent collection are the examples of prehistoric cave drawings and a marvelously reconstructed Doric frieze from the Greek temple at Selinunte, which reveals the high level of artistic culture attained by the Greek colonists in Sicily some 2,500 years ago. (To enter, use the door around the corner on Via Roma.) At the time of this writing, the museum was closed for extensive renovations, so before journeying on, phone the museum or the tourist information office to check whether it's open. ⊠ *Piazza Olivella 24, Via Roma, Olivella* ☎ 091/6116806 🔟 *€4, subject to increase when museum reopens* ☾ *Closed at time of writing; regular hrs: Tues.–Fri. 8:30–1:30 and 2:30–6:30, weekends 8:30–1; last entry ½ hr before closing.*

Palazzo Reale (*Royal Palace*). This historic palace, also called Palazzo dei Normanni (Norman Palace), was the seat of Sicily's semiautonomous rulers for centuries. The building is a fascinating mesh of abutting 10th-century Norman and 17th-century Spanish structures. Because it now houses the Sicilian Parliament, parts of the palace are closed to the public from Tuesday to Thursday when the regional parliament is sitting. The **Cappella Palatina** (Palatine Chapel) remains open. Built by Roger II in 1132, it's a dazzling example of the harmony of artistic elements produced under the Normans. Here the skill of French and Sicilian masons was brought to bear on the decorative purity of Arab ornamentation and the splendor of 11th-century Greek Byzantine mosaics. The interior is covered with glittering mosaics and capped by a splendid 10th-century Arab honeycomb stalactite wooden ceiling. Biblical stories blend happily with scenes of Arab life—look for one showing a picnic in a harem—and Norman court pageantry.

Upstairs are the royal apartments, including the **Sala di Re Ruggero** (King Roger's Hall), decorated with medieval murals of hunting scenes—an earlier (1120) secular counterpoint to the religious themes seen elsewhere. French, Latin, and Arabic were spoken here, and Arab astronomers and poets exchanged ideas with Latin and Greek scholars in one of the most interesting marriages of culture in the Western world. The Sala is always included with entry to the palace or chapel. ⊠ *Piazza*

Indipendenza, Albergheria ☎ *091/6262833* ⊕ *www.federicosecondo. org* 🎫 *Fri.–Mon. €8.50, Tues.–Thurs. €7 (on these days no admittance to Royal Apartments due to Parliamentary sessions)* ⊙ *Palazzo Reale: Mon.–Sat. 8:15–5:40, Sun. 8:15–1 (Cappella Palatina closed Sun. 9:45–11:15 for religious ceremonies). Royal Apartments: Fri.–Mon. 8:15–5:40. Last entry 40 mins before closing.*

San Cataldo. Three striking Saracenic scarlet domes mark this church, built in 1154 during the Norman occupation of Palermo. The church now belongs to the Knights of the Holy Sepulchre and has a spare but intense stone interior. If closed, inquire next door at La Martorana. ⊠ *Piazza Bellini 3, Kalsa* ☎ *091/6118168* ⊕ *www.amicimuseisiciliani. it* 🎫 *€2.50* ⊙ *Daily 9:30–12:30 and 3–6.*

San Giovanni degli Eremiti. Distinguished by its five reddish-orange domes and stripped-clean interior, this 12th-century church was built by the Normans on the site of an earlier mosque—one of 200 that once stood in Palermo. The emirs ruled Palermo for nearly two centuries and brought to it their passion for lush gardens and fountains. One is reminded of this while sitting in San Giovanni's delightful cloister of twin half columns, surrounded by palm trees, jasmine, oleander, and citrus trees. ⊠ *Via dei Benedettini 14–20, Albergheria* ☎ *091/6515019* 🎫 *€6* ⊙ *Tues.–Sun. 9–6:30, Mon. 9–1.*

Teatro Massimo. Construction of this formidable Neoclassical theater, the largest in Italy, was started in 1875 by Giovanni Battista Basile and completed by his son Ernesto in 1897. A reconstruction project started in 1974 ran into gross delays, and the facility remained closed until just before its centenary in 1997. Its interior is as glorious as ever. *The Godfather: Part III* ended with a famous shooting scene on the theater's steps. Visits, by 25-minute guided tour only, are available in four languages, including English. ⊠ *Piazza Verdi 9, at top of Via Maqueda, Olivella* ☎ *091/6053267* ⊕ *www.teatromassimo.it* 🎫 *€8* ⊙ *25-min guided tours daily 9:30–6.*

WORTH NOTING

Catacombe dei Cappuccini. The spookiest sight in all of Sicily, this 16th-century catacomb houses nearly 9,000 corpses of men, women, and young children—some in tombs but many mummified and preserved—hanging in rows on the walls, divided by social caste, age, or gender. Most wear signs indicating their names and the years they lived. The Capuchins were the founders and proprietors of this bizarre establishment (many of the corpses are Capuchin friars) from 1599 to 1911, and it's still under the auspices of the nearby Capuchin church. It was closed when an adjacent cemetery was opened, making the catacombs redundant. Although memorable, this is not a spot for the faint of heart; children might be frightened or disturbed. ⊠ *Piazza Cappuccini 1, off Via Cappuccini, near Palazzo Reale* ☎ *091/6524156* 🎫 *€3* ⊙ *Apr.–Sept., daily 9–1 and 3–6; Oct.–Mar., daily 9–12:30 and 3–5:30.*

FAMILY **Museo Internazionale delle Marionette Antonio Pasqualino.** With a collection of more than 4,000 pieces showcasing both traditional Sicilian (and other) *opere dei pupi* (puppet shows), these masterpieces with their glittering armor and fierce expressions will delight visitors of all ages.

PALERMO'S MULTICULTURAL PEDIGREE

Palermo was first colonized by Phoenician traders in the 6th century BC, but it was their descendants, the Carthaginians, who built the important fortress here that caught the covetous eye of the Romans. After the First Punic War, the Romans took control of the city in the 3rd century BC. Following several invasions by the Vandals, Sicily was settled by Arabs, who made the country an emirate and established Palermo as a showpiece capital that rivaled both Córdoba and Cairo in the splendor of its architecture. Nestled in the fertile Conca d'Oro (Golden Conch) plain, full of orange, lemon, and carob groves and enclosed by limestone hills, Palermo became a magical world of palaces and mosques, minarets, and palm trees.

It was so attractive and sophisticated a city that the Norman ruler Roger de Hauteville (1031–1101) decided to conquer it and make it his capital (1072). The Norman occupation of Sicily resulted in Palermo's golden age (1072–1194), a remarkable period of enlightenment and learning in which the arts flourished. The city of Palermo, which in the 11th century counted more than 300,000 inhabitants, became the European center for the Norman court and one of the most important ports for trade between the East and West. Eventually the Normans were replaced by the Swabian ruler Frederick II (1194–1250), the Holy Roman Emperor, and incorporated into the Kingdom of the Two Sicilies. You'll also see plenty of evidence in Palermo of the Baroque art and architecture of the long Spanish rule. The Aragonese viceroys also brought the Spanish Inquisition to Palermo, which some historians believe helped foster the protective secret societies that evolved into today's Mafia.

The plots of performances are based on the chivalric legends of troubadours of bygone times, in regular episodes to keep you coming back for more. The museum can be hard to find: look for the small alley just off Piazzetta Antonio Pasqualino 5. ⊠ *Piazzetta Antonio Pasqualino 5, near Via Butera, Kalsa* ☎ *091/328060* ⊕ *www.museomarionettepalermo.it* 🎫 *€6* ☉ *Mon.–Sat. 9–1 and 2:30–6:30. Performances generally Oct.–June, Mon. and Fri. at 5:30 pm.*

Palazzo Abatellis. Housed in this late-15th-century Catalan Gothic palace with Renaissance elements is the **Galleria Regionale.** Among its treasures are the *Annunciation* (1474), a painting by Sicily's prominent Renaissance master Antonello da Messina (1430–79), and an arresting fresco by an unknown 15th-century painter, titled *The Triumph of Death,* a macabre depiction of the plague years. Call before you visit to make sure that they're open. ⊠ *Via Alloro 4, Kalsa* ☎ *091/6230011, 091/6230047 for tickets* 🎫 *€8* ☉ *Tues.–Fri. 9–6:30, weekends 9–1.*

Piazza Pretoria. The square's centerpiece, a lavishly decorated fountain with 500 separate pieces of sculpture and an abundance of nude figures, so shocked some Palermitans when it was unveiled in 1575 that it got the nickname "Fountain of Shame." It's even more of a sight when illuminated at night. ⊠ *Piazza Pretoria.*

Quattro Canti. The "Four Corners" is the intersection of Corso Vittorio Emanuele and Via Maqueda. Four rather exhaust-blackened Baroque palaces from Spanish rule meet at concave corners, each with its own fountain and representations of a Spanish ruler, patron saint, and one of the four seasons.

Santa Caterina. The walls of this splendid Baroque church (1596) in Piazza Bellini are covered with decorative 17th-century inlays of precious marble. At the time of this writing, Santa Caterina is closed for repairs with no scheduled reopening date. ✉ *Piazza Bellini, Quattro Canti* ☎ *338/4512011* 🎟 *€2* 🕓 *Apr.–Sept., daily 9:30–1:30 and 3–7; Oct.–Mar., Mon.–Sat. 9:30–5:30, Sun. 9:30–1:30.*

WHERE TO EAT

$$ SICILIAN

🍴 **Antica Focacceria San Francesco.** Turn-of-the-20th-century wooden cabinets, marble-top tables, and cast-iron ovens characterize this neighborhood bakery. Come here for the locally beloved snacks that can be combined to make an inexpensive meal. The big pot on the counter holds the delicious regional specialty *pani ca meusa* (boiled calf's spleen with caciocavallo cheese and salt). The squeamish can opt for some chickpea fritters, an enormous *arancino* (stuffed, fried rice ball), or the outstanding cannoli. [$] *Average main: €15* ✉ *Via A. Paternostro 58, Kalsa* ☎ *091/320264* 🌐 *www.afsf.it* 🕓 *Closed 2 wks mid-Jan.*

$$ SICILIAN

🍴 **Casa del Brodo.** On the edge of the Vucciria is a restaurant that dates to 1890, one of Palermo's oldest. In winter its namesake dish, tortellini *in brodo* (in beef broth), is the specialty of the house. There's an extensive antipasto buffet, and you can't go wrong with the *fritella di fave, piselli, carciofi e ricotta* (fried fava beans, peas, artichokes, and ricotta). Most days they offer fixed-price meat (€16) and a fish (€18) menus. A mix of tourists and locals crowds the three small rooms. [$] *Average main: €15* ✉ *Corso Vittorio Emanuele 175, Vucciria* ☎ *091/321655* 🌐 *www.casadelbrodo.it* 🕓 *Closed Tues. Oct.–May, Sun. June–Sept., and July 1–15.*

$$$$ SICILIAN

Fodor's Choice ★

🍴 **Osteria dei Vespri.** This foodie paradise occupies a cozy-but-elegant space on an unheralded piazza in the historic city center. The winter menu (from November to March) is traditional osteria fare: three menus are offered at €25, €30, and €40. But in the summer months the chef offers two special tasting menus (€65 and €85) built around seasonal ingredients. Local seafood is a big draw here, so when it's offered, try the superb antipasto *cinque variazioni di crudo dal mare* (five variations of raw delicacies from the sea). Alternately, you can order the ravioli *pieni di ricotta al forno con aroma di cedro* (ricotta ravioli with a citrus fruit aroma)—sheep's-milk cheese ravioli with basil, fresh tomato, eggplant, and crispy onions adds creative depth to traditional preparation. The wine list is also one of the best in Palermo. [$] *Average main: €60* ✉ *Piazza Croce dei Vespri 6, Kalsa* ☎ *091/6171631* 🌐 *www.osteriadeivespri.it* ✍ *Reservations essential* 🕓 *Closed Sun.*

$ SICILIAN

🍴 **Pani Ca Meusa.** A civic institution facing Palermo's old fishing port, this joint has been serving its titular calf's spleen sandwich for more than 70 years. The original owner's grandsons produce this local specialty sprinkled with a bit of salt and some lemon and served with or without cheese to a buzzing crowd of Palermo's well-weathered elders. New to the menu are the *panino con panelle* (sandwich with fried chickpeas) and potato *crocche*. There's no seating, though—only counters. $ *Average main: €2* ⊠ *Via Cala 62, Porta Carbone, Kalsa* ☎ 091/323433 ⚑ *Reservations not accepted* ▭ *No credit cards* ⊘ *Closed Sun.*

$$ ✕ **Piccolo Napoli.** Founded in 1951, this is one of Old Palermo's most
SEAFOOD   esteemed seafood eateries. Locals come at midday to feast on the fresh-
Fodor'sChoice   est of fish. You can begin with a memorable buffet featuring baby
★   octopus, raw *neonata* (tiny fish resembling sardines but with a milder flavor), and chickpea fritters. Next, tuck into spaghetti with sea urchin or *casarecce* (partially rolled pasta) with swordfish and mint; then finish with glorious fresh fish or shellfish, roasted or grilled. Depending on what you select, the bill can creep up on you, but it's worth every cent. $ *Average main: €24* ⊠ *Piazzetta Mulino al Vento 4, Borgo Vecchio* ☎ 091/320431 ⚑ *Reservations essential* ⊘ *Closed Sun., and last 2 wks in Aug. No dinner Mon.*

$ ✕ **Pizzeria Ai Comparucci.** One of Palermo's best pizzerias serves deli-
PIZZA   cious Neapolitan-style pies from a big oven in the open kitchen—the genius is in the crust, which is seared in a matter of seconds. The owners make their money on a quick turnover (so don't expect a long, leisurely meal). But the pizza is delicious, and the place often serves until midnight—later than almost any other restaurant in the neighborhood. $ *Average main: €7* ⊠ *Via Messina 36e, Libertà* ☎ 091/6090467 ⊕ *www.comparucci.com* ⚑ *Reservations essential* ⊘ *Closed last 2 wks in Aug. No lunch.*

$$ ✕ **Ristorante Cin Cin.** Here you'll find lighter and more modern versions
SICILIAN   of traditional Sicilian dishes, from the exemplary ricotta casserole with pumpkin, mint, and zucchini to the ultrafresh bavettine pasta with artichoke, leek, speck, dried ricotta, and balsamic vinegar. Don't miss Clemente's signature dessert, a heavenly semifreddo that comes in rotating flavors like pistachio and cinnamon, chocolate and hazelnut, and Marsala wine and raisin. Private cooking classes with a market visit are also offered upon request (€150 per person). $ *Average main: €17* ⊠ *Via Manin 22, Libertà* ☎ 091/6124095 ⊕ *www.ristorantecincin.com* ⊘ *Closed Sun. No lunch.*

$ ✕ **Trattoria Altri Tempi.** This small and friendly "retro" restaurant is a
SICILIAN   favorite among locals who pine for the rustic dishes served by their ancestors. A meal begins when the server plunks down a carafe of the house red and a superb spread of traditional antipasti on your table. Dishes have old-fashioned names: *fave a cunigghiu* is fava beans prepared with olive oil, garlic, and remarkably flavorful oregano; and *pasta al'anciova*, with a concentrated sauce of tomatoes and anchovies. The meal ends well, too, with free house-made herbal or fruit liquors and excellent cannoli. $ *Average main: €8* ⊠ *Via Sammartino 65/67, Libertà* ☎ 091/323480 ⊕ *www.trattoriaaltritempi.it* ⊘ *Closed 3 wks in July, and Sun. in July and Aug.*

WHERE TO STAY

$ | **Centrale Palace Hotel.** A stone's throw from Palermo's main his-
HOTEL | toric sites, the Centrale Palace is the only hotel in the heart of the
Fodor'sChoice | centro storico that was once a stately private palace. **Pros:** sparkling
★ | clean; good bathrooms; convenient garage parking. **Cons:** hotel show-
ing its age; traffic noise; some rooms have no view. $ *Rooms from:*
€104 ⊠ Corso Vittorio Emanuele 327, Vucciria ☎ 091/8539 ⊕ www.
centralepalacehotel.it ↝ 95 rooms, 9 suites |○| Breakfast.

$$ | **Grand Hotel Piazza Borsa.** Cleverly constructed within Palermo's his-
HOTEL | toric stock exchange, this monastery-turned-hotel is ideally situated in
the old town, just around the corner from Focacceria San Francesco.
Pros: very convenient location; interesting architecture; wellness center
with fitness equipment, rare for Sicily hotels. **Cons:** somewhat indif-
ferent staff; no Wi-Fi in guest rooms (though free in public spaces);
building feels a bit sterile. $ *Rooms from: €168 ⊠ Via dei Cartari*
18 ☎ 091/320075 ⊕ www.piazzaborsa.it ↝ 113 rooms, 14 suites
|○| Breakfast.

$$$ | **Grand Hotel Villa Igiea.** This grande dame set in a private tropical
HOTEL | garden at the edge of the bay—a local landmark for a century, and
starting to show its age—still maintains a somewhat faded aura of
luxury and comfort. **Pros:** secluded setting; historic building with lots
of atmosphere; free shuttle to city center in the summer. **Cons:** could use
a refresh; noise and fumes from nearby marina; a bit far from Palermo
attractions. $ *Rooms from: €256 ⊠ Salita Belmonte 43, Acquasanta, 3*
km (2 miles) north of Palermo ☎ 091/6312111 ⊕ www.villa-igiea.com
↝ 106 rooms, 14 suites |○| Breakfast.

$$ | **Hotel Principe di Villafranca.** Modern art mixed with antique furnish-
HOTEL | ings, creamy marble floors, and vaulted ceilings evoke a luxurious
private home in the heart of Palermo's glitzy shopping district. **Pros:**
helpful staff; well-maintained building; central location. **Cons:** extra
charge for Wi-Fi in rooms and public areas; some bathrooms are on the
small side. $ *Rooms from: €136 ⊠ Via G. Turrisi Colonna 4, Libertà*
☎ 091/6118523 ⊕ www.principedivillafranca.it ↝ 29 rooms, 3 junior
suites |○| Breakfast.

$ | **Le Terrazze.** Though it's just steps from the bustling streets around
B&B/INN | the Cattedrale, complete calm envelops this small, beautifully restored
B&B, named for its five roof terraces, all with sublime views of Palermo's
skyline. **Pros:** convenient location; in summer, breakfast is served on
the glorious rooftop. **Cons:** parking can be difficult; books up quickly.
$ *Rooms from: €110 ⊠ Via Pietro Novelli 14, Capo ☎ 091/6520866,*
320/4328567 ⊕ www.leterrazzebb.it ↝ 2 rooms ⊟ No credit cards
|○| Breakfast.

$ | **Massimo Plaza Hotel.** Small and select, this hotel enjoys one of Pal-
HOTEL | ermo's best locations—opposite the renovated Teatro Massimo, on
the border between the old and new towns. **Pros:** central location;
low-season bargains; free Wi-Fi in rooms. **Cons:** stairs up to rooms
(no elevator); plain interiors; some noisy rooms (ask for one in the
back for more quiet). $ *Rooms from: €120 ⊠ Via Maqueda 437, Vuc-*
ciria ☎ 091/325657 ⊕ www.massimoplazahotel.com ↝ 11 rooms
|○| Breakfast.

15

NIGHTLIFE AND PERFORMING ARTS

NIGHTLIFE

Each night between 6 and 9, Palermo's youth gather to shop, socialize, flirt, and plan the evening's affairs in an epic passeggiata along Via Ruggero Settimo (a northern extension of Via Maqueda) and filling Piazza Ruggero Settimo in front of Teatro Politeama. Some trendy bars also line Via Principe del Belmonte, intersecting with Via Roma and Via Ruggero Settimo.

BARS AND CAFÉS

Kursaal Kalhesa. Truly representative of the New Palermo, this is one of the most fascinating places to drink or socialize. Down by the port and the Porta Felice, it attracts an energetic, eclectic crowd of Palermitan youth for lively jazz, coffee, and drinks inside an ancient city wall with spectacular 100-foot ceilings and an idyllic courtyard. Interesting, if pricey, Sicilian food with an Arab touch is served in the adjacent restaurant, and there's also a recently opened sushi bar. ⊠ *Foro Umberto I 21, Kalsa* ☎ *091/6162111* ⊕ *www.kursaalkalhesa.it* ⊘ *Closed Mon.*

Santa Monica. Immensely popular with the twenty- and thirtysomething crowds, who belly up to the bar for pizza, bruschetta, and, of course, excellent German-style draft beer, this pub is also a good place to watch televised soccer. ⊠ *Via E. Parisi 7, Libertà* ☎ *091/324735.*

PERFORMING ARTS

CONCERTS AND OPERA

Teatro Massimo. Teatro Massimo is truly larger than life—it's the biggest theater in Italy. Concerts and operas are presented throughout the year, though in summer concerts are usually held outdoors. An opera at the Massimo is an unforgettable Sicilian experience. ⊠ *Piazza Verdi, at top of Via Maqueda, Capo* ☎ *091/6053580 for tickets, 091/6053391 for tickets, 091/6053267 for tours* ⊕ *www.teatromassimo.it* ⊡ *Tours €8; performances €12–€125* ⊘ *Tours and box office daily 9:30–6; box office also open 1 hr before performances.*

Teatro Politeama Garibaldi. The shamelessly grandiose Neoclassical Teatro Politeama Garibaldi, home of the Orchestra Sinfonica Siciliana, stages a season of opera and orchestral works from October through June. ⊠ *Piazza Ruggero Settimo, Libertà* ☎ *091/6072532* ⊕ *www.orchestrasinfonicasiciliana.it.*

PUPPET SHOWS

FAMILY **Figli d'Arte Cuticchio Association.** Palermo's tradition of puppet theater holds an appeal for children and adults alike, and street artists often perform outside the Teatro Massimo in summer. The Figli d'Arte Cuticchio Association hosts performances most weekends (6:30 pm) from September to June. ⊠ *Via Bara all'Olivella 95, Kalsa* ☎ *091/323400* ⊕ *www.figlidartecuticchio.com* ⊡ *€8.*

SHOPPING

North of Piazza Castelnuovo, Via della Libertà and the surrounding streets represent the luxury end of the shopping scale. A second nerve center for shoppers is the pair of parallel streets connecting modern

Palermo with the train station, Via Roma and Via Maqueda, where boutiques and shoe shops become increasingly upscale as you move from the Quattro Canti past Teatro Massimo to Via Ruggero Settimo.

Most shops are open 9–1 and 4 or 4:30–7:30 or 8 and closed Sunday and on Monday morning; in addition, most food shops are closed on Wednesday afternoon.

FOOD AND WINE

Enoteca Picone. The best wine shop in town has a fantastic selection of Sicilian and national wines. Though the service can be curt, you can taste a selection of wines by the glass in the front of the store. There are tables in the back, where meats and cheeses are also served. ⊠ *Via Marconi 36, Libertà* ☎ *091/331300* ⊕ *www.enotecapicone.it* ⊙ *Closed Sun.*

I Peccatucci di Mamma Andrea. With a name that means "Mamma Andrea's small sins," this charming store sells a plethora of mouthwatering original creations, including jams, preserves, and Sicilian treats like the superb marzipan *frutta martorana.* ⊠ *Via Principe di Scordia 67, near Piazza Florio, Vucciria* ☎ *091/334835* ⊕ *www.mammaandrea.it.*

Pasticceria Alba. One of the most famous sweets shops in Italy, this is the place to find pastries such as cannoli and cassata siciliana. ⊠ *Piazza Don Bosco 7/C, off Via della Libertà near La Favorita Park, Libertà* ☎ *091/309016* ⊕ *www.pasticceriaalba.it.*

MARKETS

Ballarò Market. Wind your way through the Albergheria district and this historic market, where the Saracens did their shopping in the 11th century—joined by the Normans in the 12th. The market remains faithful to seasonal change as well as the original Arab commerce of fruit, vegetables, and grain. Although these days it sees more tourists than locals, it's still fun to experience. Go early: the action dies out by 4 pm most days. ⊠ *Albergheria.*

Bancherelle (*market stalls*). If you're interested in truly connecting with local life while searching for souvenirs, a visit to one of Palermo's many bustling markets is essential. Between Via Roma and Via Maqueda, the many bancherelle on Via Bandiera sell everything from socks to imitation designer handbags.

Vucciria Market. It's easy to see how this market got its name—*vucciria* translates to "voices" or "hubbub." Palermo's most established outdoor market, in the heart of the centro storico, is a maze of side streets around Piazza San Domenico, where hawkers deliver incessant chants from behind stands brimming with mounds of olives, blood oranges, fennel, and long-stem artichokes. One hawker will be going at the trunk of a swordfish with a cleaver, while across the way another holds up a giant squid or dangles an octopus. Morning is the best time to see the market in full swing.

15

THE TYRRHENIAN COAST

Sicily's northern shore, the Tyrrhenian Coast, is mostly a succession of small holiday towns interspersed with stretches of sand. It's often difficult to find a calm spot among the thousands of tourists and locals in high summer, though the scene quiets down considerably after August. The biggest attraction is the old town of Cefalù, with one of Sicily's most remarkable medieval cathedrals, encrusted with mosaics. The coast on either side is dotted with ancient archaeological remains and Arab-Norman buildings.

Some 48 km (30 miles) south of Cefalù, Pizzo Carbonara (6,500 feet) is the highest peak in Sicily after Mt. Etna. Piano della Battaglia has a fully equipped ski resort with lifts. The area has a very un-Sicilian aspect, with Swiss-type chalets, hiking paths, and even Alpine churches.

CEFALÙ

70 km (43 miles) east of Palermo, 161 km (100 miles) west of Messina.

The coast between Palermo and Messina is dotted with charming villages. Tindari (which dates back to the early-Christian era) and Laghetti di Maranello are two that are worth a stop, but it's Cefalù, a classically appealing old Sicilian town built on a spur jutting out into the sea, that's the jewel of the coast.

GETTING HERE AND AROUND

Trains and buses run between Palermo and Messina. Drivers can take the A20 autostrada.

VISITOR INFORMATION

Cefalù Tourism Office ✉ *Corso Ruggero 77* ☎ *0921/421050.*

EXPLORING

Duomo. Cefalù is dominated by a massive headland (*la rocca*) and a 12th-century Romanesque Duomo, which is one of the finest Norman cathedrals in Italy. Roger II began the church in 1131 as an offering of thanks for having been saved here from a shipwreck. Its mosaics rival those of Monreale. (Whereas Monreale's Byzantine Christ figure is an austere and powerful image, emphasizing Christ's divinity, the Cefalù Christ is softer, more compassionate, and more human.) The traffic going in and out of Cefalù town can be heavy in summer, so you may want to take the 50-minute train ride from Palermo instead of driving. At the Duomo you must be suitably attired—no shorts or beachwear are permitted. ✉ *Piazza del Duomo* ☎ *0921/922021* ⊕ *www.chiesadicefalu. it* ☉ *Apr.–Oct., daily 8–7; Nov.–Mar., daily 8–1 and 3:30–6; hrs subject to change, so check before visiting.*

WHERE TO EAT

$ ✕ **Al Porticciolo.** Nicola Mendolia runs two restaurants, 50 feet apart, both
SICILIAN   comfortable, casual, and faithfully focused on food. You might start with the *calamaretti piccoli fritti* (fried baby squid and octopus) and then follow with one of the chef's specials, which change weekly. Regardless, a refreshing *sgroppino* (whipped lemon sorbet with spumante) should end the meal. Dark, heavy, wooden tables create a comfortable environment

filled with a mix of jovial locals and businesspeople. $ *Average main: €14* ✉ *Via C. Ortolani di Bordonaro 66 and 86* ☎ *0921/921981, 0921/423151* ⊕ *www.alporticcioloristorante.com* ⊗ *Closed Wed. Nov.–Apr.*

THE AEOLIAN ISLANDS

Off Sicily's northeast coast lies an archipelago of seven spectacular islands of volcanic origin. The Isole Eolie (Aeolian Islands), also known as the Isole Lipari (Lipari Islands), were named after Aeolus, the Greek god of the winds, who is said to keep all the Earth's winds stuffed in a bag in his cave here. The Aeolians are a world of grottoes and clear-water caves carved by waves through the centuries. Superb snorkeling and scuba diving abound in the clearest and cleanest of Italy's waters.

Lipari provides the widest range of accommodations and is a good jumping-off point for day trips to the other islands. Most exclusive are Vulcano and Panarea: the former is noted for its black sands and stupendous sunsets, as well as the acrid smell of its sulfur emissions, whereas the latter is, according to some, the prettiest. Most remarkable is Stromboli (pronounced with the accent on the first syllable) with its constant eruptions, while the greenest island—and the one with the best hiking trails—is Salina. The remotest are Filicudi and Alicudi, where electricity was introduced only in the 1980s, and broadband Internet connections are still the stuff of pipe dreams.

The bars in the Aeolian Islands, and especially those on Lipari, are known for their granitas of fresh strawberries, melon, peaches, and other fruits. Many Sicilians on the Aeolians (and in Messina, Taormina, and Catania) begin the hot summer days with a *granita di caffè* (a coffee ice topped with whipped cream), into which they dunk their breakfast rolls. (You can get one any time of day.)

GETTING HERE AND AROUND

Car ferries and much faster hydrofoils carry passengers to and between the islands. They depart from Milazzo and Messina (on Sicily), and from Reggio di Calabria (on the mainland), with the majority stopping at Lipari before continuing on to other islands in the chain. Service is most frequent in summer. May to September, a few car ferries a week also provide overnight service to and from Naples; during that same period hydrofoils run to and from Naples, Cefalù, and Palermo. Operators' websites are the best source of information regarding schedules and fares.

Ferry and Hydrofoil Contacts N.G.I ☎ 090/9283415, 800/250000 ⊕ *www. ngi-spa.it* ▤ *No credit cards.* **Siremar** ☎ 091/7493315, 081/4972999 ⊕ *www. siremar.it* ▤ *No credit cards.* **SNAV** ☎ 081/4285555 ⊕ *www.snav.it* ▤ *No credit cards.* **Ustica Lines** ☎ 0923/873813 ⊕ *www.usticalines.it* ▤ *No credit cards.*

LIPARI

2 hrs 10 mins from Milazzo by ferry, 1 hr by hydrofoil; 60–75 mins from Reggio di Calabria and Messina by ferry.

The largest and most developed of the Aeolians, Lipari welcomes you with distinctive pastel-color houses. Fields of spiky agaves dot the northernmost tip of the island, Acquacalda, indented with pumice and obsidian quarries. In the west is San Calogero, where you can explore hot springs and mud baths. From the red-lava base of the island rises a plateau crowned with a 16th-century castle and a 17th-century cathedral.

GETTING HERE AND AROUND

Ferries and hydrofoils from Milazzo, which is 41 km (25 miles) west of Messina, stop here. There's also ferry service from Reggio di Calabria and Messina.

EXPLORING

Fodor's Choice ★ **Museo Archeologico Eoliano.** The vast, multibuilding Museo Archeologico Eoliano is a terrific museum, with an intelligently arranged collection of prehistoric finds—some dating as far back as 4000 BC—from various sites in the archipelago, as well as Greek and Roman artifacts, including an outstanding collection of Greek theatrical masks, and even interesting information on volcanoes. Basic descriptions about the exhibits are provided in English and Italian, though more comprehensive information is only in Italian. That said, there is so much to see, it's worth at least a few hours of your time. ✉ *Via Castello 2* ☎ *090/9880174* 🌐 *www.regione.sicilia.it/beniculturali/museolipari* 🎟 *€6* ⏲ *Mon.–Sat. 9–7:30 and Sun. 9–1:30.*

Fodor's Choice ★ **Vulcano.** A popular day trip from Lipari is to visit the most notorious of the Aeolian Islands: Vulcano. True to its name—and the origin of the term—Vulcano has a profusion of fumeroles sending up jets of hot vapor, though the volcano here has long been dormant. This is an island most travelers wish to visit, perhaps to soak in the strong-smelling sulfur springs, but not to stay on: when the wind is right, the odors greet you long before you disembark. The island has some of the archipelago's best beaches, though the volcanic black sand can be off-putting at first glance. Ascend to the crater (1,266 feet above sea level) on muleback for eye-popping views or take a boat ride into the grottoes around the base. From Capo Grillo you can see all the Aeolians. **Ustica Lines** has high-speed passenger vessels that make the crossing from Lipari in 10 minutes. Frequent daily departures are offered year-round, with round-trip tickets priced at €14. ☎ *0923/873813 for Ustica Lines* 🌐 *www.usticalines.it.*

WHERE TO EAT AND STAY

$$ SICILIAN Fodor's Choice ★ 🍴 **Filippino.** The views from this upper-town restaurant's outdoor terrace are a fitting complement to the superb fare featured on its menu. Founded in 1910, Filippino is rightly rated as one of the archipelago's best dining venues—you'll understand why when you sample the seafood. *Zuppa di pesce* (fish soup) and the antipasto platter of smoked and marinated fish are absolute musts. Just leave some room for the local version of cassata siciliana, accompanied by sweet malvasia wine from Salina. [$] *Average main: €18* ✉ *Piazza Mazzini Lipari* ☎ *090/9811002* 🌐 *www.filippino.it* ⏲ *Closed Mon. Oct.–Mar.*

$$ HOTEL 🏨 **Les Sables Noirs.** Named for the black sands of the beach in front, this luxury hotel is superbly sited on the beautiful Porto di Ponente. **Pros:** stunning beachfront location; delicious breakfasts; five-minute

walk to town. **Cons:** no restaurant; pesky mosquitoes; iffy Wi-Fi. $ *Rooms from: €176* ⊠ *Porto di Ponente, Vulcano* ☎ *090/9850* ⊕ *www.hotelvulcanosicily.com* ⇥ *14 rooms, 29 apartments* ⊗ *Closed mid-Oct.–Apr.* ○ *Breakfast.*

SALINA

50 mins from Lipari by ferry, 20 mins by hydrofoil.

The second largest of the Aeolians, Salina is also the most fertile—which accounts for its excellent malvasia dessert wine. Salina is the archipelago's lushest and highest island, too—Mt. Fossa delle Felci rises to more than 3,000 feet—and the vineyards and fishing villages along its slopes add to its allure. Pollara, in the west of the island, has capitalized on its fame as one of the locations in the 1990s cult movie, *Il Postino (The Postman)*, and is an ideal location for an evening passeggiata on well-maintained paths along the volcanic terrain.

GETTING HERE AND AROUND
Ferries and hydrofoils arrive here from Lipari.

WHERE TO STAY

$$
HOTEL
Hotel Solemar. In a valley between Salina's two mountains, this hotel has most of the hallmarks of Mediterranean charm—large terraces for contemplation, a location in a sleepy town, and pleasing food served on summer evenings in the restaurant. **Pros:** relaxed atmosphere; helpful staff; terrific views. **Cons:** no pool; hit-or-miss Wi-Fi in public areas; a 15-minute taxi ride from Salina's main port. $ *Rooms from: €180* ⊠ *Via Roma 8, Leni* ☎ *090/9809445* ⊕ *www.salinasolemarhotel.it* ⇥ *13 rooms* ⊗ *Closed Nov.–Mar.*

PANAREA

2 hrs from Lipari by ferry, 25–50 mins by hydrofoil; 7–9 hrs from Naples by ferry.

Panarea has some of the most dramatic scenery of the islands: wild caves carved out of the rock and dazzling flora. The exceptionally clear water and the richness of life on the sea floor make Panarea especially suitable for underwater exploration, though there's little in the way of beaches. The outlying rocks and islets make a gorgeous sight, and you can enjoy the panorama on an easy excursion to the small Bronze Age village at Capo Milazzese.

GETTING HERE AND AROUND
Ferries and hydrofoils arrive here from Lipari and Naples.

WHERE TO STAY

$$$$
HOTEL
Il Raya. Discreet, expensive, with views over the sea toward Stromboli, Il Raya is perfectly in keeping with the elite style of Panarea, most exclusive of the Aeolian Islands. **Pros:** great views of Stromboli; fashionable ambience; well-known dance club on the premises. **Cons:** snooty staff; uphill trudge to rooms; mediocre food; dance club means noise after dark. $ *Rooms from: €540* ⊠ *San Pietro* ☎ *090/983013* ⊕ *www.hotelraya.it* ⇥ *36 rooms* ⊗ *Closed mid-Oct.–mid-Apr.* ○ *Breakfast.*

STROMBOLI

3 hrs 45 mins from Lipari by ferry, 65–90 mins by hydrofoil; 9 hrs from Naples by ferry, 5 hrs by hydrofoil.

This northernmost of the Aeolians consists entirely of the cone of an active volcano. The view from the sea—especially at night, as an endless stream of glowing red-hot lava flows into the water—is unforgettable. Stromboli is in a constant state of mild dissatisfaction, and every now and then its anger flares up, so authorities insist that you climb to the top (about 3,031 feet above sea level) only with a guide. The round trip (climb, pause, and descent), usually starting around 6 pm, takes about six hours; the lava is much more impressive after dark. Some choose to camp overnight atop the volcano—again, a guide is essential. The main town has a small selection of reasonably priced hotels and restaurants, and a choice of lively clubs and cafés. In addition to the island tour, excursions might include boat trips around the naturally battlemented isle of Strombolicchio.

GETTING HERE AND AROUND

Ferries and hydrofoils arrive here from Lipari and Naples.

EXPLORING

Pippo Navigazione. Numerous tour operators have guides that can lead you up Stromboli or take you round in a boat, among them Pippo Navigazione. Rates are around €25 per person for three hours. A €20 night tour explores where the lava reaches the sea. ☎ *338/9857883, 090/986135.*

FILICUDI

30–60 mins from Salina and Lipari by hydrofoil; 2 hrs from Cefalù and Palermo, 2 hrs from Milazzo, and 10 hrs from Naples by ferry.

Just a dot in the sea, Filicudi is famous for its unusual volcanic rock formations and the enchanting Grotta del Bue Marino (Grotto of the Sea Ox). The crumbled remains of a prehistoric village are at Capo Graziano. The island, which is spectacular for walking and hiking and is still a truly undiscovered, restful haven, has a handful of hotels and pensioni, and some families put up guests. Car ferries are available only in summer.

GETTING HERE AND AROUND

Ferries and hydrofoils arrive throughout the year from Salina and Lipari, and also in summer from Palermo, Cefalù, Milazzo, and Naples.

WHERE TO STAY

$$$ HOTEL 🏨 **La Canna.** It's wonderful to wake up to the utter tranquillity that characterizes a stay on Filicudi—especially if you happen to be greeting the day at this hotel, set above the tiny port. **Pros:** relaxed setting; family-friendly atmosphere; great views. **Cons:** an uphill climb from the port; half or full board required in peak season; not much English spoken. [$] *Rooms from: €220* ✉ *Via Rosa 43, Filicudi Porto* ☎ *090/9889956* 🌐 *www.lacannahotel.it* 🛏 *14 rooms* 🕓 *Closed mid-Oct.–mid-Apr.* 🍴 *Some meals.*

SARDINIA

WELCOME TO SARDINIA

TOP REASONS TO GO

★ **Relax on idyllic beaches:** Covering more than 1,200 miles of coastline, Sardinia's beaches beckon with their turquoise waters, white sand, and rippled dunes.

★ **Discover natural beauty:** A network of trails explores Sardinia's resplendent mountains, deep gorges, lush forests, and cascading waterfalls.

★ **Explore charming towns and villages:** From coastal towns to rural villages, the island is dotted with a variety of settlements that take pride in their history and tradition. Each has its own culture, cuisine, and unique way of life.

★ **Dive or snorkel the outer reefs:** Crystalline waters, warm weather, and outer reefs make Sardinia a paradise for underwater adventurers. Sunken ships and marine reserves provide the ideal place to discover marine life.

★ **Savor Sardinian delicacies:** From pasta and prosciutto to lamb and cheese, the island's cuisine is sure to satisfy any appetite.

1 **Cagliari and the Southern Coast.** The gateway to Sardinia's spectacular coastline, Cagliari bustles with modern commercial activity while preserving ancient history as the island's capital. Along the southern coast, rural coastal villages stretch along idyllic waters, and archaeological ruins enrich the breathtaking natural beauty of the dramatic mountain peaks and rugged promontories. Pristine white-sand beaches are set against flawless sapphire seas.

2 **Su Nuraxi to the Costa Smeralda.** From the UNESCO World Heritage Site of Su Nuraxi—a mysterious complex of beehivelike stone structures near the town of Barumini—to the secluded beaches and coves and the posh towns and resorts along the northern coast, this region is a summer playground for the world's rich and famous. The iconic Porto Cervo serves as its hedonistic heart, where superyachts moor after their owners have spent sun-drenched days in Romazzino, Liscia Ruia, Capriccioli, Rena Bianca, and Del Principe. The Emerald Coast's unparalleled beauty stretches into the archipelago of La Maddalena, the site of one of the world's most important marine wildlife reserves.

GETTING ORIENTED

The lure of Sardinia lies in its spectacular natural beauty and historical roots, which date back to the Bronze Age. With Europe's highest dunes in the southwest, deepest canyons in the mountainous center, and best beaches on eastern and western coastlines, Sardinia enchants with fortified towns, open-air museums, stunning vistas, and crystalline coastal waters from north to south.

FRANCE

Santa Teresa
Gallura
Ponte Liscia
Bassacutena
La Maddalena
Palau
Porto
Cervo
Arzachena

COSTA SMERALDA

Punta Caprara

ISOLA
ASINARA

Golfo
dell' Asinara

Gulfo Aranci
Golfo di Olbia

Stintino

Castelsardo

Olbia

Porto Torres

Sedini

Telti

Monti

199

131

125

Sorso

Sassari

Chiaramonti

Padru

Oschiri

Ozieri

Budduso

Siniscola

125

Alghero

Villanova
Monteleone

Bultei

Bitti

Sas Linnas Siccas

Padria

131

Orosei

Bosa

Macomer

Orotelli

Monte
Ortobene

Nuoro

Dorgali
Cala Gonone

Golfo
di Orosei

Tresnuraghes

Abbasanta

Fonni

125

Tortoli

Cabras

Asuni

Su Nuraxi

Barumini

Bari Sardo

Tharros

Oristano

Golfo di
Oristano

Laconi

Nurallao

125

Marrubiu

Uras

Porto Palma

Guspini

Furtei

Piscinas

Samassi

San Vito

Buggerru

Villasor

Monastir

Decimomannu

Decimomannu

Iglesias

Portoscuso

Carloforte

ISOLA
SAN PIETRO

Cagliari

Golfo di
Cagliari

Villasimius

Sarroch

Sant'Antioco

ISOLA
SANT'ANTIOCO

Giba

Pula

Nora

Golfo
di Palmas

Chia
Capo Spartivento

Capo Teulada

COSTA VERDE

16

EATING AND DRINKING WELL IN SARDINIA

Wining and dining in Sardinia is not just a richly delicious experience, it's also a way to have a close-up encounter with the history, geography, and cultural traditions of the island. Sardinian food has its own culinary identity, a complex and eclectic mix that makes for mouthwatering and often revelatory dishes.

Sardinia's proximity to North Africa and its long Spanish occupation mean that elements of both cultures can be found in the island's kitchens, including couscous and paella. There are also strong regional variations within Sardinia itself, as well as a traditional division between the land-based fare of the interior and the fresh seafood on the coasts. Wherever you go here, you'll find a strong emphasis on seasonal ingredients and ancient cooking techniques.

BREADS, CHEESES, AND SWEET SPECIALTIES

Sardinia has a strong tradition of bread making, and is famous for crispy, paper-thin *pane carasau* flatbread (*carta di musica* in Italian). Famous Sardinian desserts include *sospiri* (morsels of almond dough stuffed with citrus-infused almond paste), *torrone di mandorle* (almond nougat), or *seadas* (cheese-filled pastries topped with honey, also called *sebadas*). The *candelaus*, a fruit-and-almond dessert, and sweet ricotta-stuffed *pardula* cakes are popular in Cagliari. Unmissable is *amaro di corbezzolo*, a honey with a slightly bitter and dazzlingly complex bouquet and taste that's prized around the world. It's made by bees that suck nectar from a plant known as *arbutus*, the tree strawberry.

Ever wondered about all those sheep roaming the rugged slopes of the interior? They're there to produce the raw materials for Italy's original and best pecorino. It's ubiquitous in Sardinia, and comes in various strengths and consistencies.

MEAT

The most popular meat dishes are veal, roast *agnello* (lamb), and *porcheddu* (spit-roasted suckling pig, often requiring a day's notice to be prepared). *Cavallo,* or *carne equino* (horse meat), is also commonly found on restaurant menus, particularly in Sassari, where it's generally served in the form of a *bistecca* (thin steak). Donkey (*asino*) and wild boar (*cinghiale*) are other Sardinian specialties—sometimes cinghiale is roasted on a spit or prepared using the ancient Sardinian technique of *incarralzadu,* for which it's placed in a large hole lined with fragrant myrtle leaves to extract juicy tenderness. Another option is *suppa quata,* a hearty soup historically cooked by Gallura shepherds that's made from beef broth, bread, and aged pecorino cheese.

SEAFOOD

Whole fish are best eaten roasted or grilled, though you may also find them sautéed in pasta or incorporated into *copaxa de peix,* a fish soup from Alghero. The most famous—and priciest—Alghero dish is lobster, known as

langouste or *aragosta*. Lobster doesn't appear on restaurant menus in winter—fortunately, the very time when *riccio di mare* (sea urchin), another local specialty, is best enjoyed. Winter is also the best season for *bottarga,* the dried, cured roe of gray mullet or tuna, often shaved directly onto a pasta dish or just served with crusty bread and olive oil.

STARTERS

Opt for *antipasti di mare* or *di terra* to kick off your meal. Traditional pastas include *malloreddus* (small pasta shells, sometimes flavored with saffron), *culurgiones* (ravioli), and *maccarones de busa* (thick pasta twists). Homemade pastas might be topped with a wild-boar sauce; *fregola,* a semolina pasta, is often served with *arselle* (clams).

WINE

Among the whites, the dry *torbato* of the Alghero coast and the slightly sparkling *vermentino* from Gallura are standouts. The Oristano region produces the dry, sherrylike *vernaccia* (unrelated to the Tuscan variety), Bosa produces amber-toned *malvasia,* while Barbagia is one of the best sources of *cannonau,* a pleasing red wine with an ancient pedigree. The traditional liqueur *mirto,* which makes a fine after-dinner drink, is made from native wild myrtle berries.

Updated
by Robert
Andrews

The second-largest island in the Mediterranean, Sardinia remains unique and enigmatic with its rugged coastline and white-sand beaches, dramatic granite cliffs, and mountainous inland tracts. Glamorous resorts lie within a short distance of quiet, medieval villages, and ruined castles and ancient churches testify to an eventful history. But although conquerors from all directions—Phoenicians, Carthaginians, Romans, Catalans, Pisans, Piemontese—have left their traces, no outside culture has had a dominant impact. Pockets of foreign influence persist along the coasts, but inland, a proud Sardinian culture flourishes.

As a travel destination, Sardinia's identity is split: the island has some of Europe's most expensive resorts, but it's also home to pristine terrain untouched by commercial development. Fine sand and clean waters draw summer sun worshippers to beaches that rank among the Mediterranean's best. Most famous are those along the Costa Smeralda (Emerald Coast), where the überrich have anchored their yachts since the 1960s. Less exclusive beach holidays can be had elsewhere on the island at La Maddalena, Villasimius, and Pula, and there are wonderfully intact medieval towns—Cagliari, Oristano, Sassari—on or near the water.

Apart from the glamorous shores and upscale locales found in the east, most of Sardinia's coast is rugged and unreachable, a jagged series of wildly beautiful inlets accessible only by sea. Inland, Sardinia remains shepherd's country, silent and stark. Against this landscape are the striking and mysterious stone *nuraghi* (ancient defensive structures) that provide clues to the island's ancient culture. Found only on Sardinia, these sites have been included on the UNESCO World Heritage List, described as "the finest and most complete example of a remarkable form of prehistoric architecture."

SARDINIA PLANNER

GETTING HERE AND AROUND

AIR TRAVEL

Flying is by far the fastest and easiest way to get to the island. Sardinia's major airport, Aeroporto di Elmas, is in Cagliari, with smaller ones at Alghero (Aeroporto Fertilia) and Olbia (Aeroporto Costa Smeralda).

Airport Contacts Aeroporto di Alghero ⊠ *Regione Nuraghe Biancu, 9.5 km (6 miles) north of Alghero* ☎ *079/935282* ⊕ *www.aeroportodialghero.it.* **Aeroporto di Cagliari** ⊠ *Via dei Trasvolatori, Elmas, 8 km (5 miles) northwest of city center* ☎ *070/211211* ⊕ *www.cagliariairport.it.* **Aeroporto di Olbia Costa Smeralda** ⊠ *Strada Statale Orientale Sarda, Olbia, 2½ miles southeast of city center* ☎ *0789/563444* ⊕ *www.geasar.it.*

BUS TRAVEL

Cagliari is linked with the other towns of Sardinia by a network of buses. All major cities and most local destinations are served by ARST. City buses in Cagliari, Olbia, and Sassari operate on the same system as those on the mainland: buy your ticket first, at a tobacco shop or machine, and punch it in the machine on the bus.

Contacts ARST ☎ *800/865042 in Italy (Mon.–Sat. 7 am–2 pm), 070/4098324 abroad* ⊕ *www.arst.sardegna.it.* **Cagliari Bus Station** ⊠ *Piazza Matteotti, Cagliari* ☎ *800/078870* ⊕ *www.ctmcagliari.it.*

CAR TRAVEL

Sardinia is about 270 km (167 miles) long from north to south and takes three to four hours to drive on the main roads; it's roughly 120 km (75 miles) across. Cars may be taken on board most of the ferry lines connecting Sardinia with the mainland.

Roads are generally in good condition, with clear signposting. "Superstrade" double-lane routes are well developed. Expect winding inland mountain and coastal roads with hairpin turns. Most gas stations are closed in the afternoons, at night, and on Sunday, though at those times you can still use cash to automatically gas up. Try to avoid driving at night, when mountain roads are particularly hazardous and roadside facilities are infrequent, especially in the east. Fog may be an issue in winter.

TRAIN TRAVEL

Ferrovie dello Stato (FS) is the national railway of Italy. You can plan itineraries, purchase tickets, and look for special deals online. The Stazione Centrale in Cagliari is next to the bus station on Piazza Matteotti. There are fairly good connections between Olbia, Cagliari, Sassari, and Oristano. Service on the few other local lines is infrequent and slow. The fastest train between Olbia and Cagliari takes nearly four hours. Local trains connect Sassari with Alghero (one hour). Trenino Verde della Sardegna operates tourist trains on narrow-gauge lines through the island's interior. These high-season services are slow but travel through some of Sardinia's most panoramic landscapes.

16

Contacts **Ferrovie dello Stato** ☎ 892021 in Italy, +3906/68475475 abroad ⊕ www.trenitalia.com. **Trenino Verde della Sardegna** ☎ 070/2657622 ⊕ www. treninoverde.com ⊘ June–mid-Sept.

WHEN TO GO

The best time to visit Sardinia is May through September. European vacationers flock to the island for sunshine in July and August. Expect to pay the highest rates during these two peak summer months, when roads, tourist sites, and beaches are most crowded. From September to early October, when accommodations start to shut down for the year, you'll find end-of-season deals and fewer tourists. Any other time of year, expect near–ghost towns, with closed restaurants, hotels, and shops.

RESTAURANTS

Prices in the dining reviews are the average cost of a main course at dinner, or, if dinner is not served, at lunch.

HOTELS

In Sardinia, there are numerous luxury resorts with stunning beachfront vistas, bed-and-breakfast inns in medieval villages, private villas tucked away on lush hills, modern hotels in the trendy capital, and farmhouses on tranquil mountainsides. During summer months, the most popular destination on the island is the Costa Smeralda in the east. High demand during July and August raises nightly rates to an astronomical range, above €1,500 for the most deluxe accommodations. Find more reasonable hotel rates in other parts of the island, which are equally breathtaking and less crowded. Plan dates well in advance, as many hotels close at the end of September until the following April or May.

Hotel reviews have been shortened. For full information, visit Fodors. com.

WHAT IT COSTS				
	$	**$$**	**$$$**	**$$$$**
RESTAURANTS	under €15	€15–€24	€25–€35	over €35
HOTELS	under €125	€125–€200	€201–€300	over €300

Prices in the dining reviews are the average cost of a main course at dinner, or, if dinner is not served, at lunch. Prices in the reviews are the lowest cost of a standard double room in high season.

TOURS

Federazione Nazionale di Turismo Equestre. The Federazione is the national association for group and individual horseback riding tours. ⊠ *Via Carso 35/a, Sassari* ☎ *388 165 0257 Mario Aldo Cadau, 329 378 1178 Mariolino Loddo* ⊕ *www.sardegna.fitetrec-ante.it.*

Horse Country. This resort village in the Oristano region has accommodations, restaurants, an equestrian center, meeting facilities, family activities, and a wellness center. ⊠ *Strada a Mare 27, near Oristano, Arborea* ☎ *0783/80500* ⊕ *www.horsecountry.it* ⊘ *Closed mid-Oct.–mid-Mar.*

Viaggi Orrù. Founded in 1933, this travel agent and tour operator arranges individual tours and group charters. ⊠ *Via Pola 41, Cagliari* ☎ *070/658458* ⊕ *www.viaggiorru.com.*

CAGLIARI AND THE SOUTHERN COAST

Cagliari (pronounced "*Cahl*-yah-ree") is Sardinia's capital and largest city; it contains the island's principal art and archaeology museums as well as an old cathedral and medieval towers, which have lofty views of the surrounding sea, lagoons, and mountains. East of Cagliari the coast is no less scenic, but it's more developed. Although the coast is uncommercialized for the most part in the old town, up on the hill, the coast, port area, and surrounding regions toward the airport have pockets of development and industrial zones. To the southwest is Pula, an inland town within easy reach of both good beaches and the excavated ruins at Nora.

CAGLIARI

268 km (166 miles) south of Olbia.

Known in Sardinia as Casteddu, the island's capital has steep streets and impressive Italianate architecture, from modern to medieval. This city of nearly 160,000 people is characterized by a busy commercial center and waterfront with broad avenues and arched arcades, as well as by the typically narrow streets of the old hilltop citadel (called, simply, "Castello"). The Museo Archeologico makes a good starting point to a visit. The imposing Bastione di Saint Remy and Mercato di San Benedetto (one of the best fish markets in Italy) are both musts.

GETTING HERE AND AROUND

The easiest way to arrive in Cagliari is by plane or boat. From the airport, it's easy to get into the city center by bus or taxi. You can also rent a car at the airport; prebooking before arrival is highly recommended. If you arrive by boat, travel from Trapani or Palermo (Sicily), Civitavecchia (Rome), or Naples. The port is quite near the city center. Piazza Matteotti is the terminal for Cagliari's city buses, which are operated by Consorzio Trasporti e Mobilità (CTM). Buy tickets at the kiosk here before boarding.

FESTIVALS

FAMILY

Fodor's Choice
★

Festa di Sant'Efisio. On May 1, thousands of costumed villagers parade through town during Sardinia's greatest annual festival, the Festa di Sant'Efisio, named after the martyred saint who saved the city from the plague in the 17th century. The saint's statue is carried aloft through Cagliari's flower-lined streets, part of a four-day procession from Cagliari to Nora and back again (about 40 miles round-trip), and is accompanied by colorful costumed groups from throughout the island in an enthusiastic celebration of traditional culture. Ask at local tourist offices about purchasing tickets for viewing the grand spectacle along the main route in Cagliari. ⊕ *www.comune.cagliari.it.*

16

EXPLORING

Anfiteatro Romano. Partially reopened after years of maintenance work, this substantial amphitheater arena dating from the 2nd century AD attests to the importance of this area to the Romans. Guided tours explore the seating area, subterranean passages, and beasts' pit. ■TIP➔ Call ahead to arrange a tour outside the normal operating hours, though even when the site is closed good views can be had from Viale Sant'Ignazio. ✉ *Viale Sant'Ignazio da Laconi* ☎ *339/6130531* ⊕ *www.anfiteatroromano.it* ✆*€5* ⊘ *Apr.–mid-Oct., Fri.–Sun. 10–6; mid-Oct.–Apr., weekends 10–4.*

Castello. Perched over the vast expanse of Cagliari and its port, the narrow streets of this hillside quarter hold ancient monuments and piazzas amid apartments with wash hung out to dry on elaborate wrought-iron balconies. The most impressive entrance is through the commanding late-19th-century archway of the Bastione di Saint Remy on Piazza Costituzione, though this means climbing numerous steps (walk up Viale Regina Elena to find an elevator). At the top is an impressive panorama of the cityscape and the Gulf of Cagliari. From Piazza Palazzo, holding Cagliari's Cathedral, you can walk to Piazza Indipendenza and the 14th-century limestone Saint Pancras Tower, a twin of the nearby Torre dell'Elefante. ⊕ *www.comune.cagliari.it.*

Duomo. The Cattedrale di Santa Maria, also known as the Duomo, was begun in the 12th century, but major renovations in the 17th century and reconstruction during the mid-1930s have left little of the original medieval church. The tiers of columns on the facade resemble those of medieval Romanesque Pisan churches, but only sections of the central portal, the bell tower, and the two side entrances are from the 13th century. Look for one of the most memorable features inside: the oversize marble pulpit sculpted in the 1300s and divided in half to fit into the church nave. ✉ *Piazza Palazzo* ☎ *070/663837* ⊕ *www.duomodicagliari. it* ⊘ *Mon.–Sat. 8–noon and 4–8, Sun. 8–1 and 4:30–8:30.*

Museo Archeologico. The intriguing artifacts here are all within the walls of a castle erected by Pisans in the early 1300s to ward off the Aragonese and Catalans attacking from what is now Spain. On display are bronze statuettes from the tombs and dwellings of some of Sardinia's earliest inhabitants, who remain a prehistoric enigma. Ancient writers called them the "nuraghic people," from the name of their curious stone dwellings, the *nuraghi*, which are unique to Sardinia. Archaeologists date most of the nuraghi to about 1300–1200 BC, the same time the ancient Israelites were establishing themselves in Canaan. The museum is the world's foremost authority on this particular ancient civilization. Of special interest are a pearl-laden Phoenician faience necklace, medieval gold coins, finds from the Tuvixeddu necropolis, and remnants from the archaeological site of Nora. ✉ *Cittadella dei Musei, Piazza Arsenale* ☎ *070/655911* ⊕ *www.comune.cagliari.it* ✆*€5* ⊘ *Tues.–Sun. 9–8; ticket office closes at 7:15 pm.*

Torre di San Pancrazio. Marking the edge of the Castello district, the 1305 tower of the imposing medieval Pisan defenses is just outside Cagliari's archaeological museum. You can climb up the limestone

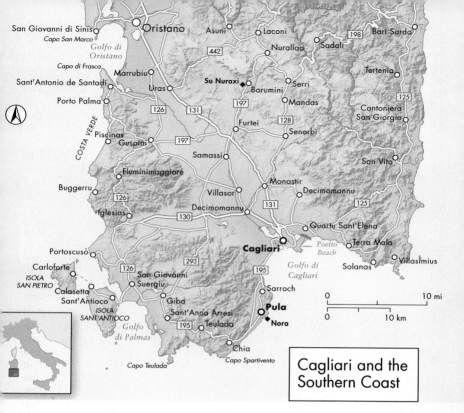

Cagliari and the Southern Coast

tower for a fabulous panorama of the city and its surroundings. As with other defensive structures of this period, the tower's back wall is missing, which allows you to see the series of wooden stairs and landings inside the cross-section without climbing a step. ✉ *Piazza Indipendenza* ⊕ *www.beniculturalicagliari.it* 🎟 *€3* ⊙ *Apr.–Sept., daily 10–7; Oct.–Mar., daily 10–5.*

Terrazza Umberto I. Excellent views of Cagliari, plus a selection of cafés and late-night bars make this a good place for a break after visiting the narrow passageways of the Castello quarter. The spacious terrazza lies atop the monumental, Neoclassical Bastione di Saint Remy, dating to 1901. ✉ *Piazza Costituzione.*

Torre dell'Elefante. This medieval fortified tower was built in 1307 by Giovanni Capula, who also designed the San Pancrazio tower. Standing 100 feet high at the seaward end of Cagliari's bastions, it was used as a prison in the 1800s and is one of the main entrances to the Castello. ✉ *Via Università* ⊕ *www.beniculturalicagliari.it* 🎟 *€3* ⊙ *June.–Sept., daily 10–7; Oct.–May., daily 10–5.*

OFF THE BEATEN PATH

San Sperate. Considered a *paese museo*, a "museum village," this small town 20 km (12 miles) northwest of Cagliari has houses whose walls have been brightened with murals by local artists and some well-known Italian painters. The murals were begun in the 1960s and continue to

be expanded, transforming the entire town into an open-air art gallery with colorful trompe-l'oeils and artistic renderings of daily life. Look for suggestive stone and bronze sculptures by the world-renowned Pinuccio Sciola that also pay tribute to the region's ancient history. ⊠ *Via Sassari, San Sperate* ⊕ *www.sansperate.net.*

WHERE TO EAT

$$
ITALIAN
✗ **Antico Caffè.** The gilded Antico Caffè once served as an intellectual haunt for famous writers like D. H. Lawrence and Grazia Deledda, who won the Nobel Prize in Literature in 1926. With its streetfront terrace and polished-wood-and-brass interior, it has anchored the base of the Bastione di Saint Remy since 1855, serving as a social center from breakfast time until well after midnight. A daily set menu (€35) features local fish and meat specialties. Pastas and salads are reliable à la carte choices. Desserts are the real attraction: try the tiramisù or one of the elaborate artisanal gelato *coupe* concoctions. A *granita di caffè con panna* is sublimely refreshing on a hot summer afternoon. $ *Average main: €17* ⊠ *Piazza Costituzione 10/11* ☎ *070/658206* ⊕ *www.anticocaffe1855.it.*

$$$
ITALIAN
✗ **Dal Corsaro.** This elegant restaurant near the port has a strong reputation for fine Italian haute cuisine. The interior shines with fine antiques and silver cutlery; the service is cordial and accommodating. A menu using local organic ingredients includes such popular dishes such as seafood antipasto, squid tagliatelle, and *porcheddu* (roast suckling pig). The wines are perfectly matched with each course, one of which includes a variety of island cheeses and honey. In August and other times of the year, the restaurant opens a branch at the seaside. ■TIP➔ **The fixed-price menus (€60 and €70) are always a good bet.** $ *Average main: €25* ⊠ *Viale Regina Margherita 28* ☎ *070/664318* ⊕ *www.stefanodeidda.it/dalcorsaro.html* ⚐ *Reservations essential* ⌂ *Jacket required* ⊘ *Closed Mon. and Jan. 1–15.*</R>

$$
ITALIAN
✗ **Su Cumbidu.** A meal at this restaurant, which is in Cagliari's lively Marina quarter, near the port, makes for a quick and affordable introduction to Sardinia's rural cuisine. The mainly meat-based dishes can be ordered as part of a fixed-price meal or à la carte. Portions are large, so go easy on the array of antipasti, in order to leave room for secondi like lamb, sausage, and the famous Sardinian porcheddu. Service is brisk and informal; choose a table on the street or within the cavernous vaulted interior. The same family runs a similar restaurant nearby, Sa Schironada, that concentrates on the island's sea-based gastronomy. $ *Average main: €15* ⊠ *Via Napoli 13* ☎ *070/670712* ⊕ *www.sucumbidu.info.*

WHERE TO STAY

$
HOTEL
▦ **Hotel BJ Vittoria.** The airy, white rooms, period-style furnishings, and ceramic flooring make this central third-floor pensione cozy and characterful. **Pros:** clean rooms; central location near port; a/c. **Cons:** no breakfast; no parking; limited amenities. $ *Rooms from: €92* ⊠ *Via Roma 75* ☎ *070/667970, 347/0683345, 349/4473556* ⊕ *www.hotelbjvittoria.it* ⇗ *18 rooms* ⦿ *No meals.*

$
B&B/INN
▦ **La Babbajola Bed & Breakfast.** This three-room bed-and-breakfast in the center of town was created on the second floor of a renovated

19th-century mansion. **Pros:** intimate charm in period house; friendly service; inexpensive room rates. **Cons:** cash only; far from beaches; few modern amenities. [$] *Rooms from: €60* ✉ *Via Giordano 13, Iglesias* ☎ *347/6144621* 🌐 *www.lababbajola.com* 🛏 *3 rooms* 💳 *No credit cards* 🍴 *Breakfast.*

$ B&B/INN 🏨 **La Ghirlanda.** These elegant apartments with tall ceilings and a cool ambience makes a quiet haven in the heart of Cagliari's bustling Marina quarter. **Pros:** affable owners; convenient location near the port and bus and train stations. **Cons:** no views from the rooms; no parking. [$] *Rooms from: €80* ✉ *Via Lodovico Baylle 7* ☎ *070/2040610, 339/8892648* 🛏 *3 rooms* 🕒 *Closed Nov.–Jan.* 🍴 *Breakfast.*

$$ HOTEL 🏨 **Hotel Panorama.** This eight-story hotel just outside downtown Cagliari is geared to businesspeople, with modern furnishings, large desks, free Wi-Fi, and soundproof windows in every room. **Pros:** nice views; bus stop across street; free parking. **Cons:** needs renovating; not very central; sparse furnishings; little English spoken. [$] *Rooms from: €125* ✉ *Viale Armando Diaz 231* ☎ *070/307691* 🌐 *www.hotelpanorama.it* 🛏 *80 rooms, 20 suites* 🍴 *Breakfast.*

$$ HOTEL Fodor's Choice ★ 🏨 **T Hotel.** In the vicinity of Parco di Monte Claro, about a 15-minute taxi or bus ride from Cagliari's center, this 15-floor, circular-shape tower holds a trendy hotel with contemporary styling and outstanding service. **Pros:** spacious designer rooms; great views from most rooms; free parking; free Wi-Fi; outstanding service. **Cons:** 4 km (2½ miles) from city center; extra fee to use indoor pool and spa; some rooms get overheated. [$] *Rooms from: €128* ✉ *Via Dei Giudicati 66* ☎ *070/47400* 🌐 *www.thotel.it* 🛏 *207 rooms* 🍴 *Breakfast.*

NIGHTLIFE AND PERFORMING ARTS

Cagliari's Teatro Lirico stages concerts with local and well-known European artists throughout the year. Contact the tourist office for information.

BARS AND CAFÉS

Caffè de Candia. Relax in the atmospheric interior or casual terrace of this café on the edge of Terrazzo Umberto I. It's a great place to enjoy a cappuccino or glass of vermentino after exploring the Castello quarter. DJs take over on Friday evenings. Caffè de Candia is open daily from 7 am until 10 pm in winter and until 2 am the rest of the year. ✉ *Bastione di Saint Remy, Via Mario de Candia 3* ☎ *070/757–2342.*

Caffè dell'Elfo. The café's central location and casual ambience attracts local professionals, who linger over good wine, Italian snacks, and conversation. ✉ *Salita Santa Chiara 4–6* ☎ *070/682399* 🕒 *Closed Sat. during the day and Sun.*

Caffè Svizzero. Entering this antique, vaulted, and frescoed bar a stone's throw from the port is like stepping back into the 19th century. Order a steaming cappuccino, a glass of the local vermentino wine, or a freshly squeezed fruit juice, and nibble on a panino, a pizzetta, or a pastry. It's all served with politeness and heaps of old-fashioned charm. ✉ *Largo Carlo Felice 6–8* ☎ *070/653784* 🕒 *Closed Sun.*

Libarium Nostrum. A dim bohemian haunt full of wooden beams and brick-lined nooks and crannies, Libarium Nostrum is one of Sardinia's coolest café-bars. It's an occasional venue for live music and DJs, but the real draw is the outdoor terrace high atop Cagliari's medieval ramparts, with lounging sofas for enjoying cocktails and the views. Panini and other snacks are available. ⊠ *Bastioni di Santa Croce 33/35* ☏ *346/5220212* ⊗ *Apr.–Oct., daily 7:30 am–2 am; Nov.–Mar., Tues.– Sun. 7:30 am–2 am.*

SHOPPING

Cagliari's two best shopping streets, full of boutiques and specialty shops for clothes, shoes, bags, and jewelry are Via Manno and Via Garibaldi, just up from the port.

ISOLA. The Istituto Sardo Organizzazione Lavoro Artigiano is a government-sponsored cooperative of artisans. Look for handmade ceramics, woven and wooden goods, baskets, metalwork, and beautiful gold filigree or precious stone jewelry. ⊠ *Via Bacaredda 176* ☏ *070/492756* ⊕ *www.isolacagliari.com*

Sapori di Sardegna. Drop into this shop for Sardinian food products, including local wines, artisanal biscuits, pecorino cheeses, carasau, honey, and olives. There's a great range of items, and the English-speaking staff are always willing to help you out. ⊠ *Vico dei Mille 1* ☏ *070/6848747* ⊕ *www.saporidisardegna.com.*

SPORTS AND THE OUTDOORS

BEACHES

FAMILY

Fodor's Choice
★

Poetto Beach. Only 3 miles southeast of the city center and easily accessible by a quick bus ride, Poetto Beach is one of the most enticing spots to relax in summer for both locals and tourists. Its shallow and clean turquoise waters stretch for some 5 miles, and the beach is lined with cafés, restaurants, shops, snack stands, and parks. Beach lounging chairs and umbrellas are available for rent for about €10 to €12. From the large sandy shores, you can admire the pink flamingos that nest in the marshy reeds of the nearby Molentargius lagoon. ■TIP→ If you're in Cagliari, this postcard setting is a must. **Amenities:** food and drink; toilets. **Best for:** swimming; walking. ⊠ *Take Viale Diaz from Cagliari to Viale Poetto.*

BOATING AND SAILING

Lega Navale Italiana. This public, state-sponsored organization has information on the island's sailing facilities, as well as everything associated with maritime activity. ☏ *079/9102120, 320/9668519* ⊕ *www. leganavale.it.*

WINDSURFING

FAMILY

Windsurfing Club Cagliari. Sardinia has some of the best windsurfing spots in Europe; the club provides advice for beginning to expert surfers. ⊠ *Viale Marina Piccola* ☏ *070/372694, 345/2225169, 333/3025583* ⊕ *www.windsurfingclubcagliari.it* ⊗ *Daily 10:30–7.*

EN
ROUTE

A drive east from Cagliari takes you through some industrial suburbs before reaching the scenic coast and beaches of Capo Boi and Capo Carbonara. **Villasimius,** 50 km (31 miles) east of Cagliari, is the chief resort here; the most beautiful beaches lie 10 km (6 miles) north of the town center, on the golden sands of the Costa Rei.

16

PULA

29 km (18 miles) southwest of Cagliari, 314 km (195 miles) southwest of Olbia.

Resort villages sprawl along the coast southwest of the capital, which has its share of fine scenery and good beaches. On the marshy shoreline between Cagliari's Aeroporto di Elmas and Pula, huge flocks of flamingos are a common sight. Beaches and lodging catering to summer crowds are concentrated 4 km (2½ miles) south of Pula, a little more than 1½ km (1 mile) south of Nora, in a conglomeration that makes up the town of Santa Margherita di Pula. South of here lies one of Sardinia's most magnificent stretches of coastline, with white-sand beaches, turquoise waters, placid coves, and powdery dunes.

GETTING HERE AND AROUND

From Cagliari, drive approximately 40 km (25 miles) on the SS195. Follow directions for Pula/Chia. From Olbia, take SS131 direction Cagliari-Sassari. Follow SS554 towards Pula/Chia. The journey is approximately 300 km (190 miles).

EXPLORING

Fodor's Choice ★ **Nora.** The narrow promontory outside Pula was the site of a Phoenician, Carthaginian, and then, later, a Roman settlement that was first settled some 2,800 years ago. Nora was a prime location as a stronghold and important trading town—Phoenician settlers scouted for good harbors, cliffs to shelter their craft from the wind, and an elevation from which they could defend themselves against attack. An old Roman paved road passes the temple ruins, which include baths, a Roman theater, and an amphitheater now reserved for summer music festivals. Extensive excavations have shed light on life in this ancient city. The channels through which hot air rose to warm the Roman baths can still be made out. Note the difference between the Carthaginians' simple mosaic pavements and the Romans' more elaborate designs in well-preserved multicolored tiles. If the Mediterranean is calm, you can peek under clear waters along the shore for more ruins of the ancient city, which are slowly submerging due to rising seas, earthquakes, and erosion. Guided tours usually begin on the hour. ✉ *3 km (2 miles) south of Pula* ☎ *070/9209138* ⊕ *www.coptur.net* 💶 *€7.50* ⊗ *Daily 10–dusk; last entrance ½ hr before closing.*

Sant'Efisio. The simple 11th-century church at the base of the Nora promontory plays a central part in one of the island's most colorful annual events. A four-day procession during the Festa di Sant'Efisio accompanies a statue of the martyred Saint Efisius all the way from Cagliari to here and back again, culminating in a huge parade down Cagliari's main avenue—it fills up with costumed Sardinians and decorated *traccas,* or ox-drawn carriages. This is a must-see if you're in southern Sardinia from May 1 to May 4. ✉ *Nora Beach, 3 km (2 miles) south of Pula* ⊗ *Summer, daily 9–dusk; winter, Sat. 4:30–7:30, Sun. 10–noon and 4:30–7:30.*

WHERE TO STAY

$$$
RESORT
FAMILY

Flamingo Hotel & Resort. The stark white buildings and the six two-story cottages of this shady beachside resort hotel are a striking contrast to the verdant parkland of eucalyptus trees, palm fronds, and miles of white-sand beach. **Pros:** excellent beach and swimming pools for adults and families; wellness center; friendly staff. **Cons:** overcrowded in high season; large facility, with business conferences hosted on occasion; some rooms in need of renovation. $ *Rooms from: €268* ⊠ *SS195, Km 33.8, 4 km (2½ miles) south of Pula* ☎ *070/9208361* ⊕ *www.hotelflamingo.it* ⤶ *180 rooms, 6 villas* ⊘ *Closed early Oct.– late Apr.* ⦿ *Breakfast.*

WORD OF MOUTH

"Unfortunately, too many travelers make the mistake of focusing on the Costa Smeralda area, which is *least* representative of Sardinia. By contrast, there are numerous interesting towns in the hinterland which are worth visiting, lovely medieval basilicas scattered about the lonely countryside, as well as beautiful Roman ruins along the coasts."   —gac

$$
HOTEL
FAMILY

Is Molas Hotel and Golf Course. If you love golf and stargazing, then the place to stay in southern Sardinia is this peaceful hotel, with 80 Mediterranean-style rooms and an 18-hole golf course. **Pros:** immediate access to golf course; freshwater pool; tranquil setting with rural views. **Cons:** old-fashioned; isolated location with poor Internet connection; beach shuttle service can be slow. $ *Rooms from: €150* ⊠ *SS195, Località Is Molas* ☎ *070/9241006* ⊕ *www.ismolas.it* ⤶ *80 rooms, 1 suite* ⊘ *Closed Nov.–Feb.* ⦿ *Multiple meal plans.*

$$$$
RESORT
FAMILY

Is Morus Relais. A luxurious enclave hidden in a large palm-filled garden with undulating paths, Is Morus sits on a sandy cove and has all the amenities of a fine beach resort. **Pros:** lovely grounds; large pool and poolside grill restaurant; free Wi-Fi in main lobby and public areas. **Cons:** restaurant and bar service slow; bathrooms need updating; very thin walls; expensive room rates. $ *Rooms from: €360* ⊠ *SS195, Km 37.4* ☎ *070/921171* ⊕ *www.ismorus.com* ⤶ *55 rooms, 18 villas* ⊘ *Closed Nov.–Apr.* ⦿ *Some meals.*

16

SU NURAXI TO THE COSTA SMERALDA

A more traditional—and wilder—Sardinia awaits the traveler who ventures into the island's mountainous interior. Inland Sardinians are hardy souls, used to living in a climate that is as unforgiving in winter as it is intolerable in summer. This is, after all, the area that popularized the *vendetta*, a claim to personal revenge against another family or individual that sometimes endured from generation to generation. Old traditions like this are softening with time but are still firmly rooted in the social fabric.

The land is hilly, barren, and beautiful. Here, rare species of wildlife share the rocky uplands with sturdy medieval churches and the mysterious nuraghi left by prehistoric people. The nuraghi were built beginning in the 19th century BC, and they vary from single beehive-shape defensive towers to multitower complexes sheltering whole communities—prehistoric versions of medieval walled towns. As you move northward, the timeless beauty of the landscape begins to show greater signs of modern development. The sunny resort of Alghero, the Spanish-influenced port on the west coast, is one of the island's premier holiday spots. Costa Smeralda, the luxury resort complex on the northeast corner of Sardinia, is considered one of the most prestigious summer destinations for Europeans and continues to attract celebrities and the wealthy.

BARUMINI

Barumini is 65 km (40 miles) north of Cagliari.

It's definitely worth a detour to the quiet village of Barumini to visit the extraordinary stone village–fortress of Su Nuraxi.

GETTING HERE AND AROUND

The best way to reach Su Nuraxi is by car. From the capital, follow SS131 to SS197. Direct buses to the site are few and far between.

EXPLORING

FAMILY

Fodor's Choice

★

Su Nuraxi. The most extensive of the island's 7,000 discovered nuraghi, Su Nuraxi's significance merits its inclusion on the UNESCO World Heritage List. Concentric rings of thick stone walls conceal dark chambers and narrow passages in a central, beehive-shape tower. The excellent guided tour (which, depending on the nature of the group and language abilities of the guide, may be available in English) allows you to explore the interior. In the ruins of the surrounding village there are benches, ovens, wells, and other Bronze Age remnants.

The specific functions of individual nuraghi remain a mystery, largely because their construction predates written history. Though this particular type of construction is unique to Sardinia in Italy, similar buildings dating from the same era are found in other parts of the Mediterranean, such as Cyprus and the Balearic islands off Spain. All visits are accompanied by a local guide, start every 30 minutes, and last approximately 50 minutes. The same ticket also allows entry to a museum and exhibition center in Barumini. ■ TIP→ **If you're driving from SS131, don't be misled to other, lesser nuraghi—follow the signs all the way to Barumini.** ✉ *SP Barumini–Tuili, 1 km (½ mile) west of Barumini* ☎ *070/9368128* ⊕ *www.fondazionebarumini.it* ✆ *€10* ⊗ *Daily 9–1 hr before sunset.*

THARROS

16 km (10 miles) west of Oristano.

Spread across a thin tongue of land that dangles off the Sinis peninsula, the archaeological site of Tharros ranks as one of Sardinia's most important Phoenician, Carthaginian, and Roman settlements. It's not hard to understand why this evocative site was selected by the ancients, given its sweeping views across the Gulf of Oristano, its defensibility, and the shelter it provides for vessels. Founded around 800 BC, the city was finally abandoned in the 11th century AD, in favor of Oristano.

GETTING HERE AND AROUND

Whether you're heading to Tharros from the north or south, follow the SS131 to Oristano. Drive through Oristano towards Cabras, branching off on SP6 for San Giovanni di Sinis and Tharros.

EXPLORING

Museo Civico di Cabras. This lakeside museum displays many of the better-preserved urns and other artifacts recovered from nearby excavation sites, including Tharros. The visit takes about an hour. Buy a combination ticket to see the Museo Civico and the ruins at Tharros. ⊠ *Via Tharros, Cabras, off SP6, 10 km (6 miles) northwest of Oristano* ☎ *0783/290636* ⊕ *www.penisoladelsinis.it* 🖾 *€5; combination ticket €8, includes Tharros* ⊙ *Apr.–Oct., Mon.–Sat. 9–1 and 4–8, Sun. 9–1 and 3–8; Nov.–Mar., Tues.–Sun. 9–1 and 3–7.*

FAMILY **Tharros.** The spectacular site of the Carthaginian and Roman city of Tharros, like Nora to the south, was chosen because it commanded the best views of the gulf and could provide an easy escape route if inland tribes threatened. The Phoenician-Punic city planning here includes sophisticated water channeling and masonry foundations. Two reconstructed Corinthian columns stand as testament to the site's Roman history, and there are baths visible and mosaic fragments from the Roman city. Look for the Cardo Maximus, the main road of the city, built to last for centuries. As at Nora, many more ruins are submerged under water. A climb up the steep hill to a Spanish watchtower affords a scenic view over the Sinis Peninsula. There's a small souvenir shop and attached café for snacks and beverages. You can buy a combination ticket that also allows entry to the **Museo Civico di Cabras,** where some of the finds are displayed, though the best items are in Cagliari's archaeological museum. ⊠ *San Giovanni di Sinis, Cabras, off SP6, 16 km (10 miles) west of Oristano, 113 km (70 miles) northwest of Cagliari* ☎ *0783/370019* ⊕ *www.penisoladelsinis.it* 🖾 *€5; combination ticket €8, includes Museo Civico di Cabras* ⊙ *Apr., May, and Oct., daily 9–6; June, July, and Sept., daily 9–7; Aug., daily 9–8; Nov.–Mar., Tues.–Sun. 9–5.*

EN ROUTE On the way to the archaeological ruins in Tharros you pass the ghost town of **San Salvatore,** revived briefly in the 1960s as a locale for spaghetti Westerns and since abandoned, except for a few days every summer, when it is the focus of a religious festival. The saloon from the movie set still stands. Among the dunes past San Salvatore are large rush huts formerly used by fishermen and now much in demand as back-to-nature vacation homes. The 5th-century church of **San Giovanni di Sinis,** on the Sinis Peninsula, is claimed to be the oldest Christian church in Sardinia.

NUORO

107 km (67 miles) northeast of Tharros, 181 km (113 miles) north of Cagliari.

The somewhat shabby provincial capital of Nuoro is on the edge of a gorge in the harsh mountainous area that culminates in Gennargentu, the island's highest massif (6,000 feet). Not much happens here; you can do some (relatively inexpensive) shopping amid strolling locals, or try the local Barbagia sausage, which is great. Just 40 km (25 miles) east of Nuoro is the coastal town of Cala Gonone. Cradled on Orosei Bay, this popular holiday destination has white-sand beaches, mountain views, and the mysterious water caves of Bue Marino.

GETTING HERE AND AROUND

From Cagliari, the drive to Nuoro takes about two hours. Take the SS131 toward Sassari/Oristano/Nuoro, then continue on SS131 DCN toward Nuoro/Olbia. After 55 km (34 miles), turn off, following signs for Nuoro Centro until you reach Nuoro.

FESTIVALS

Nuoro's **Festa del Redentore** (Feast of the Redeemer) is held on the next-to-last Sunday in August. It's the best time to view the various traditional costumes of Sardinia's interior all in one place. The culmination of the feast is the annual pilgrimage of worshippers to the bronze statue of Christ the Redeemer atop Monte Ortobene.

ESSENTIALS

Nuoro ⊠ *Piazza Italia 19* ☎ *0784/238878* ⊗ *Mon. and Wed.–Fri. 8:30–2, Tues. 8:30–2 and 3:30–7.*

EXPLORING

Monte Ortobene. About 7 km (4 miles) northeast of Nuoro is Monte Ortobene, a granite peak at 2,900 feet offering lofty views over the gulch below. Here you can also see up close the imposing bronze statue of the *Rendentore* (*Christ the Redeemer*) overlooking the city. Pilgrimages and mass take place in summer here. Picnic tables make this a favorite spot for an alfresco lunch throughout the year. ⊕ *www.comune.nuoro.it.*

Museo Etnografico Sardo (*Museum of Sardinian Life and Popular Traditions*). Also known as the Museo del Costume, or Costume Museum, this ethnographic collection is a must for anyone interested in the cultural context of Sardinia's customs and traditions. Among the 8,000 items in the museum's collection, you can view domestic and agricultural implements, splendid jewelry, traditional musical instruments, and dozens of local costumes. The nearby park on Sant'Onofrio Hill affords magnificent views over Nuoro and the surrounding country. ⊠ *Via A. Mereu 56* ☎ *0784/257035* ⊕ *www.isresardegna.org* ▭ *€3* ⊗ *Mid-June–Sept., Tues.–Sun. 9–1 and 3–7; Oct.–mid-June, Tues.–Sun. 10–1 and 3–5.*

WHERE TO EAT

$
ITALIAN
FAMILY

✕ **Il Portico.** Brotherly love (and ownership) is what makes this old-town restaurant so exceptional, in addition to the quality seafood dishes. Modern artwork, stone pillars, and arched ceilings give way to tables draped in gold linen. Appetizers created by the Ladu brothers include caviar with artichoke, octopus salad, and smoked salmon buttered with goat cheese and rolled into a crêpe. The seasonally changing menu always features local fish and might include homemade pastas such as *maccheroncini neri con calamari* (squid-ink noodles with clams, calamari, and zucchini purée). Desserts of ginger ice cream and chocolate lava cake are not to be missed. Service is attentive and welcoming.

$ *Average main: €14* ⊠ *Via Mons. Bua 13* ☎ *0784/217641* ⊕ *www. ilporticonuoro.it* ⊙ *Closed Wed., 2 wks in July and Aug., 2 wks in Jan. and Feb.*

$$
ITALIAN
FAMILY
Fodor's Choice
★

✕ **Il Rifugio.** Family-run since 1988, this local spot is packed nearly every night. The dining area is rustic with terra-cotta flooring, brick pillars, straw-base chairs, and a wood-burning stove. The service, presentation, food, and wine list are all exceptional, and only the freshest of local meats and cheeses are served. Orchestrated by chef Francesco Nanu, the menu features grilled tuna, rosemary lamb, glazed pork, and might include such delicacies as *cordedda con piselli stufati* (lamb intestines on a bed of snow peas). Everything is made from scratch, including the pizza, the pasta, and ice cream that's dribbled with honey. ■ TIP→ **The daily menu is a very good deal.** $ *Average main: €16* ⊠ *Via A. Mereu 28/36* ☎ *0784/232355* ⊕ *www.trattoriarifugio.com* ⊙ *Closed Wed.*

WHERE TO STAY

$
HOTEL

⌂ **Euro Hotel.** Centrally located, this simple, block-style hotel—more or less standard for provincial Nuoro—is ideal for a stopover. **Pros:** budget rates; ample parking. **Cons:** not much character; outdated rooms; no restaurant. $ *Rooms from: €80* ⊠ *Via Trieste 62* ☎ *0784/34071* ⊕ *www.eurohotelnuoro.it* ⇦ *54 rooms* ⦿⧵ *Breakfast.*

$
B&B/INN

⌂ **Silvia e Paolo.** Overlooking cafés and cobblestone streets, this quaint bed-and-breakfast has three spacious bedrooms. **Pros:** great location; friendly owners; excellent value. **Cons:** parking may be tricky to find; two rooms share a bathroom. $ *Rooms from: €55* ⊠ *Corso Giuseppe Garibaldi 58* ☎ *0784/31280, 329/6122897* ⊕ *www.silviaepaolo.it* ⇦ *3 rooms* ⦿⧵ *Breakfast.*

$$
HOTEL
Fodor's Choice
★

⌂ **Su Gologone.** In the foothills of the Supramonte, you'll find this luxury hotel, where the rooms are country retreats, decked out with traditional Sardinian fabrics, wood chests, paintings, and wood-beam ceilings. **Pros:** locally influenced restaurant; great location for hiking in the Supramonte valley. **Cons:** frequented by large groups; some rooms are distant from the main reception area. $ *Rooms from: €170* ⊠ *Località Su Gologone, Oliena* ☎ *0784/287512* ⊕ *www.sugologone.it* ⇦ *62 rooms, 8 suites* ⊙ *Closed Nov.–late Mar.* ⦿⧵ *Some meals.*

FONNI

30 km (19 miles) south of Nuoro, 137 km (85 miles) south of Olbia.

In the heart of the Barbagia region, Fonni is the highest town on the island. This mountainous district, including Monte Spada and the Bruncu Spina refuge on the Gennargentu Massif, is Sardinia's most primitive. Life in some villages seems not to have changed much since the Middle Ages. Here a rigidly patriarchal society perpetuates age-old customs and obedience to rural traditions. Although as a tourist you may be looked at with curiosity, a smile can go a long way. High mountain roads wind and loop through the landscape; towns are small and undistinguished, their social fabric formed in complete isolation. On feast days elaborate local costumes are worn as an explicit statement of community identity.

GETTING HERE AND AROUND

To reach Fonni, the highest town in Sardinia, drive (or hire a car and driver), or take a bus from Nuoro. There is no train service.

From Nuoro, take SS389 from the junction of Mamoiada, or from SS128 to the town of Gavoi. From Cagliari, follow SS131, exiting toward the village of Ottana. Continue on SS128, turning at Fonni. From Sassari, follow SS131 south, turning east onto SS129 at Macomer. Continue on SS128, following signs for Fonni.

FESTIVALS

You can see one of the most characteristic of the Barbagia's celebrations in local costume during the **Festa di San Giovanni,** held June 24, in honor of Saint John. Events include *palios,* or horse races, live music, and fireworks.

WHERE TO STAY

$ **Hotel Sa Orte.** Close to the highest peaks of the Gennargentu range
HOTEL   in the center of Sardinia, this hotel provides a warm welcome at any time of the year. **Pros:** generous breakfasts; affable staff; convenient for mountain excursions. **Cons:** some rooms are small and dark; few facilities; no views. $ *Rooms from: €80 ⊠ Via Roma 14 ☎ 0784/58020 ⊕ www.ristoranteilpergolato.com ⤳ 26 rooms, 1 suite ⵙ⃝ Some meals.*

16

ALGHERO

137 km (85 miles) southwest of Olbia.

A tourist-friendly town of about 45,000 inhabitants with a distinctly Spanish flavor, Alghero is also known as "Barcelonetta" ("little Barcelona"). Rich wrought-iron scrollwork decorates balconies and screened windows; Spanish motifs appear in stone portals and bell towers. The town was built and inhabited in the 14th century by the Aragonese and Catalans, who constructed seaside ramparts and sturdy towers encompassing an inviting nucleus of narrow, winding streets with honey-color palazzi. The native language spoken here is closer to Catalan than Italian, although you probably have to attend one of the masses conducted in Algherese (or listen in on stories swapped by older fishermen) to hear it.

Besides its historic architectural gems such as the cathedral and Palazzo d'Albis, the fortified city is well worth a visit to simply stroll and discover local culture on narrow cobblestone streets. The city also has a reputation for serving great food at reasonable prices.

GETTING HERE AND AROUND

Alghero International Airport is 15 km (9 miles) from the city center, which you can reach by car, taxi, or public transport. Regional buses connect the town with Sassari and local villages. The closest passenger port to Alghero is Porto Torres (approximately 40 km [25 miles] away).

ESSENTIALS

Alghero Tourism ⊠ *Piazza Porta Terra 9 ☎ 079/979054 ⊕ www.algheroturismo.it.*

EXPLORING

Capo Caccia. Head 15 km (9 miles) west of Alghero for broad sandy beaches and the spectacular heights of the imposing limestone headland of Capo Caccia. The rugged promontory, blanketed by thick *maquis* (brush), is home to Le Prigionette nature reserve and deep caves such as the Grotta di Nettuno. Close by are the beaches of Porto Ferro, Cala Viola and, on the beautiful Porto Conte inlet, Cala Dragunara.

FAMILY
Fodor's Choice ★
Grotta di Nettuno (*Neptune's Cave*). At the base of a sheer cliff, the pounding sea has carved an entrance to a vast fantastic cavern filled with stunning water pools, stalactites, and stalagmites. The dramatic cave and coves, discovered by fishermen in the 18th century, are popular tourist attractions for their sheer natural beauty. You must visit with a guide; tours start on the hour. It's possible to reach the caves by boat or by land. Between March and October, boat trips depart at regular intervals from the port of Alghero for €16 round-trip (admission to the grotto is extra). To reach the grotto by land, you can descend the 654 dizzying steps of Escala del Cabirol ("Goat Steps"), which are cut into the steep cliff here. ■ TIP→ **By public bus from Alghero's Via Catalogna, the trip to the top of the stairway takes about 50 minutes. Allow 15 minutes for the descent by foot.** ✉ *13 km (8 miles) west of Alghero* ☎ *079/946540* 🎟 *€13* ⏲ *Grotto: Apr., daily 10–6; May–Oct., daily 9–8; Nov.–Mar., daily 10–4 (weather permitting). Last entry 1 hr before closing. Bus from Alghero to stairs: year-round at 9:15; mid-June–Sept. at 9:15, 3:10, and 5:10. Bus from Capo Caccia: year-round at noon; mid-June–Sept. at noon, 4:05, and 6:05*

Torre Porta Terra. This old stone tower fortress can be climbed for good views from the terrace. Stop at the interesting city history display on the computer terminals inside the tower. There's also a rotating set of exhibits and a miniature model of Alghero's old town. ✉ *Piazza Porta Terra 2* ☎ *079/973–4045* 🌐 *www.smuovi.com* 🎟 *Free* ⏲ *Jan.–May and Oct.–Dec., Mon.–Sat. 9–1 and 4–7; June–Sept., daily 9–1 and 7–10.*

WHERE TO EAT

$
ITALIAN
🍴 **Il Ghiotto.** Handily situated in Alghero's historic Piazza Civica, and popular with locals, this casual eatery makes an ideal spot for a lunchtime or evening snack. There's a buffet for lunch, with dishes that include seafood salad, stuffed eggplant, and pastas; in the evening, there are reasonably priced meat and fish dishes. Choose between sitting at the functional tables in the piazza or in the spacious eating area within. The restaurant also sells various Sardinian specialties, from biscuits to wine. [$] *Average main: €13* ✉ *Piazza Civica* ☎ *079/974820* ⏲ *Closed Wed.*

$$
ITALIAN
🍴 **Il Pavone.** Fresh flowers on white linen tablecloths add color to the bright, glass-encased dining area of this delightful eatery on busy Piazza Sulis. Oversize wine bottles capped in wax add Italian charm, and there are gold-framed paintings covering every inch of the back wall. Although the menu changes seasonally, you're likely to find pasta and seafood dishes such as tagliatelle with shrimp, or octopus with pesto. The three-course menu for two includes an appetizer, a pasta, and a traditional dessert. ■ TIP→ **For a caffeine boost, head to the neighboring Piccolo Pavone, a plainer, cheaper version of its parent, for its**

signature Dado coffee, an espresso made with chili peppers and honey. $ *Average main: €18* ⊠ *Piazza Sulis 3* ☎ *079/979584* ⊙ *No dinner Sun. Nov.–Mar.*

$$
SEAFOOD

✕ **La Lepanto.** A covered veranda by the seafront marks out Alghero's top seafood restaurant, an expansive and sunny room complete with crustacean-filled aquarium. It's usually crowded with both locals and tourists in summer. The specialty is *aragosta* (lobster) cooked different ways, including *alla catalana* (with tomato and onions)—or try it with ricotta foam, parsley, basil, and tomato. In winter, when lobster isn't available, sample the *ricci* (sea urchins). For starters, try *fregola ai crostacei* (local semolina pasta with shellfish). $ *Average main: €17* ⊠ *Via Carlo Alberto 133* ☎ *079/979116* ⊕ *www.lalepanto.com* ⊙ *Closed Jan. and Feb., and Tues. Mar.–May and Oct.–Dec.*

WHERE TO STAY

$$$
HOTEL

🛏 **Carlos V.** On the shore boulevard opposite the Villa Las Tronas and 15 minutes from the airport, this grand, modern hotel (pronounced "Carlos Quinto") has an array of gardens and terraces, and a huge saltwater pool with sea views. **Pros:** wonderful vistas; good-size pool; a bargain in low season, when rates drop. **Cons:** large-hotel atmosphere; mediocre breakfasts; patchy Wi-Fi. $ *Rooms from: €274* ⊠ *Lungomare Valencia 24* ☎ *079/972 0600* ⊕ *www.hotelcarlosv.it* ⇱ *176 rooms, 3 suites* ⦿ *Breakfast.*

$
B&B/INN

🛏 **San Francesco.** The convent that was once attached to the church of San Francesco is a very handy hotel. **Pros:** historic ambience; central location; very tranquil. **Cons:** low-light spaces; somber, sparsely furnished rooms; not a good choice for kids. $ *Rooms from: €101* ⊠ *Via Machin 2* ☎ *079/980330* ⊕ *www.sanfrancescohotel.com* ⇱ *21 rooms* ⊙ *Closed mid-Nov.–Dec.* ⦿ *Breakfast.*

$$$$
HOTEL
Fodor'sChoice
★

🛏 **Villa Las Tronas Hotel & Spa.** Privacy, elegance, and charm are among the draws of this secluded mansion estate. **Pros:** regal setting; incredible service; exceptional views. **Cons:** very expensive; rocky beach. $ *Rooms from: €407* ⊠ *Lungomare Valencia 1* ☎ *079/981818* ⊕ *www. hotelvillalastronas.it* ⇱ *18 rooms, 6 suites* ⦿ *Some meals.*

SHOPPING

De Filippis. On the so-called Riviera del Corallo, Alghero has long been famed for its coral products, fashioned into elegant jewelry. This shop, with three outlets within a few yards of each other in the old town, has an impressive range of bracelets, brooches, and necklaces. ⊠ *Via Carlo Alberto 23* ☎ *079/979394* ⊕ *www.defilippis.it.*

NIGHTLIFE

Caffè Costantino. The elegant and historic Caffè Costantino continues to attract tourists and locals to its tables on the pretty town square. Inside, yellow flowered walls, chandeliers, classical music, and a warm crowd of distinguished, well-dressed Algherese maintain its authenticity and popularity. Stop in for a glass of local wine or macchiato; it's open until midnight. ⊠ *Piazza Civica 30* ☎ *079/976154.*

16

SASSARI

34 km (21 miles) northeast of Alghero, 212 km (132 miles) north of Cagliari.

With a population of about 130,000, Sassari, the island's second-largest city, is an important university town and administrative center, notable for its history of intellectualism and bohemian student culture, an ornate old cathedral, and a good archaeological museum. Look for downtown vendors of *fainè*, a pizzalike chickpea-flour pancake glistening with olive oil, which is a Genoese and Sassarese specialty. The mazelike old town is blissfully isolated from the chaotic traffic swirling though the newer neighborhoods—Sassari is the hub of several highways and secondary roads leading to various coastal resorts, among them Stintino and Castelsardo.

GETTING HERE AND AROUND

Sassari can be reached by plane, ferry, train, bus, or car. The nearest airport is Alghero-Fertilia, about 30 km (19 miles) from Sassari. Inexpensive buses can get you to the center of Sassari. The closest port is Porto Torres, about 20 km (12½ miles) away. Ferries connect Sassari to Genoa and Civitavecchia (Rome). Frequent bus and train services operate between Sassari and Cagliari, Olbia, and Alghero.

ESSENTIALS

Sassari ⊠ *Via Sebastiano Satta 13* ☎ *079/2008072* ⊕ *www.comune. sassari.it.*

EXPLORING

Duomo. The elegant stone Duomo is Sassari's must-see sight. The cathedral, dedicated to Saint Nicolas, Santa Claus's inspiration, took more than half a millennium to build: the foundations were laid in the 12th century, and the Spanish colonial–style facade was completed in the 18th. Of particular interest in the interior are the ribbed Gothic vaults, the 14th-century painting of the Madonna del Bosco on the high altar, and the early-19th-century tomb of Placido Benedetto di Savoia, the uncle of united Italy's first king. ⊠ *Piazza Duomo del 3* ☎ *079/233185* 🌐 *Free* ⊙ *Apr.–Oct., daily 9–noon and 5–7; Nov.–Mar., daily 9–12:30 and 4–6.*

FAMILY **Museo Sanna.** Sassari's excellent museum has Sardinia's best archaeological collection outside Cagliari, spanning nuraghic, Carthaginian, and Roman histories, including well-preserved bronze statuettes, household objects from the 2nd millennium BC, and decorated amphorae. ⊠ *Via Roma 64* ☎ *079/272203* ⊕ *www.museosannasassari.beniculturali.it* 🌐 *€4 (free 1st Sun. of month)* ⊙ *Jan.–Mar., Tues.–Sat. 9–8, Sun. 9–2; Apr.–Dec., Tues.–Sun. 9–8.*

WHERE TO EAT

$ ✕ **L'Assassino.** Get a true taste of local Sassarese cooking—and many
ITALIAN other Sardinian specialties—at this family-run restaurant in the old town. The menu is not for the squeamish or for vegetarians: horse, donkey, and *porcetto* (also spelled "porcheddu") figure prominently, as do typical Sassarese dishes such as *trippa alla parmigiana* (tripe

with Parmesan), *lumaconi in rosso* (snails in a rich tomato sauce), and *cordula con piselli* (sheep's intestines with peas). Tables are available in the buzzy, vaulted, terra-cotta-tiled dining room, or, in summer, in a courtyard. $ *Average main: €14* ⊠ *Via Pettenadu 19* ☎ *079/233463* ✆ *Closed Mon.*

CASTELSARDO

32 km (20 miles) northeast of Sassari.

The walled seaside citadel of Castelsardo holds tiny shops crammed with all kinds of souvenirs, particularly woven baskets, but also rugs and wrought iron. The **Roccia dell'Elefante** (Elephant Rock) on the road into Castelsardo was hollowed out by primitive man to be used as a burial chamber. The local name for one is *domus de janas* (literally, "fairy house").

16

GETTING HERE AND AROUND

In summer, a daily bus runs between Alghero Airport and Castelsardo. Tickets can be purchased directly from the driver. Check the ARST bus service timetable from Sassari, which operates a route with stops in Castelsardo. The trip takes about an hour. The main bus stop in Castelsardo is located in the central Piazza Pianedda. There is also a stop on the seafront by the beach.

By car, access from Alghero, heading toward Porto Torres. Follow signs for Sassari onto the SS200, merging onto the SS134. Follow signs for Santa Teresa Gallura that takes you along the beautiful coastline.

LA MADDALENA

45 km (20 miles) northwest of Olbia.

From the port of Palau you can visit the archipelago of La Maddalena, seven granite islands embellished with aromatic scrub and wind-bent pines. The most significant of the handful of sites to see here is Giuseppe Garibaldi's home and tomb. Explore the lively port (also called La Maddalena), then head to one of several picture-postcard coves, the perfect spot for a picnic and to rejuvenate after your journey to the archipelago.

GETTING HERE AND AROUND

The only way to get to this small island is by boat or ferry. From Olbia, take a bus or drive to Palau, then catch the ferry to La Maddalena. During the day, car ferries make the 3-km (2-mile) trip two to four times an hour. The town center is right in front of the dock. Local buses are available for accessing the beaches, although the island is best explored by scooter or bike.

EXPLORING

Compendio Garibaldino. Pilgrims from around the world converge on the Compendio Garibaldino, a complex on Isola Caprera that contains the restored home, a museum, and the tomb of Giuseppe Garibaldi (1807–82). The national hero and military leader who laid the groundwork for the first unification of Italy in 1861 lived a simple life as a farmer on the island that he eventually owned. Take the ferry to Isola Maddalena and then the bridge to Caprera. ✉ *Caprera, 7 km (4½ miles) east of Isola Maddalena* ☎ *0789/727162* 🌐 *www.compendiogaribaldino.it* 🎟 €6 🕒 *Mar.–Oct., Tues.–Sun. 9–1:30 and 2–8; Nov.–Feb., Tues.–Sat. 9–1:30 and 2–8, and 1st Sun. of month 9–1:30 and 2–8. Last entry at 7:15.*

PORTO CERVO

35 km (22 miles) southeast of La Maddalena, 30 km (19 miles) north of Olbia.

Sardinia's northeastern coast is fringed with low cliffs, inlets, and small bays. This has become an upscale vacationland, with glossy resorts such as Baia Sardinia and Porto Rotondo just outside the confines of the famed Costa Smeralda. Some of Italy's most expensive hotels are here, and magnificent yachts anchor in the waters of Porto Cervo. Golf courses, yacht clubs, and numerous alfresco restaurants and bars cater to those who want to see and be seen.

All along the coast, carefully tended lush vegetation surrounds vacation villages and discreet villas that have sprung up over the past decade in eclectic architectural styles best described as "bogus Mediterranean." The trend has been to keep this an enclave of the very rich. Outside the peak season, however, prices dip and the majesty of the natural surroundings shines through, justifying all the hype and the Emerald Coast's fame as one of the truly romantic corners of the Mediterranean.

GETTING HERE AND AROUND

Porto Cervo is accessible by boat, car, taxi, and bus. Buses run regularly from Olbia and Palau.

Whichever airport or port of entry into Sardinia you choose, head to Olbia. By car, follow SS125 north towards Arzachena and Costa Smeralda. After 10 km (6 miles), turn right onto SP73 towards Porto Rotondo/Porto Cervo. Continue on SP94 and turn onto SP59 to Porto Cervo. The trip takes about 30 minutes.

WHERE TO STAY

$$$$ RESORT Fodor's Choice ★ 🏨 **Cala di Volpe.** Long a magnet for the beautiful people, this hyper-glamorous five-star Starwood hotel was designed by Jacques Couëlle to resemble an ancient Sardinian fishing village, with its own covered wooden bridge. **Pros:** stunning architecture; luxurious ambience; professional staff. **Cons:** some rooms disappoint; astronomical rates for room, additional amenities, drinks, and meals; car necessary. [$] *Rooms from: €1088* ✉ *Cala di Volpe* ☎ *0789/976111* 🌐 *www.caladivolpe.com* 🛏 *100 rooms, 21 suites* 🕒 *Closed Oct.–mid-Mar.* 🍴 *Some meals.*

$$$$ HOTEL 🏨 **Cervo Hotel, Costa Smeralda Resort.** Designed in 1963 by the architect Luigi Vietti, the Cervo Hotel is an integral part of the surrounding resort.

Pros: open year-round; prime location; superb service. **Cons:** small beach; mediocre decoration; feels a little too much like a chain; very expensive. Ⓢ *Rooms from: €372* ✉ *Waterfront* ☎ *0789/931111* ⊕ *www. hotelcervocostasmeralda.com* ⤳ *89 rooms, 7 suites* ⦿ *Breakfast.*

$$
HOTEL

▢ **Nibaru.** Lush gardens and pinkish-red brick buildings with tiled roofs lend this hotel on a secluded inlet the feel of a small resort. **Pros:** courteous staff; nice pool; close to good beaches. **Cons:** you'll need a car to reach neighboring restaurants; basic décor and furnishings; crowded in summer. Ⓢ *Rooms from: €180* ✉ *Località Cala di Volpe* ☎ *0789/96038* ⊕ *www.hotelnibaru.it* ⤳ *50 rooms, 2 suites* ⊘ *Closed early Oct.–Apr.* ⦿ *Breakfast.*

SHOPPING

ISOLA. The colorful artisanal ceramics and woven items showcasing traditional craftsmanship sold here are unique and affordable. Crafted for local festivals, the wooden masks also make unusual souvenirs. This local branch of ISOLA, a state-sponsored organization promoting Sardinian handicrafts, is in the center of Porto Cervo. ✉ *Sottopiazza* ☎ *0789/94428* ⊘ *Closed Oct.–Apr.*

SPORTS AND THE OUTDOORS

BEACHES

The beaches around the Costa Smeralda are some of the most exclusive in Europe, and they don't disappoint, with fine golden sand sheltered by red cliffs and fronting azure waters. Many can only be reached by boat, and there are regular launches from Porto Cervo. Rentals of sun beds and towels are as expensive as you'd expect.

BOATING AND SAILING

Yacht Club Costa Smeralda. The Aga Khan IV and some local associates founded the yacht club in 1967 with a view to promoting nautical activities. The club provides use of its pool, restaurant, bar, and guest rooms to those with memberships at other yacht clubs. Watch for regattas from June to September, and check out the YCCS Sailing School, which organizes courses on dinghies and cabin cruisers. ✉ *Via della Marina* ☎ *0789/902200* ⊕ *www.yccs.it.*

GOLF

Pevero Golf Course. Designed by Robert Trent Jones Sr. and opened in 1972, Pevero is a world-class course with some of Europe's most beautiful fairways. Stretching nearly 4 miles between the Gulf of Pevero and Cala di Volpe (Bay of Foxes), it provides challenging playing conditions with 70 bunkers, several rocks, and vegetation. The dress code is formal in the upscale Club House. ✉ *Cala di Volpe 20* ☎ *0789/958000* ⊕ *www.peverogolfclub.com* ⤳ *€70–€120, depending on season* ⛳ *18 holes, 6700 yards, par 72.*

OLBIA

30 km (19 miles) south of Porto Cervo.

Amid the resorts of Sardinia's northeastern coast, Olbia, a town of about 60,000, is a lively little seaport and port of call for mainland ferries at the head of a long, wide bay.

16

GETTING HERE AND AROUND

The main airport, Olbia–Costa Smeralda, is only 1½ km (1 mile) from the town center. Inexpensive city buses and taxis are available outside the terminal. Trains operate between Olbia and Cagliari and take about four hours. If you're driving, main roads are clearly marked to reach the city center, outlying areas, and other major towns.

The Olbia-Isola Bianca harbor provides daily connections with the Italian mainland, less than 300 km (186 miles) away. Regular ferries arrive from Genoa, Civitavecchia, and Livorno. Most ferries take between 4 and 10 hours.

ESSENTIALS

Olbia ✉ *Municipio, Via Dante 1, at Corso Umberto I* ☎ *0789/52206* 🌐 *www.olbiaturismo.it* ✉ *Via Nanni 17/19* ☎ *0789/563444* 🌐 *www.olbiatempioturismo.it.*

EXPLORING

Basilica San Simplicio. Olbia's little Catholic basilica, a short walk behind the main Corso Umberto I and past the train station, is worth searching out if you have any spare time in Olbia. The simple granite structure dates from the 11th century, part of the great Pisan church-building program, using pillars and columns recycled from Roman buildings. The basilica has a bare, somewhat somber interior, its three naves separated by a series of arches. ✉ *Via San Simplicio, at Via Fausto Noce* ☎ *0789/23542* 🕒 *Daily 7–12:45 and 4–7.*

WHERE TO EAT AND STAY

$$ ITALIAN 🍴 **Ristorante Barbagia.** The chefs at this restaurant on a busy center street prepare traditional dishes from Sardinia's wild interior and ones that make use of seafood and other local ingredients. Antipasti might include a refreshing salad of sliced tomato and fresh cheese (called *sa t'amata chi sa frughe*) with carasau. *Maccarrones de busa* with wild-boar sauce is often on the menu, and you might find roast lamb and suckling pig in season. Pizzas and fresh pastas are also served. [$] *Average main: €15* ✉ *Via Galvani 94* ☎ *0789/51640* 🌐 *www.ristorantebarbagia.com* 🕒 *Closed Jan., and Wed. Oct.–June.*

$$ HOTEL 🏨 **Hotel Martini.** Modern and businesslike, the Hotel Martini occupies an eye-catching site on the shore of a lagoon north of town. **Pros:** lovely restaurant; friendly staff; central location. **Cons:** no room service; some small showers; expensive Wi-Fi. [$] *Rooms from: €135* ✉ *Via Gabriele D'Annunzio 21* ☎ *0789/26066* 🌐 *www.hotelmartiniolbia.com* 🛏 *68 rooms, 2 suites* 🍽 *Breakfast.*

$$$$ HOTEL 🏨 **Petra Segreta Resort and Spa.** Sea and mountain views, top-quality cuisine, and spacious guest rooms that ooze chic, modern charm are the main draws at this romantic boutique hotel outside the picturesque village of San Pantaleo. **Pros:** tranquil mountainside setting with spectacular views; blend of traditional surroundings and modern amenities; good restaurant. **Cons:** a drive from the beach; not suitable for families; very expensive. [$] *Rooms from: €378* ✉ *Strada di Buddeu, C.P. 130, Frazione San Pantaleo* ☎ *0789/1876441* 🌐 *www.petrasegretaresort.com* 🛏 *21 rooms, 3 suites* 🕒 *Closed Nov.–Mar.* 🍽 *Breakfast.*

ITALIAN VOCABULARY

ENGLISH	ITALIAN	PRONOUNCIATION

BASICS

ENGLISH	ITALIAN	PRONOUNCIATION
Yes/no	Sí/no	see/no
Please	Per favore	pear fa-**vo**-ray
Yes, please	Sí grazie	see **grah**-tsee-ay
Thank you	Grazie	**grah**-tsee-ay
You're welcome	Prego	**pray**-go
Excuse me, sorry	Scusi	**skoo**-zee
Sorry!	Mi dispiace!	mee dis-spee-**ah**-chay
Good morning/ afternoon	Buongiorno	bwohn-**jor**-no
Good evening	Buona sera	**bwoh**-na **say**-ra
Good-bye	Arrivederci	a-ree-vah-**dare**-chee
Mr. (Sir)	Signore	see-**nyo**-ray
Mrs. (Ma'am)	Signora	see-**nyo**-ra
Miss	Signorina	see-nyo-**ree**-na
Pleased to meet you	Piacere	pee-ah-**chair**-ray
How are you?	Come sta?	**ko**-may **stah**
Very well, thanks	Bene, grazie	**ben**-ay **grah**-tsee-ay
Hello (phone)	Pronto?	**proan**-to

NUMBERS

ENGLISH	ITALIAN	PRONOUNCIATION
one	uno	**oo**-no
two	due	**doo**-ay
three	tre	tray
four	quattro	**kwah**-tro
five	cinque	**cheen**-kway
six	sei	say
seven	sette	**set**-ay
eight	otto	**oh**-to
nine	nove	**no**-vay
ten	dieci	dee-**eh**-chee
twenty	venti	**vain**-tee

ENGLISH	ITALIAN	PRONOUNCIATION
thirty	trenta	**train**-ta
forty	quaranta	kwa-**rahn**-ta
fifty	cinquanta	cheen-**kwahn**-ta
sixty	sessanta	seh-**sahn**-ta
seventy	settanta	seh-**tahn**-ta
eighty	ottanta	o-**tahn**-ta
ninety	novanta	no-**vahn**-ta
one hundred	cento	**chen**-to
one thousand	mille	**mee**-lay
ten thousand	diecimila	dee-eh-chee-**mee**-la

USEFUL PHRASES

Do you speak English?	Parla inglese?	**par**-la een-**glay**-zay
I don't speak Italian	Non parlo italiano	non **par**-lo ee-tal-**yah**-no
I don't understand	Non capisco	non ka-**peess**-ko
Can you please repeat?	Può ripetere?	pwo ree-**pet**-ay-ray
Slowly!	Lentamente!	**len**-ta-men-tay
I don't know	Non lo so	non lo **so**
I'm American	Sono americano(a)	**so**-no a-may-ree-**kah**-no(a)
I'm British	Sono inglese	so-no een-**glay**-zay
What's your name?	Come si chiama?	**ko**-may see kee-**ah**-ma
My name is . . .	Mi chiamo . . .	mee kee-**ah**-mo
What time is it?	Che ore sono?	kay **o**-ray **so**-no
How?	Come?	**ko**-may
When?	Quando?	**kwan**-doe
Yesterday/today/tomorrow	Ieri/oggi/domani	**yer**-ee/**o**-jee/do-**mah**-nee
This morning	Stamattina	sta-ma-**tee**-na
This afternoon	Oggi pomeriggio	**o**-jee po-mer-**ee**-jo
Tonight	Stasera	sta-**ser**-a

ENGLISH	ITALIAN	PRONOUNCIATION
What?	Che cosa?	kay **ko**-za
What is it?	Chee cos'é?	kay ko-**zay**
Why?	Perché?	pear-**kay**
Who?	Chi?	kee
Where is . . .	Dov'è . . .	doe-**veh**
the bus stop?	la fermata dell'autobus?	la fer-**mah**-tadel ow-toe-**booss**
the train station?	la stazione?	la sta-tsee-**oh**-nay
the subway	la metropolitana?	la may-tro-po-lee-**tah**-na
the terminal?	il terminale?	eel ter-mee-**nah**-lay
the post office?	l'ufficio postale?	loo-**fee**-cho po-**stah**-lay
the bank?	la banca?	la **bahn**-ka
the hotel?	l'hotel?	lo-**tel**
the store?	il negozio?	eel nay-**go**-tsee-o
the cashier?	la cassa?	la **kah**-sa
the museum?	il museo?	eel moo-**zay**-o
the hospital?	l'ospedale?	lo-spay-**dah**-lay
the first-aid station?	il pronto soccorso?	Eel **pron**-to so-**kor**-so
the elevator?	l'ascensore?	la-shen-**so**-ray
a telephone?	un telefono?	oon tay-**lay**-fo-no
the restrooms?	il bagno?	eel **bahn**-yo
Here/there	Qui/là	kwee/la
Left/right	A sinistra/a destra	a see-**neess**-tra/a **des**-tra
Straight ahead	Avanti dritto	a-**vahn**-tee **dree**-to
Is it near/far?	È vicino/lontano?	ay vee-**chee**-no/lon-**tah**-no
I'd like . . .	Vorrei . . .	vo-**ray**
a room	una camera	**oo**-na **kah**-may-ra
the key	la chiave	la kee-**ah**-vay
a newspaper	un giornale	oon jor-**nah**-lay
a stamp	un francobollo	oon frahn-ko-**bo**-lo

ENGLISH	ITALIAN	PRONOUNCIATION
I'd like to buy . . .	Vorrei comprare . . .	vo-**ray** kom-**prah**-ray
How much is it?	Quanto costa?	**kwahn**-toe **coast**-a
It's expensive/cheap	È caro/economico	ay **car**-o/ay-ko-**no**-mee-ko
A little/a lot	Poco/tanto	**po**-ko/**tahn**-to
More/less	Più/meno	pee-**oo**/**may**-no
Enough/too (much)	Abbastanza/troppo	a-bas-**tahn**-sa/**tro**-po
I am sick	Sto male	sto **mah**-lay
Call a doctor	Chiama un dottore	kee-**ah**-mah oon doe-**toe**-ray
Help!	Aiuto!	a-**yoo**-toe
Stop!	Alt!	ahlt
Fire!	Al fuoco!	ahl **fwo**-ko
Caution/Look out!	Attenzione!	a-ten-**syon**-ay

DINING OUT

A bottle of . . .	Una bottiglia di . . .	**oo**-na bo-**tee**-lee-ahdee
A cup of . . .	Una tazza di . . .	**oo**-na **tah**-tsa dee
A glass of . . .	Un bicchiere di . . .	oon bee-key-**air**-ay dee
Bill/check	Il conto	eel **cone**-toe
Bread	Il pane	eel **pah**-nay
Breakfast	La prima colazione	la **pree**-ma ko-la-**tsee**-oh-nay
Cocktail/aperitif	L'aperitivo	la-pay-ree-**tee**-vo
Dinner	La cena	la **chen**-a
Fixed-price menu	Menù a prezzo fisso	may-**noo** a **pret**-so **fee**-so
Fork	La forchetta	la for-**ket**-a
I am diabetic	Ho il diabete	o eel dee-a-**bay**-tay
I am vegetarian	Sono vegetariano/a	**so**-no vay-jay-ta-ree-**ah**-no/a
I'd like . . .	Vorrei . . .	vo-**ray**
I'd like to order	Vorrei ordinare	vo-**ray** or-dee-**nah**-ray

ENGLISH	ITALIAN	PRONOUNCIATION
Is service included?	Il servizio è incluso?	eel ser-**vee**-tzee-o ay een-**kloo**-zo
It's good/bad	È buono/cattivo	ay **bwo**-no/ka-**tee**-vo
It's hot/cold	È caldo/freddo	ay **kahl**-doe/**fred**-o
Knife	Il coltello	eel kol-**tel**-o
Lunch	Il pranzo	eel **prahnt**-so
Menu	Il menù	eel may-**noo**
Napkin	Il tovagliolo	eel toe-va-lee-**oh**-lo
Please give me . . .	Mi dia . . .	mee **dee**-a
Salt	Il sale	eel **sah**-lay
Spoon	Il cucchiaio	eel koo-kee-**ah**-yo
Sugar	Lo zucchero	lo **tsoo**-ker-o
Waiter/waitress	Cameriere/ cameriera	ka-mare-**yer**-ay/ ka-mare-**yer**-a
Wine list	La lista dei vini	la **lee**-sta **day**-ee **vee**-nee

TRAVEL SMART ITALY

GETTING HERE AND AROUND

▌ AIR TRAVEL

Most nonstop flights between North America and Italy serve Rome and Milan, though the airports in Venice and Pisa also accommodate nonstop flights from the United States. Many travelers find it more convenient to connect via a European hub to Florence, Bologna, or another smaller Italian airport.

Flying time to Milan or Rome is approximately 8–8½ hours from New York, 10–11 hours from Chicago, and 11½ hours from Los Angeles.

Labor strikes are not as frequent in Italy as they were some years ago, but when they do occur they can affect not only air travel, but also local public transit that serves airports. Your airline will usually have details about strikes affecting its flight schedules.

Airline Security Issues Transportation Security Administration (*TSA*). The agency has answers for almost every security question that might come up. ⊕ *www.tsa.gov.*

Contact A helpful website for information (location, phone numbers, local transportation, etc.) about all of the airports in Italy is ⊕ *www.italianairportguide.com.*

AIRPORTS

The major gateways to Italy include Rome's Aeroporto Leonardo da Vinci (FCO), better known as Fiumicino, and Milan's Aeroporto Malpensa (MXP). Most flights to Venice, Florence, and Pisa make connections at Fiumicino and Malpensa or another European airport hub. You can take the Ferrovie dello Stato (FS) airport train or bus to Rome's Termini station or to Cadorna or Centrale in Milan; from the latter you can then catch a train to any other location in Italy. It'll take about 40 minutes to get from Fiumicino to Roma Termini, less than an hour to Milano Centrale.

Many carriers fly into the smaller airports. Milan also has Linate airport (LIN) and Rome has Ciampino (CIA). Venice is served by Aeroporto di Venezia Marco Polo (VCE), Naples by Aeroporto Internazionale di Napoli Capodichino (NAP), Palermo by Aeroporto di Palermo (PMO) and Cagliari by Aeroporto Elmas (CAG). Florence is serviced by Aeroporto di Firenze (FLR) and by Aeroporto di Pisa (PSA), which is about 2 km (1 mile) outside the center of Pisa and about one hour from Florence. Aeroporto de Bologna (BLQ) is a 20-minute direct Aerobus ride away from Bologna Centrale, which is 35 minutes from Florence by high-speed train.

Many Italian airports have undergone renovations in recent years and have been ramping up security measures, which include random baggage inspection and bomb-detection dogs. All airports have restaurants, snack bars, shopping, and Wi-Fi access. Each also has at least one nearby hotel. In the cases of Milan Linate, Florence, Pisa, Naples, and Bologna, the city centers are less than a 15-minute taxi or bus ride away—so if you encounter a long delay, spend it in town.

When you take a connecting flight from a European airline hub (Frankfurt or Paris, for example) to a local Italian airport (Florence or Venice), be aware that your luggage might not make it onto the second plane with you. The airlines' lost-luggage service is efficient, however, and your delayed luggage is usually delivered to your hotel or holiday rental within 12–24 hours.

Airport Information Aeroporto di Bologna (*BLQ, also called Guglielmo Marconi*). ⊠ *6 km (4 miles) northwest of Bologna* ☏ *051/6479615 (5 am–midnight)* ⊕ *www.bologna-airport.it.* **Aeroporto di Cagliari.** 7 km (4½ miles) from Cagliari ⊠ *Via dei Trasvolatori, Elmas, Cagliari* ☏ *070/211211* ⊕ *www.cagliari-airport.com.* **Aeroporto di**

Firenze (*FLR, also called Amerigo Vespucci and Peretola*). ✉ *6 km (4 miles) northwest of Florence* ☎ *055/3061300* ⊕ *www.aeroporto. firenze.it.* **Aeroporto di Milan Linate** (*LIN*). ✉ *8 km (5 miles) southeast of Milan* ☎ *02/232323* ⊕ *www.milanolinate.eu.* **Aeroporto di Palermo** (*PMO, also called Falcone e Borsellino and Punta Raisi*). ✉ *32 km (19 miles) northwest of Palermo* ☎ *091/7020111, 800/541880 in Italy (toll-free)* ⊕ *www.gesap.it.* **Aeroporto di Pisa** (*PSA, also called Aeroporto Galileo Galilei*). ✉ *2 km (1 mile) south of Pisa, 80 km (50 miles) west of Florence* ☎ *050/849300* ⊕ *www.pisa-airport.com.* **Aeroporto di Roma Ciampino** (*CIA*). ✉ *15 km (9 miles) southwest of Rome* ☎ *06/65951* ⊕ *www.adr.it.* **Aeroporto di Venezia** (*VCE, also called Marco Polo*). ✉ *6 km (4 miles) north of Venice* ☎ *041/2609260* ⊕ *www.veniceairport.com.* **Aeroporto Fiumicino** (*FCO, also called Leonardo da Vinci*). ✉ *35 km (20 miles) southwest of Rome* ☎ *06/65951* ⊕ *www.adr.it.* **Aeroporto Internazionale di Napoli** (*NAP, also called Capodichino*). ✉ *7 km (4 miles) northeast of Naples* ☎ *081/7896111 (weekdays 8–4), 848/888777 for flight info* ⊕ *www.naples-airport.com.* **Aeroporto Malpensa** (*MPX*). ✉ *45 km (28 miles) north of Milan* ☎ *02/232323* ⊕ *www. airportmalpensa.com.*

FLIGHTS

From the United States, Alitalia and Delta Air Lines serve Rome, Milan, Pisa, and Venice. The major international hubs in Italy (Milan and Rome) are also served by United Airlines and American Airlines; US Airways serves Rome as well. From June through October, the Italy-based Meridiana has nonstop flights from New York to Naples and Palermo.

Alitalia has direct flights from London to Milan and Rome, while British Airways and smaller budget carriers provide services between Great Britain and other locations in Italy. EasyJet connects London's Gatwick and Stansted airports with 13 Italian destinations. Ryanair, departing from Stansted, flies to 18 airports. Meridiana has flights between Gatwick and Olbia on Sardinia in summer. For flights within Italy, check Alitalia and

smaller airlines, such as Air One, blu-express, and Meridiana. Since tickets are frequently sold at discounted prices, it's wise to investigate the cost of flying—even one-way—as an alternative to train travel.

Airline Contacts Aer Lingus ☎ *02/43458326 from Italy, 516/6224222 from the U.S.* ⊕ *www. aerlingus.com.* **Air Berlin** ☎ *199/400737 within Italy* ⊕ *www.airberlin.com.* **Alitalia** ☎ *800/223–5730 in the U.S., 892/010 in Italy, 06/65640 for Rome office* ⊕ *www.alitalia. it.* **American Airlines** ☎ *800/433–7300, 199/257300 in Italy* ⊕ *www.aa.com.* **British Airways** ☎ *800/247–9297 in the U.S., 02/69633602 in Italy* ⊕ *www.britishairways. com.* **Delta Air Lines** ☎ *888/750–3284 for international reservations, 02/38591451 in Italy* ⊕ *www.delta.com.* **EasyJet** ☎ *+44330/3655454 from outside the UK, 199/201840 in Italy, 0330/3655000 from inside the UK* ⊕ *www.easyjet.com.* **Ryanair** ☎ *0871/2460000 in the UK (toll number), 895/8958989 in Italy (toll number)* ⊕ *www. ryanair.com.* **United Airlines** ☎ *800/864–8331 in the U.S., 02/69633256 in Italy* ⊕ *www. united.com.* **Volotea** ☎ *895/895 4404 in Italy, 0034/931220717 abroad* ⊕ *www.volotea.com.*

Domestic Carriers Air One ☎ *091/2551047 abroad, 892/444 in Italy* ⊕ *www.flyairone. it.* **blu-express** ☎ *06/98956666* ⊕ *www. blu-express.com.* **Meridiana** ☎ *866/387–6359 in the U.S., 0789/52682 in Italy, 0844/4822360 for UK call center* ⊕ *www.euroflyusa.com.*

▮ BUS TRAVEL

Italy's far-reaching regional bus network, often operated by private companies, is not as attractive an option as in other European countries, partly due to convenient train travel. Schedules are often drawn up with commuters and students in mind and may be sketchy on weekends. But, car travel aside, regional bus companies often provide the only means of getting to out-of-the-way places. Even when this isn't the case, buses can be faster and more direct than local trains, so it's a good idea to compare bus and train schedules. Lazzi operates in Tuscany and central

Italy, while BusItalia–Sita Nord covers Tuscany and Veneto. SitaSud caters to travelers in Puglia, Foggia, Matera, Basilicata, and Campania.

All major cities in Italy have urban bus services. It's inexpensive, and tickets should be purchased from newsstands or tobacconists and validated on board (some city buses have ticket machines on the buses themselves). Buses can become jammed during busy travel periods and rush hours.

Smoking is not permitted on Italian buses. All, even those on long-distance routes, offer a single class of service. Cleanliness and comfort levels are high on private motor coaches, which have plenty of legroom, sizable seats, and luggage storage, but often do not have toilets. Private bus lines usually have a ticket office in town or allow you to pay when you board.

Bus Information ANM ⊠ *Via G. Marino 1, Naples* ☏ *800/639525 in Italy (toll-free)* ⊕ *www.anm.it.* **ATAC** ⊠ *Rome* ☏ *06/46951* ⊕ *www.atac.roma.it.* **ATAF** ⊠ *Stazione Centrale di Santa Maria Novella, Florence* ☏ *800/424500, 199/104245 from mobile phone (toll number)* ⊕ *www.ataf.net.* **BusItalia–Sita Nord** ⊠ *Viale dei Cadorna, 105, Florence* ☏ *800/373760 (toll-free)* ⊕ *www.fsbusitalia.it.* **Lazzi** ⊠ *Via Mercadante 2, Florence* ☏ *0573/1937900* ⊕ *www.lazzi.it.* **SitaSud** ⊠ *Via S. Francesco D'Assisi 1, Putignano* ☏ *080/4052245* ⊕ *www.sitasudtrasporti.it.*

▮ CAR TRAVEL

Italy has an extensive network of *autostrade* (toll highways), complemented by equally well-maintained but free *superstrade* (expressways). Save the ticket you're issued at an autostrada entrance, as you'll need it to exit; on some shorter autostrade, you pay the toll when you enter. Viacards, on sale for €25 and up at many autostrada locations, let you pay for tolls in advance, exiting at special lanes where you simply slip the card into a designated slot. There is no need to purchase this, as the tollbooths also accept Visa and MasterCard.

An *uscita* is an exit. A *raccordo annulare* is a ring road surrounding a city; a *tangenziale* generally bypasses a city entirely. *Strade, strade statale, strade regionale,* and *strade provinciale* (regional and provincial highways, denoted by *S, SS, SR,* or *SP* numbers) may be two lanes, as are all secondary roads; directions and turnoffs aren't always clearly marked.

GASOLINE

You'll find gas stations on most main highways. Those on autostrade are open 24 hours. Otherwise, gas stations are generally open Monday through Saturday 7–7, with a break at lunchtime. At self-service stations the pumps are operated by a central machine for payment, which often doesn't take credit cards: it accepts bills in denominations of €5, €10, €20, and €50, and doesn't give change. Stations with attendants accept cash and credit cards. It's not customary to tip the attendant.

At this writing, gasoline (*benzina*) costs about €1.65 per liter and is available in unleaded (*verde*) and superunleaded (*super*). Many rental cars in Italy use diesel (*gasolio*), which costs about €1.52 per liter (remember to confirm the fuel type your car requires before leaving the agency).

DRIVING IN *CENTRI STORICI* (HISTORIC CENTERS)

To avoid hefty fines (which you may not be notified of until months after your departure from Italy), make sure you know the rules governing where you can and can't drive in historic city centers. You must have a permit to enter many towns, and Florence, for example, is very strict in enforcement. Check with your lodging or car-rental company to find out about acquiring permits for access.

PARKING

Parking is at a premium in most towns, especially in historic centers. Fines for parking violations are high, and towing is common. Don't think about tearing up a ticket, as car-rental companies can use your credit card to be reimbursed for any fines incurred. It's a good idea to park in a designated (and preferably attended) lot; even small towns often have a large lot at the edge of historic centers.

In congested cities, indoor parking costs €25–€30 for 12–24 hours; outdoor parking costs about €10–€20. Parking in an area signposted *zona disco* (disk zone) is allowed for short periods (from 30 minutes to two hours or more—the time is posted); if you don't have an appropriate cardboard disk (check in the glove box of your rental car) to show what time you parked, you can write your arrival time on a piece of paper. In most metropolitan areas you can find curbside *parcometro* machines; once you insert coins, it prints a ticket that you then leave on your dashboard.

RENTALS

Fiats, Fords, and Alfa Romeos in a variety of sizes are the most typical rental cars. Note that most Italian cars have standard transmission—if you need an automatic, specify one when you make your reservation. Significantly higher rates will apply.

Most American chains have affiliates in Italy, but costs are usually lower if you book a car before leaving home. Rentals at airports usually cost less than city pickups (and airport offices are open later). An auto broker such as ⊕ *www.rent.it* lets you compare rates among companies while guaranteeing the lowest price.

Most rental companies won't rent to someone under age 21. Most also refuse to rent any model larger than an economy or subcompact to anyone under 23, and, further, require customers under that age to pay by credit card. There are no special restrictions on senior citizen drivers. Any additional drivers must be identified in the contract and qualify with the age limits. There's also a supplementary daily fee for additional drivers. Expect to pay extra for add-on features, too. A car seat

(required for children under age three) will cost about €36 for the duration of the rental and should be booked in advance. In some areas, snow chains are compulsory in winter months and can be rented from €30 to €60—it may be cheaper to buy your own at the first open garage. Upon rental, all companies require credit cards as a warranty; to rent bigger cars (2,000 cc or more), you may be required to show two credit cards.

Hiring a car with a driver can simplify matters, particularly if you plan to indulge in wine tastings or explore the distractingly scenic Amalfi Coast. Search online (the travel forums at ⊕ *Fodors.com* are a good resource) or ask at your hotel for recommendations. Drivers are paid by the day, and are usually rewarded with a tip of about 15% upon completion of the journey.

All rental agencies operating in Italy require you to buy a collision-damage waiver (CDW) and a theft-protection policy, but those costs should already be included in the rates you're quoted. Verify this, along with any deductible, which can vary greatly depending on the company and type of car. Be aware that coverage may be denied if the named driver on the rental contract isn't the driver at the time of an accident. In Sicily there are some roads for which rental agencies deny coverage; ask in advance if you plan to travel in remote regions. Also ask your rental company about other included coverage when you reserve the car or pick it up. Finally, try not to leave valuables in your car, because thieves often target rental vehicles. If you can't avoid doing so—for instance, if you want to stop to see a sight while traveling between cities—park in an attended lot.

ROAD CONDITIONS

Autostrade are well maintained, as are most interregional highways. Typically, autostrade have two lanes in both directions; the left lane should be used only for passing. Italians drive fast and are impatient with those who don't. Tailgating (and flashing with bright beams to signal intent to pass) is the norm if you dawdle in the left lane—the only way to avoid it is to stay to the right.

The condition of provincial (county) roads varies, but road maintenance at this level is generally good in Italy. In many small hill towns the streets are winding and extremely narrow, so try to park at the edge of town and explore on foot.

Driving on back roads isn't difficult as long as you're on the alert for bicycles and passing cars. In addition, street and road signs are often missing or placed in awkward spots; a good map or GPS is essential. If you feel pressure from a string of cars in your rearview mirror but don't feel comfortable speeding up, pull off to the right, and let them pass.

Be aware that some maps may not use the SR or SP (strade regionale and strade provinciale) highway designations, which took the place of the old SS designations in 2004. They may use the old SS designation or no numbering at all.

ROADSIDE EMERGENCIES

Automobile Club Italiano offers 24-hour road service (☎ 803116); English-speaking operators are available. Your rental-car company may also have an emergency tow service with a toll-free phone number: keep it handy. Be prepared to report which road you're on, the *verso* (direction) you're headed, and your *targa* (license plate number). Also, in an emergency, call the police (☎ 113).

When you're on the road, always carry a good road map and a flashlight—a reflective vest should be provided with the car. A cell phone is highly recommended, though there are emergency phones on the autostrade and superstrade. To locate them, look on the pavement for painted arrows and the term "SOS."

Emergency Services American Automobile Association (*AAA*). ☎ 800/2224357 ⊕ www. aaa.com. **Automobile Club Italiano** (*ACI*). ☎ 803/116 for emergency service ⊕ www. aci.it.

RULES OF THE ROAD

Driving is on the right. Speed limits are 130 kph (80 mph) on autostrade, reduced to 110 kph (70 mph) when it rains, and 90 kph (55 mph) on state and provincial roads, unless otherwise marked. In towns, the speed limit is 50 kph (30 mph), which may drop as low as 10 kph (6 mph) near schools, hospitals, and other designated areas. Note that right turns on red lights are forbidden. Headlights are required to be on while driving on all roads (large or small) outside of municipalities. You must wear seat belts and strap young children under 4 feet 11 inches into car seats at all times. Using handheld mobile phones while driving is illegal—and fines can exceed €100. In most Italian towns the use of the horn is forbidden in many areas. A large sign, *"zona di silenzio,"* indicates a "no honking" zone.

In Italy you must be 18 years old to drive a car. A U.S. driver's license is acceptable to rent a car, but by law Italy also requires non-Europeans to carry an International Driver's Permit (IDP), which essentially translates your license into Italian (and a dozen other languages). In practice, it depends on the police officer who pulls you over whether you'll be penalized for not carrying it. The IDP costs only $15, and obtaining one is easy: see the AAA website ⊕ *www.aaa.com* for more information.

The blood-alcohol content limit for driving is 0.05% (stricter than in the United States). Surpass it and you'll face fines up to €6,000 and the possibility of one year's imprisonment. Although enforcement of laws varies depending on the region, fines for speeding are uniformly stiff: 10 kph over the speed limit can warrant a fine of up to €500; greater than 10 kph (6 mph), and your license could be taken away. The police have the power to levy on-the-spot fines.

TRAIN TRAVEL

Traveling by train in Italy is simple and efficient. Service between major cities is frequent, and trains usually arrive on schedule. The fastest trains on the Trenitalia Ferrovie dello Stato (FS)—the Italian State Railways—are Freccie Rosse Alta Velocità. Ferrari mogul Montezemolo launched the competing NTV Italo high-speed service in 2012. Bullet trains on both services run between all major cities from Venice, Milan, and Turin down through Florence and Rome to Naples and Salerno. Seat reservations are mandatory, and you'll be assigned a specific seat; to avoid having to squeeze through narrow aisles, board only at your designated coach (the number on your ticket matches the one near the door of each coach). Reservations are also required for Eurostar and the slower Intercity (IC) trains; tickets for the latter are about half the price they are for the faster trains. If you miss your reserved train, go to the ticket counter within the hour and you may be able to move your reservation to a later one (this depends on the type of reservation, so check the rules when booking). Note that you'll still need to reserve seats in advance if you're using a rail pass.

There are often significant discounts when you book well in advance. On websites, you'll be presented with available promotional fares, such as Trenitalia's "Super Economy" (up to 60% off), "Famiglia" (a 20% discount for one adult and at least one child), and "A/R" (a round trip in a day). Italo offers "Low Cost" and "Economy." The caveat is that the discounts come with restrictions on changes and cancellations; make sure you understand them before booking.

Reservations are not available on Interregionale trains, which are slower, make more stops, and are less expensive than high-speed and Intercity trains. Regionale and Espresso trains stop most frequently and are the most economical (many serve commuters). There are refreshments on long-distance trains, purchased from a mobile cart or a dining car, but not on the commuter trains.

All but commuter trains have first and second classes. On local trains, first-class fare ensures you a little more space; on long-distance trains, you also get wider seats (three across as opposed to four) and a bit more legroom, but the difference is minimal. At peak travel times a first-class fare may be worth the additional cost, as the coaches may be less crowded. In Italian, *prima classe* is first class; second is *seconda classe*.

Many cities—Milan, Turin, Genoa, Naples, Florence, Rome, and even Verona included—have more than one train station, so be sure you get off at the right station. When buying tickets, be particularly aware that in Rome and Florence some trains don't stop at all of the cities' stations and may not stop at the main, central station. When scheduling train travel online or through a travel agent, request to arrive at the station closest to your destination in Rome and Florence.

Except for Pisa, Milan, and Rome, none of the major cities have trains that go directly to the airports, but airport shuttle buses connect train stations and airports.

You can purchase train tickets and review schedules online, at travel agencies, at train station ticket counters, and at automatic ticketing machines located in all but the smallest stations. If you'd like to board a train and don't have a ticket, seek out the conductor prior to getting on; he or she will tell you whether you may buy a ticket on board and what the surcharge will be (usually €8). Fines for attempting to ride a train without a ticket are €100 (€50 if paid on the spot) plus the price of the ticket.

For trains without a reservation you must validate your ticket before boarding by punching it at wall- or pillar-mounted yellow or green boxes in train stations or at the track entrances of larger stations. If

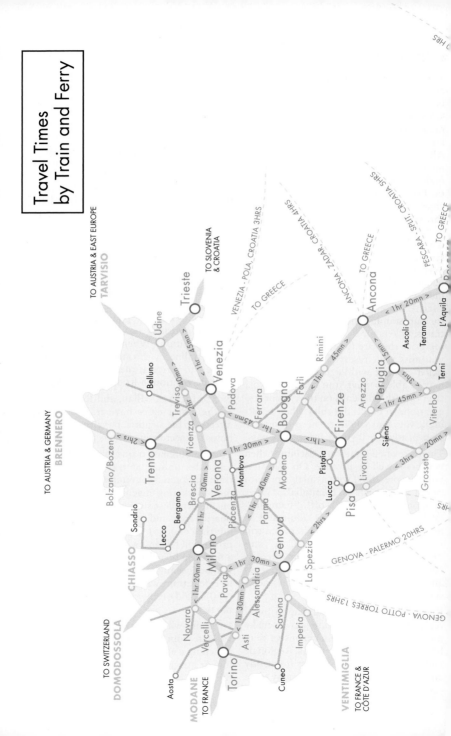

Travel Times
by Train and Ferry

you forget, find a conductor immediately to avoid a hefty fine.

Train strikes of various kinds are not uncommon, so it's wise to ensure that your train is actually running. During a strike minimum service is guaranteed (especially for distance trains); ask at the station or search online to find out about your particular reservation.

Traveling by night can be a good deal—and somewhat of an adventure—because you'll pass a night without having to have a hotel room. Comfortable trains run on the longer routes (Sicily–Rome, Sicily–Milan, Rome–Turin, Lecce–Milan); request the good-value T3 (three single beds), Intercity Notte, and Carrozza Comfort. The Vagone Letto has private bathrooms and single-, double-, or twin-bed suites. Overnight trains also travel to international destinations like Paris, Vienna, Munich, and other cities.

Information FS-Trenitalia ☎ *06/68475475 abroad (English), 892021 in Italy* ⊕ *www. trenitalia.com.* **NTV Italo** ☎ *06/0708* ⊕ *www. italotreno.it.*

TRAIN PASSES

Rail passes promise savings on train travel. But compare prices with actual fares to determine whether a pass will truly pay off. Generally, the more often you plan to travel long distances on high-speed trains, the more sense a rail pass makes.

Italy is one of 24 countries that accept the Eurail Pass, which provides unlimited first- and second-class travel. If you plan to rack up miles across the Continent, get a Global Eurail Pass (covering all participating nations). The Eurail Select Pass allows for travel in four contiguous countries. Other options are the Eurail Youth Pass (for those under 26), the Eurail Flexipass (valid for a certain number of travel days within a set period), and the Eurail Saver (aimed at two to five people traveling together).

The Eurail Regional Pass, available for non-European residents, allows a certain number of travel days within two contiguous countries over the course of two months. Four to 10 days of travel in Italy and France cost $408–$692 (1st class) or $348–$590 (2nd class). If there are two or more of you, consider the **Eurail Regional Pass Saver:** good for 4 to 10 travel days, the price per person for France-Italy is $348–$590 (1st class) or $296–$502 (2nd class); family passes offer further discounts for children under 12; kids under four travel free. **Eurail Regional Youth** (for those under 26) is second-class only and costs $267–$452 for 4 to 10 days of travel in Italy and France.

All passes must be purchased before you leave for Europe. Keep in mind that even with a rail pass you still need to reserve seats on the trains that require them.

Contacts Eurail ⊕ *www.eurail.com.* **Italia Rail** ☎ *877/375–7245 in the U.S.* ⊕ *www.italiarail. com.* **Rail Europe** ☎ *800/622–8600 in the U.S.* ⊕ *www.raileurope.com.* **RailPass** ⊕ *www. railpass.com.*

ESSENTIALS

■ ACCOMMODATIONS

Hotels in Italy are becoming increasingly distinctive. Palazzi, villas, and monasteries have been restored as luxurious lodgings, while retaining their original atmosphere, and small hotels are revamping historic buildings with contemporary décor. Famed Italian wineries are offering rooms and apartments for three-day to weeklong stays.

The lodgings we list are the cream of the crop in each price category. Properties are assigned price categories based on the rate for two people sharing a standard double room in high season, including tax and service.

APARTMENT AND HOUSE RENTALS

Renting a vacation property can be economical depending on your budget and the number of people in your group. Most are owned by individuals and managed by rental agents who advertise online; and because many properties are represented by multiple agents, one may appear on different sites under different names (hence "Chianti Bella Vista," "Tuscan Sun Home," and "Casa Toscana Sole" could all refer to the same villa). In some cases rental agents handle only the online reservation and financial arrangements; in others, the agent or owner may meet you at the property for the initial check-in.

Issues to keep in mind when renting an apartment in a city or town are the neighborhood (street noise and ambience), the availability of an elevator or number of stairs, the furnishings (including pots and linens), what's supplied on arrival (dishwashing liquid, coffee or tea), and the cost of utilities (are all covered by the rental rate?). Inquiries about countryside properties should also include how isolated the property is (do you have to drive 45 minutes to reach the nearest town?). If you're arriving too late in the day to

grocery shop, request that provisions for the next day's breakfast be supplied.

Contacts At Home Abroad ☎ 212/421-9165 ⊕ www.athomeabroadinc.com. **Barclay International Group** ☎ 800/845-6636, 516/364-0064 ⊕ www.barclayweb.com. **Bed & Breakfast Inns Online** ☎ 800/215-7365 ⊕ www.bbonline.com. **Doorways Villa Vacations** ☎ 610/520-0806, 800/261-4460 ⊕ www.villavacations.com. **Home Away** ☎ 512/493-0382 ⊕ www.homeaway.com. **Hosted Villas** ☎ 800/374-6637, 416/920-1873 ⊕ www.hostedvillas.com. **Interhome** ☎ 800/882-6864 ⊕ www.interhomeusa.com. **Italy Rents** ☎ 202/821-4273, 06/99268007 in Italy ⊕ www.italyrents.com. **Parker Villas** ☎ 800/280-2811 ⊕ www.parkervillas.com. **Rent A Villa** ☎ 877/250-4366, 206/417-3444 ⊕ www.rentavilla.com. **Summer In Italy** ☎ 800/509-8194 in the U.S., 089/8426126 in Italy ⊕ www.summerinitaly.com. **Tuscan House** ☎ 800/844-6939 ⊕ www.tuscanhouse.com. **Villas & Apartments Abroad** ☎ 212/213-6435 ⊕ www.vaanyc.com. **Villas International** ☎ 800/221-2260, 415/499-9490 ⊕ www.villasintl.com. **Villas of Distinction** ☎ 800/289-0900 ⊕ www.villasofdistinction.com. **Wimco** ☎ 800/449-1553 ⊕ www.wimco.com.

CONVENTS AND MONASTERIES

Throughout Italy tourists can find reasonably priced lodging at convents, monasteries, and religious houses. Religious orders commonly charge about €30 to €60 per person per night for rooms that are clean, comfortable, and convenient. Many have private bathrooms; spacious lounge areas and secluded gardens or terraces are standard features. A continental breakfast ordinarily comes with the room, but be sure to ask. Sometimes, for an extra fee, family-style lunches and dinners are provided, too.

Be aware of three issues when considering a convent or monastery stay: many have a curfew of 11 pm or midnight; you need to book in advance because they fill up quickly; and your best means of booking is usually email or fax—the person answering the phone may not speak English.

Contact **Hospites.it**. Information and listings for religious housing facilities throughout Italy are provided. ⊕ *www.hospites.it*.

FARM HOLIDAYS AND AGRITOURISM

Rural accommodations in the *agriturismo* category are growing in popularity among both Italians and visitors; you may have to look a little harder, though, to find an actual working farm or vineyard. Accommodations vary in size and range from luxury apartments, farmhouses, and villas to basic facilities. Agriturist has compiled *Agriturism*, which is available only in Italian, but includes more than 1,450 farms in Italy; pictures and the use of international symbols to describe facilities make the guide a good tool. Local APT tourist offices also have information.

Information **Agriturismo.com** ☎ *800/911856 (toll-free)* ⊕ *www.agriturismo. com*. **Agriturismo.net** ☎ *050/8665377* ⊕ *www.agriturismo.net*. **Agriturist-Farm Holidays** ☎ *0564/417418* ⊕ *www. byfarmholidays.com*. **Turismo Verde** ☎ *06/3240111* ⊕ *www.turismoverde.it*.

HOME EXCHANGES

With a direct home exchange you stay in someone else's home while they stay in yours. Some outfits also deal with vacation homes, so you're not really occupying someone's full-time residence, just their vacant weekend place.

Italians have historically not been as enthusiastic about home exchanges as others; however, there are many great villas and apartments in Italy owned by foreigners (Americans, English, and others) who use home-exchange services.

Exchange Clubs **Home Exchange.com**. Membership is $7.95 monthly. ☎ *800/877–8723, 310/798–3864, 0382/1861690 from Italy* ⊕ *www.homeexchange.com*. **HomeLink International**. Membership is $95 for one year,

$152 for two. ☎ *800/638–3841, 954/328–1643, 0422/815575 in Italy* ⊕ *www.homelink. org*. **Intervac Home Exchange**. One-year membership is $99. ☎ *800/756–4663* ⊕ *www. intervac-homeexchange.com*.

▮ COMMUNICATIONS

INTERNET

Getting online in Italian cities isn't difficult: public Internet stations and Internet cafés are fairly common, and Wi-Fi is widely available. Most hotels have Wi-Fi or a computer for guests to use. Many business-oriented hotels also offer in-room broadband, though some (ironically, often the more expensive ones) charge for broadband and Wi-Fi access. Note that chargers and power supplies may need plug adapters to fit European-style electric sockets (a converter probably won't be necessary).

Italy is also looking to improve city Wi-Fi access; Rome, Venice and Turin are continuing to develop and expand services, some free for now, some at a daily or weekly rate for temporary access.

Paid and free Wi-Fi hotspots can be found in major airports and train stations, and shopping centers; they're most likely to be free in bars or cafés that want your business.

Contact **Provincia Wi-Fi**. In Rome, this service offers the ability to surf the Internet for free with a daily limit of 300MB of total traffic. There is a one-time credit card fee of 50¢ to register. ☎ *06/40409434* ⊕ *www.provincia. roma.it*.

PHONES

With the advent of mobile phones, public pay phones are becoming increasingly scarce in Italy, but they can be found at train and subway stations, main post offices, and in some bars. In rural areas, town squares usually have a pay phone. These require a *scheda telefonica* (⇨ *Calling Cards*).

LOCAL DO'S AND TABOOS

GREETINGS

Upon meeting and leave-taking, both friends and strangers wish each other good day or good evening (*buongiorno, buona sera*); *ciao* isn't used between strangers. Italians who are friends greet each other with a kiss, usually first on the left cheek, then on the right. When you meet a new person, shake hands and give your name.

SIGHTSEEING

Italy's churches house significant works of art, but they're also places of worship, so remember to dress appropriately.

Shorts, tank tops, and sleeveless garments are taboo in most churches throughout the country. To avoid being denied entrance, carry a shawl or other item of clothing to cover bare shoulders.

You should never bring food into a church, and don't sip from your water bottle inside. If you have a mobile phone, turn it off before entering. Ask whether photographs are allowed—and *never use a flash*. Never enter a church when a service is in progress either, especially if it's a private affair such as a wedding, funeral, or baptism.

OUT ON THE TOWN

Table manners in Italy are quite formal. In a restaurant, be reserved and polite with your waiter—no calling across the room for attention.

When you've finished your meal and are ready to go, ask for the check (*il conto*); unless it's well past closing time, it is unlikely a waiter will put a bill on your table until you've requested it.

Italians don't have a culture of sipping cocktails or chugging pitchers of beer. Wine, beer, and other alcoholic drinks are usually consumed only as part of a meal. Public drunkenness is abhorred.

Smoking has been banned in all public establishments, much as in the United States.

DOING BUSINESS

Showing up on time for business appointments is the norm and expected in Italy. There are more business lunches than business dinners, and even business lunches aren't common, as Italians view mealtimes as periods of pleasure and relaxation.

Business cards (*biglietto da visita*) are used throughout Italy, and business attire is the norm for both men and women. To be on the safe side, it's best not to use first names or a familiar form of address until invited to do so.

Business gifts aren't the norm, but if one is given it's usually small and symbolic of your home location or type of business.

LANGUAGE

One of the best ways to connect with Italians is to learn a little of the local language. You need not strive for fluency; just mastering a few basic words and terms is bound to make interactions more rewarding.

"Please" is *per favore*, "thank you" is *grazie*, "you're welcome" is *prego*, and "excuse me" is *scusi* (or *permesso* when you need to move past someone, as on a bus).

In larger cities like Venice, Rome, and Florence, language isn't a big problem. Most hotels have English-speakers at their reception desks, and if not, they can always find someone who speaks at least a little English. You may have trouble communicating in the countryside, but expressive gestures and a good phrase book—like *Fodor's Italian for Travelers* (available at bookstores everywhere)—will go a long way. Need audio assistance? Visit ⊕ *www.fodors. com/language/italian* to hear more than 150 essential phrases.

CALLING ITALY FROM ABROAD

When telephoning Italy from North America, dial 011 (to get an international line), followed by Italy's country code, 39, and the phone number, including any leading 0. Note that Italian cell numbers have 10 digits and always begin with a 3; Italian landline numbers will contain from 4 to 10 digits and always begin with a 0. So, for example, when calling Rome, where local numbers start with 06, dial 011 + 39 + 06 + phone number; for a mobile phone, dial 011 + 39 + cell number.

CALLING WITHIN ITALY

For all calls within Italy, whether local or long-distance, you'll dial the entire phone number that starts with 0 or 3 for mobile phone numbers. Calling a mobile phone will cost significantly more than calling a landline, depending on the calling plan. Italy uses the prefix "800" for toll-free or *numero verde* (green) numbers.

MAKING INTERNATIONAL CALLS

The country code for the United States and Canada is 1 (dial 00 + 1 + area code and number).

Because of the high rates charged by most hotels for long-distance and international calls, you're better off making such calls from public phones or your mobile phone or by using an international calling card (⇨ *Calling Cards).*

Although not advised because of the exorbitant cost, you can place international calls or collect calls through an operator by dialing 170.

CALLING CARDS

Prepaid *schede telefoniche* (phone cards) are available throughout Italy for use in pay phones. Cards in different denominations are sold at post offices, newsstands, tobacco shops, and some bars. Before the first use, break off the corner of the card; then, to make a call, insert it into the phone's slot and dial. The card's credit will be displayed in the window as you chat. After you hang up, be sure not to walk off without retrieving the card.

International calling cards are different; you call a toll-free number from any phone, entering the access code found on the back of the card followed by the destination number. With calling cards offered by AT&T and MCI instructions and operator assistance are in English, avoiding language difficulties, and the charges appear on your phone bill. A reliable prepaid card for calling North America and elsewhere in Europe is the TIM Welcome card, which retails for €20, offering 200 minutes and 2GB data in 30 days and is available at TIM stores

Calling Cards AT&T Direct ☎ *800/172444* ⊕ *www.shop.att.com.* **World Access** ☎ *800/905825* ⊕ *www.worldaccessnumbers. com.* **TIM Welcome Card** ☎ *119* ⊕ *www.tim.it.*

MOBILE PHONES

Most mobile phones are now multiband (Europe and North America use different calling frequencies), so if your service provider uses the world-standard GSM network (as do T-Mobile, AT&T, and Verizon), you can use your own phone and provider abroad. But roaming fees can be steep—€0.99 a minute is considered quite low—and overseas you'll normally pay toll charges for incoming calls, too.

■TIP→ **If you're carrying a laptop, tablet, or smartphone, investigate apps and services such as Skype, Viber, and Whatsapp, which offer free or low-cost calling and texting services.**

To keep calling expenses to a minimum, consider purchasing an Italian SIM card—these can be purchased for as little as €5, depending on the provider (make sure your home service provider first unlocks your phone for use with a different SIM) and choose a prepaid service plan, topping off the credit as you go. You then have a local number and can make calls at local rates (about €0.15 per minute, and only for those made, not received), or send text messages for a reasonable fee (€0.12 per message or less). Have the service provider enable international calling;

use an international calling card with your cell for even more savings.

■TIP➜ If you're a frequent international traveler, save your old mobile phone (ask your service provider to unlock it for you) or buy an unlocked, multiband phone online. Use it as a travel phone, buying a new SIM card with pay-as-you-go service in each destination.

The cost of mobile phones is dropping: you can purchase a dual-band (Europe only) phone in Italy with a prepaid calling credit for as little as €20. Alternatively, you can buy a multiband phone that will also function in North America (European phones aren't usually "locked" to their provider's SIM, which is why they cost more). That means you can use it with your own service provider once you return home. You'll find dedicated mobile phone stores in all but the smallest towns. Service providers include TIM, Tre, Vodafone, and Wind; stop by a multivendor shop to compare offers, or check their websites. Note that you'll need to present your passport to purchase any SIM card.

Rental phones are available online prior to departure and in Italy's cities and larger towns. Shop around for the best deal. Most contracts require a refundable deposit that covers the cost of the mobile phone (€75–€150) and then set up a monthly service plan that's automatically charged to your credit card. Frequently, rental phones will be triple band with a plan that allows you to call North America. You should check the rate schedule, however, to avoid a nasty surprise on your credit card bill two or three months later. Often the local purchase with a prepaid plan will be the more cost-effective one.

■TIP➜ Beware of mobile phone (and PDA) thieves. Use your device's security code option. Keep your phone or PDA in a secure pocket or purse. Don't lay it on the bar when you stop for an espresso. Don't zip it into the outside pocket of your backpack in crowded cities. Don't leave it in your hotel room. Notify your provider immediately if it's lost or stolen; p ers can disable your SIM and give new one, copying the original's num_e_ and contents.

Contacts Cellular Abroad. This is a good source for SIM cards that work in many countries; travel-friendly phones can also be purchased or rented. ☎ 800/287–5072 ⊕ www.cellularabroad.com. **Mobal.** GSM phones that will operate in 190 countries are available for purchase (starting at $29) and rent. Per-call rates in Italy are $1.25 per minute; sending a text costs $0.80. ☎ 888/888–9162, 212/785–5800 for support ⊕ www.mobal.com. **Planet Fone.** Rental phones, with per-minute rates costing $0.99–$1.98, are available. ☎ 888/988–4777 ⊕ www.planetfone.com.

■ CUSTOMS AND DUTIES

Travelers from the United States should experience little difficulty clearing customs at any Italian airport. It may be more difficult to clear customs when returning to the United States, where residents are normally entitled to a duty-free exemption of $800 on items accompanying them. You'll have to pay a tax (most often a flat percentage) on the value of everything beyond that limit. When you shop in Italy, keep all your receipts handy, as customs inspectors may ask to see them as well as the items you purchased.

Although there's no problem with aged cheese (vacuum-sealed works best), you cannot bring back any of that delicious prosciutto, salami, or any other meat product. Fresh mushrooms, truffles, or fresh fruits and vegetables are also forbidden. There are restrictions on the amount of alcohol allowed in duty-free, too. Generally, you can bring in one liter of wine, beer, or other alcohol without paying a customs duty; visit the travel area of the Customs and Border Patrol Travel website for complete information.

Italy requires documentation regarding the background of all antiques and antiquities before these items are taken out of the country. Under Italian law, all antiquities found on Italian soil are considered state property, and there are other restrictions on antique artwork. Even if purchased from a business in Italy, legal ownership of artifacts may be in question if brought into the United States. Therefore, although they don't necessarily confer ownership, documents such as export permits and receipts are required when importing such items into the United States.

Information in Italy Dogana Sezione Viaggiatori ☎ 06/50241 ⊕ www. agenziadogane.it.

U.S. Information U.S. Customs and Border Protection ☎ 877/227–5511 ⊕ www.cbp.gov.

▮ EATING OUT

Italian cuisine is still largely regional. Ask what the specialties are—and, by all means, try spaghetti *alla carbonara* (with bacon and egg) in Rome, pizza in Naples, *bistecca alla fiorentina* (steak) in Florence, *cinghiale* (wild boar) in Tuscany, truffles in Piedmont, *la frittura* (fish fry) in Venice, and *risotto alla milanese* in Milan. Although most restaurants in Italy serve local dishes, you can find Asian and Middle Eastern alternatives in Rome, Venice, and other cities. The restaurants we list are the cream of the crop in each price category.

MEALS AND MEALTIMES

What's the difference between a *ristorante* and a *trattoria*? Can you order food at an *enoteca*? Can you go to a restaurant just for a snack or order only salad at a pizzeria? The following definitions should help.

Not long ago, *ristoranti* tended to be more elegant and expensive than *trattorie*, which serve traditional, home-style fare in an atmosphere to match, or *osterie*, which serve local wines and simple, regional dishes. But the distinction has blurred considerably, and an osteria in the center of town might now be far fancier (and pricier) than a ristorante across the street. In any sit-down establishment, however,

you're generally expected to order at least a two-course meal, such as: a *primo* (first course) and a *secondo* (main course) or a *contorno* (vegetable side dish); an *antipasto* (starter) followed by either a primo or secondo; or a secondo and a *dolce* (dessert).

There is no problem if you'd prefer to eat less, but consider an enoteca or pizzeria as an alternative, where it's more common to order a single dish. An enoteca menu is often limited to a selection of cheese, cured meats, salads, and desserts, but if there's a kitchen you can also find soups, pastas, and main courses. The typical pizzeria serves *affettati misti* (a selection of cured pork), simple salads, various kinds of bruschetta, *crostini* (similar to bruschetta, with a variety of toppings) and, in Rome, *fritti* (deep-fried finger food) such as *olive ascolane* (green olives with a meat stuffing) and *supplì* (rice balls stuffed with mozzarella).

The most convenient and least expensive places for a quick snack between sights are probably bars, cafés, and pizza *al taglio* (by the slice) spots. Pizza al taglio shops are easy to negotiate, but few have seats. They sell pizza by weight: just point out which kind you want and how much. Kebab stores are also omnipresent in every Italian city.

Note that Italians do not usually walk and eat.

Bars in Italy resemble what we think of as cafés, and are primarily places to get a coffee and a bite to eat, rather than drinking establishments. Expect a selection of panini warmed up on the griddle (*piastra*) and *tramezzini* (sandwiches made of untoasted white bread triangles). In larger cities, bars also serve vegetable and fruit salads, cold pasta dishes, and gelato. Most offer beer and a variety of alcohol, as well as wines by the glass (sometimes good but more often mediocre). A café is like a bar but typically has more tables. Pizza at a café should be avoided—it's usually heated in a microwave.

If you place your order at the counter, ask whether you can sit down. Some places charge for table service (especially in tourist centers); others don't. In self-service bars and cafés, it's good manners to clean your table before you leave. Be aware that in certain spots (such as train stations and stops along the highway) you first pay a cashier; then show your *scontrino* (receipt) at the counter to place your order. Menus are posted outside most restaurants (in English in tourist areas). If not, you might step inside and ask to take a look at the menu, but don't ask for a table unless you intend to stay.

Italians take their food as it's listed on the menu, seldom if ever making special requests such as "dressing on the side" or "hold the olive oil." If you have special dietary needs, however, make them known; they can usually be accommodated. Vegetarians should be firm, as bacon and ham can slip into some dishes. Although mineral water makes its way to almost every table, you can order a carafe of tap water (*acqua di rubinetto* or *acqua semplice*) instead—just keep in mind that such water can be highly chlorinated.

An Italian would never ask for olive oil to dip bread in, and don't be surprised if there's no butter to spread on it either. Wiping your bowl clean with a (small) piece of bread, known locally as *la scarpetta*, is usually considered a sign of appreciation, not bad manners. Spaghetti should be eaten with a fork only, although a little help from a spoon won't horrify locals the way cutting spaghetti into little pieces might. Order your caffè (Italians drink cappuccino only in the morning) after dessert, not with it. As for doggy bags, Italians would never ask for one, though eateries popular with tourists are becoming more accustomed to travelers who do.

Breakfast (*la colazione*) is usually served from 7 to 10:30, lunch (*il pranzo*) from 12:30 to 2:30, and dinner (*la cena*) from 7:30 to 10, later in the south; outside those hours, best head for a bar. Peak times are usually 1:30 for lunch and 9 for dinner. Enoteche and Venetian *bacari* (wine bars) are also open in the morning and late afternoon for *cicchetti* (finger foods) at the counter. Most pizzerias open at 8 pm and close around midnight—later in summer and on weekends. Bars and cafés are open from 7 am until 8 or 9 pm; a few stay open until midnight.

Unless otherwise noted, the restaurants listed here are open for lunch and dinner, closing one or two days a week.

PAYING

Most restaurants have a cover charge per person, usually listed at the top of the check as *coperto* or *pane e coperto*. It should be modest (€1–€2.50 per person) except at the most expensive restaurants. Whenever in doubt, ask before you order to avoid unpleasant discussions later. It's customary to leave a small cash tip (between 5% and 10%) in appreciation of good service: you will usually see a *servizio* charge included at the bottom of the check, but the server will not likely receive it.

The price of fish dishes is often given by weight (before cooking), so the price quoted on the menu is for 100 grams of fish, not for the whole dish. (An average fish portion is about 350 grams.) In Tuscany, bistecca alla fiorentina is also often priced by weight (about €4 for 100 grams or $18 per pound).

Major credit cards are widely accepted in Italy; however, cash is always preferred. More restaurants take Visa and MasterCard than American Express or Diners Club.

When you leave a dining establishment, take your meal bill or receipt with you. Although not a common experience, the Italian finance (tax) police can approach you within 100 yards of the establishment at which you've eaten and ask for a receipt; if you don't have one, they can fine you and will fine the business owner for not providing it. The practice is intended to prevent tax evasion; it's not necessary to show receipts when leaving Italy.

RESERVATIONS AND DRESS

Although we only mention reservations specifically when they're essential (there's no other way you'll ever get a table) or when they're not accepted, it's always safest to make one for dinner. For popular restaurants, book as far ahead as you can (two to three weeks), and reconfirm as soon as you arrive. Large parties should always call ahead to check the reservations policy. If you change your mind, be sure to cancel, even at the last minute.

We mention dress only when men are required to wear a jacket or a jacket and tie. But unless they're dining outside or at a seafront resort, Italian men never wear shorts or running shoes in a restaurant. The same applies to women: no casual shorts, running shoes, or rubber sandals when going out to dinner. Shorts are acceptable in pizzerias and cafés.

WINES, BEER, AND SPIRITS

The grape has been cultivated in Italy since the time of the Etruscans, and Italians justifiably take pride in their local varieties, which are numerous. Though almost every region produces good-quality wine, Tuscany, Piedmont, the Veneto, Puglia, Calabria, and Sicily are some of the more renowned areas, with Le Marche and Umbria being well reputed, too. Italian wine is less expensive in Italy than almost anywhere else, so it's often affordable to order a bottle of wine at a restaurant rather than sticking with the house wine (which is usually good but quite simple). Many bars have their own *aperitivo della casa* (house aperitif); Italians are imaginative with their mixed drinks, so you may want to try one.

You can purchase beer, wine, and spirits in any bar, grocery store, or enoteca, any day of the week, any time of the day. Italian and German beer is readily available, but it can be more expensive than wine. Some excellent microbreweries are beginning to dot the Italian beer horizon, so ask if there's a local brew available to sample.

There's no minimum drinking age in Italy. Italian children begin drinking wine mixed with water at mealtimes when they're teens (or thereabouts). Italians are rarely seen drunk in public, and public drinking, except in a bar or eating establishment, isn't considered acceptable behavior. Bars usually close by 9 pm; hotel and restaurant bars stay open until midnight. Brewpubs and discos serve until about 2 am.

▌ ELECTRICITY

The electrical current in Italy is 220 volts, 50 cycles alternating current (AC); wall outlets accept continental-type plugs, with two or three round prongs.

You may purchase a universal adapter, which has several types of plugs in one lightweight, compact unit, at travel specialty stores, electronics stores, and online. You can also pick up plug adapters in Italy in any electric supply store for about €2 each. You'll likely not need a voltage converter, though. Most portable devices are dual voltage (i.e., they operate equally well on 110 and 220 volts)—just check label specifications and manufacturer instructions to be sure. Don't use 110-volt outlets marked "for shavers only" for high-wattage appliances such as hair dryers.

Contacts Walkabout Travel Gear. Walkabout Travel Gear has a good coverage of electrical and telephone plugs around the world under "adapters." ⊕ *www.walkabouttravelgear.com.*

▌ EMERGENCIES

No matter where you are in the European Union, you can dial ☎ *112* in case of an emergency: the call will be directed to the local police. Not all 112 operators speak English, so you may want to ask a local person to place the call. Asking the operator for "*pronto soccorso*" (first aid and also the emergency room of a hospital) should get you an *ambulanza* (ambulance). If you just need a doctor, ask for "*un medico.*"

Italy has the *carabinieri* (national police force; their emergency number is ☎ 113 from anywhere in Italy) as well as the *polizia* (local police force). Both are armed and have the power to arrest and investigate crimes. Always report the loss of your passport to the carabinieri as well as to your embassy. When reporting a crime, you'll be asked to fill out *una denuncia* (official report)—keep a copy for your insurance company. You should also contact the police any time you have a car accident of any sort.

Local traffic officers, known as *vigili*, are responsible for, among other things, giving out parking tickets. They wear white (in summer), navy, or black uniforms. Should you find yourself involved in a minor car accident in town, contact the vigili.

Pharmacies are generally open weekdays 8:30–1 and 4–8, and Saturday 9–1. Local pharmacies rotate covering the off-hours in shifts: on the door of every pharmacy is a list of which pharmacies in the vicinity will be open late.

Foreign Embassies U.S. Consulate Florence ✉ *Via Lungarno Vespucci 38, Florence* ☎ *055/266951* ⊕ *florence.usconsulate.gov.* **U.S. Consulate Milan** ✉ *Via Principe Amedeo 2/10, Milan* ☎ *02/290351* ⊕ *milan.usconsulate. gov.* **U.S. Consulate Naples** ✉ *Piazza della Repubblica, Naples* ☎ *081/5838111* ⊕ *naples. usconsulate.gov.* **U.S. Embassy** ✉ *Via Vittorio Veneto 121, Rome* ☎ *06/46741* ⊕ *italy. usembassy.gov.*

General Emergency Contacts Emergencies ☎ *115 for fire, 118 for ambulance.* **National and State Police** ☎ *112 for Polizia (National Police), 113 for Carabinieri (State Police).*

▌ HOURS OF OPERATION

Religious and civic holidays are frequent in Italy. Depending on the holiday's local importance, businesses may close for the day. Businesses don't close Friday or Monday when the holiday falls on the weekend, though the Monday following Easter is a holiday.

Banks are open weekdays 8:30–1:30 and for one or two hours in the afternoon, depending on the bank. Most post offices are open Monday–Saturday 9–1:30, some until 2; central post offices are open 9–6:30 weekdays, 9–12:30 or 9–6:30 on Saturday.

Most churches are open from early morning until noon or 12:30, when they close for three hours or more; they open again in the afternoon, closing at about 6. A few major churches, such as St. Peter's in Rome and San Marco in Venice, remain open all day. Walking around during services is discouraged. Many museums are closed one day a week, often Monday or Tuesday. During low season museums often close early; during high season many stay open until late at night.

Most shops are open Monday through Saturday 9–1 and 3:30 or 4–7:30. Clothing shops are generally closed Monday mornings. Barbers and hairdressers, with certain exceptions, are closed Sunday and Monday. Some bookstores and fashion- or tourist-oriented shops in places such as Rome and Venice are open all day, as well as Sunday. Many branches of large chain supermarkets such as Standa, COOP, and Esselunga don't close for lunch and are usually open Sunday; smaller *alimentari* (delicatessens) and other food shops are usually closed one evening during the week (it varies according to the town) and are almost always closed Sunday.

HOLIDAYS

Traveling through Italy in August can be an odd experience. Although there are some deals to be had, the heat can be oppressive, and much of the population is on vacation. Most cities are deserted (except for foreign tourists) and privately run restaurants and shops are closed. The national holidays in 2016 include January 1 (New Year's Day); January 6

(Epiphany); March 27 and 28 (Easter Sunday and Monday); April 25 (Liberation Day); May 1 (Labor Day or May Day); June 2 (Festival of the Republic); August 15 (Ferragosto); November 1 (All Saints' Day); December 8 (Immaculate Conception); and December 25 and 26 (Christmas Day and the Feast of Saint Stephen).

In addition, feast days of patron saints are observed locally. Many businesses and shops may be closed in Florence, Genoa, and Turin on June 24 (Saint John the Baptist); in Rome on June 29 (Saints Peter and Paul); in Palermo on July 15 (Santa Rosalia); in Naples on September 19 (San Gennaro); in Bologna on October 4 (San Petronio); in Trieste on November 3 (San Giusto); and in Milan on December 7 (Saint Ambrose). Venice's feast of Saint Mark is April 25, the same as Liberation Day, so the Madonna della Salute on November 21 makes up for the lost holiday.

▌ MAIL

The Italian mail system has a bad reputation but has become noticeably more efficient in recent times with some privatization. Allow from 7 to 15 days for mail to get to the United States. Receiving mail in Italy, especially packages, can take weeks, usually due to customs (not postal) delays.

You can buy stamps at tobacco shops as well as post offices.

"Posta Prioritaria (for regular letters and packages) is the name for standard postage. It guarantees delivery within Italy in three to five business days and abroad in five to six working days. The more expensive express delivery, "Postacelere" (for larger letters and packages), guarantees one-day delivery to most places in Italy and three- to five-day delivery abroad. Note that the postal service has no control over customs, however, which makes international delivery estimates meaningless. Mail sent as "Posta Prioritaria

Internazionale" to the United States costs €2 for up to 20 grams, €3.50 for 21–50 grams, and €4.50 for 51–100 grams. Mail sent as "Paccocelere" to the United States costs €40 for up to 500 grams.

Reliable two-day international mail is generally available during the week in all major cities and at popular resorts via UPS and Federal Express—but again, customs delays can slow down "express" service.

SHIPPING SERVICES

Sending a letter or small package to the United States via Federal Express takes at least two days and costs about €45. Other package services to check are Quick Pack Europe (for delivery within Europe) and Express Mail Service (a global three- to five-day service for letters and packages). Compare prices with those of Paccocelere to determine the cheapest option.

If your hotel can't assist you with shipping, try an Internet café; many offer two-day mail services using major carriers.

If you've purchased antiques, ceramics, or other fragile objects, ask if the vendor will do the shipping for you. In most cases this is possible, and preferable, because many merchants have experience with these kinds of shipments. If so, ask whether the article will be insured against breakage.

▌ MONEY

Prices vary from region to region and are substantially lower in the country than in urban centers. Of Italy's major cities, Milan is by far the most expensive. Resort areas such as Amalfi, Portofino, and Cortina d'Ampezzo cater to wealthy vacationers and charge top prices. Good values can be had in the scenic Trentino–Alto Adige region of the Dolomites and in Umbria and Marche. With a few exceptions, southern Italy and Sicily also offer bargains for those who do their homework before they leave home.

ITEM	AVERAGE COST
Cup of Coffee	€0.80–€1.50
Soft Drink (glass/can/bottle)	€2–€3
Glass of Beer	€2–€5
Sandwich	€3–€4.50
2-km (1-mile) Taxi Ride in Rome	€8.50

Prices here are given for adults. Substantially reduced fees are almost always available for children, students, and senior citizens from the EU; citizens of non-EU countries rarely get discounts, but inquire before you purchase tickets, as this situation is constantly changing.

■TIP→ **U.S. banks do not keep every foreign currency on hand, and it may take as long as a week to order. If you're planning to exchange funds before leaving home, don't wait until the last minute.**

ATMS AND BANKS

An ATM (*bancomat* in Italian) is the easiest way to get euros in Italy. There are numerous ATMs in large cities and small towns, as well as in airports and train stations. Be sure to memorize your PIN in numbers, as ATM keypads in Italy won't always display letters. Check with your bank to confirm that you have an international PIN (*codice segreto*) that will be recognized in the countries you're visiting; to raise your maximum daily withdrawal allowance; and to learn what your bank's fee is for withdrawing money (Italian banks don't charge withdrawal fees).

■TIP→ **Be aware that PINs beginning with a 0 (zero) tend to be rejected in Italy.**

Your own bank may charge a fee for using ATMs abroad and for the cost of conversion from euros to dollars. Nevertheless, you can usually get a better rate of exchange at an ATM than you will at a currency-exchange office or even when changing money inside a bank with a teller, the next-best option. Whatever the method, extracting funds as you need them is safer than carrying around a large amount of cash. Finally, it's advisable to carry more than one card that can be used for cash withdrawal, in case something happens to your main one.

CREDIT CARDS

It's a good idea to inform your credit card company before you travel, especially if you're going abroad and don't travel internationally often. Otherwise, the credit card company might put a hold on your card owing to unusual activity—not a welcome occurrence halfway through your trip. Record all your credit card numbers—as well as the phone numbers to call if your cards are lost or stolen. Keep these in a safe place, so you're prepared should something go wrong. MasterCard and Visa have general numbers you can call (collect if you're abroad) if your card is lost. But you're better off calling the number of your issuing bank, because MasterCard and Visa generally just transfer you there; your bank's number is usually printed on your card.

■TIP→ **North American toll-free numbers aren't available from abroad, so be sure to obtain a local number with area code for any business you may need to contact.**

Although it's usually cheaper (and safer) to use a credit card abroad for large purchases (so you can cancel payments or be reimbursed if there's a problem), note that some credit card companies *and* the banks that issue them add substantial percentages to all foreign transactions, whether they're in a foreign currency or not. Check on these fees before leaving home, so there won't be any surprises when you get the bill. Because of these fees, avoid using your credit card for ATM withdrawals or cash advances (use a debit or cash card instead).

■TIP→ **Before you charge something, ask the merchant whether he or she plans to do a dynamic currency conversion (DCC). In such a transaction the credit card processor (shop, restaurant, or hotel, not Visa or MasterCard) converts the currency and charges you in dollars. In most** cases you'll pay the merchant a 3% fee for this service in addition to any credit card company and issuing-bank foreign-transaction surcharges.

Merchants who participate in dynamic currency conversion programs are supposed to ask whether you want to be charged in dollars or the local currency, but they don't always do so. And even if they do offer you a choice, they may well avoid mentioning the additional surcharges. The good news is that you *do* have a choice—you can simply say no. If this practice really gets your goat, you can avoid it entirely by using American Express; with its cards, DCC simply isn't an option.

Italian merchants prefer MasterCard and Visa (look for the CartaSi sign), but American Express is usually accepted in popular tourist destinations. Credit cards aren't accepted everywhere, though; if you want to pay with a credit card in a small shop, hotel, or restaurant, it's a good idea to make your intentions known early on.

Reporting Lost Cards American Express
☎ 800/528–4800 in the U.S., 905/474–0870 collect from abroad ⊕ www.americanexpress. com. **Diners Club** ☎ 800/234–6377 in the U.S., 514/877–1577 collect from abroad, 800/393939 in Italy ⊕ www.dinersclub. com. **MasterCard** ☎ 800/307–7309 in the U.S., 636/722–7111 collect from abroad, 800/870866 in Italy ⊕ www.mastercard.us. **Visa** ☎ 800/847–2911 in the U.S., 303/967–1096 from abroad, 800/819014 in Italy ⊕ usa. visa.com.

CURRENCY AND EXCHANGE

The euro is the main unit of currency in Italy. Under the euro system there are 100 *centesimi* (cents) to the euro. There are coins valued at 1, 2, 5, 10, 20, and 50 centesimi as well as 1 and 2 euros. There are seven notes: 5, 10, 20, 50, 100, 200, and 500 euros. At this writing, €1 was worth was about $1.26.

Post offices exchange currency at good rates, but employees speak limited English, so be prepared. (Writing your request can help in these cases.)

■ TIP→ Even if a currency-exchange booth has a sign promising no commission, rest assured that there's some kind of huge, hidden fee. You're almost always better off getting foreign currency at an ATM or exchanging money at a bank or post office.

▮ PASSPORTS AND VISAS

U.S. citizens need only a valid passport to enter Italy for stays of up to 90 days.

PASSPORTS

Although somewhat costly, a U.S. passport is relatively simple to obtain and is valid for 10 years. You must apply in person if you're getting a passport for the first time; if your previous passport was lost, stolen, or damaged; or if it has expired and was issued more than 15 years ago or when you were under 16. All children under 18 must appear in person to apply for or renew a passport. Both parents must accompany any child under 14 (or send a notarized statement with their permission) and provide proof of their relationship to the child.

There are 25 regional passport offices as well as 7,000 passport acceptance facilities in post offices, public libraries, and other governmental offices. If you're renewing a passport, you may do so by mail; forms are available at passport acceptance facilities and online, where you can trace the application's progress.

The cost of a new passport is $135 for adults, $105 for children under 16; renewals are $110 for adults, $105 for children under 16. Allow four to six weeks for processing, both for first-time passports and renewals. For an expediting fee of $60 you can reduce this time to two to three weeks. If your trip is less than two weeks away, you can get a passport even more rapidly by going to a passport office with the necessary documentation. Private expediters can get things done in as little as 48 hours, but charge hefty fees for their services.

■TIP→ Before your trip, make two copies of your passport's data page (one for someone at home and another for you to carry separately). Or scan the page and email it to someone at home and/or yourself.

GENERAL REQUIREMENTS FOR ITALY	
Passport	Must be valid for 6 months after date of arrival
Visa	Tourist visas aren't needed for stays of 90 days or less by U.S. citizens.
Vaccinations	None
Driving	International driver's license required. CDW is compulsory on car rentals and will be included in the quoted price.

VISAS

When staying for 90 days or less, U.S. citizens aren't required to obtain a visa prior to traveling to Italy. A recent law requires that you fill in a declaration of presence within eight days of your arrival—the stamp on your passport at airport arrivals substitutes for this. If you plan to travel or live in Italy or the European Union for longer than 90 days, you must acquire a valid visa from the Italian consulate serving your state *before you leave the United States*. Plan ahead, because the process of obtaining a visa will take at least 30 days, and the Italian government doesn't accept visa applications submitted by visa expediters.

U.S. Passport Information U.S. Department of State ☎ 877/487–2778 ⊕ travel.state.gov.

U.S. Passport Expediters A. Briggs Passport & Visa Expeditors ☎ 800/806–0581 (toll-free), 202/338–0111 ⊕ www.abriggs.com. **American Passport Express** ☎ 800/455–5166 ⊕ www.americanpassport.com. **Travel Document Systems** ☎ 800/874–5100 ⊕ www.traveldocs.com. **Travel the World Visas** ☎ 202/223–8822 ⊕ www.world-visa.com.

▌ TAXES

A 10% V.A.T. (value-added tax) is included in the rate at all hotels except those at the upper end of the range.

No tax is added to the bill in restaurants. A service charge of approximately 10%–15% is often added to your check; in some cases a service charge is included in the prices.

The V.A.T. is 22% on clothing, wine, and luxury goods. On consumer goods it's already included in the amount shown on the price tag (look for the phrase "IVA *inclusa*"), whereas on services it may not be. If you're not a European citizen and if your purchases in a single day total more than €154.94, you may be entitled to a refund of the V.A.T.

When making a purchase, ask whether the merchant gives refunds—not all do, nor are they required to. If they do, they'll help you fill out the V.A.T. refund form, which you then submit to a company that will issue you the refund in the form of cash, check, or credit card adjustment.

Alternatively, as you leave the country (or, if you're visiting several European Union countries, on leaving the EU), present your merchandise and the form to customs officials, who will stamp it. Once through passport control, take the stamped form to a refund-service counter for an on-the-spot refund (the quickest and easiest option). You may also mail it to the address on the form (or on the envelope with it) after you arrive home, but processing time can be long, especially if you request a credit card adjustment. Note that in larger cities the cash refund can be obtained at in-town offices prior to departure; just ask the merchant or check the envelope for local office addresses.

Global Blue is the largest V.A.T.-refund service with 225,000 affiliated stores and more than 700 refund counters at major airports and border crossings. Its refund form, called a Tax Free Check, is the most common across the European continent. Premier Tax Free is another company that represents more than 70,000 merchants worldwide; look for their logos in store windows.

V.A.T. Refunds Global Blue ☎ *866/706-6090 in North America, 421 232/111111 from abroad, 00800/32111111 from Italy* ⊕ *www.global-blue.com.* **Premier Tax Free** ☎ *905/542-1710 from the U.S., 06/699-23383 from Italy* ⊕ *www.premiertaxfree.com.*

■ TIME

Italy is in the Central European Time Zone (CET). From March to October it institutes Daylight Saving Time. Italy is 6 hours ahead of U.S. Eastern Standard Time, 1 hour ahead of Great Britain, 10 hours behind Sydney, and 12 hours behind Auckland. Like the rest of Europe, Italy uses the 24-hour (or "military") clock, which means that after noon you continue counting forward: 13:00 is 1 pm, 23:30 is 11:30 pm.

■ TIPPING

In restaurants a service charge of 10% to 15% may appear on your check, but it's not a given that your server will receive this; so you may want to consider leaving a tip of 5% to 10% (in cash) for good service. Tip checkroom attendants €1 per person and restroom attendants €0.50 (more in expensive hotels and restaurants). In major cities, tip €0.50 or more for table service in cafés. At a hotel bar, tip €1 and up for a round or two of drinks.

Italians rarely tip taxi drivers, which isn't to say that you shouldn't. A euro or two is appreciated, particularly if the driver helps with luggage. Service-station attendants are tipped only for special services; give them €1 for checking your tires. Railway and airport porters charge a fixed rate per bag. Tip an additional €0.25 per person, more if the porter is helpful. Give a barber €1–€1.50 and a hairdresser's assistant €1.50–€4 for a shampoo or cut, depending on the type of establishment.

On sightseeing tours, tip guides about €1.50 per person for a half-day group tour, more if they're especially knowledgeable. In monasteries and other sights where admission is free, a contribution (€0.50–€1) is expected.

In hotels, give the *portiere* (concierge) about 10% of the bill for services, or €2.50–€5 for help with dinner reservations and such. Leave the chambermaid about €0.75 per day, or about €4.50–€5 a week in a moderately priced hotel; tip a minimum of €1 for valet or room service. In an expensive hotel, double these amounts; tip doormen €0.50 for calling a cab and €1.50 for carrying bags to the check-in desk, and tip bellhops €1.50–€2.50 for carrying your bags to the room.

■ TOURS

Guided tours are a good option when you don't want to do it all yourself. You travel along with a group (sometimes large, sometimes small), stay in pre-booked hotels, often eat with your fellow travelers (the cost of meals may or may not be included in the price of your tour), and follow a set schedule. Not all guided tours are an "if it's Tuesday this must be Belgium" experience, however. A knowledgeable guide can take you places that you might never discover on your own, give you a richer context, and lead you to a more in-depth experience than you would have otherwise. They may be just the thing if you don't have the time or inclination to make travel arrangements on your own.

Whenever you book a guided tour, find out what's included and what isn't. A "land-only" tour includes all your travel (by bus, in most cases) in the destination, but not necessarily your flights to and from or even within it. Also, in most cases prices in tour promotions don't include fees and taxes. You'll also want to review how much free time you'll have, and see if that meets with your personal preferences. Remember, too, that you'll be expected to tip your guide (in cash) at the end of the tour.

Even when planning independent travel, keep in mind that every province and city in Italy has tour guides licensed by the government. Some are eminently qualified in relevant fields such as architecture and art history and are a pleasure to spend time with. Lots of private guides have websites, and you can check the travel forums at ⊕ Fodors.com for recommendations (it's best to book before you leave home, especially for major destinations, as popular guides and tours are in demand). Once in Italy, tourist offices and hotel concierges can also provide the names of knowledgeable local guides and the rates for certain services. When hiring on the spot, ask about their background and qualifications—and make sure you can understand each other. Tipping is always appreciated, but never obligatory, for local guides.

Recommended Generalists Andante ☎ 888/331–3476 ⊕ www.andantetravels. com. **Abercrombie & Kent** ☎ 800/554–7016, 630/725–3400 ⊕ www.abercrombiekent.com. **Maupin Tour** ☎ 800/255–4266, 954/653–3820 ⊕ www.maupintour.com. **Perillo Tours** ☎ 800/431–1515 ⊕ www.perillotours.com. **Travcoa** ☎ 888/979–1434, 310/730–1263 ⊕ www.travcoa.com. **Tauck** ☎ 800/788–7885 ⊕ www.tauck.com.

Biking and Hiking Tour Contacts Backroads ☎ 800/462–2848, 510/527–1555 ⊕ www. backroads.com. **Butterfield & Robinson** ☎ 866/551–9090, 416/864–1354 ⊕ www.butterfield.com. **Ciclismo Classico** ☎ 800/866–7314, 781/646–3377 ⊕ www. ciclismoclassico.com. **Genius Loci Travel** ☎ 089/791896 ⊕ www.genius-loci.it. **Italian Connection** ☎ 0932/231816 in Italy, 335/8016115 in Italy (mobile) ⊕ www.italian-connection.com.

Culinary Tour Contact Epiculinary ☎ 520/4882792 ⊕ www.epiculinary.com.

Educational Programs Road Scholar ☎ 800/454–5768, 877/426–8056 ⊕ www. roadscholar.org.

Golf Tour Contact Golf Italy ☎ 051/266277 ⊕ www.golfitaly.com.

Wine Tour Contacts Cellar Tours ☎ 310/496–8061 ⊕ www.cellartours.com. **Food and Wine Trails** ☎ 800/367–5348 ⊕ www.foodandwinetrails.com.

■ TRIP INSURANCE

Comprehensive trip insurance is valuable if you're booking an expensive or complicated trip (particularly to an isolated region) or if you're booking far in advance. Comprehensive policies typically cover trip cancellation and interruption, letting you cancel or cut your trip short because of illness (yours or that of someone back home), or, in some cases, acts of terrorism in your destination. Such policies usually also cover evacuation and medical care. (For trips abroad you should have at least medical and medical evacuation coverage. With a few exceptions, Medicare doesn't provide coverage abroad, nor does regular health insurance.) Some also cover you for trip delays because of bad weather or mechanical problems as well as for lost or delayed luggage.

Another type of coverage to consider is financial default—that is, when your trip is disrupted because a tour operator, airline, or cruise line goes out of business. Generally you must buy this when you book your trip or shortly thereafter, and it's available to you only if your operator isn't on a list of excluded companies.

Many travel insurance policies have exclusions for preexisting conditions as a cause for cancellation. Most companies waive those exclusions, however, if you take out your policy within a short period (which varies by company) after the first payment toward your trip.

Always read the fine print of your policy to make sure that you're covered for the risks that most concern you. Compare several policies to be sure you're getting the best price and range of coverage available.

Comprehensive Insurers
Allianz ☎ 866/884–3556 ⊕ www.allianztravelinsurance.com. **CSA Travel Protection** ☎ 877/243–4135, 240/330–1529 (collect) ⊕ www.csatravelprotection.com. **HTH Worldwide** ☎ 610/254–8700, 1-888/243–2358 (toll-free) ⊕ www.hthworldwide.com. **Travel Guard** ☎ 800/826–1300, 800/345–0505 (toll-free) from Italy ⊕ www.travelguard.com. **Travel Insured International** ☎ 800/243–3174, 603/328–1707 collect ⊕ www.travelinsured.com. **Travelex Insurance** ☎ 800/228–9792, 603/328–1739 (collect) ⊕ www.travelexinsurance.com.

Insurance Comparison Info Insure My Trip ☎ 800/487–4722, 401/773–9300 ⊕ www.insuremytrip.com. **Square Mouth** ☎ 800/240–0369, 727/564–9203 ⊕ www.squaremouth.com.

INDEX

PHOTO CREDITS

ABOUT OUR WRITERS

Robert Andrews specializes in southern Italy, but has a penchant for the islands, in particular Sardinia, where he resides for part of the year, and which chapter he updated for this edition. He has previously lived in Calabria, has family roots in Sicily, and likes nothing better than noisy dinner tables and still mountain landscapes.

After completing his master's degree in art history, **Peter Blackman** settled permanently in Italy in 1986. Since then he's worked as a biking and walking tour guide, managing to see more of Italy than most of his Italian friends. When he's not leading a trip, you'll find Peter at home in Chianti, listening to opera and planning his next journey. He updated the Piedmont and Valle d'Aosta chapter, the Tuscany chapter, and the introduction to Central Italy.

Lorna Holland and her husband, Dante Zambrano-Cassella, share their time between the U.S. and Italy. They live in Feltre, a village in the Veneto region, where they own a boutique tour company called VaFeltre Tours (⊕ *www.vafeltre.com*). They offer private, customizable tours of the Dolomites and Northern Italy for families and small groups. Lorna and Dante updated the Dolomites chapter.

Liz Humphreys is a recent transplant to Europe from New York City, where she spent a decade in editorial positions for media companies including Condé Nast, Time Inc., and *USA Today*. She has worked on several guidebooks for Fodor's, including Amsterdam, Germany, and Portugal, and currently writes and edits for *Fodors.com* and *Forbes Travel Guide* on locales across Europe. Liz has an advanced certificate in wine studies from the WSET (Wine & Spirit Education Trust), and Italy is a favorite destination to indulge her obsessions with food and wine, which she also chronicles on her blog, ⊕ *www.winderlust.com*. She updated the Sicily chapter, and the Milan, Lombardy, and the Lakes chapter for this edition.

Specializing in the Neapolitan art of *arrangiarsi* ("getting by"), Campania updater **Fergal Kavanagh** has dabbled in teacher training, DJ-ing, writing guidebooks, translating, and organizing cultural exchanges. He currently teaches at the University of Naples and through his website (⊕ *www.tuneintoenglish.com*) demonstrates how pop music can help students learn English. He updated the Naples and Campania chapter, as well as our introduction to Southern Italy, and Travel Smart.

Bruce Leimsidor studied Renaissance literature and art history at Swarthmore College and Princeton University, and in addition to his scholarly works, he has published articles on political and social issues in the *International Herald Tribune* and the *Frankfurter Allgemeine Zeitung*. He lives in Venice, where he teaches at the university, collects 17th- and 18th-century drawings, and is rumored to make the best *pasta e fagioli* in town. He updated the Venice and Veneto and Friuli–Venezia Giulia chapters for this edition, as well as the introduction to Northern Italy.

After a dozen trips to and a two-decade-long love affair with Liguria, Italian Riviera updater **Megan McCaffrey-Guerrera** moved to the seaside village of Lerici in 2004. Soon after, she started a personal travel concierge service. When not organizing tailor-made vacations of the area, Megan can be found hiking the trails of the Cinque Terre, sailing the Gulf of Poets, or searching for the freshest anchovies in the Mediterranean.

Journalist and editor Amanda Ruggeri returned to the United States in 2014, after nearly five years living in Rome, where she wrote about travel across Italy and Europe for the *New York Times,* the BBC, the *Globe and Mail, National Geographic Traveler, Travel + Leisure,* and *AFAR,* among other publications. Her popular blog on Rome (⊕ *www.revealedrome.com*) features tips, tricks, and things not to miss in the Eternal City. She updated our Rome chapter.

Florence resident Patricia Rucidlo holds master's degrees in Italian Renaissance history and art history. When she's not extolling the virtues of a Pontormo masterpiece or angrily defending the Medici, she's leading wine tours in Chianti and catering private dinner parties. For this edition she updated our Experience Italy, Florence, and Emilia-Romagna chapters.

Italy was to be Margaret Stenhouse's first stop on her planned world tour, but she was captivated by the art, culture and lifestyle and settled for a life in Italy instead. After a long career as a travel writer, author, newspaper correspondent and columnist, she now edits an English website recounting little-known places, traditions and events in her adopted country, with emphasis on local culture, gastronomy, wine and other typical pleasures of life. She is married, with three sons and a dog, and updated our Side Trips Rome chapter and Puglia, Basilicata and Calabria chapter, as well as the introduction to Rome and Environs.

Jonathan Willcocks, a Brit by birth with a degree from the Sorbonne, has been teaching courses in language, literature, and translation at the university in Perugia since the early 1990s. He updated our Umbria chapter.